WITHDRAWN

# Cooperative Office Systems

# Cooperative Office Systems

## Concepts and Enabling Technologies

**Alexander Schill**
*Dresden University of Technology*

**PRENTICE HALL**
London New York Toronto Sydney Tokyo Singapore Madrid Mexico City Munich

First published 1995 by
Prentice Hall International (UK) Limited
Campus 400, Maylands Avenue
Hemel Hempstead
Hertfordshire, HP2 7EZ
A division of
Simon & Schuster International Group



Printed and bound in Great Britain by
Bookcraft, Midsomer Norton

Library of Congress Cataloging-in-Publication Data

Available from the publisher

British Library Cataloguing in Publication Data

A catalogue record for this book is available from the British Library

ISBN 0-13-106097-X

1 2 3 4 5 99 98 97 96 95

# Contents

# Preface

The purpose of this book is to give an introduction to the broad area of cooperative office systems. An office system in this sense is a computer environment that generates, processes, stores, retrieves, communicates, and displays office-related data. Cooperation means that multiple activities, often controlled by several people, are involved in these operations, and that they work together to achieve a common goal. The more general, widely-used term to describe such scenarios is computer supported cooperative work (CSCW). Special characteristics of such approaches are that they involve concurrency of activities, distribution across several workstations or host systems, and complex data and document management tasks. Moreover, emerging systems apply multimedia technology to enhance functionality and user-friendliness of cooperative work.

The problem with such approaches is that they often provide a very interesting, appealing functionality but require a lot of sophisticated, technologically advanced system support. Therefore, the goals of this book are twofold. On the one hand, examples of cooperative office applications are described and classified in order to provide the required technical information from the viewpoint of a user or application developer (chapter 2). Typical applications are multiuser conference environments, group decision support systems, shared multiuser editing facilities, and hypertext and hypermedia support. Moreover, the broad area of cooperative acitivities and office task management is covered by a description of complex activity coordination systems and distributed office procedure support environments. Altogether, these applications provide the basis of advanced cooperative office systems that involve various multiuser/multiapplication interaction facilities and new solutions to complex coordination problems.

On the other hand, the core chapters of the book (chapters 3-6) focus on enabling concepts and standards in various areas. These foundations are applied to and discussed within the context of the office applications mentioned before. The enabling technologies presented are distributed systems support to enable distributed data and activity management (chapter 3), also covering advanced solutions and standards (chapter 4), document modeling, processing, management techniques and standards (chapter 5), conventional, object-oriented, and distributed database support (chapter 6), and foundations of multimedia document representation, communication, and storage (chapter 7). Finally, chapter 8 describes several example systems in more detail and in the context of enabling technology and outlines an overall integration of the approaches discussed.

For each area, the book presents mature concepts and standards that are an essential framework for today's system solutions. However, the presentation is also accompanied by a discussion of new, emerging concepts in order to outline conceptual advances, current research and development directions, and solutions that might become product-level reality within a few years. Due to this orientation, the major focus is on workstation-based solutions. PC-based environments and systems are not described in detail but are only mentioned for completeness where appropriate. Examples in the area of relatively mature, consolidated approaches are client/server computing, remote procedure call, ISO/OSI standards for distributed communication, distributed directory services, the OSF Distributed Computing Environment, the document-related standards ODA, SGML and EDIFACT, relational databases, transaction processing, and object-oriented databases. Examples of more advanced, emerging approaches are distributed object-oriented systems, cooperative document management systems, distributed document models, loosely-coupled federated databases, multimedia documents, and multimedia storage and communication techniques.

The various concepts, systems, and applications are described by numerous examples, often detailed down to the actual programming level. Moreover, many technical figures and tables help illustrate and compare complex approaches in a practical, understandable way. The description of the various concepts is mainly based on recent literature from technical journals and international conferences. However, the book does not describe the large number of relevant systems and standards completely but rather aims to give an impression of their major concepts with respect to cooperative office systems.

Most chapters are augmented with exercises to check the reader's understanding of the material and to give incentives for further in-depth studies. Many of the exercises can be solved in a short time. However, there are also some programming exercises that are intended as practical tasks to be performed in small groups and require more effort. Depending on the level of the group or class, it will be necessary to detail the given problem by providing additional programming hints. According to their nature, the exercises are labelled "basic knowledge", "conceptual design" or "implementation". Implementations can be done in any high-level procedural or object-oriented language.

The book is intended for advanced undergraduate and graduate students, for software engineers, for technical managers, and for lecturers in the areas of office automation, computer-supported cooperative work, distributed systems, databases, and software engineering. It can be used as a base for computer science classes on office automation with a special focus on enabling technology. It can also serve as additional reference material for advanced distributed systems or database classes to cover the application domain of cooperative office systems in detail. Knowledge of specific foundations or systems is not a prerequisite for understanding the book. The reader should just be familiar with basic concepts of computer science such as general operating systems approaches and high-level programming languages (C is used to illustrate some examples). The book is not intended for people who are mainly looking for a product-level orientation in the current marketplace or who are mainly focusing on systems and tools for PC-based environments.

The different chapters can generally be studied relatively independently of each other; knowledge of the other chapters is not absolutely required. However, if the book is to be studied as a whole, some mutual implications should be considered: Chapter 2 (cooperative office work) is important as the motivation for the overall topic areas of the book. Chapters 3 and 4 present material on distributed systems that is useful for an in-depth understanding of chapters 5 (especially distributed document models) and 6 (especially federated and distributed databases). Chapter 7 (multimedia) extends the foundations that have been described in chapters 3-6. Finally, chapter 8 (example systems and integration) details the approaches discussed in chapter 2 by applying the foundations of chapters 3-7. Concerning the exercises, it should be noted that some of them are dependent on the solution of exercises in previous chapters.

Finally, it should be noted that the given examples (e.g. program fragments, notations of document standards, or application of multimedia concepts) are often simplified and are sometimes based on a more understandable abstraction of the original notation. For simplicity, C++-style comments are used everywhere (instead of C-style comments, for example), and specifications of variables are sometimes simplified. Moreover, some examples (like the application of the DCE remote procedure call) are based on specific versions of system environments that might of course change in the future. The presentation is based on best efforts of the author; however, no guarantee of correctness can be given due to the rapid development of the field.

**Acknowlegements**

I would like to thank all those who contributed to this book in any way. Professor Dr. Dr. h.c. Gerhard Krüger made the book possible by providing plenty of organizational and personal support. The director of Digital Equipment's Campusbased Engineering Center in Karlsruhe, Dr. Lutz Heuser, has been generously supporting our research and development projects for many years, especially focusing on the OSF Distributed Computing Environment, on mobile computing and also on multimedia conferencing. The chair of Digital Equipment's European External Research Program, Dr. Igor Varsek, also provided significant support over many years. Professor Dr. Gerhard Barth and Dr. Norbert Diehl of the Daimler-Benz Research Center in Ulm also made new research projects possible. I would also like to thank our dean, Professor Dr.-Ing. Erwin Stoschek, for his valuable support. Professor Dr. Meyer-Wegener provided important comments on the material about the database area; his help is gratefully acknowledged.

Markus Diermann and Leszek Kotsch made additional material on document standards available. Markus Mock performed the design and implementation of a distributed object-oriented system that provided a good model for some aspects covered by this book. Jörg Nonnenmacher performed practical programming examples with the OSF Distributed Computing Environment that were important for the description of this software platform. Wito Böhmak, Robert Heß, Tino Hutschenreuther, Sascha Kümmel, Wolfgang König, and several other colleagues also provided very valuable support in this area. Reinhard Merz and Christian Zeidler helped with systems management during former projects. Nathalie Catalan also provided valuable contributions. Frank Lackermeier contributed technical examples to several chapters within his master's thesis; his support is gratefully acknowledged.

During a very nice and fruitful year with Dr. Ashok Malhotra at the IBM Thomas J. Watson Research Center, I learned a lot about object-oriented databases and computer supported cooperative work. Professor Dr. Peter C. Lockemann taught me about the importance of examples for the reader of a book during former projects. The anonymous reviewers and the publisher, in particular Viki Williams and Alison Stanford, gave lots of valuable technical and organizational support.

Finally, my wife Ursula constantly supports me with lots of care, love, and understanding.

Alexander Schill Dresden University of Technology, 1995

# Trademarks

Apollo Domain, HP-UX and Iris are trademarks of Hewlett Packard Computer Company. CODASYL is a trademark of Conference in Data Systems Language. DB2, IBM, IMS, MVS, SAA, LinkWay, OS/2, SNA, Starburst, and System R are trademarks of International Business Machines Corporation. DCE is a trademark of the Open Software Foundation. DEC, DECnet, and OpenVMS are trademarks of Digital Equipment Corporation. Encina is a trademark of Transarc Corporation. Ethernet is a trademark of Xerox Corporation. Gemstone is a trademark of Servio Corporation. Ingres and Postgres System are trademarks of INGRES Corporation. ISODE is a trademark of X-Tel Services Ltd. LAN Manager, Windows, OLE and COM are trademarks of Microsoft Corporation. MacOS, MacApp, Macintosh and HyperCard are trademarks of Apple Computer, Inc. NetWare and NetBIOS are trademarks of Novell, Inc. O2 is a trademark of Altair Inc. Objectivity/DB is a trademark of Objectivity Inc. ObjectStore is a trademark of Object Design Inc. Ontos is a trademark of Ontologic Inc. Orion is a trademark of MCC. PostScript is a trademark of Adobe Systems Inc. Proshare is a trademark of Intel Inc. Sinix is a trademark of SNI. Smalltalk, Cedar and Courier are trademarks of Xerox Corporation. SparcStation, SunOS and SUN RPC are trademarks of Sun Microsystems, Inc. Tuxedo, Unix are trademarks of AT&T Bell Laboratories. TCP/IP is a trademark of Defense Advanced Research Projects Administration. Versant is a trademark of Versant Object Technology Inc.

All other brand and product names referenced in this book are trademarks or registered trademarks of their respective holders and are used here for informational purposes only. The fact that a system or product is mentioned or has been omitted does not imply any kind of judgement concerning quality, importance, or any other criteria. Product, prototype and standards information in this book cannot be guaranteed to be current.

# 1 Introduction

## 1.1 Motivation

Office applications have a long tradition of using computer systems for supporting or even automating specific tasks. The demand for more advanced computer support in the office domain grew tremendously in the 1980s and continues to increase. Examples are *computer supported cooperative work (CSCW)* [GRU94] for goal-directed workgroup interactions, *complex office procedures* to handle routine as well as non-routine office tasks, *document management* with specific data models to represent complex office documents online, *advanced database techniques* to store mass data of office applications in a structured way, and *multimedia approaches* to support digital manipulation and communication of all kinds of mixed media that exist in the office domain.

In most of these areas, *networks and distributed systems* play an important if not even crucial role: cooperating workgroups are typically distributed across several sites; usually many distributed but interacting parties are involved in a complex office procedure; documents have to be exchanged between distributed and possibly heterogeneous sites of operation via networks; databases can be interconnected by networks in order to form a federation; multimedia data may have to be retrieved from several distributed storage sites or may be transferred between participants in an online conference.

As a result, an integration of computerized office support mechanisms, of document management and database techniques, of networking and distributed systems, and of general computing technology is required. Only in this way can today's and tomorrow's office automation requirements be satisfied by concrete systems implementations. This book presents and combines approaches, software techniques, and standards of different relevant areas in order to enable advanced, computerized office applications. It mainly focuses on advanced solutions at the borderline between the research and development domain. Based on this direction, an important goal is to present examples and technological foundations of current CSCW systems and evolutions to the reader.

In contrast, it is not the goal of the book to provide complete product overviews or to discuss the commercial impact of CSCW. It is also important to note that from the systems point of view, the workstation area is within the main focus. PC-based solutions are only mentioned for completeness where appropriate and are not discussed in detail. Moreover, the area of loosely-coupled asynchronous cooperation (as found in office procedures) is discussed in more detail than the more tightly-coupled synchronous cooperation facilities (as found in teleconferencing environments).

## 1.2 Basic Technological Advances

**Networking and distributed systems:** From the networking and distributed systems technology point of view [TAN89, COD94], recent hardware and software evolution strongly support the development of office technology. *High-speed networks* are available to provide the communication speed and service quality necessary for advanced, data-intensive office application types like multimedia-based collaboration. *Network interconnection techniques* allow subnetworks to be coupled in order to achieve an integrated distributed environment. *Standards* are evolving that enable heterogeneous computer systems to interoperate using different hardware, operating systems, and networking technology. *Distributed programming techniques*, especially *remote procedure call (RPC)*, are already widely accepted and are also being standardized. In addition, complete, vendor-independent service environments for distributed programming like the *Distributed Computing Environment* of the Open Software Foundation are becoming available.

**Database technology:** In the database area, great advances can be observed, too. *Relational databases* have become mature and are widely available as products. *Object-oriented databases* are also becoming available more and more; they provide advanced facilities for semantic data modeling - which is of great importance in the office domain. *Active databases* introduce trigger mechanisms in order to react to external events automatically. *Multimedia databases* are emerging and will provide new opportunities for multimedia applications with huge storage requirements and specific data access demands. In addition, the combination of database and distributed systems technology has already led to distributed databases with a high degree of distribution transparency. However, in CSCW environments, such transparency characteristics affect the potential for mutual cooperation and coordination - it is required to make distribution and interaction more explicit rather than hide it completely. A more recent evolution are *federated database systems* with such explicit coupling of databases at different locations. In this way, databases are loosely coupled, and a larger degree of database autonomy is provided; as shown later, this is required for many open distributed CSCW applications.

**General computing technology:** General computing technology shows similar achievements. Low-cost, high-quality workstations are emerging; their typical characteristics are: several megapixels of screen resolution, several (even up to 100 and more) megabytes of main memory, very large secondary storage capacity exploited by virtual memory mechanisms, standardized window-based user interfaces, various network integration facilities, and - in some cases - also multimedia facilities.

In summary, the relevant technological foundations for distributed office applications are emerging rapidly and are - at least partly - already available today. Many of these aspects are treated in more detail in the following chapters dealing with specific office technology.

## 1.3 Office Systems Technology

Using general computer systems, networks and distributed systems, as well as database technology, advanced computerized office applications have been developing since the early 1980s. The overall goal of this book is to give an in-depth technical survey of different office application domains and of their enabling technology. Central technological areas in today's office systems domain are summarized in figure 1-1 and are discussed below.

The figure shows the most important areas of computer supported cooperative work (CSCW). As a foundation, document modeling and underlying document storage facilities are discussed. These facilities, as well as CSCW scenarios in general, tend to be extended towards distributed systems over computer networks. This is indicated by the general distributed computing concepts on the left-hand side of the figure, and by the more office-specific distributed document management and interchange techniques on the right-hand side. All of these areas require further extensions for multimedia support; this is reflected by the overlay box with the major multimedia issues.

**Computer supported cooperative work:** CSCW subsumes many different techniques for specifying, performing, managing, and controlling complex interactions between potentially distributed office workgroups. According to [KRK88], CSCW describes *coordinated activities performed by a collection of participants supported by a computer system*. The possible types of activities range from very well-structured procedures (e.g. processing of a form within a fixed number of subsequent steps) to very unstructured group discussions (e.g. discussion of a project plan based on very little initial knowledge about project goals and project background).

The participants form a collaborating group and can be humans using computer technology (like electronic mail or group decision support systems), or they can even be fully automated servers (like a print server within a distributed office procedure). In addition, the number of participants can be fixed (as in a long-term project group) or can vary dynamically (as in an online computer conference on the Internet). Computer system support and group coordination can range from very basic inter-participant communication facilities (like e-mail) to sophisticated coordination facilities (like pre-specified, system-controlled execution of actions within an office procedure).

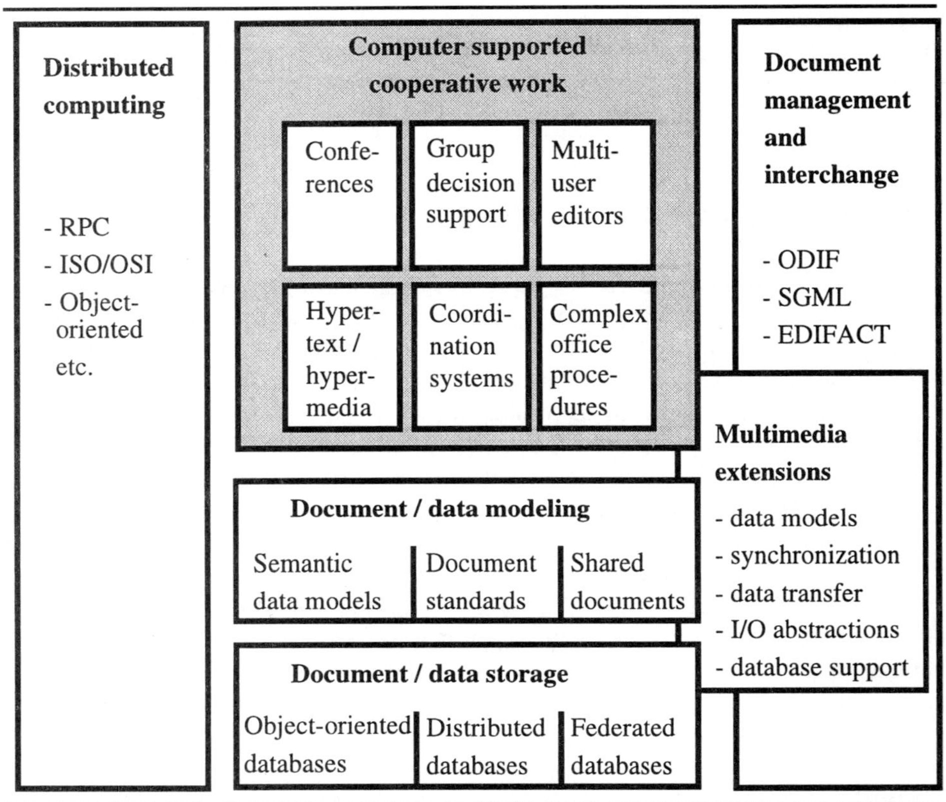


Fig. 1-1 Technological areas of office systems domain

In addition to activities, participants, and coordination support, the *information* used within CSCW is another central issue. In general, all different kinds of information found in an office environment are relevant to specific types of CSCW. For example, office documents are exchanged during group meetings, are processed within office procedures, or are jointly edited. Or, as another example, multimedia information is passed between conference participants and is used jointly within hypermedia systems. Therefore, office information management, transfer, and storage are central issues related to CSCW. Overall, CSCW is a broad area with a number of specific subdomains:

- *Conference systems* support online conferences with distributed participants. Such systems can just be based on plain text exchange but can also include extended online document transfer or even dynamic multimedia interactions including audio and video.

- *Group decision support systems* are interactive environments to facilitate the solution of complex, unstructured problems by a group of cooperating decision-makers. For example, such systems support gathering, retrieval, and exchange of decision-related information, as well as interaction and negotiation within a local or physically distributed group.
- *Multiuser editors* support cooperative document editing; example areas are joint authoring, cooperative software development and collaborative computer-aided design including joint drawing. Specific features of such editors include WYSIWIS ("what you see is what I see") functionality, concurrency control, checkout/checkin of document versions, and negotiation support concerning concurrent document changes. Access to such editors can be possible from different distributed sites. With WYSIWIS tools, all participants immediately see the data modifications that have been performed by their peer participants; this can be implemented by instantaneous propagation via a computer network.
- *Hypertext and hypermedia systems* provide a specific data model describing semantic relationships, e.g. between office documents. Such data entities are represented by nodes of a semantic network while their relationships are mapped to logical links, i.e. to arcs. Most important, browsing and navigation are supported within the semantic network. By including various different media as the contents of nodes, hypertext is extended towards *hypermedia.* Moreover, the semantic network can be stored and accessed in a distributed way leading to the notion of distributed hypermedia systems.
- *Coordination systems* enable management and control of task execution within a workgroup in general; such systems include important features of complex office procedures, of group decision support systems, and of conference systems; in particular, the corresponding distributed systems features are often adopted. However, the coordination systems approach is more flexible in that it supports very unstructured coordination problems, too. Rule-based solutions are common in order to support these kinds of tasks.
- *Complex office procedures* are relatively well-structured, typically recurring office tasks. The term *workflow* is often used as a synonym. Workflows are handled by potentially distributed agents within several sequential or parallel steps. Several languages and systems to specify, execute, and control such procedures have been developed.

In summary, it is obvious that CSCW is found in most office environments. In addition, distributed systems and database techniques as well as document management play an important role in most CSCW scenarios.

**Document and data modeling:** In most kinds of computer-supported cooperative office work, significant amounts of digital data and documents are involved. Therefore, data and document modeling, storage, and retrieval are central issues in office systems.

*Semantic data models* and especially object-oriented models have been developed in order to represent complex data structures and especially document structures in an adequate, natural way. Typical features of such models are hierarchical document structure support, document classification, and reuse of existing document classes by inheritance mechanisms. In addition, more programming-oriented data models allow for data abstraction by restricting data access to well-defined operations on objects or documents.

Moreover, *document standards* are available which allow for the development of universal tools like document structure and contents editors. Most important, documents can then be used by several different tools on heterogeneous platforms and can be exchanged via a network as long as their representation conforms to the standard. The Open Document Architecture (ODA) and the Standardized Generalized Markup Language (SGML) are examples of such standards. This book presents these and other standards, addresses document modeling in detail, and also discusses central aspects of semantic data models in the context of CSCW applications.

Finally, in CSCW environments, models for jointly operating on *shared documents* are essential. This way, several participants can work with documents simultaneously in a coordinated way. Several strategies are possible, including mutually exclusive access, arbitrary simultaneous access with application-specific coordination, and - between these two extremes - moderate access control with relaxed consistency guarantees. These and several other derived models are discussed by example.

**Document and data storage**: In principle, structured documents and other composite objects can be stored using conventional file systems. These systems can also be enhanced by relational databases for managing document contents descriptions and for supporting document retrieval [DAT90]. In contrast, *object-oriented databases (OODBs)* allow for integrated storage of document contents descriptions and of the actual contents. In addition, they support efficient retrieval of complete documents or of general complex objects, as well as of portions thereof. Therefore, this book discusses OODB approaches in the context of semantic data and document models. More conventional *relational databases* are also covered due to their practical importance for storing structured, record-oriented data.

*Distributed systems aspects* are also relevant for document modeling and storage. Extended *distributed object models* allow for interobject references which can even span node boundaries. Specific techniques are necessary to enable location-independent remote access via such references. In addition, some approaches allow for dynamic object migration between nodes. This mechanism is very appropriate for modeling dynamic document exchange. In particular, distributed object models are an ideal base for implementing distributed hypermedia systems as mentioned above. For these reasons, distributed object-oriented approaches are described in detail within this book.

*Federated database systems* are concerned with related issues; they represent a collection of interconnected autonomous databases with individual database schemas. The databases can even have heterogeneous data models or can be implemented on heterogeneous platforms. Extended distributed systems technology enables data exchange between such databases, remote access to individual databases, and specific data management policies like replication. In contrast, *distributed relational databases* present a global, universal database schema to the end user and provide a large degree of distribution transparency. They are more directed towards relatively self-contained applications like management information systems or flight reservation systems with more conventional, record-oriented data.

**Distributed computing:** Distributed computing is essential as a basic mechanism for most of the above-mentioned areas. Most important, application-level communication services and protocols are central issues for distributed office applications. The application layer of the *Open Systems Interconnection (OSI) Reference Model (RM)* of the *International Organization for Standardization (ISO)* provides such mechanisms. Examples are Message Handling Systems *(MHS* according to *CCITT X.400* and *ISO MOTIS (Message Oriented Text Interchange Systems))*, remote invocation *(ROSE),* reliable transfer *(RTSE),* distributed transaction management *(CCR (Commitment, Concurrency and Recovery)* and *TP (Transaction Processing)),* and *Remote Database Access (RDA).*

From a practical point of view, the remote procedure call *(RPC)* seems to be the predominant choice and is now also undergoing ISO standardization. It is also the central communication mechanism of the emerging *Distributed Computing Environment (DCE)* of the *Open Software Foundation (OSF).* Related aspects are naming and security; *distributed directory services* for global name management (like the *X.500* standard) and *security services* for authentication, authorization, and encryption (like the *Kerberos* system) are vital issues for production-quality distributed applications. More advanced mechanisms like distributed object interaction and migration have already been mentioned above. Such mechanisms can be used as a basis for implementing higher-level protocols, for example for distributed CSCW. It is essential that they are embedded into distributed programming languages in order to be easily accessible.

This book presents the standardized ISO/OSI communication protocols with respect to office communication and also discusses the practical usage of RPC in typical client/server office applications. The RPC of the OSF DCE is used as an important system example; naming and security solutions are presented as part of it. Based on general distributed computing facilities, distributed office applications can be built on top of them. According to relatively widely accepted terms, we define a *distributed system* [MUL89] as a collection of computing nodes (each including at least CPU and main memory) that are loosely interconnected via a general-purpose network and that do not share memory. In addition, control of the overall environment is fully decentralized. The distributed system also offers a set of basic services (like communication, remote execution or distributed file management) that are implemented by decentralized servers on different nodes.

Based on this definition, a distributed operating system and a network operating system [TAR85] offering a bunch of decentralized services based on distributed server implementations are good examples of distributed systems. In contrast, a collection of interconnected transputers is not a distributed system (no general-purpose network); neither is a shared-memory number-crunching multiprocessor (no distributed memory). Neither is a large host with a bunch of intelligent terminals attached to it via a star network a distributed system (no decentralized control), although it might be called a networked system. Therefore, we will exclude some system architectures and configurations from our discussion that are sometimes considered to belong to the area of distributed systems but do not conform to our definition.

However, concerning decentralization of control, we will use a slightly relaxed view within the context of this book. Although a system-wide centralized control is not desirable and not within the domain of a distributed system, clearly separated subsystems of a distributed CSCW environment might be organized around a central control facility. For example, a groupware system for WYSIWIS joint editing might have such a central control entity for event distribution. Nevertheless, it is discussed within the context of distributed solutions.

An example of a distributed system is shown in figure 1-2. Two hosts and three workstations are interconnected via an Ethernet (bus-based local area network (LAN) with shared medium access based on message collision detection) and a token ring (LAN with token-controlled access and ring topology). The two networks are coupled via a gateway which performs communication protocol conversions. Each computer system offers local resources (at least CPU and main memory, but possibly also printers and secondary storage). These resources can also be accessed remotely and can be shared among different computers. Resource control is performed in a decentralized and mainly autonomous way. On each computer system, a set of application processes is operating. These processes can communicate over the interconnected networks via basic communication mechanisms like message passing or remote procedure call. At this level, the underlying physical network topology is already considered to be relatively transparent.

Jointly, the application processes form a *distributed application*; in general, such an application can be defined as a global program that consists of a number of modules allocated to different nodes of an underlying distributed system. The modules usually execute independently, however, they can transfer control and data between each other based on the system-level communication mechanisms. As shown in the figure, there can be static interaction paths between modules that represent communicating peer processes. However, these interaction paths can also be installed and changed dynamically. For example, in many teleworking applications, interaction paths are very dynamic.

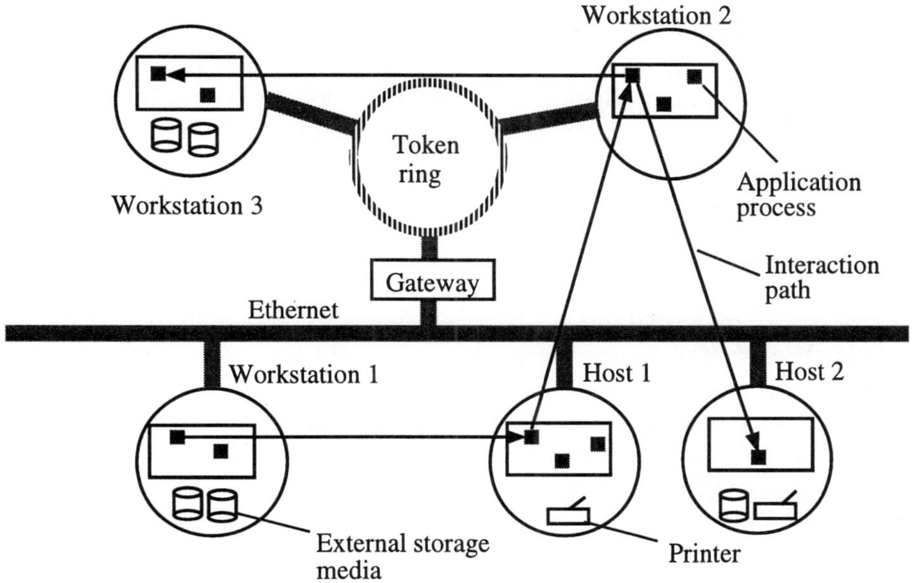


Fig. 1-2 Distributed system with communicating processes

Specific examples of distributed applications in the office domain are distributed hypertext systems, distributed office procedure support systems, and distributed coordination systems. All these applications share common characteristics; namely, they are composed of different, relatively autonomous but communicating components, they exploit underlying communication and operating system services, and there is usually no central control. The last feature, avoidance of central control, is not always shared by all office applications on top of a distributed system. For example, distributed conference systems often have a central mediator, and distributed multiuser editing facilities may have a central editor tool with remote access. For pragmatic reasons and for completeness, we also include such applications in our discussion.

**Document management and interchange:** As part of distributed computation, data and document interchange are central issues. Standardized formats are required to support transfer between heterogeneous platforms. Examples of data format description techniques are *ASN.1* of the ISO/OSI model or the *Interface Definition Language (IDL)* of the OSF DCE, each with associated transfer formats. By negotiating and using a common transfer format, different sites of a distributed office environment can interoperate but still use their own data formats locally for convenience.

For the interchange of documents, similar standards and techniques are available. Examples are the *Open Document Interchange Format (ODIF)* as part of ODA, the specific format associated with *SGML,* and the *EDIFACT* office communication service and protocol. This book presents the document interchange formats but also discusses the most relevant aspects of the above-mentioned data exchange formats.

**Multimedia extensions:** Based on an integration of the techniques mentioned above, most office application areas can be augmented with multimedia data. The basic motivation is that multimedia is a very natural way of information representation, and that multimedia data are naturally used within many office activities. Therefore, it is very desirable to integrate them seamlessly with conventional data and Rdocuments. A basic requirement for this is digital representation of multimedia data, preferably within the whole office environment. In particular, this enables computerized manipulation of multimedia information; however, it also generates huge amounts of data.

Besides the resulting requirement for high-speed mass data communication facilities and efficient mass storage techniques, some additional system and service issues arise:

- *Multimedia data models:* In order to represent multimedia data and documents in an integrated way, extended semantic data models are required. Important issues are inter-media relationships, media synchronization points, and integrated media presentation protocols. Extensions of document models like ODA towards multimedia attempt to cover these issues.
- *Multimedia synchronization:* When presenting dynamic multimedia information (e.g. audio and video), different media information streams have to be synchronized. This is especially important if the streams are supplied by different distributed sources and may therefore be delayed during transmission. Techniques to describe synchronization requirements and to enforce synchronization at runtime are required.
- *Realtime and isochronous data transfer:* Dynamic multimedia data communication leads to special quality of service requirements. Data usually has to be transferred in *realtime* in order to make timely presentation and synchronization possible at all. Therefore, upper bounds for communication delays have to be obeyed. Mostly, even *isochronous* communication is required; in this case, the time intervals between the delivery of subsequent data items have to be constant (or at least between a strict lower and upper bound). Specific resource reservation and scheduling techniques are necessary.
- *I/O abstractions:* Different hardware-supported I/O mechanisms and related tools (cameras and monitors, microphones and loudspeakers, or voice editors) are required for multimedia I/O. In order to hide various hardware-related problems from the user, uniform media and device abstrac-

tions are necessary. Ideally, all kinds of media should be handled by the same set of overloaded I/O operations.

- *Multimedia database support:* Specific database techniques are useful for multimedia data management. Mass storage, inter-media relationship support, contents-related queries and extended transaction facilities are important issues of such databases.

This book presents examples of multimedia data models including new standard proposals. It also discusses I/O abstractions and mechanisms for media synchronization and for multimedia data transmission. Moreover, it gives a survey of multimedia database support. However, as these issues are still very much at the research level, only selected examples of possible solutions and not completely mature and widely accepted generic approaches can be presented.

## 1.4 Outline of the Book

In chapter 2, the book focuses on computer supported cooperative work (CSCW) which is of growing importance in many application domains. Customized for the office domain, it will be a central term throughout this book. Therefore, chapter 2 presents important definitions of CSCW and discusses several detailed examples of CSCW support systems found in office environments. In particular, it outlines what kind of technological support by document management, distributed systems, database and multimedia techniques is required for the different kinds of CSCW applications. Corresponding approaches are later described in detail; therefore, chapter 2 can also be viewed as an overall motivation for the technical aspects described in subsequent chapters.

In chapter 3, distributed processing techniques are described as a basis for CSCW in distributed office environments; the techniques presented include application-level communication protocols, in particular remote procedure call, distributed name management, and security aspects.

Advanced distributed systems techniques such as distributed transactions, atomic broadcast protocols and distributed object-oriented systems are covered in chapter 4. Moreover, the relevant standards for open distributed systems are also discussed in that chapter. Special emphasis is placed on an emerging industry standard, the Distributed Computing Environment of the Open Software Foundation.

Chapter 5 focuses on document management as another important basis for CSCW. It first presents semantic models and standards (like ODA, SGML, and EDIFACT) for complex documents by giving concrete examples. In addition, it presents data and document interchange formats which are an essential basis for distributed office computation. Moreover, the software structure of tools like customized editors or browsers for document handling is described. Extensions towards distributed document models and requirements of multimedia documents are also outlined.

Chapter 6 is dedicated to the storage aspects of office data and documents; this is the third important basis for CSCW in office environments. In particular, the chapter presents advanced database techniques for these tasks. Specific emphasis is placed on networked, federated database systems, on distributed databases, and on object-oriented databases but also on conventional relational databases.

Chapter 7 is concerned with new techniques and extensions for multimedia office applications. It presents emerging approaches for modeling, transfer, synchronization, and storage of multimedia information. Chapter 8 presents several examples of CSCW systems for the office in more detail, based on the technological details presented in the other chapters. In particular, it outlines how some existing CSCW systems discussed in chapter 2 can be applied and extended based on document management, distributed systems, database, and multimedia support. Finally, chapter 9 gives a global summary and outlines important directions for future research and development in the office applications field.

Many examples are described throughout the book in order to illustrate complex issues practically. At the end of each chapter, a number of exercises are given in order to enable some practical feedback. Exercises labelled "basic knowledge" are just for testing the basic understanding of the text, "conceptual design" exercises are concerned with the development of concrete solutions to given practical problems, and "implementation" exercises require an actual implementation of selected solutions in a high-level programming language (such as C or C++). In addition, each chapter is augmented with a set of references in order to give pointers to further sources of information.

## 1.5 Exercises

1. [Basic knowledge]
Give a definition of computer supported cooperative work (CSCW). Give a few examples of typical cooperative office applications found in the CSCW domain.

2. [Basic knowledge]
Outline the difference between complex coordination systems and complex office procedure support environments. Give an example of a typical office application problem to be solved by each approach.

3. [Basic knowledge]
What is the difference between a hypertext and a hypermedia system? What are typical user-level operations in such environments?

4. [Basic knowledge]
Explain the difference between WYSIWYG (what you see is what you get, the typical paradigm of modern text editors) and WYSIWIS (as explained in this chapter). Give examples for system approaches where these paradigms are supported.

5. [Basic knowledge]
What is a distributed system? Which of the following systems are distributed (explain/discuss your answers):
- network operating system
- interconnected transputers
- central transaction monitor with attached terminals
- distributed file system with several decentralized servers
- flight reservation system with central database server and attached PCs
- loosely interconnected office workstations with a set of decentralized services?

6. [Basic knowledge]
Which representations are among the most appropriate ones for documents:
- standardized document models
- plain files
- semantic data models
- database relations (in relational databases)
- database objects (in object-oriented databases)?

7. [Conceptual design]
Give an example of a scenario where multimedia synchronization is important. (First consider possible media and then try to compose them to a realistic scenario.)

8. [Basic knowledge]
What is the difference between realtime traffic and isochronous traffic? Where are such service characteristics required in the multimedia area?

## 1.6 References

[COD94] Coulouris, G.F., Dollimore, J.: Distributed Systems - Concepts and Design; *Addison-Wesley, Reading, MA, 1994*

[DAT90] Date, C.J.: An Introduction to Database Systems (5th edn); *Addison-Wesley, Reading, MA, 1990*

[GRU94] Grudin, J.: CSCW: History and Focus; *Computer, Vol. 27, No. 5, May 1994, pp. 19-26*

[KRK88] Kraemer, K.L., King, J.L.: Computer-Based Systems for Cooperative Work and Group Decision Making; *ACM Comp. Surveys, Vol. 20, No. 2, June 1988, pp. 115-146*

[MUL89] Mullender, S. (Ed.): Distributed Systems; *Addison-Wesley, Reading, MA, 1989*

[TAN89] Tanenbaum, A.S.: Computer Networks; *Prentice Hall, Englewood Cliffs, NJ, 1989*

[TAR85] Tanenbaum, A.S., van Renesse, R.: Distributed Operating Systems; *ACM Comp. Surv., Vol. 17, No. 4, Dec. 1985, pp. 419-470*

# 2 Cooperative Office Work

Computer supported cooperative work is one of the most important areas of the current and future office application domain. It includes many different kinds of office applications and presents sophisticated requirements concerning communication and distributed systems support, document management and storage, and multimedia information exchange. For these reasons, we describe several CSCW areas and system examples throughout this chapter and outline their requirements concerning technological support. By way of a conclusion to this chapter, a basic CSCW classification is presented in order to structure the overall field. The most important CSCW application areas are then embedded into our classification scheme.

Subsequent chapters will then describe advanced software technology (document and data models, storage and database facilities, distributed programming techniques, document interchange standards, and multimedia extensions) providing this kind of support. Emphasis is placed on asynchronous cooperative work where participants perform joint tasks, but are not necessarily active at the same time. For example, office procedures with some loose cooperation of office workers belong to this domain. The area of synchronous cooperative work is discussed where appropriate (for example, in the context of teleconferences). However, the supporting technologies mainly address asynchronous cooperation.

**Basic definition:** As defined in chapter 1, CSCW describes *coordinated activities performed by a collection of participants supported by a computer system* [KRK88]. *Groupware* is the term describing an actual support system for CSCW, i.e. the implementation of specific tools enabling coordinated group activity [RSV94]. The tools forming such a system can range from group decision support programs (e.g. spreadsheets, statistical analysis tools, or brainstorming support) via online group communication facilities (e.g. multicast communication mechanisms or intelligent message filtering systems) to complete coordination environments (e.g. with intelligent agents that perform complex group activities in a semi-automatic way controlled via sophisticated user interfaces).

We describe several examples of groupware systems supporting different levels of coordination and different kinds of CSCW applications below.

## 2.1 CSCW Applications

We divide the overall CSCW domain into several areas, namely *conferences, group decision support, multiuser editing and drawing, shared hypertext and hypermedia, complex coordination systems,* and *complex office procedures.* For each of these areas, we discuss typical application structures and supporting tools in this section.

### 2.1.1 Conferences

Computer-supported conferences enable group meetings using advanced technology support. Basic motivations for this are as follows:

- *Participant communication:* By supporting remote communication between participants at different locations, travel costs can be reduced and meetings can be held more frequently.
- *Information access:* Significant overhead within group meetings is caused by lack of technical or managerial information relevant to detailed discussion and to decision-making. Conference support systems facilitate online access to such information during a meeting.
- *Anonymity:* Especially within heterogeneous groups with participants at different management levels, anonymous contributions are an important means of encouraging controversal discussion. Computer technology makes such contributions feasible.

In general, we can distinguish between *conference centers* and *teleconferences* using computer systems as secondary aids and *computer conferences* using computers as the central support tool.

**Conference centers:** A conference center is a meeting room equipped with special audiovisual technology (e.g. slide projectors, video projectors, and movie projectors) and with computer support for centralized meetings. Computer support is provided for controlling audiovisual tools, for accessing relevant information, and for supporting local participant interaction. The physical structure of such an environment comprises workstations for the participants and at least one shared, large-screen display. Software support is provided for remote database access, report generation, and various kinds of data analyses. Examples of traditional systems providing such support are *EIS (Executive Information Services)*, *EXPRESS*, and *XSIM* [SUM85].

More recent systems provide enhanced features including support for anonymous contributions (see above), different modes of group communication (e.g. freestyle communication, moderated communication based on token-controlled contributions, or one-party contributions similar to a talk), shared logical information spaces (e.g. an electronic blackboard), and support for distinct steps within a group session (e.g. brainstroming, idea organization and analysis, detailing of ideas, voting, and report generation). An example of an approach with these features is *GroupSystems* [NDV91] which will be discussed in more detail in the context of group decision support systems (see section 2.1.2). Such advanced systems are also called *information centers* according to [KRK88]. If specific computerized tools for decision-making are offered, too, the term *decision conference* is appropriate.

Conference and information centers lead to specific requirements concerning document management in order to support information access. They also require local and remote database access and support for document exchange and editing. If the workstations of participants do not directly share main memory or secondary storage, remote communication facilities via a local area network are necessary, too.

**Teleconferences:** These CSCW environments are primarily designed to facilitate meetings between groups at two or more locations [FKR93]. Audiovisual equipment similar to that found in a conference center is used; however, remote audio and video is added in order to enable meetings involving several conference centers. This leads to the well-known notion of the videoconference. For audio and video transfer via the emerging *Integrated Services Digital Network (ISDN)*, there are already international videoconference standards, CCITT H.261 (compression) and H.320 (interoperability). These standards are supported by most manufacturers of the enabling environment, especially of the voice/video encoders/decoders (codecs); an example of such a system is Intel's *Proshare.* Advanced systems mentioned below also exploit local area networks and wide-area high-performance networks for digital high-quality video and audio transfer.

Examples of teleconference systems are *Etherphone* [VZS91] and the *Rapport* system [AEH88]. A number of earlier systems have also been surveyed in [SAG85]. The Etherphone will be presented in more detail in section 8.1. Examples of recent multimedia teleconferencing systems are *MMC (Multimedia Collaboration)* of the German BERKOM-II project [ADH93] (see section 8.2 for details), *XTV* (X Teleconferencing and Viewing) [CJA94], and *MediaSpaces* [BHI93]. Both approaches support digital video and audio conferencing, dynamic participation in a conference, and shared use of drawing or editing tools. The *MBone* system [ERI94, MAB94] enables video and audio broadcasting over the Internet, for example to do an online transmission of conferences, workshops and other events.

It is also interesting to extend the computer-based tools of a conference center towards a distributed environment for the teleconference. This leads to an integration of teleconferences and computer conferences (see below); however, only limited system support is currently provided for this. A basic example of such an approach is the *RTCAL* system [GRS87] which integrates audio teleconferencing with a shared, computer-based blackboard.

For an evaluation of the organizational and social impacts of teleconferencing and for some more technical background information, see also [GAL92]; some of the conclusions drawn there are that teleconferencing cannot really replace face-to-face meetings and that net travel within a company does not necessarily decrease when teleconferences are available as an alternative. On the other hand, the advantages of teleconferences as an additional tool are also acknowledged.

**Computer conferences:** Within computer conferences, a distributed computer system is the basic means of group interaction. In contrast to conference centers and teleconferencing with *synchronous* interactions, computer conferences can be based on both synchronous and *asynchronous* group interaction. In the synchronous case, a request or - more generally - a message sent by a participant is followed by a response within a limited, typically relatively short time interval. Asynchronous interactions do not have these characteristics.

Typical features of a computer conference system include inter-participant message exchange facilities and a shared computerized blackboard with controlled joint access. In contrast to basic bulletin board systems, computer conferences always focus on a specific topic; multiple conferences with different topics and possibly overlapping sets of participants can coexist in the same environment. An example of groupware supporting both synchronous and asynchronous computer conferences is the *Caucus* system [OPP88]. It can support up to 16 simultaneous users (synchronously) and several hundred occasional callers (asynchronously). A special feature of the system is database support; each conference can be linked to a database which provides background technical knowledge about the given topic.

Very widespread asynchronous computer conference support is given by *Usenet News* [HOR87]. A new, more far-reaching approach is *SuperKOM* [PAT92]; the system supports simultaneous multiconference interactions, it is integrated with a directory system, and it is based on a fully distributed architecture concerning the message repository. Sophisticated solutions for phone-based asynchronous CSCW are offered by the *HyperVoice* system [RES93]. It provides a software toolkit for constructing such applications with high-level presentation formats for structured voice messages. Based on these concepts, users can execute filtering, sorting and browsing operations for advanced phone message management.

Various modified ways of computer conferencing are also found in many other environments; for example, the joint use of distributed hypertext systems or distributed joint document editing can be classified as dedicated kinds of conferences. However, these areas are discussed separately below due to their specific semantic aspects.

**Technological requirements:** The technological requirements of computer supported conferences are summarized in table 2-1. In all kinds of conferences, complex office documents are used frequently as sources of information and as a major unit of data exchange. Therefore, document models, shared document access facilities, and dedicated document database support are required. In addition, access to remote databases storing other decision-related information necessary for a conference is required.

Due to the potential distribution of participants - especially in computer conferences - high-level remote participant communication facilities are important. For conference centers with locally interconnected workstations, similar techniques are required to enable anonymous voting, for example. In addition, distributed application support is necessary for implementing a shared distributed blackboard. If not only data but also complex documents are the subject of communication and blackboard usage, standardized document interchange facilities and mechanisms for remote document database access are required.

| Technological area | Specific requirements |
|---|---|
| Document and data models | Models for shared access to complex documents |
| Document and data storage | Database support for documents used within a conference; database access to decision-related information |
| Distributed systems aspects | Remote inter-participant communication; distributed blackboard management; remote database access |
| Document interchange | Formats for inter-participant document transfer and for remote document database access |
| Multimedia extensions | Storage and exchange of static multimedia documents; multimedia conferences based on dynamic audio and video |

Table 2-1 Technological requirements of conference groupware

Moreover, all kinds of conferences can benefit from supporting documents with static multimedia data (i.e. time-independent graphics, pictures and static voice annotations). Full multimedia conference support (as found in the Etherphone environment) also requires dynamic media inclusion (i.e. audio and video).

### 2.1.2 Group Decision Support

*Group decision support systems (GDSS)* are interactive environments to facilitate the solution of complex, unstructured problems by a group of cooperating decision-makers [KRK88]. These systems can be viewed as an extension of conference systems in providing numerous tools for gathering, retrieval and exchange of decision-related information, as well as for group negotiation. Usually, each GDSS participant has a terminal or workstation offering these facilities online. Specific examples of GDSS tools are:

- *Remote database access (RDA):* Based on RDA protocols, remote databases can directly be queried for decision-relevant material interactively. In addition, other tools can have program-level query interfaces. Moreover, results of decisions are usually stored in a database and are accessed in subsequent GDSS sessions.
- *Information-gathering tools:* These tools implement distributed brainstorming and subsequent idea organization. This process can be supported by a shared electronic blackboard with controlled access and by direct inter-participant negotiation facilities. In addition, an information management tool is required; its tasks are to order information according to topics and subtopics, and to assign decision weights to different information items.
- *Tools implementing decision-analytic techniques:* Such techniques can support decisions using database input data and pre-defined decision criteria. They can also enable future projections of organizational states based on virtual decisions and on data elaboration algorithms. Examples of specific techniques are decision trees, multiattribute utility models, cost-benefit models for resource allocation, and spreadsheet models for information preparation.
- *Voting protocol tools:* These tools support optionally anonymous online voting concerning a specific decision. Usually a mediator component collects votes remotely and returns the final results to the participants. Variations are the assignment of different votes to different participants and implementation of hierarchical voting structures.

**System example:** Several GDSS are described in [KRK88]. A more recent example of a sophisticated GDSS environment is *GroupSystems* [NDV91] of the University of Arizona, Tucson. This provides one workstation per participant in a GDSS session, one or two workstations for a discussion mediator, a very large, shared screen as an electronic blackboard, various forms of audio-visual support, and a number of software tools. The mediator plans the meeting agenda in advance, provides technical support to the participants, and controls the agenda and its goals during the decision meeting. Figure 2-1 shows the components of a GroupSystems decision meeting and its supporting tools; the components and tools are discussed below.

*Session planning and management:* Session planning is supported by an *electronic questionnaire* for collecting important topics and issues of a decision meeting. Based on these topics and on the typical decision finding process, an *agenda tool* is used to develop an initial session agenda. During a decision meeting, a *tool control facility* mediates access to shared tools and initializes, starts, and ends tools dynamically. A *task assigment tool* records the different tasks of each participant. It basically maintains a task list with read-only access for the participants and read-write access for the mediator. An *output organization and storage tool* performs final report generation, information distribution to participants, and persistent storage in the organizational memory.

*Dynamic group interaction and decision finding:* Group interaction is supported by message-based electronic communication between participant workstations and by shared use of the electronic blackboard. For the latter, three modes are available: (a) *chauffeured:* only one person at a time can enter group information; (b) *supported:* all group members can enter comments; (c) *interactive:* all members can enter comments anonymously and can directly modify them via their personal workstations. Case (a) supports very structured, mediated group meetings (e.g. to develop a decision about a well-defined topic). In contrast, case (c) supports more unstructured discussions while (b) is a trade-off between (a) and (c).

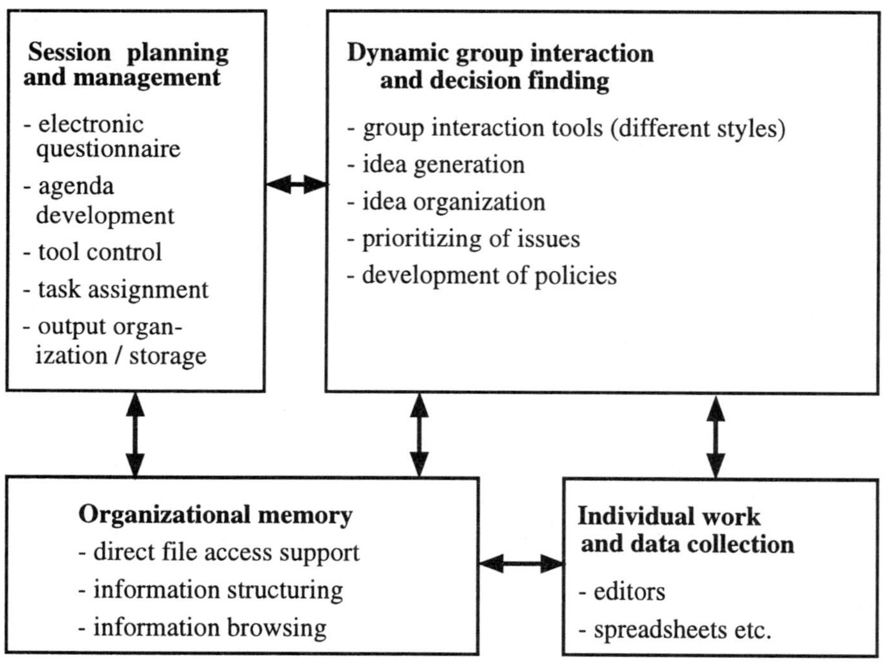


Fig. 2-1 Group decision support in GroupSystems

*Idea generation* is supported by an *electronic brainstorming tool.* It allows each participant to enter comments according to different topics, each assigned to a separate shared file. In addition, a *topic commenter* supports more structured collection of comments based on a pre-defined task framework.

*Idea organization* according to topics is performed in a supported style based on an *organizer tool.* An additional *issue analyzer* enables a more structured idea organization based on a chauffeured style. In a first phase, ideas are identified based on the brainstorming results. In a second phase, consolidation of ideas is performed based on online voting. Moreover, a *shared group editor* (see also section 2.1.3) supports joint document generation to describe ideas interactively in an integrated way.

*Prioritizing of issues* is supported by various tools; an *online voting tool* enables direct anonymous voting and chauffeured discussion of results, an *alternative evaluator* supports multicriteria evaluation of ideas with a scale for each criterion, a *group questionnaire* allows for dynamic querying of participants, and a *group matrix* supports rating of issues based on several combined criteria.

*Policy development* is supported by a tool to assess the impact of a potential policy. It works in supported mode; participants first identify individuals and organizations affected by a policy and then rate assumptions concerning the degree of policy effect. A *policy formation tool* supports agreement on the wording of a policy statement; a policy draft is created by each participant, displayed on the shared screen, discussed interactively, and redrafted thereafter.

*Organizational memory and individual work:* The *organizational memory* is a persistent storage subsystem that stores text and data files in a structured way. Files can be accessed remotely by each participant via an attribute-based access tool named *briefcase*. In addition, files can be structured as a semantic net based on a modeling tool named *enterprise analyzer*. The semantic net can also be accessed interactively based on a *graphical browsing tool*. In addition, the other tools mentioned above use the organizational memory for information storage and access, even across different decision meetings.

Individual work and data collection is supported by more conventional *editing and spreadsheet tools* that are integrated into the overall toolset concerning their data interface, i.e. they have access to the organizational memory.

A quite similar approach supporting multiple groups, the Multigroup Decision Support System (MGDSS) with the Advanced Integrated Requirements Engineering System (AIRES) has been described recently; for details refer to [PFB94].

**Technological requirements:** GDSS have similar technological requirements to those found in computer supported conference systems (see table 2-1 above). However, the document and data management aspect is more important here while the distributed systems and multimedia aspects are of less significance - at least in current environments.

Document database access, document generation and storage tools, and document interchange facilities are primary means for implementing higher-level GDSS tools as found in GroupSystems. Static multimedia document extensions are also important for facilitating rapid preparation, compression and display of decision-related information.

In future GDSS environments, conference technology will tend to be integrated with typical GDSS tools, and distributed systems will be exploited to enable decision-making among remote participants. This will lead to the same distributed systems and multimedia requirements as discussed in section 2.1.1. In addition, actually distributed and decentralized decision support tools will emerge. That is, not only remote communication and document interchange between decision-makers but also fully distributed tool implementations will be common.

### 2.1.3 Multiuser Editors and Drawing Tools

This category of CSCW applications is concerned with shared modification of documents and graphics. There are two major categories of groupware systems in this area: *Hardware-based* systems use cameras and special displays to enable sharing of remote editing and drawing facilities. Examples are Xerox PARC's *VideoDraw* and *VideoWhiteboard* [TAM91]. *Software-based* systems use computer communication software to achieve this goal. An example is the *CoDraw* system [ABD90] for joint drawing.

*ForComment* [BRO90] is a software example of a multiuser text document editor. It supports up to 16 users and has specific editing modes (e.g. for jointly adding comments and annotations to a document without altering its contents). MIT's *CES (Collaborative Editing System)* [GRS87, GRW92] is a similar approach with sophisticated support for hierarchical documents and for different locking modes. The *TeamWorkStation (TWS)* [ISM91] from the Japanese NTT Human Interface Laboratories is an example of a mixed software and hardware approach.

The basic concepts of VideoDraw, VideoWhiteboard, and CoDraw are discussed below. A more detailed description of the CES approach is given in chapter 8.

**Hardware-based solutions:** The hardware approaches usually only support an instantaneous WYSIWIS functionality between two or more peers. Any modification of a local display or whiteboard immediately materializes on the remote display or whiteboard. The information of both participants in an editing session is physically overlaid. These features are appropriate for some applications where immediate feedback and synchronous work are important. However, very little coordination support is provided; coordination is performed interactively by explicit consideration of the peer's drawing actions.

The general schematic of such an approach is illustrated in figure 2-2 by showing the VideoDraw and VideoWhiteboard drawing facilities [TAM91]. With VideoDraw, users directly draw on a video display screen using erasable whiteboard markers. A video camera is aimed at each display screen. The created marks and also the hand gestures during drawing are imaged by the camera and displayed on the other screen. The major advantage of this approach is its support for immediate joint display of changes made to a drawing.

VideoWhiteboard is a follow-on prototype which has been developed based on experiences with VideoDraw. It supports the same interaction structure based on a different physical arrangement. The video camera is now behind a semi-transparent whiteboard. Its image is displayed on the other whiteboard and overlays the actual drawing generated there. In addition, the camera transmits a shadow of the collaborator to the remote screen. An audio connection also enables the collaborators to talk with each other. The major advantages of VideoWhiteboard are that the drawing surface is much larger, and that the camera's view cannot be blocked by a collaborator. However, both tools only support very basic human coordination of joint drawing.

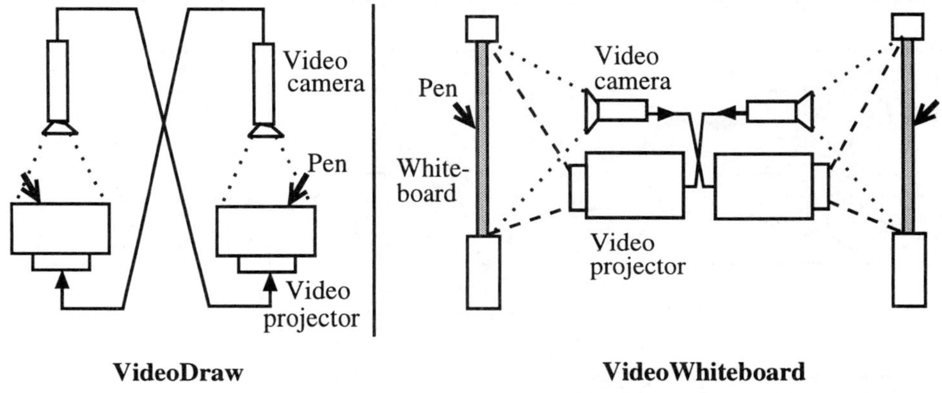


Fig. 2-2 The VideoDraw and VideoWhiteboard joint drawing tools

**Software-based solution:** The *CoDraw* system [ABD90] is a software solution supporting a group of remote users collaborating in drawing figures and graphs. The system consists of a joint drawing editor and of inter-user communication facilities to support direct user interaction. The basic architecture is shown in figure 2-3. The joint drawing editor is represented by the *master tool*. It is accessed remotely via tool windows from different collaborating users. Participant interactions are performed via the *chat windows*. Each chat window has a section for each participant. All notes typed in a participant's own section are immediately sent to all remote users and are displayed in the corresponding chat window section. The *control windows* present an interface to the *session mediator*. The mediator has the task of coordinating the overall group editing process; it handles requests to join or leave an editing session and to get exclusive access to the master tool.

Internally, inter-participant communication is implemented based on participant agents. Remote tool access is performed via tool agents. These intermediate components allow for a network-independent implementation of the end-user interface; they map remote commands to internal messages and unwrap received messages at the destination site again.

Two specific features of interest are *floor management* and *WYSIWIS implementation*. Floor management is concerned with controlling multiuser access to the master tool by a *floor passing protocol.* Usually, one of the participants possesses floor control. This participant can then be asked to "pass the floor" to someone else via the control window and the session mediator. Until responding to the request, the floor owner is allowed to continue working for some time, the *grace period.* This period can be varied from zero to indefinite; in the first case the floor owner is interrupted immediately, while in the second case a floor request may have to wait indefinitely. Appropriate trade-offs concerning the length of the grace period have to be determined in an application-dependent way.

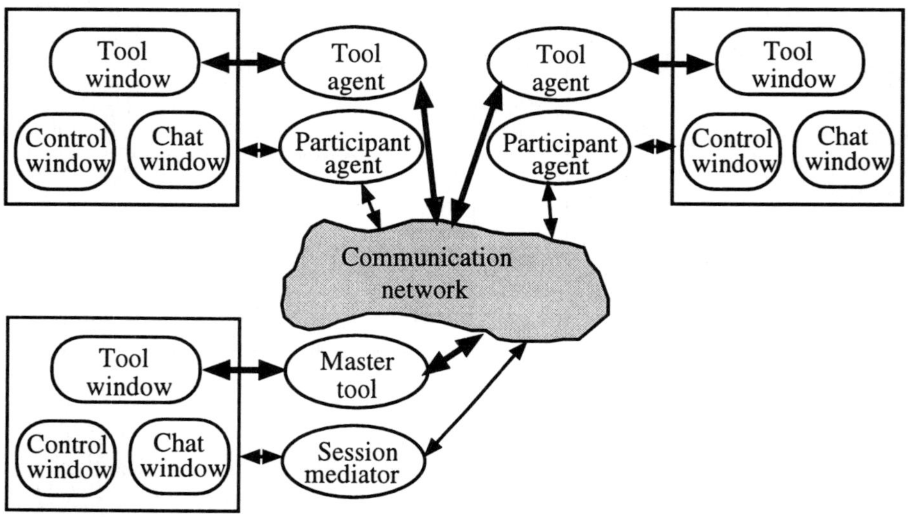


Fig. 2-3 CoDraw architecture

A WYSIWIS implementation of the editing tool can be performed in two different ways: (a) Each user command is forwarded to the master tool which performs the resulting editing operations and status changes and then forwards its complete new state to all tool agents. (b) User commands are forwarded to the master tool as in solution (a) but are then immediately distributed to all tool agents that execute them based on their own state - as does the master tool. If the initial state and the sequence of received editing commands of all tool agents are identical, all tool agents will observe the same sequence of states, guaranteeing WYSIWIS behaviour. Solution (b), however, has the advantage of generating only a very reduced message volume - instead of transferring complete states, only state change commands are transferred. However, each user agent must have full local editing functionality available. In addition, a reliable multicast mechanism is necessary to guarantee correct message delivery.

Several similar tools and systems have been built. A recent example is the *ClearBoard* system [IKG93]. This permits co-workers in two locations to draw with color markers or with electronic pens while maintaining direct eye contact. In some sense, it can be classified as being a mixture of the hardware and software approaches presented. In particular, the system seamlessly integrates a shared workspace and an interpersonal workspace. The shared workspace represents a common space for joint drawing according to the WYSIWIS principle. The interpersonal space supports the mutual exchange of gestures and facial expressions of distributed group members based on a videoconferencing environment. Very similar features are also found in the *MMC (Multimedia Collaboration)* system of the German BERKOM-II project [ADH93].

**Technological requirements:** The software-based solutions of multiuser editors and drawing tools have specific technological requirements in the sense of our discussion; the hardware-based approaches are mostly self-contained systems without significant additional requirements for external software technology support. To enable professional work with a multiuser editor, persistent document storage has to be provided by a document database. Due to the facilities for remote access to the editor, a universal document model with an associated interchange format is required. For example, this enables the WYSIWIS implementation in systems like CoDraw: the whole document or portions thereof have to be exchanged between participants after document status changes. Alternatively, a universal editing command set has to be established; this leads to the same requirement of a universal document model against which the commands are executed.

As outlined above, an approach like CoDraw represents a distributed application (however with partly centralized control); each participant agent and tool agent maintains its own state. Specific protocols (like atomic multicast) are necessary to guarantee distributed state consistency. In addition, direct synchronous communication facilities are required for implementing the chat facility.

Static multimedia extensions enable joint multimedia document editing. This leads to requirements for multimedia document model and interchange support. Even more important, the implementation of the WYSIWIS facility may have to be redesigned due to the increased cost of exchanging multimedia data; exchange of editing commands instead of state may be much more appropriate if sufficient local storage facilities are available.

### 2.1.4 Hypertext and Hypermedia

**Basic terms:** *Hypertext* is an approach to organizing and operating on text documents in a nonlinear way [CON87, NIE90]. The essential feature of hypertext systems is support for arbitrary *links* between documents. This leads to a *hypertext graph* with documents as its nodes and links as its edges. CSCW is supported by hypertext systems by allowing multiple users to access the same hypertext database and to share information in this way. By allowing multimedia objects (e.g. graphics, digitized speech and audio, digitized pictures, or video clips) as the contents of nodes, hypertext is extended towards *hypermedia*. As a conceptual base, semantic data models are an important foundation for structure-based operations on hypertext/hypermedia graphs [SLH93].

**Application areas:** Typical applications of a hypertext system are as follows:

- *Idea and design organization:* In the early stages of a project, important technical ideas and subsequently developed design data can be organized nicely as a hypertext graph. Nodes represent descriptions of central conceptual ideas and design documents. Links represent semantic relationships between ideas and between documents. Navigation in the hypertext graph is important for retrieving all information related to some discussion topic, for example.
- *Library and authoring systems:* In online libraries and authoring systems, documents (books, journals, catalogues, manuals etc.) and document annotations (e.g. publishing information, criticism, related technical material, orders etc.) can be represented by hypertext nodes. Links model inter-document references and relationships between documents and annotations. Navigation allows a reader or an author to find and access related material rapidly for a given book. Joint authoring applications especially benefit from these features.
- *Tutoring and teaching:* In teaching environments, technical background material and documents, examples, or exercises can be represented as hypertext nodes with semantic links between the material according to the usage in specific classes. Navigation features with appropriate access control are important both for teachers and for students.
- *Decision support:* Information relevant to management decisions (e.g. product descriptions, sales summaries, problem reports etc.) can be organized well as a hypertext graph. Navigation techniques enable a manager to retrieve semantically related information relevant for decision-making more rapidly than in a conventional database (cf. section 2.1.2).

Several other application areas are emerging; further examples are scientific applications, information organization in museums, or semantic information organization for applications based on artificial intelligence.

**Basic hypertext features:** A *hypertext system* typically consists of two major components:

- *Database:* A hypertext database contains information objects (mostly text documents) and pointers between these objects. The pointers are the implementation of document links.
- *User interface:* Hypertext systems usually provide a graphical user interface. This supports the display of information objects (one window per object) and of links (graphical edges between windows), manipulation of both, and interactive navigation by following links from one object to another.

Notably, there is a direct correspondence between the windows and graphical edges between windows on the one hand, and the related objects and pointers of a hypertext database (i.e. of the corresponding database subset) on the other. This is illustrated by figure 2-4. In the lower part of the figure, the contents of a small hypertext database containing objects *O1-O7* are shown. The objects have associated pointers referencing each other. The display shows a part of the database contents, namely objects *O1* and *O2*. In addition, it shows the sources of the labeled links *l1-l4* that correspond to the pointers in the database that originate from *O1* and *O2*.

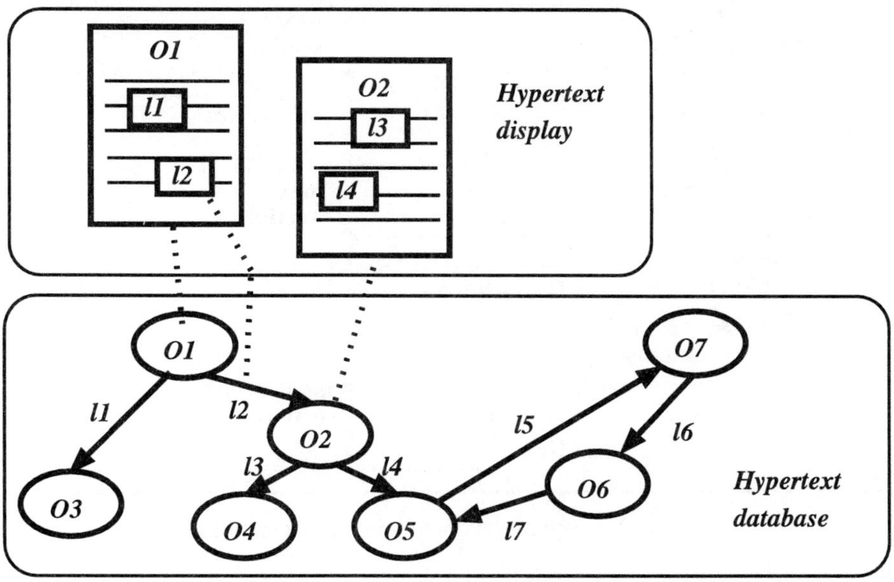


Fig. 2-4 Correspondence between hypertext database and display

As illustrated in the figure, the links originate from specific points within the document that can be defined explicitly. The destination of a link can be either a whole document or a specific point within the document. In the figure, the whole document *O2* is referenced via *l2*. The label of a link (e.g. *l2*) is not necessarily identical with the referenced object (e.g. *O2*). This has two major advantages: (a) link names do not change when the destination of a link is modified, and (b) an object can be referenced multiply from the same source object within different contexts. Graphically, a link can be represented by a link icon within the window of the source object. When a user clicks on the link icon, the referenced object may appear as an additional window on the screen or may replace the current window. Navigation in a hypertext graph is performed by repeatedly following links in this way. While this is the typical approach in many systems, other representations of links such as arrows are also found in various systems; so this is just an example and not a general principle.

**Representation of complex documents:** Based on a hypertext graph, the structure of complex documents can be represented in detail. As this aspect is important in later chapters, we give a brief example (see figure 2-5).

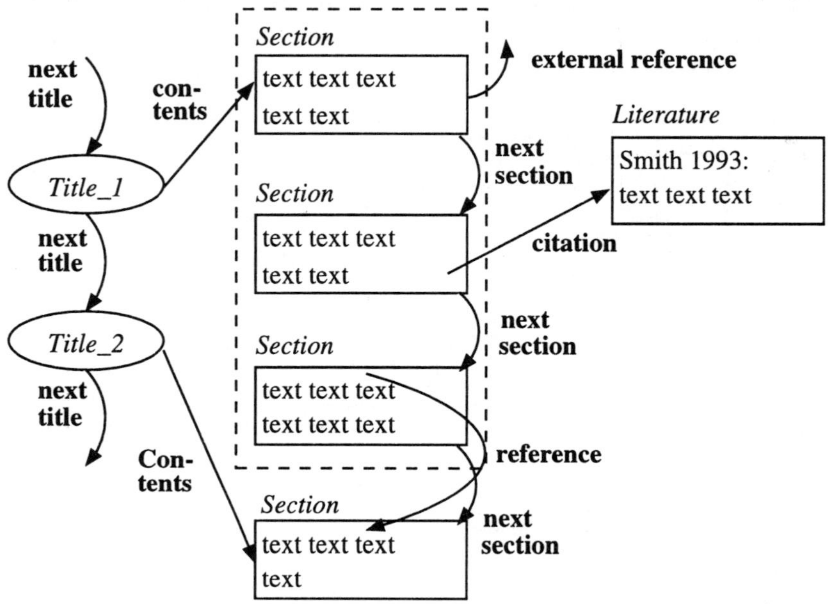


Fig. 2-5 Hypertext document representation

The document consists of several sections which are linked sequentially by hypertext links labeled *next section*. The title of selected sections is stored in separate hypertext nodes and is linked to the sections via the *contents* links. The titles are also linked with each other; this allows for fast navigation through the table of contents. Arbitrary references can exist between sections as indicated by the *reference* link. Each section can have some literature associated with it; citations are modeled as links between a section and the literature. In addition, external references may exist; they are modeled as external inter-document links.

**Typical system features:** In addition to the general concepts of a hypertext database and user interface, a typical hypertext system should support the following features:

- *Object and window manipulation:* Windows can be opened for existing and for newly created objects in the hypertext database; objects can be created and deleted if permitted by the access rights of a given user. In addition, windows can be resized and iconized in the usual ways.
- *Link manipulation:* Links can be created (subject to access control) by creating a link icon within a window (source object) and clicking on the

destination object. Links can be followed by clicking on the link icon within the window of a source object; the window for the referenced object is then displayed. In order to facilitate navigation, link icons can contain a textual description of the referenced object. Some systems also support navigation via predefined paths in order to facilitate the most common tours through a hypertext graph.

- *Queries:* Navigation can also be supported by simple queries against the nodes of a hypertext graph for keywords or attribute values. The objects matching a query are displayed as windows. Of course the facilities for plain text search in large hypertext databases are limited due to performance problems.
- *Browsing:* Link following can easily lead to disorientation in a large hypertext graph. Therefore, many systems provide a browsing facility to display parts of the hypertext database entirely as a graph instead of only displaying objects and link icons.
- *Multiuser access:* Large applications require multiuser access to a hypertext database. Therefore, systems have to support access control and access synchronization as found in database environments.

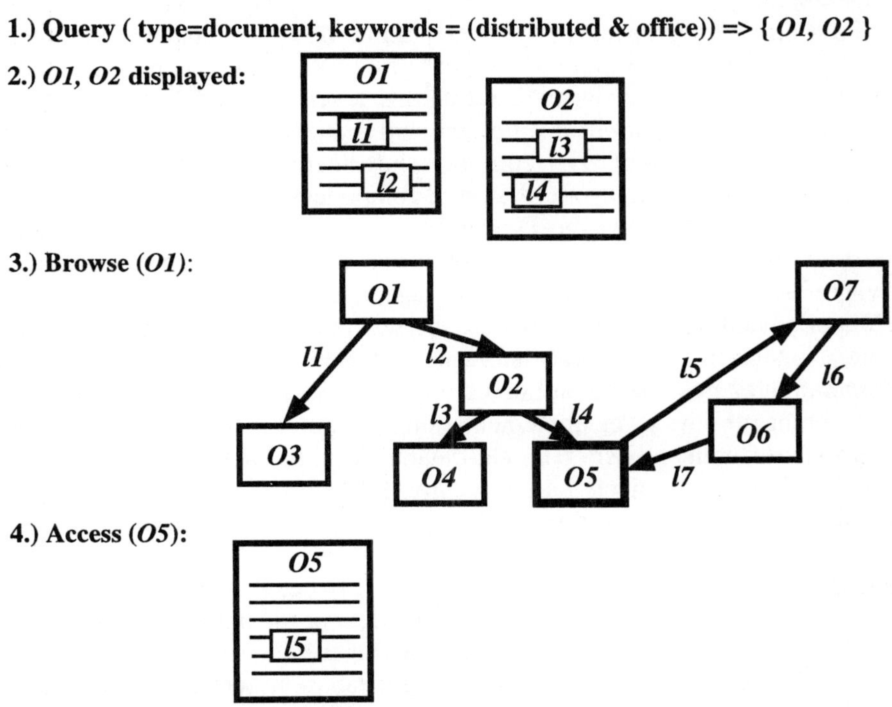


Fig. 2-6 Queries, browsing, and navigation

Figure 2-6 shows an example of queries, browsing, and navigation corresponding to the example given above. First, a user issues a query looking for documents with the keywords "distributed" and "office". This results in the two documents *O1* and *O2* with the intermediate link *l2*; they are displayed as windows with a link icon for *l2* in *O1* and with other link icons. However, in order to achieve a better orientation, the user requests display of the entire *browsing graph* originating from *O1* in browsing mode; the result is shown in the lower part of the figure. Afterwards, the user clicks on the icon of *O5* in the browsing graph and a window opens displaying the contents of *O5*.

**Dexter Reference Model:** As a result of a hypertext standardization effort, the *Dexter Reference Model (DRM)* has been developed [HAS94]. It unifies the vaious concepts of existing hypertext systems into a single framework. The model consists of three layers:

- The *storage layer* describes a repository for hypertext components. *Atomic components* contain the actual data such as text or graphics. *Composite components* enable the aggregation of atomic components, and *link components* implement inter-component references. All components have associated manipulation operations such as creation, deletion, modification, and search operations.
- The *runtime layer* specifies the presentation of components and the interaction between the user and the system at runtime. Components of the storage layer are fetched and instantiated at this level. The actual presentation is guided by a *presentation specification* that is attached to every component.
- The *within-component layer* comprises information about the actual internal structure and storage layout of atomic components. Therefore, it is a base of the storage layer. However, Dexter does not determine any specific storage format. It rather enables the integration of arbitrary storage representations via referencing *anchors* within the storage layer.

The major advantages of this model are the separation of functionality, the facility for integrating different storage representations, and the explicit representation of links based on link components. This way, it is possible to provide different runtime layer implementations on top of a single storage layer, to use various different repositories and databases within a single system, and to manipulate links and objects independently. [GRT94] presents a hypertext system conforming to the Dexter model.

**Existing systems:** Numerous systems have already been developed in the hypermedia area. We briefly discuss and compare a few of the more common systems. We will also give a more detailed description of the *Intermedia* environment in chapter 8, including distributed systems and database aspects. A good overview of PC-based hypertext solutions is given in [NIE90]; some examples are *IBM LinkWay*, *Apple HyperCard*, *Cognetics Hyperties,* and *Guide* from Office Workstations Ltd. However, we will focus instead on workstation-based hypertext systems in the following comparison.

*Intermedia:* The *Intermedia* system [YHM88, HKR92] was developed at the Institute for Research in Information and Scholarship of Brown University. It is a hypermedia system including the basic hypertext features discussed above. The system offers several editors for different media types. Within a document, *blocks* can be defined that are the content portions to be mapped to hypermedia nodes (see figure 2-7). Blocks are interconnected by *links*; both intra-document links (between blocks of a single document) and inter-document links are supported. All links are bidirectional; therefore, link destinations are also indicated by link icons and links can be followed in both directions during navigation.

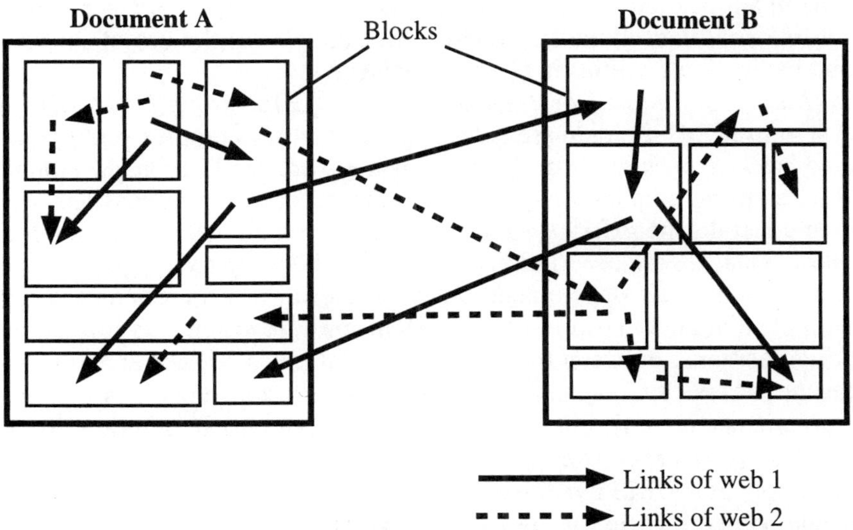


Fig. 2-7 Hypermedia model of the Intermedia system

A set of interconnected blocks and links is called a *web* and is a hypertext graph in terms of our definitions. Different webs with shared documents can coexist in an Intermedia database. That is, different blocks of a specific document can occur in several webs. Blocks within a document can overlap concerning their contents and are basically independent (unless they are connected via inter-document links).

In addition to several tools for hypermedia access and management (e.g. the *Finder* tool for hierarchical document organization), the Intermedia *Web View* tool [UTY89] is most notable. For each web that a user accesses by opening a document block within it, Web View maintains and manages browsing information dynamically and displays it via a *Web View window*. This information consists of a *path*, a *map,* and a *scope line*. The path is the history of navigation actions of the user within the web. The map consists of the set of documents linked to the current document. The path and map give the user additional orientation as discussed above in the context of browsing. Moreover, they allow for *shortcut* navigation: any document within the path or map can be opened immediately without further navigation operations. Path and map are always updated dynamically.

The scope line indicates the approximate number of documents and links in the web. It gives the user some basic impression of the search space and complexity of the hypermedia graph. Together, the facilities of the Web View tool address the problem of potential disorientation by additional support for context information. The web concept itself helps to control complexity by separating different aspects of document relationships (e.g. technological relationships and design relationships of a set of products) into different webs.

The main application area of Intermedia is the organization of teachware, e.g. of lesson material and of student reports. An example for the use of Intermedia webs and navigation facilities is given in chapter 8.

*Issue-Based Information Systems (IBIS):* The gIBIS (*group-based* IBIS) hypertext system [COB88] addresses idea organization for complex problem areas (so-called *wicked problems*) in the area of software application development. Therefore, a strong emphasis is placed on support for group discussions and on CSCW in general. The gIBIS system supports three kinds of pre-defined hypertext nodes: (1) *issues* are descriptions of open problems related to a design aspect of an application under develoment (stated in the form of questions); (2) *positions* are potential answers to issues; (3) *arguments* are statements supporting or disproving positions. Between these nodes, several kinds of links are defined: issues can be related by *specialization* and *generalization*. Positions *respond-to* issues, arguments *support, question* or *object-to* positions. In addition, the general relationships *refers-to* and *replaces* are also available.

An example of a gIBIS hypertext graph is shown in figure 2-8. The graph represents the general issue of new hypertext approaches, and especially the problem of distributed hypertext implementations. Two positions are made concerning this problem: distributed object-oriented systems and the use of standards are considered to be appropriate high-level solutions for distributed hypertext systems. The first position is supported by the arguments of distribution transparency and natural data representation but is objected to by the argument of lack of maturity. Further discussion and extension of the hypertext graph is required to address these concerns appropriately. The position of using standards is supported by the desire for heterogeneous interoperability but is objected to by concerns about performance of standards implementations. The further discussion might raise new issues (e.g. how to implement inter-object communication or how to move hypertext objects between different databases) and might also create new positions (e.g. use of RPC-based systems or use of federated database products).

As opposed to other hypertext systems, the set of predefined node and link types in gIBIS suggests a special method for using the system; this reflects the goal of supporting idea organization stated above. A typical scenario consists of stating an issue, finding positions which address the issue, and finding arguments supporting or disproving the positions. During this process, new issues may be uncovered, and positions and arguments may have to be revisited.

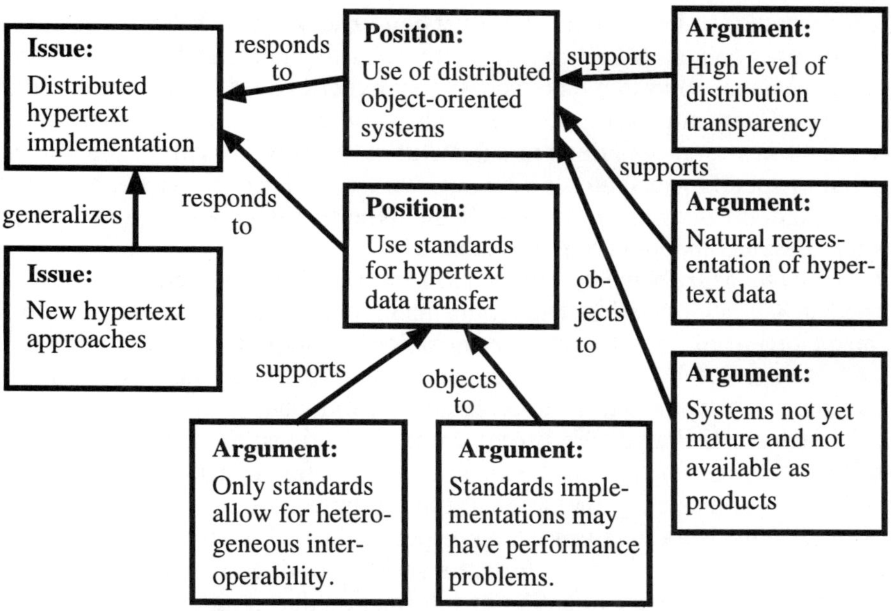


Fig. 2-8 Example of a gIBIS hypertext graph

*NoteCards:* The Xerox PARC *NoteCards* system [HMT87] is a support tool for information analysts. It helps gather information about a given topic and produce analytic reports based on that information. The information is organized on computerized note cards as known from conventional paper-based techniques. In addition to the typical hypertext features, the system supports multiple media and is open for higher-level application programs on top of it. Pre-defined media node types include text, video, animation, graphics, and actions; an action is represented by LISP code which is evaluated dynamically when the action node is activated during navigation. The system has a programming interface for LISP programs which can access the hypermedia database. This way, new node types can also be created by programming their functionality in LISP.

*Neptune:* The *Neptune* system [DES86] of Tektronix is based on a Smalltalk user interface and a transaction-based database server (named *Hypertext Abstract Machine*). It specifically addresses the organization of CAD data but can be classified as a general hypertext system. The separation of user interface and database is very strict according to our initial model. The system offers several browsing tools including (1) a *graph browser* providing a self-contained view of an entire subgraph of nodes and links to improve orientation; (2) a *document browser* allowing for browsing hierarchical documents with special support for hierarchical abstraction; (3) a *node browser* displaying individual hypertext nodes in detail; (4) a *node difference browser* supporting differential analyses of similar nodes.

The system also keeps a complete version history for each object, with direct access to any version. A link can explicitly refer to a dedicated version of an object. The system supports remote access to a hypertext database from distributed workstations with transaction-based crash recovery facilities and multiuser access synchronization. Queries are supported in Neptune based on the values of application-specific attributes associated with an object. However, the system does not support distributed storage of the hypertext database - as does none of the other systems mentioned in this subsection.

*Knowledge Management System (KMS):* The KMS system [AMY88] developed at Carnegie-Mellon University and by Knowledge Systems addresses the management of knowledge in organizations. A hypermedia object is called a *frame*. Each frame has a title, a descriptive text, a set of frame-specific menu items called *selections,* and a set of standard commands (like editing the frame) associated with it. Frames are linked via the selections; therefore, navigation is performed by choosing one of the menu items of a frame. The structure given by the selections is basically hierarchical but can also include general links. Only one frame is displayed at a time, i.e. no specific browsing support is provided. It is also possible to specify that a program should be triggered when a selection is activated. Thus dynamic evaluation of information during navigation can be supported. Major applications of the system include information management for an aircraft carrier, joint authoring, code management, and bulletin board implementations.

*PlaneText:* The PlaneText system [CON87] developed at MCC in Austin is also a general hypertext system. It makes intensive use of the Unix file system. Each hypertext object is mapped to a Unix file. Links between objects are stored in separate files. Therefore, the file contents of objects are not affected by the definition or modification of links. This principle also allows for the integration of existing files with arbitrary contents (e.g. mail distribution lists, source code, $\LaTeX$ files etc.). In addition, it makes the Unix directory hierarchy directly available for modeling hierchical structures among hypertext objects.

**System comparison:** The systems are compared in table 2-2 according to several criteria. Most systems support typed links instead of just general links. The major advantages of this are: (a) type checking can be performed by the system in order to avoid links referring to objects of incompatible type, and (b) link icons can be augmented with an indication of the link type to improve orientation.

In the Intermedia, Neptune and NoteCards systems, objects (and in the first two systems links, too) can have associated attributes and attribute values. This allows for specifying the characteristics of objects and links in a formalized way. In addition, attributes enable querying based on their values and facilitate browsing this way. KMS and Neptune support versioning of nodes and links; Neptune provides a very sophisticated versioning scheme. IBIS allows for versioning of links but not of nodes. Versioning of hypertext elements supports the maintenance of design histories and is important in development projects, for example.

In the NoteCards, Neptune, and KMS systems, procedures, or - more generally - executable code can be attached to objects. This allows for dynamic evaluation during navigation and provides important facilities for higher-level application programs (e.g. integration of database retrieval or report generation with hypertext operations). Most systems support queries - an important feature for establishing appropriate entry points for a dedicated navigation operation. Browsing in hypertext subgraphs is explicitly supported by Intermedia, NoteCards, Neptune, and PlainText. Intermedia provides the most sophisticated support for browsing based on the Web View tool. The systems just mentioned (Intermedia, NoteCards, Neptune, PlainText) also support other media than text and are therefore real examples of *hypermedia* systems.

| | Typed links | Attributes | Versions | Procedures | Queries | Browsing | Other media |
|---|---|---|---|---|---|---|---|
| Intermedia | Yes | Yes | No | No | Yes | Yes | Yes |
| gIBIS | Yes | No | By link | No | No | No | No |
| NoteCards | Yes | Objects | No | Yes | Yes | Yes | Yes |
| Neptune | Yes | Yes | Yes | Yes | Yes | Yes | Yes |
| KMS | Yes | No | Yes | Yes | Yes | No | No |
| PlaneText | No | No | No | No | Yes | Yes | Yes |

Table 2-2 Comparison of hypertext systems

**World Wide Web System:** Finally, the widely available World Wide Web system (WWW or W3) has become the *de facto* standard for distributed wide-area hypermedia in the Internet. It was developed by the European CERN research center, and is a large-scale distributed hypertext system [LEE93, BCL94, VSW94]. The WWW system consists of nodes (documents) and links. As usual, links enable graphical browsing in the hypertext graph. In addition, *indexes* are offered. These are special documents with links to other documents that support explicit search operations. The user can supply keywords or other search criteria.

All nodes are addressed using a special *URL (Uniform Resource Locator)* syntax. A URL includes an access path that may also refer to remote documents, and contain an Internet ftp address, for example. For accessing remote documents, *HTTP (HyperText Transfer Protocol)* has been specified as an Internet standard. The WWW system is very important from a practical point of view due to its broad availability and rich functionality. It is currently being extended in a backward-compatible way to add multimedia facilities.

Recently, attention has also been drawn to the problems of hypertext application design. As a representative example, [GPS93] describes a novel model for authoring-in-the-large as a basis for an overall design method. The *HDM* approach *(Hypertext Design Model)* presented allows the system-independent description of overall classes of information elements and navigational structures of complex applications without much concern with implementation details. All details of link and object structures are derived automatically from a conceptual-design-level description.

**Technological requirements:** The technological requirements of hypertext and especially hypermedia systems are summarized in table 2-3.

| Technological area | Specific requirements |
|---|---|
| Document and data models | Complex document model with extensions for attributed hypermedia links |
| Document and data storage | Persistent document storage; attribute-based querying of hypermedia objects; multiuser access control |
| Distributed systems aspects | For distributed hypermedia: transparent remote object access; dynamic object migration |
| Document interchange | For distributed hypermedia: standardized interchange formats to implement hypermedia object migration |
| Multimedia extensions | Static multimedia document support with specific extensions for links between content portions |

Table 2-3 Technological requirements of hypermedia groupware

Database technology is most important for hypermedia systems. In particular, object-oriented databases are suitable for storing hypertext databases and controlling multiuser access. In addition, attribute-based querying facilities can be used to implement hypermedia queries at a higher level. Existing document models have to be extended in order to be suitable for a hypermedia environment. For example, hypermedia links between documents can have attributes - a feature that is usually not supported by general document models. Multimedia extensions become relevant when extending hypertext to hypermedia. Most important, static multimedia documents have to be supported. In addition, such multimedia models have to support link sources and destinations within the content portion of different kinds of media.

A hypertext database is often very large and frequently consists of information relevant at different locations. Therefore, it is reasonable to distribute hypertext nodes within a distributed system and to support remote links and remote link following between hypertext nodes. In this case, distributed systems aspects and document interchange become important when extending an environment to a distributed hypermedia system. In particular, transparent remote hypermedia object access during browsing, distributed access synchronization, and dynamic hypermedia object migration are central features. Migration facilitates relocation of hypermedia objects according to expected access patterns; this way, access costs can be reduced by saving remote communication. In addition, migrating a copy of a hypermedia object to a browsing site presents a simple way of remote hypermedia object transfer. We will focus on the technical details of this area in the context of distributed object-oriented systems (see chapter 3).

### 2.1.5 Complex Coordination Systems

Groupware supporting complex coordination addresses very general kinds of group interaction and provides means to structure them. Typical examples of coordination problems are activity management, especially joint execution of relatively unstructured tasks and weakly structured workflows, time and calendar management, and intelligent message management in a large system. A central feature of such systems is the combination of advanced user interfaces and some kind of knowledge-based support. Because of the huge variety of problems and solutions in this area, it is hard to describe such systems by a set of general features; we instead discuss specific groupware examples for the three areas mentioned above.

**Activity management: The Coordinator:** Activity management is addressed by *The Coordinator* [WIN88]. This system implements a coordination model for peer-to-peer activity scenarios; these can also be applied to group activities by dividing them into sets of interrelated peer-to-peer interactions.

The general interaction model is based on speech-act theory, an approach that basically considers language as a series of actions [WIF87]. The resulting Coordinator model is represented by a state machine in figure 2-9. It consists of an activity request from party A to B followed by a promise by B to A to perform the activity, and eventually by a notification from B to A that the activity has been completed; finally, A declares satisfaction with the result. Several exceptions to this basic scenario are possible: B can decline the request or can make a counter-offer of a modified activity to A. In the latter case, A can accept or can again counter etc. After the completion message from B, A can reject the work done instead of declaring satisfaction. In this case, B can work on the activity again and eventually signals completion to A again; this might be accepted by A (satisfaction) or be rejected once more etc. In each phase, both peers can also cancel the activity.

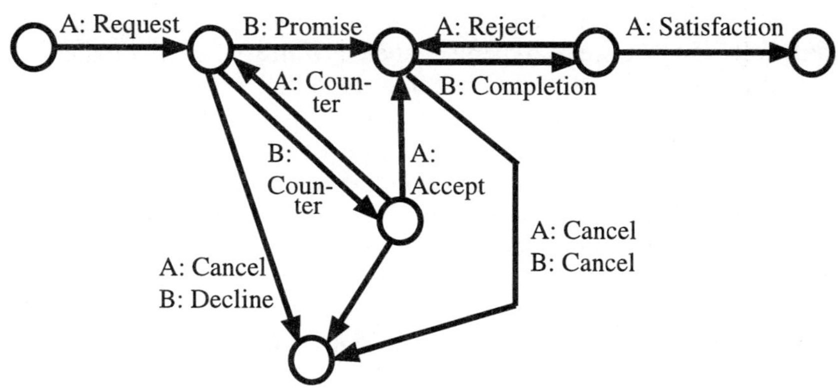


Fig. 2-9 State machine for the Coordinator model

Based on this model, many kinds of basic activities can be represented. For example, an interaction of a manager requesting a project report from an employee would fit nicely into the model. In contrast to automated office procedures without human intervention, several alternative actions are supported in each state and are selected interactively. This leads to the flexibility required for unstructured office tasks.

Activity messages can comprise enclosures, for example data objects that are necessary for performing an activity. In addition, each activity can be associated with a pre-defined deadline. System support is provided for remote message interaction between participants based on the coordination model, for managing a collection of different ongoing activities (e.g. list of activities, selection of specific activities requiring action, control of activity deadlines), and for automatically keeping records of completed activities.

Group activities are supported in two ways: (a) several activity requests can be issued simultaneously; this is important when assigning different subtasks of a complex activity to several group members; (b) within an activity, a request can be delegated to a subordinate group member; a subactivity is started for that.

The activity model of The Coordinator has already been adopted within several other approaches due to its relative generality and flexibility. New approaches also attempt to extend the basic coordination concepts by allowing the integration of arbitrary application-specific interaction protocols. For example, the *Strudel* environment [SMK90] and the *Conversation Builder* [KAC92] belong to this category of systems.

**Activity management: ObjectLens and Envoy:** The *ObjectLens* system [LMY88] provides several building blocks for general CSCW applications, and especially for coordination problems.

In particular, it offers facilities for representing information about people, tasks, products, and messages in a high-level way, and for executing actions based on these objects in a semi-automatic way. Three major kinds of objects are provided: *semi-structured objects* represent passive information like text documents; *folders* are aggregations of such elements forming complex information objects; and *semi-autonomous agents* are active entities that are triggered by events and apply actions to passive objects.

*Semi-structured objects* are defined and displayed as forms using a template-based interface. A form comprises a pre-defined set of fields (dependent on the object type) with optional default values and value alternatives. In addition, fields can also hold links to other objects instead of pure data values. This results in a simple kind of hypertext system. Object types are part of an inheritance hierarchy according to object-oriented programming techniques. Therefore, new types can be defined in terms of existing types by reusing their properties based on inheritance. The objects are semi-structured in the sense that their fields are virtually untyped and can hold variable length data.

A *folder* is a collection of objects (e.g. groups of people or e-mail messages from a specific sender). It can be displayed as a table with a row for the attributes of each object or as a hypertext graph showing the links between the objects.

A *semi-autonomous agent* consists of a set of rules. Each rule specifies a trigger event and several conditions in its *if* part, and a set of resulting actions in its *then* part. When an event that is part of an agent specification is triggered, the corresponding *if* part is evaluated. If the given condition holds, the actions of the *then* part are executed on one or several objects. Typically, actions lead to the exchange of e-mail messages with remote peers and these messages may then cause triggering of events at the remote site. The agents are only *semi*-autonomous in the sense (a) that actions can involve human interaction and (b) that the rules of an agent can be modified interactively and dynamically.

An example of an ObjectLens application is shown in figure 2-10. Two semi-autonomous agents cooperate. One represents the tools of a design engineer and the other implements an archival server for CAD-based designs. The rules of the design engineer are applied to a folder named *Designs* which stores the designs that are subject to current design work. When the state of a design is *Finished*, it is extracted from the folder and sent remotely to the archival server. When the state is *OpenProblem*, an open issue arises and the design is moved to the folder *ToDiscuss*. Other rules are required to send designs stored in this folder to colleagues in order to instigate technical discussion of open problems.

The archival server has rules for handling e-mail stored in the *NewMail* folder. If there is an urgent action deadline stated in received mail, the object is moved to the *Urgent* folder and has to be handled by additional rules. If mail comes from the design engineer (and is not urgent), it is moved to the *Archive* folder. System support is provided for event and trigger handling, folder and object access (especially navigation via links), and object and object-type definition.

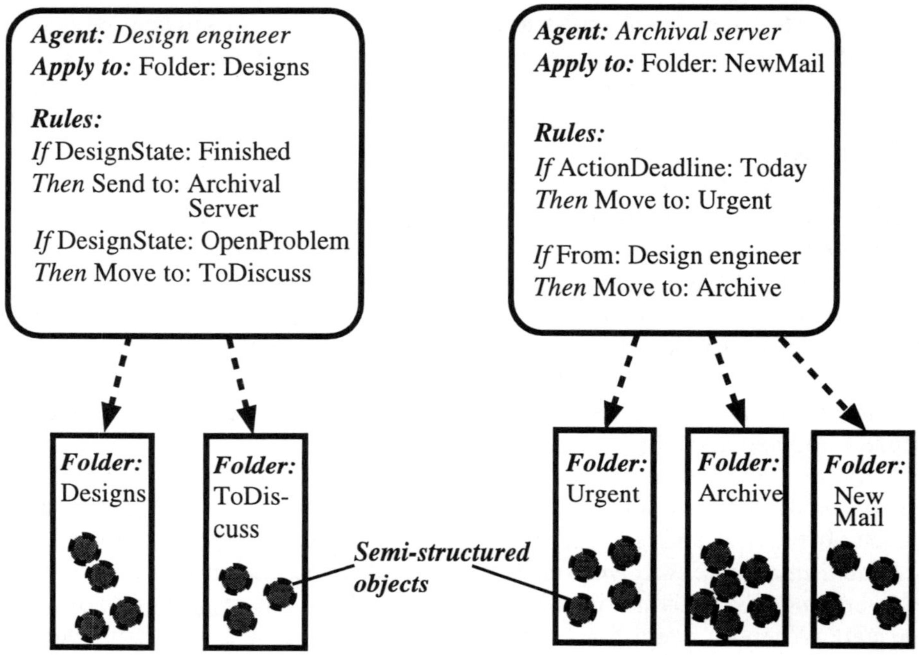


Fig. 2-10 Example of an ObjectLens application

Based on the *ObjectLens* approach, various distributed office tasks can be performed in a semi-automatic way. Thereby, a typical office environment consists of a set of semi-autonomous agents, each managing a collection of folders with semi-structured objects. Complex activities and inter-agent coordination problems can be supported by an appropriate rule base for each agent. For example, agents jointly representing a project group could offer rules for handling activity requests from other group members (with project data and documents in folders) or for negotiating group meetings (with electronic calendars represented by semistructured objects). A more detailed example of ObjectLens is presented in chapter 8.

An extended approach has been developed within the *Envoy Framework* [PYF92]. This provides support for computer-based assistants or agents that operate for the user. Envoys carry out missions for users by invoking envoy-aware applications called operatives and inform users of mission results via so-called informers. The operatives can be distributed across a heterogeneous networked environment. An envoy plays the role of a coordinator by scheduling, tracking, and dispatching all the missions of a particular user. A script language for specifying the functionality of an envoy in a high-level way is available. Existing software can be converted for use in the Envoy environment based on a set of application programmer's interfaces. Compared with *ObjectLens,* the *Envoy Framework* provides more flexible ways to solve relatively unstructured problems based on distributed activities.

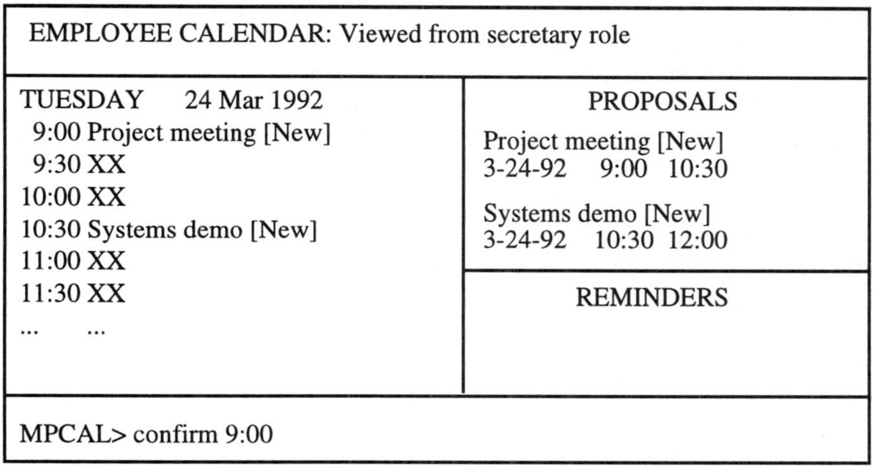


Fig. 2-11 Display for MPCAL calendar management

**Time and calendar management: MPCAL:** The *MPCAL* system [GRS87] addresses another kind of coordination problem: time and calendar management. The system offers several kinds of calendars representing the schedules of persons, of common resources (e.g. seminar rooms), or of special events (e.g. conferences). Each calendar has a set of role definitions associated with it; the roles control access to a calendar. For example, anyone might be allowed to manipulate a resource calendar by inserting reservations as long as no conflicts arise. In contrast, only the owners of a personal calendar are allowed to insert appointments but may overbook their own schedule.

An important example for joint use of calendars with MPCAL is scheduling of a meeting. A user creates a proposal for an appropriate date and time and names the potential participants. The system then inserts the meeting, marked as *unconfirmed,* into the calendars of all named participants. The appropriate role within these calendars must be available to the initiator, e.g. to a secretary. Participants are notified about the meeting proposal when they next look at their calendar. They can then accept the proposal or reject it. In the first case the meeting is marked *confirmed,* in the second case the calendar entry is removed. As a third alternative, they may put the meeting on hold and decide later about participation. The responses are returned to the calendar of the initiator. The example can be extended by integrating resource calendars; they could be used for reserving meeting rooms and would probably be contacted before notifying potential participants.

Figure 2-11 shows an example of an MPCAL display. It is divided into several major sections. The header shows which calendar is used and which role of the calendar is accessed. The main section shows the calendar entries that are accessible for that role. In addition, there is a separate section displaying the entries that are still only proposals. A special section shows reminders for important appointments. User commands are entered in the lower section; in the example, the project meeting proposal is being confirmed.

Recently, the area of intelligent software agents performing complex coordination tasks has become quite popular. Based on artificial intelligence techniques, these approaches are very flexible. For an overview and example system, see [MIR94, MAE94].

**Technological requirements:** The technological requirements of complex coordination systems are summarized in table 2-4. Complex coordination systems are inherently distributed applications; the different instances being coordinated usually reside at different nodes, are acting autonomously, and are communicating explicitly. The ObjectLens system is a good example. Therefore, distributed systems aspects are most important concerning support technology in this area. In particular, high-level remote communication facilities and directory system support for locating remote instances are required. In addition, the data objects involved can be stored in a distributed way, too. Therefore, transparent remote object access as discussed in the context of hypermedia is also a requirement. In order to enable document transfer in systems like ObjectLens, document interchange formats are important.

| **Technological area** | **Specific requirements** |
|---|---|
| Document and data models | Specific document model for dedicated form types (like semi-structured objects) |
| Document and data storage | Persistent document storage; attribute-based document access and browsing |
| Distributed systems aspects | High-level remote communication facilities; directory system support; transparent remote object access |
| Document interchange | Standardized interchange formats for document transfer between coordinated instances |
| Multimedia extensions | Optional static multimedia document support |

Table 2-4 Technological requirements of coordination systems

Specific document models and associated database storage facilities are required to support the ObjectLens approach, for example. In this way, each folder can be mapped to a database supporting semi-structured objects. Flexible attribute-based access and browsing facilities are important for implementing the trigger/action model of ObjectLens or for handling the calendar entries of MPCAL.

Multimedia extensions are not a specific requirement of complex coordination systems; they are relatively orthogonal to the basic coordination protocols. However, for some specific applications (like coordination of computer-aided design processes), they are an essential issue. In most cases, static multimedia document support will be sufficent.

### 2.1.6 Complex Office Procedures

Complex office procedure support systems can be classified as being a specialization of coordination systems. In contrast to general coordination problems, a complex office procedure is usually very well structured. The term *workflow* is often used as a synonym for this kind of task structure. We first describe the area of office procedures in general terms based on experience with a personal system design. Then, we give a comparison of existing systems for handling complex office procedures (often called *workflow management systems (WFMS)),* including an own approach. The office procedure specification notation of our system is described by a detailed example in chapter 8.

**Basic terms and concepts:** An example of an office procedure implementing travel expense processing is shown in figure 2-12.

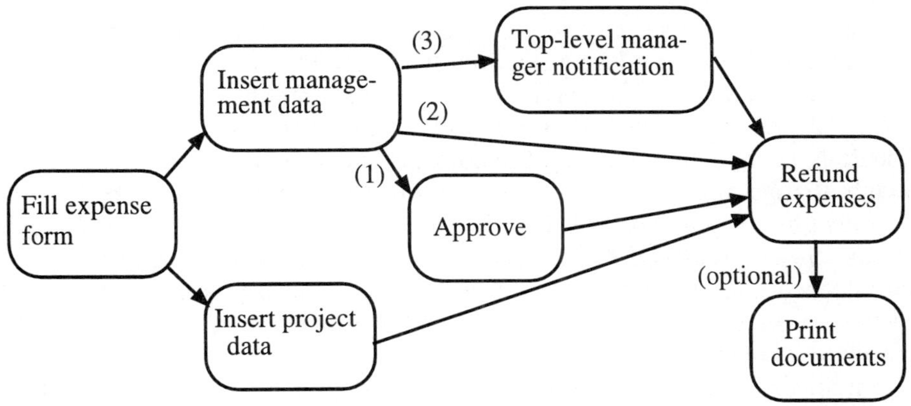


Fig. 2-12 Example of an office procedure

An office procedure consists of several parallel and sequential steps or *service requests* according to its *execution graph*. In addition, *conditions* can be attached to edges in order to control alternative execution of specific paths (indicated by (1)-(3) in the example). Moreover, edges can also be marked as being *optional;* if they point to services that are not executed for some reason, the overall office procedure still succeeds. The execution graph is a directed graph with explicit start and end nodes. The graph may contain loops in order to model repeated execution of a specific step.

Each node of the graph represents a *basic service request*. At runtime, each basic service request is mapped to a *server* offering the service. In our example, the servers would be interactive tools used by human office workers; however, many examples of fully automated services can be found, too (consider stepwise image processing, for example). Servers are typically distributed throughout a networked environment; therefore, the resulting notion of *distributed* office procedure execution has to be supported. An object representing an office procedure moves conceptually between the selected servers. In some systems, this is also reflected by the actual implementation - in this case, a dedicated object representing the office procedure moves dynamically between network nodes.

Service requests can sometimes be augmented with specific binding and control attributes. Examples are *application-level characteristics* that have to be supported by a selected server (e.g. speed of a print server), *cost measures* that are evaluated in order to select one out of several servers, *server instance preferences* to give hints to specific server instances to be used, or *timeouts* to control the overall service execution time.

*Data handling:* An office procedure accesses, modifies, and generates data during its execution. In most environments, these data correspond to office documents. In our example, a travel expense form would belong to the office procedure.

Therefore, the support system has to provide means for document management during office procedure execution. Important facilities are: (1) definition of typed slots within an office procedure to manage references to attached documents; (2) remote access to referenced documents during office procedure execution; (3) dynamic transfer of documents between execution servers; and (4) reliable storage of attached documents after important processing steps.

*Execution support:* A typical office procedure execution consists of several runtime phases. Within the *initiation phase*, an office procedure object is created and attached data objects are initialized. This is typically performed via a user interface offered by special control stations. At the end of this phase, the office procedure is submitted to the first execution server.

Within the *main execution phase*, several steps are executed repeatedly for each service: the execution graph is analyzed for conditional and parallel paths in order to determine the next service(s) to be performed (*routing*). The next server(s) is/are determined by contacting a directory service and evaluating the service request attributes (*binding*). The office procedure and attached data are then shipped to the selected server site(s) (*migration*). With parallel execution, additional techniques are necessary. Either office procedure object and attachments have to be replicated under explicit replication and update control, or the object and its attachments have to be split according to their specified use by the selected servers. In the second case, the execution graph has to be extended by a specification of the required data objects or data slots for each service request. Then the service is invoked and the required slots of the data section are accessed (*invocation*). Finally, result data are written into appropriate slots of the data section (*output handling*). Afterwards, the routing step is performed again until the final service is completed. In the *termination phase*, the initiator is notified and the result data are stored according to the termination section of the office procedure specification.

*Execution control:* Office procedures may have very long execution times (in the order of days to weeks). Therefore, online execution control is important. Some approaches offer specific features for remote control; thus a user can access and analyze office procedures that were initiated by him or her or that require personal attention. Typical operations required for this task are as follows: (1) *Retrieval functions:* office procedures must be accessible by logical names globally within the whole distributed system; as a result, a unique identifier is delivered that enables remote, location-independent access to an office procedure. (2) *Status enquiries:* a retrieved office procedure can then be analyzed concerning its execution history (e.g. list of visited servers), its current binding, and its current location. (3) *Data access:* attached data can be accessed and possibly modified remotely. (4) *Continuous execution monitoring:* in this mode, a user is always notified by an event whenever an office procedure moves to a new server; he or she can thus keep track of the ongoing execution.

**System architecture:** We give an impression of a system architecture for implementing the characteristics summarized above based on personal experience. The architecture is shown in figure 2-13 and consists of several distributed systems components. The upper part of the figure represents office procedure specification and development, the lower part represents runtime execution.

Initially, the office service and server environment and the types of available office procedures are specified using a declarative notation. The specifications are transformed into an internal representation which is accessible via a global directory service. In addition, the office procedure specifications are available to the nodes involved in office procedure execution, i.e. the nodes hosting servers and the nodes hosting *control stations*. Control stations offer user interfaces to perform initiation and monitoring of office procedure execution. Each node has basic runtime mechanisms for office procedure management and distributed object interaction mechanisms available.

At runtime, the components interact as follows: a control station initiates an office procedure execution, contacts the directory service in order to locate the first execution server, invokes a handler operation of that server and transfers the office procedure and its attached data objects to the server by object migration. After having performed the service, the server acts similarly: it locates the next server via the directory service and transfers control and office procedure data to it. At any time, a control station can invoke control operations on an office procedure or on a server by remote object invocation.

The architecture is based on a completely decentralized approach. Except for the directory service, no logically centralized component is included. Even the directory service can be implemented in a physically decentralized way by dividing name management into several subdomains assigned to different servers (see chapter 3). These properties are very important for scalability. The notation used for office procedure specification are described in chapter 8.

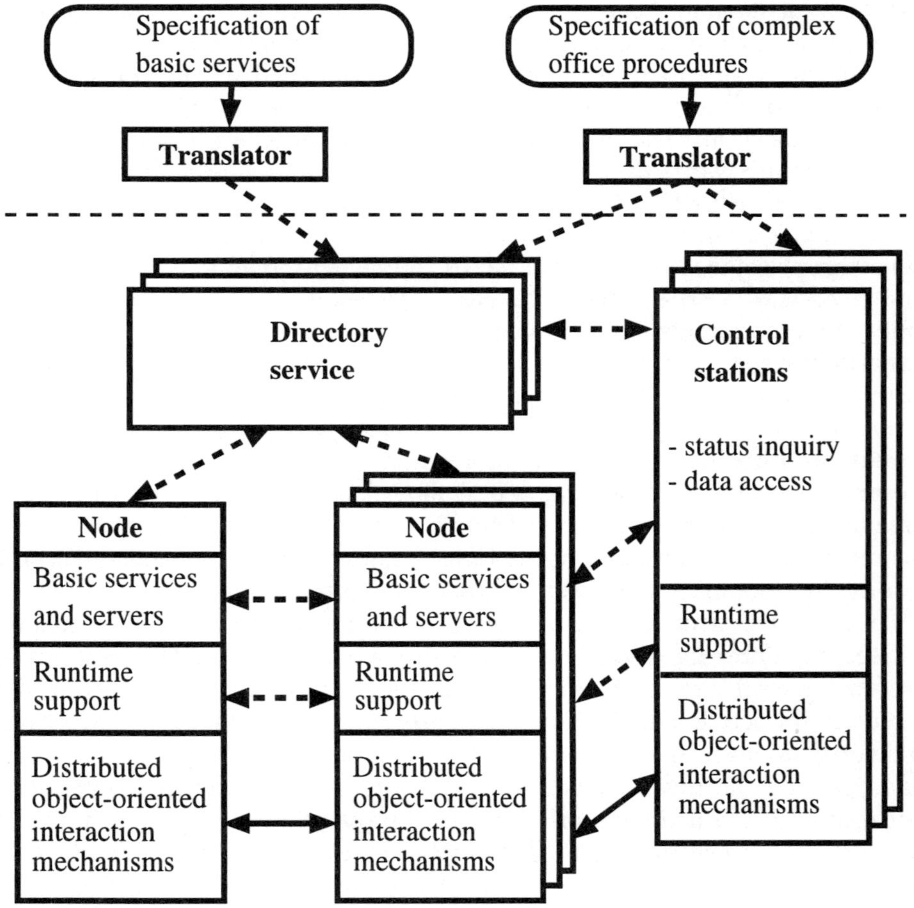


Fig. 2-13 Architecture of distributed office procedure support system

**System comparison:** In the area of distributed office procedures, several existing systems including our own *IPSO* approach [SCH91] are compared below.

*Action Paths:* The *Action Paths* approach [ART90] of DEC Littleton introduces a distributed systems architecture and sophisticated binding facilities for complex distributed services and office procedures. An *action path* corresponds to an instance of an office procedure. The basic services are provided by so-called *principals*. Each node of an action path is called an *action stop*. For each action stop (i.e. service request), either an abstract *role* can be given which is dynamically bound to a principal at runtime, or an instance of a principal can be specified directly. Service execution can be controlled by timeouts; after timeout expiry, the executing principal is reminded by special messages. Special aspects of the approach are the use of a reliable distributed directory service, support for persistent checkpoints of attached data before executing a service, implementation of termination actions after termination of an office procedure, and exception handling in case of unexpected outcome of a service execution.

As opposed to our basic conceptual description, the approach does not specify the explicit operations to be performed by each principal but only the principals or their roles. That is, the principals themselves decide which operations to perform. This may improve flexibility but can also lead to lack of control, especially in very well-structured office procedures.

*PAGES/DIMUN:* The *PAGES* system [HEA90] within project *DIMUN* was developed at the University of Helsinki. It supports migrating forms that move between distributed operational agents. Each agent handles a dedicated set of form types; resulting type restrictions have to be obeyed when requesting migration of forms. Agents are implemented in a high-level language which includes specification of form forwarding. For local office procedure coordination, agents can maintain data structures of a special class named *project*. An object of this class manages all local history information of a given office procedure. However, no explicit global representation of an overall office procedure is supported; office procedures result implicitly from distributed agent cooperation.

Special features of the approach are graphical support for form editing, a facility for defining new form classes dynamically, and an event/trigger mechanism to activate agent programs based on time or e-mail events. Agent autonomy is emphasized by the fact that each agent is free to define subclasses of form classes to handle arriving forms in a customized way. For example, a manager could define a subclass of travel expense form which has an operation to check whether given expense limits were exceeded.

*Electronic Circulation Folders (ECF):* The *ECF* approach [KRW90] of the Munich Technical University implements so-called electronic circulation folders that move between processing sites. An ECF comprises a complete execution graph with explicit specification of the locations where the requested services should be performed. Each ECF has an explicit representation at runtime and can also have attached documents.

Special features of the system are facilities for starting new ECFs during ECF execution (e.g. to refine tasks), time conditions for execution control, and support for graphical specification of ECFs. In addition, special operations for execution control are offered; these include delegation of service execution, refusing of execution, or canceling of overall ECFs.

*Message Management System (MMS):* The *MMS* system [MAL84] of the University of Toronto supports the specification of complex message routing between so-called *processing sites* in a distributed environment. A high-level specification notation is offered for this. Based on these facilities, office procedures can be implemented on top of it.

The specification notation allows for complex conditions to control execution of alternatives. For example, conditions can include the number of message iterations or the arrival of other specific messages at a processing site. At runtime, it is possible to track message routing remotely. A pre-defined message routing (specified in the high-level notation) can also be modified before starting a message instance. Overall, the system provides a high level of flexibility and can also be used to implement less structured office procedures.

*Intelligent Routers:* The *Intelligent Routers* system [WVF89] of Siemens Corporate Research is based on a very different computational model: the implementation of basic services is shipped together with an office procedure (called *router*) to the distributed processing sites. This is made possible by using an interpreted notation (*Manufacturing Programming Language 1, MPL.1*). A router program comprises the basic services and the rules which control the migration steps. The notation is executed by *interpreters* which can be located on *heterogeneous* network nodes, especially with different operating systems (Unix, OpenVMS and Windows). In contrast, most other system only support office procedures in homogeneous environments. Routers can also be replicated in order to achieve a limited level of fault tolerance.

*OTM:* The *OTM* approach [LHW88] of the University of Toronto supports the specification of hierarchical office tasks based on an object-oriented model of computation. A *task* or *subtask* can access documents in hierarchical *folders*. Therefore, hierarchy is supported both for office procedures and for attached data. A high-level language named *Officeaid* supports retrieval and reuse of existing task definitions. Persistent data management is provided by the OZ+ database system. However, the system does not explicitly address *distributed* computation.

*EuroCoOp:* The *EuroCoOp* activity coordination model and toolkit [HKE92] supports both strongly and weakly structured office procedures. The basic construct is a *task* that can be decomposed into subtasks in a hierarchical way. Each task has a set of attributes associated with it, for example an actor (the person responsible for the task), a deadline, an expected duration, a start and end condition, and a current status. Each task executes within a logical context that describes the participants involved, resources (e.g. accessed data objects), and external human observers. Task execution can be distributed among several network nodes, using X.400 message handling and X.500 directory services (see chapter 3). Task descriptions can even be changed dynamically at runtime, making the approach very flexible.

*IPSO:* Our own approach [SCH91] provides a high-level notation for office procedure specification (see chapter 8). Specific features of the notation are attribute-based service binding requests, conditional service execution, extended facilities for attached data handling, and strict separation of types and instances of servers and office procedures. Distributed runtime support is provided according to the system architecture described above. Specific runtime features are dynamic service binding based on heuristics, exception handling, timeout control, and remote execution control.

| | Execution graph | Conditional execution | Exceptions | Time control | Hierarchies | Heterogeneity | Database support |
|---|---|---|---|---|---|---|---|
| Action Paths | explicit | not directly | yes | yes | no | no | checkpoints |
| PAGES | implicit | yes | no | yes | server hierarchies | no | yes |
| ECF | explicit | yes | yes | yes | hierarchical execution graph | no | yes |
| MMS | explicit | yes | yes | yes | no | no | central log |
| Intelligent Routers | implicit | yes | no | no | no | yes | no |
| OTM | implicit | yes | yes | yes | hierarchical execution graph | no | yes |
| Euro-CoOp | implicit | not directly | no | yes | hierarchical execution graph | no | knowledge base |
| IPSO | explicit | yes | yes | yes | no | no | yes |

Table 2-5 Comparison of office procedure support systems

The different systems are compared in table 2-5. Some systems offer explicit representations of the execution graph; this facilitates office procedure specification but may limit flexibility in the case of less structured tasks. Conditional service execution is supported directly by most systems; in the Action Paths and EuroCoOp approaches, conditional execution can be implemented in an application-specific way. Most systems provide some kind of execution control based on exception handling or time control for basic service execution.

Hierarchical abstraction facilities are offered by PAGES, ECF, OTM, and EuroCoOp; this is especially important for large applications. As discussed above, the problem of heterogeneous systems is only addressed directly by the Intelligent Routers approach. Finally, some systems offer database support for persistent management of attached data. The Action Paths and MMS approaches support persistent data storage and recovery based on checkpoints and logs, respectively. The EuroCoOp system stores persistent context information about people, roles, and resources in a knowledge base.

**Technological requirements:** The technological requirements of complex office procedure support systems are very similar to the requirements of complex coordination systems (see table 2-4 above). Both approaches represent inherently distributed applications. With distributed office procedures, locating and binding of services to servers is even more important. Therefore, a more flexible distributed directory and trading service is required. Most important, it should be implemented by a collection of completely decentralized servers in order to guarantee a high degree of availability. In addition, distributed replication techniques are required if the data portion of an office procedure is submitted to several servers in parallel.

Document interchange formats are relevant if not only basic forms but also complex documents are transferred as part of the data section. Document and data interchange within such an environment can be nicely implemented by object migration. Moreover, location-independent object invocation is an important means to implement basic service invocation during office procedure execution.

Database and multimedia support is of similar importance as in complex coordination systems. At least some basic persistent storage facilities are necessary to enable storage of office procedure results and implementation of intermediate checkpoints. Static multimedia documents may be required in an application-specific way.

## 2.2 Classification of CSCW

The different CSCW areas and supporting systems can be classified according to several criteria. We first describe our classification scheme and then embed into it the areas discussed.

## 2.2.1 Classification Scheme

Several CSCW classifications can be found in the literature (see [CON87], [KRK88], and [ROB92], for example); we try to integrate, extend and adapt them in order to provide a relatively complete classification scheme (see figure 2-14) with respect to our main focus areas:

- *Coordination support:* The complexity of coordination support between the participants in a CSCW application can be *low* (basically only interactive coordination based on human interaction), *medium* (explicit support for specific, pre-defined execution/interaction patterns), or *high* (full system control of task execution).
- *Kind of coordination:* Coordination can be *guiding* (suggestion of specific task/action alternatives in advance) or *controlling* (control after task/action execution whether it conforms to an intended schedule).
- *Participants:* The participants in a CSCW application can either be *humans* (as in a conference), *human interaction tools* (e.g. for browsing in shared hypermedia applications), or *fully automated servers* (as in some distributed office procedures).
- *Data involved:* The data involved in CSCW can be conventional *digital data, conventional complex documents,* or *multimedia data* and *documents.*
- *Tasks involved:* The task that is subject to CSCW can be *highly structured* (like complex office procedures), *weakly structured* (like complex coordination problems), or *relatively unstructured* (like computer conferences).

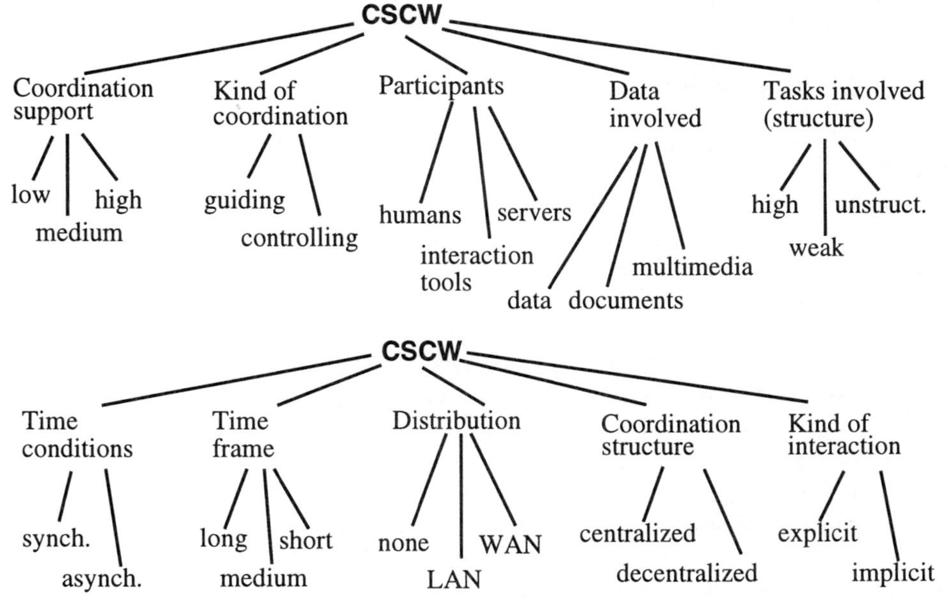


Fig. 2-14 Classification scheme for CSCW

- *Time conditions of interactions:* Interactions can be *synchronous* (i.e. they cause an explicit response within a limited time interval), or *asynchronous* (without the necessity of a response).
- *Time frame:* The overall time frame can be *long* (activities of long duration, i.e. days or weeks), *medium* (duration in the order of hours), or *short* (typically less than an hour).
- *Distribution:* An application may run on a *centralized,* local computer system, on a collection of workstations interconnected via a *local area network (LAN)*, or on a globally distributed system across a *wide area network (WAN).* The distinction between the latter two kinds becomes less important with the development of high-speed metropolitan area networks covering wide distances.
- *Coordination structure:* Coordination can be performed in a *centralized* way (usually implemented by a central instance in a distributed system) or in a *decentralized* way (distributed among several control instances).
- *Kind of interaction:* Interactions between participants can be *explicit* (based on message exchange) or *implicit* (based on access to locally or remotely shared data). This distinction is often related to the underlying interaction medium; explicit interactions are usually performed via a computer network while implicit interactions may be based on a locally shared computer system. However, this is not always necessarily true: explicit interactions can also be performed via local messages, and implicit interactions can be based on distributed and globally shared memory.

Finally, different applications can also be classified according to their overall *goal* (e.g. complex task execution, human coordination, decision finding etc.).

### 2.2.2 Classification of CSCW Approaches

The different CSCW approaches summarized in the previous sections are compared in table 2-6 according to our classification scheme.

*Coordination support* for cooperative work is most sophisticated in complex coordination systems and in office procedure support systems. In such systems the typical kind of computer supported coordination is concerned with the relationship between many different office activities and provides ways to manage their causal order or their explicitly parallel execution. Group decision support applications, multiuser editors, and multiuser hypertext/hypermedia systems usually provide less sophisticated coordination support; this is typically concerned with controlling multiuser access to shared data and with supporting basic user-to-user interactions. Most conference support systems provide only basic coordination support and often rely on human coordination.

The *kind of coordination* is controlling in most CSCW applications; for example, a multiuser hypertext system makes sure that no conflicting updates of the hypermedia graph can be performed by different users concurrently. However, in complex coordination and office procedure systems, an advanced kind of guiding coordination can be found: the system proposes and/or enforces subsequent steps of a complex activity or of a complex interaction protocol. In some group decision support systems, this kind of guidance is present, too, especially when stepwise decision finding is supported explicitly.

The *participants* in a cooperation group are mostly humans who are supported by interactive cooperation tools in some cases (e.g. for descision finding in GDSS or for coordinated browsing in hypertext). In contrast, fully or patly automated servers are also found in complex coordination and office procedure systems.

| | Conferences | GDSS | Multiuser editors | Hypertext | Complex coord. | Office proc. |
|---|---|---|---|---|---|---|
| Coordination support | low to medium | medium | medium | medium | high | high |
| Kind of coordination | control | guiding | control | control | guiding | guiding |
| Participants | humans | humans / tools | humans | humans / tools | tools / servers | tools / servers |
| Data involved | audio, video, doc. | data, documents | doc., static media | doc., static media | data, doc. | documents |
| Tasks involved | unstructured | weak | weak | weak | high or weak | high |
| Time conditions | synch. or asynch. | synch. or asynch. | synch. or asynch. | asynch. | asynch. | asynch. |
| Time frame | short to medium | medium explicit | medium implicit | short implicit | medium explicit | long explicit |
| Distribution | central. or LAN/WAN | centralized or LAN | LAN | LAN | LAN or WAN | LAN |
| Coordination structure | centralized | centralized | centralized | partially decentral. | decentralized | decentralized |
| Kind of interaction | explicit | explicit | implicit | implicit | explicit | explicit |
| Overall goal | collecting opinions / results | finding decisions | coordinated data manipul. | retrieval/ structuring of data | solving complex problems | solving structured problems |

Table 2-6 Classification of CSCW approaches

The *data involved* are mostly structured documents. Pure digital data are also relevant for controlling cooperative work and for generating derived document contents (e.g. via spreadsheets). Many CSCW applications also tend to be enhanced with multimedia data; in teleconferences, dynamic audio and video are important while other applications are mostly limited to static media like graphics and still images.
The *tasks involved* are usually highly structured in office procedure support systems. Less structured tasks can be partly automated by complex coordination systems. Multiuser editing, joint use of a hypertext system, and GDSS tasks are usually much less structured, while computer supported conferences are of very unstructured nature.

The *time conditions* of interactions are asynchronous in most applications; although there are causal dependencies betweeen different user actions, there is no *synchronous* reaction by different users in hypertext or office procedure systems etc. Only in conferences and in some kinds of group decision support systems are synchronous interactions found. The instantaneous remote display of changes in multiuser editors is a simple kind of synchronous interaction, too.

The overall *time frame* of CSCW is rather long in distributed office procedures (consider long-duration activities involving many cooperating peers). In contrast, a typical hypertext navigation or computer supported conferences may last only for a short time. The other applications usually have a medium time frame.

Concerning *distribution,* most applications are executed on a local area network; conferences and GDSS can also be of purely centralized, local nature. Some of the complex coordination systems can be used in a wide area network environment, too. In the future, most CSCW applications will tend to be used in larger networks as the gap between LAN and WAN performance narrows.

The *coordination structure* follows these characteristics; in networked hypertext, coordination, and office procedure environments, it is more decntralized than in conferences, GDSS, and multiuser editors. For example, distributed office procedure execution is controlled by autonomous servers, each deciding upon the next steps of execution of a particular office procedure. Similarly, in distributed hypertext systems, the server hosting a particular hypertext subgraph controls navigation within that subgraph autonomously.

The *kind of interaction* is implicit by accessing and modifying shared data in multiuser editors and shared hypertext. In contrast, explicit interaction is typical in most other CSCW applications.

Finally, the *overall goal* associated with CSCW varies depending on the application. Opinion and decision finding is typical in conferences and GDSS. Coordinated data manipulation, structuring, and retrieval is the major goal of multiuser editors and hypertext systems, while coordinated joint problem-solving is the major goal of complex coordination and office procedure approaches.

## 2.3 Exercises

1. [Basic knowledge]
Define the following terms:
- CSCW
- groupware
- group decision support
- hypertext.

2. [Basic knowledge]
Outline the differences between teleconferences and computer conferences with respect to the following criteria:
- synchronous/asynchronous interactions
- computer interaction (actual involvement of a computer system)
- number of participants (typical participant population)
- multimedia support (concerning transferred data).

3. [Conceptual design]
Develop the structure of a group decision support session based on the GroupSystems approach. The participants in the session are to decide whether to introduce a new product within a company. The decision itself shall be based on costs, potential market, competitor products, existing personnel resources, and existing production resources. Participants in the session are a sales manager, a production engineer, the head of the development department, and the head of the marketing department. Consider in particular the following issues:
- session planning (structure of a questionnaire, task identification, and task assignment)
- dynamic group interaction (selection of interaction modes for specific tasks, evaluation of alternatives concerning product marketing, development of a final policy concerning product introduction)
- organizational memory and individual work (structure of information files concerning various product-related aspects, appropriate tools for individual work on several tasks).

4. [Implementation]
Design and implement data structures and basic operations for a simple hypertext system. The data model is to consist of hypertext nodes with a name, up to five links to other nodes, and a pointer to arbitrary text data. User-level operations must support definition of nodes, retrieval of a "current" node by name, display of the text contents and of the names of the neighbor nodes of the current node, navigation along a link to a named neighbor node (new "current" node), and return via a link to the previous node.

5. [Implementation]
Extend the simple hypertext system to support pre-defined navigation paths. New operations are the definition of a named path originating from a hypertext node to a destination node via several intermediate nodes, the step-by-step following of a path (with display of each node's contents), the direct or step-by-step

return via the same path, and the concatenation of two paths to create a new, extended path.

6. [Conceptual design]
Apply the Coordinator model to the following example: A company named "SoftwareLab" issues an order to a company named "PrintEngine" to print 1000 copies of a reference manual. A first offer by "PrintEngine" to do the work for $3000 is rejected by "SoftwareLab", leading to a second request from "SoftwareLab" to get the work done for $2000. After "PrintEngine" accepts the order based on the modified conditions and completes the work, "SoftwareLab" is not satisfied with the quality of the last 100 copies. "PrintEngine" prints these copies again and "SoftwareLab" is finally satisfied. Draw all occurring state transitions of the Coordinator model.

7. [Conceptual design]
Define a semi-autonomous ObjectLens agent representing a sales manager's support system. The agent has three folders, named "letters", "salesOffers", and "oldCorrespondence". Formulate rules to express the following transactions:
- old letters (older than four weeks) shall be moved from "letters" to "oldCorrespondence"
- completed letters with the sales manager as their sender shall be sent to the mailroom agent
- completed sales offers shall be sent to the agent of the boss for approval if their amount is greater than $10 000.

(Use a rule notation "if <cond1> [and <cond2>] then <action>".)

8. [Conceptual design]
Develop an execution graph for an office procedure "introduction of new product". Typical steps of the procedure may be:
- market analysis
- general decision-making
- product design
- production tool design
- production planning
- marketing planning
- start of production
- start of marketing activities
- sales support
- analysis of initial marketing success.

Decide which steps can be performed in parallel (e.g. product planning and marketing planning), and which are conditional (e.g. production tool design and production planning are only relevant if the company itself produces the product). Also consider additional steps (like third-party subcontracting of the actual production) and incorporate them into your design.

9. [Basic knowledge]
Explain the following criteria of office procedure support based on the office procedure example "introduction of new product":

- explicit / implicit execution graph (show how both approaches would appear in your example)
- exceptions (give possible examples)
- hierarchies (give an example of hierarchical decomposition of the execution graph)
- time control (give realistic deadlines and resulting exception handling actions for some of the basic services).

10. [Implementation]

Design and implement data structures and an algorithm for an office procedure emulation system. Each node of an execution graph should comprise a name, a set of pointers to successors with optional conditions (for conditional execution), and a pointer to a procedure to be called to execute the basic service. An office procedure under execution should be represented as a data structure with several integer values (to be interpreted in an application-specific way for conditional execution) and with a pointer to the current basic service(s) to be executed (node of the execution graph). The conditions can be limited to simple value comparisons and should be represented in a form like "INTEGER1 LessThan INTEGER2", referring to the integer values of the office procedure's data structure. The algorithm should execute an office procedure according to a given execution graph, i.e. it should implement an interpreter for office procedures (concurrent execution must be replaced by stepwise execution unless a thread package is available on your system). Test the system implementation using the office procedure example "introduction of new product".

11. [Basic knowledge / conceptual design]

Discuss the classification of CSCW approaches given in this chapter with respect to mixed system solutions like:
- a mixed teleconference / computer conference approach
- multiuser read/write editing access to a hypertext system
- office procedure support for weakly structured tasks, involving the use of interactive GDSS tools between agents.

Do these approaches fit neatly into the classification? Discuss your opinions and modify or extend the classification schema if appropriate. Find more examples and classify them, too.

## 2.4 References

[ABD90] Abdel-Wahab, H.M.: Multiuser Tools Architecture for Group Collaboration in Computer Networks; *Computer Communications, Vol. 13, No. 3, April 1990, pp. 165-169*

[ADH93] Altenhofen, M., Dittrich, J., Hammerschmidt, R., Käppner, T., Kruschel, C., Kückes, A., Steinig, T.: The BERKOM Multimedia Collaboration Service; *ACM Conf. on Multimedia, 1993*

[AEH88] Ahuja, S.R., Ensor, J.R., Horn, D.N.: The Rapport Multimedia Conferencing System; *ACM Conf. on Office Information Systems, 1988, pp. 1-8*

[AMY88] Akscyn, R., McCracken, D., Yoder, E.: KMS: A Distributed Hypermedia System for Managing Knowledge in Organizations; *Comm. of the ACM, Vol. 31, No. 7, July 1988, pp. 820-835*

[AND94] Anderson, R.J.: Why Cryptosystems Fail; *Comm. of the ACM, Vol. 37, No. 11, Nov. 1994, pp. 32-40*

[ART90] Artsy, Y.: Routing Objects on Action Paths; *10th IEEE Int. Conf. on Distributed Computing Systems, Paris, 1990, pp. 572-579*

[BCL94] Berners-Lee, T., Cailliau, R., Luotonen, A., Nielsen, H.F., Secret, A.: The World-Wide Web; *Comm. of the ACM, Vol. 37, No. 8, Aug. 1994, pp. 76-82*

[BHI93] Bly, S.A., Harrison, S.R., Irwin, S.: MediaSpaces: Bringing People Together in a Video, Audio, and Computing Environment; *Comm. of the ACM, Vol. 36, No. 1, Jan. 1993, pp. 29-47*

[BRO90] Broderbund Software: ForComment; *Broderbund Software, Inc., San Rafael, CA, 1990*

[CJA94] Chung, G., Jeffay, K., Abdel-Wahab, H.: Dynamic Participation in a Computer-Based Conferencing System; *Computer Communications, Vol. 17, No. 1, Jan. 1994, pp. 7-16*

[COB88] Conklin, J., Begeman, M.: gIBIS: A Hypertext Tool for Exploratory Policy Discussion; *ACM Trans. on Office Information Systems, Vol. 6, No. 4, Oct. 1988, pp. 303-331*

[CON87] Conklin, J.: Hypertext: An Introduction and Survey; *IEEE Computer, Vol. 20, No. 9, Sept. 1987, pp. 17-41*

[DES86] Delisle, N., Schwartz, M.: Neptune: A Hypertext System for CAD Applications; *ACM SIGMOD Int. Conf. on the Management of Data, Washington, DC, 1986, pp. 132-143*

[ERI94] Eriksson, H.: MBone: The Multicast Backbone; *Comm. of the ACM, Vol. 37, No. 8, Aug. 1994, pp. 54-60*

[FKR93] Fish, R.S., Kraut, R.E., Root, R.W., Rice, R.E.: Video as a Technology for Informal Communication; *Comm. of the ACM, Vol. 36, No. 1, Jan. 1993, pp. 49-61*

[GAL92] Gale, S.: Desktop Video Conferencing: Technical Advances and Evaluation Issues; *Computer Communications, Vol. 15, No. 8, Oct. 1992, pp. 517-526*

[GPS93] Garzotto, F., Paolini, P., Schwabe, D.: HDM - A Model-Based Approach to Hypertext Application Design; *ACM Trans. on Information Systems, Vol. 11, No. 1, Jan. 1993, pp. 1-26*

[GRS87] Greif, I., Sarin, S.: Data Sharing in Group Work; *ACM Trans. on Office Information Systems, Vol. 5, No. 2, April 1987, pp. 187-211*

[GRT94] Gronbaek, K., Trigg, R.H.: Design Issues of a Dexter-Based Hypermedia System; *Comm. of the ACM, Vol. 37, No. 2, Feb. 1994, pp. 40-49*

[GRW92] Greif, I., Seliger, R., Weihl, W.: A Case Study of CES: A Distributed Collaborative Editing System Implemented in Argus; *IEEE Trans. on Software Engineering, Vol. 18, No. 9, Sept. 1992, pp. 827-839*

[HAS94] Halasz, F.G., Schwartz, M.: The Dexter Hypertext Reference Model; *Comm. of the ACM, Vol. 37, No. 2, Feb. 1994, pp. 30-39*

[HEA90] Hammainen, H., Eloranta, E., Alasuvanto, J.: Distributed Form Management; *ACM Trans. on Information Systems, Vol. 8, No. 1, Jan. 1990, pp. 50-76*

[HKE92] Hennessy, P., Kreifelts, T., Ehrlich, U.: Distributed Work Management: Activity Coordination within the EuroCoOp Project; *Computer Communications, Vol. 15, No. 8, Oct. 1992, pp. 477-488*

[HKR92] Haan, B.J., Kahn, P., Riley, V.A., Coombs, J.H., Meyrowitz, N.K.: IRIS Hypermedia Services; *Comm. of the ACM, Vol. 35, No. 1, Jan. 1992, pp. 36-51*

[HMT87] Halasz, F.G., Moran, T.P., Trigg, T.H.: NoteCards in a Nutshell; *ACM Conf. on Human Factors in Computing Systems, Toronto, Canada, April 1987*

[HOR87] Horton, M.: Standard for Interchange of Usenet Messages; *Networking Group RFC 1036, Dec. 1987*

[IKG93] Ishii, H., Kobayashi, M., Grudin, J.: Integration of Interpersonal Space and Shared Workspace: ClearBoard Design and Experiments; *ACM Trans. on Information Systems, Vol. 11, No. 4, Oct. 1993, pp. 349-375*

[ISM91] Ishii, H., Miyake, N.: Toward an Open Shared Workspace: Computer and Video Fusion Approach of TeamWorkStation; *Comm. of the ACM, Vol. 34, No. 12, Dec. 1991, pp. 36-50*

[KAC92] Kaplan, S.M., Carroll, A.M.: Supporting Collaborative Processes with Conversation Builder; *Computer Communications, Vol. 15, No. 8, Oct. 1992, pp. 489-501*

[KRK88] Kraemer, K.L., King, J.L.: Computer-Based Systems for Cooperative Work and Group Decision Making; *ACM Comp. Surveys, Vol. 20, No. 2, June 1988, pp. 115-146*

[KRW90] Karbe, B., Ramsperger, N., Weiss, P.: Support of Cooperative Work by Electronic Circulation Folders; *ACM Conf. on Office Information Systems, Cambridge, MA, 1990, pp. 109-117*

[LEE93] Berners-Lee, T.: Protocol for the Retrieval and Manipulation of Textual and Hypermedia Information; *Technical Report, CERN, 1993*

[LHW88] Lochovsky, F.H., Hogg, J.S., Weiser, S.P., Mendelzon, A.O.: OTM: Specifying Office Tasks; *ACM Conf. on Office Information Systems, Palo Alto, CA, 1988, pp. 46-53*

[LMY88] Lai, K.-Y., Malone, T.W., Yu, K.-C.: ObjectLens: A Spreadsheet for Cooperative Work; *ACM Trans. on Office Information Systems, Vol. 6, No. 4, Oct. 1988, pp. 332-353*

[MAB94] Macedonia, M.R., Brutzman, D.P.: MBone Provides Audio and Video Across the Internet; *Computer, Vol. 27, No. 4, April 1994, pp. 30-36*

[MAE94] Maes, P.: Agents that Reduce Work and Information Overhead; *Comm. of the ACM, Vol. 37, No. 7, July 1994, pp. 30-40*

[MAL84] Mazer, M.S., Lochowsky, F.H.: Logical Routing Specification in Office Information Systems; *ACM Trans. on Office Information Systems, Vol. 2, No. 4, Oct. 1984, pp. 303-330*

[MIR94] Minsky, M., Riecken, D.: A Conversation with Marvin Minsky About Agents; *Comm. of the ACM, Vol. 37, No. 7, July 1994, pp.* 22-29

[NDV91] Nunamaker, J.F., Dennis, A.R., Valacich, J.S., Vogel, D.R., George, J.F.: Electronic Meeting Systems to Support Group Work; *Comm. of the ACM, Vol. 34, No. 7, July 1991, pp. 40-61*

[NIE90] Nielsen, J.: Hypertext und Hypermedia; *Academic Press, Inc., Boston, 1990*

[OPP88] Opper, S.: A Groupware Toolbox; *Byte, Vol. 13, No. 13, Dec. 1988, pp. 275-282*

[PAT92] Palme, J., Tholerus, T.: SuperKOM - Design Considerations for a Distributed, Highly Structured Computer Conferencing System; *Computer Communications, Vol. 15, No. 8, Oct. 1992, pp. 509-516*

[PFB94] Palmer, J.D., Fields, J.A., Brouse, P.L.: Multigroup Decision-Support Systems in CSCW; *Computer, Vol. 27, No. 5, May 1994, pp. 67-72*

[PYF92] Palaniappan, M., Yankelovich, N., Fitzmaurice, G., Loomis, A., Haan, B., Coombs, J., Meyrowitz, N.: The Envoy Framework: An Open Architecture for Agents; *ACM Trans. on Information Systems, Vol. 10, No. 3, July 1992, pp. 233-264*

[RES93] Resnick, P.: Phone-Based CSCW: Tools and Trials; *ACM Trans. on Information Systems, Vol. 11, No. 4, Oct. 1993, pp. 401-424*

[ROB92] Rodden, T., Blair, G.S.: Distributed Systems Support for Computer Supported Cooperative Work; *Computer Communications, Vol. 15, No. 8, Oct. 1992, pp. 527-538*

[RSV94] Reinhard, W., Schweitzer, J., Völksen, G., Weber, M.: CSCW Tools: Concepts and Architectures; *Computer, Vol. 27, No. 5, May 1994, pp. 28-36*

[SAG85] Sarin, S., Greif, I.: Computer-Based Real-Time Conferencing Systems; *Computer, Vol. 18, No. 10, Oct. 1985, pp. 33-45*

[SCH91] Schill, A.: Distributed System and Execution Model for Office Environments; *Computer Communications, Vol. 14, No. 8, Oct. 1991, pp. 478-488*

[SLH93] Schnase, J.L., Leggett, J.J., Hicks, D.L., Szabo, R.L.: Semantic Data Modeling of Hypermedia Associations; *ACM Trans. on Information Systems, Vol. 11, No. 1, Jan. 1993, pp. 27-50*

[SMK90] Shepherd, A., Mayer, N., Kuchinsky, A.: Strudel - An Extensible Electronic Conversation Toolkit; *CSCW '90 Conf., Los Angeles, 1990*

[SUM85] Sumner, M.: Organization and Management of the Information Center: Case Studies; *21st Annual Computer Personnel Research Conference, Wetherbe, J.C. (Ed.), May 1985, ACM, New York, pp. 38-49*

[TAM91] Tang, C.J., Minneman, S.L.: VideoWhiteboard: Video Shadows to Support Remote Collaboration; *Conf. on Human Interaction (CHI), New Orleans, 1991, pp. 315-322*

[UTY89] Utting, K., Yankelovich, N.: Context and Orientation in Hypermedia Networks; *ACM Trans. on Information Systems, Vol. 7, No. 1, Jan. 1989, pp. 58-84*

[VSW94] Vetter, R.J., Spell, C., Ward, C.: Mosaic and the World Wide Web; *Computer, Vol. 27, No. 10, Oct. 1994, pp. 49-57*

[VZS91] Vin, H.M., Zellweger, P.T., Swinehart, D.C., Rangan, P.V.: Multimedia Conferencing in the Etherphone Environment; *Computer, Vol. 24, No. 10, Oct. 1991, pp. 69-79*

[WIF87] Winograd, T., Flores, F.: Understanding Computers and Cognition; *Addison-Wesley, Reading, MA, 1987*

[WIN88] Winograd, T.: Where the Action is; *Byte, Vol. 13, No. 13, Dec. 1998, pp.* 255-258

[WVF89] Wolfson, C.D., Voorhees, E., Flatley, M.M.: Intelligent Routers; *9th Int. Conf. on Distributed Computing Systems, Newport Beach, 1989, pp. 371-376*

[YHM88] Yamkelovich, N., Haan, B., Meyrowitz, N., Drucker, S.: Intermedia: The Concept and the Construction of a Seamless Information Environment; *IEEE Computer, Vol. 21, No. 1, 1988, pp. 81-96*

# 3 Distributed Office Computation

Office computation in open distributed environments requires specific techniques and standards as a foundation. Examples are standardized document interchange formats or office database systems with remote access facilities. Such issues will be described in detail in later chapters. First, we focus on basic techniques required for distributed computing, namely communication services and suplemental system services. Based on these services, higher-level distributed office computation can be implemented as shown by several examples.

In general, our considerations are based on the definition of a distributed system given in chapter 1, i.e. a collection of loosely interconnected nodes. Distributed office computation is a kind of distributed application on top of such a system, consisting of a number of autonomous but cooperating software modules or processes.

In the area of communication techniques, this chapter discusses message handling systems, interprocess message passing, and remote procedure call (RPC) facilities. It then outlines how these mechanisms are augmented with distributed name management and security services. It illustrates how such techniques can be used to locate servers, for example within an office procedure, and to ensure that only authorized service invocations can be performed. More advanced distributed systems techniques and important standards are then discussed in chapter 4.

## 3.1 Basic Communication Techniques

The foundation of any distributed system is the ability to communicate between network nodes. We assume that basic end-to-end communication mechanisms of the transport layer are available; examples are the TCP/IP and the OSI TP4 transport protocols and services. Based on these services, inter-process message passing facilities can be built as described in this section. However, from an office computing point of view, higher-level communication mechanisms on top of such protocols are more important. As an example, we initially also present the X.400 message handling standard in this section.

### 3.1.1 X.400: Interpersonal Message Handling

The most basic way of communication in cooperative office systems is user-level message passing based on electronic mail. Although rather simple, this approach is one of the most important communication techniques in today's office systems. Moreover, advanced group communication mechanisms and CSCW layers can be built on top of a basic interpersonal message passing environment. For these reasons, we describe this approach first, focusing on the *X.400 standard* for *Message Handling Systems (MHS)*. A similar approach used in the Internet is *SMTP (Simple Mail Transfer Protocol)* with the recent extension *MIME (Multipurpose Internet Mail Extensions)*. X.400 has been chosen here to illustrate the overall architectural model in a generic way.

**Overview and Architectural Model:** The CCITT X.400 MHS standard (X.400-X.430) is an important base for interpersonal message passing in heterogeneous environments. It conforms to the *MOTIS (Message Oriented Text Interchange Systems)* standard of the ISO [ISO89] and to the *MIDA (Message Interchange Distributed Application)* standard of the ECMA. The standard has evolved from earlier MHS recommendations of 1984 that were improved and extended in 1988, with slight additional modifications in 1992.

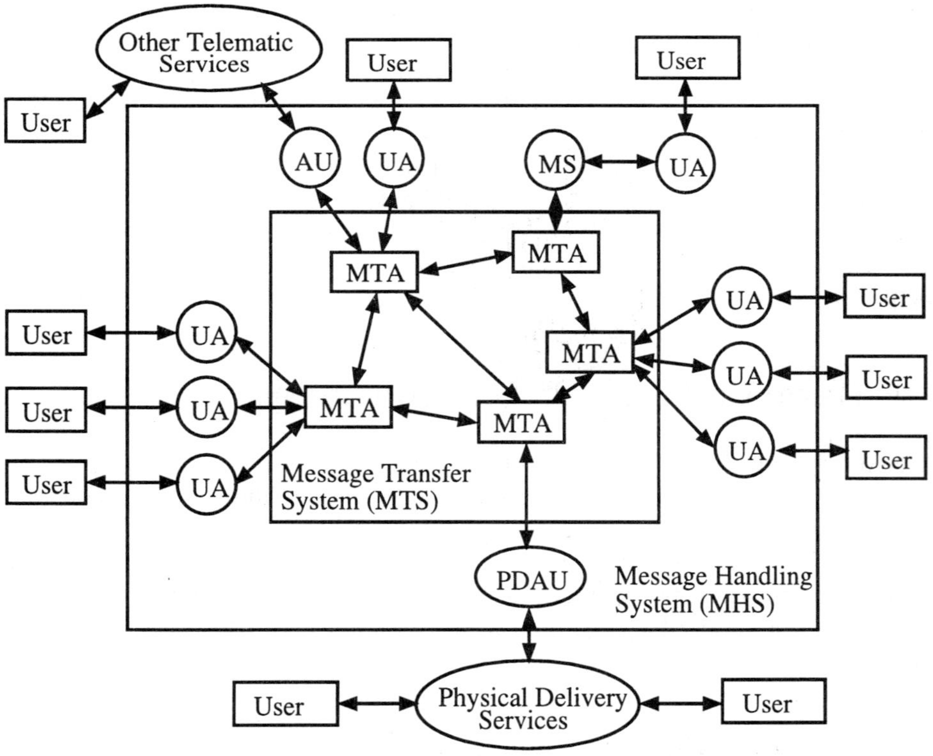


Fig. 3-1 MHS architectural model with sample configuration

MHS is based on a systems architecture as shown in figure 3-1. Message passing within a network is implemented by *Message Transfer Agents (MTAs)* based on the *Message Transfer Protocol P1* of the MHS standard. This protocol applies a store-and-forward technique for sending a message from a given system via the MTAs of several intermediate nodes to the receiver's site. If the destination system or an intermediate node is currently unavailable, message delivery is retried after a set time interval; MHS implements a reliable delivery service.

End users interact with MTAs via *User Agents (UAs)*. This separation enables decoupling of end users from network access mechanisms. In practise, UA and MTA can be implemented within the same node or even the same operating system process, or can be distributed across several nodes. For example, several UAs at various PCs can access an MHS system via a common MTA located on a host system. In this case, the *MTS Access Protocol P3* of MHS is used for UA/MTA communication.

As shown in figure 3-1, services other than interpersonal messaging can be integrated into an MHS environment. First, general *Access Units (AUs)* enable access to MHS from other Telematics services, for example from *Teletex* and *Telex*. The standard defines special access protocols for this, for example protocol *P5* for Teletex access. Second, a *Physical Delivery Access Unit (PDAU)* provides an interface to conventional mail services for forwarding MHS messages as conventional letters. An additional *Message Store (MS)* between MTA and UA can support message archiving functions. It is usually implemented on a host or workstation system with large storage capacity and may be co-located with the MTA. It mainly stores received messages when the UA system is unavailable and can also store messages to be sent if the network is currently not accessible. MS support is especially important for UA systems with limited capacity and availability.

For basic communication, MHS uses standardized ISO/OSI application layer services described in section 4.5.3, namely *ACSE, ROSE,* and *RTSE*. To retrieve the destination addresses of peer users, MHS exploits the *X.500* directory service standard (X.500-X.521). This service basically maps hierarchical logical names like */.../C=UK/O=OSF/OU=Dept1/CN=Peter* to network addresses. Its functionality is described in closer detail in section 3.3.1.

**Interpersonal Messaging Service:** A UA offers an *Interpersonal Message Service (IPM)* to the end user on top of MTS based on the *Interpersonal Messaging Protocol P2* of MHS. It provides service elements for sending and receiving messages. A message consists of a header including address information and a body including the actual message text. Detailed service elements are available for controlling message transfer. These can be selected via specific header fields of an X.400 message. Table 3-1 gives an overview of some important service elements.

| Service elements | Semantic meaning |
|---|---|
| IP-Message-ID | Globally unique identifier of message |
| Originator Indication | Sender address shown to receiver |
| Authorizing Users Indication | Names of people who authorized the sender |
| Primary and Copy Recipients | Primary receiver and receivers of copy (cc:) |
| Blind Copy Recipients | Other receivers remaining anonymous |
| Reply Request Indication | Request for a reply by given deadline |
| Receipt Notification | Request for a receipt acknowledgement |
| Non-receipt Notification | Notify if message is undeliverable |
| Replying IP-Message Indication | Message is a reply to a previous message |
| Obsoleting Indication | Declare previous messages as obsolete |
| Cross-referencing Indication | Cross-reference to other message via ID |
| Subject Indication | Subject description of message |
| Expiry Date Indication | Specifies expiry of given message |
| Importance Indication | Specifies importance level of message |
| Sensitivity Indication | Specifies sensitivity level of message |
| Auto-forwarded Indication | Message was forwarded automatically |

Table 3-1 Service elements for X.400 messages

The service elements are specified by filling the associated header fields of an X.400 message with appropriate values. Basically, the header specifies all control information required for message transfer. Each message has a globally unique *Interpersonal Message Identifier (IPM-ID)*, usually generated by the sender's UA. The IPM-ID is mainly used for message cross-referencing and for relating replies to previous messages. The *Originator Indication* contains the sender address that is shown to the receiver. For sensitive messages, specific users who authorized the sender can also be given; this option might be used when a secretary sends a message by order of her boss to some other manager. Moreover, regular recipients of a copy (the usual *cc:* option) and recipients of a copy whose names are not shown to the other recipients *(blind copy recipients)* can be specified.

The sender can specify a request for a reply within a given time frame, can request a basic acknowledgement of receipt, and can also request to be informed when the message cannot be delivered. Messages can be interrelated in several ways: a message can be a reply to a previous message; a message can declare former messages as obsolete; and it can contain an application-specific cross-reference to another message.

As usual, each message can have a subject indication. Moreover, an expiry date and time for the message can be given if its contents are only of temporary validity. Finally, several levels of importance and sensitivity can be specfied to guide message handling at the receiver's site. An auto-forwarded indication gives the receiver the information that the message was directed to someone else and was auto-forwarded by the system. Auto-forwarding can be specified by users while they are absent from their office.

The body of an IPM typically contains ASCII text based on the ISO IA5 alphabet. However, other *body types* are also supported by the standard, although not all X.400 implementations enable their transfer. Body type examples are Teletex documents and full ODA (Open Document Architecture) documents (see chapter 5). ODA documents can contain structured text as well as graphics and bitmaps. The X.400 body parts can be encrypted if sensitive information is transferred; encryption is indicated by an additional *Body Part Encryption Indication.*

**Use of MHS in Cooperative Office Environments:** MHS offers an easy-to-use interpersonal messaging service for heterogeneous computer systems. In office environments, it can be used for basic information transmission up to complex document transfer based on ODA. By building automatic message handling tools on top of MHS user interfaces, some of the CSCW applications discussed in chapter 2 can even be implemented directly.

For example, complex office procedure requests can be transferred between office agents via X.400. An X.400 message must contain some application-specific encoding of the requested task, of a given deadline, of related data and document information, and of other control data. Similarly, complex coordination systems with application-dependent message forwarding can be implemented by operating system shell programs on top of X.400.

However, X.400 only serves as a very basic communication mechanism. It does not support any semantic context regarding the given CSCW application. For example, it is completely application-dependent in interpreting received messages. Moreover, the integration of automatic servers (like print servers or document servers) into an MHS environment is difficult and cannot really be implemented efficiently. Direct inter-process communication as required in distributed multiuser editors or distributed hypermedia systems must be based on other system-level communication mechanisms. For these reasons, we focus on RPC as the primary mechanism in this area but also discuss interprocess message passing in the following sections.

### 3.1.2 Message Passing between Processes

Interprocess message passing mechanisms serve as direct program-to-program interaction techniques; basically, a process sends a message to a remote location where the receipt of the message triggers a program-level action of a peer process. Within this approach, many variations exist; a coarse-grained classification can be made into direct and indirect message passing techniques.

**Direct message passing:** With *direct message passing*, untyped one-way messages are directly sent to a peer process or to several processes (*multicast* or *broadcast*) as pure bytestreams. The destination address of a message consists of the destination node and of a process identifier within that node. The receiver can either perform an anonymous receive operation, willing to receive messages from anyone, or can also give the address of the desired sender explicitly. An example of direct message passing between processes *P1* (example: conference participant) and *P2* (example: conference manager) is given by the following code (P1 and P2 are full process addresses):

| **Process P1** (conference participant): | **Process P2** (conference manager): |
|---|---|
| send <message> to P2 | receive <message> [ from P1 ] |

The major problem of direct message passing is the lack of reconfigurability. For example, if P2 at server machine S2 is replaced by P3 at server machine S3, P1 will not be able to get its messages redirected to P3 transparently. The implementation of P1 would have to be changed, a fact that is undesirable for large office applications.

A *multicast send* operation with direct message passing has several destination processes as its argument. Similarly, a receive operation can give several processes indicating that the receiver is willing to accept messages from any of these peers (*multi-receive*). A *broadcast send* operation does not need a destination specification; the message is just sent to any reachable process. Examples of multicast, multi-receive, and broadcast are as follows:

| **Process P1:** | **Process P2:** |
|---|---|
| send <message> to P2, P3, P4 | receive <message> from P1, P6 |
| broadcast <message> // to all receivers | |

Direct message passing is the most basic communication mechanism and can generally be used for all kinds of remote interactions in cooperative office environments. Examples are messages between participants in a distributed conference or decision support systems or messages between office procedure servers. However, this very basic communication level is not an adequate abstraction from the software engineering point of view. Higher-level mechanisms described below facilitate implementation and evolution of cooperative office systems significantly.

**Indirect message passing:** The reconfiguration problem of direct message passing can be addressed by introducing an additional level of indirection between peers who wish to communicate. Existing approaches can be classified as *mailbox-* and *port-*based.

A *mailbox* is an intermediate communication buffer between two or more processes. It can physically be implemented at any site but is often co-located with a receiver process. Mailboxes are addressed by shared names both by senders and by receivers. Therefore, processes do not name communication peers explicitly but rather specify the well-known mailbox name for send and receive operations:

**Process P1:** **<mailbox>** **Process P2:**
send <message> to <mailbox> ------> | ------> receive <message> from <mailbox>

The well-known mailbox name can be established by hard-coding it, or, more flexibly, by querying it from a name service based on descriptive information (e.g. mailbox for establishing a communication session within "*area = department 1*").

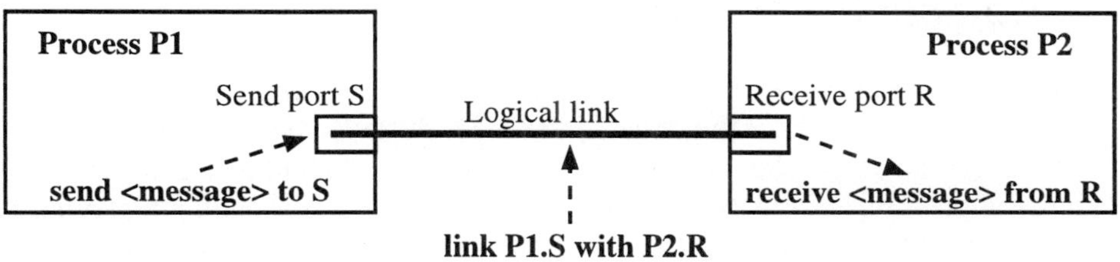


Fig. 3-2 Port-based indirect communication

The *port-based* approach introduces local communication ports for each process, often divided into *send ports* and *receive ports* (see figure 3-2). Send and receive ports of different processes are linked explicitly by application management commands, establishing *logical links*. A message submitted to a local send port is automatically forwarded via such a logical link to a remote receive port. Therefore, destination addressing is performed implicitly based on a pre-defined application configuration specified by a system/application manager.

After the ports are created (not shown here), they are linked by the indicated *link* command. Now messages can be exchanged just by specifying the send or receive port local to the respective process. Some systems offer an additional *test* operation for the receiver in order to test whether a message is available without becoming blocked. In systems like *Conic* [KMS89] (cf. section 4.4), ports and messages can also be *typed;* that is, it can be specified which types of messages a port can handle, and which structure the message layout has. The major advantage is that the system can check whether a logical link is established between type-compatible ports and can refuse any other kinds of links.

In summary, mailbox-oriented message passing is suitable for distributed applications with more dynamically-coupled cooperating processes; the relationships between processes and mailboxes can be established and modified dynamically and directly by the application. Port-based message passing is based on a more static configuration with explicit inter-port links. Although dynamic reconfigurations are possible, they usually require explicit management operations. This approach is more suitable for relatively self-contained distributed applications.

In the context of cooperative office applications, a distributed computer conference with dynamic group membership can be well supported by mailbox communication. In contrast, a relatively fixed server population jointly offering a complex office procedure service can benefit from port-based communication with a pre-defined, relatively static configuration. In addition to an explicit configuration representation, message-type consistency of communicating peers is enforced, and facilitates coupling of distributed processes.

## 3.2 Remote Procedure Call

A common system model in cooperative office environments is the *client/server model* of distributed processing (see figure 3-3). A server typically offers a service to a population of clients (e.g. a service such as "document formatting" or "document printing"). A client can make use of a service by sending a service request message to a suitable server. The server performs its service and finally sends a service response back to the client. The request can comprise input parameters (like a document to be formatted) and the response can contain output parameters (like a status indication).

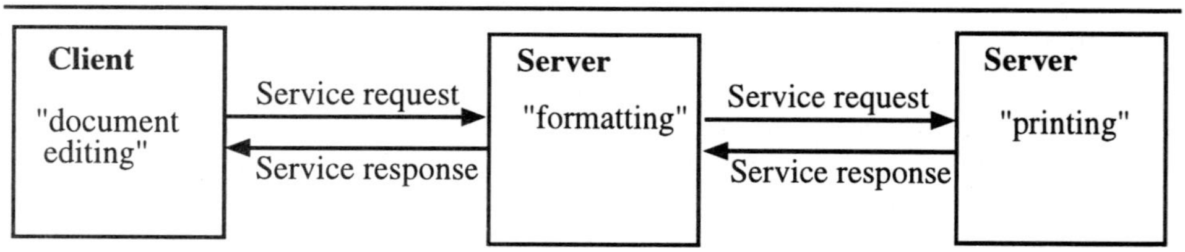


Fig. 3-3 Client/server model with delegation

As shown in the figure, a server can also act as a client of another service. For example, the document formatting server could request a print service in order to offer complete document processing functionality to its client; This mode is called *delegation*.

In this section, the *remote procedure call (RPC)* as an important implementation base of the client/server model is described in more detail. After some basic foundations and a definition, we present a typical RPC system architecture, interface definition facilities, important runtime aspects, and a comparison of several existing systems.

### 3.2.1 Foundations and Definition

The *remote procedure call (RPC)* is the most common implementation of client/server interactions. A service offered by an RPC server consists of a bunch of procedures that represent the interface of a service. Service request and response correspond to remote procedure invocation and return. Syntactically, a remote procedure call is almost identical to a local procedure invocation. The system maps an invocation onto flat communication messages, transparently sends them to the server site, and handles the response in the same way. The major abstractions of RPC as opposed to basic message passing are transparent handling of parameters, transparent procedure invocation at the server site, and automatic association of request and response at the client site.

More precisely, RPC has been defined as a "*synchronous language-level transfer of control between programs in disjoint address spaces whose primary communication medium is a narrow channel*" [NEL81]. As a synchronous mechanism, RPC in its basic form blocks the caller until an invocation is completed, i.e. until the server has returned the results. The existence of separate address spaces linked via a narrow communication channel (with limited throughput) emphasizes that a loosely-coupled distributed system is the typical target environment of RPC (as opposed to a tightly coupled multiprocessor with shared memory or with high-speed bus links).

Due to the importance and wide use of the RPC, we present its conceptual foundations and its implementation in some detail. In particular, we discuss basic RPC system architecture, procedure interface definitions, server initialization, RPC binding, and call semantics. The RPC of the OSF Distributed Computing Environment (DCE) [OSF94a] is used as an example system (see section 4.5.1 for an architectural description of the OSF DCE). We also compare several other RPC approaches and later discuss related standardization efforts.

In cooperative office systems, RPC facilitates the implementation of all kinds of office servers. For example, each basic service of a distributed office procedure environment can be mapped onto an RPC server, using delegation for forwarding service requests between servers. As another example, interactions between clients and a multiuser document editor can be implemented via RPC; the service consists of a set of editing procedures and the server synchronizes concurrent RPC invocations. For instance, a very simple interaction between client and server to open a document could have the following structure (including an operation to locate a suitable server for RPC binding):

| **Client:** | **Server:** |
|---|---|
| server = locate ("SharedDocumentEditor"); | |
| openDocument (server, "my_document"); | openDocument (...) {...} |
| // invocation | // implementation |

In the following, we discuss how this interaction can be supported by concrete system architectures and runtime mechanisms.

### 3.2.2 RPC System Architecture

A typical RPC system consists of the following components:

- *Interface definition support:* An interface definition notation is offered to specify the procedure interface of an RPC server. Usually, a compiler is available for this notation that generates code for preparing RPC invocations for network transmission.
- *Runtime support* (see figure 3-4; cf. [BIN84]): At runtime, an RPC invocation of an application program is encoded by the client and transferred to the server site, executed by a server process within the server program, and finally returned with the results to the client. The encoding/decoding phases are performed by so-called *stub components* of client and server, generated by the compiler of the interface definition language. The server stub also allocates processes for executing procedures at the server site; multithreaded servers with several such processes can serve multiple clients concurrently. The actual network transmission is performed by a dedicated *communication component* at both sites.
- *Directory service:* In order to support dynamic binding of servers to client requests, a directory service is required. Such a service maps logical names and optional descriptive attributes to network addresses of matching entities. In order to support such a mapping request (*import* operation) of a client, a server must *export* its identity and characteristics to the directory service beforehand.

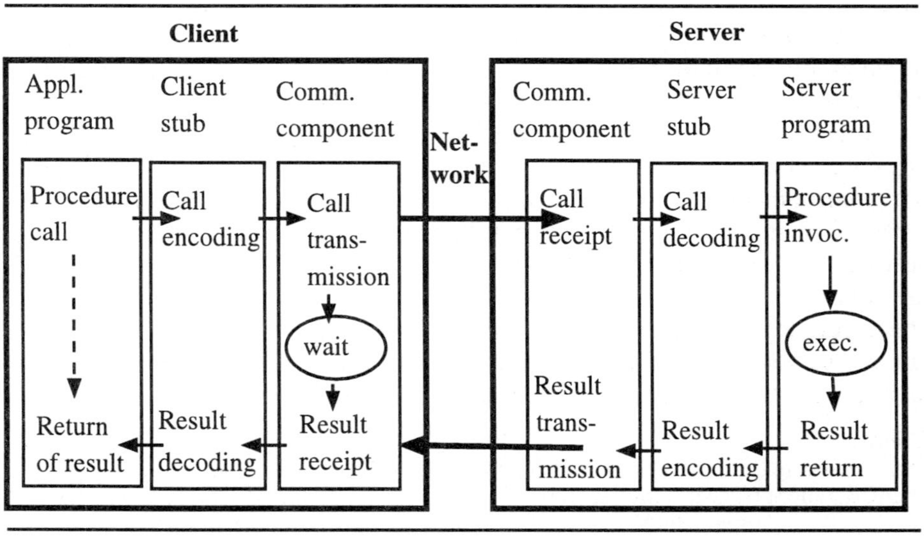


Fig. 3-4 General structure of RPC runtime support

In the following, we give examples of the interface definition language, for RPC runtime functions, and of export/import operations based on DCE RPC. Details of robust directory service implementation are discussed in section 3.3.1.

### 3.2.3 Interface Definition and Stub Generation

An RPC interface definition must specify all types of parameters used in procedures invoked remotely, and the exact signature of these procedures. In addition, RPC-specific attributes can exist that specify details of how to handle an RPC, e.g. concerning node and network faults, or concerning transfer of nested parameter structures. High-level programming languages already support many of these issues within their declarative part. However, some syntactic and semantic details have to be added.

The interface definition language (*IDL*) of the OSF DCE is based on C but introduces additional attributes and conventions. The following example specifies a simplified interface of a conference management server. It supports operations for joining an online conference, for leaving it, and for querying for a list of participants:

```
[
uuid(F418EB9C-A6A1-11CB-9185-08002B1C5088),
version(1.0)
]
interface Conference                    // Interface for conference management
  {
  import "globaldef.idl";               // Import of general IDL definitions

  const long maxMembers = 20;           // Maximum number of members
  typedef [string] char *String;        // Data type for character strings

  typedef struct {                      // Data type for conference participant
     String name;                       // Participant name
     long position;                     // Professional position of participant
     long deptNo;                       // Department number
  } Participant;

  typedef struct {                      // Data type for conferences
     String name;                       // Name of conference
     String subject;                    // Conference subject
     Participant *members [maxMembers]; // Members of conference (participants)
  } Conference;

  void joinConference (                 // RPC operation to join a conference
     [in] Conference *c;                // Conference to be joined
     [in] Participant *p;               // Participant wishing to join conference
     [out] long *status );              // Status return value

  void leaveConference (                // RPC operation to leave a conference
     [in] Conference *c;                // Conference to be left
```

```
    [in] Participant *p;                  // Participant wishing to leave conf.
    [out] long *status );                 // Status return value

  [idempotent] void getParticipants (     // RPC op. to get list of participants
    [in] Conference *c;                   // Conference to be queried
    [out] Participant *p[maxMembers];     // Returned list of participants
    [out] long *status );                 // Status return value
}
```

The interface definition first consists of a header. It specifies a global identity of the interface (*uuid = universal unique identifier)*, and a version number controlling compatible upgrades to new software versions. Several other global attributes are supported by IDL.

The actual interface body introduces C constants and data types for strings, participants, and conferences. A string type (null-terminated string) is explicitly distinguished from a general memory pointer by the attribute "*[string]*". The conference management operations are basically C-style definitions; however, input ("*[in]*") and output ("*[out]*") parameters are explicitly distinguished and full type information is given. Moreover, the *getParticipants* operation is marked as having *idempotent* semantics; this allows for a more efficient implementation. In particular, invocations can be repeated after network failures without having to eliminate duplicates; an idempotent operation does not have side-effects when invoked multiply. Other attributes like *maybe* for operations without a return value are also supported.

Most other RPC systems are based on a similar approach. For example, the *SUN RPC* offers the interface definition language *RPCL* [COR90], and an RPC on top of the *MACH* distributed operating system uses the *Matchmaker* language [JOR86]. The latter approach also supports the definition of *exceptions* within a procedure interface.

### 3.2.4 Runtime Aspects

In addition to the interface definition and stub generation facilities, dedicated runtime support is required both for the client and the server. Moreover, the possible failure characteristics of network communication have to be considered in detail. These aspects are discussed in this subsection.

**Server initialization:** The server part of an RPC application has to perform some initializations before being able to perform remote RPC communication. In particular, the server must get access to underlying network protocols, register its procedure interface with the RPC runtime system, and *export* its interface to a directory service. This enables the client to *import* the interface and retrieve the server address, and to perform actual RPC invocations. In general, both parties must access the directory service in order to perform dynamic binding; this is summarized in figure 3-5.

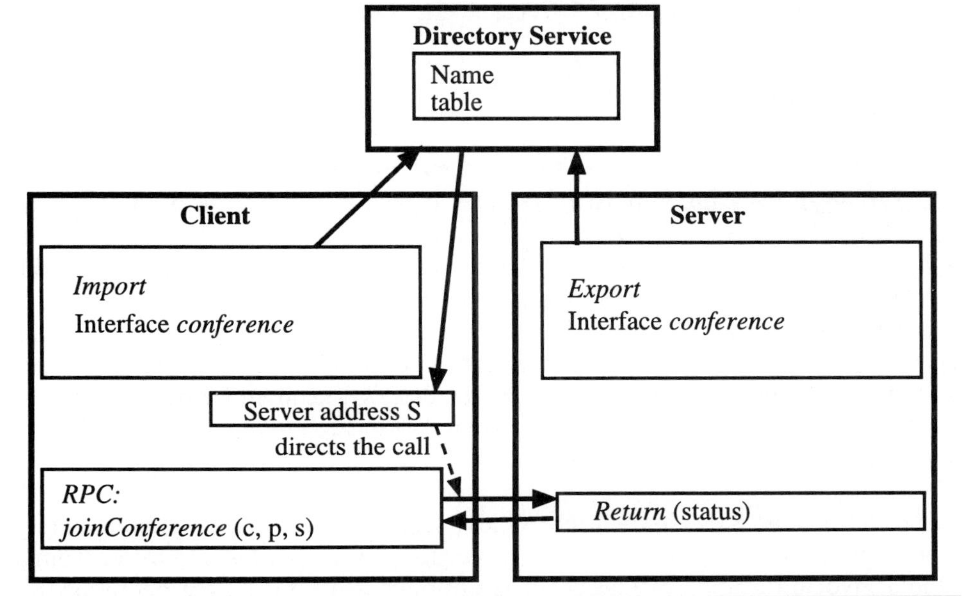


Fig. 3-5 RPC binding and invocation

The server address returned from the directory service is internally used for directing the invocation to the correct node and process. With DCE RPC, this information is embedded in so-called *binding handles*. The following code shows details of a typical server initialization with DCE RPC:

```
#include "conference.h"                      // Generated by the IDL compiler

#define entryName "/.:/ConferenceServer"    // Name of server's directory entry
#define maxConcCalls 5                       // Max. number of concurrent invoc.

main ()
  {
  unsigned status;                           // Return status
  rpc_binding_vector_t *bVec;                // Vector of binding handles

  // *** Perform some local initializations (not detailed here)

  // *** Get the actual vector of binding handles: ***
  rpc_server_inq_bindings (&bVec, &status);

  // *** Register the interface with a machine-local RPC manager process: ***
  rpc_ep_register (Conference_v1_0_s_ifspec, bVec, NULL, NULL, &status);
```

```
// *** Export the interface to the directory service under the given name: ***
rpc_ns_binding_export (rpc_c_ns_syntax_default , entryName,
        Conference_v1_0_s_ifspec, bVec, NULL, &status);

// *** Now be ready to accept incoming invocations concurrently: ***
rpc_server_listen (maxConcCalls, &status);
}
```

After some local initializations, the acquired binding handle of the interface *(rpc_server_inq_bindings)* must be registered with a system process local to the server's machine (*rpc_ep_register; ep = "endpoint")*; this process dispatches actual invocations to server processes later. Then the binding information for the interface is exported to the directory service (*rpc_ns_binding_export*) and is stored in a name table there. Finally, the server is ready to accept invocations (*rpc_server_listen*). Internally, a multithreaded server implementation is provided by DCE, with a maximum number of threads specified by *maxConcCalls*. Concurrent invocations exceeding this limit are stored intermediately before being served.

**Client setup and RPC invocation:** Client setup with DCE RPC is comparably simple; basically, client code for local invocations does not have to differ from a remote invocation implementation. It is only necessary to tell the operating system under which name to locate the server during binding. Under Unix, this is achieved by initializing a dedicated environment variable with the server name:

```
setenv RPC_DEFAULT_ENTRY "/.:/ConferenceServer"
```

An actual invocation can then be performed by a simple, self-explaining C program; for simplicity, the actual terminal input of participant and conference data is not shown but is embedded in a local application-specific routine:

```
#include "conference.h"                    // Interface definition header file

main ()
  {
  Participant p;                           // New participant
  Conference c;                            // Conference to be joined
  long status;                             // Status value
  inputData (&c, &p);                      // Application-specific input routine
  joinConference (&c, &p, &status);        // RPC invocation
  // ... check status value and handle errors
  }
```

DCE RPC also operates in heterogeneous environments between machines of different vendors with different data representation formats (like ASCII vs. EBCDIC for character strings). This functionality is achieved by the "*receiver makes right*" principle, i.e. the receiver of an RPC message converts the sender's data representation into its local format. An alternative approach based on a universal transfer representation is described in section 4.5.3.

**RPC Call Semantics:** RPC systems offer different kinds of semantics in the case of node and network failures. An overall classification has been described in [SPE82] (see table 3-2) and shall be discussed here.

In general, a given RPC implementation supports one or several of these semantic classes with possible variations. "*Call*" means how often an invocation is performed at the server site, "*result*" means how often a result for a given invocation is delivered to the client. In general, multiple calls or result deliveries are possible due to call repetition after timeout.

*Maybe* semantics does not give any guarantee whether a call is actually executed in the case of failures. The client does not get status information after a failure. This semantics is useful for RPCs of low importance, e.g. to disseminate general conference status information periodically.

*At least once* semantics guarantees that temporary network failures with lost messages are tolerated; however, more than one execution and result may be generated. This semantics is appropriate for procedures with idempotent behaviour without side-effects (e.g. read access to remote documents). The *idempotent* mode of DCE RPC belongs to this class.

| Kinds of faults / Semantic class | Fault free | Lost messages | Server failure | Client failure |
|---|---|---|---|---|
| **Maybe** | Call: 1<br>Result: 1 | Call: 0/1<br>Result: 0/1 | Call: 0/1<br>Result: 0/1 | Call: 0/1<br>Result: 0/1 |
| **At least once** | Call: 1<br>Result: 1 | Call: >= 1<br>Result: >= 1 | Call: >= 0<br>Result: >= 0 | Call: >= 0<br>Result: 0 |
| **At most once** | Call: 1<br>Result: 1 | Call: 1<br>Result: 1 | Call: 0/1<br>Result: 0/1 | Call: 0/1<br>Result: 0 |
| **Exactly once** | Call: 1<br>Result: 1 | Call: 1<br>Result: 1 | Call: 1<br>Result: 1 | Call: 1<br>Result: 1 |

Table 3-2 RPC call semantics

*At most once* semantics guarantees that temporary network failures are tolerated without generating duplicate invocations. This is the usual default semantics of most RPC systems, including DCE RPC. Finally, *exactly once* semantics tolerates all kinds of failures, including client and server node failures. However, it can only be implemented based on distributed transactions (see section 4.1) and is associated with significant additional runtime overhead. Nevertheless, this kind of semantics is required for consistency-sensitive distributed office applications, e.g. in the banking domain.

**Variation: Rendezvous:** A variation of RPC is the *rendezvous* concept. In contrast to RPC, a server does not accept all kinds of invocations at any time; it rather signals explicitly when it is available to serve a specific kind of invocation. As client and server conceptually have to "meet" concerning procedure invocation and acceptance, the term "rendezvous" is used. The given example would have the following structure with rendezvous:

| **Client:** | **Server:** |
|---|---|
| server = locate ("SharedDocumentEditor"); | |
| openDocument (server, "my_document"); | accept (openDocument); |
| | // now the operation is invoked |

The advantage of the rendezvous concept is the explicit synchronization of service requests at the server site. In addition, a server can act autonomously; it can delay acceptance of service requests or can even reject requests selectively. Therefore, the concept is suitable for open office environments where servers must be able to decide explicitly whether to accept requests from foreign clients. For example, a distributed office procedure environment spanning multiple departments is part of this application category.

### 3.2.5 Comparison of Existing Systems

Table 3-3 shows a comparison of some existing RPC systems (cf. also [TAA90]). *DCE RPC* [OSF94a-d] and *SUN RPC* [SUN90], [COR90] are among the most important current systems for industrial use. *Xerox Courier RPC* [XER81] and *Cedar RPC* [BIN84] were two of the earliest sophisticated implementations of RPC. *Modula/V RPC* [ALM86] is based on *System V*, developed at Standford University, and provides exceptionally high performance exploiting a special transport protocol.

All systems support synchronous, blocking calls; DCE RPC and SUN RPC also enable non-blocking calls based on concurrent threads at the client site. Moreover, SUN RPC explicitly provides an option to broadcast invocations to multiple servers. With the other systems, non-blocking calls can also be implemented by using an additional thread package.

The call semantics is usually at most once; some systems allow for selecting other kinds of semantics explicitly, e.g. based on procedure attributes of DCE RPC. With SUN RPC, call semantics depends on the transport protocol used below (with TCP/IP, at most once semantics can be achieved). Binding is usually dynamic, based on a directory service. With SUN RPC, a static binding mode can also be selected for efficiency. For interface definition, different languages are offered. IDL, from DCE RPC, has the advantage of being directly based on C; therefore, existing C applications can easily be adapted for running in a distributed environment. DCE and SUN RPC use standard transport protocols; DCE RPC even runs on an increasing number of different multivendor protocols. The other systems use dedicated protocols for performance improvements.

| Characteristics / Systems | Call mode | Call semantics | Binding | Interface descr. | Transport protocol |
|---|---|---|---|---|---|
| DCE RPC | blocking non-blocking | Maybe At least once At most once | dynamic | IDL | UDP/IP TCP/IP etc. |
| Xerox Courier | blocking | At most once | dynamic | Courier notation | XNS SPP |
| Xerox Cedar | blocking | At most once | dynamic | Mesa | Special protocol |
| SUN RPC | blocking non-blocking broadcast | depends on transport protocol | static dynamic | RPCL | TCP/IP UDP/IP |
| Modula/V RPC | blocking | At least once At most once | dynamic | Modula-2 | VMTP |

Table 3-3 Comparison of existing RPC systems

In summary, a number of mature RPC systems exist that provide rich and flexible functionality. They cover all major architectural issues discussed above and are available today for implementing cooperative office applications. RPC provides a high degree of distribution transparency and is relatively easy to use. Some additional mechanisms discussed below, in particular distributed name management and distributed security services, are required for rich RPC functionality. Other extensions concerning distributed transactions, broadcast protocols, and distributed object-oriented programming are also discussed later.

As discussed above, an RPC system as offered by DCE can be used for many different aspects of office environments. Examples are remote access to documents, distributed conference management, or server access in distributed office procedures. Concerning standardization, DCE RPC seems to be among the most promising candidates in practise (see also section 4.5.1). Another ISO standardization effort is also under way and is briefly described in section 4.5.3.

## 3.3 Distributed Directory Services

The communication mechanisms presented are the basis for peer-to-peer interactions in cooperative office environments. However, advanced distributed system services are required in order to implement a complete distributed processing environment. Most important, distributed directory services are relevant for identifying and locating RPC entities such as office servers, but also documents and general computer systems.

### 3.3.1 Basic Characteristics

As discussed above, a *directory service* or *name service* is necessary to enable mapping of RPC servers to client requests dynamically at runtime [COP89]. Basically, the input to such a service is a structured name (e.g. *schill@cs.tu-dresden.de*) with additional optional description information; the output is the address of a server, network node, or other resource (represented by a binding handle in DCE). Several issues, however, require advanced name management features:

- *Name structures:* In order to manage large name spaces, hierarchical names reflecting organizational boundaries (e.g. country, organization, department etc.) must be supported.
- *Replicated name management:* A directory service is crucial for the functionality of many office services (e.g. e-mail, resource access, remote service calls). Therefore, it must be readily available. This is achieved by replicating name information throughout several name servers.
- *Distributed name queries:* Name information can be split over several directory servers (e.g. according to the structural levels of the name space, with replication at each level). Therefore, name queries to resolve a given name must be implemented by a distributed algorithm to locate the appropriate servers.
- *Attributes and name entries:* A name entry, i.e. the information stored with a name, can consist of structured data with application-specific attributes. Examples are telephone number, address, or position of a person with a given name. The directory service must be able to return attribute information for a given name, and, ideally, to perform attribute-based search operations in the name space.

In the following, we discuss how these requirements are addressed by directory services in practise. In particular, we discuss the Cell Directory Service and the Global Directory Service of the OSF DCE as a concrete system example.

### 3.3.2 Contexts and Name Spaces

For structured (e.g. hierarchical) names, the name interpretation conceptually consists of several steps. Each step interprets a component of the name according to a corresponding *context* and returns information on how further to interpret the remaining part of the name. A context basically is the set of existing names at a givel level (e.g. the names of all countries or the names of all organizations within a country etc.). A *name space* can then be informally defined as the unification of all such contexts. An example is given in figure 3-6.

The hierarchical name */.../C=DE/O=TU-Dresden/OU=ComputerScience* with the global name prefix "/..." is to be interpreted. The name structure conforms to the X.500 directory service standard [ISO88]. The first interpretation step resolves the *country* component (such as *DE* for Germany) by querying a global directory server. The result is a reduced name and the address of a second directory server that is responsible for the *organization* context within the country. The top level directory server then resolves the organization name component and returns the address of another directory server for the organizational units with the given organization (such as *TU-Dresden* for Dresden University of Technology). This process is continued until the name is resolved completely; in the given example, a node or server address for the Computer Science department is eventually returned.

The correspondence of contexts to directory servers need not be one-to-one; a directory server might also manage several contexts. The context nesting level can also vary; however, a typical depth is 3-6.

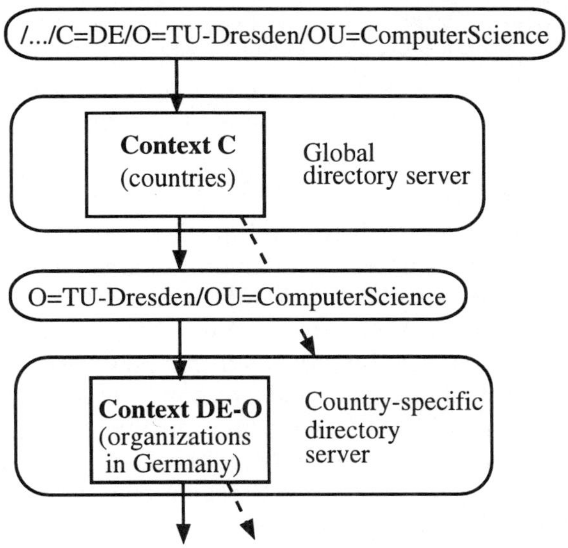


Fig. 3-6 Contexts and name interpretation

**Different kinds of name spaces:** As opposed to hierarchical name spaces with several nested contexts, a *flat name space* consists of only a single context. Flat name spaces are easy to handle but are limited to small naming domains, for example for local, autonomous name management within a department.

The names in a *routing-oriented name space* specify a route how to access or locate a named entity in a distributed environment. An example is *host1!host2!host3/peter*. Name interpretation proceeds according to the predefined route; this technique is also called *source routing*. An entity may have different names according to the given source (*peter* at *host3* might also be reachable via *host10* and *host11* (*host10!host11!host3!peter*) when accessed from *host7*, for example). In office environments, routing-oriented name spaces can be used for specifying routing of distributed office procedures. However, for general naming purposes, hierarchical name spaces are more appropriate; in particular, they support location-independent naming.

**Other kinds of names:** Up to now, the names discussed were usually *absolute*; they specify a named entity in a globally unique way. Within a given context, *relative* names are also useful as a shorthand for an absolute name. An example of a relative name was *O=TU-Dresden/OU=ComputerScience* within the context *DE-O*. Moreover, *synonym names* can be defined for entities with an existing absolute name. In this way, a user can establish his or her private name space. For example, user *peter* could define the name *myprinter* as a synonym for */.../C=DE/O=TU-Dresden/OU=ComputerScience/lps_20*. Finally, *group* or *multicast names* are useful for naming a set of entities. For example, the name */.../C=DE/O=TU-Dresden/OU=ComputerScience/workgroup_X* may denote several users (e.g. *peter, nathalie, walter, ben, lydia*) and finally return their e-mail addresses. Group names are useful in cooperative office environments for managing conferences or group decision support systems.

### 3.3.3 Distributed Directory Service Implementation

An efficient and fault tolerant distributed directory service implementation requires replication of name entries, distribution of name interpretation tasks, and caching of interpretation results. A specific characteristic of names is their relatively slow change. For example, the department structure of a company, the set of employees or the set of print servers of a department does not change as rapidly as other business data do (e.g. accounts, receipts, orders, billing material etc.). This characteristic can be exploited by the implementation; in particular, the probability that a cached name interpretation result is correct is relatively high. Moreover, read accesses are much more frequent than write accesses to names; therefore, replication also has performance advantages.

*Replication:* Figure 3-7 shows a replicated directory server structure for the hierarchical name space discussed above. At the highest level, two servers *S1* and *S2* replicate the context of all countries. At the next level, *S3* and *S4* both manage the organizational contexts for France (*FR-O*) and for Germany (*DE-O*). At the lowest level, no replication is applied; in the example, distinct servers manage the contexts of the organizational units for the French *INRIA* research institute, and for the German research institutions *TU-Dresden* and *GMD*, respectively.

The name */.../C=DE/O=TU-Dresden/OU=ComputerScience* could be interpreted by (S1, S3, S6), (S1, S4, S6), (S2, S3, S6), or (S2, S4, S6). Therefore, single server faults at the two upper levels can be tolerated. For updating replicas after changes, *lazy replication* techniques are often used. These techniques do not immediately update all replicas but only guarantee that a consistent replica state is gradually achieved. This is enabled by associating time stamps with update requests to implement a distributed protocol where all replicating servers eventually perform the same update sequences. Temporary, relatively unlikely inconsistencies between replicas might lead to problems with name interpretation; however, this can usually be tolerated by the application. An early example implementation of such a lazy replication technique has been performed within the *Grapevine* system (see [BLN82] and [SBN84] for further details).

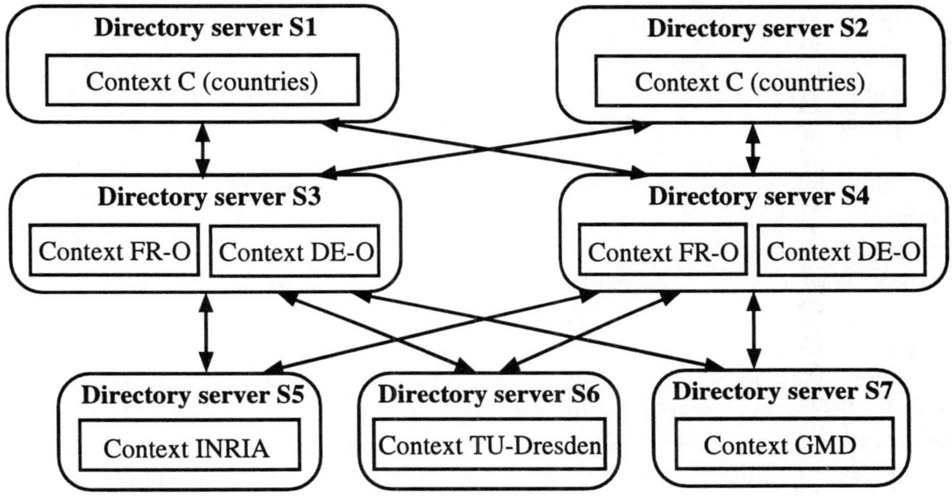


Fig. 3-7 Replicated directory server structure

***Caching:*** For a name space with $n$ names, the cost of name interpretation in terms of messages between servers is in the order of $O(\log n)$. However, name interpretation need not start at the highest level. A querying client may have a reference to a directory server at a lower level. For example, if *S5* is known to a client within the TU-Dresden, any name within INRIA can be directly interpreted without having to query other servers. In contrast, if a client within the GMD asks S7 for the same name, server S7 has to forward the request up the hierarchy to S3 or S4 who forward it up to S1 or S2, then leading to the same downward interpretation as discussed above.

The behavior can thus be improved by caching techniques at different levels. For example, the TU-Dresden client may cache the fact that the name */.../C=FR/O=INRIA/OU=Dept1* has eventually been interpreted by S5 and may directly query S5 for other names within INRIA later; the cache entry would be (*/.../C=FR/O=INRIA, S5*). If the server structure is modified or if the name context is deleted, the cache would be inconsistent. However, the probability for such structural changes is relatively low compared to the frequency of name queries. The same cache data could also be stored by S6 or S7 in order to direct queries for names within INRIA directly to the appropriate server. In contrast to client-specific caching, this technique has the advantage that all clients can benefit from it automatically. In general, caching is more important at the lower levels of the name space, while replication is typically used at the higher levels for making relatively global directory servers fault-tolerant.

### 3.3.4 Standards

**X.500:** The CCITT X.500 standard (more precisely: X.500-X.521) is almost identical to the ISO standard ISO-9594 (ISO 9594-1 to 9594-8) [ISO88] and specifies services and protocols for the ISO/OSI directory service. The hierarchical name structure (the so-called *Directory Information Tree, DIT*) is based on an ordered set of typed attributes; some of them have already been described above (country, organization, organizational unit). Different types of names (e.g. personal name or mailbox name) can be defined based on different attribute combinations. Each possible combination is defined by a name class. Classes are part of an inheritance hierarchy according to object-oriented programming techniques. Therefore, it is possible to specialize existing name classes by reusing and refining their attributes. Attributes can also be multivalued; thus group names are explicitly supported.

Names are managed by distributed directory servers (*Directory System Agents, DSAs*; see figure 3-8); the servers jointly implement the global *Directory Information Base (DIB)*. They are accessed by clients (*Directory User Agents, DUAs*) via a standardized *Directory Access Protocol (DAP)*. This enables heterogeneous systems interoperability concerning name interpretation. Different DSAs may cooperate in resolving a given name. For such DSA interaction, the standardized *Directory System Protocol (DSP)* is used. DUAs and DSAs may also apply caching for performance reasons; however, such implementation-level aspects (also including replication) are not part of the current standard. Nevertheless, X.500 defines a flexible directory standard that seems to be gaining wide acceptance.

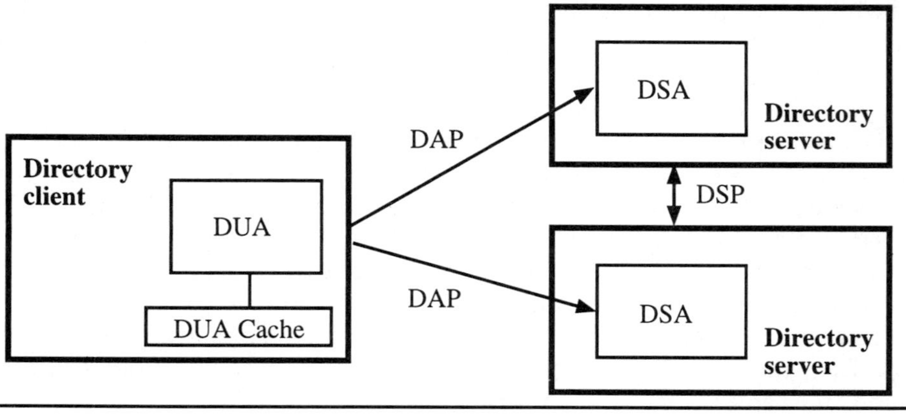


Fig. 3-8 X.500 configuration

**DNS:** The *Domain Name System (DNS)* [COM88] is widely used in the *Internet.* DNS names are also hierarchical with a typical depth of 3-4. As opposed to X.500 names, the name components are untyped; an example of a node name has been mentioned above (*cs.dresden.de*). The highest-level component of the name is standardized; usually, it specifies a country code. Within the USA, a more detailed distinction is made; for example, *COM* stands for commercial, *EDU* for educational, *GOV* for government, and *NET* for network management institutions.

DNS uses sophisticated caching and replication techniques at several levels of the distributed directory server hierarchy. Due to its widespread implementation and use, it tends to be one of the most important naming environments.

### 3.3.5 Naming Examples in Cooperative Office Applications

Distributed name management is important for virtually all cooperative office applications. Following our survey in chapter 2, we discuss general applications in different CSCW domains:

- *Conferences and GDSS:* In conference systems and GDSS environments, naming is important for identfying and locating remote participants, for getting access to remote conferences, and for locating data and documents to be submitted to other participants. Group names and synonyms are especially useful in such environments. Similar requirements hold for complex multi-user editing tasks.
- *Hypermedia:* In hypermedia systems, naming is required for identifying and locating databases and for following links. Typically, a link between remote databases in distributed hypermedia systems is represented by a logical name that has to be mapped to an appropriate server address. Browsing can also be supported by attribute-based naming, for example to search for dedicated hypermedia nodes that match specific attributes.
- *Coordination systems and office procedures:* In such environments, cooperative activities are performed by distributed agents. Naming is important for forwarding requests between agents, for retrieving office procedures of long duration, and for accessing folders and documents required by coordination tasks or office procedures.

Distributed name management is also relevant for basic interaction support, for example to locate X.400 communication peers, message mailboxes, or RPC servers. In summary, a flexible distributed directory service is essential for large cooperative office environments; *ad hoc* solutions based on simple name tables usually do not enable the required efficiency, scalability, and fault tolerance.

# 3.4 Distributed Security Techniques

Another important aspect of open distributed office environments is security. Compared to non-distributed systems, the potential risks concerning denied access and manipulation of data and services is much higher in networked environments. Typical offenses are unauthorized copying or modification of data within a system or in transit, artificial generation and insertion of communication messages, replay of copied messages, and gathering of statistical data based on global analyses (e.g. concerning the frequency of messages exchanged between communication peers). In client/server environments, additional offenses are unauthorized invocation of services/servers.

Most of these offenses can be prevented by distributed security techniques, namely by authentication, encryption, and authorization. Especially in office environments, such mechanisms are important due to the significant value, importance and confidentiality of many business data and documents. Nevertheless, significant security problems still remain [AND94].

In the following, we describe these techniques based on the Security Service of the OSF DCE, which itself uses MIT's *Kerberos* system [SNS88]. In particular, we focus on how to apply such techniques to achieve a secure RPC mechanism; an early implementation of a similar approach has been described in [BIR85].

## 3.4.1 Authentication and Encryption

Authentication is basically a mechanism to verify the identity of a person, server or other entities. In non-distributed systems, this is usually based on a secret password; by typing the password, a user confirms that he or she is actually the person to whom a given account belongs. In distributed environments, this is not sufficient as machines can usually not trust each other. Therefore, advanced mechanisms are required based on encryption techniques.

Encryption is based either on private or on public keys. In the first case, a key distribution center is required for managing the secret keys of all participants. In the second case, non-invertible one-way functions are used for generating a public encryption key from a secret, non-public decryption key. We first describe the private key approach which is also used in DCE and then compare the structure of public key mechanisms with it.

**Private key approaches:** Figure 3-9 shows a simplified authenticated and encrypted RPC scenario based on private keys. The notation *{<data>}K* means that the given data are encrypted with key *K*. A client C with private key *kC* wishes to communicate with a server S with private key *kS*. The client first sends a request for a common *conversation key* to the key distribution center (*KDC*), that is implemented by a specific system server or by multiple servers. The KDC generates an arbitrary conversation key *kCS*. It first encrypts the conversation key with *kS*, and then the result and also kCS once more with kC, and sends the encrypted data back to the client with a reply message. Encryption in Kerberos is based on the *Data Encryption Standard (DES)* of the US Department of Defense.

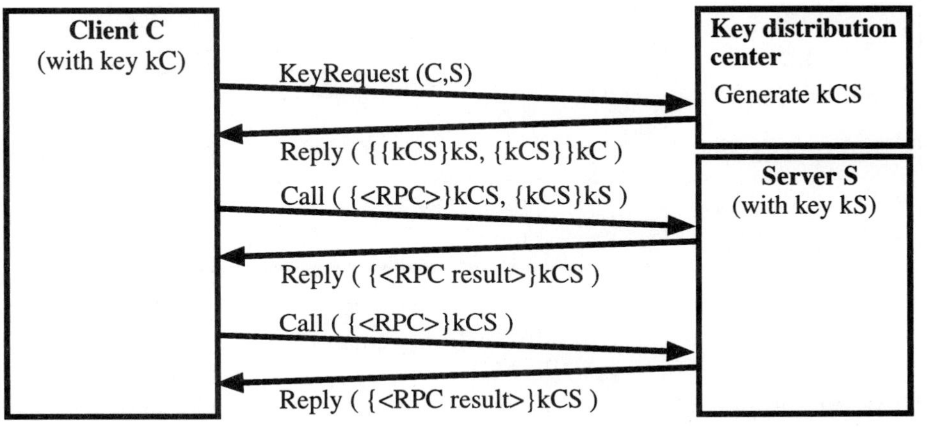


Fig. 3-9 Authenticated and encrypted RPC (simplified)

The client is able to decrypt kCS with kC and can set up a secure RPC message encrypted with kCS now. The version of the conversation key still encrypted with kS is appended to the message and is sent to server S. The server is now also able to decrypt kCS using kS; hence, both parties possess the conversation key and can communicate securely using kCS from now on.

Mutual authentication has been performed implicitly: the client could not have sent *{kCS}KS* to the server if it had not known kC. Similarly, the server could not have decrypted kCS if it had not known kS. However, the simplified protocol must be extended in practise in order to guarantee full security. For example, time stamps must be added to communication messages in order to detect and prevent message replay by third parties. Moreover, message checksums or similar mechanisms are required for client and server in order to test whether the communication peer was really able to decrypt correctly; details can be found in [OSF94c].

In DCE, authenticated RPC is offered via additional interface functions. With *rpc_server_register_auth_info*, a server registers its name with the key distribution center. The client specifies that an RPC shall be authenticated using the function *rpc_binding_set_auth_info;* it augments the binding handle for a server with authentication information. The client can also select different protection levels. For example, authentication can be performed only once during client/server binding or for each RPC invocation separately. Moreover, different encryption levels can be specified. This allows for a trade-off between security and efficiency. In office applications, sensitive interactions involving confidential data of course require a high security level. In contrast, public conferences or simple office procedures may be performed without security mechanisms at all.

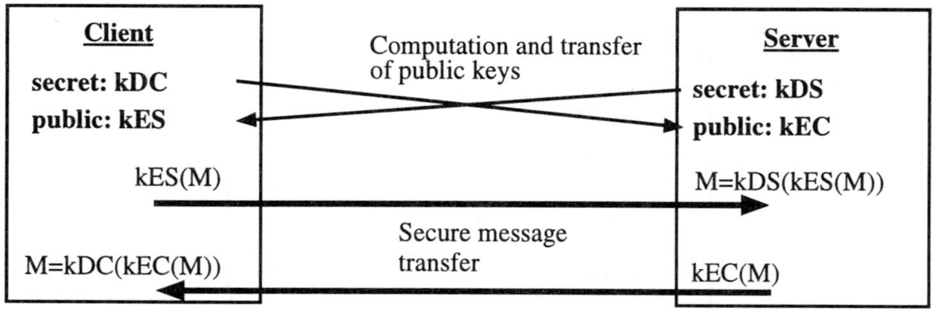


Fig. 3-10 Public key approach

**Public key approaches:** A public key encryption approach is shown in figure 3-10. Initially, the client possesses a secret key *kDC* for decryption of received messages, and the server possesses *kDS* for the same purpose. Both parties now compute public encryption keys *kEC* and *kES* from kDC and kDS, respectively, by applying a one-way function to the secret keys. The encryption keys are then transferred to the communication peers. Public key transfer does not have to be secure due to the property that the decryption key cannot be computed from the encryption key.

Now communication between client and server can start. All messages are encrypted with the peer's public key, i.e. with kES and kEC, respectively. Only the correct receiver can decrypt the message with its corresponding secret key. The one-way function is implemented by a non-reversible prime number decomposition. Public key approaches have the major advantage that no secure key distribution center is required. Moreover, digital signatures can only be performed based on a public key system. However, private key encryption is significantly more efficient. Therefore, advanced systems use a combination of public and private key approaches; a private key is generated for every remote interaction and is first exchanged safely based on public key encryption. Thereafter, user-level payload data can be encrypted efficiently with the private key that is now known by both partners. Nevertheless, no key distribution center is necessary, and keys are modified frequently. Future versions of the Security Service of DCE may include such a facility, too.

### 3.4.2 Authorization

Authentication makes sure that cooperating peers cannot pretend to have a wrong identity. In addition, authorization checks are required to restrict the access rights of correctly authenticated entities. For example, a regular employee must not be able to initiate management-level decision support conferences, while a manager or his or her secretary may be granted that right. Access restrictions to documents of different levels of confidentiality are another straightforward example.

In general, authorization is based on an access control matrix with accessing *subjects* (e.g. users) as its rows, accessed *objects* (e.g. servers, files etc.) as its columns, and concrete rights as the matrix field entries. An example is shown in figure 3-11. In a real distributed system, the matrix should not be stored at a central site but has to be implemented in a decentralized way by row or by column. The first approach leads to *capabilities*, i.e. lists of access rights for a number of objects stored with a given subject. The second approach results in *access control lists*, i.e. lists of subjects with specific access rights stored with a given object. Both approaches can be found in distributed systems. For example, the *Amoeba* system [TKR91] is known for its capability approach. Capabilities have the advantage that they can be forwarded between authorized subjects in a controlled way, and that they can easily be retracted by changing the identity of the respective object.

| **objects** / **subjects** | **Printer_1** | **DocumentServer** | **Department Database** |
|---|---|---|---|
| Peter | print, fastPrint | read, write, delete | read, write, delete |
| Bob | print, reboot | read | --- |
| Mary | print | read | read, write |
| Ben | print | --- | --- |

Fig. 3-11 Example of an access control matrix

Access control lists (ACLs) facilitate implementation of common rights for a whole group of users. Moreover, access checking is purely a task of the server site holding the ACLs. The ACL approach has been implemented as part of the DCE Security Service. For each object, a list of pre-defined entries for specific subject classes is available. Within each entry, object-specific rights can be specified. An example showing the document server's ACL according to the matrix of figure 3-11 is given in figure 3-12.

**CDS-Name:** /.:/DocumentServer

| | | |
|---|---|---|
| **user_obj** | /.:/sec/principal/Peter | : rwd |
| **user** | /.:/sec/principal/Bob | : r ---- |
| **user** | /.:/sec/principal/Mary | : r ---- |
| **group_obj** | /.:/sec/group/Department_1 | : r---- |

Fig. 3-12 Example of an access control list

The *user_obj* entry specifies the rights of the object's owner, *Peter*; in addition to read/write, a separate delete right is also given. The two other users, *Bob* and *Mary* are granted the read right only. *Ben* is not mentioned and is therefore not granted any rights. However, a user group, *Department_1*, is also granted read access to the document server. Other entries are offered by DCE Security to specify (usually restricted) rights for users of foreign cells and for unauthenticated users. ACLs are checked by RPC servers and other servers whenever an invocation or request arrives; a server must implement a so-called *ACL manager* for this task. Of course, ACL checking can be omitted for servers without security requirements in order to improve performance.

## 3.5 Exercises

1. [Conceptual design]
A client wishes to access a remote document print server. Model this scenario using the various communication techniques described in this chapter (especially direct/indirect message passing and RPC). The client request includes a plain text representation of the document. The server response consists of a simple integer status value. Describe the resulting messages or higher-level interactions in as much detail as possible (using pseudo-code or C code where appropriate).

2. [Conceptual design]
Outline an MHS/X.400 configuration for a company with a head office and four satellite offices. The head office supports up to 20 users and also telex and teletex access. Each satellite office supports up to five users with associated message stores. Each office has a reliable host system hosting its MTA. The user agents are placed on (less reliable) PCs (decide where to allocate the message stores).

3. [Conceptual design]
Define an X.500 name space for this company (assume it is a US company named "CoolProducts" with the offices as its major organizational units). Also propose a replicated directory server structure so that the head office has local access to all names while each satellite office has local access to its own names and to the main office's names. Draw graphical diagrams of your name space and directory server design.

4. [Conceptual design / optional implementation]
Develop an RPC server interface (using DCE's IDL) for a hypertext navigation server as implemented within the exercises of chapter 2. As described there, the following operations are to be considered: retrieval of a hypertext node by name, display of node contents and of neighbor nodes, following of a link, and return via a link. Consider in particular the following aspects: What are appropriate parameter data types or structures? What are input, and what are output parameters of each operation? Are there any idempotent operations? Moreover, if DCE should be available to you, study the DCE RPC reference manuals and try to implement your approach as a distributed client/server application.

5. [Basic knowledge / conceptual design]
Consider the RPC example of the hypertext server again:
- If messages frequently get lost, which call semantics should be provided?
- If the hypertext server is also unreliable, would the semantics still be sufficient?
- Each hypertext server is now to serve several clients concurrently (as a multithreaded server). How can this be achieved easily with DCE RPC?

6. [Basic knowledge]
What is the difference between private and public key encryption? Which approach is more appropriate if there is no single trustworthy computer system within a network (not even a trustworthy system server)?

7. [Conceptual design]
Outline a capability data structure and its component values that represents the access control matrix example of section 3.4.2.

## 3.6 References

[ALM86] Almes, G.: The Impact of Language and System for Remote Procedure Call Design; *6th Int. Conf. on Distributed Computing Systems, 1986, pp. 414-421*

[BIN84] Birrell, A.D., Nelson, B.J.: Implementing Remote Procedure Calls; *ACM Trans. on Comp. Syst., Vol. 2, No. 1, Feb. 1984, pp. 39-59*

[BIR85] Birrell, A.D.: Secure Communication Using Remote Procedure Calls; *ACM Trans. on Comp. Syst., Vol. 3, No. 1, Feb. 1985, pp. 1-14*

[BLN82] Birell, A.D., Levin, R., Needham, R.M., Schroeder, M.: Grapevine: An Exercise in Distributed Computing; *Comm. of the ACM, Vol. 25, No. 4, April 1982, pp. 250-273*

[COM88] Comer, D.E.: Internetworking with TCP/IP; *Prentice Hall, Englewood Cliffs, NJ, 1988*

[COP89] Comer, D.E., Peterson, L.L.: Understanding Naming in Distributed Systems; *Distrib. Comp., No. 3, 1989, pp. 51-60*

[COR90] Corbin, J.R..: The Art of Distributed Applications; *Springer, New York, 1990*

[ISO88] ISO: Open Systems Interconnection - The Directory: Parts 1-7; *ISO 9594/1-7, 1988*

[ISO89] ISO: MOTIS - System and Service Overview; *ISO/IEC IS 10021-1, 1989*

[JOR86] Jones, M.B., Rashid, R.F.: Mach and Matchmaker: Kernel and Language Support for Object-Oriented Distributed Systems; *ACM OOPSLA '86, Portland, OR, ACM 1987, pp. 67-77*

[KMS89] Kramer, J., Magee, J., Sloman, M.: Constructing Distributed Systems in CONIC; *IEEE Trans. on Softw. Eng., Vol. 15, No. 6, June 1989, pp. 663-675*

[NEL81] Nelson, B.J.: Remote Procedure Call; *Ph.D. Dissertation, Carnegie-Mellon University, May 1981*

[OSF94a] Open Software Foundation: Introduction to OSF DCE; *Open Software Foundation, Cambridge, MA, USA, 1994*

[OSF94b] Open Software Foundation: DCE User's Guide and Reference; *Open Software Foundation, Cambridge, MA, USA, 1994*

[OSF94c] Open Software Foundation: DCE Application Development Guide; *Open Software Foundation, Cambridge, MA, USA, 1994*

[OSF94d] Open Software Foundation: DCE Application Development Reference; *Open Software Foundation, Cambridge, MA, USA, 1994*

[SBN84] Schroeder, M.D., Birrel, A.D., Needham, R.M.: Experience with Grapevine: The Growth of a Distributed System; *ACM Trans. on Comp. Syst., Vol. 2, No. 1, Feb. 1984, pp. 3-23*

[SNS88] Steiner, J.G., Neuman, B.C., Schiller, J.I.: Kerberos: An Authentification Service for Open Network Systems; *Usenix Winter 1988 Conf., Dallas, TX, 1988, pp. 191-202*

[SPE82] Spector, A.Z.: Performing Remote Operations Efficiently on a Local Computer Network; *Comm. of the ACM, Vol. 25, No. 4, April 1982, pp. 246-260*

[SUN90] SUN Microsystems: Remote Procedure Call Specification; *SUN Microsystems, Inc., 1990*

[TAA90] Tay, B.H., Ananda, A.L.: A Survey of Remote Procedure Calls; *Operating Syst. Rev., Vol. 24, No. 3, July 1990, pp. 68-79*

[TKR91] Tanenbaum, A.S., Kaashoek, M.F., v. Renesse, R., Bal, H.E.: The Amoeba Distributed Operating System - a Status Report; *Computer Communications, Vol. 14, No. 6, July 1991, pp. 324-335*

[XER81] Xerox Corporation: Courier: The Remote Procedure Call Protocol; *Xerox System Integration Standard 038112, Xerox OPD, Dec. 1981*

# 4 Advanced Distributed Systems Techniques and Standards

While the communication mechanisms and supplemental services discussed above provide the required framework for building cooperative office systems, many applications benefit from higher-level distributed interaction techniques. As examples, we discuss distributed transactions and multiparty interaction primitives to achieve increased reliability and recoverability, and distributed object-based systems to enable a more flexible interaction model than given by RPC. Furthermore, we give a basic impression of how the distributed programming mechanisms presented are supported by dedicated languages.

As an integrated system platform for open distributed applications, we describe the OSF Distributed Computing Environment (DCE), as well as related open distributed systems environments. Moreover, the ISO/OSI standardization efforts with their services and protocols are also discussed. Finally, we outline the use of the Open Distributed Processing (ODP) approach for overall structuring of CSCW applications.

## 4.1 Distributed Transactions

### 4.1.1 Foundations

Transactions are a well-known approach found in database systems. They guarantee so-called *ACID* semantics (*atomicity, consistency, isolation,* and *durability*) [HÄR83]. Atomicity means that an operation is only performed as a unit; either it is fully completed (*commit*) or its effects do not become visible at all (*abort*). Consistency means that a transaction transforms data from a consistent state into another consistent state. Based on isolation, concurrent transaction execution is semantically identical to execution in a sequential system. In particular, a transaction *T1* will never see any intermediate state of data caused by another transaction *T2* before *T2* is completed. Finally, durability means that the effects of a transaction (data manipulations etc.) remain persistent after transaction completion; for example, they do not get lost after a system crash.

A simple example illustrates these properties: a funds transfer shall be performed between two bank accounts *A1* and *A2* managed by different network nodes; a given amount shall be subtracted from A1 and added to A2. Due to obvious consistency constraints, the operations (invoked as RPCs from a coordinating site) must be embedded in a distributed transaction:

```
begin_distributed_transaction
subtract (A1, amount);
add (A2, amount);
end_distributed_transaction
```

If both operations complete successfully and no other failure (such as system or network errors) occurs, the transaction completes and actually updates both accounts. Otherwise, the account modifications are aborted and both accounts are left in their former state.

The transaction properties have proven very useful for implementing processing functionality with strict consistency requirements (like credit/debit transactions as discussed above). Therefore, extensions of the basic concept to distributed systems have been developed. Some of them are based on RPC or distributed object interactions, others on pure message passing. The distributed transaction model is also an important means of implementing consistent distributed processing in cooperative office environments. Basically, all remote interactions with node-spanning consistency requirements have to be embedded in distributed transactions. An example is a distributed office procedure that should either complete successfully or leave no results at any participating node.

### 4.1.2 Basic Technique: Two-Phase Commit

Distributed transactions augment conventional remote interactions (RPC, remote object invocations etc.) with the transactional ACID semantics discussed above. In addition to the usual locking and commit techniques known from conventional database systems, the two-phase commit protocol is important for making sure that all participants in a transaction jointly commit or jointly abort [CER84]. It is controlled by a *coordinator process* (see figure 4-1).

To complete a transaction, the coordinator first sends a "prepare" message to all participants in the distributed transaction. Upon receipt of this message, each participant stores all data manipulated by itself persistently. The former version of these data is also still kept in persistent storage. Each participant then acknowledges with a "ready" message. However, if a local failure occurs (e.g. computation error, persistent storage failure etc.), a participant responds with an "abort" message.

The coordinator collects all messages. If there has been at least one abort message (or if the coordinator has to abort itself for local reasons), it directs all participants to abort, i.e. to roll back their state to the former version of data. Otherwise, the coordinator sends a "commit" message to all participants who then replace the old data version by the new one. Even if node or communication failures should happen after a participant responds with "commit", the transaction can still be completed; the modified data are already stored persistently. Therefore, the coordinator can make its global commit/abort decision merely based on the responses and does not have to take further failures into consideration.

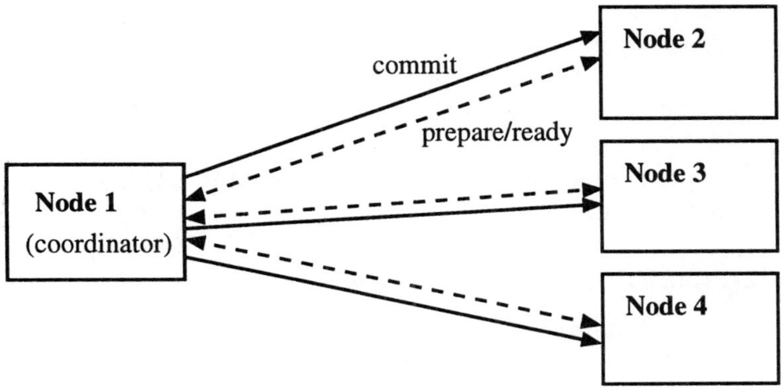


Fig. 4-1 Two-phase commit protocol

Figure 4-2 summarizes the protocol behavior by giving a state machine for a scenario with one coordinator and one participant. Each state transition arc is annotated with the received message(s) leading to the transition, and with the message sent as a result of it (notation: <received_message> / <sent_message>). For example, the coordinator moves from the "wait" state to the "aborted" state if it receives an "abort" message or if it receives a "ready" message but locally decides to abort. In both cases, it sends an "abort" message.

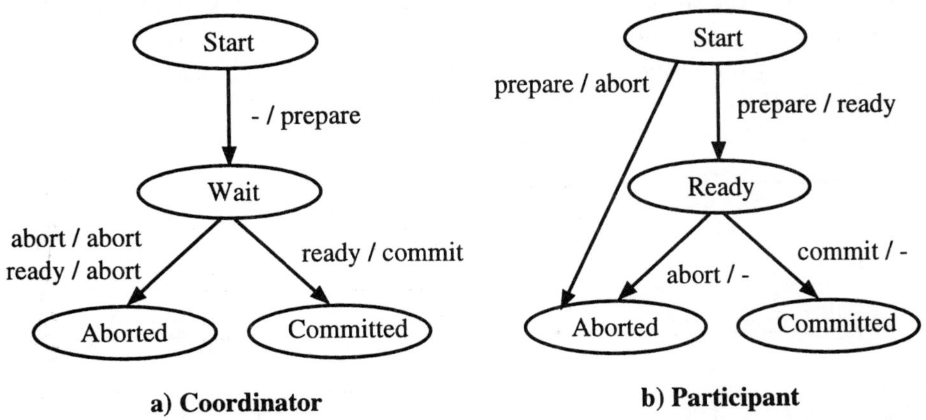


Fig. 4-2 State diagram for coordinator and participant

As discussed in section 4.1, this model can be applied to almost all cooperative office applications in a distributed environment, whenever consistency of manipulated data is a critical issue. However, the two-phase commit protocol is rather expensive to execute due to the messages required. Moreover, distributed transactions can be blocking for quite a long time if a node crashes just after the prepare phase [MOS82]. For these reasons, a reasonable trade-off between consistency and efficiency is necessary in many cases. Extensions of distributed transactions also attempt to address other problems: in their basic form, distributed transactions limit concurrency of their component actions, and, more important, if a single action has to abort, all computed results are lost entirely and have to be recomputed.

### 4.1.3 Nested Distributed Transactions

*Nested distributed transactions* improve the situation described above [MOS82]; they increase the potential for concurrency and limit the amount of work to be rolled back. A nested transaction consists of hierarchical component transactions that form a dynamic transaction tree. An example representing an office procedure as a nested transaction is shown in figure 4-3.

The example does not emphasize parallelism among subtransactions; virtually all operations have to be executed sequentially due to mutual dependencies. First, the expense form is edited by the employee, then converted into a transmission format, sent to the manager, signed, converted, sent to the travel expense office, checked for the actual expenses, and a refund finally made. However, selective abort and retry of subtransactions is an important feature exploited by the example. If the expense form has already been filled by the employee, but the approval fails due to a system shutdown at the manager's site, no global abort is required. Rather, the results of the actions taken by the employee can be maintained and only the manager's operations must be rolled back and restarted after system recovery. Similarly, a network failure during electronic funds transfer does not affect the employee's or the manager's previously completed actions. As a general rule, an abort of a subtransaction does not necessarily affect superior transactions or transactions within other parts of the tree.

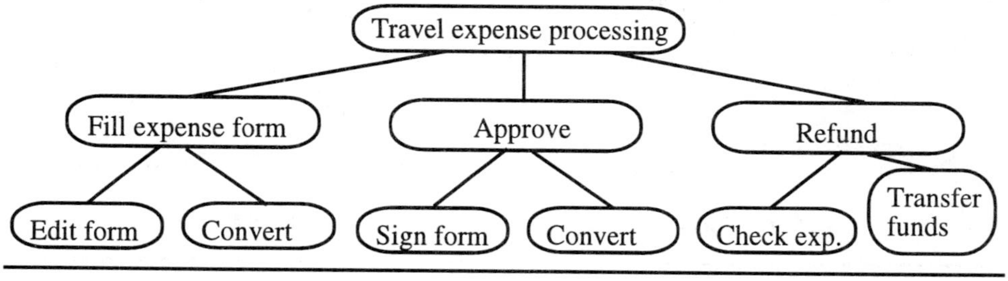


Fig. 4-3 Nested transaction

However, if a subtransaction cannot complete at all (not even after retry), it is possible to abort the whole transaction. For example, if the expense office detects that the employee tried to exaggerate his or her expenses, it is possible to perform a global abort, including the approval and the employee's actions. Therefore, a commit of a subtransaction must always be conditional until the global transaction actually commits. For these reasons, the previous version of all modified data must be maintained in stable storage until global commit. Moreover, at each level of the transaction hierarchy, a two-phase commit is required to complete the subtransactions of the next level below.

### 4.1.4 Standards and Existing Implementations

Meanwhile, there are several emerging product-level implementations of distributed transactions that conform to new standards (see also [GRR93]). Most notably, the X/Open consortium has defined the *X/Open Distributed Transaction Processing (DTP)* application programming interface named *XA* [XDT92]. This approach is designed to work with standardized ISO/OSI transaction protocols, namely CCR and TP (see section 4.5.3). The procedural interface of XA allows the following transaction execution sequence, for example (detailed parameters of function calls are omitted):

```
do_transaction ()
{
int rc;                      // return code

xa_open ();                  // open connection to a remote site
xa_start ();                 // start a transaction
...                          // application-specific transactional operations
xa_end ();                   // complete execution of transactional operations
rc = xa_precom ();           // ask remote site to do a prepare-to-commit
if (rc) xa_commit ();        // actually initiate commit
else xa_abort ();            // transaction has to abort
xa_close ();                 // close connection to remote site
}
```

There is also a higher-level *TX interface* available that encapsulates these internal XA calls (for example, the *xa_end, xa_precom,* and *xa_commit* sequence is embedded in a single call *tmcommit*).

Conforming to the XA standard, there are several implementations available. The *Tuxedo* system [TUX92] of Unix System Laboratories was the prototype that served as a model for the XA standardization. It is available on numerous hardware platforms and operating systems. The system consists of a transaction monitor, Tuxedo System/T, that offers the basic transaction processing functionality, and of a relational database, Tuxedo System/D, that can be accessed by System/T. However, these components can interoperate with other database systems and with other XA-based transaction processing components, respectively.

As another example, the *Encina* transaction processing system [ENC92] of Transarc also conforms to the XA standard. The system runs on top of the OSF

Distributed Computing Environment (see section 4.5.1) and uses threads, RPC, the security service, and the directory services of DCE. Transaction functionality is embedded in a high-level C programming interface on top of XA. As an example, an extended version of the credit/debit program fragment of section 4.1 can be expressed as follows:

```
main ()
{
unsigned A1, A2; // account numbers
unsigned amount; // amount to be added/subtracted

scanf ("%d%d%d", A1, A2, amount);

transaction {                    // start a transaction
  add (A1, amount);
  subtract (A2, amount);
  if (negativeBalance (A2)) abort ("Negative balance not allowed");
  }

onCommit                         // action if transaction commits
  printf ("Transaction committed successfully.\n");

onAbort                          // action if transaction aborts
  printf ("Transaction aborted.\n");
}
```

The transaction is aborted explicitly with an error message when the balance of the second account has become negative. As an extension, it is also possible to create several concurrent subtransactions; this is enabled by the keyword *subTran*. To implement concurrency, DCE threads are used.

**Research prototypes:** A prominent example implementation of the distributed transaction approach has also been performed within the *Argus* prototype [LIS88]. Interactions are RPC-based and the modified data correspond with the status information of RPC servers (so-called *guardians*). Subtransactions can be executed in parallel when possible; however, the superior transaction blocks until all subtransactions have completed. This allows for a simple lock management; a subordinate transaction can inherit locks from its superior transaction on demand.

For example, if the "fill expense form" transaction locks the form object, the "edit form" transaction can access it nevertheless. When a subtransaction commits, it passes all locks held by it (including newly acquired locks) back to the superior transaction. This way, a strict two-phase locking protocol for avoiding nested rollbacks can be implemented. However, when a subtransaction aborts, all locks acquired by it are released. Potential deadlocks are handled by a timeout-based lock operation with subtransaction abort after timeout. Other systems implementing nested distributed transactions are *Camelot* [EPS89], *Eden* [PUN87], and *ZMOB* [LIG85], for example. For further technical details concerning extended commit protocols, locking strategies, optimized transaction models, and deadlock detection and prevention refer to the extensive discussion in [GRR93]. A discussion of advanced locking techniques that allow explicit cooperation during joint document access is also given in chapter 5.

## 4.2 Broadcast and Multiparty Interactions

Cooperative office applications often require interactions between more than two peers. For example, a voting protocol within a decision support conference consists of a 1:*n* request for votes from all participants. Or a screen update of a multiuser drawing tool may require a multicast message to all tool users to update their local views. Although such functionality can be implemented by a set of regular messages or by a bunch of RPCs, an explicit multiparty interaction primitive has two major advantages: (1) it can be implemented more efficiently by exploiting the multicast functionality of the physical network (e.g. Ethernet), and (2) specific delivery semantics for group messages can be guaranteed. The following sections introduce *atomic broadcast protocols* to achieve higher-level group message delivery semantics.

### 4.2.1 Broadcast and Multicast

A broadcast protocol provides a mechanism for sending a message from one sender to a set of receivers; if this set is explicitly denoted, the term *multicast* is used, while *broadcast* in its original form means that every process able to receive the message will actually receive it. Some possible linguistic mechanisms for broadcast/multicast have already been discussed in section 3.1:

```
send <message> to P2, P3, P4             // multicast to receivers given explicitly
send <message> to ConferenceGroup        // multicast to group
                                         // (receivers given implicitly)
broadcast <message>                      // broadcast to all receivers
```

These operations enable multicast to a set of processes, to a group specifying such a set implicitly by a group name, or broadcast to all receivers. The distinction between multicast and broadcast will not be maintained in the following as it is not of primary importance from the semantics point of view.

**Atomic broadcast:** An *atomic broadcast* protocol guarantees the atomicity property of message delivery: a message is either received by all operable destinations or by none of them. That is, even if the sender fails after having sent some of the messages, either all remaining messages are sent, too, or no received message becomes visible to any participant at all. The important property of such protocols from a practical point of view is: whenever a receiver gets an atomic broadcast message, it knows that all other receivers got or will get the same message, and will eventually perform the same action upon it. For example, with a multiuser drawing tool, a participant who contacts another participant directly will know that the peer will actually have the same information on screen (maybe after some slight time delay). This simple property can facilitate many distributed protocol implementations, for example the management of replicas of data items at different nodes.

An implementation of atomic broadcast that is simple but also expensive in terms of communication and storage would be as follows (see figure 4-4 for an example with three receivers):

**Sender:**
send <message> to <group>

**For each receiver** (receiving <message>)**:**
if <message> has not been received yet
  send copy of <message> to <group>
  deliver <message> to application program

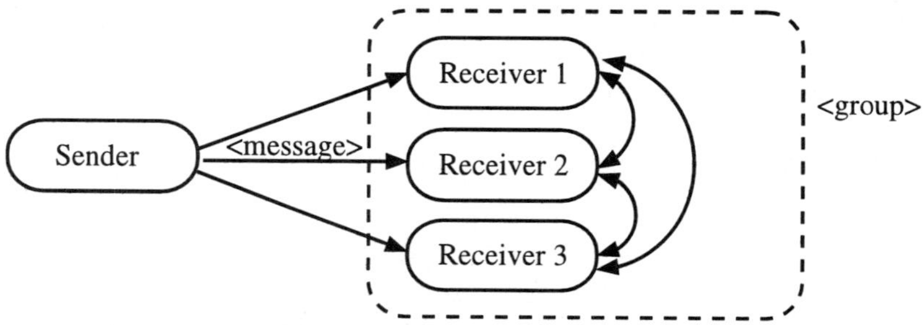


Fig. 4-4 Simple atomic broadcast protocol

The protocol guarantees that all recipients remaining operable will eventually get the message. Only if the sender fails before the first message is sent at all will nobody receive anything. Otherwise, the message is forwarded to all operable receivers even if the sender fails after sending some of the messages. Of course, the protocol sends an unnecessarily large number of messages even in the fault-free case. Moreover, messages must be stored intermediately to detect received duplicates until all receivers get an acknowledgement (not shown here). An improved protocol could detect sender failure explicitly by some means of messages and would only retransmit messages between the receivers in this case.

### 4.2.2 Ordered Broadcast Protocols

The protocol discussed above does not have message ordering properties. In particular, messages of subsequent broadcasts may arrive in different order at different receiver sites. This causes problems with non-commutative operations, for example with mutually dependent updates of a shared drawing. For these reasons, *ordered atomic broadcast* protocols have been developed as an extension of basic atomic broadcast. They guarantee that subsequent messages from the same sender arrive in the same order at all receivers. For example, the *ISIS* system [BIJ87] with its *ABCAST* protocol is known for such an improved approach.

The protocol implementation is rather complex and naturally generates more message overhead than basic broadcast protocols. It is based on a time stamp negotiation between the receivers and the sender that is implemented as a kind of handshake protocol. As a result of the protocol, all messages in the receivers' queues get globally agreed and ordered time stamps and are eventually delivered to the application in time stamp order. Details can be found in [BIJ87].

For cooperative office applications, ordered atomic broadcast protocols can be very important if coordinated group operations must be supported in a distributed environment. However, commercially available systems like the OSF DCE do not yet offer such protocols; the protocols are still at a prototype level. Moreover, the increased message overhead is significant; therefore, as with distributed transactions, a trade-off between consistency requirements and runtime overhead must be achieved in practise.

## 4.3 Distributed Object-Oriented Approaches

A recent extension of RPC are distributed object-based systems. These are often implemented as extensions of programming languages like *C++*, *Smalltalk*, *Modula-2+* or *Eiffel*. Fine-grained objects (data structures with associated operations) are the basic units of placement. Communication is performed by RPC-style location-independent object invocations where interacting objects can reside at different nodes. The fine-grained model allows for a very natural representation of applications.

### 4.3.1 Basic Characteristics

Distributed object-oriented approaches have several distinguishing basic characteristics. Instead of invoking heavyweight servers implemented by operating system processes, objects of arbitrarily fine grain are the most basic units of invocation and computation. In contrast to RPC, with its call-by-value parameter semantics, object references (i.e. pointers to objects) can also be passed remotely, leading to call-by-object-reference semantics. The resulting approach is more flexible than RPC and, in particular, enables a more natural modeling of cooperative office applications. Moreover, objects can be mobile and can therefore be relocated dynamically between nodes. In this way, communicating objects can be co-located in order to reduce communication costs.

For example, the office procedure object approach discussed can be directly mapped to a distributed environment in this way [ART90] (see figure 4-5 for a simplified illustration). Distributed office procedures can be represented as task objects transferred between server objects. Typical operations on task objects are start, stop, suspend, and status inquiry. Typical operations on servers are actual service invocations, status enquiries, and accounting functions. Data/document objects attached to an office procedure can also be modeled as objects. Examples of operations on data objects are global read/write editing mechanisms, and object-specific computations, e.g. for spreadsheets.

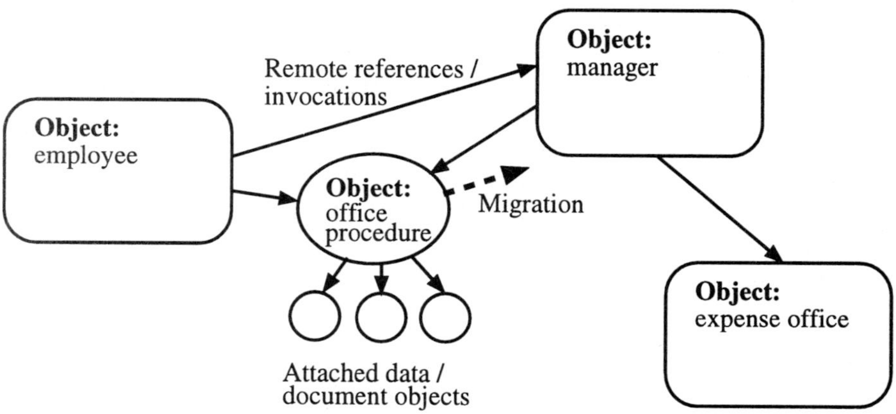


Fig. 4-5 Distributed object-oriented office procedure modeling

More concretely, the software tools of an employee, of his or her manager, and of a travel expense office are modeled by objects in the example, each placed and fixed at a different node of a distributed system. The office procedure and its attached data and documents are mobile objects; they currently move from the employee's site to the manager's site in order to enable local access by the manager. Inter-object references between employee, manager, and expense office enable remote invocations of the referenced entities. Moreover, the employee has a remote object reference to the office procedure, enabling status checks in case of an unexpectedly long duration, for example. The manager also has direct access to that object in order to retrieve and manipulate data moving with it. The expense office will eventually get an object reference to the office procedure when the manager forwards it. A typical invocation of the manager's object that specifies that the office procedure object should be co-located with it during operation execution might look as follows:

**Employee object:**

```
manager->approve (move office_procedure);
        // invocation
```

**Manager object:**

```
approve (...) {...}
        // implementation
```

The distributed object model has actually been implemented by a number of prototype systems and currently seems to move toward a mature stage, with an already visible influence on product development. In the following, we outline how location-independent object invocations and object mobility can be realized conceptually. Moreover, existing prototype approaches are discussed.

### 4.3.2 Object Addressing and Location-Independent Invocation

In order to implement location-independent invocation, objects must get globally unique, location-independent identifiers. This can easily be achieved by concatenating the node identifier (e.g. an Internet address) of the node creating an object ("*birthnode*") and a locally unique identifier. All objects can then be referenced systemwide via such global identifiers. An intermediate level of indirection is required to map such identifiers to memory addresses for local objects and to network addresses for remote objects. This is typically achieved via an extended object table per node and does not require any kind of central location server; due to the fine grain and relatively large number of objects, it would be a bad idea to register all objects with a directory service, for example.

The address information for remote objects is usually represented by so-called *proxies*, i.e. local representatives of remote objects. A proxy basically implements a remote object reference, giving either a location hint or the exact location of the referenced object. It usually does not contain actual object data itself, although some advanced approaches attempt to perform some limited data caching within the proxy. An example of proxies for the office procedure object is shown in figure 4-6; the object is now located at the node of the travel expense office (*node3*).

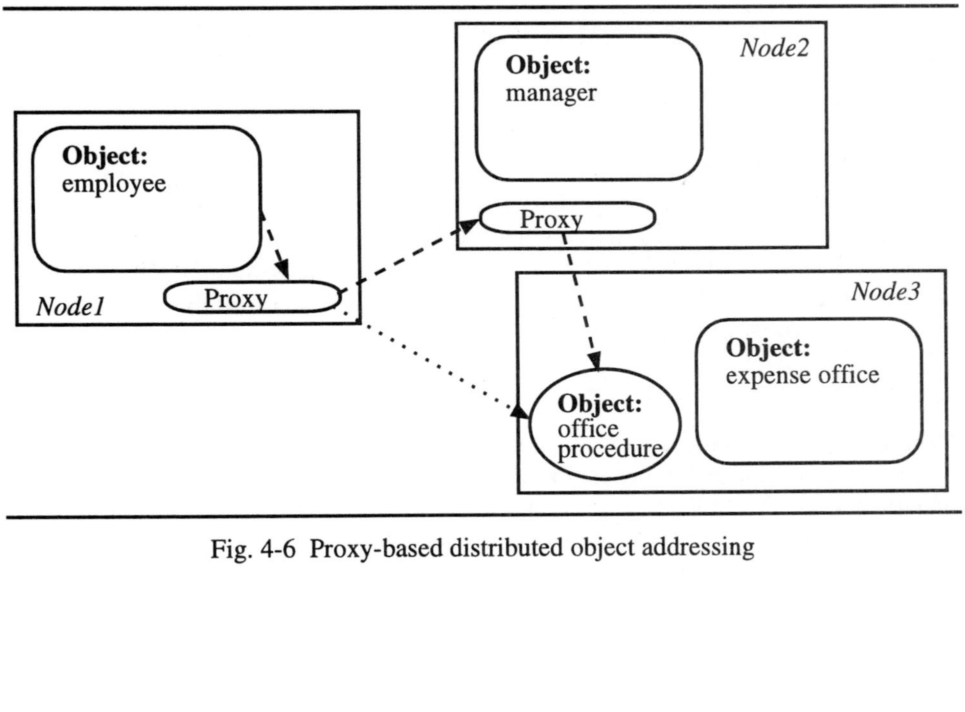


Fig. 4-6 Proxy-based distributed object addressing

**Location algorithm:** The employee can locate the object by following the resulting proxy chain from *node1* to *node2* to *node3 (forward addressing)*. After an invocation of the object, the chain can be compressed by informing *node1* about the current location of the object (indicated by a shortcut from the first proxy to the object in the figure). Some systems keep the location information of proxies constantly up to date. However, this requires additional update messages when an object moves and is not appropriate for very large systems.

A different modification of the location algorithm is to keep the birthnode of an object constantly up to date concerning the object's location. This is less expensive and easy to implement, as the birthnode address is part of the object identifier itself. However, a third-party node *X* needs at least two messages to access an object (message from *X* to birthnode to current location). The original forward addressing approach is more efficient after the indicated shortcut has been performed. However, both approaches can also be combined: up to a maximum length of the proxy chain (say 3), an object is located by following the chain. Afterwards, the birthnode is contacted when necessary. This policy is reflected conceptually by the following recursive algorithm:

```
const maxLength = 3;

Location *locate (Location *nodeAsked, ObjectId object, int pathLength)
 {
 if (Local (object)) return nodeAsked;        // object is local
 if (pathLength <= maxLength)                 // path length is still small enough
   return (locate (LocationHint (object), object, pathLength+1)); // forward via proxy
 else return (locate (BirthNode (object), object, pathLength+1)); // now ask birthnode
 }

// Initial invocation:
objectLocation = locate (localNode, object, 0); // check at the local node first
```

The *locate* function can be implemented by RPC (see section 3.2) with the first parameter controlling the location where it is to be invoked. The macros *Local, LocationHint,* and *BirthNode* access the local object table and the object identifier for the required information. In practise, the location algorithm can of course be implemented more efficiently by asynchronous message passing.

Actual object invocations, after having located an object, are performed like an RPC. In particular, parameter encoding/decoding based on stubs is required according to section 3.2. Moreover, new proxies must be installed at a site whenever a new remote object reference is passed there.

### 4.3.3 Object Mobility

Object migrations at runtime are useful for co-locating interacting objects dynamically (e.g. the office procedure object and its attached data with the expense office object), for balancing computational load, or just as an easy-to-use data transfer mechanism. In most systems, the destination of a migration is specified explicitly by the application. Only few higher-level automatic migration policies have yet been implemented. An object migration basically consists of the following steps:

- *Synchronization with invocations:* First, the migration request must be synchronized with ongoing invocations. In most systems, an object may only move when it is not currently invoked. Therefore, mutual exclusion of invocations and migration requests on objects is required.
- *Encoding of object data:* Like an RPC request, the data of an object must be encoded into a flat transfer format.
- *Proxy installation:* The object is replaced by a proxy with the new location information at the source node. Optionally, other proxies may get informed about the new location (see above).
- *Object transfer:* The object is then shipped to the given destination via a message or RPC and is decoded there.
- *Object installation:* Finally, the object's data structure is installed at the destination node, the object is registered within the object table, and invocations of the object can be accepted again. As a specific requirement, a proxy must be installed for each remote object reference originating from the migrated object.

Some systems support whole clusters of objects as units of migration. Thus larger data entities can be represented as a single unit of placement [JLH88]. An example are related documents of an office procedure. Moreover, object migration can be combined with remote parameter passing; while very large objects (like complex documents) may be passed by remote object reference, small data objects (like a small table) are better passed by moving them to the callee's site together with the invocation. This technique is termed *call-by-move* [BHJ87].

### 4.3.4 Existing Systems

Several distributed object-oriented prototype systems have been implemented; a survey is given in [CHC91]. Many recent systems extend existing object-oriented programming languages toward distribution.

For example, distributed *C++* extensions have been implemented by the *Amber* system [CAL89], by the *Amadeus* system [HOC91] within the European ESPRIT project *COMANDOS*, and by the *Arjuna* system [SDP91]. A similar approach has been the basis of the *ANSA* project [ANS89], leading to the *ANSAware* system. A distributed C++ extension of the author's research group is described in [SCM93]. These systems have in common that they only introduce modest extensions of C++ or even maintain the language as it is. Most functionality is offered via system classes from which application-specific classes are derived. The functionality of various systems differs significantly; for example, Amber supports parallel multiprocessor-based computations in addition to remote interactions, and Arjuna offers distributed transactions in addition to regular RPC-style interactions. Virtually all systems assume that object class implementations are available wherever necessary; in particular, no dynamic code installation is performed as a consequence of migrations. Some relatively common functionality is represented by a class definition for distributable objects according to [SCM93]:

```
class DistributedObject {
 // ... Instance variables like location, size etc.
 public:
  DistributedObject (Location*);        // Constructor to create at a given location
  ~DistributedObject ();                // Destructor
  Location *locate ();                  // Locate the object
  boolean move (Location*);             // Move to a given location
  boolean fix ();                       // Fix at current location
                                        // (prevent from moving)
  boolean unfix ();                     // Release for migrations
  void Invoke (//...);                  // Perform generic invocation
 };
```

Methods are available for creating objects at a given location, for deleting them, for locating them, and for moving them to a given destination. Moreover, an object can be prevented from being moved by the *fix* operation. For example, this is useful for keeping documents at a location where they are currently accessed. Fixed objects can be released by *unfix*. Finally, a location-independent generic invocation operation is available that is based on the location algorithm. Subclasses add application-specific operations for remote invocation.

Other systems extend the *Smalltalk* environment toward distribution, for example *Distributed Smalltalk* [BEN90]. A distributed extension of *Modula-2+* is described in [BLA90]; the *Action Paths* approach applicable to complex office procedures (see chapter 2) has been implemented on top of it, providing an environment as discussed above. *DOWL* extends Digital Equipment's object-oriented Trellis language to distribution with all features mentioned above [ACH93]. Associated design methods and tools for distributed applications were developed in the related *DOCASE* project [MGH93].

Finally, completely new distributed object-oriented programming languages have been implemented within the *Emerald* system [BHJ87, JLH88], and within the *COMANDOS* project (language *Guide* [KMN90]). These approaches embed the functionality discussed above directly in the language; for example, Emerald offers an explicit linguistic *move* primitive. Such a language-based approach also allows for extended programming models. For example, both systems enable multiple heterogeneous implementations of the same object class. This is especially useful in heterogeneous networks where operations must be implemented differently according to different physical resources; a concrete example is a *print* operation with access to different kinds of printers.

In summary, distributed object-oriented approaches provide a very powerful, easy-to-use model for cooperative applications in a distributed environment. Compared with RPC, the programming model is more flexible due to fine-grained objects, remote object references, and object mobility. It is especially appropriate for modeling cooperative office environments; many "real" office objects like documents or desktops can directly be mapped to corresponding implementation objects. However, it will probably take years yet before the distributed object paradigm will be as mature as some RPC systems already are today.

## 4.4 Language Integration of Communication

The communication features and the additional distributed system services discussed above can either be offered as function or class libraries, or be directly embedded into *programming languages for distributed systems*. The first approach is easy to implement and does not require the software developer to learn any new language. For example, the OSF DCE offers all services as C functions. The language approach, however, can enable more detailed static checking of semantics by a compiler. Moreover, it can support advanced syntactic abstractions. In the following, typical language primitives are discussed and a comparison of some existing programming languages for distributed systems is given (cf. [BST89] for further information on a large number of such languages).

Programming languages for distributed systems typically support concurrency within an address space by lightweight processes, remote communication by message passing, by RPC, or by distributed transactions, and, optionally, logical interconnection mechanisms for establishing communication channels between processes or mailboxes. In addition to such specific language primitives, the usual linguistic features like control structures and arithmetic operations are offered, of course.

### 4.4.1 Example: Conic

A concrete example of the *Conic* programming language for distributed systems [KMS89] will illustrate the implementation of an interacting process using port-based communication.

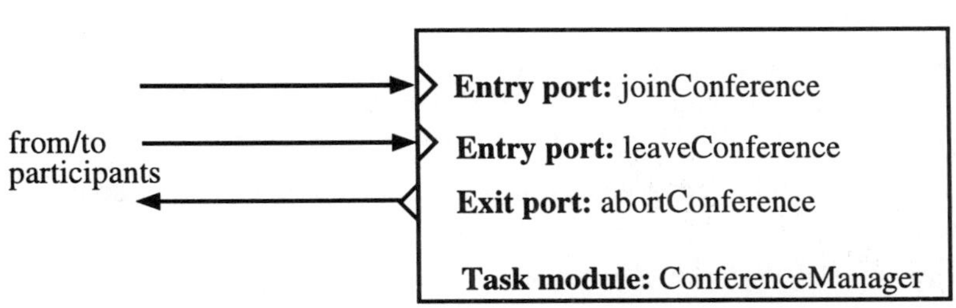


Fig. 4-7 Task module example in Conic

The process *(task module)* represents a simple conference manager with a functionality similar to the example in section 3.2 (see figure 4-7). It has an interface consisting of several entry ports for receiving and exit ports for sending messages. The process body is an infinite loop for handling received messages (some type definitions and internal functions (like *Participant* or *insertMember)* are assumed to exist already; Conic keywords are printed in bold face):

```
task module ConferenceManager;                 // module for conference management
 entryport joinConference: Participant p;      // for receiving conference join requests
          leaveConference: Participant p;      // for receiving req. to leave conference
 exitport abortConference: AbortMessage m;     // for signaling abort of conference

begin
 loop                                          // infinite loop
  select                                       // selective receive
    receive p from joinConference              // handle join request
      => insertMember (p);
    or receive p from leaveConference          // handle leave request
      => removeMember (p);
    or receive InterruptNotification           // handle internal interrupt; abort conf.
      => setupMessage (m); send m to abortConference;
  end;
 end;
end;
```

The process within the task module performs a *selective receive*; it listens both to input ports and to internal interrupts concurrently and handles the first event that occurs. This is a specific feature of Conic that is also offered by several other languages. If a message at one of the entry ports arrives, a participant is added to or removed from an internal list. If an internal interrupt notification occurs, a conference abort message is sent to the exit port and is eventually delivered to all participants this way.

Conic offers an additional *configuration language* for specifying interconnections of exit and entry ports of communicating modules in a declarative way. This allows for explicit management of the overall structure of a distributed application. For example, a participant's ports could be linked with the conference manager's ports as follows:

```
link Participant[1].joinRequests to ConferenceManager.joinConference;
link Participant[1].leaveRequests to ConferenceManager.leaveConference;
link ConferenceManager.abortConference to Participant[1].abortSignal;
```

Conic also offers additional primitives for process management and inter-process synchronization. It is a rich language with support both for computational and for structural aspects of distributed applications.

### 4.4.2 Comparison of Existing Languages

Table 4-1 gives a comparison of various programming languages for distributed systems. Important criteria are the kind of communication mechanism offered (different message passing modes (see section 3.1.2), RPC (see section 3.2), rendezvous, transactions (see section 4.1), or object interactions (see section 4.3)), the kind of concurrency support (static number of processes or dynamically adaptable number), support for selective receive of messages, and fault tolerance mechanisms offered to handle node failures (reconfiguration, exception handling, transaction recovery, and object migration).

*CSP (Communicating Sequential Processes)* [HOA78] was one of the first languages for concurrent/distributed systems. It is based on synchronous message passing with direct addressing; the sender is blocked until the receiver is ready to accept the message. Concurrency is supported by dynamic processes with static interaction paths (channels). A selective receive operation is explicitly provided. CSP is mainly intended as a language for formally reasoning about concurrency. A closely related implementation language for parallel computing is Occam with special implementations on transputer systems.

*Conic* [KMS89] supports asynchronous messages between ports with indirect addressing as discussed above. It enables dynamic process creation and provides the select primitive described. Fault tolerance techniques can be implemented by dynamic reconfiguration mechanisms; for example, a module can easily be replaced by a substitute after a node failure. *Lady* [WYB90] basically supports similar features.

| Language | Comm. mechanism | Concurrency | Selective receive | Fault tolerance |
|---|---|---|---|---|
| CSP | synchronous messages, direct | dynamic processes | select primitive | |
| Conic | asynchronous messages, indirect | dynamic processes | select primitive | dynamic reconfiguration |
| Lady | asynchronous messages, indirect | dynamic processes | | dynamic reconfiguration |
| ADA | rendezvous | static or dyn. processes | select primitive | exception handling |
| Argus | RPC/transactions | dynamic processes | | transaction recovery |
| Emerald | object interaction | dynamic processes | | object migration |

Table 4-1 Programming languages for distributed systems

*ADA* [USD83] is also suitable for implementing distributed applications. It is based on rendezvous communication (see section 3.1) and explicitly supports exception handling; thus fault tolerance mechanisms can be implemented in an application-specific way. *Argus* [LIS88] provides distributed transactions as discussed in section 4.1. Fault tolerance can therefore be achieved by transaction recovery. Finally, *Emerald* [BHJ87] uses distributed object interactions as its communication mechanism. Object migrations can be applied to handle expected system failures in advance by moving objects to substitute nodes.

The languages discussed provide sophisticated support for application-level distributed programming. However, most of them (except ADA, of course) are just prototype implementations with a limited application scope. For industrial applications, a procedural or class-based add-on of distributed communication features like RPC to more conventional programming languages like C or C++ currently seems to be more accepted practise.

## 4.5 Standardization

Many of the techniques presented are currently undergoing standardization or are already part of standardized software environments for distributed systems. We discuss some of the most prominent standardization efforts, the OSF Distributed Computing Environment, the Object Management Group's Object Management Architecture, the application-level ISO/OSI standardization, ISO's Distributed Office Applications Model, and ISO's Open Distributed Processing Approach. Finally, industry standards for PC networks are also mentioned for completeness.

### 4.5.1 The OSF Distributed Computing Environment

This section describes the architecture of the OSF Distributed Computing Environment (DCE) [OSF94a-d] as a major practical basis for building distributed applications. Some components of DCE have already been mentioned above from a technical point of view (namely RPC, Directory Service, and Security Service). DCE is becoming an industry standard for Distributed Processing; most of the major computer vendors are members of the OSF and support DCE on their platforms.

Originally, the OSF issued requests for technology (*rft*) for important distributed systems functionality. Hardware and software vendors as well as research institutes responded with technical submissions of operable prototypes. The OSF selected one or multiple systems for each required functionality based on technical criteria and on maturity. Then, the OSF integrated all the selected components and determined standardized C programming interfaces for them. Finally, the source code of the resulting DCE was offered to vendors for porting to their platforms. OSF DCE is commercially available on most major Unix systems, but also under MS Windows, OS/2, and various mainframe operating systems. Interoperability of DCE applications on these systems is guaranteed by common programming and communication interfaces, and by automatic data translation between heterogeneous data formats. For these reasons, DCE is of major importance in the distributed systems area. In marked contrast to other standards, the implementation existed first, and standardization was undertaken thereafter. This seems to have major advantages concerning the resulting functionality and time frame.

**DCE Architecture and Services:** Figure 4-8 shows the overall architecture of the OSF DCE. All DCE components are based on local operating system services (e.g. Unix) and transport services (e.g. TCP/IP). Distributed applications make explicit use of *fundamental DCE services* (in *italics* in the figure) via C programming interfaces. The other DCE services are used implicitly via the fundamental services or via modified operating system services.

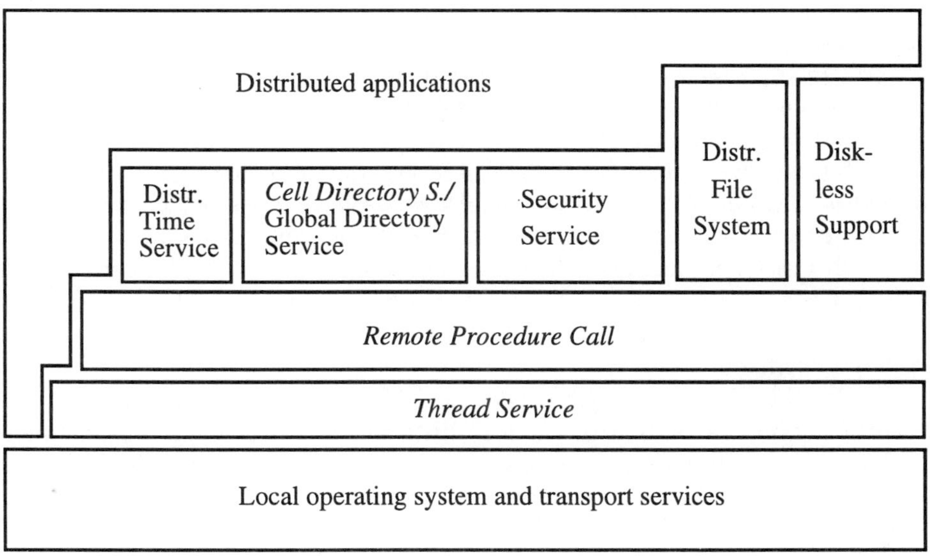


Fig. 4-8 DCE architecture

The *Thread Service* provides a portable implementation of lightweight processes (*threads*) according to *POSIX Standard 1003.4a*. Threads enable concurrent processing within a shared address space, and are especially used by RPC for implementing asynchronous invocations and multithreaded servers.

The *DCE RPC* [OSF94c-d] has already been discussed in section 3.2. It is the basis of heterogeneous systems communication with DCE. It offers significant functionality, including the C-based *Interface Definition Language (IDL)*, explicitly selectable call semantics, nested parameter structures, secure RPC with authentication and authorization based on the DCE Security Service, global (up to worldwide) naming of servers based on the X.500 directory service standard, backward calls from servers to clients, and bulk data transfer based on typed pipes (logical channels). The overall functionality is quite rich, and DCE RPC seems to be increasingly accepted as a *de facto* standard in practise. Most important, it is operable here and now. Like all other DCE components, it is based on an existing implementation that was submitted after an OSF request for technology; this implementation was part of the *Network Computing System (NCS)* of HP/Apollo and DEC. The OSF adapted the system and determined a set of interface procedures for RPC usage.

The *Cell Directory Service (CDS)* supports distributed name management as discussed in section 3.3.1. It is the basis for RPC binding and its functionality is integrated into the DCE RPC programming interface via *NSI (Name Service Interface)*. As mentioned above, it provides a robust and efficient directory service implementation for DCE cells, i.e. for domains consisting of logically related network nodes. CDS exploits replication and caching to achieve this functionality. An advanced CDS programming interface is offered by the standardized *X/Open Directory Service Interface.*

The *Global Directory Service (GDS)* extends CDS by global, cross-cell naming. As discussed in section 3.3.1, it is based on the X.500 directory service standard. Therfore, it enables interoperability not only with other DCE directory servers but also with other arbitrary X.500 servers worldwide. As an alternative, the *Internet Domain Name Service* can also be used for cross-cell naming.

The *Security Service* implements authentication, authorization, and encryption as discussed in section 3.4. These mechanisms are tighly integrated with DCE RPC; for example, RPC clients and servers can be mutually authenticated, servers can perform ACL-based access control, and all RPC messages can be encrypted on demand.

Finally, the *Distributed Time Service (DTS)* implements distributed clock synchronization, a common problem in distributed environments. It guarantees that local clocks of participating nodes are synchronized within a given interval. Moreover, synchronization with exact external time sources (e.g. with radio clocks) is supported. This functionality is important for implementing time-stamp-based distributed algorithms; it is directly exploited by other DCE components, for example by time-stamp-based name update synchronization.

The *Distributed File System (DFS)* implements cell wide transparent distributed file management. Files can be stored at different servers and can also be replicated. Clients, i.e. application programs, can access files by location-transparent names as in a local Unix file system. File access is quite efficient based on whole-file caching at the client site. This technique also supports scalability by offloading work from file servers to clients during file access. Interoperability with the widely used *Network File System* is enabled via an *NFS/DFS interface.* DFS is augmented with a *Diskless Support* component; it provides boot, swap, and file services for diskless workstations; they can thus be integrated into a DCE environment.

In summary, DCE provides very rich and integrated functionality for distributed and cooperative applications. The usage and benefits of such functionality, namely of RPC, name management, and security techniques, for cooperative office applications have already been demonstrated above. Moreover, DCE supports heterogeneous systems interoperability and is available as a product. In addition to all major Unix platforms and OpenVMS, it is also offered for host operating systems such as IBM/MVS, and for Windows and Windows NT. The RPC implementation with the IDL compiler is available in the public domain.

DCE can already simplify distributed programming significantly. However, several extensions of DCE seem to be desirable in the near future. For example, support for distributed object-oriented programming, for distributed transactions, and for atomic broadcast would be important for many applications. Another relevant question is to what extent DCE will support other standards, namely of the ISO (see section 4.5.3), or whether such standards will eventually converge.

### 4.5.2 OMG CORBA

In addition to OSF DCE, there are other emerging industry standards for open distributed environments; these are also defined joinly by hardware vendors, software developers, research institutes, and related organizations. Most notable is the *Object Management Architecture (OMA)* of the *Object Management Group (OMG)*. In particular, the *Common Object Request Broker Architecture (CORBA)* is OMA's advanced remote object interaction mechanism.

The Object Management Architecture aims at providing support for distributed object interaction in a heterogeneous environment. A main part of it is the *Object Services Architecture* [OMG93] that offers the required services with a very broad spectrum of functionality. In general, these services are at a higher level than the DCE services and cover a broader technological area. Examples are database- and transaction-oriented services, version control of software objects, concurrency control, and distributed object replication.

Distributed object interactions are supported by CORBA [OMG92], which is another part of the overall approach. CORBA supports mechanisms for identifying, locating, and accessing objects in a distributed environment. The most important characteristics of the architecture are:

- *Dynamic interfaces:* In addition to static compile-time interface definitions, interfaces can also be specified dynamically at runtime. Thus a server can export an interface on demand or can configure a specific interface according to dynamic interactive query facilities, for example. A client can take conforming actions in order to access a dynamic interface.
- *Interface repository:* All interface information can be stored in a global interface repository. This is similar to the functionality of a directory service, but additionally includes explicit type information for all interfaces. This enables clients to browse complete interface definitions and assemble dynamic interfaces accordingly.

The overall architecture also includes services that are comparable to DCE such as threads, directory, security, and time synchronization. Interoperability with DCE is provided to some extent, but standardization has not yet been completed. The Object Management Architecture has not yet reached the same level of maturity as DCE has. Its overall set of services is also much more complex and it will probably take significant effort and time to provide an overall integrated implementation. However, parts of the architecture, namely CORBA, are already available from selected vendors. Recently, the heterogeneous interoperability concept *Unified Network Objects (UNO)* on top of TCP/IP was approved by the OMG as a base for CORBA version 2.0.

### 4.5.3 Higher-Level ISO/OSI Protocols and Services

As part of the Reference Model for *Open Systems Interconnection (OSI)*, the *International Organization for Standardization (ISO)* has specified several application-level services and protocols for distributed communication [ISO84], [ISO87]. Their scope of application is comparable to the RPC approaches discussed above, i.e. application-level interprocess communication is the main focus. However, the ISO/OSI services aim at providing more generic, language- and system-independent mechanisms.

As opposed to the OSF DCE, standardization of ISO/OSI protocols started with conceptual draft papers that were discussed and further developed up to the level of a standard by the ISO. Only then did major implementations of the specified standards begin. While this may lead to wider-spectrum, system-independent mechanisms, the radically different DCE approach emphasizes well-engineered solutions with real and efficient implementations. At the moment, it is not clear how the evolution of both approaches will look and whether a synthesis can be achieved. This will mainly be a question of practical acceptance and also of strategic issues like vendor support.

Table 4-2 gives an overview of the major services of the OSI application and presentation layers. The presentation layer is responsible for data format conversions between heterogeneous systems. The application layer provides end-to-end communication services between application entities (e.g. office servers, user processes etc.). Communication is based on logical connections, the so-called application associations *(ACSE, Association Control Service Elements)*, and is actually performed via remote operation invocation *(ROSE, Remote Operations Service Elements)*, *Reliable Data Transfer (RTSE)*, or remote procedure call *(RPC)*. Specific support is provided for distributed transactions *(CCR, Commitment, Concurrency and Recovery*, and *TP-ASE, Transaction Processing Application Service Elements)*. These services are called *Common Application Service Elements (CASE)*.

Moreover, *Specific Application Service Elements (SASE)* are available for dedicated distributed systems functionality, including *Remote Database Access* (*RDA*), File Transfer, Access and Management *(FTAM)*, job transfer and manipulation (*JTM*), and message handling systems *(MHS)*; cf. section 3.1.1. In the following we discuss the presentation layer and some of the common application service elements.

| Layer | Service / notation | Functionality |
|---|---|---|
| Application (Common Services) | ACSE | Basic application-level associations |
| | ROSE | Remote operation invocation |
| | RTSE | Reliable data transfer (exactly-once semantics) |
| | RPC | Remote Procedure Call (draft level) |
| | CCR/TP | Distributed transaction support |
| Application (Specific Services) | RDA | Remote database access |
| | FTAM | File transfer, access, and management |
| | JTM | Job transfer and manipulation |
| | MHS | Message handling systems |
| Presen-tation | ASN.1 Presentation Context | Data transformation between heterogeneous data formats (mapping between local syntax and transfer syntax) |

Table 4-2 ISO/OSI application and presentation layer services

**Presentation Layer:** The presentation layer offers the following concepts for handling data conversions for heterogeneous systems communication:

- *Abstract syntax:* This syntax defines a language- and system-independent representation of data types within communication messages. It is based on the *Abstract Syntax Notation One (ASN.1)*, a standardized data description language [ISO85].
- *Transfer syntax:* The transfer syntax provides a concrete bit-level representation of communicated data items; it mainly represents the information "on the wire".
- *Encoding/decoding rules:* The mapping from a local representation described by an abstract syntax to a transfer syntax, and vice versa, is defined by basic encoding rules. For example, the rules may specify how an abstract string is mapped to a null-terminated ASCII character stream.
- *Presentation context:* Such a context associates exactly one specific transfer syntax with an abstract syntax. The context can be negotiated during connec-

tion establishment between two peers. It can also be changed dynamically, i.e. a different transfer syntax can be selected at runtime.

Figure 4-9 summarizes the relationship among these concepts based on a data conversion scenario. Two peers with different local data representations (e.g. strings as ASCII or EBCDIC) communicate. A string is described as *IA5STRING* in an abstract way. A concrete ASCII representation is selected via the presentation context as the transfer syntax for strings. The actual mapping of the local representation to the transfer syntax and vice versa is guided by encoding/decoding rules.

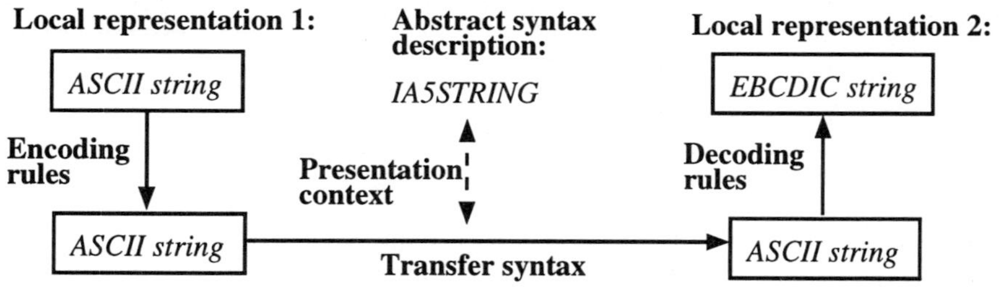


Fig. 4-9 Data conversion based on presentation layer concepts

A simple example of an ASN.1 representation of a document data structure with an optional subdocument according to section 3.2 would be as follows (embedded into a set of office environment data definitions):

```
OfficeEnvironment DEFINITIONS ::= BEGIN
 Document ::= SEQUENCE {
            name                     IA5STRING,
            contents                 IA5STRING,
            subdocument Subdocument  OPTIONAL,
            owner                    Person
            }
END
```

The notation supports many other features, for example operation declarations, C-style unions with an explicit selector, or selective repetition of data items. Translators from ASN.1 to C exist and are important for the practical use of the language. Nevertheless, an approach like the C-based IDL of DCE RPC seems to be more straightforward for practical use if language heterogeneity is not a requirement. In general, however, the ASN.1 approach is very flexible and is used by several other ISO/OSI services for data representation purposes.

**Application Layer:** *ACSE* is the basic mechanism for establishing associations between application-level communication peers. It is a prerequisite to have an established ACSE association before submitting other communication service requests. Basically, ACSE offers service primitives for establishing an association (*A-Associate*), for terminating it (*A-Release*), for signaling a system/provider-initiated abort of an association (*A-PAbort*), and for signaling a user-initiated abort (*A-UAbort*). These primitives have the usual addressing information and some additional control data as their parameters.

*ROSE* [ROP86] provides service primitives for synchronous and asynchronous remote operation invocation. It basically works like RPC but does not provide sophisticated language bindings. Input and output parameters of ROSE invocations are described by ASN.1 and are handled by the presentation layer mechanisms. Important service primitives are *R-Invoke* to perform invocations, *R-Result* to deliver the results of an operation, *R-Reject* to reject operation execution, and *R-Error* to signal execution or transmission errors. ROSE supports interactions according to the client/server model. However, it is possible that a communication partner acts both as a client and as a server. In this way, nested remote operations and backward invocations from a former server to a client are enabled.

*RTSE* [BFZ90] provides a reliable data transfer mechanism with exactly-once semantics. It is offered via a confirmed service primitive, *RT-Transfer*. In particular, RTSE masks temporary node and network failures during data transfer. Only if a transfer operation cannot be completed due to a permanent failure is it aborted, and the application is informed explicitly by an exception. To achieve this functionality, an RTSE protocol implementation must have access to stable storage in order to realize transaction-based recovery mechanisms. In general, RTSE can be classified to provide atomicity and durability for data transfer operations.

*ISO/ECMA RPC:* The International Organization for Standardization (ISO) is also working towards an RPC standard [ISO93], based on existing proposals of the European Computer Manufacturers Association (ECMA). The standard proposal defines an RPC service and protocol, and an interface definition notation (*IDN*). The functionality of IDN is comparable with the IDL of the DCE but the language is not tightly integrated with a common programming language as IDL is with C. Moreover, the proposed RPC functionality does not cover asynchronous RPCs or security aspects yet, although these issues shall be addressed by future extensions. Most important, however, no running, consolidated implementation of the ISO/ECMA RPC exists. For these reasons, it will probably take some time until it becomes clear whether this standard will be accepted in practise.

*CCR* and *TP-ASE* provide a basic protocol framework for distributed transactions [CCR86]. The major service primitives are *C-Begin* to initiate a new transaction, *C-Prepare*, initiated by a coordinator to run the prepare-to-commit phase, *C-Ready* to inform a coordinator that a prepare-to-commit was successful, *C-Refuse* to request an abort due to a failed prepare-to-commit, *C-Commit* to initiate a final commit, and *C-Rollback* to initiate a final abort. *TP* provides an extended transaction processing framework. It mainly supports full coordination of the commit phase, without requiring any explicit intermediate actions from the application; with basic CCR, the application must determine explicitly how to react to a *C-Refuse,* for example. For these reasons, TP only needs the service primitives *TP-Begin, TP-Commit*, and *TP-Abort* (plus some auxiliary primitives), but no intermediate *Prepare, Ready,* or *Refuse*. TP explicitly handles node failures, network partitions, and communication timeouts. It is even possible to select a new transaction coordinator dynamically. In summary, TP simplifies transaction handling significantly compared to basic CCR.

Of the other services, RDA is discussed in more detail in chapter 6, and MHS has already been presented in section 3.1.1. FTAM and JTM are somewhat outside the scope of our discussion and are only established to a limited degree in practise.

In summary, the services and protocols of the ISO/OSI application layers provide various peer-to-peer communication mechanisms to be used directly by applications. Some standards like MHS, ASN.1, and RDA have been accepted pretty well in practise already. However, acceptance of some of the other ISO standards is still very limited - and some important standards like RPC are still under development. Moreover, the lack of language bindings and advanced system support as found in DCE - for example, for threads, replicated name management, security techniques, and time synchronization - makes it an open question when and to what extent these standards will find their way into industrial practise.

The *ISO Development Environment (ISODE)* [ROR91] is currently the most important implementation of the already standardized ISO/OSI application layer services. It has been developed jointly by several software engineers from various American and European insitutions, supported by several companies. ISODE mainly supports ASN.1, ACSE, ROSE, RTSE, FTAM, and X.500.

The environment is well documented and has been used in several research and development projects. It is important that it provides a relatively complete implementation of the standards. Whether ISODE or comparable environments will gain major acceptance in practise will mainly depend on future vendor support and on experiences with industrial software development projects. For cooperative office applications, ISODE provides the required set of basic communication services. However, its current functionality and usability does not seem to reach the level of OSF DCE.

### 4.5.4 Distributed Office Applications Model

On top of basic client/server interactions supported by the remote operations service element, the ISO has also standardized an office-specific model, the *Distributed Office Applications Model (DOAM)* [ISO89]. The model specifies basic client/server processing functionality in office environments and includes a number of supplemenatal services. In particular, it comprises the following components:

- *Referenced Data Transfer (RDT):* This service supports the remote transfer of document references, without necessarily copying the referenced document. For example, site A might have a reference to a document stored at site B. If A passes the reference to site C, C can access the document remotely but does not necessarily get a copy of the document instantaneously. The basic concept is similar to passing object references in distributed object-oriented systems (see section 4.3).

- *Document Filing and Retrieval (DFR):* This service provides the capability for large-capacity non-volatile document storage to multiple users in a distributed office system. Document retrieval and browsing are controlled by document-specific attributes. The standard does not define a dedicated database architecture for document storage but mainly the interaction protocol between clients and document filing servers.
- *Document Printing Application (DPA)*: The print application provides a facility for shared access to high-quality printers in order to print structured documents. This includes name management of printers, authorization and authentication of users, and actual document transfer.
- *Message Transfer Application*: This component supports interpersonal message transfer based on MHS / MOTIS, i.e. the X.400 standard (see section 3.1.1). It also includes the message store facility discussed in section 3.1.1.

DOAM is interrelated with, and represents a common framework for, several other standards, including the document architectures discussed in chapter 5. However, it does not provide or define a support environment for actual office applications. Therefore, it will be the task of vendors and software developers to provide such technology based on DOAM. In this book, we have already discussed selected DOAM services, namely MHS, and will also focus on other aspects like document management later. In addition, we will often try to outline practical solutions and systems that are not directly related to such standards in order to give concrete examples whenever possible.

### 4.5.5 Open Distributed Processing

In order to address the full scope of distributed application development, the ISO and the ECMA have also developed a more general approach covering all major aspects of distributed applications, and not only the communication issues as the OSI model does.

**ODP model:** The approach is called *Open Distributed Processing (ODP)* [ODP89] and mainly provides a description model for distributed applications. It is hardly supported by actual tools yet but serves as a technique for decomposing applications according to different *viewpoints* defined by the model:

- The *enterprise viewpoint* defines the business environment of an application, i.e. business activities and policies, management and administrative structures, and business-oriented constraints.
- The *information viewpoint* describes the information structure and information flow of an application, i.e. the information types and values, the information processing units, and the time dependence of information.

- The *computation viewpoint* defines actual software structures and interfaces of a modular application, i.e. application components and component relationships.
- The *engineering viewpoint* defines the functional requirements of an application, i.e. processing, memory, and communications requirements, as well as performance aspects and dependability issues.
- The *technology viewpoint* describes the physical hardware and system software structures used by an application.

The definition of these viewpoints has been influenced by work within the ANSA project in the UK, which resulted in the ANSAware environment for distributed processing [ANS89]. The viewpoints provide a conceptual framework for application and tool development. However, their definition is at a relatively high and abstract level. Nevertheless, they can provide an interesting basis for distributed application development.

**Application of the ODP approach to complex office procedures:** A complex office procedure environment for concrete office procedures as discussed in chapter 2 could be described by the ODP model as summarized in table 4-3.

| Viewpoint | Described aspects of the application |
|---|---|
| Enterprise | Set of required office procedures<br>Set of servers/agents involved<br>Time and security restrictions |
| Information | Types of documents/forms involved<br>Office procedure data structures |
| Computation | Server/agent interfaces<br>System component interfaces<br>(e.g. directory service) |
| Engineering | Resource requirements of servers (e.g. printer access, CPU requirements for long-term computations) |
| Technology | Hardware system structure (involved host systems, workstations, and PCs), system software used (e.g. DCE or ISODE) |

Table 4-3 ODP-based description of office procedure support

The enterprise viewpoint describes the set of required office procedures as found in the former, non-computerized environment, as well as the set of office clerks (agents) or automatic servers involved. Moreover, specific restrictions concerning task deadlines, security requirements regarding involved documents, and other aspects like monetary constraints are described. The information viewpoint provides specifications of the documents and forms involved (e.g. travel expense forms, order forms etc.). Moreover, it describes the data structures for representing office procedures themselves (like an execution graph).

The computation viewpoint describes the software outline for implementing the system. The main issues are the concrete functional interfaces of office servers and agents, and the interfaces of underlying system components (like a directory service, a remote execution service, or a document storage system).

The engineering viewpoint describes the resource requirements of office servers to perform dedicated services like printing, intensive computations, or persistent document management. Finally, the technology viewpoint is concerned with the hardware involved, for example focusing on heterogeneity aspects of various hosts, workstations, and PCs. Moreover, the applied system software, for example for distributed communication support, is a concern of this viewpoint.

**ODP trading:** A specific component defined by the ODP model is the ODP Trader [ISO92]. This can be characterized as an extended kind of directory service that maps RPC servers to client requests in an "intelligent" way. The idea is summarized in figure 4-10.

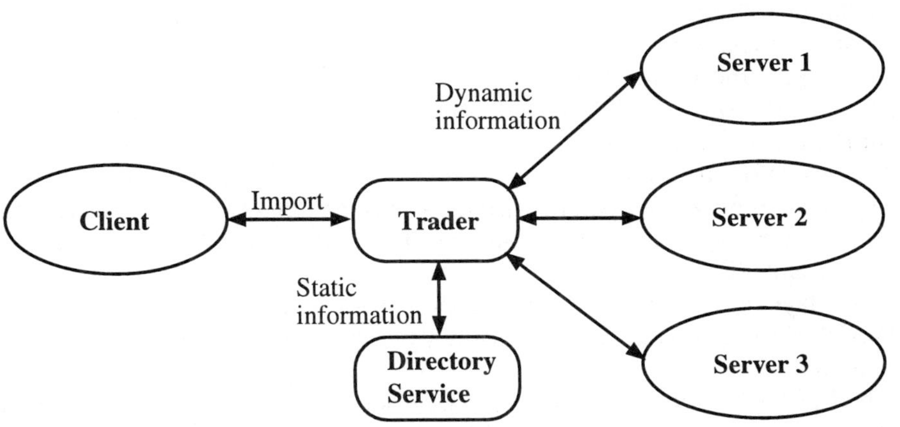


Fig. 4-10 ODP Trading approach

A client specifies an RPC request, giving a description of the required server interface (see section 3.2), and passes the request to the trader. The trader first contacts a directory service to evaluate all static information about the existing servers. This is identical with traditional directory-supported RPC binding. The result is a list of potential servers that can execute the client request. Afterwards, however, the trader first contacts all servers or a selected subset of them to ask for dynamic information about their status - this may include their availability, their current request queue, or their interpolated CPU load, for example. Based on this information, the trader performs a heuristic optimization and finally binds the client to the most appropriate server. ODP trading can therefore be classified as being a higher-level service on top of a directory service.

In the office procedure example, the ODP trading support can obviously be used to optimize the mapping from basic service requests to implementing servers within office procedure execution. However, the main problem of the overall ODP approach seems to be the lack of a universal linguistic representation of the viewpoint issues, together with computer-assisted development tools for transforming and integrating information of different viewpoints. A promising approach would be to offer a wide-spectrum design language with dedicated parts for addressing different viewpoints. Tool support would be required for stepwise refinement of such an approach and for design information management during various phases down to implementation and maintenance. The current ODP approach can only serve as a basic description technique for organizing an application design.

### 4.5.6 Industry Standards for PC Networks

In the area of personal computers, there are also a number of important *de facto* industry standards. Although the major emphasis of this book is put on CSCW in workstation settings, some approaches in the PC area shall also be mentioned here for completeness.

Among the most important systems are *Novell Netware, Microsoft LAN Manager,* and *Banyan VINES.* Novell Netware is a file-server-based network operating system. It supports a multiuser and multitasking mode. All important resources can be managed by the file server and are accessed by client PCs. The clients can run different operating systems such as OS/2, MS DOS or MS Windows. Communication is based on the IPX (Internetwork Packet Exchange Protocol) and SPX (Sequenced Packet Exchange Protocol) at the network and transport layers, respectively. It also supports the standard LAN interface, Novell NetBIOS. Recent versions of the system also support sophisticated directory and security features.

The MS LAN Manager is based on OS/2 but is also available for DOS. It also supports server-based resource management. Interprocess communication is based on so-called *named pipes.* These communication facilities are independent of the location of interacting processes. On top of it, various RPC mechanisms are available. Like the other systems, *Banyan VINES (Virtual Network System)* also supports the coexistence of different networks and low-level communication mechanisms. In particular, bridging facilities for heterogeneous networks are part of the system. Due to its close relationship with Unix, it is also suited for medium to large environments with several hundred systems.

In summary, all these three approaches, and numerous related systems, support interconnection and communication within PC networks, and partially also integration with workstation environments. Therefore, they can provide a suitable base for CSCW applications on PC platforms. However, due to the limited resources and operating system functionality of PCs, most of the advanced CSCW environments in the research domain have been built on top of Unix workstations. Therefore, the major focus, as in the context of distributed systems, has been put on this area.

## 4.6 Exercises

1. [Conceptual design]

Model the office procedure "introduction of new product" from the exercises in chapter 2 as a distributed transaction. (First perform a decomposition into hierarchical subtasks, then outline the nested transaction tree; indicate which transactions have to be executed sequentially or are executed conditionally.)

2. [Implementation]

Design and implement an emulation environment for locating mobile objects. Design the following data structures or object classes:

- MobileObject (with a global identifier, a location, and operations to move it to a new node and to locate it)
- Proxy (representing forward addresses left after migrations)
- Node (representing a simple emulation of physical nodes).

Hints:

- Each node must have a list of its local objects and proxies available.
- A proxy must be installed when an object migrates.
- A proxy is replaced by the object itself again when the object moves back to a previous location.
- A recursive location algorithm as described in this chapter may be applied; however, extesions and details like object access via the birthnode may be omitted.
- Proxy chains may be compressed after locating an object; in particular, the requesting node may update its proxy.

3. [Basic knowledge]

Consider the OSF DCE technology components. Which components could have been (or actually have been) used throughout the previous exercises and how? Consider office system examples where specific services like the distributed file system are useful.

4. [Basic knowledge]

Explain the following ISO/OSI terms:

- Abstract syntax
- Transfer syntax
- Encoding rules

- Presentation context
- ACSE
- ROSE.

5. [Conceptual design]

Apply the ODP trading approach to a client/print server scenario. A client selects a print server based on the server's interface, availability, expected response time, distance, costs, and paper reserve. Which of these parameters are better handled by an underlying directory service, and which of them by the servers themselves?

6. [Implementation]

Implement a simple trader emulation for this example. (Develop data structures for a directory service table, for a print server, and for a client request; ignore the actual distribution of servers in your emulation; test the implementation with a scenario involving a client and about five print servers.)

## 4.7 References

[ACH93] Achauer, B.: The DOWL Distributed Object-Oriented Language; *Comm. of the ACM, Vol. 36, No. 9, Sept. 1993, pp. 48-55*

[ANS89] Advanced Network Systems Architecture (ANSA): ANSA Reference Manual; *APM Ltd., 24 Hills Road, Cambridge CB2 IJP, UK (March 1989)*

[ART90] Artsy, Y.: Routing Objects on Action Paths; *10th IEEE Int. Conf. on Distributed Computing Systems, Paris, 1990, pp. 572-579*

[BEN90] Bennett, J.K.: Experience with Distributed Smalltalk; *Software - practise and Exp., Vol. 20, No. 2, Feb. 1990, pp. 157-180*

[BFZ90] Blumann, W., Fauth, D., Zok, H.: Considerations of the OSI Reliable Transfer Service; *Comp. Comm., Vol. 13, No. 3, April 1990, pp. 143-148*

[BHJ87] Black, A., Hutchinson, N., Jul, E., Levy, H., Carter, L.: Distribution and Abstract Types in Emerald; *IEEE Trans. on Softw. Eng., Vol. 13, No. 1, Jan. 1987, pp. 65-75*

[BIJ87] Birman, K.P., Joseph, T.A.: Reliable Communication in the Presence of Failures; *ACM Trans. on Computer Systems, Vol. 5, No. 1, Feb. 1987, pp. 47-76*

[BLA90] Black, A., Artsy, Y.: Implementing Location Independent Invocation; *IEEE Trans. on Parallel and Distributed Systems, Vol. 1, No. 1, Jan. 1990, pp. 107-119*

[BST89] Bal, H.E., Steiner, J.G., Tanenbaum, A.S.: Programming Languages for Distributed Computing Systems; *ACM Comp. Surv., Vol. 21, No. 3, Sept. 1989, pp. 261-322*

[CAL89] Chase, J.S., Amador, F.G., Lazowska, E.D., Levy, H.M., Littlefield, R.J.: The Amber System: Parallel Programming on a Network of Multiprocessors; *12th ACM Symp. on Operating Systems Principles, Litchfield Park, AZ, 1989, pp. 147-158*

[CCR86] ISO: DIS8649, Service Definition for Common Application Service Elements - Part 3 - Commitment, Concurrency and Recovery; *Information Processing Systems - Open Systems Interconnection (1986)*

[CER84] Ceri, S.: Distributed Databases; *McGraw-Hill, New York, 1984*

[CHC91] Chin, R.S., Chanson, S.T.: Distributed Object-Based Programming Systems; *ACM Comp. Surv., Vol. 23, No. 1, March 1991, pp. 91-124*

[ENC92] Encina Transaction Processing System; *Transarc Corp., Pittsburgh, PA, 1992*

[EPS89] Eppinger, J.L., Spector, A.Z.: Transaction Processing in Unix: A Camelot Perspective; *Unix Review, Vol. 7, 1989, pp. 58-67*

[GRR93] Gray, J., Reuter, A.: Transaction Processing - Concepts and Techniques; *Morgan Kaufmann Publishers, San Mateo, CA, 1993*

[HÄR83] Härder, T., Reuter, A.: Principles of Transaction-Oriented Database Recovery; *ACM Computing Surveys, Vol. 15, 1983, pp. 287-317*

[HOA78] Hoare, C.A.R.: Communicating Sequential Processes*; Comm. of the ACM, Vol. 21, No. 8, Aug. 1978, pp. 666-677*

[HOC91] Horn, C., Cahill, V.: Supporting Distributed Applications in the Amadeus Environment; *Comp. Comm., Vol. 14, No. 6, July/Aug. 1991, pp. 358-365*

[ISO84] ISO: Open Systems Interconnection - Basic Reference Model*; ISO Int. Standard 7498, ISO 1984*

[ISO85] ISO: Open Systems Interconnection - Specification of Basic Encoding Rules for Abstract Syntax Notation One (ASN.1); *ISO/DIS 8825, ISO 1985*

[ISO87] ISO: Open Systems Interconnection - Application Layer Structure*; ISO Draft Proposal 9545, ISO 1987*

[ISO89] ISO: Information Processing - Text Communication - Distributed Office Applications Model; *ISO/IEC JTC 1/SC18/WG 4 N 965, 1989*

[ISO92] International Organization for Standardization: ODP Trader; *ISO/IEC JTC1/SC21, 1992*

[ISO93] ISO: Open Systems Interconnection - Remote Procedure Call*; ISO/IEC JTC1/SC21/WG6, Working Draft, 1993*

[JLH88] Jul, E., Levy, H., Hutchinson, N., Black, A.: Fine-Grained Mobility in the Emerald System*; ACM Trans. on Comp. Syst., Vol. 6, No. 1, Feb. 1988, pp. 109-133*

[KMN90] Krakowiak, S., Meysembourg, M., Van Nguyen, H., Riveill, M., Roisin, C., Rousset de Pina, X.: Design and Implementation of an Object-Oriented, Strongly Typed Language for Distributed Applications*; J. of Object-Oriented Programming, Vol. 3, No. 3, 1990, pp. 11-22*

[KMS89] Kramer, J., Magee, J., Sloman, M.: Constructing Distributed Systems in CONIC*; IEEE Trans. on Softw. Eng., Vol. 15, No. 6, June 1989, pp. 663-675*

[LIG85] Lin, K.-J., Gannon, J.D.: Atomic Remote Procedure Call; *IEEE Trans. on Software Engineering, Vol. 11, 1985, pp. 1126-1135*

[LIS88] Liskov, B.: Distributed Programming in Argus; *Comm. of the ACM, Vol. 31, No. 3, March 1988, pp. 300-312*

[MGH93] Mühlhäuser, M., Gerteis, W., Heuser, L.: DOCASE: A Methodic Approach to Distributed Programming; *Comm. of the ACM, Vol. 36, No. 9, Sept. 1993, pp. 127-138*

[MOS82] Moss, J.E.: Nested Transactions and Reliable Distributed Computing; *2nd Symp. on Reliability in Distributed Software and Database Systems, Pittsburgh, PA, July 1982, pp. 33-39*

[ODP89] European Computer Manufacturers Association (ECMA): Support Environment for Open Distributed Processing; (SE-ODP) *ECMA/TC32-TG2/89/67, Final Draft (July 1989)*

[OMG92] Object Management Group: The Common Object Request Broker: Architecture and Specification; *OMG, 1992*

[OMG93] Object Management Group: Object Services Architecture; *OMG, 1993*

[OSF94a] Open Software Foundation: Introduction to OSF DCE; *Open Software Foundation, Cambridge, MA, USA, 1994*

[OSF94b] Open Software Foundation: DCE Users Guide and Reference; *Open Software Foundation, Cambridge, MA, USA, 1994*

[OSF94c] Open Software Foundation: DCE Application Development Guide; *Open Software Foundation, Cambridge, MA, USA, 1994*

[OSF94d] Open Software Foundation: DCE Application Development Reference; *Open Software Foundation, Cambridge, MA, USA, 1994*

[PUN87] Pu, C., Noe, J.D.: Design and Implementation of Nested Transactions in EDEN; *6th Symp. on Reliability in Distributed Software and Database Systems, 1987, pp. 126-136*

[ROP86] DP9072, Remote Operations - Part 1: Model, Notation and Service Definition; *Information Processing Systems - Text Communication - MOTIS (1986)*

[ROR91] Rose, M.T., Onions, J.P., Robbins, C.J.: The ISO Development Environment; *X-Tel Services Ltd., Nottingham, UK, 1991*

[SCM93] Schill, A., Mock, M.: DC++: Distributed Object-Oriented System Support on top of OSF DCE; *Distributed Systems Engineering Journal, Vol. 1, 1993, pp. 112-125*

[SDP91] Shrivastava, S.K., Dixon, G.N., Parrington, G.D.: An Overview of the Arjuna Distributed Programming System; *IEEE Software, Jan. 1991, pp. 66-73*

[TUX92] Tuxedo System Transaction Manager, Unix System Laboratories, 1992

[USD83] US Department of Defense: Reference Manual for the ADA Programming Language; *ANSI/MIL-STD-1815A, DoD, Washington, DC, Jan. 1983*

[WYB90] Wybranietz, D., Buhler, P.: The LADY Programming Environment for Distributed Operating Systems; *Future Generation Comp. Syst., Vol. 6, No. 3, Dec. 1990, pp. 209-223*

[XDT92] X/Open Distributed Transaction Processing; *X/Open Ltd., Reading, Berkshire, UK, 1992*

# 5 Cooperative Document Management

This chapter outlines how document management in advanced office applications is supported by current computing technology. Specific aspects discussed are models for structured documents, standards for uniform document representation and transmission, specific data and document models for shared and distributed environments, and requirements concerning multimedia document extensions.

The basic concepts described are applied to selected CSCW office applications. For example, we show how document models are related to hypertext and hypermedia environments, or how distributed document management can be exploited by data management facilities of distributed office procedures.

## 5.1 Motivation and Foundations

### 5.1.1 Characteristics of Document Management

Chapter 2 has described the area of computer supported cooperative work. It became clear that applications such as GDSS, complex coordination systems, and complex office procedures impose specific requirements concerning cooperative document management. In particular, the data manipulated by such applications are mostly online documents or parts thereof. Therefore, distributed office computation techniques as described in chapter 3 are not sufficient as the sole basis for CSCW. Specific support for cooperative document management is required; this is a specialization of cooperative/distributed data management. As opposed to pure data, documents have special characteristics (see figure 5-1):

- *Structure:* Documents typically consist of a nested, *complex* structure. They comprise dedicated parts like chapters, sections, subsections, references, footnotes etc. Usually, this structure has to conform to given guidelines; for example, a subsection should only occur within a section.
- *Contents:* The contents of a document mainly consist of text but may also comprise other media like graphics, images, or tables. The different content portions must be explicitly associated with the structural elements of a document. Structure and contents representation is supported by dedicated *document models*.
- *Processing model:* As opposed to general data with associated arbitrary processing functions, a more specific processing model can be defined for

documents. Typical processing phases are document editing, device-independent document formatting, and device-dependent formatting.

- *Layout:* As a result of document formatting, a specific document layout is generated. This depends on the logical structure of the document, on specified formatting options, and on device-dependent formatting requirements.
- *Document access and transfer:* Between their processing phases, documents may be transferred between potentially heterogeneous computer systems. Moreover, in order to use documents in a cooperative office environment, they must be accessible both locally and remotely; this allows document sharing among participants in CSCW applications.

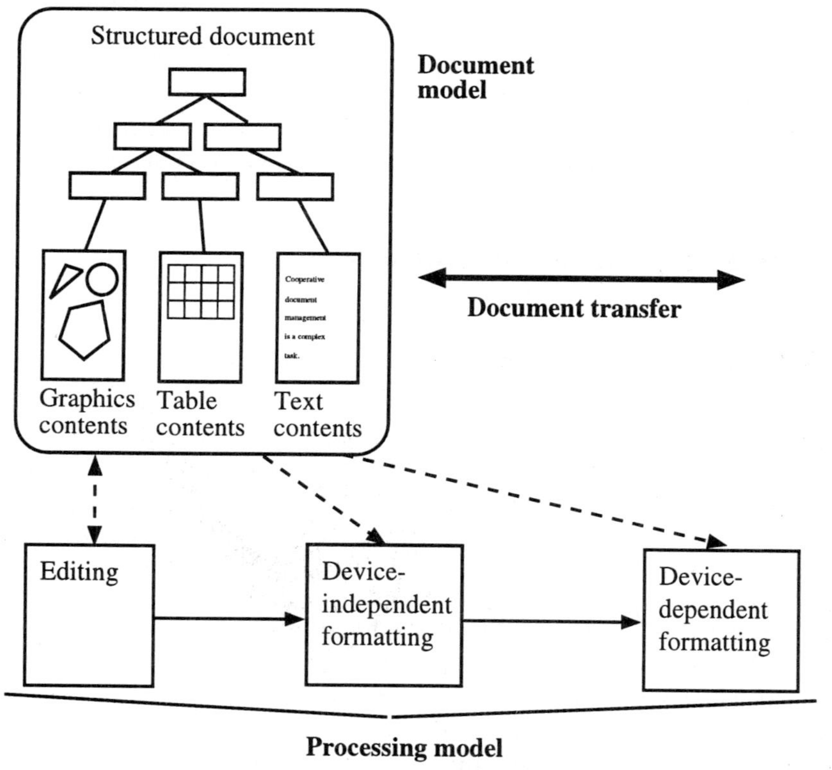


Fig. 5-1 Important aspects of document management

Several requirements arise from these characteristics:

- *Document representation:* Description notation and corresponding data structures are required in order to represent the complex structure of documents. An explicit structural representation facilitates the implementation of comfortable document editors. Moreover, it allows for specifying structural restrictions that specific documents have to conform to. For example, forms within a complex office procedure usually consist of a dedicated, pre-defined sequence of data entries. An explicit structural representation is also required to guide data conversions when documents are transferred between heterogeneous computer systems. In addition to the structure of a document, its layout should also be represented explicitly.

- *Document structure and contents classification:* In order to define and manage application-specific document structures, *document classes* or *types* must be supported. A given document class (e.g. travel expense form, memo, technical report etc.) represents a template for a set of document instances with common structural characteristics. Likewise, a pre-defined set of contents classes (e.g. text, graphics, and images) should be offered. This way, the different content portions and their media can be supported by dedicated tools like editors or communication facilities.
- *Document transfer mechanisms:* For document exchange between distributed and potentially heterogeneous sites, some common document transfer representation must exist in order to enable interoperability. Moreover, a distinction should be made between transfer of the logical structure and contents of a document, and transfer of its layout structure.

In order to meet these requirements, a semantic document model is required that supports explicit document representation.

### 5.1.2 Semantic Data Models: A Basis for Document Models

Semantic data models are a major conceptual basis for existing document models. A brief overview, taken from [PEM88] and [POT88], should be sufficient to serve as a basic introduction to this area.

A semantic data model is a representation scheme that allows more semantic content to be expressed than more traditional models like the relational database approach. This is achieved by a combination of several features (see figure 5-2):

- *Object and relationship representation:* The basic units of a semantic data model are objects (data entities) with explicit relationships between them. As opposed to object-oriented programming languages, an object need not necessarily have operations associated with it although some semantic data models support them. Relationships can be augmented with characteristics like cardinality. Whole documents and document components can be modeled as objects linked by relationships.
- *Object classification:* Similar objects are grouped into classes as discussed in chapter 3. A class defines the data attributes that an object may have. Examples of document classes are reports, memos, and various types of forms. Documents are instances of such pre-defined classes, similar to the class/instance relationship in object-oriented programming systems.
- *Unstructured objects:* Advanced semantic data models support objects with large quantities of unstructured data as their contents. This property is im-

portant for representing multimedia documents with text, graphics, bitmaps, and audio content portions.

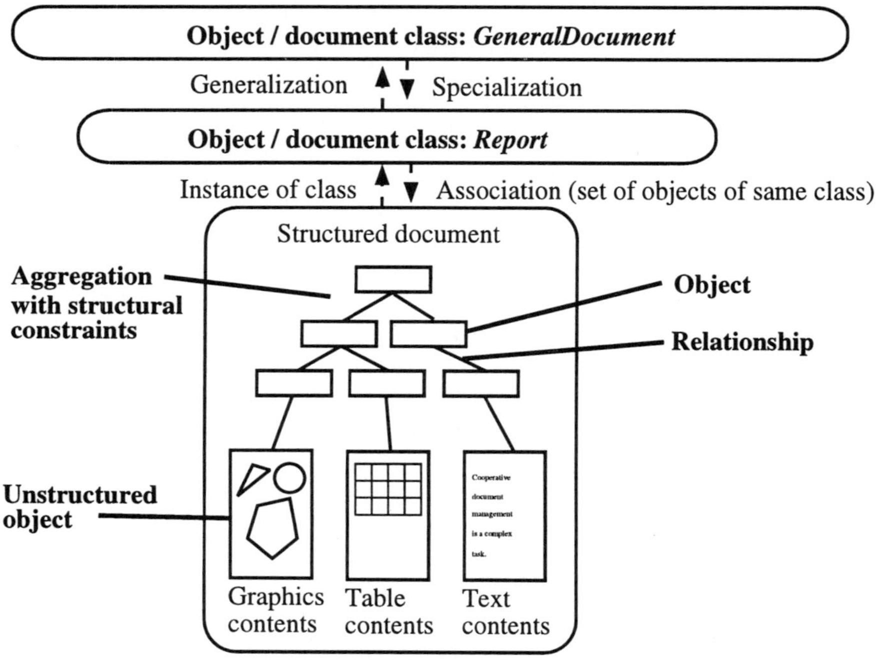


Fig. 5-2 Aspects of semantic data models applied to documents

- *Generalization / specialization:* Classes can be embedded into an inheritance hierarchy (single inheritance) or lattice (multiple inheritance). A superclass is a generalization of its subclassses while a subclass is a specialization of its superclass(es). For example, a travel expense form may be a subclass of a general expense form which may be a subclass of a general form.
- *Aggregation:* An object can be composed of a hierarchy of component objects. This aggregation mechanism allows complex objects to be represented as a logical unit. A document as an aggregation of components like sections, subsections, and figures can be edited, stored, and transferred as a unit.
- *Association:* An association is a set of objects of the same class. The set abstraction especially supports content- or descriptor-based search operations on documents. It is also useful for transmitting folders of related documents or forms as a unit.
- *Constraints and dynamic aspects:* Some advanced semantic data models allow for explicit specification of semantic constraints on data objects. An example from the document area is the restriction that a subsection can only

occur within a section. Moreover, some models support representation of dynamic aspects by offering operations or database transactions on objects.

These characteristics are a basic foundation of document models. Most important are object and relationship representation, object classification, unstructured object representation, and aggregation. In conjunction with object-oriented modeling, generalization and specialization are also relevant elements.

One of the first approaches with semantic data modeling facilities was the *Entity-Relationship Model* [CHE76]. An example of a concrete semantic data model offering most of the properties discussed is the *SDM* model [HAM81]. More recent implementations of semantic data models can be found in the object-oriented database area discussed in chapter 6. The standardized document models presented in more detail below are dedicated kinds of semantic data models for documents.

### 5.1.3 Models for Cooperative Document Management

In addition to models for document structures, related models are required to manage documents in a distributed environment cooperatively. Depending on the application, different approaches of increasing complexity can be taken:

1. *Transfer of documents as unstructured files:* In the simplest case, documents are represented as unstructured files and are exchanged between cooperating sites via basic file transfer (e.g. using *ftp* or *e-mail*). A common example is the transfer of $T_EX$ source files or of formatted *PostScript* files. The major drawback of this approach is the lack of structural document representation and the lack of system-controlled coordination between participants. Although the approach is viable for simple applications, we will not discuss it further.
2. *Transfer of structured documents:* A higher level of abstraction is achieved by representing the complex structure of documents explicitly and by supporting transfer of such structures. The major advantage is that editors and other tools can exploit the structural representation. However, coordination is still left to the application.
3. *Shared access to structured documents:* A more advanced functionality is achieved by supporting controlled and shared remote access to structured documents. This includes locking documents for editing, fetching cached copies of documents, and coordinating access and updates via explicit inter-user protocols. Multiuser document editors implement such functionality (see section 2.1.3). Most operations are eventually mapped down to basic document transfer mechanisms.
4. *Distributed document models:* Finally, document components can themselves be stored in a distributed way at different sites. In addition to shared access facilities, remote inter-document references and dynamic relocation of document components by object migration are supported. Examples of such approaches are distributed hypermedia systems, and, to a limited degree concerning data modeling, distributed object-oriented systems.

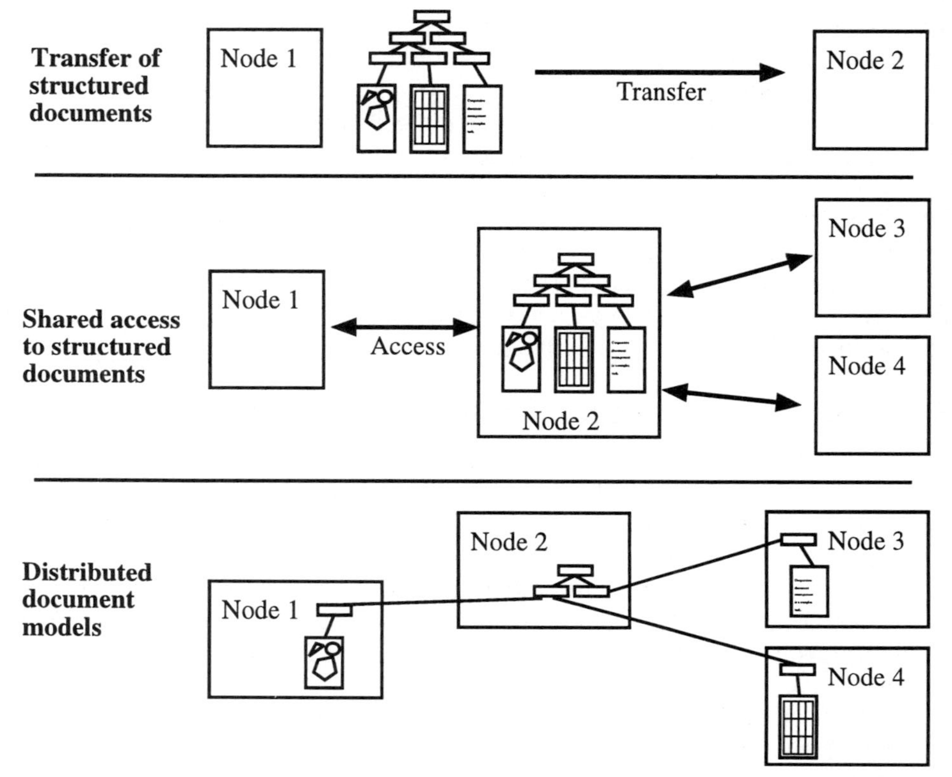


Fig. 5-3 Models for cooperative document management

Figure 5-3 summarizes approaches 2, 3, and 4. As an example of structured document transfer, a complex document with different content portions is shipped from node 1 to node 2 using a common transfer format. The second example illustrates shared document access; a structured document is stored at node 2 and is concurrently accessed from nodes 1, 3, and 4. Finally, the document itself is distributed among different nodes 1-4 in the third example. The different structural parts and content portions are linked via node-spanning remote references. In the following, we first discuss structured document modeling and transfer in detail and then outline extensions toward the other two scenarios.

### 5.1.4 The Need for Standards

In relatively small, homogeneous office environments, *ad hoc* approaches to cooperative document management may be sufficient. However, when computer systems and application software are heterogeneous, such approaches cannot provide a base for interoperability. It then becomes necessary to introduce standards with globally-agreed document formats. Although local and implementation-specific document structures may still exist, all systems can transform them into a universal structure for cooperation and document transfer purposes.

In the following sections, we discuss three standardized techniques for representing and transferring structured documents, namely the *Open Document Architecture and Interchange Format (ODA/ODIF),* the *Structured Generalized Markup Language (SGML), and EDIFACT (Electronic Data Interchange for Administration Commerce and Transport).* We mainly focus on ODA due to its conceptual richness and give a shorter discussion of the other two standards. Based on these approaches, we then show how such facilities can be conceptually extended to shared and distributed document management.

## 5.2 Open Document Architecture

The *Open Document Architecture (ODA)* (cf. e.g. [HKN89]) is a standard for representation and interchange of structured documents. The standard [ISO88] consists of eight parts, namely introduction (1), open document architecture (2), document layout and imaging process (3), document profile (4), Open Document Interchange Format *(ODIF)* (5), character content architectures (6), raster graphics content architecture (7), and geometric graphics content architecture (8).

Part 2 defines the structural representation of office documents, part 3 is concerned with document layout generation, part 4 defines techniques for specifying document classes based on so-called profiles, part 5 describes the interchange format for document transfer, and parts 6-8 specify the representation of text, raster graphics (bitmaps), and geometric graphics (line-oriented drawings). The following ODA overview focuses on the logical and layout structure of ODA documents, and on ODA document processing and transfer.

### 5.2.1 ODA Document Representation

ODA represents documents as tree structures. A document is an aggregation of objects. It is described by a *logical structure.* This structure subdivides it into objects such as sections, subsections, paragraphs, figures, and footnotes, for example. Structural objects can also be defined in an application-specific way; further examples are address labels, logos, and sales tables. According to the standard, an object is called a *composite logical object* if it consists of part objects; the leaf objects are called *basic logical objects.* Moreover, the top-level object is called the *document logical root.*

The visual appearance of a formatted document is separated from its logical structure. It is defined by a *layout structure.* This consists of *page sets, pages, frames* within a page, and, eventually, basic *blocks.*

Within both structures, only the leaves of the trees hold the actual contents of a document, i.e. text or graphics. The two structures are interrelated for a given document: they share the same content portions. For example, a paragraph of the logical structure has some text associated with it which is mapped to one or several blocks of the layout structure. In many cases, this mapping is even one-to-one, i.e. the contents of a basic logical structure element are mapped directly to a single layout block. However, different mappings are possible; for example, the contents of a long paragraph could be split over two layout pages, and would therefore be mapped to several blocks eventually.

An example of the correspondence of the ODA logical and layout structures is given in figure 5-4. The example represents a travel expense form used in a complex office procedure implementing travel expense processing. The form is structured into a travel description consisting of a list of costs with date, textual description, and total costs for each item, an employee field (applicant for expenses refund) with name, number, and signature, and an approval field with the same information for the approving manager.

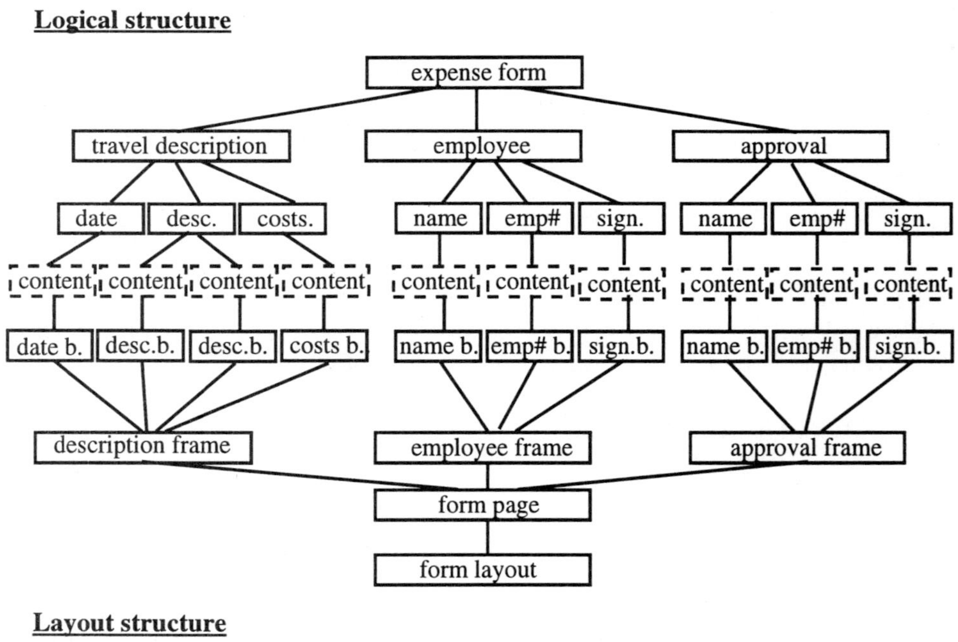


Fig. 5-4 Correspondence of logical and layout structures of ODA

The travel description can be a repetition of several items describing the expenses of several days. However, in the example given, only one item is shown.

For all other fields, only one instance can exist within one form. Each field has a content portion associated with it which is mapped to a block (abbreviated as *b.*) of the layout structure. As an exception, the textual travel description is split into two content portions which are mapped to two different blocks. Thus the display of the description can be split into two columns, for example. Corresponding to the logical structure, the blocks are mapped to frames which are then mapped onto a single page of the form. A possible visual appearance of the form with sample data added is shown in figure 5-5.

The exact positioning of the blocks is not specified by the given layout structure but by additional attributes. The visual appearance could be changed significantly if the allocation of content portions to blocks were modified. For example, the travel description text could be laid out in more than two columns or in only one column. Similarly, the first and last name of the employee could be allocated to different blocks.

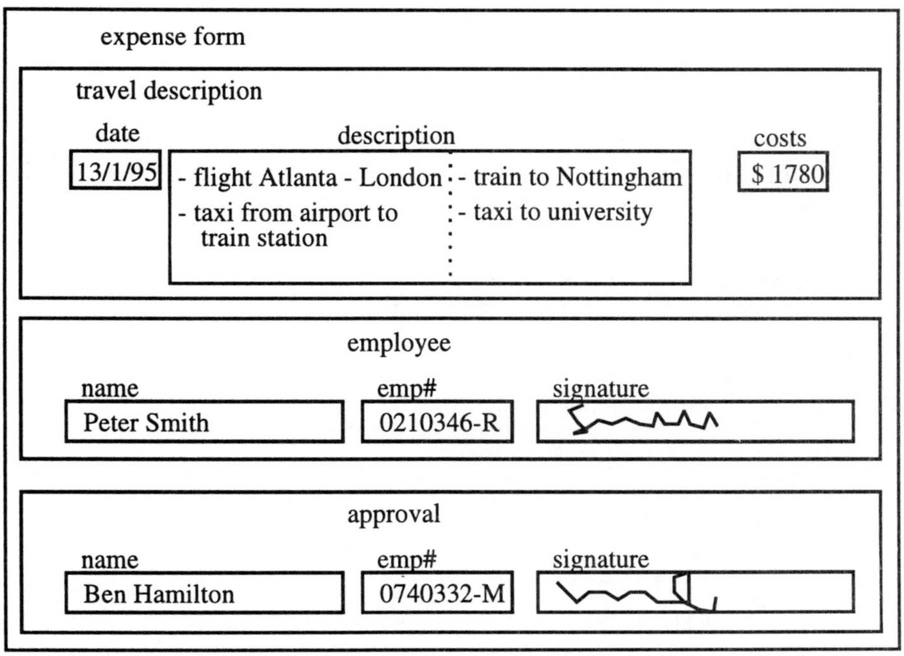


Fig. 5-5 Possible layout of a travel expense form

### 5.2.2 Generic and Specific Structures

The given document structure describes an actual form. In ODA, such a *specific* document is derived from a *generic* structure; this is a template specifying the rules for generating valid document structures. In terms of programming languages, a generic structure corresponds with the type or class of a document while a specific structure represents a document instance. More concretely, the generic structures specify the types and combinations of logical objects (sections, subsections, fields etc.) and of layout objects (pages, frames, and blocks) allowed for a particular document type. Document editors can then guide the document development process according to the given document type (see section 5.2.4). In summary, four document structures are part of the ODA standard, i.e. generic logical and layout, and specific logical and layout (see table 5-1).

| | Generic | Specific |
|---|---|---|
| **Logical** | Structural document template | Template for document formatting |
| **Layout** | Document instance | Formatted document |

Table 5-1 ODA Document structures

In the following, we introduce a (simplified) textual ODA representation of these structures. Each structure is modeled as a set of object class definitions (generic structure) or object instance definitions (specific structure).

| | |
|---|---|
| **OPT** | Optional (0 or 1 occurrence) |
| **REQ** | Required (exactly 1 occurrence); default |
| **REP** | Repetetive (1 or more occurrences) |
| **SEQ** | Sequence (ordered collection) |
| **AGG** | Aggregate (unordered collection) |
| **CHO** | Choice (one element of collection to be selected) |

Table 5-2 Options for generator for subordinates

**Generic structure:** A generic ODA structure is basically a tree of object classes that is a template for the object trees of the specific structures. The tree does *not* specify an inheritance hierarchy but describes a potential object aggregation. By allowing a class to be reused throughout the tree, the tree structure is generalized into a lattice of object classes. Each object class has a set of attributes associated with it; some of the most important attributes are the *object type* (e.g. *composite* logical object or *basic logical* object; or *page, frame,* or *block*), the *object class identifier* (a number that is unique within the document), the *user-visible name* (a textual name for the class), the *generator for subordinates* of composite objects (rules for generating a specific object tree), and the *content architecture class* (valid kinds of content portions associated with a specific object class). The generator for subordinates allows some degree of freedom concerning the creatable document and layout structures (see table 5-2). First, components can be declared as optional, required, or repetetive. Second, ordered sequences, unordered aggregates, and selective choices of components can be defined.

These options can also be combined, so that *OPT REP* stands for 0, 1 or more occurrences. As an example, possible component sequences of *SEQ (OPT c1 REQ c2 REP c3)* include *[c1 c2 c3], [c2 c3], [c2 c3 c3],* and *[c1 c2 c3 c3 c3].* Based on these explanations, we can now give a textual example of the generic logical and the generic layout structure of the expense form.

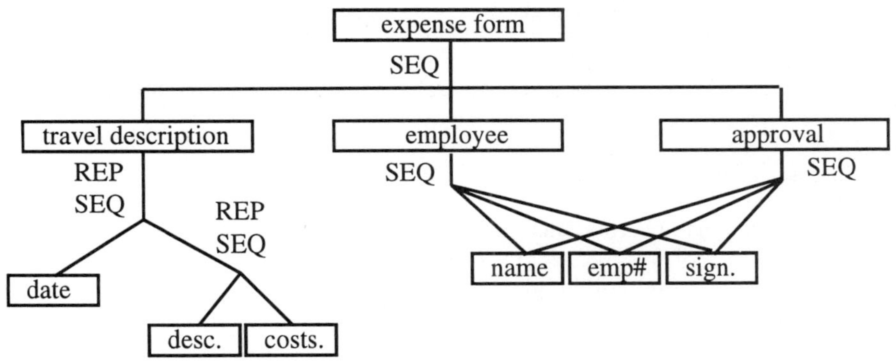


Fig. 5-6 Example of generic logical structure

The generic logical structure is represented graphically in figure 5-6 (the default option *REQ* is not explicitly represented). The corresponding notation used below is a simplified ODIF structure; for local document management, implementation-specific notation and data structures can be used. By ODA/ODIF convention, the identifiers for logical object classes start with *2*, and the identifiers for layout object classes start with *0*. For subordinate components, a hierarchical numbering scheme is used (notation simplified):

object type: document logical root
object class identifier: [2]
user-visible name: expense form
generator for subordinates: SEQ [20] [21] [22]

object type: composite logical
object class identifier: [20]

user-visible name: travel description
generator for subordinates: REP ( SEQ ( [200] REP (SEQ ( [201] [202] ))))

object type: composite logical
object class identifier: [21]
user-visible name: employee
generator for subordinates: SEQ ( [210] [211] [212] )

object type: composite logical
object class identifier: [22]
user-visible name: approval
generator for subordinates: SEQ ( [210] [211] [212] )

object type: basic logical
object class identifier: [200]
user-visible name: date
content architecture class: formatted processable character content architecture

object type: basic logical
object class identifier: [201]
user-visible name: description
content architecture class: formatted processable character content architecture

object type: basic logical
object class identifier: [202]
user-visible name: costs
content architecture class: formatted processable character content architecture

object type: basic logical
object class identifier: [210]
user-visible name: name
content architecture class: formatted processable character content architecture

object type: basic logical
object class identifier: [211]
user-visible name: emp#
content architecture class: formatted processable character content architecture

object type: basic logical
object class identifier: [212]
user-visible name: signature
content architecture class: formatted processable raster graphics content architecture

Most of the object class definitions are relatively straightforward. However, some characteristics are worth mentioning. The travel description may consist of a repetition of items; each item consists of a date and of one or more description and costs tuples. Informally, the travel expenses for several days can be specified and the date has to be given only once for a list of several expenses for the same day. The classes *name*, *emp#*, and *signature* are used within the classes *employee* and *approval* in the generator for subordinates. Informally, an employee and an approving manager are characterized by the same kinds of data. Finally, the basic logical object classes have content architecture classes associated with them. Most components have character contents; only the signature is represented as a raster graphic.

The generic layout structure is defined in a similar way using the attributes introduced above. In contrast to the *specific* layout structure, it does *not* include blocks; the lowest-level object class is a frame. Blocks within frames are only generated during the layout process (see section 5.2.4). An example of the generic layout specification of the expense form is shown in figure 5-7 and is described textually below.

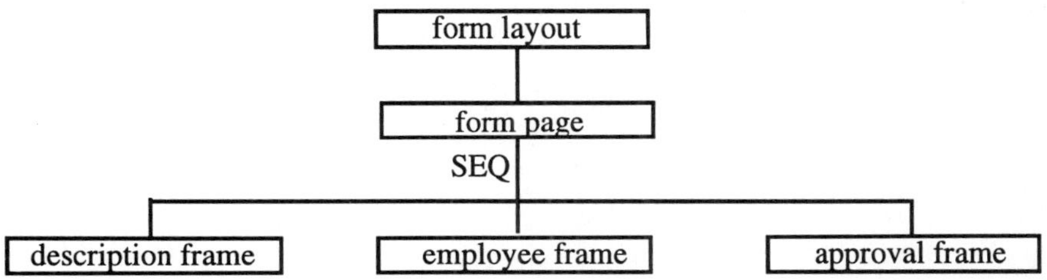


Fig. 5-7 Example of generic layout structure

object type: document layout root
object class identifier: [0]
user-visible name: form layout
generator for subordinates: [00]

object type: composite or basic page
object class identifier: [00]
user-visible name: form page
generator for subordinates: SEQ ([000] [001] [002])

object type: frame
object class identifier: [000]
user-visible name: description frame

object type: frame
object class identifier: [001]
user-visible name: employee frame

object type: frame
object class identifier: [002]
user-visible name: approval frame

Both for the generic logical and layout structure, additional object class attributes are supported and are relevant, especially for guiding the document formatting process. Further discussion is given in section 5.2.4.

**Specific structure:** The object tree of the specific logical and layout structures is generated by a document editor or formatter, respectively. The generation process is guided by the generic structures; the specific structures have to conform to the "generator for subordinates" rules of the generic structures. The textual representation of the specific structures of our example of figures 5-4 and 5-5 is similar to the representation of the generic structures. Therefore, we only give an extract of a few objects of the logical and layout structures:

*Logical objects:*

| object type: | composite logical |
|---|---|
| object identifier: | [30] |
| object class identifier: | [20] |
| user-visible name: | travel description |
| generator for subordinates: | [300] [301] [302] |

| object type: | basic logical |
|---|---|
| object identifier: | [300] |
| object class identifier: | [200] |
| user-visible name: | date |
| content portions: | [3000] |

| content identifier logical: | [3000] |
|---|---|
| content information: | 13/1/95 |

*Layout objects:*

| object type: | frame |
|---|---|
| object identifier: | [100] |
| object class identifier: | [000] |
| user-visible name: | description frame |
| generator for subordinates: | [1000] [1001] [1002] |

| object type: | block |
|---|---|
| object identifier: | [1000] |
| object class identifier: | [0000] |
| user-visible name: | date block |
| content portions: | [3000] |

The partial description of the specific structures specifies the travel description and date object with the actual date as its information content. The corresponding layout frame has been augmented with a layout block holding the date content portion. It should be mentioned that the specific structures naturally do not contain any generator options (*SEQ* etc.) as they describe an actual, fixed structure. The attribute "*object identifier*" specifies the identifier of the logical or layout object; the "*object class identifier*" refers to the corresponding object class of the generic structures. The specific logical and layout structures are connected via the "*content portions*" attribute referring to shared content objects.

### 5.2.3 Overall ODA Document Model

The four structures presented form the center of the ODA model. In addition, a complete ODA document comprises a *document profile* and a set of *style definitions*. The overall model is summarized in figure 5-8.

**Document profile:** The document profile consists of a set of attributes describing characteristics of the overall document. First, it can be specified whether all other parts of the document are present or not. For example, a document may lack a generic logical structure if no more editing is to be carried out. Or a formatted document may only have a specific layout structure if its logical structure is not required any more (e.g. if a document will only be printed but not be reformatted). The profile also specifies characteristics of a document such as the required fonts or the version of ODA associated with it. Moreover, some management attributes are part of the profile. They are mainly informal descriptive data (like title, abstract, keywords, authors, or language) and may be used for retrieval purposes, for example.

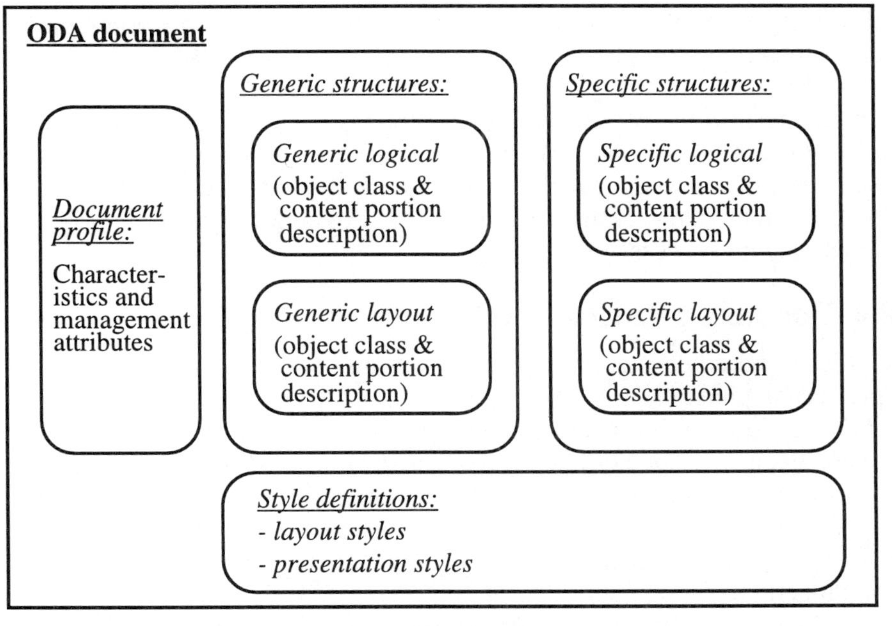


Fig. 5-8 Overall ODA document model

**Content portions and architectures:** Within their leaves, the generic and specific structures refer to content architectures and content portions, respectively. Within the ODA standard, currently three content architecture classes are defined: the character content, the raster graphics content, and the geometric graphics content classes. Each content architecture class specifies actual content elements, presentation attributes, and encoding techniques. The character content architecture is able to represent all kinds of text, including characters of foreign languages like Japanese, Hebrew, and Arabic. The raster graphics content architecture represents two-dimensional images as a pixel array. The geometric graphics content architecture supports line-oriented graphics and is based on the *Computer Graphics Metafile (CGM)* standard [ANS86]. In summary, ODA documents can include graphics and bitmaps but ODA does not support any time-dependent media as yet (ODA extensions are discussed later).

**Style definitions:** An ODA document also comprises a set of style definitions controlling the layout process. The *layout styles* control the *document layout process*, namely the allocation of pages and frames. A layout style is also defined by attributes; some of them are directly attached to logical and layout objects. For example, a logical object can have the attributes *layout object class* and *layout categories* associated with it. *Layout object class* specifies that a whole logical object (e.g. a field of a form) must be mapped to a single layout object (e.g. to a frame). *Layout category* associates a logical category name with a logical leaf object. Such an object can then only be mapped to a layout object that specifies the same category as one of the values of its *permitted categories* attributes.

The *presentation styles* define representations of the different contents architectures, for example fonts to be used for character contents. These styles guide the *content layout process* which is concerned with the allocation and positioning of blocks within frames. Parts of this style information are also used during the document layout process.

## 5.2.4 Document Processing Model

The ODA standard defines not only the structure of documents but also their major processing phases:

- *Editing:* The editing phase is concerned with document generation and update. It consists of editing the logical document structure and editing the document contents. Both tasks are supported by dedicated editor tools described below. Content editing is dependent on the content architecture class; for example, a graphical editor is required for the geometric graphics content architecture.
- *Layout process:* The layout process has a formatted but device-independent document as its result. It is guided by the specific logical and generic layout structures and by the styles.

- *Imaging process:* The imaging process finally performs device-dependent formatting, e.g. for an *X*-terminal or for a specific printer.

In addition, document transfer is an important part of ODA document processing and especially of cooperative office applications. This aspect is discussed in more detail in section 5.2.5.

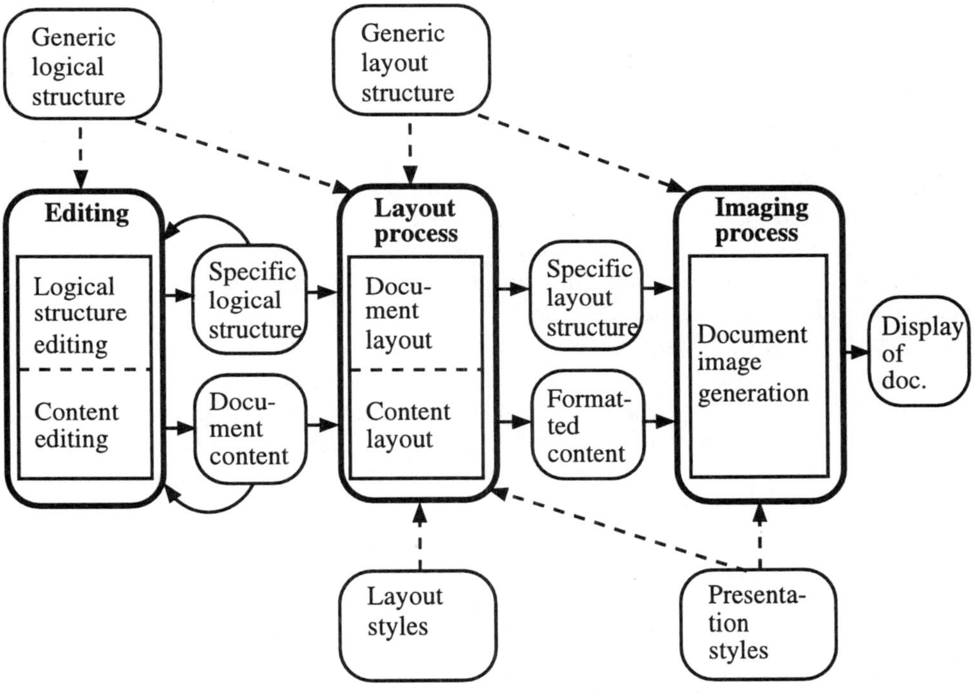


Fig. 5-9 ODA document processing model

Figure 5-9 summarizes the three major document processing phases. Document editing is controlled by the generic logical structure and produces a corresponding specific logical structure as well as the actual document content. Both parts can of course be subject to further editing.

As discussed above, the layout process consists of document and content layout. Document layout associates basic logical objects with layout objects. This task is controlled by the generic structures and by the layout styles. As a result, the specific logical structure is transformed into a specific layout structure. In a second step, the content layout process formats the content portions using the presentation styles.

The resulting device-independent document layout is finally prepared for displaying or printing on a dedicated device by the imaging process. A relatively detailed description of the layout and imaging process can be found in [RSM91], for example. We will concentrate further on supporting editing tools [MAZ87].

**ODA document editing:** Editing of ODA documents has to be supported by dedicated editors. According to the different structures, corresponding editing facilities have to be offered. Since the standard was established in 1988, several projects have focused on the development of such tools and have lead to relatively mature solutions.

Typically, the generic document structures are already given when the editing process starts. That is, editing the generic structures - defining the valid structure for document classes - is assumed to be a task for experts. It is therefore separated from the day-to-day task of editing actual document instances. For example, the format of a travel expense form is determined once and changed only after a significant amount of time, while actual expense forms are filled every day. Generic structure editing is therefore supported by advanced editors with an emphasis on flexibility rather than simplicity. Editors for the specific structures can be divided in two major categories:

1. *Top-level ODA editors:* These editors accept any document class, i.e. any generic logical and layout structure as a basis for the editing process. They are very flexible but are more difficult to implement. Specific document classes are usually represented by attributed grammars that are loaded dynamically.
2. *Low-level ODA editors:* These editors are dedicated to specific document classes. The generator for subordinate rules of the generic structures of these classes is simply hardcoded within the editor.

Figure 5-10 shows the architecture of a top-level ODA editor with an additional document class editor as developed in several projects (e.g. *PODA* [KLL86]).

The common user interface integrates the different components of the editor architecture and provides a uniform command shell. Two dedicated command shells can be accessed, one for controlling the document class editor and one for editing document instances (the ODA editor shell). The output of a document class definition mainly consists of an attributed grammar for the generic logical and layout structures. According to the document class desired, such grammars are loaded by the logical and layout structure editors and control the editing process. The user interface of these two editors provides two views of the document:

- *Global logical view:* One window shows the overall logical structure of the document, either graphically as a tree or textually as a structure table. This window is used for editing the global structure and for performing global structural changes. An example of this kind of view was given in figure 5-4.
- *Formatted content view:* The other window shows the formatted document and acts as a WYSIWYG editor; the user can directly edit content portions and can perform minor structural changes there. A corresponding example of this view was shown in figure 5-5.

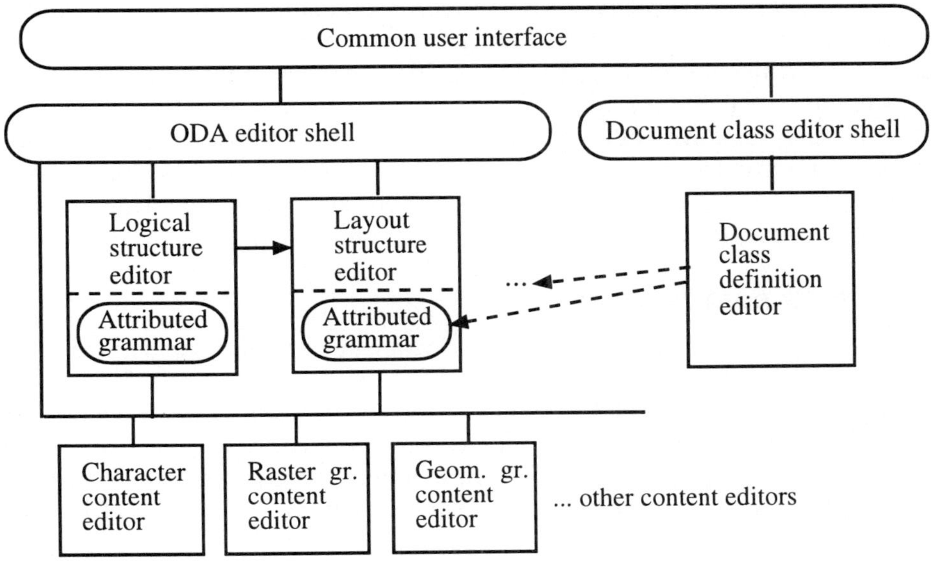


Fig. 5-10 Architecture of an ODA document editor

Both views correspond with each other; for example when the structure is changed in the global logical view window, the formatted content view window is immediately updated. Due to the WYSIWYG nature of this window, the layout process has to be performed for a current portion of the document immediately after changes.

Whenever a specific content portion is to be edited, the corresponding content editor is invoked automatically. The software integration of the different editors is implemented by the ODA editor shell. Other content editors can be added when desired without major global architectural changes.

The architecture described can be classified as a *two-view document editor* with a language-based source representation of the structure and a WYSIWYG representation of the content. The advantage of such an approach is the suitability of different representations for different tasks (global changes versus local content editing). Two-view document editors have also been developed within different organizational contexts. For example, the *Lilac* editor [BRO91] supports a WYSIWYG document representation for general editing and, synchronized with it, source-language representation for sophisticated editing tasks like definition of chemical symbols. Existing commercial products of WYSIWIG document editors emphasize the formatted view of a document. The logical structure can usually be modified only indirectly by changing the chapter sequence, for example.

Similar editing facilities are available on PCs. Typical architectural bases are Microsoft's *OLE (Object Linking Environment)* and publish and subscribe. OLE enables application programs, including text processing tools, to be logically connected and integrated. Together with *COM (Component Object Model)*, OLE also supports the definition of remote communication interfaces between different tools. Thus document editors and other document and office processing tools can be interconnected across distributed machines. However, these mechanisms still have to be integrated with official document interchange standards in order to support a more general open multiapplication interaction.

### 5.2.5 Document Transfer

For cooperative document management, document transfer between heterogeneous systems is an essential facility. ODA provides support for this task by offering a common transfer format, *ODIF (Open Document Interchange Format)*. It is based on the *ASN.1* notation (see section 4.5.3) and therefore uses a non-textual bytestream representation. In addition, the ODA standard defines a textual transfer format, *ODL (Open Document Language)*. This format is based on *SGML* (see section 5.3).

ODIF-based document exchange can be implemented using dedicated message passing protocols, but in practise it is often performed by using X.400 MHS as a base (see section 3.1.1).

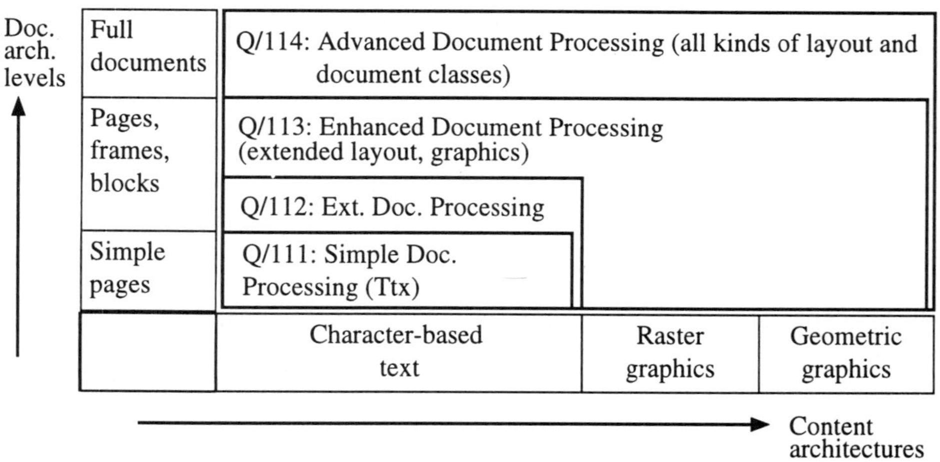


Fig. 5-11 Family of ODIF transfer formats

**ODIF and ODL:** An ODA document can be transformed into the ODIF transmission format by an ODA/ODIF translator. Such a tool basically works like an

RPC stub generator (see chapter 3) and produces a flat ASN.1 representation of the different parts of an ODA document as its output. On the receiver's site, an inverse transformation regenerates the ODA document. While the implementation of the ODA representation may vary from system to system (e.g. concerning byte ordering), the ODIF representation is a common format for all cooperating systems. If new ODA tool implementations with different data representations are introduced, only their ODA/ODIF conversion functions have to be added while all other systems remain unaffected.

The ODA standard defines a family of ODIF transfer formats with different encoding schemes supporting various content architectures and document architecture levels (see figure 5-11). Each format belongs to a so-called *document application profile.* The simplest format, *Q/111,* is functionally compatible with Teletex. It only supports simple documents consisting of a set of paragraphs but without a higher-level structure. The extended format *Q/112* supports structured documents, and *Q/113* adds facilities for transfer of graphics. Only *Q/114* supports the definition and transfer of new document classes with newly defined generic logical and layout structures. This format is most suitable for advanced cooperative office applications.

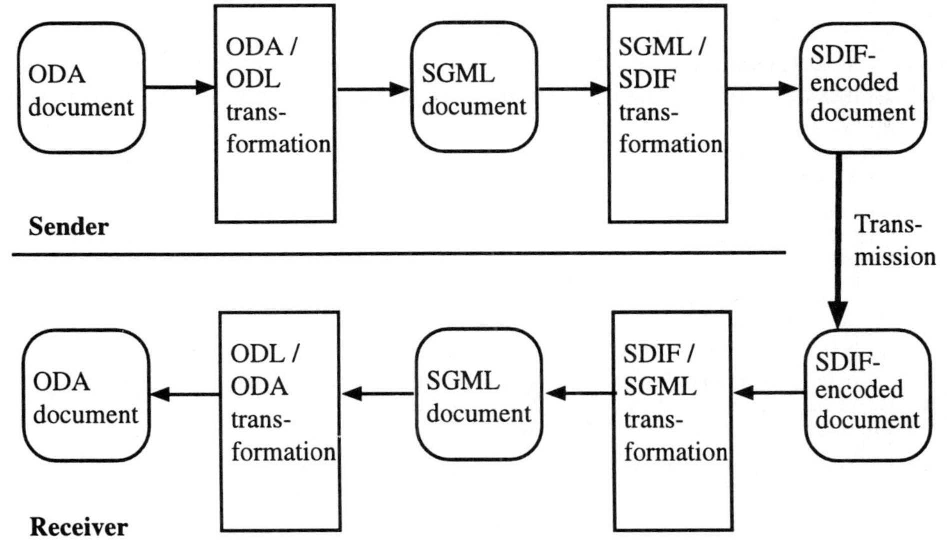


Fig. 5-12 Document transfer based on ODL

*ODL* is an SGML representation of an ODA document. In order to transfer a document in this way, it is first transformed from an ODA to ODL as a subset of SGML (see section 5.3). It is then mapped to the SGML transfer format, *SDIF*, and is transmitted thereafter. On the receiver's site, the inverse transformations are performed. The transformation and transmission process is summarized in figure 5-12. The ODL and SDIF representations enable interoperability of ODA- and SGML-based systems and therefore support cooperative office applications in mixed document processing environments.

ODA document editors should directly provide a document communication interface to send edited documents to other sites and to load received documents into the editor tool. Such functionality can be integrated into the editor shell discussed above; the end user can then stay in the same, familiar environment for editing and document interchange. Current prototype implementations support this functionality in a limited way. The exact notations and internal bytestream or text representations of both ODIF and ODL are found in [ISO88] and related standards documents.

**Document architecture classes:** An important principle of ODA is that the receiver of a document does not need any existing context information in order to operate on the document. That is, all information required to work with a document in a particular way must be transmitted together with it. Depending on the amount of information available for a document according to its document profile (e.g. generic structures, specific structures etc.), different operations are possible. In accordance with these considerations, ODA defines three *document architecture classes*, summarized in table 5-3. The sender of a document can specify which class the transmitted document should belong to. These architecture classes are valid for all ODIF transfer formats of the family described above.

| Document archit. class | Required (and optional) components |
|---|---|
| Formatted | profile, specific layout structure<br>(generic layout structure, layout and presentation styles) |
| Processable | profile, specific logical structure<br>(generic logical and layout structure, layout and presentation styles) |
| Formatted processable | profile, specific logical and layout structure<br>(generic logical and layout structure, layout styles, presentation styles) |

Table 5-3 Document architecture classes

A document of the architecture class *formatted* can only be displayed or printed but cannot be edited or otherwise processed further. The specific layout structure is sufficient for that. If the generic layout structure and the styles are also available, the imaging process can be performed for different kinds of devices.

A *processable* document can be edited based on the available specific logical structure. However, only if the generic logical structure is also available, the editor can enforce conformance to the structural template. If the generic layout structure and the styles are present, the layout process can be performed. Otherwise, the document cannot be laid out at the given network node.

Finally, a *formatted processable* document belongs to the most general architecture class. It consists of the specific logical structure and of both layout structures. The specific logical structure can be edited; editing can be controlled by the generic logical structure if it is available. The specific layout structure represents the formatted document. If available, the generic layout structure and the styles allow for reformatting after changes and for device-dependent formatting.

Section 5.6 discusses the concrete use of these document architecture classes in a sample cooperative document management application. In summary, ODA offers a rich document architecture that supports detailed structural representation of documents including semantic aspects, e.g. concerning layout of different document components. Moreover, a standardized document transfer representation for all parts of a document is provided.

## 5.3 Standardized General Markup Language

### 5.3.1 Overview

The *Standard Generalized Markup Language (SGML)* [SMI89] is also an ISO standard [ISO86] and has a lot in common with the ODA approach. It is also used to define document types and instances and it provides the *SDIF* document transfer format mentioned above. However, the SGML standard does not support a detailed layout specification. A reason for that is that SGML is mainly used for exchanging documents between authors and publishers and that publishers usually wish to apply their own formatting conventions. Moreover, SGML does not represent a document structure as a tree of objects but directly embeds the structural description into the document contents. This more pragmatic approach is enabled by descriptive markups, the so-called *markup tags*. A document type consists of *markup declarations*; these specify the permitted ordering of markup tags for associated document instances.

In the following, we describe the markup approach of SGML by means of an example. A comparison of ODA, SGML, and EDIFACT is given in section 5.5.

### 5.3.2 Markup Approach of SGML

As in ODA, an SGML representation of a document consists of a type and an instance description.

**SGML document type definition:** An SGML document type definition (DTD) consists of a list of composite or basic elements specified by markup declarations. As in ODA, rules are given for generating instances of composite elements. Table 5-4 gives an overview of the most important parts of the SGML notation. A whole markup declaration is enclosed in "<!...>", a specific document processing instruction is embedded in "<?...>". The rules for the permitted elements that are part of a composite element are specified in a way similar to ODA using the notation shown in the table. For basic elements, the types of associated content portions are specified by reserved keywords (e.g. "*#CDATA*" for character data and "*#NDATA*" for other data that are not interpreted by SGML itself).

<table>
<tr><th>Notation</th><th>Semantics</th></tr>
<tr><td><!...></td><td>Markup declaration</td></tr>
<tr><td><?...></td><td>Processing instruction</td></tr>
<tr><td>,</td><td>Elements separated by commas in given sequence</td></tr>
<tr><td>&</td><td>Elements in arbitrary sequence</td></tr>
<tr><td>|</td><td>Choice of exactly one element</td></tr>
<tr><td>?</td><td>Optional element</td></tr>
<tr><td>+</td><td>One or more occurrences of an element</td></tr>
<tr><td>*</td><td>0, 1 or more occurrences of an element</td></tr>
</table>

Table 5-4 Part of the SGML notation

The expense form type specified in ODA as shown in figure 5-6 can be specified in SGML as follows:

```
<!ELEMENT expense form          (travel description, employee, approval)>
<!ELEMENT travel description    (date, (description, costs)+ )+ >
<!ELEMENT date                  (#CDATA)>
<!ELEMENT description           (#CDATA)>
<!ELEMENT costs                 (#CDATA)>
<!ELEMENT  employee             (name, emp#, signature)>
<!ELEMENT name                  (#CDATA)>
<!ELEMENT emp#                  (#CDATA)>
<!ELEMENT signature             (#NDATA)>
<!ELEMENT approval              (name, emp#, signature)>
```

The potential structure of the associated form instances is the same as with the ODA definition. However, no semantics is associated with the different elements. That is, SGML does not specify the meaning and layout of form fields or chapters, it just describes the structure.

**SGML document instance definition:** In an SGML document instance, the structural elements specified by the type definition are used as *markup tags* to describe the document structure. They are directly embedded into the text contents using a depth-first scheme. The start of a logical structure level is indicated by a *start tag* with its name enclosed in "<...>"; the end is indicated by an end tag with the same name enclosed in "</...>". External data that instantiate the "*#NDATA*" basic elements are referenced by logical names with leading "&". The logical structure of the form instance of figures 5-4 and 5-5 has the following representation (markup tags in bold face):

**<expense form><travel description><date>**13/1/95**</date><description>**flight Atlanta - London - taxi from airport to train station - train to Nottingham - taxi to university**</description><costs>**$1780**</costs></travel description>**
**<employee><name>**PeterSmith**</name><emp#>**0210346R**</emp#>**
**<signature>**&emp_sig**</signature></employee>**
**<approval><name>**Ben Hamilton**</name> <emp#>**0740332-M**</emp#>**
**<signature>**&app_sig**</signature></approval></expense form>**

For the signatures, references to external graphics files (*emp_sig* and *app_sig*) are specified. This is a possible way of embedding non-character data (*#NDATA*) into SGML documents. Alternatively, SGML offers explicit graphics interfaces to the *Computer Graphics Metafile (CGM)* based on SGML syntax [CHG87].

The markup tag specification can be *minimized* by omitting redundant markup tags. For example, the end tags *</date>* or *</costs>* are not necessarily required; the end of the corresponding text elements is implicitly specified by the subsequent start tags according to the document type definition. Such minimization simplifies document representation and document editing.

### 5.3.3 SGML Document Processing and Transfer

**Tool support:** To generate an SGML document description, special SGML editors can be used that enforce consistency of markup tags and markup declarations. To process an SGML document, an *SGML parser* is required. Such tools, however, are application-specific. Only their input - the SGML document - is based on the standard. Their processing functionality and their output depends on the implementation. For example, a parser could transform a document into a $\mathrm{T_EX}$ source representation so that it could be formatted by a $\mathrm{T_EX}$ formatter; an implementation of this concept is described in [SCH86]. The transformation or, more generally, a layout process can be controlled in a limited way by attributes that can be attached to markup tags and have to be defined within markup declarations. However, the semantic interpretation of these attributes is implementation-specific.

An SGML document can also be subdivided into document parts by *marked sections*; a marked section encloses a document part by means of special tags. For each marked section, *status specifications* can be given. These specify

whether a document part should be included in processing by a parser (*INCLUDE*) or not (*IGNORE*). In this way, different document components can be selected for different application programs.
**Document transfer:** SGML documents are transferred via a network using the *SDIF* format. However, in contrast to ODA documents, the semantics of different document components, e.g. concerning their layout, is not part of the document specification. Therefore, global agreements concerning different document types between cooperating peers have to be established before any document transfer and cooperative document management phases. Due to this requirement, SGML user groups are typically more closed and self-contained. However, various global document type definitions for different application domains exist; examples are *book, paper, slides, letter*.

**Advanced standardization:** The lack of document semantics specification in SGML has lead to advanced standardization initiatives. In particular, a specific notation named *DSSSL (Document Style Semantics and Specification Language)* is being developed and standardized [ISO91]. This language offers rich layout specification facilities. In particular, it addresses page layout, block layout, basic text formatting, and positioning relationships between different text portions. The DSSSL directives are conceptually separated from the logical SGML structure specification.

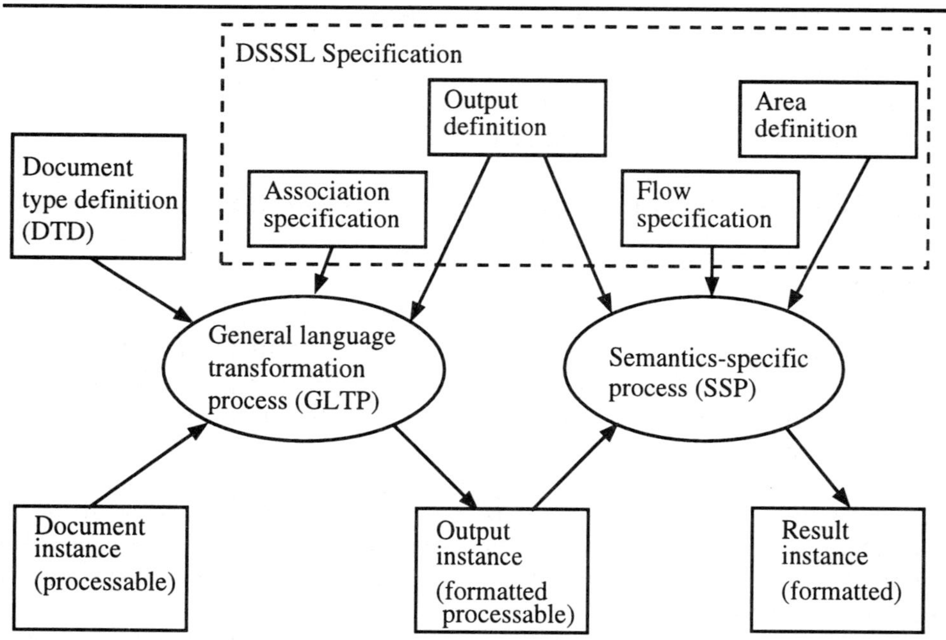


Fig. 5-13 DSSSL document processing model

Figure 5-13 gives an overview of the extended document processing model defined by DSSSL [ISO92]. The *general language transformation process (GLTP)* performs some format-independent document transformations like suppression, replacement, replication, reordering, and regrouping of source document objects. The GLTP is intended to be used as a tool to prepare the document content for straightforward processing by the semantics-specific formatting process. Input to the GLTP is constituted by the actual source document, the document type definition, and the *association specification* and *output definition* of DSSSL. The association specification consists of a set of mutually dependent transformations of source to output objects. The output definition defines the possible objects and structure that can occur in the output instance, using the SGML notation.

The semantics-specific process (SSP) actually formats an SGML document; it maps logical SGML objects to layout areas. It is guided by the output specification, too. Its main input - in addition to the output document instance of the GLTP - is a *flow specification* and an *area definition* of DSSSL. The flow specification describes how objects from the output instance are mapped to layout areas, using so-called *flow rules*. The area definition provides templates for the layout areas that can finally occur in the formatted result document instance.

In summary, SGML provides a straightforward mechanism for representing and transferring complex document structures. Together with DSSSL and its associated processing model, document layout specification and document formatting are also enabled in a way similar to ODA.

## 5.4 EDIFACT

*EDIFACT (Electronic Data Interchange for Administration Commerce and Transport)* [BER89] is a standard for representation and exchange of structured business data like forms, bills, receipts, customs declarations etc. This section describes the basic concepts of this approach and gives examples.

### 5.4.1 Overview

EDIFACT emphasizes business data transfer much more than document representation. It is more dedicated to well-structured forms than to weakly-structured documents. Moreover, data transmitted using EDIFACT are usually the input and output of application programs and are often not directly accessed by end users.

The basic concept of EDIFACT is to map such business data of a pre-defined structure onto flat *EDIFACT transmission files* which are then transmitted via a network and consist of a set of *EDIFACT messages*. The standard defines character sets for character content encoding. It also specifies the structure of EDIFACT transmission files. Contents other than text are not supported. However, due to its relative simplicity and usability, EDIFACT is apparently becoming more and more accepted by the business user community. Standardization efforts are under way to define EDIFACT message types for various application domains. Like ODIF, EDIFACT messages can be exchanged by using X.400 as a message transfer service (see section 3.1.1).

## 5.4.2 Structure and Contents of EDIFACT Messages and Files

An EDIFACT message is a structured character stream representing the contents of business documents or forms. The standard defines two character sets used for encoding the data:

- The type A character set consists only of printable characters and is therefore not suited for representing arbitrary binary data but only for text and digits.
- The type B character set also includes non-printable characters according to the 7-bit code ISO 646 or the 8-bit codes ISO 8859 or 6937.

An EDIFACT message consists of a start delimiter, a set of *segments,* and an end delimiter. Each segment starts with a segment identifier and can then contain a set of data elements with values or *data element groups.* A group also consists of a set of data elements but introduces a logical association between them. For example, it make sense to group a currency specification (e.g. *$*) and a currency value (e.g. *1780*). Several EDIFACT messages can be embedded into an *EDIFACT transmission file* and can also be grouped logically. Figure 5-14 summarizes the resulting structure graphically.

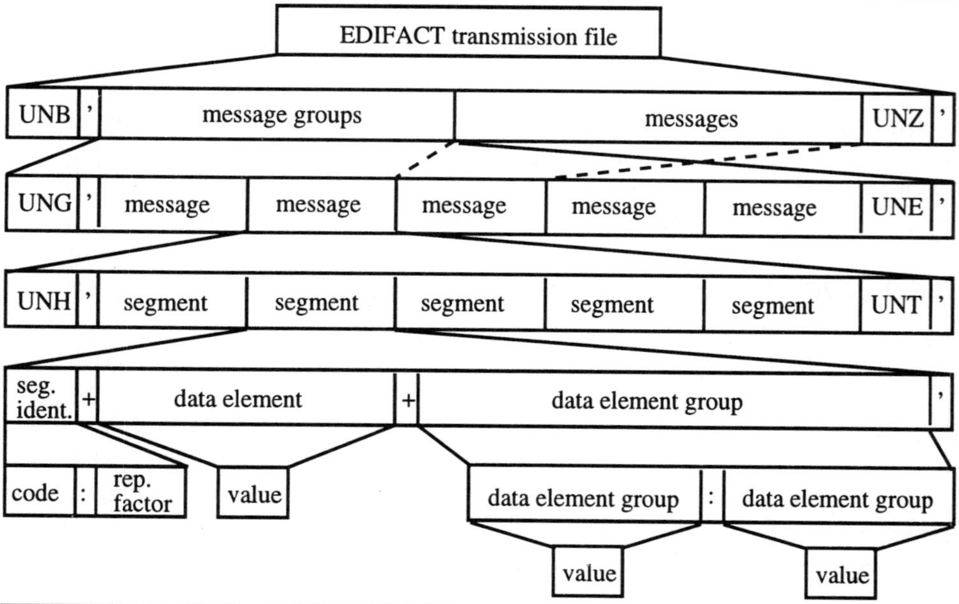


Fig. 5-14 Structure of an EDIFACT transmission file

The special codes *UNB / UNZ* represent the beginning and end of a file, *UNG / UNE* the beginning and end of a message group, and *UNH / UNT* the header and trailer of a message. Every code is terminated with a "'" character. Segment identifiers and data elements are separated by "+" signs, different data element groups are separated by *":"*. A segment has a repetition factor that indicates how many of its instances follow.

For dedicated application domains, EDIFACT message types can be specified; they determine the kinds of allowed segment identifiers and associated maximum repetition factors, for example. EDIFACT messages and message types, however, only specify the structure of data but not the semantics or layout. As in the basic SGML approach, this is left to the application.

The expense form of figure 5-5 can be specified as an EDIFACT transmission file as follows; we assume that a message type exists that specifies segment identifiers for the travel description (*TDC*), for the employee (*EMP*), and for the approving manager (*APP*), with special codes in bold face:

**UNB'UNG'UNH'TDC:1+**10/5/94+flight Atlanta - London - taxi from airport to train station - train to Nottingham - taxi to university+$:1780**'EMP+**Peter Smith+0210346-R+signed**'APP+**Ben Hamilton+0740332-M+signed**'UNT'UNE'UNZ**

The travel description can be repeated for different dates. In the example, only a repetition factor of 1 is used. The other segments are not repetitive. The substructure within the segments that has been represented explicitly in ODA and SGML is now only reflected by a set of data elements. The data element group concept has been used to specify the actual travel expenses (*$ 1780*).

An obvious limitation is the lack of arbitrarily defined hierarchical structures in EDIFACT. This is expressed in the example as follows: Although it is possible to represent several date/claim groups (by using a corresponding TDC repetition factor), it is not possible to represent several claims for the same date. The signature can also not be represented using EDIFACT. Therefore, all that is indicated is whether the signature or approval has already been given ("*signed*").

### 5.4.3 EDIFACT Message Types

More than 50 EDIFACT message types (for example *invoice, purchase order,* and *customs declaration*) have already been standardized. Message type standardization is performed by major EDIFACT boards for North America, Europe, and Australia. The European board consists of eight working groups *MD1-MD8* concerned with industry, transport, customs and public administration, banking, real estate, statistics, insurance, and tourism.

Standardized message types are documented in the universal *EDIFACT Data Message Directory*. Their components are described by the *Data Segment Directory* and the *Data Element Directory*. Segment definitions can be reused within different message definitions. The directories are available in digital form and can be used for controlling converter software. Such converters transform an external, application-specific data representation into EDIFACT messages.

In summary, EDIFACT is a relatively simple yet flexible transfer format for business data. As opposed to SGML and ODA, it is not used to represent the structure of documents in a general way but is only applied for actual transmission purposes. Therefore, it is at the same level as ODIF or SDIF but has a simpler structure. Notably, it does not support arbitrary hierarchies of document components and does not provide facilities for graphics integration. Nevertheless, it is practical and is therefore used in many application domains.

## 5.5 Comparison

Table 5-5 compares the document representation and transfer standards ODA, SGML and EDIFACT.

| Functionality | ODA | SGML | EDIFACT |
|---|---|---|---|
| Complex logical structure description | yes | yes | no |
| Layout structure description | yes | by DSSSL extension | no |
| Document classes/ types and semantics | yes | yes | yes (message types) |
| Representation of document semantics | yes | no | no |
| Graphics support | yes | yes | no |
| Interchange format | ODIF | SDIF | EDIFACT transmission file |
| Document architecture classes | "processable" / "formatted" | only "processable" | only "processable" |
| Interoperability with other approaches | ODL/SGML interface | ODL/SGML interface | no |
| Complexity of tool implementation | high | medium | low |
| Major application domains | General office document transfer | Publishing industry | Business data transfer |

Table 5-5 Comparison of the approaches

The description of arbitrary documents with complex, nested structures is only supported by ODA and SGML; EDIFACT only allows for representation of relatively fixed structures with limited degrees of freedom. A layout structure representation is only supported by ODA, except that DSSSL extensions for layout description with SGML are under way. Document classes can be defined with all three approaches (*message types* in EDIFACT). However, only ODA supports transfer of self-describing documents including their type information. In contrast, cooperating users must negotiate document classes and semantics in advance when using SGML or EDIFACT.

Document contents other than text are supported by ODA and SGML, especially focusing on graphics. Other media can be integrated via external references but such advanced functionality is not part of the current standards. The interchange formats used are ODIF, SDIF and the EDIFACT transmission file, respectively. With ODA, SDIF can also be used for document interchange; this is enabled by the ODA/ODL/SGML interface. Therefore, ODA/SGML interoperability is supported explicitly. Only ODA explicitly supports different document architecture classes according to the processing state (processable, formatted, or both) of a document. The other approaches generally transfer processable documents.

Due to the richer functionality, implementation of supporting tools (editors, parsers, transformation tools etc.) is most complex for ODA and least complex for EDIFACT.

The major application domain of ODA is the general transfer of arbitrary office documents. ODA is therefore applicable to a wide range of situations throughout the whole office domain. SGML is mostly used in the publishing industry; its development and evolution have been strongly influenced by American publishers. EDIFACT is applied to relatively well-structured business data transfer rather than for general document management.

In summary, ODA functionality is quite rich and general. SGML is more limited but seems to enjoy better acceptance, especially in the publishing area. SGML tool implementations and converters from other representations are available today, while this is hardly the case for ODA. EDIFACT is the most specific approach and can be recommended for transfer of forms and relatively fixed document structures.

## 5.6 Document Exchange in Office Procedures

In the following, we discuss conceptually an example of a small cooperative document management application exploiting ODA. We mainly focus on the document interchange facilities and on the use of the document architecture classes.

Figure 5-15 shows the structure of the example scenario, a version of travel expense processing discussed already, i.e. a complex office procedure. We assume that all relevant tasks are supported by standards-based tools as shown in the figure.

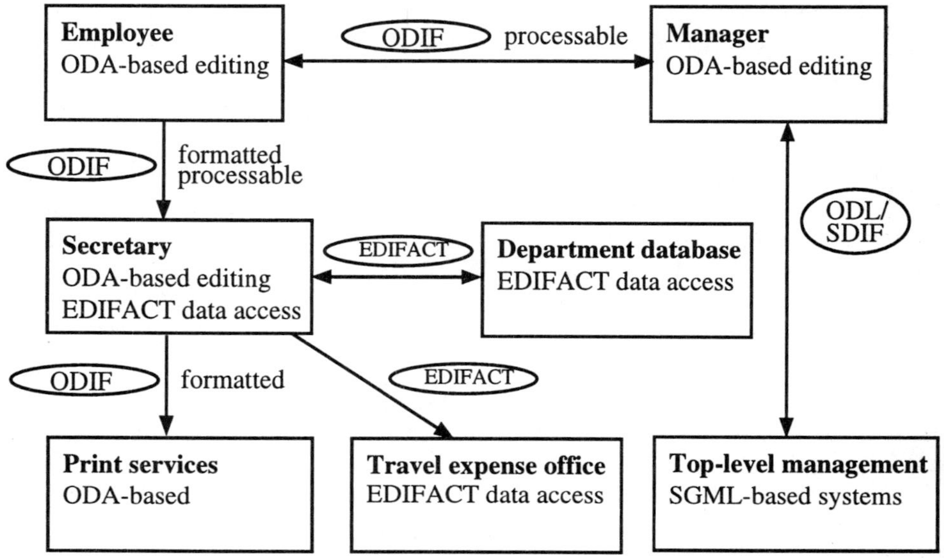


Fig. 5-15 Cooperative document management using standards

First, a travel expense form is filled by an employee using an ODA editor according to an existing document class for such forms. ODA allows arbitrary structured text to be added in order to provide additional explanations or to give a description of travel details. The result is a processable document that is shipped to the responsible manager for approval, using ODIF. The document architecture class *processable* is sufficient; the manager will modify portions of the document but will not need any sophisticated layout, i.e. no *formatted* document. Afterwards, however, the modified document is formatted by the employee and is transferred to the secretary based on the *formatted processable* architecture class using ODIF. This allows for further editing (e.g. to add project data or accounting information) but also specifies a device-independent document format already. Concerning ODIF, the *extended document processing format* is sufficient if no graphics or images are involved. Otherwise, the *advanced document processing format* would be required.

The secretary has access to the department database and may gather additional business data from there. Due to the structured nature of these data, EDIFACT is used as a transfer format. The resulting EDIFACT messages are further processed using dedicated software at the secretary's site and are made available via a user interface. In this way, the secretary can integrate such data (e.g. a summary of previous expenses of the given employee) into the ODA document manually. After this phase, she finally formats the document and transfers it to a print service. This service performs the device-dependent document imaging phase and prints the document on a high-quality printer.

Moreover, the secretary creates an EDIFACT message that contains the expense data of the ODA travel expense form; those data represent the subset of the travel expense form that is relevant to the refund (e.g. total expenses, purpose of trip, dates of expenses, account number of employee etc.). All other explanatory material may be omitted. The resulting EDIFACT message is sent to the travel expense office and is received and processed semi-automatically there. In this way, the final refund is initiated.

In special cases, the manager may have to contact the top-level management for discussion or approval. If we assume that this management level uses SGML-based document processing tools for historical reasons, interoperability would still be possible via ODL. The manager initiates an ODA/ODL conversion and then transfers the document using SDIF. At the receiver's site, the document can be processed by an SGML editor; however, there must exist an agreement concerning the matching of document classes and concerning the corresponding formatting information. In summary, the example has illustrated several aspects:

- *Use of document architecture classes:* The different architecture classes supported by ODA can be used for representing documents for different purposes adequately, e.g. for contents and structure modification, for complete processing including formatting, and for printing or displaying an already formatted document.
- *Use of different document management standards:* Applications may benefit from using different standards in an integrated way; for example, ODA is suitable for weakly structured textual explanations and descriptions while EDIFACT better supports access to and transfer of well-structured business data.
- *Interoperability:* Tools based on different standards can basically interoperate; explicit support is provided by ODL while interoperability of EDIFACT and ODA has to be explicitly enabled by additional software.

The use of standards for document exchange becomes even more important if a more open environment is addressed. For example if different departments or even different corporations collaborate, document standards are a vital prerequisite.

## 5.7 Related Approaches

The three approaches discussed above seem to be most important from the standardization and interoperability point of view; therefore, our discussion has focused on them. For completeness, we mention some related, mostly vendor-specific approaches but do not go into details.

The *Digital Document Interchange Format (DDIF)* [DEC90] of the Digital Equipment Corporation is based on an early version of ODA but has diverged from ODA during its development. It offers similar document structuring facilities to ODA but provides advanced support for multimedia documents. The *Document Content Architecture (DCA)* [IBM83] of IBM is a common document format for IBM word processors. It only supports character-based text. Finally, the *Rich Text Format (RTF)* [AND87] of Microsoft and other companies is used for encoding structured text and graphics for transfer between DOS and the Apple Macintosh.

These approaches are usually limited to a dedicated machine or operating system domain. Some of them also show diverging implementations that may only support a subset of the industry standard.

There are also other standards for exchange of formatted documents, so-called *page description languages*. Best-known and most widely used is the *PostScript* language of Adobe Systems Inc. Another example is *Interpress* of Xerox Corp. There is also an ISO standard page description language (*SPDL*) [ROS89] that provides a device-independent specification of non-revisable, formatted documents. Like PostScript, an SPDL document can include complex graphics and text of arbitrary fonts. Finally, there is a *font information interchange* standard [SBS89] for the exchange of font information used in the document preparation process of the standards described.

## 5.8 Shared and Distributed Document Models

In section 5.1.3, we outlined four different levels of document management in cooperative environments. These can be implemented up to the second level, i.e. transfer of unstructured and of structured documents, based on the techniques described. However, shared access to structured documents (level 3) and distributed document models (level 4) require additional extensions that are discussed below. As only a few prototype systems support such functionality as yet, we describe basic concepts rather than complete systems. Parts of the material are based on personal work on cooperative object management described in [SCH92].

### 5.8.1 Shared Access to Structured Documents

Access to structured documents in shared mode is usually based on an architectural model as shown in figure 5-16. A current copy of the whole document is stored at a selected node, a *document server*. As an alternative to a central server, different nodes of a distributed system can act as document servers according to the client population (*server nodes* $S_1, \dots, S_n$ in the example); for example, one document server could be allocated for each segment of an internetworked LAN environment. However, in contrast to distributed document models (see below), such an implementation does not support mutual and explicit relationships between documents stored at different servers.

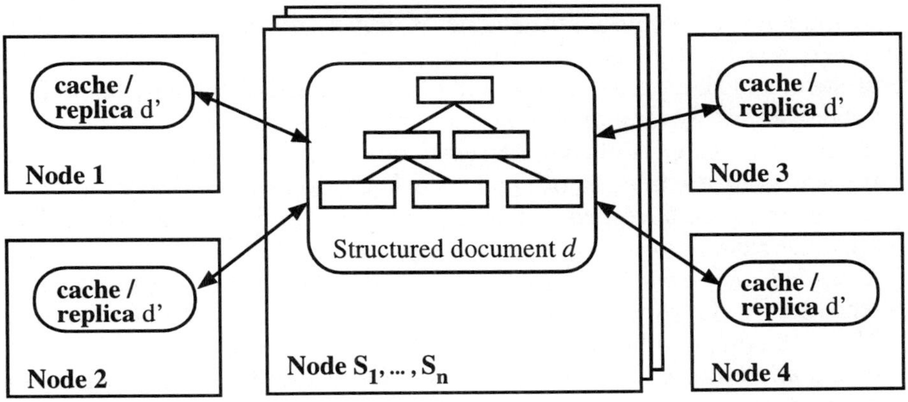


Fig. 5-16 Shared access to a structured document

**Basic access operations:** Clients at remote nodes (*nodes 1-4* in the example) can now request access to a structured document stored at a document server. First the server storing the desired document must be located and then the document must be opened for access. This can be supported by the following example operations:

```
Server = LocateDocument ("SalesTables");
SalesDocumentId = AccessDocument ("SalesTables", Server);
```

The operation *LocateDocument* should be implemented by a directory service like CDS of the OSF DCE (see chapter 3). The basic name-to-address mapping of such a service can be augmented with an attribute-based search facility (e.g. to locate all documents where the value of the owner attribute equals *Brown*). Moreover, a directory service can offer the mapping function in a robust way by replicating the name tables at several directory servers transparently.

The *AccessDocument* operation takes the given document name and the discovered server address, performs a remote procedure call at the selected document server and opens the document for access. The requesting client receives a document identifier that can later be used for accessing the document directly. The identifier is implemented like a proxy in distributed object-based systems (see chapter 3); it is globally unique and can internally be mapped to a location hint for the document server. In addition to *AccessDocument,* a separate operation *CreateDocument* with the same parameters must be supported to create new documents. The document server should register all documents with the directory service after creation.

**Document cache/replica management:** As a side effect of *AccessDocument*, the client may receive a cached copy or replica of the document or of a document portion (indicated by *d'* in the example). The required transfer of the document can be implemented based on the standards discussed, such as ODA and SGML, using their transfer formats ODIF or SDIF, respectively. However, the central issue of document sharing is management of the installed client copy in the face of multiclient access. Several options are possible, including:

- *Exclusive locking:* A client receives a copy of the document and has exclusive access to it while the original is locked. Modified copies are eventually sent back to the document server updating the original, or are discarded on client demand.
- *Extended lock compatibility:* The trivial read/write lock modes can be extended by a *dirtyRead*, and by a *checkoutRead* and *checkoutUpdate* mode. The lock compatibility is discussed in more detail below. It mainly allows a potentially outdated copy to be accessed for read-only purposes with limited consistency requirements (*dirtyRead*), and it supports long-term document checkout operations with explicit notification if other access requests are pending (*checkoutRead* and *checkoutUpdate*).
- *Application-specific coordination:* With this method, any requesting client immediately receives a replica of the document or of a selected portion. Updates are synchronized by an application-specific inter-client protocol. Based on a distributed negotiation protocol, one client is granted control and can perform document updates. Control is passed to another client based on explicit requests, timeouts or voting approaches, for example. It is sufficient to replay update operations at all client sites due to their explicit serialization.

Different combinations and variations of these approaches are possible and can be found in distributed systems. As a concrete system example, MIT's *CES (Collaborative Editing System)* [GRW92] shall be mentioned. The system implements a joint document editing facility for a set of distributed participants. It uses a combination of extended lock compatibility and application-specific coordination: document portions can always be accessed in read mode without any synchronization; this may lead to inconsistent views but not to inconsistencies of the stored document itself. Write access is exclusive and is controlled by a token in an application-specific way. The token can be requested by co-workers explicitly and can also be revoked based on a timeout interval. More details can be found in section 8.3.

Similar application-specific lock management facilities have already been discussed in section 2.1.3 in the context of the *CoDraw* multiuser editing tool. A floor passing protocol transfers control between clients based on client requests that have to be satisfied after a pre-defined period of time. The time period can be adjusted from zero to infinite. In the first case, control is immediately revoked upon request. The second case is equal to the checkout notification. Typically, a trade-off with a timeout in the order of several seconds to minutes seems to be most practical.

Below, we discuss the more interesting coordintation mechanisms, i.e. extended lock compatibility and application-specific coordination, more closely.

**Extended lock compatibility:** Table 5-6 shows the compatibility table for the extended locking modes. In contrast to the usual locking rules, an update lock is compatible with a dirty read lock; that is, a dirty read lock guarantees a stable document state at the time it is acquired but it does not prevent the original document from being modified, neither is the cached copy updated when the original changes. This locking mode is suitable if a client accesses a document to extract some slowly-changing information or if a client just wishes to create an independent copy of the document. The implementation of *dirtyRead* must only guarantee that the document is not being changed while the cached copy is generated but does not impose any restrictions thereafter.

| 1. \ 2. | **dirtyRead** | **read** | **write** | **checkout Read** | **checkout Write** |
|---|---|---|---|---|---|
| dirtyRead | ok | ok | ok | ok | ok |
| read | ok | ok | conflict | ok | conflict |
| write | ok | conflict | conflict | conflict | conflict |
| checkoutRead | ok | ok | notification | ok | notification |
| checkoutWrite | ok | notification | notification | notification | notification |

Table 5-6 Extended lock compatibility for shared document access

The *checkoutRead* and *checkoutWrite* lock modes basically behave like the *read* and *write* modes. However, if a write or checkoutWrite lock is requested for an object with an existing lock on one of the checkout lock modes, the lock-holder is notified by a signal as indicated by the following code; this code is executed by the client requesting the lock:

```
if (UpdateRequest (object)) {
  while (CheckoutWrite (object)) {
    lockingEntity = getLockingEntity (object);
    notifySignal (lockingEntity);
    wait (delayTime);
    }
  lock (object);
  lockingEntity (object) = myself;
  }
```

The selected semantics emphasizes a relatively conservative solution: The requesting client blocks when it encounters an existing checkoutWrite lock. By converting the signal into a visual notification (e.g. via the user interface of a shared document editor), an end user can be requested to release such a "long lock" prematurely. However, the lockholder is not obliged to actually release the lock immediately. Some systems - such as CES mentioned above - implement such an enforcement based on timeouts. Finally, existing checkoutRead locks do not affect other clients that request a write lock.

This approach is comparable to caching with automatic callback in the context of distributed file systems like DFS of the OSF DCE. However, after a callback due to a conflicting file access request, the cached copy is released immediately and the file is accessed remotely. Such an automatic approach is hardly feasible in a cooperative document management environment.

The checkout locking modes mainly support cooperative document editing in a relatively closed user environment. For example if joint authors jointly write a technical paper, an author can notify a colleague that he or she is ready to spend some more time editing the document. If the colleague is able to interrupt his or her activity at that time, the other author can get control of the document. However, as the first author is not obliged to release document control, social rules are required to enable practical cooperation; such rules are mostly found in closed user populations.

The checkout lock implementation can be extended by issuing periodic notifications if control is not released immediately. Another enhancement enables temporary granting of control; in this case, a client with a former checkout lock receives control again once the other client releases the document. Many other extensions and variations of this scheme are possible; for example, lock hierarchies can be introduced, locking can be combined with versioning, and semi-automatic merging of related but inconsistent versions can be supported. An extensive discussion of such approaches is given in [BAK91].

**Application-specific coordination:** Client access to a shared document can also be coordinated by an application-specific protocol; this can also be classified as a generalization of the extended checkout lock modes. Typically, one client has control over the document and is allowed to modify it. Control is passed by a distributed protocol; notification of clients with checkout requests is only one example of this.

Examples of other possible coordination protocols are classified in figure 5-17 and are discussed below. First, a distinction between structured and unstructured coordination can be made. In the first case, how and to whom control is passed next is well defined, either by a logical control token circulating between the clients or by a dedicated mediator deciding whom to grant control.

The token-controlled approach can be compared with the token-passing protocol of the token bus LAN; a logical ring is established between the clients and each client knows his successor. After a client has completed document modifications, he passes control to the successor by forwarding the logical token by a special network message or RPC invocation. If a client has no need for document control, he forwards a received token immediately. The token holding time, i.e. the time a client is granted control, can be controlled by an upper timeout limit. Special protocols are necessary for integrating new clients, for leaving the logical ring, and for handling node failures. The token-controlled approach has the advantage that it is decentralized and deterministic. However, it does not allow for interrupting a client holding the token.

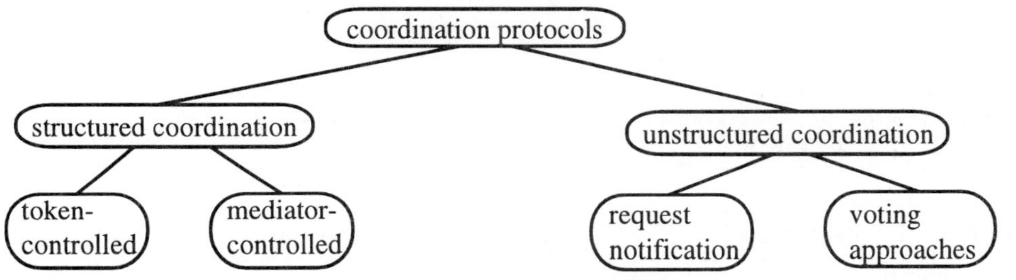


Fig. 5-17 Coordination for cooperative document management

The mediator-controlled approach is based on a central mediator and is often found in teleconferences or computer conferences (see chapter 2). Typically, document access requests have to be issued to the mediator who grants control when possible. Different clients may have different priorities and the mediator may select a client based on application-specific criteria (like urgency of request or frequency of requests in the past). The major advantage of the mediator-controlled approach is its flexibility concerning the applied coordination protocol; the major disadvantage is its dependence on a central instance.

With *unstructured coordination,* more competetive control mechanisms are applied. For example, the request notification of the checkout lock modes can be classified to belong to this category. Control can directly be passed between any two clients upon request. The main advantage of this approach is its ability to react on request and immediately.

Finally, *voting* can also be applied to controlling document access in a decentralized way. Usually, this mechanism is used for low-level access synchronization in distributed systems, but it can also be exploited for use in interactive distributed CSCW environments. A client requesting document control has to collect a majority of all votes of the client population. A special policy must be established to control how a client votes in a given situation. Most important, a client may only vote once until control is transferred again. In this way, no two "majorities" can result at any time. Figure 5-18 shows an example of a voting scenario when *node 1* and 2 both request access. Node 1 and S vote for node 1, nodes 2-4 vote for node 2. Hence, node 2 gets control.

The voting protocol itself must be implemented based on distributed communication techniques like RPC but typically requires a broadcast facility for efficient propagation of voting requests. In general, the voting approach only seems suitable for a highly interactive and relatively closed environment. It can also be combined with voting support found in decision support systems as discussed in chapter 2.

| | **Votes for node 1** | **Votes for node 2** |
|---|---|---|
| Vote of node 1 | x | |
| Vote of node 2 | | x |
| Vote of node 3 | | x |
| Vote of node 4 | | x |
| Vote of node S | x | |
| Total votes | 2 | **3** |

Fig. 5-18 Example of voting-controlled document access

Many other application-specific document access coordination protocols are possible; examples are random selection of a controlling client, selection according to recent group communication patterns between clients, or selection based on the role of a participant and the intended document manipulation operation. The coordination mechanisms are not only applied to multiuser document editors in practise, but are also useful for synchronous conference systems with joint data access or for joint calendar management.

Therefore, such coordination facilities have a broad impact on all kinds of synchronous CSCW systems. For example, shared document models are also found in several hypermedia systems discussed in chapter 2; examples are *Intermedia*, *Neptune*, and *KMS*. These systems are based on a client/server architecture with a single server storing hypermedia documents and several clients having access to them. Typically, synchronization is performed by a relatively straightforward locking scheme, sometimes extended by a facility similar to the checkout lock modes.

## 5.8.2 Distributed Document Models

With shared document access, whole documents are still the basic units of placement, i.e. a document is stored as a whole at a selected node. An exception might be caching of document portions. However, this is only an optimization technique for reducing the amount of transferred information. The document models themselves do not support document portions as general units of placement. More important, they do not support relationships between remote documents or document portions.

**Basic concepts of distributed document models:** *Distributed document models* address these issues. Such models are often based on distributed object-oriented systems [CHC91] and limited prototypes have already been implemented in the context of distributed hypermedia systems; examples are *PlaneText* [CON87], *Distributed Hypertext* [NOS91], and *Virtual Notebook System* [SHI89]. An important advantage of such systems is their ability to store data in a distributed way according to expected access patterns. For example, documents can be allocated to different departmental databases but can still be interrelated explicitly. Another advantage is the ability to integrate formerly separate document servers. In this way, cooperative and global access to documents is facilitated.

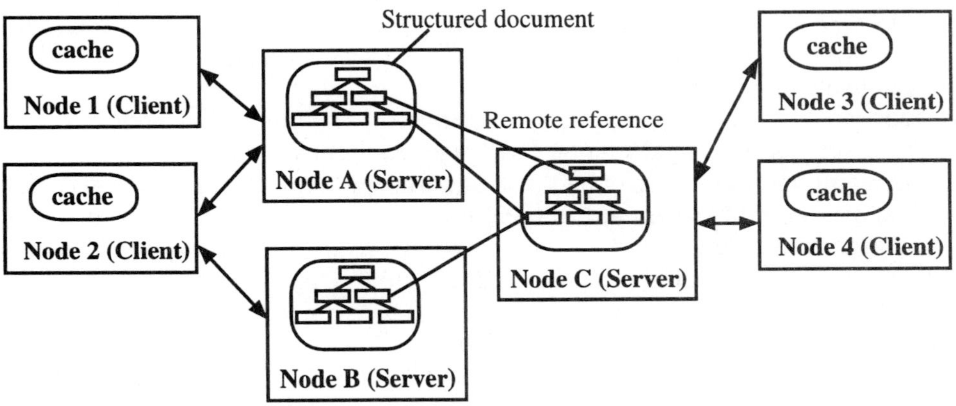


Fig. 5-19 Distributed document management model

Typically, such distributed document management systems are based on an architectural model similar to distributed object-oriented systems discussed in chapter 3 (see also figure 5-19). Document components or whole documents are modeled as objects, inter-document references or links are mapped to inter-object references. The objects are stored by different document or hypermedia servers *(nodes A-C* in the example). Objects can be accessed by clients (*nodes 1-4* in the example) remotely via location-independent invocations. Such invocations are also performed between servers, e.g. to access a remotely referenced document. Typical operations are *browsing* through the global object space and *editing* particular objects/documents. For a complete system, several additional technical issues arise:

- *Document data transfer and caching:* When a client accesses distributed documents, document components must be transferred to the client's site and cached there in order to enable editing. Even for browsing, the different inter-document links must be made available at the client's site in order to enable interactive selection of the links actually to follow.

- *Server autonomy:* Each server participating in a distributed document environment must be able to act autonomously. In particular, a server must have the ability to restrict access to its documents and to export only a limited subset of all its documents to other servers and to clients.
- *Heterogeneity:* Especially in formerly separate server environments, different document servers tend to be heterogeneous in terms of hardware, storage system, and document model. Common data and document formats and communication protocols are required for interoperability.
- *Transactions:* In contrast to single-server document environments, a client can now manipulate interrelated documents at several sites within a logical sequence of operations. In order to keep documents consistent, such operations must be embedded into atomic distributed transactions.
- *Document migration:* According to the expected access patterns, it might be desirable to relocate documents between servers. Basically, this can be implemented by object migration; however, additional issues like data conversion between heterogeneous formats, synchronization with ongoing transactions, and consideration of storage requirements arise.

These requirements can partly be satisfied by integrating existing approaches described already. Standardized document transfer formats can serve as a base for heterogeneous document interchange between servers, access control lists and explicit export operations as found in RPC systems can address the server autonomy issue, distributed transactions based on two-phase commit can solve the global consistency problem, and extended object migration facilities can implement dynamic document relocation. However, these techniques have not yet been completely integrated in an existing distributed document management system. Therefore, we describe a system with limited distributed document management facilities although it does not cover the complete scope of requirements stated above.

**Example system:** The *DHT (Distributed Hyptertext)* system [NOS91] integrates different heterogeneous document servers via a network or via several interconnected networks. Its architecture is shown in figure 5-20.

Documents of relatively static structure are stored in an object-oriented database (OODB) and in an Ingres relational database. They represent hypertext objects. Links between these objects are either local and are then implemented directly within the database or can also be remote, i.e. span different databases. Remote links are implemented by a *link server* associating objects at different sites. That is, links are not necessarily stored together with the linked objects. The advantage of this approach is that links can be easily manipulated without the need to access potentially large objects. Moreover, the link implementation can be optimized more easily; the system uses B-trees to retrieve links for particular objects efficiently. The disadvantage of the approach is that the link server may become a bottleneck and that additional network messages are required to traverse a link between two documents.

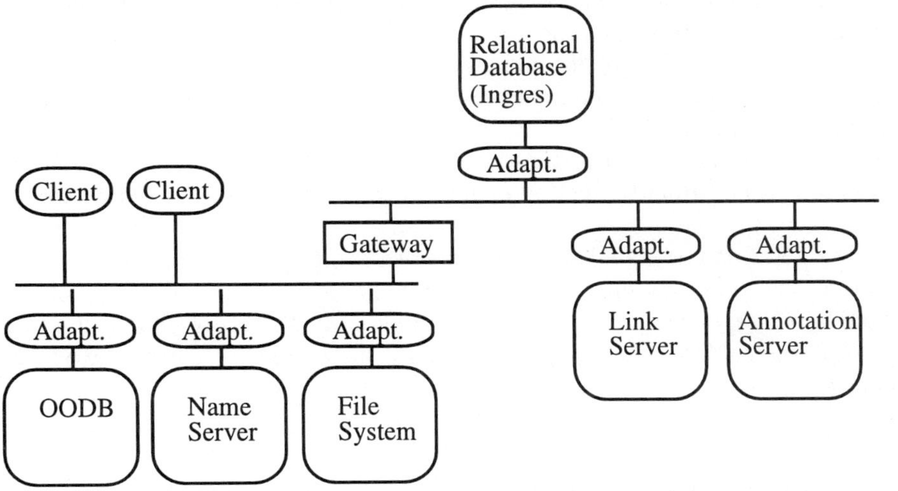


Fig. 5-20 Architecture of the Distributed Hypertext System

An *annotation server* stores additional annotations (e.g. textual comments) linked to hypertext objects. A *Unix file system* is used for storing unstructured data in flat files. A *directory server* enables location of other servers, for example to find the address of the link server initially. Clients access the system from workstations with a window-based browser/editor tool.

Each server component has an adaptation component; its major task is to map the local storage representation of documents and links to a universal, global representation, and to map global operations onto local database access. This architecture facilitates system extensions; to integrate a new document server, only a new adaptation component must be implemented while the existing servers remain unaffected.

Distributed traversal of links between documents (originating from a document *d1* and using the well-known directory server) is performed as indicated by the following program fragment:

```
ls = locate_link_server (name_service);     // locate the link server
                                            // (mesage to directory server)
links = retrieve_links (ls, d1);            // retrieve links originating from d1
                                            // (message to link server)

link_subset = filter (links, filter_description);           // filter the resulting list
link = select_link (link_subset);                           // select one particular link
check_object_type_and_resources (link.destination);         // check if object can be stored
fetch_object (link.destination);                            // fetch object
                                                            // (message to doc. server)
```

First, the link server is located by querying the directory service. The link server is then asked for a list of links originating from the given document. The result is filtered according to application-specific criteria (e.g. "select only links related to a project context"). Out of the remaining links, a particular one is selected. Before fetching the destination object, its object type and storage/resource requirements are checked. As the system also supports multimedia objects like audio, this is important in order to guarantee that the client is able to store and access the object. Finally, a copy of the object is physically fetched to the client site.

The operations to actually access an object (e.g. *fetch_object*) are mapped to database operations by the adaptation component. For example, to select a form named *travel_expense_form_1* within a folder named *expense_folder,* the following SQL query (see also chapter 6) would be issued to access the relational database:

```
SELECT *
FROM form
WHERE name = "travel_expense_form_1"
AND folder = "expense_folder"
```

Different access operations would be generated for the OODB or for other storage devices. The database access can be embedded into local transactions for atomic update operations; however, distributed transactions are not supported. Therefore, no global rollback can be performed for undoing changes to several objects managed by different document servers. The system also does not address migration of documents or of their components between servers directly. Although migration can be emulated in general by fetching a document, storing it at a different server, and deleting it at the original site, an explicit migration facility would provide enhanced support for locating mobile objects, and could be implemented more efficiently.

In summary, the DHT system covers the document transfer, server autonomy, and heterogeneity requirements. It only provides limited support for transactions and migration.

### 5.8.3 Application to Distributed Office Procedures

A shared or distributed document model can be exploited by many CSCW applications; we discuss the example of distributed office procedures. Obviously, document models are suitable for managing the data/document portions attached to an office procedure. In contrast, forwarding of control between participants in the overall procedure is better implemented by explicit message passing or remote procedure call.

Applying a shared document model means that all data related to an office procedure are stored by one or multiple document servers and that only references to these data are passed as part of office procedure control transfer. While a participant performs his or her dedicated task within the overall procedure (e.g.

filling in of a travel expense form by an employee or approval by a manager), he or she interacts with the document server remotely. Finally, he or she passes a reference to the modified form to the next party (e.g. to a secretary) who also accesses the document server. An example of the resulting messages passed between the different sites is shown diagrammatically in figure 5-21.

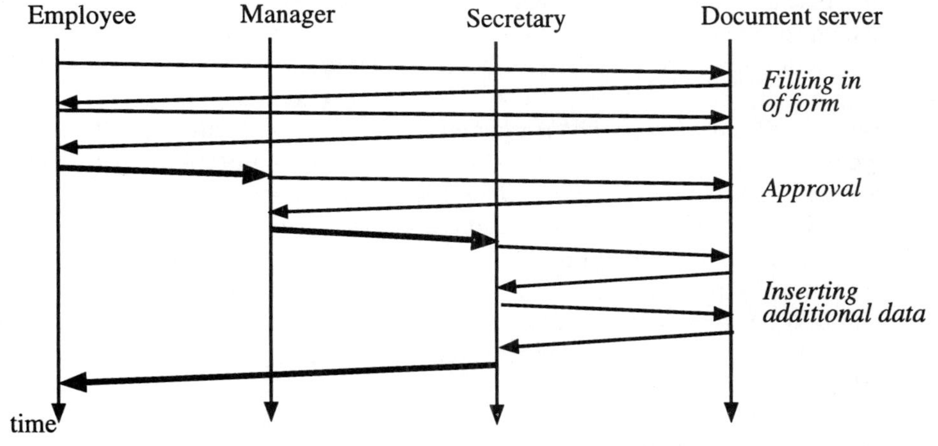


Fig. 5-21 Messages in an office procedure with shared documents

First, the employee interacts several times with the document server to edit the travel expense form. Then office procedure control is forwarded to the manager (bold arrow) who accesses the document server to approve the form. Afterwards, control is transferred to the secretary who also accesses the server multiply in order to complete a number of form entries. Finally, the employee is informed as to process completion.

The shared document model facilitates implementation of an office procedure support system. In particular, communication messages become much simpler and even a straightforward e-mail system can be used for a basic implementation of control transfer. All document storage and access tasks are covered by the document management system. However, the amount of messages to be passed may increase and it may not be reasonable to manage very simple data objects at the document server site. Therefore, a combination of distributed object-oriented programming and a shared or distributed document model seems more promising.

By applying a distributed document model, a similar scenario to that discussed above can be implemented. However, loosely related documents can be stored at different server sites according to existing locality of reference. For example, all travel expense forms would be managed by a dedicated server while all order forms would be stored at a different server. Nevertheless, both kinds of forms could be involved in a common office procedure; for a client, it is possible to access them jointly as discussed in the context of the DHT system above.

## 5.9 Extension: Multimedia Document Requirements

Current research and development efforts are focusing on extending the approaches described, especially ODA, to multimedia. This area will be discussed in more detail in chapter 7; here, we merely summarize the resulting requirements:

- *Representation of multimedia content portions:* Multimedia document management requires a standardized digital representation of all kinds of content portions. In addition to still graphics and images supported by the ODA standard, time-dependent video and audio and other media must be represented.
- *Transfer formats:* For transfer of multimedia documents, standardized formats must be provided, too. An important issue is compression of transferred data in order to reduce communication bandwidth requirements. An example of an emerging standard for transfer of non-revisable multimedia data is *MPEG.*
- *Synchronization:* Time-dependent multimedia data have to be synchronized during their presentation. Especially when different document components are fetched from different servers, varying delay times can occur that complicate synchronization. *HyTime* and *HyperODA* are emerging standards for a description notation for the required sychronization.
- *Hypermedia links:* Multimedia documents typically have complex interdependencies between document components, exceeding the hierarchical structuring concept. For this reason, hypermedia links between document components must be supported, preferably in a standardized way. Both *HyTime* and *HyperODA* address this issue.
- *Document processing:* In addition to document representation and transfer, an extended processing model is required. For example, editing of various kinds of media with dedicated editors and browsing through media content portions must be supported. Moreover, the formatting process changes; some media (like voice) have no direct meaning for various devices like printers, and the formatting process for other devices must evaluate the stated synchronization requirements.

We discuss these issues and emerging standards in chapter 7, dividing our treatment into the aspects of multimedia object and document models, multimedia communication and synchronization, and multimedia storage systems and databases.

## 5.10 Exercises

1. [Basic knowledge]
What are the main differences between record-oriented conventional data structures and documents? Why should the structure of complex documents be represented explicitly?

2. [Basic knowledge]
Consider a travel expense form as a dedicated kind of form with several predefined fields (such as travel description, requesting employee etc.) and attachments (like receipts). Concrete form instances might exist for a trip by Bob to Boston and for a trip by Mary to New York. Based on this example, explain the semantic data model terms "generalization", "specialization", "instance", "association", and "aggregation".

3. [Basic knowledge]
Classify the following approaches according to the models described for cooperative document management:
- document transfer by ftp protocol in the Internet
- distributed hypermedia system
- ODA/ODIF-based document transfer
- multiuser editor
- SGML/SDIF-based document transfer.

4. [Conceptual design]
Extend the generic logical ODA structure of the travel expense form in section 5.2 so that the trips of several employees can be represented on a single form (there should be one travel description and employee object for each employee, but only a single approval object for the whole form). Outline the result in graphical form and in the pseudo-notation given in this chapter.

5. [Conceptual design]
Extend the generic layout structure accordingly so that there is a dedicated description and employee frame for each employee.

6. [Basic knowledge]
Explain the difference between the layout process and the imaging process. Which are the advantages of separating both processes from each other?

7. [Basic knowledge]
Explain the following ODA terms:
- document profile
- raster graphics content architecture
- top-level / low-level editor
- document architecture class
- ODL.

8. [Conceptual design]
Repeat the structural extensions of the travel expense form carried out for ODA (several employees on a single form) for the SGML representation as well.

9. [Basic knowledge]
Select the most appropriate of the document-related standards ODA, SGML, or EDIFACT for each of the following tasks:
- preparation of a book for publication
- editing and printing of a complex text document
- transfer of sales tables of regular structure
- transfer of a formatted mixed text/graphics document.

10. [Conceptual design]
Using a system for shared document access with extended lock compatibility as described in section 5.8.1, the following scenario is to be modeled:
- Peter browses through document A, just to get a first impression of its overall structure.
- Mary opens documents A and B in order to copy a table from B to A.
- Bob opens document B to perform some global changes that involve the whole document and may take several hours.
- John wants to replace a chapter in document B by a version of his own.

Which access operation (dirtyRead, read, write, checkoutRead, checkoutWrite) is most appropriate for each of these operations? Draw a table with rows and columns labeled Peter, Mary, Bob, and John and indicate the resulting conflicts / notifications among these operations (consider any possible sequence of operations).

11. [Implementation]
Implement a simple distributed hypertext system as an example of a basic distributed document model. As a basis, combine the solutions to the simple hypertext implementation exercise (chapter 2) and to the distributed object emulation system (chapter 3). The system is to offer the following facilities:
- hypertext browsing operations according to chapter 2, now between distributed hypertext nodes (with emulated distribution)
- relocation of hypertext nodes between network nodes (with emulated distribution).

Note: The implementation involves major detailed design decisions and may require significant time to be completed.

## 5.11 References

[AND87] Andrews, N.: Rich Text Format Makes Transferring Text Easier; *Microsoft Systems Journal, March, 1987, pp. 63-70*

[ANS86] ANSI X3.122-1986: Metafile for the Storage and Transfer of Picture Description Information; *American National Standards Institute, 1986*

[BAK91] Barghouti, N.S., Kaiser, G.E.: Concurrency Control in Advanced Database Applications; *ACM Computing Surveys, Vol. 23, No. 3, Sept. 1991, pp. 269-317*

[BER89] Berge, J.: EDIFACT - A Technical Introduction; *In: Gifkins, M. (Ed.): EDI Technology, London, 1989, pp. 63-78*

[BRO91] Brooks, K.P.: Lilac: A Two-View Document Editor; *Computer, Vol. 24, No. 6, June 1991, pp. 7-19*

[CHC91] Chin, R.S., Chanson, S.T.: Distributed Object-Based Programming Systems; *ACM Comp. Surv., Vol. 23, No. 1, March 1991, pp. 91-124*

[CHE76] Chen, P.: The Entity-Relationship Model: Towards a Unified View of Data; *ACM Trans. on Database Systems, Vol. 1, No. 1, March 1976, pp. 9-36*

[CHG87] Chamberlin, D.D., Goldfarb, C.F.: Graphics Applications of the Standard Generalized Markup Language (SGML); *Computer Graphics, Vol. 11, 1987, pp. 343-358*

[CON87] Conklin, J.: Hypertext: An Introduction and Survey; *IEEE Computer, Vol. 20, No. 9, Sept. 1987, pp. 17-41*

[DEC90] Digital Equipment Corporation: Digital Technical Journal; *Technical Report Vol. 2, No. 1, 1990 (discussion of Compound Document Architecture including DDIF)*

[GRW92] Greif, I., Seliger, R., Weihl, W.: A Case Study of CES: A Distributed Collaborative Editing System Implemented in Argus; *IEEE Trans. on Software Engineering, Vol. 18, No. 9, Sept. 1992, pp. 827-839*

[HAM81] Hammer, M., McLeod, D.: Database Description with SDM: A Semantic Database Model; *ACM Trans. on Database Systems, Vol. 6, No. 3, Sept. 1981, pp. 351-386*

[HKN89] Hunter, R., Kaijser, P., Nielsen, F.: ODA: A Document Architecture for Open Systems; *Computer Communications, Vol. 12, No. 2, April 1989, pp. 69-78*

[IBM83] International Business Machines Corporation: Document Content Architecture: Revisable-Form-Text Reference; *IBM, 1983*

[ISO86] ISO/DIS 8879: Information Processing - Text and Office Systems - Standard Generalized Markup Language; *International Organization for Standardization, 1986*

[ISO88] ISO/DIS 8613: Information Processing - Text and Office Systems - Open Document Architecture, Parts 1-8; *International Organization for Standardization, 1988*

[ISO91] ISO/IEC JTC1/SC18 N2837 - CD10179: Information Technology - Document Style Semantics and Specification Language (DSSSL); *International Organization for Standardization, 1991*

[ISO92] ISO/IEC JTC1/SC18/WG8 N1427, Paula Angerstein: Summary of the Document Style Semantics and Specification Language (DSSSL) Draft International Standard 10179; *International Organization for Standardization, 1992*

[KLL86] Krönert, G., Lauber, G., Lörscher, J., Meynieux, E., Postl, W., Schneider, U., Seisen, S., Tombre, K.: Document Editing and Entry Based on the Standardized Open Document Architecture; *ESPRIT '86: Results and Achievements, North-Holland, 1987, pp. 107-126*

[MAZ87] Ma, Z.: New Tools to Support ODA and ODIF; *Computer Communications, Vol. 10, No. 1, Feb. 1987, pp. 15-20*

[NOS91] Noll, J., Scacchi, W.: Integrating Diverse Information Repositories: A Distributed Hypertext Approach; *IEEE Computer, Vol. 24, No. 10, Dec. 1991, pp. 38-45*

[PEM88] Peckham, J., Maruanski, F.: Semantic Data Models; *ACM Computing Surveys, Vol. 20, No. 3, Sept. 1988, pp. 153-189*

[POT88] Potter, W.D., Trueblood, R.P.: Traditional, Semantic, and Hyper-Semantic Approaches to Data Modeling; *Computer, Vol. 21, No. 6, June 1988, pp. 53-63*

[ROS89] Robinson, P.J., Strasen, S.M.: Standard Page Description Language; *Computer Communications, Vol. 12, No.2, April 1989, pp. 85-92*

[RSM91] Rosenberg, J., Sherman, M., Marks, A., Akkerhuis, J.: Multi-Media Document Translation: ODA and the Express Project; *Springer, New York, 1991*

[SBS89] Smura, E.J., Beeton, B., Savage, K., Griffee, A.: Font Information Interchange Standard ISO/IEC 9541; *Computer Communications, Vol. 12, No.2, April 1989, pp. 93-96*

[SCH86] Scheller, A.: Integrated Processing of Text and Graphics within the German Research Network; *Computer Graphics, Vol. 10, 1986, pp. 133-142*

[SCH92] Schill, A.: Migration, Caching and Replication in Distributed Object-Oriented Systems: An Integrated Framework; *IFIP Int. Conf. on Information Networks and Data Communication, Helsinki, Finland, March 1992; Tienari, M., Khakhar, D. (Eds), North Holland, Amsterdam, 1992, pp. 309-329*

[SHI89] Shipman III, F.M.: Distributed Hypertext for Collaborative Research: The Virtual Notebook System; *Proc. Hypertext '89, ACM, New York, 1989, pp. 29-35*

[SMI89] Smith, J.M.: Standard Generalized Markup Language and Related Standards; *Computer Communications, Vol. 12, No.2, April 1989, pp. 80-84*

# 6 Database Support for Cooperative Office Systems

While the previous chapters were mainly concerned with modeling techniques for office documents and distributed execution aspects of office applications, this chapter is dedicated to persistent data management techniques for office environments, in particular to databases supporting such persistent storage.

First, a classification of data models and of distributed database extensions is given. Then we discuss the major concepts of relational and object-oriented databases, giving an integrated example for both areas. In particular, we show how data within a department database can be managed and how hypertext systems can benefit from object-oriented database concepts.

Concerning distributed extensions of database approaches, we discuss remote database access, especially the RDA standard, distributed database systems with a distribution-transparent data model, and emerging federated database systems with a more flexible model, only partially hiding distribution. We show how such distributed approaches can be applied to an office procedure environment. In particular, we illustrate how the results of an office procedure stored at various databases can be accessed and assembled using extended distributed technology. Further extensions to multimedia databases are described in chapter 7.

## 6.1 Database Approaches: Overview

The following sections give a basic overview of the most important traditional and modern database approaches.

### 6.1.1 Functionality Offered

Databases [DAT90] support persistent storage of data, surviving the termination of process executions. In contrast to persistent storage based on traditional files, they enable a much more enhanced functionality:

- *Representation of typed data:* Databases embed data into a type system. Each data item has to conform to a type that has been defined within the database in advance. The set of all types of a given database application is called the *schema* of the database.
- *Consistency:* Data held within a database conforms to consistency constraints found in real-world applications. For example, a database might

guarantee that a salary value is always a positive number or that the department referenced by employee data must actually exist.

- *Transactions:* Data within a database are modified by transactions with their atomicity, consistency, isolation, and durability characteristics discussed in section 4.1. For applications, this asserts a well-defined semantics of operations on data.
- *Multiuser access:* Based on transactions, multiuser / multiprogram access to a database is synchronized; a particular user may act as if he or she were in a single-user environment. Nevertheless, cooperation by using shared data is possible. Access control, a central issue in multiuser systems, is also implemented by the system.
- *Query support:* Access to data items is supported by high-level query languages, facilitating selection of data according to user-level criteria. With conventional files, data access has to be implemented by complex programs in an *ad hoc* way.
- *Access optimization:* Data access can be optimized for frequent access patterns. This is supported by the definition of access paths for which special data structures like hash tables are installed by the system. Moreover, queries are generally mapped to efficient internal execution sequences by optimization algorithms.
- *Recovery:* Databases support consistent recovery after system failures. This is achieved by rolling back and restarting transactions. Moreover, recovery of storage media failures can be supported by dedicated online backup mechanisms.
- *Data independence:* A database represents an intermediate layer between the physical storage system and the application programs. Thus applications become independent of the physical data representation. This enables storage reorganization without affecting the application and improves portability.
- *Application programming interfaces:* For non-trivial data management tasks, most databases offer specific programming interfaces, for example to languages such as C or C++. In addition to the programming language functionality, the query mechanisms of the database are available as a language embedded feature.

In cooperative office environments, databases are useful for storage and retrieval of documents, of record-oriented business data, and of all other kinds of long-living information. Most database approaches discussed later offer the above functionality at least in a basic version.

### 6.1.2 Databases and Data Models

The major database approaches and systems can be categorized according to their data model [SSU91]. Figure 6-1 gives an overview with an example that uses a pseudo-notation to represent employees, documents, and projects as persistent data within a department.

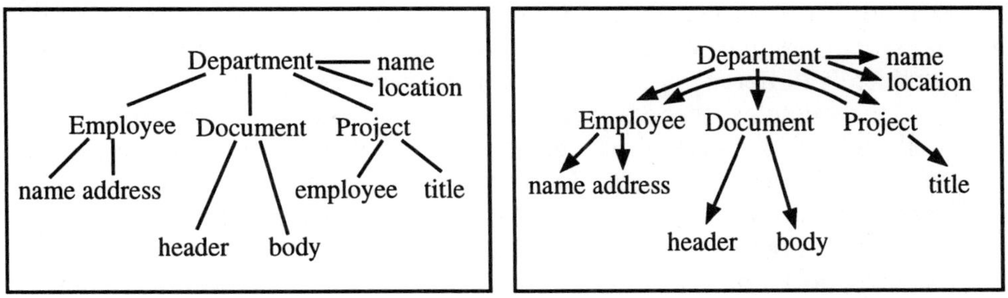


a) Hierarchical

b) Network

Department (DP#, name, location)

Employee (E#, name, address, DP#, P#)

Document (DO#, header, body, DP#)

Project (P#, title, DP#)

c) Relational

Department (name, location,
employees, projects, documents)

Employee (name, address, department,
project)

Document (header, body, department)

Project (title, department)

d) Object-oriented

Fig. 6-1 Overview of data models

Accordingly, the following major data model categories and types of databases can be classified:

- *Hierarchical databases:* With the hierarchical model, all data records are assembled into collections of information trees. Some records (e.g. representing a department in figure 6-1a) are root records while all other records (e.g. an employee or a document) have unique parent records. The query languages of such databases support navigation from a root record to selected records below it, accessing one record at a time. A traditional example is IBM's Information Management System (IMS) [IBM91]. Major disadvantages of the hierarchical model are the restrictive tree representation of data and the lack of set-oriented data access facilities.
- *Network databases:* This approach, standardized by the Conference on Data Systems Languages (CODASYL), extends the hierarchical data model towards a directed graph of data. Therefore, a more flexible modeling of applications is enabled. For example, the project records in figure 6-1b can directly refer to existing employee records in a non-hierarchical way, without replicating employee records. However, application programs still have to

navigate through data on a record-by-record basis. In addition to the programming effort required for this, maintenance of application programs is difficult due to various dependencies on the data representation graph.

- *Relational databases:* This model, introduced by *E.F. Codd,* is based on a completely different approach. It conceptually represents all data by flat tabular structures (called relations). Data access is performed by non-procedural, declarative query languages; a query describes *what* the user expects as a result and not *how* the result shall be computed, i.e. no navigation through data is specified. Relationships between records are expressed by using unique numbers or other unique *keys* to refer to related records. For example, the employee record in figure 6-1c names the number of the department and project of which an employee is a member. The relational approach facilitates database application programming and end user access to databases significantly. Examples of relational database systems are *System R, Ingres*, and *DB2*.
- *Object-oriented databases (OODBs):* The recent generation of OODBs has evolved from the observation that relational databases have deficiencies in modeling complex data objects like documents or CAD objects. Such data would have to be split into numerous relations, and would have to be reassembled when querying for an entire complex object, a frequent operation. OODBs support modeling and storage of entire, nested objects. For example, the department object in figure 6-1d directly contains the associated set of employees, projects and documents as component objects. Similarly, the other objects contain direct mutual references based on built-in pointers (such as *Document -> Department).* In this sense, OODBs can also be classified as being a successor of network databases with more general semantic modeling facilities. OODBs support encapsulation of objects based on well-defined interfaces, strong typing of objects, and inheritance/reuse of existing types for defining new, derived types of objects. Some examples of OODBs are *ObjectStore, Versan*t, and *O2*.

The relational approach is more mature and products have been available since the mid-seventies. However, meanwhile, there are also a growing number of OODB products available, especially for workstation environments. In the medium term, there will probably be some coexistence of both approaches, each with its specific target domain. We discuss both approaches in subsequent sections but do not go into details of the older network and hierarchical systems.

### 6.1.3 Distributed Systems Support

Databases can also be classified in terms of their support for distributed systems environments. Figure 6-2 shows the main categories based on a simple schematic example with three nodes; each node hosts a database, and potentially accesses the other databases remotely.

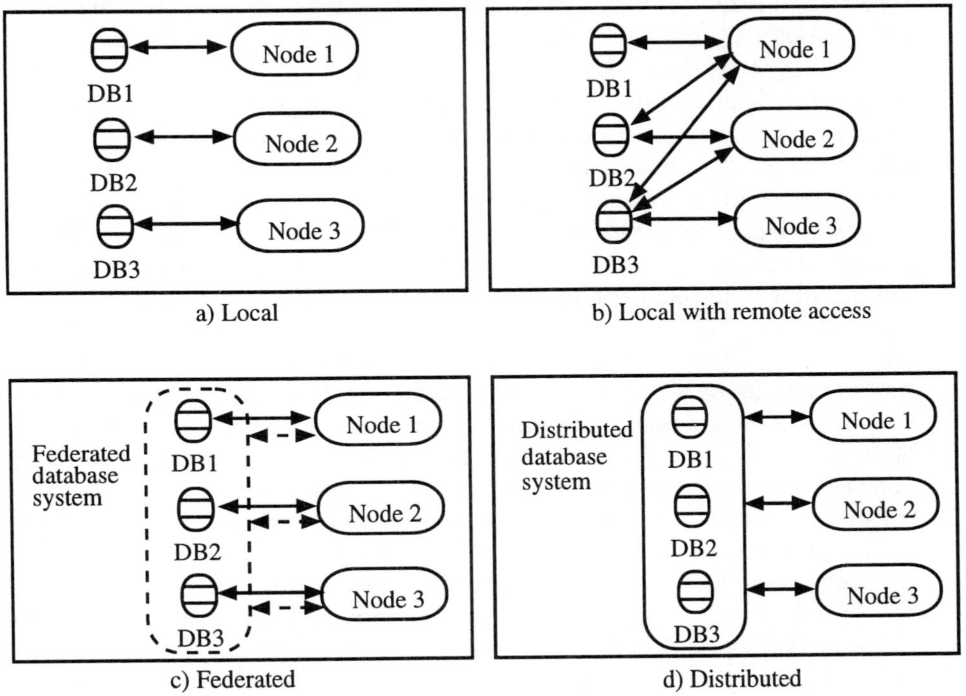


Fig. 6-2 Database models and distribution

These categories can be summarized as follows:

- *Local databases:* This is the most widespread type in today's office environments; a local database with one of the above data models resides on a large host and is accessed from terminals connected to that host; in our example in figure 6-2a, nodes 1-3 would have terminals attached and each node would only access its own database. Alternatively, smaller local databases might also result on workstations or even PCs but still be used only from the same system, i.e. by local workstation or PC programs or via respective user interfaces.
- *Local databases with remote access:* The local database paradigm can be extended to a client/server model by providing a remote database access interface and a corresponding access protocol. In this way, workstation or PC clients can access remote databases on hosts or other workstations. In our example in figure 6-2b, node 1 is able to access databases 2 and 3 in addition to its own database. Node 2 has access to database 3, too.
- *Federated database systems:* This model aims at loosely coupling various heterogeneous local databases via a network in order to integrate their data and functionality. Most important, there is usually no single database

schema, i.e. no global type system, but rather a collection of mutually related schemata. Therefore, distribution and heterogeneity are explicitly visible in many cases. Although this introduces additional complexity for application developers, it also provides enhanced flexibility especially in large systems: the distinct databases remain relatively autonomous in matters of administration, access control, and schema modification. This is indicated by the direct access arrow of each node to its local database in our example (figure 6-2c). Access to the federation as a logical unit is also supported for each node.

- *Distributed database systems:* A distributed database system provides logically centralized but physically distributed management of data by several tightly integrated local databases. During data access and modification, the actual distribution (and possible replication) of data is completely transparent; this is achieved by a global, uniform schema that is mapped to local data representations by the system. Nevertheless, fault tolerance, locality of access, and organizational decoupling of data can be achieved by defining an appropriate physical distribution of data in advance. However, distributed databases also have their costs in terms of complexity of systems management and overhead of distributed protocol execution. In our example (figure 6-2d), each node accesses the distributed database as a self-contained unit, without being able to access distinct databases directly. This is especially a problem for CSCW applications where cooperation is explicit, and locations of involved data and documents should therefore also be explicitly known and managed by the participants.

### 6.1.4 Relationship with Cooperative Office Systems

In today's cooperative office environments, the relational and object-oriented data models are most important. A relational data representation is more suitable for well-structured, record-oriented data (like payroll data, lists of employees etc.) while an object-oriented model is appropriate for weakly-structured, complex data like documents.

Within a cooperative office environment, distributed systems support is also important for data management. Remote database access facilities, preferably by dedicated protocols but possibly also by *ad hoc* mechanisms using RPC are a first step toward distribution. For example, with complex office procedures, each agent that offers a basic service might have access to a local database. With remote database access, the enhanced facility of passing remote document references as office procedure parameters can be implemented: the referenced documents can be accessed at other database locations remotely. Another example is a decision support system with remote access to several management information databases.

Federated database systems enable advanced facilities. For example, an authorized agent within an office procedure can access databases of other agents in an integrated way. This makes it possible to browse through data generated during previous office procedure steps.

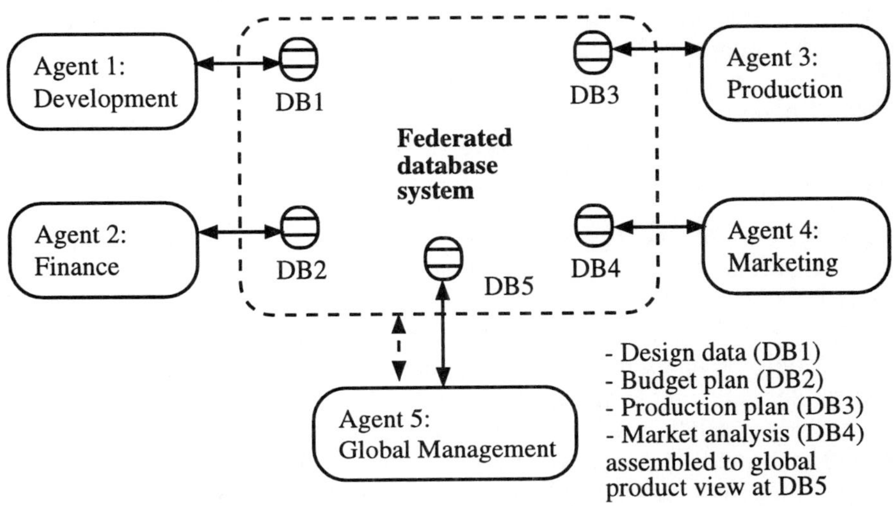


Fig. 6-3 Federated databases and office procedures

Figure 6-3 shows a concrete example. An office procedure implements the introduction of a new product within a company. Several departments have to cooperate, for example product development (e.g. product design), finance (e.g. budget planning), production (e.g. production planning and actual production), and marketing (e.g. market analysis). After various office procedure steps have been completed successfully, global management decides whether the product really should be introduced. Thus a global view of all product-related data is desirable. However, each department has its own database for autonomy and security reasons. For reasons of historical development, the databases might even be heterogeneous. Nevertheless, a federated database system allows for the construction of a (limited) global view of all product-related data at the global management site. The resulting approach can also serve as a basis for a global decision support system, considering data spread throughout the company.

With a distributed database, an even tighter integration can be achieved, based on an agent- or department-spanning global schema. However, autonomy of local databases is then sacrificed for integration and for distribution transparency.

## 6.2 Relational Databases

Relational databases are a major success due to their clarity and simplicity. They are most suited for organizing record-oriented mass data.

### 6.2.1 Structure of Relations

As discussed above, relational databases offer a straightforward data model based on flat relations. A relation is a set of data records with a common structure; in figure 6-1c, several relations have already been given. Each record consists of a set of named and typed attributes. For example, the employee record can be described more closely as follows:

Employee (E#: Integer, name: String, address: String, DP#: Integer, P#: Integer)

Within a relation, all records must be distinct from each other as a relation is a set and not a list of records. The minimal set of attributes to identify a record uniquely is called the *primary key*. For example, the unique employee number *E#* is the primary key of the *Employee* relation. The attribute combination *(Name, Address)* would be an alternative way to identify a record uniquely, a *secondary key*. Attributes referring to the keys of other relations are called *key candidates*. In the *Employee* relation, *DP#* and *P#* are foreign keys, referring to records of the *Department* and *Project* relations, respectively. The set of all relation definitions with their associated attributes within a database is called the *database schema*.

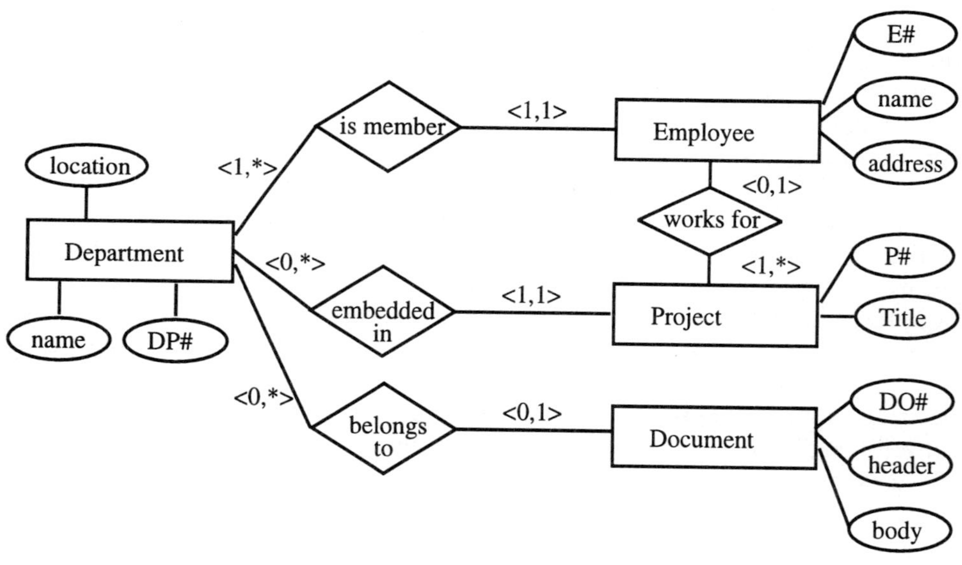


Fig. 6-4 Entity-Relationship schema representation

In our small example, the schema consists of the *Department, Employee, Document,* and *Project* relations. It is represented in more detail by the associated *entity-relationship* representation in figure 6-4. Each relation (*entity*) is represented by a rectangle with associated (oval) attribute representations. *Rela-*

*tionships* between relations (based on foreign keys within a relational implementation) are modeled explicitly (e.g. employee *is member* of a department, later represented by the foreign key *DP#* within the *Employee* relation).

The numbers given at the edges are constraints concerning the minimum and maximum number of related entities. For example, a document can belong to at most one department but may also belong to no department at all (represented by *<0,1> (=<min, max>)*). Conversely, a department may have many documents belonging to it or may have no documents of its own at all (represented by *<0,*>*). These constraints are not directly captured by the relational model but can be added to the schema in some database systems; for example, it is possible to represent the cardinality constraint *<1,*>* by using the *NOT NULL* attribute. In the following, we give an example of sets of records for the given relations:

**Department relation:**

| DP# | name | location |
|---|---|---|
| 134 | Marketing | Building_13 |
| 147 | Development | Building_15 |
| 183 | Finance | Building_1 |
| 201 | Personell | Building_2 |

**Employee relation:**

| E# | name | address | DP# | P# |
|---|---|---|---|---|
| 17 | Smith | 15 W21 St. | 147 | 12 |
| 18 | Cole | 13 E13 St. | 147 | 14 |
| 19 | Rogers | 18 Bench Rd. | 147 | 14 |
| 20 | Miller | 1 Horward Dr. | 201 | --- |
| 21 | Wang | 13 4th Av. | 183 | --- |

**Document relation:**

| DO# | header | body | DP# |
|---|---|---|---|
| 124 | DesignDoc | ... | 147 |
| 133 | SalesTable | ... | 134 |
| 134 | BudgetPlan | ... | 183 |
| 135 | ProjReport | ... | 147 |

**Project relation:**

| P# | title | DP# |
|---|---|---|
| 12 | OpenDatabaseSupport | 147 |
| 13 | DocumentStandards | 147 |
| 14 | DCEApplications | 147 |

As the example shows, each record is identified by a unique primary key. However, only in some cases is this number significant for the application itself. While departments and employees usually have unique organizational numbers, this will rarely be the case for documents. Thus the example shows that some unnatural attributes may be required in order to enable cross-references via foreign keys. With object-oriented databases, unique object identifiers are already built into the system and replace such unnatural keys. In addition to optimized storage facilities, this is one of the important advantages of OODBs over relational databases. For details on such issues and on the design of relations and schemata, see [DAT90], for example.

### 6.2.2 Database Queries and Transactions

Operations on relational data are expressed via *queries* formulated in a dedicated, declarative *query language.* For relational databases, the *SQL* query language has been standardized [ANS92]. It allows for set-oriented queries involving multiple relations. Most queries can be expressed in a straightforward way, a feature that has been one of the major reasons for the success of relational databases. We do not describe SQL in detail but give some brief examples based on the above relations to illustrate the flavor of the language; this query identifies the names of all employees working in the development department on the *DCEApplications* project:

```
select Employee.name
from   Department, Employee, Project
where  Department.name = "Development"
and    Project.title = "DCEApplications"
and    Employee.DP# = Department.DP#
and    Employee.P# = Project.P#;
```

The query *selects* matching records from the *Department* and *Project* relations and performs a *join* of the results with the records of the employee relation, matching the department and project numbers. The result is a large temporary relation which is finally reduced to the names of the employees sought. This temporary relation contains the following records (employee address field omitted for simplicity):

| DP# | DP.name | location | P# | title | E# | E.name |
|---|---|---|---|---|---|---|
| 147 | Development | Building_15 | 14 | DCEAppl. | 18 | Cole |
| 147 | Development | Building_15 | 14 | DCEAppl. | 19 | Rogers |

A final internal *projection* reduces the result as desired:

Cole
Rogers

It is obvious how simple general queries can be expressed; it is necessary simply to specify the desired result (*select* clause), the set of relations involved *(from* clause), and the selection criteria (*where* clause). It is even possible to omit the relation name in front of an attribute if attribute names are unique. Much more complex queries can also be expressed; however, this sometimes leads to complex nested query statements.

For data modification, similar language constructs are available. The main operations are *insert, delete*, and *update* of records. Within these operations, selection clauses can be used to identify the set of records to be updated or to be deleted, for example. All data access and modification operations can be embedded into *transactions* with ACID semantics as discussed in section 4.1; a transaction guarantees *atomicity* (fully completed or fully aborted), *consistency* (transformation from one consistent data state to another), *isolation* (concurrency control), and *durability* (committed modifications never get lost).

The following example changes the department number of all employees in department *147* to number *900*, e.g. due to an organizational restructuring:

```
update Employee
set DP# = 900
where DP# = 147;
commit work;
```

The whole operation is embedded into a transaction that is started implicitly and is committed explicitly at the end. This transaction is undone automatically if anything should fail.

### 6.2.3 Required System Support

The appealing model of flat relations with a declarative query language requires sophisticated system support. We summarize the basic mechanisms but cannot discuss their implementation details here:

- *Query optimization:* Declarative queries must be mapped to procedural statements that operate on the internal database representation. An efficient mapping is non-trivial and must be supported by special mechanisms. Typically, the schema designer specifies *access paths* (*indexes*) for one or several attributes of each relation. The database system implements the attributes based on hash tables or variations of B-trees in order to enable efficient access. Moreover, the database system computes an efficient access strategy for each query, exploiting indexes but also reordering commutative query operations. The major goal is to reduce the set of records to be evaluated as early as possible during query processing.
- *Transaction management:* Transaction support requires concurrency control based on various kinds of locking strategies (usually the *two-phase* locking protocol with a distinct lock and release phase). Moreover, transactions must be abortable until they are committed. This requires complex logging mechanisms such as *shadow storage* techniques in order to maintain the previous version of a record during non-committed modifications.
- *Schema management:* The database schema of a given application must be defined by a schema designer. Most databases offer a dedicated *data definition language (DDL)* for that task. The database system must store schema information (so-called *metadata*) online (in a so-called *data dictionary*) in order to enable query processing and control of data modifications. More-

over, dynamic schema modifications should also be supported in order to allow for schema evolution. This may require physical reorganization of the internal storage representation. For example, if an additional attribute *JobPosition* was introduced for the *Employee* relation, the extended records might not fit into their previous storage locations any more.

- *Physical storage management:* All relations must actually be mapped to physical storage, typcially using an underlying file system. The mapping is usually structured into several layers, mainly the *record layer* and the *segment layer*. The record layer maps set-oriented relations onto ordered data structures with associated navigation operations, resembling e.g. the network data model. The segment layer performs the mapping of these structures onto byte sequences that are assembled into logical database segments.

Within each of these areas, sophisticated algorithms and data structures are required; this leads to a very high overall complexity of database system implementations. The resulting global architectural structure of an entire database environment is represented by figure 6-5 from [LKK93].

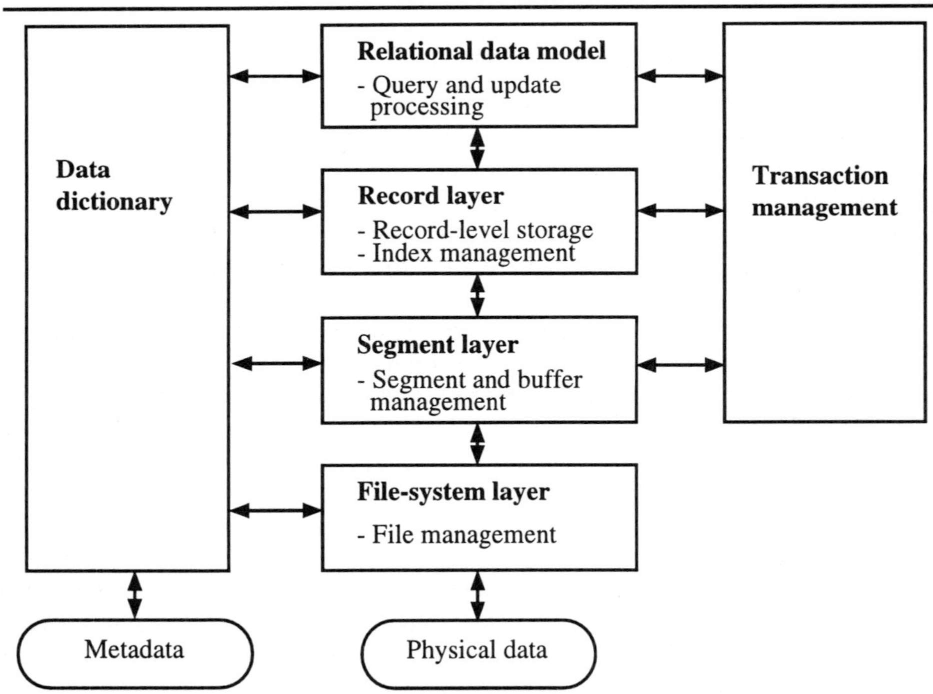


Fig. 6-5 Architectural structure of a database environment

The relational data model is mapped to records, segments, and eventually flat files that store physical data. Queries and other database operations are controlled and optimized based on metadata at the various levels. Transaction management is implemented by multiple, mutually interacting techniques at the upper three layers (e.g. locking of records, logging of change operations, shadow storage etc.).

In summary, the relational database approach is suitable for cooperative office applications due to its simple model and rich functionality. As a special feature, concurrency control of database transactions is an important issue in large cooperative multiuser environments. However, the modeling capacities of relational databases are rather limited when dealing with complex, unstructured documents. The object-oriented approach that provides an alternative solution in this area is discussed below in section 6.3. Local relational databases also provide only modest support for cooperative office applications in a distributed environment. The required distribution extensions are discussed in sections 6.4 to 6.6. Finally, multimedia database extensions are presented in chapter 7.

## 6.3 Object-Oriented Databases

Object-oriented databases have entered the marketplace more recently. They provide enhanced facilities for semantic modeling of complex data and are therefore most suited for application domains such as desktop publishing or document management.

### 6.3.1 Motivation

Relational databases offer a nice and simple model with reasonable efficiency for "standard", record-oriented applications. However, they do not satisfy all the requirements of advanced, non-standard applications as found in cooperative office systems. More precisely, the following problems can be identified:

- *Modeling power:* Advanced semantic data models (see section 5.1.2) are required for modeling data of complex structure, i.e. documents, hypermedia graphs, or multimedia data. The simple relational model only provides modest support for representing such semantics. Extended type systems with type inheritance, data encapsulation, and data aggregation are important features of improved solutions.
- *Queries and access facilities:* Although declarative queries are an essential feature of modern databases, new applications also have a demand for navigational, non-set-oriented data access. For example, browsing through a hypermedia graph or through a complex document can be implemented more efficiently based on direct navigation rather than by using indirect, name-based set-oriented queries as in relational databases.
- *Impedance mismatch:* Most real applications require the use of a conventional programming language in addition to a declarative database query language. However, it is hard to integrate both paradigms in a seamless way; most important, set-oriented data returned from a query must be processed in

an iterative style within the programming language. Moreover, database data structures usually have a different layout compared with programming language data structures. Complex mapping problems result from this.

Other requirements, some not directly related to OODBs, are support for advanced transaction models (allowing for concurrent data sharing in cooperative environments), and type evolution (supporting dynamic modification of the structure of persistent data). OODBs address many of these problems. They are based on an object-oriented data model with advanced data processing mechanisms.

### 6.3.2 Basic Concepts

Object-oriented databases are based on the following concepts [BEM91, JTT91, KIM90, LOO90]:

- *Object identity:* All data entities are represented as objects that have a unique, attribute-independent, and immutable identity to identify them.
- *Encapsulation:* Objects are usually accessed by operations (methods) instead of direct attribute access. This way, data encapsulation and abstraction are supported.
- *Classification:* Similar objects are grouped by types or classes. A type/class specifies the data structure and operations of its objects.
- *Inheritance:* Types are embedded into an inheritance lattice or hierarchy. A subtype inherits data structures and operations of a supertype above it in the hierarchy/lattice. This corresponds to the concept of specialization (subtyping) and generalization (represented by supertypes).
- *Aggregation:* Complex objects that consist of component objects can be represented as a unit for purposes of data storage and access. This mainly improves the performance of entire object retrieval.
- *Navigation:* In addition to set-oriented data access as found in relational databases, navigation from object to object by following inter-object references is supported directly.
- *Seamless integration:* Based on the object approach, a relatively seamless integration with (object-oriented) programming languages is achieved. Database objects can be directly mapped to programming language objects.

In addition, basically all conventional database techniques including persistent data management, transactions, access optimization, and schema management are supported by OODBs. Many object-oriented databases have been developed as prototypes, and a number of products are available. Most of them are based on existing object-oriented programming languages and augment them with database-oriented constructs, e.g. for persistence, transactions, and queries.

Data modeling itself is also often based on programming language object representations. As C++ is the most common object-oriented language today, it has become the typical base for OODBs, too. This is definitely not an ideal choice due to the numerous low-level constructs of this language and due to its mix of conventional-style, procedural programming and object-oriented extensions. However, reality is different from the pure conceptual view, and there are pragmatic reasons for using C++ as a base. Most important, existing C++ and also C programs can easily interact with the database, and C++ objects can be made persistent without major additional programming effort. For these reasons, we also present some simplified C++-based examples.

### 6.3.3 Details and Examples

The abstract concepts discussed above are best illustrated by an example; we represent the organizational model introduced above using OODB techniques. We use the programming interface of the ObjectStore database for pragmatic reasons but could in fact use any other OODB.

**Class/schema definition:** The schema definition is based on C++ class definitions, making use of inheritance; for example, the *Department* class is derived from a generic class for organizational units, inheriting its characteristics.

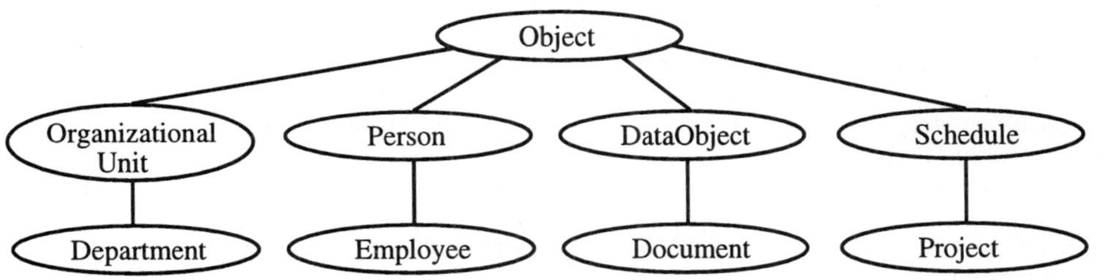


Fig. 6-6 Inheritance graph of schema classes

The inheritance graph is shown in figure 6-6; a generic superclass *Object* contains operations common to all objects. Of course, the superclasses (e.g. *DataObject*) can also be used to derive other specific subclasses like *Form* or *Spreadsheet* from them. The syntactical representations of the subclasses are as follows:

**Department class:**

```
class Department : public OrganizationalUnit {
 public:
  unsigned DPno indexable;              // department number
  String name indexable;                // department name
  String location;                      // department location
  set<Employee*> employees inverse_member Employee::department;
                                        // who works for dep.
  set<Document*> documents inverse_member Document::department;
                                        // documents of department
```

```
 set<Project*> projects inverse_member Project::department;
                                        // projects of department
 void printDepartmentInformation ();    // print all information
 void displayProjectSummary ();         // print summary of all projects
};
```

**Employee class:**

```
class Employee : public Person {
 public:
  unsigned Eno indexable;               // employee number
  String name indexable;                // employee name
  String address;                       // home address
  Department *department indexable inverse_member Department::employees;
                                        // department
  Project *project indexable inverse_member Project::members;
                                        // member of project
  void changeSalary (int);              // adapt salary
  int notify (Message);                 // send a message
};
```

**Document class:**

```
class Document : public DataObject {
 public:
  String header;                        // document header
  DocBody *body;                        // actual body
  Department *department inverse_member Department::documents;
                                        // belongs to department
  void print ();                        // print document on default device
  void edit ();                         // edit document with default editor
};
```

**Project class:**

```
class Project : public Schedule {
 public:
  String title indexable;               // title of project
  Department *department inverse_member Department::projects; // belongs to dep.
  set<Employee*> members inverse_member Employee::project;  // work for project

  void checkStatus ();                  // check current project status
  void cancel ();                       // cancel project
};
```

In contrast to the relational model, objects/classes have operations associated with them. For example, the department class offers operations for printing out its data or for displaying a summary of all of its projects. Operations are also inherited; for example, operations for associating organizational units with internal keys or numbers are inherited by the department class. They can be used within the subclass as if they were defined there.

Another important feature is the explicit representation of bidirectional inter-object relationships. This is achieved by declaring pointers or typed sets of pointers to related elements. A bidirectional implementation is supported by the keyword *inverse_member*; this specifies the instance variable of the peer class containing the backward reference. For example, a department references its employees, also specifying the inverse member *department* of the employee class. The latter class contains the corresponding definition. The important feature is that the system maintains *referential integrity* for such references; whenever an object reference to object B is inserted into an instance variable of object A, A's identity is inserted into the corresponding instance variable of B. Similar referential consistency mechanisms are implemented for modification and deletion of references. Inter-object references are also the means for implementing aggregation; for example, a document object references its body object via the *body* instance variable. Additional definitions are available to specify that such aggregates should be clustered together in physical storage in order to access them efficiently as a unit.

The keyword *indexable* specifies that an index can be defined based on the associated instance variable for access optimization.

**Queries and navigation:** Based on the given schema, a query for the names of all employees of the development department and the *DCEApplications* project (see section 6.2.2) could be expressed by the following extended C++ program fragment (definition of variables omitted):

```
set<Employee*> result = employees [: department->name == "Development" &&
                                      project->title == "DCEApplications" :];

foreach (Employee *e, result) cout << e->name;
```

The actual query is embedded into "*[: ... :]*"; the query statements are applied to the given set of employees. The resulting selection is assigned to the *result* set. Finally, the names of the queried employees are displayed by interation over the set, using the *foreach* operator that is offered by the database environment. The join operations of the relational approach are replaced by direct access to the values of the referenced department and project objects. It would have been possible to invoke operations on these objects within a query, too.

The query can be optimized by defining an index for the attributes involved. Indexes can be installed and removed dynamically:

```
employees.add_index (pathof (Employee*, department->name));
employees.add_index (pathof (Employee*, project->title));
```

The system installs an index for the given access paths; it is possible to specify a whole path (see figure 6-7) rather than only a single attribute for which access should be optimized. The department update operation discussed in section 6.2.2, embedded into a transaction, has the following outline (simplified):

```
transaction::begin ();
set<Employee*> result = employees [: department->DPno == 147 :];
Department *otherDepartment = departments [: DPno == 900 :];
foreach (Employee *e, result) e->department = otherDepartment;
transaction::commit ();
```

In contrast to the relational implementation, the object that represents the other department first has to be identified explicitly. This is necessary as the employee objects to be updated contain object references to departments rather than just pure numbers. The transaction mechanism is offered via static member methods of a C++ transaction class. It would also be possible to create explicit transaction objects in order to distinguish between different, possibly nested transactions.

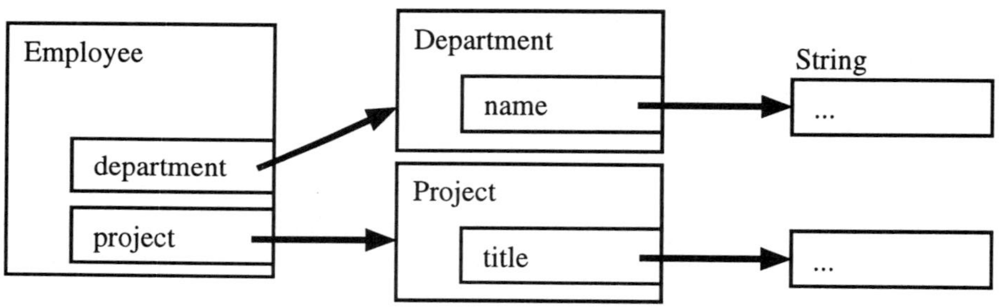


Fig. 6-7 Example of access paths

The above query was based on set-oriented access as found in relational databases. Navigational access is also supported, just by using conventional programming-level navigation between object structures.

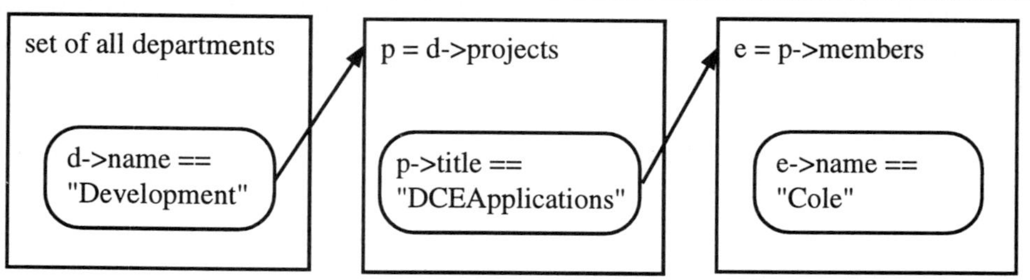


Fig. 6-8 Navigation example

Such facilities are of course not new, but it is important that they are operating on persistent database objects. Moreover, higher-level facilities like hypertext navigation can easily be built on top. As an example, here is a small program navigating from the *Development* department to the *DCEApplications* project to the project member *Cole* (see figure 6-8):

```
Department *d = departments [: name == "Development" :];
Project *p = d->projects [: title = "DCEApplications" :];
Employee *e = p->members [: name = "Cole" :];
```

The navigational approach can also be used to implement the above update operation by explicit iteration:

```
transaction::begin ();
Department *otherDepartment = departments [: DPno == 900 :];
foreach (Employee *e, employees)
  if (e->department->DPno == 147) e->department = otherDepartment;
transaction::commit ();
```

**Basic hypertext scenario:** Based on the given document class, we also outline what a basic (very simplified) hypertext extension could look like. Document objects will now consist of part objects and also have a set of arbitrary bi-directional links to other document objects. Moreover, they will have some associated hypertext operations:

```
class Document : public DataObject {
 public:
  String name;
  String header;
  DocBody *body;
  set<Document*> componentDocuments inverse_member parentDocument;
                                        // components
  Document *parentDocument inverse_member componentDocuments;
                                        // backward pointer
  set<Document*> linksTo inverse_member linksFrom; // arbitrary links
  set<Document*> linksFrom inverse_member linksTo; // backward pointers

  void print ();                        // print document
  void edit ();                         // edit document
  void browse ();                       // show the hypertext graph around the object
  Document* followLink (String);        // follow named hypertext link
  Document* returnFromLink ();          // return from link to previous document
 };
```

Based on these definitions, the following scenario from section 2.1.4 can be implemented (see figure 6-9):

```
Document *O1 = documents [: header.contains("office", "distributed") :];
O1->browse ();
Document *O2 = O1->followLink ("Object2");
Document *O3 = O2->followLink ("Object3");
O3->print ();
O2 = O3->returnFromLink ();
O1 = O2->returnFromLink ();
```

A user selects the first document with the keywords *distributed* and *office* found in the header, given a method that tests for string containment. Then the hypertext graph surrounding this document, *O1,* is displayed using the *browse* method. Thereafter, the user follows links to *O2* and then to *O3* by navigation methods. After displaying *O3*, the user returns to *O1*.

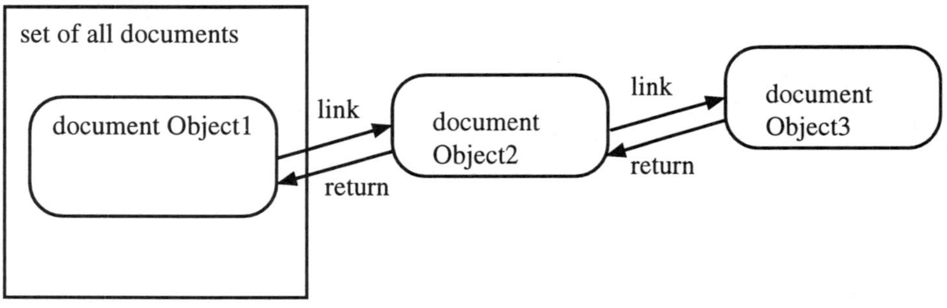


Fig. 6-9 Hypertext navigation on persistent objects

The *returnFromLink* operation must be supported by an internal stack of return addresses. This must be part of the process that accesses the objects; due to possible concurrency, the stack cannot be implemented within the objects themselves. Therefore, it is not reflected by any components or instance variables of the object. Such a stack-based history feature is found in many existing hypertext systems. Of course, the hardcoded link-following approach would have to be replaced by a flexible, interactive control mechanism in practise. Moreover, links themselves should be modeled by explicit objects in order to improve link browsing. Such mechanisms can actually be built on top of the basic methods for link following. Most important, all document objects are managed persistently without adding any significant code.

**Summary:** In summary, the example has shown some of the most important features of an OODB briefly in a simplified way. Object identity is exploited by using object identifiers as a base for inter-object references. Classification and inheritance are used for modeling the application domain in a natural way, reusing existing definitions. Aggregation is found within the document class definition, containing references to part objects. The navigation approach has been exploited to move through the object graph in order to identify a member within a specific department and project directly, and to move through a hypertext graph.

Encapsulation has not been of direct use for this relatively simple example; however, its benefits become obvious when the interface methods of each class are applied to selected objects (e.g. to print document or department information based on a single method call). Finally, seamless integration with a programming language (C++) has been achieved by adding a few set-oriented processing features.

### 6.3.4 Existing Systems

The following existing OODBs are among the most important ones from a practical point of view: Ontologic's Ontos [ONT92], Servio Corp.'s Gemstone [BOS91, PSM87], MCC's Orion (available as ITASCA) [KGB90], HP's Iris (available as OpenDB) [WLH90], Altair's O2 [DEU91], ObjectDesign's ObjectStore [LLO91], Versant Object Technology's Versant [VER92], and Objectivity's Objectivity/DB [OBJ92]. Moreover, several extensible relational database systems with object-oriented features were developed; examples of these so-called third generation databases are IBM's Starburst [LLP91] and Berkeley Postgres [SRH90]. This list is by no means exhaustive; many other interesting prototypes and systems have been developed and numerous approaches are under development today. A good survey is [JTT91]. Most of these systems are available commercially. Iris, Postgres, and Starburst are research prototypes. In the early 1980s, predecessors of today's OODBs were also built as extensions of relational databases; an example is the R2D2 system of IBM. However, the disavantage of such extensions has been their limited performance due to the extended layering of functionality.

All systems support user-defined data types with associated operations. Complex objects (aggregation), inheritance, declarative queries, and transactions are also enabled by all systems at least in a basic way. Most systems provide a client/server architecture with remote workstation clients having access to a database server. To implement this feature, proprietary protocols are used in general; as an alternative, a standard for remote database access is discussed in section 6.4.

The systems differ in their implementation details, in the programming and query languages they support, and in their architecture; most systems are native object-oriented implementations while a few are based on an existing relational database. An extended relational architecture can of course be implemented more easily; object identifiers are mapped to system-level attributes of relations and complex objects and inter-object relationships are modeled by joining relations via these attributes. The major disadvantage of this approach is efficiency; relational join operations can hardly be implemented as efficiently as direct navigation via object references. Although some encouraging results on implementing objects on top of relational systems are reported in [PBR90], for example, native OODBs will perform better in general.

Table 6-1 gives a brief overview of the existing OODBs mentioned above. Most systems offer C++ and C programming interfaces and enable a relatively seamless integration of C++ objects and persistence. Declarative queries are usually provided by language extensions or by dedicated class libraries. A corresponding C++ extension has been demonstrated by the ObjectStore example in section 6.3.3. Versant and Objectivity/DB offer similar approaches. Other systems like Ontos use SQL or an extension of SQL as a base for declarative queries. Most systems built on top of a relational database also exploit the existing SQL features. Postgres, a follow-on system to the Ingres relational database uses an extension of the QUEL query language. The Gemstone system mainly supports Smalltalk as a programming language with embedded query support; OPAL, the language offered by Gemstone, is basically a superset of Smalltalk.

Several specific features are worth noting. Ontos provides flexible locking techniques for long transactions. These features can be exploited by cooperating groups working on a joint design document, for example (see section 5.8.1). Moreover, optimistic concurrency control techniques are offered that are more efficient if concurrent access conflicts are rare.

| System | Progr. Language | Query Language | Relational extension | Notable features |
|---|---|---|---|---|
| Ontos | C++, C | Embedded SQL | no | various locking / concurrency control mechan. |
| Gemstone | Smalltalk/OPAL, C, C++ | OPAL query support | no | replication / authorization |
| Orion | Common LISP with object-oriented extensions | special query extensions | no | |
| Iris | C with embedded SQL | extended SQL | yes | on top of Allbase relational DB |
| O2 | O2 C, C++ | O2 Query | no | |
| Postgres | Postgres language | QUEL extensions | yes | rule support |
| Starburst | C and SQL | SQL extensions | yes | trigger rules |
| Object Store | C++, C | C++ extensions | no | virtual memory architecture, tool support |
| Versant | C++, C | C++ extensions | no | tool support |
| Objectivity/DB | C++, C | C++ extensions | no | tool support |

Table 6-1 Comparison of OODBs

Gemstone supports mechanisms for replicating objects at workstations that access an object database. Moreover, several strategies for moving objects between workstations and the database for access performance optimization are proposed. Dedicated authorization protocols for access control are supported. Postgres and Starburst provide various support for *rules* stored within the database. Rules specify trigger conditions and resulting actions, for example to maintain consistency constraints within a database. For example, a rule to update the department of employee "Smith" whenever the department of employee "Cole" changes, looks as follows in Postgres (using the syntax described in [STK91]):

**on new** Employee.department **where**
Employee.name = "Cole"
**then do replace**
E (department = new.department)
**from** E **in** Employee
**where** E.name = "Smith"

ObjectStore provides transparent access to persistent objects via a special virtual memory architecture. Basically, a page fault occurs when an accessed object is not in virtual memory but on disk. The object is transparently fetched by the extended virtual memory implementation. This approach is quite efficient and completely transparent at the application level. Other systems implement transparent object access via intermediate software-level pointer indirections. The commercial systems, especially ObjectStore, Versant, and Objectivity/DB, offer a rich set of tools to the application developer. Examples are a graphical schema designer, a class browser, or interactive high-level query support. Tool support currently tends to be enhanced rapidly from version to version; in practise, it seems very important to evaluate in detail the tools offered when deciding which OODB to use.

In the area of standards, efforts are under way to extend SQL with object-oriented concepts, for example to query for aggregated objects, and to consider class inheritance hirarchies. This extension is called SQL3. In the area of object-oriented databases themselves, the standardization proposal ODMG-93 (Object Database Management Group) [ODM94] has been launched, but is still at a rather early stage.

## 6.4 Remote Database Access

Remote Database Access (RDA) is a standardized service and protocol of the ISO/OSI application layer [ISO90] (see also section 4.5.3). It is based on the client/server model; a database acts as a server and is accessed by one or several remote clients.

### 6.4.1 Architectural Model

Figure 6-10 summarizes the underlying architectural model of RDA. A client application program and a server process (with local access to a database) interact via the RDA application programming interface (API). The actual RDA service is offered via the RDA service interface by an RDA service provider instance at each node. The service providers interact remotely based on the RDA protocol, using the underlying services of the ISO/OSI layers 1-7, for example ROSE, ACSE, and ASN.1 (see section 4.5.3).

In practise, the client passes a generic database query to the server via RDA who receives it and maps it to its local database environment for execution. Finally, results are passed back to the client using a generic format again. Specifics of the given database are hidden by the server and do not therefore propagate via the network to clients.

The RDA standard is divided into two parts. Part 1 specifies the generic, data-model-independent RDA service and protocol. Part 2 is concerned with specializations according to various concrete data models; so far, only a specialization for the relational model using SQL has been defined. Remote access support to object-oriented databases is not yet provided by RDA. However, the separation into generic and specific parts allows for extensions of RDA by adding other specific parts while the generic protocol can be maintained.

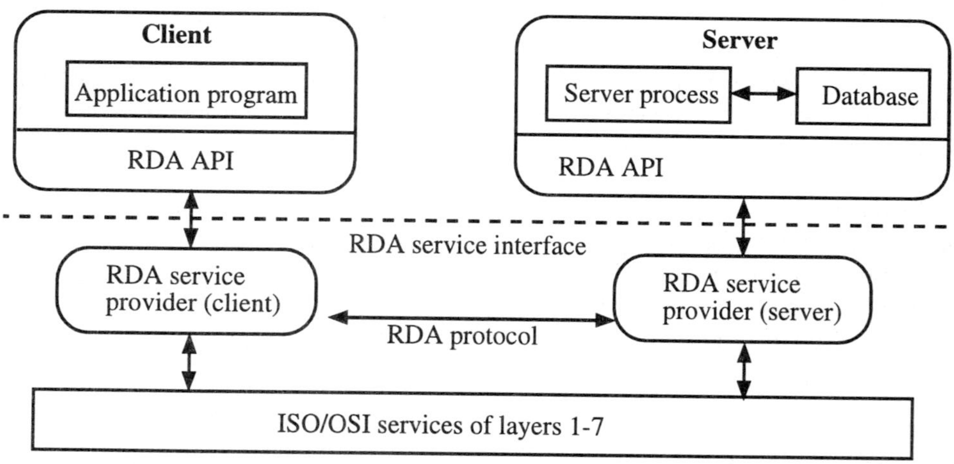


Fig. 6-10 Architectural model of RDA

RDA implementations are offered by various companies, including DEC, HP, NCR, Tandem, and Teradata; see [ACG91] for a discussion.

## 6.4.2 RDA Services

An RDA interaction between a client and a database server is based on several dedicated services offered to the client. These are summarized in table 6-2 and are discussed below. They are not directly visible at the API but are provided internally at the RDA service interface. The API offers a higher-level interface, usually embedded into SQL (see section 6.4.3).

**Dialog and resource management:** First, a logical RDA relationship (*dialog*) must be established. The client invokes the *R-Initialize* service, giving the name/address of the server and a set of specific parameters (e.g. database language, kind of transaction management). After the relationship has been established, it is acknowledged internally and the client gets some associated context information. The client/server relationship is maintained until it is explicitly terminated by *R-Terminate* by either site.

Moreover, before starting the actual database access, the client must request that the required resources be allocated or opened, using *R-Open*. Resources within this context are the database itself as well as organizational partitions thereof. A resource is released or closed by *R-Close*.

| Service | Semantics |
|---|---|
| R-Initialize | Dialogue establishment with parameter negotiation |
| R-Terminate | Termination of a dialog |
| R-Open | Open a resource at the server site for the client |
| R-Close | Close a resource at the server site |
| R-ExecuteDBL | Execute a given DBL statement with parameters |
| R-DefineDBL | Pre-define a DBL statement at the server for later execution |
| R-InvokeDBL | Invoke a pre-defined DBL statement |
| R-DropDBL | Remove a pre-defined DBL statement |
| R-BeginTransaction | Start a new transaction |
| R-Commit | Commit a transaction |
| R-Rollback | Abort a transaction |
| R-Status | Enquire the status of the server executing DBL statements |
| R-Cancel | Cancel an ongoing DBL execution at the server |

Table 6-2 RDA services offered to the client

**Database access:** Actual access to a remote database can then be performed by *R-ExecuteDBL*. This service has the database operations to be executed as a parameter. The database language (DBL) must have been negotiated during dialogue establishment; in current implementations, it is trivially SQL. As mentioned above, the remote interaction is of RPC style with a final response and result delivery from the server to the client (see also section 3.2). Input parameters and results are transmitted in a generic format, using ASN.1 as a definition base.

Obviously, *R-ExecuteDBL* leads to transmission and interpretation of the database query statements. As a more efficient and reusable alternative, the client can also install query code for later execution at the server's site. This is achieved by calling *R-DefineDBL*, giving the respective code as a parameter. Such code can later be invoked by *R-InvokeDBL* and can be removed from the server by *R-DropDBL*.

**Transaction management:** RDA in its basic form also supports local transactions at the server, with the usual ACID transaction characteristics (see section 4.1). A transaction is started from the client site by *R-BeginTransaction* and is committed by *R-Commit* or aborted by *R-Rollback*. Using these features, transactional one-to-one interactions between a client and a server can be implemented. However, a client cannot interact with multiple databases within the same transaction.

Extensions of the RDA standard address this issue by incorporating the CCR and TP services of ISO/OSI (see section 4.5.3). These services offer the framework for the required two-phase-commit protocol and for complete distributed transaction execution, respectively.

**Status enquiry:** As a control mechanism, the client can enquire the status of an RDA execution at the server site, using the service *R-Status*. If a database operation takes too long or if its results are not required any more, the operation can be aborted by the client by *R-Cancel*.

### 6.4.3 Example

As an example, we model remote database access within the office procedure application of figure 6-3 (introduction of a new product, e.g. a refrigerator). In particular, the global management accesses several databases of the development, finance, marketing, and production departments remotely in order to retrieve product-related data (see figure 6-11).

The following program fragment sets up a context with DB1, retrieves design data, closes this context, opens a new one with DB4, selects the corresponding project plan, and closes this context again. Both database access operations are embedded into transactions that are started implicitly and are committed explicitly. Finally, an application-specific evaluation routine is invoked.

The RDA functionality is accessed via an extended SQL interface. The RDA services that are invoked internally are shown on the right-hand side of the following program fragment (with simplified parameters):

| **Client invocations (extended SQL)** | **Corresponding RDA services** |
|---|---|
| **connect to** agent1DB **as** mgrDB1 **user** paul; | R-Initialize (agent1DB, paul)<br>R-Open (agent1DB) |
| **select** * **into** RefrigeratorDesign **from** DesignData<br>**where** product = CoolRefrigerator; | R-BeginTransaction<br>R-ExecuteDBL (select ...) |
| commit work;<br>disconnect mgrDB1; | R-Commit (transaction ...)<br>R-Close (agent1DB)<br>R-Terminate (agent1DB) |
| **connect to** agent3DB **as** mgrDB3 **user** paul; | R-Initialize (agent3DB, paul)<br>R-Open (agent3DB) |
| **select** ***into** RefrigeratorProduction **from** ProductionPlan<br>**where** product = CoolRefrigerator; | R-BeginTransaction<br>R-ExecuteDBL (select ...) |
| **commit work**;<br>**disconnect** mgrDB3; | R-Commit (transaction ...)<br>R-Close (agent3DB)<br>R-Terminate (agent3DB) |
| evaluate (RefrigeratorDesign, RefrigeratorProduction); | |

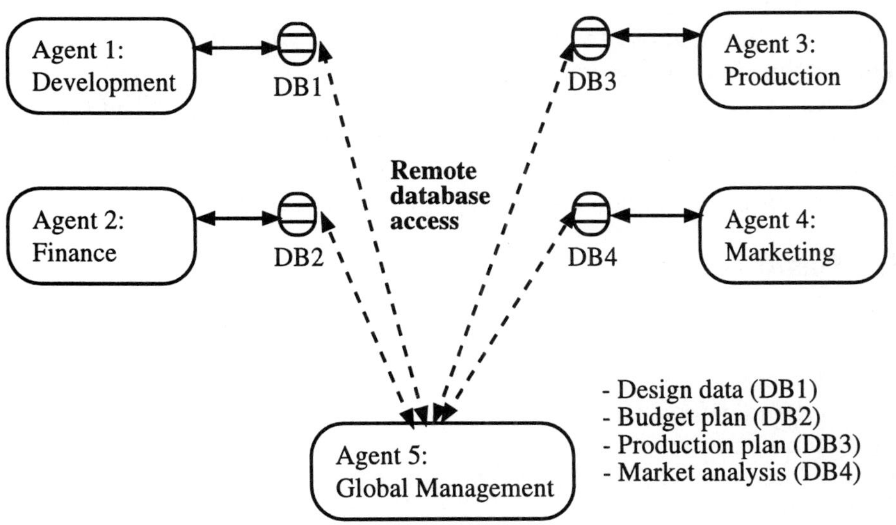


Fig. 6-11 RDA within an office procedure

The example has shown that remote SQL database access is quite straightforward using RDA. However, major limitations of RDA are also obvious. It is not possible to operate on several databases within a single transaction (without using SQL extensions). Inter-data references across databases cannot be supported.

At the user level, no database-spanning schema is available; it is the task of the user to integrate data retrieved from both databases within the *evaluate* operation, for example. Moreover, access to heterogeneous databases with different data models is not yet supported by RDA.

## 6.5 Federated Database Systems

Federated database systems [RAM91, ELP90] provide extended solutions for coupling and accessing a set of databases. They aim at providing support for the following, partially conflicting goals:

- *Integration:* Several heterogeneous databases are integrated at the user/application programming level. In particular, location-independent database access is enabled, heterogeneity of databases is hidden, and various schemata are (at least partially) integrated.
- *Autonomy:* On the other hand, each singular database remains autonomous concerning access control, schema modification, and general database administration. In particular, existing local applications can be maintained without modification, local schemata can coexist with partially integrated, database-spanning schemata, and heterogeneity of databases is the rule, rather than the exception.

RDA does not address the first goal sufficiently while distributed databases do not support database autonomy. Therefore, federated database systems can be classified as a trade-off between a simple remote access facility and a fully integrated distributed database system. Of course, the functionality and advantages of federated database systems require an additional software layer with high system-level implementation complexity.

### 6.5.1 Basic Terms and Concepts

The following terms are used in this area: A *federated database management system (FDBMS)* comprises the overall distributed management techniques and tools required for integrating several databases. The resulting environment is called a *federated database system (FDBS)*, or, more concisely, a *federated database.* In the literature, *multidatabase* is often used as a synonym for federated database. These terms are illustrated by figure 6-12.

The figure shows that the component database systems can have different data models (e.g. relational, network, or object-oriented) that are integrated by the FDBMS. This issue is of particular importance in cooperative office systems; typical database configurations in today's companies consist of heterogeneous systems that are not integrated or are at most connected by *ad hoc* mechanisms. Federated databases support a tighter integration, enabling distributed cooperative applications as discussed in section 6.1.4 (e.g. management access to office procedure results at various agent databases).

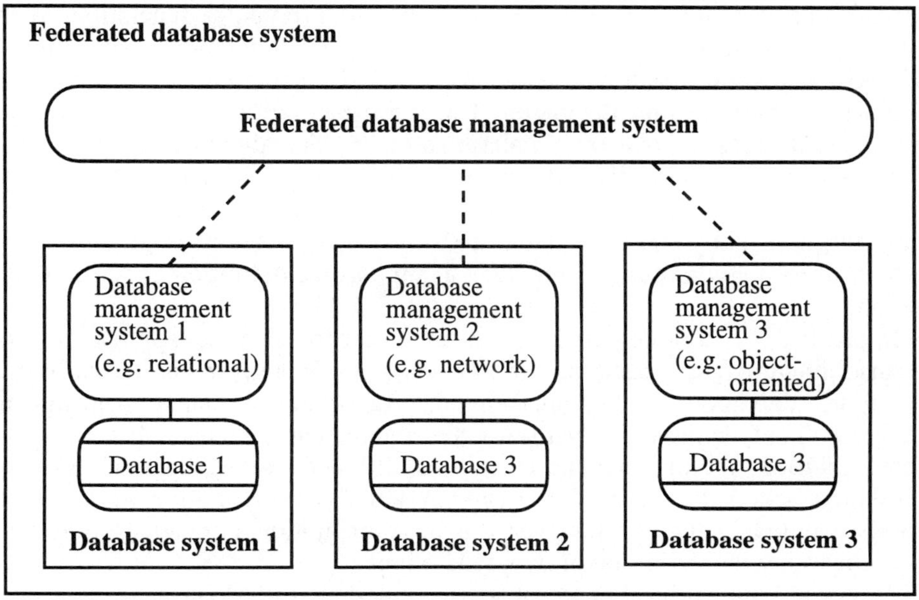


Fig. 6-12 Federated database management system architecture

**Aspects of database autonomy:** Autonomy of databases within a federation can be divided into several areas. *Design autonomy* means that each database schema can be developed without regard to other schemata. Therefore, schema design is independent of data models, query languages, and naming and semantics of data found in other databases. Of course, this may lead to inconsistent naming of similar data items and to related problems. Such aspects, however, are handled by the FDBMS.

*Federation autonomy* means that each database can decide autonomously with whom to cooperate, i.e. in which federations to participate. For example, a database can restrict the set of its peer databases and can reject communication requests issued from other databases. *Execution autonomy* gives each database the right to control execution of transactions in a completely autonomous way. In particular, a database can determine the sequence of its transaction executions, and it can reject specific transaction requests.

These areas of autonomy guarantee database independence whenever necessary. Of course, specific problems may result, for example, conventional transaction semantics may be in conflict with autonomy, and it is difficult to make any guarantees concerning accessibility of remote databases. Such problems are addressed by practical conventions and by advanced technical solutions like extended transaction paradigms.

**Levels of integration:** Database integration within an FDBS can be *tight* or *loose*. Within a *tightly integrated FDBS*, the configuration of federations is the task of a database administrator. He or she specifies federations and defines a *federated schema* for each federation. A federated schema integrates component schemata of participating databases. The tight integration approach resembles distributed databases; however, database autonomy is maintained. Each database keeps its own schema locally and remains autonomous as discussed above.

A *loosely integrated FDBS* is based on a partial *ad hoc* integration of schemata; this is usually the task of the end user or application programmer. The system offers a *multidatabase language* to support the definition of schema integration.

In practise, tightly integrated FDBSs are easier to use at the application level because integrated schemata are already available. Moreover, they usually support update operations on the underlying databases; updates can be mapped from the pre-defined integrated schema to the component schemata. Loosely integrated FDBSs require advanced user skills and knowledge of different distributed schemata. Moreover, many systems only support read access to loosely coupled databases. However, the loose integration approach is more flexible concerning the definition of new federations.

A typical application domain of loosely integrated FDBSs would be a large software development company: software engineers with the required expert knowledge can configure their personal federations in a flexible way. In contrast, a government finance office or the upper-level management of a company would more likely benefit from a tightly integrated FDBS with pre-defined federated schemata.

### 6.5.2 System Architecture and Database Integration

Most existing FDBMSs conform more or less to a generic layered system architecture as shown in figure 6-13 (see also [SHL90]). This consists of several lower levels where local database schemata are exported, and of upper levels where exported schemata are combined to federations.

**Schema export:** At the lowest layer, the local database systems with their local schemata are found. These schemata are mapped to *component schemata* of a common FDBS data model for each database. The mapping is performed by a command transformation mechanism. As an example, consider a relational, SQL-based common data model which is mapped onto another relational schema, onto an object-oriented schema, and onto a network schema (see figure 6-12). This mapping is the basic way to hide database heterogeneity from users of an FDBS. [SHL90] recommends the usage of a *semantic data model* (see section 5.1.2) at the component schema level in order to enable a complete representation of various kinds of underlying data models by the common data model.

Each database can now export selected subsets of its component schema for use by the FDBS. This results in one or more *export schemata* per database. An access control component makes sure that only information offered via the export schema can actually be accessed remotely. As databases are autonomous, they are free to determine the actual portion of data to be exported. In figure 6-13, database 2 exports two schemata (2a and 2b), while the other databases export only one schema.

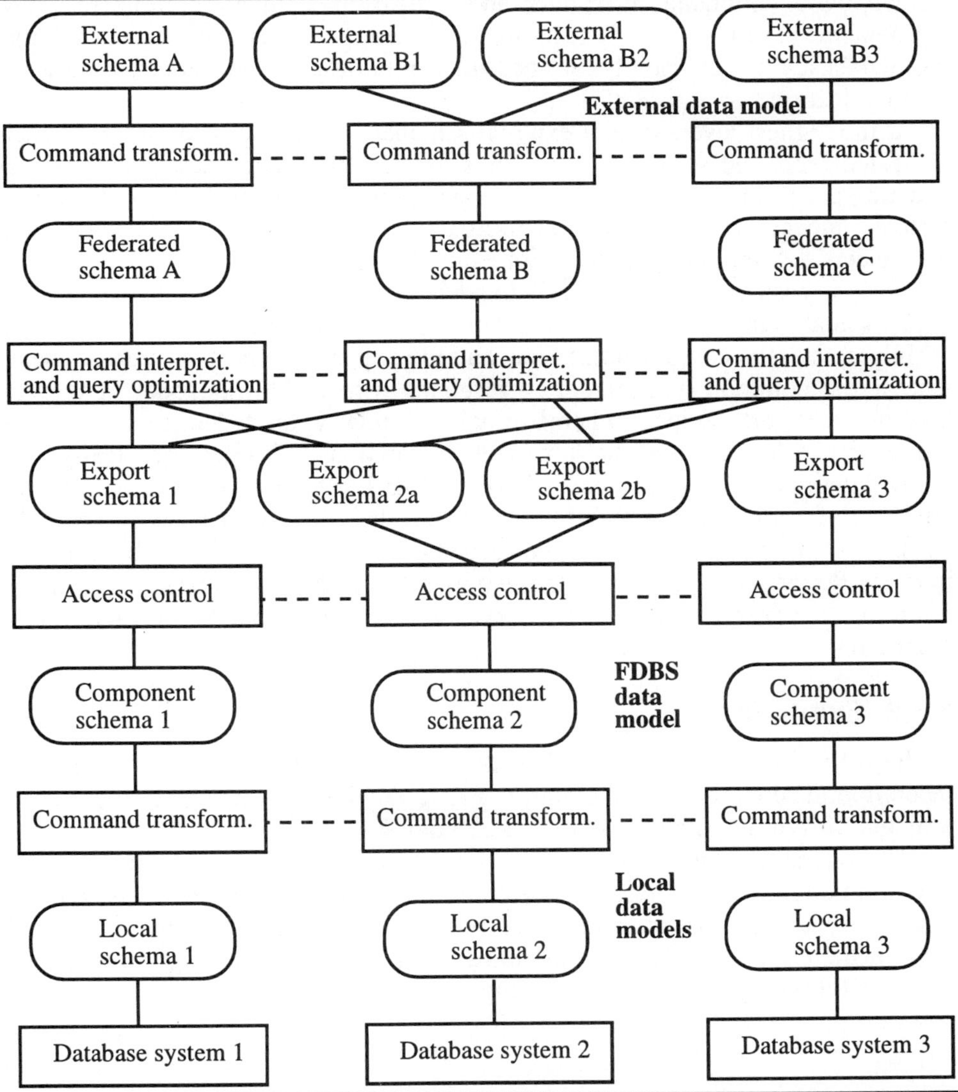


Fig. 6-13 Generic system architecture of FDBMSs

**Federated schema configuration:** Above the level of export schemata, schema configuration is driven by applications rather than by singular databases. For example, the federated schema A as a partial distributed schema integration is defined by combining the export schemata 1 and 2a. Federated schema C combines the export schemata 2a, 2b, and 3. As discussed above, the definition of federated schemata is a task of the administrator in tightly coupled systems, and of the user in loosely coupled environments.

At runtime, the mapping from federated schemata to export schemata is performed by a command interpreter and a distributed query optimizer. These mechanisms have the task of executing combined queries on the various underlying databases as efficiently as possible, minimizing the required network communication.

At the highest level, several external schemata can be defined on top of each dedicated federated schema. This allows for adapting or restricting the schema structure according to dedicated user requirements. Moreover, it allows for transforming the common data model used at the federated schema level into a user-specific *external data model*. For example, a user of an object-oriented database might wish to transform a relational federated schema into his or her local object-oriented representation. This requires a command transformation again.

In practise, the component schema and the export schema can often be identical. If the common data model corresponds with the local model, it is even possible to export the local schema directly. Similarly, the federated schema and the external schema can be the same with applications of limited complexity.

To integrate existing databases into an FDBS, a bottom-up approach can be applied. First, the schema transformation into the common data model must be defined, resulting in the component schema. Then the portion to be exported must be determined, leading to the export schema. Now the database administrator or the user can access the export schema in order to configure new federations.

### 6.5.3 Example

In the following example, several local schemata shall be integrated to form a federation. The example (see figure 6-14) resembles the office procedure environment of figure 6-3, also discussed in section 6.4.

The federated schema shall be used by the management for decision-making. For simplicity, only one federation is configured, the external schema is identical with the federated schema, and only three component databases are considered. Two of them are relational and the third one is object-oriented. We assume we have the following local schemata (simplified):

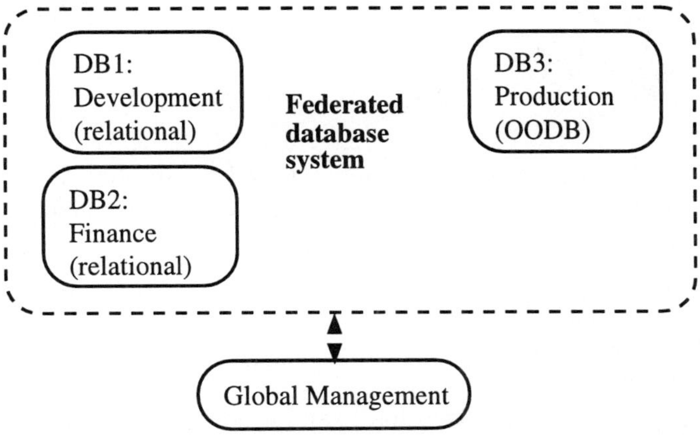


Fig. 6-14 Federated database: Integration example

**DB1 (Development):**

Employee (E#, name, address, DP#)
Document (DO#, header, body, DP#)
DesignData (PR#, product, design)

**DB2 (Finance):**

Budget (productNumber, year, totalBudget)
DevelopmentCosts (productNumber, costs, costCenter)
MarketingCosts (productNumber, costs, period)

**DB3 (Production):**

```
class ProductionPlan : Schedule {
 public:
  Product *product;
  set<Action*> requiredActions;
  void createProductionSchedule ();
  void printProductionSchedule ();
 };

class Product {
 public:
  int productNo;
  String description;
  void printAll ();
 };
```

```
class Action {
 public:
  int actionNo;
  String description;
  String responsibleEmployee;
  void notifyAboutAction ();
 };
```

The component schemata shall be relational; therefore, the first two schemata are maintained. The third schema has to be transformed into a relational representation, for example leading to the following result:

ProductionPlan (PR#, A#)
Product (PR#, description)
Action (A#, description, E#)
Employee (E#, name)

An auxiliary relation for employees has been introduced in order to manage them separately based on their numbers. Now the export schemata are determined by the database administrators:

**DB1 (Development):**

DesignData (PR#, product, design)

**DB2 (Finance):**

DevelopmentCosts (productNumber, costs)
MarketingCosts (productNumber, costs, period)

**DB 3 (Production):**

ProductionPlan (PR#, A#)
Action (A#, description)
Product (PR#, description)

Obviously, only a subset of the relations, and only a subset of the attributes within a relation are exported. For example, the employees and the documents of the development department are not made visible externally. Similarly, the budget or the cost centers are not shown externally by the finance department.

Now we assume we have a loosely-coupled system with a multidatabase language to specify the federated schema. The major task is to combine the given relations appropriately and to resolve potential semantic and naming conflicts among attributes. Using the relational model, we can use an extended SQL *view* mechanism as our multidatabase language, corresponding to the language *MSQL* [LMR90]. A view basically consists of a new relation that is mapped to the original relations by SQL selection clauses. When creating a view, it is possible to rename or ignore attributes, to join several relations, and to apply other SQL operations. Here is our federated schema as a view on the existing export schemata:

```
create view ProductInformation (PR#, name, description, design, developCosts) as
select DB1.DesignData.PR#, DB1.DesignData.product, DB3.Product.description,
       DB1.DesignData.design, DB2.DevelopmentCosts.costs
from   DB1.DesignData, DB2.DevelopmentCosts, DB3.Product
where  DB1.DesignData.PR# = DB2.DevelopmentCosts.productNumber
and    DB1.DesignData.PR# = DB3.Product.PR#;

create view ProductionInformation (PR#, name, action)
select DB1.DesignData.PR#, DB1.DesignData.product, DB3.Action.description
from   DB1.DesignData, DB3.ProductPlan, DB3.Action
where  DB1.DesignData.PR# = DB3.ProductionPlan.PR#
and    DB3.ProductionPlan.A# = DB3.Action.A#;
```

The two views describe products and their production steps. They are generated by join operations over distributed relations. For each relation, the database hosting it must be specified explicitly. However, within subsequent queries against the federated schema, no location information has to be given. For example, a manager might request all information related to the refrigerator product:

```
select * from ProductInformation
where ProductInformation.name = CoolRefrigerator

select * from ProductionInformation
where ProductionInformation.name = CoolRefrigerator
```

The example shows that data integration of heterogeneous databases can be achieved at the federated schema level. Moreover, queries against the federated schema are location-transparent and are almost identical with conventional local queries. However, with the view-based MSQL mechanism described, no update operations would be possible at the federated schema level. It is also important to note that the definition of the federated schema can become rather complex. The simple example presented above has already shown that detailed database configuration information and knowledge of the semantics of various attributes are required.

Of course, a rather sophisticated system implementation is required at the FDBMS level. While things still look simple at the application level, complex attribute mappings, query optimizations, and authorization checks are required below. Numerous technical problems arise from this (see section 6.5.5). Moreover, basic distributed communication support must be provided as discussed in chapter 3.

### 6.5.4 Case Study and System Comparison

**Example system:** As a concrete FDBS example, we discuss the *Amoco Distributed Database System (ADDS)* [BOT86, TTC90]. Although the system name might suggest a distributed database architecture (see section 6.6), it is actually a tightly integrated federated database system.

Local databases within ADDS can be heterogeneous; relational, network, and hierarchical databases are currently supported under the MVS, VM, and Unix operating systems. In particular, SQL/DS, DB2, Ingres, RIM, FOCUS, and IMS databases can be integrated. Remote communication is based on a *network interface facility (NIFTY),* applying OSI and SNA communication protocols.

The common data model for component schemata and for federated schemata is an extended relational model, using SQL and other relational query extensions. No distinction is made between export schemata and component schemata. At the application level, an interactive, menu-based interface and an application programming interface are offered for location-independent queries. Both read and update operations are supported at the federated schema level, at least within a prototype version of the system.

Local databases remain autonomous. Interactions from remote databases are mapped to a local database only via the conventional local query interface. No manipulation of the underlying database implementations is necessary.

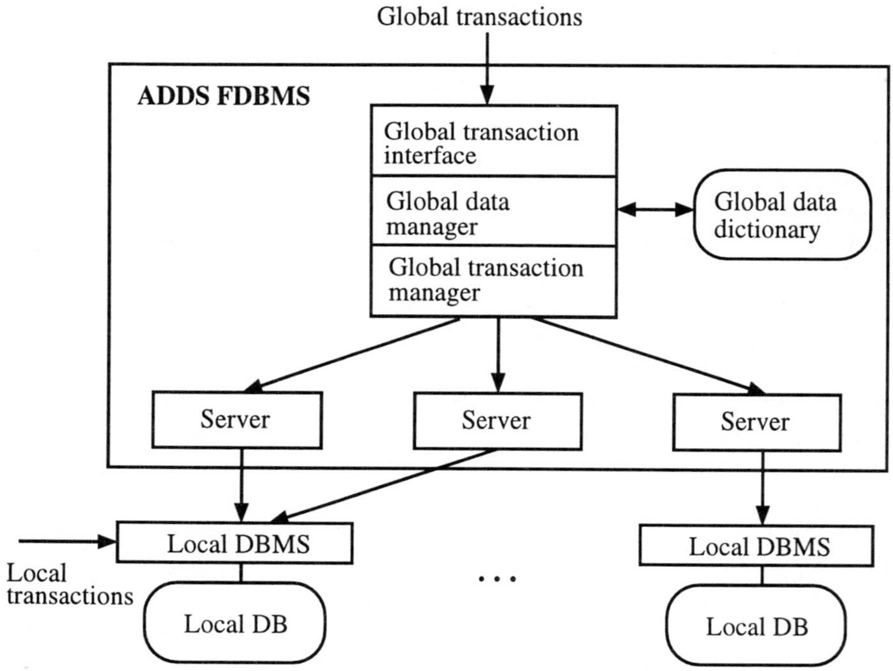


Fig. 6-15 System architecture of the ADDS FDBMS

The internal system architecture of ADDS is shown in figure 6-15. Global transactions can consist of several read or update operations against multiple databases. They are passed to the *global transaction interface*; this checks queries for syntactical correctness and generates a global execution plan for the transaction. This plan optimizes query processing by compiling queries into an internal format and by computing a distributed query strategy that minimizes remote communication. The *global data manager* determines the locations of data involved and stores intermediate data that have been generated during query execution. It has access to a *global data dictionary*; this comprises the definitions of all relations of each federated schema. This information is used for planning and controlling distributed transaction execution.

The *global transaction manager* allocates server processes to perform global subtransactions. That is, a global transaction is split into components that can again work on several databases. Each server process interfaces locally or remotely with local DBMSs. All local data items required by a server process remain locked until transaction completion (strict two-phase locking). Transformation of queries at the component schema level into local queries is performed by the server processes. Global transaction semantics is achieved by a two-phase commit protocol (see section 4.1) run by the server processes. Therefore, true transaction semantics is provided. In contrast, more loosely-coupled FDBSs do not necessarily provide traditional transaction semantics. Due to a large degree of autonomy of component databases, a strict two-phase commit behavior cannot be enforced. Therefore, relaxed consistency guarantees have to be tolerated; in addition to improved autonomy, another advantage is also the potential for extended runtime optimization.

In summary, the ADDS prototype provides a practical integration of heterogenous distributed databases across a network. It applies sophisticated query optimization and transaction processing techniques to achieve the described functionality. Moreover, it enables real autonomy of local databases by separating the FDBMS layer completely from the local DBMS, leaving the local implementation unaffected.

**Comparison of other systems:** Several other prototypes and some products are available in the federated database area. Table 6-3 gives a comparison and names references for more information on each system (see also [TTC90] and [SHL90] as well as current product documentation). Most systems are based on the relational data model with SQL as their query language. As a consequence, most local DBMSs supported within a federation are relational. Both loose and tight integration approaches are found in practise.

Concerning transactions, only a limited set of systems support distributed update operations on multiple databases. Some systems limit remote updates to a single database, and some others only enable remote read operations. The major reason for such limitations is that distributed update operations require two-phase commit protocols that are not possible with all underlying databases without significant extensions. Moreover, relational views are often used for definition of the federated schemata, and update operations on views are known to be very limited.

The DATAPLEX and IMDAS systems are dedicated to the manufacturing application area; they mainly manage production data in a distributed heterogenous environment. IMDAS uses a semantic data model similar to object-oriented models. This allows for integration of object-oriented databases like GBASE, too. Sybase uses an RPC client/server approach to access multiple databases within a federation. It is possible to write system-specific servers in order to integrate new types of databases into the environment.

| System | Integ-ration | Common data model | Query language | Local DBMS | Transact. support |
|---|---|---|---|---|---|
| ADDS [BOT86] | tight | extended relational | SQL | IMS, RIM, SQL/DS, Ingres, DB2, FOCUS | read and update |
| DATAPLEX [CHU90] | tight | relational | SQL | IMS, Ingres, DB2 | read, single DB update |
| IMDAS [KSL87] | tight | semantic | SQL-like | RTI/Ingres, BCS/RIM, GBASE, AMRF | read and update |
| Mermaid [TBC87] | tight | relational | SQL | Ingres, Oracle, IDM | read, single DB update |
| Ingres/Star [TTC90] | tight | relational | SQL | RMS, RDB, DB2, IMS, SQL/DS | read, single DB update |
| Sybase [TTC90] | loose | relational | SQL | Sybase, other systems via API | read and update |
| Calida [LIZ88] | loose | relational | universal DELPHI | most kinds of systems | read and update |
| DQS/ Multistar [BEL88] | loose | relational | SQL-like | IMS/VS, IDMS, ADABAS, RODAN, VSAM-files | read |
| ADMS+- [LIZ88] | loose | relational | special lang. | Ingres, Oracle, Sybase | read and update |

Table 6-3 Comparison of FDBS

This brief overview should illustrate that there are several real federated database systems available and that this approach is practical. It also makes clear that federated database systems still focus on the more traditional data models and, as yet, have scarcely begun to incorporate emerging object-oriented approaches. This will definitely be an important issue for future developments; especially in the office area, applications can benefit from distributed heterogeneous object databases.

### 6.5.5 Special Technical Problems and Open Issues

When integrating arbitrary heterogeneous databases into a federation, numerous difficult problems have to be solved. These issues might have looked simple in the limited example given above; however, in large applications, the integration is actually a hard problem. Some of the reasons are:

- *Semantic heterogeneity:* Due to design autonomy, some databases are semantically heterogeneous. Examples are identical data elements with different names, elements with the same name but different semantic meaning, different types for the same semantic aspects, and different attributes for the same characteristics of a data element. Schema transformation techniques have to be applied and have to be further developed to resolve these problems [LMR90].
- *Command transformation:* While it is possible to transform SQL into a procedural, navigational execution sequence efficiently, it is not clear how new object-oriented query languages or conventional navigational approaches could be mapped to SQL in general. Therefore, general command transformation between arbitrary kinds of systems is not possible. Further research in this area is required.
- *Query optimization:* As mentioned above, distributed query optimization to implement queries efficiently is important in FDBS. The main goal is to reduce the number of communication messages required. This problem is similar to query optimization in distributed databases. However, due to autonomy, local query optimization can vary within different databases and global knowledge about current system characteristics is not readily available. Most existing systems perform an *ad hoc* partitioning of a global transaction into several local transactions at a coordinator site; this site reassembles results, too. More sophisticated approaches might help to improve query efficiency.
- *Distributed transaction management:* Most existing systems implement distributed transactions using a two-phase commit protocol (see section 4.1). However, this limits autonomy of component databases. It is not possible for a local database to abort autonomously any more after its has responded positively to a prepare-to-commit request. As a more specialized issue, it is not possible to abort local transactions remotely for deadlock resolution. This would violate autonomy even more severely. New transaction models are required to address such problems (see [GRR93] for an extensive discussion).
- *Operating systems heterogeneity:* In addition to databases, the underlying operating systems and communication protocols are also heterogeneous, in general. Therefore, all the approaches and standards required in general distributed heterogeneous systems (see chapter 3) are also necessary here.

In summary, it is obvious that a federated database environment is very complex to build and to manage. However, such an environment can provide many benefits in large cooperative office systems. Most important, global data integration can be achieved without very significant application-level programming effort.

## 6.6 Distributed Database Systems

A *distributed database system (DDBS)* [BEG92, CEP84, ÖZV91] can be classified as a tightly integrated, homogeneous version of federated database approaches. However, existing systems in this area were available long before the development of FDBS.

### 6.6.1 Overview and Comparison

Major characteristics of distributed databases are:

- *Distribution transparency:* Distribution of component databases is hidden at the application level. Queries against a DDBS are identical to local queries. There is usually no support for independent local queries; local database access is just a special case of a global DDBS query.
- *Global schema:* In contrast to FDBSs, there is a single global schema. It is visible to all component databases.
- *System management:* DDBSs are managed in a partially centralized way. For example, schema modifications have to be coordinated globally. However, local database administrators have some autonomy concerning physical storage configuration, for example.

Table 6-4 compares FDBSs and DDBSs based on these criteria. FDBSs have the advantage of a high degree of database autonomy, and of good extendibility. Depending on the kind of query presented, they can also work more efficiently as they do not have to keep all data items globally consistent; many data items are only relevant within a limited federated schema. Moreover, FDBSs integrate heterogeneous databases and not only homogeneous systems. For many CSCW applications, FDBSs seem to be a better solution than DDBSs: They enable an explicit view of distributed participants and documents, especially if cooperation among various distributed organizations is required.

| | **Autonomy of databases** | **Distribution transparency** | **Global schem a** | **Local / global queries** | **Integration of new databases** |
|---|---|---|---|---|---|
| **FDBS** | high | limited | no | separate | relatively easy |
| **DDBS** | low | full | yes | uniform | significant effort |

Table 6-4 Comparison of FDBS and DDBS

DDBSs provide a higher degree of distribution transparency at the end-user level. The uniform treatment of all queries might be an attractive solution for non-expert users. Fault tolerance and access efficiency can be improved by replicating data at various locations. Replica consistency is maintained by the system. Data distribution can be specified at a grain finer than a whole relation; records can be distributed according to a selection criterion (horizontal fragmentation), and relations can be split into component relations at different locations (vertical fragmentation).

Finally, global query optimization involving many databases can be implemented in a more sophisticated way; this is enabled by systems homogeneity and by the availability of global data about the characteristics of the databases involved (e.g. concerning the actual data distribution). From the CSCW point of view, a distributed database can serve as a global data repository independent of the CSCW application itself. Cooperation should be implemented by other mechanisms presented in the context of distributed systems. For explicit modeling of data-oriented cooperation, FDBSs seem to be more appropriate.

Examples of distributed databases are SDD-1, R*, Distributed Ingres, and DB2 with distributed extensions [LHM84, DAT90, BEG92]. Most existing DDBSs are based on the relational data model.

Major issues in distributed database systems are data distribution (how to distribute data among databases adequately), distributed query optimization, and distributed transaction management. In the following subsection, we give an example of data distribution. The other topics are discussed briefly later.

### 6.6.2 Data Distribution: Example

As an example of distributing data across databases in a DDBS, we investigate how the schema of our example application can be partitioned. In contrast to the federated approach, we start from the global schema that might look as follows (simplified):

Employee (E#, name, address, DP#)
Document (DO#, header, body, DP#)
Product (PR#, description)

DesignData (PR#, product, design)

Budget (PR#, year, totalBudget)
DevelopmentCosts (PR#, costs, costCenter)
MarketingCosts (PR#, costs, period)

ProductionPlan (PR#, A#)
Action (A#, description, E#)

We decide that the global management database (DB5) should store the first three relations. In addition, a vertical partition of the employee relation with number and name shall be replicated at each database. This can be specified as follows (using a pseudo-notation based on SQL):

**allocate** Employee, Document, Product **to** DB5;
**define partition as select** E#, name **into** EmployeePartition **from** Employee;
**replicate** EmployeePartition **at** *;

The design data relation shall be stored by the development department database (DB1) and the next three relations shall be allocated to the finance department (DB2). However, the product budgets of previous years shall be stored within the global management database (DB5); only the current budget is stored within the finance department. This can be achieved by a horizontal partition. The corresponding definitions are as follows:

**allocate** DesignData **to** DB1;

**define partition as**
**select** * **into** CurrentBudget **from** Budget
**where** year = currentYear;

**allocate** CurrentBudget, DevelopmentCosts, MarketingCosts **to** DB2;

**define partition as**
**select** * **into** PastBudget **from** Budget
**where** year < currentYear;

**allocate** PastBudget **to** DB5;

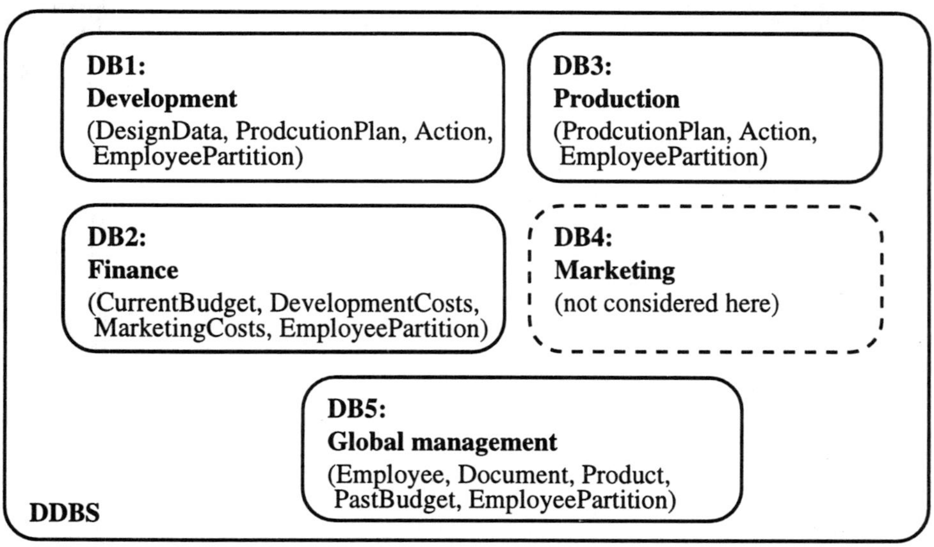


Fig. 6-16 Data distribution example in DDBS

Finally, the production plans and associated actions are stored by the production department (DB3). In addition, a replica of both relations is allocated to the development department (DB1):

**allocate** ProductionPlan, Action **to** DB3;
**replicate** ProductionPlan, Action **at** DB1;

The resulting data distribution is shown in figure 6-16. It is now possible to issue queries against the global schema. For the user or application program, it is then absolutely transparent how data have been distributed. The mapping from the global query to physical data access is performed entirely by the system. For example, consider the following query, issued at DB1:

**select** * **from** Budget, Product
**where** Product.PR# = Budget.PR#
**and** description = Refrigerator;

As a possible scenario, this query might involve the interactions of figure 6-17:

1. The product numbers of all refrigerators are fetched from DB5 to DB1 by applying the given selection to the product relation stored at DB5.
2. The join operation for the current budget partition of the budget relation is performed at DB2; the results are sent to DB1.
3. The join operation for the remaining previous budgets is performed at DB5; the results are again sent to DB1.
4. The results are assembled and output at DB1.

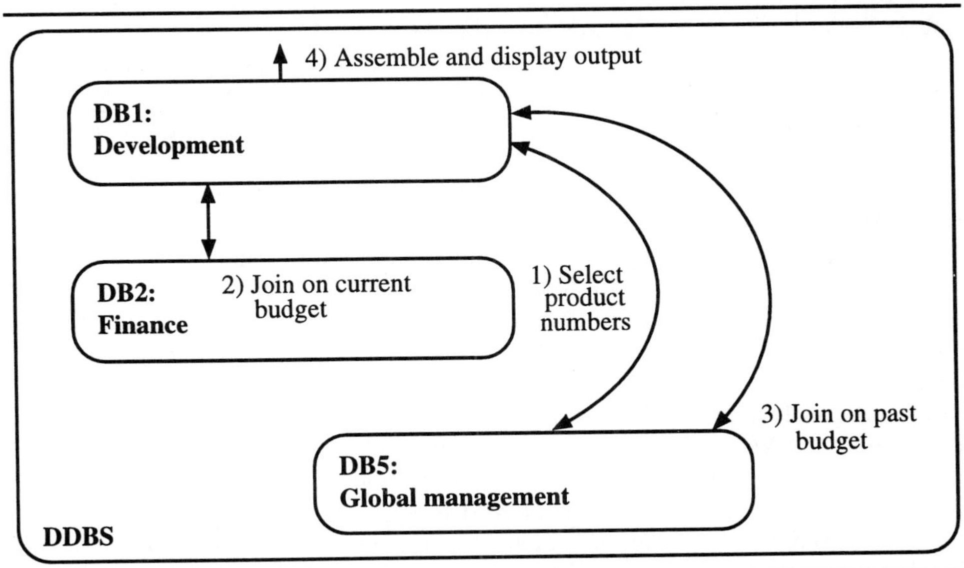


Fig. 6-17 Internal interactions during query processing

Obviously, several optimizations could have been performed; for example, the selection and the join could have been combined at DB5. The scenario might also seem inefficient concerning the partitioning of the budget data, leading to two different join operations. However, if other operations are considered, the advantages of that approach become obvious: the global management department can perform analyses and comparisons of previous budgets without contacting the finance department.

Similarly, the finance department can perform current budget calculations without any remote interaction. The replication of the employee partition offers other advantages, too. Any department can find out the name of any employee, giving his or her number, and vice versa, without requiring any remote communication. Moreover, this can be done independently of the potential failure of other network nodes.

This simple example should have illustrated some of the benefits of distributed databases. It has also shown that a top-down approach is usually used for distributed database design; a global schema is partitioned and allocated to databases in a stepwise way. In contrast, federated databases encourage a bottom-up approach, integrating diverse schemata.

### 6.6.3 Other Technical Issues

The technical problems found in DDBSs and FDBSs are similar to a large degree. In the DDBS area, more sophisticated and mature concepts have already been developed and implemented. Two of the most important issues, discussed below, are query optimization and distributed transaction management.

**Query optimization:** As mentioned above, the goal of distributed query optimization is to reduce the required communication overhead. Moreover, local query optimization is important for minimizing the secondary storage access required.

The global optimization process is divided into several steps: (1) First, a global query is transformed into possible internal query plans. During this procedure, possible sequences of query operations that might lead to a high number of communication messages are removed. For example, it would have been a bad idea to perform the two join operations on budget data first before doing the selection; unnecessary records for other products would have been transmitted. (2) Now a global optimization for the candidate query plans is performed. This comprises a heuristic cost evaluation for several query plan alternatives. Moreover, for each alternative, additional choices are possible: most important, join operations can be implemented at different locations and sometimes only the affected parts of a relation have to be transmitted, leading to the notion of so-called *semijoins*. (3) Finally, each affected database performs a local optimization for the local query statements to be executed. The major goal is to reduce secondary storage access and to make use of existing indexes.

In summary, query optimization in distributed databases is a complex problem with numerous parameters and trade-offs to be considered. However, in practise, pragmatic and workable solutions have been developed. Their internal functionality is completely transparent to the application programmer and user.

**Distributed transactions:** To implement ACID transactions in a distributed environment, two-phase commit protocols are required (see section 4.1). In the first phase, a coordinator node requests all participating databases to store data modifications in stable storage (prepare-to-commit), and to acknowledge whether they are able to commit successfully. In the second phase, the actual commit is performed if all nodes voted positively. Otherwise, a global abort is done.

Locking of data items must consider all replicas. A straightforward approach is to lock all replicas of a data item or relation for write access and to lock an arbitrary copy for read access. Obviously, all write/write and read/write conflicts are detected then. Another issue are deadlocks among distributed transactions. A deadlock is equal to a cyclic wait relation between processes that intend to lock data with mutual dependencies. Distributed deadlock detection is more difficult than local detection and requires sophisticated distributed algorithms; the basic idea is to analyze for local wait relations at each node, and to send a compressed result to a coordinator site that performs a global deadlock analysis by combining the results.

These and other distributed database aspects like security, recovery, and distributed schema evolution cannot be covered in detail here. For further information on technical details of distributed databases and their implementation, specific books on this topic like [CEP84] or [BEG92] should be consulted. Distributed transaction processing is addressed in sophisticated detail in [GRR93]. Additional database requirements for multimedia support are discussed in chapter 7. Major issues are complex multimedia object modeling, media-specific storage support, representation of spatial and temporal intermedia relationships, consideration of realtime conditions within transactions, and content-based query support for various media.

## 6.7 Exercises

1. [Basic knowledge]

Compare the functionality of a database system with a network file system you are familiar with (like NFS) with respect to the criteria summarized at the beginning of this chapter.

2. [Basic knowledge]

What are the differences:
- between hierarchical and network databases
- between relational and object-oriented databases
- between federated and distributed databases?

3. [Conceptual design]

Based on the relations given in section 6.2 for modeling departments, employees, documents, and projects, give an SQL representation for the following query: "select all documents that belong to the department running the project named 'DocumentStandards'".

4. [Conceptual design / optional implementation]
Develop a C++-based object-oriented database schema for your hypertext system implementation of the exercises in chapter 2. Design an implementation of the hypertext node selection operation using a set-oriented query, optimized by an index. If a C++-based OODB is available to you, implement your design.

5. [Basic knowledge]
What are the advantages and disadvantages of OODBs on top of relational DBs versus native OODB system implementations?

6. [Conceptual design]
Design an RDA implementation (client site) for the query in exercise 3; the whole database is to be stored at node "departmentDB" and accessed by client "user5". Which RDA services are invoked internally?

7. [Basic knowledge]
Explain the following FDBS terms:
- local schema
- component schema
- export schema
- federated schema
- external schema.

8. [Conceptual design]
Extend the federated database example of section 6.5.3 by an additional federated schema; this schema is to represent specific product information, including design, marketing costs per period, and the whole production plan of all products with product numbers between 100 and 200.

9. [Conceptual design]
Consider the distributed database example of section 6.6.2. The following query shall be stated by the finance department's database:

```
select * from Product, DesignData, MarketingCosts
where Product.PR# = DesignData.PR#
and Product.PR# = MarketingCosts.PR#
and Product.description = "Refrigerator";
```

Which of the databases will be involved in processing the query based on the given distribution of the relations? In which order should the query operations be executed to keep network data transfer small? Discuss possible alternatives and potential modifications of the allocation of relations to databases.

## 6.8 References

[ACG91] Arnold, D., Cannata, P., Glasson, L.A., Hallmark, G., McGuire, B., Newman, S., Odegard, R., Sabharwal, H.: SQL Access: An Implementation of the ISO Remote Database Standard; *Computer, Vol. 24, No. 12, Dec. 1991, pp. 74-78*

[ANS92] ANSI X3H2 - Database Language SQL; *ANSI X3.135, 1992*

[BEG92] Bell, D., Grimson, J.: Distributed Database Systems; *Addison-Wesley, Wokingham, England, 1992*

[BEL88] Belcastro, V.: An Overview of the Distributed Query System DQS; *Int. Conf. on Extending Database Technology, Venice, 1988, pp. 170-189*

[BEM91] Bertino, E., Martino, L.: Object-Oriented Database Management Systems: Concepts and Issues; *Computer, Vol. 24, No. 4, April 1991, pp. 33-47*

[BOS91] Butterworth, P., Otis, A., Stein, J.: The Gemstone Object Database Management System; *Comm. of the ACM, Vol. 34, No. 10, Oct. 1991, pp. 64-77*

[BOT86] Breitbart, Y.J., Olson, P.L., Thompson, G.R.: Database Integration in a Distributed Heterogeneous Database System; *IEEE Int. Conf. on Data Engineering, Los Angeles, CA, Feb. 1986, pp. 301-310*

[CEP84] Ceri, S., Pelagatti, G.: Distributed Databases: Principles and Systems; *McGraw-Hill, New York, 1984*

[CHU90] Chung, W.C.: DATAPLEX: An Access to Heterogeneous Distributed Databases; *Comm. of the ACM, Vol. 33, No. 1, Jan. 1990, pp. 70-80*

[DAT90] Date, C.J.: An Introduction to Database Systems (5th edn); *Addison-Wesley, Reading, MA, 1990*

[DEU91] Deux, O.: The O2 System; *Comm. of the ACM, Vol. 34, No. 10, Oct. 1991, pp. 34-48*

[ELP90] Elmagarmid, A.K., Pu, C. (Eds): Special Issue on Heterogeneous Databases; *ACM Comp. Surveys, Vol. 22, No. 3, Sept. 1990*

[GRR93] Gray, J., Reuter, A.: Transaction Processing - Concepts and Techniques; *Morgan Kaufmann Publishers, San Mateo, CA, 1993*

[IBM91] IBM: Information Management System - General Information; *IBM, San Jose, CA, 1991*

[ISO90] ISO: Remote Database Access - Parts 1 and 2; *ISO/IEC JTC1/C21 WG3 N996, 1990*

[JTT91] Joseph, J.V., Thatte, S.M., Thompson, C.W., Wells, D.L.: Object-Oriented Databases: Design and Implementation; *Proc. of the IEEE, Vol. 79, No. 1, Jan. 1991, pp. 42-64*

[KGB90] Kim, W., Garza, J.F., Ballou, N., Woelk, D.: Architecture of the ORION Next Generation Database System; *IEEE Trans. on Knowledge and Data Engineering, Vol. 2, No. 3, March 1990, pp. 109-124*

[KIM90] Kim, W.: Architectural Issues in Object-Oriented Databases; *Journal of Object-Oriented Programming, March/April 1990, pp. 29-38*

[KSL87] Krishnamurthy, V., Su, S.Y., Lam, H., Mitchell, M., Barkmeyer, E.: A Distributed Database Architecture for an Integrated Manufacturing Facility; *IEEE Int. Conf. on Data and Knowledge Systems for Manufacturing and Engineering, Oct. 1990, pp. 4-13*

[LHM84] Lindsay, B.G., Haas, L.M., Mohan, C., Wilms, P.F., Yost, R.A.: Computation and Communication in R*: A Distributed Database Manager; *ACM Trans. on Computer Systems, Vol. 2, No. 1, Feb. 1984, pp. 24-38*

[LIZ88] Litwin, W., Zeroual, A.: Advances in Multidatabase Systems; *European Teleinformatics Conf. - Eutoce 1988, pp. 1137-1151*

[LKK93] Lockemann, P.C., Krüger, G., Krumm, H.: Telekommunikation und Datenhaltung; *Hanser-Verlag, Munich, 1993*

[LOO90] Loomis, M.E.: OODBMS: The Basics; *Journal of Object-Oriented Programming, May/June 1990, pp. 77-81*

[LLO91] Lamb, C., Landis, G., Orenstein, J., Weinreb, D.: The ObjectStore Database System; *Comm. of the ACM, Vol. 34, No. 10, Oct. 1991, pp. 50-63*

[LLP91] Lohman, G.M., Lindsay, B., Pirahesh, H., Schiefer, K.B.: Extensions to Starburst: Objects, Types, Functions, and Rules; *Comm. of the ACM, Vol. 34, No. 10, Oct. 1991, pp. 94-109*

[LMR90] Litwin, W., Mark, L., Roussopoulos, N.: Interoperability of Multiple Autonomous Databases; *ACM Computing Surveys, Vol. 22, No. 3, Sept. 1990, pp. 267-293*

[OBJ92] Objectivity Inc.: Objectivity/DB System Overview; *Objectivity Inc., Menlo Park, CA, 1992*

[ODM94] Cattel, R. (Ed.): The Object Database Standard: ODMG-93 Release 1.1; *Morgan Kaufmann, New York, 1994*

[ONT92] Ontologic Inc.: Ontos System Documentation; *Ontologic, Billerica, MA, 1992*

[ÖZV91] Özsu, M.T., Valduriez, P.: Distributed Database Systems: Where are we now?; *Computer, Vol. 24, No. 8, Aug. 1991, pp. 68-78*

[PBR90] Premeriani, W.J., Blaha, M.R., Rumbaugh, J.E., Varwig, T.A.: An Object-Oriented Relational Database; *Comm. of the ACM, Vol. 34, No. 11, Nov.1991, pp. 99-111*

[PSM87] Purdy, A., Schuchardt, B., Maier, D.: Integrating an Object Server with Other Worlds; *ACM Trans. on Office Information Systems, Vol. 5, No. 1, Jan. 1987, pp. 27-47*

[RAM91] Ram, S. (Ed.): Heterogeneous Distributed Database Systems; *Computer, Vol. 24, No. 12, Dec. 1991*

[SHL90] Shet, A.P., Larson, J.A.: Federated Database Systems for Managing Distributed, Heterogeneous, and Autonomous Databases; *ACM Computing Surveys, Vol. 22, No. 3, Sept. 1990, pp. 183-236*

[SRH90] Stonebraker, M., Rowe, L., Hirohama, M.: The Implementation of Postgres; *IEEE Trans. on Knowledge and Data Engineering, Vol. 2, No. 3, March 1990, pp. 125-141*

[STK91] Stonebraker, M., Kemnitz, G.: The Postgres Next-Generation Database Management System; *Comm. of the ACM, Vol. 34, No. 10, Oct. 1991, pp. 78-92*

[SSU91] Silberschatz, A., Stonebraker, M., Ullman, J.: Database Systems: Achievements and Opportunities; *Comm. of the ACM, Vol. 34, No. 10, Oct. 1991, pp. 110-120*

[TBC87] Templeton, M., Brill, D., Chen, A., Dao, S., Lund, E., Macgregor, R., Ward, P.: Mermaid: A Front-end to Distributed Heterogeneous Databases; *Proc. IEEE, Vol. 75, No. 5, May 1987, pp. 695-708*

[TTC90] Thomas, G., Thompson, G.R., Chung, C., Barkmeyer, E., Carter, F., Templeton, M., Fox, S., Hartman, B.: Heterogeneous Distributed Database Systems for Production Use; *ACM Computing Surveys, Vol. 22, No. 3, Sept. 1990, pp. 237-266*

[VER92] Versant Object Technology: Versant Object Database Management System; *Versant Object Technology, Menlo Park, CA, 1992*

[WLH90] Wilkinson, K., Lyngboek, P., Hasan, W.: The Iris Architecture and Implementation; *IEEE Trans. on Knowledge and Data Engineering, Vol. 2, No. 3, March 1990, pp. 63-75*

# 7 Multimedia Extensions

This chapter presents extensions of basic office technology to multimedia. We first discuss techniques for multimedia modeling and outline how multimedia documents can be represented. This is also related to the issue of extended multimedia document standards like *HyTime* and *HyperODA* that are also illustrated.

Other issues are multimedia data transfer and sychronization. In particular, we discuss how multimedia documents can be communicated and how dynamic media (audio, video) can be transferred based on limited network capacities. Synchronization of multimedia data streams from different sources is a related problem. We classify the required synchronization techniques and illustrate them by concrete examples.

Finally, the chapter presents an overview of multimedia database concepts. These emerging approaches are important for storing and retrieving multimedia documents in office environments. Special multimedia products that appear in the PC area at the moment are not covered in detail as they tend to be rather specific and sometimes short-lived; instead, we focus on the more general concepts.

**Basic Concepts and Requirements:** *Multimedia data* can be divided into time-dependent and time-independent media. Examples of time-independent media are text, graphics, and still images. Time-dependent media are for example audio, video, and visual animation sequences. *Multimedia systems* support the generation, processing, presentation, storage, and communication of both time-independent and time-dependent media [BRS91, DAN91, FOX91]. The different media must be processable in an independent way. Based on this definition, a WYSIWIG text editor with graphics facilities is not a multimedia application; it only supports time-independent media. Neither is an analog video system a multimedia application; video and audio are tighly coupled there and cannot be processed independently. In contrast, a system supporting documents with voice annotations [MRT91], a digital videoconference environment [ZIW90], and a dynamic graphical animation as a sequence of images [LIG90b] are examples of multimedia applications.

Other application domains are multimedia e-mail [PFK88], hypermedia systems (see section 2.1.4), multimedia-based medical systems, multimedia-supported teaching, and virtual reality simulation systems. In cooperative office systems, document processing, conferencing, and e-mail applications are most important today [NAF90, WIB94]. Multimedia support in cooperative office systems imposes new demands on the underlying system support:

- *Data modeling:* In addition to offering data representation models for different media, temporal and spatial relationships between media must be represented. This leads to new requirements concerning semantic data models and time-dependent data representation. Moreover, such models should be integrated with existing document representation techniques such as ODA or SGML.
- *Synchronization:* During presentation of multimedia data, the specified temporal relationships must be evaluated dynamically. At given synchronization points, the presentation of various media must be coordinated.
- *Communication:* Transfer of multimedia data imposes high bandwidth requirements due to the large data sizes, especially of images and video. The time dependencies of various media also impose realtime constraints that have to be addressed by advance reservation of communication resources.
- *Storage support:* Multimedia data require mass storage support. In many cases, special storage media like optical disks are necessary as conventional storage systems do not offer sufficient capacity. Moreover, media-dependent data access techniques have to be provided that are not offered by general-purpose databases.
- *Tool support:* Specific media-dependent tools like video editing facilities [MAD89] or text-to-speech conversions [OMA90] are required for managing multimedia data.
- *Software engineering:* New software-level abstractions are necessary to deal with multimedia data. For example, an object-oriented, high-level representation of storage and I/O devices, and of multimedia data themselves can facilitate the implementation of multimedia applications significantly.

These requirements are detailed in the following sections. Technical solutions are outlined for dealing with them and are illustrated by examples.

## 7.1 Characteristics of Multimedia Data

Multimedia data are characterized by large data size, complex structure, media interrelationships, and spatial and temporal dependencies. These characteristics apply to arbitrary multimedia information as well as to multimedia documents in cooperative office systems. In the following, we discuss some of these issues in more detail and present several ways of modeling multimedia data.

### 7.1.1 Representation and Storage Requirements of Multimedia

Multimedia data can be classified into low-cost and high-cost media according to their size of data and the resulting storage and transmission requirements [LIG90a, DAN91]. Examples of the first category (low-cost) are text and vector graphics, while digital bitmap images, audio and video belong to the second category (high-cost). The different media are represented digitally as follows:

- *Text* is usually defined as characters using a standardized code (e.g. ASCII or EBCDIC).
- *Vector graphics* are not stored as a direct representation of the corresponding image but rather as a list of instructions for redrawing the image. As an example, the *Computer Graphics Metafile (CGM)* representation is frequently used in practise.
- *Bitmap images* correspond to a matrix representation of the pixels to be displayed on the screen.
- *Voice* and general audio are stored as a sequence of digitally encoded samples. For each sample, the corresponding tone is represented as a digital value. The quality of the regenerated audio signal depends on the frequency of samples. For voice, a much lower quality is acceptable than for high fidelity audio.
- *Video* is also represented by encoded samples, where each sample corresponds to a digitized image. Video quality of course also depends on the sample frequency.

| **Medium** | **Storage requirements (uncompressed)** | **Storage requirements (compressed)** |
|---|---|---|
| Text (1 page; small font) | ~ 10 kb | ~ 3 kb (ratio up to 3:1) |
| Vector graphics (1 page; 500 graphical lines) | ~ 3 kb | ~ 1 kb (ratio up to 3:1) |
| Bitmap image (1 page) | ~ 0.5-8 Mb | ~ 10-160 kb (ratio up to 50:1) |
| Low-quality audio (1 second) | ~ 8 kb | ~ 0.05 kb (ratio up to 160:1) |
| Hifi-quality audio (1 second) | ~ 80-90 kb | ~ 0.5 kb (ratio up to 160:1) |
| Video (1 second; 30 frames/second) | ~ 30-200 Mb | ~ 0.2-1.2 Mb (ratio up to 160:1) |

Table 7-1 Storage requirements of multimedia data

**Storage requirements:** In table 7-1, some general approximations of the storage capacities required for these media in uncompressed and compressed form are given. While a page of text and also a page of vector graphics require only a few kilobytes, a typical uncompressed bitmap image is already in the range of several megabytes. One second of phone-quality audio requires about 8 kb of storage (sample rate of 8 kHz with 8 bits per sample) [STR90]; a reasonable audio sequence of several minutes therefore requires several megabytes of storage. High-quality audio increases these requirements by a factor of about 10. Digital video imposes much higher requirements, leading to a necessary storage capacity of more than 30 Mb for an uncompressed 1-second clip, or several gigabytes for a reasonable video sequence of a few minutes.

These requirements can be reduced significantly by applying compression techniques. A loss-free compression ratio of 3:1 is possible for text and vector graphics. For the other media, much higher ratios can be achieved (up to 160:1 for video), albeit with an associated loss of quality. This can be tolerated by many applications, but there are special scientific applications that cannot really make use of significant compression levels. Nevertheless, even with compression, a few minutes of high-quality video still require many megabytes of storage.

For bitmap images, the standardized compression technique *JPEG (Joint Photographics Expert Group)* offers compression ratios of 24:1, 15:1, and 6:1, depending on the desired quality. The *MPEG* standard *(Moving Picture Coding Experts Group)* for video compression offers a compression ratio of 100:1; this is achieved by storing only inter-sample differences rather than full video samples. The successor *MPEG-2* enables integrated compression and encoding of digital audio and video.

### 7.1.2 Spatial and Temporal Inter-Media Relationships

Multimedia data, especially within documents, are often interrelated in various ways. Most important, a distinction between *spatial relationships* (describing how mutually to position data during presentation) and *temporal relationships* (specifying how to synchronize time-dependent data during presentation) can be made.

**Spatial relationships:** An example of a multimedia document with associated spatial block composition operations is shown in figure 7-1. The document consists of several overlaid blocks of text, graphics, voice, and images. The image block is generated by another recursive overlay operation of two encoded bitmap images. The voice annotation is configured from an encoded video sequence of which some parts have been cut away using an audio editor tool. The graphics block is generated from a CGM graphics file. The graphics has been scaled so that it fits into the appropriate physical space within the document.

The spatial relationships can be represented in detail by annotating the tree of layout blocks with relative or absolute positions within a coordinate system. The layout definitions of ODA discussed in chapter 5 provide such annotation facilities within the layout structure.

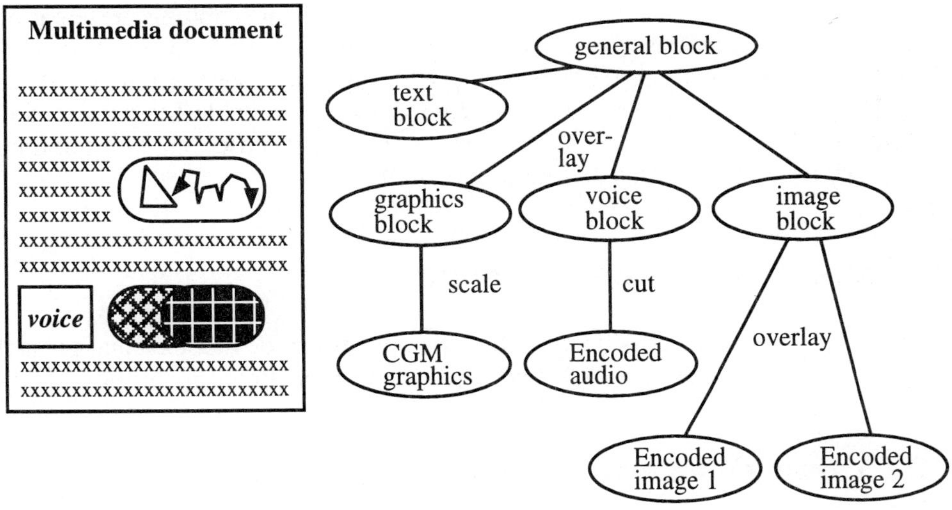


Fig. 7-1 Spatial composition of multimedia data

**Temporal relationships:** Imagine that the components of the above document are to be presented in a given order: the overall document with its text and graphics must be displayed for 30 seconds. During the first 20 seconds, the voice annotation must be played. Moreover, during the first 10 seconds, only the first image must be shown, and during the remaining 20 seconds, both images must be overlaid. This can be represented by a time/media diagram as shown in figure 7-2.

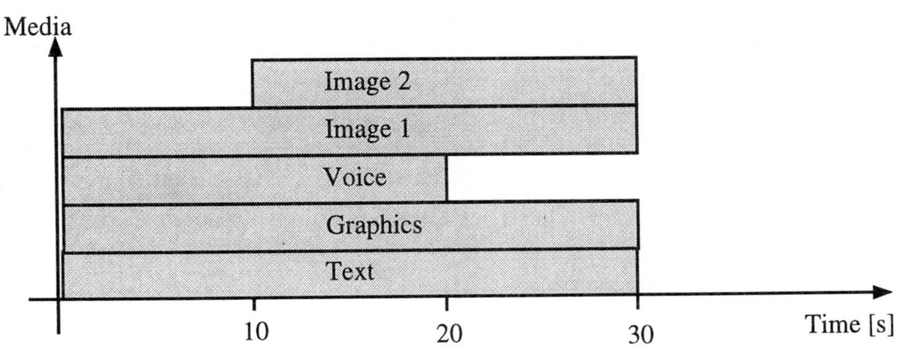


Fig. 7-2 Temporal composition: Time/media diagram

Such temporal relationships must be specified together with the layout representation of the document or multimedia object. Moreover, they must be interpreted at display time in order to determine the corresponding presentation schedule. In a distributed environment where components of a document can reside at different locations (see section 5.1.3), specific transmission schedules must be computed in order to have multimedia data available for presentation just in time. For capturing and structuring audio with specific temporal relationships, new concepts can also be found in [HSH93].

## 7.2 Multimedia Data Modeling

In the following, we discuss how multimedia objects can be modeled and present a concrete system example. We also survey the modeling capabilities of extended multimedia document standards.

### 7.2.1 Object-Orientated Approaches as a Base

Most existing multimedia approaches are based on an object-oriented data model [KNS90, STF92]. This allows for a natural representation of multimedia documents as a set of component objects with inter-object relationships. Moreover, objects can be ordered by classes, with different pre-defined classes for different media. Depending on its class, an object might select an appropriate operation/method, for example to display itself or to synchronize with other object presentations.

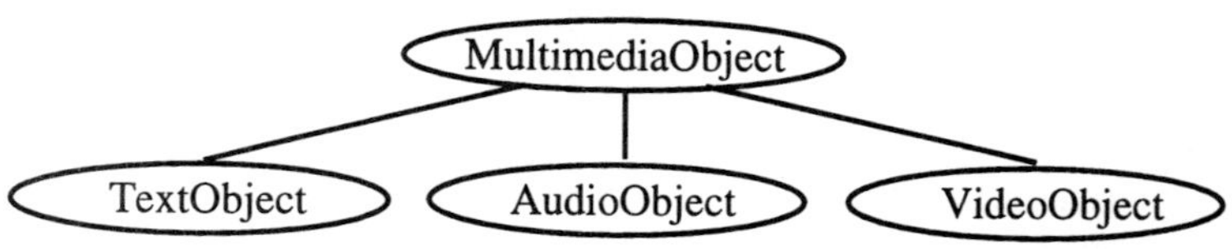


Fig. 7-3 Multimedia object classes

For example, consider the following simplified C++ class definition fragments for general multimedia with subclasses for text, audio, and video objects (see figure 7-3):

```
class MultimediaObject {
 void *data;  // pointer to data portion
 public:
  virtual void display ();      // display the object;
                                // operation to be implemented by subclasses
  // ... other general methods
 };
```

```
class TextObject : public MultimediaObject {
 public:
  void display ();            // medium-specific display operation
  // ... other methods
 };

class AudioObject : public MultimediaObject {
 public:
  void display ();
  // ... other methods
 };

class VideoObject : public MultimediaObject {
 public:
  void display ();
  // ... other methods
 };

// method implementation fragments:

TextObject::display () { TextDisplay (data); }
AudioObject::display () { AudioDisplay (data); }
VideoObject::display () { VideoDisplay (data); }

// operation to display arbitrary objects; each object decides how to display itself:

ShowAll (MultimediaObject *mmo)
 {
 mmo->display ();
 }
```

The example function *ShowAll* does not care about which multimedia object it gets passed as a parameter; it merely calls the virtual *display* method of the multimedia object class. Based on the actual subclass of which the object is a member, a different implementation of *display* is selected at runtime. Using this software structure, a simple algorithm to display a whole tree or graph of multimedia objects can be implemented. Even if new media (e.g. music) are added, no general software changes are required; only a new subclass has to be added.

An object-oriented representation is also found in current document standards, at least in a limited way: although logical or layout objects in ODA do not have application-specific operations associated, they are typed and they have inter-object relationships. In general, object-oriented multimedia document representations can be mapped onto extensions of existing document standards.

Another advantage of the object-oriented approach is that a multimedia environment with its devices and tools can be modeled in a uniform way similar to the actual multimedia data being manipulated. In this sense, a distinction between *primary* (actual) multimedia data objects and *secondary* multimedia tool objects can be made. Examples of secondary objects are a scanner, a camera, a CD player, an audio recorder, and a display. As a concrete example of a secondary object class definition, consider the following fragment of a camera class:

```
class Camera : public SecondaryMultimediaObject {
 public:
   void start ();              // start the camera
   void stop ();               // stop the camera
   void zoom (int factor);     // zoom up or down
   void rotate (int angle);    // rotate camera by given angle
   // ... other control methods
 };
```

Multimedia office application programs can exploit such class abstractions for configuring concrete scenarios without having to take care of device-dependent specifics.

### 7.2.2 Representation Example: Active Media Objects

As a concrete system example, we discuss the multimedia representation model of *active objects* introduced in [GIB91]. This defines multimedia objects as active entities that provide or consume multimedia data of specific types at given data rates. An object is active in that it initiates activities without external stimulation. However, it can also react to external invocations. Moreover, each object has a state that is manipulated by operations as usual.

The producer/consumer relationship between multimedia objects is modeled by interconnected output and input *ports* associated with each object. According to their ports, objects are classified into sources (output ports only), filters (both input and output ports), and sinks (input ports only). The ports of different multimedia objects can be interconnected in order to configure a multimedia presentation scenario. For example, a special multimedia filter object that overlays two images could be introduced; its input ports would be interconnected with the image objects, and its output port with a display device object.

It is important to note that such a configuration of interconnected multimedia objects is only valid for a given time interval and might change thereafter. For example, new sources may be integrated or new filters may be activated to combine different media.

**Example:** As an example, the presentation of a multimedia document as discussed in section 7.1 could be modeled as shown in figure 7-4; the special symbols represent connected input and output ports. The given configuration is valid for the time interval [10s, 20s] where all media are active and images 1 and 2 are overlaid by a filter object.

The behavior of each output port of multimedia objects is described by an entry within an overall time/media diagram as discussed in section 7.1.2. Extending figure 7-2, the output port of the image overlay filter would be represented by a time/media block within the interval [10s, 20s].

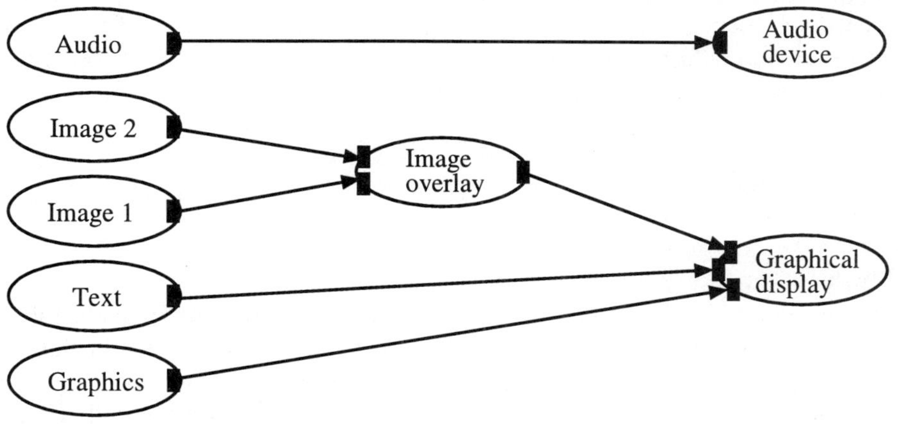


Fig. 7-4 Interconnected active multimedia objects

**Multimedia object classes:** Internally, active multimedia objects are implemented by a class hierarchy. Its superclass is *ActiveObject* with methods for starting, stopping, pausing, and resuming an object, i.e. its producer/consumer behavior:

```
class ActiveObject {
 public:
  void start ();              // start the activity of the object
  void stop ();               // stop the activity
  void pause ();              // suspend the activity until explicitly resumed
  void resume ();             // resume the activity
 };
```

Derived from this class, a generic multimedia object superclass is defined. This mainly provides methods for positioning the object within a time system, and for controlling multimedia data generation. Some of the most important methods are shown below based on concepts found in [GIB91]:

```
class MultimediaObject : public ActiveObject {
 public:
  void translate (int time);  // position the object's start time in the time system
  void setTime (int time);    // set the object's internal time
  void scale (int value);     // scale presentation time
                              // (<1 means faster; >1 means slower)
  void invert ();             // invert presentation direction (backward/forward)
  void synch (int time);      // synchronization
 };
```

Using these methods, the audio object presentation could be modified as follows: after a delay of 30 seconds, it is presented in reverse at half of its actual speed.

The object's start time is first positioned at 30 seconds, its internal time is set to the end of the audio duration, the presentation time is scaled by a factor of 2, and the direction is inverted. Then the object is activated. The object itself is of class *AudioObject*, a subclass of *MultimediaObject* and *ActiveObject*. It is generated and initialized with data fetched from a CD player:

```
AudioObject audio (CDPlayer);
audio.translate (30);
audio.setTime (20);
audio.scale (2);
audio.invert ();
audio.start ();
```

The configuration and presentation of active multimedia objects can also be controlled by a higher-level language, so-called *scripts*. Basically, a script defines the overall execution of a multimedia object presentation, in particular the configuration of multimedia objects and the start times and presentation characteristics of each object. It is also possible to express arbitrary interobject synchronization conditions (see also section 7.3).

In summary, the active multimedia object approach provides a uniform framework for multimedia object modeling and presentation. This allows for high-level specification of synchronization and configuration constraints.

Several other models have been developed; for example in [KNS90], an object-oriented multimedia document modeling approach is described. It allows weakly-structured documents to be represented. Specific features are data sharing among different documents, multimedia object versioning, presentation of objects in several alternative ways etc. However, the approach mainly addresses time-independent media and does not support synchronization. The *Mode* system [BLA90, BHL92] introduces a distinction between multimedia information, presentation, and transport objects in a distributed environment. In this way, flexible conversions involving compression and various presentation qualities can be expressed. Much emphasis is placed on synchronization of multimedia presentation (see section 7.3).

### 7.2.3 HyTime

The international standard *HyTime (Hypermedia and Time-based Structuring Language)* [ISO92a, GOL91] is an extension and application of SGML (see chapter 5) for modeling multimedia documents. It defines new SGML element types and attributes to support multimedia and hypermedia. The functionality offered by HyTime covers two major areas:

- *Hyperlinks:* A document can consist of multimedia objects that can have arbitrary links between them. Moreover, inter-document links are supported, too. These links can serve as a basis for hypermedia applications as discussed in section 2.1.4.
- *Synchronization:* HyTime allows for describing inter-object synchronization constraints for presentation of multimedia information. In this way, time-

dependent presentation schedules as discussed in section 7.1.2 can be specified.

HyTime is divided into several mutually dependent modules that are shown in figure 7-5. The *base module* offers general document management and identification mechanisms. The *location address module* provides several document addressing modes that are exploited by various HyTime modules. The *hyperlinks module* implements inter-document links. The *scheduling module* controls spatial and temporal composition of multimedia objects. It is supported by the *measurement unit module* that defines measuring units (such as seconds), and by the *rendition module* that controls the actual presentation. We discuss some of the more interesting aspects of the location address module, the hyperlinks module, and the scheduling module.

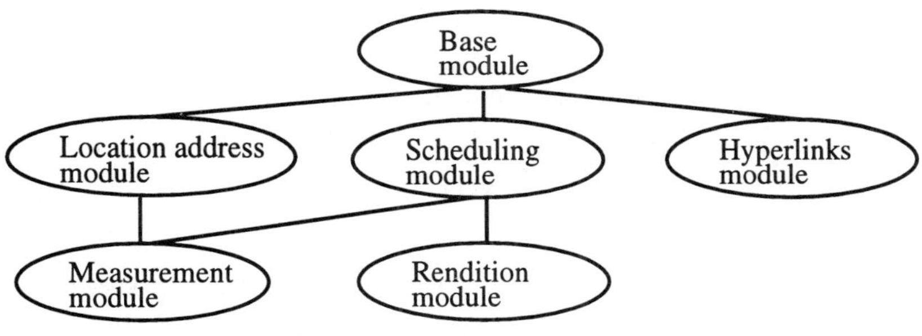


Fig. 7-5 HyTime modules

**Location address module:** This module specifies several HyTime document addressing methods that are exploited for intra- and inter-document links:

- *Name-based addressing:* This addressing mode refers to a named SGML entity. The entity can either be within the same document or within an external document. An example is "the figure named 'HyTime modules'".
- *Coordinate-based addressing:* This mode allows for addressing an entity within an arbitrary virtual coordinate system, e.g. over space or time. The entity is identified by its relative or absolute position within the system. An example is "the image to be displayed after 5 seconds".
- *Semantic addressing:* This way of addressing refers to semantic characteristics of an entity, defined by its attributes. An example is "the chapter with subject attribute 'Databases'".

These mechanisms provide flexible ways of addressing within multimedia document components and across documents.

**Hyperlinks module:** This module mainly offers two kinds of links:

- *Independent links* can connect an arbitrary number of document elements. They are independent of the actual elements and are not stored directly to-

gether with them. Moreover, even if there is only read access to an element, it can become part of an independent link. An example of its use is the definition of a set of arbitrary hypermedia links between several documents.
- *Contextual links* are embedded into the context of one element and refer to exactly one other element. As an example, a contextual link might refer from a piece of text to a voice annotation.

HyTime links are defined as SGML elements; as discussed above, the SGML notation is applied for specifying the extended HyTime functionality. Just to give an impression of the structure of such a definition, the contextual link element specification [ISO92a] is given below (a detailed explanation of the notation cannot be given here as it would require much more background information on SGML):

```
                      <!-- Contextual Link -->
<! element clink      -- Contextual link --
                      -- Constraint: content must be valid in the context
                         in which the contextual link occurs, with
                         respect to both the DTD and the meta-DTD --
                      - 0        (%HyBrid;)* >

<! attlist clink      HyTime     Name        clink
                      id         ID          #IMPLIED  -- Default: none --
                      linkend    -- Link end --
                                 -- Constraint: No HyTime reftype
                                             constraints --
                                 IDREF       #REQUIRED >
```

**Scheduling module:** This module specifies event scheduling, alignment, and synchronization within a complex multimedia document, especially for guiding multimedia object presentation. This is achieved by establishing a temporal unit (such as seconds or minutes) as the system of measurement for a virtual coordinate axis, and by specifying the address of an event as a function of the coordinate address of another event (such as "*event2(display(image2)) = event1(display(image1))+10*") [GOL91]. Each event can also have an associated duration so that scenarios as given in figure 7-2 above can be modeled.

In summary, HyTime is an enabling standard for hypermedia and multimedia document modeling. It offers the foundations required for specifying hyperlinks and for expressing time-dependent inter-object synchronization constraints. However, HyTime is just a basic specification framework. It does not provide tools, language integrations, or an overall system architecture. These facilities will be offered by vendors when the standard is accepted in practise. The important issue is that HyTime enables interoperability and data exchange facilities between heterogeneous multimedia systems.

### 7.2.4 HyperODA

HyperODA is the multimedia extension of ODA with a functionality that mainly corresponds with the features of HyTime: it supports *temporal relations* between hypermedia objects [ISO92b] and enables *nonlinear structures* of such objects, i.e. hypermedia links [ISO92c]. Different media are added to ODA by defining new content architectures. In the following, we discuss these features in more detail and give an overview of the audio content architecture as an example [ISO92d].

**Temporal relations:** Such relations are defined over *actions* that correspond to the presentation of a document constituent, i.e. a basic or composite ODA object [ISO92b]. When an action completes, it triggers an event that may initiate other actions. HyperODA classifies relationships between actions into *sequential* (actions in sequence), *parallel* (parallel execution of actions), and *cyclic* (limited or unlimited number of repetitions of an action). Parallel actions are further distinguished according to the time when the termination event is generated:

- *Parallel-last:* An event is issued when all parallel actions have terminated.
- *Parallel-first:* An event is issued when the first parallel action has terminated; the other actions may continue their execution.
- *Parallel-selective:* An event is generated when a specific, explicitly given action has terminated.

For each action, a *start time delay* and a *duration constraint* can optionally be specified. A start time delay specifies the time between the event that initiates a new action and the actual start of action execution. A duration constraint specifies the maximum time for which an action may execute.

All these properties (order of action execution, start time delay, duration constraint) can be applied hierarchically; an object within an ODA document can specify such relationships and constraints for its subordinate objects, and so on.

As an example, here is the specification of a sequential presentation of three ODA layout objects (numbered 100-102) that are subordinate to another object where the specification is given. For the second object, a start time delay and a maximum duration are provided. For the third object, a start time delay is specified, too, and its presentation is to be repeated ten times.

```
synchronization-type sequential
subordinate-set
 [100]

 [101]
 start-time 10
 duration 100

 [102]
 start-time 5
 cyclic 10
```

**Nonlinear structures:** The ODA extension for nonlinear structures within HyperODA [ISO92c] is similar to the features offered by the HyTime hyperlinks module. It supports independent links and contextual links between document nodes. A node in this sense can be a whole document, a document fragment, or a selected region within one of these. An independent link is specified separately from the interconnected nodes, while a contextual link is defined within the context of the source node.

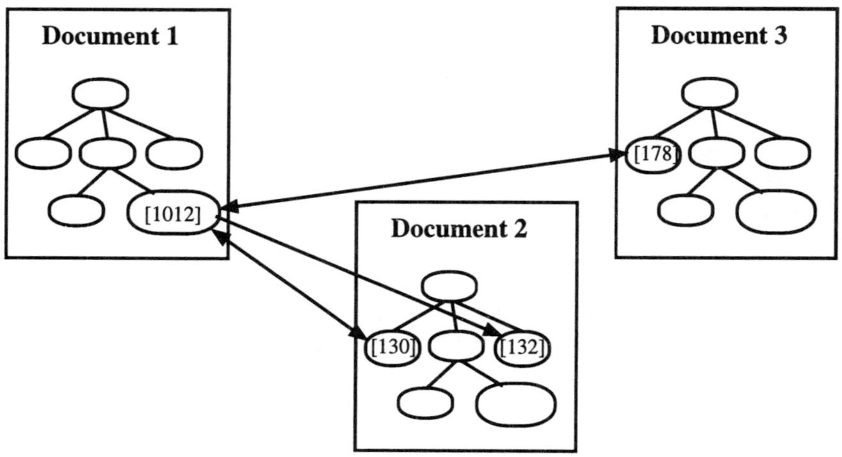


Fig. 7-6 HyperODA link example

As an example, here is the definition of an independent link from one node within document *d1* to three other nodes within documents *d2* and *d3* (see figure 7-6):

```
address-type                one-to-many
application-comments        "hyperlink"
user-readable-comments      "hypermedia link to three documents"
link-type
  direction                 return
  invocation                user
source                      {d1}.[100]
destination
  target                    {d2}.[130]
  target                    {d2}.[132]
  link-type
    direction               one-way
  target                    {d3}.[178]
```

The document identifiers are given explicitly in a pseudo-notation that has not yet been specified in detail within HyperODA; the required extensions are under development. The link type specifies that the link is bidirectional ("*direction: return*"); at runtime, the link can be followed in both directions. Moreover, it specifies that the link is not followed automatically (within the layout process) but only upon explicit user request ("*invocation: user*"). For the second destination, a different specification is given, overriding this default; the corresponding link is only one-way.

The nonlinear structure extensions of HyperODA also define a number of additional document attributes and a special hypermedia document profile. Additional standardization work is required to refine addressing techniques and other details.

**Audio content architecture:** As its first time-dependent medium, ODA includes an audio content architecture [ISO92d]. Using this extension, any node within an ODA document, i.e. any logical or layout objects, can be of type audio. Most importantly, the standard specifies new *presentation attributes* for audio contents:

- *Time units:* This attribute specifies a number of basic units of time per realtime second. It is used for introducing a notion of virtual time.
- *Clipping* specifies the virtual start and end time of the audio presentation. Only the audio portion within this time interval is actually presented.
- *Attenuation* defines the loudness of the presentation; positive values decrease the presentation level, negative values increase it.
- *Temporal envelope:* This attribute consists of a set of time and attenuation pairs. At the given instants in time, the loudness of the presentation is adjusted dynamically according the the attenuation values.
- *Frequency envelope:* This attribute consists of a set of frequency band and attenuation values. It specifies the increase or decrease in loudness according to different frequency levels.
- *Duration* gives the total original duration of the audio object.

As an example, here is the specification of an audio sequence in a pseudo-notation:

```
time units: 100              // 100 virtual time units per realtime second
clipping:
  start time: 200            // start at virtual time position 200
  finish time: 3000          // finish at virtual time position 3000
attenuation: 0.5             // presentation with twice the original loudness
temporal envelope:
  time: 1000
  attenuation: 1.0           // original loudness again from time 1000
duration: 10000              // original duration of audio sequence
```

The example specifies an audio of duration 10 000 [virtual time units] whereby 100 time units correspond to one realtime second. Only the audio portion from 200 to 3000 [virtual time units] will be played. Initially, twice the original loudness will be used; after 1000 virtual time units, the loudness is reset to the original value. A frequency envelope has not been used.

The audio content architecture also specifies some additional *audio content portion attributes*. For example, the *type of coding* attribute specifies the audio encoding schema used (such as J.41 stereo).

In order to support full multimedia applications, similar content architecture classes will have to be defined for video and for other time-dependent media.

In summary, the HyTime and HyperODA extensions of current document standards enable representation of multimedia/hypermedia documents. HyTime has undergone further development and HyTime-based system and tool implementations will soon be available. It will probably be some time yet before HyperODA achieves the status of a full standard. In terms of their functionality, both approaches seem to be quite similar. Both support hypermedia links and temporal relationships. Like SGML, HyTime does not support layout specifications itself. However, the DSSSL extension of HyTime (see section 5.3) provides this feature.

## 7.3 Multimedia Synchronization

We have repeatedly already mentioned the issue of multimedia synchronization. This section classifies existing synchronization approaches more exactly and describes details of a selected synchronization technique.

### 7.3.1 Classification of Techniques

Multimedia synchronization techniques can be based on a *time axis*, can be *hierarchical,* or can be based on *inter-object timing relations* [BHL92].

**Synchronization based on time axis:** In section 7.1.2, synchronization was defined using a time axis: the start time of each multimedia object presentation was given as a time offset along a virtual time axis. A more complex example is shown in figure 7-7.

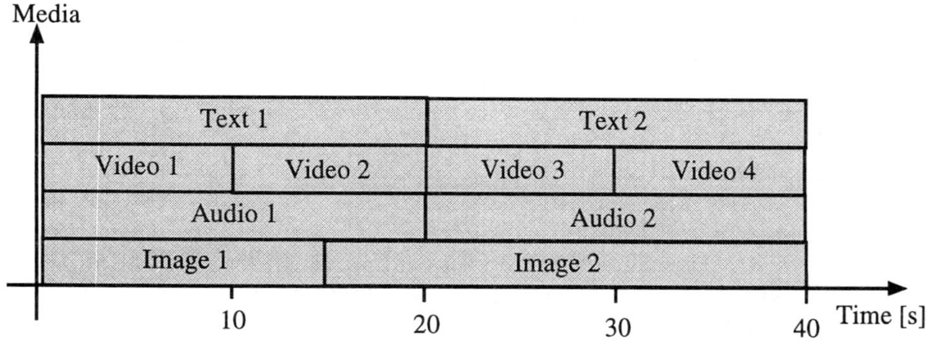


Fig. 7-7 Synchronization based on time axis

The given multimedia presentation displays three sequential video clips of 10 seconds each. In parallel, two audio sequences, each lasting for 20 seconds, are played. The videos are accompanied by two static text segments, each shown for 20 seconds. Finally, two different images are overlaid with the presentation, the first one during the first 15 seconds, and the second one for the remaining time. A time-axis-based synchronization definition would give the start time of each multimedia object presentation:

(Text 1: 0, Video 1: 0, Audio 1: 0, Image 1: 0, Video 2: 10, Image 2: 15, Text 2: 20, Video 3: 20, Audio 2: 20, Video 4: 30)

This simple approach, however, has the disadvantage that direct inter-media synchronization cannot be specified. This is a particular problem if the duration of some presentation sequences is not known in advance; for example, this may be the case with interactive applications.

**Hierarchical synchronization:** With this approach, the overall presentation of a complex multimedia object is divided into sequential and parallel presentation actions recursively. Hierarchical synchronization is used within HyTime and HyperODA, as well as in many other systems. For the example given above, a hierarchical synchronization specification is shown in figure 7-8.

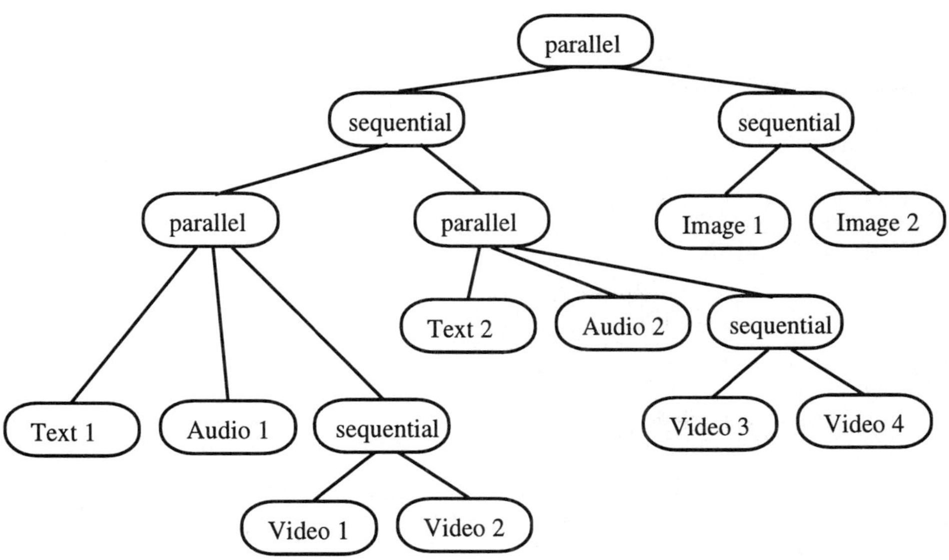


Fig. 7-8 Hierarchical synchronization

At the highest level, it specifies that the presentation of the text, audio, and video sequences should start in parallel with the display of the images. Then it specifies that there are sequential presentation components within each part of the tree. The first component defines the subsequent text, audio, and video presentation within the first 20 and within the subsequent 20 seconds. The other sequential component at the second level in the tree specifies the subsequent presentation of the two images. The text, audio, and video synchronization is further refined, specifying that all media are presented in parallel, and that the video presentation is divided into two subsequent steps (and another two subsequent steps later).

Obviously, the hierarchical technique enables direct inter-media synchronization. Moreover, it can be well represented by traditional approaches like Petri nets, for example (see section 7.3.2). It is easy to map a hierarchical specification into a presentation algorithm at runtime; the following recursive algorithm is an example of the handling of binary synchronization trees (from [LIG90b]):

```
typedef struct node {
  char kind;          /* kind of synchronization node (SEQ./PAR./TERMIN.) */
  Node *left;         /* left subtree                                      */
  Node *right;        /* right subtree                                     */
  char *contents;     /* data contents of terminal nodes                   */
  int duration;       /* presentation duration of terminal nodes           */
  } Node;

void presentation (Node *node)
{
if (node->kind != TERMINAL) {
  if (node->kind == SEQUENTIAL) {
    presentation (node->left);
    presentation (node->right);
    }
  else { /* parallel */
    Thread *t1 = startThread (presentation (node->left));
    Thread *t2 = startThread (presentation (node->right));
    wait (t1, t2);
    }
  }
else { /* terminal node */
  display (node->contents, node->duration);
  }
}
```

In the algorithm, we assume we have lightweight threads available that are created by *startThread* and are synchronized by *wait*. The algorithm can easily be extended to general trees.

A disadvantage of the hierarchical approach is that synchronization can only be expressed at the begin and end of an object's presentation. With the time-axis approach, intermediate synchronization points can also be expressed.

**Inter-object timing relations:** This approach [BHL92, STE90] is similar to the time-axis technique, but it does not refer to time explicitly. It rather specifies *reference points* at the beginning or end of an object presentation, or even in between, and establishes synchronization relationships between these reference points. More preceisely, synchronization is specified by giving *synchronization points* as sets of reference points that denote simultaneous presentation. For the example of figure 7-7, the following synchronization points could be specified:

Synch1 (Text1.start, Video1.start, Audio1.start, Image1.start)
Synch2 (Video1.end, Video2.start)
Synch3 (Image1.end, Image2.start)
Synch4 (Text1.end, Video2.end, Audio1.end, Text2.start, Video3.start, Audio2.start)
Synch5 (Video3.end, Video4.start)

This approach has the advantage that synchronization can be specified at various levels of granularity. For example, it would be possible to provide additional synchronization points within the audio and video sequences in order to enable a more fine-grained synchronization. In contrast to the time-axis approach, no reference to explicit time is necessary. This enables synchronization of objects with a duration that is not known in advance.

In practise, hierarchical synchronization is most widely used. However, the other techniques, especially inter-object timing relations, seem to be equally important from a conceptual point of view.

### 7.3.2 Example: Object Composition Petri Nets

A way to express inter-media synchronization based on extended Petri nets is described in [LIG90b, LIG91]; the approach is called *object composition Petri nets (OCPN)*. The technique can be classified as being based on the hierarchical approach but also has conceptual elements from inter-object timing relations, albeit at a coarse level of granularity.

The presentation of a multimedia object corresponds to a place in a Petri net; synchronization is modeled by transitions. Each place has an execution time (=object presentation duration) and a set of resource requirements associated with it; these requirements may guide presentation location selection in distributed systems.

A Petri net token within a place is locked until the execution time has expired. A transition "fires" when each incoming place has an unlocked token available. Then one token is removed from each input place and one token is added to each output place. As a special property, each place has exactly one incoming and one outgoing arc; this leads to deterministic behavior of the Petri net. Moreover, the Petri net is guaranteed to have the liveness property (no deadlocks are possible), and the one-boundedness property (not more than one token can be in any place).

Synchronization within our multimedia presentation example can be expressed by the Petri net shown in figure 7-9 (presentation time and resource requirements omitted).

The first transition fires immediately due to the available token in the start place. After the first video has been presented, the second one is displayed. A major synchronization point is given by the next transition. It synchronizes the text, video, and audio presentation before entering the second phase. Image synchronization is independent of this, represented by a different transition in the lower part of the figure.

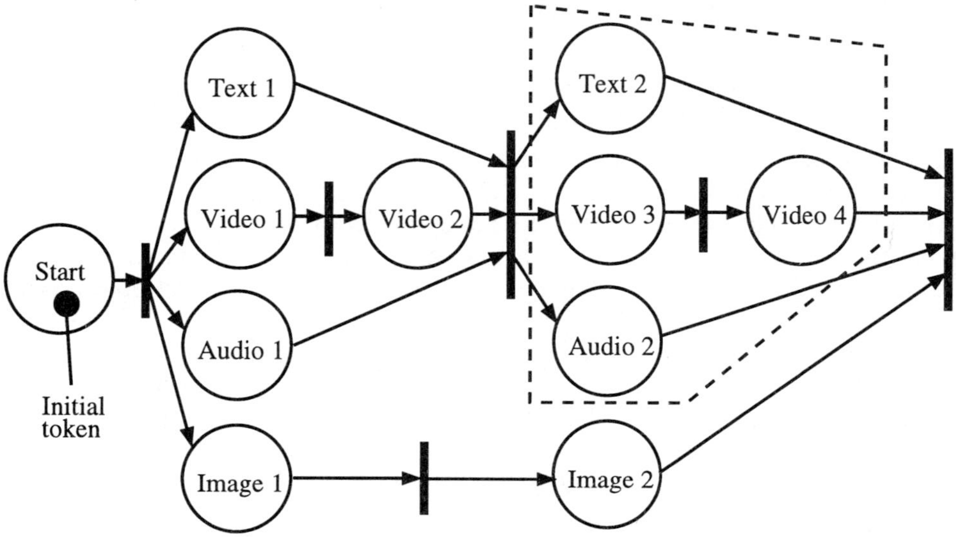


Fig. 7-9 Hierarchical synchronization using Petri nets

It is also possible to subcompose the Petri net into component networks hierarchically. For example, the dotted region in the figure could be assembled into a single place that consists of the given subnet internally. Using such decompositions and some auxiliary mechanisms (like dummy places with null delays), a hierachical synchronization model as discussed above can be derived. Moreover, in [LIG90b] it is shown that all basic temporal relations between object presentation intervals (such as "before", "meets", "during" etc.) can be modeled by the approach. A similar mapping from such relations expressed by path expressions onto Petri nets is presented in [HOE92].

## 7.4 Multimedia Communication

Just like cooperative office systems in general, multimedia office applications tend to be distributed: multimedia data are generated or stored at some network nodes and displayed on others, multimedia objects are relocated between nodes dynamically, and their components can even reside on different nodes. This leads to multimedia communication requirements with selected quality-of-service characteristics that have to be met by modern networking technology [NIC90]:

- *Throughput:* The overall end-to-end communication throughput must be in the range of several up to several hundred megabits per second. For example, a single video channel (with compression) requires a throughput of almost 10 megabits per second. Due to congestion by several channels, much higher throughput values are required within a network.
- *Delay:* For interactive applications like videoconferences, the end-to-end delay of data transfer must be short, preferably below a second. More important, the delay should have an upper bound in order to enable realtime transmission. This is required to achieve synchronization of multimedia presentation at the destination.
- *Jitter:* The delay jitter, i.e. the variation of delay values, should be minimal. This is necessary for synchronization purposes, too. Otherwise, large amounts of early data would have to be buffered until they are to be presented, or late data would have to be ignored. Network traffic with zero or approximately zero jitter is called isochronous.

These requirements can only be met by emerging high-performance networks and by dedicated network- and transport-level protocols on top of them.

### 7.4.1 High Performance Communication Networks

Traditional local area networks such as *Ethernet (IEEE 802.3)* and the *Token Ring (IEEE 802.5)* can only provide a throughput of up to 10 and 4 Mbits/s, respectively. For multimedia applications, new high-performance networks are more appropriate (see figure 7-10).

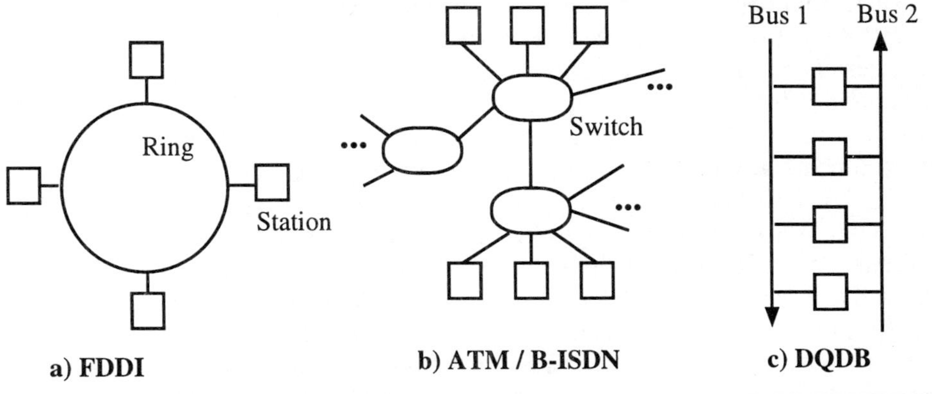


Fig. 7-10 High-performance networks

The most important current approach in industry is the *FDDI (Fiber Distributed Data Interface)* token ring. However, the dominant network of the future will be based on *ATM (Asynchronous Transfer Mode)*. This technique is the basis for emerging broadband ISDN networks, but also for local high-performance networks. Finally, *DQDB (Distributed Queue Dual Bus)* must be mentioned. This is classified as a metropolitan area network and is based on a slotted medium access technique.

FDDI (ANSI X3T9.5, IS 9314-2) [ROS89, MIK93] is based on a token ring architecture using an optical fiber medium. Access to the ring for data transmission is controlled by a circulating token. The ring offers a throughput of 100 Mbits/s. A distinction between realtime traffic (synchronous transmission) and non-realtime traffic (asynchronous transmission) can be made. The FDDI token ring access protocol guarantees that the network access delay for synchronous traffic is bounded by a pre-specified upper time. An extension of the original FDDI proposal, FDDI-II, also supports isochronous traffic with a constant access delay to the ring. This is achieved by pre-allocating portions of the overall bandwidth, so called *wide band channels (WBCs),* of 6.144 Mbits/s each. However, FDDI-II has not been a breakthrough in practise due to its incompatibility with the original FDDI.

ATM [CCI91, BOU92] is based on asynchronous time division multiplexing. The unit of multiplexing is a fixed-size cell of 53 bytes. Unlike FDDI or DQDB, no ring or bus network topology is used; instead, stations are interconnected in a rather arbitrary way via a collection of ATM switches. To establish an end-to-end connection between two stations, a *virtual channel* is established over a selected route via the switches. Each switch stores a mapping of an input to an output channel identifier belonging to a virtual channel. Each cell contains a channel identifier, too, indicating to which channel it belongs. The bandwidth of a channel can range from 64 kbits/s up to 155 Mbits/s and more. Within a switch, a much higher total bandwidth is available and can be allocated dynamically to the different channels. ATM supports synchronous and isochronous traffic based on different *AAL (ATM Adaptation Layer)* classes, as well as fixed and variable bit rates. It has been selected as the transfer mode to be used within *B-ISDN (Broadband Integrated Services Digital Network)*. Local ATM networks are also available so that ATM presents a uniform networking technique for all kinds of environments. It will probably be the major networking technology of the future.

DQDB (IEEE 802.6) [MOL88] is a standard for metropolitan area networks. Each station/node is connected to two buses operating in opposite directions. Depending on the location of the receiver, a data packet is sent on one of the two buses. Data packets are allocated to fixed-size transmission slots for data transfer. Before being able to transmit, a station must put a reservation request on the opposite bus; this informs the upstream stations that they have to delay transmission and have to pass empty transmission slots downstream on the other bus. DQDB also supports synchronous realtime traffic and isochronous traffic, also using a reservation technique.

Basically, all three approaches can be used for multimedia communication. FDDI has been available for the longest. However, in the medium term, ATM-based networks will become more and more important as they are used both for very long-distance links and for local area networks. Interconnectivity of different networks, e.g. FDDI with ATM, will also become a very important issue.

### 7.4.2 Network- and Transport-Level Protocols

On top of such networks as discussed above, network-level and transport-level communication protocols are required [DTH92]. Traditional protocols such as TCP/IP are not well suited to multimedia communication. Most important, they do not guarantee any time constraints of data transfer. New protocols offer resource reservation techniques in order to provide such guarantees.

**Network-level protocols:** As an example of a network-level protocol for multimedia data communication, we consider *ST-II (Stream Protocol Version II)* [EXP90, DHH94]. The protocol is based on so-called streams; a stream is a virtual tree from a sender to several receivers via intermediate nodes. This of course includes the special case of a linear stream from one sender to one receiver. Associated with a stream are specific service guarantees concerning packet sizes and packet transmission rates, leading to an end-to-end throughput guarantee.

To establish a stream, the sender initiates a routing function to find a path to the given receivers. Moreover, the sender specifies the required total bandwidth. Each intermediate node reserves buffers and other resources to enable the required quality of service. If the requirements cannot be satisfied completely, the actual quality-of-service parameters that can be achieved are adjusted. Then the request is forwarded to the next node(s) until it reaches the receiver. Finally, sender and receiver check the actual quality of service provided and can accept or reject the stream. Based on the stream concept, ST-II supports multicast facilities; this is useful for *n*-party communication as found in videoconferences.

Figure 7-11 shows a schematic example of resource reservation when streams are established. Both nodes 1 and 2 wish to initiate a stream to node 6, each stream with a throughput of 50 Mbits/s (according to the requests Req1 and Req2). Each node has a given throughput capacity (shown in italics) depending on its own buffer capacities and on its physical network links. Nodes 3 and 4 have to reduce the actual throughput that can be offered from 50 to 30 Mbits/s according to their capacity. Node 5 has to handle both streams and has a capacity of 50 Mbits/s available. Therefore, the first stream can be granted 30 Mbits/s while the second stream can only get the remaining 20 Mbits/s. These numbers are passed to node 6 that can satisfy them easily. Finally, node 6 and nodes 1 and 2 jointly decide whether to accept the reduced transmission capacities or whether to reject them.

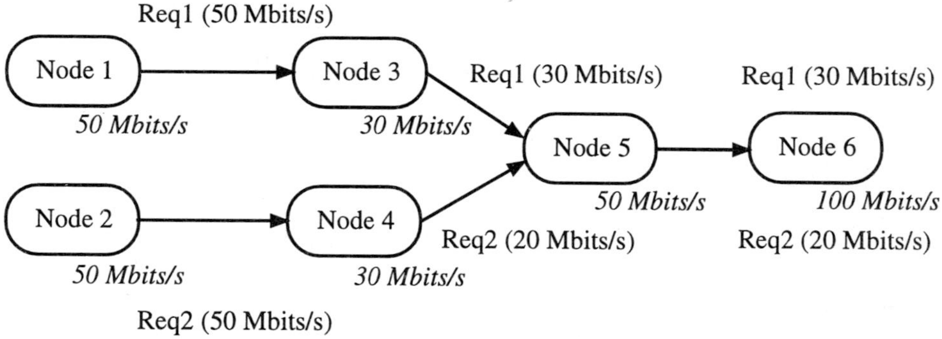


Fig. 7-11 Resource reservation example

In practise, the reservation protocol is of course more complex and involves several different resources, not just a single throughput value. However, the example should have given a basic impression of the functionality. A recent receiver-driven reservation protocol is *RSVP*. It allows more flexibility for managing quality of service according to the individual receiver's capabilities, especially in multicast settings.

**Transport-level protocols:** While network-level protocols provide a basic end-to-end communication facility, transport-level protocols augment this with additional features such a transmission error recovery and flow control. An example of a new transport protocol suitable for multimedia communication on top of ATM is *XTP (eXpress Transport Protocol)* [XTP90, SDW92, KUS93]. Although it offers both network- and transport-level services, it is also possible to use only its transport-level parts together with another network protocol such as ST-II.

XTP has been designed to be implemented efficiently in hardware. It supports traditional transport communication services like TCP does, but also provides a realtime datagram service. Error recovery is based on a selective retransmission scheme (for lost packets), and on a resequencing scheme (for packets arriving out of order). Flow control is based on rate adjustment mechanisms, dynamically adjusting the transmission rate of the sender when the receiver is in danger of overflowing. XTP also supports multicast for 1:*n* communication.

Using these protocols on top of high-performance networks, the required quality of communication service for multimedia data transfer can be achieved. Implementations of these protocols are already available today. However, significant research is going on in order to improve these protocols and to provide enhanced quality-of-service characteristics. It can also be expected that the current TCP/IP protocol suite will be enhanced by such concepts.

### 7.4.3 Distributed Synchronization Techniques

On top of multimedia communication protocols, higher-level policies are necessary for coordinated distributed multimedia processing. Most important, the synchronization techniques presented must be extended in order to incorporate network delays. In [LIG92], a proposal for a way to enhance the OPCN synchronization model discussed in section 7.3.2 is described. We briefly sketch this approach as an example.

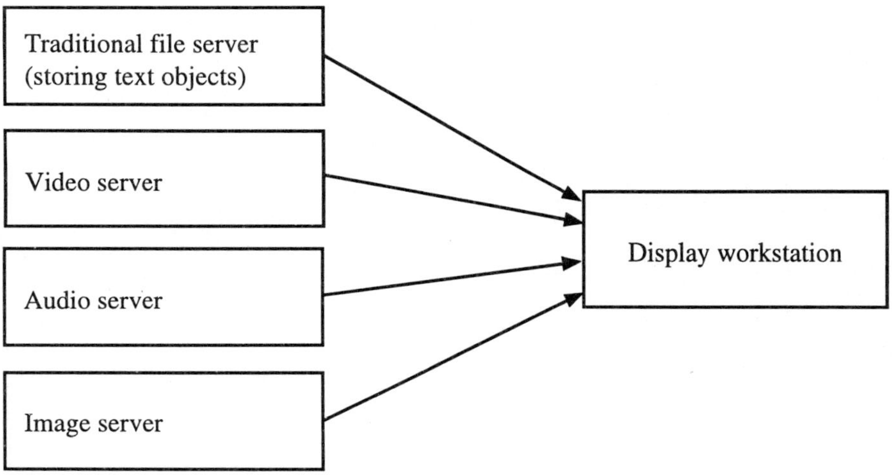


Fig. 7-12 Distributed multimedia system configuration

The assumed system configuration is shown in figure 7-12. It consists of different media servers that are connected with a display workstation via a high-performance network. The same display scenario as discussed in section 7.3 will be achieved at the display workstation. However, all multimedia data have to be fetched via the network first. The goal is to fetch data as late as possible but still early enough to maintain synchronization.

The basic idea is to compute a *fetch time* $F$ for each multimedia object so that a required *presentation time* $P$ can be achieved when incorporating the *network delay* D, i.e. $F+D <= P$ for each object. The delay consists of the time $s$ required to put the data onto the network (depending on the transmission rate), the physical propagation delay $X$ (depending on the distance between stations), and a possible delay $C$ due to network congestion, i.e. $D = S+X+C$. With perfect isochronous traffic support, the congestion delay should be zero; in practise, however, some congestion can hardly be avoided.

For the example in figure 7-7, we compute the fetch times based on the following assumptions: The end-to-end transmission rate of the network (including all protocol overheads) is 1 Mb/s, the physical latency is 0.1 ms (according to a distance of 30 km), the expected congestion delay is constant (due to almost sufficient resource reservation) at about 1 ms, and compressed multimedia data sizes are 1 kb for each text object, 200 kb for each 20-second audio object, 10 Mb for each 10-second video object, and 100 kb for each digital image. Moreover, we assume that we must have each multimedia object available entirely before its presentation can begin.

The computation of the fetch times must begin at the end of an overall presentation schedule if variable congestion delays are to be considered (for a detailed algorithm, see [LIG92]). For simplicity, we can start at the beginning of the schedule due to our constant congestion delay. This results in the following fetch times:

| $Object_i$ | $F_i = P_i - S_i - X_i - C_i$ |
|---|---|
| Text 1: | $F_1$ = 0 - 0.001 Mb / 1 Mb/s - 0.0001 s - 0.001 s = -0.0021 s |
| Video 1: | $F_2$ = 0 - 10 Mb / 1 Mb/s - 0.0001 s - 0.001 s = -10.0011 s |
| Audio 1: | $F_3$ = 0 - 0.2 Mb / 1 Mb/s - 0.0001 s - 0.001 s = -0.2011 s |
| Image 1: | $F_4$ = 0 - 0.1 Mb / 1 Mb/s - 0.0001 s - 0.001 s = -0.1011 s |
| Video 2: | $F_5$ = 10 - 10 Mb / 1 Mb/s - 0.0001 s - 0.001 s = -0.0011 s |
| Image 2: | $F_6$ = 15 - 0.1 Mb / 1 Mb/s - 0.0001 s - 0.001 s = 14.8989 s |
| Text 2: | $F_7$ = 20 - 0.001 Mb / 1 Mb/s - 0.0001 s - 0.001 s = 19.9979 s |
| Video 3: | $F_8$ = 20 - 10 Mb / 1 Mb/s - 0.0001 s - 0.001 s = 9.9989 s |
| Audio 2: | $F_9$ = 20 - 0.2 Mb / 1 Mb/s - 0.0001 s - 0.001 s = 19.7989 s |
| Video 4: | $F_{10}$ = 30 - 10 Mb / 1 Mb/s - 0.0001 s - 0.001 s = 19.9989 s |

The result is represented approximately by the fetch time schedule for each multimedia object in figure 7-13. It is obvious that the fetch time schedule is very different from the presentation schedule due to transmission times varying according to the size of different multimedia objects. Earlier fetch times may result if high congestion delays are considered, especially when the large video objects are sent.

For unexpected delays or for objects arriving too early, additional techniques are required. Most important, video presentations can be delayed artificially by repeating the same image several times or by increasing the time between the presentation of two images. Similar tricks can be applied for audio. If the change in presentation rate is not significant, it might not even be noticeable by a human observer. By applying this technique, a presentation can be delayed until a required object from another data stream arrives. Alternatively, presentation can be accelerated by omitting video images or audio samples, or by reducing the display interval. In this way, the presentation of a delayed medium can catch up with other media once the required data have arrived. In [ANH91], a detailed algorithm for controlling artificial acceleration or delay of presentation is described.

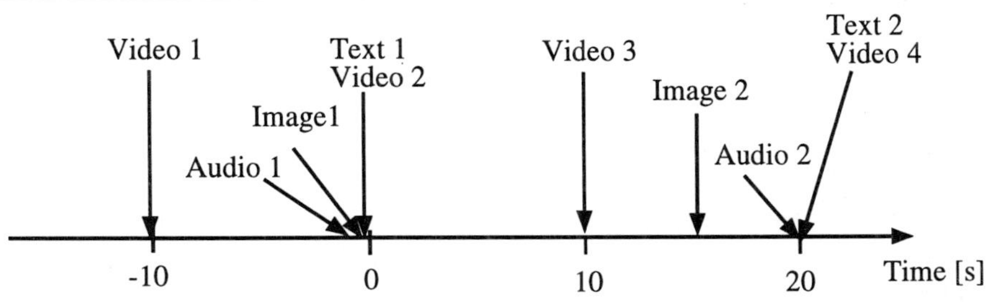


Fig. 7-13 Fetch time schedule

In addition to the network congestion problem, several other issues must be considered for distributed multimedia processing. For example, distributed clocks must be synchronized, multimedia data may have to be converted between different storage formats in heterogeneous systems, and resource reservation may also be necessary at the application level rather than only at the transport communication level. For details on such problems, the references given and the emerging research literature should be consulted.

## 7.5 Multimedia Database Support

In addition to synchronization and communication, multimedia objects and documents impose new requirements on database support. Meanwhile, there are a number of dedicated multimedia database approaches available. However, technology has not yet reached the product level. In this section, we survey requirements, techniques and an existing system in the multimedia database area.

### 7.5.1 Requirements

Multimedia databases must satisfy the following requirements [LOC90, MEY92, ODD91]:

- *Storage capacity:* Multimedia objects consist of large amounts of data; therefore, multimedia databases must offer huge storage capacities. New technologies like optical disks are required.
- *Complex object storage:* Multimedia documents tend to be composed of component objects of different media. A database must be able to model

such complex object structures and to retrieve them efficiently. As discussed in chapter 6, object-oriented databases are most appropriate to meet these requirements.

- *Database integration:* Different media tend to be stored within different databases, each tailored to specific media-dependent characteristics. For example, a video server may use an optical disk while text objects may be stored within a traditional database. Therefore, different databases must be logically integrated for managing complex multimedia objects. In particular, inter-object relationships across databases must be modeled. This requirement is similar to the characteristics of the federated database approach in distributed systems (see chapter 6).
- *Synchronization:* As discussed above, multimedia synchronization is one of the central issues in this area. Synchronization can even be provided within a database during object retrieval. If synchronization is performed externally, a database should at least provide the retrieval performance required to maintain synchronization properties.
- *Queries:* In addition to conventional attribute-based queries, multimedia databases should support content-based queries for images, video, and audio sequences.
- *Transactions:* Multimedia applications tend to be highly interactive and cooperative. Therefore, traditional transaction models with concurrency control by mutual exclusion are overly restrictive. New models that support enhanced sharing of information are required.

These requirements are only partially satisfied by current technology. In the following subsections, we present an architectural model for multimedia databases to address these requirements and outline an example of an associated system implementation. First, a discussion of the required high-volume storage media is given.

### 7.5.2 High-Volume Storage Media

As discussed in section 7.1, multimedia data tend to be of very large size. Images, audio, and video objects in particular require several megabytes of storage (aussuming a realistic duration of audio or video sequences in the range of several minutes). To reduce these requirements, the compression techniques discussed in section 7.1 are important - both for multimedia communication and for multimedia storage.

Nevertheless, even with compression, conventional magnetic disks with storage capacities of say 1 to 10 Gb are hardly sufficient for data-intensive multimedia objects. For example, a 1 Gb disk would be able to store about 10-20 minutes of compressed high-quality video. In large cooperative office systems, however, thousands of multimedia documents with images and audio and video annotations may occur. Moreover, the cost of storage per megabyte on a magnetic disk is still relatively high. Therefore, other storage media, namely *CD-ROMs (compact disk read-only memory)* [KOP94], with much higher storage capacities are more appropriate. These belong to the category of optical storage media. An international standard (*ISO 9660*) specifies the storage characteristics of CD-ROMs so that such optical disks can be managed by any CD-ROM drive in a uniform way. Complete hardware support is provided by *CD-I (Compact Disk Interactive)* products; the standardized environment consists of a CD player, a microprocessor, an audio processing unit, audio and video decoders, a clock, a pointing device, and a special realtime operating system [FOX91].

*DVI (Digital Video Interactive)* is an even more far-reaching approach; it supports video and audio compression conceptually based on the MPEG standard, special pixel processors, and machine-independent software interfaces to such media. It is especially dedicated to the PC area.

A major disadvantage of CD-ROMs, however, is that they are not erasable. This is not a problem for large image or video archives that are just used for multimedia object retrieval. Many applications, for example in the publishing area, in the more general domain of document archiving, or in the hypermedia area, can live with such an approach. However, for highly interactive multimedia applications (like office procedures with multimedia support or joint multimedia authoring systems), writeable storage systems are required. Writeable optical disks are already available today although they are still comparably expensive; these enable much larger, data-intensive interactive multimedia applications to be implemented than with conventional disk technology.

For multimedia database systems, the requirement of integrating different storage media (e.g. CD-ROMs, writeable optical disks and magnetic disks) within a single logical schema becomes obvious.

### 7.5.3 Architectural Model

Based on the above considerations, an architectural model for multimedia databases must include a storage layer and a media integration layer. The storage layer masks the differences in heterogeneous storage devices used for different media. The media integration layer assembles component objects into complex multimedia objects or multimedia documents. An architectural proposal in [KNS90] introduces an additional layer, the presentation layer. This is responsible for presenting multimedia documents in various ways and also includes synchronization issues as discussed above. The overall architectural model is shown in figure 7-14.

The objects offered at the storage layer interface are usually single-media objects; however, they should already conform to a global schema. This facilitates media integration at the next highest layer. At the presentation layer, different representations of a multimedia object are possible. For example, a text object can be presented with different alternative fonts or can even be converted into an audio object by speech synthesis. This makes multimedia object presentation quite flexible.

A concrete system that conforms to this architecture, the *MULTOS* environment [MRT91, BRG88], is presented in chapter 8. It supports storage and contents-based retrieval of most kinds of media. Moreover, it integrates magnetic and optical storage media and supports ODA/ODIF as its document model. Other prototypes supporting similar features are *MINOS* [CTP86], *ISR* [BDB89], *Diamond* [CVL84], and *CCWS* [PGC85], for example. The interested reader can also find a discussion of principles for optimizing storage and retrieval of delay-sensitive multimedia data in [GEC92].

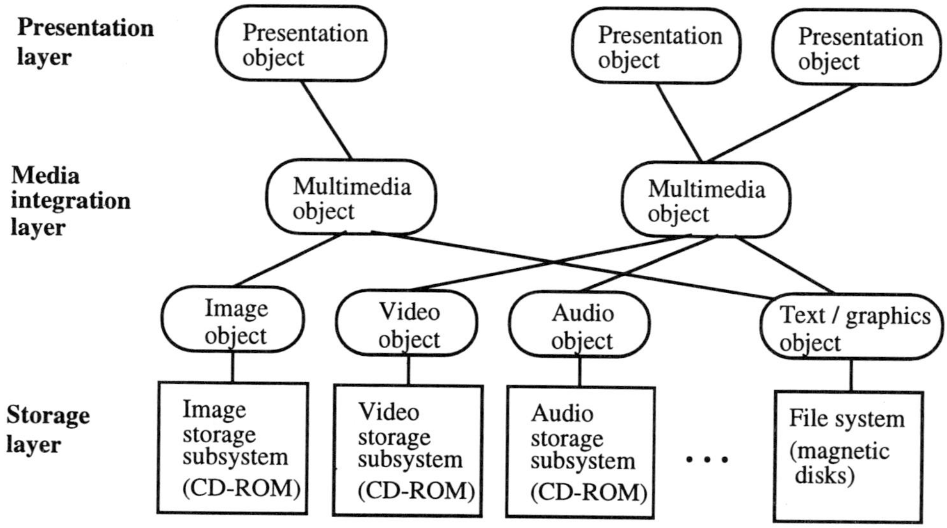


Fig. 7-14 Multimedia database architecture

Of course, many features of such existing approaches could be improved; examples are read/write storage support for all media, fully automatic classification of arbitrary images for retrieval purposes, database-integrated audio/video synchronization, and new transaction models for cooperative work. This requires new hardware technology, improved image processing algorithms, preferably also with hardware support, and integration of the synchronization techniques discussed. Current research addresses most of these issues; however, sophisticated products in this area will still be a medium-term issue.

### 7.5.4 Multimedia Document Queries

Queries against a multimedia document database can include conventional, SQL-like query statements, but also content-based query operations on images or audio. As an example, we describe the query facilities of the MULTOS multimedia database system [BRG88]. In this system, conceptual (semantic) structures of documents can be specified explicitly; they form the basis for content-related document queries. For example, consider the conceptual structure of a multimedia mail document given in figure 7-15. Such a conceptual structure is specified in MULTOS using a *conceptual structure definition notation (CSD)*. The various conceptual structure elements are associated with specific logical structure portions of the document; therefore, the conceptual structure is a way to make the logical structure more explicit and accessible to queries.

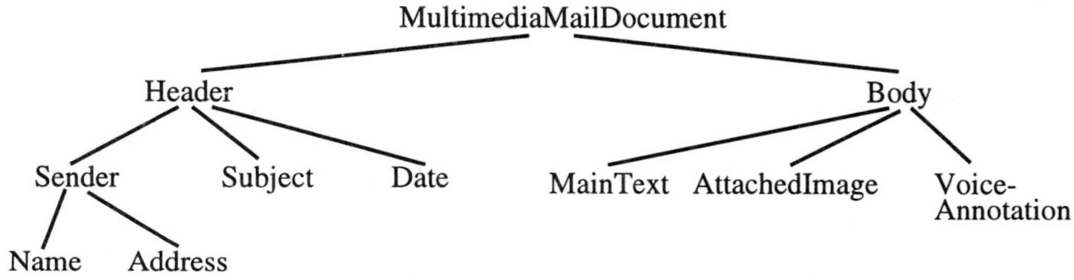


Fig. 7-15 Conceptual document structure

In the example, each document contains a conventional header structure indicating the sender, the subject, and the date when it was sent. The document body comprises a main section of text but can also have an attached image and an optional voice annotation.

A query against the given conceptual structure might ask for all received documents sent by Peter after January 1, 1995 that contain the words "product description" in their main text part, that have an image of a refrigerator attached, and that have a voice annotation:

```
FIND MultimediaMailDocument WHERE
Header.Date > 1/1/1995 AND
Header.Sender = "Peter" AND
Body.MainText CONTAINS "product description" AND
IMAGE Body.AttachedImage MATCHES
  (DOMAIN ProductPictures OBJECTS Refrigerator) AND
WITH Body.VoiceAnnotation;
```

The first few components of the query are straightforward. The *CONTAINS* operator performs a basic pattern matching on a text block. The *MATCHES* operator works on digital images and checks whether an image within the document matches another pre-defined image within the database (stored in a logical domain named *ProductPictures* under the name *Refrigerator*). The image matching is tested by comparing image classifications for similarity. The degree of required similarity can be controlled by optional probability measures within a query. The *WITH* operator just checks whether a document component exists at all, in this case the voice annotation.

## 7.6 Summary

This chapter has outlined solutions for modeling, synchronizing, communicating, and storing multimedia documents. Although a number of prototypes in these areas exist already, the field is still developing rapidly and it will take some time until product-level quality systems are widely available.

To provide fully distributed multimedia office systems support, the various technological aspects discussed in this chapter must be integrated into a single environment - such a complete integration has still to be put into practise. Moreover, in each technological area - document modeling, communication and synchronization, and database support, further research and development efforts are necessary. Examples are the integration of standardized document models, database schemata, and language interfaces, the development of user-friendly synchronization specification techniques, the development of synchronization algorithms for heterogeneous distributed systems, and the design and implementation of new high-performance communication protocols with flexible quality-of-service characteristics.

## 7.7 Exercises

1. [Basic knowledge / conceptual design]

A multimedia document with 100 pages of text, 30 simple vector graphis, 10 images, and a 5-minute high-quality voice annotation is to be stored in compressed form. Give an approximation of the required storage space (using worst-case assumptions). How would these requirements increase with an additional 5-minute video clip attached to the document?

2. [Basic knowledge]

Define the terms "multimedia data" and "multimedia system".

3. [Conceptual design]

Give a time/media diagram for a slide show taking 20 minutes. Each slide is displayed for 1 minute, accompanied by a voice annotation that starts after 10 seconds and takes 40 seconds. Moreover, during the first 10 minutes, an additional text ("text1") is to be shown, and during the remaining 10 minutes a different text ("text2") is to be displayed. The small time intervals required to change slides can be neglected.

4. [Conceptual design]

Give a possible configuration of the "active media objects" approach for the slide scenario at the time instant "1 minute after start". Possible media objects are slides, voice objects, text objects, a slide projector, a loudspeaker, and a monitor for text display.

5. [Basic knowledge]

Explain the following HyTime / HyperODA terms:
- contextual links

- independent links
- temporal relations / scheduling.

In addition, describe the general representation of these features within both approaches.

6. [Conceptual design]

Give a hierarchical synchronization representation for the above slide show example.

7. [Conceptual design]

Give an OCPN synchronization representation for the slide show.

8. [Basic knowledge]

What are the topology differences between
- FDDI
- DQDB
- B-ISDN / ATM.

9. [Conceptual design]

Consider the distributed synchronization example of section 7.4.3. Assume that only a *single* video, audio, or image object may be under transmission on the network at any given time (text objects are not affected by this restriction). Based on this assumption, compute new possible fetch times so that the given presentation times can be maintained. (Start at the end, i.e. compute the fetch time for the last video object (video 4) first. Then take *min(fetch_time(video4), presentation_time(audio2))* as the starting point for computing the fetch time for audio 2 etc. Try different schedules (e.g. first fetching audio 2 or first video 3 etc.) in order to perform some heuristic optimization (so that the first fetch time is as late as possible)).

10. [Basic knowledge]

Why do multimedia databases have to integrate different storage media? What are the advantages of optical and of magnetic disks?

11. [Conceptual design]

Consider the multimedia document query of section 7.5.4. Modify/simplify the query so that all documents with the given date and sender condition that have either a voice annotation or an attached image of some kind or that contain the keyword "cost summary" in their main text section match.

## 7.8 References

[ANH91] Anderson, D.P., Homsy, G.: A Continuous Media I/O Server and its Synchronization Mechanism; *Computer, Vol. 24, No. 10, Oct. 1991, pp. 51-57*

[BDB89] Brolio, J., Draper, B.A., Beveridge, J.R., Hanson, A.R.: ISR: A Database for Symbolic Processing in Computer Vision; *Computer, Vol. 22, No. 12, Dec. 1989, pp. 22-30*

[BHL92] Blakowski, G., Hübel, J., Langrehr, U., Mühlhäuser, M.: Tool Support for the Synchronization and Presentation of Distributed Multimedia; *Computer Communications, Vol. 15, No. 10, Dec. 1992, pp. 611-618*

[BLA90] Blakowski, G.: Supporting Multimedia Information Presentation in a Distributed, Heterogeneous Environment; *2nd IEEE Int. Workshop on Future Trends in Distributed Computing Systems, Cairo, Sept. 1990, pp. 29-35*

[BOU92] Boudec, J.-Y.: The Asynchronous Transfer Mode - A Tutorial; *Computer Networks and ISDN Systems, Vol. 24, 1992, pp. 279-309*

[BRG88] Bertino, E., Rabitti, F., Gibbs, S.: Query Processing in a Multimedia Document System; *ACM Trans. on Office Information Systems, Vol. 6, No. 1, Jan. 1988, pp. 1-41*

[BRS91] Brackenbury, I., Sachar, H.: The Road to Multimedia; *Future Generation Computer Systems, Vol. 7, 1991, pp. 91-96*

[CCI91] CCITT Recommendations I.121, I.150, I.311, I.321, I.327, I.361, I.362, com. XVIII, CCITT, Geneva, 1991

[CTP86] Christodoulakis, S., Theodoridou, M., Ho, F., Papa, M., Pathria, A.: Multimedia Document Presentation, Information Extraction, and Document Formation in MINOS: A Model and System; *ACM Trans. on Office Information Systems, Vol. 4, No. 4, Oct. 1986, pp. 345-383*

[CVL84] Christodoulakis, S., Vanderbroek, J., Li, J., Li, T., Wan, S., Wang, Y., Papa, M., Bertino, E.: Development of a Multimedia Information System for an Office Environment; *10th Int. Conf. on Very Large Databases, 1984, pp. 261-271*

[DAN91] Davies, N.A., Nicol, J.R.: Technological Perspective on Multimedia Computing; *Computer Communications, Vol. 14, No. 5, June 1991, pp. 260-272*

[DHH94] Delgrossi, L., Herrtwich, R.G., Hoffmann, F.O., Schaller, S.: Receiver-Initiated Communication with ST-II; *Multimedia Systems, Vol. 2, No. 4, 1994, pp. 141-149*

[DTH92] Dupuy, S., Tawbi, W., Horlait, E.: Protocols for High-Speed Multimedia Communications Networks; *Computer Communications, Vol. 15, No. 6, July/Aug. 1992, pp. 349-358*

[EXP90] Experimental Internet Stream Protocol, Version 2 (ST-II); *Network Working Group, RfC: 1190, IEN-119, CIP Working Group, 1990*

[FOX91] Fox, E.A.: Advances in Interactive Digital Multimedia Systems; *Computer, Vol. 24, No. 10, Oct. 1991, pp. 9-21*

[GEC92] Gemmell, J., Christodoulakis, S.: Principles of Delay-Sensitive Multimedia Data Storage and Retrieval; *ACM Trans. on Information Systems, Vol. 10, No. 1, Jan. 1992, pp. 51-90*

[GIB91] Gibbs, S.: Composite Multimedia and Active Objects; *ACM OOPSLA Conf. 1991, pp. 97-112*

[GOL91] Goldfarb, C.F.: HyTime: A Standard for Structured Hypermedia Interchange; *Computer, Vol. 24, No. 8, Aug. 1991, pp. 81-84*

[HOE92] Hoepner, P.: Synchronizing the Presentation of Multimedia Objects; *Computer Communications, Vol. 15, No. 9, Nov. 1992, pp. 557-564*

[HSH93] Hindus, D., Schmandt, C., Horner, C.: Capturing, Structuring and Representing Ubiquitious Audio; *ACM Trans. on Information Systems, Vol. 11, No. 4, Oct. 1993, pp. 376-400*

[ISO92a] ISO/IEC JTC1/SC18/WG8 N1421 - CD 10744: Information Technology - Hypermedia/Time-based Structuring Language (HyTime); *International Organization for Standardization, 1992*

[ISO92b] ISO/IEC JTC1/SC18/WG3 N3621: Information Technology - Text and Office Systems - Open Document Architecture (ODA) and Interchange Format - Amendment 7:

HyperODA - Extensions for Temporal Relationships; *International Organization for Standardization, 1992*

[ISO92c] ISO/IEC JTC1/SC18/WG3 N3621: Information Technology - Text and Office Systems - Open Document Architecture (ODA) and Interchange Format - Amendment 8: HyperODA - Extensions for Nonlinear Structures; *International Organization for Standardization, 1992*

[ISO92d] ISO/IEC JTC1/SC18/WG3 N3621: Information Technology - Text and Office Systems - Open Document Architecture (ODA) and Interchange Format - Part 9: Audio Content Architecture; *International Organization for Standardization, 1992*

[KNS90] Klas, W., Neuhold, E.J., Schrefl, M.: Using an Object-Oriented Approach to Model Multimedia Data; *Computer Communications, Vol. 13, No. 4, May 1990, pp. 204-216*

[KOP94] Korst, J., Pronk, V.: Compact Disc Standards: An Introductory Overview; *Multimedia Systems, Vol. 2, No. 4, 1994, pp. 157-171*

[KUS93] Kure, O., Sortenberg, I.: XTP over ATM; *Computer Networks and ISDN Systems, Vol. 26, 1993, pp. 253-262*

[LIG90a] Little, D.C., Ghafoor, A.: Network Considerations for Distributed Multimedia Object Composition and Communication; *IEEE Network Magazine, Vol. 4, No. 6, Nov. 1990, pp. 32-49*

[LIG90b] Little, D.C., Ghafoor, A.: Synchronization and Storage Models for Multimedia Objects; *IEEE J. on Selected Areas in Communications, Vol. 8, No. 3, April 1990, pp. 413-427*

[LIG91] Little, D.C., Ghafoor, A.: Spatio-Temporal Composition of Distributed Multimedia Objects for Value-Added Networks; *Computer, Vol. 24, No. 10, Oct. 1991, pp. 42-50*

[LIG92] Little, D.C., Ghafoor, A.: Scheduling of Bandwidth-Constrained Multimedia Traffic; *Computer Communications, Vol. 15, No. 6, July/Aug. 1992, pp. 381-387*

[LOC90] Lockemann, P.C.: Multimedia Databases: Paradigm, Architecture, Survey and Issues; *Research Report, Naval Postgraduate School, Monterey, CA, 1990*

[MAD89] Mackay, W.E., Davenport, G.: Virtual Video Editing in Interactive Multimedia Applications; *Comm. of the ACM, Vol. 32, No. 7, July 1989, pp. 802-810*

[MEY92] Meyer-Wegener, K.: Multimedia Databases: Integrated Storage and Retrieval of Text, Images, Sound and Video; *University of Erlangen-Nürnberg, Technical Report, Vol. 25, No. 12, Nov. 1992*

[MIK93] Mirchandani, S., Khanna, R.: FDDI - Technology and Applications; *John Wiley, New York, 1993*

[MOL88] Mollenauer, J.F.: Standards for Metropolitan Area Networks; *IEEE Network Magazine, Vol. 26, No. 4, April 1988, pp. 20-28*

[MRT91] Meghini, C., Rabitti, F., Thanos, C.: Conceptual Modeling of Multimedia Documents; *IEEE Computer, Vol. 24, No. 10, Oct. 1991, pp. 23-30*

[NAF90] Naffah, N.: Multimedia Applications; *Computer Communications, Vol. 13, No. 4, May 1990, pp. 243-249*

[NIC90] Nicolaou, C.: An Architecture for Real-Time Multimedia Communication Systems; *IEEE J. on Selected Areas in Communications, Vol. 8, No. 3, April 1990, pp. 391-400*

[ODD91] O'Docherty, M.H., Daskalakis, C.N.: Multimedia Information Systems - The Management and Semantic Retrieval of all Electronic Data Types; *The Computer Journal, Vol. 34, No. 3, 1991, pp. 225-238*

[OMA90] O'Malley, M.H.: Text-to-Speech Conversion Technology; *Computer, Vol. 23, No. 8, Aug. 1990, pp. 10-15*

[PFK88] Postel, J., Finn, G., Katz, A., Reynolds, J.: An Experimental Multimedia Mail System; *ACM Trans. on Office Information Systems, Vol. 6, No. 1, Jan. 1988, pp. 63-81*

[PGC85] Poggio, A., Garcia Luna Aceves, J., Craighill, E.J., Moran, D., Aguilar, L., Worthington, D., Hight, J.: CCWS: A Computer-Based Multimedia Information System; *IEEE Computer, Vol. 18, No. 10, Oct. 1985, pp. 92-103*

[ROS89] Ross, F.: An Overview of FDDI: The Fiber Distributed Data Interface; *IEEE J. on Selected Areas in Communications, Vol. 7, No. 7, Sept. 1989, pp. 1043-1051*

[SDW92] Strayer, W.T., Dempsey, B.J., Weaver, A.C.: XTP: The Xpress Transfer Protocol; *Addison-Wesley, Reading, MA, 1992*

[STE90] Steinmetz, R.: Synchronization Properties in Multimedia Systems; *IEEE J. on Selected Areas in Communications; Vol. 8, No. 3, April 1990, pp. 401-412*

[STF92] Steinmetz, R., Fritzsche, J.C.: Abstractions for Continuous-Media Programming; *Computer Communications, Vol. 15, No. 6, July/Aug. 1992, pp. 396-402*

[STR90] Strathmeyer, C.R.: Voice in Computing: An Overview of Available Technologies; *Computer, Vol. 23, No. 8, Aug. 1990, pp. 10-15*

[WIB94] Williams, N., Blair, G.S.: Distributed Multimedia Applications: A Review; *Computer Communications, Vol. 17, No. 2, Feb. 1994, pp. 119-132*

[XTP90] XTP Protocol Definition; *Protocol Engines Inc., PEI 90-120, 1990*

[YHM88] Yamkelovich, N., Haan, B., Meyrowitz, N., Drucker, S.: Intermedia: The Concept and the Construction of a Seamless Information Environment; *IEEE Computer, Vol. 21, No. 1, 1988, pp. 81-96*

[ZIW90] Ziegler, C., Weiss, G.: Multimedia Conferencing on Local Area Networks; *Computer, Vol. 23, No. 9, Sept. 1990, pp. 52-61*

# 8 System Examples and Technology Support

This chapter embeds the technological foundations presented in previous chapters into the context of dedicated CSCW system examples.

In particular, we discuss the multimedia facilities of the *Etherphone* teleconference system, the specific communication and synchronization aspects of the *CES* collaborative editing system, the hypermedia approach of the *Intermedia* environment, the complex coordination system *ObjectLens*, the architecture and linguistic support of our *IPSO* complex office procedure approach, and the structure of the multimedia document storage system *MULTOS*.

After describing each approach from an architectural point of view, we discuss how specific distributed programming, database, and document management techniques are used or could be used within the system. In this way, it should become obvious that such kinds of supporting technology are a fundamental issue in the cooperative office systems domain.

## 8.1 Teleconference: Etherphone

Xerox PARC's *Etherphone* [VZS91] is an example of a teleconference system with digital audio data transfer that has already been operating for some time. However, the system is not fully digital; according to the given reference, it uses a hybrid approach by exploiting analog video transfer and storage facilities. This is due to communication and computing resources that are still limited. The system comprises the following features:

- *Multimedia conferencing:* Teleconferences based on digital audio and analog video can be established dynamically and can basically involve an arbitrary number of participants. Several options such as participation in multiple conferences are supported.
- *Multimedia storage and editing:* Video and audio objects can be stored persistently and can be modified by video and audio editors.
- *Multimedia e-mail:* Text or general documents can be augmented with audio and video annotations and can be transferred between participants using an extended e-mail facility.

The architecture of the system is shown in figure 8-1 from [VZS91]. The equipment of an end user comprises a camera for video capturing, a monitor for video display, and a workstation (SparcStation under Unix) which is connected to audio I/O devices and can handle digital audio.

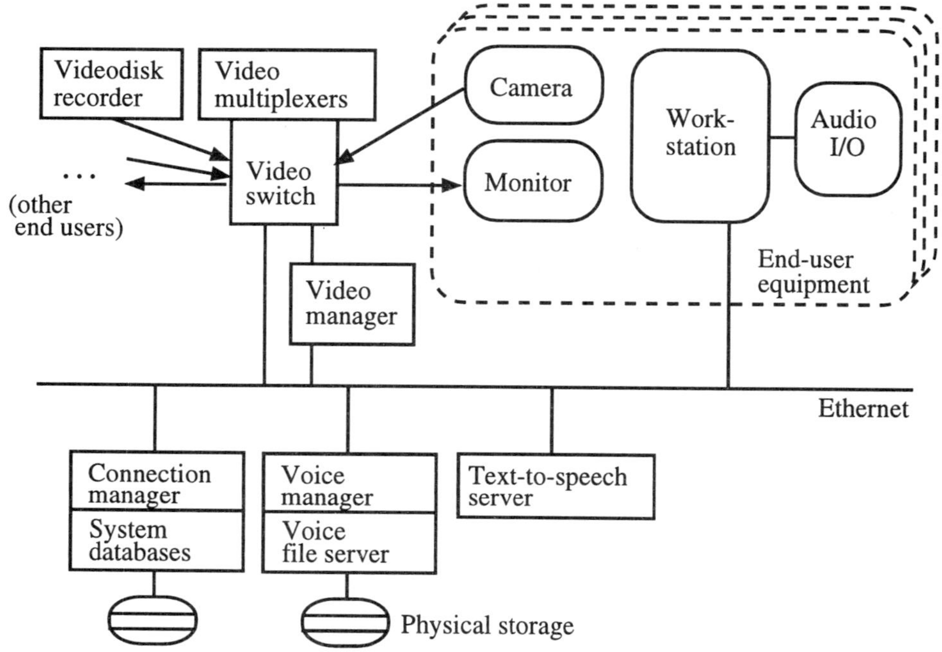


Fig. 8-1 Etherphone architecture

***Data and voice transmission:*** Conventional data and voice are transmitted directly via the Ethernet. For voice, a special audio protocol is used. It supports physical multicast of voice streams to all participants, and some basic jitter control mechanisms in order to tolerate limited amounts of transmission delay time jitter. Every participant receives audio streams from all other participants, and the system software merges them at the receiver's site; this allows adjustment of the volume level and other parameters of selected voice streams individually.

***Conference establishment:*** Conferences (so-called *conversations*) are established by a *control agent* running on each workstation. An initiator can set up a new conversation by calling the *CreateConversation()* function of the remote *connection manager*; thereafter, he or she can invite other participants to join the conversation by calling the *Alert()* function of the connection manager; this notifies other participants so that they may decide autonomously whether actually to join the conversation. Communication between the control agents and the connection manager is based on SUN RPC. The connection manager makes use of system databases that store directory information about the potential participants.

Whenever a participant becomes a member of a conversation, his or her audio devices are logically connected to the Ethernet via the intermediate workstation. In addition, the *video switch* component of the system is instructed via an RPC to the *video manager* to create analog connections for the camera and monitor of the participant. Switching is actually implemented by analog video multiplexers. Basically, a video multiplexer connects *n* camera input lines to *n* monitor output lines. The video manager has a software interface to invoke the physical hardware operations of the video switch component. The operations *ReserveMultiplexer()* and *FreeMultiplexer()* reserve a multiplexer for a given conversation and release it again after termination of the conversation. Cameras and monitors are connected to a multiplexer by the operations *ConnectCamera()* and *ConnectMonitor()*.

***Conference management:*** Participants can join and leave a conference dynamically. A participant can also go "on hold". In this case, all devices are disconnected temporarily but can be reconnected later; the participant's workstation and the connection manager maintain all necessary status information. Moreover, a participant can also move from the usual "active" state into a "receive only" state; in this case, the camera and the audio input (microphone) are disconnected so that the participant's site only receives multimedia data but does not generate such data. All other participants in a conversation are informed of such status changes via the state transition operation *AdvanceState()* of the connection manager, leading to a *ProgressReport()* invocation at each workstation.

A participant can be an active member of only one conversation but can be a passive (receive only) member of any number of other conversations. For example, a participant can establish a "subconference" with other participants for private discussion purposes and can become passive within the main conference in the meantime. Alternatively, a participant can also establish a conference with outside peers while being passive within the main conference.

***Special services:*** In addition to inter-participant conferencing, each participant can also make use of a set of special services. Most important, recorded voice and video can be accessed, manipulated, transferred, and attached to documents. The required storage functionality is supported by a digital voice file server and by an analog videodisk recorder. Access to these storage services from workstations is enabled by the voice manager and by the video manager, respectively. In addition, a commercial speech synthesizer is integrated as a text-to-speech server into the system.

***Technology support:*** The Etherphone system makes use of message-based distributed communication for audio transfer and of RPC communication for all control and resource management interactions between components. Basic directory service functionality is exploited by the connection manager to locate participants and to set up inter-participant connections. Moreover, distributed security techniques are indicated as an area of future work in [VZS91]; in particular, various levels of control of access to conversations are envisaged.

Document management is only relevant within the context of supplemental tools, namely concerning voice and video annotations to documents and concerning a simple means of e-mail-based document transfer. Conventional database techniques are exploited by the connection manager for persistent management of system-level information. Voice storage support is based on a regular file system. Multimedia functionality is offered for voice transmission, storage, and annotation. Of the multimedia techniques presented in this book, a type of active media object modeling approach is applied (with software objects like camera, monitor, audio device etc.), and a limited isochronous multimedia communication protocol is provided.

In summary, the Etherphone system provides a flexible teleconferencing environment, but is still based on limited technology for pragmatic and historical reasons. Extensions of this approach make use of high-performance networks, provide digital video support with inter-media synchronization, apply standardized application-level communication services, and include standardized document models. The following section presents an example of such a current approach.

## 8.2 Teleconference: Multimedia Collaboration

As an example of a current multimedia teleconferencing system, we discuss the *Multimedia Collaboration (MMC)* approach [ADH93]. This system has been developed as part of the BERKOM project of the German Telekom. The project represents an important broadband ISDN trial. Its main goal is to enable heterogeneous broadband applications in high-performance networks with a special focus on multimedia. Major project partners are Digital Equipment, Hewlett-Packard, IBM, Siemens, Liebing & Ullfors (a Berlin-based software house), the GMD (Gesellschaft für Mathematik und Datenverarbeitung, a government-based research association), and the Technical University of Berlin.

**System functionality:** The MMC system offers a fully digital video / audio conferencing facility via local or wide area networks. In addition, it supports distributed application sharing among conference participants based on a shared X windows implementation. Among the supported operating system platforms are DEC OSF/1, SUN's Solaris, Hewlett-Packard's HP-UX, SNI's Sinix, IBM AIX, MS Windows, and Apple's MacOS. Multimedia communication is performed via a special MultiMedia Transport (MMT) system that is being developed within the project. It is based on ST-II, the Internet Stream Protocol, and is operable via Ethernet, Token Ring, ATM, and FDDI. This transport system provides guaranteed quality of service, namely throughput and delay.

Cooperative work of the conference participants is based on the application sharing component. The output of an application (for example, the current status of a CAD session) is displayed to all participants, but only one participant at a time can provide input. The right to work on a shared application is controlled by a logical token based on a floor management policy. The token can be requested and can be passed explicitly to peer participants.

A conference is being established by an initiator. He or she is free to invite other users to join the conference. User groups are also supported and can participate as a whole. During a conference, participants can assume the roles of chairperson (privileged conference management), token holder (with write access to the shared application and the right to start new applications), and observer (everybody else). Roles can be assigned dynamically, for example based on passing the token.

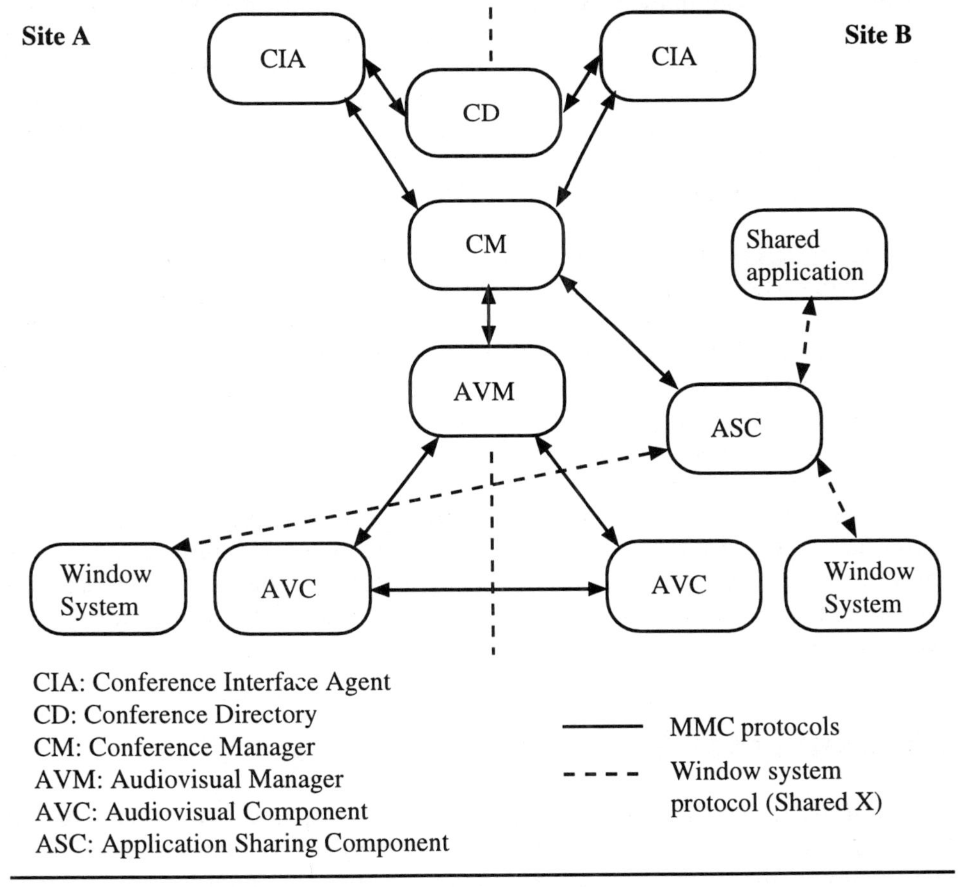


Fig. 8-2 MMC architecture

**System architecture:** The architecture of the MMC system is shown in figure 8-2, from [ADH93], based on a simple scenario with two participants at site A and B, respectively. The *Conference Manager (CM)* is the core component for conference administration. There is at least one CM in a system, possibly one per conference. The *Conference Interface Agents (CD)* serve as user interfaces to MMC with one per user machine. The *Conference Directory (CD)* is an auxiliary component for managing all conference-related administrative data. It comprises a logically centralized repository of users, user groups, and conferences. It is implemented in a physically decentralized way based on the X.500 directory service.

The *Audiovisual Manager (AVM)* coordinates the establishment of communication channels among the participants and is co-located with the CM. For example, MMT audio and video connections are established by AVM for a participant upon joining a conference. The *Audiovisual Component (AVC)* represents the counterpart of AVM on the user machines. The *Application Sharing Component (ASC)* enables applications to be viewed and accessed by several users. There will be at least one ASC per conference, and potentially one ASC per user who submits applications to be shared. Among the components, various protocols are executed according to the arrows in the figure. These protocols were implemented based on ISO application-level services (ROSE - Remote Operations Service Elements) in RPC style.

**Technology support:** MMC is based on high-performance communication facilities. Moreover, for the control part, it makes use of client/server interactions based on the RPC paradigm. Directory services are incorporated in the architecture. Document management techniques are not directly relevant to the system although shared editing of arbitrary documents is possible based on the application sharing component. Concerning multimedia, compression techniques (based on a motion JPEG approach) are of major importance. Moreover, quality-of-service aspects are observed by the multimedia transmission facilities.

In summary, MMC represents a flexible, up-to-date solution for teleconferencing and application sharing. In addition, a multimedia mail system (MMM) has been developed as part of the project. It is based on the X.400 standard and augments it with the facility to transfer e-mail with multimedia attachments in a heterogeneous environment.

## 8.3 Distributed Multiuser Editor: CES

*CES (Collaborative Editing System)* [GRW92], developed at MIT, is an example of a cooperative, distributed multiuser editor. The system allows for shared document editing by a number of physically distributed authors. It has been implemented in *Argus*, an RPC- and transaction-based programming language for distributed systems.

**Document management and access:** Documents in CES have an explicit structure representation, consisting of a set of sections with text contents. Each section has an owner and is stored locally at the owner's site; therefore, the contents of a whole document can be distributed across multiple network nodes. The global structural representation of a document, however, is replicated at all nodes to improve performance and availability. Shared document access has the following concurrency control semantics:

- *Read access* to any section is possible at any time, regardless of intermediate changes to the section. This may lead to slightly outdated versions, but increases concurrency.
- *Write access* is exclusive. Document sections are the units of locking. As an extension of this conventional approach, so-called *tickle locks* are introduced (see also section 5.8.1 for a general discussion of lock management). These are released if there is a conflicting access request and if the lock holder has been idle for at least a pre-defined time interval. In this way, users are prevented from keeping a lock for an unnecessarily long time, for example if they have been disturbed during their work and yet did not release the lock.

All changes to a document are embedded into Argus *atomic actions*; an atomic action is serializable (i.e. concurrency is controlled in such a way that concurrent execution of actions is equivalent to serial execution), and is recoverable (an action is either successfully committed or is aborted and then leaves no effects at all). When a modification action commits, the screens of remote users are also updated when necessary. The granularity of actions is kept low so that only very limited changes may get lost when a tickle lock is released after timeout (which leads to the abort of an action). Based on these properties, consistency of documents after changes can be guaranteed, even if multiple users are involved remotely. The recoverability property of distributed actions is achieved by a two-phase commit protocol.

Altogether, the use of the distributed action approach has facilitated the implementation of remote editing operations significantly; remote access to document sections of a foreign user is location-independent, consistent, and still relatively efficient.

The system also offers a special *undo* feature. Modified sections do not replace the previous version immediately but are stored as a new version; this may lead to a whole stack of versions after several modifications. In this way, an undo functionality can be provided by "popping" an older version from the stack if it is necessary to refer back to it.

**System architecture:** The architecture of CES is shown in figure 8-3. It consists of a set of *Argus guardians*; a guardian basically is a resilient process that communicates via transactional RPC and can be recovered after system failures. Each end-user editing system comprises three guardians: the *display management guardian* is responsible for updating the user's screen with the current document view; the *document section management guardian* stores and accesses the sections owned by the local user; and the *document structure management guardian* is responsible for storing and updating the replicated representation of the global document structure.

Moreover, several other guardians implement a replicated system configuration management and directory service. They mainly provide the necessary facilities for locating other users and machines and for reconfiguring the environment dynamically. They are replicated for fault-tolerance reasons.

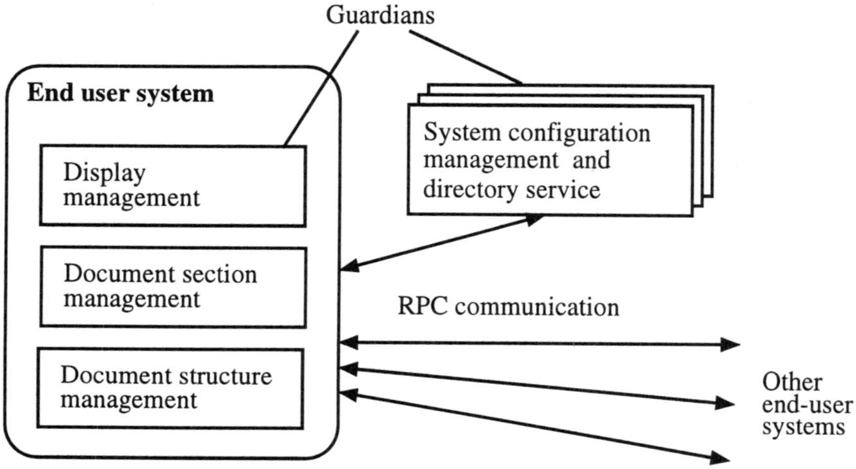


Fig. 8-3 CES architecture

Internally, several subtle problems have had to be solved; some of them still require further attention [GRW92]. For example, the display management guardian must refresh the screen quickly after an action aborts; timely notification has been an implementation problem. An example of another problem is the potentially abnormal behavior after remote section modifications. In particular, after changes have been committed remotely, a subsequent read operation may still reveal the old version of the section object due to update propagation delays. For a different user, this is no problem - it conforms to the concurrent read/write access semantics - but for the user who actually performed the changes it may be surprising.

In summary, the system enables distributed collaboration between authors based on a flexible document sharing model and is an interesting distributed application of Argus.

**Technology support:** The system uses RPC invocations as its basic interaction mechanism - guardians of other end users and also system service guardians offer RPC interfaces. The RPC functionality is augmented with distributed transactions (*Argus atomic actions*) that are based on a two-phase commit protocol and can also be nested. These features are embedded into a specific programming language for distributed systems. A directory service is used for locating remote users and machines. To a limited degree, the underlying Argus system also offers distributed object-based mechanisms; guardians as well as the data managed by them are based on a dedicated object model, and guardians can be invoked in a location-independent way - just like distributed objects in many other systems. However, object mobility is not supported, and the object model is not uniform in the sense that different kinds of objects are used for coarse-grained processes and for fine-grained data, respectively.

CES introduces its own document model. Although not directly based on standards such as ODA or SGML, the model allows for an explicit structural representation and for structure editing. CES is also an example of a shared document management approach with a sharing functionality similar to the one discussed in section 5.1.3. The evironment does not use a separate database system but implements persistent storage and transaction support on its own. Multimedia documents are not addressed by the described implementation yet.

## 8.4 Hypermedia: The Intermedia System

The *Intermedia* system [YHM88, HKR92] of Brown University is a hypermedia environment that also provides a rich set of tools. Its basic mechanism offers the facility to define hypermedia *links* between various kinds of multimedia documents. A link originates at an *anchor* within a source document and terminates at another anchor within a destination document. Anchors and links are stored in a separate database system, making the linked objects and the links themselves independent of each other.

The tools offered include a graphical browser for link information (*Web-View*), and direct-manipulation editors for text, graphics, animations, and video data. The system has been implemented under Unix, with the Macintosh user interface functionality, *MacApp*.

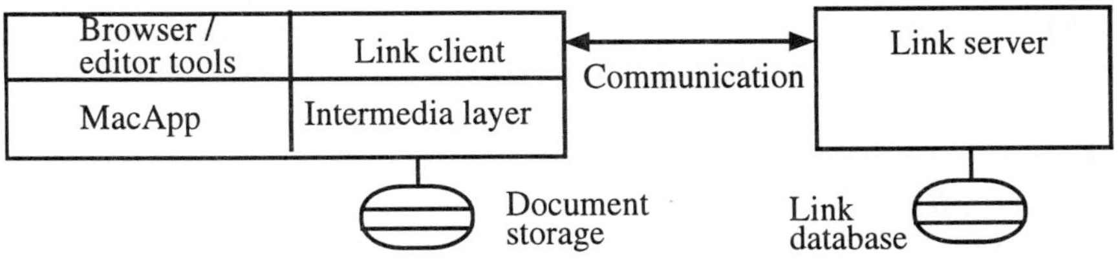


Fig. 8-4 Intermedia architecture

**System architecture:** The coarse-grained architecture of the system is shown in figure 8-4. It is based on a general client/server paradigm. The client site (of which many instances may exist) stores documents within a conventional Unix file system. It also offers the tools and the user interface. All link and anchor information is stored in a separate link database managed by a *link server* process. Links are kept consistent by the system itself; for example, when a document is deleted, the related links are automatically deleted, too. The linked documents may reside on different client workstations, so that Intermedia actually can be classified as being a distributed hypermedia system (however, the link storage itself is not distributed).

When links are followed or manipulated, the *link client* of the client site contacts the link server. Both processes may be co-located on the same machine (in this case, local Unix sockets are used for interprocess communication) or may be distributed across different machines (then Internet socket communication is applied). Extensions also address higher-level communication mechanisms based on an object-oriented RPC extension. The link client, the link server, and the link database together are called the *link engine.*

The *intermedia layer* extends the object-oriented MacApp user interface framework with the required linking capabilities. Several new object classes provide facilities for displaying anchors, for highlighting anchor-related data, and for initiating hypermedia operations (such as creating new links or following links).

*Link database:* To store links, a relational database approach is applied for pragmatic reasons - as the authors say [HKR92], an object-oriented database would have been more suitable, but was not available when work on the project started. Relations are mainly defined for *documents* (with document identifier, name, and file system access path), for *document lock management* (concurrency control), for *anchors* (associating an anchor with a document and with some attributes), and for *links* (assembling anchors and documents). Object identifiers that are required for unique document, anchor, and link identification are generated based on an auxiliary relation.

*Organization of links:* Links and anchors can be organized in so-called *webs.* A web is a logical unit or domain and improves user orientation; it reduces the global view of the entire hypermedia object space to a manageable subset. This organizational subdomain is also reflected by the WebView browser. As mentioned in chapter 2, the browser offers specific orientation mechanisms within a web, such as display of a navigation history and of a hypermedia node neighborhood map. A given user can only open one web at a time.

*Multiuser support:* Multiple users can concurrently access links and documents from different workstations. They can even be active within the same web. While several users can browse a document, editing in write mode can only be done by a single user at a time. However, in the meantime, other users may continue browsing a read-only copy of the document. In the case of concurrent changes by another user, the read-only copy is refreshed only after reopening the document. Links involving the same document can be defined concurrently by multiple users. This is possible due to the separation of document and link storage. Multiuser access is controlled by dedicated access rights for read, write, and link definition ("annotate").

**Technology support:** The system makes use of message-based communication between link clients and servers. Higher-level, object-oriented communication mechanisms are addressed by system extensions. The approach comprises features of distributed object-oriented systems: documents and links have a globally unique object identity and links can be followed in a location-independent way (this is similar to performing a location-independent invocation on the destination document).

The system uses a specific hypermedia interchange format, the *Dexter Interchange Format* for hypermedia object transfer between workstations. In [HKR92], it is remarked that this format can also be mapped to HyTime, leading to a standardized representation. Relational database support is exploited by the link server; an object-oriented database would have been an alternative solution. Moreover, extensions to a more decentralized link storage facility as discussed in [HKR92] might benefit from federated database techniques. Finally, multimedia modeling and spatial composition techniques are applied by the system; temporal media relationships and media synchronization are addressed only in a limited way.

## 8.5 Coordination: ObjectLens

MIT's *ObjectLens* system [LMY88] is an example of a complex coordination system. It assists a user in handling tasks with various levels of structure. In particular, it provides facilities for handling incoming e-mail in a semi-automatic way. An enhanced version of the system is now also available as a product named OPAL. Similar features are also supported by advanced intelligent e-mail systems.

**Basic building blocks:** As discussed in chapter 2, the system is based on three major concepts:

- *Semi-structured objects* represent all kinds of data found within an office, for example documents, forms, or e-mail messages. These objects have an application-specific set of data fields (such as *name, id* etc.), but can also comprise untyped data such as large text portions. Moreover, the objects can have links between them as in a hypertext system.
- *Folders* are collections of semi-structured objects and are used for organizing the personal object space of a user.
- *Semi-autonomous agents* are active entities that perform actions upon folders and objects, such as moving an object into a new folder or sending an object via e-mail. The actions are triggered when pre-defined rules apply.

It is possible to define types and instances of these elements in an application-specific way. This enables the implementation of arbitrary CSCW applications. For each object, a customized display format can be defined to support interactive applications. The objects offer a set of generic operations (such as *Hardcopy* to create a hardcopy, *Save* to store the object data persistently, and *AddLink* to add a link between objects), as well as some type-specific operations (such as *Send, Answer*, and *Forward* for e-mail message objects). Operations can be invoked interactively or by agents. An example of rule-based triggering of agent operations has already been presented in chapter 2.

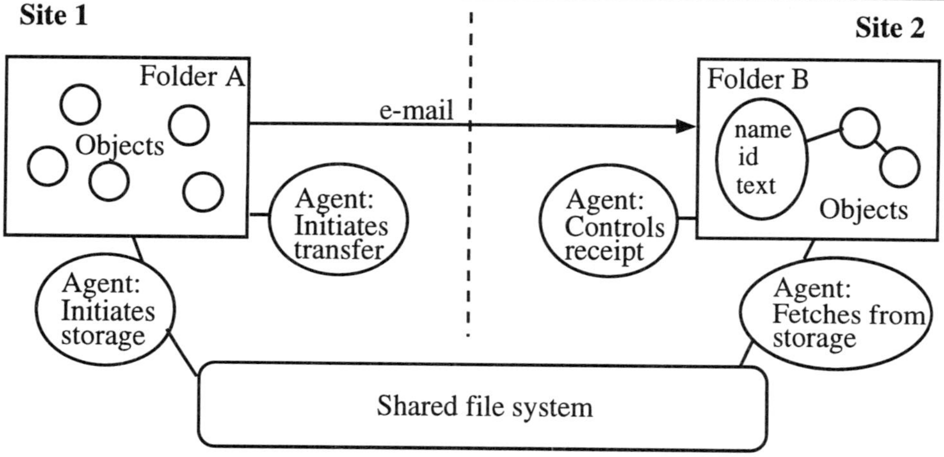


Fig. 8-5 Object transfer in ObjectLens

**Object transfer:** Objects can be transferred between the machines of different users. This can be done by e-mail or by shared files (see figure 8-5). In the first case, a message object is sent. This object may contain additional embedded objects of arbitrary types. These objects are automatically converted into a flat text representation and are reinstalled at the destination site. The transfer and receipt actions are controlled by agents that are triggered upon pre-defined events. Extensions of the approach attempt to pass objects not only as copies but also by remote reference similar to distributed object-oriented systems.

With the shared files approach, a user saves an object on disk, while a peer user loads the same named object into his or her workspace. This procedure can actually be automated by the system: a user can define an agent that stores objects periodically - or based on an explicit event - and the peer user specifies an agent that fetches objects automatically from disk, also in a trigger-controlled way. As a simple example, the objects representing sales data of an external office could be stored every evening and would be fetched by a central site with shared file access at midnight.

**Application examples:** Examples of typical applications of the system as discussed in [LMY88] are task tracking, e-mail message sorting, database retrieval, and hypertext features. Tasks to be performed by an employee can be tracked by moving all task-related message objects into one or several common folders (performed automatically by an agent), and by querying the folder(s) for selected task information. Electronic mail messages can be sorted into appropriate folders (or even be discarded) by agents that act upon message receipt and perform some basic message object evaluation. Simple database retrieval functionality can be implemented by agents scanning a set of given folders for objects that match predefined criteria; for matching objects, an agent can create links in a new folder that thus functions like a temporary result relation. Finally, hypertext features can also be supported based on the inter-object links. Agents can be defined that perform automatic link following and that may also generate new links.

Altogether, the system provides numerous possibilities for implementing higher-level cooperative office applications. However, the model seems to be limited as far as the possible complexity of office problems is concerned; more complex solutions may require additional conventional programming effort. Efficiency considerations may also give rise to a need for the application of more conventional programming techniques.

**Technology support:** The system makes use of simple e-mail-based message passing. It adds presentation layer services to this approach; objects are automatically converted into a universal transmission format that can also be applied between heterogeneous systems. Based on advanced distributed object-oriented techniques, the functionality can be enhanced. For example, references to remote objects can be passed easily and can be exploited for follow-on invocations. The e-mail interaction mechanism can also be augmented with directory service support for locating distant peer systems.

Documents are modeled by a system-specific approach; standards are not applied here. Concurrent document management is enabled by the agent approach; an agent can access documents jointly with other agents and higher-level cooperation mechanisms can be implemented on top. Modest database support is exploited for persistent object and folder storage.

## 8.6 Office Procedures: IPSO Model

As an example of a complex office procedure approach, we discuss the author's *IPSO model* [SCH91] that has already been mentioned in chapter 2. The approach aims at automating well-structured office tasks. A task or office procedure consists of a set of sequential and concurrent *basic service requests* that are represented by a pre-defined *execution graph*. An example of an execution graph for travel expense processing was given in figure 2-12 of chapter 2; a more detailed representation is shown in figure 8-6.

At runtime, the graph is interpreted in a distributed way; each service request is mapped to a server of a distributed office system. After having completed a basic service execution, the office procedure (an object representing it) is forwarded to the site of the subsequent service. This is repeated until the whole execution graph has been processed.

The approach offers a high-level, declarative notation to specify the execution graph of a given office procedure and to define the service and server environment. Runtime execution is based on a distributed object-oriented system. Servers, office procedure instances, and their data attachments are modeled as objects with location-independent invocation facilities. Office procedure objects are mobile; they move between the server sites during office procedure execution.

**Example of execution graph specification:** The following example specifies the execution graph of the travel expense processing office procedure. First, a data object, the travel expense form, is declared as an attachment. Thereafter, the different basic service requests and their logical interrelationships are defined:

```
DATA f: TravelExpenseForm;  // data object of pre-defined type

SERVICE FillExpenseForm START                                   // initial activity
  LINKS_TO InsertManagementData, InsertProjectData;             // parallel
SERVICE InsertManagementData                                    // alternative
  LINKS_TO Approve IF f.costs > 100 AND f.costs <= 5000;
           RefundExpenses IF f.costs <= 100;
           ToplevelManagerNotification IF f.costs > 5000;
SERVICE InsertProjectData, Approve, ToplevelManagerNotification // n:1 link
  LINKS_TO RefundExpenses;
SERVICE RefundExpenses LINKS_TO PrintDocuments;
SERVICE PrintDocuments OPTIONAL END;                 // final service (optional)
```

After *InsertManagementData* has been executed, a condition is evaluated to guide further execution. Depending on the costs recorded on the attached form, different subsequent services are executed. Very low costs do not require approval, and very high costs require a top-level manager notification. The last service is optional; for example, it is possible to decide interactively about its execution. A service request can be augmented with attributes as shown below; the *PrintDocuments* service should be completed within 30 minutes (keyword *TIMEOUT*); otherwise, an exception is signaled at the server. In addition, the server to be selected must have the format attribute *PostScript* (keyword *ATTRIBUTES*). The server selection is based on *MEASURES* that are calculated based on the pre-defined printing costs and the estimated waiting time (depending on the input queue).

```
SERVICE PrintDocuments
 TIMEOUT: 30 minutes REMIND;                  // execution time control
 ATTRIBUTES: Format = PostScript;             // required attribute of the service
 MEASURES: 0.8 * PrintCosts+ 0.2 * ExpectedWaitingTime;   // for server selection
```

**Specification of service and server environment:** A small example that illustrates the notation to specify basic services and servers is shown below. Several services can be offered by a *server type*. The server type can have attributes which match service request attributes. In addition, status enquiry methods can be provided to be invoked remotely by control stations. A server instance specification is based on existing server types and can include a placement specification.

```
SERVER_TYPE PrintServer                                        // type definition
 SERVICES PrintDocuments                                       // service interface
  (d: SET OF Document, OPTIONAL ControlData, OUT Status);
 ATTRIBUTES Format = PostScript, PrintCosts = 100;             // service-specific attributes
 STATUS_INQUIRY ExpectedWaitingTime, Availability;  // status enquiry methods
END_SERVER_TYPE

SERVER Printer_1: PrintServer;                                 // instance definition
  ALLOCATION: Host_A;                                          // placement specification
END_SERVER
```

In our example, a print server type and instance offering the service *PrintDocuments* are defined; this service has been requested within the execution graph shown above.

**Execution model:** The overall office procedure execution consists of the phases of initiation, main execution, and termination (see figure 8-6). Within the *initiation phase*, an office procedure object is created and attached data objects are initialized by a control station. The office procedure is then submitted to the first execution server.

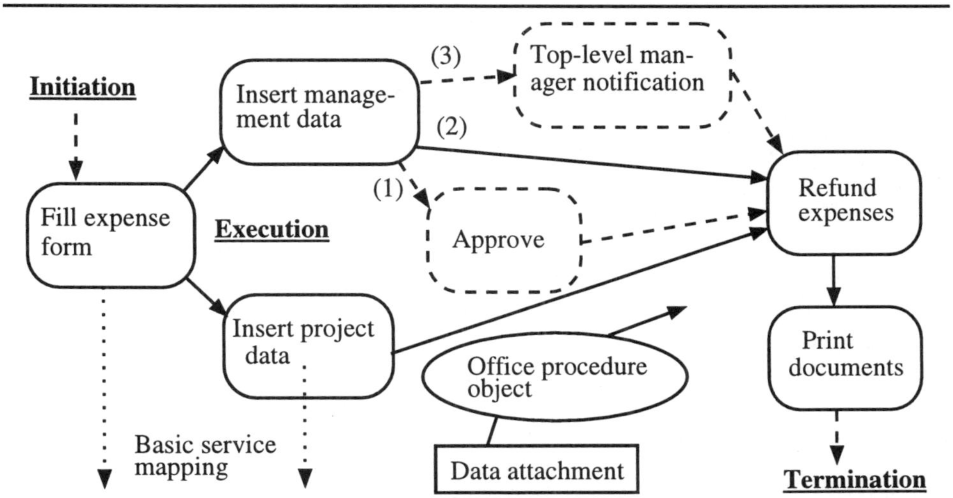


Fig. 8-6 Office procedure execution model

Within the *main execution phase*, several steps are executed repeatedly for each service: the execution graph is analyzed for conditional and parallel paths in order to determine the next service(s) to be performed; in the figure, the services that are not executed due to condition evaluation are shown with dotted lines. After a service has completed, the next server(s) is/are determined by contacting a directory service and evaluating the service request attributes (basic service mapping; indicated by vertical dotted arrows in the figure). The office procedure and attached data are then shipped to the selected server site(s) (by object migration); in the figure, the objects are currently moved from a site executing *InsertProjectData* to a site perfoming *RefundExpenses*. Then, the service is invoked and attached data objects can be accessed by the server. Afterward, these steps are repeated until the final service is completed.

In the *termination phase*, the initiator of the office procedure is notified and the result data are stored according to a pre-defined termination section of the office procedure specification.

Office procedures can be supervised by control stations. A set of remote control commands are offered for this. Existing office procedures can be globally retrieved by logical names, specific office procedures can then be analyzed concerning their execution history (e.g. list of visited servers) or concerning their current location, attached data can be accessed remotely, and continuous monitoring can be requested; in this case, a control station is always notified by an event whenever an office procedure moves to a new server.

**Technology support:** The approach is based on a distributed object-oriented system; it uses location-independent object invocation for service calls, and object migration for forwarding office procedure objects. A simplified prototype has actually been implemented with a distributed extension of C++ on top of the RPC of the OSF Distributed Computing Environment. An object invocation is mapped to an RPC; however, the mechanism for locating mobile objects extends the RPC approach significantly.

For basic service mapping, a dedicated directory service has been built; as an alternative, a simple mapping functionality could have been implemented with DCE's Cell Directory Service, too. Viewed from a different perspective, the type of service mapping provided can even be classified as a trading service due to complex attribute evaluations and due to querying of dynamic parameters like server availability. A document model has not been used in the small prototype; however, the approach could easily be extended to incorporate transfer of standardized documents, e.g. using ODA/ODIF. The same holds for database and multimedia support. In fact, within a related IBM project named *Business Procedures*, an object-oriented database (*ObjectManager*) has been used to manage persistently the data objects involved in an office procedure.

## 8.7 Multimedia Document Storage: MULTOS

Finally, the *MULTOS* system [MRT91], developed within a European ESPRIT project, is an example of a database for multimedia documents. The approach is not a typical CSCW application but more a kind of enabling technology; nevertheless, we discuss it here as it exploits other technological foundations and offers mechanisms for remotely accessing shared documents within higher-level CSCW applications.

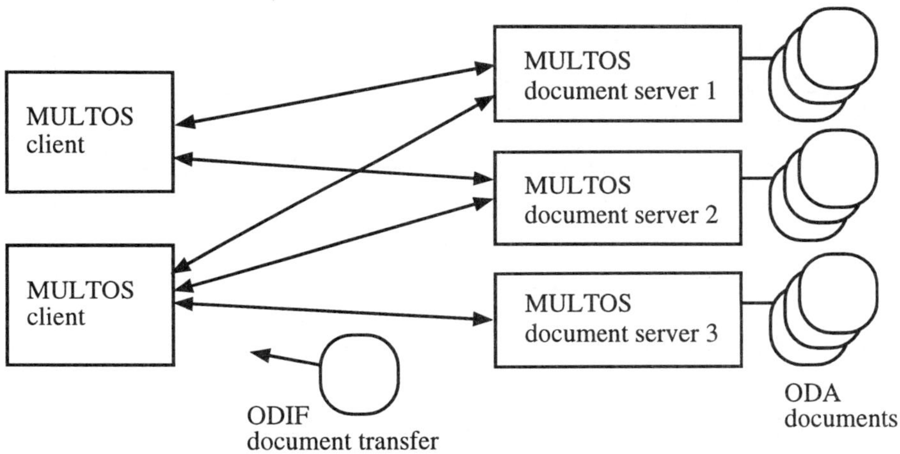


Fig. 8-7 MULTOS architecture

**System characteristics and architecture:** MULTOS supports storage of complex multimedia documents on various physical media. As already discussed in section 7.5.4, it also enables content-based queries. The system supports all media discussed in chapter 7 except video. As its document model it uses ODA, augmented with multimedia support and with a conceptual model for representing document content semantics.

The system is based on a distributed client/server architecture (see figure 8-7; compare also [BCG90]). Multiple clients can access multiple servers using RDA-style interactions (see section 6.4). Documents and their components are transferred between servers and clients using the ODIF representation.

**Document server structure:** Each document server consists of several components and processes as shown in figure 8-8. The *dialog manager* is responsible for handling all client/server communication; for example, it receives query requests from a client, forwards them to the *server controller* process, and finally sends the results back to the client. The *status broadcaster* informs clients periodically about the actual availability of the server, and about server status parameters like the amount of free storage. Based on this information, a client can decide whether to contact a given server or use an alternative server. However, the servers do not implement a full distributed database functionality with features such as transparent document replication. Therefore, a client may actually be dependent on a specific server that stores particular documents.

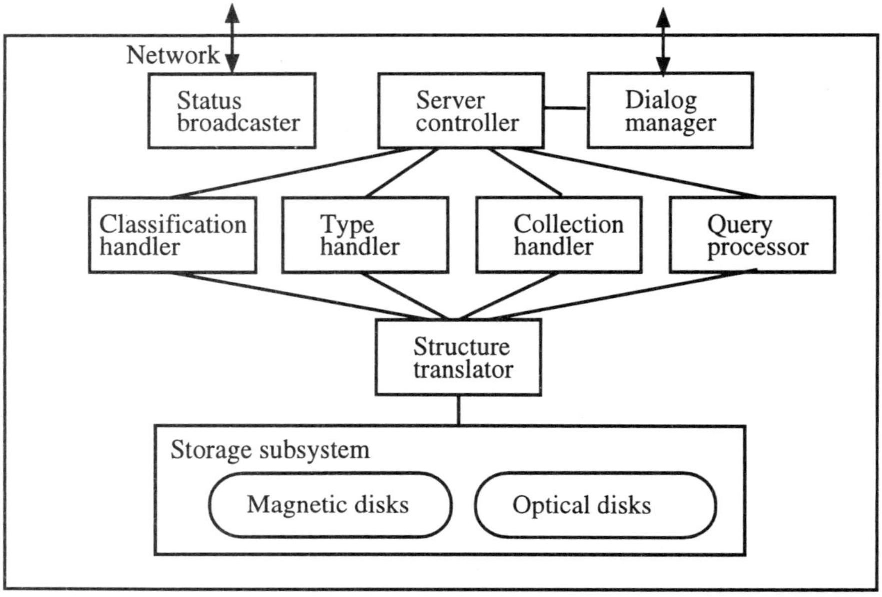


Fig. 8-8 MULTOS server structure

Depending on the type of request, the server controller process contacts different peer processes. Conventional and content-based queries are served by the *query processor*; it checks queries for correctness and performs query optimization during execution. The *collection handler* supports operations on document groups or collections, for example browsing or set-oriented queries. Document collections can be established explicitly, for example to manage all documents of a specific project. The *type handler* manages document type definitions (according to the ODA generic structures) and supports operations on document types, for example structural queries. The *classification handler* is responsible for managing the conceptual document structures mentioned above. More concretely, a conceptual structure is an explicit representation of document content semantics. For text documents, it might be given by a list of keywords. For images of limited complexity, the conceptual structure can be generated by image analysis, for example by extracting well-known graphical symbols.

The *structure translator* corresponds to the interface between the storage subsystem layer and the media integration layer discussed in section 7.5.3. It maps

ODA documents and their components onto internal storage formats of the *storage subsystem*. Different physical storage media are supported; for example, both magnetic and optical disks are integrated into the storage subsystem. The structure translator also maps basic query and storage commands onto the storage systems. To perform an efficient mapping, access paths based on B-trees for conventional data and on signatures for image and audio data are exploited.

**Technology support:** The system makes use of an RPC-style interaction mechanism between clients and servers, and provides a message-based document transmission facility. More important, the whole approach is based on ODA for document modeling, using ODIF as the document transfer representation. Shared document access during cooperative work is possible; however, it is based on a more conventional locking approach. Advanced database support - including content-based multimedia retrieval - is provided by the system itself. Moreover, concerning multimedia, some of the modeling techniques for complex multimedia objects as discussed in chapter 7 are exploited.

## 8.8 Exercises

1. [Conceptual design / basic knowledge]
Which techniques of chapter 7 would be required to extend the described Etherphone approach to digital audio? Consider in particular synchronization, communication, and storage aspects.
2. [Basic knowledge]
Explain the functionality of the Conference Manager and of the Audiovisual Manager of the Multimedia Collaboration system.
3. [Conceptual design]
The CES document editing system updates the screens of remote users when a section is modified at a given site. How could this update task benefit from atomic broadcast as described in chapter 3? Which properties would result in the case of node and network failures?
4. [Conceptual design]
The Intermedia system stores all link information at a central database server. Which problems may result from that concerning performance and fault tolerance? Outline a coarse-grained design for a more decentralized approach based on a distributed object-oriented system as discussed in chapter 3. Represent links as explicit objects and use location-independent invocation for link following.
5. [Conceptual design]
Based on chapter 6, design a C++-based object-oriented database schema for the major ObjectLens entities, i.e. for folders, semi-structured objects, and semi-autonomous agents. Consider that folders contain objects, that semi-structured objects may contain arbitrary text portions, and that agents may have rules that

involve objects and folders. The rules themselves should be represented as regular unstructured text; rule interpretation is outside the scope of this design.

6. [Conceptual design]
Specify the routing graph of the office procedure example of exercise 8 in chapter 2 (introduction of a new product into a company) using the notation of the IPSO approach. Detail one service request more precisely according to the example given in this chapter.

7. [Basic knowledge]
Describe the execution path of typical MULTOS multimedia database operations based on the server components of the system: the first operation stores a new image that also has to be classified; the second operation issues a content-based query against the database in order to retrieve a specific image.

## 8.9 References

[ADH93] Altenhofen, M., Dittrich, J., Hammerschmidt, R., Käppner, T., Kruschel, C., Kückes, A., Steinig, T.: The BERKOM Multimedia Collaboration Service; *ACM Conf. on Multimedia, 1993*

[BCG90] Berra, P.B., Chen, C.Y., Ghafoor, A., Lin, C.C., Little, T.D., Shin, D.: Architecture for Distributed Multimedia Database Systems; *Computer Communications, Vol. 13, No. 4, May 1990, pp. 217-230*

[GRW92] Greif, I., Seliger, R., Weihl, W.: A Case Study of CES: A Distributed Collaborative Editing System Implemented in Argus; *IEEE Trans. on Software Engineering, Vol. 18, No. 9, Sept. 1992, pp. 827-839*

[HKR92] Haan, B.J., Kahn, P., Riley, V.A., Coombs, J.H., Meyrowitz, N.K.: IRIS Hypermedia Services; *Comm. of the ACM, Vol. 35, No. 1, Jan. 1992, pp. 36-51*

[LMY88] Lai, K.-Y., Malone, T.W., Yu, K.-C.: ObjectLens: A Spreadsheet for Cooperative Work; *ACM Trans. on Office Information Systems, Vol. 6, No. 4, Oct. 1988, pp. 332-353*

[MRT91] Meghini, C., Rabitti, F., Thanos, C.: Conceptual Modeling of Multimedia Documents; *IEEE Computer, Vol. 24, No. 10, Oct. 1991, pp. 23-30*

[SCH91] Schill, A.: Distributed System and Execution Model for Office Environments; *Computer Communications, Vol. 14, No. 8, Oct. 1991, pp. 478-488*

[VZS91] Vin, H.M., Zellweger, P.T., Swinehart, D.C., Rangan, P.V.: Multimedia Conferencing in the Etherphone Environment; *Computer, Vol. 24, No. 10, Oct. 1991, pp. 69-79*

[YHM88] Yamkelovich, N., Haan, B., Meyrowitz, N., Drucker, S.: Intermedia: The Concept and the Construction of a Seamless Information Environment; *IEEE Computer, Vol. 21, No. 1, 1988, pp. 81-96*

# 9 Conclusion

Having presented examples of cooperative office systems and having given an extensive discussion of their technological foundations, we conclude this book with an overall summary and try to outline potential future trends in the area of cooperative office environments.

## 9.1 Summary

As we have shown throughout this book, cooperative office systems cover many different areas, ranging from multiuser document editors and conference support to hypermedia environments and complex distributed activity coordination systems. These are only a few examples of the broad domain; many other approaches can be imagined and some of them can actually already be found in today's research and development labs - consider emerging virtual reality approaches, for example. All these systems and applications have two important characteristics in common:

- They provide support for cooperatively working toward a common goal.
- They make heavy use of enabling technology from various areas.

The first issue was discussed in chapter 2 and illustrated in chapter 8; it is the basic motivation for introducing and for actually using cooperative office systems in real-world environments. Moreover, the notion of cooperation is actually the feature that distinguishes such approaches from conventional computerized office systems; such systems either have enabled single-user office work (consider conventional spreadsheets or text-processing systems), or they have supported strictly controlled exclusive access to shared resources in multiuser environments (consider conventional database systems and transactions). In contrast, cooperative office systems as discussed in this book enable information and activity sharing based on a much wider range of cooperation paradigms and offer much greater higher-level functionality.

The second issue - technological support - was the subject of chapters 3 to 7 and is a vital issue for building and for understanding cooperative office systems. Most technological approaches discussed in this book are found in almost all emerging cooperative office environments. Distributed systems techniques enable physical distribution of office activities while maintaining global interconnectivity and interoperability; the latter features are a major prerequisite for systemwide cooperation. Document standards and document management techniques are concerned with the data part of cooperative office systems - they support computerized document modeling, distributed document interchange, and shared document manipulation. Database techniques augment this area with persistent storage and transaction and query support for documents but also for all other kinds of office data. Moreover, multimedia techniques are a prerequisite for natural modeling of all kinds of real-world data and for offering more user-friendly environments. Their impact is found within all kinds of supporting technology. Some final messages of this book are the following:

- Cooperative office systems offer a functionality which is interesting, rich, and important in practise.
- Such systems are difficult to build, requiring in-depth knowledge of a broad range of technological foundations.
- The whole area has only just begun to emerge; for researchers and for practitioners, it is vital to keep track of the current rapid development of the field and to be aware of the increasing movement of research-level solutions into actual products.

The contents of this book constitute merely a structured snapshot of the current status in the cooperative office systems domain. In the final section, we attempt to project this snapshot a small step into the future.

## 9.2 Future Trends

As mentioned above, the cooperative office systems area is emerging rapidly. This move is guided by several developments:

- *Application demands:* There is an increasing demand for cooperative office solutions stated by end users. For example, many companies are attempting partial automation of their office tasks and are looking for new CSCW solutions; shared access to documents and other office data is becoming a common requirement; and conference and group decision support systems are already used within larger, physically distributed companies. This evolution leads to new product demands, and it also generates incentives to turn prototype-level solutions into actual products.
- *Technological evolution:* The second supporting development is the rapid evolution taking place in the enabling technology. Examples are high-performance networks, standardized distributed application platforms, multimedia document support, emerging object-oriented and federated database solutions, and general techniques for managing high-capacity, time-dependent multimedia data. This makes it feasible to develop complex CSCW products with an acceptable performance, and, more important, it opens the field to numerous new application areas.
- *Research activities:* Finally, researchers are always curious to work in new fields. For those involved in CSCW research, this means that the approaches described in this book will be outstripped by much more far-reaching solutions in the near future. Examples are new artificial intelligence techniques

for managing weakly-structured office tasks, global multimedia support for documents, office activities, and personal interactions, and distributed multimedia-based virtual reality systems for modeling decentralized office environments with thousands of nodes in an integrated way. Research will actually be the leading force in opening the field to such new domains.

It is a difficult and vague task to speculate upon such developments, and we do not attempt any arbitrary, non-technical speculations here. However, some developments guided by the technological evolution can already be foreseen today in a relatively concrete way:

*High-performance network support:* New networks like ATM/B-ISDN, as discussed in chapter 7, will soon be commonplace. Most importantly, they offer the transmission rates necessary for high-capacity multimedia data transfer, and they also provide other relevant quality-of-service characteristics, such as isochronous traffic support. Therefore, widely distributed multimedia systems could soon become a reality. Moreover, other distributed applications that were not practicable due to performance limitations will also be enabled by such networks - consider complex distributed algorithms, widely distributed information systems, or distributed multiuser interactions in realtime. Communication speed will even increase from about 100 Mbits/s in today's high-performance networks to several gigabits per second - research prototypes with these characteristics already exist today. Moreover, new mobile communication networks will evolve, also supporting increasing communication speeds.

*Standardized distributed environments:* Networks alone are by no means sufficient - they provide basic connectivity but not application-level interoperability. With the advent of standardized distributed environments such as OSF's Distributed Computing Environment or OMG's Object Management Architecture, global application-level interoperability in heterogeneous distributed systems becomes a reality. For cooperative office systems, this means that it becomes easier to build them in a distributed way, that the underlying platforms can actually be heterogeneous, and that new communication technology can be incorporated without difficulty; for example, an RPC application is hardly affected when the underlying transport protocol or physical network technology changes. Even higher-level mechanisms such as distributed transactions become available as products based on industry standards.

*New document standards:* As discussed in this book, existing document standards are being extended to multimedia and hypermedia. This makes it possible to interchange arbitrary multimedia documents within cooperative office systems. This way, almost all CSCW applications can benefit and enhance their functionality. Moreover, hypermedia systems will be based on standards and will therefore be globally interoperable.

*Emerging storage technology:* Conventional magnetic disks are already accompanied by optical storage systems today. In the near future, much more far-reaching perspectives can become reality; huge-capacity optical storage media in the order of terabits may become arbitrarily writeable, and disk access times will be reduced further. Main memory capacities will increase in parallel into the gigabit range. This will open the field for new multimedia databases, and also for very efficient in-memory databases (with much of the database content cached in main memory). The field of multimedia CSCW applications can be enhanced in this way by providing fast-access, persistent digital storage for all media. Moreover, CSCW applications based on conventional media will benefit from improved storage access performance.

*New database technology:* With the introduction of new object-oriented and of emerging federated databases into the marketplace, modeling and processing facilities of databases are being improved significantly. Object-oriented databases support integrated modeling, storage, and retrieval of complex objects - an issue that is very important for office documents but also for all other office data with nested structure. Federated databases extend distributed systems and database technology with facilities for heterogeneous database integration - an issue of major importance in large office systems with heterogeneous equipment.

Other developments that will have impact on cooperative office systems are advanced user interface and interaction paradigms, new operating systems architectures and services, and new processor hardware, including parallel processing environments. It can be anticipated that performance, modeling capacities, user-friendliness, and general functionality of cooperative office systems will be improved significantly based on such approaches.

We would like to encourage the reader to keep track of these developments, to engage in the use of new cooperative office paradigms, and to promote the overall field in academia and practise.

# Index

# The Venomous Reptiles of Latin America

# The Venomous Reptiles of Latin America

JONATHAN A. CAMPBELL and WILLIAM W. LAMAR

*Department of Biology, The University of Texas at Arlington*



Comstock Publishing Associates | A DIVISION OF CORNELL UNIVERSITY PRESS
ITHACA AND LONDON

First published 1989 by Cornell University Press.

*Library of Congress Cataloging-in-Publication Data*

Campbell, Jonathan A.
The venomous reptiles of Latin America / Jonathan A. Campbell, William W. Lamar.
p. cm.
Bibliography: p.
Includes index.
ISBN 0-8014-2059-8
1. Poisonous snakes—Latin America. 2. Poisonous animals—Latin America. 3. Reptiles—Latin America. I. Lamar, William W., 1950– . II. Title.
QL665.C36 1989
597.96'0469'098—dc19 88-47934

Printed in the United States of America.
Color and black-and-white plates printed in Hong Kong.

*The paper in this book is acid-free and meets the guidelines for permanence and durability of the Committee on Production Guidelines for Book Longevity of the Council on Library Resources.*

# Contents

# Tables

# Preface

There has long been a need for a comprehensive work dealing with the venomous reptiles that inhabit Latin America. This group of reptiles is important for medical reasons, and to most people—layperson and herpetologist alike—it represents a fascinating component of the animal world.

The goals of this book are modest: (1) to facilitate the identification of various reptile species of the region that are potentially dangerous, (2) to describe these species and to delimit their distributions, (3) to provide a broad overview of the various kinds of natural habitats found in the countries south of the United States, and (4) to present information relevant to the treatment of human envenomation. Knowledge of which species probably occur in a given region may allow some caution to be exercised by anyone undertaking certain activities or entering particular habitats.

The geographic scope of this work includes the New World tropics as well as the temperate regions of Mexico and Argentina; thus we encompass all of what is known as Latin America. The term Latin America refers to those parts of the Americas that lie south of the United States; it does not imply that all its inhabitants are of Latin origin. Almost all of the venomous reptile species that occur in the United States and Canada occur also in Latin America. With very little effort, we could have expanded this book to "The Venomous Reptiles of the Americas." We chose not to do so primarily for two reasons. First, both of us have spent considerable time in Latin America conducting field studies (more than 20 years, collectively), and we think it prudent to emphasize the area we know best and to which we can perhaps make the greatest contribution. Second, the lands north of Mexico are well known herpetologically and are adequately covered in a number of sources.

The assembling and synthesis of all the materials that have gone into the preparation of this book have at times been tedious, frustrating, and maddening. We have engaged most of our spare time over the past 12 months in its production; nevertheless, we have come away with a heightened interest in and appreciation for these reptiles. Because circumstances have combined to create significant obstacles to conducting fieldwork in Latin America, and this at a time when critical habitats are vanishing before they can even be identified, it is only through the collective concern of many individuals that crucial data (specimens, photographs, field notes) can be obtained. It is our hope that this book will stimulate such activities, enabling us to reduce the mystery that still surrounds the venomous reptiles of Latin America. If we accomplish nothing else but to encourage others to learn more about this subject, we will have succeeded beyond any of our original goals.

Many individuals assisted us in some way during the preparation of this manuscript, and we attempt here to acknowledge all of them. Regrettably, there probably are omissions, and for this we apologize.

We thank particularly Edmund D. Brodie, Jr., Chairman of the Department of Biology at The University of Texas at Arlington; without his support this project could not have been completed. Among the curators and staff who kindly allowed us access to many collections, we are especially grateful to Charles W. Myers, American Museum of Natural History (AMNH); Edmund V. Malnate, Academy of Natural Sciences of Philadelphia (ANSP); C. J. McCoy, the Carnegie Museum (CM); Hymen Marx and Robert F. Inger, Field Museum of Natural History (FMNH); William E. Duellman, Darrel R. Frost, and John E. Simmons, Museum of Natural History, University of Kansas (KU); John W. Wright and Robert L. Bezy, Los Angeles County Museum of Natural History (LACM); Douglas A. Rossman, Louisiana State University Museum of Zoology (LSUMZ); Pere Alberch, Ernest E. Williams, and José Rosado, Museum of Comparative Zoology, Harvard University (MCZ); Harry W. Greene, Museum of Vertebrate Zoology, University of California at Berkeley (MVZ); Arnold Kluge and Ronald A. Nussbaum, University of Michigan Museum of Zoology (UMMZ); and W. Ronald Heyer, Roy W. McDiarmid, and Ronald I. Crombie, National Museum of Natural History, Smithsonian Institution (USNM). We have been particularly fortunate to have been associated with the University of Texas at Arlington Collection of Vertebrates (UTA), and its ample facilities have been made fully available to us.

Drs. George Watt and David L. Hardy generously responded to questions concerning the clinical effects of venom and graciously prepared the sections relevant to snakebite which bear their names.

Our forays into the literature consistently benefited from the exhaustive bibliographies compiled by Hobart M. Smith, Rozella B. Smith, and Paulo E. Vanzolini. Portions of the manuscript were reviewed by Augusto Shinya Abe, Charles M. Bogert, Darrel R. Frost, Harry W. Greene, Roy W. McDiarmid, James B. Murphy, Douglas A. Rossman, Ivan Sazima, and Norman J. Scott. Their comments and criticisms have been helpful. However, any mistakes in logic or fact assuredly remain our responsibility.

We acknowledge the following individuals who have assisted us by providing specimens, locality data, literature, translations, or other favors: Kraig K. Adler, Anthony Alexander, Aida Luz Aquino, David G. Barker, Paolo Bettella, David Blody and the staff of the Fort Worth Zoological Park, Hans Boos, Julius Boos, Robert Burleson, Ed Chapman, Jr., Linda Chapman, Joseph T. Collins, Roger Conant, Jack Cover, Ronald I. Crombie, John L. Darling, John de Bruin, James R. Dixon, Maureen A. Donnelly, Lee Fitzgerald, Marcos A. Freiberg, Antonio Freire L., Darrel R. Frost, Charles M. Fugler, Anthony Garel, Stephan Gorzula, Kenneth L. Gosner, Rick Green, David L. Hardy, Marinus S. Hoogmoed, Ken Hovey, Germán A. Ibarra, Riena Kondo, Victor Kondo, Ligia Krause, Enrique La Marca, Lionel Landry, David Lazcano, Jean-Claude LeJosne, Mark J. Lucas, Mark M. Lucas, C. J. McCoy, Hugh K. McCrystal, Roy W. McDiarmid, Sherman A. Minton, Joep M. Moonen, James B. Murphy and the staff of the Dallas Zoo, Peter Nguyen, R. Andrew Odum, Alfredo Paolillo, Louis Porras, William F. Pyburn, Hugh Quinn and the staff of the Houston Zoological Gardens, Miguel T. Rodrigues, Aldemaro Romero, José Rosado, Richard Sage, Jay K. Salser, Jay M. Savage, Ivan Sazima, Norman J. Scott, Augusto Shinya Abe, John E. Simmons, Eric N. Smith, Jim Stout, Christine Strüssmann, John H. Tashjian, Mac Tidwell, Jay P. Vannini, Ernest Wagner, John E. Werler, Anne V. Winter, John W. Wright, and Claudio Zamprogno.

The breadth of photographic coverage in the book exceeds our initial expectations, and such a pleasant situation would not have existed without the enthusiastic generosity of the following contributors: Albertus Abuys, Federico Achával, Rudolf Arndt, David G. Barker, Richard D. Bartlett, Charles M. Bogert, Hans Boos, Julius Boos, Jim Bridges, Edmund D. Brodie, Jr., T. L. Brown, John de Bruin, Benjamín Busto, John E. Cadle, Ed Cassano, Fernando Castro, Joseph T. Collins, Jack Cover, Ronald I. Crombie, David M. Dennis, James R. Dixon, William E. Duellman, William A. Dunson, Michael Franzen, Paul Freed, Marcos A. Freiberg, Saul Friess, Thomas H. Fritts, Robert Godshalk, Stephan Gorzula, George Grall, Harry W. Greene, Paul Gritis, Robert W. Hansen, David L. Hardy, Dennis M. Harris, Terry L. Hibbitts, David M. Hillis, Marinus S. Hoogmoed, Peter Janzen, Ligia Krause, Gerhard Kuehnhanss, Enrique La Marca, Abdem Ramón Lancini, the late F. Carlos Lehmann, Thales de Lema, Ernest A. Liner, John D. Lynch, the late Scott J. Maness, Peter P. Marra, Ricardo Martori, Hymen Marx, Gerald Marzec, James R. McCranie, Roy W. McDiarmid, Brian Mealey, Ute Meede, Anibal Melgarejo, Sherman A. Minton, the late Kenneth Miyata, Joep M. Moonen, John C. Murphy, Charles W. Myers, Lawrence E. Naylor, Janet Nehrbass, R. Andrew Odum, Dennis Paulson, Dieter Pfistner, Louis Porras, Ken Preston-Mafham, William F. Pyburn, Juan Manuel Renjifo, Miguel Rodrigues, Janis A. Roze, Fernando Sandner-Montilla, Ivan Sazima, Thomas S. Schulenberg, Norman J. Scott, Gustavo Scrocchi, John E. Simmons, Pekka Soini, Pascual Soriano, Gail Stone, John H. Tashjian, Ismael diTada, Ludwig Trutnau, R. Wayne Van Devender, Terry Vandeventer, John Visser, Laurie J. Vitt, Richard C. Vogt, Harold Voris, Enrique Yústiz, and Barbara Zimmerman.

The photographic expertise of Edward Watkins and Mary Jones of Slides Unlimited, Inc., Dallas, Texas, resulted in illustrations of consistently high quality. Uncredited photographs were taken by us.

We were fortunate to have the skilled services of Ty Kubin and Clay M. Garrett, who executed the line drawings. Linda Bigham and Pamela Temple stoically and competently attended to many of the typing chores associated with the various drafts of the manuscript.

The topographic map of Mexico is redrawn and modified from *Atlas of Mexico* by Stanley A. Arbingast et al. (1975) with permission of the Bureau of Business Research, The University of Texas at Austin, copyright 1975, Board of Regents, The University of Texas System. The vegetation map of Mexico is redrawn and modified from *Wildlife of Mexico* by A. Starker Leopold (1959) with permission of the University of California Press. The vegetation map of South America is redrawn and modified from "Vegetation Map of South America," 1:5,000,000 (1980) with permission of UNESCO.

Several individuals were especially helpful throughout the course of our writing; all of them graciously responded to our repeated requests for advice, data, or materials and thus made the task more pleasant. Accordingly, we thank Edmund D. Brodie, Jr., Ronald I. Crombie, James R. Dixon, Roy W. McDiarmid, Anibal Melgarejo, Louis Porras, Ivan Sazima, and John H. Tashjian.

Two herpetologists whose comments on the manuscript would have been a source of delight and chagrin to us both unfortunately passed away before they could exercise the opportunity. It was our good fortune to have benefited from the tutelage and support of Federico Medem and L. C. Stuart, and our approach to herpetology will always be a product of their influence.

Production costs for this book were defrayed in part by the Herpetologists' League. To its officers, especially Roy W. McDiarmid, we are grateful.

The inconveniences, irritations, and scheduling constraints inherent in producing lengthy publications are nowhere felt more than by loved ones. Our wives, Tanya G. Dowdey and Nancy F. Lamar, have endured all of these while managing to maintain the bonds of matrimony. For them we reserve our deepest thanks, with apologies for ever having thought such gestures cliché.

Jonathan A. Campbell and William W. Lamar

*The University of Texas at Arlington*
*Arlington, Texas*

# The Venomous Reptiles of Latin America

# Introduction

The venomous reptiles of Latin America include a great number of species and some systematically complex groups. We recognize herein a total of 145 species of dangerously venomous snakes in Latin America. Of these, 55 species are proteroglyphs (coral snakes and sea snakes), and the remainder are solenoglyphs (lanceheads, bushmaster, rattlesnakes, and other pitvipers). Much work remains to be done before any reasonably complete systematic or ecological picture may emerge for many of these species or groups of species.

Contrary to centuries of lurid tales, however, the tropics are not a haven for great numbers of individual snakes. In fact, with some local exceptions, snakes are uncommon in Latin America. The richness of snake species is quite another matter; there are many more kinds of snakes in tropical areas than there are in temperate zones, but members of most species tend not to exist in great numbers.

The varied snake fauna of Latin America includes some of the smallest (blind snakes) and some of the largest (boas and anacondas) species—the majority of which are inoffensive. Like all animals, snakes prefer to stay out of harm's way, and thus are not likely to engage in aggression toward humans. As a means of escaping detection, many snakes resort to simply remaining still until danger has passed, their shape and coloration allowing them to blend with their surroundings.

The primary function of snake venom is to aid in obtaining prey; of secondary importance is its role in defense. Bites are nearly always the result of accidental or careless contact, with the snake striking in response to pain or fear. Many accidents involve individuals who go out of their way to kill a snake. Reports of extreme aggression (on the part of the snake) are almost invariably exaggerated. It is important to remember that cases of snakebite that have received adequate first aid measures and subsequent medical treatment are almost never fatal. Venomous snakes inject their venom by means of a pair of hollow or grooved fangs (Figs. 19, 253) located at the front (or occasionally the rear) of the mouth. No snake is capable of stinging, nor can any Latin American snake "spit" its venom.

Harmless reptiles outnumber venomous species by a large margin in most parts of Latin America, both in number of species and overall abundance, and thus one is more likely to encounter an inoffensive variety. Many venomous species include rodents in their diets and hence are attracted to areas in which rats and mice abound. The propensity for humans to place garbage in close proximity to their living quarters provides an attraction for rats, mice, and often the snakes that seek them.

Although snake activity cycles may vary by season, by species, and by individual, some generalities still apply. Most lowland pitvipers tend to be nocturnal, venturing forth from their resting places to seek food after nightfall. Because temperatures in the highlands may fall drastically at night, many of the upland pitvipers are active by day. Coral snakes are less easy to characterize, and we have found them active at all hours. However, they seem to be discovered most often at dawn, at twilight, or after dark. Rainfall, temperature fluctuation, season, and numerous other factors can cause alterations in the trends just mentioned. Unless the identity of an individual is known with certainty, it is prudent to regard any snake encountered at any time as potentially venomous.

Collectively, Latin American venomous snakes can be found in nearly every kind of habitat. Coral snakes tend to stay on or under the ground, and many kinds occupy the leaf litter on forest floors. Not surprisingly, coral snakes are seldom encountered by humans. Lowland pitvipers often take shelter in brush piles or beneath debris at the bases of trees. Still others occupy a saxicolous habitat and live in crevices or under rocks. Consult the species accounts for more information.

## REGIONAL ACCOUNTS AND KEYS TO VENOMOUS SNAKES

The use of accent marks on names of countries and localities is largely a matter of individual preference. Advocates, writing in English, may be found who suggest their total abolition (Stuart, 1963), restricted or modified usage (Myers et al., 1978), or wholesale use (Wilson and Meyer, 1985). For this book we have followed the usage suggested by *Webster's New Geographical Dictionary* (1984 ed.) and have also used Rand McNally (1984) as a principal source of geographic information.

We have attempted to provide a brief description of the "lay of the land" that includes notes on the vegetation, physiography, and climate for each country. This may be useful to those who want not only to identify a particular species, but also to know something about where it lives. In preparing these accounts, we have profited from our field experience—which includes every mainland Latin American country except Argentina, Guyana, Suriname, and French Guiana.

We have not been totally consistent when describing different kinds of vegetation and have used various schemes for different countries. For example, we have found Leopold (1950) useful for delineating different habitats in Mexico and parts of northern Central America. In other parts of Central America we have used the Holdridge (1964) system of classification and the excellent series of maps that have been prepared for countries of the region using his system. For some of the South American countries we found the series of maps prepared by the Central Intelligence Agency or the vegetation map published by UNESCO (1981) useful. Regional works such as those prepared by the Instituto Geográfico "Augustín Codazzi" (1977a, 1977b, 1977c) for Colombia have been helpful.

Using multiple sources when dealing with the complex vegetation of the Neotropics may have its advantages because it has been pointed out that "we have yet to devise a systematic classification of forest types that we can apply uniformly from region to region. In other words, we have yet to learn how to describe these forests in consistent fashion" (N. Myers, 1984). It would have been inappropriate to have attempted a thorough zoogeographic treatise in this volume, as many systematic problems remain to be solved.

One of the most thankless and tedious tasks undertaken by systematists (but one for which there is an urgent need) is the assessment of geographic variation in wide-ranging species. In addition to elucidating fundamental biological principles, this type of study greatly facilitates our understanding of relationships among species and the construction of meaningful identification keys for a particular region. In constructing some of the identification keys we have resorted to using only the variation present in the particular population inhabiting the country under consideration. Therefore, the information contained in a species account may often encompass a far greater amount of variation than is evident in the keys. Unfortunately, for many species we do not have a clear picture of geographic variation, or we would have been able to differentiate more sharply among some of the species in the keys. We usually have made no effort to describe sexual dimorphism of certain characteristics such as the number of ventral and subcaudal scales; males generally average fewer of the former and more of the latter than females, although the amount of overlap is often considerable.

Many venomous snake species exhibit so much variability, especially over their total distribution, that finding a single, easily recognizable characteristic to distinguish among similar species is difficult. As a result, some species are multiple keyed, that is, they appear more than once in a particular key—not as tidy a situation as could be hoped for. This simply confirms the notion that a little ignorance goes a long way. We have, on occasion, found it desirable to reinforce characteristics given in the keys by recourse to distribution. We realize that in some instances the provenance of a preserved or captive specimen may not be known, and we have not used geographic characteristics by themselves.

Because animals do not recognize political boundaries, there is considerable overlap in the composition of the venomous reptile fauna for some countries, and portions of the identification keys may be redundant. However, we decided at the outset in preparing this book that this situation was preferable to the alternative, which would be to construct a single long key for all the venomous species that occur throughout Latin America. Although the preparation of such a key would be no more difficult (probably less so, actually) than what we present herein, to use a single key would require a considerably greater amount of expertise on the part of the user, and it would provide more opportunities for incorrect identifications.

To identify a snake, it is usually necessary to have the specimen at hand. We wish to emphasize, however, that one of the best ways we know of to prevent snakebite is to refrain from pursuing and attempting to kill every snake encountered in the field. Snakes, even venomous ones, should not be killed unless they present a real hazard or have been involved in an accident. One of the best ways to dispatch a snake is by a blow *behind* the head. If possible, try not to damage the head, as this may obscure features that will be helpful in identification. The surest way to establish whether a dead snake is dangerously venomous is to check for the presence of enlarged teeth (hollow fangs) on the front end of the maxillae (Figs. 19, 253). Some people may be reluctant to become this intimate with a snake, and for good reason. Common sense should prevail—make sure the snake is dead and do not use fingers to open a snake's mouth; that is usually easily accomplished by grasping a dead snake behind the head with forceps and using a probe to examine the inside of the mouth. Another feature that readily distinguishes the largest group of venomous reptiles in Latin America, the pitvipers, is the presence of a deep pit in the loreal region (on the side of the head behind the nostril but in front of the eye; see Figs. 133, 162, 264, 421).

A word of caution about species not covered in this book: in Latin America there are numerous so-called rear-fanged colubrid snakes. This term means, simply, that these snakes have several enlarged teeth on the posterior ends of the maxillae. These enlarged teeth often have grooves, which aid in conducting a mild toxin into their prey. Although members of this group of snakes are rarely dangerous to humans, individual reactions to bites from these snakes may vary greatly, and we know nothing of the venom of some species (see discussion in Snakebite Treatment and First Aid and in Mimics of Venomous Snakes).

Many persons are reluctant to use keys, complicated and technical as they may seem to the novice. Instead they proceed immediately to the photographs for the purpose of identification. Actually, the photographs, used in conjunction with the distribution maps, will frequently yield the correct identification for some of the more distinct species. However, photographs and maps are meant to be used as a supplement to, not in lieu of, the keys. The organization and use of a key can be clearly understood in a few minutes. Most keys are artificial and dichotomous—artificial in that they are not intended to reflect any phylogenetic patterns; dichotomous in that they are composed of a series of paired choices. To use a key, simply begin at the first couplet, select the more appropriate of the two choices, proceed to the next couplet indicated, and so on, until an identification is reached. (Most terms unfamiliar to the user are defined in the Glossary.) It is prudent to compare this tentative identification with the description, figures, and distribution map to help confirm if it is correct. The keys in this book are designed to aid in the identification of typical adult examples of a given species (living or recently so); as all variation cannot possibly be accounted for, judgment must be exercised. If a snake cannot be identified, it may be injected liberally throughout its length with a solution of 9 parts water to 1 part stock formalin (37%) and stored in a bottle containing the same liquid until it can be sent to a reputable museum or herpetologist for identification.

## GENERIC AND SPECIES ACCOUNTS

In any work dealing with a large number of poorly known species, taxonomic decisions must be made, even though systematics in itself may not be the main objective. We have made a number of these decisions based on our own opinions and the available literature. For example, we have recognized as full species populations that often are afforded only subspecific status (e.g., *Micrurus ruatanus*); we have reduced to subspecific rank some populations that usually are regarded as having attained full specific status (e.g., *Bothriopsis taeniata lichenosa, Crotalus durissus unicolor, C. d. vegrandis*); we have proposed new combinations, altering the current ideas concerning the relationships of some populations (e.g., *Crotalus molossus oaxacus*); we have tentatively recognized some species, but have questioned their validity (e.g., *Bothriopsis alticola, Bothrops roedingeri, B. xanthogrammus*); and we have placed a few names into the synonymy of others (e.g., *Bothriechis ornatus*). Still other species (e.g., *Bothrops eneydae, B isabelae, Crotalus pifanorum*) are considered too poorly described for diagnosis or synonymy. Our reasons for such actions are contained within the appropriate species accounts.

We have partitioned the large, widespread group of snakes previously placed in the genus *Bothrops* (*sensu lato*). As partitioned herein, five genera are recognized:

- *Bothriechis:* the palm-pitvipers; 7 species; mostly Central American in distribution, but 1 species ranging into northwestern South America.
- *Bothriopsis:* the forest-pitvipers; 8 species; mostly northern South American, but one species ranging into eastern Panama.
- *Bothrops (sensu stricto):* the lanceheads; 31 species; mostly South American, but 1 species widely distributed in Middle America (Mexico plus Central America).
- *Ophryacus:* the Mexican horned pitviper; 1 species; southern Mexican highlands (north of the Isthmus of Tehuantepec).
- *Porthidium:* the hognosed and montane pitvipers; 14 species; mostly Middle American but 3 species in northern South America.

Recognition of these five genera is not original with us, having been proposed by Burger in 1971 in a dissertation undertaken at the University of Kansas. This dissertation was never published, except in abstract form (Burger, 1972); because the published abstract neither defined nor gave the composition of these genera, this arrangement was not valid under the rules of the International Code of Zoological Nomenclature (Ride et al., 1985). Recently, however, in a rather shrewd action to validate the arrangement proposed by Burger, the portion of his dissertation that contains the keys with these genera was published verbatim by Pérez-Higareda, Smith, and Juliá-Zertuche (1985) in their description of *Porthidium olmec*. (Therefore, as these authors correctly point out, credit for this generic arrangement of Neotropical pitvipers should now be cited as Burger, in Pérez-Higareda et al., 1985.)

Our listings of local names are certainly not complete; widely distributed species often have many more names than we have been able to enumerate, many names undoubtedly remain unknown outside of restricted regions or tribes, and names we have included may be invalid or no longer in use. Nevertheless, knowledge of local names can be of great use to those working in particular regions. The name fer-de-lance, often employed outside of Latin America, is usually applied to *Bothrops asper* or *B. atrox*. This name was coined to apply to an Antillean species, *B. lanceolatus*, but is not used by native inhabitants of any Latin American country. We list names published previously as well as those we have encountered during fieldwork. Several words, often misapplied, enjoy especially wide usage in Latin America and are worth knowing by persons interested in venomous reptiles:

- *Cantil:* used widely in Middle America, refers to *Agkistrodon bilineatus* and often also to harmless species having a relatively large head such as cat-eyed snakes, genus *Leptodeira*.
- *Cascabel, cascabela, cascavel:* refers to the various species of rattlesnakes, genera *Crotalus* and *Sistrurus*; casabela muda means "mute rattlesnake" and refers to the bushmaster, *Lachesis muta*, which lacks a rattle. In Peru (especially the oriente), cascabel refers to juvenile *Bothrops*, owing perhaps to the pale tail tip.
- *Cobra:* Portuguese for any kind of snake.
- *Coral, coralillo, coralilla:* refers to almost any coral snake, genus *Micrurus*, or false coral snake with bright colors of red and/or yellow.
- *Cuatronarices:* Spanish, meaning "four nostrils," referring to the presence of paired nostrils plus a pair of loreal pits in pitvipers; this term is used in Mexico primarily for *Bothrops asper*, and in parts of South America for species such as *Bothriopsis punctata, B. taeniata*, and *Bothrops atrox*.
- *Culebra:* Spanish for any kind of snake.
- *Escorpión:* the name for both the Gila monster (*Heloderma suspectum*) and the beaded lizard (*H. horridum*) throughout their ranges in Latin America; however, this term is also widely used in reference to many

species of harmless lizards that are feared and presumed venomous by local inhabitants.

*Jararaca, jararacussu* (plus derivatives): general terms used in Brazil, Paraguay, and Argentina for many species of pitvipers but especially *Bothrops jararaca* and *B. jararacussu*, respectively. The name jararacussu is often applied to large specimens of any lancehead.

*Jergón:* applied to pitvipers in southeastern Colombia (*Porthidium hyoprora*) and eastern Peru (a variety of species).

*Mapanaré* (plus derivatives): general terms applied to *Bothrops asper*, *B. atrox*, and a variety of other venomous and nonvenomous species in Colombia and Venezuela.

*Nauyaca:* general term used in southern Mexico for many species of pitviper, including the eyelash palm-pitviper (*Bothriechis schlegelii*) and the terciopelo (*Bothrops asper*).

*Tamagás, tamagá:* general term used in Central America for many species of small to moderate-sized pitvipers of diverse genera, including *Bothriechis aurifer* (tamagás verde) and *Porthidium godmani*.

*Tommygoff:* probably a corruption of tamagás; used for several species of pitvipers in Belize, and in parts of Honduras for such species as *Bothriechis schlegelii* (green tommygoff) and *Porthidium nummifer* (jumping tommygoff).

*Víbora:* Spanish, meaning "viper," but often applied to nonviperid snakes as well.

Laypersons sometimes find common names easier to deal with than scientific names. However, for some species of Latin American snakes more than one name is in current use. We have selected only one name, the one we think is the most appropriate for whatever reason. In many instances we proposed an English name (although not necessarily in the English language) because there is not one in current use. There are many advantages to standardizing common names; hopefully, herpetological common names will someday reach the stability already achieved by ornithologists for common name usage. However, we are guilty of not strictly following the common names proposed for North American (U.S. and Canadian) species by Collins et al. (1982). Our reasons are succinctly pointed out by Rossman et al. (1978). Also, the use of the name eastern coral snake for *Micrurus fulvius* seems a little gringocentric considering all of the species of coral snakes, and we have thus adopted the name harlequin coral snake for this taxon. In cases where a local name is of widespread usage and has been employed often in the literature published in English, we suggest that the name be adopted as the standard name in English (e.g., cantil and terciopelo).

We have attempted to give as accurate and detailed a notion of the overall distribution of various species as permitted by the literature and museum specimens. In most instances we provide the first distribution maps available for a particular species. Future studies and field investigations will no doubt greatly alter our concepts of relationships and distributions of many of these species. No attempt has been made to delimit the distributions of venomous reptiles north of Mexico; a number of excellent field guides are readily available that cover the United States, including Conant (1975), Smith and Brodie (1982), and Stebbins (1985).

It is usually helpful to have some notion of the habitat of a particular species. This enables one to predict which snakes might be encountered and also helps narrow the number of possibilities when one is trying to identify a specimen. We have given in general terms the primary forest types in which particular species are found. As previously mentioned, vegetation types have not been classified in any consistent manner throughout Latin America. The term "rainforest" may imply "coastal," but this is not necessarily the case; many snakes may occur along the upper portion of this type of habitat and not descend below 300–500 m in elevation (e.g., *Bothriechis bicolor*, *Micrurus latifasciatus*). Also, "evergreen," as used here, means nondeciduous, not coniferous.

Unless stated otherwise, colors used in the species descriptions and keys are life colors. When using descriptions of pattern or color, bear in mind that many of their aspects are subject to individual, ontogenetic, sexual, and geographic variation. In some accounts, the description provided will accurately portray the majority of individuals, in others it will provide but a general overview for the species.

Except for this brief introduction, Snakebite Treatment and First Aid, and Mimics of Venomous Snakes, we have not used in-line citations, but a list of references follows each species account. Each section that contains in-line citations is followed by a list of literature cited; in addition, a comprehensive list of references for the species accounts is included at the end of the book. We have made no attempt to list all available references for each species; however, some of those listed are rather esoteric and others may have contributed as little as a single locality record used in preparing the account. References do not follow the generic accounts; the collective references for the species in a particular genus can be consulted for an overview of that genus.

### *Literature Cited*


Burger, W. L. 1972. Genera of pitvipers (Serpentes: Crotalidae). Diss. Abstr. B32:6119.

Burger, W. L. 1985. Pp. 103–104 in G. Pérez-Higareda, H. M. Smith, and J. Juliá-Zertuche. A new jumping viper, *Porthidium olmec*, from southern Veracruz, Mexico (Serpentes: Viperidae). Bull. Maryland Herpetol. Soc. 21:97–106.

Collins, J. T., R. Conant, J. E. Huheey, J. L. Knight, E. M. Rundquist, and H. M. Smith. 1982. Standard common and current scientific names for North American amphibians and reptiles. 2d ed. SSAR Herpetol. Circ. no. 12. Pp. 1–28.

Conant, R. 1975. A field guide to reptiles and amphibians of eastern and central North America. Boston, Houghton Mifflin Co. 429 pp.

Holdridge, L. R. 1964. Life zone ecology. San José, Costa Rica, Tropical Science Center. 187 pp.

Instituto Geográfico "Augustín Codazzi." 1977a. Atlas de Colombia. Bogotá, Colombia.

Instituto Geográfico "Augustín Codazzi." 1977b. Carta Ecológica de Colombia. 1:500,000. Bogotá, Colombia. 20 sheets.

Instituto Geográfico "Augustín Codazzi." 1977c. Zonas de vida o formaciones vegetales de Colombia; memoria explicativa sobre el mapa ecológico. Bogotá, Colombia.

Leopold, A. S. 1950. Vegetation zones of Mexico. Ecology 31:507–518.

Myers, C. W., J. W. Daly, and B. Malkin. 1978. A dangerously toxic new frog (*Phyllobates*) used by Emberá Indians of western Colombia, with discussion of blowgun fabrication and dart poisoning. Bull. Am. Mus. Nat. Hist. 161:307–366.

Myers, N. 1984. The primary source. N.Y., W. W. Norton and Co. 399 pp.

Pérez-Higareda, G., H. M. Smith, and J. Juliá-Zertuche. 1985. A new jumping viper, *Porthidium olmec*, from southern Veracruz, Mexico (Serpentes: Viperidae). Bull. Maryland Herpetol. Soc. 21:97–106.

Rand McNally. 1984. The new international atlas. Chicago, Ill.

Ride, W. D. L., C. W. Sabrosky, G. Bernardi, and R. V. Melville, ed. committee. 1985. International Code of Zoological Nomenclature. 3d ed. Berkeley, Univ. of California Press. 388 pp.

Rossman, D. A., H. R. Mushinsky, and H. C. Dessauer. 1978. Letter to the editor regarding common names list. Herpetol. Rev. 9:146.

Smith, H. M., and E. D. Brodie, Jr. 1982. A guide to field identification, reptiles of North America. N. Y., Western Publishing Co. 240 pp.

Stebbins, R. C. 1985. A field guide to western reptiles and amphibians. 2d ed., rev. Boston, Houghton Mifflin Co. 336 pp.

Stuart, L. C. 1963. A checklist of the herpetofauna of Guatemala. Misc. Publ. Mus. Zool. Univ. Michigan no. 122. Pp. 1–150.

UNESCO. 1981. Vegetation map of South America. 1:5,000,000, Paris. 2 sheets.

Wilson, L. D., and J. R. Meyer. 1985. The snakes of Honduras. 2d ed. Milwaukee, Wis., Milwaukee Pub. Mus. 150 pp.

# Snakebite Treatment and First Aid

George Watt, M.D.

The first aid treatment and medical management of snakebite victims are among the most neglected and poorly studied areas of medicine. Some authors have suggested that the management of snakebite is still in the Dark Ages (Warrell, 1983). The varied and often contradictory advice found in articles and textbooks results from a lack of controlled clinical studies. Countless treatments have been proposed, some extremely aggressive, prompting one observer to comment that it was surprising anyone survived the medical treatment of snakebite!

Advances in medical management have potential benefit for snakebite victims. Modern ventilators and arterial blood gas monitoring could be of great use in the management of respiratory paralysis due to neurotoxic venoms. Refinements already made in peritoneal and hemodialysis could be lifesaving in renal failure—an important cause of snakebite fatalities in Latin America. The intensive care unit treatment of shock with pulmonary artery wedge pressure measurements could improve the treatment of pitviper bites. Pitviper bites can cause both hypovolemic renal tubular damage and noncardiogenic pulmonary edema, a combination of events that makes fluid management difficult. Unfortunately, the majority of snakebite patients cannot benefit from these techniques. Most snakebites occur in the rural tropics, far from medical facilities, and only a minority of snakebite victims are hospitalized.

Nevertheless, some advances have been made and there are grounds for optimism. Among the medical community aggressive first aid measures, such as incision, suction, and the application of tight tourniquets have been deemphasized. Coupled with accentuated primary health care in the rural tropics, this deemphasis could permeate to the village level and decrease morbidity. It is hoped that an awareness of the need for more information on snakebite will stimulate properly conducted studies leading to sound treatment recommendations based on scientific evidence.

The therapeutic suggestions presented herein pertain to bites occurring in Latin America; appropriate treatment may differ in other parts of the world. The care to be given at peripheral ("first-line") medical facilities is stressed, but therapeutic modalities available in sophisticated tertiary referral centers are also discussed.

Several people made invaluable contributions to this chapter. Drs. David L. Hardy, Sherman Minton, and David Warrell reviewed the manuscript and made numerous helpful suggestions. Drs. Rolando de la Guardia, Steven Wignall, and J. P. Chippaux provided clinical insights stemming from their personal observations of snakebites in Latin America. Finally, special thanks are due Gloria Nuguid of NAMRU-2 for her technical assistance and ability to decipher illegible handwriting.

**Table 1**
Conflicting first aid advice for snakebite (from a survey of American literature 1970–1979)

| |
|---|
| Catch the snake and kill it; bring it with you to the hospital. |
| Get away from the snake as fast as possible to avoid the risk of additional bites. |
| Apply a tourniquet proximal to the bite. |
| Always loosen the tourniquet every 10 minutes. |
| Never loosen the tourniquet until arrival at the hospital. |
| Never use a tourniquet. |
| Pack the bitten extremity in fresh-water ice. |
| Never pack the extremity in ice of any kind. |
| Immediately apply incision and suction to the bite. |
| Do not attempt incision and suction. |
| Keep moving to encourage spread of the venom from the wound and minimize bite site necrosis. |
| Avoid all unnecessary movement. |

*Source:* Modified from Stewart et al., 1981, courtesy of *Annals of Emergency Medicine.*

## FIRST AID

First aid consists of those measures taken for the patient between the time of the bite and the time the patient arrives at a treatment facility. Few subjects in medicine are as controversial (Table 1). An adequate discussion of the advantages and disadvantages of various first aid measures would be protracted and would give undue importance to these measures. Early and effective medical treatment, not first aid, should be emphasized when managing the snakebite victim.

Only a few first aid measures are generally accepted. Reassure the patient. Many patients believe that death after a snakebite is rapid and inevitable, and thus may be extremely frightened. Emphasize to snakebite victims that treatment is available and effective.

Immobilize the bitten limb as much as is practical with a splint or sling. Muscular contraction promotes the absorption of venom through lymphatic channels. Remove rings, bracelets, or other potentially constrictive devices.

Transport the patient to a place that provides medical

attention as quickly as possible (see below for problems during transport). Restrict physical activity on the part of the patient to a minimum.

Avoid harmful procedures and medicines. Incision and suction ("slash and suck") and the application of ice to the bite site (cryotherapy) can be dangerous and are of no proven value. The application of an electric current to the bite site is the latest aggressive measure to be recommended on the basis of anecdotal reports (Guderian et al., 1986). The demonstration of efficacy by controlled studies is necessary before this potentially hazardous procedure can be advocated.

Avoid aspirin and intramuscular injections. Aspirin can aggravate bleeding tendencies, and intramuscular injections can cause large hematomas in patients with blood-clotting abnormalities. Oral acetaminophen or codeine phosphate are safe analgesics.

If possible, prior to transport, establish an intravenous line with isotonic fluid ($D_5W$, normal saline, Ringer's lactate). During transport, watch for the following problems:

Vomiting increases the risk of asphyxiation from blocked airways in a comatose patient or one with glossopharyngeal palsy. Place such a patient on his or her side to avoid aspiration of vomitus. To control persistent vomiting, prochlorperazine (Compazine) may be tried: 20 mg added to an intravenous infusion, 5–10 mg by slow intravenous injection, or 25 mg by rectal suppository. Carefully monitor the patient for possible drug-induced hypotension. An alternative is Trimethobenzamide (Tigan), 200 mg by rectal suppository.

Airway obstruction in patients bitten by snakes with neurotoxic venom (e.g., some South American populations of *Crotalus durissus*, Neotropical rattlesnake, or *Micrurus* and *Micruroides*, coral snakes) may be caused by paralysis of the jaw and tongue. Lay such a patient on his or her side, insert an oral airway, and hyperextend the neck.

If either cardiac or respiratory arrest occurs, perform standard cardiopulmonary resuscitation (CPR).

Antivenom should not ordinarily be administered in the field. It should be given only by someone who is familiar with its use and has emergency drugs available to treat possible adverse reactions. If transporting the patient is impossible or no treatment facility is available, and definite evidence of serious envenoming is present, the field administration of antivenom should be part of the overall management of the patient, as described later in this chapter.

The routine application of tight (arterial) tourniquets is not recommended. In addition to being painful, their use risks ischemic damage and even gangrene (Fig. 1A). Local venom effects can be enhanced and acute systemic toxicity can occur if the tourniquet is suddenly released. An argument can be made for recommending the use of a tourniquet in certain very specific circumstances; however, these circumstances do not exist in Latin America. Splinting combined with a tight-fitting ace bandage is an alternative and perhaps carries less risk (Sutherland et al., 1979); further assessment of this method in human snakebite victims is necessary before it can be recommended. The impact of this technique in the Americas is likely to be minimal even if it is found to be effective. In this region, the only species of snakes for whose bites this "crepe-bandaging" technique would be advocated are the coral snakes (*Micrurus* and *Micru-*

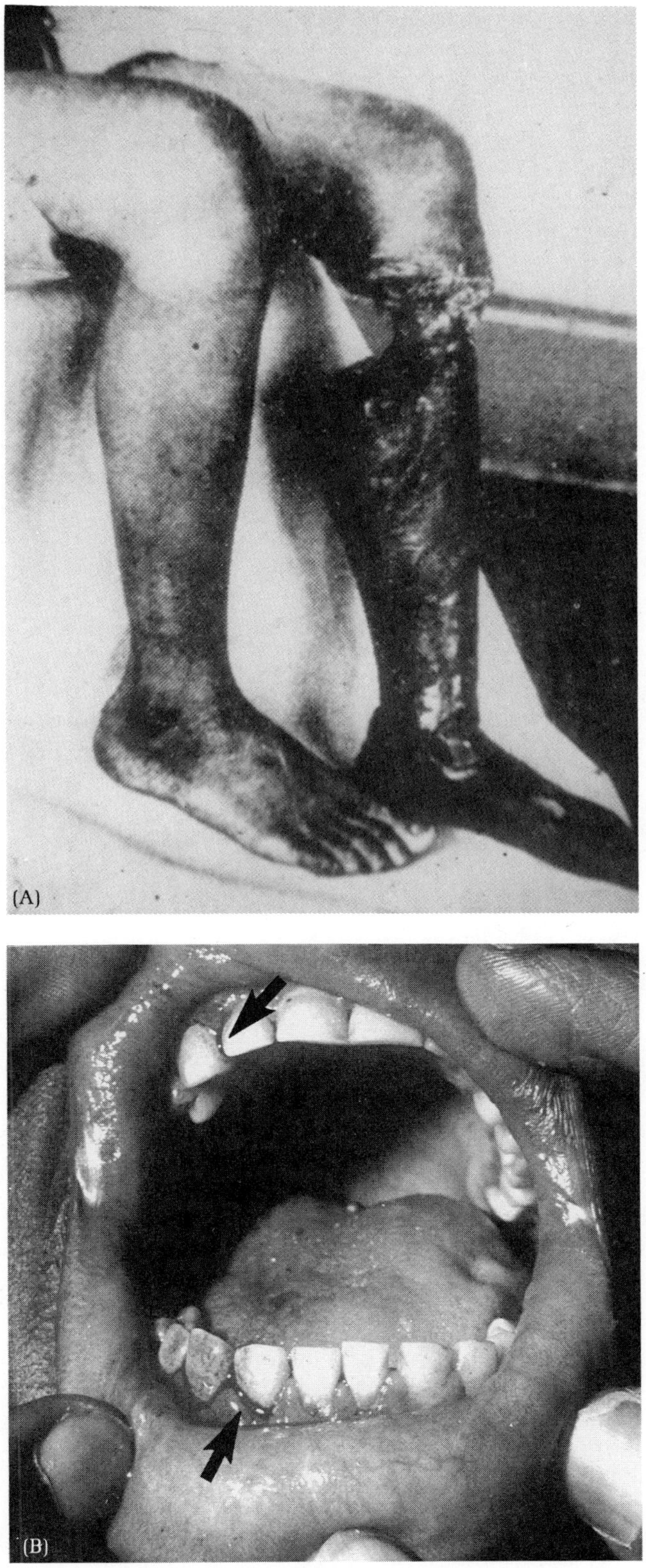


Fig. 1. (A) Severe local necrosis following the prolonged application of a tourniquet. Courtesy of the Japan Snake Institute, Tokyo. (B) Bleeding from the gums (*arrows*), the site where the hemorrhagic effects of snake venom are most frequently seen. Courtesy of D. A. Warrell.

*roides*), and their bites are rare. In addition, the necessary materials are unlikely to be found in the rural, often isolated areas where coral snake bites usually occur.

Occasionally patients develop shock before arrival at the treatment facility, usually because of decreased circulating blood volume. Clinical manifestations include altered sensorium, hypotension, rapid heart rate and respiration (tachycardia and tachypnea, respectively), weak or absent pulses, pallor, sweating, and cool skin. Give these patients oxygen if available; volume expansion with crystalloid (i.e., normal saline or Ringer's lactate) is indicated, provided there is no evidence of pulmonary congestion. A rarer cause of hypotension is anaphylactic shock due to the autopharmacological effects of venom. The clinical manifestations are angioneurotic edema, severe abdominal pain, and diarrhea; the best treatment is intravenous antihistamine (e.g., 50 mg diphenhydramine hydrochloride, Benadryl).

Bring the biting snake to the treatment facility if this can be done without risk. Identification of the snake permits optimum treatment to be given to those bitten by venomous species and prompts reassurance to those bitten by nonvenomous ones. However, because its biting reflex can persist after death, venom can be injected by a recently killed snake. Careless attempts to kill a snake that has already bitten one victim can result in further bites.

## TREATMENT AT THE HOSPITAL OR DISPENSARY

All patients bitten by a snake known or suspected of being venomous should be observed for a minimum of 24 hours and their vital signs monitored frequently. An intravenous infusion should be started or maintained to provide ready access for medication should the patient need it; this measure also reassures frightened patients.

In Latin America as a whole, bites by snakes of the genus *Bothrops*, the large terrestrial lanceheads, have the greatest medical importance. The Neotropical rattlesnake, *Crotalus durissus* subsp., presents a serious snakebite problem in South America. Bites by other venomous species occur and may cause death or serious injury, but their impact on human health is far less than that of the lanceheads and the Neotropical rattlesnake; therefore, the discussion emphasizes medical treatment for the bites of those snakes.

Other species may be important in circumscribed areas but not throughout the region. *Agkistrodon bilineatus* bites are said to be a problem in Nicaragua and parts of Mexico, and *Lachesis muta* (bushmaster) bites are a problem in certain heavily forested areas. In Mexico, *Bothrops asper* is the only lancehead; it and the rattlesnakes (genus *Crotalus*) represent the chief snakebite problems. Snakebites in northern Mexico are almost entirely caused by rattlesnake species found in the southwestern United States, the clinical features of which have been described in the U.S. literature (see Russell, 1983, and Hardy, 1986).

Coral snake (*Micrurus* and *Micruroides*) bites are rare but can be serious. Although bites by rear-fanged colubrids may cause pain and swelling, no species in Latin America have been implicated in human deaths. See Mimics of Venomous Snakes for more information on mildly venomous snakes. Gila monster (*Heloderma suspectum*) bites occur occasionally in northern Mexico, and those of the beaded lizard (*H. horridum*) occur in western Mexico and northern Central America; however, documented fatalities have not occurred. Readers interested in more information are referred to Albritton et al. (1970), Bogert and Martín del Campo (1956), Russell and Bogert (1981), and Streiffer (1986).

### Antivenom

Antivenom is the only proven treatment for envenoming (sometimes called envenomation). For example, untreated bites by *Crotalus durissus* (Neotropical rattlesnake) are said to carry a 72% case fatality rate. This is reduced to 12% with the use of antivenom (Rosenfeld, 1971). Sources of antivenom are listed at the end of this section.

Antivenom should be given *only* to patients with symptoms and signs of envenoming. Not only is it often in limited supply, but its indiscriminate use needlessly exposes patients to the risk of antivenom reactions. Many patients are bitten by nonvenomous snakes, and even if the biting snake is venomous, venom (or a significant quantity of venom) is not always injected. It is estimated that 30% of (Old World) viper bites do not lead to envenoming (Reid, 1973).

Contrary to popular opinion, snakebite rarely produces sudden death. The average interval between the time of a pitviper bite and death is measured in days, not hours. Those treating a snakebite patient have time to observe the patient for specific indications for antivenom. Although some authorities recommend that antivenom be given to any patient bitten by an identified highly venomous snake, no solid evidence supports this practice. Once definite signs of envenoming are apparent, however, antivenom should be administered promptly; every effort should be made to detect the signs, discussed below, as early as possible.

#### INDICATIONS FOR ANTIVENOM

Any spontaneous bleeding distant from the site of the bite should be noted. Always examine carefully for bleeding from the gums (Fig. 1B); bleeding may also occur from the nose, gastrointestinal tract, urinary tract, venipuncture and incision sites, or elsewhere.

Look for signs of cardiovascular involvement, including hypotension, bradycardia, and arrhythmias, or an abnormal electrocardiogram. Hypotension or wide fluctuation in blood pressure readings may be the first sign of serious trouble in pitviper bites.

Check for renal involvement. Oliguria (less than 400 ml urine/24 hr), raised serum creatinine and blood urea nitrogen (BUN) levels, or blood in the urine (hematuria) is a sign of nephrotoxicity and an indication for antivenom. Hemoglobinuria and myoglobinuria (discussed below) may also be associated with kidney damage.

Investigate signs of nervous system involvement,

which may include drooping of the eyelids (ptosis), difficulty in moving the eyes (opthalmoplegia), difficulty in swallowing or talking, and difficulty in breathing. Weakness or paralysis of the arms and legs are late signs.

View massive local swelling—that is, swelling involving more than half the bitten limb or swelling accompanied by blister formation—as an indication that significant envenoming has occurred.

Look for evidence of abnormal blood clotting or hemolysis. If the treatment facility has a well-equipped laboratory, standard blood-clotting tests should be performed (PT, PTT, etc.). However, simple whole-blood-clotting tests that can be performed at the bedside often give quicker results and can be more useful for monitoring response to therapy (Fig. 2A) (Warrell et al., 1977). Failure of the patient's blood to clot if placed in a clean dry glass tube and left for 20 minutes is an indication for antivenom.

Bites by some snakes, particularly some populations of *Crotalus durissus* (Neotropical rattlesnake) (Rosenfeld, 1971), can result in hemolysis, the breaking up of red blood cells. Laboratory evidence of hemolysis includes increased levels of unconjugated ("indirect") bilirubin and decreased or absent haptoglobin. If hemolysis is substantial, the patient may be jaundiced. The presence of dark urine suggests hemoglobinuria. The plasma of patients with hemoglobinuria has a reddish brown color. The presence of laboratory evidence of hemolysis, acquired jaundice, or hemoglobinuria are indications for antivenom.

Myonecrosis and myoglobinuria probably occur in some *C. durissus* subsp. bites (Azevedo-Marques et al., 1985) and possibly in *Micrurus* sp. bites (Gutiérrez et al., 1983). The coexistence of dark urine with normal-colored plasma suggests this complication. Elevated values of serum creatinine phosphokinase (CPK), aldolase, lactate dehydrogenase (LDH), and oxaloacetic transaminase (SGOT) are found if these tests are available. The detection of myoglobin in the serum and urine is confirmatory, but tests are done only in a few highly specialized centers.

Fever, leukocytosis, and vomiting are useful non-specific signs that envenoming may have occurred, although they are not by themselves indications for antivenom. Lymphangitis or tender regional lymphadenophathy are also useful clues to envenoming, particularly in pitviper bites.

Note these precautions when attempting to diagnose envenoming. Minor local swelling limited to the area around the bite is *not* an indication for antivenom. Generalized paresthesias and numbness are often signs of hyperventilation, not neurotoxicity. These and other manifestations of anxiety, including dizziness, breathlessness, palpitations, and sweating, are indications for reassurance and sometimes for a mild sedative, *not antivenom*.

Indications for the use of antivenom after coral snake bites are unlike those for other species. Although rare, bites by these snakes can be followed by a long asymptomatic period and a sudden onset of paralytic symptoms that can be difficult to reverse with antivenom (Parrish and Khan, 1967). Therefore, antivenom should be given if there is a high index of suspicion of coral snake bite and skin punctures are present, even before there are signs of neurotoxic envenoming. Useful non-specific symptoms are numbness or weakness in the bitten extremity, lack of local swelling, and severe abdominal pain.

### CONTRAINDICATIONS TO ANTIVENOM

Snakebite with envenoming should be considered a medical emergency. There is no absolute contraindication to antivenom treatment. However, individuals with a history of allergy to horse serum have an increased risk of developing severe antivenom reactions and should be given antivenom only if the risk of death from envenoming is high. Epinephrine, antihistamines, and corticosteroids can be given to these patients beforehand. Rapid desensitization is not recommended. Antivenom should be administered with increased caution to patients with a history of hay fever, asthma, or eczema.

### CHOICE OF ANTIVENOM

If the species of biting snake is known, antivenom specific for that snake should be used (monovalent antivenom). Otherwise, antivenoms effective against several species of snakes are indicated (polyvalent antivenom). The description of the snake and knowledge of those species found in a particular locality can help to identify the biting snake. Table 2 gives a rough guide for distinguishing the clinical effects of bites by the most important groups of snakes in Latin America.

An antivenom for one species in a genus may not effectively neutralize the venom of another species, so it is important to read carefully the antivenom insert provided by the manufacturer. Wyeth produces a polyvalent antivenom (Crotalidae) that the company says may be used in the treatment of all pitviper bites in the New World; unfortunately, its cost prohibits widespread distribution and use. Occasionally, only antivenom already past its indicated expiration date is available; however, if it has been stored appropriately, it may still be effective. Opaque or cloudy antivenom should not be used. Precipitation of protein indicates loss of activity and increased risk of antivenom reactions.

### ADMINISTRATION OF ANTIVENOM

*Dosage.* Unfortunately, variables such as differing amounts of venom introduced by the snake and varying rates of absorption of venom from the site of the bite make it impossible to predict how much antivenom will be required for an individual patient. The appropriate initial dose of antivenom has been established in very few cases. The manufacturer's recommendations are usually based on mouse-protection tests, which may not reflect the real-life situation. In the vast majority of cases there is adequate time to monitor the patient's response; some antivenom should be given initially, and more can

**Table 2**

Effects of bites by some medically important snakes of Latin America

| | *Local signs* | *Abnormal bleeding* | *Renal complications* | *Neurologic signs* |
|---|---|---|---|---|
| Lanceheads (*Bothrops*) | +++ | +++ | +++ | − |
| Neotropical rattlesnake (*Crotalus durissus* subsp.)[1] | +− | + | ++++ | ++ |
| Bushmaster (*Lachesis muta*) | ++++ | ++ | ++ | +− |
| Coral snakes (*Micrurus* or *Micruroides*) | − | − | − | +++ |

*Source:* Compiled, in part, from Rosenfeld, 1971.
*Note.* −, does not occur; +−, can be present or absent; +, ++, +++, ++++, increasing degrees of severity.
1. The bites of Central American and some northern South American populations of the Neotropical rattlesnake (*C. durissus*) do not produce renal or neurologic complications.

then be given according to the response of the patient. Choose the initial dose according to the manufacturer's recommendations; 50 ml is an average dose. Children must be given the same or larger doses than adults because the volume of venom injected is distributed in a smaller body fluid volume. Give patients with severe envenoming a large initial dose as soon as possible.

*Monitoring of response to antivenom.* With an adequate neutralizing dose of antivenom, spontaneous systemic bleeding usually stops within 1 hour. The return of blood coagulability to normal usually takes longer, and the simple whole-blood-clotting test repeated at 6-hour intervals is a very convenient way to monitor the effectiveness of therapy (Fig. 2A). Clearing of hemoglobinuria or myoglobinuria can be seen easily in a catheterized patient. The stabilization of blood pressure and pulse and return to normal of electrocardiographic changes indicate a good response to antivenom in patients who are hemodynamically unstable or who have cardiotoxic signs. Lessening of ptosis and increase in the number of seconds that upward gaze can be maintained signify improvement of neurotoxicity. If no response to antivenom is seen, an increased dose should be tried. If signs of envenoming are not controlled, antivenom can be administered every 1–2 hours.

*Route of administration.* Antivenom should always be given intravenously. Ideally, it is diluted in up to 500 ml of isotonic fluid and given by intravenous infusion over 1–2 hours. The volume of dilution should be reduced in small children or infants. If doubt exists that the patient can be closely observed throughout the time of infusion, an alternative method is to give undiluted antivenom by slow intravenous push over 10–15 minutes. Infiltrating antivenom at the bite site is not indicated; only if intravenous access is not possible should the intramuscular or subcutaneous route be used.

*Timing of antivenom treatment.* It is never too late to try antivenom, as long as the indications for its use are present. Blood coagulability has been restored 10 days or more after some viper bites! If a patient who has a tourniquet in place is to be treated and there is evidence of envenoming, give antivenom *before* releasing the tourniquet. If signs of envenoming are absent, place a blood pressure cuff above the tourniquet and inflate it to greater than the diastolic blood pressure. With an intravenous line in place and antivenom at the bedside, release the tourniquet and deflate the blood pressure cuff *very* gradually. *Never* rapidly remove the tourniquet of a snakebite victim without taking these precautions.

*Reactions to antivenom.* Early reactions usually begin with 1–20 minutes of starting an intravenous injection of undiluted antivenom and within 30–180 minutes of starting an intravenous infusion of antivenom. (These reactions are also referred to as "anaphylaxis" or "anaphylactoid," although their pathophysiology is unclear and may not have an allergic basis.) Skin and conjunctival testing are unreliable predictors of early reactions and can be dangerous (Malasit et al., 1986). *Do not perform skin testing* unless it is required for medicolegal reasons.

Warning symptoms include palpitations, a feeling of heat, restlessness, cough, itching of the scalp, nausea, and vomiting. Later, urticaria, generalized itching, fever, and tachycardia become evident. *Rarely*, severe, potentially fatal manifestations occur, including hypotension, bronchospasm, and airway obstruction.

**Epinephrine is the treatment of choice for early reactions and should be easily available any time antivenom is used.** If warning symptoms develop, stop antivenom and give 0.3–0.5 mg epinephrine subcutaneously. Diphenhydramine (Benadryl) 25–50 mg can be administered intravenously to shorten the duration of the reaction and prevent relapses. Antivenom can then be restarted slowly.

If asthma, upper airway swelling, or hypotension occur, discontinue antivenom and administer epinephrine intravenously. If signs of severe envenoming persist and more antivenom must be given, the antivenom drip can be restarted slowly; ensure that epinephrine is by the bedside. An alternative is to restart the antivenom while giving epinephrine (1:1000) by constant infusion (1 ml in 250 ml $D_5W$). Airway patency and blood pressure must be maintained by the normal methods. Antihistamines should be given for 24 hours after an early reaction occurs.

Serum sickness reactions may develop 5–24 days after antivenom has been given. Urticaria, fever, and joint pains are the most common symptoms and are easily controlled by a short course of antihistamines and steroids (e.g., prednisone 40 mg/day tapered off over 3–4

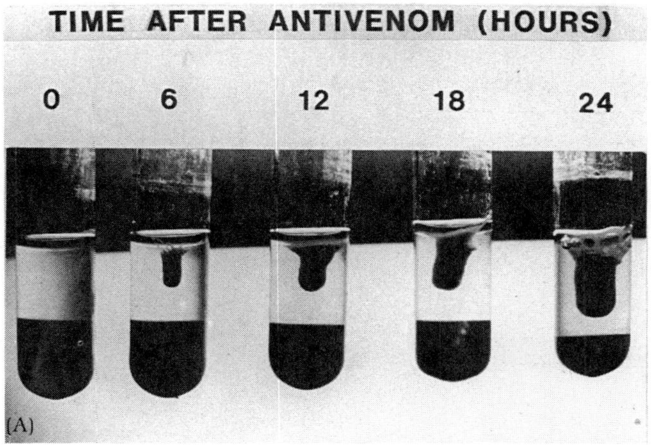


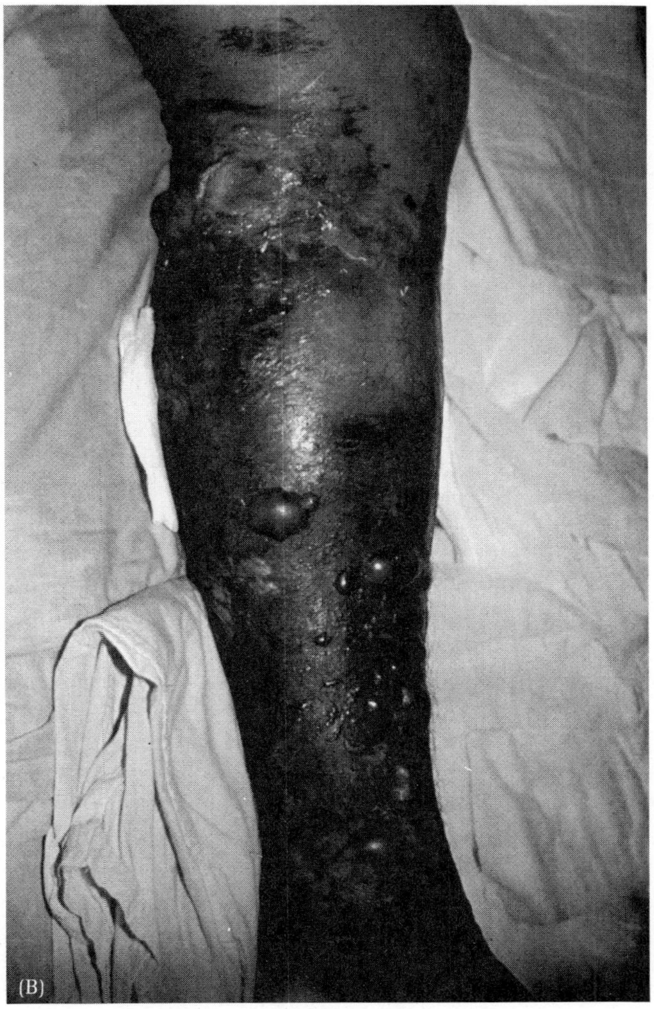


Fig. 2. (A) Restoration of normal blood clotting following the administration of antivenom. Clotting was restored at 6 hours after antivenom administration and then progressively improved at 12, 18, and 24 hours. Courtesy of D. A. Warrell. (B) Extensive early necrosis and bullae formation after a bite by *Bothrops atrox*. Courtesy of R. L. Gay.

days). This is the only established indication for the use of corticosteroids in the treatment of snakebite.

## Supportive Treatment

Effective nonspecific treatment measures must be combined with antivenom if a good result is to be obtained. Most symptomatic snakebite cases can be managed effectively without having to resort to extremely specialized techniques or equipment. Management of some of the rarer complications of snakebite are not discussed in detail here, because this chapter is written primarily for those who initially treat the snakebite patient. It is assumed that patients developing severe or unusual complications would be transferred for more specialized care.

### CARE OF THE BITE SITE AND BITTEN LIMB

In uncomplicated cases keep the bite site clean and uncovered. Elevate bitten limbs that are swollen, and leave blisters undisturbed. Prophylactic antibiotics are not indicated; however, tetanus prophylaxis or a booster should be given unless the patient is known to have been reliably immunized.

Severe cases are seen especially after bites by *Bothrops* (lanceheads) (Fig. 2B) and *Lachesis muta* (bushmaster). Severe local necrosis should be treated by surgical debridement, immediate split skin grafting, and antibiotics, such as metronidazole (Flagyl), effective against gram-negative bacilli as well as anaerobes. Careful, prompt surgical management is the key to minimizing damage in cases complicated by necrosis.

Tense edema in the bitten limb rarely leads to vascular compromise and necrosis. A decision to perform pressure-relieving fasciotomy should be made only if raised tissue pressure or severe narrowing of a major vessel can be demonstrated by doppler, angiography, or measurement of subfascial pressure. Clinical signs can be misleading in intensely swollen limbs. Fasciotomy should be done only after the blood has become coagulable. This can be speeded up by administering fresh whole blood or clotting factors 30–60 minutes after an adequate dose of antivenom.

### SHOCK

Patients can leak large amounts of plasma and blood into swollen limbs. Antivenom usually effectively stops further fluid loss as well as bleeding from other sites. However, if circulatory collapse develops or is already present, adequate tissue perfusion sometimes must be achieved rapidly with whole fresh blood, a plasma expander, normal saline, or Ringer's lactate. Antivenom alone is not sufficient. Shock may develop after *C. durissus* subsp. (Neotropical rattlesnake) bites despite lack of local swelling.

### RENAL INVOLVEMENT

Envenoming by both *Bothrops*, (lanceheads) and *Crotalus durissus* (Neotropical rattlesnake) can cause acute renal failure (Da Silva et al., 1979). Although multifactorial, most cases of renal failure after *Bothrops* bites are secondary to hemorrhagic shock and hypovolemia. Many times this complication can be prevented by careful attention to maintaining adequate circulating blood volume and fluid balance. Skilled medical management is necessary for treating established renal failure, and occasionally dialysis may be required in cases that do not respond to conservative therapy. However, peritoneal dialysis in the rural hospital setting is commonly complicated by secondary infection and bleeding, and the mortality is high. The indications for dialysis in the rural tropics are, therefore, more limited than they would be in a more sophisticated hospital setting. Hemodialysis is rarely available in areas where snakebite incidence is high.

Intravascular hemolysis may occur after bites by *C. durissus terrificus* (Rosenfeld, 1971). Red blood cell pigments filtered by the kidneys not only give the urine a reddish brown color but increase the risk of renal failure. *Crotalus durissus terrificus* venom also has a direct nephrotoxic effect and possible myotoxic effect; myoglobinuria adds to kidney damage. Alkalinization of the urine is desirable in the presence of myoglobinuria and probably should also be attempted in hemoglobinuria. Renal failure is the major cause of death after bites by this snake.

#### NEUROTOXIC ENVENOMING

Patients with paralysis of the muscles of the jaw and tongue as well as paralysis of the muscles of coughing and swallowing are at high risk for aspiration pneumonia and asphyxiation from blocked airways. These patients should be nursed on their sides and have frequent suctioning. Insert an oral airway and hyperextend the neck. Although mild neurotoxic signs are frequently seen after *Crotalus durissus* subsp. (Neotropical rattlesnake) bites, severe neurotoxicity is most likely to follow *Micrurus* or *Micruroides* (coral snake) bites.

If respiratory paralysis develops, *maintain adequate ventilation by whatever means are available.* Patients have recovered from respiratory paralysis after being manually ventilated by relays of relatives and nurses for up to 10 days. Supportive care is particularly important in cases of *Micrurus* or *Micruroides* bites, where neurotoxic symptoms may be unresponsive to antivenom. Endotracheal intubation or tracheostomy are dangerous if there is inadequate supervision to ensure frequent suctioning and adequate humidification. These measures should be approached with extreme caution in the rural hospital setting and only instituted if respiratory dysfunction is present.

Edrophonium chloride (Tensilon) is a safe drug that can benefit some patients with neurotoxic snakebite. A Tensilon test is therefore recommended for any snakebite patient with signs of neuromuscular paralysis (Watt et al., 1986). Atropine sulphate (0.6 mg for adults, 50 μg/kg for children) is given by intravenous injection, followed by Tensilon (10 mg for adults, 0.25 mg/kg for children). If improvement occurs, the patient can then be maintained on a longer acting anticholinesterase preparation, such as neostigmine methyl sulfate. An average initial dose is 25 μg/kg/hr given by constant intravenous infusion, but the exact amount to be given must be titrated according to the patient's clinical response. Anticholinesterase side effects, such as abdominal cramps, can be readily controlled by administering atropine.

**Table 3**
Envenoming site of 563 snakebites in Brazil

| *Site* | *Percentage of cases* |
|---|---|
| Foot and lower leg | 76.7 |
| Hand | 17.2 |
| Thigh | 1.6 |
| Forearm | 1.6 |
| Upper arm | 0.8 |
| Head | 0.2 |
| Others/unknown | 1.9 |

*Source:* Compiled from Rosenfeld, 1971.

#### COAGULOPATHY

The most effective method of reversing coagulopathy is antivenom therapy. *Bothrops* bites sometimes produce gradual disseminated intravascular coagulation, resulting in fibrinolysis and occasionally thrombocytopenia. Even if available, cryoprecipitates have a shorter beneficial effect in treating this syndrome than has antivenom. The use of heparin is not recommended (Warrell et al., 1976).

### Conclusion

Bites by *Bothrops* (lanceheads), and *Crotalus durissus* (Neotropical rattlesnake) cause most snakebite mortality and morbidity in Latin America. Antivenom is the most important treatment available for bites by these snakes. However, it should be used only when specific indications exist and when epinephrine is readily available to treat early antivenom reactions. Nonspecific supportive therapy is also important and may be lifesaving in some cases.

## PREVENTION OF SNAKEBITE

Simple precautions will prevent snakebite in most instances. Boots and long trousers should be worn when walking in areas known to harbor venomous snakes, and a light should be used at night. Venomous snakes should not be kept by amateurs as pets or as performing animals. Snakes should never be handled in the wild, even if they look dead or are thought to be harmless. Many bites by *Micrurus* or *Micruroides* species (coral snakes) result from their being handled in the mistaken belief that they are harmless (see the discussion of false coral snakes in Mimics of Venomous Snakes). Climbing or moving rocks with bare hands, collecting firewood, climbing trees with dense foliage, and swimming in lakes or rivers may result in snakebite. Reaching into holes with bare hands or a stick is particularly dangerous.

Unfortunately, these precautions are impractical for those most likely to be bitten by snakes—rural farmers. Most bites occur on the legs and feet, and many bites occur when snakes are inadvertently stepped on (Table 3). In many instances, however, wearing boots is neither practical nor affordable. Vaccination against snakebite in high-risk groups is not yet available. One snake vaccine study has been completed (Sawai et al., 1969) and other preliminary studies with venoids are in progress (Burma, 1986), but the degree of protection conferred by vaccination has not yet been established.

*Literature Cited*


Albritton, D. C., H. M. Parrish, and E. R. Allen. 1970. Venenation by the Mexican Beaded Lizard (*Heloderma horridum*): Report of a case. South Dakota J. Med. 1970:9–11.

Azevedo-Marques, M. M., P. Cupo, T. M. Coimbra, S. E. Hering, M. A. Rossie, and C. J. Laure. 1985. Myonecrosis, myoglobinuria and acute renal failure induced by South American Rattlesnake (*Crotalus durissus terrificus*) envenomation in Brazil. Toxicon 23:631–636.

Bogert, C. M., and R. Martín del Campo. 1956. The Gila Monster and its allies. The relationships, habits and behavior of the lizards of the family Helodermatidae. Bull. Am. Mus. Nat. Hist. 109:1–238.

Burma, D. M. R. 1986. Trial of Russell's Viper venoid. II. Human immunization with venoid. Working group on clinical trial of Russell's Viper venoid. Trans. R. Soc. Trop. Med. Hyg. 1986: 423–428.

Da Silva, D. A., M. Lopez, and P. Godoy. 1979. Intensive care unit treatment of acute renal failure following snake bite. Am. J. Trop. Med. Hyg. 28:401–407.

Guderian, R. H., C. D. Mackenzie, and J. F. Williams. 1986. High voltage shock treatment for snake bite. Letter to the editor. Lancet ii:229.

Gutiérrez, J. M., B. Lomonte, E. Portilla, L. Cerdas, and E. Rojas. 1983. Local effects induced by coral snake venoms: Evidence of myonecrosis after experimental inoculations of venoms from five species. Toxicon 21:777–783.

Hardy, D. L. 1986. Fatal rattlesnake envenomation in Arizona: 1969–1984. J. Toxicol. Clin. Toxicol. 24:1–10.

Malasit, P., D. A. Warrell, P. Chanthavanich, C. Vivavan, J. Mongkolsapaya, B. Singhthong, and C. Supich. 1986. Prediction, prevention and mechanism of early (anaphylactic) antivenom reactions in victims of snake bites. Br. Med. J. 294:17–20.

Parrish, H. M., and M. S. Khan. 1967. Bites by coral snakes: Report of 11 representative cases. Am. J. Med. Sci. 253:561–568.

Reid, H. A. 1973. Clinical aspects of animal toxins. Pp. 957–983 in A. deVries and E. Kochva, eds. Toxins of animal and plant origin. Vol. 3. London, Gordon and Breach.

Rosenfeld, G. 1971. Symptomatology, pathology, and treatment of snakebites in South America. Pp. 345–384 in W. Bucherl and P. Buckley, eds. Venomous animals and their venoms. Vol. 2. New York, Academic Press.

Russell, F. E. 1983. Snake venom poisoning. Great Neck, N.Y., Scholium International.

Russell, F. E., and C. M. Bogert. 1981. Gila monster: Its biology, venom, and bite—a review. Toxicon 19:341–359.

Sawai, Y., Y. Kawamura, T. Fukuyama, T. Okonogi, and I. Ebisawa. 1969. Studies on the improvement of treatment of habu (*Trimeresurus flavoviridis*) bites. VIII. A field trial of prophylactic immunization of habu venom toxoid. Japanese J. Exp. Med. 39:147.

Stewart, M. E., S. Greenland, and J. R. Hoffman. 1981. First aid treatment of poisonous snakebite: Are currently recommended procedures justified? Ann. Emerg. Med. 10:331–335.

Streiffer, R. H. 1986. Bite of a venomous lizard, the Gila monster. Postgrad. Med. 79:297–299.

Sutherland, S. K., A. R. Coulter, and R. D. Harris. 1979. Rationalization of first aid measures for elapid snakebite. Lancet i:183–186.

Warrell, D. A. 1983. [Review of] Snake venom poisoning, by F. E. Russell (1983). Trans. R. Soc. Trop. Med. Hyg. 75:909–910.

Warrell, D. A., N. McD. Davidson, B. M. Greenwood, D. Ormerod, H. M. Pope, B. J. Watkins, and C. R. M. Prentice. 1977. Poisoning by bites of the Saw-Scaled or Carpet Viper (*Echis carinatus*) in Nigeria. Q. J. Med., n.s. 46:33–62.

Warrell, D. A., H. M. Pope, and C. R. M. Prentice. 1976. Disseminated intravascular coagulation caused by the Carpet Viper (*Echis carinatus*): Trial of heparin. Br. J. Haematol. 33:335–342.

Watt, G., R. D. G. Theakston, C. G. Hayes, M. L. Yambao, R. Sangalang, C. P. Ranoa, E. Alquizalas, and D. A. Warrell. 1986. Positive response to Edrophonium in patients with neurotoxic envenoming by cobras (*Naja naja philippinensis*). New England J. Med. 315:1444–1449.

# Annotated Bibliography of Snakebite in Latin America

*David L. Hardy, M.D.*

This bibliography includes the recent literature on clinical effects and treatment of envenoming by Latin American snakes. It may be of use to those treating snakebites throughout this region as well as to clinicians and others wherever these snakes are maintained in captivity. References are primarily from the literature of the past 25 years but also include older works of significance. Some papers dealing with laboratory studies of antivenoms are included, but the voluminous literature of nonclinical effects of venoms has been omitted. Titles dealing with Mexican species that have extensive ranges within the United States—for example, *Crotalus atrox*, *C. molossus*, *C. scutulatus*, and the lizard *Heloderma suspectum*—have been omitted except when present in the Mexican literature. Annotations are provided, particularly when species involved or locality are not evident from the title. Scientific names used in the annotations conform to the present work and may differ from those used in the article. The most comprehensive works in the recent literature are Cardoso and Brando (1982) and Rosenfeld (1971) for South America, Bolaños (1982, 1984) for Central America, and Tay et al. (1981) for Mexico.


Abalos, J. W. 1964. Que sabe usted de víboras? Buenos Aires, Libros del Cominante.

Abalos, J. W., and I. Pirosky. 1963. Venomous Argentine serpents, ophidism and snake antivenin. Pp. 363–371 in H. L. Keegan and W. V. MacFarlane, eds., Venomous and poisonous animals and noxious plants of the Pacific region. Oxford, Pergamon Press. (*Bothrops*, *Crotalus*, Micrurus)


I thank the following persons for sending me the articles I requested: Jonathan A. Campbell, João Luis Cardoso, Luis G. Cerdas Fallas, Jean-Philippe Chippaux, José María Gutiérrez, Aura S. Kamiguti, William W. Lamar, Sherman A. Minton, Carmen M. Rojas G., Juan Silva Haad, and George Watt. To Daina Wasson, who prepared many drafts of the manuscript, goes my sincere gratitude.


Albritton, D. C., H. M. Parrish, and E. R. Allen. 1970. Venenation by the Mexican beaded lizard (*Heloderma horridum*): Report of a case. South Dakota J. Med. 1970:9–11.

Alfaro Brianso, B., and A. Boza Mora. 1983. Ofidismo en hospital rural del Pacífico Sur durante 1981. Acta Med. Costarric. 26:24–27. (*Bothriechis schlegelii*, *Bothrops asper*; Costa Rica)

Alvarez del Toro, M. 1982. Los reptiles de Chiapas. 3d ed. Publicación del Instituto de Historia Natural. Chiapas, Mexico, Tuxtla Gutiérrez.

Amaral, A. do. 1966. Venom and antivenin specificity: Modern concept. Mem. Inst. Butantan Simp. Internac. 33:293–303. (*Bothrops atrox*; Colombia)

Amaral, C. F. S., O. A. Da Silva, P. Godoy, and D. Miranda. 1985. Renal cortical necrosis following *Bothrops jararaca* and *B. jararacussu* snakebite. Toxicon 23:877–885. (Minas Gerais, Brazil)

Amaral, C. F. S., O. A. Da Silva, M. López, and E. R. Pietra Pedroso. 1980. Afibrinogenemia following snake bite (*Crotalus durissus terrificus*). Am. J. Trop. Med. Hyg. 29:1453–1455. (Belo Horizonte, Brazil)

Amaral, C. F. S., N. A. De Rezende, O. A. Da Silva, M. M. F. Ribeiro, R. A. Magalhaes, R. J. Dos Reis, J. G. Carneiro, and J. R. S. Castro. 1986. Insuficiencia renal aguda secundaria a acidentes afídicos botrópico e crotálico. Analise de 63 casos. Rev. Inst. Med. Trop. São Paulo 28:220–227.

Ambrose, M. S. 1956. Snakebite in Central America. Pp. 323–329 in E. E. Buckley, and N. Porges, eds. Venoms. Washington, D.C., American Association Advancement Science. (Western Panama)

Amorim, M. F., and R. F. Mello. 1952. Nefrose do nefron intermediário no envenenamento crotálico humano. Estudio anátomo-patológico. Mem. Inst. Butantan 24:281.

Amorim, M. F., and R. F. Mello. 1954. Intermediate nephrosis from snake poisoning in man. Am. J. Pathol. 30:479–499. (*Crotalus durissus terrificus*; São Paulo, Brazil)

Anonymous. 1974. Tratamiento para las mordeduras por serpientes. Coronado, Costa Rica, Instituto Clodomiro Picado.

Anonymous. 1984. Wyeth antivenin (Crotalidae) polyvalent. Marietta, Penn., Wyeth Laboratories Inc. (biological product package insert pamphlet)

Antivenom Index. 1986. American Association of Zoological Parks and Aquariums and American Association of Poison Control Centers, Oglebay Park, Wheeling, W.V. 26003. (source book for antivenoms and their location in the United States)

Arnold, R. E. 1984. Treatment of venomous snakebites in the western hemisphere. Mil. Med. 149:361–365.

Arroyo, O., R. Bolaños, and G. Muñoz. 1980. The bacterial flora of venoms and mouth cavities of Costa Rican snakes. Bull. Pan. Am. Health Organ. 14:280–285.

Ayerbe, S. 1979. Estudio retrospectivo sobre ofidiotoxicosis en el Departamento del Cauca. Pautas para el manejo de las mordeduras de serpiente. Cuadernos Med. Popayán 4:46–55. (Colombia)

Ayerbe, S., L. M. Otero, D. Gálvez, and A. Paredes. 1977. Estudio retrospectivo sobre ofidiotoxicosis en el Departamento del Cauca. la. parte. Cuadernos Med. Popayán 2:1–7. (Colombia)

Ayerbe, S., A. Paredes, and D. Gálvez. 1979. Estudio restrospectivo sobre ofidiotoxicosis en el Departamento del Cauca. Segunda parte: Aspectos clínicos, epidemiológicos y complicaciones. Cuadernos Med. Popayán 4:33–45. (*Bothriechis schlegelii*, *Bothrops asper*, *Micrurus mipartitus*; Colombia)

Azevedo, A. P., and J. C. Teixeira. 1938. Intoxicação por veneno de cobra: Necrose symétrica da córtex renal. Mem. Inst. Oswaldo Cruz 33:23–37. (*Bothrops jararaca*; Brazil)

Azevedo-Marques, M. M., P. Cupo, T. M. Coimbra, S. E. Hering, M. A. Rossi, and C. J. Laure. 1985. Myonecrosis, myoglobinuria and acute renal failure induced by South American rattlesnake (*Crotalus durissus terrificus*) envenomation in Brazil. Toxicon 23:631–636.

Banton, H. J. 1930. A snake doctor of the Mosquito Coast. Mil. Surg. 67:474–478. (*Bothrops*, *Micrurus*; Nicaragua)

Barrantes, A., V. Solís, and R. Bolaños. 1985. Alteración de los mecanismos de la coagulación en el envenenamiento por *Bothrops asper* (terciopelo). Toxicon 23:399–407. (Costa Rica)

Belluomini, H. E., E. L. Cembranelli, and M. P. Autuori. 1976/77. Wildlife rescue, capture of snakes and establishment of antiophidic stations in flooded area destined for Brazilian hydroelectric power plants. Mem. Inst. Butantan 40/41:129–154.

Berthold, G. 1959. Algunas consideraciones sobre el tigre mariposa (*Bothrops medusa*), su veneno y mordedura. Mem. Soc. Cienc. Nat. La Salle 52:17–22. (*Bothriopsis medusa*; Venezuela)

Bolaños, R. 1971. Nuevos recursos contra el ofidismo en Centroamérica. 2d ed. San José, Ministerio de Salud, Universidad de Costa Rica.

Bolaños, R. 1982. Las serpientes venenosas de Centro América y el problema del ofidismo. Primera Parte. Aspectos zoológicos, epidemiológicos y biomédicos. Rev. Costarric. Cienc. Med. 3:165–184.

Bolaños, R. 1984. Serpientes, venenos y ofidismo en Centroamérica. San José, Editorial Universidad de Costa Rica.

Bolaños, R., and L. Cerdas. 1978. The production and control of anti-venoms sera. Dev. Biol. Stand. 41:109–116.

Bolaños, R., and L. Cerdas. 1980. Producción y control de sueros antiofídicos en Costa Rica. Bol. Of. Sanit. Panam. 88:189–196.

Bolaños, R., L. Cerdas, and J. W. Abalos. 1978a. Veneno de *Micrurus* (serpiente de coral). Un antiveneno multivalente de valor panamericano. Bol. Of. Sanit. Panam. 84:128–133.

Bolaños, R., L. Cerdas, and J. W. Abalos. 1978b. Venoms of coral snakes (*Micrurus* spp.): Report on a multivalent antivenin for the Americas. Bull. Pan. Am. Health Organ. 12:23–27.

Bolaños, R., L. Cerdas, and R. Taylor. 1973. Estudios inmunológicos de los venenos de las principales *Micrurus* de Norte América, Centro América, Panamá y Colombia. Antioquia Med. 23:9–10.

Bolaños, R., L. Cerdas, and R. Taylor. 1975. The production and characteristics of a coral snake (*Micrurus mipartitus hertwigi*) antivenin. Toxicon 13:139–142. (*M. multifasciatus*)

Bolaños, R., A. Flores, R. T. Taylor, and L. Cerdas. 1974. Color patterns and venom characteristics in *Pelamis platurus*. Copeia 1974:909–912.

Bolaños, R., O. Marín, E. Mora Medina, and E. A. Alfaro. 1981. El accidente ofídico por cascabela (*Crotalus durissus durissus*) en Costa Rica. Acta Med. Costarric. 24:211–214.

Bolaños, R., G. Muñoz, and L. Cerdas. 1978. Toxicidad, neutralización e inmunoelectroforesis de los venenos de *Lachesis muta* de Costa Rica y Colombia. Toxicon 16:295–300.

Bolaños, R., O. Rojas, and C. E. Ulloa Flores. 1982. Aspectos biomédicos de cuatro casos de mordedura de serpiente por *Lachesis muta* (Ophidia: Viperidae) en Costa Rica. Rev. Biol. Tropical 30:53–58.

Brunker, T., and B. Fernández. 1974. Clostridios aislados de culebras costarricenses. Acta Med. Costarric. 17:147–152.

Bücherl, W. 1963. Uber die Ermittlung von Durchschnitts-und Höchst-Giftmengen bei den haüfigsten Giftschlangen Südamerikas. Pp. 67–120 in Die Giftschlangen der Erde. Behringwerk-Mitteilungen Sonderband. Marburg/Lahn, N. G. Elwert Universitäts-und Verlags-Buchhandlung. (*Micrurus frontalis*)

Bulletin of the Antivenin Institute of America. 1927–1932. Antivenin Institute of America, Mulford Biological Laboratories, Glenolden, Pennsylvania. Vols. 1–5. Reprinted 1973. Athens, Ohio, Society for the Study of Amphibians and Reptiles.

Caño Avila, G., J. Estada, and J. P. García. 1980. Picados de víbora de cascavel. (Revisión de casos atendidos en el Hospital General del Estado.) Plana Med. 17:35–46. (*Crotalus*; Sonora, Mexico)

Cardoso, J. L. C. 1985. Snakebites at Hospital Vital Brazil. A study of 2,908 cases. Abstract. Toxicon 23:558.

Cardoso, J. L. C., and R. B. Brando. 1982. Acidentes por animais peçonhentos clínica e tratamento. São Paulo, Livraria e Editória Santos.

Carr, A. 1969. A naturalist at large. Nat. Hist., New York 78:18–24, 68–71. (*Bothrops asper*; Costa Rica)

Cato David, J., and S. Fernandez Martinez. 1976. Serpientes venenosas de Venezuela. Diagnóstico, pronóstico y tratamiento del accidente ofídico. Caracas, Venezuela, Edit. Latorre.

Cerdas, L., A. Cornavaca, and R. López. 1986. Ofidismo en la región Atlántica de Costa Rica: Análisis de 164 casos. Acta Med. Costarric. 29:113–117.

Chippaux, J.-P. 1987 [dated 1986]. Les serpents de la Guyane Française, in vol. 27: Coll. Faune Tropicale. Paris, Éditions de L'Orstrom. 165 pp. (epidemiology of snakebite in French Guiana)

Chippaux, J.-P., J. Galtier, and J. F. Lefait. 1984. Epidemiologie des envenimations en Guyane Française. Bull. Soc. Pathol. Exp. 77:206–215.

Chippaux, J.-P., and M. Goyffon. 1983. Producers of antivenomous sera. Toxicon 21:739–752.

Clark, H. C. 1942. Venomous snakes. Some Central American records. Incidence of snake bite accidents. Am. J. Trop. Med. 22:37–49.

Cohen, P., W. H. Berkeley, and E. B. Seligmann, Jr. 1971. Coral snake venoms: *in vitro* relation of neutralizing and precipitating antibodies. Am. J. Trop. Med. Hyg. 20:646–649. (*Micrurus carinicauda* = *M. dumerilii*, *M. frontalis*, *M. mipartitus*, *M. nigrocinctus*, *M. spixii*; Central America and Colombia)

Cohen, P., J. H. Dawson, and E. B. Seligmann, Jr. 1968. Cross-neutralization of *Micrurus fulvius fulvius* (coral snake) venom by anti-*Micrurus carinicauda dumerilii* serum. Am. J. Trop. Med. Hyg. 17:308–310. (*Micrurus carinicauda* = *M. dumerilii*)

Colwell, R. K. 1985. A bite to remember. Nat. Hist., New York 94:2–8. (*Bothrops asper*; Costa Rica)

Cook, D. G. 1984. A case of envenomation by the Neotropical colubrid snake *Stenorrhina freminvillei*. Toxicon 22:823–827.

Dao, L. 1971. Emponzoñamiento ofídico en el Estado Lara. Gac. Med. Caracas. 79:383–400.

De Franco Montalvan, D., I. Alvarez Trejos, and L. A. Mora Watler. 1983a. Mordedura de ofidios venenosos en niños en la región Pacífico Sur. Análisis de ciento sesenta casos. Acta Med. Costarric. 26:61–70.

De Franco Montalvan, D., I. Alvarez Trejos, and L. A. Mora Watler. 1983b. Terapia de la mordedura de ofidios venenosos en niños en la región Pacífico Sur. Análisis en ciento sesenta casos. Acta Med. Costarric. 26:76–80. (*Bothriechis lateralis*, *Bothriechis schlegelii*, *Bothrops asper*, *Micrurus nigrocinctus*, *Porthidium godmani*; Costa Rica)

Díaz, O. 1971. Accidentes por animales ponzoñosos. Trib. Med. 42:6–12. (Colombia)

Ekenbäck, K., J. Hulting, H. Persson, and I. Wernell. 1985. Unusual neurological symptoms in a case of severe crotalid envenomation. Clin. Toxicol. 23:357–364. (*Crotalus durissus terrificus*)

Fonseca, F. da. 1949. Animais peçonhentos. São Paulo, Instituto Butantan. (Summary of 6,601 snakebite reports, 1902–1945)

Garrido, O. H. 1980. Notas sobre mordidas de jubo, *Alsophis* (Serpentes: Colubridae) Misc. Zool. La Habana 11:2–3.

Ghitis, J., and V. Bonelli. 1963. Fibrinogenopenia in snake bite. Ann. Intern. Med. 59:737–739. (*Bothrops atrox*; Colombia)

Glass, T. G., Jr. 1971. Mordedura de serpientes. Trib. Med. Venez. 33:1–14.

Guderian, R. H., C. D. Mackenzie, and J. F. Williams. 1986. High voltage shock treatment for snakebite. Letter to the editor. Lancet 2:229. (*Bothriechis*, *Bothriopsis*, *Bothrops*, *Lachesis*; Ecuador)

Guevara, I. T., and E. Mendez. 1978. Acción neurotóxica del veneno de *Crotalus d. durissus*. Tesis, Facultad de Farmacia, Universidad de Costa Rica Ciudad Universitaria, Costa Rica.

Gutiérrez, J. M. 1986. Myonecrosis induced by *Bothrops asper* venom: Pathogenesis and treatment. Proceedings Second American Symposium of Animal, Plant and Microbial Toxins. Tempe, Ariz. Pp. 27–39.

Gutiérrez, J. M., and R. Bolaños. 1980. El problema de los efectos hemorragico y mionecrotico por mordeduras de serpiente en el continente americano. Bol. Of. Sanit. Panam. 89:149–158.

Gutiérrez, J. M., L. Cerdas, O. Arroyo, E. Rojas, B. Lomonte, and J. E. Gené. 1982. Patogénesis y neutralización de los effectos locales inducidos por veneno de la serpiente terciopelo (*Bothrops asper*). Acta Med. Costarric. 25:225.

Gutiérrez, J. M., F. Chaves, R. Bolaños, L. Cerdas, E. Rojas, O. Arroyo, and E. Portilla. 1981. Neutralización de los effectos locales del veneno de *Bothrops asper* por un antiveneno polivalente. Toxicon 19:493–500. (Costa Rica)

Gutiérrez, J. M., J. A. Gené, G. Rojas, and L. Cerdas. 1985. Neutralization of proteolytic and hemorrhagic activities of Costa Rican snake venoms by a polyvalent antivenom. Toxicon 23:887–893.

Gutiérrez, J. M., G. Rojas, B. Lomonte, J. A. Gené, and L. Cerdas. 1986. Comparative study of the edema-forming activity of Costa Rican snake venoms and its neutralization by a polyvalent antivenom. Proceedings Second American Symposium on Animal, Plant and Microbial Toxins. Tempe, Ariz. P. 61.

Haas, J. 1966. Die corticosteroide Therapie nach Intoxikation mit Schlangengiften, sowie eigene Beobachtungen beider Behandlung eines Bisses von *Bothrops nasutus*. Z. Tropenmed. Parasitol. 17:26–35.

Hardy, D. L. 1982. Envenomation by the Mexican lance-headed rattlesnake *Crotalus polystictus*: A case report. Toxicon 20:1089–1091.

Hardy, L. M., and R. W. McDiarmid. 1969. The amphibians and reptiles of Sinaloa, Mexico. Univ. Kan. Publ. Mus. Nat. Hist. 18:39–252. (*Leptophis diplotropis*)

Heatwole, H., and I. B. Banuchi. 1966. Envenomation by the colubrid snake, *Alsophis portoricensis*. Herpetologica 22:132–134.

Hulin, A., Ochoa, and J. M. Desbordes. 1982. Envenimations par des crotalides en Guyane Française. Med. d'Afrique Noire 29:249–253.

Jaume, M. L. 1983. Notas sobre mordeduras tóxicas de serpientes (Reptilia-Serpientes-Colubridae). Rev. Cubana Med. Trop. 35:224–230.

Jaume, M. L., and O. H. Garrido. 1980. Notas sobre mordeduras de jubo *Alsophis cantherigerus* Bibron (Reptilia-Serpentes-Colubridae) en Cuba. Rev. Cubana Med. Trop. 32:145–148.

Jiménez, E. 1977. Tratamiento de las mordeduras de serpiente. P. 575 in R. Loria, ed. Normas Pediátricas. San José, Editorial Universidad de Costa Rica.

Jiménez, E., and J. García. 1969. Análisis de 86 casos de ofidismo en niños. Rev. Med. Hosp. Nacion. Niños 4:91–99.

Jiménez Porras, J. M., M. A. Gómez Leiva, J. A. Rodriguez Barquero, S. A. Minton, Jr., J. J. Graydon, and A. do Amaral. 1973. Reptile Toxins. Pp. 697–723 in Biology data book. Vol. 2. Federation of American Societies for Experimental Biology (FASEB). (*Bothrops alternatus, B. atrox, B. jararaca, Crotalus durissus, Lachesis muta, Micrurus corallinus, Porthidium nummifer*)

Johanbocke, M. M. 1974. Effects of a bite from *Conophis lineatus* (Squamata: Colubridae). Bull. Philadelphia Herpetol. Soc. 22:39.

Johanbocke, M. M. 1976. Effects of a bite by a Godman's viper, *Bothrops godmani*. Bull. Philadelphia Herpetol. Soc. 24:10–12.

Juliá Zertuche, J. 1981. Reptiles mexicanos de importancia para la salud pública y su distribución geográfica. Salud Pública (México) 23:329–343.

Jutzy, D. A., S. H. Biber, N. W. Elton, and E. C. Lowry. 1953. A clinical and pathological analysis of snake bites on the Panama Canal Zone. Am. J. Trop. Med. Hyg. 2:129–141.

Kamiguti, A. S., S. Matsunaga, M. Spir, I. S. Sano Martins, and L. Nahas. 1985. Changes of blood coagulation following human accidental inoculation of *Bothrops* venom. Abstract. Toxicon 23:579. (*B. jararaca*)

Kamiguti, A. S., S. Matsunaga, M. Spir, I. S. Sano Martins, and L. Nahas. 1986. Alterations of the blood coagulation system after accidental human inoculation by *Bothrops jararaca* venom. Brazilian J. Med. Biol. Res. 19:199–204.

Koba, K. 1969. Introductory notes on Brazilian venomous snakes and the Instituto Butantan. Snake 1:23–24.

Lancini, A. R. 1979. Serpientes de Venezuela. Caracas, Talleres de Gráficas Armitano, C. A.

Larrick, J. W., J. A. Yost, and J. Kaplan. 1978. Snake bite among the Waorani indians of eastern Ecuador. Trans. R. Soc. Trop. Med. Hyg. 72:542–543.

Larrick, J. W., J. A. Yost, and J. Kaplan, G. King, and J. Mayhall. 1979. Patterns of health and disease among the Waorani indians of eastern Ecuador. Med. Anthropol. 3:147–189.

Leiva Herdoiza, G., P. Franco De Oliveira, S. Godoy Marks, M. Braz Zanolli, E. Podolan, P. Piazza Branco, A. Soares Mulinari, A. Laffitte, and J. G. Rocha de Carvalho. 1983. Alterações electrocardiográficas em ofidismo. Arq. Bras. Cardiol. 40:319–323. (*Bothrops, Crotalus*; Brazil)

Leon Luzardo, M. 1961. Aspectos hemorrágicos de las mordeduras de serpientes. Rev. Venez. Sanid. Asist. Soc. 26:913–922.

Lomonte, B. 1985. Edema-forming activity of bushmaster (*Lachesis muta stenophrys*) and Central American rattlesnake (*Crotalus durissus durissus*) venoms and neutralization by a polyvalent antivenom. Toxicon 23:173–176. (Costa Rica)

López, M., L. G. Foscarini, J. M. Alvares, I. Diniz Filho, U. D. Marra, and N. M. M. Procópio. 1972. Tratamento intensivo das complicações do acidente ofídico. Rev. Asoc. Med. Minas Gerais 23:107–112. (*Bothrops*)

Magalhaes, R. A., M. M. F. Ribeiro, N. A. De Rezende, and C. F. S. Amaral. 1986. Rabdomiólise secundária a accidente ofídico crotálico (*Crotalus durissus terrificus*). Rev. Inst. Med. Trop. São Paulo 28:228–233.

Malasit, P., D. A. Warrell, P. Chanthavanich, C. Viravan, J. Mongkolsapaya, B. Singhthong, and C. Supich. 1986. Prediction, prevention, and mechanism of early (anaphylactic) antivenom reactions in victims of snake bites. Br. Med. J. 292:17–20.

Martén, E. 1976. Tratamiento quirúrgico de las mordeduras de serpiente. P. 129 in Filosofía y lógica de la cirugía pediátrica. Costa Rica, Imprenta Universal.

Martén, E. 1978. The surgical treatment of snake bites. Pp. 471–475. P. Rosenberg ed., Toxins—animal, plant and microbial. Oxford, Pergamon Press. (*Bothrops asper*; Costa Rica)

Mekbel, S. T., and R. Céspedes. 1963. Las lesiones renales en el ophidismo. Acta Med. Costarric. 6:111–118.

Minton, S. A., Jr. 1979. Beware: Nonpoisonous snakes. Nat. Hist., New York 87:56–61.

Minton, S. A., Jr. 1979. Beware: Nonpoisonous snakes. Clin. Toxicol. 15:259–265.

Minton, S. A., Jr. 1982. Snakebite. Pp. 283–300, in J. H. Steele, ed. CRC Handbook series in zoonoses. Vol. 3: Parasitic zoonoses. Boca Raton, Fla., CRC Press.

Minton, S. A., Jr., H. G. Dowling, and F. E. Russell. 1965. Poisonous snakes of the world. Washington, D.C., U.S. GPO.

Minton, S. A., Jr. and D. Mebs. 1978. Vier bissfälle durch Colubriden. Salamandra 14:41–43. (*Coniophanes, Cyclagras = Hydrodynastes, Leptophis ahaetulla*)

Monroy Velasco, J. 1966. Inyección in situ de antisuero en el tratamiento de la intoxicación por mordedura de serpiente. Mem. Inst. Butantan Simp. Internac. 33:857–860.

Nickerson, M. A., and R. W. Henderson. 1976. A case of envenomation by the South American colubrid, *Philodryas olfersi*. Herpetologica 32:197–198.

Oden, L. H., Jr. 1975. Historia de una mordedura de ofidio. Consulta 2:41–46. (Colombia)

Oostburg, B. F. J. 1973. Case report. A snakebite in Surinam. Trop. Geogr. Med. 25:187–189. (*Bothrops atrox*)

Parrish, H. M. 1966. Bites by foreign venomous snakes in the United States. Am. J. Med. Sci. 251:150–155. (*Bothriechis schlegelii*)

Pellegrini Filho, A., and O. Vital Brazil. 1976. Origem da paralisia respiratória causada pela peçonha de *Micrurus frontalis*. Cienc. Cult. 28:199.

Peña Chavarría, A., V. M. Villarejos, and M. Zomer. 1970. Clinical importance of prothrombin time determination in snake-venom poisoning. Am. J. Trop. Med. Hyg. 19:342–344. (*Bothrops asper*; Costa Rica)

Perez De La Mora, S., A. Pérez-Miravete, and G. García P. 1972. Estudios de protección cruzada entre sueros y venenos de las especies más communes de serpientes mexicanas. Rev. Invest. Salud Pública (México) 32:145–157.

Pesce, H., and H. Lumbreras. 1956. Ofidismo en Lima por *Bothrops picta*. Am. Fac. Med., Lima 39:1152–1188.

Pettigrew, L. C., and J. P. Glass. 1985. Neurologic complications of a coral snake bite. Neurology 35:589–592. (*Micrurus laticollaris*; Mexico)

Picado, C. 1931. Serpientes venenosas de Costa Rica. Sus venenos, seroterápia antiofídica. San José, Imprenta Alsina. Reprinted 1976. San José, Editorial Universidad de Costa Rica.

Pickwell, G. V. 1973. Production, toxicity and preliminary pharmacology of venom from the sea snake, *Pelamis platurus*, with observations on its probable threat to man along middle America. Pp. 247–265 in L. R. Worthen ed. Food-drugs from the sea. Conference proceedings 1972. Washington, D.C., Marine Technology Society.

Restrepo, M. 1969. Mordeduras por serpientes. Antioquia Med. 19:459–469.

Roboz, L. 1959. Mordeduras de serpientes. Estudio clínico patológico y apuntes sobre su tratamiento. Rev. Med. Costarric. 2:134–138.

Rosado-López, L., and F. A. Laviada-Arrigunaga. 1977. Accidente ofídico. Communicación de 38 casos. Prensa Med. Mex. 42:409–412. (*Bothrops, Crotalus*; Mexico)

Rosenfeld, G. 1964. Accidentes por animais peçonhentos (Serpentes, aranhas e escorpiões). Pp. 872–887 in R. Veronesi, ed. Doenças infecciosas e parasitárias. 2d ed. Rio de Janeiro, Editorial Guanabara-Koogan.

Rosenfeld, G. 1965. Moléstias por venenos animais. Pinheiros Terapeut. 17:3–15.

Rosenfeld, G. 1966. Mordeduras de serpientes venenosas. Abbottempo 4:8–10.

Rosenfeld, G. 1971. Symptomatology, pathology, and treatment of snake bites in South America. Pp. 345–384 in W. Bücherl and E. E. Buckley, eds. Venomous animals and their venoms. Vol. 2. New York, Academic Press.

Rosenfeld, G. 1972. Animais peçonhentos e tóxicos do Brasil. Pp. 430–375 in Lacaz et al., eds. Introdução á geografia médica do Brasil. São Paulo, EDUSP.

Rosenfeld, G. 1979. Envenenamentos por picadas de animais peçonhentos. P. 821 in W. Cossermelli, R. V. Saldanha, and L. G. C. C. de Serro Azul, eds. Terapêutica clínica. Rio de Janeiro, Guanabara-Koogan.

Rosenfeld, G., and E. M. A. Kelen. 1966. Cross neutralization of the coagulant activity of some snake venoms by antivenins. Toxicon 4:7–15.

Rosenfeld, G., and E. M. A. Kelen. 1969. Bibliography of animal venoms, envenomations and treatments (period 1500–1968). São Paulo, Instituto Butantan.

Rosenfeld, G., E. M. A. Kelen, and L. Nahas. 1958. Regeneration of fibrinogen after defibrination by bothropic venom in man and dogs. Relationship with clotting and bleeding times. Rev. Clin. São Paulo 34:36–44.

Russell, F. E. 1967. Bites by the Sonoran coral snake *Micruroides euryxanthus*. Toxicon 5:39–42.

Russell, F. E. 1979. The clinical problem of crotalid snake venom poisoning. Pp. 978–996. in Handbook of experimental pharmacology. Vol. 52. Snake venoms, ed. C.-Y. Lee (ed.). Berlin, Springer-Verlag.

Russell, F. E. 1980. Snake venom poisoning. Philadelphia, J. B. Lippincott Co.

Russell, F. E. 1983. Snake venom poisoning. Great Neck, N.Y., Scholium International.

Russell, F. E., and R. S. Scharffenberg. 1964. Bibliography of snake venoms and venomous snakes. West Covina, Calif., Bibliographic Associates. (Eighty-eight titles are from South and Central America through 1964)

Saavedra, D., A. Restrepo and N. Caro. 1975. Ofidiotoxicosis bothrópica en Colombia. Parte 1: Aspectos clinicos y hematológicos. Antioquia Méd. 25:13–26. (*Bothriechis schlegelii*, *Bothriopsis punctata*; *Bothrops asper*; Medellín)

Sandner-Montilla, R., and R. Garcia Lopez. 1962. Estudio bioquímico y electroforético de las ponzoñas de las principales serpientes de la Familia Crotalidae venezolanas y su actividad biológica en el hombre. Mem. Soc. Cienc. Nat. La Salle 22:5–33.

Sass, J. K. 1979. Snake bite in the Canal Zone: An update with review of cases from September 1975 to August 1978. Lab. Med. 10:77–81. (*Bothrops*; central Panama)

Schenone, H., and H. Reyes. 1965. Animales ponzoñosos de Chile. Bol. Chil. Parasitol. 20:104–108. (*Tachymensis peruviana*)

Schmutz, J., and E. Stahel. 1985. Anaphylactoid reactions to snakebite. Letter. Lancet 2:1306. (*Crotalus durissus*)

Seib, R. L. 1980. Human envenomation from the bite of an aglyphous false coral snake *Pliocercus elapoides* (Serpentes: Colubridae). Toxicon 18:399–401. (Mexico)

Shaw, C. E. 1971. The coral snakes, genera *Micrurus* and *Micruroides*, of the United States and northern Mexico. Pp. 157–172 in W. Bücherl and E. E. Buckley, eds. Venomous animals and their venoms. Vol. 2. N.Y., Academic Press.

Silva, M. V. da, and M. A. Buononato. 1984. Relato clínico de envenenamiento humano por *Philodryas olfersi*. Mem. Inst. Butantan 47/48:121–126.

Silva, O. A. da, M. López, and P. Godoy. 1979. Bilateral cortical necrosis and calcification of the kidneys following snakebite: A case report. Clin. Nephrol. 11:136–139. (*Bothrops*; Brazil)

Silva, O. A. da, M. López, and P. Godoy. 1979. Intensive care unit treatment of acute renal failure following snakebite. Am. J. Trop. Med. Hyg. 28:401–407. (*Bothrops jararaca*, *Crotalus d. terrificus*; Brazil)

Silva Haad, J. 1982a. [dated 1980/81]. Accidentes humanos por las serpientes de los géneros *Bothrops y Lachesis*. Mem. Inst. Butantan 44/45:403–423. (*Bothriopsis bilineata*, *Bothrops atrox*; Leticia, Colombia)

Silva Haad, J. 1982b. Las serpientes del género *Bothrops* en la Amazonia colombiana. Amazonia/82 Comando Unificado del Sur 1982:45–50.

Silva Haad, J., and R. A. Rodriguez. 1985. Las serpientes *Micrurus* de la Amazonia colombiana. Amazonia/85 Comando Unificado del Sur 1985:26–28.

Solórzano, A., and L. Cerdas. 1986. A new subspecies of the bushmaster, *Lachesis muta*, from southeastern Costa Rica. J. Herpetol. 20:463–466.

Stahel, E., and G. A. Marbet. 1983. Snakebite and coagulation disturbances. (In German.) Schweiz. Med. Wochenschr. 133:970–976. (*Bothrops atrox*)

Sutherland, S. K., A. R. Coulter, and R. D. Harris. 1979. Rationalisation of first-aid measures for elapid snakebite. Lancet 1:183–186. (pressure/immobilization first aid method)

Swaroop, S., and B. Grab. 1954. Snakebite mortality in the world. Bull. W. H. O. 10:35–76.

Tay, J., L. Castillo, and R. Romero-Cabello. 1981. Tratamiento de las mordeduras por serpientes ponzoñosas. Salud Pública (México) 23:457–572.

Tay, J., L. Castillo, R. Romero-Cabello, J. Juliá-zertuche, and C. O. Velasco. 1980. Accidentes por mordeduras de animales ponzoñosos. Rev. Fac. Med. (México) 23:7–8.

Theakston, R. D. G., H. A. Reid, D. Iddon and J. W. Larrick. 1983. Protective effect of snake venom antibodies in sera of previous snakebite victim Ann. Trop. Med. Parasitol. 77:311–314. (Waorani Indians, Ecuador)

Theakston, R. D. G., H. A. Reid, J. W. Larrick, J. Kaplan, and J. A. Yost. 1981. Snake venom antibodies in Ecuadorian indians. J. Trop. Med. Hyg. 84:199–202.

Tinoco, R. C. 1972. Picada de cobra (uso de heparina como substituto de soro antiofídico). J. Brasil Med. 23:109–114.

Vallejo-Freire, A. 1967. Informe sobre condiciones para la elaboración de sueros antiofídicos y programas correlativos en Costa Rica. Washington, D.C., Organ. Panam. Sal., Offic. Sanit. Panam.

Vital Brazil, O. 1980. Venenos ofídicos neurotóxicos. Rev. Assoc. Med. Brasil. 26:212–218. (*Crotalus durissus terrificus*, *Micrurus*)

Vital Brazil, O. 1987. Coral snake venoms: Mode of action and pathophysiology of experimental envenomation. Rev. Inst. Med. Trop. São Paulo 29:119–126.

Wajchenberg, B. L., J. Sesso, and T. Inague. 1954. Feiçôes clínico-laboratoriais do envenenamento crotálico humano. Rev. Assoc Med. Brasil. 1:1979.

Weinstein, S. A., S. A. Minton, and C. E. Wilde. 1985. The distribution among ophidian venoms of a toxin isolated from the venom of the Mojave rattlesnake (*Crotalus scutulatus scutulatus*). Toxicon 23:825–844. (*Crotalus durissus*)

Wolff, H. 1958. Insuficiencia hipofisaria anterior por picada de ofidio. Arq. Brasil. Endocrinol. Metabol. 7:25–47. (*Bothrops jararacussu*)

Zethelius, M., and M. J. Balick. 1982. Modern medicine and shamanistic ritual: A case of positive synergistic response in the treatment of a snakebite. J. Ethnopharmacol. 5:181–185. (*Bothrops* "montañosa"; Colombia)

Zugaib, M., A. C. S. D. de Barros, R. E. Bittar, E. de A. Burdmann, and B. Neme. 1985. Abruptio placentae following snake bite. Am. J. Obstet. Gynecol. 151:754–755. (*Bothrops jararaca*; Brazil)

# Producers of Antivenoms for Venomous Snakes of Latin America

*David L. Hardy, M.D.*

A number of institutions in the Western Hemisphere produce antivenoms useful in the treatment of venomous snakebite in North, Central, and South America. These antivenoms and the institutions that produce them are listed along with the species against which they have been prepared. This information is based on Chippaux and Goyffon (1983) and previous compilations. As of 1985, antivenom was no longer available from Syntex do Brasil, São Paulo. It should be noted that Wyeth International indicated its antivenom may be used in the treatment of all New World pitviper bites.

| INSTITUTION | ANTIVENOM | SPECIES |
|---|---|---|
| Wyeth International Ltd.<br>P. O. Box 8299<br>Philadelphia, PA 19101<br>USA | Wyeth Antivenin (Crotalidae) Polyvalent | *Crotalus adamanteus, C. atrox, C. durissus terrificus*<br>*Bothrops atrox* (probably includes *B. asper*), |
| | Wyeth Antivenin (*Micrurus fulvius*), North American coral snake | *Micrurus f. fulvius* |
| Laboratorios "MYN" S.A.<br>Av. Coyoacán 1707<br>México 12, D. F., Mexico | "Snake Antivenin" | *Agkistrodon bilineatus, Bothrops asper, Porthidium nummifer*<br>*Crotalus atrox, C. molossus nigrescens, C. tigris, C. durissus* |
| Instituto Nacional de Higiene, Csda.<br>Gerencia General de Biológicos y Reactivos<br>M. Escobedo 20, C. P. 11400<br>México 12, D. F., Mexico | Anti-*Crotalus*<br>Anti-*Bothrops* | |
| Instituto Clodomiro Picado<br>Universidad de Costa Rica<br>Ciudad Universitaria "Rodrigo Facio"<br>San José, Costa Rica | "Polyvalent serum" | *Bothrops asper, Crotalus d. durissus, Lachesis muta stenophrys* |
| | "Anti-Coral" polyvalent | *Micrurus nigrocinctus, M. f. fulvius, M. dumerilii* |
| | Panamerican anti-coral polyvalent serum | *Micrurus fulvius, M. nigrocinctus, M. carinicauda* (=*dumerilii*), *M. frontalis, M. corallinus, M. spixii, M. mipartitus* (=*multifasciatus*), *M. alleni, M. lemniscatus* |
| | "Anti-Laquesico" monovalent | *Lachesis muta stenophrys* |
| | "Anti-Coral" monovalent | *Micrurus multifasciatus* |
| Instituto Nacional de Salud<br>Av. Eldorado con Carrera 50, Zona 6<br>Bogotá D. E., Colombia | "Polyvalent" (Suero Antiofídico) | *Bothrops asper/Bothrops atrox, Crotalus durissus* subsp. |
| Laboratorios Behrens<br>Av. Principal de Chapellin<br>Apartado 62<br>Caracas 101, Venezuela | Polyvalent ("Antibothròpico") | *Bothrops atrox/ Brothrops asper, B. venezuelensis, Crotalus durissus* subsp. |
| | Bi-valent | *B. atrox/B. asper, B. venezuelensis* |
| | Monovalent ("Anticrotálico") | *Crotalus durissus* subsp. |

| INSTITUTION | ANTIVENOM | SPECIES |
|---|---|---|
| Instituto Butantan<br>Caixa Postal 65<br>São Paulo, São Paulo<br>Brazil | Sôro antibothrópico | *Bothrops alternatus, B. cotiara, B. jararaca, B. jararacussu, B. moojeni, B. neuwiedi, B. pradoi* |
| | Sôro anticrotálico | *Crotalus durissus terrificus, C. d. collilineatus* |
| | Sôro antielapidico | *Micrurus frontalis, M. corallinus* |
| | Sôro antiofídico polivalente | *Bothrops* spp., *Crotalus* sp. |
| | Sôro antilaquético | *Lachesis muta* |
| | Sôro antibotrópico-laquético (a combination of these sera) | |
| Institutos Vital Brazil S. A.<br>Caixa Postal 28<br>Niteroi, Rio de Janeiro<br>Brazil | Sôro antiofídico polivalente | *Bothrops* spp., *Crotalus* sp. |
| | Sôro antibotrópico | *Bothrops* spp. |
| | Sôro anticrotálico | *Crotalus d. terrificus* |
| Fundação Ezequiel Dias<br>Rua Conde Pereira<br>80-Gameleira 30550<br>Belo Horizonte-MG<br>Brazil | Sôro antibotrópico | *Bothrops jararaca, B. jararacussu, B. alternatus, B. neuwiedi* |
| | Sôro anticrotálico | *Crotalus d. terrificus* |
| Instituto Nacional de Higiene y Medicina Tropical "Leopoldo Izquieta Pérez"<br>Casilla 3961<br>Guayaquil, Ecuador | Monovalent antivenom | *Bothrops asper* |
| Institutos Nacionales de Salud<br>Departamento de Animales Venenosos<br>Calle Capac Yupanqui 1400<br>Apartado 451<br>Lima, Peru | Suero antibotrópico polivalente | *Bothriopsis bilineata smaragdina, B. brazili, B. castelnaudi* (=*Bothriopsis taeniata*), *B. pictus, Bothrops atrox* |
| | Suero anti-crotálico | *Crotalus d. terrificus* |
| | Suero anti-lachésico | *Lachesis muta* |
| Instituto Nacional de Microbiología "Dr. Carlos G. Malbran"<br>Av. Velez Sarsfield 563<br>Buenos Aires, Buenos Aires<br>Argentina | Antibothrops bivalente | *Bothrops alternatus, B. neuwiedi diporus, B. ammodytoides* |
| | Antibothrops tetravalente | *Bothrops alternatus, B. neuwiedi, B. jararaca, B. jararacussu* |
| | Anticrótalus | *Crotalus d. terrificus* |
| | Antimicrurus | *Micrurus frontalis, M. corallinus* |
| Ejército Argentino<br>Campo de Mayo, Batallon 601<br>Provincia de Buenos Aires<br>Argentina | Antibothrops bivalente<br>Antimicrurus | |
| Centro de Zoología Aplicada<br>Universidad de Córdoba<br>Provincia de Córdoba<br>Argentina | Antibothrops bivalente<br>Anticrótalus | *Crotalus d. terrificus* |

REGIONAL ACCOUNTS AND KEYS TO VENOMOUS SNAKES

# Mexico and Central America

The land mass situated between the contiguous United States and the continent of South America is composed of the territory of Mexico, most of which falls within biotic North America, and Central America, which comprises seven of the smallest countries of Latin America: Belize, Guatemala, Honduras, El Salvador, Nicaragua, Costa Rica, and Panama.

Mexico is the third largest Latin American country and is roughly one-quarter the size of the contiguous United States. It is the second most populous country in Latin America, with about 67 million inhabitants as of 1980.

Physiographic Central America extends from the Isthmus of Tehuantepec (Mexico) in the north to the Darién lowlands in the south; its total area approximates that of the state of Texas. The low but rugged Nicaraguan Depression separates the two major mountain systems of the region into Nuclear Central America, which extends from southern Mexico to northern Nicaragua, and Isthmian Central America, which stretches from southern Nicaragua to Panama. The population of Central America totals almost 25 million and is concentrated primarily in urban areas.

Much of Mexico and Central America contains cone-shaped volcanoes, extensive mountain ranges, or high plateaus. More than 50% of Mexico is at an elevation exceeding 1,000 m above sea level. All of the countries have at least one seacoast; coastal lowlands tend to be extensive along the Atlantic Ocean, narrow along the Pacific. Xeric and semiarid regions occur primarily in Mexico, although dry habitats prevail in scattered locales throughout Central America, principally along the Pacific Coast or in rainshadow valleys. Numerous types of tropical forest can be found, distributed chiefly according to elevation and humidity. Humidity is greatly affected by the convection currents of northeast trade winds and by the position of mountain ranges.

Much of Mexico and Central America has been cleared for agriculture, thus creating areas of secondary growth that provide suitable habitat for such venomous snake species as *Bothrops asper*. This abundant species of large pitviper is the principal cause of snakebite envenomation throughout its range. The rattlesnakes (genera *Crotalus* and *Sistrurus*) undergo their maximum radiation in Mexico, with a total of 26 species found in that country. They constitute a second important source of snakebite envenomation. The region also contains the world's only venomous lizards (genus *Heloderma*), which are found in Mexico and Guatemala; the range of one species, however, extends into the United States. Bites from these lizards are rare. For specific information refer to country accounts, distribution tables, and identification keys.

## MEXICO

Mexico is the northernmost of the Latin American countries and one of the largest, encompassing 1,972,547 km$^2$. It is bounded on the north by the United States and on the south by Belize and Guatemala. Mexico has 2,780 km of coastline on the Atlantic Ocean and 7,360 km on the Pacific and the Gulf of California.

Physiographically, Mexico is exceedingly complex. For purposes of delimiting snake distributions, it may be divided conveniently into the following general regions: (1) the Mexican Plateau, (2) the Sierra Madre Oriental, (3) the Sierra Madre Occidental, (4) the Transverse Volcanic Cordillera, (5) the Sierra Madre del Sur and associated highlands, (6) the Pacific coastal lowlands, (7) the Rio de las Balsas Basin, (8) the Gulf coastal lowlands, (9) the Yucatán Peninsula, (10) the Isthmus of Tehuantepec, (11) the highlands of southern Mexico, and (12) the Peninsula of Baja California.

The Mexican Plateau is the largest physiographic province in Mexico and extends from the U.S.-Mexican border southward to the east-west axis of tall volcanoes that stretches across central Mexico. The Mexican Plateau is bounded by three mountain systems: the Sierra Madre Oriental to the east, the Sierra Madre Occidental to the west, and the Transverse Volcanic Cordillera to the south. The northern two-thirds of the plateau is relatively arid, and this portion, which is characterized by elevations averaging 1,000 m above sea level, is often referred to as the Mesa del Norte or Altiplanicie Septentrional. The most conspicuous features of the landscape of the Altiplanicie Septentrional are the internally drained basins called *bolsones*. The plateau gradually gains elevation to the south, and many areas, particularly from central Jalisco across to western Hidalgo, may exceed 2,000 m above sea level. This more highly elevated southern third of the Mexican Plateau is known as the Mesa Central or Altiplanicie Meridional. The southern portion of the Altiplanicie Meridional dips into a shallow basin called the bajío in the region of Guanajuato. Similar to the northern part of the Mexican Plateau, much of the Altiplanicie Meridional is characterized by a dry climate and desertlike vegetation. However, many of the higher mountain ranges possess more mesic, luxuriant forests. In many areas the landscape is dotted with numerous cinder cones called *xalapazcos* ("dry cinder cones") or *axalapazcos* ("with small lakes"). Many lakes of internal drainage are scattered across the southern part of the Mexican Plateau, including the lakes of Xochimilco, Cuitzeo, Pátzcuaro, Zacapu, Sayula, and Magdalena.

The Sierra Madre Oriental is a series of rather tightly folded ridges, most of which run in a north-south direction. This mountain system borders the eastern side of the Mexican Plateau and extends southward to about the Cerro Zempoaltepec region in the northern Oaxacan highlands. In the north the Sierra Madre Oriental bifurcates, with one arc of east-west trending ranges reaching into the northern portion of the Mexican Plateau and terminating near the point were the borders of Coahuila, Zacatecas, and Durango come together, and the other arc extending northwestward into the Big Bend region of Texas. Much of the crest of the Sierra Madre Oriental ranges from 2,000 to 3,000 m in elevation and may exceed 4,000 m.

The Sierra Madre Occidental extends in the north from the southwestern New Mexico and southeastern Arizona-Mexican border southward to the Río Grande de Santiago in Jalisco. Most of this range rises to a maximum of 2,500–3,000 m. A series of deeply incised canyons, called *barrancas*, characterizes the western side of the Sierra Madre Occidental and makes this one of the most rugged regions in Mexico.

The Transverse Volcanic Cordillera comprises a series of large volcanoes distributed in an east-west axis across central Mexico. The larger volcanoes (Nahuatl name is given in parentheses) and their elevations, from east to west, are Orizaba (Citlaltépetl) at 5,700 m (the highest point in Middle America), the Cofre de Perote (Nauchampatepetl) at 4,280 m, Malinche (Matlalcueyatl) at 4,461 m, Popocatépetl at 5,400 m, Iztaccíhuatl at 5,286 m, Nevado de Toluca (Zinantecati) at 4,392 m, Tancítaro at 3,842 m, and the Nevado de Colima at 4,265 m. The Sierra de Ajusco to the south of the Valley of Mexico is part of this region. The southern escarpment of the Transverse Volcanic Cordillera drains into the Río de las Balsas Depression.

To the southeast of the Transverse Volcanic Cordillera, the isolated volcanic Sierra de los Tuxtlas arises out of the Gulf coastal lowlands to a maximum elevation of about 1,600 m at the summit of the Volcán San Martín Tuxtla. The extinct volcanoes Volcán Santa Marta and Volcán Martín Pajapan exceed 1,200 m in elevation. Lake Catemaco is located within this range. Whether or not this range is geologically a part of the Transverse Volcanic Cordillera or represents an unrelated tectonic event is a matter of dispute.

The Sierra Madre del Sur and associated highlands are located south of the Río de las Balsas. The Sierra Madre del Sur is a particularly rugged area with few flatlands; it extends from Guerrero in the west into south-central Oaxaca. Cerro Teótepec is the highest elevation in Guerrero, at about 3,810 m. Average elevations of mountain crests in the Sierra Madre del Sur are between 1,800 and 2,000 m. To the north of the main crest of the Sierra Madre del Sur in Oaxaca is a series of extremely rugged ranges; between a few of these lie structural basins such as that containing the city of Oaxaca. This region is known as the Mesa del Sur, but it forms a continuous highland with the Sierra Madre del Sur. One of the highest peaks of the Mesa del Sur is Cerro San Felipe, which reaches 3,110 m. Northwest of the city of Oaxaca several portions of the Continental Divide exceed 3,000 m.

The Pacific coastal lowlands tend to be narrow throughout most of Mexico. They are widest to the north, in Sonora. In the vicinity of San Blas, Nayarit, mountainous spurs extend to the coast. Other than the Río de las Balsas, the major river systems are the Río Yaqui, Río Mayo, Río del Fuerte, Río Culiacán, Río Grande de Santiago (or Río Lerma), and the Río Verde.

The Río de las Balsas forms a great inland basin that is mostly hot, low, and dry hilly country. Extending to the west-northwest from its confluence with the Río de las Balsas, the Río Tepalcatepec winds through southern Michoacán and is the major tributary of the Río de las Balsas. The Río de las Balsas Depression separates the Mexican Plateau and Transverse Volcanic Cordillera from the highlands of Oaxaca and Guerrero. This basin breaks through the mountains near the Pacific Ocean along the border of Guerrero and Michoacán and is not broadly connected with the Pacific lowlands.

The Gulf coastal lowlands extend from the Río Grande in the north to the Yucatán Peninsula in the south. The width of these lowlands varies from about 300 km in northern Tamaulipas and Nuevo León to practically nothing in central Veracruz near Punta Delgada, where a spur of mountains from the Sierra Madre Occidental extends eastward to the coast. Most of the Gulf coastal region consists of a series of gently rolling hills. In southern Veracruz the aforementioned Sierra de los

Tuxtlas dramatically rises out of the Gulf coastal plain and is isolated from other highland areas. The major river systems draining into the Gulf of Mexico are the Río Pánuco, Río Papaloapan, and Río Grijalva.

The Yucatán Peninsula is continuous with the Gulf coastal lowlands. The northern part of the peninsula is almost level, with maximum elevations of only about 50 m above sea level. This region is characterized by the absence of surface streams. To the south the peninsula becomes hilly, with the highest elevation about 350 m above sea level and a number of surface drainages. The peninsula as a whole is composed mostly of limestone with a karstic surface. Shallow depressions, called *aguadas*, are widespread, particularly in the north, as are *cenotes*, which are sinkholes resulting from the caving in of portions of subterranean stream channels.

In the Isthmus of Tehuantepec region the Mexican land mass narrows to a width of about 200 km between the Gulf of Mexico and the Pacific Ocean. The maximum elevation of the east-west trending ridge that extends across the isthmus is only about 250 m. This tropical lowland depression separates the highlands of central Oaxaca from those of extreme southeastern Oaxaca and Chiapas and presents a formidable barrier to the dispersal of highland-adapted species.

The highlands of southern Mexico east of the Isthmus of Tehuantepec extend from extreme southeastern Oaxaca through Chiapas. There are two major regions that are separated by the Río Grijalva Valley. The northern Chiapan highlands vary from the plateaulike terrain of the Meseta Central of Chiapas near San Cristóbal de Las Casas at 2,300 m to the broken, rugged peaks north of Tuxtla Gutiérrez. The Sierra Madre de Chiapas to the south of the Río Grijalva extends from Cerro Baúl in the west to Volcán Tacaná on the Mexico-Guatemalan border at 4,093 m. This steep escarpment, with the majority of peaks ranging from 2,000 to 3,100 m, overlooks the Pacific Ocean.

The Peninsula of Baja California extends southward some 1,300 km from the U.S.-Mexican border. It is separated throughout most of its length from the mainland of Mexico by the Gulf of California. A number of islands within the gulf are inhabited by rattlesnakes. A continuous backbone of mountains extends the length of the peninsula, which is oriented from north-northwest to south-southeast. In the north the Sierra de Juárez, with elevations exceeding 2,000 m, is a continuation of the Laguna Mountains of southern California. Just to the south of the Sierra de Juárez, the Sierra San Pedro Mártir reaches about 3,000 m above sea level. Elevations gradually decline to the south as far as the Sierra San Lázaro, but some peaks reach 1,500 m. In the cape area of the peninsula some peaks in the Sierra San Lázaro reach 1,800 m. The peninsula does not have extensive lowlands; the most extensive lowland region is the Vizcaino Desert on the western drainage near the center of the peninsula.

Despite its geographic location, only about 30% of Mexico is tropical, whereas 70% is subject to temperate climates and supports vegetation typical of a temperate region. As a broad generality, northern Mexico—including the northern portion of the Gulf Coast, the Mexican Plateau, and the Pacific Coast to the Isthmus of Tehuantepec—is relatively dry. Parts of northwestern Mexico and the Peninsula of California receive less than 100 mm of precipitation per year. The interior valleys and plateau region of central Mexico receive varying amounts of rainfall, generally 1,000–2,500 mm a year. Another somewhat isolated dry region is the northern part of the Yucatán Peninsula, which receives less than 1,000 mm annual precipitation. Southern Mexico—including the central and southern portions of the Gulf Coast, the high mountain ranges from Guerrero and Oaxaca southward, and the Pacific Coast from just east of the Isthmus of Tehuantepec—is relatively wet. The most humid region in Mexico is along the Caribbean drainage, where the trade winds are forced up mountain slopes; more than 6,000 mm of rain may fall in a year. Even though the Pacific Coast tends to be dry over much of its extent, mountain escarpments overlooking the coast may be quite wet: the Sierra Madre del Sur in Guerrero and Oaxaca, and the Sierra Madre de Chiapas near the Guatemalan border, receive more than 4,000 mm of rainfall per year.

Features of topography greatly complicate this simplified picture and many windward slopes and high mountains in the central portion of the country receive abundant rainfall. In a mere 30-km transect over a mountain a tremendous difference in rainfall and temperature may be evident: climates may vary along different portions of the transect from hot and wet tropical to cool and wet temperate, cold alpine, cool and dry temperate, or hot and dry desertlike conditions.

Precipitation in most of Mexico is seasonal, with most falling from May through October. On most of the Mexican Plateau, the southern mountains, and the Pacific Coast, over 80% of the annual rainfall is received during this period. The humid eastern versant also receives most of its rain during these months, but precipitation is distributed more evenly, with some rain generally falling every month.

Much of the Mexican Plateau is covered by mesquite-grassland. This plant community usually has a ground cover dominated by grasses interspersed with various shrubs and small trees, the dominant one being mesquite (*Prosopis*). Mesquite-grassland is also characteristic of the lower Río Grande Valley and the northern part of the Gulf Coast in Mexico; this particular region has been referred to as the Gulf Coast bluestem prairie.

The central portion of the Mexican Plateau from San Luis Potosí northward to Texas and Arizona is occupied by the Chihuahuan Desert. The western portion of Sonora and most of the Peninsula of Baja California are covered by the Sonoran Desert.

The mountains fringing the Mexican Plateau—the Sierra Madre Oriental, the Sierra Madre Occidental, and the Transverse Volcanic Cordillera—are covered largely by pine-oak forest. The loose term "pine-oak forest" refers to a number of vegetational associations including tall dense stands of pine forest, pine-oak woodland, piñon-juniper woodland, and oak scrub. At least three dozen species of pines and many species of oaks occur in Mexico. Many isolated pine-oak forests occur in the mountain ranges scattered across the southern portion of the Mexican Plateau, the outlying ranges of the Sierra Madre Oriental and Sierra Madre Occidental, and the higher elevations of the northern mountains of the Peninsula of Baja California. Pine-oak forests are characteristic of most of the highlands of the Sierra Madre del Sur and Mesa del Sur in Guerrero, Oaxaca, and eastern Puebla; in the southern Mexican highlands, pine-oak forest occurs in the northern Chiapan highlands and the Sierra Madre de Chiapas.

On the windward escarpments of peaks and ridges, cloud forests often are present above about 1,300 m. This vegetation type is characterized by a great variety of hardwoods, epiphytes, and tree ferns. A series of isolated cloud forests occurs along the Atlantic escarpment in the states of Tamaulipas, San Luis Potosí, Hidalgo, Puebla, Veracruz, Oaxaca, and Chiapas; on the Pacific versant cloud forests occur in Guerrero, Oaxaca, and Chiapas. On the leeward side of mountains, cloud forests generally tend to grade into pine-oak forests.

Boreal forest associations in Mexico consist primarily of some combination of firs, pines, alders, and junipers, and often have a heavy understory of bunch grasses called *zacate* or *zacatón*. Boreal forests occur only on the highest portions of the Transverse Volcanic Cordillera from the Volcán de Colima in the west to the Volcán de Orizaba in the east, on the highest peaks in the northern portions of the Sierra Madre Oriental and Sierra Madre Occidental, and on the crest of the Sierra San Pedro Mártir in the northern portion of the Peninsula of Baja California.

In Mexico a chaparral formation occurs only along the Pacific Coast of the northern portion of the Peninsula of Baja California to the west of the Sierra de Juárez and the Sierra San Pedro Mártir. This vegetation type is characterized by shrubs such as manzanita (*Arctostaphylos*), coyote bush (*Baccharis*), chamise (*Adenostoma*), wild lilac (*Ceanothus*), sage (*Artemisia*), and scrub oaks (*Quercus*).

As its name implies, most of the vegetation composing tropical deciduous forest tends to lose its leaves during the dry season. A corridor of tropical deciduous forest extends along the lower Pacific drainage from the Río Yaqui system in Sonora southward to the Isthmus of Tehuantepec, where it extends northward across the Continental Divide and thence eastward up the Río Grijalva Valley into Guatemala. This type of vegetation often occurs just below the pine-oak belt and generally does not extend to the coast except in hilly regions. Other tracts of tropical deciduous forest are not as extensive as that along the Pacific foothills; nevertheless, large areas covered with this type of forest are present in southern Tamaulipas, northeastern San Luis Potosí, and northern Veracruz. Tropical deciduous forest is also found around the periphery of the Río de las Balsas Basin, in some of the interior valleys of Oaxaca, in part of the lower portion of the Peninsula of Baja California, and in a 20–40-km-wide strip extending from the east to west across the northern Yucatán Peninsula.

Thorn forest occurs in some of the more arid regions of Mexico. This forest is generally contiguous with tropical deciduous forest, and like it, also loses its leaves during the dry season. The dominant vegetation of thorn forest consists of thorny leguminous trees, particularly acacias; organ cacti also are often present. A narrow corridor of thorn forest extends along the Pacific Coast from central Sonora to south-central Guerrero, broken only by an occasional savanna. Thorn forest also occurs along the northern coast of the Yucatán Peninsula and in southeastern Tamaulipas and northern Veracruz.

Rainforest occurs in southern lowland regions receiving heavy rainfall. It is characterized by several hundred species of broad-leaved trees, many of which attain a gigantic size and have buttressed roots, including zapote (*Achras*), mahogany (*Swietenia*), and *ramón* (*Brosimum*). Rainforest is distributed in southeastern Mexico from along the Atlantic drainage in the Sierra de los Tuxtlas across the northern portion of Chiapas and southern Tabasco, thence northward, occupying the southern half of the Yucatán Peninsula. This type of forest also occurs along the lower piedmont of the Sierra Madre de Chiapas.

Tropical evergreen forest occurs along the Caribbean coast from northern Veracruz, extending inland as far as Cuidad de Valles in San Luis Potosí, southward to about the city of Veracruz, thence inland along the Atlantic foothills to northwestern Chiapas. An east-west strip of tropical evergreen forest extends across most of the northern third of the Yucatán Peninsula and is transitional between rainforest to the south and tropical deciduous forest to the north. Many of the same species of trees characteristic of rainforest are also found in tropical evergreen forest.

Arid tropical scrub covers the lower elevations of the Río de las Balsas Basin, and a few isolated patches occur in rainshadow valleys in the Atlantic drainages of southern Puebla and northern Oaxaca. Organ cacti, prickly pear cacti, and thorny leguminous shrubs, particularly acacias, are prevalent in this vegetational association. Arid tropical scrub is characterized by much sparser, lower vegetation than thorn forest and occurs in regions receiving less precipitation.

Isolated tropical savannas occur along flat coastal plains of the Pacific Ocean and Caribbean Sea in Mexico. The most extensive savannas are in the south, especially southern Veracruz and most of Tabasco. On the Pacific Coast, savannas predominate from southeastern Oaxaca through Chiapas. Dominant plants are coarse tropical grasses, palms, and palmettos.

Mexico possesses a larger number of dangerously venomous snakes (59 species) than any other country in the New World; in addition, the only two species of venomous lizards (*Heloderma*) in the world occur within its borders. Included in its fauna are practically every species of venomous snake occurring in the United States and most of those known from Guatemala and Belize. A few species presently known only to the south of Mexico may eventually be found within its borders, but this is unlikely. Possible candidates are *Micrurus hippocrepis*, *M. stuarti*, and *Porthidium ophryomegas*. The distributions of the species of dangerously venomous reptiles in Mexico are presented by physiographic region and vegetation type in Tables 4 and 5, respectively.

**Table 4**

Distributions by physiographic region of venomous reptiles in Mexico

| Species | Mexican Plateau | Sierra Madre Oriental | Sierra Madre Occidental | Transverse Volcanic Cordillera | Sierra Madre del Sur | Pacific coastal lowlands | Río de las Balsas Basin | Gulf coastal lowlands | Yucatán Peninsula | Isthmus of Tehuantepec | Southern Mexico highlands | Peninsula of California |
|---|---|---|---|---|---|---|---|---|---|---|---|---|
| *Pelamis platurus*[1] | | | | | | | | | | | | |
| *Micruroides euryxanthus* | | | X | | | X | | | | | | |
| *Micrurus bernadi* | | X | | | | | | | | | | |
| *M. bogerti* | | | | | | X | | | | | | |
| *M. browni* | | | | | X | X | | | | X | X | |
| *M. diastema* | | X | | | | | | X | X | | | |
| *M. distans* | | | X | | | X | | | | | | |
| *M. elegans* | | X | | | | | | | | | X[2] | |
| *M. ephippifer* | | | | | X | | | | | X | | |
| *M. fulvius* | X[3] | X | | | | | | X | | | | |
| *M. laticollaris* | | | | | | X | X | | | | | |
| *M. latifasciatus* | | | | | | | | | | | X[4] | |
| *M. limbatus* | | | | | | | | X[5] | | | | |
| *M. nigrocinctus* | | | | | | X | | | | | X[4] | |
| *M. proximans* | | | | | | X | | | | | | |
| *Agkistrodon bilineatus* | | | | | | X | X | X | X | | | |
| *A. contortrix* | X[3] | | | | | | | | | | | |
| *Bothriechis aurifer* | | | | | | | | | | | X[2] | |
| *B. bicolor* | | | | | | | | | | | X[4] | |
| *B. rowleyi* | | | | | | | | | | | X | |
| *B. schlegelii* | | | | | | | | X | | | | |
| *Bothrops asper* | | | | | | X[6] | | X | X | X | | |
| *Ophryacus undulatus* | | X | | | X | | | | | | | |
| *Porthidium barbouri* | | | | | X[7] | | | | | | | |
| *P. dunni* | | | | | | X | | | | X | | |
| *P. godmani* | | | | | | | | | | | X | |
| *P. hespere* | | | | | | X | | | | | | |
| *P. melanurum* | | | | | X | | | | | | | |
| *P. nasutum* | | | | | | | | X | X[8] | | | |
| *P. nummifer* | | X | | | X[2] | | | | X[8] | | X | |
| *P. olmec* | | | | | | | | X[5] | | | | |
| *P. tzotzilorum* | | | | | | | | | | | X[9] | |

**Table 4—*continued***

| Species | Mexican Plateau | Sierra Madre Oriental | Sierra Madre Occidental | Transverse Volcanic Cordillera | Sierra Madre del Sur | Pacific coastal lowlands | Río de las Balsas Basin | Gulf coastal lowlands | Yucatán Peninsula | Isthmus of Tehuantepec | Southern Mexico highlands | Peninsula of California |
|---|---|---|---|---|---|---|---|---|---|---|---|---|
| *P. yucatanicum* | | | | | | | | | X[10] | | | |
| *Crotalus atrox* | X[3] | X | X | | | X | | X | | | | |
| *C. basiliscus* | | | X | | X | X | | | | | | |
| *C. catalinensis* | | | | | | | | | | | | X[11] |
| *C. cerastes* | | | | | | X | | | | | | X |
| *C. durissus* | | X | X | | X | X | X | X | X | X | X | |
| *C. enyo* | | | | | | | | | | | | X |
| *C. exsul* | | | | | | | | | | | | X[12] |
| *C. intermedius* | | X | | | X | | | | | | | |
| *C. lannomi* | | | | X | | | | | | | | |
| *C. lepidus* | X | X | X | | | | | | | | | |
| *C. mitchellii* | | | | | | | | | | | | X |
| *C. molossus* | X | X | X | X | X | | X[13] | | | | | |
| *C. polystictus* | X | | | X | | | | | | | | |
| *C. pricei* | | X | X | | | | | | | | | |
| *C. pusillus* | | | | X | | | | | | | | |
| *C. ruber* | | | | | | | | | | | | X |
| *C. scutulatus* | X | X | X | X | | X[14] | | | | | | |
| *C. stejnegeri* | | | X | | | | | | | | | |
| *C. tigris* | | | | | | X | | | | | | |
| *C. tortugensis* | | | | | | | | | | | | X[15] |
| *C. transversus* | | | | X[16] | | | | | | | | |
| *C. triseriatus* | X | X | X | X | | | | | | | | |
| *C. viridis* | X[3] | | | | | | | | | | | X[17] |
| *C. willardi* | | | X | | | | | | | | | |
| *Sistrurus catenatus* | X[18] | X[19] | | | | | | | | | | |
| *S. ravus* | X[20] | X | | X | X | | | | | | | |
| *Heloderma horridum* | | | X | | | X | | | | X | X[21] | |
| *H. suspectum* | | | X | | | X | | | | | | |

1. Pacific marine habitat.
2. Atlantic drainage.
3. Altiplanicie Septentrional.
4. Sierra Madre de Chiapas.
5. Sierra de los Tuxtlas region, occurring at relatively high elevations.
6. Chiapas only.
7. Guerrero only.
8. Southern mesic portion.
9. Meseta Central of Chiapas.
10. Northern xeric portion.
11. Isla de Santa Catalina, Gulf of California.
12. Isla de Cedros, off west coast of Baja California.
13. Upper tributaries.
14. Sonora only.
15. Isla de Tortuga, Gulf of California.
16. Sierra de Ajusco.
17. Including Isla Coronado del Sur.
18. Known only from Bolsón de Cuatro Ciénegas, central Coahuila.
19. Known only from near Aramberri, Nuevo León.
20. Altiplanicie Meridional.
21. Rio Grijalva Depression.

**Table 5**

Distributions by vegetation type of venomous reptiles in Mexico

| Species | Pine-oak forest | Boreal forest | Cloud forest | Mesquite-grassland | Desert | Chaparral | Rain-forest | Tropical evergreen forest | Savanna | Tropical deciduous forest | Thorn forest | Arid tropical scrub |
|---|---|---|---|---|---|---|---|---|---|---|---|---|
| *Pelamis platurus*[1] | | | | | | | | | | | | |
| *Micruroides euryxanthus* | X | | | X | X | X | | | | X | X | |
| *Micrurus bernadi* | | | X | | | | | | | | | |
| *M. bogerti* | | | | | | | | | | X | | |
| *M. browni* | X | | X | | | | | | | X | | |
| *M. diastema* | X | | X | | | | X | X | X | X | X | |
| *M. distans* | X | | | | | | | | | X | X | |
| *M. elegans* | X | | X | | | | | | | | | |
| *M. ephippifer* | X | | | | | | | | | X | | |
| *M. fulvius* | X | | | X | X | | | | | | X | |
| *M. laticollaris* | | | | | | | | | | X | | X |
| *M. latifasciatus* | | | X | | | | X | | | | | |
| *M. limbatus* | | | | | | | X | X | | | | |
| *M. nigrocinctus* | X | | X | | | | | | X | | | |
| *M. proximans* | | | | | | | | | | X | X | |
| *Agkistrodon bilineatus* | | | | | | | | | X | X | X | |
| *A. contortrix* | | | | | X[2] | | | | | | | |
| *Bothriechis aurifer* | X[3] | | X | | | | | | | | | |
| *B. bicolor* | | | X | | | | X[4] | | | | | |
| *B. rowleyi* | X | | X | | | | | | | | | |
| *B. schlegelii* | | | X[5] | | | | X | | | | | |
| *Bothrops asper* | | | X[5] | | | | X | X | X | X | | |
| *Ophryacus undulatus* | X | | X | | | | | | | | | |
| *Porthidium barbouri* | X | | X | | | | | | | | | |
| *P. dunni* | | | | | | | | | | X | | |
| *P. godmani* | X | | X | | | | | | | | | |
| *P. hespere* | | | | | | | | | | X | | |
| *P. melanurum* | X | | | | | | | | | X[6] | | X[7] |
| *P. nasutum* | | | | | | | X | | | | | |
| *P. nummifer* | X | | X[8] | | | | X | | | | | |
| *P. olmec* | | | X | | | | X | | | | | |
| *P. tzotzilorum* | X | | | | | | | | | | | |
| *P. yucatanicum* | | | | | | | | X | | X[9] | | |

**Table 5—*continued***

| Species | *Pine-oak forest* | *Boreal forest* | *Cloud forest* | *Mesquite-grassland* | *Desert* | *Chaparral* | *Rain-forest* | *Tropical evergreen forest* | *Savanna* | *Tropical deciduous forest* | *Thorn forest* | *Arid tropical scrub* |
|---|---|---|---|---|---|---|---|---|---|---|---|---|
| *Crotalus atrox* | X | | | X | X | X | | | | X | X | |
| *C. basiliscus* | X | | | | | | | | X | X | X | |
| *C. catalinensis* | | | | | X | | | | | | | |
| *C. cerastes* | | | | | X | | | | | | | |
| *C. durissus* | X[10] | | | | | | X[11] | X | X | X | X | X |
| *C. enyo* | | | | | X | X | | | | X | | |
| *C. exsul* | | | | | X | | | | | | | |
| *C. intermedius* | X | | X | | | | | | | | | X[12] |
| *C. lannomi* | X[13] | | | | | | | | | | | |
| *C. lepidus* | X | | | X | X | | | | | | | |
| *C. mitchellii* | X | | | | X | X | | | | X[14] | | |
| *C. molossus* | X | X | | X | X | X | | | | X | ? | X |
| *C. polystictus* | X | | | X | | | | | | | | |
| *C. pricei* | X | X | | | | | | | | | | |
| *C. pusillus* | X | | | | | | | | | | | |
| *C. ruber* | X | | | | X | X | | | | X[14] | | |
| *C. scutulatus* | X | | | X | X | | | | | | | |
| *C. stejnegeri* | X[13] | | | | | | | | | X | | |
| *C. tigris* | X | | | X | X | | | | | X[15] | X[15] | |
| *C. tortugensis* | | | | | X[16] | | | | | | | |
| *C. transversus* | | X[17] | | | | | | | | | | |
| *C. triseriatus* | X | X | | X | X[18] | | | | | | | |
| *C. viridis* | X | | | X | X | | | | | | | |
| *C. willardi* | X | | | X[19] | | | | | | | | |
| *Sistrurus catenatus* | | | | X[20] | X[21] | | | | | | | |
| *S. ravus* | X | X | X | | | | | | | | | X[7] |
| *Heloderma horridum* | X | | | | | | | | | X | X | |
| *H. suspectum* | X | | | X | X | | | | | | | |

1. Pacific marine habitat.
2. Several sightings and museum specimens bearing precise locality data are now available for northern Coahuila and Chihuahua.
3. Humid forests of Atlantic drainage of Chiapas.
4. Pacific versant of Chiapas at minimum elevation of about 500 m.
5. Barely entering this forest type along lower border.
6. At elevations above 1,600 m.
7. Sierra de Acatepec in southern Puebla and near Cacaloapan, Puebla.
8. At elevations less than 1,600 m.
9. Drier portions only.
10. Localized in Querétaro; Sierra de Coalcomán, Michoacán; and near Comitán, Chiapas.
11. Generally in open areas or savannas.
12. In the vicinity of Cacaloapan, Puebla; also occurring locally in dry habitats near Pachuca, Hidalgo, and Perote, Veracruz.
13. Ecotone between pine-oak and tropical deciduous forests.
14. Lower Baja California.
15. In southern Sonora.
16. Isla de Tortuga, Gulf of California.
17. Sierra de Ajusco, Morelos; probably also adjacent state of México and the Federal District; possibly Cerro Tancítaro, Michoacán.
18. Southern San Luis Potosí.
19. Uncommon in this habitat.
20. Isolated population reportedly from near Aramberri, Nuevo León; also northern Tamaulipas.
21. Isolated population from vicinity of Bolsón de Cuatro Ciénegas, Coahuila; possibly northern Sonora and Chihuahua.

## Key to Venomous Snakes of Mexico

1. No loreal pit between eye and nostril; loreal scale absent (Fig. 100); dorsal scales smooth; fangs permanently erect (Fig. 19); Elapidae. ................................2
   A loreal pit between eye and nostril (Fig. 320); loreal scale(s) present; dorsal scales keeled; fangs fold back (Fig. 253); Viperidae ................................18
2. Tail strongly flattened laterally (Fig. 110); marine habitat; usually a longitudinal black-and-yellow pattern (Fig. 111). ................................*Pelamis platurus*
   Tail round in cross section; pattern consisting of some combination of black, yellow, or red rings or spots ................................3
3. Pale parietal or nuchal ring followed by a red ring (Figs. 108–109) ................................*Micruroides euryxanthus*
   Pale parietal or nuchal ring followed by a black ring ................................4
4. Black body rings arranged in triads (Fig. 65) ................................5
   Black body rings not arranged in triads (Fig. 36) ................................6
5. Yellow or white rings on body bisected with black pigment dorsally and laterally, forming short "double" rings ½–1 scale long (Fig. 45); pale head ring narrow and incomplete dorsally (Fig. 13); temporals 1 + 1 (Fig. 13) ................................*Micrurus elegans*
   Center black ring of each triad set off from other black rings by relatively long (2–3 scales) yellow rings not bisected with black; pale head ring long and uninterrupted (Fig. 65); temporals 1 + 2 (Fig. 15)..........*Micrurus laticollaris*
6. A bicolored dorsal pattern consisting of alternating red and black rings or spots, or body mostly red ................................7
   A tricolored pattern consisting of black, yellow, and red rings ................................9
7. Dorsum of body with 24–42 transversely elongated black blotches on red ground color; western Hidalgo to northern Puebla (Figs. 27, 28) ................................*Micrurus bernadi*
   Pattern not as described; from Veracruz southward or Yucatán Peninsula......8
8. Black head cap including all or most of parietals; more than 25 black body rings or spots (Figs. 72, 73) ................................*Micrurus limbatus*
   Black head cap including less than anterior half of parietals; or fewer than 10 black body rings (Figs. 36–38)................................*Micrurus diastema*
9. Red body rings, usually interrupted dorsally with black (Figs. 46–48) ................................*Micrurus ephippifer*
   Red body rings not interrupted dorsally with black ................................10
10. Fewer than 10 black body rings (Fig. 66)......................*Micrurus latifasciatus*
    More than 10 black body rings ................................11
11. Most red scales black tipped................................12
    Most red scales not black tipped................................15
12. Black nape ring not involving posterior tips of parietals; pale spot on snout involving rostral and/or internasals, anterior supralabials pale or with pale spots (Fig. 41) ................................*Micrurus distans*
    Black nape ring involving posterior tips of parietals; snout (including rostral, internasals, and anterior supralabials) entirely black ................................13
13. Dorsally red body rings one to one and a half times as long as black body rings (Fig. 29)................................*Micrurus browni*
    Dorsally red body rings nearly two times or more as long as black body rings ................................14
14. Yellow rings 1½ dorsal scales long on anterior part of body; supra-anal keels absent in males; coastal Oaxaca ................................*Micrurus bogerti*
    Yellow rings never more than 1 dorsal scale long on anterior part of body; supra-anal keels present in males; Pacific versant of Chiapas, barely reaching mountains of extreme southeastern Oaxaca (Fig. 90) ...........*Micrurus nigrocinctus*
15. Lower part of anterior supralabials pale; usually a pale rostral-internasal spot; lower jaw mostly pale with mottling on the border of the first infralabials and anterior chinshields; Nayarit and Jalisco (Fig. 41) ...............*Micrurus distans*
    Snout entirely black, including anterior infralabials ................................16
16. Red rings more than twice as long as black rings; Atlantic drainage, Veracruz southward (Figs. 36, 37)................................*Micrurus diastema*

Red rings not more than twice as long as black rings, often very nearly equal in length ........................................17

17. Supra-anal keels present in males; south of 18°N latitude (Fig. 29) ........................................ *Micrurus browni*
Supra-anal keels absent; north of 18°N latitude (Figs. 56, 57) ........................................ *Micrurus fulvius*

18. Tail terminating in rattle or button........................................19
Tail not terminating in rattle........................................50

19. Dorsum of head covered with 9–11 large plates (Fig. 439) ........................................20
Dorsum of head covered with more than 11 scales ........................................21

20. Head with distinct markings; upper preocular in contact with postnasal; sharp canthus (Figs. 437, 438)........................................*Sistrurus catenatus*
Head without distinct markings; upper preocular not in contact with postnasal; rounded canthus (Figs. 439–443)........................................*Sistrurus ravus*

21. Supraoculars extended into distinctly raised, flat, hornlike processes (Figs. 326, 327)........................................*Crotalus cerastes*
Supraoculars not extended into hornlike processes ........................................22

22. Subcaudals more than 30 ........................................23
Subcaudals fewer than 30........................................24

23. Intersupraoculars 4 or fewer (Fig. 356)........................................*Crotalus lannomi*
Intersupraoculars 5 or more (Fig. 410)........................................*Crotalus stejnegeri*

24. Tip of snout raised into a sharp ridge; usually distinct pale facial stripes extending from about nostril to angle of mouth (Figs. 431–436, 458, 459)........................................ *Crotalus willardi*
Tip of snout not raised into a sharp ridge; no distinct pale stripes extending from about nostril to angle of mouth ........................................25

25. Prenasals generally separated from rostral by small scales; upper preoculars often divided horizontally, vertically, or both (Figs. 371–379)........................................ *Crotalus mitchelii*
Prenasals in contact with rostral; upper preocular usually not divided, or divided only vertically ........................................26

26. Body pattern of crossbands........................................27
Body pattern of dorsal blotches ........................................29

27. Dark body crossbands 34 or fewer (Figs. 357–359, 363) .........*Crotalus lepidus*
Dark body crossbands 35 or more ........................................28

28. Supralabials 10 or fewer; infralabials 9 or fewer; ventrals 155 or fewer (Fig. 415) ........................................*Crotalus transversus*
Supralabials 11 or more; infralabials 11 or more; ventrals 156 or more (Figs. 411, 412)........................................*Crotalus tigris*

29. Anterior subocular contacting at least one supralabial (Fig. 452)................30
Anterior subocular separated from all supralabials (Fig. 444) ....................35

30. Upper preocular divided vertically, the anterior portion higher than the posterior and extending over the edge of the canthus in front of the supraocular (Figs. 357–370, 454 ........................................*Crotalus lepidus*
Upper preocular usually single or, if divided, not as described..................31

31. One upper loreal; midbody scale rows usually 23 or fewer ........................32
Two upper loreals; midbody scale rows 25 or more (Figs. 392, 393)........................................ *Crotalus polystictus*

32. No prefoveals (Figs. 352–355, 452) ............................*Crotalus intermedius*
One or more prefoveals........................................33

33. Sixth or seventh supralabial below posterior edge of eye; midbody scale rows usually 23 ........................................34
Fifth supralabial below posterior edge of eye; midbody scale rows usually 21 (Figs. 394–399) ........................................*Crotalus pricei*

34. Canthals (prefrontals) expanded to contact each other at midline (Figs. 400, 401) ........................................*Crotalus pusillus*
Canthals separated from each other by at least one or two scales (Figs. 416–427, 456)........................................*Crotalus triseriatus*

35. Rattle matrix shrunken or poorly developed, no loose rattle segments (Fig. 325) ....................36
Rattle matrix normal, usually one or more loose rattle segments ....................37

36. First infralabial not transversely divided; ventrals generally less than 186; Isla Santa Catalina, Gulf of California (Fig. 324).................*Crotalus catalinensis*
First infralabial transversely divided; ventrals 186 or more; Isla San Lorenzo del Sur, Gulf of California (Figs. 405, 406). ................*Crotalus ruber*

37. Usually more than 2 scales between the nasals in contact with rostral (Figs. 428–430, 451)................*Crotalus viridis*
Two scales between the nasals in contact with rostral....................38

38. Upper preocular usually divided vertically, the anterior portion situated higher than the posterior and extending over the edge of the canthus in front of the supraocular (Fig. 454); dorsal body markings occupying less longitudinal space than the interspaces (Figs. 357–369) ................*Crotalus lepidus*
Upper preocular not divided vertically or, if divided, the anterior portion not conspicuously higher than the posterior and not extending over the edge of the canthus; dorsal body markings occupying more longitudinal space than the interspaces ....................39

39. Ventral scales 161 or fewer; scales on dorsum of head flat and without keels (Figs. 416–427, 457)................*Crotalus triseriatus*
Ventral scales 162 or more; or, if less than 162, then scales on dorsum of head knobby with definite keels ....................40

40. No alternating, strongly contrasting dark and pale tail rings....................41
Tail with alternating, strongly contrasting dark and pale rings ....................45

41. A pair of longitudinal paravertebral dark stripes on the neck (Figs. 329, 332, 341, 343)................*Crotalus durissus*
No pair of longitudinal paravertebral dark stripes on the neck....................42

42. A pair of large flat internasals that contact each other at midline; a pair of large flat prefrontals (canthals) that contact each other at midline (Fig. 447) .......43
Internasals not in contact with each other; prefrontals (canthals) not in contact with each other; scales on dorsum of head knobby with definite keels (Figs. 347–349)................*Crotalus enyo*

43. Tail dark brown or black, usually with no pale crossbars in evidence posteriorly (Figs. 380, 381, 384–389) ................*Crotalus molossus*
Tail gray with pale gray crossbars in evidence posteriorly ....................44

44. Ventrals fewer than 177 in males and 184 in females; number of body blotches usually less than 30; Oaxaca and Puebla (Figs. 390, 391) ................*Crotalus molossus*
Ventrals more than 177 in males and 183 in females; number of body blotches usually greater than 30; central Michoacán northward (Figs. 319–321) ................*Crotalus basiliscus*

45. Top of head anterior to supraoculars and frontal region usually covered by 4–6 large flat plates including paired internasals and prefrontals (canthals) (Figs. 319–321)................*Crotalus basiliscus*
Top of head anterior to supraoculars and frontal region covered by numerous irregularly arranged plates ....................46

46. First pair of infralabials usually not divided transversely ....................47
First pair of infralabials usually divided transversely....................48

47. Upper preocular usually in contact with the postnasal (Fig. 444), or such contact prevented by an upper loreal (Figs. 317, 318)................*Crotalus atrox*
Upper preocular usually not in contact with postnasal, and no upper loreal present (Figs. 413, 414) ................*Crotalus tortugensis*

48. Interchinshields usually absent; prenasals generally in contact with first supralabials; dark tail rings equal to or shorter than pale tail rings....................49
A pair of interchinshields usually present; generally no contact between prenasal and first supralabial; dark tail rings broader than pale tail rings (Figs. 350, 351) ................*Crotalus exsul*

49. Ground color of tail ash gray or white, with distinct black rings, both in sharp contrast with the *posterior* body color (Figs. 402–404) ................*Crotalus ruber*

Ground color of tail essentially the same as that of the body posteriorly, with dark brown or black rings (Figs. 407–409)......................*Crotalus scutulatus*

50. Dorsum of head with 9 large plates.......................................................51
Dorsum of head with 11 or more plates or scales.....................................52

51. A pair of prominent pale lines extending posteriorly from the rostral on each side of head (Figs. 113–116)...................................*Agkistrodon bilineatus*
No pale lines as described (Fig. 119, 120) ...................*Agkistrodon contortrix*

52. Subcaudals paired (Fig. 316)...............................................................53
Subcaudals single (Fig. 316) ...............................................................54

53. Supraoculars extended into soft, hornlike processes (Fig. 261); intersupraoculars more than 15 (Fig. 260); dorsal pattern a zig-zag stripe (Figs. 254–256) ..................................................................*Ophryacus undulatus*
Supraoculars flat (Fig. 175); intersupraoculars fewer than 10 (Fig. 176); dorsal pattern of X-shaped (triangular laterally) blotches (Figs. 184, 185)................ ...........................................................................*Bothrops asper*

54. Supraoculars extended into soft spinelike or hornlike processes.................55
Supraoculars flat.......................................................................56

55. Nine or fewer supralabials (Fig. 165); 21 midbody scale rows; arboreal, tail prehensile; Chiapas (Fig. 138) .................................*Bothriechis schlegelii*
Ten or more supralabials (Fig. 308); usually 23 midbody scale rows; terrestrial, tail not prehensile; highlands of Puebla and Oaxaca (Fig. 277–280) ............. ..................................................................*Porthidium melanurum*

56. Snout noticeably turned up (Figs. 312, 314); pattern of pale middorsal line with alternating or opposite blotches on either side.......................................57
Snout not noticeably turned up; pattern not as described ..........................60

57. Rostral usually about one and a half (or more) times higher than wide (Figs. 281, 282) ...................................................................*Porthidium nasutum*
Rostral usually less than one and a half times higher than wide .................58

58. Dorsal scale rows 21 on posterior part of body; Yucatán Peninsula (Figs. 298, 299) ..............................................................*Porthidium yucatanicum*
Dorsal scale rows fewer than 21 on posterior part of body; western Mexico .........................................................................................59

59. Middle preocular not divided vertically; intercanthals comprised of 4 equal-sized scales; dorsal scale rows 17 on posterior part of body; Colima and probably Michoacán (Fig. 272)............................................*Porthidium hespere*
Middle preocular divided vertically (Fig. 312); intercanthals comprise 2 large scales, or 2 large scales separated by smaller scales (Fig. 313); dorsal scale rows usually 19 on posterior part of body; Oaxaca and Chiapas (Figs. 267, 268) Chiapàs (Figs. 267, 268) ...............................................*Porthidium dunni*

60. Ground color green .........................................................................61
Ground color brown, gray, tan, or rust...................................................63

61. Seven or more intersupraoculars; dorsal scale rows at midbody 21; Pacific versant of Chiapas (Figs. 123, 124)................................*Bothriechis bicolor*
Five or fewer intersupraoculars (Fig. 164); dorsal scale rows at midbody generally 19 ...........................................................................................62

62. Generally a well-defined black postocular stripe (Fig. 122); black-and-yellow dorsal markings; northeastern highlands of Chiapas (Fig. 121)..................... ........................................................................*Bothriechis aurifer*
No black postocular stripe (Fig. 135); markings, if present, generally pale blue or purple (Figs. 134–137)...............................................*Bothriechis rowleyi*

63. Supraoculars extremely narrow or divided into small scales (Fig. 305); more than 7 intersupraoculars (Fig. 305); scales in internasal and prefrontal regions strongly keeled...........................................................................64
Supraoculars large and well differentiated from other head scales; 7 or fewer intersupraoculars; dorsal scale rows 23 or fewer at midbody....................65

64. Usually 2 or fewer nasorostrals per side; more than 115 ventrals; usually 25 anterior dorsal scale rows; usually most of the lateral body blotches separated from the dorsal blotches by 1–2 scales; Sierra Madre Oriental, southeastern Oaxaca, Tabasco, and Chiapas (Figs. 286–289) ...........*Porthidium nummifer*

Usually 3 nasorostrals per side; fewer than 115 ventrals; usually 27 anterior dorsal scale rows; usually most of the lateral body blotches coalesced with the dorsal blotches or separated by no more than 1 scale; Sierra de los Tuxtlas in Veracruz (Figs. 290, 291) ............................................ *Porthidium olmec*

65. Dorsal scale rows at midbody 19 or fewer (Figs. 263–266, 300, 301) .............. ........................................................................ *Porthidium barbouri*

Dorsal scale rows at midbody 21 or more .............................................66

66. Most lateral body blotches encompassing an area no greater than 2–3 scales (Figs. 295–297) ................................................ *Porthidium tzotzilorum*

Most lateral body blotches encompassing an area equal to 5–7 scales (Figs. 269, 270) ................................................................ *Porthidium godmani*

## GUATEMALA

Guatemala is the northernmost Central American republic and encompasses 108,889 km$^2$. It is bounded on the north and west by Mexico, on the south by about 260 km of coastline on the Pacific Ocean, on the southeast by Honduras and El Salvador, and on the northeast by Belize and about 90 km of shoreline on the Gulf of Honduras. Guatemala can be divided into three broad regions: (1) the Pacific coastal plain, (2) the highlands, and (3) the extensive northern lowlands.

The Pacific coastal plain is narrow, extending inland only 40–50 km before reaching a sharply elevated piedmont, and the coastline is relatively straight with no natural harbors. The beaches are of black sand and many of the adjacent inland waters are bordered by mangrove forests. The coastal plain is now mostly denuded of its original forests owing to agricultural development; it is largely open savanna interspersed with tall trees, including the Ceiba (Bombacaceae), the national tree of Guatemala. The southern highlands paralleling the Pacific Coast are mostly of volcanic origin and consist in part of some 30 volcanoes, several of which are still active. The highest point in the country is Volcán Tajumulco, which reaches 4,220 m. Six other volcanoes in the western portion of the southern volcanic highlands exceed 3,500 m. Lying on the Guatemalan tableland to the north of the volcanic axis are several isolated basins containing the lakes of Atitlán, Amatitlán, and Ayarza.

The central and northern highlands are composed of the Sierra de los Cuchumatanes in the northwest, which has a continuous highland connection of over 1,500 m with the southern volcanic highlands via the Guatemalan Plateau, and the Sierra de Chuacús, which extends eastward from the plateau and forms a continuous ridge above 1,500 m with the Sierra de las Minas. The latter range gradually loses elevation as it extends eastward, and in the region just to the south of Lago de Izabal it is little more than low, rolling foothills. The isolated Montañas del Mico in eastern Guatemala reach elevations in excess of 1,000 m. Several poorly explored ranges, the Sierra de Chamá in central Alta Verapaz and the Sierra de Santa Cruz to the north of Lago de Izabal, represent the northeasternmost highlands.

Between the southern volcanic highlands and the highlands to the north, several deeply entrenched Atlantic drainage systems dissect and isolate various highland regions; chief among these are the valleys of the upper Río Grijalva, Río Negro, Río Motagua, and Río Polochic. Portions of some of these valleys are notable in that they possess an extremely dry climate because the high ranges to the north create rainshadow conditions.

The extensive Petén lowlands of northern Guatemala are physiographically part of the Yucatán Platform; this region is composed predominantly of limestone with many underground drainages, and for the most part lies 150–225 m above sea level.

The Pacific Coast, much of the southern volcanic highlands, and the Guatemalan Plateau experience a well-defined wet or rainy season during the *invierno* ("winter"), which extends from about mid-May through October, when the prevailing winds are from the south. From November to May winds are predominantly from the north, and there is little precipitation. This dry season is called the *verano* ("summer"). Most of this region receives about 1,500–2,500 mm of precipitation annually. In contrast to most of the highlands, the Caribbean-facing slopes are exposed to the prevailing rain-bearing northeastern trade winds and may receive between 4,000 and 5,000 mm annual precipitation; rain may fall every month of the year, and there is no marked dry season. The Atlantic slopes, and also the upper Pacific piedmont on the larger volcanoes of the southern highlands, sequester much of the moisture from the prevailing winds coming off the oceans, so that by the time this air reaches the interior valleys it is quite dry. In these valleys most of the rainfall is limited to a 3–4 month period and may not exceed 500 mm annually. The Petén lowlands and lower Río Motagua Valley receive more rainfall than the Pacific Coast; their dry season is not as well defined and is of shorter duration.

Temperature is largely a function of altitude. The average annual temperature ranges from 24 to 27°C in the lowlands, or *tierra caliente* ("hot country"), with average daytime highs of 29–32°C. At moderate to intermediate elevations of 1,200–2,000 m, the *tierra templada* ("temperate country"), the average annual temperatures range from 15 to 22°C with daytime highs of 16–28°C. At elevations exceeding 3,000 m, the *tierra fria* ("cold country"), mean annual temperatures drop to below 10°C, but daytime maxima may be as high as 24°C.

Vegetation is dependent on a number of complex factors, including physiography and climate. Most of the highlands are covered by lower montane dry forest that consists predominantly of pines and oaks. However, those portions of the Atlantic and Pacific slopes that receive heavy precipitation are covered with luxuriant montane wet forest or cloud forest. On the Atlantic slope this type of vegetation cover is present in portions of the Sierra de los Cuchumatanes, Sierra de Chuacús, Sierra de las Minas, and Sierra de Chamá; on the Pacific side cloud forest is present on south-facing volcanic slopes from the Mexican border to about south-central Guatemala.

The rainshadow valleys of the upper Río Grijalva, Río Negro, and middle Río Motagua support a xerophytic thorn forest or desert. A dry tropical deciduous forest extends from the Zacapa region southward through the low foothills of southeastern Guatemala into El Salvador. High montane forests and meadows occur mainly in the Sierra de los Cuchumatanes, Sierra de Cuilco, the Guatemalan Plateau, and also on the peaks of the highest volcanoes. Lowland rainforest is most widespread in northern Guatemala, but is found also in the lower Río Motagua Valley and along the lower Pacific piedmont from western Guatemala to about the latitude of Escuintla. Interspersed in the rainforest of northern Guatemala is a series of isolated savannas that extends from just southwest of Lago Petén Itza eastward into Belize, where they become replaced by open grasslands with scattered pines (*Pinus caribaea*).

It is probable that *Bothriechis marchi* occurs in extreme northeastern Guatemala in the Montaña Espíritu Santo (sometimes called Sierra de Merendón); it has been taken from the eastern side of this range in Honduras. The distributions by vegetation type of the species of dangerously venomous reptiles in Guatemala are given in Table 6.

**Table 6**

Distributions by vegetation type of venomous reptiles in Guatemala

| *Species* | *Lowland rainforest* | *Lowland dry forest* | *Thorn forest, savannas* | *Lower montane wet forest, cloud forest* | *Lower montane dry forest* | *High montane forests and meadows* |
|---|---|---|---|---|---|---|
| *Pelamis platurus*[1] | | | | | | |
| *Micrurus browni* | | | X[2] | X | X | |
| *M. diastema* | X | | X | X[3] | X[3] | |
| *M. elegans* | | | | X | X | |
| *M. hippocrepis* | X | | | | | |
| *M. latifasciatus* | X[4] | | | X | | |
| *M. nigrocinctus* | X | X | X | X | | |
| *M. stuarti* | | | | X | | |
| *Agkistrodon bilineatus* | X | X | X[5] | | | |
| *Bothriechis aurifer* | | | | X | | |
| *B. bicolor* | X[6] | | | X | | |
| *B. schlegelii* | X | | | X[7] | | |
| *Bothrops asper* | X | X | | X[7] | | |
| *Crotalus durissus* | X | X | X[5] | | | |
| *Porthidium godmani* | | | | X | X | X |
| *P. nasutum* | X | | | | | |
| *P. nummifer* | X | | | X | X | |
| *P. ophryomegas* | | X | X[5] | | | |
| *Heloderma horridum* | | X | X[5] | | | |

1. Pacific marine habitat.
2. Extreme western Guatemala.
3. At elevations of less than 1,300 m.
4. At elevations exceeding 300 m.
5. Dry interior valleys.
6. At elevations exceeding 500 m.
7. Generally at elevations of less than 1,000 m.

## Key to Venomous Snakes of Guatemala

1. No loreal pit between eye and nostril; loreal scale absent (Fig. 100); dorsal scales smooth; fangs permanently erect (Fig. 19); Elapidae ................................2
   A loreal pit between eye and nostril (Fig. 124); loreal scale(s) present; dorsal scales keeled; fangs fold back (Fig. 253); Viperidae ..................................9
2. Tail strongly flattened laterally (Fig. 110); marine habitat; usually a longitudinal yellow and black (or brown) pattern (Figs. 111, 112) ...........*Pelamis platurus*
   Tail round in cross section; terrestrial habitat; pattern usually ringed and consisting of some combination of black, yellow or white, and/or red..............3
3. Triads of black rings on body (Fig. 45) ..............................*Micrurus elegans*
   Pattern not composed of triads...............................................................4
4. Fewer than 10 black rings on body (Fig. 66) .................*Micrurus latifasciatus*
   More than 10 black rings on body, although some may not be complete dorsally ..........................................................................................5

5. Tip of snout pale ........................................................................6
Tip of snout generally uniformly black........................................................7
6. Black rings on body 10–24; red scales without black tipping or other black markings (may be dusky) (Figs. 60, 61) .......................*Micrurus hippocrepis*
Usually 25 or more black rings on body; black tipping or other black markings on red scales (Fig. 37) ................................................*Micrurus diastema*
7. Most red rings more than 13 dorsal scales long; temporals usually 1 + 2 ...............................................................................*Micrurus stuarti*
Most red rings less than 13 dorsal scales long; temporals variable ................8
8. Black rings on body 25 or more (Fig. 39) ..........................*Micrurus diastema*
Black rings on body fewer than 25........................................................9
9. Temporals 1 + 1 (Figs. 13, 90) ..................................*Micrurus nigrocinctus*
Temporals usually 1 + 2 (Figs. 15, 29)...............................*Micrurus browni*
10. Tail terminating in rattle or button.................................*Crotalus durissus*
Tail not terminating in rattle..............................................................11
11. Dorsum of head covered with 9–15 scales, often regularly arranged; distinctive pair of stripes on side of head (Figs. 113, 117, 118).....*Agkistrodon bilineatus*
Dorsum of head covered with more than 15 scales, often irregularly arranged; pattern on side of head not as described...............................................12
12. Subcaudals mostly paired (Figs. 184–186, 316)......................*Bothrops asper*
Subcaudals mostly single (Fig. 316) .......................................................13
13. Green ground color, with or without dorsal pattern; arboreal, with prehensile tail ...........................................................................................14
Tan, brown, or grayish ground color, but never green, always with some dorsal pattern; terrestrial, without prehensile tail.............................................16
14. Raised superciliary scales giving appearance of eyelashes (Fig. 165); venter stippled, mottled, or otherwise darkly pigmented (Fig. 138)........................ ...................................................................*Bothriechis schlegelii*
No superciliary scales; venter uniformly yellowish green ..........................15
15. Dorsum uniformly green, without black middorsal markings; no dark postocular stripe; 21 midbody scale rows; 7–11 intersupraoculars (Figs. 123, 124) ..............................................................................*Bothriechis bicolor*
Dorsum with middorsal black-and-yellow markings; dark postocular stripe present; generally 19 midbody scale rows; 1–5 intersupraoculars (Figs. 121, 122, 164) ................................................................*Bothriechis aurifer*
16. Midbody scale rows 21 (Figs. 269, 270).........................*Porthidium godmani*
Midbody scale rows 23 or more...........................................................17
17. Supraoculars extremely narrow or divided into small scales (Fig. 305); more than 9 scales between orbits (Fig. 305); body scales extremely rugose; dorsal blotches not separated by pale middorsal line (Figs. 288, 289)...................... ...................................................................*Porthidium nummifer*
Supraoculars large and well differentiated from other head scales; generally 7 or fewer intersupraoculars; body scales keeled, but not rugose; dorsal blotches often separated by pale middorsal line .................................................18
18. Tip of snout strongly upturned, forming a free flap (Fig. 314); one canthal scale on each side (Fig. 315); ventrals fewer than 150 (Figs. 281, 282) .................. ...................................................................*Porthidium nasutum*
Tip of snout not strongly upturned (Fig. 310); 2 canthal scales on each side (Fig. 311); ventrals more than 150 (Fig. 292).................*Porthidium ophryomegas*

**BELIZE**

Belize, formerly British Honduras, is known as Belice in other Central American countries and Mexico. It covers 22, 963 km$^2$ and is the only country in Central America without a Pacific coastline. It is bounded by Mexico to the north, Guatemala to the west and south, and the Caribbean Sea to the east. About 25 km offshore, a major barrier reef extends the length of the coast.

The northern half of the country is composed of low-lying, gently undulating hills, flat plains, and swamps; elevations generally do not exceed 100 m above sea level. A dissected plateau with several major ridge systems occupies the southern half of the country. Most of the plateau lies between 350 and 750 m above sea level. In this region the Caribbean coastal plain is relatively narrow and gradually rises above the 300-m contour within 25 km of the coast. The Maya Mountains fringe the eastern side of the plateau; the main axis of these mountains runs in a southwest-northeast direction. Most of the crest of the Maya Mountains lies above the 700-m contour, and several peaks exceed 900 m in elevation. These are, from south to north, Richardson Peak at 1,040 m, Mount Mossy at 975 m, and Mount Margaret at 945 m. The Cockscomb Range extends as an eastern spur of the Maya Mountains and contains Victoria Peak, which at 1,122 m is the highest point in the country. Mountain Pine Ridge, which includes the Bald Hills, borders the northern portion of the plateau. The major crest of Mountain Pine Ridge trends generally from east to west, but in the west the system gradually loses elevation and arcs to the southwest.

The northwest portion of the country is drained by a number of small to moderate sized sluggish rivers, most of which flow in a northerly or northeasterly direction. Numerous freshwater lagoons and swamps dot the landscape. Drainage patterns are more complex in the south owing to the various ridge systems. To the east of the main divide of the Maya Mountains, numerous small rivers flow directly to the Caribbean Sea. The western slopes of the Maya Mountains, as well as the southern portion of Mountain Pine Ridge, are dissected by tributaries that eventually become confluent to the north of the plateau to form the Belize River, which thence flows to the northeast. Farther down its course the Belize River becomes confluent with other tributaries that drain the northern slopes of Mountain Pine Ridge. A small portion of the western side of the southernmost extension of the Maya Mountains contains the upper tributaries of the Río Usumacinta; this is the only region in Belize draining into the Gulf of Mexico.

The climate of Belize is punctuated by two well-defined seasons: a rainy period that extends from June to October, and a dry period from February to April. The transitional month of May may be wet or dry depending on location and yearly fluctuations. From November to January much of the country receives relatively little rain owing to the "northers," prevailing winds that bring cool, dry air. The general pattern of rainfall is clinal with greater amounts of precipitation in the south. Corozal, located in the north on the coast of Chetumal Bay, receives 1,320 mm of rainfall per year, while Barranco, located in the south on the coast of the Gulf of Amatique, receives 4,570 mm. Most of the country is subject to more-or-less equitable year-round temperatures. Monthly means at Belize City range from about 23°C in December to about 28°C in July.

Much of Belize is covered by rainforest; however, because of the clinal variation of rainfall from north to south and the mountain ridges that intercept much of the incoming moisture from the Gulf of Honduras, distinctive vegetation associations occur in different parts of the country. Within the rainforest, groves of cohune palms (*Orbignya*) are frequently encountered. These palms often form a closed canopy, and little undergrowth is present. In the north, many of the trees are deciduous, and this seasonally dry forest extends a considerable distance down the coast. The vegetation consists of trees less than 5 m in height interspersed with taller trees. Some of the dominant trees in this region are sapote (*Achras*) and caoba or mahogany (*Swietenia*). Scattered savannas are abundant in the northeastern part of the country. Over much of the plateau region in the south the most important timber tree is the Santa María (*Calophyllum*). The coast south and inland from Belize City is characterized by grass savannas with oaks, pines, and palmetto palms (*Paurotis*). A dense forest dominated by red and black mangroves (*Rhizophora* and *Avicennia*, respectively) fringes much of the coast. Mountain Pine Ridge is characterized by a dense ground cover of grasses and numerous pines (*Pinus caribaea*) with a few oaks in some areas. On the windward side of the higher peaks in the Maya Mountains and Cockscomb Range, cloud forest conditions prevail.

The numerous cays lying offshore from the coast of Belize have not been well collected. The majority of these are probably not inhabited by venomous snakes, but it would not be surprising to find coral snakes (*Micrurus*) or the "yellow-jaw" tommygoff (*Bothrops asper*) on a few of these islands.

A list of the species of dangerously venomous snakes of Belize and their distributions is given in Table 7. A single specimen (USNM 61781) from Benque Viejo, Cayo District, has been identified by different herpetologists as either *Porthidium nasutum* or *P. yucatanicum*. We have not examined the specimen, but on ecologic and geographic grounds it appears more likely that this specimen represents the former species. Therefore, we tentatively do not recognize *P. yucatanicum* as part of the Belizean herpetofauna and have omitted it from Table 7.

**Table 7**

Distributions by district of venomous snakes in Belize

| *Species* | *Corozal* | *Orange Walk* | *Belize* | *Cayo* | *Stann Creek* | *Toledo* |
|---|---|---|---|---|---|---|
| *Micrurus diastema* | X | X | X | X | X | |
| *M. hippocrepis* | | | | X | X | X[1] |
| *M. nigrocinctus* | | | X | | X | X[1] |
| *Agkistrodon bilineatus* | X | | | | | |
| *Bothriechis schlegelii* | | X | | X | X[2] | X[1] |
| *Bothrops asper*[3] | X | X | X | X | X | X |
| *Crotalus durissus* | X | X | X | X | X | X[4] |
| *Porthidium nasutum* | | | | X | | X[1] |
| *P. nummifer* | | | | X | X | X |

*Source:* Compiled, in part, from Henderson and Hoevers, 1975.
1. This species has not been collected in this district, but is known from adjacent Guatemala.
2. We suspect this species occurs throughout the wetter portions of the Maya Mountains.
3. Primarily along riparian habitats in drier areas.
4. Only on coast.

Key to Venomous Snakes of Belize

1. No loreal pit between eye and nostril; loreal scale absent (Fig. 100); dorsal scales smooth; fangs permanently erect (Fig. 19); Elapidae .................................2
   A loreal pit between eye and nostril (Fig. 141); loreal scale(s) present; dorsal scales keeled; fangs fold back (Fig. 253); Viperidae ..................................4
2. Tip of snout pale; 10–24 black rings on body, often not complete dorsally; red scales may be dusky, but not black tipped or marked with black; temporals 1 + 2 (Figs. 60, 61) ..................................................... *Micrurus hippocrepis*
   Tip of snout generally uniformly black, or rostral pale; most black rings on body complete dorsally; red scales black tipped or marked with black; temporals variable .....................................................................................3
3. Black rings on body 25 or more; red dorsal scales may be mottled with black, but not uniformly (Fig. 37) ................................................ *Micrurus diastema*
   Black rings on body fewer than 25; red dorsal scales uniformly tipped with black (Figs. 87, 88) ...................................................... *Micrurus nigrocinctus*
4. Tail terminating in rattle or button (Fig. 343) ...................... *Crotalus durissus*
   Tail not terminating in rattle .................................................................5
5. Dorsum of head covered with 9–15 often regularly arranged plates (Figs. 117, 118) ............................................................... *Agkistrodon bilineatus*
   Dorsum of head covered with more than 15 scales, often irregularly arranged .........................................................................................6
6. Most subcaudals paired (Figs. 184, 185, 316) ......................... *Bothrops asper*
   Most subcaudals single (Fig. 316) ..........................................................7
7. Green ground color with brown dorsal pattern; raised superciliary scales giving appearance of eyelashes (Fig. 165); aboreal, with prehensile tail (Fig. 138) ................................................................... *Bothriechis schlegelii*
   Tan, brown, or gray ground color; no raised superciliaries; terrestrial, tail not prehensile ..................................................................................8
8. Snout not upturned (Fig. 304); supraoculars divided into small scales or reduced to long narrow scale; more than 9 scales between orbits (Fig. 305); body scales extremely rugose; dorsal blotches not separated by pale middorsal line (Fig. 288) ........................................................... *Porthidium nummifer*
   Snout strongly upturned (Fig. 314); supraoculars large and well differentiated from other head scales; generally 7 or fewer intersupraoculars (Fig. 315); body scales keeled, but not rugose; dorsal blotches often separated by pale middorsal line (Figs. 281, 282) ................................................ *Porthidium nasutum*

## HONDURAS

Honduras is the second largest Central American republic, encompassing 112,088 km$^2$; it is roughly triangular in shape. The Caribbean coastline in the north extends 644 km from the Río Motagua in the west to the Río Coco at Cabo Gracias a Dios in the east. About 80 km of Pacific coastline borders the Gulf of Fonseca. Nicaragua lies to the southeast of Honduras, its boundary in part defined by the Río Coco (or Río Segovia). To the west, Honduras is bordered by Guatemala and to the south by El Salvador. The political boundaries of Honduras include several islands; however, only two of these, Roatán, located about 50 km off the north coast, and Zacate Grande in the Gulf of Fonseca, are known to be inhabited by venomous snakes.

Honduras may be divided into three general physiographic regions: (1) the Caribbean lowland region, which tends to be narrow but merges with the alluvial plains of some of the major rivers—including the Motagua, Ulúa, Chamelecón, Comayagua, Aguán, Negro, Patuca, and Coco—thus extending inland up to 150 km; (2) the Pacific lowland region, which extends inland 15–40 km and is traversed by three major rivers, the Goascorán, Nacaome, and Choluteca; and (3) the Serranía region, which may be further divided into two subregions—the southwest-northeast trending northern cordilleras and the southern mountains, which are prolonged toward the north or northwest. Many peaks in Honduras exceed 2,000 m, and two of them exceed 2,700 m. Although mountains in the southern part of the country are of volcanic origin, there are no active volcanoes.

In much of the country the rainy season extends from

May to late November, with a short dry period (*canícula*) occurring in late July and early August. The dry season is less pronounced along the northern and eastern alluvial plains of the Caribbean Coast, and generally at least 100 mm of rainfall is received during each of the drier months from March to June. The higher elevations are not subject to harsh dry periods, and frequent cloud cover and mists occur throughout the year.

Below 600 m, mean annual temperatures range from 26 to 28°C; however, northers reaching the north coast from October to April may sharply reduce monthly means. From 600 to 1,500 m, mean annual temperatures are mild and range from 18 to 24°C. A relatively cool environment prevails above 1,500 m; the mean annual temperature is less than 18°C and may drop to less than 14°C at elevations above 2,000 m.

As in all mountainous tropical countries, the forests of Honduras are exceedingly varied, and strongly contrasting vegetation types may be closely interdigitated owing to topographic, climatic, and edaphic (soil condition) factors.

In the lowlands (sea level to about 600 m) tropical moist forest predominates on much of the Caribbean versant, with trees that are continuously green, a vertical stratification of three to four layers, and an upper canopy as high as 60 m. In northeastern Honduras the lowlands are covered with open pine savanna consisting mainly of grasses and the conspicuous *Pinus caribaea*. Edaphic factors rather than climate may be responsible for the presence of this distinctive vegetation type, which may extend inland from the coast some 100 km.

Between 600 and 1,500 m above sea level most of the highlands of the interior of Honduras are covered with subtropical moist forest, which receives 1,000–2,000 mm of precipitation annually. This region is characterized by a rather harsh dry season, and *Pinus oocarpa* is frequently the dominant tree. At this elevation on the Caribbean versant, the amount of rainfall received is 2,000–4,000 mm per year, and a lusher subtropical wet forest prevails. Some of the characteristic trees, at least at the higher elevations, are oaks (*Quercus*) and sweetgum (*Liquidambar*). Especially on the leeward side of mountains in higher portions of interior valleys from about 600 to 1,000 m, a subtropical dry forest is present. These areas receive 500–1,000 mm annual precipitation and have a vegetation cover of agaves, thorny scrub, short grasses, and scattered trees up to 15 m in height.

Most of the interior valleys of Honduras, including those of the river valleys of Ulúa, Chamelecón, Aguán, Negro, and Patuca, are covered with tropical dry forest that receives 1,000–2,000 mm of rainfall per year. This vegetation type is also present on the Pacific lowlands and may reach heights of 10–25 m. The drier portions of some of these valleys receive only 500–1,000 mm of rainfall annually, and tropical dry forest is replaced by tropical arid scrub characterized by tall columnar cacti.

The higher elevations of the Caribbean versant from 1,500 to 2,700 m and above are subject to 2,000–4,000 mm of rainfall per year, and a spectacular, verdant cloud forest or lower montane wet forest is present. This type of forest contains much epiphytic growth, and giant trees may reach 50 m in height. On the leeward side of these mountains, generally on the Pacific versant, a drier type of forest is present that receives 1,000–2,000 mm of precipitation annually. The canopy is lower than that of the lower montane wet forest, but many of the same species are present, such as oaks, sweetgum, and tree ferns.

Finally, above 2,700 m on the summit of Cerro Santa Bárbara, a montane rainforest exists consisting of numerous epiphytes, bryophytes (mosses), and lower vascular plants. This forest often is enshrouded by mist during the day and receives up to 4,000 mm or more of precipitation annually. Firs and cypresses are among the dominant trees.

It is probable that *Micrurus alleni* occurs in extreme eastern Honduras; this species has been reported from near Cabo Gracias a Dios in Nicaragua. The distributions by vegetation type of the species of dangerously venomous snakes in Honduras are given in Table 8.

**Table 8**

Distributions by vegetation type of venomous snakes in Honduras

| Species | *Tropical wet and moist forests* | *Lowland dry forest* | *Thorn forest, savannas* | *Lower montane wet forest, cloud forest* | *Lower montane dry forest* | *High montane forest* |
|---|---|---|---|---|---|---|
| *Pelamis platurus*[1] | | | | | | |
| *Micrurus diastema* | X | X | X | X | X | |
| *M. nigrocinctus* | X | X | X | X | X | |
| *M. ruatanus* | X[2] | | | | | |
| *Agkistrodon bilineatus* | | X[3] | | | | |
| *Bothriechis bicolor* | | | | X | | X[4] |
| *B. marchi* | X[5] | | | X | | |
| *B. schlegelii* | X | | | X[6] | | |
| *Bothrops asper* | X | X[7] | | X | X[7] | |
| *Crotalus durissus* | X | X | X | | X | |
| *Porthidium godmani* | | | | X | X | X |
| *P. nasutum* | X | X[7] | | | | |
| *P. nummifer* | X | | | X[6] | X | |
| *P. ophryomegas* | | X | X | | X[8] | |

*Source:* Adapted from Wilson and Meyer, 1985, courtesy of the Milwaukee Public Museum.

1. Pacific marine habitat.
2. Restricted to Isla de Roatán.
3. Pacific drainage and Isla Zacate Grande.
4. Not known definitely from this habitat in Honduras.
5. Reportedly occurring as low as "from near sea level."
6. At elevations of less than 1,300 m.
7. Primarily along river courses.
8. At elevations of 850 m or less.

### Key to Venomous Snakes of Honduras

1. No loreal pit between eye and nostril; loreal scale absent (Fig. 100); dorsal scales smooth; fangs permanently erect (Fig. 19); Elapidae ........ 2
   A loreal pit between eye and nostril (Fig. 124); loreal scale present; dorsal scales keeled; fangs fold back (Fig. 253); Viperidae ........ 6
2. Tail strongly flattened laterally; marine habitat; usually a longitudinal black (or brown) and yellow pattern (Figs. 110–112) ........ *Pelamis platurus*
   Tail round in cross section; terrestrial habitat; pattern consisting of some combination of red, yellow, and black rings ........ 3
3. Dorsal pattern of red and black rings only ........ 4
   Dorsal pattern of red, black, and yellow rings ........ 5
4. More than 31 black rings ........ *Micrurus ruatanus*
   Fewer than 31 black rings (Fig. 88) ........ *Micrurus nigrocinctus*
5. Tip of snout with pale pigment; more than 25 black rings (Fig. 39) ........ *Micrurus diastema*
   Tip of snout completely black; fewer than 25 black rings (Fig. 87) ........ *Micrurus nigrocinctus*
6. Tail terminating in rattle or button (Fig. 328) ........ *Crotalus durissus*
   Tail not terminating in rattle ........ 7
7. Dorsum of head covered with 9–15 often regularly arranged plates; distinctive yellow lateral stripes on head (Fig. 113) ........ *Agkistrodon bilineatus*
   Dorsum of head covered with more than 15 scales, often irregularly arranged; no distinctive yellow lateral head stripes ........ 8
8. Subcaudals mostly paired (Figs. 186, 316) ........ *Bothrops asper*
   Subcaudals mostly single (Fig. 316) ........ 9
9. Green or yellow ground color; with or without dorsal pattern; arboreal, with prehensile tail ........ 10
   Tan, brown, or gray ground color, always with some dorsal pattern; terrestrial, tail not prehensile ........ 12
10. Raised superciliary scales giving appearance of eyelashes (Fig. 165); venter generally spotted, mottled, or otherwise darkly pigmented (except in yellow or "oropel" phase) (Figs. 138–141) ........ *Bothriechis schlegelii*
    No superciliary scales; venter uniformly colored ........ 11
11. Intersupraoculars usually fewer than 7 and smooth (Fig. 164); usually 19 midbody dorsal scale rows (Figs. 129–131) ........ *Bothriechis marchi*
    Intersupraoculars usually more than 7 and keeled; 21 midbody dorsal scale rows (Figs. 123, 124) ........ *Bothriechis bicolor*
12. Midbody dorsal scale rows 21 (Figs. 269, 270) ........ *Porthidium godmani*
    Midbody dorsal scale rows 23 or more ........ 13
13. Supraoculars extremely narrow or divided into small scales (Fig. 305); more than 9 scales between orbits; body scales extremely rugose; dorsal blotches not separated by pale middorsal line (Fig. 288) ........ *Porthidium nummifer*
    Supraoculars large and well differentiated from other head scales; generally 7 or fewer intersupraoculars; body scales keeled, but not rugose; dorsal blotches often separated by pale middorsal line. ........ 14
14. Tip of snout strongly upturned, forming a free flap (Fig. 314); one canthal scale on each side (Fig. 315); ventrals fewer than 150 (Figs. 281, 282) ........ *Porthidium nasutum*
    Tip of snout not strongly upturned (Fig. 310); two canthal scales on each side (Fig. 311); ventrals more than 150 (Fig. 292) ........ *Porthidium ophryomegas*

## EL SALVADOR

El Salvador is the smallest mainland country in the Western Hemisphere, encompassing 21,041 km$^2$, and it is the only Central American country without a Caribbean coastline. This country is bounded to the north and east by Honduras, to the west by Guatemala, and to the south by about 275 km of coastline on the Pacific Ocean.

El Salvador is divisible into four general physiographic regions: (1) The mountainous regions in the north are often referred to as the *tierra fria*. (2) The southern volcanic highlands include more than 20 cone-shaped volcanoes that stretch from west to east across the country. Most of these volcanoes attain elevations between 1,200 and 2,300 m; Volcán Santa Ana at 2,355 m is the highest in the country. Four of these volcanoes are still active. (3) The broad plateaulike area between the northern mountains and the southern volcanic highlands is drained by the Río Lempa and Río San Miguel. Most of this region lies between 200 and 1,000 m above sea level and is referred to as the *tierra templada*. (4) The Pacific coastal plain and foothills extend inland 8–25 km from the coastline and include the lower portions of the Río Lempa and Río San Miguel.

Mean monthly temperatures along the Pacific Coast and in most other low-lying regions vary from 22 to 29°C; at about 1,500 m mean monthly temperatures vary from 16 to 22°C. During the rainy season, which extends from May through October, heavy rainfall occurs most days and monthly averages of more than 250 mm are common in some areas. Occasional rainy periods that last for several days to several weeks, characterized by persistently overcast days and marked by intermittent but heavy downpours, are known as *temporales* and most frequently occur in June and September. Average rainfall for most localities ranges from about 1,400 to 2,300 mm per year. In general, the Pacific lowlands receive about 1,700–1,800 mm annual precipitation, the higher windward elevations of the northern mountains and the southern volcanoes receive 2,000–3,000 mm, and some of the plateau region and interior valleys are subject to a rainshadow effect and receive only 1,000–1,500 mm.

The vegetation of the northern mountains—especially in the Departamento de Santa Ana and Departamento de Chalatenango, and at the moderate elevations on the volcanoes—is predominantly lower montane dry forest consisting of oaks and pines. Lower montane wet forests or cloud forests occur in small isolated patches at the highest elevations in the northwestern portion of the country and on the peaks of the highest volcanoes. The plateau region is covered by lowland dry forest containing small deciduous trees and bushes. Cut-over lowland dry forests, thorn forests, savannas, and fields characterize most of the Pacific Coast.

It is possible that *Bothriechis bicolor* occurs in cloud forest habitats in El Salvador. We are unfamiliar with any reports of the wide-ranging *Bothrops asper* from El Salvador, but this species may occur in some of the more mesic riparian forests of the Pacific lowlands, as it does in adjacent Guatemala. *Micrurus latifasciatus* has been taken along the Pacific slopes of Guatemala less than 50 km from the El Salvador border, and its discovery in El Salvador would not be surprising. Also, there is a slight possibility that the range of *Heloderma horridum* extends into this country. The distributions by vegetation types of the species of dangerously venomous snakes in El Salvador are given in Table 9.

### Key to Venomous Snakes of El Salvador

1. No loreal pit between eye and nostril; loreal scale absent (Fig. 100); dorsal scales smooth; fangs permanently erect (Fig. 19); Elapidae ................................ 2
   A loreal pit between eye and nostril; loreal scale present; dorsal scales keeled; fangs fold back (Fig. 253); Viperidae ................................ 3
2. Tail strongly flattened laterally; marine habitat; usually a longitudinal black (or brown) and yellow pattern (Figs. 110–112) ................ *Pelamis platurus*
   Tail round in cross section; terrestrial habitat; pattern consisting of red, yellow, and black rings (Fig. 90) ................ *Micrurus nigrocinctus*
3. Tail terminating in rattle or button (Fig. 328) ................ *Crotalus durissus*
   Tail not terminating in rattle ................................ 4
4. Dorsum of head covered with 9–15 often regularly arranged plates; distinctive yellow lateral stripes on head (Fig. 113) ................ *Agkistrodon bilineatus*
   Dorsum of head covered with more than 15 scales; no distinctive yellow lateral stripes on head ................................ 5
5. Midbody dorsal scale rows 21 (Figs. 269, 270) ................ *Porthidium godmani*
   Midbody dorsal scale rows 23 or more ................................ 6
6. Ventrals fewer than 150; supraocular long and narrow (Fig. 305); extremely stout body with rugose scales; no pale vertebral line (Figs. 288, 289) ................ *Porthidium nummifer*
   Ventrals more than 150; supraoculars large and broad (Fig. 311); relatively slender body with keeled, but not rugose, scales; usually a pale vertebral line evident (Fig. 292) ................ *Porthidium ophryomegas*

**Table 9**

Distributions by vegetation type of venomous snakes in El Salvador

| *Species* | *Lowland dry forest* | *Thorn forest, savannas* | *Lower montane wet forest* | *Lower montane dry forest* |
|---|---|---|---|---|
| *Pelamis platurus*[1] | | | | |
| *Micrurus nigrocinctus* | X[2] | X[2] | X | |
| *Agkistrodon bilineatus* | X | X | | |
| *Crotalus durissus* | X | X | | |
| *Porthidium godmani* | | | X[3] | X[3] |
| *P. nummifer*[4] | | | X | |
| *P. ophryomegas*[5] | X | X | | |

1. Pacific marine habitat.
2. Usually in more mesic portions of forest near watercourses.
3. Known in El Salvador at elevations exceeding 1,800 m.
4. Mertens (1952b) reported that this species occurred at 2,700 m in El Salvador, but this location is higher than any point in the country.
5. Distribution disjunct in Pacific lowlands; most frequently encountered in relatively dry areas.

## NICARAGUA

Nicaragua is the largest country in Central America, encompassing 130,000 km². It is bordered by Honduras to the north and Costa Rica to the south. There are about 480 km of coastline on the Caribbean Sea and about 320 km on the Pacific Ocean.

Nicaragua can be divided conveniently into four physiographic regions: (1) The volcanic mountains and hills are located adjacent to the Pacific coastal plain. This region includes an axis of young volcanoes that runs between the Gulf of Fonseca and Lago de Nicaragua; many of these volcanoes are still active. Much of this terrain is gently rolling, such as the Rivas Isthmus, which separates the Lago de Nicaragua from the Pacific Ocean. The higher peaks generally do not exceed 600 m; however, Volcán Cerro Negro to the west of Lago de Managua reaches 675 m, and several volcanoes in the Diriamba highlands and on the Isla de Ometepe in the Lago de Nicaragua exceed 1,300 m. The drainage system of this region consists of many short, relatively fast-flowing rivers that discharge into the Pacific Ocean. (2) The great structural rift that runs from the Gulf of Fonseca to the Río San Juan drainage contains the largest freshwater lakes in Central America. These are the Lago de Nicaragua, which is 161 km long and 75 km wide, and the Lago de Managua, which is 56 km long and 24 km wide. These two great lakes are connected by the Río Tipitapa. Much of this land is composed of low plains drained by short rivers flowing into the lakes. (3) The rugged central highlands extend from Honduras southeastward to the Río San Juan drainage. This region is composed of a series of mountain ridges, ranging from 900 to 1,800 m above sea level, and steep valleys with long rivers that drain primarily eastward into the Caribbean Sea. Some of the major ranges include the Cordillera Isabelia, which forms a broad arc in the north, the Cordillera Chontaleña, which flanks the Lago de Nicaragua to the east and northeast, and the Serranís Huapí, which consist of a series of broken ridges in central Nicaragua. (4) East of the central highlands lies the Caribbean lowland region, composed of the coastal plain, with many swamps, lagoons, and gently undulating foothills. Several eastern spurs of the central highlands extend into these lowlands, and in the region just north of the Río San Juan Basin there is practically no coastal plain. The principal rivers in the region are the Río Coco, forming part of the border with Honduras; the Río Grande de Matagalpa and Río Escondido, draining much of the central highlands; and the Río San Juan, connecting the Lago de Nicaragua with the Caribbean Sea and forming part of the boundary with Costa Rica.

The Caribbean lowland region of Nicaragua is the wettest place in Central America and has no well-defined dry season. The region is basically hot and rainy year-round owing, in part, to the effects of the northeast trade winds. The amount of precipitation falling annually is clinal, with 2,540 mm reported on the Río Coco in the north and an impressive 6,500 mm registered near San Juan del Norte (Greytown) in the south. There is little seasonal variation in mean annual temperatures in the eastern lowlands; recordings from most stations fall between 25 and 28°C. Mean monthly temperatures in the western lowlands are slightly higher, 26–30°C. The coastal plains are the *tierra caliente* of Nicaragua and localities from sea level to about 750 m experience daytime temperatures of 30–33°C and nightly lows of 21–24°C. The piedmont and eastern slopes of the central highlands are subject to heavy rainfall, but the western slopes of the central highlands—as well as the rift and Pacific lowlands regions—are much drier and experience a well-defined dry season. This extends from about November or December through April, when 1,000–1,500 mm of precipitation falls at most localities in the Pacific lowlands and rift regions, and 1,500–2,200 mm falls in the central highlands. The terrain lying between 750 and 1,600 m in the central highlands is known as *tierra templada* and has daytime highs of 24–27°C and nightly lows of 15–21°C. Only a few crests and peaks exceed 1,600 m in Nicaragua; these are considered *tierra fria*.

The broad Caribbean lowlands of northeastern Nicaragua are covered by tropical moist forest consisting largely of pines (*Pinus caribaea*) and palm savannas.

This type of vegetation extends inland through most of the Río Coco Depression and southward as far as the Laguna de Perlas. From this lagoon southward to the Río San Juan, the coastal lowlands are dominated by tropical wet forest (rainforest), although an eastern spur of mountains restricts the extent of this forest to the immediate coast in the vicinity of Punta Mono. The eastern slopes of the central highlands are covered primarily by lower montane (subtropical) wet and moist forests; the western slopes of the central highlands and the slopes of the Pacific volcanic range are mostly covered by subtropical dry forests consisting of deciduous hardwoods and grasses. Pines reach their southernmost limit in the northern portion of the eastern lowlands and central highlands. Tropical dry and tropical arid forests predominate in the rift region surrounding the great lakes and in the Pacific lowlands. The western lowlands also possess numerous savannas with deciduous gallery forests.

The distribution and occurrence of some venomous snake species have been poorly documented in Nicaragua. *Bothriechis marchi* was reported only once, and the specimen is now lost, so its identity cannot be confirmed (see footnote 5, Table 10). The presence of *Bothriechis lateralis* is based on one specimen purportedly from the Diriamba highlands. No additional specimens have been found despite extensive collecting in the area, and the accuracy of the locality data for this specimen is doubtful. *Lachesis muta* is well known from adjacent Costa Rica, and there is no reason to doubt its existence in Nicaragua; unfortunately, all specimens collected there either have been lost or bear questionable or imprecise locality data. *Laticauda colubrina* reportedly has been sighted at several localities off the west coast of Central America, including San Juan del Sur in Nicaragua, but no specimens have reached scientific collections. The distributions by vegetation type of species of dangerously venomous snakes in Nicaragua are given in Table 10.

**Table 10**

Distributions by vegetation type of venomous snakes in Nicaragua

| Species | *Tropical wet forest* | *Tropical moist forest* | *Subtropical wet and moist forests* | *Subtropical dry forest* | *Tropical dry and arid forests* |
|---|---|---|---|---|---|
| *Pelamis platurus*[1] | | | | | |
| *Micrurus alleni*[2] | X | X | X | | |
| *M. multifasciatus*[2] | X | | X | | |
| *M. nigrocinctus*[3] | X | X | X | X | X |
| *Agkistrodon bilineatus* | | | | | X[4] |
| *Bothriechis marchi* | | | X[5] | | |
| *B. schlegelii*[2] | X | X | X | | |
| *Bothrops asper*[2] | X | X | X[6] | | X[7] |
| *Crotalus durissus*[4] | | | | X | X |
| *Lachesis muta*[8] | X | X | | | |
| *Porthidium godmani* | | | X[9] | | |
| *P. nasutum* | X | X | X[6] | | X[7] |
| *P. nummifer* | | | X[10] | | |
| *P. ophryomegas* | | | | X[11] | X |

*Source:* Compiled, in part, from Villa, 1984.
1. Pacific marine habitat.
2. Caribbean drainage.
3. Also found on Isla del Maíz Grande.
4. Pacific lowlands and rift region.
5. The status of this species is uncertain; its presence in Nicaragua is based on a single specimen now lost, reportedly collected in the Departamento de Nueva Segovia.
6. Usually at elevations of less than 900 m.
7. In gallery forests.
8. Poorly documented in Nicaragua.
9. Known only from northern highlands.
10. Known only from the slopes of the central highlands.
11. At elevations of less than 850 m; rarely encountered in more humid environments.

## Key to Venomous Snakes of Nicaragua

1. No loreal pit between eye and nostril; loreal scale absent (Fig. 100); dorsal scales smooth; fangs permanently erect (Fig. 19); Elapidae .................................2
   A loreal pit between eye and nostril (Fig. 141); loreal scale present; dorsal scales keeled; fangs fold back (Fig. 253); Viperidae ...........................................5
2. Tail strongly flattened laterally; marine habitat; usually a longitudinal black (or brown) and yellow pattern (Figs. 110–112)........................*Pelamis platurus*
   Tail round in cross section; terrestrial habitat; pattern consisting of black, red, and/or yellow or white rings ...............................................................3
3. A bicolored dorsal pattern consisting of black rings alternating with white, yellow, pink, or red rings; black head cap generally involving only anterior edges of supraoculars and frontal scale, if at all (Fig. 81) ............................ ....................................................................*Micrurus multifasciatus*
   A tricolored dorsal pattern consisting of black, yellow or white, and red or pink

rings; black head cap involving a substantial portion of the supraoculars and frontal scale, sometimes extending onto parietals ....................................4

4. Black head cap barely reaching parietals, if at all (Figs. 85, 86, 89) ................ ........................................................................ *Micrurus nigrocinctus*
   Black head cap extending posteriorly at least along interparietal suture (Fig. 20) ........................................................................ *Micrurus alleni*
5. Tail terminating in rattle or button (Fig. 328)...................... *Crotalus durissus*
   Tail not terminating in rattle ..............................................................6
6. Dorsum of head covered with 9–15 often regularly arranged plates; distinct yellow stripes on side of head (Figs. 114, 115) ...........*Agkistrodon bilineatus*
   Dorsum of head covered with more than 15 scales, often irregularly arranged; side of head without distinctive yellow stripes ......................................7
7. Posterior subcaudals finely divided (Figs. 252, 316) ................*Lachesis muta*
   Posterior subcaudals single or paired (Fig. 316) ........................................8
8. Most subcaudals paired (Figs. 186, 316) ...............................*Bothrops asper*
   Most subcaudals single (Fig. 316)...........................................................9
9. Green or yellow ground color, with or without dorsal pattern; arboreal, with prehensile tail ..........................................................................10
   Tan, brown, or gray ground color, always with some dorsal pattern; terrestrial, tail not prehensile..........................................................................12
10. Raised superciliary scales giving appearance of eyelashes (Fig. 165); venter distinctly mottled or ground color brilliant yellow (Figs. 139–141) .............. .................................................................... *Bothriechis schlegelii*
    No raised superciliary scales; venter green ............................................11
11. Distinct yellow paraventral stripes on first scale row; alternating or opposite yellow paravertebral vertical bars usually present; usually 23 midbody scale rows (Figs. 125–128) ...............................................*Bothriechis lateralis*
    No yellow paraventral stripes on first scale row; dorsum without yellow paravertebral vertical bars; usually 21 midbody scale rows (Figs. 129–131).......... ........................................................................ *Bothriechis marchi*
12. Midbody dorsal scale rows 21 (Figs. 269, 270)................*Porthidium godmani*
    Midbody dorsal scale rows 23 or more ..................................................13
13. Supraoculars narrow or divided into small scales (Fig. 305); more than 9 scales between orbits; body scales extremely rugose; no pale vertebral line (Fig. 288) .................................................................... *Porthidium nummifer*
    Supraoculars broad and well differentiated from other head scales; usually 7 or fewer intersupraoculars; body scales keeled, but not rugose; usually a pale vertebral line present .......................................................................14
14. Tip of snout strongly upturned, forming a free flap (Fig. 314); fewer than 150 ventrals (Figs. 281, 282) ..........................................*Porthidium nasutum*
    Tip of snout not strongly upturned (Fig. 310); more than 158 ventrals (Fig. 292) ................................................................ *Porthidium ophryomegas*

## COSTA RICA

At 51,100 km², Costa Rica is the third smallest country in Central America; only El Salvador and Belize are smaller. Costa Rica is oriented on a northwest-southwest axis between Nicaragua to the north and Panama to the south, and it possesses long coastlines on both the Caribbean Sea and the Pacific Ocean.

Costa Rica can be divided into four broad physiographic regions: (1) In the north the Caribbean lowlands extend inland from the coast for about 120 km, but become progressively more narrow in the south, where mountainous spurs penetrate to within 5 km or less of the coast. Some of these lowlands, especially in the north and near the coast, are nearly flat and are subject to flooding. A number of large rivers that have their origins in the high mountains of the interior snake their way across the lowlands and flow into the Caribbean Sea. These include Río San Carlos and Río Sarapiquí, both major tributaries of the Río San Juan; the Río Reventazón; and the Río Chirripó del Atlántico. (2) The interior highlands, which form a backbone that runs the length of the country, are composed of four major ranges: Cordillera de Guanacaste, Cordillera de Tilarán, Cordillera Central, and Cordillera de Talamanca. The Cordillera de Guanacaste is volcanic in origin and has five peaks exceeding 1,500 m; Volcán Miravalles is the highest within this range at 2,020 m. The Cordillera de Tilarán is nonvolcanic and somewhat lower than the Cordillera de Guanacaste, but its crest exceeds the

1,500-m contour for about 40 km. The Cordillera Central is of volcanic origin, and its tall volcanoes dominate the landscape of central Costa Rica, with Volcán Poás at 2,705 m, Volcán Barba at 2,906 m, Volcán Turrialba at 3,328 m, and Volcán Irazú at 3,432 m. Of these, Poás and Irazú are still active volcanoes. The Cordillera de Talamanca extends from central Costa Rica into Panama. This nonvolcanic range has 10 peaks exceeding 3,000 m in elevation, including Chirripó Grande; this is the highest point in the country, 3,820 m. A large interior high valley, known as the Valle Central, is formed where the southeastern portion of the Cordillera Central runs north of, and parallel to, the northwestern portion of the Cordillera de Talamanca. A part of the Valle Central is relatively flat and is called the Mesa Central. It is within the Mesa Central that several basins containing the major population centers of Costa Rica are located. The Cartago Basin is subject to Caribbean winds and receives more rainfall than the San José Basin. (3) The plains of Guanacaste, including the Valle de Tempisque and northern province of Puntarenas, and the hilly terrain of the Nicoya Peninsula, form a geographic region that is especially hot and dry. (4) The plains and hills of the southeastern Osa Peninsula, the southeastern Cordillera Costeña, and upper Río Grande de Térraba Basin are relatively wet, in contrast to the northwestern portion of the country. One of the major tributaries of the Río Grande de Térraba, the Río General, drains the valley between the coastal range and the Cordillera de Talamanca. Most of this upland valley, the Valle del General, lies between 200 and 1,000 m above sea level. Most of the rivers that flow to the Pacific Ocean, with the exception of the Río Grande de Térraba, are short and relatively precipitous. The Pacific coastal plain of southeastern Costa Rica is narrow to almost nonexistent, except for the peninsulas flanking the Gulf of Dulce.

The Caribbean lowlands possess a warm climate with mean annual temperatures of 22–27°C for most localities below 600 m in elevation. Rain falls throughout the year in some areas; others experience a brief drought. From 3,000 to 6,000 mm of precipitation falls annually, with rainfall higher in the north.

At moderate elevations in the cordilleras, a wet seasonal climate prevails that is transitional between that of the wet Atlantic lowlands and the dry lowland climates of the Pacific Coast or the climates that occur at higher elevations in the cordilleras. This wet seasonal climate extends from the Llanuras de los Guatusos in northwestern Costa Rica southward along the lower Caribbean slopes to Panama and along the Pacific Coast from the tip of the Nicoya Peninsula and northern province of Puntarenas southward to Panama, including all of the Osa Peninsula. There is a 2–4 month dry period that falls sometime between January and May, depending on locality: nevertheless, total annual rainfall (2,500–4,000 mm) may be as high as or higher than that of the Atlantic lowlands.

The Llanos de Guanacaste and all but the southern tip of the Nicoya Peninsula have a dry lowland climate in which there is a harsh dry season extending for at least 5, and as many as 8, months (October to May). This type of climate extends up the Pacific slopes to about 800 m; the mean annual precipitation is from 1,300 to 2,300 mm, and mean annual temperatures range from 22 to 28°C.

An Atlantic slope upland climate extends from about 600 to 1,600 m. Cool temperatures from 16 to 22°C prevail, and 2,500–5,000 mm of precipitation is received annually. The Pacific slope upland climate ranges from about 800 to 1,600 m and is generally drier than that of the Atlantic, with 1,500–2,500 mm of rainfall per year. Temperatures on the Pacific side are usually warmer than those at corresponding elevations on the Atlantic side.

A highland climate prevails at elevations above 1,600 m, primarily in the Cordillera Central and the Cordillera de Talamanca. Temperatures are decidedly cool, ranging from 10 to 16°C. Although some areas may experience dry periods, frequent surface-level clouds often create extremely humid conditions.

Vegetation associations are largely determined by climate, and because complex climatic patterns are present in Costa Rica, the vegetation is correspondingly varied. For convenience, the following major vegetation types may be recognized.

Tropical rainforest (tropical wet and moist forest) extends from the Llanura de los Guatusos and the Río San Juan plains southward in the Caribbean lowlands to Panama. On the Pacific side this type of forest also extends from about the Río Tulín in northern province of Puntarenas southward through the Osa Peninsula to Panama. Rainforest is especially wet in the northeastern Caribbean lowlands and the region north and east of the Gulf of Dulce on the Pacific side. In the drier portions of rainforest (tropical moist forest) a few trees may be deciduous, but most are evergreen. The dominant trees in rainforest may attain a height of 30–50 m, often have buttressed roots, and possess many epiphytes and lianas. A prominent understory of small palms is typically present.

Lowland (tropical) dry forest predominates in much of northwestern Costa Rica. This forest type extends from about the Río Grande de Tárcoles drainage northwestward along the Pacific Coast and foothills, including the Nicoya Peninsula, to Nicaragua. Most trees do not exceed 15 m in height and are deciduous during the dry season except along river courses.

Along the lower slopes and piedmont a premontane forest prevails (premontane moist, wet, and rainforest). These forests may be extremely humid year-round or may experience a dry period for several months each year. The hardwood trees that make up these forests are slightly lower in stature than those in the wet lowlands. These forests extend from the Cordillera de Guanacaste through the Cordillera de Talamanca.

At moderate to intermediate elevations the forest is composed primarily of broad-leaved hardwoods (lower montane moist, wet, and rainforests). In some areas a rather persistent low-lying cloud cover causes these forests to be cool, wet, and dark. There is an abundance of epiphytes. This type of forest is found primarily in the Cordillera Central and the Cordillera de Talamanca.

**Table 11**

Distributions by vegetation type of venomous snakes in Costa Rica

| Species | *Tropical wet and moist forests* | *Tropical dry forests* | *Premontane forests* | *Lower montane moist, wet, and rainforests* | *High montane forests* |
|---|---|---|---|---|---|
| *Pelamis platurus*[1] | | | | | |
| *Micrurus alleni*[2] | X | | X | | |
| *M. clarki* | X[3] | | | | |
| *M. multifasciatus* | X | X[4] | X | X | |
| *M. nigrocinctus* | X | X | X | X | |
| *Agkistrodon bilineatus* | | X | | | |
| *Bothriechis lateralis* | | | | X | |
| *B. nigroviridis* | | | | X | X |
| *B. schlegelii* | X | | X | X[5] | |
| *Bothrops asper* | X | X[6] | X | X[7] | |
| *Crotalus durissus* | | X | | | |
| *Lachesis muta* | X | | X | | |
| *Porthidium godmani* | | | | X[8] | X |
| *P. nasutum* | X | | X | | |
| *P. nummifer* | X | | X | X[5] | |
| *P. ophryomegas* | | X | X | | |
| *P. picadoi* | X | | X | X[5] | |

1. Pacific marine habitat.
2. Most records for southeastern lowlands.
3. Only one specimen with locality data is known from Costa Rica; it was collected about 1 km from the Panamanian border in the lowlands of extreme southeastern Costa Rica.
4. Known from the vicinity of Liberia, Guanacaste.
5. Generally below 1,500 m.
6. Along watercourses.
7. Generally below 1,200 m.
8. Generally above 1,500 m.

At high elevations humid montane forest generally prevails (montane wet and rainforests). The trees are shorter than in lower montane forests, and there is less epiphytic growth. Various species of oaks are common, and bamboo thickets are often encountered. Montane forests occur on the higher volcanoes of the Cordillera Central and the high crest of the Cordillera de Talamanca.

In a few small areas above 3,000 m in the Cordillera de Talamanca a subalpine *páramo* is present that is dominated by grasses and short shrubs. Costa Rica is the northernmost location for this kind of vegetation, which is characteristic of the high Andes in South America.

Costa Rica is relatively well collected herpetologically; it is improbable that any new venomous snake species will be added to its fauna other than by elevating presently known populations to full species status. The distributions by vegetation type of species of dangerously venomous snakes in Costa Rica are given in Table 11.

## Key to Venomous Snakes of Costa Rica

1. No loreal pit between eye and nostril; loreal scale absent (Fig. 100); dorsal scales smooth; fangs permanently erect (Fig. 19); Elapidae ................................2
   A loreal pit between eye and nostril (Fig. 133); loreal scale present; dorsal scales keeled; fangs fold back (Fig. 253); Viperidae ..........................................6
2. Tail strongly flattened laterally; marine habitat; usually a longitudinal black (or brown) and yellow pattern (Figs. 110–112)........................*Pelamis platurus*
   Tail round in cross section; terrestrial habitat; pattern consisting of some combination of black, red, and/or yellow rings .............................................3
3. A bicolored dorsal pattern consisting of alternating rings of black with white, yellow, pink, or red; black head cap usually involving only anterior edges of supraoculars and frontal scale, if at all (Fig. 81) ........*Micrurus multifasciatus*
   A tricolored dorsal pattern usually consisting of black, yellow or white, and red or pink rings; black head cap involving a substantial portion of the supraoculars and frontal scale, sometimes extending onto parietals .........................4
4. Black head cap entirely covering parietals; mental and infralabials pale with some dark stippling; pale lateral head scales outlined by black (Fig. 30) ....................................................................................................*Micrurus clarki*
   Black head cap generally not entirely covering parietals; *if* cap does completely cover parietals, *then* mental and anterior infralabials are mostly black, and pale lateral head scales are not outlined by black ...........................................5
5. Black head cap barely reaching parietals, if at all (Figs. 85, 86, 89) ................ .........................................................................*Micrurus nigrocinctus*

Black head cap extending posteriorly at least along interparietal suture (Fig. 20) ........................................................................................... *Micrurus alleni*

6. Tail terminating in rattle or button (Fig. 328) ...................... *Crotalus durissus*
   Tail not terminating in rattle ................................................................ 7
7. Posterior subcaudals finely divided (Figs. 250, 252, 316) .......... *Lachesis muta*
   Posterior subcaudals single or paired (Fig. 316) ....................................... 8
8. Dorsum of head covered with 9–15 plates, often regularly arranged; distinctive yellow stripes on side of head (Figs. 114, 115) ........... *Agkistrodon bilineatus*
   Dorsum of head covered with more than 15 scales, often irregularly arranged; side of head without distinctive yellow stripes ...................................... 9
9. Subcaudals paired (Figs. 186, 316) ...................................... *Bothrops asper*
   Subcaudals single (Fig. 316) ............................................................ 10
10. Green or yellow ground color, with or without dorsal pattern; arboreal, with prehensile tail ........................................................................... 11
    Tan, brown, or gray ground color, always with some dorsal pattern; terrestrial, tail not prehensile ........................................................................ 13
11. Raised superciliary scales giving appearance of eyelashes (Fig. 165); venter distinctly mottled or ground color brilliant yellow (Figs. 139–141) .............. ....................................................................... *Bothriechis schlegelii*
    No raised superciliary scales; venter greenish, mottled with black or not ..... 12
12. Dorsum strongly mottled with black, black-bordered pale green dorsal blotches may be present; no yellow paraventral stripe; iris black; generally fewer than 158 ventrals; generally 19 midbody scale rows (Figs. 132, 133) .................... ...................................................................... *Bothriechis nigroviridis*
    Dorsum not mottled with black, alternating or opposite yellow paravertebral vertical bars usually present; distinct yellow paraventral stripes on first scale row; iris yellow; usually more than 158 ventrals; usually 23 midbody scale rows (Figs. 125–128) ............................................... *Bothriechis lateralis*
13. Midbody scale rows 21 (Figs. 269–271) ......................... *Porthidium godmani*
    Midbody scale rows 23 or more ........................................................... 14
14. Fewer than 138 ventrals; supraoculars divided into small scales (Fig. 305); more than 9 scales between orbits; body scales extremely rugose (Figs. 288) .......... ....................................................................... *Porthidium nummifer*
    More than 138 ventrals; supraoculars well differentiated from other head scales (although elongated in *P. picadoi*); generally 7 or fewer intersupraoculars; body scales keeled, but not rugose (Figs. 293, 294) ................................. 15
15. More than 158 ventrals (Fig. 292) .......................... *Porthidium ophryomegas*
    Fewer than 158 ventrals ..................................................................... 16
16. Tip of snout strongly upturned, forming a free flap (Figs. 281–283) ............... ...................................................................... *Porthidium nasutum*
    Tip of snout not upturned (Figs. 293, 294) ...................... *Porthidium picadoi*

## PANAMA

Panama is the most southern and eastern Central American country and is the link between Middle and South America. It is shaped like a sigmoid curve oriented on a more-or-less east-west axis. The width of the country varies from 48 km near the Panama Canal to about 185 km across the Azuero Peninsula. Panama is bordered on the west by Costa Rica, on the east by Colombia, on the north by 1,246 km of Atlantic coastline, and on the south by 1,634 km of Pacific coastline. The country encompasses 77,082 km$^2$. The territory of Panama includes the 366 Islas de San Blas off its eastern Atlantic Coast and some 1,000 islands off the Pacific Coast, including the Islas de las Perlas, Coiba, and Taboga.

The central backbone of mountains that forms the Continental Divide is the dominant feature of the landscape. The highest mountains are those of western Panama, which are extensions of the same uplift that formed the mountain chains of eastern Costa Rica. These include the Cordillera de Talamanca with Volcán Baru (Volcán de Chiriquí), the highest point in the country at 3,454 m, and the Serranía de Tabasará with Cerro Santiago, the highest point in the range at 2,810 m. Geographers sometimes refer to the Cordillera de Talamanca and the Serranía de Tabasará together as the Cordillera Central because they make up a narrow backbone that is unbroken up to the 1,200-m contour. To the east the

Serranía de Tabasará gradually loses elevation toward the central province of Coclé, where it is composed only of low foothills. A small isolated group of mountains with ridges and peaks exceeding 1,000 m is present in the western portion of the province of Panamá. The Azuero Peninsula on the southern side of the isthmus possesses an isolated highland with a few peaks reaching 1,500 m.

East of the Canal Zone uplifts tend to be extensive but low, and except for the region near the Colombian border, few peaks exceed 800 m. The Cordillera de San Blas and Serranía del Darién form the Continental Divide, which is close to the Atlantic Coast. Elevations along the divide average less than 500 m for the most part, but near the Colombian border the Continental Divide swings southward and the Altos de Limón includes peaks exceeding 1,500 m. Cerro Tacarcuna, at 1,875 m, is the highest point in the region. Along the eastern edge of the province of Panama the isolated Serranía de Cañazas (sometimes called the Serranía de Maje) is located near the Pacific Coast and exceeds 1,200 m in places. Several other major ranges arise out of the Pacific lowlands of the eastern portion of the province of Panama, including the Serranía de Pirre, which reaches about 1,540 m, and the Serranía de Jungurudó, which exceeds 1,600 m. The ranges of eastern Panama seem to be associated with the Andean orogeny rather than the mountains to the north in Central America.

The rivers of the Atlantic drainage tend to be relatively short and precipitous, whereas those of the Pacific drainage are longer and more sluggish. Of the more than 300 rivers flowing into the Pacific Ocean, the Río Tuira is the longest, flowing into the Gulf of San Miguel.

Some regions of Panama receive abundant rainfall during most of the year. However, from about late December to April much of the lowlands and moderate elevations are subject to a dry period. Five climatic types may be recognized in Panama on the basis of rainfall distribution and elevation.

Several regions on the Atlantic Coast are especially wet and receive sufficient rainfall throughout the year to be classified as possessing a tropical wet climate. These regions are the Atlantic Coast of western Panama and the Portobelo area of central Panama. The majority of the lowland regions have a tropical monsoon climate in which the total annual amount of precipitation may equal that of the tropical wet climate, but it is not so evenly dispersed and a definite dry season occurs sometime between December and April. Tropical monsoon climates are found in most of the Atlantic lowlands, the extreme southwestern lowlands, the western portion of the Azuero Peninsula, most of the eastern Pacific lowlands, and the Isla Coiba. Some portions of the Pacific lowlands are subject to rainshadow effects and have a tropical wet and dry climate with an extended and harsh dry season.

Tropical wet and dry climates characterize much of the Pacific Coast and the foothills of western Panama around the city of David, the region from about the Río San Pablo in the province of Veraguas eastward to the western edge of the Bay of Panama and southward along the eastern and southeastern portions of the Azuero Peninsula, and the area from about Panama City to east of the mouth of the Río Chepo. This type of climate also prevails on the major islands in the Bay of Panama. The highlands are cooler and may or may not have rainy periods that alternate with a pronounced dry season.

A temperate wet and dry climate is present in the highlands along the southern escarpment of the high ranges in western Panama, which tend to have alternating rainy and dry seasons. The northern slopes of the Cordillera de Talamanca and the Serranía de Tabasará, and the higher elevations of the Serranía de Cañazas, Cerro Tacarcuna, Serranía de Pirre, and Serranía de Jungurudó have a temperate wet climate in which precipitation is more evenly distributed throughout the year than in temperate wet and dry climates.

Tropical rainforest is present in most of the lowlands of Panama, including all of the Atlantic coastal region, the extreme southwestern portion of the Pacific Coast, the lowlands bordering the northeastern portion of the Gulf of Chiriquí and western portion of the Azuero Peninsula, and much of the eastern Pacific lowlands. Tropical dry forests are restricted to several regions of the Pacific Coast and foothills including the vicinity of David in western Panama, central province of Veraguas eastward almost to the Canal Zone and southward through the western portion of the Azuero Peninsula, and from near Panama City eastward some 100 km. Rather extensive regions in eastern Panama sometimes are considered to be transitional between tropical dry forest and tropical rainforest.

Wet subtropical forests are widespread along the foothills of the western Panamanian highlands, the western slopes of the highlands of the Azuero Peninsula, and the highlands of eastern Panama. Lower montane wet forest extends along the crest of the Cordillera de Talamanca and Serraniá de Tabasará from the Costa Rican border to about the province of Veraguas. This type of forest is also present at higher elevations in eastern Panama in the Serranía de Cañazos, Serranía de Jungurudó, Serranía de Pirre, and Cerro Tacarcuna. High montane wet forest occurs only on the highest peaks of the Cordillera de Talamanca.

Many regions of Panama, especially those in the eastern part of the country, remain poorly explored. Several venomous snake species known from Colombia (see Table 13) may enter the province of Darién, including *Micrurus dumerilii*. The Neotropical rattlesnake *Crotalus durissus* is curiously absent from Panama, although it occurs in neighboring Costa Rica and Colombia. The distributions by vegetation type of the species of dangerously venomous snakes in Panama are given in Table 12.

**Table 12**

Distributions by vegetation type of venomous snakes in Panama

| Species | *Tropical rainforest* | *Tropical dry forest* | *Subtropical wet forest* | *Lower montane wet forest* | *Montane wet forest* |
|---|---|---|---|---|---|
| *Pelamis platurus*[1] | | | | | |
| *Micrurus alleni* | X | X[2] | X | X | |
| *M. ancoralis* | X | | X | | |
| *M. clarki* | X | X[2] | X | | |
| *M. dissoleucus* | X | X[2] | | | |
| *M. mipartitus* | X | | | | |
| *M. multifasciatus* | X | | X | X | |
| *M. nigrocinctus* | X | X | X | X | |
| *M. stewarti* | | | X | X | |
| *Bothriechis lateralis* | | | | X | X |
| *B. nigroviridis* | | | | X | X |
| *B. schlegelii* | X | | X | X[3] | |
| *Bothriopsis punctata*[4] | X | | X | X | |
| *Bothrops asper* | X | X[2] | X[5] | | |
| *Lachesis muta* | X | | X[5] | | |
| *Porthidium godmani* | | | | X[6] | X |
| *P. lansbergii* | X | X | | | |
| *P. nasutum* | X | | X[5] | | |
| *P. nummifer* | X | | X | X | |
| *P. ophryomegas* | | X | | | |
| *P. picadoi* | | | | X | |

1. Pacific marine habitat; may also occur off Atlantic Coast.
2. Probably in moist riparian situations.
3. Generally below 1,500 m.
4. The distribution of this species in Panama is poorly documented; vegetation types inhabited by this snake largely deduced using data from Colombian specimens.
5. Generally below 1,000 m.
6. Above 1,500 m.

## Key to Venomous Snakes of Panama

1. No loreal pit between eye and nostril; loreal scale absent (Fig. 100); dorsal scales smooth; fangs permanently erect (Fig. 19); Elapidae ....2
   A loreal pit between eye and nostril (Fig. 133); loreal scale present; dorsal scales keeled; fangs fold back (Fig. 253); Viperidae ....12
2. Tail strongly flattened laterally; marine habitat; usually a longitudinal yellow and black (or brown) pattern (Figs. 110–112) ....*Pelamis platurus*
   Tail round in cross section; terrestrial habitat; pattern consisting of some combination of black, yellow, and/or red rings ....3
3. Triads of black rings on body ....4
   No triads on body ....5
4. First *complete* triad posterior to and not involving black ring on nape (Fig. 40) ....*Micrurus dissoleucus*
   Black ring on nape comprising anteriormost black ring of first *complete* triad (Fig. 23) ....*Micrurus ancoralis*
5. A bicolored dorsal pattern consisting of black rings alternating with rings of white, yellow, pink, or red ....6
   A tricolored dorsal pattern consisting of black, yellow or white, and red or pink rings ....9
6. Head and tail have orange (or red) rings, generally black and white or yellow rings on body (Fig. 77) ....*Micrurus mipartitus*
   Generally black and red or pink rings on body ....7
7. More than 46 black rings on body (Fig. 81) ....*Micrurus multifasciatus*
   Fewer than 46 black rings on body ....8
8. More than 22 black rings on body (Figs. 85, 86, 89) ....*Micrurus nigrocinctus*
   Fewer than 22 black rings on body ....*Micrurus stewarti*
9. Black cap covering all of parietals ....10
   Black cap only partially covering parietals, if at all ....11
10. Mental and several anterior infralabials mostly black; lateral head scales not outlined by black (Fig. 20) ....*Micrurus alleni*

Mental and infralabials not covered with black, some dark speckling often present; lateral head scales outlined with black (Fig. 30)........*Micrurus clarki*

11. Black head cap barely involving parietals, if at all (Figs. 85, 86, 89)........................................................................................*Micrurus nigrocinctus*

    Black head cap extending posteriorly along interparietal suture (Fig. 20) ....................................................................................*Micrurus alleni*

12. Posterior subcaudals finely divided (Figs. 252, 316)................*Lachesis muta*

    Posterior subcaudals single or paired (Figs. 316).....................................13

13. Subcaudals mostly paired (Fig. 316).....................................................14

    Subcaudals mostly single (Fig. 316).....................................................15

14. More than 78 subcaudals; dorsum of head tan with symmetrically arranged dark brown markings; arboreal, tail prehensile (Fig. 157).......*Bothriopsis punctata*

    Fewer than 78 subcaudals; dorsum of head uniformly brown; terrestrial, tail not prehensile (Fig. 186).......................................................*Bothrops asper*

15. Green or yellow ground color; with or without dorsal pattern; arboreal, with prehensile tail..............................................................................16

    Tan, brown, or gray ground color, always with some dorsal pattern; terrestrial, tail not prehensile...........................................................................18

16. Raised superciliary scales giving appearance of eyelashes (Fig. 165); venter distinctly mottled or ground color yellow (Figs. 139–144)..........................................................................................*Bothriechis schlegelii*

    No raised superciliary scales; venter green, mottled with black or not .........17

17. Dorsum strongly mottled with black; black-bordered pale green dorsal blotches may be present; no yellow paraventral stripe; iris black; usually fewer than 158 ventrals; usually 19 midbody scale rows (Figs. 132, 133)..........................................................................................*Bothriechis nigroviridis*

    Dorsum not mottled with black; alternating or opposite yellow paravertebral vertical bars usually present; distinct yellow paraventral stripes on first scale row; iris yellow; usually more than 158 ventrals; usually 23 midbody scale rows (Figs. 125–128)...............................................*Bothriechis lateralis*

18. Midbody scale rows 21 (Figs. 269–271).........................*Porthidium godmani*

    Midbody scale rows 23 or more...........................................................19

19. Distinct middorsal blotches, sometimes merging to form zig-zag stripe........20

    Alternate or opposite paravertebral blotches, generally rectangular or triangular in shape and separated by a pale vertebral line.....................................21

20. Supraoculars divided into small scales (Fig. 305); ventrals fewer than 138 (Fig. 288)..................................................................*Porthidium nummifer*

    Supraoculars elongated (Fig. 294), but clearly differentiated from head scales; ventrals more than 138 (Figs. 293, 294) .........................*Porthidium picadoi*

21. Ventrals plus subcaudals more than 195; snout not sharply elevated (Figs. 292, 310)...........................................................*Porthidium ophryomegas*

    Ventrals plus subcaudals fewer than 195; snout moderately to strongly elevated ...........................................................................................22

22. Usually fewer than 146 ventrals; outer edges of supraoculars forming a distinct ridge (Figs. 281–284)...............................................*Porthidium nasutum*

    Usually more than 146 ventrals; outer edges of supraoculars rounded (Figs. 274, 275)..................................................................*Porthidium lansbergii*

# The Caribbean Islands

With the exception of inshore islets that are territorial possessions of Latin American countries (such as Isla de Margarita, Venezuela), only six Caribbean islands are known to harbor venomous snakes. These islands include part of the Windward group of the western Lesser Antilles, Aruba, the Islas Los Testigos, and Trinidad. Conflicting reports exist regarding the occurrence of *Bothrops* on the island of Tobago, but the most recent information is that the island lacks dangerously venomous snakes.

## THE WINDWARD ISLANDS

The Windward group of islands, part of the western Lesser Antilles, lies in a north-south chain in the Caribbean Sea north of the Paria Peninsula of Venezuela. There are two islands in the chain known to harbor dangerously venomous snakes.

### *Saint Lucia*

The island of Saint Lucia lies at 14°N latitude and 60°W longitude, 32 km south of Martinique and 40 km north of St. Vincent. It has an area of 603 km² and is of volcanic origin. The highlands are concentrated in a central ridge in the island's interior; the highest peak is Mt. Gimie (958 m). There are lateral extensions of this ridge, most notably Gros Piton (798 m) and Petit Piton (750 m), which abut the sea near Soufrière on the west coast.

The east coast is deeply incised, and there are numerous xeric islets adjacent to it. The coast and plains on the northern and southern ends of the island are xeric and covered with scrubby thornbush. The highlands are forested, and the humid interior receives the island's maximum rainfall (3,500 mm). Precipitation averages about 1,500 mm over much of the rest of the island. Rainfall is concentrated from May to August, with some activity in December as well; the dry season extends from January to April. The climate is influenced by the northeast trade winds, and the mean annual temperature averages 26°C.

The single species of dangerously venomous snake, *Bothrops caribbaeus*, is confined principally to the coastal lowlands and is most common at elevations below 200 m. It is found from near Castries south to Canaries on the west coast and from Marquis to Micoud on the east coast.

### *Martinique*

The mountainous island of Martinique is situated 32 km north of Saint Lucia and 40 km south of Dominica. It comprises 1,101 km² and is of volcanic origin, with numerous mountains. The southern portion of the island contains the Vauclin (504 m) and Diamant mountains; Les Pitons du Carbet (1,196 m) are located in central Martinique. The island's highest point is the volcano Montagne Pelée (1,397 m) in the northwest.

Martinique was once extensively covered with tropical rainforest; however, the forest has been cleared for agriculture and little, if any, virgin forest remains. The southern portion of the island is lower and drier and covered with scrub woodland. The upper slopes of Montagne Pelée and Les Pitons du Carbet possess a luxuriant secondary growth of wet broad-leaved forest. Temperatures average 26°C, with the warmest months, June to November, receiving the greatest amount of rainfall (about 2,000 mm annually). The dry season extends from December to May; February is the driest month.

The single species of dangerously venomous snake, *Bothrops lanceolatus*, is found in humid uplands in the northern and southern portions of the island.

## THE NETHERLANDS ANTILLES

The Netherlands Antilles, also known as the Dutch Leeward Islands, are part of the eastern Lesser Antilles and lie on an east-west chain in the Caribbean Sea north of the Venezuelan coast. Only one island in the chain is known to harbor dangerously venomous snakes.

### *Aruba*

With an area of 184 km² and lying just 25 km north of the Paraguaná Peninsula of Venezuela, Aruba is the smallest and most westerly of the Dutch Leeward Island chain. In January of 1987, Aruba became politically independent. The region is arid, with mostly cacti and thorn scrub throughout its interior. Average annual precipitation is 444 mm, less than any other of the Leeward Islands. The mean temperature is 27.5°C, with northeast trade winds providing constant cooling. Temperatures reach their peak during August to September and their low during January and February. Rainfall is concentrated from October to January.

The soil is poor, and the island, with its salty trade

winds and prolonged dry spells, does not provide a suitable environment for abundant vegetation. On the northeast (windward) coast, conditions are especially extreme and only salt-resistant ground cover such as *Lithophila muscoides* (yerba di cusinchi), *Batis maritima*, and *Sesuvium portulacastrum* (banana di rif) survive there. Coastal shrubs in sandy areas are usually *Tournefortia gnaphaloides* (cocorobana). Isolated *Coccoloba uvifera* are virtually the only trees, although *Hipponame mancinella* (manzanilla) exists in limited numbers.

The leeward side of the island is fringed by mangroves (*Rhizophora*, *Laguncularia*, and *Conocarpus*). The interior consists of rolling terrain characterized by clusters of diorite boulders, shrubs, cacti, succulents, and scattered trees of many varieties: *Caesalpinia coriaria* (dívi divi; watapana), *Prosopis juliflora* (kwihi; indju), *Acacia tortuosa* (hubada; wabi), and many others.

The Aruba Island rattlesnake, *Crotalus durissus unicolor*, is the island's only dangerously venomous snake.

## ISLAS LOS TESTIGOS

The Islas Los Testigos are a group of five tiny islets (the largest is only 2.5 km²) situated in the Caribbean Sea approximately 16 km north of Venezuela's Paria Peninsula. The vegetation and topography resemble that of Aruba, with xeric scrub covering a rocky landscape. Two of the islands, Morro de la Iguana (100 m elevation; 0.66 km²) and Tamarindo (200 m elevation; 2.5 km²), reportedly have populations of the Neotropical rattlesnake, *Crotalus durissus*.

## TRINIDAD

Trinidad, 4,542 km² in area, is the southernmost of the Caribbean islands, situated only 16 km from the coast of Venezuela. The island is roughly rectangular, with prominent peninsular extensions in the southwestern and the northwestern corners. The southwestern peninsula closely approaches the Paria Peninsula of Venezuela, with which Trinidad is associated geologically.

The dominant topographic features in Trinidad are three ranges of hills: the Northern and Southern ranges, which run in an east-west direction, and the Central Range, which traverses the island diagonally. The Northern Range, which is an extension of Venezuela's Cordillera de la Costa, includes the highest elevations in Trinidad—El Cerro del Aripo at 940 m, and El Tucuche at 936 m. Mount Tamana (307 m) in the Central Range and the Trinity Hills in the Southern Range (304 m) are the only other areas higher than 300 m.

There are three brackish water swamps in western Trinidad: the Caroní, South Oropouche, and Cedros. Significant freshwater swamps include the North Oropouche and Nariva in the east and Erin on the southern part of the island. Numerous small islands are associated with Trinidad but only Gaspar Grande (or Gaspareé) is known to harbor dangerously venomous snakes (*Micrurus psyches*).

Trinidad supports very humid tropical forest, swamp forest, mangrove woodland, marsh, and savanna. Much of the vegetation has been altered by agricultural and commercial interests. Seasonal temperatures for most localities on the island range between 21° and 30°C, with occasional drops in upland regions and higher temperatures during the rainy season. Precipitation is concentrated from May to December but usually is interrupted by a brief dry spell (*petit carême*) in September or October. The highest rainfall occurs on the eastern portion of the Northern Range (up to 2,540 mm). To the west and south, precipitation diminishes; the northwestern and southwestern peninsulas receive 1,270 mm or less annually. Prevailing winds are from the northeast during the dry season and from the southeast in the rainy season.

Only four dangerously venomous snake species are known from Trinidad. Two species of *Micrurus* occur throughout the island, but they are most abundant in forests and swampy lowlands. The bushmaster (*Lachesis muta*) and *Bothrops asper* are found in forested regions, particularly in the uplands. See appropriate generic and species accounts for further information.

While other taxa of venomous snakes have not been found on Trinidad, a specimen of *Bothrops venezuelensis* (see Key to Venomous Snakes of Venezuela) has been taken from the nearby Paria Peninsula (Sucre) of Venezuela.

### Key to Venomous Snakes of Trinidad

1. No loreal pit between eye and nostril; loreal scale absent (Fig. 100); scales on top of head enlarged into plates (Fig. 16); dorsal scales smooth; fangs permanently erect (Fig. 19); pattern consisting of black, red, and/or yellow or white rings; Elapidae ........ 2
   A loreal pit between eye and nostril (Fig. 162); loreal scale present; scales on top of head small and numerous; dorsal scales keeled; fangs fold back (Fig. 253); pattern variable, but never ringed; Viperidae ........ 3
2. Black rings on body form triads, sometimes only visible ventrally (Figs. 68, 69) ........ *Micrurus lemniscatus*
   Black rings on body not in form of triads (Fig. 93) ........ *Micrurus psyches*
3. Posterior subcaudals finely divided (Fig. 316); keels on middorsals conical; 9 or 10 supralabials (Fig. 249) ........ *Lachesis muta*
   Posterior subcaudals all or mostly paired (Fig. 316); keels on middorsals normal; 7 or 8 supralabials (Fig. 192) ........ *Bothrops asper*

# South America

Continental South America includes thirteen countries: Argentina, Bolivia, Brazil, Chile, Colombia, Ecuador, Paraguay, Peru, Uruguay, Venezuela, Guyana, Suriname, and French Guiana (or Guyane). The area comprises 17,770,000 km$^2$ and ranges from Brazil, the world's fifth largest country, to tiny French Guiana, scarcely one-sixth the size of France. The continent of South America has twice the area of the contiguous United States. South America's population, of which Brazil contains over half, exceeds 231 million people. In general, areas of concentrated settlement include highlands, coastal plains, and port cities; the interior lowlands have low population densities.

The continent is characterized by four major topographic features: (1) mountains, the Andes principal among them; (2) a vast expanse of lowland rainforest; (3) extensive river systems, especially the Amazon, Orinoco, and Paraná; and (4) coastal plains—all but two countries have a seacoast and Colombia has two. Significant xeric regions include the Sechura and Atacama deserts along the Pacific Coast and the La Guajira Peninsula in the Caribbean Sea. A multitude of vegetation types may be found in South America, and venomous snakes occupy all but those occurring at extremely high altitudes or those in the far southern part of the continent where Antarctic breezes create cold conditions. The only country lacking dangerously venomous snakes is mainland Chile; *Pelamis* occurs within the territorial waters of Chile, specifically, those around Isla de Pascua (Easter Island).

Considerable clearing of forest for agricultural purposes has taken place throughout South America. With few exceptions, it is in these regions that most venomous snakebites occur. Major offenders in serious envenomation of humans are *Bothrops asper* in northwestern South America; *B. atrox* in the Orinoco and Amazon basins and the Guianas; *B. jararaca* and *B. jararacussu* from central Brazil southward; and, to a lesser extent, *Crotalus durissus* at scattered localities throughout its range. In southern South America, *B. alternatus* and *B. neuwiedi* are locally important causes of snakebite. For specific information refer to country accounts, distribution tables, and identification keys.

## COLOMBIA

Colombia comprises 1,138,914 km$^2$ and is situated in the tropical zone in extreme northwestern South America. The country is roughly square in shape, with a northeasterly extension terminating in the desertic La Guajira Peninsula, and a narrow arm that reaches the Amazon River in the southeast. Colombia shares boundaries with Panama on the northwest, Venezuela and Brazil on the east, and Peru and Ecuador on the south. In addition, Colombia is the only country in South America with both Atlantic and Pacific coastlines.

The dominant topographic features in Colombia are the Andes mountains, consisting of three major and dissimilar ranges: the Cordillera Oriental, the Cordillera Central, and the Cordillera Occidental, each of which runs in a north-south direction through the country. The latter two mountain chains arise from the Nudo de Pasto formation on the Ecuadorian border; the Cordillera Central is divided at the Garzón Massif to form the Cordillera Oriental. The southern Andean region in Colombia has numerous peaks exceeding 4,000 m, the Nevados de Chiles and Cumbal being principal among them. The Cordillera Oriental continues northward into Venezuela while the Serranía del Darién (up to 1,900 m) forms the Colombia-Panamanian border and represents the geologic continuation of the Cordillera Occidental into Panama. The Cordillera Central is the highest range and averages 3,000–3,500 m in elevation, followed in descending order by the Cordillera Oriental and the Cordillera Occidental.

Peripheral, but important, mountain systems include the Serranía del Baudó and Serranía de los Saltos, both rugged basaltic ranges on the Pacific Coast; the Sierra Nevada de Santa Marta in northern Colombia, which contains the highest peak (Pico Cristóbal Colón at 5,775 m) and largest snowfield in the country; and the Serranía de la Macarena, which lies just north of the Río Guayabero/Guaviare. The Serranía de la Macarena represents an older orogeny than the Andes, and it is located east of the Andes in south-central Colombia. The Serranía de Macuira (850 m) is situated in the arid La Guajira Peninsula.

The Orinoco and Amazon watersheds drain all of Colombia east of the Andes. The Arauca, Casanare, Meta, and Guaviare are among the rivers that drain the Cordillera Oriental across a vast savannah called the Llanos Orientales before eventually emptying into the Orinoco along the Venezuelan border. South of the Guaviare, the Vaupés, Caquetá, Putumayo, and innumerable smaller rivers flow through rainforest into the Negro/Amazon drainage. North of the Río Caquetá there are several isolated cerros (hills) of sandstone-conglomerate composition that, like the Serranía de la Macarena, are of Guianan Shield orogeny. The three Andean cordilleras are interdigitated by the large river valleys of the Magdalena, Cauca, and Sinú, each of which drains northward to the Caribbean Sea, and by the Patía, which drains to the Pacific Ocean.

Colombian territory includes various islands in both oceans, but only one, Isla Gorgona, is known to support a dangerously venomous snake species. Isla Gorgona is located in the Equatorial Zone, 56 km west of the Colombian mainland in the Pacific Ocean. The island is approximately 44 $km^2$ in size and close to a tiny islet, Gorgonilla. Owing to their proximity, it is likely that Gorgonilla also is inhabited by venomous snakes.

Vegetation zones are broadly diverse in Colombia but major trends are as follows: (1) rainforests and very humid tropical forests dominate the Pacific equatorial lowlands (Chocó region) and the Amazon Basin; (2) savannas (interspersed with gallery forest) are primarily confined to the Llanos Orientales; (3) tropical thorn forests and lowland dry forests are typical of the Caribbean coastal plain; (4) the lower elevations of the intermontane valleys are composed of dry to very humid tropical forests, which are replaced at intermediate and high elevations by cloud forests. The eastern versant of the Cordillera Oriental is covered by humid to very humid tropical forests. Above the timberline a moist grassy plain called *páramo* prevails. There are no records of Colombian venomous snakes from above 3,000 m, and it would be unusual to find one much above 2,500 m.

Seasonal temperatures in Colombia are subject to the major influence of the northeast and southeast trade winds, which, in turn, are related to winter in the Northern and Southern Hemispheres, respectively. Prevailing winds are further modified by the presence of the Andes, evapotranspiration, and other factors, thus creating numerous smaller localized climates. Temperature ranges are also greatly influenced by elevation, and some of the upper reaches of the Andes are perpetually snowbound. Low-lying areas are characterized by fluctuations in rainfall, which may be pronounced or not, depending on the region.

In general, there are marked wet and dry seasons in the Llanos Orientales and the Caribbean lowlands; in the Andean region each type of season occurs twice annually. Fluctuation in precipitation is much less noticeable in the Amazon Basin and the Chocó region; portions of the latter receive in excess of 10,000 mm of rain annually. At the other extreme, the La Guajira Peninsula receives less than 300 mm of rainfall per year.

Our knowledge of reptile distribution in South America is still very incomplete. Thus, venomous snake species might eventually be discovered that have not yet been recorded for Colombia. Some possibilities are *Micrurus alleni* (Fig. 20; see Key to Venomous Snakes of Panama), which may enter Colombia in the Darién region; *M. steindachneri* (Figs. 102, 103; see Key to Venomous Snakes of Ecuador), which may enter Colombia in the southern Andes; *M. stewarti* (see Key to Venomous Snakes of Panama), which may enter Colombia in the Darién region; and *Bothrops xanthogrammus* (Figs. 247, 248; see Key to Venomous Snakes of Ecuador), which may enter Colombia in the southern Andes. The distributions by vegetation type of the species of dangerously venomous snakes in Colombia are given in Table 13.

**Table 13**

Distributions by vegetation type of venomous snakes in Colombia

| Species | Lowland rainforest | Lowland dry forest, thorn forest | Savanna, gallery forest | Lower montane wet forest, cloud forest | Lower montane dry forest |
|---|---|---|---|---|---|
| *Pelamis platurus*[1] | | | | | |
| *Micrurus ancoralis* | X[2] | | | X | |
| *M. clarki* | X[2] | | | | |
| *M. dissoleucus* | | X | | | X |
| *M. dumerilii* | | X | | | X |
| *M. filiformis* | X[3] | | | X[4] | |
| *M. hemprichii* | X[3] | | X | | |
| *M. isozonus* | | X | X | X[4] | |
| *M. karlschmidti* | X[3] | | | | |
| *M. langsdorffi* | X[3] | | | | |
| *M. lemniscatus* | X[3] | | | X[4] | |
| *M. mipartitus*[5] | | | | X | |
| *M. multiscutatus* | | | | X | |
| *M. narduccii* | X[3] | | | | |
| *M. nigrocinctus* | X[2] | | | | |
| *M. psyches* | X[3] | | X | X[6] | |
| *M. putumayensis* | X[3] | | | | |
| *M. sangilensis* | | | | | X |
| *M. spixii* | X[3] | | X | | |
| *M. spurrelli* | X[2] | | | | |
| *M. surinamensis*[7] | X[3] | | X | | |
| *Bothriechis schlegelii* | X[2] | | | X[8] | |
| *Bothriopsis bilineata* | X[3] | | | | |
| *B. punctata* | X[2] | | | X[6] | |
| *B. taeniata* | X[3] | | | X | |
| *Bothrops asper*[5] | X[2] | X | | X[6] | X |
| *B. atrox* | X[3] | | X | X[6] | |

**Table 13—*continued***

| Species | Lowland rainforest | Lowland dry forest, thorn forest | Savanna, gallery forest | Lower montane wet forest, cloud forest | Lower montane dry forest |
|---|---|---|---|---|---|
| *B. brazili* | X[3] | | | | |
| *B. microphthalmus* | | | | X[6] | |
| *B. pulcher* | X[2] | | | | |
| *Crotalus durissus* | | X | X | | X |
| *Lachesis muta* | X[2,3] | | X | | |
| *Porthidium hyoprora* | X[3] | | | | |
| *P. lansbergii* | | X[9] | | | |
| *P. nasutum* | X[2] | | | | |

1. Pacific marine habitat.
2. Western lowlands.
3. Amazon Basin.
4. Generally at elevations of 500 m or less.
5. Also on Isla Gorgona.
6. Generally at elevations of 1,000 m or less.
7. Found in aquatic situations.
8. Up to 2,700 m.
9. Caribbean lowlands.

## Key to Venomous Snakes of Colombia

1. No loreal pit between eye and nostril; loreal scale absent (Fig. 100); scales on top of head enlarged into plates (Fig. 16); dorsal scales smooth; fangs permanently erect (Fig. 19); Elapidae ........ 2
   A loreal pit between eye and nostril (Fig. 162); loreal scale present; scales on top of head small and numerous; dorsal scales keeled; fangs fold back (Fig. 253); Viperidae ........ 23
2. Tail strongly flattened laterally (Fig. 110); marine habitat; usually a longitudinal black (or brown) and yellow pattern (Figs. 111, 112) ........ *Pelamis platurus*
   Tail round in cross section; nonmarine habitat; pattern consisting of some combination of black, yellow, or red; generally ringed or spotted ........ 3
3. Black rings arranged in triads, separated by yellow and/or red, sometimes visible only ventrally ........ 4
   Color pattern not forming triads ........ 13
4. Anal plate divided; black rings may be longer or shorter than pale rings........ 5
   Anal plate entire; all black rings three or more times longer than pale rings (Figs. 58, 59) ........ *Micrurus hemprichii*
5. Black ring on nape comprising anteriormost black ring of a pair or of first complete triad (Figs. 99–101, 104, 105) ........ 6
   Black ring on nape single, followed by first complete triad (Fig. 40) ........ *Micrurus dissoleucus*
6. First body triad usually represented by two black rings ........ 7
   First body triad complete, consisting of three black rings ........ 9
7. Ten or more triads on body; dorsum of head black, including parietals; western and inter-Andean Colombia ........ 8
   Fewer than 10 triads on body; dorsum of head not black; east of the Andes (Figs. 99–101) ........ *Micrurus spixii*
8. Fewer than 14 triads on body; supra-anal keels present in males (Figs. 42–44) ........ *Micrurus dumerilii*
   More than 14 triads on body; no supra-anal keels present ........ *Micrurus sangilensis*
9. Several supracephalic scales black or spotted with black, but not outlined in black; frontal wider than supraocular; eye in contact with third and fourth supralabials (Fig. 15) ........ 10
   All supracephalic scales red, outlined in black; frontal not wider than supraocular; 6–9 complete triads on body; eye in contact with fourth supralabial only (Figs. 17, 104, 105) ........ *Micrurus surinamensis*
10. First triad normal, first white ring not oblique ........ 11
    First two black rings in first triad form an anchor shape, outlining oblique first white ring, the latter interrupted or nearly so on middorsal line; 12–24 black body triads (Figs. 21–23) ........ *Micrurus ancoralis*
11. No red ring on parietals or, if so, red *and* white rings on supracephalic scales; first nuchal black ring usually not covering parietal tips; snout black, with a yellow ring crossing it; ventrals usually 230 or more ........ 12

Single red ring or spot on parietals; some pale spots occasionally on snout; first nuchal black ring usually covers parietal tips, at times with spotlike extensions onto them; snout dirty white, crossed by a black ring; ventrals 231 or fewer (Fig. 63) .......... *Micrurus isozonus*

12. Ventrals 268 or fewer; 8–13 body triads; reaches large size (Figs. 70, 71) .......... *Micrurus lemniscatus*
    Ventrals 266 or more; usually more than 13 body triads; size small and slender (Fig. 49) .......... *Micrurus filiformis*

13. Pattern consisting of yellow or orange spots on venter, usually not crossing dorsum; normally, uniform black above except for a yellow or orange ring crossing head and orange rings occasionally present on tail; first pair of infralabials not in contact behind mental .......... 14
    Pattern not as above; first pair of infralabials in contact behind mental (Fig. 14) .......... 15

14. From 261–382 ventrals, usually more than 270 (Figs. 83, 84) .......... *Micrurus narduccii*
    From 219–270 ventrals .......... *Micrurus karlschmidti*

15. Black head cap including part or all of parietals, no pale ring interrupting black cap .......... 16
    Black reduced on head, not or barely reaching parietals, or at least one pale ring on head, on or anterior to parietals .......... 20

16. Solid black head color reaches beyond parietals, usually including one or more dorsal scale rows, all temporals, and almost all upper labials; red or yellow scales have black tips, or may be obscured by black; pattern consists of two colors (Fig. 96) .......... *Micrurus putumayensis*
    Black head color usually not covering all temporals, or with some pale spots on supracephalic scales, or black on posterior part of parietals reduced; only a few supralabials black; red scales with or without black tips; pattern consists of two or more colors .......... 17

17. All anterior infracephalic scales pale, usually outlined with salt-and-pepper borders; 13–20 black body rings (Fig. 30) .......... *Micrurus clarki*
    Some infracephalic scales always black, especially infralabials .......... 18

18. Supra-anal keels present on adult males and some females; both coasts and inter-Andean valleys (Figs. 42–44) .......... *Micrurus dumerilii*
    Supra-anal keels absent; occurring east of the Andes .......... 19

19. Narrow white rings usually present on body, delimiting black rings; no small white supracephalic spots, but snout occasionally paler than rest of head (Figs. 92, 94) .......... *Micrurus psyches*
    Black rings, occasionally replaced by yellow or brown, delimited dorsally by transverse rows of white specks; some small white spots usually present on supracephalic scales, particularly supraoculars (Fig. 64) .......... *Micrurus langsdorffi*

20. Fewer than 30 black rings on body (Figs. 85, 86) .......... *Micrurus nigrocinctus*
    More than 30 black rings on body .......... 21

21. Subcaudals 36 or more; usually 2 pale rings crossing dorsal head scales anterior to first black nuchal ring .......... *Micrurus spurrelli*
    Subcaudals fewer than 36; only 1 pale ring crossing dorsal head scales anterior to first black nuchal ring .......... 22

22. Red rings confined to head and tail, body pattern composed of alternating black and white or yellow rings (Figs. 77–79) .......... *Micrurus mipartitus*
    Pattern consisting of alternating black and red rings (Fig. 82) .......... *Micrurus multiscutatus*

23. Tail terminating in a rattle or button (Figs. 333, 334) .......... *Crotalus durissus*
    Tail not terminating in a rattle .......... 24

24. Posterior subcaudals finely divided; keels on middorsals conical (Figs. 249–252, 316) .......... *Lachesis muta*
    Posterior subcaudals single or paired; keels on middorsals normal (Fig. 316) .......... 25

25. Most subcaudals single (Fig. 316); snout not strongly upturned; a row of cream spots or a cream stripe along juncture of dorsals and ventrals .......... 26

Subcaudals single or paired (Fig. 316); snout may or may not be strongly upturned; no cream spots along juncture of dorsals and ventrals (but a stripe present on *Bothriopsis bilineata*) ........................................................27

26. Raised superciliary scales giving appearance of eyelashes (Fig. 165); ventrals fewer than 170; cream spots or cream stripe at juncture of dorsals and ventrals (Figs. 142–146) ..................................................... *Bothriechis schlegelii*
    Superciliaries absent; ventrals more than 200; a row of cream spots, but never a stripe, at juncture of dorsals and ventrals (Figs. 158–162)........................... ................................................................................ *Bothriopsis taeniata*

27. Most subcaudals single (Fig. 316); snout upturned, forming a flaplike process ..................................................................................................28
    Most subcaudals paired (Fig. 316); snout normal.....................................30

28. Ventrals more than 160; Caribbean lowlands (Figs. 274, 275) ........................ ................................................................................ *Porthidium lansbergii*
    Ventrals fewer than 151; absent in Caribbean lowlands .............................29

29. Fewer than 40 subcaudals; outer internasals in contact or separated by 1 scale (Fig. 315); pale middorsal line usually present; Pacific lowlands (Figs. 281–285) ................................................................... *Porthidium nasutum*
    Usually more than 40 subcaudals; outer internasals separated by two or more scales (Fig. 307); pale middorsal line absent; Amazon Basin (Fig. 273)........... ................................................................................ *Porthidium hyoprora*

30. Ventrals usually less than 180..............................................................31
    Ventrals usually more than 180............................................................33

31. Prelacunal not fused with second upper labial (i.e., lacunolabial absent); postorbital stripe present (Figs. 229, 230) ...................... *Bothrops microphthalmus*
    Prelacunal fused with second upper labial (i.e., lacunolabial present); postorbital stripe absent or faint ..................................................................32

32. Dorsal scale rows at midbody 23–29; 8 or more supralabials; outer internasals in contact; Amazon Basin (Figs. 201–205) .............................. *Bothrops brazili*
    Dorsal scale rows at midbody 22 or 23; 7 supralabials; outer internasals separated by 1–2 scales; Pacific lowlands (Fig. 242)................. *Bothrops pulcher*

33. Dorsum pale green with black speckling; creamy yellow stripe at juncture of dorsals and ventrals (Fig. 151)................................... *Bothriopsis bilineata*
    Dorsum variable in color, but never green; no stripe at juncture of dorsals and ventrals.......................................................................................34

34. Subcaudals usually 78 or more; tail prehensile, posterior half pale even in adults; 16–22 paired dark brown dorsal blotches with irregular borders; dark brown spots on scale rows 4–7; top of head with ornate pattern; Pacific drainage (Fig. 157)......................................................... *Bothriopsis punctata*
    Subcaudals usually fewer than 78; tail not prehensile, posterior half not pale in adults; dark dorsal blotches with relatively straight vertical or diagonal borders, may be single or paired; top of head not ornately patterned; Pacific or Atlantic drainage..........................................................................35

35. Lateral borders of dorsal blotches more-or-less diagonal (as opposed to vertical); dorsal ground color grayish brown; dark postorbital stripe bordered above by a pale stripe 2 scales wide; last 1–2 supralabials usually enter dark postorbital stripe (Fig. 175); Pacific and Caribbean lowlands and inter-Andean valleys (Figs. 187–190) ............................................................ *Bothrops asper*
    Lateral borders of dorsal blotches more-or-less vertical (as opposed to diagonal); dorsal ground color dark yellowish brown to olive; dark postorbital stripe not distinctly pale bordered above; last 3 supralabials enter postorbital stripe (Fig. 177); Orinoco and Amazon basin (Figs. 193, 194) ................. *Bothrops atrox*

## VENEZUELA

Venezuela encompasses 912,050 km² and is situated in northern South America on the Caribbean Coast. It is bounded by 2,813 km of shoreline on the north, by Guyana on the east, by Colombia on the west, and by Brazil on the south. Venezuela broadly comprises four different regions: (1) The Venezuelan highlands extend along the northern coast and also occur in the extreme northwest. These include the Serranía de Perijá (NW), the Sierra Nevada de Mérida (NW), the Segovia highlands (NW), the Cordillera de la Costa (including the Central highlands) to the north, and the Northeastern highlands of the Paria and Araya peninsulas. (2) The Maracaibo lowlands are situated in the northwest corner of Venezuela between the Serranía de Perijá and the Sierra Nevada de Mérida. (3) The Llanos del Orinoco encompass 180,000 $km^2$ in the central part of the country. (4) The Guayana highlands comprise more than 50% of the country; these highlands extend over the southeastern portion of the country and include isolated *tepuis* along the Brazilian border.

The Venezuelan highlands are an Andean extension, and include five peaks (in the Sierra Nevada de Mérida) nearly or above 5,000 m in elevation. The Guiana Highlands are considerably older and consist of rolling hills and table-topped tepuis. Auyán Tepuy (2,950 m) gives rise to Angel Falls, which at 979 m is the tallest waterfall in the world. The Sierra de la Neblina at 3,014 m is the tallest of the Venezuelan tepuis.

The Río Orinoco bisects the entire country, and its drainage system includes all of Venezuela's major rivers, among them the Ventuari, Cinaruco, Arauca, Apure, Caura, and Caroní. These are set in a vast savanna known as the *llanos*.

The Brazo Casiquiare, in southern Venezuela, provides periodic connection between the upper Orinoco and the Río Negro system. Rivers not draining into the Orinoco include the Cuyuni, which flows northeastward from the Guiana Highlands into Guyana, and the Chama, Santa Ana, Catatumbo, and Escalante, which empty into Lake Maracaibo. The lake itself lies in a 85,000-$km^2$ basin with high mean temperatures and low annual rainfall.

The Isla de Margarita, a Venezuelan possession lying north of the Araya Peninsula, supports three species of dangerously venomous snakes. There are also four species found on the Paraguaná Peninsula, which juts into the Caribbean Sea east of Lake Maracaibo (Table 14).

Vegetation zones in Venezuela are diverse, but several major trends are apparent. Rainforest and very humid tropical forest dominate the lowlands of the Amazon Basin and the Orinoco Delta; lower elevations of the intermontane valleys and coastal foothills are composed of dry to very humid tropical forest, which is replaced at intermediate and high elevations by cloud forest. Above the timberline a moist grassy plain called *páramo* prevails; the highest areas are perpetually snowbound. The La Guajira Peninsula and the Falcón coastal desert (both north of, and adjacent to, Lake Maracaibo) are xerophytic; the *llanos* and adjacent Sabanas de Yuruarí are grasslands interspersed with gallery forest. The Guiana Highlands are covered by semideciduous forest and savanna.

Annual precipitation and mean temperatures vary from less than 1,000 mm and over 28°C in some of the Caribbean arid lowlands to more than 2,500 mm and 24°C in the Amazon Basin and Orinoco Delta. The *páramo* regions are subject to periodic hail and prolonged cold temperatures.

In general, there are alternating wet and dry seasons in the *llanos*, the Caribbean lowlands and, to a lesser extent, in the highland regions. Fluctuations in precipitation are less pronounced in the Amazon Basin.

Our knowledge of reptile distribution in South America is far from complete. Thus, it would not be surprising to encounter a venomous snake species as yet unrecorded for Venezuela. Some possibilities are *Micrurus averyi* (Fig. 26; see Key to Venomous Snakes of Guyana), which may enter Venezuela in the southeast; *M. filiformis* (Fig. 49; see Key to Venomous Snakes of Colombia), *M. karlschmidti* (see Key to Venomous Snakes of Brazil), *M. langsdorffi* (Fig. 64; see Key to Venomous Snakes of Colombia), and *M. narduccii* (Figs. 83, 84; see Key to Venomous Snakes of Colombia), which may enter extreme southern Venezuela; *Bothrops microphthalmus* (Figs. 229, 230; see Key to Venomous Snakes of Colombia), which may exist in the western Andes; and *Porthidium hyoprora* (Fig. 273; see Key to Venomous Snakes of Colombia), which may enter extreme southern Venezuela (a single unverified report exists). The distributions by vegetation type of the species of dangerously venomous snakes in Venezuela are given in Table 14.

### Key to Venomous Snakes of Venezuela

1. No loreal pit between eye and nostril; loreal scale absent (Fig. 100); scales on top of head enlarged into plates (Fig. 16); fangs permanently erect (Fig. 19); Elapidae .......... 2
   A loreal pit between eye and nostril (Fig. 162); loreal scale present; scales on top of head small and numerous; fangs fold back (Fig. 253); Crotalidae .......... 12
2. Pattern consisting of black, red, and/or yellow or white rings; chinshields separated from mental scale (Fig. 14) .......... 3
   Pattern primarily black dorsally, with yellow bands on the venter covering the first 2–3 rows of dorsals; 1 red ring on neck; tail with red rings or red bands underneath; anterior chinshields in contact with mental scale (Figs. 31, 32) .......... *Micrurus collaris*
3. Black rings arranged in triads, separated by red and/or yellow rings (sometimes visible only ventrally) .......... 4
   Color pattern not forming triads .......... 9
4. Anal plate entire; all black rings three or more times longer than pale rings (Fig. 58) .......... *Micrurus hemprichii*
   Anal plate divided; black rings may be slightly longer, equal to, or shorter than

pale rings ........................................................................................5

5. Black ring on nape comprising anteriormost member of a pair or of first complete triad (Figs. 99–101, 104, 105) .......................................................6
   Black ring on nape single, followed by first complete triad (Fig. 40) .............. ....................................................................*Micrurus dissoleucus*
6. Fewer than 24 subcaudals; first black neck ring also serving as *second* triad ring, and elongated to form a blotch; white rings heavily marked with black (Figs. 99–101)................................................................*Micrurus spixii*
   More than 24 subcaudals; black nape ring comprising anteriormost member of first *complete* triad ..........................................................................7
7. Head scales red, bordered with black (Fig. 18); only the fourth supralabial in contact with the eye (Fig. 17); frontal not wider than supraocular; usually found in aquatic habitat (Figs. 104, 105) ..................*Micrurus surinamensis*
   Some head scales black, pale head scales not outlined in black; eye in contact with third and fourth supralabial (Fig. 15); frontal wider than supraocular...8
8. Single red ring or spot on parietals; some pale spots occasionally present on snout; first black neck ring usually covering parietal tips, at times with spotlike extensions onto them; snout dirty white with a black band (Fig. 63)............. ......................................................................*Micrurus isozonus*
   No red ring or, if so, red and white rings on supracephalic scales; first black neck ring usually not covering parietal tips; snout black with a yellow ring (Figs. 68–71)...............................................................*Micrurus lemniscatus*
9. At least some red rings on body or tail...................................................10
   No red rings present (Fig. 92).........................................*Micrurus psyches*
10. Red rings confined to head and tail, body with 30 or more black rings that alternate with white (or yellow) rings (Figs. 78, 80).........*Micrurus mipartitus*
    Red rings on trunk of body .................................................................11
11. Black head color covering parietals and feebly separated from first black neck ring; no supra-anal keels; first temporal scale reduced in size (Fig. 93).......... ......................................................................*Micrurus psyches*
    Black head color covering about half of parietals and distinctly separated from first black neck ring; supra-anal keels present in males; first temporal scale is normal (Fig. 42).......................................................*Micrurus dumerilii*
12. Tail terminating in a rattle or button (Figs. 333, 334, 337, 346) ..................... ......................................................................*Crotalus durissus*
    Tail not terminating in a rattle (Fig. 316)................................................13
13. Tail terminating in a spine, subcaudals finely divided posteriorly (Fig. 316); keels on dorsals conical (Fig. 249)......................................*Lachesis muta*
    Tail normal, subcaudals single or paired (Fig. 316); keels normal ...............14
14. Subcaudals single (Fig. 316); superciliaries form spinelike processes (Figs. 142–144, 165) .........................................................*Bothriechis schlegelii*
    Subcaudals single or paired (Fig. 316); superciliaries absent ......................15
15. Most subcaudals single, at least proximally (Fig. 316)..............................16
    Most subcaudals paired (Fig. 316)........................................................18
16. Snout normal, but a distinct canthal ridge sometimes present; subcaudals more than 41; lacunolabial present (Fig. 177) ...............................................17
    Snout upturned, forming a flaplike process (Fig. 314); subcaudals 41 or fewer; lacunolabial absent (Figs. 274–276, 312) ...................*Porthidium lansbergii*
17. Subcaudals 62 or fewer; midbody dorsal scale rows 21 (Fig. 152).................. ....................................................................*Bothriopsis medusa*
    Subcaudals 66 or more; midbody dorsal scale rows 25–29 (Figs. 158–162) ..................................................................*Bothriopsis taeniata*
18. Dorsum mostly green, sometimes with orange-tan dorsal spots; a creamy yellow stripe at juncture of dorsals and ventrals (Figs. 149, 150)............................ ..................................................................*Bothriopsis bilineata*
    Dorsum variable, but never green; no stripe at juncture of dorsals and ventrals ........................................................................................19
19. Postorbital stripe absent or faint (Fig. 203); venter predominately pale (Figs. 201–205)..................................................................*Bothrops brazili*
    Postorbital stripe well defined; venter heavily pigmented, at least posteriorly ........................................................................................20

20. Postorbital stripe usually bordered above by a pale stripe 2 scales wide; last 1–2 supralabials usually enter dark postorbital stripe (Fig. 175); supralabials usually without dark spotting; dorsal blotches X-shaped (triangular laterally); generally north of the Río Orinoco (Figs. 188–192) ................*Bothrops asper*
    Postorbital stripe not usually bordered above by pale stripe; last three supralabials usually enter dark postorbital stripe (Fig. 177); supralabials usually with dark spots and/or specks; dorsal blotches square; if north of the Río Orinoco, then generally in the Cordillera de la Costa ..............................21
21. Postorbital stripe edged narrowly with white pigment; snout obtusely rounded; canthal and labial region usually with darker speckling, not spots; venter usually dark anteriorly; restricted to the Cordillera de la Costa (Figs. 243–246) ....................................................................*Bothrops venezuelensis*
    Postorbital stripe usually without white edging; snout slightly acuminate; supralabials usually bear 3 dark spots; venter may be pale anteriorly, generally south of the Río Orinoco (Figs. 193–196)..............................*Bothrops atrox*

**Table 14**

Distributions by vegetation type of venomous snakes in Venezuela

| *Species* | *Lowland rainforest* | *Lowland dry forest, thorn forest* | *Savanna, gallery forest* | *Lower montane wet forest, cloud forest* | *Lower montane dry forest* |
|---|---|---|---|---|---|
| *Micrurus collaris* | X | | | | |
| *M. dissoleucus*[1] | | X[2,3] | | | X |
| *M. dumerilii*[1] | | X[3] | | | X |
| *M. hemprichii* | X | | X | X[4] | |
| *M. isozonus*[1,5] | | X | X | | |
| *M. lemniscatus* | X | | X | X[6] | |
| *M. mipartitus*[7] | | | | X[8] | |
| *M. psyches* | X | | | | |
| *M. spixii* | X | | | X[4] | |
| *M. surinamensis* | X[9] | | | | |
| *Bothriechis schlegelii* | X | | | X[8] | |
| *Bothriopsis bilineata*[10] | X[4] | | | | |
| *B. medusa*[7] | | | | X[11] | |
| *B. taeniata* | X | | | X[8] | |
| *Bothrops asper*[1] | X | X | X | X[8] | X |
| *B. atrox* | X | X | X | X[8] | X |
| *B. brazili*[10] | X[4] | | | | |
| *B. venezuelensis*[7] | | | | X[8] | X |
| *Crotalus durissus*[1,5] | | X[3] | X | X[11] | X |
| *Lachesis muta* | X | | | X[6] | |
| *Porthidium lansbergii*[1,5] | | X[2,3] | | | |

1. Primarily north of the Rio Orinoco.
2. Coastal lowlands.
3. Range includes the Paraguaná Peninsula.
4. Generally at elevations of 500 m or less.
5. Also found on the Isla de Margarita.
6. Generally at elevations of 1,000 m or less.
7. Northern highlands.
8. Up to 2,000 m or more.
9. Found in aquatic situations.
10. Amazon Basin.
11. Up to 2,500 m or more.

## GUYANA

The country of Guyana (formerly known as British Guiana) is roughly oval in shape and covers 214,969 km². It is situated on the northern coast of South America and is bounded on the west by Venezuela, on the south by Brazil, on the east by Suriname, and on the north by 320 km of Caribbean Coast.

The dominant topographic features in Guyana are the highlands in the Roraima region, which lies in the eastern portion of the country, and the upland savanna of the Rupununi and Kanuku mountains in the southwest. The remainder of the country is rolling forest with the exception of a narrow coastal strip, much of which is below sea level and maintained by dikes, and is heavily populated and cultivated.

The entire country slopes toward the Caribbean Sea, into which its river systems drain. Among the major rivers are the Cuyuni, Mazaruni, Essequibo, Rupununi, Demerara, Corantyne, and Berbice. The Pakaraima Mountains in the west include the highest peak (Mt. Roraima at 2,771 m) in Guyana. The Rupununi savanna comprises 60,000 km², of which 13,000 km² lie in Guyana. The savanna is divided from east to west by the Kanuku Mountains, which reach their highpoint at Mt. Ilamikipang (957 m).

Precipitation and mean temperatures vary somewhat but the country has basically two rainy seasons: from mid-April to mid-August and from mid-November through January. The coastal region receives an average of 2,300 mm of rainfall per year. The mean annual temperature throughout the lowlands of the country is about 27°C.

Over 85% of Guyana is covered by rainforest or very humid tropical forest. Grassland and scrubby deciduous forest prevail on the Rupununi savanna, and some lower montane wet forest and cloud forest exist in the Roraima region.

A few species of dangerously venomous snakes that potentially occur in Guyana, but which are not recorded with certainty, include *Micrurus filiformis* (Fig. 49; see Key to Venomous Snakes of Brazil), which may enter southern Guyana; *M. isozonus* (Fig. 63; see Key to Venomous Snakes of Venezuela), which may enter western Guyana; *M. spixii* (Figs. 99–101; see Key to Venomous Snakes of Brazil), which may enter western Guyana; and *Porthidium hyoprora* (Fig. 273; see Key to Venomous Snakes of Colombia), which may enter southern Guyana. The distributions by vegetation types of species of dangerously venomous snakes in Guyana are given in Table 15.

## Key to Venomous Snakes of Guyana

1. No loreal pit between eye and nostril; loreal scale usually absent (Fig. 100); scales on top of head enlarged into plates (Fig. 16); dorsal scales smooth; fangs permanently erect (Fig. 19); Elapidae .......... 2
   A loreal pit between eye and nostril (Fig. 203); loreal scale present; scales on top of head small and numerous; dorsal scales keeled; fangs fold back (Fig. 253); Viperidae .......... 7
2. Pattern consisting of black, red, and/or yellow or white rings; chinshields separated from mental scale (Fig. 14) .......... 3
   Pattern without rings except for pale collar; dorsum uniformly black or brown; venter with a series of white, yellow, or red spots extending onto sides; chinshields in contact with mental scale (Figs. 31, 32) .......... *Micrurus collaris*
3. Black rings arranged in triads, sometimes visible only ventrally .......... 4
   Black rings not forming triads .......... 6
4. Anal plate divided .......... 5
   Anal plate single (Fig. 58) .......... *Micrurus hemprichii*
5. Only fourth supralabial in contact with eye (Fig. 17); head scales red, outlined in black (Fig. 18); often found near water (Figs. 104, 105) .......... *Micrurus surinamensis*
   Third and fourth supralabials in contact with eye (Fig. 15); head scales not outlined in black (Figs. 68, 69) .......... *Micrurus lemniscatus*
6. Red rings long (a single one covering 12–18 ventrals), usually immaculate; black nuchal ring absent; black rings short (Fig. 26) .......... *Micrurus averyi*
   Red rings absent or reduced, tipped with black when present; black nuchal ring present; black rings nearly as long as red ones (Figs. 92, 93) .......... *Micrurus psyches*
7. Tail terminating in a rattle or button (Figs. 333–337) .......... *Crotalus durissus*
   Tail not terminating in a rattle .......... 8
8. Posterior subcaudals finely subdivided (Fig. 316); keels on middorsals conical (Fig. 249) .......... *Lachesis muta*
   Posterior subcaudals single or paired; keels on middorsals normal .......... 9
9. A well-defined dark postorbital stripe present .......... 11
   Postorbital stripe absent, faint, or pale .......... 10
10. Dorsum pale green with scattered tan markings; postorbital stripe absent or tan; creamy yellow stripe at juncture of dorsals and ventrals; more than 190 ventrals (Figs. 149, 150) .......... *Bothriopsis bilineata*
    Dorsum variable but never green; postorbital stripe absent or faint; no stripe at juncture of dorsals and ventrals; fewer than 190 ventrals (Figs. 201–205) .......... *Bothrops brazili*
11. Most subcaudals single (Fig. 316); tail prehensile; iris heavily speckled; a row of cream spots along juncture of dorsals and ventrals (Figs. 158–162) .......... *Bothriopsis taeniata*
    Most subcaudals divided (Fig. 316); tail normal; iris not heavily speckled; no cream spots at juncture of dorsals and ventrals (Figs. 195, 196) .......... *Bothrops atrox*

**Table 15**

Distributions by vegetation type of venomous snakes in Guyana

| Species | *Lowland rain-forest* | *Savanna, gallery forest* | *Lower montane wet forest, cloud forest* |
|---|---|---|---|
| *Micrurus averyi* | X | | X[1] |
| *M. collaris* | X | | |
| *M. hemprichii* | X | X | X[1] |
| *M. lemniscatus* | X | | X[1] |
| *M. psyches* | X | | X[1] |
| *M. surinamensis* | X[2] | | |
| *Bothriopsis bilineata* | X | | |
| *B. taeniata* | X | | X |
| *Bothrops atrox* | X | X | X |
| *B. brazili* | X | | |
| *Crotalus durissus* | | X | |
| *Lachesis muta* | X | | X[1] |

1. Generally at elevations of 1,000 m or less.
2. Found in aquatic situations.

**Table 16**

Distributions by vegetation type of venomous snakes in Suriname

| Species | *Lowland rainforest* | *Savanna, gallery forest* | *Lower montane wet forest* |
|---|---|---|---|
| *Micrurus averyi* | X | | |
| *M. collaris* | X | | |
| *M. hemprichii* | X | X | |
| *M. ibiboboca*[1] | | X | |
| *M. lemniscatus* | X | | X |
| *M. psyches* | X | | X |
| *M. surinamensis* | X[2] | | |
| *Bothriopsis bilineata* | X | | X |
| *B. taeniata* | X | | X |
| *Bothrops atrox* | X | X | X |
| *B. brazili* | X | | |
| *Crotalus durissus* | | X | |
| *Lachesis muta* | X | | X |

1. See Remarks under species account.
2. Aquatic habitat.

## SURINAME

Suriname (formerly known as Dutch Guiana) encompasses 163,265 km² and is situated in northern South America. It is bounded on the west by Guyana, on the south by Brazil, on the east by French Guiana, and on the north by 370 km of Atlantic Coast. The country is nearly square in shape and can be divided into three major physiographic regions: highlands, savanna, and lowlands.

The lowlands are confined to a narrow swampy coastal strip that is bordered toward the interior of the country by a belt of rainforest and a belt of savannas. These give way to the interior highlands, which do not exceed 1,280 m in elevation. With the exception of scattered small savannas and a large one on the upper Sipaliwini River in southern Suriname, the interior highlands are forested.

There are nine mountain ranges and a number of isolated peaks as well as several elevated plateaus. Most of the mountain ranges run in a north-south direction, as do the major rivers. The most important rivers are the Courantyne, Nickerie, Coppename, Saramacca, Suriname, Commewijne, and Marowijne.

Virtually all of Suriname is covered by rainforest or very humid tropical forest. Exceptions are the coastal swamps (and mangroves) and the savannas interspersed with scrub forest. Seasonal rains occur from May to July and December to January, with accumulations in excess of 2,500 mm annually in some areas. Suriname is constantly exposed to northeast trade winds, and mean monthly temperatures do not vary much from the annual average (27°C).

Species of venomous snakes not known from Suriname but that might occur there include *Micrurus spixii* (Figs. 99–101; see Key to Venomous Snakes of Venezuela), which may enter the southwestern portion of the country, and *Porthidium hyoprora* (Fig. 273; see Key to Venomous Snakes of Colombia), which may enter southern Suriname. The distributions by vegetation type of the species of dangerously venomous snakes in Suriname are given in Table 16.

### Key to Venomous Snakes of Suriname

1. No loreal pit between eye and nostril; loreal scale usually absent (Fig. 100); scales on top of head enlarged into plates (Fig. 16); dorsal scales smooth; fangs permanently erect (Fig. 19); Elapidae ....... 2
   A loreal pit between eye and nostril (Fig. 203); loreal scale present; scales on top of head small and numerous; dorsal scales keeled; fangs fold back (Fig. 253); Viperidae ....... 8
2. Pattern consisting of black, red, and/or yellow or white rings; chinshields separated from mental (Fig. 14) ....... 3
   Pattern lacks rings except for pale collar; dorsum uniformly black or brown; venter with a series of white or red spots extending onto sides; chinshields in contact with mental (Figs. 31, 32) ....... *Micrurus collaris*
3. Black rings forming triads ....... 4
   Black rings not forming triads ....... 7
4. Anal plate divided ....... 5
   Anal plate single (Fig. 58) ....... *Micrurus hemprichii*
5. Only fourth supralabial in contact with eye (Fig. 17); head scales red, outlined in black (Fig. 18); often found near water (Figs. 104, 105) ....... *Micrurus surinamensis*

Third and fourth supralabial in contact with eye (Fig. 15); head scales not outlined in black ........ 6

6. Subcaudals fewer than 30, usually fewer than 25; 7–10 triads (Fig. 62) ........ *Micrurus ibiboboca*

   Subcaudals more than 28, usually in excess of 30; 8 or more triads present (Figs. 68, 69) ........ *Micrurus lemniscatus*

7. Red rings present or absent; if present, then 13–30 black body rings; usually some black stippling in red rings (Figs. 92, 95) ........ *Micrurus psyches*

   Red rings always present; 8–13 black body rings; red rings immaculate (Fig. 26) ........ *Micrurus averyi*

8. Tail terminating in a rattle or button (Figs. 335, 336, 338) ........ *Crotalus durissus*

   Tail not terminating in a rattle ........ 9

9. Posterior subcaudals finely subdivided (Fig. 316); keels on middorsals conical (Fig. 249) ........ *Lachesis muta*

   Posterior subcaudals single or paired (Fig. 316); keels on middorsals normal ........ 10

10. A well-defined dark postorbital stripe present ........ 12

    Postorbital stripe absent, faint, or pale ........ 11

11. Dorsum pale green with scattered tan markings; postorbital stripe absent or tan; creamy yellow stripe at juncture of dorsals and ventrals; more than 190 ventrals (Figs. 149, 150) ........ *Bothriopsis bilineata*

    Dorsum variable but never green; postorbital stripe absent or faint; no stripe at juncture of dorsals and ventrals; fewer than 190 ventrals (Figs. 201–205) ........ *Bothrops brazili*

12. Most subcaudals single (Fig. 316); tail prehensile; iris heavily speckled (Fig. 169); a row of cream spots along juncture of dorsals and ventrals (Figs. 158–162) ........ *Bothriopsis taeniata*

    Most subcaudals divided (Fig. 316); tail not prehensile; iris not heavily speckled; no cream spots at juncture of dorsals and ventrals (Figs. 195, 196) ........ *Bothrops atrox*

## FRENCH GUIANA

French Guiana, also known as Guyane, encompasses 91,000 km² and is situated in northern South America. It is bounded on the west by Suriname, from which it is separated by the Maroni-Itany River. On the south it is bounded by Brazil, with which it shares the Tumuc-Humac Mountains. The eastern frontier is also with Brazil, along the Oyapock River. To the north lies 320 km of Atlantic coastline.

French Guiana has little topographic diversity, with coastal lowlands gradually giving way to higher slopes that are dotted with savannas. The coastal lowlands form a band about 80 km in width. The more elevated regions reach a maximum height of only 800 m above sea level. The Tumuc-Humac Mountains are the only range of importance. Higher peaks in French Guiana include Mounts Mitarka, LeBlond, Temorairem, and Temotakem (on the Brazilian border to the south).

The entire region is traversed by numerous rivers that enter the Atlantic Ocean. Among them are the Approuague, Cayenne, Mana, Maroni, Oyapock, and Sinnamary/Courcibo. Approximately 8 million hectares of the inland region are forested. Virtually all of this is rainforest or very humid tropical forest. Exceptions are the coastal swamps (and mangroves) and the savannas, which are grassland interspersed with scrub forest.

Seasonal rains occur from November to July, with an occasional dry spell in February and March; the heaviest rainfall is in May. The average temperature is 27°C at sea level and somewhat less at higher elevations.

The distributions of the species of dangerously venomous snakes occurring in French Guiana are given in Table 17; they broadly overlap as the country encom-

**Table 17**

Distributions by vegetation type of venomous snakes in French Guiana

| Species | *Lowland rainforest* | *Savanna, gallery forest* | *Lower montane wet forest* |
|---|---|---|---|
| *Micrurus collaris* | X | | X |
| *M. hemprichii* | X | X | X |
| *M. ibiboboca*[1] | | X | |
| *M. lemniscatus* | X | X | X |
| *M. psyches* | X | | X |
| *M. surinamensis* | X[2] | | |
| *Bothriopsis bilineata* | X | | |
| *B. taeniata* | X | | X |
| *Bothrops atrox* | X | X | X |
| *B. brazili* | X | | X |
| *Crotalus durissus* | | X | |
| *Lachesis muta* | X | | X |

1. See Remarks under species account.
2. Aquatic habitat.

passes a relatively small area without great topographic diversity. Biologically, French Guiana is poorly known and venomous snake species in addition to those listed in Table 17 may occur within its borders. Some possibilities are *Micrurus averyi* (Fig. 26; see Key to Venomous Snakes of Guyana), *M. filiformis* (Fig. 49; see Key to Venomous Snakes of Brazil), and *M. spixii* (Figs. 99–101; see Key to Venomous Snakes of Brazil).

### Key to Venomous Snakes of French Guiana

1. No loreal pit between eye and nostril; loreal scale usually absent (Fig. 100); scales on top of head enlarged into plates (Fig. 16); dorsal scales smooth; fangs permanently erect (Fig. 19); Elapidae ....................2
   A loreal pit between eye and nostril (Fig. 203); loreal scale present; scales on top of head small and numerous; dorsal scales keeled; fangs fold back (Fig. 253); Viperidae ....................7
2. Pattern consisting of black, red, and/or yellow or white; chinshields separated from mental (Fig. 14) ....................3
   Pattern usually lacks rings except for pale or red collar; dorsum uniform black or brown; venter with a series of white to red spots extending onto sides; chinshields in contact with mental (Figs. 31, 32) ....................*Micrurus collaris*
3. Black rings forming triads, sometimes visible only ventrally; red rings present; white head ring, if present, complete ....................4
   Black rings not forming triads; red rings absent; white head ring interrupted dorsally (Fig. 92) ....................*Micrurus psyches*
4. Anal plate divided ....................5
   Anal plate single (Fig. 58) ....................*Micrurus hemprichii*
5. Only fourth supralabial in contact with eye (Fig. 17); head scales red, outlined in black (Fig. 18); often found near water (Figs. 104, 105) ....................*Micrurus surinamensis*
   Third and fourth supralabials in contact with eye (Fig. 15); head scales not outlined in black ....................6
6. Subcaudals fewer than 30, usually fewer than 25; 7–10 triads (Fig. 62) ....................*Micrurus ibiboboca*
   Subcaudals more than 28, usually in excess of 30; 8 or more triads (Figs. 68, 69) ....................*Micrurus lemniscatus*
7. Tail terminating in a rattle or button (Figs. 335, 336) ....................*Crotalus durissus*
   Tail not terminating in a rattle ....................8
8. Posterior subcaudals finely subdivided (Fig. 316); keels on middorsals conical (Fig. 249) ....................*Lachesis muta*
   Posterior subcaudals single or paired (Fig. 316); keels on middorsals normal ....................9
9. A well-defined dark postorbital stripe present ....................11
   Postorbital stripe absent, faint, or pale ....................10
10. Dorsum pale green with scattered tan markings; postorbital stripe absent or tan; creamy yellow stripe at juncture of dorsals and ventrals; more than 190 ventrals (Figs. 149, 150) ....................*Bothriopsis bilineata*
    Dorsum variable, but never green; postorbital stripe absent or faint; no stripe at juncture of dorsals and ventrals; fewer than 190 ventrals (Figs. 201–205) ....................*Bothrops brazili*
11. Most subcaudals single (Fig. 316); tail prehensile; iris heavily speckled; a row of cream spots along juncture of dorsals and ventrals (Figs. 158–162) ....................*Bothriopsis taeniata*
    Most subcaudals divided; tail normal; iris not heavily speckled; no cream spots at juncture of dorsals and ventrals (Figs. 195, 196) ....................*Bothrops atrox*

## BRAZIL

Brazil is the fifth largest country in the world, comprising 8,456,508 km$^2$ (8,511,965 km$^2$ according to some authorities), about half of the landmass of South America. It is situated in the east-central portion of the continent and, along a 15,700-km frontier, borders all other mainland South American countries except Ecuador and Chile. The eastern border consists of about 7,500 km of Atlantic coastline.

Brazil can be divided into five major physiographic zones: (1) the Central highlands (Plateau of Brazil), (2) the Guiana Highlands, (3) the Amazon lowlands, (4) the La Plata Basin, (5) and the coastal plain. Brazil's great span of latitude, elevational diversity, and various prevailing wind patterns lead to a variety of climatic and vegetation regions.

The escarpment comprising the Central highlands lies south of the Amazon River. It is inclined westward and northward and contains three significant mountain ranges: the Serra do Mar/Serra dos Orgãos, the Serra da Mantiqueira, and the Serra do Espinhaço. Sometimes the latter two ranges are referred to collectively as the Serra Geral. The Serra do Mar/Serra dos Orgãos stretches north from Santa Catarina to Rio de Janeiro along the coast and then turns inland to Espírito Santo. The average elevation above sea level is about 1,500 m, with Pedra Açu reaching 2,318 m.

The Serra da Mantiqueira is farther inland and is the most rugged range in the Central highlands, reaching 2,898 m at Pico da Bandeira, the second highest point in Brazil. The Serra do Espinhaço runs in a north-south direction and divides the Rio São Francisco drainage from smaller rivers that empty into the Atlantic Ocean.

Aside from these isolated ranges, the Central highlands may be characterized as rolling terrain with low rounded hills (300–900 m) and savannas scattered throughout. There are numerous mountain ranges but they do not attain significant elevations. The Central highlands traverse many vegetation zones: to the west and north are tropical rainforest and semideciduous forest (the Cerrado region); to the northeast are transitional palm forest and dry thorn scrub (the Caatinga); to the east and south tropical rainforest and semideciduous forest (known as the Eastern Tropical Forest) grade into araucaria forest and grassland; and in the central region lie vast savannas that are seasonally inundated in some southern areas (the Pantanal).

The Guiana Highlands make up about 2% of the total area of the country and are situated to the north of the Negro/Amazon river system. The area is rugged and highly dissected by numerous streams that drain southeastward to the Amazon River. The crests of these ranges collectively represent much of the southern border of a large plateau that drains northward into the Rio Orinoco or the Atlantic Ocean through Venezuela and the Guianas. The median elevation is higher than that of the Central highlands, and Pico da Neblina in the Serra Imeri is Brazil's highest peak at 3,014 m. Other ranges in the Guiana Highlands of Brazil include the Serra Parima, Serra Pacaraima, and Serra Tumucumaque, all delineating part of Brazil's northern border. The entire region is composed of tropical rainforest and semideciduous forest.

The Amazon lowlands are a vast region lying mostly below 250 m in elevation and constituting more than one-third of the country. The topography is gently undulating, such that the higher ground (*terra firma*) drains into countless streams that feed the large rivers associated with the Amazon itself. The collective flood plains (*várzeas*) contain fertile soil and originally supported great concentrations of evergreen forest. There are regions of rolling savanna to the northwest (and irregularly throughout the basin), but nearly all of the Amazon lowlands are equatorial rainforest.

The La Plata Basin is a lowland region (including the Pantanal) that represents a northward extension of the Gran Chaco into the Brazilian states of Mato Grosso and Mato Grosso do Sul. Large sections of the states of São Paulo, Paraná, Santa Catarina, and Rio Grande do Sul are drained by the La Plata system. The Pantanal region is very wet and low, with an average elevation of about 150 m; it contains many streams that, together with the Rio Cuiabá, give rise to the Rio Paraguai. Much of the Pantanal area is permanent or seasonal swamp or marshland with interspersed patches of gallery forest on higher ground. Other parts of the basin include tropical forest and grassland.

The Atlantic coastal plain constitutes 8% of Brazil's total area and extends as a narrow strip along the entire length of the Atlantic seaboard. Along its northern reaches, from the Amazon Basin to the Rio São Francisco, the vegetation is tropical rainforest and semideciduous forest, with a mangrove-dune ecotone on the coast itself. The Atlantic coastal plain narrows south of Cabo de São Roque, and the forests become progressively more subtropical in character. The encroachment of the Serra Geral at times reduces the coastal plain to 100 km or less in width, and in a few locations the Serra do Mar rises directly from the sea. In southern Brazil the Atlantic coastal plain expands into rolling grassland more typical of the Uruguayan Pampas.

Brazil's river systems are extensive, the Amazon being the world's largest. Together with its more than 200 tributaries, the Amazon drains 60% of the country. There are 18 major rivers that empty into the Amazon, and 10 of these are longer than the Mississippi River in the United States. Primary among these tributaries are the Rio Negro, Rio Madeira, Rio Xingu, Rio Tapajós, and the Rio Araguaia-Tocantins-Pará. Significant rivers that drain directly into the Atlantic Ocean include the Rio Paranaíba, Rio São Francisco, Rio Doce, and Rio Paraíba do Sul. Many rivers with origins near the coast flow westwardly, owing to the inclination of the Central highlands plateau, and empty into the Rio Paraná. The Paraná, together with the Rio Paraguai, Rio Iguaçú, and Rio Uruguai, constitute the Brazilian portion of the Rio de la Plata Basin, which drains the southern part of the country.

There are many Brazilian islands in the Atlantic Ocean, and a number of these are situated quite near the mainland; several of them harbor venomous snake species. Of particular concern are the Ilha de Marajó at the mouth of the Amazon; the Ilha Queimada Grande, a 1-km$^2$ island of very rugged terrain off the coast of the state of São Paulo, about 64 km southwest of the Baía de Santos; and the Ilha de São Sebastião, a 350-km$^2$ island located 3.3 km from the coast of São Paulo.

The Ilha de Marajó is an immense tract of land in the Amazon Delta, in the state of Pará, with a venomous snake fauna essentially identical to the surrounding mainland. The Ilha Queimada Grande is of continental origin and is separated from the mainland by a shallow sea. This rocky island is of low elevation (not exceeding

206 m) and covered with humid woodland and grassy areas. It is of interest to us because an endemic lancehead, *Bothrops insularis*, exists in great numbers on the island and possesses a venom of extraordinary potency. The Ilha de São Sebastião is mountainous (the Pico de São Sebastião attains 1,370 m) with wooded hills and interior valleys surrounded by coastal grassland. Its fauna is similar to that of the adjacent mainland and includes three species of venomous snakes: *Micrurus corallinus*, *Bothrops jararacussu*, and *B. jararaca*.

There are numerous climatic conditions in Brazil, but they can be broadly grouped into three major regions: (1) The North, the Atlantic coastal plain as far south as the state of Rio de Janeiro, and the northern half of the Central highlands are tropical and are subject to high daily temperatures and receive abundant rainfall. (2) In the Central highlands of southeastern Brazil and along the Atlantic coastal plain as far south as the state of São Paulo subtropical conditions prevail, primarily owing to oceanic breezes and the proximity of the uplands. (3) Southern Brazil is affected by Antarctic air currents and at its extreme is predominantly temperate in character, with occasional frosts.

Rainfall cycles are seasonal and largely a function of latitude and elevation. The heaviest precipitation occurs during the months of December to February, which are also accompanied by the highest temperatures. The hottest regions of Brazil are in the northeast (the Caatinga and coastal plain) and the Amazon Basin. Seasonal fluctuations of temperature are most extreme in the temperate south. In tropical Brazil annual temperatures may average 24–27°C with daily maxima of 40°C, whereas in the south the temperatures are similar to those of the southern United States. The rainy season in the southeast extends from October to March, in the northeast from April to October, and in the Amazon region from January to June. Precipitation averages 1,000–2,000 mm annually over much of the country, but this figure is much higher for the Amazon Basin and Guiana Highlands. Some areas receive as much as 3,750–5,000 mm annually. In contrast, the thorn scrub of the Caatinga region (Sertãos) in northeastern Brazil is subject to droughts and receives less than 1,000 mm of rainfall annually.

The distributions of the species of dangerously venomous snakes in Brazil by major physiographic region and by vegetation type are given in Tables 18 and 19, respectively. Our interpretation of these distributions may be expected to change dramatically as more data become available.

**Table 18**

Distributions by physiographic region of venomous snakes in Brazil

| Species | *Guiana Highlands* | *Amazon lowlands* | *Central highlands* | *La Plata Basin* | *Coastal plain* |
|---|---|---|---|---|---|
| *Micrurus annellatus*[1] | | X(NW) | | | |
| *M. averyi* | X(C) | X(NC) | | | |
| *M. collaris*[1] | X | | | | |
| *M. corallinus* | | | | X | X |
| *M. decoratus* | | | X(SE) | | X(SE) |
| *M. filiformis* | | X | | | |
| *M. frontalis* | | | X(S) | X(S) | X(S) |
| *M. hemprichii* | X | X | | | X(N) |
| *M. ibiboboca* | | X(E) | X(NE) | | X(NE) |
| *M. karlschmidti* | X(NW) | | | | |
| *M. langsdorffi* | | X(NW) | | | |
| *M. lemniscatus* | X | X | X | X(N,E) | X(NE) |
| *M. narduccii* | | X(NW) | | | |
| *M. psyches*[2] | X(NW) | X(E) | | | X(N) |
| *M. putumayensis* | | X(NW) | | | |
| *M. spixii* | X[3] | X | | | X(N) |
| *M. surinamensis*[4] | X | X | | | |
| *Bothriopsis bilineata* | X | X | | | X(N,E,SE) |
| *B. taeniata* | X | X | | | X(N) |
| *Bothrops alternatus* | | | X(SE,S) | X | |
| *B. atrox* | X | X | X(NW,W) | | X(N) |
| *B. brazili* | X | X | | | X(N) |
| *B. cotiara* | | | X(S) | | |
| *B. erythromelas* | | | X(NE) | | X(NE) |
| *B. fonsecai* | | | X[5] | | |
| *B. iglesiasi* | | | X(NE) | | |
| *B. insularis* | | | | | X[6] |
| *B. itapetiningae* | | | X(SE) | X(S) | |
| *B. jararaca* | | | X(S,SE) | X[3] | X(S,SE,E) |
| *B. jararacussu* | | | X(S) | X(SW) | X(S,SE) |
| *B. leucurus* | | | | | X(E) |
| *B. marajoensis*[7] | | X | | | X(N) |
| *B. microphthalmus* | | X[1] | | | |
| *B. moojeni* | | | X | X | |
| *B. neuwiedi* | | | X | X | X(SE) |
| *B. pirajai* | | | X(E) | | X(E,SE) |

**Table 18—*continued***

| Species | *Guiana Highlands* | *Amazon lowlands* | *Central highlands* | *La Plata Basin* | *Coastal plain* |
|---|---|---|---|---|---|
| *B. pradoi* | | | | | X(E,SE) |
| *Crotalus durissus* | X(N) | X[8] | X | X | X(N) |
| *Lachesis muta* | X | X | X(N) | | X(N,E) |
| *Porthidium hyoprora* | | X(W) | | | |

*Note.* C, central; E, eastern; N, northern; S, southern; W, western; NE, northeastern; SE, southeastern; SW, southwestern; NW, northwestern; NC, north-central.

1. Needs confirmation for Brazil.
2. Includes *M. donosoi* and *M. paraensis*; see species account.
3. Presence questionable.
4. Aquatic habitat.
5. Minas Gerais, São Paulo, and Rio de Janeiro (southeastern Brazil).
6. Ilha Queimada Grande.
7. Ilha de Marajó and coast of Maranhão; also Amapá.
8. Isolated savannas.

**Table 19**

Distributions by vegetation type of venomous snakes in Brazil

| Species | *Equatorial rainforest* | *Transitional palm forest* | *Cerrado* | *Pantanal* | *Caatinga* | *Eastern tropical forest* | *Araucaria Plateau* | *Grassland* | *Mangrove-dune forest* |
|---|---|---|---|---|---|---|---|---|---|
| *Micrurus annellatus*[1] | X(W) | | | | | | | | |
| *M. averyi* | X(C)[2] | | | | | | | | |
| *M. collaris*[1] | X[2] | | | | | | | | |
| *M. corallinus*[3] | | | | | | X(S,SE) | X | | X(SE) |
| *M. decoratus* | | | | | | X(SE) | | X(S)[1] | |
| *M. filiformis* | X | | | | | | | | |
| *M. frontalis* | | | X(S,SE) | X | | X(S,SE) | X | X | |
| *M. hemprichii* | X | | | | | | | | |
| *M. ibiboboca* | | X | | | X | | | | |
| *M. karlschmidti* | X(NW) | | | | | | | | |
| *M. langsdorffi* | X(W) | | | | | | | | |
| *M. lemniscatus*[4] | X | | | X[1] | | X(S) | | | |
| *M. narduccii* | X(W) | | | | | | | | |
| *M. psyches*[5] | X(NE)[2] | | | | | | | | |
| *M. putumayensis* | X(NW) | | | | | | | | |
| *M. spixii* | X | | | | | | | | |
| *M. surinamensis*[6] | X | | | | | | | | |
| *Bothriopsis bilineata*[7] | X | | | | | X | | | |
| *B. taeniata* | X | | | | | | | | |
| *Bothrops alternatus* | | | | X[1] | | X | X | X | |
| *B. atrox* | X | | X(W) | | | | | | |
| *B. brazili* | X | | | | | | | | |
| *B. cotiara* | | | | | | | X | | |
| *B. erythromelas* | | | | | X | | | | |
| *B. fonsecai* | | | | | | X(SE)[7] | | | |
| *B. iglesiasi*[8] | | X | | | | | | | |
| *B. insularis*[9] | | | | | | X | | | |
| *B. itapetiningae* | | | X | | | | X(N) | | |
| *B. jararaca*[3] | | | | | | X(S,SE) | X | X | X(SE) |
| *B. jararacussu*[3] | | | | X | | X(S,SE) | | | X(SE) |
| *B. leucurus*[10] | | | | | | X | | | X |
| *B. marajoensis*[11] | X(NE) | | | | | | | | |
| *B. microphthalmus*[1] | X(W) | | | | | | | | |
| *B. moojeni* | | | X(C,SE) | | | | X(C) | | |
| *B. neuwiedi*[12] | | X | X | X | X | X | | X | |
| *B. pirajai* | | | | | | X[7] | | | |
| *B. pradoi* | | | | | | X[7] | | | |
| *Crotalus durissus*[13] | | | X | | X | | | X | |
| *Lachesis muta*[4] | X | | | | | X | | | |
| *Porthidium hyoprora* | X(NW) | | | | | | | | |

*Note.* C, central; N, northern; S, southern; W, western; NE, northeastern; NW, northwestern; SE, southeastern.

1. Of questionable occurrence in the stated zone or country.
2. Guiana Highlands.
3. Found also on Ilha de São Sebastião and probably other islands.
4. Amazon Basin and Atlantic forest.
5. Includes *M. donosoi* and *M. paraensis*; see species account.
6. Aquatic habitat.
7. Atlantic forest.
8. Known only from Piaui.
9. Known only from Ilha Queimada Grande.
10. Known only from coastal Bahia; see species account.
11. Known only from Amapá, Ilha Marajó SE to Maranhão.
12. Largely restricted to open formations; an isolated population in Amazon Basin.
13. Largely in southern and central Brazil with isolated populations in the Guiana highlands.

## Key to Venomous Snakes of Brazil

1. No loreal pit between eye and nostril; loreal scale usually absent (Fig. 100); scales on top of head enlarged into plates (Fig. 16); dorsal scales smooth; fangs permanently erect (Fig. 19); Elapidae ........ 2
   A loreal pit between eye and nostril (Fig. 203); loreal scale present; scales on top of head small and numerous; dorsal scales keeled; fangs fold back (Fig. 253); Viperidae ........ 20
2. Black rings arranged in triads, separated by red rings on body, sometimes only visible ventrally ........ 3
   Color pattern not forming triads ........ 10
3. Several supracephalic scales entirely black; frontal wider than supraocular; supralabials 3 and 4 in contact with eye (Fig. 15); supra-anal keels absent in males ........ 4
   All supracephalic scales red, outlined in black; frontal not wider than supraocular (Fig. 18); only fourth supralabial in contact with eye (Fig. 17); supra-anal keels present in males (Figs. 104, 105) ........ *Micrurus surinamensis*
4. Anal plate divided; usually more than 192 ventrals ........ 5
   Anal plate single; 191 or fewer ventrals (Figs. 58, 59) ........ *Micrurus hemprichii*
5. Parietal tips touched by red or pale ring ........ 6
   Parietal tips black ........ 9
6. Ventrals 266 or more; limited to Amazon Basin (Fig. 49) ........ *Micrurus filiformis*
   Ventrals usually fewer than 266 ........ 7
7. Black nape ring not the anteriormost black member of the first complete black body triad (Fig. 35); southeastern Brazil ........ *Micrurus decoratus*
   Black nape ring the anteriormost member of the first complete black body triad ........ 8
8. Subcaudals 26 or more, usually more than 30; body triads 7–17 (Figs. 67–71) ........ *Micrurus lemniscatus*
   Subcaudals usually 26 or fewer, never more than 30; body triads 8–10 (Fig. 62) ........ *Micrurus ibiboboca*
9. Longest rings on body usually red; central to southern Brazil (Figs. 50–52) ........ *Micrurus frontalis*
   Red rings on body equal to or shorter than yellow (or white) body rings; northern Brazil (Figs. 97–101) ........ *Micrurus spixii*
10. Few, if any, rings present on body ........ 11
    Body all or mostly ringed ........ 14
11. Chinshields in contact with mental; 215 or more ventrals ........ 12
    Chinshields not in contact with mental (Fig. 14); fewer than 215 ventrals ........ *Micrurus psyches*
12. Parietals all or mostly black; northern Brazil. (Figs. 31–32) ........ *Micrurus collaris*
    Parietals mostly pale; northwest Brazil ........ 13
13. From 261 to 382 ventrals, usually more than 270; possibly found also in Acre (Figs. 83, 84) ........ *Micrurus narduccii*
    From 219 to 270 ventrals; state of Amazonas ........ *Micrurus karlschmidti*
14. Parietals, including tips, all or mostly black; pattern bicolored or tricolored ........ 15
    Parietals crossed by narrow pale ring, usually including tips (Fig. 24); pattern usually tricolored, at least ventrally (Fig. 25); northwestern Brazil ........ *Micrurus annellatus*
15. Pattern bicolored ........ 16
    Pattern tricolored, at least ventrally ........ 17
16. Entire head black, with symmetrically arranged white spots sometimes forming a broken band; 75–91 short pale rings ........ *Micrurus langsdorffi*
    Pale markings on posteriormost labials and gulars, and usually in the occipital region; fewer than 20 long, pale rings, heavily stippled with black pigment (Fig. 96) ........ *Micrurus putumayensis*
17. Red pigment visible, at least ventrally, on tail ........ 18
    Red pigment not present on tail ........ 19
18. Black body rings occasionally replaced by yellow or brown rings; 36–60 black,

yellow, or brown rings; red rings stippled with black or heavily melanized (Fig. 64) ........ *Micrurus langsdorffi*

Black body rings never replaced by yellow or brown rings; 8–13 black rings on body; red rings lack dark pigment (Fig. 26) ........ *Micrurus averyi*

19. Black body rings 3 middorsals long; little or no black stippling dorsally on red rings; lower Amazon (Fig. 95) ........ *Micrurus psyches*

    Black body rings 3–5 middorsals long; uniform black stippling dorsally on red rings; southeastern to southern Brazil (Figs. 33, 34) ........ *Micrurus corallinus*

20. Tail terminating in a rattle or button (Figs. 330, 331, 335–340, 342) ........ *Crotalus durissus*

    Tail not terminating in a rattle (Fig. 316) ........ 21

21. Posterior subcaudals finely divided (Fig. 316); keels on middorsals conical (Figs. 249, 251) ........ *Lachesis muta*

    Posterior subcaudals single or paired (Fig. 316); keels on middorsals not conical ........ 22

22. Subcaudals all or mostly single (Fig. 316) ........ 23

    Subcaudals all or mostly divided (Fig. 316) ........ 24

23. Snout normal (Fig. 169); a row of cream spots paraventrally; 203–254 ventrals (Figs. 158–162) ........ *Bothriopsis taeniata*

    Snout upturned, forming a flaplike process (Fig. 306); no cream spots paraventrally; 124–141 ventrals (Fig. 273) ........ *Porthidium hyoprora*

24. Dorsal pattern consists of pale green color, sometimes with orange-tan dorsal spots, and a distinct white or yellow ventrolateral line (Figs. 149–151) ........ *Bothriopsis bilineata*

    Dorsal pattern variable, but not including green and lacking ventrolateral lines ........ 25

25. Prelacunal usually fused with second supralabial (Fig. 177) ........ 35

    Prelacunal usually discrete from second supralabial (Fig. 173) ........ 26

26. Usually fewer than 33 subcaudals; southeastern and south-central Brazil (Fig. 216) ........ *Bothrops itapetiningae*

    Usually more than 33 subcaudals ........ 27

27. Intersupraoculars smooth; midbody dorsal scales usually 21 or fewer; northeastern Brazil (Fig. 210) ........ *Bothrops erythromelas*

    Intersupraoculars usually keeled; midbody dorsal scales usually more than 21 ........ 28

28. Top of head with ornate pattern ........ 29

    Top of head not ornately patterned ........ 32

29. Venter primarily or entirely black ........ 30

    Venter primarily or entirely pale ........ 31

30. Intersupraoculars 8–10; postorbital stripe hook shaped posteriorly (Figs. 211–213) ........ *Bothrops fonsecai*

    Intersupraoculars 11–14; postorbital stripe not hook shaped posteriorly (Figs. 208, 209) ........ *Bothrops cotiara*

31. Anterior part of venter with a dark median stripe; rostral with distinctive dark vertical marking; intersupraoculars 8–13; postorbital stripe broad, passing beneath eye (Figs. 179, 180) ........ *Bothrops alternatus*

    Anterior part of venter lacking dark median stripe; rostral without dark marking; intersupraoculars 6–9; postorbital stripe moderate in extent, not passing beneath eye (Figs. 233–237) ........ *Bothrops neuwiedi*

32. Venter heavily spotted or mottled with dark pigment ........ 33

    Venter only slightly marked with dark pigment ........ 34

33. Subcaudals 35–43; state of Piauí ........ *Bothrops iglesiasi*

    Subcaudals 44–56 (Figs. 229, 230); possibly found in extreme northwestern Brazil ........ *Bothrops microphthalmus*

34. Dorsal pattern indistinct or absent; postorbital stripe often indistinct; 48–65 subcaudals; restricted to Ilha Queimada Grande (Figs. 214, 215) ........ *Bothrops insularis*

    Dorsal pattern variable but always distinct; postorbital stripe always distinct; 37–53 subcaudals (Figs. 233–237) ........ *Bothrops neuwiedi*

35. Postorbital stripe weakly defined or absent ............................................36
Postorbital stripe well defined..............................................................38

36. Supraoculars large; pattern often obscure and never bold; Amazon Basin (Figs. 201–205)....................................................................*Bothrops brazili*
Supraoculars narrow; pattern variable; eastern or southeastern Brazil .........37

37. Pattern includes prominent black markings; elongated outer internasals usually not in contact with each other; 155–167 ventrals................*Bothrops pirajai*
Pattern usually ill defined; elongated outer internasals usually in contact with each other; 171–195 ventrals; Ilha Queimada Grande (Figs. 214, 215)........... ......................................................................*Bothrops insularis*

38. Top of head with ornate pattern .........................................................39
Top of head not ornately patterned ......................................................41

39. Intersupraoculars 10 or more ............................................................40
Intersupraoculars fewer than 10 (Fig. 227) .......................*Bothrops leucurus*

40. Ventrals 151–173; intersupraoculars 11–14; subcaudals 34–52 (Figs. 208, 209) ..........................................................................*Bothrops cotiara*
Ventrals 191–207; intersupraoculars 10; subcaudals 56–70 (Fig. 241)............ ..........................................................................*Bothrops pradoi*

41. Elongated outer internasals separated from one another by one or more smaller internasals...........................................................................42
Elongated outer internasals in contact with each other.............................43

42. Postorbital stripe encroaches on 3 posteriormost supralabials; gular region and venter usually heavily spotted with dark pigment (Figs. 218, 219) ............... ........................................................................*Bothrops jararaca*
Postorbital stripe encroaches on 2 posteriormost supralabials; gular region and venter usually sparsely spotted with dark pigment (Figs. 231, 232) .............. ........................................................................*Bothrops moojeni*

43. Intersupraoculars 10 or more ............................................................44
Intersupraoculars fewer than 10 .........................................................45

44. Dorsal pattern usually heavily spotted; a pair of undulating black-bordered pale markings on neck; nostril often contained within a brown spot; Espírito Santo and southern Bahia (Fig. 241) .........................................*Bothrops pradoi*
Dorsal pattern includes spots, but not usually in profusion; no pair of undulating black-bordered pale markings on neck; nostril not contained within a brown spot; from Mato Grosso and Pará northwestward in northern Brazil (Figs. 193–199) ..........................................................*Bothrops atrox*

45. Venter heavily pigmented; snout acuminate; supralabials generally 7..........46
Venter pale or with scattered dark punctuations; snout obtusely rounded; supralabials 8 (Figs. 220, 221).....................................*Bothrops jararacussu*

46. Supralabials usually with some dark spotting (Fig. 177); dorsal markings indistinct and tend to form transverse bands; lateral accessory blotches absent or indistinct (Figs. 193–199) ................................................*Bothrops atrox*
Supralabials usually immaculate; dorsal markings distinct and usually do not tend to form transverse bands; lateral accessory blotches usually distinct...47

47. Ventrals 195–225; intersupraoculars more than 6; Bahia (Fig. 227)................ ........................................................................*Bothrops leucurus*
Ventrals 176–194; intersupraoculars fewer than 6; Amapá, Pará, and possibly Maranhão (Fig. 228) ..............................................*Bothrops marajoensis*

## ECUADOR

Ecuador encompasses 283,561 km$^2$ and is situated on the western coast of South America. It is bounded on the north by Colombia, on the east and south by Peru, and on the west by 685 km of Pacific coastline. Ecuador broadly comprises three regions: (1) Pacific Coast (La Costa), (2) Andean highlands (La Sierra), and (3) eastern lowlands (El Oriente). The Galápagos Islands, an Ecuadorian possession lying 970 km offshore, contains no dangerously venomous snakes.

The Pacific coastal lowlands are approximately 100 km wide and consist of low rolling hills and regions of swampy ground. Most of the lowlands are below 300 m in elevation. Much deforestation has occurred and the area is heavily agricultural. Rainforest still exists to the north, and some mangroves remain as well.

The Andean highlands sharply abut the Pacific lowlands and comprise two principal ranges: the Cordillera Oriental and the Cordillera Occidental. These are separated by 10 intermontane basins that collectively form the 400-km long Valle Central, which varies in width from 40 to 65 km and in elevation from 1,800 to 3,000 m.

More than 30 volcanic cones, most of them extinct, dot the eastern and western rims of the Valle Central. Among them are Chimborazo, which at 6,270 m is the highest peak in the country, and Cotopaxi, which at 5,896 m is the world's highest active volcano. The principal rivers dissecting the valley rims are the Guaillabamba-Esmeraldas and the Patía, which drain westward, and the Napo and Pastaza, which empty into the Amazon. East of the Cordillera Oriental the mountains drop off sharply into forested plains of the Amazon Basin. Other important rivers draining Amazonian Ecuador are the Zamora, Tigre, and Coca.

The major Ecuadorian vegetation zones include rainforest and very humid tropical forest in the northern coastal lowlands and the Amazon Basin; tropical thorn forest, lowland dry forest, and savanna along the central and southern coastal plain; dry to humid montane forest and cloud forest at intermediate elevations; and *páramo* (moist grassland) above the timber line. Along the coast, mangroves are restricted to the extreme north and the extreme south.

Seasonal rains occur in one or two annual cycles in the north and throughout the highlands and eastern lowlands; the time of arrival, duration, and number of seasons vary by location. The Santa Elena Peninsula and southwestern coast near Peru receive only minimal precipitation.

Our knowledge of the Ecuadorian herpetofauna is incomplete. Time may reveal taxa of venomous snakes as yet undescribed or unrecorded from the country. In the latter category some likely candidates include *Micrurus clarki* (Fig. 30; see Key to Venomous Snakes of Panama), which may occur in the northwest lowlands; *M. margaritiferus* (Figs. 74, 75; see Key to Venomous Snakes of Peru), which probably exists in southeastern Ecuador; *M. multiscutatus* (Fig. 82; see Key to Venomous Snakes of Colombia), which may occur in the northwest lowlands; *M. peruvianus* (Fig. 91; see Key to Venomous Snakes of Peru), which possibly occurs in the Cordillera

**Table 20**

Distributions by vegetation type of venomous snakes in Ecuador

| *Species* | *Lowland rainforest* | *Lowland dry forest, thorn forest* | *Savanna* | *Lower montane wet forest, cloud forest* | *Lower montane dry forest* |
|---|---|---|---|---|---|
| *Pelamis platurus*[1] | | | | | |
| *Micrurus ancoralis* | X[2] | | | | |
| *M. annellatus* | | | | X[3] | |
| *M. bocourti* | | X[2] | | | X |
| *M. dumerilii* | X[2] | | | | |
| *M. filiformis* | X[4] | | | | |
| *M. hemprichii* | X[4] | | | X[4] | |
| *M. karlschmidti* | X[4] | | | | |
| *M. langsdorffi* | X[4] | | | | |
| *M. lemniscatus* | X[4] | | | X[4] | |
| *M. mertensi* | | X[2] | X[2] | | |
| *M. mipartitus* | | | | X[3] | |
| *M. narduccii* | X[4] | | | X[4] | |
| *M. petersi* | | | | X[3] | |
| *M. spixii* | X[4] | | | X[4] | |
| *M. steindachneri* | | | | X[3] | |
| *M. surinamensis* | X[5] | | | | |
| *M. tschudii* | | | | | X[2,6] |
| *Bothriechis schlegelii* | X[2] | | | X[3] | |
| *Bothriopsis albocarinata* | | | | X[7] | |
| *B. alticola* | | | | X[7] | |
| *B. bilineata* | X[4] | | | | |
| *B. punctata* | X[2] | | | X[8] | |
| *B. taeniata* | X[4] | | | X[6] | |
| *Bothrops asper* | X[2] | X[2] | X | X[8] | X |
| *B. atrox* | X[4] | | | X[8] | |
| *B. brazili* | X[4] | | | | |
| *B. lojanus* | | | | | X[7] |
| *B. microphthalmus* | | | | X[3] | |
| *B. pulcher* | X[2] | | | X[7] | |
| *B. xanthogrammus* | | | | X[3] | |
| *Lachesis muta* | X[2,4] | | | X[6] | |
| *Porthidium hyoprora* | X[4] | | | | |
| *P. nasutum* | X[2] | | | | |

1. Pacific marine habitat.
2. Western lowlands.
3. Up to 2,000 m.
4. Amazon Basin.
5. Found in aquatic situations.
6. Generally at elevations of 500 m or less.
7. Up to 2,000–3,000 m.
8. Generally at elevations of 1,000 m or less.

del Condor; *M. putumayensis* (Fig. 96; see Key to Venomous Snakes of Peru), which probably exists in eastern Ecuador; and *Bothrops barnetti* (Fig. 200; see Key to Venomous Snakes of Peru), which probably exists in the upper Río Catamayo Valley of southern Ecuador. The distributions by vegetation type of species of dangerously venomous snakes in Ecuador are given in Table 20.

### Key to Venomous Snakes of Ecuador

1. No loreal pit between eye and nostril; loreal scale absent (Fig. 100); scales on top of head enlarged into plates (Fig. 16); dorsal scales smooth; fangs permanently erect (Fig. 19); Elapidae ........ 2
   A loreal pit between eye and nostril (Fig. 162); loreal scale present; scales on top of head small and numerous; dorsal scales keeled; fangs fold back (Fig. 253); Viperidae ........ 19
2. Tail strongly flattened laterally; marine habitat; longitudinal black (or brown) and yellow pattern (Figs. 110–112) ........ *Pelamis platurus*
   Tail round in cross section; nonmarine habitat; pattern consisting of black, red, and/or yellow-to-white rings or blotches ........ 3
3. Black rings arranged in triads that are separated by red rings on the body, the latter sometimes visible only ventrally ........ 4
   Black rings not arranged in triads ........ 11
4. Anal plate divided ........ 5
   Anal plate not divided (Fig. 59) ........ *Micrurus hemprichii*
5. First *complete* triad posterior to and not involving black ring on nape ........ 6
   Black ring on nape comprising anteriormost black ring of first *complete* triad ........ 7
6. Tail bicolored; 32–49 subcaudals ........ *Micrurus bocourti*
   Tail tricolored; 15–24 subcaudals (Figs. 99–101) ........ *Micrurus spixii*
7. Several supracephalic scales entirely black; frontal wider than supraocular; third and fourth supralabials in contact with eye (Fig. 15) ........ 8
   All supracephalic scales red, outlined by black; frontal not wider than supraocular; only the fourth supralabial in contact with eye (Fig. 17); 6–9 complete triads on body (Fig. 104) ........ *Micrurus surinamensis*
8. First triad normal; first white ring not oblique ........ 9
   First two black rings in first triad anchor shaped, outlining oblique first white ring, the latter interrupted or nearly so on middorsal line; 16–24 black triads (Figs. 21, 22) ........ *Micrurus ancoralis*
9. Ventrals usually more than 218; first nuchal black ring usually not covering parietal tips; snout black, with a yellow ring crossing it; Amazon Basin ........ 10
   Ventrals usually fewer than 218; first nuchal black ring usually covering parietal tips; snout spotted; Río Catamayo Valley (Fig. 107) ........ *Micrurus tschudii*
10. Ventrals fewer than 268; usually 9–13 triads; reaches large size (Figs. 70, 71) ........ *Micrurus lemniscatus*
    Ventrals 266 or more; usually more than 13 triads; size small and slender (Fig. 49) ........ *Micrurus filiformis*
11. Black head cap present, including part or all of parietals; no pale band interrupting black cap ........ 15
    Black reduced on head, not or barely reaching parietals, or at least one pale ring crossing head on or anterior to parietals ........ 12
12. Dorsum uniformly black with a yellow (or orange) ring on head; venter with a series of yellow-to-orange spots extending somewhat onto the sides, rarely crossing dorsum; first pair of chinshields in contact with mental ........ 13
    Pattern includes rings on body; chinshields not in contact with mental (Fig. 14) ........ 14
13. From 261 to 382 ventrals, usually more than 270 (Figs. 83, 84) ........ *Micrurus narduccii*
    From 219 to 270 ventrals ........ *Micrurus karlschmidti*

14. Pale parietal ring long; red rings confined to head and tail; body with alternating black and white rings (Fig. 79) .................................... *Micrurus mipartitus*
Pale parietal ring short; red rings not confined to head and tail (Figs. 24, 25) ..................................................................... *Micrurus annellatus*
15. Dorsally red rings immaculate or slightly stippled with black, but always clearly discernible on body; Pacific versant ..................................................... 16
Dorsally red rings often heavily pigmented with black, or totally obscured from view; Amazonian slopes and lowlands ................................................ 17
16. Black body rings 11–21; ventrals 183–217; males with supra-anal keels; northwestern Ecuadorian lowlands (Figs. 43, 44) ..................... *Micrurus dumerilii*
Black body rings 18–30; ventrals 210–236; males lack supra-anal keels; southwestern Ecuadorian lowlands ....................................... *Micrurus mertensi*
17. Lacking pale supracephalic spots; short white rings present on body; red pigment usually obscured or only visible laterally ...................................... 18
Pale supracephalic spots present; white body rings each reduced to a thin line of specks delimiting black rings; red pigment absent or heavily melanized (Fig. 64) ..................................................................... *Micrurus langsdorffi*
18. Snout dark; 22–42 black rings on body (Figs. 102, 103) ..................................................................... *Micrurus steindachneri*
Snout pale; 21 black rings on body .................................... *Micrurus petersi*
19. Posterior subcaudals finely divided (Fig. 316); keels on dorsals conical (Figs. 249, 252) ..................................................................... *Lachesis muta*
Posterior subcaudals single or paired (Fig. 316); keels on dorsals normal ..... 20
20. Subcaudals all or mostly single (Fig. 316) ............................................. 21
Subcaudals all or mostly divided (Fig. 316) ............................................ 24
21. Slightly raised superciliary scales giving appearance of eyelashes (Figs. 145, 146, 165) ............................................................ *Bothriechis schlegelii*
Superciliaries absent ........................................................................ 22
22. Snout normal (Fig. 169); a row of cream spots along juncture of dorsals and ventrals (Figs. 158–162) ............................................ *Bothriopsis taeniata*
Snout upturned, forming a flaplike process; lateral row of cream spots absent ..................................................................................... 23
23. Fewer than 40 subcaudals; outer internasals in contact with each other or separated by 1 scale; pale middorsal line usually present; Pacific lowlands and foothills (Figs. 284, 285) ........................................... *Porthidium nasutum*
Usually more than 40 subcaudals; outer internasals separated from each other by 2 or more scales; pale middorsal line absent; Amazon Basin (Fig. 273) ..................................................................... *Porthidium hyoprora*
24. Postorbital stripe absent or feebly indicated ........................................... 25
Postorbital stripe well defined ............................................................. 27
25. Ventrals 192 or more; dorsum green with yellow paraventral stripe (Fig. 151) ..................................................................... *Bothriopsis bilineata*
Ventrals 190 or fewer; dorsum variable, but not green; paraventral stripes lacking ............................................................................. 26
26. Supralabials 8 or more; elongated outer internasals in contact with each other; usually 5 or 6 intersupraoculars; ventrals usually more than 160; Amazon Basin (Figs. 201–205) ................................................... *Bothrops brazili*
Supralabials 7; outer internasals separated from each other by 1 or 2 scales; intersupraoculars 4 or fewer; ventrals fewer than 160; Pacific drainage (Fig. 242) ..................................................................... *Bothrops pulcher*
27. Intersupraoculars smooth ................................................................... 28
Intersupraoculars keeled .................................................................... 29
28. Ventrals 196; subcaudals 54; midbody dorsal scale rows 27 (Figs. 247, 248) ..................................................................... *Bothrops xanthogrammus*
Ventrals 155 or fewer; subcaudals 46 or fewer; midbody dorsal scale rows 23 or fewer (Fig. 226) ......................................................... *Bothrops lojanus*
29. Lacunolabial present (Fig. 177) .......................................................... 30
Lacunolabial absent (Figs. 229, 230) ...................... *Bothrops microphthalmus*

30. Midbody dorsal scale rows 21 or fewer (Figs. 147, 148) ................................................................................ *Bothriopsis albocarinata* or *B. alticola*
Midbody dorsal scale rows 23 or more ................................................... 31
31. Tail prehensile, posterior half pale even in adults; top of head with ornate pattern; usually more than 75 subcaudals (Fig. 157)....... *Bothriopsis punctata*
Tail not prehensile, posterior half dark in adults; top of head not ornately patterned; usually fewer than 75 subcaudals ......................................... 32
32. Lateral borders of dorsal blotches more or less diagonal (as opposed to vertical); dorsal ground color grayish brown; dark postorbital stripe bordered above by a pale stripe 2 scales wide; last 1–2 supralabials usually enter dark postorbital stripe (Fig. 175); supralabials usually without dark spotting; Pacific drainage (Fig. 187) ...................................................................... *Bothrops asper*
Lateral borders of dorsal blotches more or less vertical (as opposed to diagonal); dorsal ground color dark yellowish brown to olive; dark postorbital stripe not distinctly pale bordered above; last 3 supralabials enter postorbital stripe (Fig. 177); supralabials usually bear several dark spots (Fig. 197) ....*Bothrops atrox*

## PERU

Peru is the third largest country in South America, encompassing 1,285,216 km$^2$; only Argentina and Brazil are larger. Peru is borderd on the north by Ecuador and Colombia, on the east by Brazil, on the southeast by Bolivia, on the south by Chile, and on the west by 2,414 km of Pacific coastline.

Three broad physiographic regions are generally recognized: (1) La Costa, which includes the Pacific Coast and foothills up to about 2,000 m; (2) La Sierra, which includes the mountainous central backbone of the Andes; and (3) La Montaña, consisting of the heavily forested eastern Andean versant—with its associated deeply incised valleys and foothills—and the plains of the eastern portion of the country.

In the coastal region rain seldom falls, and stark desert conditions prevail; most of the terrain along the lower elevations of the Pacific Coast is essentially barren, except along the few streams traversing the area which support riparian vegetation. This desert, a northern extension of the Atacama, is a region of rugged foothills with little flat land. Of the more than 50 rivers that have their origins in the Andes and that discharge into the Pacific Ocean, most are relatively short and flow in a generally westward direction; only 10 have water all year.

The climate of this region is dominated by the cold offshore oceanic current (the Humboldt) coming up from the south. The prevailing inshore winds pick up little moisture from these cold waters, and rain is a rare phenomenon on the western slopes of the Andes below the 1,500-m contour. However, from June to October a rather static cloud blanket bathes moderate elevations of the western Andes; these clouds provide a fine mist known as the *garúa*.

Between about 800 and 1,400 m on the Pacific slopes sufficient moisture is received from the *garúa* to support isolated zones with abundant growth of grasses and other small plants from June to October; these areas are generally referred to as the *lomas*. The higher slopes receive more moisture, some in the form of rainfall, and a more complete covering of grasses and shrubs is present.

Mean annual temperatures in the lowlands of the coastal region range from 18.8 to 22.7°C; these temperatures are about 5°C less than those of corresponding latitudes on the Atlantic Coast in Brazil.

No rain falls most years along most of the Pacific Coast, but rarely during the summer a warm current of water called *El Niño* is displaced by strong winds to the south of its normal position. These warm waters override the cold Humboldt current, and winds coming across them pick up abundant moisture. During these periods the coastal desert may receive exceptionally heavy rainfall.

From the Pacific Coast the Andes rise rather abruptly, whereas the eastern slopes gain elevation more gradually. The Andes in Peru are about 210 km wide at the latitude of Lima, even narrower in the north, and widen to about 480 km in the southern part of the country. Near the Ecuadorian border the highlands are not only narrower, but most of the high-level surface disappears, and low passes of only about 2,100 m form part of the Continental Divide. The highlands of Peru consist of many complex range systems. Some of these run more or less parallel to each other, but others may be oriented at right angles to the main axis of the Andes, and numerous ridge systems interconnect most of the ranges. Ten peaks in Peru exceed 6,000 m. The Cordillera Blanca is the highest ridge system, and its 6,768-m peak, Huascarán, is the highest in the country.

The most conspicuous feature of the highland hydrography is Lake Titicaca located in the southern portion of the country along the border with Bolivia. The surface of this lake lies at 3,809 m. Lago Lauricocha, just north of the Cerro de Pasco, gives rise to one of the major tributaries of the Amazon, Río Marañón, hence this lake is often considered to be the source of the Amazon.

Most inter-Andean valleys experience rainshadow conditions to some degree, although some of the northern valleys and some of the valleys that lie between the

Cordillera Oriental and the ranges to the west may receive ample rainfall. Over much of La Sierra region the rainy period extends from September to April. Rainfall is heaviest in the north and gradually decreases to the south. The eastern slopes of the Cordillera Azul receive about 4,000 mm of rain annually.

Highland temperatures are largely correlated with elevation. At elevations of over 3,500 mm mean annual temperatures are less than 10°C, with little variation between the warmest and coldest months. However, the daily range between day and night temperatures is dramatic, and differences of 20–28°C may exist between places in the sun and in the shade. The snowline occurs at elevations above 5,000–5,800 m.

The wetter northern highlands are covered with tall bunchgrass and elfin shrubs comprising *páramo* vegetation. Most of the other highlands are also covered by grasses and small plants, but rainfall is less abundant and the grass cover is shorter than 15 cm at maturity. This *puna* vegetation type prevails over much of the central and southern highlands. Many of the interior valleys support, at best, a mixture of shrubs and short trees, except in the north, where many of the valleys and ridges support a luxuriant rainforest.

La Montaña (the forest) region of eastern Peru is usually divided into two zones on the basis of elevation. The lower zone, below 1,000 m, is referred to as *la selva* (the jungle) and includes the tropical Amazonian rainforest. About 2,500–3,000 mm of rain falls in this region per year; rainfall is distributed rather evenly throughout the year, with more than 200 rainy days and no marked dry season. At Iquitos the average temperature for the warmest month is 25.7°C; there is not much variation of monthly means throughout the year, but daily maxima may approach 35°C.

The upper zone lies above 1,000 m and extends along the eastern escarpment of the Andes. This region, the *ceja de la montaña* ("eyebrow of the forest"), ranges from 80 to 160 km in width and is extremely varied and rugged. This forest extends up to 3,000–3,350 m; above this level the highlands are covered by grasses and shrubs. A dense forest of relatively short trees comprises the upper portion of this forest, and luxuriant cloud forest occurs at moderate and intermediate elevations in the zones of greatest rainfall.

The drainage systems in eastern Peru are extensive. Rivers originate high in the Andes and flow into the Amazon Basin. Some of the major tributaries of the upper Amazon drainage system that flow through eastern Peru include the Río Napo, Río Marañón, Río Ucayali, and Río Madre de Dios.

Because of its geographic location and diversity of terrain, Peru has not been adequately collected herpetologically; some regions have not been explored at all. It is reasonable to assume that a number of dangerously venomous snake species that are known from other countries will ultimately prove to exist in Peru. Some species whose ranges may include parts of Peru include *Micrurus bocourti* (see Key to Venomous Snakes of Ecuador) in the northwest, *M. frontifasciatus* (Fig. 55, see Key to Venomous Snakes of Bolivia) in the southeast, and *M. mipartitus* (Fig. 79; see Key to Venomous Snakes of Ecuador), *M. petersi* (see Key to Venomous Snakes of Ecuador), and *M. steindachneri* (Figs. 102, 103; see Key to Venomous Snakes of Ecuador) in the northern Andes. Because of the cold, north-flowing Humboldt current off the Pacific Coast, it is unlikely that *Pelamis platurus* (Figs. 110–112; see Key to Venomous Snakes of Ecuador) occurs in Peruvian waters; however, owing to the southward deflection of warm ocean currents, the species does occur around the Isla de Pascua about 4000 km west of the coast of Chile even farther to the south. It is possible that *Bothrops neuwiedi* (Fig. 233, see Key to Venomous Snakes of Bolivia) enters Peru in the Yungas region; its northward extent in Bolivia is not well known, but it exists definitely in the Departamento de Cochabamba. The distributions of species of dangerously venomous snakes in Peru by physiographic regions are given in Table 21.

**Table 21**

Distributions by physiographic region of venomous snakes in Peru

| | *La Costa* | | | *La Montaña* | |
|---|---|---|---|---|---|
| *Species* | *Lower* | *Lomas* | *La Sierra* | *La Ceja* | *La Selva* |
| *Micrurus annellatus* | | | | X | X[1] |
| *M. bocourti* | X[2] | | | | |
| *M. filiformis* | | | | | X[3] |
| *M. hemprichii* | | | | | X |
| *M. karlschmidti* | | | | X | X |
| *M. langsdorffi* | | | | X | X |
| *M. lemniscatus* | | | | X | X |
| *M. margaritiferus* | | | | X[4] | X |
| *M. mertensi* | X | | | X | X |
| *M. narduccii* | | | | X | X |
| *M. peruvianus* | | | X[5] | | |
| *M. putumayensis* | | | | | X[3] |
| *M. spixii* | | | | X | X |
| *M. surinamensis* | | | | | X |
| *M. tschudii* | X | X | | | |
| *Bothriopsis albocarinata* | | | | | X[6] |
| *B. bilineata* | | | | X | X |
| *B. oligolepis* | | | | X | |
| *B. peruviana* | | | | X[7] | |

**Table 21—*continued***

| Species | La Costa | | La Sierra | La Montaña | |
|---|---|---|---|---|---|
| | Lower | Lomas | | La Ceja | La Selva |
| *B. taeniata*[3] | | | | X | X |
| *Bothrops andianus* | | | | X[8] | |
| *B. atrox* | | | | X | X |
| *B. barnetti* | X[2] | | | | |
| *B. brazili* | | | | | X[3] |
| *B. microphthalmus* | | | | X | X[1] |
| *B. pictus* | X | X | | | |
| *B. roedingeri* | X[9] | | | | |
| *Crotalus durissus* | | | X[10] | | |
| *Lachesis muta* | | | | X[4] | X |
| *Porthidium hyoprora* | | | | | X[3] |

1. Apparently restricted to uplands; may not descend below 1,000 m (see species account).
2. Probably only in extreme northern coastal area.
3. Northeastern Peru.
4. Upper vertical distribution unknown; may not exceed 1,000 m.
5. Northern Andes of Peru in Departamento de Cajamarca.
6. According to Meneses (1974b); we regard this record with skepticism.
7. Known only from southeastern Peru in the northern portion of the Departamento de Puno.
8. Known only from the Departamento de Cuzco and the Departamento de Puno.
9. Known only from southern coastal region.
10. Known in Peru only from inter-Andean valleys in the south; these are better considered as fingerlike projections of *la ceja de la montaña*.

## Key to Venomous Snakes of Peru

1. No loreal pit between eye and nostril; loreal scale absent (Fig. 100); scales on top of head enlarged into plates (Fig. 16); dorsal scales smooth; fangs permanently erect (Fig. 19); Elapidae ....................2
   A loreal pit between eye and nostril (Fig. 150); loreal scale present; scales on top of head small and numerous; dorsal scales keeled; fangs fold back (Fig. 253); Viperidae ....................17
2. Tail strongly flattened laterally; marine habitat; longitudinal black (or brown) and yellow pattern (of doubtful occurrence in Peru) (Figs. 110–112) .................... *Pelamis platurus*
   Tail round in cross section; nonmarine habitat; pattern consisting of black, red, and/or yellow-to-white rings or blotches ....................3
3. Black rings arranged in triads separated by red rings on the body, sometimes visible only ventrally ....................4
   Black rings not arranged in triads ....................10
4. Anal plate not divided (Fig. 59) ....................*Micrurus hemprichii*
   Anal plate divided ....................5
5. First *complete* triad posterior to and not involving black ring on nape ....................6
   Black ring on nape comprising anteriormost black ring of first *complete* triad ....................7
6. Fewer than 10 triads on body; tail tricolored (Figs. 99–101).....*Micrurus spixii*
   Usually 10 or more triads on body; tail bicolored....................*Micrurus bocourti*
7. Several supracephalic scales entirely black; frontal wider than supraocular; supralabials 3 and 4 in contact with eye (Fig. 15) ....................8
   All supracephalic scales red, outlined by black; frontal not wider than supraocular (Fig. 18); only fourth supralabial in contact with eye (Figs. 17, 104) ....................*Micrurus surinamensis*
8. Parietal tips black; west of Andes (Figs. 106, 107) ....................*Micrurus tschudii*
   Parietal tips red; east of Andes....................9
9. Ventrals usually fewer than 266; 7–17 triads; reaches large size (Figs. 70, 71) ....................*Micrurus lemniscatus*
   Ventrals 266 or more; 11–20 triads; size small (Fig. 49) ......*Micrurus filiformis*
10. Parietal ring does not include parietal tips (Figs. 24, 25)...*Micrurus annellatus*
    Pale parietal ring, if present, includes parietal tips ....................11
11. Dorsally uniform black with a yellow (or orange) ring on the head; venter with a series of yellow-to-orange spots extending somewhat onto sides, rarely crossing dorsum; first pair of infralabials not in contact with each other behind mental ....................12
    Pattern includes rings on the body; first pair of infralabials in contact with each

other behind mental (Fig. 14)...............................................................13

12. From 261 to 382 ventrals, usually more than 270 (Figs. 83, 84)......................
.........................................................................*Micrurus narduccii*
From 219 to 270 ventrals.........................................*Micrurus karlschmidti*

13. Black body rings 30 or more ...............................................................14
Black body rings fewer than 30 ..........................................................15

14. Black body rings 68 or more; no rings on head; pattern usually bicolored (Figs. 74–76) ..........................................................*Micrurus margaritiferus*
Black body rings 36–60; pale supracephalic spots present; pattern bicolored or tricolored, including rings of yellow, brown, or black (one of these colors only) alternating with red rings and white spots (Fig. 64) ........*Micrurus langsdorffi*

15. Black body rings fewer than 16; pattern bicolored (Fig. 96) ..........................
................................................................*Micrurus putumayensis*
Black body rings 16 or more; pattern usually tricolored............................16

16. Body pattern occasionally bicolored; tail always *bicolored*; ventrals 178–211 (Fig. 91)..............................................................*Micrurus peruvianus*
Body pattern tricolored; tail *tricolored*; ventrals 210–236....*Micrurus mertensi*

17. Tail terminating in a rattle or button (Figs. 339, 340)...........*Crotalus durissus*
Tail not terminating in a rattle (Fig. 316).................................................18

18. Posterior subcaudals finely divided (Fig. 316); keels on middorsals conical (Fig. 249) ......................................................................*Lachesis muta*
Posterior subcaudals single or paired (Fig. 316); keels on middorsals not conical
..........................................................................................19

19. Subcaudals all or mostly single (Fig. 316) ..............................................20
Subcaudals all or mostly divided (Fig. 316)............................................21

20. Snout normal (Fig. 169); a row of cream spots along juncture of dorsals and ventrals; 203–254 ventrals (Figs. 158–162) ..................*Bothriopsis taeniata*
Snout upturned, forming a flaplike process (Fig. 306); no cream spots laterally; 124–141 ventrals (Fig. 273) .....................................*Porthidium hyoprora*

21. Dorsal color pattern usually with a considerable amount of green, with or without dark or pale markings ...........................................................22
Dorsal color pattern variable, but *not* including green..............................25

22. Midbody dorsal scale rows 23 or more ..................................................23
Midbody dorsal scale rows 19–21 (Figs. 147, 148).....*Bothriopsis albocarinata*

23. Dorsal pattern consists of pale green color with no crossbands, a distinct white or yellow ventrolateral line (Fig. 151).........................*Bothriopsis bilineata*
Dorsal pattern consists of green to grayish green color with crossbands .......24

24. Dorsal pattern includes 32–40 black crossbands; snout bluntly rounded (Figs. 153, 154, 167, 168)................................................*Bothriopsis oligolepis*
Dorsal pattern includes fewer than 20 *pale* crossbands; snout obtusely acuminate (Figs. 155, 156)..............................................*Bothriopsis peruviana*

25. Dorsum with irregular median blotches or spots, often forming a zig-zag pattern; restricted to arid regions on the west coast from the Departamento de La Libertad south to Arequipa................................................................26
Dorsum with lateral triangular or inverted C-shaped blotches, often arranged on either side so as to coalesce across the midline of the dorsum; or dorsum with irregular dark bands; north of the Departamento de La Libertad, if on the west coast.........................................................................................27

26. Ventrals 152–173; infralabials 9–13 (Figs. 238–240).............*Bothrops pictus*
Ventrals 179–185; infralabials 13 or 14 .........................*Bothrops roedingeri*

27. Prelacunal fused with second supralabial, forming a lacunolabial (Fig. 177)
..........................................................................................28
Prelacunal discrete from second supralabial (Figs. 229, 230) ........................
...............................................................*Bothrops microphthalmus*

28. Postocular stripe broad and well defined ..............................................29
Postocular stripe absent, narrow, or ill defined (Figs. 201–205) ....................
...........................................................................*Bothrops brazili*

29. Subcaudals 48 or more; high montane regions or east of the Andes............30
Subcaudals fewer than 48; west of the Andes in northern Peru (Fig. 200)

..............................................................................Bothrops barnetti

30. Fewer than 178 ventrals; each infralabial usually with distinct pale spot in center; highlands above 1,800 m in southern Peru (Figs. 182, 183)............... ...........................................................................*Bothrops andianus*

More than 178 ventrals (in Peruvian specimens); infralabials without distinctive pale markings; widespread in Amazon Basin up to about 1,200 m on the eastern versant of the Andes (Figs. 197–199) ........................*Bothrops atrox*

## BOLIVIA

Bolivia is an inland South American country encompassing 1,098,581 km². It is bordered on the north and east by Brazil, on the southeast by Paraguay, on the south by Argentina, on the southwest by Chile, and on the northwest by Peru.

Physiographically and geographically Bolivia is divisible into three broad regions: (1) the eastern lowlands, (2) the Valles region, and (3) the highland region. Owing in part to its diverse topography, this country possesses a great variety of climates and vegetation, ranging from tropical lowlands to alpine and arctic environments.

The eastern lowlands, often referred to as El Oriente, represent the most sparsely populated region in Bolivia and include about 60% of the country. This region includes not only the eastern part but also the northern part of the country and is composed of swamps, alluvial plains, and low rolling hills. The eastern lowlands may be subdivided into three subregions: 1. The northern rainforest subregion extends from Bolivia's northern border through the Departamento de Pando to the northern half of the Departamento del Beni. This subregion is part of the Amazon Basin and is covered with tropical rainforest that is subject to heavy precipitation with some rain falling during every month of the year; but rainfall is somewhat seasonal, with a wet season occurring from November to April and a relatively dry period extending from May to October. During the wet season much of the subregion is inundated, particularly in the north.

2. The humid Santa Cruz central subregion occupies the northern two-thirds of the Departamento de Santa Cruz and is transitional between the wet tropical rainforest to the north and the semiarid subregion to the south. This area is composed of gently rolling to flat terrain that is well drained and free from flooding. The vegetation consists of savannas or low thorny scrub interspersed with tropical riparian forests or forest islands.

3. The Chaco subregion extends from southeastern Bolivia into Argentina and Paraguay. This low, level region drains slowly to the east and has strongly contrasting seasons with alternating floods and droughts. During the wet season this subregion is one of the wettest, hottest places in South America, with swamps covering much of the land and temperatures frequently reaching 37–38°C. During the dry season, the area becomes parched and most of the vegetation desiccates. Extensive savannas dotted with isolated patches of forest that consist of mimosas, acacias, other deciduous trees, and palms characterize this subregion.

To the west of the eastern lowlands lies the Valles region, sometimes called the Montañas region. Topographically this is an extremely rugged area; it is composed of deep valleys and high mountain spurs. In general, most of the Valles region has a warm climate, but may have moderate variations in the monthly means of both temperature and rainfall. The northern part of this region, more specifically the valleys east of the Cordillera Real, is referred to as the Yungas and has a mild warm climate with an annual mean temperature of about 25°C. Rain occurs throughout the year east of the Cordillera Oriental, with mean annual averages varying from 800 to 1,300 mm, although precipitation may be much greater locally. Along the headwaters of some valleys a distinctly temperate climate prevails at elevations of 2,500–3,500 m, with occasional frosts in winter. Some of these valleys are subject to rainshadow conditions, whereas other are covered by dense cloud forest, called *ceja de la montaña*, down to an elevation of about 1,500 m. Cloud forest is prominent on the eastern slopes of the Cordillera Real.

The highland region, often referred to as the Puna, includes the western part of Bolivia. Most of this region lies at elevations of 3,300–4,500 m and it includes the Central Plateau of Bolivia. These highlands are composed of three subregions: (1) the Cordillera Occidental, (2) the Altiplano, and (3) the Cordillera Real. To the west of the Cordillera Occidental, the amount of precipitation is scant and occurs mostly during the summer. The amount of rainfall is clinal from north to south, with 500–600 mm in the north and even less to the south, where the terrain is bleak and barren. The region overall is characterized by a harsh, cold, and windy climate all year, although temperatures may be warm in some areas during the daytime. There is little seasonal fluctuation in temperature, but dramatic variations occur on a daily basis. Much of the region has a mean annual temperature around 10°C, but mountains rising from the Altiplano reach 6,400 m, and areas above 5,500 m are covered by perpetual snow. The plateau is primarily a grassland with a conspicuous bunch grass (*Stipa ichu*) that extends up to the snowline.

Most of the eastern lowlands and the Valles region are drained by major tributaries of the Amazon River system, the Río Beni, Río Mamoré, and Río San Miguel. The southern portion of the country is drained by tributaries of the Río de la Plata, including the Río Pilcomayo. The Central Plateau represents an extensive inland basin. In the north, Lake Titicaca is the most dominant element of this internal drainage system. This lake is located on the Bolivia-Peru border and is 175 km long and 75 km wide. Lake Titicaca is drained by the Río Desaguadero, which flows into Lake Poopó and in turn is connected to the

Salar (Saltmarsh) de Coipasa by the Río Lacajahuira. The southern portion of the system is independent from the rest and drains into the Salar de Uyuni.

Biologically, Bolivia is very poorly known, and the distributions of dangerously venomous snakes within this country are not well understood. A number of species have not been reported for Bolivia but may occur within its borders: *Micrurus langsdorffi* (Fig. 64; see Key to Venomous Snakes of Peru) in the northeast, *Bothriopsis peruviana* (Figs. 155, 156; see Key to Venomous Snakes of Peru) and *Bothrops andianus* (Figs. 182, 183; see Key to Venomous Snakes of Peru) in the northern Valles region, *Bothrops moojeni* (Fig. 232; see Key to Venomous Snakes of Paraguay) in the eastern lowland region, and *Bothrops pulcher* (Fig. 242; see Key to Venomous Snakes of Ecuador) in the northern rainforest.

The distributions of the species of dangerously venomous snakes in Bolivia by the physiographic regions and subregions outlined above are given in Table 22. Our interpretation of the distributions of venomous snakes as outlined in this table may be expected to change dramatically as this country becomes more thoroughly explored.

**Table 22**

Distributions by physiographic region of venomous snakes in Bolivia

| | *Eastern Lowland Region* | | | | *Highland Region* | | |
|---|---|---|---|---|---|---|---|
| | *Northern rainforest* | *Santa Cruz* | *Chaco* | *Valles Region* | *Cordillera Real* | *Altiplano* | *Cordillera Occidental* |
| *Micrurus annellatus* | | | | X | | | |
| *M. frontalis* | | X | | | | | |
| *M. frontifasciatus* | | | | X | | | |
| *M. hemprichii* | X | | | X | | | |
| *M. lemniscatus* | X | | | X | | | |
| *M. narduccii* | | | | X | | | |
| *M. spixii* | X | X | | | | | |
| *M. surinamensis*[1] | X | | | | | | |
| *M. tschudii* | | | | | | | X[2] |
| *Bothriopsis bilineata* | X | | | | | | |
| *B. oligolepis* | | | | X | X | | |
| *B. taeniata* | X | | | | | | |
| *Bothrops atrox* | X | | | | | | |
| *B. brazili* | X | X | | | | | |
| *B. jararacussu* | | X | | X[3] | | | |
| *B. microphthalmus* | X | | | | | | |
| *B. neuwiedi* | | X | X | X[4] | | | |
| *B. sanctaecrucis* | X | | | | | | |
| *Crotalus durissus* | | X | X | | | | |
| *Lachesis muta* | X | | | | | | |
| *Porthidium hyoprora* | X | | | | | | |

1. Aquatic habitat.
2. Not definitely confirmed from Bolivia.
3. Possibly occurs in extreme southern portion.
4. Known from the Departamento de Cochabamba.

## Key to Venomous Snakes of Bolivia

1. No loreal pit between eye and nostril; loreal scale absent (Fig. 100); scales on top of head enlarged into plates (Fig. 16); dorsal scales smooth; fangs permanently erect (Fig. 19); Elapidae ........................................ 2
   A loreal pit between eye and nostril (Fig. 162); loreal scale(s) present; scales on top of head small and numerous; dorsal scales keeled; fangs fold back (Fig. 253); Viperidae ........................................ 10
2. Black rings arranged in triads separated by red rings on body, sometimes visible only ventrally ........................................ 3
   Black rings not arranged in triads ........................................ 9
3. Anal plate not divided; 5–8 triads on body; 191 or fewer ventrals (Fig. 59) ........................................ *Micrurus hemprichii*
   Anal plate divided; number of triads on body variable; usually more than 190 ventrals ........................................ 4
4. First *complete* triad usually posterior to and not involving black ring on nape (Figs. 99–101) ........................................ *Micrurus spixii*
   Black ring on nape comprising anteriormost black ring of first *complete* triad ........................................ 5

5. Several supracephalic scales entirely black; frontal wider than supraocular (Fig. 16); supralabials 3 and 4 in contact with eye (Fig. 15) ..............................6
All supracephalic scales red, outlined in black; frontal not wider than supraocular (Fig. 18); only fourth supralabial in contact with eye (Figs. 17, 104)......... ..................................................................*Micrurus surinamensis*
6. Posterior temporals enlarged, reaching beyond the parietal tips (Fig. 51); ........................................................................*Micrurus frontalis*
Posterior temporals not enlarged, not reaching beyond the parietal tips.........7
7. Parietals red, including tips (Figs. 70, 71).....................*Micrurus lemniscatus*
Parietals not, or only partially, red; parietal tips black ...............................8
8. Body triads 8–11; more than 30 subcaudals (Fig. 55).................................. ..................................................................*Micrurus frontifasciatus*
Body triads 12–22; fewer than 30 subcaudals (Fig. 106).......*Micrurus tschudii*
9. Body pattern includes rings; a short pale ring crosses parietals; first pair of infralabials in contact with each other behind mental (Figs. 14, 24, 25) .......................................................................*Micrurus annellatus*
Body pattern usually lacks rings; a long pale ring includes parietals; first pair of infralabials not in contact with each other behind mental (Figs. 83, 84) .......................................................................*Micrurus narduccii*
10. Tail terminating in a rattle or button (Figs. 339, 340)...........*Crotalus durissus*
Tail not terminating in a rattle ...........................................................11
11. Posterior subcaudals finely divided (Fig. 316); keels on middorsals conical (Fig. 249) ........................................................................*Lachesis muta*
Posterior subcaudals single or paired (Fig. 316); keels on middorsals not conical .........................................................................................12
12. Subcaudals all or mostly single (Fig. 316) ..............................................13
Subcaudals all or mostly divided (Fig. 316)............................................14
13. Snout normal (Fig. 169); a row of cream spots along juncture of dorsals and ventrals; 203–254 ventrals (Figs. 158–162) ..................*Bothriopsis taeniata*
Snout upturned, forming a flaplike process (Fig. 306); no cream spots laterally; 124–141 ventrals (Fig. 273) .....................................*Porthidium hyoprora*
14. Dorsal color pattern usually includes a considerable amount of green, with or without dark markings ...................................................................15
Dorsal pattern variable, but does not include green .................................16
15. Dorsal pattern consisting of pale green color with no crossbands, a distinct white or yellow ventrolateral line; ventrals 192 or more (Fig. 151) ............... ..................................................................*Bothriopsis bilineata*
Dorsal pattern consisting of green to grayish green color with dark crossbands; ventrals fewer than 193 (Figs. 153, 154, 167, 168) ........*Bothriopsis oligolepis*
16. Prelacunal fused with second supralabial forming lacunolabial (Fig. 177)....18
Prelacunal discrete from supralabials, no lacunolabial (Fig. 171) ...............17
17. Dorsum of head usually unpatterned; ventrals usually 165 or fewer; supralabials usually 7; venter contains dark pigment; northern rainforest region (Figs. 229, 230)............................................................*Bothrops microphthalmus*
Distinct paired parietal or occipital markings usually present; ventrals 163 or more; supralabials 8 or 9, rarely 7; venter white or nearly so; not found in northern rainforest region (Fig. 233)..............................*Bothrops neuwiedi*
18. Postorbital stripe absent or, if present, narrow ........................................19
Postorbital stripe broad and well defined ...............................................20
19. Usually fewer than 180 ventrals; 10–12 infralabials; usually 6 or fewer intersupraoculars; robust in form (Figs. 201–205).......................*Bothrops brazili*
Usually more than 180 ventrals; 9 or 10 infralabials; 6–9 intersupraoculars; somewhat slender in form ....................................*Bothrops sanctaecrucis*
20. Usually 7 supralabials; venter with numerous dark markings forming paraventral spots; dorsal pattern variable, but usually somewhat muted; northern rainforest (Figs. 198, 199).................................................*Bothrops atrox*
Eight supralabials; venter mostly unmarked and paraventral spots not conspicuous; dorsal pattern variable, but usually prominent and contrasting; southern Valles region (Figs. 220, 221) ....................................*Bothrops jararacussu*

## PARAGUAY

Paraguay, an inland South American country, encompasses 406,752 km$^2$. It is bordered to the northwest by Bolivia, to the north and east by Brazil, and to the south and west by Argentina. The Río Paraguay divides the country into two parts: (1) The Chaco comprises 246,950 km$^2$ of flat, sparsely inhabited, seasonally flooded grassy plains, palm groves, and dry scrubby forest. The region is drained principally by the marshy Río Pilcomayo. (2) Eastern Paraguay extends over 159,800 km$^2$, is bordered by the Río Alto Paraná and Río Apa to the east and north. It is divided into two subregions: (a) a region of gently rolling hills extending from the Río Paraguay eastward to the edge of the Paraná Plateau (300–600 m in elevation)—a vast forested region rimmed by high cliffs on the west and bordered by the Río Paraguay and Río Alto Paraná; and (b) the flat plains south of the plateau (Ñeembucú and Misiones), which are treeless, covered with coarse grass, and seasonally inundated.

Most of Paraguay is interior lowland, and there are no mountains attaining any appreciable elevation. The greatest elevations are found in the northeast, where the Paraná Plateau is crossed by the Río Paraná. In this region the Serranía de Maracajú and the Montañas de Aracanguy crest at about 600 m. The Río Alto Paraná slices deeply into the volcanic matrix of the plateau, creating deep canyons and the spectacular falls of Iguazú and, prior to their inundation, Sete Quedas (Guaíra).

Vegetation zones in Paraguay coincide approximately with the major subregions outlined above. The Chaco is parkland of palm savannas, scrubby forest thickets, and isolated trees interspersed with grassland, with local patches of thorn bush and halophytic vegetation. East of the Río Paraguay the precipitation is heavier, but dense forest is basically restricted to river courses and to two ranges of rolling hills, one running from the cliffs of the Paraná Plateau west to the Río Paraguay north of Concepción, and the other an extension of the plateau forest reaching the Río Paraguay at the level of Asunción. The Paraná Plateau itself basically is covered with subtropical forest.

**Table 23**

Distributions by physiographic region of venomous snakes in Paraguay

| Species | Chaco | Eastern Paraguay: Río Paraguay plains | Eastern Paraguay: Paraná Plateau |
|---|---|---|---|
| *Micrurus corallinus* | | | X |
| *M. frontalis* | X | X | X |
| *Bothrops alternatus* | X[1] | X | X |
| *B. jararaca* | | | X[2] |
| *B. jararacussu* | | X | X |
| *B. moojeni* | X[3] | | X[3] |
| *B. neuwiedi* | X | X | X |
| *Crotalus durissus* | X | X | X |

1. In extreme northwestern Chaco.
2. Southeastern portion only.
3. Northeastern portion only.

Eastern Paraguay and the Paraná Plateau receive a greater amount of annual precipitation (1,500–2,000 mm) than elsewhere in the country, and rainfall is concentrated during the spring and summer (October to April). Daily temperatures range from 5 to 43°C in different parts of the country but average 16–22°C in the east. The period from April to June is mild with cold nights; July through September are the coldest months.

The distributions by physiographic region of the species of dangerously venomous snakes in Paraguay are listed in Table 23. Several additional species of dangerously venomous snakes may occur within the borders of Paraguay, but as yet are not definitely recorded from this country. These include *Micrurus lemniscatus* (Figs. 67–71; see Key to Venomous Snakes of Brazil), which may enter east-central Paraguay; *Bothrops cotiara* (Figs. 208, 209; see Key to Venomous Snakes of Brazil) in relictual *Araucaria* forest in eastern Paraguay; and *Bothrops itapetiningae* (Fig. 216; see Key to Venomous Snakes of Brazil), the range of which approaches the Paraguay border in the northeast.

### Key to Venomous Snakes of Paraguay

1. No loreal pit between eye and nostril; loreal scale absent (Fig. 100); scales on top of head enlarged into plates (Fig. 16); dorsal scales smooth; fangs permanently erect (Fig. 253); pattern consisting of black rings in combination with red and yellow or white; Elapidae .......... 2
   A loreal pit between eye and nostril (Fig. 203); loreal scale(s) present; scales on top of head small and numerous; dorsal scales keeled; fangs fold back (Fig. 253); pattern variable but never ringed; Viperidae .......... 3
2. Black rings on body arranged in triads, some visible only ventrally (Fig. 52) .......... *Micrurus frontalis*
   Pattern not composed of triads (Figs. 33, 34) .......... *Micrurus corallinus*
3. Tail terminating in rattle or button (Figs. 339, 340) .......... *Crotalus durissus*
   Tail not terminating in a rattle .......... 4
4. Prelacunal discrete from second supralabial, no lacunolabial present (Fig. 171) .......... 5
   Prelacunal fused with second supralabial forming a lacunolabial (Fig. 177) ... 6
5. Intersupraoculars 8–13; supraoculars long and narrow; dorsolateral blotches usually in contact with lateral blotches, the latter tending to be C-shaped and resembling a telephone receiver, with well-defined, pale cross-shaped centers;

a pale transverse band or spot on top of head between eyes; dorsals 28 or more; large, heavy bodied (Figs. 179, 180) ............................ *Bothrops alternatus*

Intersupraoculars 6–9; supraoculars relatively broad; dorsolateral blotches usually not in contact with lateral blotches, triangular in shape, pale centers absent or ill defined; head with small blotches, lacking pale transverse band between eyes; dorsals 21–27; medium sized, moderately slender (Figs. 233, 234) ........ ....................................................................... *Bothrops neuwiedi*

6. Supralabials usually 8 or more; postorbital stripe crosses portions of last 3 supralabials ........................................................................................ 7

   Supralabials 7; postorbital stripe crosses portions of last 2 supralabials (Figs. 231, 232) ................................................................ *Bothrops moojeni*

7. Elongated outer internasals in contact with each other medially; pale borders of dorsal blotches frequently unite to form a chainlike pattern; prominent pale border above postorbital stripe; ventrals 166–186; 4–8 intersupraoculars; size large; low-lying wet areas (Figs. 220, 221) .................... *Bothrops jararacussu*

   Elongated outer internasals separated from each other by 1 or more scales; pale borders of dorsal blotches, if present, do not form chainlike pattern; no prominent pale border above postorbital stripe; ventrals 181–195; 5–12 intersupraoculars; size moderate; southeastern Paraguay only, usually occupying higher ground (Figs. 217–219) ............................................... *Bothrops jararaca*

## URUGUAY

Uruguay encompasses 176,215 km² and is located in south-central South America on the Atlantic Coast. Uruguay is bordered on the north by Brazil and on the west and south by Argentina. On the south the broad estuary of the Río de la Plata separates Uruguay from Argentina.

The topography of Uruguay is fairly uniform with no high elevations. The only significant concentrations of hills are the Cuchilla de Haedo in the north-northwest and the Cuchilla Grande in east-central Uruguay. However, none of the upland peaks or ridges exceeds 600 m in elevation.

The western boundary with Argentina is delineated by the Río Uruguay, which forms an alluvial plain (in conjunction with the Río de la Plata) stretching from Fray Bentos southeast to Colonia Department. The rest of the country may be characterized as undulating, grassy slopes that are transitional between the two coastal plains and the low hills of the interior.

Forest is primarily confined to the river courses and a region at the juncture of the Río Negro (which divides the country into two parts) and the Río Uruguay. The entire region is temperate, with both deciduous and evergreen forests, the latter characterized by dense stands of *Araucaria* trees.

The climate in Uruguay is affected strongly by breezes from the Atlantic Ocean, and the entire region is humid and windy. During the winter season (June to September) mean monthly temperatures average 14–16°C, although daily lows occasionally fall to well below freezing. Snow is a rare phenomenon in this country. Mean monthly summer (December to March) temperatures are 22–26°C, but nights are cool; there are usually dry periods during this season. The greatest rainfall occurs during July and August, and precipitation varies from about 1,200 to 1,500 mm per year, with the higher amounts falling in the north.

*Micrurus corallinus* (see Key to Venomous Snakes of Argentina) has not been definitely recorded from Uruguay, but it has been cited by some authors as occurring in the extreme northwestern portion of the country. The distributions by physiographic region of other species of dangerously venomous snakes in Uruguay are given in Table 24.

**Table 24**

Distributions by physiographic region of venomous snakes in Uruguay

| | *Northern Uruguay (N. of Río Negro)* | | | *Southern Uruguay (S. of Río Negro)* | | | |
|---|---|---|---|---|---|---|---|
| *Species* | *Río Uruguay/ Río Quaraí Basin* | *Cuchillo de Haedo region* | *Río Negro Basin N.* | *Río Negro Basin S.* | *Cuchillo Grande region* | *Coastal plain* | *Lower Río Uruguay* |
| *Micrurus corallinus* | X[1] | | | | | | |
| *M. frontalis*[2] | X | X | X | | X | X | X |
| *Bothrops alternatus*[2] | X | | X | X | X | X[3] | X |
| *B. neuwiedi*[2] | | X | | | X[4] | X | |
| *Crotalus durissus* | | X | | | | X[5] | |

1. Of questionable occurrence in Uruguay.
2. Probably countrywide.
3. Records from Montevideo are not reflective of natural distribution.
4. South to Montevideo; another population in San José; favors rocky regions (such as the Sierra de Animas, Maldonado).
5. Scarce in Uruguay; known from Laguna Merín and the Montevideo region (Pan de Azúcar) in dry forest and open areas.

### Key to Venomous Snakes of Uruguay

1. No loreal pit between eye and nostril; loreal scale absent (Fig. 100); scales on top of head enlarged into plates (Fig. 16); dorsal scales smooth; fangs permanently erect (Fig. 19); pattern consisting of black rings in combination with red and yellow or white; Elapidae .......... 2
   A loreal pit between eye and nostril (Fig. 203); loreal scale(s) present; scales on top of head small and numerous; dorsal scales keeled; fangs fold back (Fig. 253); pattern variable, but never ringed; Viperidae .......... 3
2. Black rings arranged in triads on body, sometimes visible only ventrally (Fig. 52) .......... *Micrurus frontalis*
   Pattern not composed of triads; of questionable occurrence in Uruguay (Figs. 33, 34) .......... *Micrurus corallinus*
3. Tail terminating in rattle or button (Figs. 339, 340) .......... *Crotalus durissus*
   Tail not terminating in a rattle .......... 4
4. Supraoculars relatively narrow; dorsolateral blotches usually in contact with lateral blotches, the latter tending to be C-shaped and resembling a telephone receiver, with well-defined pale cross-shaped centers; a pale transverse band or spot on top of head between eyes; postorbital stripe broad, passing beneath eye; dorsals 24–37; large, heavy bodied (Figs. 179, 180) .......... *Bothrops alternatus*
   Supraoculars relatively broad; dorsolateral blotches usually not in contact with lateral blotches, trapezoidal in shape, pale centers absent or ill defined; head with small blotches, lacking transverse band between eyes; postorbital stripe moderate, not passing beneath eye; dorsals 21–29; medium sized, moderately slender (Fig. 236) .......... *Bothrops neuwiedi*

## ARGENTINA

Argentina is the second largest country in South America, with an area of 2,776,889 km$^2$. Argentina is bordered on the north by Bolivia, Paraguay, Brazil, and Uruguay, on the northeast by the estuary of the Río de la Plata, and on the east by 2,575 km of Atlantic Coast. The western and part of the southern boundaries are formed by Chile. The southernmost limit of Argentina is the Beagle Channel, which lies between Tierra del Fuego and Chile. Tierra del Fuego is separated from contiguous Argentina by the Estrecho de Magallanes (Straits of Magellan).

A land of broadly diverse topography and climate, Argentina can be broken into five physical regions: the Andes, the Chaco, the Littoral-Mesopotamia, the Pampas, and Patagonia.

The Andes occur as high cordilleras from Patagonia northward along the western frontier with Chile. In the northwest, from the crest of the mountains eastward to the Río Paraguay, there is the high xeric Altiplano that joins the Puna, heavily dissected by rivers flowing into the lowlands. The entire area comprises a strip about 400 km wide and includes all the northwest provinces as far south as Tucumán. The Altiplano and Puna average 3,350 m and 4,000 m in altitude, respectively, with isolated ranges in the Puna reaching elevations in excess of 5,800 m. The Puna is covered with scattered shrubs and has forest along its peripheral ranges and eastern face.

East of the Puna a series of north-south trending hilly ridges separate the Puna from the Chaco. The valleys between these hills are covered by scrub forest typical of the Chaco. This region ends at Tucumán, with parched salt flats and swamps surrounding the Sierras de Córdoba.

The Chaco is bordered on the east by the Rio Paraná and comprises the southern end of the Gran Chaco, which includes parts of Bolivia and Paraguay. The southern terminus of the Chaco in Argentina is the Río Dulce, which originates in the Sierra de Aconquija and is one of four major streams draining the region. The Pilcomayo, Bermejo, and Salado are the other three rivers, and all empty into the Río Paraná. The Río Pilcomayo forms the northern border of Argentina with Paraguay. The Río Dulce discharges into the Mar Chiquita, a vast lake in an internally drained basin.

The Argentine Chaco is a lowland swampy region formed by alluvium from the Andes and covered with grassy savanna and thorn scrub, the latter occurring as dense thickets or isolated patches. The entire region, especially to the east, is subject to summer inundation, when rainfall is greatest. In general, precipitation varies from an average of 510 mm in the west to more than 1,220 mm in the east. Summer temperatures are quite high, making the Chaco one of the hottest and, for humans, least hospitable regions on the continent. Evaporative rates are extremely high in some parts of the Chaco, creating xeric conditions.

The Mesopotamia region lies to the northeast between the Río Paraná and the Río Uruguay. The province of Misiones, in the extreme northeast, is a hilly region that is part of the Paraná Plateau. Its northern boundary is the Río Iguazú, which forms a high waterfall (the Saltos de Iguazú) at its confluence with the Río Paraná. The area is covered with pine, cedar, and deciduous trees forming a dense subtropical forest with heavy rainfall (more than 3,000 mm).

In the Littoral region the terrain is marshy with dense woodland and grassy hills interspersed. Precipitation

**Table 25**

Distributions by physiographic region of venomous snakes in Argentina

| *Species* | *Andean region* | *Chaco* | *Littoral-Mesopotamia* | *Pampas* | *Patagonia* |
|---|---|---|---|---|---|
| *Micrurus corallinus* | | X[1] | X | | |
| *M. frontalis* | | X | X | | |
| *Bothrops alternatus* | | X | X | X | |
| *B. ammodytoides* | X | | | X | X |
| *B. cotiara* | | | X[2] | | |
| *B. jararaca* | | | X | | |
| *B. jararacussu* | | | X[3] | | |
| *B. neuwiedi* | X | X | X | | |
| *Crotalus durissus* | X | X | X | X | |

1. Existence in this region not confirmed.
2. *Araucaria* forest in province of Misiones.
3. Low-lying areas along river courses in province of Misiones.

varies from 1,500 to 2,000 mm annually and is very unequally distributed; local droughts are not uncommon. It is a region of mild winters and hot summers.

The Pampas make up one-fifth of the land area of Argentina and chiefly consist of a huge expanse of flat plains that lies south of the Chaco, east of the Andes, west of the Mesopotamia region, and north of Patagonia. The eastern portion (Pampa Húmeda) receives more precipitation than the western portion (Pampa Seca); the range is from 400 to 1,020 mm. The only vertical relief is in the Sierras de Córdoba (1,400 m), the Sierras de Tandil (500 m), and the Sierra de la Ventana (1,200 m). There are some large sand dunes to the south and very few rivers. Primary among the rivers are the Salado (not of the Chaco) and the Carcarañá. Aside from some stands in the west, the only trees in the Pampas have been planted by humans. The winters are mild and the summers are hot, with both seasons varying in accordance with latitude. The growing season is 300 days in the north but only 145 days in the south.

With the exception of the Andes to the west, Patagonia comprises all of southern Argentina south of the Río Colorado and includes the territory of Tierra del Fuego. Like the Pampas, Patagonia is basically treeless except in the north and the Andean foothills. The Andes are lower in this region than they are in the north and are heavily glaciated. A series of lakes border the foot of the Andes from above 40°S latitude to below 50°S latitude in the Parque Nacional los Glaciares. Precipitation falls mostly during the winter, and amounts to only 200–250 mm. The climate is affected strongly by westerly winds that arise in the Atlantic Ocean and create a cloud of dust in the summer (or mud in the winter). Mean monthly temperatures in the summer range from 10°C at Tierra del Fuego to 15–24°C along the northern border. There is little variation in annual temperature extremes throughout the region; winter temperatures average above freezing even in Tierra del Fuego, although locally severe drops can occur anywhere in Patagonia.

In an area as large and diverse as Argentina, it is difficult to characterize the climate. In general, the country is subtropical in the north, temperate in the central zones, and sub-Antarctic at its southern tip. With some local variation, summer is roughly from December to March and winter from June to August.

Argentina does not have a diverse venomous snake fauna, and the herpetogeography of the country is relatively well known. Nevertheless, it is possible that *Bothrops moojeni* (Figs. 231, 232; see Key to Venomous Snakes of Brazil) might occur in extreme northern Misiones. The distributions by physiographic region of the species of dangerously venomous snakes known to inhabit Argentina are given in Table 25.

### Key to Venomous Snakes of Argentina

1. No loreal pit between eye and nostril; loreal scale absent (Fig. 100); scales on top of head enlarged into plates (Fig. 16); dorsal scales smooth; fangs permanently erect (Fig. 19); pattern consisting of black rings in combination with red and/or yellow or white; Elapidae .......... 2
   A loreal pit between eye and nostril (Fig. 203); loreal scale(s) present; scales on top of head small and numerous; dorsal scales keeled; fangs fold back (Fig. 253); pattern variable, but never ringed; Viperidae .......... 3
2. Black rings arranged in triads on body, sometimes visible only ventrally (Figs. 50–55) .......... *Micrurus frontalis*
   Pattern not composed of triads (Figs. 33, 34) .......... *Micrurus corallinus*
3. Tail terminating in a rattle or button (Figs. 339, 340) .......... *Crotalus durissus*
   Tail not terminating in a rattle .......... 4
4. Prelacunal fused with second supralabial, forming a lacunolabial (Fig. 177) .......... 8
   Prelacunal not fused with second supralabial, both of these scales discrete (Fig. 173) .......... 5

5. Snout normal (Fig. 171) ........................................................................6
Snout upturned (Figs. 173, 181) ............................*Bothrops ammodytoides*

6. Postorbital stripe broad, passing beneath eye; supraoculars relatively narrow (Fig. 172) ........................................................................7
Postorbital stripe moderate in extent, not passing beneath eye; supraoculars large and relatively broad (Fig. 234) ..............................*Bothrops neuwiedi*

7. Dorsolateral blotches usually in contact with lateral blotches, the latter tending to be C-shaped and resembling a telephone receiver, with well-defined pale cross-shaped centers; a pale transverse band or spot on top of head between eyes; dorsals 24–37, usually 29–35; intersupraoculars 8–13 (Figs. 179, 180) ........................................................................*Bothrops alternatus*
Dorsolateral blotches usually not in contact with lateral blotches, instead forming a series of irregular trapezoids; no pale transverse band or spot on top of head between eyes, although tan ground color forms a spearpoint on top of head; dorsals 25–29; intersupraoculars 11–14 (Figs. 208, 209) ........................................................................*Bothrops cotiara*

8. Elongated outer internasals in contact with each other medially; pale borders of dorsal blotches frequently unite to form chainlike pattern; prominent pale border above postorbital stripe; ventrals 166–186; intersupraoculars 4–8; size large; low-lying wet areas (Figs. 220, 221) ...................*Bothrops jararacussu*
Elongated outer internasals separated from each other by 1 or more smaller medial internasals; pale borders of dorsal blotches, if present, do not form chainlike pattern; no prominent pale border above postorbital stripe; ventrals 170–214; intersupraoculars 5–12; size moderate; widespread, but generally occupying higher ground (Figs. 217–219) ........................*Bothrops jararaca*

# Gila Monster and Beaded Lizard

## Genus *Heloderma* Wiegmann, 1829

As presently understood, the family Helodermatidae comprises four genera. Three of these include extinct species, and the fourth consists of two extant species, *Heloderma horridum*, the beaded lizard, and *H. suspectum*, the Gila monster, as well as an extinct form, *H. texanum*. The name *H. texanum* was applied in 1977 to fossils found in early Miocene deposits in Big Bend National Park in Texas. The ancestry of the family is believed to extend at least as far back as the Upper Cretaceous period in North America. Fragments of lizard skulls found in Wyoming deposits suggest that a lizard named *Paraderma* may have been an ancestor of the Gila monster and beaded lizard.

Members of the genus *Heloderma* are distributed from the southwestern United States (lower Colorado River drainage) southward along most of the Pacific slope of Mexico to southeastern Guatemala, crossing over into the Atlantic drainages in the Mexican state of Chiapas and in Guatemala (see individual species accounts and Maps 1 and 2 for more precise delimitation of ranges).

These are robust, large lizards, usually reaching total lengths of between 250 and 700 mm; *H. horridum* is occasionally even longer. The head is large, with a bluntly rounded snout, and the lower lips bulge conspicuously to the sides. Movable eyelids cover relatively small, somewhat protuberant eyes, and no parietal eye or foramen is in evidence. The tail is usually thick, especially in *H. suspectum*, but it may be slender in emaciated individuals. The tail does not break readily as in many other lizard species, and the stump apparently does not regenerate if the tail is detached. The length of the fourth toe scarcely exceeds that of the third, and all of the digits possess strong, recurved claws.

The tongue is thick but distally bifid. As an individual ambles along, it frequently protrudes its tongue and sometimes the paired tips touch the substrate. The tongue, in conjunction with the Jacobson's organ in the roof of the mouth, is important in chemoreception. The teeth are long and recurved, and may be grooved on both the anterior and posterior surfaces; if present on both surfaces, grooves tend to be more strongly developed anteriorly. The largest and most deeply grooved teeth are found on the dentary bone in the lower jaw, which bears 8–10 teeth, numbers 4–7 being the longest. However, some of the 6–9 maxillary teeth are also grooved, despite the fact that the venom glands, which are modified inferior labial glands, are confined to the lower jaw. Each gland (one on each side) is multilobed, with a separate duct leading from each lobe to an orifice that discharges close to the base of a dentary tooth. At the time of discharge, venom flows, in part, along the grooved surfaces of a tooth by means of capillary action.

The scales are nonimbricate, and those covering the dorsum of the head, body, and tail, and much of the gular region and limbs are rounded and convex. Scales on the top of the head, the back and sides of the body and tail, the limbs, and the ventral surface of the preanal region are underlain by small bony elements called osteoderms; usually there is a one-to-one correspondence between scales and osteoderms in these regions. The venter is covered with rows of rectangular scales. (See Table 26 for other details of scutellation.)

The color pattern consists of a dark brown to black reticulum or ground color, usually with some combination of yellow, pink, or orange dots, spots, bars, bands, rings, or blotches (see individual species accounts).

These lizards are most active during the cooler periods of the day—at dusk, after dark, or during the late afternoon—and on overcast days. They normally move somewhat slowly but can twist and turn quickly.

A case of envenomation by *H. horridum* resulted in swelling and extremely severe pain locally. The pain was not relieved by a large dose of meperidine (150 mg

**Table 26**
Variation of selected scale characteristics in members of the genus *Heloderma*

| *Scale characteristic* | *H. horridum* | *H. suspectum* |
|---|---|---|
| Postrostrals | 2 (sometimes 1, rarely 3 or 4) | 2 (sometimes 3) |
| Internasals | 2 (rarely 3) | 2 (sometimes 3) |
| Canthals | 3 (infrequently 2, rarely 4) | 3 (rarely 1, 2, or 4) |
| Superciliaries | 3 (rarely 1, 2, or 4) | 3 (sometimes 4, rarely 5) |
| Dorsals between posterior superciliaries | 6–9 (usually 7 or 8) | 6–8 |
| Scales between internasals and occiput | 7–12 | 11–15 (usually 12 or 13) |
| Loreals | 2 (sometimes 1 or 3) | 2–4 (rarely 5) |
| Lorilabials | 4–7 | 4–9 |
| Preoculars | 2 (sometimes 1) | 2 (sometimes 1, rarely 3) |
| Supralabials | 10–13 (mode 11) | 10–14 (mode 12) |
| Infralabials | 11–15 (mode 13) | 12–16 (mode 14) |
| Pairs of chinshields along mental groove | 3 (sometimes 2) | 3 (sometimes 4) |
| Scales around midbody | 49–60 | 56–62 |
| Scales between gular fold and vent | 59–73 | 62–72 |
| Scales between axilla and groin | 45–57 | 48–59 |
| Scales around proximal portion of tail | 24–35 | 26–31 |
| Scales from vent to tip of tail | 73–87 | 48–62 |
| Subdigital lamellae on fourth toe | 11–15 (mode 13) | 8–14 (mode 11) |

*Source:* Adapted, in part, from Bogert and Martín del Campo, 1956.
*Note.* For additional information refer to individual species accounts.

IV). The victim was nauseated and vomited, but his vital signs remained stable and he recovered without event. Bites by *H. suspectum* have produced similar effects.

Unless molested, these lizards are inoffensive to humans. They are protected by law throughout their ranges (United States, Mexico, and Guatemala) and should be left alone.

### *Heloderma horridum* (Wiegmann)

(Figs. 3–8; Map 1)

LOCAL NAMES Guatemala: escorpión. Mexico: escorpión; heloderma negro, lagarto enchaquirado (Chiapas); talachini, tole-chini, (Zapotec Indians of Oaxaca); galwemma (Chontal Indians of Oaxaca); ciyx, siy (Cora Indians of Nayarit); acaltetepon, caltetepon, temacuilcahuya (Indian names in west-central Mexico); guchachigishe (Tehuantepec); silafica.

ENGLISH NAME Beaded lizard.

DISTRIBUTION Mexico and Guatemala. *Heloderma horridum* occurs in low and moderate elevations of the Pacific foothills of Mexico from southern Sonora to Chiapas, and along Pacific drainages in southeastern Guatemala in the Departamento de Santa Rosa. A hiatus in distribution apparently occurs in southeastern Chiapas and southwestern Guatemala. *Heloderma horridum* inhabits two Atlantic drainages: the Río Grijalva Valley through central Chiapas into extreme western Guatemala (the Río Lagartero Depression), and the Río Motagua Valley of eastern Guatemala from about El Rancho to Gualán. The distribution of this species appears to be continuous from the foothills of southern Oaxaca through the Río Grijalva Valley; we have taken several *H. horridum* from near the crest of the Continental Divide near Rizo de Oro, Chiapas (UTA R-5715; Fig. 4). The population in the Río Motagua Valley is isolated from that of the Río Lagartero Depression by some 230 km of mountainous terrain; however, the distribution of this species appears to be continuous between the Río Motagua Valley and the dry foothills of southeastern Guatemala whose drainages flow to the Pacific Ocean (Map 1). The vertical distribution is from about sea level to about 1,500 m.

HABITAT This species is most widely distributed in tropical deciduous forest, but also occurs in thorn forest and tropical scrub, and enters the lower portion of pine-oak forest. The middle Río Motagua Valley is quite arid with desertlike vegetation.

DESCRIPTION This is a large, stout lizard that usually reaches a maximum adult size of no more than 700 mm, but rarely may approach 1 m in total length.

The second supralabial is usually separated from the nasal and prenasal by a lorilabial, and the supranasal is almost always separated from the postnasal by the first canthal, except in specimens from the northern periphery of the range. In the northern part of the range, the mental possesses distinct lateral indentations, which become inconspicuous in the south. The mental in specimens from the Río Grijalva Valley is wedge shaped. For other features of scutellation see the generic account and Table 26.

The color pattern is highly variable within and among populations, and is subject to distinct ontogenetic changes. Members of populations in the northern part of the range tend to become paler with age, whereas specimens from the Río Grijalva Valley in the south tend to have the pale pattern obscured with dark pigment. In juveniles the pattern consists of a ground color that is black or dark brown with spots and bars of yellow. The head and neck, including the infralabials and gular area, are dark. The limbs are mostly dark, but sometimes may have pale blotches. The tail is distinctly ringed or

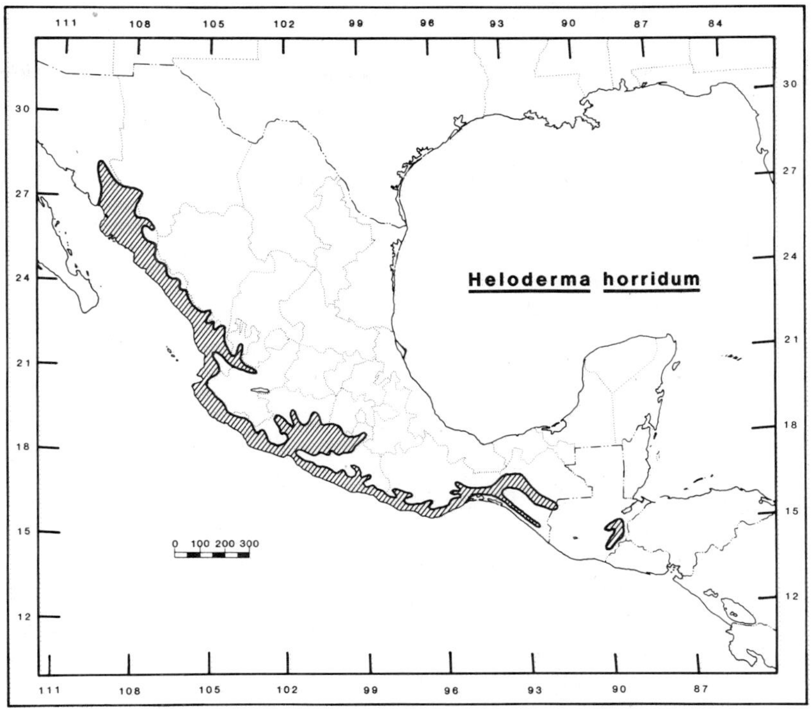


**Map 1.** Distribution of *Heloderma horridum* in Mexico and Guatemala. This species occurs in valleys of the Atlantic watershed only in the southern portion of its range (the Río Grijalva and Río Motagua systems).

banded with alternating dark and yellow bands; there are 5–7 dark bands.

In the Río Grijalva drainage of central Chiapas and western Guatemala, adults are mostly dark brown or slate gray; pale markings, if present at all, are much reduced and dingy. However, juveniles of this population closely resemble juveniles from elsewhere and possess a contrasting pattern of yellow and dark pigment. Throughout most of the rest of the range, adults are mostly dark brown, but with distinct yellow markings. In some individuals, the pattern is somewhat reticulate with an irregular network of dark scales enclosing the pale markings. In southern Sonora and northern Sinaloa, the extent of the pale coloration often exceeds that of the dark, and the pale coloration may be slightly pink. In adults, the number of dark rings on the tail varies somewhat clinally from none in specimens from central Chiapas, which have a uniformly dark tail, to more than 20 in specimens occurring near the northern terminus of the range. In populations along most of the west coast of Mexico, the pale tail rings of juveniles become bisected by dark pigment, resulting in adults with 5–7 pairs of pale rings on a tail that is mostly dark.

SIMILAR SPECIES *Heloderma horridum* appears to be sympatric with *H. suspectum* in southern Sonora and northern Sinaloa, although to our knowledge the two species have yet to be taken from the same hillside, and there may be subtle habitat differences that preclude their coexistence. These two species are most easily distinguished from one another by relative tail length. In *H. horridum* the tail comprises at least 65% of the snout-vent length, and there are 73–87 scales along the ventral midline from the vent to the tip of the tail; in *H. suspectum* the tail comprises no more than 55% of the body length, and there are 48–62 scales from the vent to the tip of the tail. *Heloderma horridum* has no enlarged preanal scales (except for some specimens from the Río Motagua Valley of Guatemala), and the first two pairs of infralabials are usually in contact with the anterior pair of chinshields. *Heloderma suspectum* has several (usually 2) conspicuously enlarged preanal scales, and usually only the first pair of infralabials reaches the anteriormost chinshields.

Many nonvenomous species of lizards that may appear dangerous to the inexperienced observer are totally harmless, except that they may be capable of biting with some resolve if handled improperly. In members of the family Iguanidae, the top of the head is covered with scales considerably larger than those on the neck and body, and a parietal eye is usually evident. Many genera of the larger iguanids (*Ctenosaura*, *Enyaliosaurus*, *Iguana*) have a conspicuously enlarged row of scales or spines down the middorsum. Members of the family Xenosauridae have a fourth toe on the hindfoot that is about three times longer than the fifth (toes subequal in *Heloderma*), dorsal scales consisting of large tubercles surrounded by granular scales, and no enlarged chinshields. Members of the family Anguidae either have perfectly smooth cycloid scales (*Celestus*) or a granular ventrolateral fold along the sides of the body (*Abronia*, *Barisia*, *Gerrhonotus*). *Lepidophyma flavimaculatum*, in the family Xantusiidae, has a slender tail, lacks movable eyelids, and has enlarged dorsal tubercles surrounded by small granular scales.

REMARKS Four subspecies of *H. horridum* have been described: *H. h. alvarezi* (Figs. 5, 6) from the Río Grijalva Depression of central Chiapas and extreme western Guatemala, *H. h. charlesbogerti* (Fig. 8) from the Río Motagua Valley and adjacent foothills of eastern Guatemala, *H. h. exasperatum* (Fig. 7) from southern Sonora and northern Sinaloa, and *H. h. horridum* (Figs.

3, 4) from the remainder of the species' range along the Pacific drainages of Mexico.

Although generally mild in disposition, *H. horridum* should be treated with respect. When aroused, these lizards may move with surprising agility, biting and retaining their grip with bulldog tenacity. Bites are reported to be extremely painful and are potentially life-threatening.

*Heloderma horridum* may be active by day or at night; however, usually it appears to retreat to a hiding place during the hotter time of the day. We have encountered four specimens by day in Jalisco and Colima; in three instances, individuals were found during the late morning as they lay at or near the entrance of a burrow that descended beneath a large rock. During the early rainy season in Oaxaca and Chiapas we have found *H. horridum* up to 5 m above the ground in trees. When we were traversing the Río Grijalva Valley by vehicle during the late 1960s and early 1970s, this species almost predictably could be found lumbering across the Pan American Highway (Mex. Hwy. No. 190) in the late afternoon after a heavy summer shower. Such is no longer the case, and this lizard has now become much more scarce owing to massive habitat destruction.

REFERENCES Albritton et al., 1970; Alvarez del Toro, 1983; Arrington, 1930; Baird, 1859, 1875; Beddard, 1907; Bellairs, 1969; Bocourt, 1875, 1876, 1878; Bogert, 1956, 1959; Bogert and Martín del Campo, 1956; Bogert and Oliver, 1945; Boulenger, 1885, 1891; Burt and Myers, 1942; Camarillo Rangel et al., 1985; Cameron, 1898; Camp, 1923; Campbell and Vannini, 1988; Cendrero et al., 1972; Cope, 1869, 1870, 1887, 1900; Croulet, 1963; Cuesta Terron, 1930b; Davis and Dixon, 1961; Ditmars, 1928a; Duellman, 1954, 1958, 1961, 1965b; Dugès, 1869, 1878, 1891, 1896, 1897, 1899a, 1899b, 1901; Dunn, 1951; Fugler and Dixon, 1961; Gadow, 1905; Garman, 1884b; Gray, 1845; Greene, 1972; Günther, 1885–1902; Hallowell, 1854b; Hardy and McDiarmid, 1969; Hartweg and Oliver, 1940; Hoffstetter, 1962; C. F. Kauffeld, 1943; Kaup, 1865; Loeb et al., 1913; Malkin, 1956, 1958; Martín del Campo, 1935, 1979; McDiarmid, 1963; Mebs, 1968; Mertens, 1963; F. Müller, 1882; Odermatt, 1940; Oliver, 1937; Ottley, 1981a; J. A. Peters, 1954; Pregill et al., 1986; Reyes, 1889; Russell and Bogert, 1981; Schmidt and Shannon, 1947; Shaw, 1964b; H. M. Smith, 1935, 1939, 1946b, 1970; H. M. Smith and Grant, 1958; H. M. Smith and Langebartel, 1949; H. M. Smith and Taylor, 1950a, 1966; H. M. Smith and Van Gelder, 1955; Stuart, 1963, 1964, 1966; Sumichrast, 1864a, 1864b, 1870, 1873, 1875, 1880, 1881–1882, 1882; E. H. Taylor, 1938b; Tinkham, 1971a, 1971b; Troschel, 1853, 1860; Trutnau, 1970; Webb, 1984; Wiegmann, 1834; Zweifel and Norris, 1955.

### *Heloderma suspectum* Cope

(Figs. 9, 10; Map 2)

LOCAL NAME Escorpión.

ENGLISH NAME Gila monster.

DISTRIBUTION The United States and Mexico. In the United States, this species occurs from extreme southwestern Utah, southern Nevada, and eastern San Bernardino County, California, southward through western, central, and southern Arizona to southwestern New Mexico; in Mexico, it occurs throughout most of Sonora, exclusive of the northwestern coastal region and the mountains in the eastern portion of the state, to about the Río del Fuerte in northern Sinaloa (Map 2). A single specimen (AMNH 90786) is known from El Dorado in west-central Sinaloa. This site is about 280 km to the south of the closest locality to the north, and it is unlikely that the range of this species is continuous through northern Sinaloa. However, this specimen suggests that small relictual populations may occur as far south as central Sinaloa. The vertical distribution is from near sea level to about 1,500 m.

HABITAT This species is most widely distributed in desert and mesquite-grassland, but also occurs in pine-oak forest, tropical deciduous forest, and thorn forest. It is usually found in rocky foothill regions and avoids open flats.

DESCRIPTION *Heloderma suspectum* usually attains an adult size of 250–350 mm, but occasionally exceeds 500 mm in overall length. The largest specimens tend to come from the eastern portion of the range.

The rostral is variable in shape, may possess irregular sutures, or may be divided into 3 scales. The anteriormost canthal extends forward to intervene between the supranasal and postnasal. The lorilabials are often in a single row, but some scales are sometimes split horizontally, producing 2 rows. The second supralabial is usually in contact with the nasal; infrequently these two scales are separated from one another by the anteriormost lorilabial. The mental is small and subtrapezoidal, and its blunt apex may slightly separate the first pair of chinshields along the midline. For other features of scutellation see the generic account and Table 26.

Pattern and coloration are subject to ontogenetic, geographic, and individual variation. Juveniles have a pattern consisting of 5 black saddles or crossbands (1 on the neck, and 4 posterior to the axilla and anterior to the insertion of the hindlimbs). The interiors of these dark saddles have 4–9 pale spots arranged in a single vertical series. The pale pigment of juveniles is usually yellow or pale orange. In juveniles the tip of the snout, the top of the head to a level about equal with the posterior margins of the eyes, the side of the head, the venter of the head including the gular region, and most of the limbs, are black. The tail in juvenile specimens has 4–5 rings. As an individual ages, there is a considerable alteration in pattern, with some areas that were previously dark becoming pale and others that were pale becoming melanic. This causes the pattern to become more reticulate. The pale pigment of adults is most frequently pink, but may be also orange or, rarely, yellow.

The pattern may show some consistency with regard to geographic region. For example, lizards from northeastern Sonora tend to have a broad, black reticulated pattern with relatively few pale scales, whereas specimens from southwestern Pima County, Arizona, and perhaps from contiguous northwestern Sonora, tend to retain most of the black coloration of juveniles, including the black limbs. Overall, these specimens appear to have an irregular pale pattern of spots and blotches on a black background and are some of the darkest specimens known.

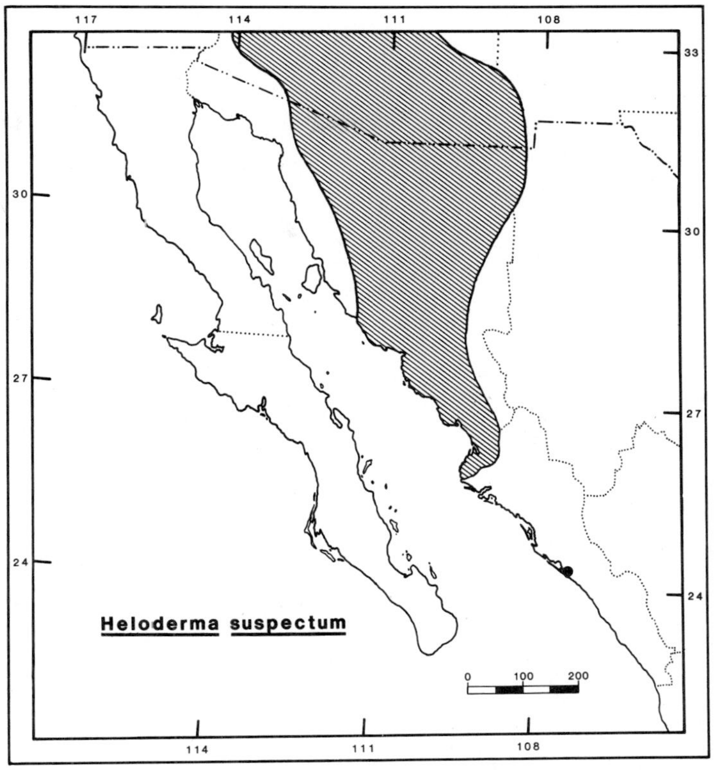


**Map 2.** Distribution of *Heloderma suspectum* in northwestern Mexico and the adjacent United States. The dot represents an isolated record for El Dorado, Sinaloa.

SIMILAR SPECIES The only venomous lizard other than *H. suspectum* occurring in Mexico is *H. horridum*, in which the tail length is at least 65% of the snout-vent length (the tail is less than 55% of the body length in *H. suspectum*). This proportion is reflected in the number of scales found along the longitudinal midline from the vent to the tip of the tail: 74–87 in *H. horridum*, and 48–62 in *H. suspectum*. In *H. suspectum* there are several (usually 2) conspicuously enlarged preanal scales (none are present in *H. horridum* throughout the northern part of its range), and usually only the first pair of infralabials reaches the anteriormost chinshields (first two pairs in *H. horridum*). For distinguishing characteristics of other lizard families that potentially may be confused with *Heloderma*, see Similar Species in the species account of *H. horridum*.

REMARKS Of the two subspecies of *H. suspectum* recognized, only one, *H. s. suspectum* (Figs. 6, 7), is found within the geographic limits of this work.

*Heloderma suspectum* sometimes appears deceptively sluggish and tame. Although these lizards are not aggressive toward humans, they nevertheless should be treated with respect. If molested, an individual can turn quickly to bite, and a bite from this species, although rarely fatal to humans, is by all accounts extremely painful and may result in severe lacerations. It should be noted that this species is protected throughout its range and should never be purposely killed.

Members of this species are capable of climbing and we have found specimens at considerable heights (5–7 m) in trees, although the species is primarily terrestrial. Whether *H. suspectum* is sympatric in the southern portion of its range with *H. horridum* has been a matter of some speculation. Certainly, if the two species are not sympatric, they are closely parapatric in portions of southern Sonora and northern Sinaloa.

REFERENCES M. J. Allen, 1933; Anonymous, 1870; Arrington, 1930; Baird, 1859; Bogert, 1956, 1959; Bogert and Martín del Campo, 1956; Bogert and Oliver, 1945; Boulenger, 1885, 1891; Cameron, 1898; Camp, 1923; Cendrero et al., 1972; Cochran, 1943; Cope, 1869, 1896, 1900; Coues, 1875; Cowles and Bogert, 1936; Cross and Rand, 1979; Cuesta Terron, 1930b; Dice, 1939; Ditmars, 1928a; Dixon and Medica, 1965; Funk, 1966; Gadow, 1905; Garman, 1884b, 1891; Gates, 1956b, 1957; Gehlbach, 1956; Gloyd, 1937; Günther, 1885–1902; Hahn and May, 1972; Hallowell, 1854b; Hardy and McDiarmid, 1969; Hensley, 1949; Koster, 1951; Linsdale, 1940; Lowe, 1955, 1964; Lowe et al., 1986; Malkin, 1956, 1962; Martín del Campo, 1935; Mertens, 1963; Minton and Minton, 1980; Odermatt, 1940; Ortenburger and Ortenburger, 1927; Ottley, 1981b; Pregill et al., 1986; Russell and Bogert, 1981; Ruthven, 1907; Shannon, 1953; Shaw, 1964b; H. M. Smith, 1946b; H. M. Smith and Taylor 1950a, 1950b, 1966; P. W. Smith and Hensley, 1958; Stebbins, 1985; Stejneger, 1893; Storer, 1931; E. H. Taylor, 1938a; Tinkham, 1971a, 1971b; Van Denburgh, 1922a, 1924; Woodbury, 1931.

# Coral Snakes

## Genus *Micrurus* Wagler, 1824

Currently the genus *Micrurus* (family Elapidae) is thought to contain 53 species. Member species are distributed from the southeastern United States through Mexico, Central America, and most of South America to central Argentina, and they occur in a variety of habitats, ranging from desert to cloud forest. Diminutive species may total less than 700 mm in length, whereas other species may exceed an impressive 1.5 m.

Many features of lepidosis are remarkably consistent within the genus. There is a typical complement of 9 large supracephalic head scales that includes 2 internasals, 2 prefrontals, 2 supraoculars, 1 frontal, and 2 parietals. Generally there are 1 preocular, 2 postoculars, 7 supralabials, 7 infralabials, and 15 smooth dorsal scale rows throughout the body; a few species have 17 dorsal scale rows anteriorly. Most coral snakes have 1 + 1 or 1 + 2 temporals; combinations of 0 + 1 (*M. collaris, M. decoratus, M. mipartitus, M. peruvianus, M. psyches*) are less frequently found. *Micrurus surinamensis*, the species with the most variable combinations of temporals, may have 1 + 3 or 2 + 2. The loreal is absent in all species. With the exception of *M. collaris, M. karlschmidti*, and *M. narduccii*, the first pair of chinshields is not in contact with the mental, being separated from it by the first pair of infralabials. Two pairs of chinshields are present and the medial suture between the first pair of infralabials is considerably shorter than that between the first pair of chinshields. The number of ventrals and subcaudals varies from 159 to 333 and from 12 to 62, respectively. Typically, the anal plate is divided in all species except *M. hemprichii*; rarely, an anomalous individual of another species will show this condition. Adult males of some species possess supra-anal keels (sometimes called tubercles), which are rarely present in adult females. The subcaudals most frequently tend to be divided (paired), but some specimens have many undivided subcaudals. The eyes are relatively small with subcircular pupils. The third and fourth supralabials are in contact with the eye in all species except *M. surinamensis*, in which usually only the fourth supralabial makes narrow contact. For the variations in selected characters in the members of the genus *Micrurus* see Table 27.

Most species possess a color pattern of some combination of red, yellow, and black rings. Usually a pale parietal or nuchal ring is followed by a *black* ring. The most common color pattern in coral snakes is represented by body rings in a red-yellow-black-yellow-red sequence. Many South American species, and a few in Central America and Mexico, have black rings disposed in triads, resulting in body rings in a red-black-yellow-black-yellow-black-red sequence. Other rarer color patterns include alternating rings of black and red (pink), black and white (yellow), yellow and red, brown and red, a red dorsum with a series of black crossbands or oval blotches, a dark dorsum with white flecks disposed in rings, and a black dorsum with incomplete pink to orange rings encroaching ventrally. In some individuals or species the yellow rings may be white or cream colored.

The maxillae of coral snakes are short, extending posteriorly to only about the level of the suture between supralabials 4 and 5. Each maxilla normally bears two fangs (one functional, one nonfunctional) that are situated at about the level of the suture between supralabials 2 and 3.

Preliminary examination of selected species suggests that coral snakes may be divided into two distinctive groups on the basis of hemipenial characteristics. One group, which includes *M. fulvius, M. browni*, and *M. nigrocinctus*, closely resembles the condition present in *Micruroides*. This group possesses long, slender, strongly bifurcate organs that extend from 8 to 15 subcaudals. The length of the lobes is equal to about one-half that of the base. A deep naked furrow extends parallel to the sulcus spermaticus from the base of the organ to the base of a lobe. This furrow is situated dorsomedially when the organ is inverted. In these species the sulcus spermaticus bifurcates at the level of the 5th to 10th subcaudal and extends to the apices. Each lobe is tapered (strongly attenuated in *M. browni*), and spinulate awns that terminate in a papilla are present in *M. fulvius*. Proximally the organ possesses tiny spines (naked on the asulcate side in some species) that gradually increase in size distally. The proximal halves of the lobes bear long slender spines that diminish in size toward the apices. The crotch and the areas flanking each branch of the sulcus on the proximal portion of each lobe are naked.

The other group of coral snakes, which includes *M. spixii* and *M. isozonus*, has short rotund hemipenes that extend about 5 subcaudals. The lobes are correspondingly short and account for one-fourth to one-third the length of the base. A deep naked furrow, so conspicuous in the aforementioned group, is absent. The sulcus spermaticus is bifurcated and extends to the apices. All but the proximal portion of the base of the organ, which has tiny spinules, is covered by moderate-sized, subequal spines.

**Table 27**
Variation of selected features in members of the genus *Micrurus*

| *Species* | *Color and pattern* | *Temporals* | *Ventrals* | *Subcaudals* | *Supra-anal keels in males** | *Maximum known size (mm)* |
|---|---|---|---|---|---|---|
| *M. alleni* | Tricolored, without triads; black, yellow (white), and red rings; 13–26 black body rings; red rings may be melanic dorsally | 1 + 1 | 214–237 | 47–59 | Present | 1,068 |
| *M. ancoralis* | Tricolored, with black rings forming 12–24 triads on body | 1 + 1 or, rarely, 1 + 2 | 248–290 | 30–37 | — | 1,510 |
| *M. annellatus* | Bicolored, with 17–83 black rings alternating with either red (orange) or white rings; or tricolored with yellow rings that are short dorsally | 1 + 1 or, rarely, 1 + 2 | 193–225 | 26–48 | Absent | 730 |
| *M. averyi* | Tricolored, without triads; lacks a black nuchal ring; black, yellow (white), and red rings; 8–13 black body rings | 1 + 1 or 1 + 2 | 190–220 | 28–48 | Absent | 715 |
| *M. bernadi* | Red ground color with 24–42 black dorsal spots | 1 + 1 | 203–228 | 37–48 | Absent | 826 |
| *M. bocourti* | Tricolored, with black rings forming 4⅔–14⅔ triads on body; tail bicolored yellow and black | 1 + 1 | 194–223 | 32–50 | Absent | 283 |
| *M. bogerti* | Tricolored, without triads; black, yellow, and red rings; 16–19 black body rings | 1 + 1 | 213–224 | 41–56 | Absent | 350 |
| *M. browni* | Tricolored, without triads; black, yellow, and red rings; 10–30 black body rings | 1 + 1 or 1 + 2 | 204–238 | 34–59 | Present | ca. 1,000 |
| *M. clarki* | Tricolored, without triads; black, yellow, and red rings; 13–20 black body rings | 1 + 1 | 192–208 | 35–58 | Absent | ca. 700 |
| *M. collaris* | Black or dark brown dorsal ground color; venter dark brown to black with up to 50 oval white, yellow, or orange-red blotches | 0 + 1 or, rarely, 1 + 1 | 212–250 | 12–30 | — | 600 |
| *M. corallinus* | Tricolored, without triads; black, white, and yellow rings; 13–27 black body rings; tail bicolored white and black | 1 + 1 | 194–231 | 24–51 | Absent | 950 |
| *M. decoratus* | Tricolored, with black rings forming 12–19 triads on body | 0 + 1 or, rarely, 1 + 1 | 196–226 | 16–37 | — | 670 |
| *M. diastema* | Tricolored, with black, yellow, and red rings; or bicolored with black and red rings; or with mostly red dorsum; 0–62 black body rings | 1 + 1 or 1 + 2 | 188–228 | 28–62 | Absent | ca. 850 |
| *M. dissoleucus* | Tricolored, with black rings forming 6⅓–11⅓ triads on body | 1 + 1 | 171–230 | 17–28 | — | 650 |
| *M. distans* | Tricolored, without triads; black, yellow, and red rings; 6–20 black body rings | 1 + 1 | 197–235 | 38–55 | Absent | 1,000+ |
| *M. dumerilii* | Tricolored, with or without triads; up to 14 triads, or 10–27 black rings on body | 1 + 1 | 170–217 | 31–58 | Present | 775 |
| *M. elegans* | Tricolored, with black rings forming 14–19 triads; black, white (broken), and orange rings | 1 + 1 | 188–228 | 29–49 | Present | 1,000+ |
| *M. ephippifer* | Tricolored, without triads; black, yellow, and red rings; red rings often melanic dorsally; 13–26 black body rings | 1 + 1 or 1 + 2 | 210–237 | 30–56 | Absent | 900+ |

**Table 27—*continued***

| Species | Color and pattern | Temporals | Ventrals | Subcaudals | Supra-anal keels in males* | Maximum known size (mm) |
|---|---|---|---|---|---|---|
| *M. filiformis* | Tricolored, with black rings forming 11–20 triads on body | 1 + 1 | 262–333 | 30–45 | Absent | 960+ |
| *M. frontalis* | Tricolored, with black rings forming 5–19 triads on body | 1 + 1 | 194–244 | 15–32 | — | 1,350 |
| *M. frontifasciatus* | Tricolored, with black rings forming 8–11 triads on body | 1 + 1 | 222 | 31 | — | 1,040 |
| *M. fulvius* | Tricolored, without triads; black, yellow, and red rings; 13–25 black body rings | 1 + 1 | 182–232 | 26–55 | Absent | 1,213 |
| *M. hemprichii* | Tricolored, with black rings forming 5–10 triads on body | 1 + 1 | 156–191 | 22–34 | Absent | 900 |
| *M. hippocrepis* | Tricolored, without triads; black, yellow, and red rings; 10–24 black body rings, often incomplete dorsally or ventrally | 1 + 1 or 1 + 2 | 199–226 | 37–57 | Absent | 655 |
| *M. ibiboboca* | Tricolored, with black rings forming 7–10 triads on body | 1 + 1 | 210–243 | 19–30 | — | 920 |
| *M. isozonus* | Tricolored, with black rings forming 8–13 triads on body | 1 + 1 | 199–231 | 24–32 | Absent | ca. 1,500 |
| *M. karlschmidti* | Dark brown to black dorsally and ventrally, with 26–38 orange-red rounded blotches on the venter | 1 + 1 | 219–270 | 21–27 | — | 335 |
| *M. langsdorffi* | Polychromatic; tricolored, without triads, or bicolored; 36–91 yellow, brown, or black body rings | 1 + 1 or, rarely, 1 + 2 | 195–231 | 30–56 | — | 761 |
| *M. laticollaris* | Tricolored, with black rings forming 6–9 triads on body | 1 + 2 | 207–225 | 35–47 | Absent | 800+ |
| *M. latifasciatus* | Tricolored, without triads; black, yellow, and red rings; 6–9 long black body rings | 1 + 1 | 192–214 | 37–55 | Present | 1,000+ |
| *M. lemniscatus* | Tricolored, with black rings forming 7–17 triads on body | 1 + 1 | 210–268 | 25–43 | Absent | 1,450 |
| *M. limbatus* | Bicolored; 25–41 black rings separated by red or orange rings; or a red dorsal ground color with middorsal black spots | 1 + 1 | 190–205 | 25–37 | Absent | ca. 650 |
| *M. margaritiferus* | Bicolored dorsally, with 68–141+ irregular transverse rows of white dots on a black ground color; venter may be bicolored black and white, or tricolored black, white, and brown | 1 + 1 | 205–225 | 33–48 | — | 773 |
| *M. mertensi* | Tricolored, without triads; black, yellow, and red rings; 18–30 black body rings | 1 + 1 or 1 + 2 | 210–236 | 31–51 | Absent | 880 |
| *M. mipartitus* | Bicolored, with 34–80 black body rings alternating with white or yellow rings; parietal and caudal rings red-orange | 1 + 1, 1 + 2 or, rarely, 0 + 1 | 197–303 | 20–35 | Absent | 1,200 |
| *M. multifasciatus* | Bicolored, with 40–65 black body rings alternating with red, pink, cream, or white rings; in black and white ringed snakes, parietal ring and subcaudals may be red or pink | 1 + 1 or 1 + 2 | 233–311 | 23–33 | Present | 1,130 |
| *M. multiscutatus* | Bicolored, with 59–66 black body rings alternating with red rings | 1 + 1 | 295–329 | 24–30 | — | 842 |

**Table 27—*continued***

| Species | Color and pattern | *Temporals* | *Ventrals* | *Subcaudals* | *Supra-anal keels in males** | *Maximum known size (mm)* |
|---|---|---|---|---|---|---|
| *M. narduccii* | Body black with a yellow-to-orange supraocular ring and 37–62 oval ventral blotches that encroach laterally and may meet dorsally | 1 + 1 or, rarely, 1 + 2 | 261–382 | 15–35 | — | 1,117 |
| *M. nigrocinctus* | Tricolored, without triads, or bicolored, in which the yellow rings may be present or absent, respectively; 10–29 black body rings | 1 + 1 or 1 + 2 | 180–230 | 31–58 | Present | 1,000+ |
| *M. peruvianus* | Usually tricolored, without triads; some snakes are bicolored black and yellow owing to melanic red rings; 16–27 black body rings | 1 + 1 or 0 + 1 | 178–211 | 39–42 | Absent | 415 |
| *M. petersi* | Tricolored, without triads; red rings obscured with black pigment creating a somewhat bicolored aspect; 21 black body rings | 1 + 1 | 232 | 31 | — | 667 |
| *M. proximans* | Tricolored, without triads; black, yellow, and red rings; 18–22 black body rings | 1 + 1 or 1 + 2 | 205–237 | 36–40 | Present | 800+ |
| *M. psyches* | Highly variable; bicolored, tricolored, or uniformly black dorsally; black rings never in triads | 1 + 1 or, less frequently, 1 + 2 or 0 + 1 | 179–231 | 29–52 | Absent | 910 |
| *M. putumayensis* | Bicolored, with 7–14 black body rings alternating with yellow (perhaps red) rings | 1 + 1 or, rarely, 1 + 2 | 192–226 | 32–51 | — | 805 |
| *M. ruatanus* | Bicolored, with 33–45 black body rings alternating with dark red rings | 1 + 1 | 183–204 | 34–46 | Present | 620 |
| *M. sangilensis* | Tricolored, with black rings forming 17–22 triads on body; tail bicolored with 5–10 black rings separated by yellow | 1 + 1 or 1 + 2 | 190–217 | 33–53 | Absent | 545 |
| *M. spixii* | Tricolored, with black rings forming 4–9 (rarely 10) triads on body | 1 + 1 or, rarely, 1 + 2 | 200–229 | 15–24 | Absent | 1,602 |
| *M. spurrelli* | Bicolored, with about 52 black body rings alternating with white rings; pale caudal rings red | 1 + 1 | 232–244 | 36–37 | — | 270 |
| *M. steindachneri* | Tricolored, without triads; 22–42 black body rings; yellow rings greatly reduced; red rings may be melanic dorsally | 1 + 1 | 200–234 | 29–49 | Absent | 860 |
| *M. stewarti* | Bicolored, with 13–21 black body rings alternating with red rings; 2–5 black tail rings | 1 + 1 or 1 + 2 | 197–223 | 40–55 | Present | 666 |
| *M. stuarti* | Tricolored, without triads; black, yellow, and red rings; 13–19 black body rings; 3–4 black tail rings alternating with brown (in preservative) | 1 + 2 | 210–231 | 37–48 | Present | ca. 600 |
| *M. surinamensis* | Tricolored, with black rings forming 5–8⅔ triads on body | 1 + 1 or 1 + 2; rarely, 1 + 3 or 2 + 2 | 160–215 | 27–40 | Present | 1,262+ |
| *M. tschudii* | Tricolored, with black rings forming 10–22 triads on body | 1 + 1 | 188–232 | 25–29 | — | ca. 880 |

*Note.* For additional information refer to individual species accounts.
* —, condition unknown.

*Micrurus collaris*, *M. karlschmidti*, and *M. narduccii* are included in the genus *Leptomicrurus* by some authors. Inasmuch as several other species of *Micrurus* appear to be more closely related to these three than they are to other members of the genus *Micrurus*, such recognition of the genus *Leptomicrurus* would make the genus *Micrurus* paraphyletic.

The signs and symptoms of envenomation by *Micrurus* are the result of progressive skeletal muscle paralysis by a postsynaptic blockade at the myoneural junction (but see Vital Brazil, 1980, for possible dual blockade). The onset of effects usually occurs in the first 2–6 hours, and it can take up to 48 hours for the maximum effect to be reached. The earliest symptom is double vision; the earliest sign is palpebral ptosis. These are followed by oculoplegia, dysarthria, dysphagia, and generalized muscle weakness. Eventually, in severe envenomation, respiratory arrest and death occur unless the victim is given artificial ventilation. Of nine cases of *Micrurus* envenomation reported in one study from Costa Rica and South American countries, two were fatal (*M. clarki*, *M. mipartitus*; Colombia) owing to lack of availability of either antivenom or artificial ventilation.

The habits of coral snakes are difficult to categorize. These snakes are often described as being diurnal, and they frequently are encountered abroad during the early morning or late afternoon hours, or after a rainstorm; however, many species are just as likely to be active after dark or, in the case of deep forest species, at midday.

### ***Micrurus alleni*** **(Schmidt)**

(Fig. 20; Map 3)

LOCAL NAME Coral.

ENGLISH NAME Allen's coral snake.

DISTRIBUTION This species is found from the Cabo Gracias a Dios in extreme northeastern Nicaragua southward in Atlantic drainages to northwestern Panama, apparently extending onto the Pacific versant in the vicinity of Tilarán, province of Guanacaste, Costa Rica; also on the Pacific Coast from southeastern Costa Rica to southwestern Panama. Isolated populations occur in Pacific drainages of central Costa Rica and in the Darién lowlands of eastern Panama (Map 3). Throughout most of its range this species generally inhabits elevations well below 1,000 m, but several specimens have been reported from as high as 1,200 m near San José, Costa Rica, and a single snake is purported to have come from 2,000 m in the Cordillera de Talamanca in Costa Rica.

HABITAT Lowland rainforest (tropical wet and moist forest), subtropical wet forest, and occasionally tropical dry forest in moist riparian situations.

DESCRIPTION *Micrurus alleni* is a moderately large coral snake; males reach a total length of about 800 mm, and females attain a maximum of 1,068 mm.

This generally tricolored species has black, yellow (or white), and red rings. The black head cap covers the top of the head and projects posteriorly onto the parietals along the interparietal suture in a linear, ovate, oblong, or lanceolate shape. Few, if any, of the scales in the yellow or white nuchal ring are outlined in black. The black nuchal ring is posterior to the parietals and extends 5–11 dorsal scale lengths. The mental and several anterior infralabials are generally black. There are 13–26 black body rings and 4–9 black tail rings.

Several differences in color pattern distinguish Atlantic versant specimens from those of the Pacific versant in southeastern Costa Rica and southwestern Panama. The black nuchal ring extends only 6–8 (mode 6) scale lengths in the Pacific population, whereas it is 7–11 (mode 9) in the Atlantic population. With the exception of some specimens from the province of Bocas del Toro, Panama, Atlantic specimens have predominantly white rings; specimens from the Pacific versant (and Bocas del Toro, Panama) have yellowish rings that are especially bright in snakes from extreme southeastern Costa Rica. There is a tendency for the dorsal portion of the red rings to become obscured with black in large specimens from the Pacific versant, thus the snake may appear black and yellow when viewed from above; red is apparent ventrally although it may be heavily mottled with black pigment. No such obfuscation of red rings occurs in specimens from the Atlantic versant.

Supra-anal keels are present in adult males and large adult females, and there are 1 + 1 temporals, 214–237 ventrals, and 47–59 subcaudals. Other characteristics of lepidosis are typical of the genus *Micrurus*.

SIMILAR SPECIES *Micrurus alleni* is sympatric with several other species of *Micrurus*. *Micrurus multifasciatus* may be distinguished from *M. alleni* in that it possesses a bicolored pattern of black and white (or red, pink, or cream), and it has a black head cap that involves only the rostral, nasals, and prefrontals, and rarely the anterior portions of the supraoculars and frontal, but does not reach the parietals. *Micrurus multifasciatus* has more than 40 black body bands, whereas *M. alleni* has 26 or fewer.

The several tricolored species with which *M. alleni* is sympatric may be distinguished by features of lepidosis and pattern. *Micrurus clarki* has a black head cap that extends posteriorly to *completely* cover the parietals, the scales of the pale nuchal ring are all outlined in black, and supra-anal keels are absent. *Micrurus nigrocinctus* has a black head cap that involves most or all of the supraoculars and frontal and sometimes encroaches on the anterior edges of the parietals, but does not project posteriorly along the interparietal suture. In the region of sympatry in the Atlantic lowlands of Nicaragua and Costa Rica there are fewer than 259 ventrals plus subcaudals in *M. nigrocinctus* and more than 258 in *M. alleni*, and usually there are fewer than 16 black body bands in *M. nigrocinctus* and more than 15 in *M. alleni*. Where the species coexist in the Pacific lowlands of southeastern Costa Rica and southwestern Panama, *M. nigrocinctus* has a total of 237–244 ventrals plus subcaudals, whereas *M. alleni* has 256–272.

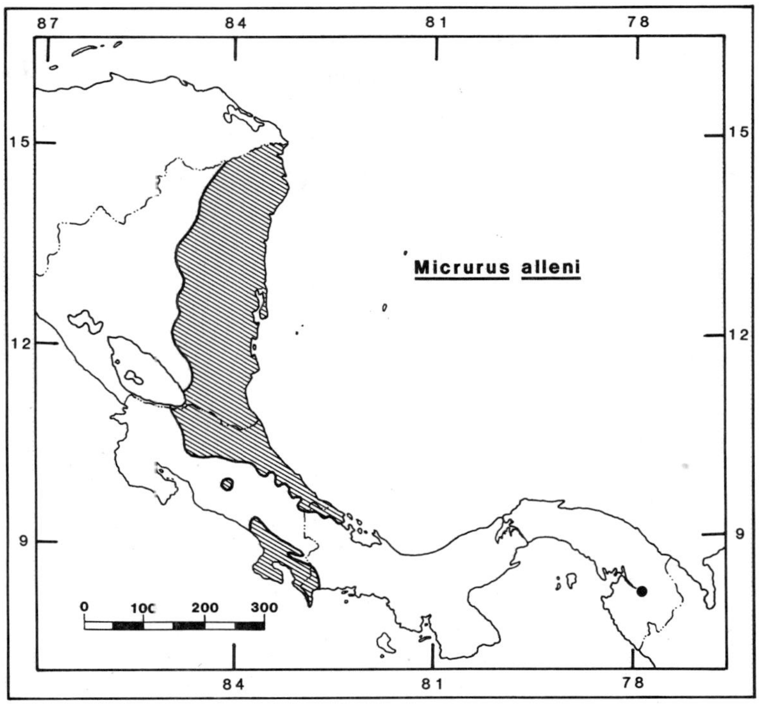


**Map 3.** Distribution of *Mircrurus alleni* in lower Middle America. The dot represents an isolated record for El Real de Santa María, Darién, Panama.

For the identification and distribution of some of the colubrid snakes from lower Central America that possess ringed patterns refer to the Key to Latin American Genera Containing False Coral Snakes in Mimics of Venomous Snakes, and Table 33; these genera include *Erythrolamprus, Lampropeltis, Liophis, Oxyrhopus, Pliocercus, Rhinobothryum, Scaphiodontophis, Scolecophis,* and *Tantilla.*

REMARKS A case might be made for considering the allopatric Pacific population of *M. alleni* a distinct species from the Atlantic versant population. The oldest available name for the Pacific population is *M. nigrocinctus yatesi*, thus it would become *M. yatesi* under the rules of nomenclature.

The single specimen of *M. alleni* known from eastern Panama (El Real de Santa María, province of Darién) possesses fewer black body rings (13) than any other known *M. alleni*; also the number of scales included in the black nuchal ring is less (5) than any other (minimum of 6 for representatives of the Pacific population).

REFERENCES Bolaños, 1983, 1984; Dunn, 1942; Gaige et al., 1937; Greene and McDiarmid, 1981; Grocott and Sadler, 1958; Roze, 1967, 1983; Savage and Vial, 1974; Schmidt, 1936b; Scott, 1969; E. H. Taylor, 1951, 1954; R. T. Taylor et al., 1974; Villa, 1984.

### *Micrurus ancoralis* (Jan)

(Figs. 21–23; Map 4)

LOCAL NAMES Coral, coralilla, gargantilla. Colombia: coral rey, coral.

ENGLISH NAME Regal coral snake.

DISTRIBUTION Pacific lowlands of eastern Panama and western Colombia south to southern Ecuador (Map 4). The vertical distribution probably does not exceed 1,500 m, although there are unverified reports of its occurrence up to 2,300 m in Colombia.

HABITAT Tropical rainforest and low montane wet forest.

DESCRIPTION *Micrurus ancoralis* is a large coral snake that averages 600–800 mm in overall length, but lengths as great as 1,510 mm have been reported.

This species is tricolored and has the black body rings arranged in 12–24 triads on the body plus 1 or 2 more on the tail. Frequently, pattern anomalies occur: for example, a red ring may be reduced (or melanized), causing triads to coalesce and form groups of 5–7 black rings (Fig. 21). The triad rings of the more northerly race (*M. ancoralis jani*) tend to have the central annulus longest, while in the nominate form they are usually more equal in size. The triads are often separated from one another by subequal red rings that are approximately the length (4–6 dorsals) of the adjacent black rings (*M. a. ancoralis*), or as much as twice the length of the adjacent black rings (*M. a. jani*). The white rings are considerably smaller (1–3 dorsals) and heavily stippled and spotted with black pigment, especially in the northern race. There is usually some black pigment in the red rings but the extent varies; we have seen Colombian specimens with practically none and Ecuadorian specimens in which over half of each red scale was black. Generally, the red and white rings are immaculate ventrally, although there are often scattered black spots along the paraventrals. The head and neck markings are diagnostic for this species; the tip of the snout to the anterior edge of the parietals is basically bright red. This includes all labials and the chin and gular region. Some specimens, particularly from the southern part of the range, may have the rostral and internasals black. The supracephalic scales contain numerous irregular black

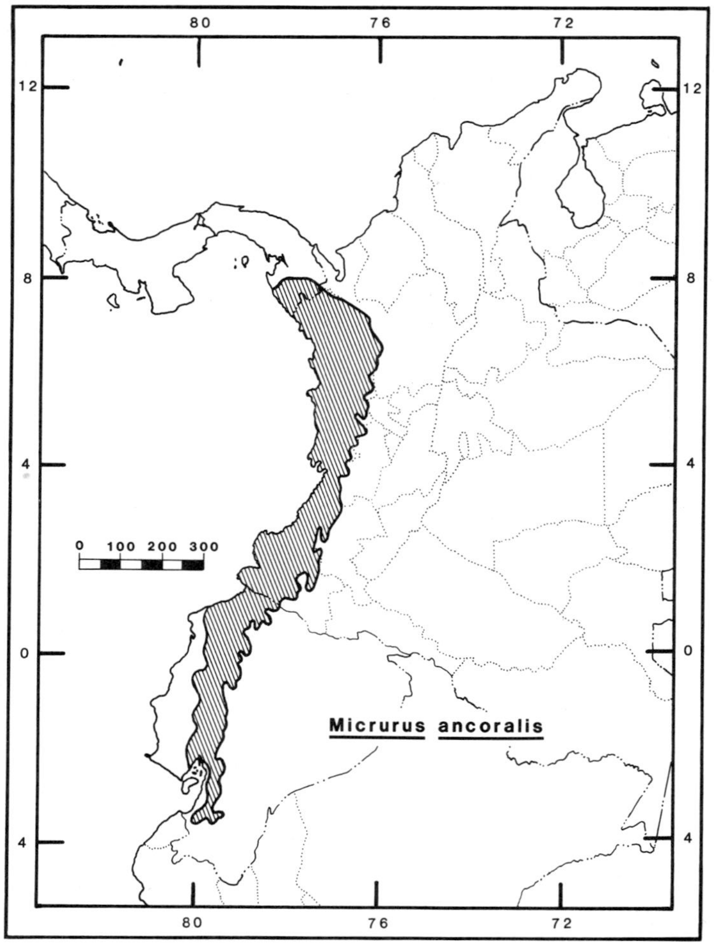


**Map 4.** Distribution of *Micrurus ancoralis* in eastern Panama and northwestern South America.

spots and specks arranged in a symmetrical fashion. The largest of these is a teardrop-shaped spot on the frontal with accessory spots on the prefrontals that may coalesce; this is especially true of the northern race, *M. a. jani*. The nuchal black ring has an irregular anterior border as it invades the parietals and follows the outline of their sutures. The first white body ring may be complete or broken middorsally. Alternatively, it may curve forward anteriorly with each respective half opening onto a parietal, cleaving the black nuchal ring into two anchor-shaped lateral markings. These anchor-shaped markings are very consistent on *M. a. jani*. In many specimens the white rings are oblique (especially the first one) and they often widen considerably on the sides. The head is somewhat flattened and flared anteriorly; in combination with the unusual color pattern this gives the species a strikingly unique appearance.

There are 1 + 1 (rarely 1 + 2) temporals, 248–290 ventrals, and 30–37 subcaudals. Other features of lepidosis are typical of the genus *Micrurus*.

SIMILAR SPECIES *Micrurus ancoralis* may be distinguished from all sympatric congeners by the presence of a triad pattern of body rings including all 3 rings of the first triad. The only other *Micrurus* species within the range of *M. ancoralis* that has the triad pattern is *M. dissoleucus*, in which only the last black ring of the first body triad is present. The head pattern of *M. ancoralis* is also unique for the genus. See Mimics of Venomous Snakes for a discussion of false coral snakes.

REMARKS Two subspecies are recognized: *M. a. jani* (Fig. 23) from eastern Panama through the Pacific lowlands of Colombia to the Río Saija drainage, where it intergrades with *M. a. ancoralis* (Figs. 21, 22), which ranges southward into northwestern Ecuador. *Micrurus a. jani* has 12–16 triads and long red body rings, while the nominate form has 16–24 triads and short red body rings. A Panamanian specimen was reported with only 2 black rings in the first triad. This species has been cited as occurring along the eastern versant of the Andes in Ecuador, but we are unaware of any specimens from that region.

REFERENCES Amaral, 1925b, 1927d, 1931b; Angel, 1983; Boulenger, 1898b; Castro et al., 1982; Daniel, 1949; Dunn, 1942, 1944a; Grocott and Sadler, 1958; Jan and Sordelli, 1870–1881; Medem, 1969; Miyata, 1982; Nicéforo-María, 1942; Orcés, 1943, 1948; Pérez-Santos and Moreno, 1986; J. A. Peters, 1955, 1960a; Roze, 1967, 1983; Schmidt, 1936a, 1955; Tiedemann and Haupl, 1980.

## *Micrurus annellatus* (Peters)

(Figs. 24, 25; Map 5)

LOCAL NAMES Coral. Perú: naca-naca.

ENGLISH NAME Annellated coral snake.

DISTRIBUTION Ecuador to Bolivia. This species occurs at moderate elevations of the Amazonian slopes of

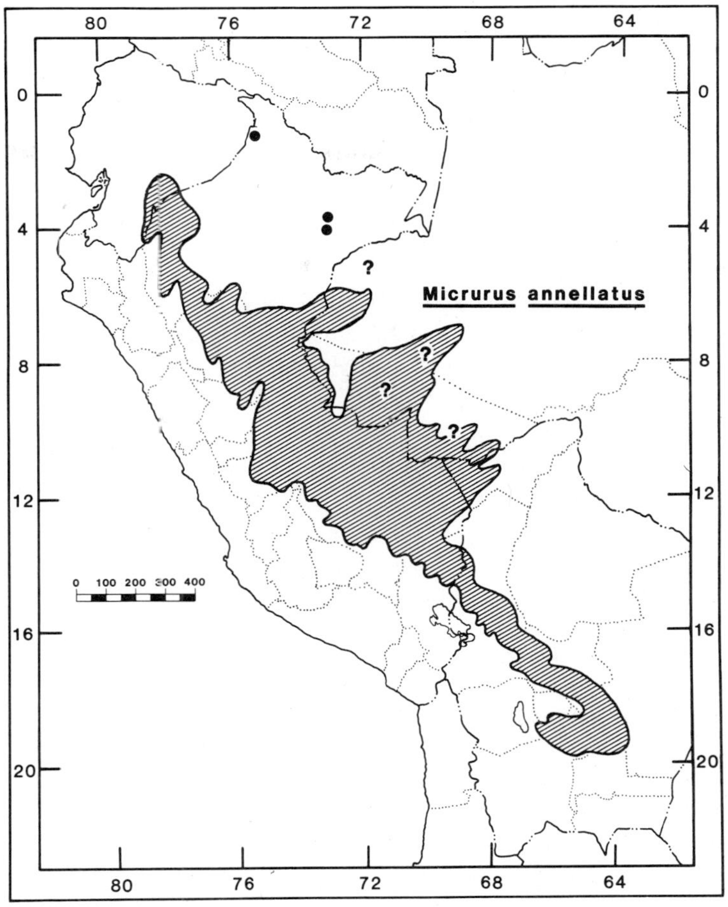


Map 5. Distribution of *Micrurus annellatus* in western South America. The dots in the north represent isolated records from near Iquitos and Pucallpa, Peru; these require verification. Question marks represent possible areas of occurrence.

the Andes, from southern Ecuador through Peru south to central and western Bolivia. There is an isolated record from Amazonas, Brazil, and unverified records exist from Iquitos and Pucallpa, Peru (Map 5). The vertical distribution is to at least 2,000 m.

HABITAT Inhabiting lower montane wet forest and cloud forests, and possibly tropical rainforest, *M. annellatus* may also be found in lower montane dry forest in Bolivia.

DESCRIPTION The reported size range for *M. annellatus* is generally 195–500 mm with a maximum overall length of 730 mm.

This species may appear either bicolored or tricolored; if tricolored, the black rings are not arranged in triads. Black-and-red as well as black-and-white specimens have been reported. In some bicolored specimens, it appears that either the red or white rings have become obscured by black pigmentation. There are 17–83 black or black plus melanized red rings (see Remarks) on the body with an additional 5–9 on the tail. In tricolored specimens, the yellow rings are extremely narrow dorsally. Because of this tendency toward melanization, some specimens may appear black and orange. The most distinctive aspect of the pattern of *M. annellatus* is the narrow-to-moderate parietal ring that traverses the temporals, the posterior 2–3 supralabials and infralabials, and the anterior ends of the posterior chinshields. Occasionally this ring is slightly interrupted middorsally. The entire head anterior to the parietal ring is black.

There are 1 + 1 temporals (occasionally one side will have 1 + 2), 193–225 ventrals, and 26–48 subcaudals, nearly all divided. Supra-anal keels are absent. Other features of lepidosis are typical of the genus *Micrurus*.

SIMILAR SPECIES *Micrurus annellatus* may be distinguished from all sympatric congeners by the relatively narrow pale parietal ring that directly traverses the parietal scales.

REMARKS Three subspecies are recognized: *M. a. annellatus* (Fig. 24), characterized by a relatively high number of black or black plus melanic red body rings, two postoculars, and a short parietal ring, occurs from southern Ecuador to southeastern Peru; *M. a. balzani* (Fig. 25), characterized by having 1 rather than 2 postoculars and distinctive red body rings, is found in the Amazonian slopes of the Andes in the Madre de Dios region of Peru and in western Bolivia; and *M. a. bolivianus*, characterized by having a relatively low number of black or black plus red body rings and a relatively long white parietal ring, occupies the eastern Andes and upper Amazonian valleys of central Bolivia in Cochabamba and Chuquisaca. Recently *M. a. montanus* has been considered synonymous with the nominate form. *Micrurus annellatus* is a confusing species that needs to be reevaluated critically in the light of more material.

REFERENCES Amaral, 1931b; Boulenger, 1898a, 1902b; Carrillo de Espinoza, 1983; Duellman, 1979; Golay, 1985; Hoge and Romano, 1969; Meneses, 1974a; Miyata, 1982; J. A. Peters, 1960a; W. C. H. Peters, 1871; Roze, 1967, 1983; Schmidt, 1936a, 1954; Schmidt and Walker, 1943a; Soini, 1974b.

### *Micrurus averyi* Schmidt

(Fig. 26; Map 20)

LOCAL NAMES Unknown, but presumably typically the same as those for other coral snakes in the region.

ENGLISH NAME Black-headed coral snake.

DISTRIBUTION Guyana and Brazil (see Remarks). *Micrurus averyi* is known from the type locality, Courantyne District, southern Guyana, and the region around Manaus, Amazonas, Brazil (see Map 20). Its vertical distribution is to at least 610 m.

HABITAT Lowland rainforest and possibly lower montane wet forest.

DESCRIPTION *Micrurus averyi* is a moderately slender, medium-sized coral snake that reaches at least 715 mm in total length.

It has rings of black, yellow or white, and red. The pattern does not consist of triads. The head is almost entirely black (sometimes with faint red markings on the snout) with a narrow white or pale yellow marking that partially covers the last 2–4 supralabials and the temporals, and borders the parietals. This pale marking may be red in some specimens; occasionally it may be interrupted by black. The black head coloration is present after the pale head ring but cannot be said to constitute a nuchal ring, an arrangement unique for the genus. The black color is predominant on the venter of the head, being interrupted by a narrow yellow or white border just behind the chinshields and by an irregular yellow or white spot on each anterior chinshield. This pattern varies, and the venter of the head may be all black, and may or may not be in contact with the sixth infralabial and dorsal head cap. There are 8–13 black body rings, 2 middorsals long, on the body. These are bordered narrowly by yellow or white rings that are interrupted frequently so that they form series of spots. There are 4–7 black tail rings. The long red body rings (12–28 ventrals in length) are very intense in color and usually lack all traces of black stippling. On the tail the red rings are heavily melanic and shorter than the black rings; the yellow or white rings usually remain sharply demarcated, but may be obscured.

There are 1 + 1 or 1 + 2 temporals, 190–220 ventrals, 28–48 subcaudals, and no supra-anal keels. One aberrant specimen with an undivided anal plate has been reported. Other features of lepidosis are characteristic of the genus *Micrurus*.

SIMILAR SPECIES The only sympatric *Micrurus* species with red rings and a pattern not forming triads is *M. psyches*. Red body rings on *M. psyches*, if present, are shorter and may be tipped with black (long and unicolored in *M. averyi*), and the black body rings are longer (very short in *M. averyi*). *Micrurus psyches* lacks red pigment on the head. See Mimics of Venomous Snakes for a discussion of false coral snakes.

REMARKS *Micrurus averyi* has been reported from Suriname, evidently in a region of a boundary dispute with Guyana.

REFERENCES Abuys, 1987a, 1987b; Brongersma, 1967; Hoge and Romano-Hoge, 1981a; Roze, 1967, 1983; Schmidt, 1939; Vanzolini, 1985.

### *Micrurus bernadi* (Cope)

(Figs. 27, 28; Map 30)

LOCAL NAMES Coral, coralillo.

ENGLISH NAME Blotched coral snake.

DISTRIBUTION Mexico. This species frequents moderate and intermediate elevations of the Atlantic drainages of western Hidalgo southward to northern Puebla, and possibly portions of northwestern Veracruz (see Map 30). Its vertical distribution appears to fall between 1,400 and 2,100 m.

HABITAT Cloud forest.

DESCRIPTION This medium-sized coral snake reaches a total length of at least 826 mm.

The color pattern consists of 24–42 black dorsal spots on a red ground color; yellow is lacking in the pattern. Black covers the entire snout including the frontal, the supraoculars, both postoculars, at least the first 4 supralabials, and the anterior tips to practically all of the parietals. The pale parietal ring is highly variable and may extend across the center of the parietals and include the posterior portion of the primary temporals, the anterior portions of the secondary temporals, and portions of supralabials 5 and 6, or it may be reduced to pale spots on the posterior of the parietals and adjacent scales. The black nuchal ring extends posteriorly 4–5 middorsal scale lengths from the parietals; it is complete ventrally, and sometimes the first black dorsal spot following the nuchal ring forms a partial ring that is incomplete dorsally. The black dorsal spots are in the form of transverse oval bands extending 5–11 scale rows across the dorsum and 2–3 dorsal scale lengths wide; in some specimens these spots may extend to the second or third scale row, but are not complete ventrally. Most dorsal black spots are separated from one another by 2–3 red scales, and a few, especially anteriorly, may be broken dorsally. There is generally a black oval spot followed by 5–12 black tail rings.

There is no trace of supra-anal keels, and there are 1 + 1 temporals, 203–228 ventrals, and 37–48 subcaudals. Other features of lepidosis are typical of the genus *Micrurus*.

SIMILAR SPECIES The population of *Pliocercus elapoides* in northern Puebla has a spotted pattern similar to that of *M. bernadi*. See also Mimics of Venomous Snakes for a discussion of *Lampropeltis triangulum*.

REMARKS A rare species, *M. bernadi* has been reported from only three localities: Zacualtipán in Hidalgo, Necaxa in Puebla, and San José Acateno in Veracruz. In the literature, the name *M. bernadi* is frequently misspelled *M. bernardi*.

REFERENCES Cope, 1887; Ferrari-Perez, 1886; Greene and McDiarmid, 1981; Martín del Campo, 1935, 1950; Neill, 1963; Roze, 1967, 1983; Schmidt, 1933a, 1958; H. M. Smith, 1941b; H. M. Smith and Taylor, 1945.

### *Micrurus bocourti* (Jan)

(Map 34)

LOCAL NAMES Coral, coralillo.

ENGLISH NAME Ecuadorian coral snake.

DISTRIBUTION Pacific lowlands of Ecuador and possibly northwestern Peru (see Remarks; Map 34). The vertical distribution is to at least 1,456 m.

HABITAT Recorded localities place this species in coastal lowland dry forest and thorn forest and lower montane dry forest. It may be found to extend into more humid regions as well.

DESCRIPTION The only published length for this species is 283 mm. It is presumably of typical size and body build for the genus *Micrurus* (300–700 mm).

*Micrurus bocourti* has a pattern of 4⅔–14⅔ or more triads (usually 10 or more) on the body. The tail is bicolored yellow and black. The head is black dorsally with a yellow occipital ring that passes posterior to the parietals, includes some or all of the posterior temporals, and some or all of the posterior 5 supralabials. Ventrally this yellow occipital ring expands to include virtually all of the lower jaw except the first 3 infralabials and mental, which are black. There are scattered but symmetrically arranged smudges of black pigment on the chinshields and posterior infralabials. The rostral and mental may be slightly stippled with yellow or red. The first black body ring is the middle of the first triad, which is thus only two-thirds present. The central black ring of each triad is the longest, the outer two being very weakly developed and little more than 1 dorsal scale in length. The yellow rings are 1½–2½ dorsal scales in length. The apical portions of all red scales are tinged with black pigment; red body rings are 5–13 dorsals in length. Ventrally the accessory (outer) black rings of each triad are poorly developed and often incomplete or present as smudges of black pigment. Black pigment also is scattered throughout the ventral portions of the red rings. The tail is bicolored, with 5–7 pairs of short white or yellow rings that are expanded ventrally such that the intervening black rings may appear as rounded ventral blotches. The tail tip is usually pale.

There are usually 1 + 1 temporals, 194–223 ventrals, and 32–50 subcaudals. Supra-anal keels are absent. Other features of lepidosis are typical of the genus *Micrurus*.

SIMILAR SPECIES *Micrurus bocourti* is unique in that the first body triad is represented by only two black rings, a condition not found among sympatric congeners. The only other *Micrurus* species with triads that might be sympatric with *M. bocourti* are *M. ancoralis*, in which the first triad is invariably complete and a black head cap is absent, and *M. tschudii*, in which the first triad is complete, the tail tricolored, and there are 25–29 subcaudals (vs. 32–50 in *M. bocourti*). See also the discussion of false coral snakes in Mimics of Venomous Snakes.

REMARKS We are unaware of specimens from Peru; the occurrence of *M. bocourti* there requires verification. In some specimens the accessory triad rings may be reduced or nearly absent. This species is cited frequently as *M. ecuadorianus* in the older literature.

REFERENCES Jan and Sordelli, 1870–1881; Miyata, 1982; Orcés, 1943, 1948; Parker, 1938; J. A. Peters, 1955, 1960a; Roux-Esteve, 1983; Roze, 1967, 1970b, 1983; Schmidt, 1936a.

### *Micrurus bogerti* Roze

(Map 24)

LOCAL NAMES Coral, coralillo.

ENGLISH NAME Bogert's coral snake.

DISTRIBUTION Mexico. Low elevations of the Pacific Coast of Oaxaca, from about Puerto Angel to Tapanatepec (see Map 24). The vertical distribution is restricted to near sea level.

HABITAT Tropical deciduous forest.

DESCRIPTION This is a small species of coral snake, not known to exceed 350 mm in total length.

It has a pattern of black, yellow, and red rings; the black rings are not disposed in triads. The 16–19 black body rings are narrowly bordered by yellow. Except for the first black ring, which may be longer, the black body rings are 3–4 dorsals long middorsally, reduced to 2–2½ scales laterally, and about 2 or 3 ventrals long. There are 3–6 black rings on the tail that are more than twice as long as the yellow rings that separate them. The first 2 red rings are about 10 dorsals long; more posteriorly, most are 6–8 dorsals long. The red scales are not tipped with black, but a few black spots may be present. The yellow rings are 1½ scales long on the anterior part of the body, decreasing to about one-half a scale length posteriorly. The snout is uniformly black and this black coloration extends to the anterior margins of the parietals, covering the frontal and upper postoculars, anterior part of the lower preocular, and anterior three-fourths of the fourth supralabials. The black nuchal band is 6–7 scales long and extends forward dorsally to cover the posterior tips of the parietals and laterally to include a part of the seventh supralabial. The mental and first 3 infralabials are black, the rest are pale; there is a dark spot on the tip of each chinshield.

Males lack supra-anal keels. There are 1 + 1 temporals, 213–224 ventrals, and 41–56 subcaudals, a few of which may be undivided. Other features of lepidosis are characteristic of the genus *Micrurus*.

SIMILAR SPECIES The other coral snakes known from Oaxaca, Mexico, include *M. elegans*, *M. diastema*, *M. browni*, and *M. ephippifer*. Of these, only the latter two occur in the Pacific lowlands. *Micrurus bogerti* may be distinguished from *M. browni* by its longer red rings (anteriorly, about 10 middorsal scale lengths; 6 or 7 posteriorly) and by the absence of supra-anal keels in males; and from *M. ephippifer* in having red rings that are not melanic dorsally, shorter black body rings (2 ventrals long), and red scales not tipped with black.

REMARKS This species is known from only a few specimens and nothing is known of its habits. It is probably nocturnal, as are most other lowland species of coral snakes that inhabit relatively dry regions.

REFERENCES Golay, 1985; Roze, 1967, 1983.

### *Micrurus browni* Schmidt and Smith

(Fig. 29; Map 6)

LOCAL NAMES Mexico and Guatemala: coral, coralillo, coral de cañutos (Chiapas), víbora de coral (Guerrero)

ENGLISH NAME Brown's coral snake.

DISTRIBUTION Mexico and Guatemala. Low, moderate, and intermediate elevations from the state of México southward through southern Puebla, Oaxaca, Guerrero, and Chiapas, Mexico, to the mountains of south-central Guatemala (Map 6). The vertical distribution is from near sea level to over 2,000 m.

HABITAT Tropical deciduous forest, pine-oak forest, and cloud forest.

DESCRIPTION A medium-sized coral snake, *M. browni* may approach 1 m in length but is usually less than 600 mm.

It is tricolored with black, yellow, and red rings. The snout is entirely black, including the rostral, supralabials 1–3 and most of 4, both postoculars, all but the posterior tips of the frontal, the supraoculars, and the anterior tips of the parietals. All or most of the mental and infralabials 1–2, and sometimes 3–4, are black; the anterior chinshields often have gray or brown mottling. The black nuchal ring involves the posterior part of the parietals, secondary temporal, and seventh supralabial; inferiorly it involves all of the seventh and parts of the sixth and sometimes fifth infralabials, and extends anteriorly to reach the posterior portions of the posterior chinshields, and posteriorly to the first 1 or 2 preventrals. There are 10–30 black body rings usually covering 3–5 (rarely up to 11) scale lengths dorsally, decreasing to about 2–3½ (rarely up to 10) scale lengths laterally, and extending 2–4 (rarely up to 11) ventrals. The 3–8 black tail rings are 5–11 dorsals and 4–10 subcaudals long. The yellow parietal ring generally extends across, but does not entirely cover, the parietals; it involves at least the posterior tip of the frontal, all of the anterior and part of the posterior temporals, and supralabials 5–6 and part of 4 and 7. The yellow body rings are from ½ to 1½ dorsals long, not more than 1 ventral long, and may be incomplete ventrally. Yellow rings on the tail are 1–3 dorsal scale lengths and usually 2–4 subcaudals long. The scales of the 11–29 red body rings are generally dusky and often have black tips; the length of the red body rings varies from 3–6 scales middorsally, increasing to 4–7 scales laterally, and covers 3–8 ventrals.

Supra-anal keels are present in adult males and may be present, although generally not strongly developed, in large females. There are 1 + 1 or 1 + 2 temporals, 204–238 ventrals, and 34–59 subcaudals, the most proximal few of which may not be divided. Other features of lepidosis are characteristic of the genus *Micrurus*.

SIMILAR SPECIES *Micrurus browni* is sympatric with *M. diastema*, *M. elegans*, and *M. nigrocinctus* in southeastern Oaxaca and western Chiapas, Mexico. *Micrurus bogerti*, *M. distans*, *M. ephippifer*, and *M. laticollaris* are geographically narrowly separated from, if not actually sympatric with, *M. browni*. *Micrurus elegans* and *M. laticollaris* are distinguished most readily from *M. browni* by the presence of black body rings disposed in triads. In the areas of sympatry, the following characteristics serve to distinguish other species of *Micrurus* from *M. browni*: *Micrurus diastema* has a black head cap that usually does not involve the anterior tips of the parietals, a pale spot is often present on the snout, and males lack supra-anal keels. *Micrurus nigrocinctus* has a lower number of ventrals, 208 or fewer in males and 224 or fewer in females, and the black body rings are shorter. *Micrurus distans* has 6–11 black body rings, the black nuchal ring begins behind the parietals, and males lack supra-anal keels; *M. bogerti* possesses a black nuchal band 6–7 scales long, the first 2 red rings are generally about 10 dorsals long, the yellow rings are about 1½ scales long anteriorly, decreasing to about ½ scale posteriorly, and males lack supra-anal keels. *Micrurus ephippifer* has red rings that are melanic dorsally, and males lack supra-anal keels.

REMARKS Some members of this species in the highlands of Oaxaca and Puebla vary somewhat from the above description. They are characterized by relatively brighter colors, shorter red and black body rings, a longer yellow parietal ring, and longer yellow rings on the body. All of the parietals, the posterior portions of the supraoculars, all of the anterior and posterior tem-

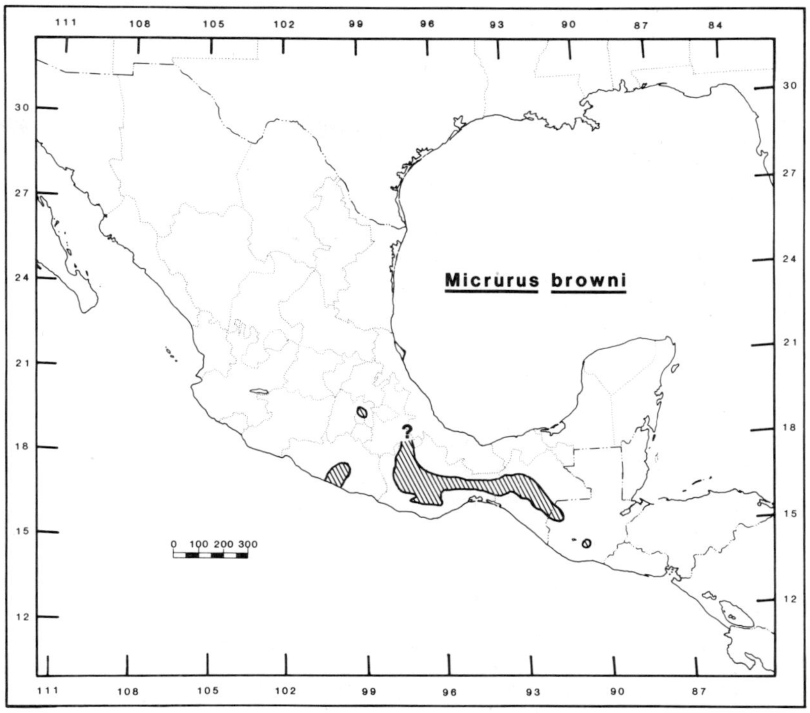


**Map 6.** Distribution of *Micrurus browni* in Mexico and Guatemala. The distribution and ecological relationships of this species are very poorly known, with populations occurring in widely divergent habitats at disparate elevations. The presence of this species near Mexico City is questionable. Question mark represents possible area of occurrence.

porals, and most or all of the postoculars, may be yellow. The red scales are not always dusky, and may be black tipped or immaculate; red ring length varies and it may be 1–4 scales dorsally, 1–4 scales laterally, and 3–5 ventrals. The yellow rings are 1–2 dorsals long and involve ½–1½ ventrals. The lengths of the black rings are 4 or 5 scales dorsally, decrease to 3 or 3½ scales laterally, and involve 2–4 ventrals.

Three subspecies are recognized: *M. b. browni* (Fig. 29), characterized by a relatively low number (less than 53) of subcaudals, occurs from the states of México and Guerrero, Mexico, southward to the mountains of western Guatemala; *M. b. taylori*, characterized by relatively few (10–17) black body rings, is known only from the vicinity of Acapulco, Guerrero, Mexico; and *M. b. importunus* is found in the Antigua Basin, Sacatepéquez, Guatemala.

REFERENCES Alvarez del Toro, 1983; Blaney and Blaney, 1978; Casas-Andreu and López-Forment, 1978; Davis and Dixon, 1959; Golay, 1985; Gutiérrez et al., 1988; Lynch and Smith, 1966; Martín del Campo, 1950; Mittleman and Smith, 1949; Muñoz Alonso, 1988; Roze, 1967, 1983; Schmidt and Smith, 1943; H. M. Smith, 1947a; H. M. Smith and Taylor, 1945, 1966; E. H. Taylor, 1940.

### *Micrurus clarki* Schmidt

(Fig. 30; Map 34)

LOCAL NAMES Coral, coralilla, gargantilla.

ENGLISH NAME Clark's coral snake.

DISTRIBUTION The distribution of this species is apparently discontinuous. It occurs in the Pacific lowlands of extreme southeastern Costa Rica and southwestern Panama; and on the Atlantic versant from about central Panama to western Colombia, extending into the Pacific lowlands in the area of the Canal Zone and eastern Panama and most of western Colombia (see Map 34). The presence of this species in the Atlantic lowlands of western Panama has not been established, but is probable (see Remarks). Its vertical distribution is from near sea level to about 700 m.

HABITAT Most specimens have come from tropical wet forest (rainforest), but the species apparently enters drier areas that are transitional between tropical wet forest and tropical dry forest along moist riparian situations.

DESCRIPTION This medium-sized coral snake reaches a maximum total length of about 700 mm.

It has a tricolored pattern of black, yellow, and red rings; the black body rings are not disposed in triads. The black head cap extends to the posterior tips of the parietals and covers all or most of these scales. The scales of the pale nuchal ring are outlined in gray or black. The anterior infracephalic scales are characteristically pale, although some may be peppered with black and they are generally gray or black margined. The black nuchal ring does not reach the parietals; it extends 3–6 middorsal scale lengths and is narrower ventrally. There are 13–20 black body rings, 2–3 ventrals long, and 5–9 black rings on the tail. Each scale of the red and yellow body rings is marked uniformly with black at the tip; these rings are generally immaculate below. The yellow rings are about 1 scale length long dorsally. The black tail rings are separated by yellow rings that are marked with black above but are immaculate ventrally.

Supra-anal keels are absent, the anal is divided, and there are 1 + 1 temporals, 192–208 ventrals, and 35–58 subcaudals. Other features of lepidosis are typical of the genus *Micrurus*.

SIMILAR SPECIES *Micrurus multifasciatus*, *M. mipartitus*, and *M. stewarti* occur within the range of *M. clarki* but are distinguished easily by having a bicolored rather than tricolored pattern of rings. Two species of coral snakes found in eastern Panama, *M. ancoralis* and *M. dissoleucus*, possess a pattern of black body rings disposed in triads. Two other species of coral snakes, *M. alleni* and *M. nigrocinctus*, are sympatric in some regions with *M. clarki* and possess a similar tricolored pattern with black body rings not arranged in triads. *Micrurus alleni* differs from *M. clarki* in having (1) a black head cap that extends posteriorly along the interparietal suture but does not cover most of the parietal scales, (2) scales of the pale nuchal ring that are not gray or black margined, (3) several black infracephalic scales, generally the mental and several anterior infralabials, and (4) strongly developed supra-anal keels in males. *Micrurus nigrocinctus* may be distinguished from *M. clarki* by the presence of (1) a black head cap that covers most or all of the frontal and supraoculars and may occasionally extend to the anterior edge of the parietals, but does not completely cover the parietal scales, (2) scales in the pale nuchal ring that are not outlined in gray or black, (3) several infracephalic scales, generally the mental and several anterior infralabials, that are black, and (4) a nuchal ring that *sometimes* involves the posterior tips of the parietals. In western Colombia *M. clarki* is sympatric with *M. dumerilii*, to which it may bear a strong resemblance; however, *M. dumerilii* has distinctly dark infracephalic scales, principally the anterior infralabials, and supra-anal keels are present in males.

Many species of harmless snakes with brightly ringed patterns occur within the range of *M. clarki*. Members of the genera *Erythrolamprus*, *Lampropeltis*, *Liophis*, *Oxyrhopus*, *Pliocercus*, *Rhinobothryum*, *Scaphiodontophis*, *Scolecophis*, and *Tantilla* may sometimes be mistaken for coral snakes; for a discussion of false coral snakes see Mimics of Venomous Snakes.

REMARKS Little is known concerning the venom of this species, but a fatality in Colombia from the bite of this snake was reported. The southern limits of distribution for *M. clarki* are unknown, but suitable habitat exists in northwestern Ecuador.

REFERENCES Bolaños, 1984; Castro et al., 1982; H. C. Clark, 1942; Dunn, 1942, 1949; Dunn and Bailey, 1939; Grocott and Sadler, 1958; Roze, 1967, 1970b, 1983; Savage and Vial, 1974; Schmidt, 1936b; Scott, 1969; Solórzano and Cerdas, 1984; E. H. Taylor, 1951.

## *Micrurus collaris* (Schlegel)

(Figs. 31, 32; Map 20)

LOCAL NAMES Coral. Suriname: kraalslang, krarasneke. Venezuela: la negra.

ENGLISH NAME Guianan black-backed coral snake.

DISTRIBUTION This species is known from southeastern Venezuela and the Guianas. It occurs in French Guiana and undoubtedly northern Brazil in the Guianan region (see Map 20). There is a disputed record from Pará, Brazil. It has been recorded from low to moderate elevations, up to 700 m.

HABITAT Lowland rainforest and lower montane wet forest.

DESCRIPTION The maximum length for *M. collaris* is unknown, but it has been recorded to be 350–600 mm in overall length.

It possesses a distinctive pattern of up to 50 oval white, yellow, or orange-red blotches on a black or dark brown venter. These blotches are 2–4 ventrals in length, usually extend laterally to the first or second dorsal scale row, but are not known to meet middorsally. The head and dorsum are black or very dark brown. There is a white, yellow, or red ring around the neck, passing just posterior to the parietals or occasionally touching them. In some specimens there are faint spots on the head. The underside of the tail bears 1 or 2 yellow-to-red blotches that may meet middorsally; these may coalesce ventrally.

There are 0 + 1 or 1 + 1 temporals, 212–250 ventrals, and 12–30 subcaudals. The first pair of chinshields is in contact with the mental. Other features of lepidosis are characteristic of the genus *Micrurus*.

SIMILAR SPECIES There are no coral snakes that lack body rings and are known to be sympatric with *M. collaris*. The only two species of *Micrurus* lacking body rings (in addition to *M. collaris*) have a 1 + 1 temporal formula and a cephalic ring that passes anterior to or directly on the parietals (see Remarks). *Micrurus collaris* differs in both of these features. It is possible to encounter a melanistic *Micrurus* specimen, but in most members of the genus the chinshields do not contact the mental, whereas in *M. collaris* they do.

REMARKS Two other species, *M. karlschmidti* and *M. narduccii*, are very similar to *M. collaris*. These are not thought to be sympatric with *M. collaris*. Material is insufficient for firm conclusions regarding the relationships among this group.

Much of the earlier literature refers to this snake under the genus *Leptomicrurus* (see genus account, *Micrurus*) Roze and Bernal-Carlo (in press) recognize two subspecies of *M. collaris*.

REFERENCES Brongersma, 1966, 1967; Chippaux, 1987; Cunha and Nascimento, 1978; Hoge and Lancini, 1962; Hoge and Romano, 1966; Hoogmoed, 1983; Lancini, 1970, 1979; Rivero Blanco and Dixon, 1979; Romano, 1972; Roux-Esteve, 1983; Roze, 1966a, 1983; Roze and Bernal-Carlo, in press; Roze and Trebbau, 1958; Sandner-Montilla, 1985b; Schmidt, 1937; Thompson, 1913; Vetencourt Finol., 1960.

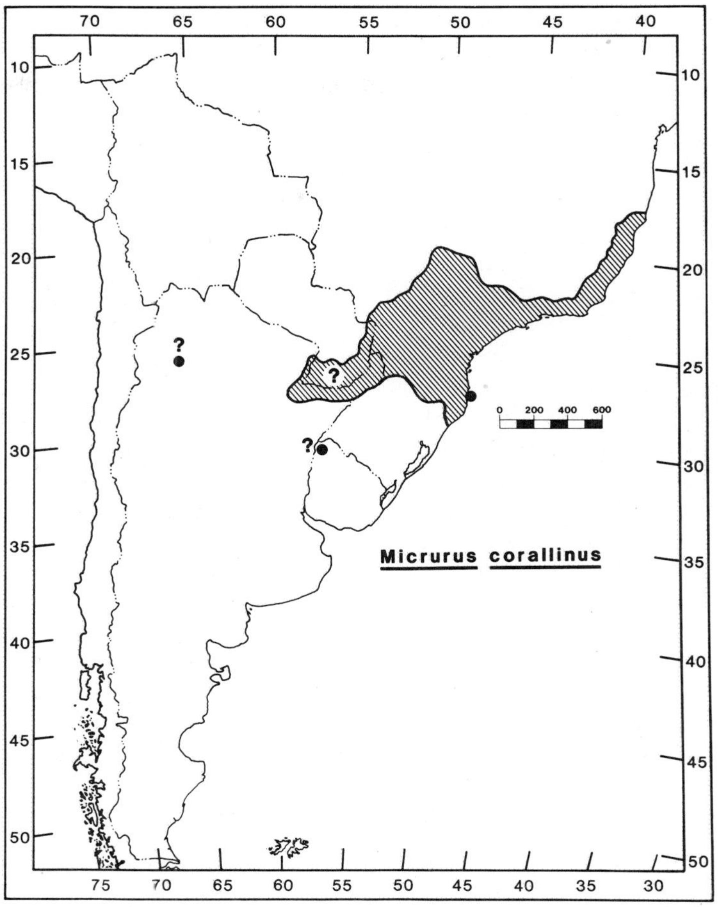


Map 7. Distribution of *Micrurus corallinus* in southeastern South America. The record off the coast of Brazil is for Ilha de São Sebastião. Questionable records exist for Uruguay and northwestern Argentina. The westward extent of the range in Paraguay is not established, and this species may not occur in the southern plains region.

## *Micrurus corallinus* (Merrem)

(Figs. 33, 34; Map 7)

LOCAL NAMES Argentina: Víbora de coral, mbói-chumbé (Guaraní tribal name). Brazil: cobra-coral, coral, boi-corá, ibiboboca, ibiboca. Paraguay: mbói-chumbé, mbói-yvyvovó. Uruguay: víbora de coral.

ENGLISH NAME Painted coral snake.

DISTRIBUTION Brazil, Paraguay, Uruguay, and Argentina. This species occurs south of the Amazon Basin in Brazil (including the Ilha de São Sebastião) and in the Littoral-Mesopotamia region of Argentina (Map 7). In eastern Paraguay, it is common around Puerto Stroessner in the Departamento de Alto Paraná. There are reports of *M. corallinus* in the Argentine Chaco and in northern Uruguay, but these need further substantiation. Its vertical distribution is unknown, but this species is found mostly at low to intermediate elevations.

HABITAT Tropical deciduous and evergreen forest.

DESCRIPTION *Micrurus corallinus* averages 500–700 mm in overall length but may reach 950 mm.

It is a tricolored snake with a pattern of 13–27 (average 18–21) black body rings plus 3–8 black rings on the tail. The snout is black to a point just posterior to the eyes and including the first 4 supralabials, the internasals, prefrontals, preoculars, supraoculars, frontal, and all (sometimes) or most of the parietals. The black pigment usually tapers to a point at the posterior end of the interparietal suture. A white occipital ring passes around the edge of the parietals, extending anteriorly on the sides of the head to a point just behind the eyes and including part of the postoculars, both temporals, and the posterior 3–3½ supralabials. In some specimens the white color extends onto the parietals and blends with the black pigment somewhat; in others the parietals are entirely black, uniting posteriorly with the black nuchal ring. The black nuchal ring is generally 3–6 middorsals and 4–6 ventrals in length. The venter of the head is white (an expansion of the white occipital ring) with black pigment usually on the mental and adjacent infralabials. The black nuchal ring is posteriorly bordered by a narrow white ring not more than 1½ middorsals in length and sometimes only barely evident. The black body rings are of fairly uniform length, about 3–5 middorsals, but are subject to numerous irregularities including disjunctures, fusions, and absence of one-half or all of a ring. The black caudal rings are usually slightly longer than the black body rings. The red rings vary greatly in length but are always the longest of the rings and are uniformly tinged with gray or black on the apices. The white rings, which flank each black ring, are 1½–2½ middorsals in length and somewhat expanded laterally; each scale bears black pigment on the apex. The last body ring is white. The tail is bicolored, lacking red rings, and the white caudal rings are somewhat larger than the white body rings.

There are 1 + 1 temporals, 194–231 ventrals (doubtful reports exist of specimens having 179 and 186 ventrals), 24–51 subcaudals, and no supra-anal keels. Other features of lepidosis are typical of the genus *Micrurus*.

SIMILAR SPECIES There are three species of *Micrurus* known to be sympatric with *M. corallinus*: *M. decoratus*, which lacks a black head cap and possesses a pattern of triads; *M. frontalis*, which possesses 32 or fewer subcaudals, a pale snout, and a pattern of triads; and *M. lemniscatus*, which lacks a black head cap and possesses a pattern of triads. There are four other species of *Micrurus* whose ranges may approach that of *M. corallinus* although sympatry is doubtful: *M. langsdorffi*, which may lack red body annuli; *M. ibiboboca*, which has a pattern of triads, lacks a black cap, and has a low number (19–30) of subcaudals; *M. psyches donosoi*, which lacks rings (black dorsally) and has 192–193 ventrals; and *M. spixii*, which possesses a pattern of triads and a low number of subcaudals (24 or fewer). See also the discussion of false coral snakes in Mimics of Venomous Snakes.

REMARKS Throughout most of its range this is a well-known and common coral snake. The name *Micrurus corallinus* appears frequently in older accounts from throughout Central and South America, and it may refer to any of a number of species.

REFERENCES Abalos and Mischis, 1975; Amaral, 1925b, 1926d, 1930b, 1948a, 1948b, 1974; Azevedo, 1964; Bertoni, 1914, 1939; Cei, 1987; Cendrero et al., 1972; Devincenzi, 1925; Fernández Barrán and Freiberg, 1951; Freiberg, 1968, 1984; Gatti, 1955; Gliesch, 1925; Gomes, 1918a; Günther, 1859; Lema, 1983; Lema and Fabián-Beurmann, 1977; Machado, 1945a; Merrem, 1820; Migone, 1929; L. Müller, 1927; P. Müller, 1968, 1971; Prado, 1945; Roze, 1966b, 1983; Santos, 1981; Schmidt, 1936a; Schouten, 1931, 1937; Talbot, n.d.; Vanzolini, 1985; Vaz-Ferreira and Sierra de Soriano, 1960; Wied-Neuwied, 1820.

### *Micrurus decoratus* (Jan)

(Fig. 35; Map 8)

LOCAL NAME Cobra-coral.

ENGLISH NAME Brazilian coral snake.

DISTRIBUTION Southern Brazil from the state of São Paulo, southern Minas Gerais, and Rio de Janeiro south to Santa Catarina and northeastern Rio Grande do Sul (Map 8). The vertical distribution is from near sea level to at least 1,500 m.

HABITAT Tropical deciduous forest, and lower montane wet forest along the southeastern and southern fringes of the Central highlands.

DESCRIPTION This is a small species not known to exceed 670 mm in overall length.

It is tricolored with a pattern of 12–19 triads on the body plus 1–1⅔ on the tail. The tip of the snout is black, including the rostral, anterior portion of the nasals, internasals, and portions of the first 1–3 pairs of supralabials. This is followed by a yellow band that may include some or all of the second and third supralabials, part of the nasals, the anterior half of the preocular, most of the prefrontals, and the anterior edge of the supraoculars and frontal. The yellow band is succeeded by a black ocular band that includes the remainder of the supraoculars and frontal, the postoculars, portions of 3–6 pairs of supralabials, and the anterior edge of the parietals. In some specimens, the black snout coloration fuses laterally with the black ocular band, reducing the yellow prefrontal band to a blotch. A red parietal ring includes the remainder of the dorsum of the head, extending over 1½–3 rows of dorsals and including most of the venter of the head. The mental, anterior chinshields, and first 3 or 4 infralabials generally bear some black pigment and may be entirely darkened. Alternatively, some specimens have tinges of yellow and/ or red around the infralabial edges. The neck pattern is variable but most frequently consists of a black ring 3–6 middorsals in length representing the *median* ring of the first body triad (i.e., first triad two-thirds complete). Frequently there is yellow pigment anterior to this ring, especially on the venter, and at times this forms a ring. There is usually some black pigment on the first dorsals, just posterior to the parietals, and some specimens may bear a vestigial black ring at this point. The pale yellow rings are generally 1½–3 middorsals long. The median black triad rings are slightly longer than the accessory black rings, averaging 3–4 and 2–3 middorsals, respectively, with the latter reduced ventrally. The red rings are the longest, averaging 7–15 middorsals and bearing black pigment on the apical tips. The vent is situated beneath the anterior edge of a red ring. The tail tip may be black or red. Generally the pale yellow rings are immaculate, although some widely scattered black pigment may be evident. Red and yellow rings are immaculate ventrally. The eye is relatively large, the head slender, and the tail thickset.

There are 0 + 1 temporals (rarely 1 + 1, and if so, usually on one side only), 196–226 ventrals, and 16–37 subcaudals (usually fewer than 25). Other features of lepidosis are typical of the genus *Micrurus*.

SIMILAR SPECIES *Micrurus decoratus* is or may be sympatric with three species of coral snakes: *M. corallinus* has a black head cap and lacks triads; in *M. frontalis* the posterior half of the parietals is heavily pigmented with black (red in *M. decoratus*) and the pattern includes a complete triad on the neck (two-thirds present in *M. decoratus*); *M. lemniscatus* possesses more than 226 ventrals (vs. 196–226 in *M. decoratus*) and the pattern includes a complete triad on the neck. *Micrurus decoratus* may be distinguished further from sympatric congeners by its 0 + 1 temporal condition—most *Micrurus* species have 1 + 1 or 1 + 2 temporals. See Mimics of Venomous Snakes for a discussion of false coral snakes.

REFERENCES Amaral, 1921a, 1922, 1926e, 1930b, 1978; Azevedo, 1962a; Günther, 1859; Hoge and Romano, 1973; Hoge and

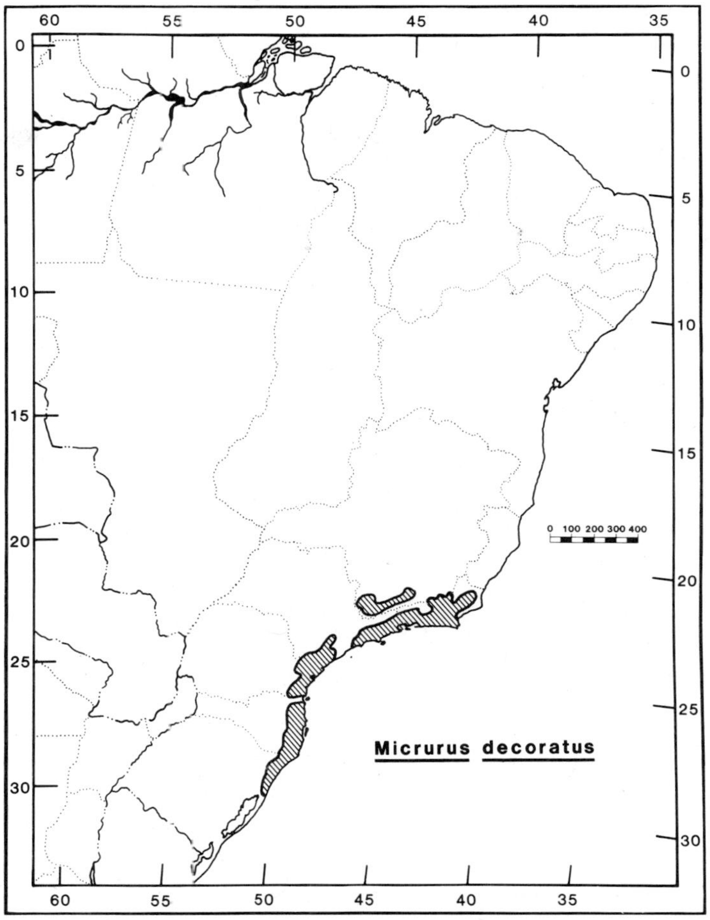


**Map 8.** Distribution of *Micrurus decoratus* in southeastern Brazil.

Romano Hoge, 1981b; Jan, 1858; Lema, 1971a; Lema and Azevedo, 1969; Lema et al., 1980; Lutz and Mello, 1922, 1923; Prado, 1945; Roze, 1983; Santos, 1981; Schmidt, 1936a.

## *Micrurus diastema* (Duméril, Bibron, and Duméril)

(Figs. 36–39; Map 9)

LOCAL NAMES Coral, coralillo. Belize: coral snake, coralillo. Guatemala: cantil coral, gargantilla. Mexico: coral anillado.

ENGLISH NAME Variable coral snake.

DISTRIBUTION Low and moderate elevations of the Atlantic drainage from central Veracruz, northern Oaxaca, and the Yucatán Peninsula, Mexico, southward through Belize and northern Guatemala to northwestern Honduras (Map 9). The vertical distribution is from near sea level to about 1,250 m.

HABITAT Tropical rainforest, tropical evergreen forest, tropical deciduous forest, lower cloud forest, and pine-oak forest.

DESCRIPTION A medium-sized coral snake, *M. diastema* occasionally reaches an overall length of about 850 mm.

This snake possesses an exceedingly variable color pattern that may make identification difficult. The black head cap often reaches, but does not encroach on, the parietals; it includes one or both postoculars and generally the first 2 or 3 and often the upper part of the fourth pair of supralabials. A pale spot on the snout may or may not be present. The number of black body rings ranges from 0 to 62; individual rings cover 1–6 ventrals. Black rings most frequently completely encircle the body but may be broken dorsally or ventrally. There are 0–16 black tail rings. Yellow rings, if present, cover ½–2 dorsal scale lengths. The black nape ring is several scales broader than the other black body rings and frequently involves the posterior tips of the parietals; it may be interrupted ventrally. The scales in the red rings may be uniformly tipped with black pigment, or the black pigment may be either concentrated into small irregular blotches covering one to several scales, or concentrated between black rings forming ill-defined accessory rings. Frequently, the red ventrals are spotted or mottled with black.

Supra-anal keels are absent in this species and there are 1 + 1 or 1 + 2 temporals, 188–228 ventrals, and 28–62 subcaudals, most or all of which are divided. Other features of lepidosis are typical of the genus *Micrurus*.

SIMILAR SPECIES Because *M. diastema* is wide-ranging and variable in color pattern, it may be confused

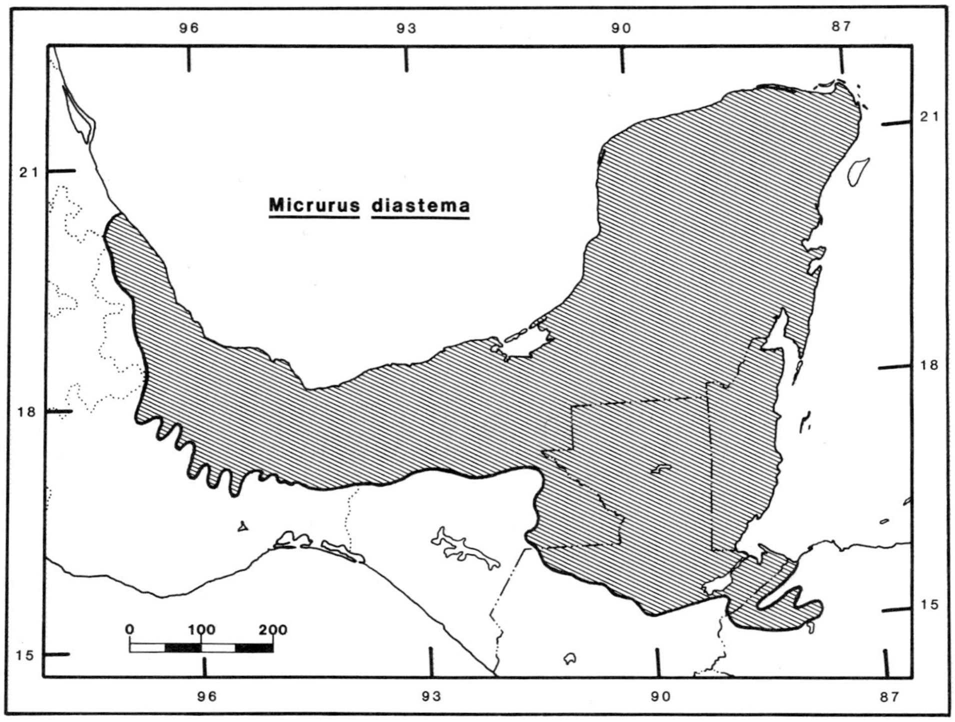


**Map 9.** Distribution of *Micrurus diastema* in southern Mexico and northern Central America. This species is confined to the Atlantic watershed.

with a number of other coral snakes and harmless species. Its range may overlap with five species of the genus *Micrurus*. These species may be distinguished from *M. diastema* in the regions of sympatry by the following characteristics: *M. limbatus* is bicolored with black and red, and has more numerous black rings or spots (25–41); *M. elegans* has black body rings disposed in triads and a pale parietal ring that is incomplete dorsally; *M. browni* has red scales that are dusky but not black tipped and males and some females have supra-anal keels; *M. nigrocinctus* has a completely black snout and males have supra-anal keels; and *M. hippocrepis* has fewer black rings (10–24) that are often incomplete dorsally and no black tipping on the red scales.

Many harmless snakes have brightly colored rings or patterns; *Pliocercus* so closely resembles *M. diastema* that careful scrutiny is necessary to distinguish it. See Mimics of Venomous Snakes for a discussion of *Erythrolamprus*, *Lampropeltis*, *Ninia*, and *Scaphiodontophis*. The unusual color morph found in some *M. diastema* specimens from the Yucatán Peninsula—blackish head, with or without nape ring, and mostly red body and tail—closely resembles the coloration of juvenile *Clelia* (Fig. 466) and occasional specimens of *Lampropeltis* found in the same region.

REMARKS Seven subspecies are sometimes recognized, primarily on the basis of pattern, but this species is so variable and exhibits so much discordant variation that recognition of these subspecies on any basis other than geographic distribution is often difficult. The various subspecies have the following ranges: *M. d. diastema* (Fig. 36), central Veracruz to western Tabasco, Mexico; *M. d. affinis*, Atlantic versant of northern Oaxaca, Mexico; *M. d. macdougalli*, Atlantic slopes of the highlands of extreme southeastern Oaxaca, Mexico; *M. d. sapperi* (Fig. 37), southern portion of the Yucatán Peninsula, including Campeche and northern Chiapas, Mexico, and northern Guatemala and Belize; *M. d. alienus* (Fig. 38), northern portion of the Yucatán Peninsula, including Yucatán and northeastern Quintana Roo, Mexico; *M. d. apiatus*, Atlantic versant of the uplands of northern Guatemala and eastern Chiapas, Mexico; and *M. d. aglaeope* (Fig. 39), northwestern Honduras.

Particular combinations of pattern, coloration, and squamation characterize certain populations. For example, specimens from central Veracruz tend to have a relatively low number of black rings on the body and tail, a heavy concentration of black pigment on the red scales, and, in most specimens, a black nape ring that is incomplete ventrally. Snakes from southern Veracruz and southeastern Oaxaca likewise have extremely heavy black pigmentation on the red scales, and almost one-half of the specimens from the latter region have an interrupted black nape ring.

In the northern Yucatán snakes tend to have a relatively low number of black rings; a few specimens may lack black and yellow body rings altogether, except for a black nape ring, and even this may be absent. Most snakes from this population generally also have an interrupted nape ring, 1 + 2 temporals, and red ventrals that lack black pigment. The black nape ring usually does not reach the parietals or covers only a small portion of the posterior tips in snakes from the Yucatán and southeastern Oaxaca.

The northern Petén Department of Guatemala has snakes that usually are characterized by 1 + 2 temporals and a pale spot on the snout involving the rostral and internasals. In the southern portion of the Petén Department of Guatemala, as well as northeastern Chiapas and southeastern Tabasco, snakes tend to have a relatively high number of black rings. Furthermore, the southern Petén Department snakes tend to have black pigment concentrated in the middle of the red rings, almost all have a pale spot on the snout, most have 1 + 2 temporals and lack or have only traces of yellow rings, and frequently the black body rings are interrupted.

Snakes from Alta Verapaz, Guatemala, and Honduras have black pigment that is concentrated on the red rings about half way between the black rings and invariably seem to have pale spots on the snout. Alta Verapaz specimens are further characterized by an especially high number of black rings, most lack or have only traces of the yellow rings, all are without black spotting on the ventrals, and they frequently have black nape and body rings that are interrupted.

REFERENCES Ahl, 1927; Alvarez del Toro, 1983; Andrews, 1937; Barrera, 1963; Blaney and Blaney, 1978, 1979; Cendrero et al., 1972; Cope, 1859, 1870, 1885b, 1887; Duellman, 1965a; Dugès, 1885, 1896; Dundee et al., 1986; Ferrari-Perez, 1886; Flores Villela et al., 1987; Fraser, 1964, 1973; Gadow, 1905; Gaige, 1936; Garman, 1884a, 1884b; Gehlbach, 1972; Greene and McDiarmid, 1981; Günther, 1859; Gutiérrez et al., 1988; Henderson and Hoevers, 1975; Jan, 1858; Lee, 1980; Martín del Campo, 1935, 1950; Meyer, 1969; Mocquard, 1908–1909; Neill, 1960; Neill and Allen, 1959a; Pérez-Higadera [*sic*] et al., 1987; Pérez-Higareda, 1980; J. A. Peters, 1953; W. C. H. Peters, 1869; Ramírez-Bautista et al., 1981; Roze, 1967, 1983; Ruthven, 1912; Schmidt, 1933a, 1936b, 1941; Schmidt and Andrews, 1936; Schmidt and Smith, 1943; H. M. Smith, 1938, 1960b; H. M. Smith and Taylor, 1945; Stuart, 1934, 1935, 1948, 1950, 1958, 1963; E. H. Taylor, 1940; Tiedemann and Haupl, 1980; Werler and Smith, 1952; Werner, 1903; Wilson, 1983; Wilson and Meyer, 1985.

## *Micrurus dissoleucus* (Cope)

(Fig. 40; Map 10)

LOCAL NAMES Coral, coralilla, gargantilla. Colombia: candelilla, coral común, coralillo, coralito. Venezuela: coral, coral llanera.

ENGLISH NAME Pygmy coral snake.

DISTRIBUTION This species is found from the Canal Zone in Panama east into the Chocó region of Colombia, the Caribbean coastal region, lower Magdalena Valley and north-central portions of Colombia (Cesar, Norte de Santander, and La Guajira), and extends into adjacent coastal regions of Venezuela to the Orinoco Delta. It occurs inland in Venezuela primarily north of the Río Orinoco (Map 10). It is known to occur at elevations up to 900 m in the vicinity of Caracas but this is a lowland form, generally encountered at elevations of 500 m or less.

HABITAT This species frequents xeric to semi-arid or seasonally dry regions: lower montane dry forest, dry tropical forest, tropical deciduous and thorn forests, and savanna.

DESCRIPTION *Micrurus dissoleucus* is perhaps the smallest member of the genus, averaging 250–400 mm, with a known maximum of 650 mm in overall length.

It is a tricolored snake with a pattern consisting of ⅓ + 6 to ⅓ + 11 black triads on the head plus body. There are ⅔–1⅔ black triads on the tail. The nuchal black ring represents the posterior ring of the first triad, giving a fractional count overall. The head is black from the snout to the occipital region; frequently the black color extends posteriorly as far as the first 2–5 rows of dorsals. The snout is slightly acuminate. There is a white band or ring crossing the dorsum of the head just posterior to the eyes that usually includes all or part of the postoculars, part of the parietals, and part (or none) of the supraoculars and frontal, the anterior temporals, and from 1 to all of the fourth, fifth, sixth, and seventh pairs of supralabials. In some specimens, the white color does not extend onto the infralabials; in others it occurs only as isolated spots on the posterior chinshields. Alternatively, it may expand laterally, traversing virtually the entire venter of the head except for scattered black pigment on the first two infralabials, the mental, and along various scale sutures. The black nuchal ring is continuous from the midparietal region through several rows of dorsals; its posterior border often forms a slight apex pointing away from the snout. Black pigment is often present along the sutures of cephalic scales included in the white parietal ring. In many (especially Colombian) specimens, the nuchal ring is incomplete ventrally.

The black nuchal ring is followed by a red ring 5–7 middorsals in length. In general, the median black ring of each triad is slightly longer (average, 7–8 middorsals) than the outer black rings (average, 6–7 middorsals). The black rings are separated by white rings 3–4 middorsals in length that are distinctly outlined in black and sometimes bear black apices. The triads are separated by red rings 4–11 middorsals long and thinly outlined in darker pigment. In some specimens the red rings bear scattered black pigment or stippling, while in others they are immaculate. The tail, which is extremely short and thickset, is normally tipped in black. The ventral colors tend to be immaculate, except for some scattered black pigment present in the white rings.

There are 1 + 1 (sometimes fused) temporals, 171–230 ventrals and 17–28 subcaudals. Other features of lepidosis are typical of the genus *Micrurus*.

SIMILAR SPECIES There are six tricolored species of coral snakes with which *M. dissoleucus* is at some point sympatric. Of these, *M. clarki*, *M. nigrocinctus*, and *M. psyches* lack triads. *Micrurus ancoralis* has a red head and the first triad, although incomplete, consists of two or more black rings (only one ring present in *M. dissoleucus*). *Micrurus isozonus* possesses a red parietal ring (white in *M. dissoleucus*) and the first body triad is complete. Throughout most of its range *M. dumerilii* lacks triads; however, in the lower Magdalena Valley of Colombia, the accessory rings are developed such that triads do exist in this species. They are poorly defined as compared with *M. dissoleucus* and they are separated by red rings more than twice the length of the triads (red rings are only slightly longer than black rings in *M. dissoleucus*). See also the discussion of false coral snakes in Mimics of Venomous Snakes.

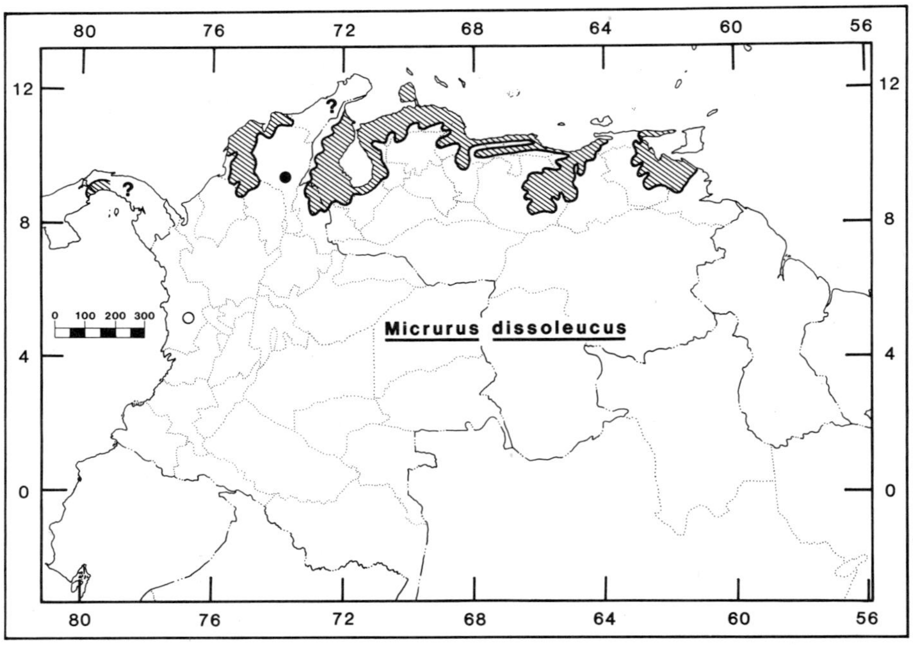


**Map 10.** Distribution of *Micrurus dissoleucus* in northern South America. The distribution of this species may actually encompass more of the Guajira Peninsula than is shown. Question marks represent possible areas of occurrence. An apparently isolated record (*open circle*) exists in the Departamento de Chocó; this remains unverified. Solid circle represents an apparently isolated record in northern Colombia.

REMARKS There are four races of *Micrurus dissoleucus*: In *M. d. dissoleucus* (Fig. 40)—found from northeastern Colombia in the Departamento del Cesar and Departamento de Norte de Santander to the Orinoco Delta of eastern Venezuela—the males possess 23 or more subcaudals and the females fewer than 213 ventrals. In *M. d. dunni* the males possess 23 or more subcaudals and the females more than 212 ventrals. There are 8–11 triads on the body. It occurs in the Canal Zone of Panama east into the Colombian Chocó, and reportedly as far south as Andagoya, but the distribution merits further investigation, as the habitat diverges from that which is considered typical. *Micrurus d. melanogenys* is known only from the vicinity of Santa Marta, Departamento de Magdalena, in northern Colombia. The males possess 23 or fewer subcaudals, and there are 6–9 triads on the body. In *M. d. nigrirostris*—found in the Río Magdalena Delta in the Departamento de Bolívar, and the Departamento de Magdalena, northern Colombia—the males possess 23 or more subcaudals and the females 212 or more ventrals. There are 6–8 triads on the body. A considerable distributional hiatus exists between the race from Panama (*M. d. dunni*) and *M. d. nigrirostris*. The latter form is separated distributionally from *M. d. melanogenys* by the Ciénaga Grande. The nominate race is separated from the Colombian coastal forms by the Sierra de Perijá. Intergradation between the races has not been documented.

This small coral snake is commonly encountered throughout its range and frequently occurs around human habitation.

REFERENCES Amaral, 1925b, 1928, 1931b; Angel, 1983; Barbour, 1923; Barbour and Amaral, 1924; Castro et al., 1982; Cendrero et al., 1972; Cope, 1860b, 1860c; Daniel, 1949; Dugand, 1975; Dunn, 1944a, 1949; Evans, 1947; Griffin, 1916; Grocott and Sadler, 1958; Hoge and Lancini, 1962; Lancini, 1970, 1979; Marcuzzi, 1950; McCoy and Richmond, 1966; Medem, 1969; Milá de la Roca, 1932; P. Müller, 1973; Nicéforo-María, 1942; Pérez-Santos, 1986a; Rivero-Blanco and Dixon, 1979; Roze, 1955, 1966a, 1967, 1970a, 1983; Ruthven, 1922; Sandner-Montilla, 1985b; Schmidt, 1933b, 1936a, 1955; Swanson, 1945; Tiedemann and Haupl, 1980; Vellard, 1941; Vetencourt Finol., 1960.

## *Micrurus distans* (Kennicott)

(Fig. 41; Map 11)

LOCAL NAMES Coral, coralillo.

ENGLISH NAME West Mexican coral snake.

DISTRIBUTION Mexico. This species occurs at low and moderate elevations from southwestern Chihuahua and southern Sonora, southward on the Pacific drainage through Sinaloa, Nayarit, Jalisco, Colima, and Michoacán to Guerrero (Map 11). Its range within the Río de las Balsas Basin probably includes portions of several other states as well. Its vertical distribution is from near sea level to about 1,300 m.

HABITAT Tropical deciduous forest and thorn forest.

DESCRIPTION A medium-sized coral snake, *M. distans* reaches a length of more than 1 m.

The pattern of this wide-ranging species is variable, but always consists of black, yellow, and red rings. There are 6–20 black rings on the body; specimens from the Río de las Balsas Basin tend to have 6–11, those from southern Nayarit and Jalisco have 19–20, and other populations fall somewhere in between. The black body rings generally cover 3 or 4 dorsal scales and involve 3 ventrals. There are 3–6 black rings on the tail and, except for snakes from the Colima region, these black rings tend to be longer than the pale rings that separate them.

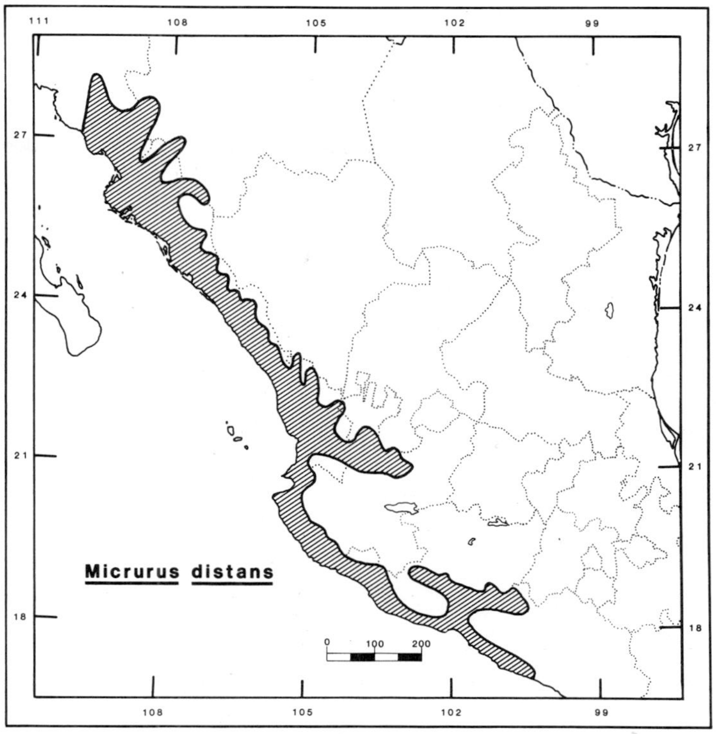


**Map 11.** Distribution of *Micrurus distans* in western Mexico.

The black nuchal ring begins *behind* the parietals and extends 6–8 dorsal scale lengths, decreasing to 2–3 scales ventrally. The yellow rings are 1–2 dorsals long. The black head cap extends to the anterior one-third to one-half of the parietals, covering the frontal, preoculars, and upper anterior part of the first temporal. In a few snakes from Colima it may also include the first 3 supralabials and upper part of the fourth, making the snout uniformly black, but most snakes in other parts of the range possess pale spots on the lower portions of the anterior supralabials or the supralabials are entirely pale. A pale spot may be present on the tip of the snout that involves the rostral, at least the anterior part of the internasals, and the first pair of supralabials. The lower jaw is pale with varying amounts of dark mottling on the mental, anteriormost infralabials, and anterior chinshields; pigment tends to be concentrated along the borders of scales, especially the chinshields. The red rings are 5–6 dorsals long at midbody and, except for snakes from southern Nayarit and Jalisco, there is no dark pigment on the tips of the red scales.

Supra-anal keels are absent, and there are 1 + 1 temporals, 198–235 ventrals, and 38–55 subcaudals. Other features of lepidosis are typical of the genus *Micrurus*.

SIMILAR SPECIES This species is sympatric over portions of its range with *M. laticollaris*, *M. proximans*, and *M. browni*. *Micrurus laticollaris* is distinguished easily on the basis of its distinctive pattern, consisting of black rings disposed in triads. Distinguishing *M. proximans* and *M. browni* from *M. distans* is more difficult, but the black nuchal ring in *M. distans* does not involve the posterior portion of the parietals, whereas it does in *M. proximans* and *M. browni*.

REMARKS Several geographic races are recognized: *M. d. distans* (Fig. 41) from southwestern Chihuahua, through southern Sonora and Sinaloa to northwestern Nayarit; *M. d. zweifeli* in central and southern Nayarit and adjacent Jalisco; *M. d. oliveri* in Colima and adjacent Jalisco; and *M. d. michoacanensis* in the Río de las Balsas Basin of Michoacán and Guerrero.

REFERENCES Bogert and Oliver, 1945; Casas-Andreu, 1981; Croulet, 1963; Duellman, 1954, 1958, 1961, 1965b; Dugès, 1891, 1896; Echternacht, 1973; Garman, 1884a; Golay, 1985; Hardy and McDiarmid, 1969; Kennicott, 1860; Martín del Campo, 1935; Mocquard, 1899; Oliver, 1937; Roze, 1967, 1983; Schmidt 1933a, 1936b; Schmidt and Shannon, 1947; Schmidt and Smith, 1943; H. M. Smith and Chrapliwy, 1958; H. M. Smith and Necker, 1944; H. M. Smith and Taylor, 1945, 1966; Tanner, 1985; E. H. Taylor, 1938b; Zweifel, 1959b; Zweifel and Norris, 1955.

### *Micrurus dumerilii* (Jan)

(Figs. 42–44; Map 12)

LOCAL NAMES Coral, coralilla.

ENGLISH NAME Dumeril's coral snake.

DISTRIBUTION This species occurs in the western lowlands of Colombia, extending south into northern Ecuador (west of the Andes); the lower slopes and inner valleys of the Colombian Andes, including the western versant of the Cordillera Oriental; the Caribbean lowlands of Colombia east to the Sierra Nevada de Santa Marta region, continuing through the Departamento del Cesar and the Departamento de Norte de Santander into the Maracaibo Basin of Venezuela and the northwestern coastal lowlands as far east as Caracas and the state of Miranda (Map 12). Its range in Venezuela is north of the Río Orinoco and Río Apure. A specimen (Fig. 43) exists from the Panamanian-Colombian border; the species is

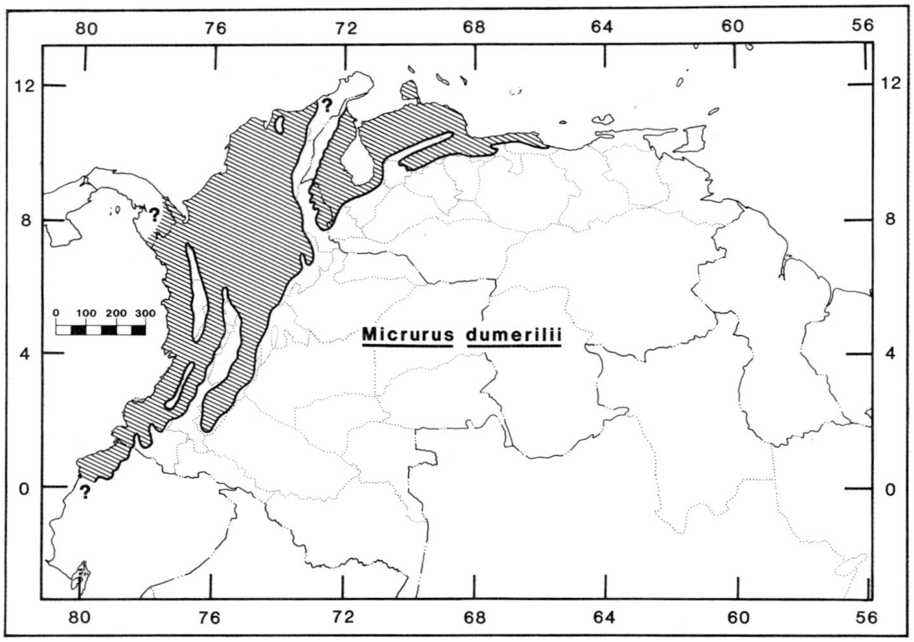


**Map 12.** Distribution of *Micrurus dumerilii* in northern South America. The range of this species into eastern Panama, coastal Ecuador, and the Guajira Peninsula is not known. Question marks represent possible areas of occurrence.

likely to turn up in southeastern Panama. It would not be surprising to find this species on forested islands. It is primarily a lowland inhabitant frequenting regions up to 600 m in elevation. However, *M. d. antioquiensis* is found as high as 1,800 m above sea level, and *M. d. colombianus* extends to at least 2,133 m elevation in the Sierra Nevada de Santa Marta of Colombia.

HABITAT Lower montane wet forest, tropical rain forest, dry tropical forest, and thorn forest. It generally prefers more humid locales and thus frequents riparian situations.

DESCRIPTION *Micrurus dumerilii* averages 500–700 mm in overall length; the maximum reported is 775 mm.

It is a tricolored species with a variable pattern involving 10–27 single black rings (Fig. 42) or up to 14 body triads (see Remarks). The snout and dorsum of the head are black; this includes all or nearly all of the parietals, the sides of the snout, and the first 2–3 pairs of supralabials. The dorsal that abuts the parietal tips is often black. The black snout and head cap are followed by a yellow or white occipital ring that may include parts of supralabials 2–5, some or all of the temporals, supralabials 6–7, and the adjacent dorsals bordering the parietals. The ring may encroach upon the posterior edges (or half) of the parietals or lighten the pigment posteriorly; it may be divided by the parietals; or it may include as many as the first 3 rows of dorsals. The occipital ring tends to expand laterally and may include all or most of the chin and infralabials, although the tip of the jaw and some infralabials are usually black. The scales of the occipital ring vary from immaculate, to outlined in black, to heavily pigmented with black. When heavily pigmented, the concentration is usually greatest middorsally and over the temporals. A black nuchal ring 3–6 middorsals long is usually present. This ring may be incomplete or replaced by red in *M. d. antioquiensis* (see Remarks).

When present, triads are poorly developed, the outer black rings being little more than concentrations of black pigment at the edges of the red rings. Median black triad rings (or simply black rings if triads are not present) tend to be fairly uniform in size and approximate the nuchal ring in length. White or yellow rings are ½–3 middorsals long. Red rings are two to three or more times as long as the black rings (or triads). The tail is patterned differently from the body and may be white-and-black bicolored or the white caudal rings may contain concentrations of black and/or red pigment. Generally the black caudal rings are longest. The ventral pattern closely approximates that of the dorsum. All red and white scales are lightly to heavily stippled with black dorsally; this pigmentation is often concentrated toward the ends of the red rings. See Remarks for further details.

There are 1 + 1 equal-sized temporals, 170–217 ventrals, and 31–58 subcaudals. Adult males and some females possess well-developed supra-anal keels. Other features of lepidosis are typical of the genus *Micrurus*.

SIMILAR SPECIES In parts of its range, *M. dumerilii* is sympatric with eight tricolored congeners. *Micrurus ancoralis* possesses triads and a red head, and *M. bocourti* and *M. isozonus* possess triads, while sympatric populations of *M. dumerilii* lack triads and have a black head cap. *Micrurus clarki* lacks supra-anal keels and has pale (or partially pale) anterior infracephalic scales; *M. dumerilii* has supra-anal keels and a distinctly dark black snout. *Micrurus dissoleucus* possesses triads of equal or subequal black rings; sympatric populations of *M. dumerilii* either lack triads or, if they are present, the outer black rings are much narrower than the median black rings. *Micrurus nigrocinctus* lacks the black head cap found in *M. dumerilii*. *Micrurus psyches circinalis* is virtually indistinguishable from *M. dumerilii* except that adult males lack supra-anal keels, possess narrower red rings, and have hetero-

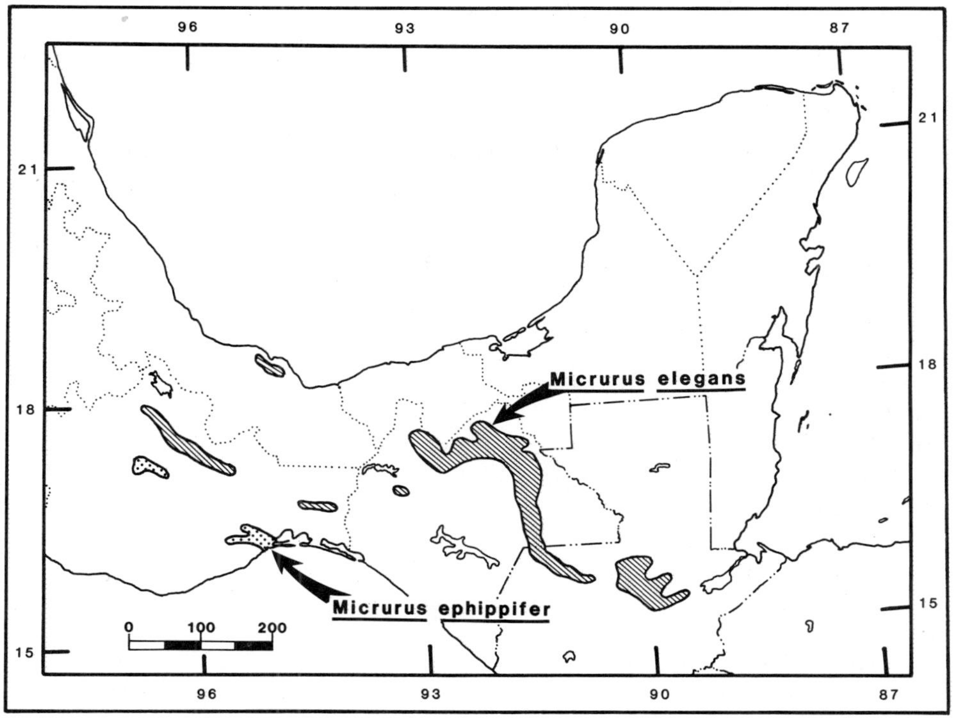


**Map 13.** Distributions of *Micrurus elegans* (*diagonal lines*) and *M. ephippifer* (*stipples*) in southern Mexico and Guatemala.

geneous temporals; the temporals tend to be subequal in *M. dumerilii.* The two species evidently are sympatric along the eastern extremity of the range of *M. dumerilii. Micrurus sangilensis* possesses 17–22 triads (vs. 14 or fewer in *M. dumerilii*) and lacks supra-anal keels. See Mimics of Venomous Snakes for a discussion of false coral snakes.

REMARKS There are currently five inadequately distinguished races of *Micrurus dumerilii*: *M. d. dumerilii*, which occurs in Colombia from the lower Magdalena Valley to Norte de Santander, possesses a pattern of up to 11 poorly developed triads plus 5–9 black caudal annuli. The black nuchal ring is not part of a complete triad. Males have more than 189 ventrals, females more than 208. *Micrurus d. antioquiensis*—found in Colombia in the middle Magdalena Valley and adjacent versants of the Cordillera Central and Cordillera Oriental, and on the western versant of the Cordillera Central—possesses a pattern of 10–17 black body rings, not disposed in triads. The black nuchal ring is usually absent (replaced by red), but may be present as a band, a blotch, or a ring. *Micrurus d. carinicauda*, found from the Norte de Santander region of northeastern Colombia through the Maracaibo Basin and eastward to Caracas and the state of Miranda, Venezuela, possesses a pattern of 14–27 black body rings, not disposed in triads, and 4–10 black caudal rings. *Micrurus d. colombianus*, which occupies northern Colombia in the Sierra Nevada de Santa Marta region, possesses a pattern of 9–14 triads plus 4–10 black caudal rings. Males have 170 or more ventrals, and females have 203–207 ventrals. *Micrurus d. transandinus* (Figs. 43, 44) is found in western Colombia in the Departamento del Chocó and western Antioquia, and probably in extreme southern Panama as well; its range extends southward into the western lowlands of Ecuador. It possesses a pattern of 11–21 black rings, not disposed in triads, and 5–9 black caudal rings.

REFERENCES Alemán, 1953; Amaral, 1925b, 1928, 1931b; Angel, 1983; Castro et al., 1982; Daniel, 1949; Dugand, 1975; Dunn, 1944a, 1944b; Griffin, 1916; Hoge and Lancini, 1962; Jan, 1858; Lancini, 1970; 1979; Marcuzzi, 1950; McCoy and Richmond, 1966; Medem, 1969; Miyata, 1982; Mocquard, 1908–1909; P. Müller, 1973; Nicéforo-María, 1942; Orcés, 1942, 1943, 1948; Pérez-Santos, 1986a, 1986b; Pérez-Santos and Moreno, 1986; J. A. Peters, 1960a; Rendahl and Vestergren, 1940; Roux-Esteve, 1983; Roze, 1955, 1966a, 1967, 1970b, 1983; Ruthven, 1922; Sandner-Montilla, 1985b; Schmidt, 1936a, 1955; Tiedemann and Haupl, 1980; Vetencourt Finol., 1960.

## *Micrurus elegans* (Jan)

(Fig. 45; Map 13)

LOCAL NAMES Guatemala: coral, coralillo. Mexico: coralillo, coral punteado (Chiapas).

ENGLISH NAME Elegant coral snake.

DISTRIBUTION Moderate and intermediate elevations of the Caribbean versant in Mexico from central Veracruz, northern Oaxaca, and the Sierra de los Tuxtlas, southeastward through southern Tabasco, northern Chiapas, and the Atlantic drainage of the northern mountains of Guatemala to the Sierra de las Minas (Map 13). The vertical distribution is from about 1,000 to 1,830 m.

HABITAT Lower montane dry forest, largely pine-oak; lower montane wet forest; cloud forest; and rarely tropical deciduous forest in areas of dense canopy.

DESCRIPTION This large coral snake may reach a total length of over 1 m but is usually less than 700 mm.

*Micrurus elegans* possesses a distinctive pattern of 14–19 triads of black rings on the body; the center black ring of each triad is set off from other black rings in the triad by irregular or broken *double* rows of yellow or white scales, and triads are separated from one another by orangish rings. The triads are more apparent ventrally, where the yellow or white coloration is continuous and there is no black suffusion on the red scales. There are 4–12 black rings on the tail. The pale head band is incomplete middorsally; the upper part of the head is entirely black except for yellow vertical bars behind the eyes that extend from the margins of the lips to the center of the parietals. These yellow bars involve all, or parts of, supralabials 5 and 6, and sometimes 4; the primary and sometimes secondary temporal; often the posterior edges of both postoculars; and the lateral portions of the parietals (Fig. 13). The mental and first 3 infralabials are marked with some black pigment, followed by 2 infralabials with some yellow. Portions of the anterior chinshields, medial portions of the first pair of infralabials, and the posterior part of the mental are also yellow.

Adult males possess well-defined supra-anal keels. There are 1 + 1 temporals, 188–228 ventrals, and 29–49 subcaudals, many of which may be undivided. Other features of lepidosis are characteristic of the genus *Micrurus*.

SIMILAR SPECIES Inasmuch as *M. elegans* is the only coral snake within its range that has black rings in triads, it is easily distinguished from other species with which it may overlap, namely, *M. browni*, *M. diastema*, *M. limbatus*, and *M. nigrocinctus* (see individual species accounts). In some parts of its range, *Pliocercus* may possess triads and closely resemble *M. elegans*. Very rarely *Lampropeltis* from the Meseta Central of Chiapas may possess triads.

REMARKS Two subspecies are recognized: *M. e. elegans* in the north and *M. e. veraepacis* (Fig. 45) to the south. Snakes in the south reputedly have more numerous ventrals and subcaudals and a relatively shorter frontal (less than one and one-half times longer than wide) than snakes occurring in the northern portion of the range.

These snakes are quick to bite when restrained; they appear to be most active at dusk or after dark, but have been found crawling in leaf litter by day.

REFERENCES Alvarez del Toro, 1983; Alvarez del Toro and Smith, 1956; Baker et al., 1971; Blaney and Blaney, 1978; Cope, 1861, 1887; Cuesta Terron, 1932; Flores Villela et al., 1987; Gadow, 1905; Garman, 1884a, 1884b; Greene and McDiarmid, 1981; Gutiérrez et al., 1988; Jan, 1858, 1859a; Jan and Sordelli, 1870–1881; Martín del Campo, 1950; Mocquard, 1908–1909; Ocaranza, 1930; Pérez-Higadera [*sic*] et al., 1987; Ramírez-Bautista et al., 1981; Roze, 1967, 1983; Schmidt, 1933a, 1936b, 1958; H. M. Smith, 1941b, 1942; H. M. Smith and Landy, 1965; H. M. Smith and Taylor, 1945; Stuart, 1948, 1950, 1963; Sumichrast, 1881–1882; Werner, 1896.

### *Micrurus ephippifer* (Cope)

(Figs. 46, 47; Map 13)

LOCAL NAMES Coral, coralillo.

ENGLISH NAME Oaxacan coral snake.

DISTRIBUTION Mexico. Low, moderate, and intermediate elevations of the Pacific drainage of Oaxaca, from the Continental Divide in central Oaxaca to the lowlands and foothills of the Isthmus of Tehuantepec (see Map 13). The vertical distribution is from near sea level to over 2,300 m.

HABITAT Tropical deciduous forest and pine-oak forest.

DESCRIPTION A medium-sized coral snake, *M. ephippifer* reaches a total length of over 900 mm.

This species possesses black, yellow, and red rings, but the pattern is unusual in that the red rings are heavily suffused with black pigment forming black dorsal saddles; red rings may form a narrow fringe in front of and behind these saddles or they may be contiguous with the yellow rings. The entire snout is black, including all or most of the frontal, the anterior tips of the parietals, and the anterior 3 or 4 pairs of supralabials. The black nuchal ring reaches the posterior tips of the parietals and extends 6–9 dorsal scale lengths; it is complete ventrally. There are 13–26 black body rings 4–7 dorsals long and 4–7 ventrals long. The tail has 4–7 black rings. The yellow body rings are 1½–2 dorsals long and 1–2 ventrals long. The red rings, interrupted dorsally with black, are 2–9 dorsals long and 2–10 ventrals long. The ventrals are marked with black.

Supra-anal keels are absent and there are 1 + 1 or 1 + 2 temporals, 210–237 ventrals, and 30–56 subcaudals, a few of which may be undivided. Other features of lepidosis are characteristic of the genus *Micrurus*.

SIMILAR SPECIES *Micrurus bogerti* and *M. browni* may be sympatric with *M. ephippifer* and are most easily distinguished from this species by the absence of black dorsal saddles. *Micrurus bogerti* is further distinctive in having shorter black body rings (2 ventrals long) and red scales not tipped with black; in males of *M. browni* supra-anal keels are present.

It is notable that *Pliocercus elapoides* has been reported within 70 km of the known range of *M. ephippifer*; specimens from this population of *P. elapoides* possess a similar pattern with middorsal darkening of the red body rings. Also see the discussion of *Lampropeltis triangulum* in Mimics of Venomous Snakes.

REMARKS Most specimens of this snake have been found in two general regions: the lowlands near Tehuantepec and the highlands to the north and west of the city of Oaxaca. However, it is probable this species occurs in much of the Pacific drainage of the state of Oaxaca.

REFERENCES Cope, 1865, 1886, 1887; Greene and McDiarmid, 1981; Lynch and Smith, 1965; Martín del Campo, 1935; Roze, 1967, 1983; Schmidt, 1933a, 1958; H. M. Smith, 1943; H. M. Smith and Langebartel, 1949; H. M. Smith and Taylor, 1945; Woodbury and Woodbury, 1944.

### *Micrurus filiformis* (Günther)

(Fig. 49; Map 14)

LOCAL NAMES Coral. Brazil: cobra-coral. Peru: nacanaca.

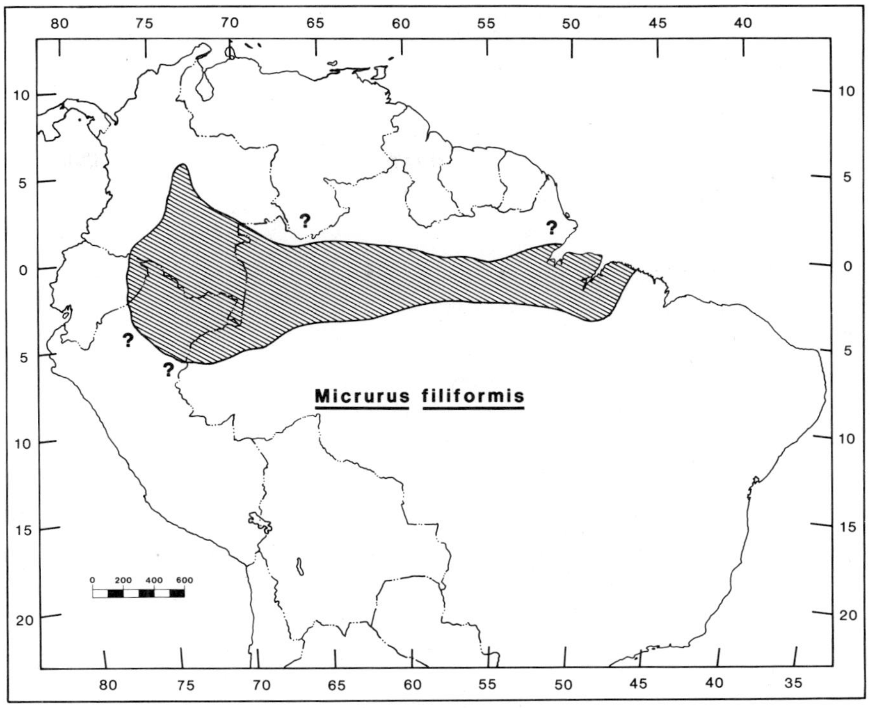


**Map 14.** Distribution of *Micrurus filiformis* across the Amazon Basin of South America. The range of this species may be considerably more extensive than is presently known. Question marks represent possible areas of occurrence.

ENGLISH NAME Slender coral snake.

DISTRIBUTION This species is found from Maranhão and Pará, Brazil, westward along the Amazon River through northeastern Peru and eastern Ecuador, southeastern and east-central Colombia throughout the Amazon watershed and north as far as Villavicencio along the Orinoco drainage of the eastern Andes (Map 14). It is undoubtedly present in southern Venezuela as well and it may exist in Guyana and French Guiana. Most localities are lowland and this species has not been observed at elevations over 400 m. See Remarks.

HABITAT Lower montane wet forest, gallery forest, and primary and secondary rainforest situations, usually near a watercourse.

DESCRIPTION *Micrurus filiformis* is a very slender species averaging 300–550 mm in overall length. It may reach a total length of over 960 mm.

A tricolored species with 11–20 body triads and 1⅔–2⅔ tail triads, it has a black snout, followed by a white prefrontal ring that sometimes has a posterior extension dorsally onto the frontal. The white prefrontal ring fails to completely encircle the head on some specimens due to extensions of black pigment from the tip of the snout posteriorly along the first 3–6 infralabials. A black ring covers all or some of the frontal and the anterior portion of the parietals, extending downward to cover the eyes and anterior temporals; it sometimes includes the last 2 supralabials but is usually interrupted by the red infralabials. The black ring is followed by a long red ring that includes the remainder of the head and the first several dorsal scale rows. The venter of the head is red, except for the mental and 3–6 infralabials, which are black. The body triads are typical in that the central black ring is slightly larger than the others. The white rings are shortest and the intervening red rings usually are the longest. The colors are especially intense and basically immaculate except for a few scattered black flecks in the red rings. The tongue is bluish gray with pale tips.

There are 1 + 1 temporals 262–333 ventrals, 30–45 subcaudals. Supra-anal keels are absent. Other features of lepidosis are typical of the genus *Micrurus*.

SIMILAR SPECIES *Micrurus lemniscatus* is very similar to *M. filiformis* but may be distinguished from it on the basis of fewer ventrals (210–268 vs. 262–333 in *M. filiformis*) and fewer body triads (up to 17, but usually 13 or fewer, vs. usually 13–20). *Micrurus surinamensis* has a red head with black scale outlines and the eye is in contact with only the fourth supralabial (the head is ringed and the eye is in contact with the third and fourth supralabials in *M. filiformis*). *Micrurus spixii* has fewer than 10 triads on the body, as does *M. hemprichii*, which also has an undivided anal plate. *Micrurus isozonus*, which is sympatric with *M. filiformis* in the upper Río Meta region of Colombia, has a white snout and the parietal tips are usually covered by the first black nuchal ring (the snout is black and the parietal scales red in *M. filiformis*). All other sympatric coral snakes lack triads. See also the discussion of false coral snakes in Mimics of Venomous Snakes.

REMARKS Two subspecies are traditionally recognized: *Micrurus f. filiformis*, which occurs from the Manaus vicinity eastward to the mouth of the Amazon River and Pará, Brazil, is distinguished by usually having 1 postocular and 280–333 ventrals. *Micrurus f. subtilis* (Fig. 49) is found from the Manaus vicinity westward along the Amazon River through northern Peru and eastern Ecuador, southern and east-central Colombia throughout the Amazon watershed, and north as far as Villavicencio along the Orinoco drainage of the eastern Andes. Intergrades have been found along the middle reaches of the Rio Negro. This subspecies possesses 2 postoculars and 262–279 ventrals. Recently, based on

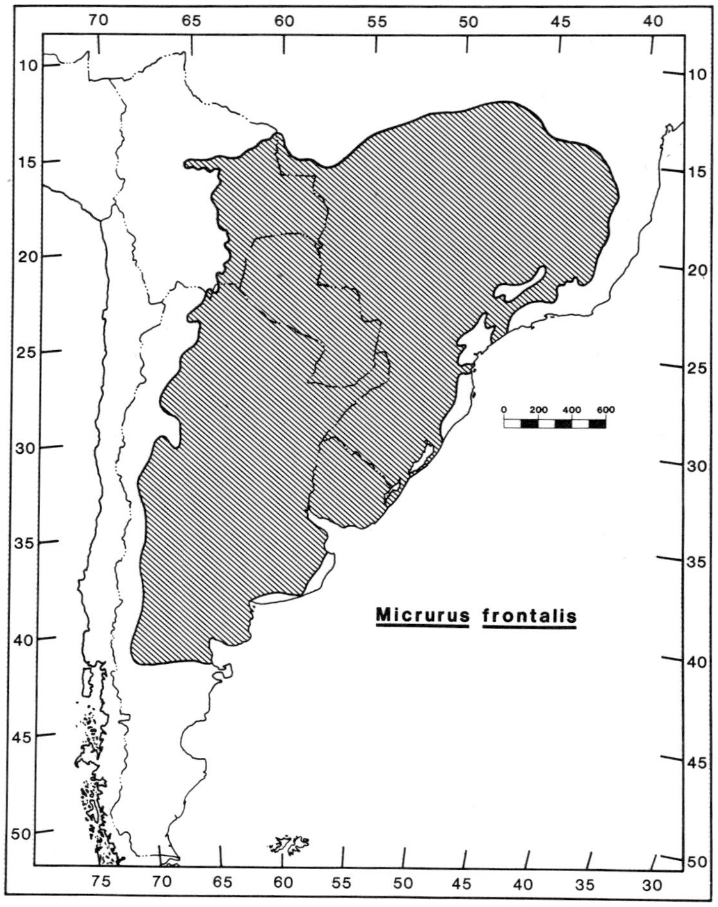


**Map 15.** Distribution of *Micrurus frontalis* in southern South America.

specimens with low ventral counts from Pará and Maranhão, the validity of *M. f. subtilis* has been called into question. With its ample distribution along the Rio Negro, we postulate the occurrence of *M. filiformis* in western Guyana along the upper Rio Tacutú.

In spite of its small size, *Micrurus filiformis* defends itself vigorously. We have observed this species flatten itself dorsoventrally, raise and curl the tail, and strike and bite violently while thrashing to and fro, sometimes with enough force to raise the snake off the ground. The species is locally common around human habitations and not infrequently enters the water, although it is not a good swimmer.

REFERENCES Amaral, 1925b, 1930a, 1930b, 1931b, 1948b; Carrillo de Espinoza, 1983; Chippaux, 1987; Cope, 1860b; Cunha and Nascimento, 1973, 1978, 1982a; Daniel, 1949; Dixon and Soini, 1986; Dunn, 1944a; Greene, 1973; Günther, 1859; Hoge and Romano, 1973; Hoge et al., 1973; Machado, 1945a; Meneses, 1974a; Miyata, 1982; Mocquard, 1908–1909; Nicéforo-María, 1942; Orcés, 1943, 1948; Pérez-Santos and Moreno, 1986; J. A. Peters, 1960a; Prado, 1945; Roze, 1967, 1983; Santos, 1981; Schmidt, 1936a, 1955; Silva Haad and Rodríguez R., 1985; Soini, 1974b.

## *Micrurus frontalis* (Duméril, Bibron, and Duméril)

(Figs. 50–54; Map 15)

LOCAL NAMES Argentina: mbói-chumbé-guazú, mil colores, tres colores, víbora de coral. Bolivia: coral venenosa. Brazil: cobra-coral, boipinima (Iguacú region). Paraguay: mbói-chumbé, mbói-yvyvovó. Uruguay: coral, víbora de coral.

ENGLISH NAME Southern coral snake.

DISTRIBUTION This species is found in south-central Brazil (see Remarks) in the states of Mato Grosso, Goiás, Minas Gerais, and Bahia southward into Uruguay, Paraguay, central Argentina, and southern and southeastern Bolivia (Map 15). At its distributional limit in Argentina, this species is the southernmost member of the genus (see Remarks). This is primarily a lowland form, although it has been found as high as 1,350 m above sea level.

HABITAT Lower montane wet forest, tropical and subtropical deciduous forest, savannah, secondary growth such as pasture and farm land, sandy or rocky areas, and temperate forests.

DESCRIPTION *Micrurus frontalis* averages 700–900 mm in overall length, reaching a maximum of 1,350 mm (there is a vague report of 1,500 mm).

It is a tricolored species with 5–19 triads of black rings on the body and 1–1⅔ triads on the tail. There are numerous races of *M. frontalis* (see Remarks) with many variations involving the head pattern. The head may be nearly black, black with pale lines along the sutures, black with pale internasals and prefrontals, or creamy yellow with black pigment along the sutures. Invariably, the supraoculars, frontal, and parietals contain black pigment; it is usually the predominant color. The supracephalic scales are irregularly invaded by yellow spots, specks, or streaks as well as red; alternatively, they may be entirely black. There is a red occipital band or ring which may border the parietals, may include nearly half of them, or may divide them with a narrow sinuous crossband. Some dorsals usually are included in the red occipital ring and these may be heavily suffused with black pigment. The postoculars, anterior temporals, and adjacent supralabial are usually tinged with yellow or cream color. The venter of the head may be entirely black, black with pale marks along the scale sutures, bicolored black and red, or tricolored as an extension of the dorsal head pattern. The red occipital ring may be incomplete dorsally such that the black parietal tips contact the black nuchal ring. When complete, it varies from 1–2 to as many as 9 middorsals in length.

The first triad is complete and the median black ring may be expanded anteriorly such that it encroaches upon the black nuchal ring. The black triad rings may be equal, subequal, or have an enlarged median ring. In some specimens the outer black triad rings may be slightly larger than the median ring. The white rings are 2–4 middorsals in length, are heavily stippled with black, and may be expanded laterally. They may be smaller than, equal to, or larger than the adjacent black rings. The red rings are the longest body rings and generally vary from 6–15 or more middorsals in length. They may be lightly or heavily stippled with black, or they may be immaculate. The juncture between red and black rings is often jagged and irregular. Pattern anomalies involving fusion of triads or absent rings are known. The tail is patterned similarly to the body but contains fewer than two triads due to its shortness. Ventrally the pattern is a continuation of the dorsum, although some specimens show a tendency toward fusion of black rings. Red rings generally lack black pigment ventrally.

There are usually 1 + 1 temporals, 194–244 ventrals, and 15–32 (mostly divided) subcaudals. There is a report of a specimen with an undivided anal but this is not the normal condition. Some specimens may have enlarged posttemporals that extend posteriorly beyond the parietal tips (see Remarks). Other features of lepidosis are typical of the genus *Micrurus*.

SIMILAR SPECIES Despite its variability, *M. frontalis* is distinctive in that the parietals are heavily (or totally) suffused with black pigment and the tail is very short. *Micrurus frontalis* is or may be sympatric with eight tricolored coral snake species at some point in its distribution: *Micrurus annellatus* and *M. corallinus* lack a triad pattern. In *M. decoratus* the posterior half of the parietals is red and only 2 black rings are present in the most anterior triad. The temporals in *M. frontifasciatus* are normal rather than expanded, and the median black triad ring is only slightly longer than the outer accessory rings (both features distinguish it from Bolivian *M. frontalis*). *Micrurus hemprichii* has orange rather than red rings, long black triad rings, and an undivided anal plate. *Micrurus ibiboboca* possesses 8–10 triads, whereas nearby or sympatric populations of *M. frontalis* possess 10 or more triads. *Micrurus lemniscatus* possesses a yellow band or ring anterior to the eyes and a red parietal ring that includes the parietal tips. *Micrurus spixii* may be sympatric in Bolivia, but in this species the parietals are normally red and, in populations sympatric with *M. frontalis*, the first triad is usually incomplete. *Micrurus surinamensis* possesses red cephalic scales bordered in black and only the fourth supralabial is in contact with the eye (third and fourth in all other *Micrurus* species). See Mimics of Venomous Snakes for a discussion of false coral snakes.

REMARKS There are eight rather poorly defined races recognized currently: *Micrurus f. frontalis* (Figs. 50, 51) is found in southern Brazil from São Paulo and Minas Gerais westward into southern Mato Grosso, Paraguay, and Argentina in the Mesopotamia region. It is characterized by a black snout, a parietal color occasionally fused with the black nuchal, a red occipital ring not extending beyond 1–3 middorsals, red rings stippled or shaded with black, 10–14 black body triads, and over 210 ventrals in males.

In *M. f. altirostris* (Figs. 52, 53)—found in southern Brazil in Rio Grande do Sul, Uruguay, and extreme northeastern Misiones, Argentina—the snout is black, the parietal color is separate from the black nuchal, a red occipital ring does not extend beyond 1–3 middorsals, the anterior portion of the parietals has a pale irregular mark, the head is black ventrally, there are 11–15 black body triads, and there are fewer than 209 ventrals in males. There is a male specimen reported from Pernambuco, Brazil (a dubious locality) with 215 ventrals.

*Micrurus f. baliocoryphus* occurs in southern Brazil in western Santa Catarina and in Argentina in southern Misiones, Corrientes, and Entre Ríos. The snout is nearly all black, the distinctive angular parietal ring is separate from the black nuchal, a red occipital ring does not extend beyond 1–4 middorsals, and the median black triad ring is considerably larger than the accessory triad rings.

*Micrurus f. brasiliensis*—which occupies south central Brazil in Goiás, Minas Gerais, Mato Grosso, and Bahia—possesses a pale snout with some dark pigment, a parietal color separate from the black nuchal, a red occipital ring not extending posteriorly beyond 1–3 middorsals, 11–14 black body triads, and black and white rings that are equal or slightly subequal. Females have 16–18 subcaudals (vs. 19–25 in female *M. f. frontalis*).

*Micrurus f. diana*, found in Bolivia in the Serranía de Santiago, Departamento de Santa Cruz, possesses a pale snout with some dark pigment, a parietal color fused middorsally with the black nuchal, red body rings that lack black pigment, a whitish interparietal line, 9–10 black body triads, and large posttemporals that reach beyond the parietal tips.

*Micrurus f. multicinctus* (Fig. 54) occurs in Brazil; an uncertain distribution possibly includes southeastern São Paulo south into northern Rio Grande do Sul. The snout is black, but it is sometimes flecked with yellow. The white rings are shorter than the black rings and there are 9–19 black body triads. This subspecies has been known to evert the hemipenes when threatened.

*Micrurus f. pyrrhocryptus* ranges from Brazil in southern Mato Grosso do Sul to Paraguay and the northern

Argentine Chaco west of the Rio Paraná and Río Paraguay, continuing westward into southern Bolivia in the Departamento de Santa Cruz and south through San Luis and Mendoza into northern Chubut, Argentina; this is the southernmost region inhabited by *Micrurus*. The snout is black with yellow pigment along scale sutures. There are 5–9 body triads, the median ring in each being two to three times the length of the outer rings, and there are frequently fusions in the pattern.

*Micrurus f. tricolor*, which occurs in Brazil in southwestern Mato Grosso do Sul and adjacent Paraguay, possesses a black snout, a red occipital ring extending 5–9 middorsals in length, 8–11 black body triads, and a first white ring that lacks black stippling.

There is considerable intergradation among the races of this complex species, and the distribution of subspecies is poorly defined. An adequate analysis of variation will probably alter the present arrangement. See also the discussion of false coral snakes in Mimics of Venomous Snakes.

REFERENCES Abalos, 1961, 1977; Abalos and Bucher, 1970; Abalos and Mischis, 1975; Abalos and Nader, 1962; Abalos et al., 1964; Achával, 1976; Achával et al., 1976, 1978; C. E. Allen, 1940; Amaral, 1925b, 1926d, 1930b, 1944c, 1944d, 1948a, 1974, 1978; Azevedo, 1960, 1962a, 1962b; Barrio and Miranda, 1967a; Bertoni, 1914, 1939; Cei, 1979, 1987; Cendrero et al., 1972; Cope, 1860b, 1860c, 1862; Cordeiro and Hoge, 1974; Devincenzi, 1925; Duméril et al., 1854; Fernández Barrán and Freiberg, 1951; Freiberg, 1968, 1984; Gallardo, 1977, 1979; Gehlbach, 1972; Gliesch, 1925; Günther, 1859; Hoge, 1956; Hoge and Lancini, 1960; Hoge and Romano, 1973; Hoge and Romano-Hoge, 1981b; Hoge et al., 1975; Ihering, 1911; Kempff-Mercado, 1975; Klappenbach and Orejas-Miranda, 1969; Koslowsky, 1895, 1898; Laurent and Teran, 1981; Lema, 1971b; Lema and Fabián-Beurmann, 1977; Lema et al., 1980; Machado, 1945a; Mertens, 1956, 1957; Migone, 1929; Minton et al., 1968; P. Müller, 1971; Roux-Esteve, 1983; Roze, 1967, 1970b, 1983; Santos, 1981; Schmidt, 1936a; Schouten, 1931, 1937; Scott and Lovett, 1975; Shreve, 1953; Talbot, n.d.; Vanzolini, 1948, 1953; Vaz-Ferreira and Sierra de Soriano, 1960.

## *Micrurus frontifasciatus* (Werner)

(Fig. 55; Map 25)

LOCAL NAME Coral.

ENGLISH NAME Bolivian coral snake.

DISTRIBUTION This species is known only from the eastern versant of the Andes in Bolivia (see Map 25); we are aware of a single specimen from Aiquile, Cochabamba. The type locality is unknown. It would not be surprising to encounter *M. frontifasciatus* southeastern Peru. The vertical distribution is to at least 2,150 m.

HABITAT Unknown. This species might be an occupant of either lower montane wet or dry forest or open formations.

DESCRIPTION The only reported length is that of the holotype, which measures 1,040 mm.

*Micrurus frontifasciatus* is a tricolored species with a pattern of triads. The snout is black, followed by a broken white ring on the prefrontals and the adjacent lower jaw. A black ring crosses the frontal, supraoculars, anterior ½–⅔ of the parietals, anterior temporal, and supralabials 3–5. There are black spots (sometimes fused into a single blotch) at the posterior edge of the parietals, the posterior portion of which, along with the remainder of the head, is red. There are 8–11 body triads plus 1⅓–1⅔ on the tail. The median black triad rings are 4–8 middorsals in length, and the black accessory rings measure 3–5 middorsals. The pale intervening rings were described as yellow with black stippling (see Remarks). On the holotype the rostral, internasals, prefrontals, and first pair of supralabials are black. On the Aiquile specimen (Fig. 55) the pale intervening rings are red with heavy black stippling middorsally. Black pigment is present on the posterior half of each scale included in the white rings. The snout is slightly acuminate. The tail is short, thickset, and tipped in black. On the holotype, there are 1 + 1 temporals, 222 ventrals, and 31 divided subcaudals. Other features of lepidosis are typical of the genus *Micrurus*.

SIMILAR SPECIES There are seven species of tricolored *Micrurus* that are or may be sympatric with *M. frontifasciatus*: *Micrurus annellatus* lacks triads and possesses a distinctive pale parietal ring. In *M. frontalis* the snout is rounded, the parietals are all or mostly black, and the posttemporals are enlarged, reaching beyond the parietal tips. In *M. hemprichii* the anal plate is undivided. *Micrurus lemniscatus* possesses red parietal tips, and the first 4 pairs of infralabials are black. *Micrurus spixii* has 24 or fewer subcaudals, and the first body triad is usually incomplete. In *M. surinamensis* the head is red with black pigment along scale sutures, and only the fourth supralabial is in contact with the orbit (third and fourth in all other *Micrurus* species). *Micrurus tschudii*, which is of doubtful sympatry with *M. frontifasciatus*, has 10–22 triads and 29 or fewer subcaudals.

REMARKS Until recently, this species was regarded as a race of *M. lemniscatus*, with which it is apparently sympatric. We have not examined the holotype of *M. frontifasciatus*, and the description is insufficient for an adequate understanding of this species. We presume the original description was made from a preserved specimen, so it is probable it possessed red rings stippled with black.

REFERENCES Roze, 1967, 1983; Werner, 1927.

## *Micrurus fulvius* (Linnaeus)

(Figs. 56, 57; Map 16)

LOCAL NAMES Coral, coralillo.

ENGLISH NAME Harlequin coral snake.

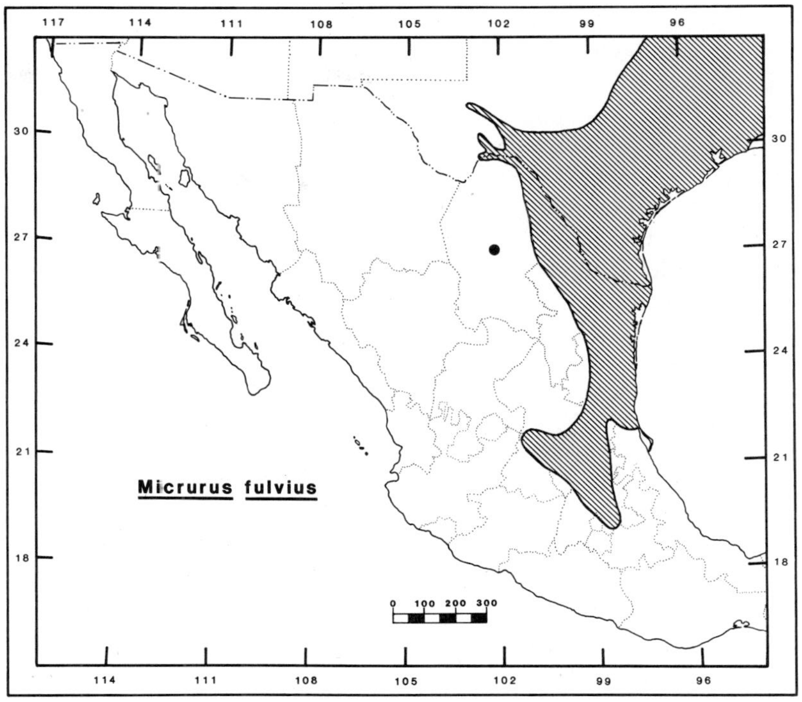


**Map 16.** Distribution of *Micrurus fulvius* in central and northern Mexico and the adjacent United States. The dot represents a record for Cuatro Ciénegas, Coahuila.

DISTRIBUTION This species is found in Mexico at low, moderate, and intermediate elevations from Morelos northward through the mountains and high plains of Hidalgo, Querétaro, eastern Guanajuato and San Luis Potosí, and southern Tamaulipas; hence along the Gulf coastal plain of Tamaulipas, Nuevo León, and the Río Grande (Río Bravo del Norte) drainage to northern Coahuila (Map 16). It has a considerable extralimital range in the southern United States. Its vertical distribution is from near sea level to over 2,000 m.

HABITAT Within its Latin American range, *M. fulvius* may be found in mesquite-grassland, pine-oak forest, thorn forest, and desert.

DESCRIPTION This medium-sized coral snake may exceed 1 m in length (1,213 mm), but is generally less than 800 mm long.

The pattern lacks triads and consists of black, yellow, and red rings. The snout is entirely black, including all or most of the frontal, supraoculars, anterior ⅒–½ of the parietals, the upper and generally all or a portion of the lower postoculars, supralabials 1–3, and sometimes part or all of 4. The mental and part or all of infralabials 1–3, and sometimes 4, are black. The black nuchal ring extends 5–7 scale lengths and involves the posterior tips of the parietals and the posterior ⅓–½ of the seventh supralabial; most frequently it does not encroach on the secondary temporal. Inferiorly, the black nuchal ring is complete and involves all of the preventrals (2 or 3) and 2 or 3 ventrals. The yellow parietal ring covers all of the primary and generally most if not all of the secondary temporals, part or all of supralabials 4 and 5, all of 6, and the anterior part of 7. The 13–25 black body rings are 2½–6 dorsal scale lengths and cover 3½–7 ventrals. There are 3–7 black tail rings that are 5–11 dorsals and 4–9 subcaudals long. The yellow body rings are ½–2 dorsals and ½–1½ ventrals long; most of these are complete. On the tail, yellow rings are 1–3 dorsals and 1–4 subcaudals long. The red scales of the 12–24 red body rings are tipped with black and black pigment is sometimes concentrated, with several blotches covering 1–6 scales; the ventrals are often pigmented with black. Entirely melanistic specimens have been reported. The red body rings are 2–10 dorsals and 2–10 ventrals long.

Supra-anal keels are absent and there are 1 + 1 temporals, 182–232 ventrals, and 26–55 subcaudals. Other features of lepidosis are typical of the genus *Micrurus*.

SIMILAR SPECIES *Micrurus fulvius* is not known to be sympatric with any other species of coral snake, but its geographic range closely approaches those of *M. bernadi*, *M. diastema*, and *M. laticollaris*. *Micrurus bernadi* has a distinctive pattern of a dorsal series of black spots. *Micrurus diastema* possesses more ventrals than the population of *M. fulvius* in southern Tamaulipas (193–220 in males and 207–226 in females vs. 182–189 in males and 202–205 in females, respectively), and the black body rings are shorter (1–2 vs. 4–5 scale lengths, respectively). *Micrurus laticollaris* possesses black body rings disposed in 6–9 triads. Other species that may be confused with *M. fulvius* within its range are *Rhinocheilus lecontei* (Fig. 521), which has undivided subcaudals, has a red snout, and does not have complete rings ventrally; *Sonora semiannulata* (Fig. 531), which has dorsal crossbands that are not complete ventrally and lacks a black snout; *Lampropeltis triangulum*, in which the yellow and red rings are separated by black; and *Pliocercus elapoides*, which has a loreal scale, 17 dorsal scale rows, and more numerous subcaudals.

REMARKS This species has a peculiar distribution. In northern Mexico it occurs at elevations of generally less than 500 m in mesquite-grassland, thorn forest, and desert. In southern Tamaulipas it reaches 900 m in oak-savanna, and in the southern portion of its range it appears to be restricted to elevations of over 800 m in pine-oak forests and mesquite-grassland.

Until recently, the southern populations of *M. fulvius* were considered to be a separate species, *M. fitzingeri*. Four subspecies of *M. fulvius* are currently recognized in Mexico: *M. f. fitzingeri* from Guanajuato and Querétaro to Morelos, and possibly Zacatecas, Aguascalientes, and southern Coahuila (not mapped); *M. f. maculatus* from the vicinity of Tampico, Tamaulipas; *M. f. microgalbineus* (Fig. 56) from southern and southwestern Tamaulipas and central and eastern San Luis Potosí to central Guanajuato; and *M. f. tener* (Fig. 57) from northern Coahuila and Nuevo León to central Tamaulipas.

This snake appears to be mainly crepuscular or nocturnal, but may be active in the early morning or on overcast days.

REFERENCES Baird, 1859; Baird and Girard, 1853; Booth, 1959; B. C. Brown and Brown, 1967; B. C. Brown and Smith, 1942; Cendrero et al., 1972; Cohen and Seligmann, 1967; Cope, 1860c, 1879, 1887, 1892; Cuesta Terron, 1932; Dixon et al., 1972; Dugès, 1885, 1890, 1896; Fraser, 1973; Gehlbach, 1972; Gloyd, 1938; Greene, 1972; Greene and McDiarmid, 1981; Günther, 1859; Hensley and Smith, 1962; Jan, 1858; Jan and Sordelli, 1870–1881; Liner and Chaney, 1974; Martin, 1958; Martín del Campo, 1935, 1950, 1953, 1955; McCoy, 1984; Milstead, 1960a; Milstead et al., 1950; Minton and Cervantes, 1977; Minton de Cervantes and Minton, 1975; Roze 1967, 1983; Roze and Tilger, 1983; Schmidt, 1933a; Schmidt and Owens, 1944; H. M. Smith and Buechner, 1947; H. M. Smith and Taylor, 1945; Stejneger, 1895; Stejneger and Barbour, 1943; E. H. Taylor, 1940, 1949, 1950; Tennant, 1984; Velasco, 1890a; Werler, 1967; Wright and Wright, 1957.

### *Micrurus hemprichii* (Jan)

(Figs. 58, 59; Map 17)

LOCAL NAMES Brazil: cobra coral. Colombia: coral verdadero, coralillo. Colombia and Venezuela: coral. Peru: naca-naca. Suriname: kraalslang, krarasneke.

ENGLISH NAME Hemprich's coral snake.

DISTRIBUTION This species occupies the Amazonian slopes of the Andes (see Remarks) in Colombia, Ecuador, Peru, and Bolivia; the upper Amazon Basin, Guiana Highlands, and upper Orinoco region from Vichada in eastern Colombia through southern Venezuela eastward, including Guyana, Suriname, and French Guiana as well as all of Brazil north of the Amazon River in Amazonas, and probably Roraima, and Amapá (it has not been recorded from these latter two regions). It exists on both sides of the Amazon River in Pará, Brazil, and undoubtedly has a wider distribution in the Amazon Basin than has been recorded (Map 17). There is a single report of this species from Ilha de Marajó, Brazil, and it is known from Maranhão. Its vertical distribution probably does not exceed 1,000 m; all records are from the lowlands.

HABITAT Lower montane wet forest, seasonally dry gallery forest, and primary rain forest. This species is a denizen of moist leaf litter on the forest floor.

DESCRIPTION *Micrurus hemprichii* is a medium-sized coral snake that averages 500–600 mm in overall length with a reported maximum of 900 mm.

The snout and top of the head to the posterior edge of the parietals, the mental, and the first infralabials are black. This is followed by an orange occipital ring that covers the postoculars, temporals, last 2–3 labials, first few dorsals, and gular region; this ring occasionally encroaches upon the parietals themselves. It is followed by 5–10 triads on the body plus ⅔–2 more on the tail. These triads are composed of exceptionally long black rings (often 10 middorsals or more), the outer two of which are longest; the black rings are separated by short (4–5 middorsals) orange rings. The triads contain very short (2–3 middorsals) white rings. The red scales are outlined faintly in black and white scales are present on many specimens as well. A long red ring traverses the cloacal region, and it is sometimes interrupted by a black blotch. Occasionally a red ring is melanized, resulting in the coalescing of two triads into a quinquad. The most distinctive feature in *M. hemprichii* is the presence of an undivided anal plate, a condition unique in the genus.

There are 1 + 1 temporals, 156–191 ventrals and 22–34 subcaudals, nearly all divided. Supra-anal keels are absent. Other features of lepidosis are typical of the genus *Micrurus*.

SIMILAR SPECIES Three features in combination distinguish *M. hemprichii* from all sympatric congeners: the presence of orange rather than red body rings; a low number of triads characterized by exceptionally long black rings; and an undivided anal plate (unique in the genus *Micrurus*). See Mimics of Venomous Snakes for a discussion of false coral snakes.

REMARKS Two subspecies are recognized: *M. h. hemprichii* (Fig. 58) in eastern Colombia, southern Venezuela, the Guianas, and northeastern Brazil (Pará); and *M. h. ortoni* (Fig. 59) along the Orinocoan and Amazonian slopes of the Andes in Colombia, Ecuador, Peru and Bolivia. It is possible that *M. h. ortoni* occupies a more elevated habitat than does *M. h. hemprichii*. The nominate form has a lower number of ventrals (156–182 vs. 179–191) and, in males, subcaudals (26–29 vs. 29–34), and a higher number of body triads.

*Micrurus hemprichii* has been recorded only from one locality in Bolivia but is known also from adjacent Madre de Dios, Peru. It should exist in all of the Amazonian versant of Bolivia.

REFERENCES Abuys, 1987b; Amaral, 1925b, 1930b, 1931b, 1948b; W. Beebe, 1946 (under *M. psyches*); Boulenger, 1898a; Brongersma, 1967; Carrillo de Espinoza, 1983; Chippaux, 1987; Cope, 1860b; Cunha and Nascimento, 1973, 1978, 1982a; Daniel, 1949; Dixon and Soini, 1986; Dunn, 1944a; Gasc and Rodrigues, 1980; Hoge and Lancini, 1962; Hoge and Romano, 1971b; Hoge and Romano-Hoge, 1981b; Lancini, 1970, 1979; Machado, 1945a; Men-

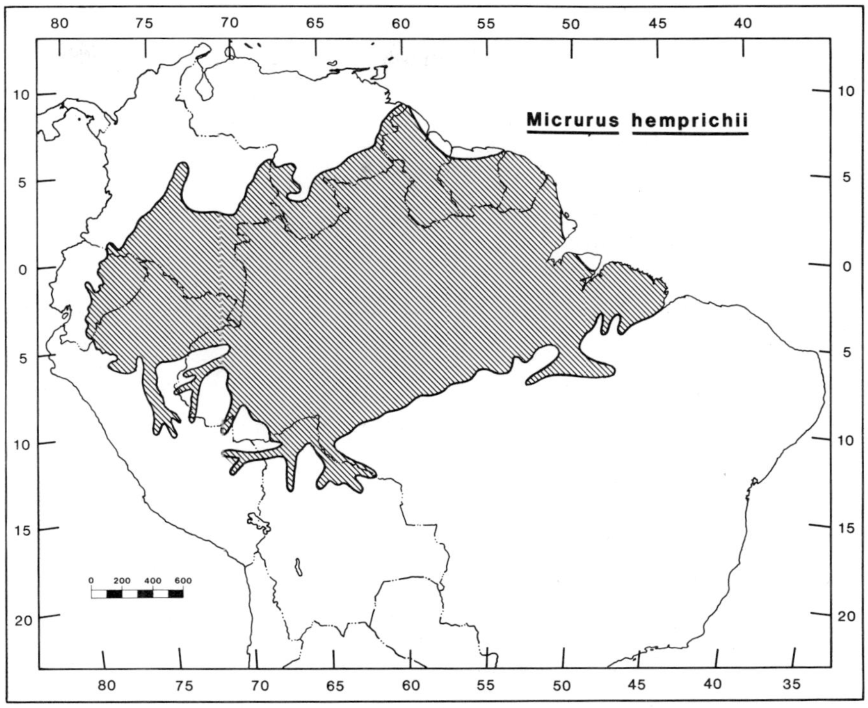


**Map 17.** Distribution of *Micrurus hemprichii* in Amazonian South America. This species undoubtedly has a more extensive range in Bolivia and possibly along the Guianan coast.

eses, 1974a; Miyata, 1982; Mocquard, 1908–1909; Nascimento et al., 1987; Nicéforo-María, 1942; Orcés, 1943, 1948; Parker, 1935; J. A. Peters, 1960a; Roze, 1954, 1955, 1957, 1966a, 1967, 1983; Sandner-Montilla, 1985b; Santos, 1981; Schmidt, 1936a, 1953a, 1955; Schmidt and Walker, 1943a; Silva Haad and Rodríguez R., 1985; Soini, 1974b; Vetencourt Finol., 1960.

## *Micrurus hippocrepis* (Peters)

(Figs. 60, 61; Map 24)

LOCAL NAMES Coral, coral snake, coralillo.

ENGLISH NAME Mayan coral snake.

DISTRIBUTION *Micrurus hippocrepis* occupies low and probably moderate elevations of the Atlantic drainages from Stann Creek District in Belize southward to the Río Motagua in eastern Guatemala (see Map 24). The distribution of this snake is poorly known; although it has been taken at localities near sea level, these have been in well-drained regions of moderately rugged foothills and we suspect this species is absent from flat coastal plains or swampy areas. Therefore, we envision the range of this species as extending from the northern foothills of the Maya Mountains (known from Middlesex) southwestward to the Sierra de Santa Cruz (known from several localities near Puerto Santo Tomás, also known as Puerto Matías de Gálvez) and the lower Río Motagua Valley (known from Quiriguá), and probably the eastern slopes of the Sierra de las Minas. The species is not known south of the Río Motagua. All records of this species are from below 500 m in elevation, but access onto the higher slopes of the aforementioned mountain ranges is extremely limited and future collections may reveal its presence at considerably higher elevations.

HABITAT Tropical wet and moist forests (lowland rainforest).

DESCRIPTION This is a small coral snake; males reach a maximum total length of about 500 mm, females 655 mm.

This species is tricolored black, yellow, and red. The tip of the snout, including the rostral, the internasals, the anterior portion of the prefrontals, the prenasals, and the first supralabials, is yellow. The black head cap involves the posterior portions of the prefrontals and some to all of the frontal, supraoculars, and postoculars, and sometimes the anterior margins of the parietals. The black head cap may extend laterally to the margin of the lip and involve all of supralabials 2 and 3 and portions of 1 and 4; or it may extend to only just below the eye, and then all the supralabials are yellow—except sometimes the posteriormost one, which is involved in the black nuchal ring. The yellow parietal ring is immaculate, as are most of the infracephalic scales. The black nuchal ring generally begins posterior to the parietals, but in a few specimens it may involve the posterior tips of these scales; it is 2–4 middorsals long. There are generally 10–24 black body rings, 2–3 middorsals long. Some or all of the black body rings are incomplete dorsally or ventrally in about one-half of the specimens. Snakes have been reported with other pattern anomalies, including lateral portions of black body bands absent and the number of black body bands reduced to 3, 2 on the neck and 1 on the tail. The yellow body rings are 1½–2 middorsals long. The red and yellow dorsals have dusky tips and there are a few irregularly scattered black spots in the red rings, but these scales are not uniformly black tipped or spotted, as is characteristic of many species in the genus *Micrurus*. There are 4–7 black tail rings that are 3–6 subcaudals long; these are separated by yellow rings 4–8 subcaudals long.

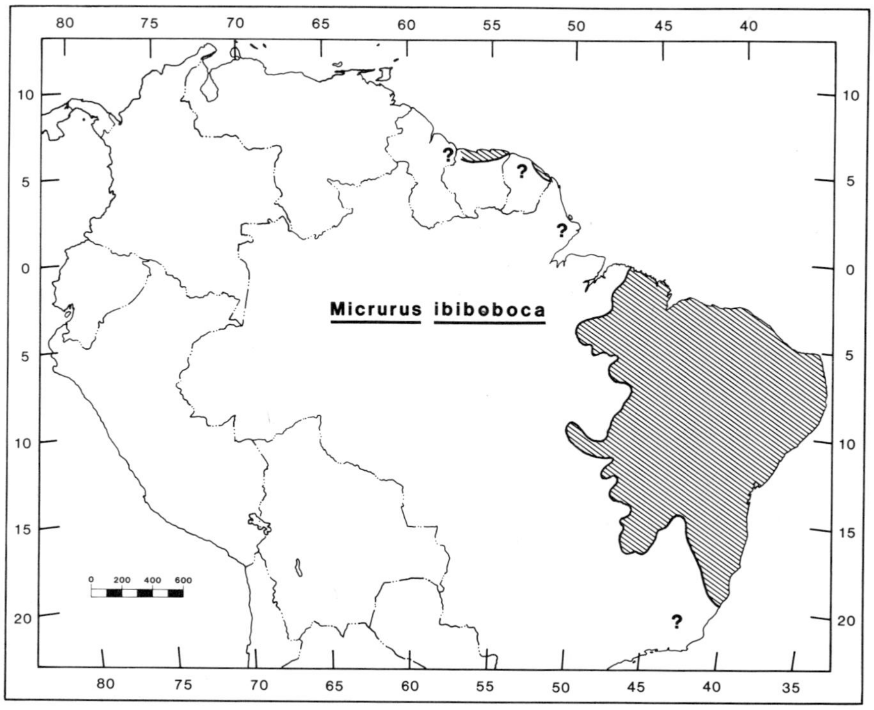


**Map 18.** Distribution of *Micrurus ibiboboca* in eastern South America. The distribution of this species along coastal portions of Suriname, French Guiana, and Amapá, Brazil, is poorly known. The southern limits of its distribution in Brazil are not clearly established. Question mark represents possible area of occurrence.

Supra-anal keels are absent and there are 1 + 1 or 1 + 2 temporals, 199–226 ventrals, and 37–57 subcaudals.

SIMILAR SPECIES Only two other species of coral snakes occur in Belize and eastern Guatemala, *M. diastema* and *M. nigrocinctus*. *Micrurus diastema* has often been confused with *M. hippocrepis*; this species is so variable throughout its range that it encompasses much of the variation found in *M. hippocrepis*. *Micrurus diastema* appears to be most easily distinguished in the area of sympatry by a combination of characters: (1) usually 25 or more black body rings, (2) relatively heavy black tipping on red dorsals, (3) black tail rings generally one and one-half to two times longer than the yellow rings dividing them, and (4) yellow rings on the body either absent or very narrow, generally less than 1 middorsal long. In the region of sympatry, *M. nigrocinctus* may be distinguished from *M. hippocrepis* by having (1) relatively heavy black tipping on red dorsals, (2) yellow body rings not more than 1 middorsal long, (3) an entirely black snout, and (4) supra-anal keels in adult males.

Sympatric populations of the harmless snake *Pliocercus elapoides* may bear an amazing resemblance to the various pattern morphs of *M. hippocrepis* (compare Figs. 514 and 515 with Figs. 61 and 60, respectively), but differ from this species in having a loreal scale, more numerous subcaudals, and a proportionately longer tail with red rings. Other genera of ringed or brightly colored snakes occurring within the range of *M. hippocrepis* include *Lampropeltis* (Figs. 493, 496), *Ninia* (Fig. 501), *Oxyrhopus* (Figs. 505, 506), and *Scaphiodontophis* (Fig. 522).

REMARKS The reports of *M. hippocrepis* from the Río Negro Gorge in the Departamento de Alta Verapaz, Guatemala, and from near Baking Pot, Cayo District, Belize, appear to be based on specimens of *M. diastema*.

We have found *M. hippocrepis* active during the cooler periods of the day (early morning and late afternoon) and after dark.

REFERENCES Gutiérrez et al., 1988; Henderson and Hoevers, 1975; Lee, 1980; McCoy, 1971; P. Müller, 1973; Neill, 1965; Neill and Allen, 1959a; W. C. H. Peters, 1861; Roze, 1967, 1983; Schmidt, 1933a, 1936b, 1941; Stuart, 1948, 1963.

### *Micrurus ibiboboca* (Merrem)

(Fig. 62; Map 18)

LOCAL NAMES Brazil: cobra de coral, coral, ibiboboca. Suriname: kraalslang, krarasneke.

ENGLISH NAME Caatinga coral snake.

DISTRIBUTION This species occurs in eastern Brazil in the states of Maranhão, Piauí, Ceará, Rio Grande do Norte, Paraíba, Pernambuco, Alagoas, Sergipe, and Bahia (Map 18). The southern extent of its range in Brazil is not established. An apparently disjunct population exists in Suriname and French Guiana (see Remarks). The vertical distribution is unknown, but this is primarily a lowland form.

HABITAT This is a species principally of semi-arid xerophytic regions in the Caatinga region of northeastern Brazil, but records also exist for the mesic forest of eastern coastal Brazil. In the eastern Guianas it would be expected in savanna or thorn forest habitats.

DESCRIPTION *Micrurus ibiboboca* is a medium to large coral snake, averaging 700–800 mm in overall length with a maximum reported length of 920 mm.

It is a tricolored species with a triad pattern consisting of 7–10 body triads plus 1–1⅔ caudal triads. The first body triad is complete. The tip of the snout is irregularly spotted with black pigment and is followed by a white to

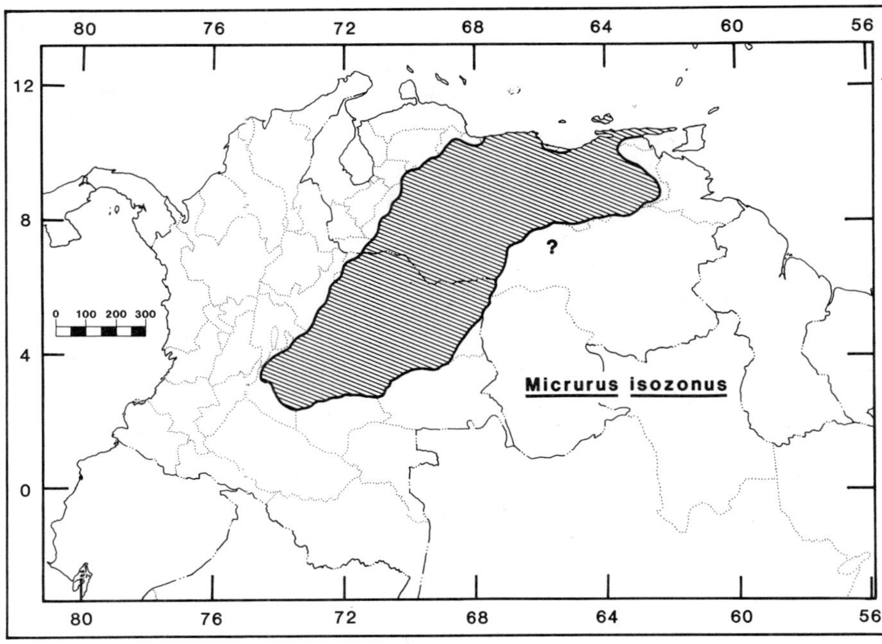


**Map 19.** Distribution of *Micrurus isozonus* in the Río Orinoco Basin of northern South America. Suitable habitat exists in southeastern Venezuela and adjacent Brazil, but we are unaware of specimens from this area.

reddish brown band which may be a mixture of these colors that occupies the first two supralabials and a variable portion of the nasals and prefrontals. This band is followed by a black band that involves supralabials 3–5 and covers the frontal, occupying varying portions of the posterior prefrontals and anterior parietals. This band is separated from the first body triad by a red ring spotted with black and reddish brown that covers the posterior parietals, the first 3–5 dorsals, the temporals (except the anterior portion), and the last 2 supralabials. The venter of the head is red except for an occasional blackish blotch in the symphysial region. The black triad rings are of approximately equal length (3–5 dorsal scale lengths), although in some specimens the median black ring is somewhat longer than the outer rings. The white to reddish brown triad rings are pigmented with black on the apical portions of each scale and may be totally melanic in some specimens. They approximate the black rings in length. The red to reddish brown rings are stippled with black and vary in length from the size of the triad rings to as much as twice their length.

There are 1 + 1 temporals, 210–243 ventrals, and 19–30 subcaudals, nearly all divided. Other features of lepidosis are typical of the genus *Micrurus*.

SIMILAR SPECIES In Suriname and French Guiana the coral snake most similar to *M. ibibiboca* is *M. lemniscatus*, which differs in having a higher number of subcaudals (25–43 vs. 19–30) and generally a higher number of body triads (7–17 vs. 7–10). In the Caatinga region of northeastern Brazil there are no sympatric *Micrurus* species, although *M. ibibiboca* may occur in Minas Gerais, where it could come into contact with *M. frontalis*, and a specimen of *M. frontalis* has been recorded from Pernambuco, although this may be an error. Sympatric populations of *M. frontalis* have 10 or more body triads (vs. 7–10 in *M. ibibiboca*).

REMARKS *Micrurus ibiboboca* has had a muddled taxonomic history, being frequently confused with *M. lemniscatus*, which, in turn, has been confused with *M. frontalis*. Thus, *M. ibibiboca* has been cited as occurring in Paraguay and other extralimital areas. The specimens from the Guianan region that seem to represent *M. ibiboboca* may in fact be a distinct population. It seems certain that there are close relationships to be clarified among *M. ibibiboca*, *M. isozonus*, *M. frontalis*, and *M. lemniscatus*.

REFERENCES Abuys, 1982, 1987b; Amaral, 1925b, 1926d, 1944d; Azevedo, 1962a; Bertoni, 1939; Chippaux, 1987; Cordeiro and Hoge, 1974; Gatti, 1955; Günther, 1859; Hoge and Romano, 1973; Hoge and Romano-Hoge, 1981b; Hoge et al., 1981; Hoogmoed, 1979; Merrem, 1820; Prado, 1945; Roze, 1966a, 1967, 1983; Schmidt, 1936a, 1957; Schmidt and Inger, 1951; Talbot, n.d.; Vanzolini, 1948; Vanzolini et al., 1980; Wied-Neuwied, 1820.

### *Micrurus isozonus* (Cope)

(Fig. 63; Map 19)

LOCAL NAMES Coral, coralillo, culebra coral. Colombia: acavai (Guahibo tribe), huayamacaicha (Cuiva tribe). Venezuela: coral, coral norteño.

ENGLISH NAME Venezuelan coral snake.

DISTRIBUTION *Micrurus isozonus* occurs in semiarid and seasonally dry regions in Colombia from east of the Andes throughout the Llanos Orientales eastward, including similar regions of northern and central Venezuela and the Isla de Margarita (Map 19). At least one authority has reported this species as existing throughout Venezuela, but it appears to occur primarily north of the Río Orinoco and to be absent in mountainous western Venezuela and humid southern and eastern portions of the country, although suitable habitat exists in the Gran Sabana region of Venezuela and Brazil. Its vertical distribution is to at least 1,400 m.

HABITAT This species frequents lower montane wet forest, tropical deciduous forest, tropical thorn woodland, savanna, and gallery forest. It is encountered commonly in pasture and other open or semi-open secondary growth, but we have collected individuals in forested situations along the Andean foothills in Meta, Colombia.

DESCRIPTION *Micrurus isozonus* averages 500–600 mm in overall length but it may exceed 1 m, especially in central Colombia, where we have seen specimens approaching 1,500 mm in length.

This coral snake is a tricolored form with a pattern of 8–13 black body triads plus 1, 1⅓, or 2 triads on the tail. The triads are separated by bright red-orange rings that are usually longer than the individual triad rings. The median black triad rings are slightly longer than the outer triad rings in most specimens; the three may be subequal, however. The snout is black, and this color may extend posteriorly as far as the eyes, supraoculars, and frontal. This black zone is usually interrupted by gray or dirty white irregular spots that sometimes coalesce to form a band crossing the prefrontals and anterior edges of the frontal, supraoculars, and supralabials 2 and 3. Sometimes the snout is primarily gray or dirty white, the black being reduced to smudges of pigment along the scale sutures. A black band covers the eyes, the third and fourth supralabials, the supraoculars, and all or most of the frontal. This band is closely bordered posteriorly by a long red parietal ring, which may encroach upon the supraoculars and frontal. Normally the black frontal appears as a cuneiform posterior extension entering this parietal ring. The parietal ring usually includes the remaining supralabials (the fifth supralabial may be partially gray), the temporals, and the parietals excluding the posterior parietal tips, which are black. The first nuchal black ring follows and normally includes the posterior parietal tips. We have seen specimens in which these tips contain anterior oblong extensions of the black nuchal ring. Alternatively, the red parietal ring may have a cuneiform posterior extension including the posterior parietal tips and portions of the adjacent occipitals, although the parietal tips may remain tinged with black. The venter of the head is almost entirely red and white with some black pigment on the mental and between the chinshields.

The first nuchal black ring is the first ring of the first body triad. The margins of the triad rings are somewhat irregular (jagged), owing to the size of the dorsals, which are large in this species. The white rings are heavily pigmented with black on the apical tips of the scales and generally effect a pale gray coloration. These rings occupy 3–5 dorsals and are as long or longer than the black rings. The red rings are usually 4–9 dorsals long and are stippled apically with black pigment; in large specimens, these may take on a rusty hue. Some specimens have extremely bright red to red-orange rings, while in others the color is more subdued owing to extensive gray pigment overlying the red.

There are 1 + 1 temporals, 199–231 ventrals, and 24–32 subcaudals. Supra-anal keels are absent. Other features of lepidosis are typical of the genus *Micrurus*.

SIMILAR SPECIES There are six coral snakes bearing triads that are sympatric with *M. isozonus* in some area of its range. In *M. dissoleucus* the black nuchal ring does not form part of the first complete triad. *Micrurus filiformis* has a much higher number of ventrals (262–333) than *M. isozonus*. *Micrurus hemprichii* has an undivided anal and long black triad rings. *Micrurus spixii* is extremely similar to *M. isozonus*, especially in central Colombia; in many specimens of *M. spixii* the first body triad is only two-thirds represented, but this is not always the case. In *M. spixii* the median black ring of the first body triad is greatly extended anteriorly, sometimes fusing with the first black triad ring (if present). Individuals of *M. spixii* occurring in the zone of sympatry with *M. isozonus* normally have 8 or fewer body triads, 200–229 ventrals, and 15–23 subcaudals, several of which are entire. *Micrurus lemniscatus* has a long red cephalic ring covering the parietal tips and the first 4 rows of dorsals, and a well-defined bright white or yellow ring or band anterior to the eyes. *Micrurus surinamensis* has a distinctive red head with black pigment outlining most of the cephalic scales, and only the fourth supralabial is in contact with the orbit (third and fourth in other species of *Micrurus*).

REMARKS *Micrurus isozonus* is common throughout most of its range and should be considered a potential health risk. It frequently raises and curls the tail when disturbed. We have collected large specimens at night and found them capable of vigorous defense. This species has been erroneously cited as occurring in Peru. Its relationship to *M. frontalis* is worthy of investigation. See also the discussion of false coral snakes in Mimics of Venomous Snakes.

REFERENCES Boulenger, 1920; Cope, 1860b, 1876b; Günther, 1859; Hoge and Lancini, 1962; Lancini, 1962c, 1970, 1979; Marcuzzi, 1950; Medem, 1969; P. Müller, 1973; Rivero-Blanco and Dixon, 1979; Roux-Esteve, 1983; Roze, 1952, 1955, 1964, 1966a, 1967, 1970a, 1983; Sandner-Montilla, 1985b; Schmidt, 1936b; Test et al., 1966; Vellard, 1941 (in part, under *Elaps lemniscatus* and *E. spixii*); Vetencourt Finol., 1960.

### *Micrurus karlschmidti* (Hoge and Romano)

(Map 20)

LOCAL NAMES Cobra-coral, coral.

ENGLISH NAME Pygmy black-backed coral snake.

DISTRIBUTION This species is known from Brazil, Colombia, Ecuador, and Peru; most localities fall within a 350-km radius of Iquitos, Peru (Map 20). There are two specimens reported from Amanavén, Guainía, Colombia. The vertical distribution is to at least 850 m (see Remarks).

HABITAT Pluvial forests of the extreme northwest Amazon Basin.

DESCRIPTION Because *M. karlschmidti* is known from very few specimens, its maximum size has not been established; two specimens measured 286 mm and 335 mm, respectively.

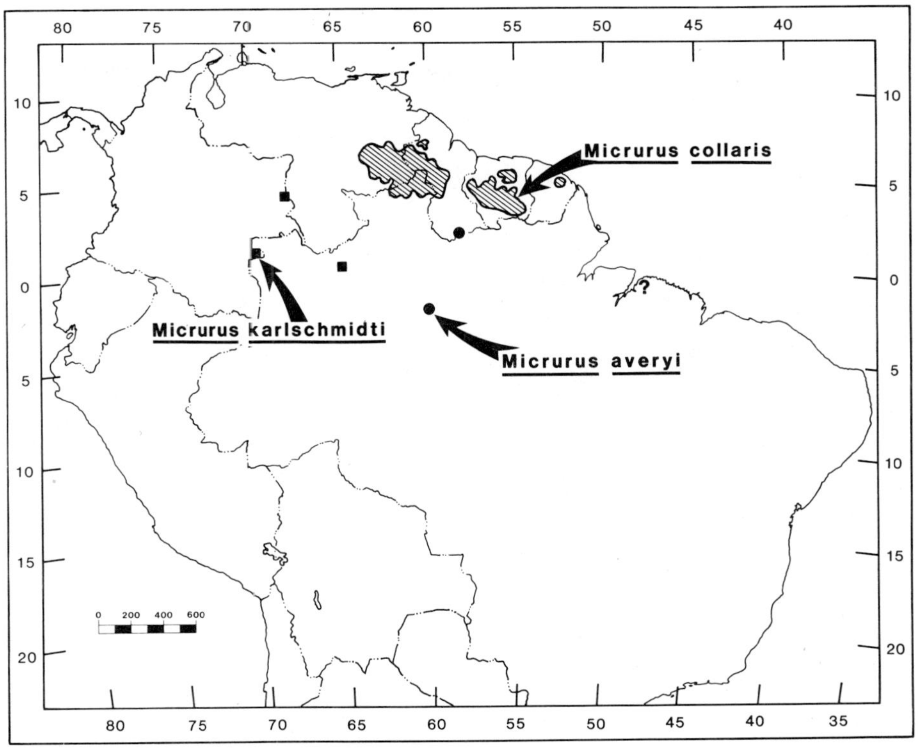


**Map 20.** Distributions of *Micrurus averyi* (dots), *M. collaris* (diagonal lines), and *M. karlschmidti* (squares) in northern South America. The question mark refers to an unverified record for *M. collaris* in Pará, Brazil.

This snake is patterned much like *M. narduccii*: it is dark brown to black, both dorsally and ventrally, with 26–38 orange-red rounded blotches on the venter. In some specimens, these ventral blotches may be connected by weak dorsal bands. There is a white ring (see Remarks) around the parietal region, just posterior to the eyes, that extends nearly to the end of the seventh supralabial. There is a white ring (see Remarks) near the tail tip, which is black.

There are 1 + 1 temporals, 219–270 ventrals, and 21–27 subcaudals. The first pair of infralabials are not in contact with each other behind the mental, thus the chinshields contact the mental. Other features of lepidosis are characteristic of the genus *Micrurus*.

SIMILAR SPECIES *Micrurus karlschmidti* essentially lacks body rings, a condition that distinguishes it from all but one sympatric congener, although a melanistic specimen of another species could be encountered. The only similar species is *M. narduccii* (see Remarks).

REMARKS The relationship between *Micrurus narduccii* and *M. karlschmidti* is very close. The color patterns are nearly identical (the "white" cephalic ring of *M. karlschmidti* was probably yellow or orange in life, but features of lepidosis scarcely overlap (*M. narduccii* has 261–382 ventrals). A specimen from Vaupés, Colombia (UTA R-3845), tentatively referrable to *M. karlschmidti*, had red tail rings in life. Unfortunately, the anterior portion of the specimen is missing so its identification remains uncertain. In a forthcoming publication, Roze and Bernal-Carlo (in press) will present evidence that an older name has priority over *M. karlschmidti*.

REFERENCES Cope, 1870; Dixon and Soini, 1986; Hoge and Romano, 1966; Romano, 1972; Roze, 1967, 1983; Roze and Bernal-Carlo, in press; Sandner-Montilla, 1985b.

## *Micrurus langsdorffi* Wagler

(Fig. 64; Map 21)

LOCAL NAMES Coral, coralillo. Peru: naca-naca, serpiente de coral. Brazil: cobra-coral.

ENGLISH NAME Langsdorff's coral snake.

DISTRIBUTION This species occupies the northwest Amazin Basin in Colombia, Brazil, Ecuador, Peru, and probably Bolivia. A specimen (UTA R-3857) from Vaupés, Colombia, leads us to surmise the presence of *M. langsdorffi* in southern Venezuela. In Brazil, the species exists in Amazonas, Rondônia/Mato Grosso, and possibly Acre. Single records for Pará and Bahia remain unsubstantiated. In Ecuador, *M. langsdorffi* is found east of the Andes, extending eastward into the adjacent Departamento de Loreto, Peru, and south in Loreto to at least the Río Aguaytía and Río Pachitea (see Remarks). Its vertical distribution is to at least 1,500 m.

HABITAT Lower montane wet forest and lowland rainforest.

DESCRIPTION *Micrurus langsdorffi* reaches a known maximum overall length of 761 mm but averages 450–650 mm.

It is tricolored or bicolored and the dorsal pattern lacks triads. Its coloration is confusing in that polychromatic populations exist. Thus, a specimen may possess rings of yellow, brown, or black (one of these colors only) that alternate with red rings, each ring being separated from the others by a narrow row of 5–8 white spots on the dorsum that becomes a narrow band (sometimes interrupted) ventrally. The red rings are frequently melanic and may appear entirely black. The snout is usu-

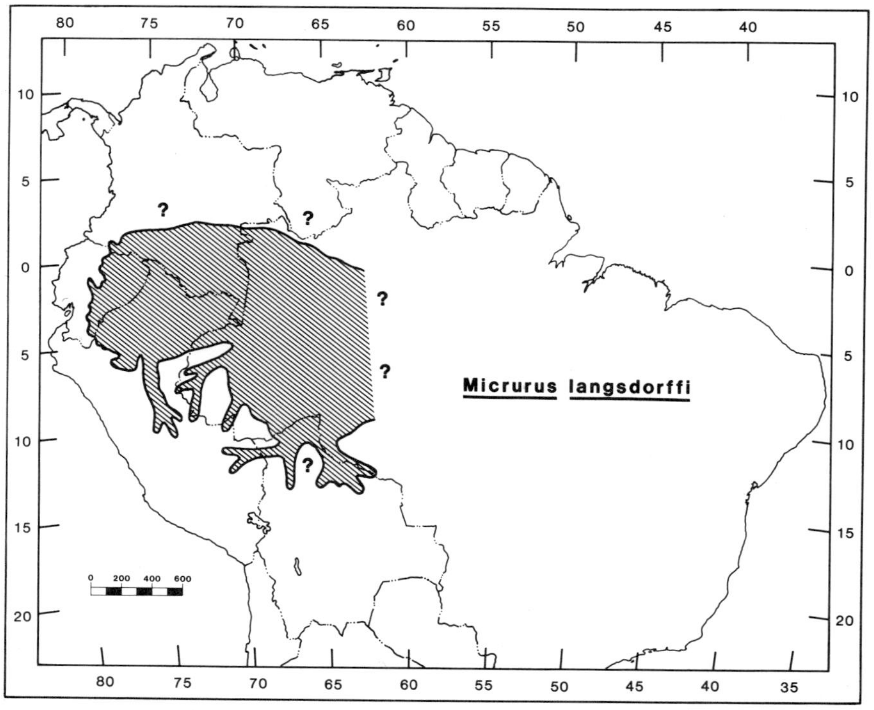


**Map 21.** Distribution of *Micrurus langsdorffi* in the upper Amazon Basin of South America. The distribution of this species, especially to the east and north, is poorly known. Question marks represent possible areas of occurrence.

ally black, but may be brown or yellow, and this coloration often includes the first 2–4 pairs of supralabials, the frontal, supraoculars, postoculars, and parietals. Alternatively, some specimens possess a red band or a series of spots that crosses the parietal or occipital region. A pair of white spots may be present, usually on the supraoculars or prefrontals, but sometimes also including each internasal, each anterior temporal, and each sixth supralabial. The temporals and posterior 2–3 supralabials are generally red with extensive black pigmentation. Ventrally the mental, chinshields, gulars, and first 3–4 pairs of infralabials are black, brown, or a yellowish cast, at times with a white spot on the chinshields; the remainder of the venter of the head is red. The black nuchal ring follows the parietals and is frequently incomplete or reduced to a dorsal blotch. There are 18–44 red rings on the body plus 5–11 on the tail; they are 2–10 middorsals long and are heavily stippled in black. There are 36–91 yellow, brown, or black rings and these measure 2–4 middorsals long. The white body rings are a single dorsal or ventral long; they are frequently interrupted dorsally or ventrally by the intervention of black dorsal scales. The tips of the white scales are usually pigmented with black. The posteriormost body ring is red and may be incomplete or nearly absent in males. Red rings on the tail are reduced to 1–3 middorsal scale lengths, while the alternate rings (whether black, brown, or yellow) are 2–6 middorsals long. Ventrally the white caudal rings are amplified, sometimes eliminating the red rings. On many specimens the red rings and dark rings are subequal, creating a striking effect in combination with the stark white rings. In spite of its variability, *M. langsdorffi* is a distinctive species.

There are 1 + 1 temporals (occasionally 1 + 2), 195–231 ventrals, and 30–56 subcaudals. Other features of lepidosis are typical of the genus *Micrurus*.

SIMILAR SPECIES All tricolored coral snakes with which *M. langsdorffi* is or may be sympatric are of the triad pattern with three exceptions: *M. petersi*, which lacks red pigment on the ventrals and in which the venter of the head is primarily white; *M. steindachneri*, which lacks pale spots on cephalic plates; and *M. peruvianus*, which has a bicolored tail without red rings and possesses a sharp snout and a foreshortened frontal. There are several usually bicolored forms that also bear a resemblance to melanized specimens of *M. langsdorffi*: *M. annellatus*, which possesses a pale narrow parietal ring (lacking in *M. langsdorffi*); *M. margaritiferus*, which lacks pale spots on the snout and possesses 68–141 or more black body rings (usually 60 or fewer when present in *M. langsdorffi*); *M. mipartitus*, an allopatric species that lacks red body rings but has a red parietal ring lacking black pigment (if present in *M. langsdorffi*, it is pigmented heavily with black); and *M. putumayensis*, which lacks red body rings and has long yellow rings.

REMARKS *Micrurus langsdorffi* is the only coral snake known to have polychromatic populations. There are two subspecies recognized, somewhat tenuously, by the different number of black body rings. *Micrurus l. langsdorffi* (Fig. 64) occupies the northern portion of the species' range in southeast Colombia, probably southern Venezuela, northwest Brazil, eastern Ecuador, and adjacent Peru. It has 38 or fewer black body rings and tends to have the red rings replaced by another color. *Micrurus l. ornatissimus* generally has 39 or more black body rings; however, some specimens of this subspecies have as few as 30 black body rings. In this subspecies the black, white, and red colors are supposedly constant. This subspecies inhabits the Amazonian slopes of the Andes in Colombia, Ecuador, and Peru.

Specimens reported by Schmidt and Walker from the Madre de Dios region of Peru are actually *M. annellatus*.

The species *M. albicinctus* was recently synonymized with *M. ornatissimus*, the latter being considered a separate species from *M. langsdorffi*. The evidence for the synonymy seems sufficient, but the case presented for the separation of *M. langsdorffi* and *M. ornatissimus* is not convincing.

Further study should elucidate relationships between *M. langsdorffi* and similar forms that exist in the Amazonian slopes of the Andes in Colombia and Ecuador.

REFERENCES Amaral, 1926c, 1930b, 1935, 1937a, 1948a, 1948b, 1978; Bertoni, 1939; Boulenger, 1896; Carrillo de Espinoza, 1983; Cope, 1868, 1876b; Cunha and Nascimento, 1982b; Daniel, 1949; Dixon and Soini, 1986; Duellman, 1978; Dunn, 1944a, 1946; Fugler and Walls, 1978; Greene and McDiarmid, 1981; Günther, 1859, 1868; Hoge and Romano, 1973; Hoge and Romano-Hoge, 1981a; Hoogmoed and Gruber, 1983; Jan, 1858, 1859b; Jan and Sordelli, 1870–1881; Machado, 1945a; Medem, 1969; Meise, 1938; Meneses, 1974a; Miyata, 1982; Nicéforo-María, 1942; Orcés, 1943, 1948; Orton, 1876; Peters, 1960a; Prado, 1945; Rendahl and Vestergren, 1941; Roze, 1967, 1983; Santos, 1981; Schmidt, 1936a, 1955; Schmidt and Walker, 1943a; Silva Haad and Rodríguez R., 1985; Soini, 1974a, 1974b; Talbot, n.d.; Wagler, 1824.

### *Micrurus laticollaris* (Peters)

(Fig. 65; Map 30)

LOCAL NAMES Coral, coralillo.

ENGLISH NAME Balsan coral snake.

DISTRIBUTION This species is endemic to Mexico and occupies low, moderate, and intermediate elevations in portions of the basins of the Río de las Balsas and Río Tepalcatepec in Michoacán, Guerrero, Jalisco, Morelos, Puebla, Oaxaca, and probably México. Its range extends northwestward along the coastal foothills of Colima and Jalisco (see Map 30). The vertical distribution is from 500 to about 1,800 m.

HABITAT Tropical deciduous forest and arid tropical scrub forest.

DESCRIPTION This coral snake reaches a length of over 800 mm.

It possesses a distinctive tricolored pattern with black rings disposed in 6–9 triads on the body. The first and last of these triads are represented by only 2 black rings. The central black ring of each triad is separated from the other black rings by yellow rings 3–4 scales long; the black rings generally are reduced on the ventrals. The red rings are 6½–9 dorsals long and each red scale has an irregular black tip or small dot. A long nuchal ring or band extends more than 10 dorsal scale lengths. Two or 3 long black rings are present on the tail, which lacks red pigment. The black on top of the head usually covers all of the frontal and a portion of the parietals, but often there are a few pale spots on the supralabials, and some specimens have an almost entirely pale snout. The lower jaw is completely pale with faint grayish mottling on the mental, first few infralabials, and chinshields.

Supra-anal keels are absent, and there are 1 + 2 temporals, 207–225 ventrals, and 35–47 subcaudals. Other features of lepidosis are characteristic of the genus *Micrurus*.

SIMILAR SPECIES The only other coral snake in Mexico possessing black body rings disposed in triads is *M. elegans*, whose range does not overlap that of *M. laticollaris*. These two species are easily distinguishable on the basis of color and pattern. In *M. elegans* the pale rings tend to be whitish, double, and very narrow, not more than 1 scale long; whereas in *M. laticollaris* the yellow rings occur singly and are 3–4 scales long. Moreover, the tail of *M. laticollaris* is bicolored black and yellow. There are 6–9 triads in *M. laticollaris* and 14–19 in *M. elegans*. Other *Micrurus* species occurring within or close to the range of *M. elegans* include *M. browni*, *M. distans*, and *M. ephippifer* (see individual species accounts). Members of the genus *Lampropeltis* in this region have rings in a yellow-black-red sequence, the black rings are not arranged in triads, and 8 or more infralabials are present on each side.

REMARKS Two subspecies are recognized: *M. l. maculirostris* (Fig. 65) differs from the nominate subspecies, *M. l. laticollaris*, in having higher subcaudal counts in males and females, pale spots on the base of the first pair of supralabials and rostral (usually black in the nominate form), and black on the snout that extends posteriorly to cover all of the frontal and ½–¾ of the parietal (in *M. l. laticollaris* the black on top of the head covers less than one-half of the parietals, and occasionally even the posterior of the frontal is pale).

The only reported bite of this snake resulted in severe symptoms.

REFERENCES Davis and Smith, 1953; Dixon and Webb, 1965; Duellman, 1958, 1961, 1965b; Frost and Aird, 1978; Garman, 1884a, 1884b; Martín del Campo, 1935; W. C. H. Peters, 1869; Pettigrew and Glass, 1985; Roze, 1967, 1983; Schmidt, 1933a, 1936b, 1958; H. M. Smith and Taylor, 1945; E. H. Taylor, 1940; Webb, 1966.

### *Micrurus latifasciatus* Schmidt

(Fig. 66; Map 22)

LOCAL NAMES Coral, coralillo.

ENGLISH NAME Broad-ringed coral snake.

DISTRIBUTION Low and moderate elevations of the Pacific versant from southeastern Oaxaca, Mexico, southeastward through Chiapas, Mexico, to eastern Guatemala (Map 22). The vertical distribution is from about 300 to 1,280 m.

HABITAT Lowland rainforest and lower montane wet forest.

DESCRIPTION A medium-sized coral snake, *M. latifasciatus* reaches an overall length of a little over 1 m.

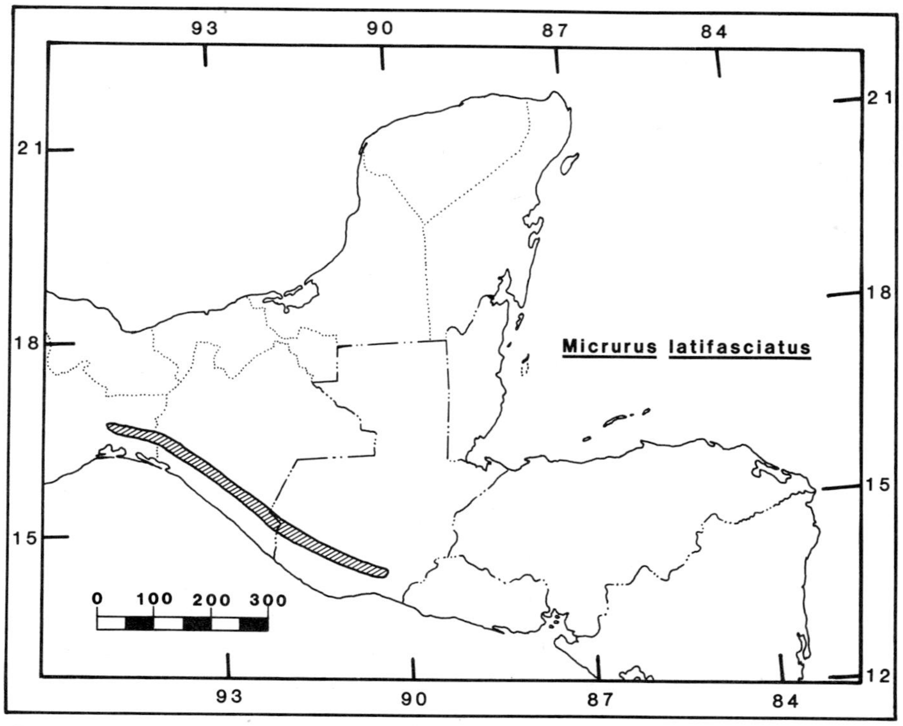


Map 22. Distribution of *Micrurus latifasciatus* in southern Mexico and Guatemala. This species is restricted to the slopes of the Pacific versant.

This is a tricolored species with alternating rings of black, yellow, and red. The snout is black, and the black pigment extends posteriorly to cover most or all of the supraoculars and frontal. The yellow parietal ring is immaculate, as are the infracephalic scales, except that the mental and anterior 2–3 infralabials are black. The black nuchal ring begins posterior to the posterior tips of the parietals and extends 10–12 middorsal scale lengths. The black and red body rings, especially, are characteristically long, covering 2–11 and 17–26 ventrals, respectively. There are 6–9 black body rings; the red dorsals are uniformly black spotted, and the red ventrals usually are immaculate or have light irregular mottling toward their lateral margins. The yellow rings are well developed, about 2–3 middorsals long, but shorter than adjacent rings. Two to 3 long black rings are present on the tail; these are separated by yellow rings less than one-half as long.

Adult males and large females possess supra-anal keels. There are 1 + 1 temporals, 192–214 ventrals, and 37–55 subcaudals, a few of which are sometimes undivided. Other features of lepidosis are characteristic of the genus *Micrurus*.

SIMILAR SPECIES This species may be sympatric with *M. browni*, *M. elegans*, *M. ephippifer*, and *M. nigrocinctus* in various portions of its range. All of these species may be distinguished from *M. latifasciatus* in having more numerous black body rings (disposed in triads in *M. elegans*) and black tail rings, and usually having shorter red body rings. With the exception of *M. ephippifer*, with which *M. latifasciatus* may not be sympatric, the alternative species have red dorsals that may be dusky but are not distinctly tipped with black.

REMARKS Previously, specimens of *M. latifasciatus* from the western part of the range in Oaxaca and Chiapas, Mexico, were recognized as a separate species, *M. nuchalis*. Additional material has revealed that representatives of these populations cannot be distinguished from Guatemalan specimens and are probably conspecific with *M. latifasciatus*.


REFERENCES Alvarez del Toro, 1983; Greene and McDiarmid, 1981; Landy et al., 1966; Lynch and Smith, 1966; Martín del Campo, 1935, 1950; Roze, 1967, 1983; Schmidt, 1933a, 1958; Schmidt and Smith, 1943; H. M. Smith and Taylor, 1945; Stuart, 1963; Tiedemann and Haupl, 1980.


### *Micrurus lemniscatus* (Linnaeus)

(Figs. 67–71; Map 23)

LOCAL NAMES Coral, coralillo. Bolivia: coral venenosa. Brazil: boi-corá, boichumbéguaçu (Mato Grosso and state of Amazonas), ibiboboca, ibiboca. Guyana: maccourracourra (Indian name). Peru: naca-naca (northeast). Suriname: kraalslang, krarasneke. Trinidad: corail, coral snake, large coral.

ENGLISH NAME South American coral snake.

DISTRIBUTION This species occupies the Amazonian slopes of the Andes in Bolivia, Peru, and Ecuador; the Amazonian and Orinocoan watersheds of Colombia; southern and eastern Venezuela; Trinidad; the Guianas; and the entire Amazon Basin south to the Brazilian states of Paraná and Mato Grosso do Sul (Map 23). In northeastern Brazil it is reported from Minas Gerais, north Rio Grande do Norte, and Ceará; we regard these reports as questionable. This species may also occur in Paraguay. Its vertical distribution is to at least 1,000 m.

HABITAT *Micrurus lemniscatus* frequents lowland rainforest and lower montane wet forest. It is found in

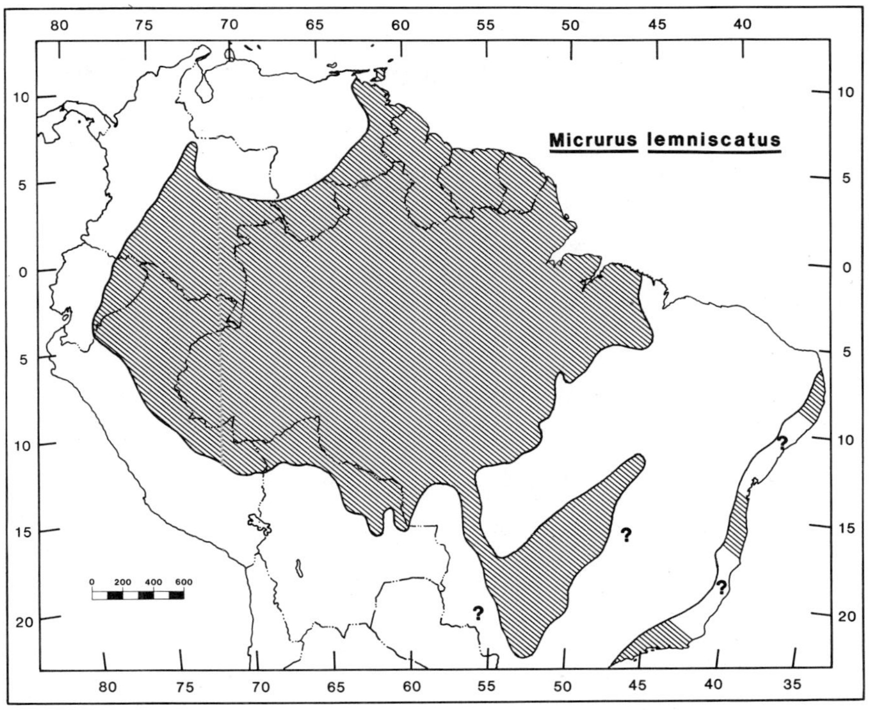


**Map 23.** Distribution of *Micrurus lemniscatus*, a widespread species in South America, including Trinidad. A disjunct segment of the range occurs along coastal southeastern Brazil, although it is unknown if the distribution is continuous. Question marks represent possible areas of occurrence.

savanna and gallery forest associations, secondary forest, cleared areas, rocky regions, and lowland floodplains. It is also frequently found near human habitations and in humid or aquatic situations.

DESCRIPTION *Micrurus lemniscatus* is a large, moderately slender coral snake averaging 600–900 mm in total length. It has been reported to be up to 1,450 mm long, and we have encountered specimens approximating this length in east-central Colombia.

This is a brightly marked, tricolored species with a pattern of 7–17 body triads plus ⅔–2 (usually 1⅔) triads on the tail. The tip of the snout and first supralabials are black, followed by a white, cream, or yellow ring that passes anterior to the eyes and usually just posterior to the nostrils, covering the postnasals, the prefrontals, the second and part of the third supralabials, and part of the frontal; this may be reduced to a dorsal spot in some specimens. There is occasionally a cuneiform posterior extension onto the frontal. The mental and first 3–4 infralabials are black. A black band covers the eyes, the anterior three-fourths of the parietals, and the anterior temporals, usually terminating below the eye on the adjacent supralabials but occasionally continuing ventrally to form a ring; rarely, it may be incomplete dorsally. A long red ring covers the posterior parietal tips and the first 4 rows of dorsals. The remainder of the venter of the head is usually red. Red rings in this species may be stippled (or even spotted) with black or they may be immaculate (see Remarks). White rings may be stippled (or spotted) with black or they may be immaculate. Generally the red and white rings are immaculate ventrally. The black rings are longer than the white rings they enclose, but they are generally shorter than the red rings. In most specimens the central black ring of each triad is longer than the two outer black rings, but in some they are nearly equal. Sometimes the black rings are angled sharply into the red zones (on the sides). Triads occasionally are fused, forming quinquads. The eyes of this species are notably small.

There are 1 + 1 temporals, 210–268 ventrals, and 25–43 subcaudals. Supra-anal keels are absent. Other features of lepidosis are typical of the genus *Micrurus*.

SIMILAR SPECIES The most distinctive feature of *M. lemniscatus* is its cephalic pattern, which includes a pale ring, band, or spot anterior to the eyes and a long red ring covering the parietal tips and first 4 rows of dorsals. *Micrurus filiformis* has virtually the same pattern but has 262 or more ventrals (vs. 268 or fewer) and a higher number of body triads. In *M. isozonus* the nuchal black ring usually covers the parietal tips and often has spotlike extensions onto them (parietal tips are red in *M. lemniscatus*). Both *M. frontalis* and *M. ibiboboca* usually have 26 or fewer subcaudals (as opposed to 25 or more in *M. lemniscatus*). *Micrurus frontifasciatus* has only the first pair of infralabials black and at least part of the parietals are black (first 3–4 infralabials are black and parietals are red in *M. lemniscatus*). Other sympatric *Micrurus* species are either highly distinctive in head pattern (*M. surinamensis*) or lack a complete first body triad on the neck. See also the discussion of false coral snakes in Mimics of Venomous Snakes.

REMARKS Four subspecies are currently recognized: *Micrurus l. lemniscatus* is a form possessing 224 or more ventrals in males, 229 or more ventrals and usually 33 or more subcaudals in females, and 12–17 body triads (a single report of 9). It is found from northern Guyana through Suriname, French Guiana, and northeastern Brazil in Amapá, Pará, and Maranhão. *Micrurus l. carvalhoi* (Fig. 67) is a subspecies possessing more than 226 ventrals in males, 234 or more ventrals and 33 or fewer subcaudals in females, and 9–16 body triads. The white body rings are narrow and heavily pigmented with black. It is found from northeastern and central Brazil south to Paraná and southern Mato Grosso do Sul and possibly Paraguay. *Micrurus l. diutius* (Figs. 68, 69) possesses fewer than 227 ventrals in males, fewer than 243 ventrals in females, and 7–13 body triads. It is found in Trinidad, eastern and southeastern Venezuela, and southern Guyana, Suriname, French Guiana, and probably Brazil. *Micrurus l. helleri* (Figs. 70, 71) is a subspecies possessing more than 226 ventrals in males, 234 or more ventrals and usually more than 33 subcaudals in females, and 9–11 body triads. It is found from the Amazonian slopes and Orinocoan watershed of Colombia south through the eastern portions of Ecuador, Peru, and Bolivia; southern Venezuela, and northwest Brazil. This race is barely, if at all, distinguishable from the nominate form.

Variation in *M. lemniscatus* is poorly understood and relationships among the races can be expected to change upon thorough analysis. Along the eastern versant of the Andes there is a marked change in the length of white body rings, with the northern population more closely resembling *M. l. diutius*, with long white rings, while more southerly populations have very short white rings. This species has traditionally been confused with *M. frontalis*, and thus is recorded in the literature as existing in regions that are actually extralimital. *Micrurus lemniscatus* has caused death in humans.

REFERENCES Abuys, 1987b; Amaral, 1925b, 1926d, 1930b, 1931b, 1937b, 1944c, 1944d, 1948b, 1974; Andersson, 1899; Bancroft, 1769; W. Beebe, 1946; Bertoni, 1914, 1939; Bolaños, 1983; Boos, 1975, 1984b; Boos and Quesnel, 1968; Brongersma, 1967; Burger, 1955; Carrillo de Espinoza, 1983; Cendrero et al., 1972; Chippaux, 1987; Cope, 1860c, 1870, 1876b; Cunha and Nascimento, 1973, 1978, 1982a; Cunha et al., 1985; Daniel, 1949; Dixon and Soini, 1986; Duellman, 1978; Dunn, 1944a; Emsley, 1977; Fugler and Walls, 1978; Gasc and Rodrigues, 1980; Gatti, 1955; Gliesch, 1925; Gomes, 1918b; Gray, 1829; Günther, 1859; Hoge, 1953a, 1967; Hoge and Lancini, 1962, 1970, 1979; Hoge and Romano, 1973; Kempff-Mercado, 1975; Klemmer, 1963; Lancini, 1979; Machado, 1945a; Marcuzzi, 1950; Medem, 1969; Meneses, 1974a; Mertens, 1956; Milá de la Roca, 1932; Miyata, 1982; Mole, 1914, 1924; Moonen et al., 1978; P. Müller, 1973; Nicéforo-María, 1933, 1942; Orcés, 1942, 1943, 1948; Parker, 1935; Pérez-Santos and Moreno, 1986; J. A. Peters, 1960a; Prado, 1945; Quelch, 1898; Rivero-Blanco and Dixon, 1979; Roze, 1955, 1966a, 1967, 1983; Sandner-Montilla, 1985b; Santos, 1981; Schmidt, 1936a, 1955, 1957a; Schmidt and Inger, 1951; Schmidt and Schmidt, 1925; Schmidt and Walker, 1943a; Schouten, 1931, 1937; Silva Haad and Rodríguez R., 1985; Soini, 1974b; Talbot, n.d.; Tiedemann and Haupl, 1980; Vanzolini, 1948; Vellard, 1941; Verteuil, 1884; Vetencourt Finol., 1960; Wehekind, 1960; Welch, 1980; Werner, 1900.

## *Micrurus limbatus* Fraser

(Figs. 72, 73; Map 24)

LOCAL NAMES Coral, coralillo.

ENGLISH NAME Tuxtlan coral snake.

DISTRIBUTION This snake is found in low and moderate elevations of the Sierra de los Tuxtlas in southern Veracruz, Mexico (Map 24). It is known from the south slope of Volcán San Martín, Coyame, near Tebanca, and the vicinity of La Palma. Its vertical distribution is from 160 to 1,050 m.

HABITAT Lowland rainforest and lower montane wet forest.

DESCRIPTION This snake is known to reach a total length of about 650 mm.

A distinctive bicolored pattern of black and red or orange with no trace of yellow rings characterizes this species. The black usually is disposed in 25–41 rings on the body that average 3 scale lengths middorsally; these rings may completely encircle the body or may be interrupted laterally. Some specimens have bold middorsal black spots rather than rings (Fig. 72). There are 4 or 5 black rings on the tail that are 4–5 subcaudals long. No black spotting is present on the ventral plates. The red dorsals are outlined distinctly with black. Two-thirds to all of the frontal and supraoculars are covered with black, and black pigment extends posteriorly along the interparietal suture; the remainder of the parietals may or may not be irregularly mottled with dark pigment. Black extends from the rostral to the fourth supralabial and postocular; the first 2½–3 infralabials and mental are irregularly mottled, and the chinshields are nearly immaculate. The nape ring varies from 3½ to 5 scales long middorsally.

Supra-anal keels are absent and there are 1 + 1 temporals, 190–205 ventrals, and 25–37 subcaudals. Other features of lepidosis are characteristic of the genus *Micrurus*.

SIMILAR SPECIES The only other coral snakes in central or southern Veracruz are *M. diastema* and *M. elegans*; both are readily distinguishable from *M. limbatus* on the basis of pattern. *Micrurus elegans* possesses black rings disposed in triads and *M. diastema* in this region is tricolored, with clearly definable yellow rings, and fewer than 24 black rings on the body. For information on false coral snakes occurring in southern Veracruz see the discussion of *Lampropeltis* and *Pliocercus* in Mimics of Venomous Snakes.

REMARKS This snake bites readily when restrained. It has been found under logs and in leaf litter.

REFERENCES Flores Villela et al., 1987; Fraser, 1964, 1973; Greene, 1973; Greene and McDiarmid, 1981; Greene and Pyburn, 1973; Pérez-Higadera [*sic*] et al., 1987; Pérez-Higareda, 1980; Ramírez-Bautista et al., 1981; Roze, 1967, 1983; H. M. Smith and Taylor, 1966.

## *Micrurus margaritiferus* Roze

(Figs. 74–76; Map 25)

LOCAL NAMES Coral. Peru: naca-naca.

ENGLISH NAME Speckled coral snake.

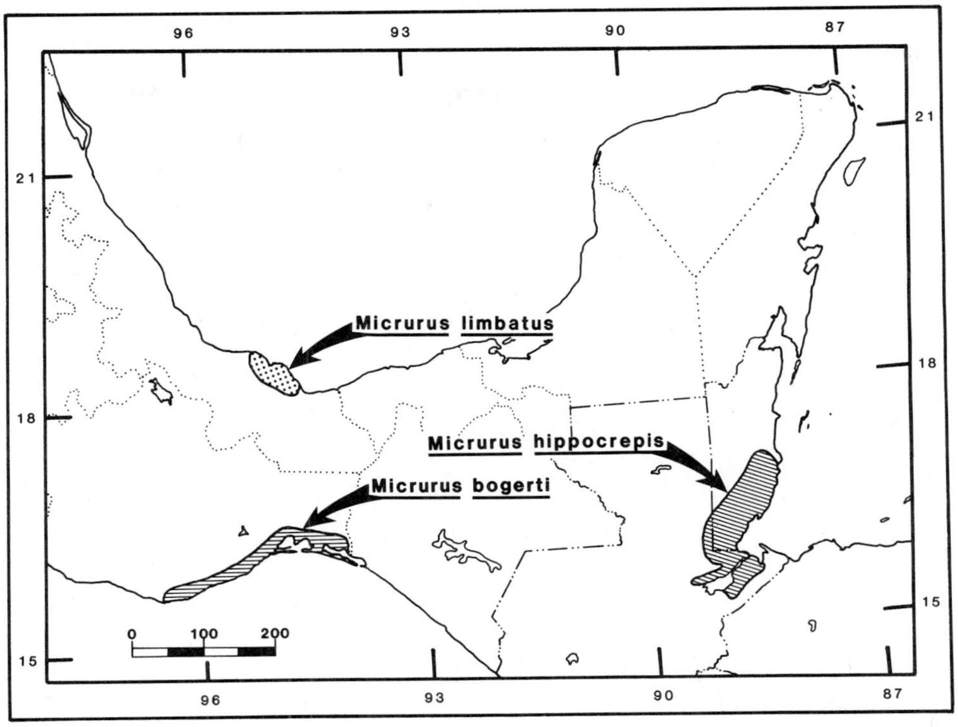


**Map 24.** Distributions of *Micrurus bogerti* (*horizontal lines*), *M. hippocrepis* (*diagonal lines*), and *M. limbatus* (*stipples*) in southern Mexico, Guatemala, and Belize.

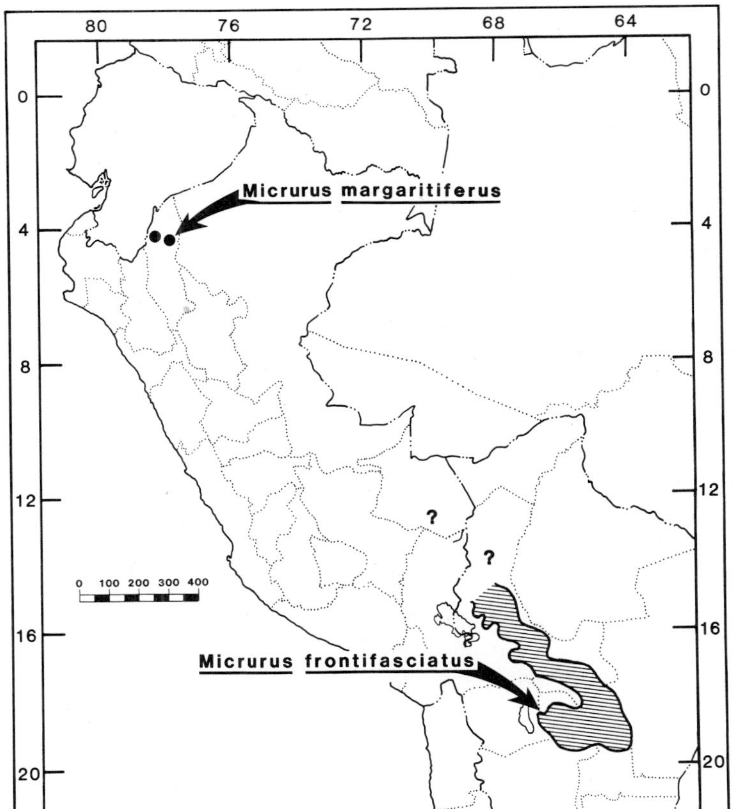


**Map 25.** Distributions of *Micrurus frontifasciatus* (*diagonal lines*) and *M. margaritiferus* (*dots*) in Bolivia and Peru, respectively. The distribution of *M. frontifasciatus* may extend into Peru. Question marks represent possible areas of occurrence of *M. frontifasciatus*.

DISTRIBUTION This species occupies the Amazonian slopes of the Andes in northern Peru; it is known only from the vicinity of the confluence of the Rió Santiago and Río Marañón, Amazonas, Perú (Map 25). It is likely that this species will be found to exist in similar habitats in eastern Ecuador. Its vertical distribution is unknown but probably does not exceed 1,000 m.

HABITAT Lower montane wet forest and tropical rainforest.

DESCRIPTION *Micrurus margaritiferus* is a small to medium-sized species; the largest recorded size is 773 mm.

This is a bicolored species, although some individuals have three colors on the venter. Dorsally the body is covered by 68–141 or more black rings plus 10 or more on the tail; all are offset by irregular transverse rows of white dots that are frequently interrupted on some specimens, more regular on others. These extend across the venter as solid to partially white single ventrals. The head is black with irregular white spots on the temporals and occipitals; these spots are especially evident on the posterior supralabials and infralabials. Ventrally the mental, anterior chinshields, and most labials are black. There is an irregular white mark at the level of the posterior chinshields. In some specimens the venter is tricolored with bands as follows: black-white-brown-white-black. Dorsally these brown bands become black, although it is not inconceivable that specimens might exist with a tricolored dorsum. On the tail, both dorsally and ventrally, the white rings become less well defined, appearing as scattered spots.

There are 1 + 1 temporals, 205–225 ventrals, and 33–48 subcaudals. Previously published information on lepidosis is for a single female specimen. Other features are typical of the genus *Micrurus*.

SIMILAR SPECIES *Micrurus margaritiferus* may be distinguished from all sympatric congeners by its (usually) bicolored dorsum, very high number of black body rings (68–141 or more), and the absence of any sort of ring on the head. *Micrurus annellatus* may be bicolored, but has a much lower body ring count and invariably possesses a pale (white or orange) parietal ring. Both *M. mertensi*, which is probably strictly coastal, and *M. peruvianus* have much lower black body ring counts (30 or fewer). The most similar species is *M. langsdorffi*, which occurs to the east of *M. margaritiferus* and differs in that it possesses 91 or fewer black body rings and has pale spots on the internasals and prefrontals. The relationship between the latter two species merits further study. See also the discussion of false coral snakes in Mimics of Venomous Snakes.

REFERENCES Carrillo de Espinoza, 1983; Greene and McDiarmid, 1981; Meneses, 1974a; Soini, 1974b; Roze, 1967, 1983.

## *Micrurus mertensi* Schmidt

(Map 32)

LOCAL NAMES Coral, coralillo.

ENGLISH NAME Mertens' coral snake.

DISTRIBUTION From southern Ecuador (in the Catamayo Valley) south in western Peru to the Departamento de La Libertad, in semi-arid coastal regions. The vertical distribution is to over 1,600 mm.

HABITAT Tropical deciduous forest, dry tropical forest, and thorn scrub. This species is most likely to be encountered in riparian situations.

DESCRIPTION The only reported size for this species is 880 mm, although specimens probably approach or slightly exceed 1,000 mm in length.

*Micrurus mertensi* is a tricolored coral snake without triads. The snout and top of the head are black, including all of the parietals; this black area is sometimes connected with the black nuchal ring via 1 black dorsal at the posterior parietal tips. The temporal region of the head is yellow. The body pattern consists of 18–30 black rings, 3–4 middorsals in length, that are bordered by yellow rings 1 middorsal in length. These rings alternate with red rings 5–6 middorsals long that are stippled strongly with black pigment on their apices. There are an additional 5–9 black rings on the tail.

There are 1 + 1 or 1 + 2 temporals, 210–236 ventrals, and 31–51 subcaudals. Males lack supra-anal keels. Other features of lepidosis are typical of the genus *Micrurus*.

SIMILAR SPECIES *Micrurus mertensi* is or may be sympatric with three species of coral snakes: *M. ancoralis*, *M. bocourti*, and *M. tschudii*. All three of these species possess a pattern of triads, whereas *M. mertensi* does not. See Mimics of Venomous Snakes for a discussion of false coral snakes.

REMARKS Relationships between *M. mertensi*, *M. peruvianus*, and *M. clarki* remain unclear. *Micrurus mertensi* is a poorly known species; its pattern characteristics resemble those of coral snakes from the nearby Río Marañón Valley east of the continental divide.

REFERENCES Carrillo de Espinoza, 1983; Meneses, 1974a; Miyata, 1982; P. Müller, 1973; Orcés, 1948; Parker, 1938; J. A. Peters, 1960a; Roze, 1967, 1983; Schmidt, 1936a; Schmidt and Walker, 1943b; Tiedemann and Haupl, 1980.

## *Micrurus mipartitus* (Duméril, Bibron, and Duméril)

(Figs. 77–79; Map 26)

LOCAL NAMES Coral, coralillo, gargantilla. Colombia: candelilla, coral cabeza de chocho, coral rabo de ají,

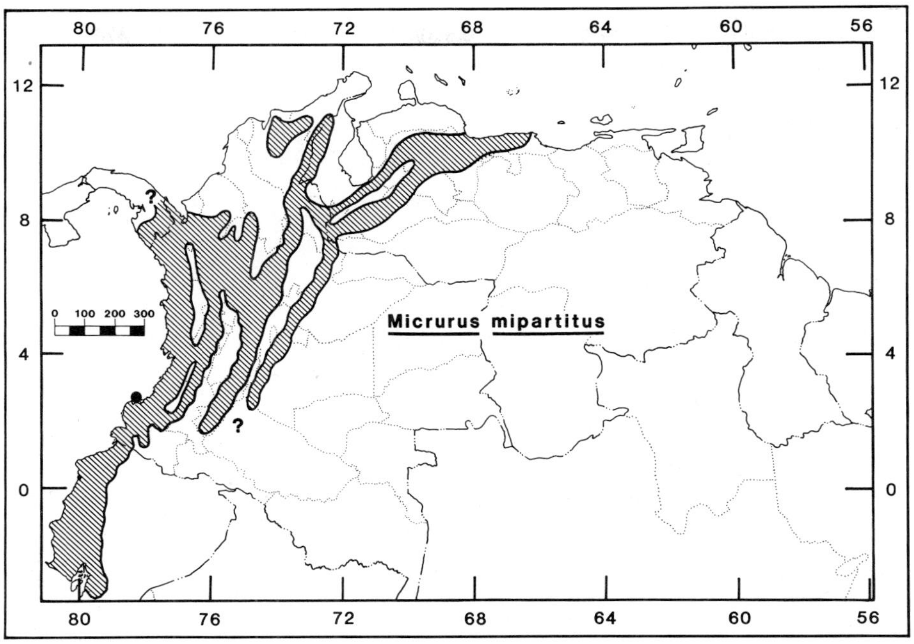


**Map 26.** Distribution of *Micrurus mipartitus* in northern and northwestern South America. The dot represents a record for Isla Gorgona off the Pacific coast of Colombia. The extent of its distribution in eastern Panama and zone of sympatry (if any) with *M. multifasciatus* (see Map 27) is not well understood. This species has been reported from northern Peru, but we are unaware of any specimens. Question marks represent possible areas of occurrence.

coral rabo de candela, gargantilla, matagatos. Venezuela: coral, coral montañera.

ENGLISH NAME Red-tailed coral snake.

DISTRIBUTION Panama, Colombia, Ecuador, and Venezuela. This species occupies the Darién region of Panama, the Pacific lowlands of Colombia (including Isla Gorgona), the Cordilleras Occidental, Central, and Oriental of the Colombian Andes (including the inter-Andean valleys and the eastern versant of the Cordillera Oriental), extending north and west into the Sierra Nevada de Santa Marta of Colombia and the Mérida Andes and Cordillera de la Costa of Venezuela (see Remarks and Map 26). *Micrurus mipartitus* ranges south into western Ecuador at least as far as the Río Catamayo Valley, and it has been suggested that it occurs in Peru, but this remains unconfirmed. Its vertical distribution is from near sea level to at least 2,410 m.

HABITAT *Micrurus mipartitus* is found in a variety of habitats, including lower montane wet forest and cloud forest. It frequently is encountered in coffee groves and other secondary areas, often in close association with human settlements (see Remarks).

DESCRIPTION This is a slender species that averages about 600–750 mm but reportedly reaches 1,200 mm in overall length.

There is conflicting information regarding the color of *M. mipartitus*, but it is usually, if not exclusively, black and white or black and yellow with a bold red-orange parietal ring and 2–7 red-orange caudal rings. There are 34–80 black body rings plus 1–6 black caudal rings. The snout is black, and this color may extend posteriorly to include the eyes and anterior portion of the supraoculars and frontal, or sometimes be restricted to the internasal-prefrontal region. The red-orange parietal ring covers the remainder of the head, including the temporals, posterior 3–3½ supralabials, and all of the parietals (sometimes the black encroaches upon the tips of the parietals). The red-orange parietal ring lacks all traces of black pigment. The black nuchal ring measures 4–7½ middorsals and is followed by a white or yellow ring 1–2½ middorsals long.

Black body rings vary from about 3 to 6 middorsals in length, are more-or-less regular, and usually are larger than the intervening white rings, although they may be nearly subequal in some specimens (see Remarks). White body rings generally contain black pigment, which varies in amount from scattered stippling to enough to cause a grayish shade to predominate. The posteriormost body ring (over the cloaca) is black and may be incomplete. The tail is invariably black and red-orange ringed (sometimes blotched); the tail terminus may be either of these colors. The tail itself is short and rather thick. Ventrally the dorsal colors are constant, although the red-orange parietal ring may be faded or absent. Generally the white rings lack black pigment ventrally. The underside of the head is cream to red, with black pigment scattered on the mental, chinshields, and infralabials. In some specimens the black nuchal ring is incomplete ventrally. Occasional specimens, especially large adults, will have the white body rings heavily obscured by black, gray, or brownish pigment such that they are not readily visible middorsally.

There are 1 + 1 (sometimes 0 + 1 or 1 + 2) temporals, 197–303 ventrals, and 20–35 subcaudals, usually divided. Supra-anal keels are absent. Other features of lepidosis are typical of the genus *Micrurus*.

SIMILAR SPECIES Five bicolored coral snakes share parts of the range of *M. mipartitus*: *Micrurus multifasciatus*, in Panama, is extremely similar to *M. mipartitus* in most features, but adult males possess weak supra-anal keels (lacking in *M. mipartitus*) and pale body rings are not always white (as in *M. mipartitus*). *Micrurus stewarti*, in Panama, is a black-and-red snake with a maximum of 223 ventrals, a minimum of 40 subcaudals, and 13–21 black body rings (*M. mipartitus* is black and white or yellow with 197–303 ventrals, 20–35 subcaudals, and 34–80 black body rings). *Micrurus multiscutatus*, in western Colombia, is a *black-and-red* snake with 295–329 ventrals (*M. mipartitus* is a *black-and-white* snake with 197–303 ventrals). *Micrurus spurrelli*, in western Colombia, possesses 232–244 ventrals, a white or red prefrontal band or ring, and 36–37 subcaudals (*M. mipartitus* has 197–303 ventrals, lacks a prefrontal ring, and has 20–35 subcaudals. *Micrurus psyches*, in Colombia and Venezuela, possesses a black parietal cap (parietals are red-orange in *M. mipartitus*).

REMARKS Four poorly defined subspecies are recognized on the basis of ventral and subcaudal counts and distribution. In *M. m. mipartitus* (Fig. 77), which occurs from eastern Panama to western Colombia, males have 240 or more ventrals, and females have more than 251 ventrals and 25–30 subcaudals, and the black snout coloration is reduced. *Micrurus m. anomalus* (Fig. 78) ranges from eastern Colombia in the Cordillera Oriental north to the Sierra Nevada de Santa Marta, the Serranía Perijá, and probably in the Mérida Andes of western Venezuela (a report of the nominate form in Táchira, Venezuela, is probably referrable to *M. m. anomalus*). In this subspecies males have 224–247 ventrals, and females have 244–287 ventrals and usually more than 25 subcaudals. *Micrurus m. decussatus* (Fig. 79) ranges from the Andes of western and central Colombia and the southern part of the Colombian Cordillera Oriental south into adjacent western Ecuador; its southern limitus remains unknown. It has also been taken on Isla Gorgona off the Colombian Pacific Coast. Males possess 250–275 ventrals, and females possess 276–303 ventrals and usually more than 25 subcaudals. In *M. m. semipartitus* (Fig. 80), which occurs in the Cordillera de la Costa and adjacent parts of northern Venezuela, including the Caracas region, males possess 197–220 ventrals, and females possess 221–258 ventrals.

The race of *M. mipartitus* occurring in the Mérida Andes of western Venezuela is of uncertain status and may represent either *M. m. anomalus* or *M. m. semipartitus*. The barrier effects of the Barquisimeto Depression and the San Cristóbal Depression could be limiting factors in the distributions.

*Micrurus mipartitus* has killed humans. It defends itself vigorously and is not uncommon around human habitations. It is often active during the day.

REFERENCES Acosta-Solís, 1944; Alemán, 1953; Amaral, 1925b, 1926c, 1927d, 1928, 1930a, 1931b; Angel, 1983; Ayerbe, 1979; Ayerbe et al., 1977, 1979; W. Beebe, 1947; Boulenger, 1896, 1902a, 1913; Breder, 1946; Carrillo de Espinoza, 1983; Castro et al. 1982; Cendrero et al., 1972; Cope, 1868; Daniel, 1949; Díaz-Gómez, 1971; Duellman, 1979; Dugand, 1975; Duméril et al., 1854; Dunn, 1944a, 1944b; Dunn and Bailey, 1939; García 1896; Golay, 1985; Greene and McDiarmid, 1981; Griffin, 1916; Grocott and Sadler, 1958; Hoge and Lancini, 1962; Jan, 1858; Lancini, 1962c, 1970, 1979; Marcuzzi, 1950; Medem, 1965, 1969, 1979; Milá de la Roca, 1932; Miyata, 1982; Mocquard, 1908–1909; Nicéforo-María, 1933, 1942; Orcés, 1942, 1943, 1948; Parker, 1926, 1938; Pérez-Santos, 1986b; Pérez-Santos and Moreno, 1986; J. A. Peters, 1955, 1960a; Rendahl, 1937; Rendahl and Vestergren, 1940; Roux-Esteve, 1983; Roze, 1952, 1955, 1966a, 1967, 1970a, 1983; Ruthven, 1922; Sandner-Montilla, 1975, 1985b; Schmidt, 1933b, 1936a, 1955; Test et al., 1966; Vellard, 1941; Vetencourt Finol., 1960; Werner, 1900, 1901a, 1903, 1927.

## *Micrurus multifasciatus* (Jan)

(Fig. 81; Map 27)

LOCAL NAMES Coral, coralilla, gargantilla.

ENGLISH NAME Many-banded coral snake.

DISTRIBUTION This species occupies the Caribbean versant in central Nicaragua, crosses the Continental Divide, and ranges into the Pacific lowlands in northwestern Costa Rica and central Panama (Map 27). Its vertical distribution is from near sea level to about 1,200 m.

HABITAT Lowland moist and wet forests (rainforest), subtropical wet forest, and lower montane wet forest. In northwestern Costa Rica this species ranges into tropical dry forest.

DESCRIPTION This is a long, slender species averaging 500–800 mm in total length, but reaches a maximum of at least 1,130 mm.

The snout is black and the black pigment includes most or all of the prefrontals and supralabials 1–4, sometimes part of 5; this coloration sometimes extends posteriorly to include the anterior portions of the supraoculars, frontal, and postoculars. Although this snake often is bicolored, the color pattern varies. The pale parietal ring is usually red, but may be pink, white, or cream suffused with red or not. The pale rings on the body may also be red, pink, cream, or white, and a few irregular dark flecks may be present on the scales of these rings. Large adult specimens are known that are completely black and white, except for the venter of the tail, which is red or pink. It is not unusual to encounter specimens with red or pink tail rings, a nuchal ring of the same color, and white or cream rings encircling the rest of the body. Juveniles tend to be more brightly colored than adults and are generally red and black. The black nuchal ring begins *behind* the posterior tips of the parietals and extends 4–8 middorsal scale lengths. The infracephalic scales are generally the same color as the pale nuchal ring and may or may not have darker markings. There are 40–65 black body rings, 4–6 middorsals long, which are separated by pale rings 2–3 middorsals long. The tail has 2–5 black rings.

Supra-anal keels are developed weakly in adult males, and there are 1 + 1 or 1 + 2 temporals, 233–311 ventrals, and 23–33 subcaudals. Other features of lepidosis are typical of the genus *Micrurus*.

SIMILAR SPECIES *Micrurus multifasciatus* is not likely to be confused with tricolored species such as *M.*

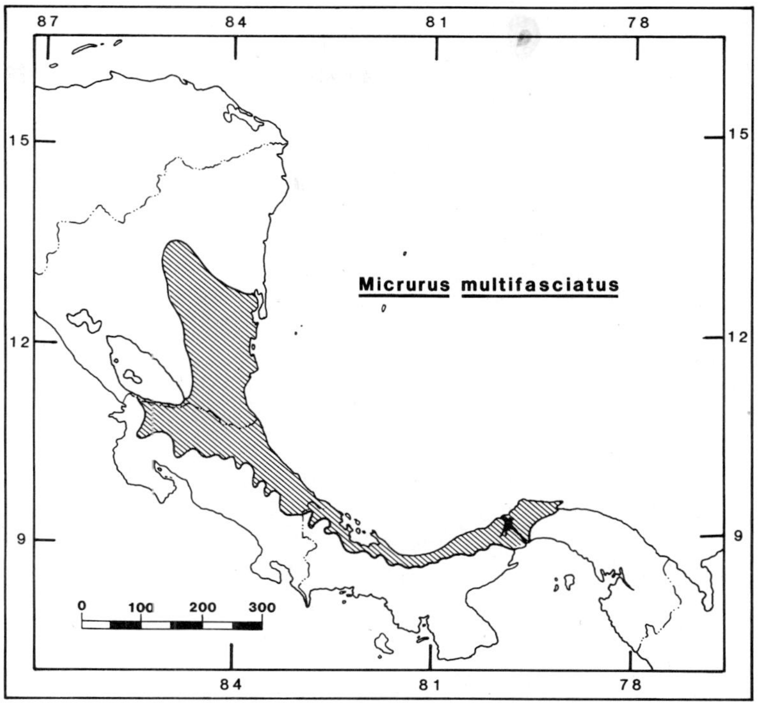


**Map 27.** Distribution of *Micrurus multifasciatus* in lower Central America. Except for small regions in northwestern Costa Rica and central Panama, this species is restricted to the Atlantic watershed. It may extend into eastern Panama for a greater distance than is shown.

*alleni, M. clarki,* or *M. nigrocinctus.* Although some specimens of *M. alleni* from the Pacific versant have an ontogenetic darkening of the red rings so as to become an essentially bicolored species dorsally, this species is tricolored ventrally, has a black cap that extends posteriorly to completely cover the parietals, and possesses only 13–26 black body rings. In eastern Panama, *M. ancoralis* and *M. dissoleucus* have black body rings disposed in triads.

There are only two bicolored species of coral snakes in lower Central America other than *M. multifasciatus*: *Micrurus stewarti* of central Panama differs from *M. multifasciatus* in having fewer (13–21) black body rings that tend to be longer, particularly the black nuchal ring (10–15 ventrals) and the first black tail ring (10–18 subcaudals). *Micrurus mipartitus* of eastern Panama differs from *M. multifasciatus* in that adult males lack supra-anal keels and invariably have white body rings (see Remarks).

Harmless bicolored snakes occurring within the range of *M. multifasciatus* include members of the genera *Lampropeltis* (some adults; see Figs. 495, 496), *Liophis* (Fig. 499), *Oxyrhopus* (Figs. 505, 506), and *Scolecophis* (Fig. 526); also see Mimics of Venomous Snakes.

REMARKS Until recently, the Central American bicolored populations of coral snakes, exclusive of *M. stewarti*, were considered to be conspecific with *M. mipartitus* of eastern Panama and Andean South America. We can offer no good evidence for either the conspecifity or distinctness of these populations and therefore follow the most recent reviewer. Two subspecies of *M. multifasciatus* are currently recognized and may be distinguished on the basis of the number of ventrals: In *M. m. hertwigi* (Fig. 81) of Nicaragua, Costa Rica, and eastern Panama, the males have 233–244 and the females 256–269. In *M. m. multifasciatus* of central Panama, the males have 247–265 and the females 278–311. The distributional extent of this species in eastern Panama has not been well documented.

This species has been found active during the early morning and late afternoon. It is reported to be nervous and to bite readily.

REFERENCES Amaral, 1926c; Bates, 1928; Bolaños, 1971, 1983, 1984; Cendrero et al., 1972; Cope, 1876a, 1886, 1887; Dunn, 1940a; Garman, 1877; Golay, 1985; Greene and McDiarmid, 1981; Grocott and Sadler, 1958; Jan, 1858; C. W. Myers and Rand, 1969; Picado, 1931; Roze, 1967, 1983; Savage, 1980; Savage and Vial, 1974; Schmidt, 1928a; Scott, 1969; E. H. Taylor, 1951, 1954; R. T. Taylor et al., 1974; Trejos, 1937; R. W. Van Devender, 1980; Villa, 1972a, 1984; Werner, 1897; Wettstein, 1934.

### *Micrurus multiscutatus* Rendahl and Vestergren
(Fig. 82; Map 36)

LOCAL NAMES Coral, rabo de ají.

ENGLISH NAME Cauca coral snake.

DISTRIBUTION This species is known only from two localities in the Departamento de Cauca, Colombia: El Tambo (type locality), and Quebrada Guanguí, Río Saija drainage (see Map 36). Its vertical distribution is from 100 to 1,745 m.

HABITAT Lowland moist and wet forests (rainforest), subtropical wet forest, and lower montane wet forest.

DESCRIPTION This is a medium-sized species; the longest recorded specimen is the holotype, which is 842 mm long.

*Micrurus multiscutatus* is a red-and-black bicolored species (the parietal ring is sometimes yellow) with 59–66 black body rings plus 3–4 black rings on the tail. The snout is black, including the first 4 supralabials, the eyes, the preoculars, and the internasals. A red or yellow ring covers the head, including the fifth, sixth, and anterior part of the seventh supralabial, the temporals, the frontal, and the parietals (excluding the tips). The head is red or yellow ventrally, with scattered black pigment. The black nuchal ring is about 5–6 middorsals in length, covers the parietal tips, and shifts anteriorly on the sides of the head to encroach upon the posterior half of the seventh supralabial. This produces a curved posterior border to the red parietal ring. The red rings are 2–4 middorsals in length and contain scattered black spots. The black rings are slightly larger than the red rings, being 3–5 middorsals in length.

There are 1 + 1 temporals (the anterior temporal is sometimes weakly divided longitudinally), 295–329 ventrals, and 24–30 subcaudals. Other features of lepidosis are typical of the genus *Micrurus*.

SIMILAR SPECIES There are only two species of bicolored coral snakes that are or may be sympatric with *Micrurus multiscutatus*: *M. mipartitus* and *M. spurrelli*. Neither of these species is known definitely to possess red body rings, as does *M. multiscutatus*. The white body rings of *M. mipartitus* are more regularly and profusely spotted with black than the red rings of *M. multiscutatus*. *Micrurus spurrelli* has a lower number of ventrals (232–244 vs. 295–329), a white or red prefrontal band or ring (lacking in *M. multiscutatus*); and a higher number of subcaudals (36–37 vs. 24–30). See also the discussion of false coral snakes in Mimics of Venomous Snakes.

REMARKS *Micrurus multiscutatus* is a member of a confusing assemblage of bicolored coral snakes that show considerable overlap in scale and pattern features. The validity of currently recognized forms can only be ascertained with additional material and accurate color descriptions of living specimens.

REFERENCES Amaral, 1930a; Pérez-Santos and Moreno, 1986; Rendahl and Vestergren, 1940; Roze, 1967, 1983; Schmidt, 1955.

### *Micrurus narduccii* (Jan)

(Figs. 83, 84; Map 28)

LOCAL NAMES Coral, coralillo. Peru: culebra de dos cabezas, naca-naca.

ENGLISH NAME Andean black-backed coral snake.

DISTRIBUTION *Micrurus narduccii* occupies low to moderate elevations of the Amazonian slopes of the Andes in southern Colombia (see Remarks), Ecuador, Peru, and Bolivia. It ranges widely in the lowlands of the northwest Amazon Basin in the aforementioned countries and Brazil, in the states of Amazonas and Acre (Map 28). Its vertical distribution is from 100 to at least 1,500 m.

HABITAT Lowland rainforest and lower montane wet forest.

DESCRIPTION This species averages 300–600 mm and has been recorded to be up to 1,117 mm in total length.

It possesses a distinctive pattern of 37–62 oval orange, red, or yellow blotches, 2–4 ventrals in length, on a black venter. These blotches may extend laterally to the fourth or fifth dorsal scale row, but some may meet dorsally to form rings. The head is black with a yellow-to-orange ring crossing the supraoculars, frontal, and parietals. There are 1½–4 orange blotches on the venter of the tail; 1 or more may extend to encircle it, and they may coalesce ventrally. Otherwise, the dorsal and ventral color is black. In specimens that have ventral blotches complete middorsally, the dorsal portion is heavily suffused with black.

There are 1 + 1 (sometimes 1 + 2) temporals, 261–382 ventrals, and 15–35 subcaudals. The first pair of infralabials are not in contact with each other behind the mental, thus the chinshields are in contact with the mental. Other features of lepidosis are characteristic of the genus *Micrurus*.

SIMILAR SPECIES Throughout most of its range, *M. narduccii* lacks body rings (a ring is present only on the head, and sometimes 1 or 2 are present on the tail tip). This feature distinguishes it from all but 1 species of coral snake with which it may be sympatric, although melanistic individuals of other species could be encountered. Moreover, ringed specimens of *M. narduccii* have not been encountered with more than 8 body rings, a feature not found in sympatric bicolored or tricolored coral snake species (see Remarks). *Micrurus karlschmidti* closely resembles *M. narduccii*; but *M. karlschmidti* has 219–270 ventrals.

REMARKS Most Colombian records for *M. narduccii* are referred to *M. karlschmidti* based on locality. The considerable range of variation in pattern and scutellation reported for *M. narduccii* may be a result of misidentifications by previous investigators, or, alternatively, *M. narduccii* may be a composite species. Roze and Bernal-Carlo (in press) recognize two subspecies of *M. narduccii*. Recently captured specimens have been observed to raise and curl the tail.

REFERENCES Amaral, 1925b, 1930b, 1948b; Angel, 1983; Carrillo de Espinoza, 1983; Cendrero et al., 1972; Cope, 1870, 1876b; Daniel, 1949; Dixon and Soini, 1986; Duellman, 1978; Dunn, 1944a, 1946; Golay, 1985; Gomes, 1918a; Griffin, 1916; Hoge and Romano, 1966; Kempff-Mercado, 1975; Medem, 1969; Miyata, 1982; Nicéforo-María, 1942; Orcés, 1943, 1948; J. A. Peters, 1960a; Romano, 1972; Roze, 1967, 1983; Roze and Bernal-Carlo, in press; Santos, 1981; Schmidt, 1936a; Silva Haad and Rodríguez R., 1985; Soini, 1974b; Thompson, 1913; Werner, 1901a.

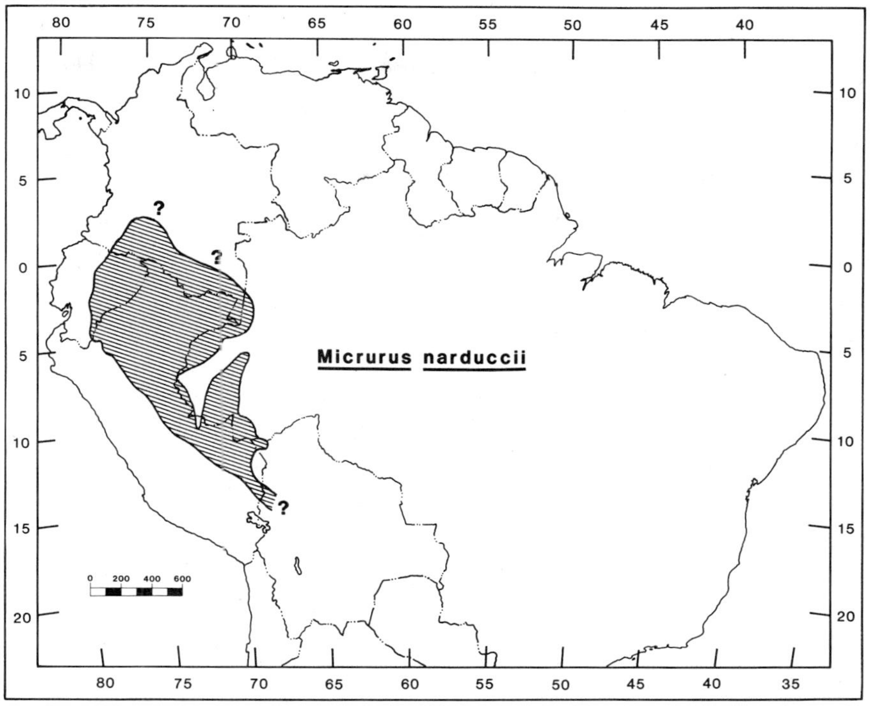


**Map 28.** Distribution of *Micrurus narduccii* in northwestern South America. The range of *M. narduccii* may be more limited than is indicated because this species has been confused with *M. karlschmidti*. Question marks represent possible areas of occurrence.

## *Micrurus nigrocinctus* (Girard)

(Figs. 85–90; Map 33)

LOCAL NAMES Coral, coralillo, gargantilla (Mexico to Colombia). Nicaragua: babaspul (Great Corn Island).

ENGLISH NAME Central American coral snake.

DISTRIBUTION This species occupies the Pacific versant of southeastern Oaxaca and Chiapas, Mexico, and Atlantic drainage of east-central Belize, southeastward through Central America, excluding the highlands, to northwestern Colombia. It also occurs on Great Corn Island, Nicaragua, and the islands of San José, San Miguel, Coiba, and Taboga, Panama (see Map 33). There are questionable records from Andagoya and Isla de Providencia, Colombia. Its vertical distribution ranges from near sea level to about 1,300 m.

HABITAT Lowland rainforest, lowland dry forest, thorn forest, lower montane wet forest, and lower montane dry forest.

DESCRIPTION A medium-sized coral snake, it may exceed 1 m in total length; a specimen (UTA R-21815) from near Palín, Guatemala, was 994 mm long.

This species is generally tricolored with black, yellow, and red rings, but it may be bicolored red and black. The snout is entirely black, but the extent of the black pigment is highly variable: it may cover only the internasals and prefrontals or may extend to cover most or all of the supraoculars, frontal, and supralabials 1–4. Generally, the mental and several infralabials are all or partially black. The location of the anterior border of the black nape ring varies from the posterior half of the parietals to 2 dorsal scale lengths behind the parietals; it extends posteriorly 4–13 scale lengths. The extent of the pale parietal ring varies according to the conformation of the black cap and black nuchal ring, but generally involves at least the posterior tip of the frontal, the anterior two-thirds of the parietals, and most of the lower preocular, as well as several supralabials and infralabials. Yellow body rings may be present or absent; if present, they usually are narrow, not more than two dorsals or two ventrals long (rarely, three or four), and they are frequently incomplete ventrally. There are 10–29 black body rings and 3–8 black rings on the tail. The pale tail rings and the parietal ring are most frequently yellow, but may be red in some specimens. The red rings are two to four times broader than the black rings. Red scales are heavily marked with black in most snakes throughout the range, with the exception of snakes from the Pacific versant of Mexico, Guatemala, and El Salvador, in which red scales may be either immaculate or tipped with tiny black dots. A snake from Necoclí, Antioquia, Colombia, was red and black dorsally with the red rings becoming yellow ventrally.

Supra-anal keels are present in adult males. There are 1 + 1 or 1 + 2 temporals, 180–230 ventrals, and 31–58 subcaudals, a few of which may be entire. Other features of lepidosis are characteristic of the genus *Micrurus*.

SIMILAR SPECIES Owing to its great variability and extensive distribution, *M. nigrocinctus* may be easily confused with many different species of coral snakes throughout its range. In Mexico and the Pacific drainages of Guatemala and El Salvador, *M. nigrocinctus* varies from *M. diastema*, *M. latifasciatus*, and *M. stuarti* in having red scales not tipped with black; it further differs from *M. latifasciatus* in almost always having more than 10 black body rings. *Micrurus nigrocinctus* differs from *M. browni* and *M. stuarti* in having a lower number of ventrals (208 or fewer in males and 224 or fewer in females) and narrower black body rings.

In Belize and the Atlantic drainages of Guatemala and Honduras, *M. nigrocinctus* usually may be distinguished from most *M. diastema* and *M. ruatanus* (Isla de Roatán) by possessing 29 or fewer black body rings; *M. diastema* and *M. hippocrepis* are further distinguished from *M. nigrocinctus* by the presence of a yellow snout and the absence of supra-anal keels in males.

In Nicaragua, Costa Rica, and Panama, *M. multifasciatus* differs from *M. nigrocinctus* in having rings of only two colors on the dorsal part of the body and a black head cap that barely reaches the supraoculars, if at all; *M. alleni* may be distinguished by the presence of a black head cap that extends posteriorly along the interparietal suture or covers most of the parietals. In Costa Rica and Panama, *M. clarki* differs in having pale lateral head scales bordered by black, parietal shields completely included in the black head cap, and a mental and infralabials that may be finely stippled with dark pigment, but are pale overall.

In Panama and Colombia, *M. dissoleucus* and *M. ancoralis* may be distinguished from *M. nigrocinctus* in having black rings forming triads on the body; *M. dumerilii* may or may not have triads; if not, it differs from *M. nigrocinctus* in having a black head cap that extends posteriorly to include all or most of the parietals.

A large number of harmless snakes have patterns and colors similar to coral snakes; see Mimics of Venomous Snakes.

REMARKS At least six subspecies of *M. nigrocinctus* are often recognized based upon the condition of the black nuchal ring, number of ventrals, or number of black body rings: *M. n. zunilensis* (Fig. 90) from the Pacific drainages of southern Mexico, Guatemala, El Salvador, and Honduras; *M. n. divaricatus* (Figs. 87, 88) from central Belize and the Atlantic drainage of Honduras; *M. n. mosquitensis* (Fig. 89) from the Atlantic drainage of Nicaragua, Costa Rica, and northwestern Panama; *M. n. nigrocinctus* (Figs. 85, 86) from the Pacific drainages of Nicaragua and Costa Rica, and most of Panama, including Isla de Taboga and northwestern Colombia; *M. n. babaspul* from Great Corn Island (Isla del Maíz Grande), Nicaragua; and *M. n. coibensis* from Coiba Island, Panama. A recent report of *M. nigrocinctus* from the department of Tolima, Colombia, is in error (Pérez-Santos, 1986b).

REFERENCES Alvarez del Toro, 1983; Amaral, 1927c; Barbour, 1906; Barbour and Loveridge, 1929c; Bates, 1928; Bolaños, 1972, 1982, 1983, 1984; H. C. Clark, 1925, 1942; Cochran, 1946; Cope, 1860c, 1874, 1876a, 1886; Dugès, 1885; Dunn, 1933, 1944a, 1947, 1949, 1951; Elton, 1948; Evans, 1947; Ferrari-Perez, 1886; Fonseca, 1949; Garman, 1877, 1884a; Gehlbach, 1972; Greene, 1972; Greene and Seib, 1983; Grocott and Sadler, 1958; Gutiérrez and Bolaños, 1979, 1981; Hallowell, 1861; Henderson and Hoevers, 1975; Heyer, 1967; Landy et al., 1966; Lee, 1980; Martín del Campo, 1950; Mertens, 1941, 1952b; Meyer, 1969; Mittleman and Smith, 1949; C. W. Myers and Rand, 1969; Neill, 1965; Nemuras, 1967; Nicéforo-María, 1942; Pérez-Santos, 1986b; Picado, 1931; Roze, 1967, 1970b, 1983; Savage, 1980; Savage and Vial, 1974; Schmidt, 1928a, 1932, 1933a, 1933b, 1936b, 1955; Schmidt and Smith, 1943; Scott, 1969; Slevin, 1939; H. M. Smith, 1943; H. M. Smith and Taylor, 1945, 1966; Stuart, 1963; Swanson, 1945; E. H. Taylor, 1951, 1954; R. T. Taylor et al., 1974; Tiedemann and Haupl, 1980; Timmerman and Hayes, 1981; Troschel, 1855; R. W. Van Devender, 1980; Villa, 1962, 1972b, 1984; Wettstein, 1934; Wilson, 1983; Wilson and Meyer, 1972, 1985.

### ***Micrurus peruvianus*** **Schmidt**

(Fig. 91; Map 29)

LOCAL NAMES Coral. Peru: naca-naca, serpiente de coral.

ENGLISH NAME Peruvian coral snake.

DISTRIBUTION This species is known only from the northern Andes of Peru in the Departamento de Cajamarca and Departamento de Amazonas, Río Marañón drainage (Huancabamba Depression). It has been reported from Perico and Bellavista, in Cajamarca, and a specimen exists from Bagua Grande, Amazonas (Map 29). Its occurrence in Ecuador along the Cordillera del Condor would not be surprising (see Remarks). Its vertical distribution is from about 500 to at least 1,500 m.

HABITAT Lower montane dry forest in the semi-arid foothills of the interandean basins.

DESCRIPTION *Micrurus peruvianus* appears to be a small species, probably not exceeding 600 mm in total length. The maximum reported size is 415 mm.

This coral snake is usually tricolored but on some specimens the red rings are completely melanic. The pattern does not include triads. There are 16–27 black rings on the body and 4–9 on the tail. The snout and top of the head are completely black, including the eyes, anterior temporals (when present), one-half of the posterior temporals, and all or nearly all of the parietals. A white to pale yellow ring borders the parietal cap, covers the remainder of the temporals, and 1–2 rows of dorsals. On some specimens the anterior edges of the dorsals bordering the parietals are black. The dorsal that abuts the parietal tips is often black, providing a narrow connection with the black nuchal ring—which is 4–9 middorsals long. Aside from the nuchal, black rings are usually 3–6 middorsals long. The venter of the head is white or pale yellow with black spots in the mental region and scattered elsewhere. The yellow rings vary from 1½ to 3 middorsals in length; usually all the yellow scales are tipped with black spots, although they may be immaculate. Red rings are 3½–6 middorsals long, and usually all the red scales have black apices. The tail is bicolored, with 4–9 black rings separated by shorter white or pale yellow rings. Ventrally the white rings tend to be immaculate but the red rings contain much scattered black pigment. Generally, all rings are complete, but in one specimen only alternate black rings were complete, the others having been invaded paraventrally by pale yellow rings, leaving a black blotch ventrally. In entirely bicolored specimens the melanic red rings may be distinguished from the black rings by their smaller size. The tail tip and tongue are black.

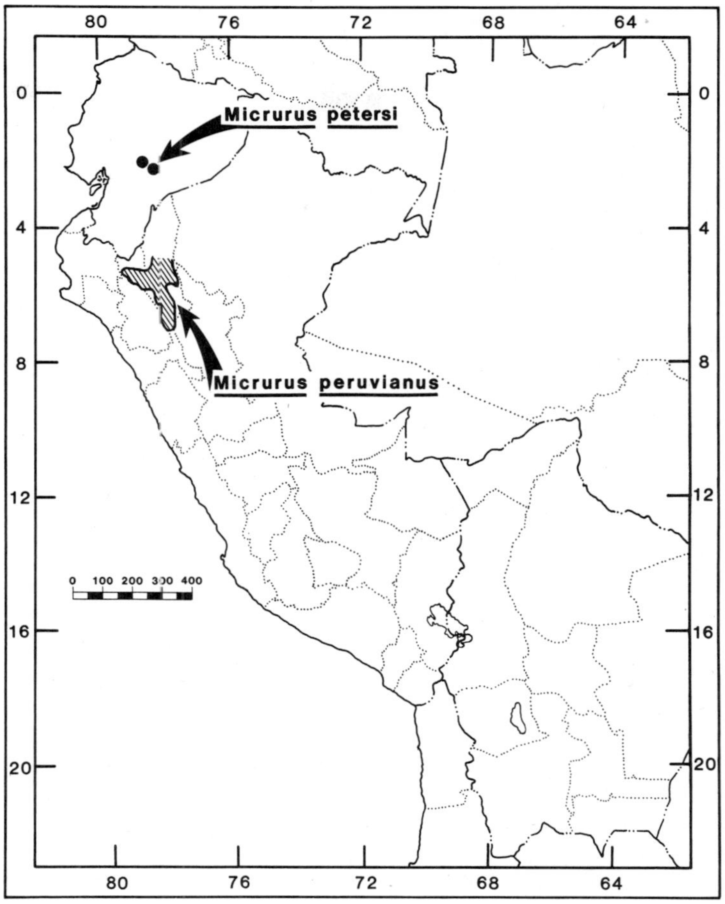


**Map 29.** Distributions of *Micrurus peruvianus* (*diagonal lines*) and *M. petersi* (*dots*) in Peru and Ecuador, respectively. The distribution of *M. peruvianus* may extend northward in Peru and into Ecuador.

There are 1 + 1 or 0 + 1 temporals, 178–211 ventrals, and 39–42 subcaudals, mostly divided. Supra-anal keels are absent. Other features of lepidosis are typical of the genus *Micrurus*.

SIMILAR SPECIES There are nine coral snakes with which *M. peruvianus* is or may be sympatric: *Micrurus annellatus* possesses a narrow ring that traverses the parietals (the parietals are black in *M. peruvianus*). *Micrurus bocourti* possesses a pattern of triads (lacking in *M. peruvianus*) and is found only in western lowlands. *Micrurus langsdorffi* is of varying color, often lacks black rings, and usually has red rings on the tail (*M. peruvianus* varies in color but always possesses black rings and has a yellow-and-black tail). *Micrurus margaritiferus* possesses more than 67 black body rings (16–25 in *M. peruvianus*). *Micrurus mertensi* possesses 210–236 ventrals (vs. 178–211) and occurs in the western lowlands. *Micrurus mipartitus* possesses a constant pattern of black and white body rings with red rings on head and tail, and the parietals are at least partially red (*M. peruvianus* lacks red in the tail and parietals). *Micrurus petersi* has a pale snout (black in *M. peruvianus*). *Micrurus steindachneri* possesses 22–42 black body rings (16–27 in *M. peruvianus*). *Micrurus tschudii* possesses a pattern of triads (single black rings in *M. peruvianus*) and occurs in the Western lowlands. See also the discussion of false coral snakes in Mimics of Venomous Snakes.

REMARKS *Micrurus peruvianus* is a poorly known species, both in terms of variation and distribution. It is quite similar to *Micrurus mertensi*, from which it is separated by the Continental Divide. The Huancabamba Depression, where *M. peruvianus* occurs, is host to a number of endemic forms as well as others that reach their northern or southern distributional limit in the region. It is possible that *M. peruvianus* will be found to have a broader range than currently known. Alternatively, it may be a composite of endemic species. This species was cited tentatively as occurring in Colombia; the specimen on which this report was based is not allocatable to *M. peruvianus*. As recognized, *M. peruvianus* possesses a distinctive head shape with a sharp snout and foreshortened frontal; in this it is similar to *M. clarki* and *M. mertensi*.

REFERENCES Carrillo de Espinoza, 1983; Duellman, 1979; Dunn, 1923; Meneses, 1974a; Roze, 1967, 1983; Schmidt, 1936a; Shreve, 1947b.

### *Micrurus petersi* Roze

(Map 29)

LOCAL NAME Coral.

ENGLISH NAME Peters' coral snake.

DISTRIBUTION This species is known on the basis of two specimens from the Río Upano Valley region,

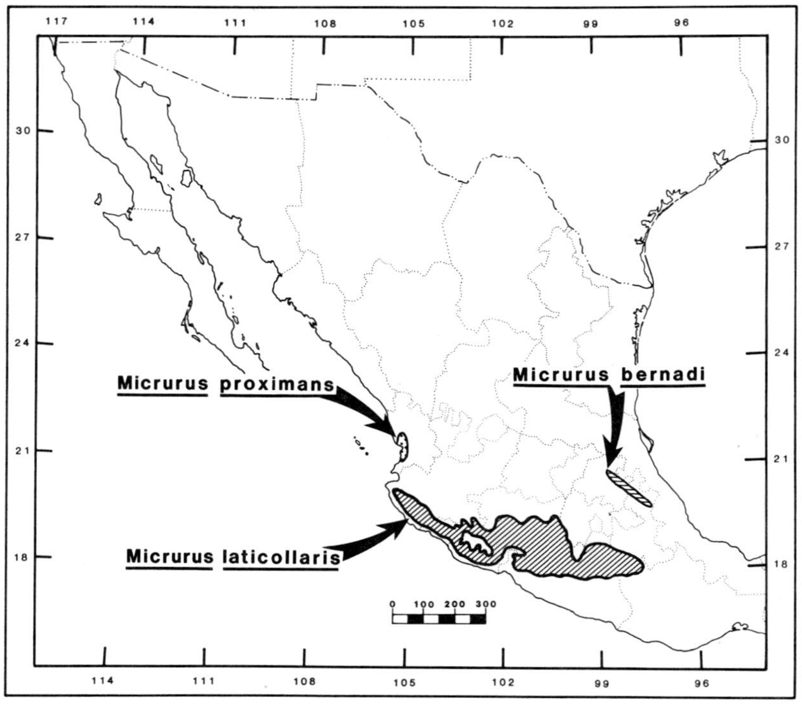


**Map 30.** Distributions of *Micrurus bernadi* (horizontal lines), *M. laticollaris* (diagonal lines), and *M. proximans* (stipples) in Mexico.

Morona-Santiago Province, Ecuador (see Map 29). It is likely to occur along the Amazon slopes of the Andes in suitable habitat in eastern Ecuador and perhaps Colombia and Peru. The two collection sites are situated at elevations of 1,000 and 1,706 m.

HABITAT Cloud forest and lower montane wet forest.

DESCRIPTION *Micrurus petersi* appears to be a medium-sized species. The holotype measures 667 mm in overall length.

This is a tricolored coral snake with a bicolored aspect owing to the obscuring of red body rings with black pigment; triads are lacking in the pattern. Only on the first row of dorsals is red pigment discernible. The snout and first 4 supralabials are bluish gray to dirty white. There is a black cap which covers the posterior prefrontals, the supraoculars, frontal, and parietals. There is some black pigment along the prefrontal-internasal suture. A white occipital ring borders the parietals and covers the temporals and posterior supralabials. The head is white ventrally except for the first 3 supralabials, which are black. The black nuchal ring is 4 dorsals in length and is barely separated from the black head cap (parietals). There are 21 black body rings 5–6 dorsals and 2–3 ventrals in length. The black rings are bordered by weak yellow rings 1½ dorsals long; these rings are interrupted by black scales dorsally. There are 21 red body rings 5–7 dorsals in length, but they are virtually obscured dorsally with black or dark gray pigment. The tail is black and yellow with 3 long black rings (8–9 dorsals long) and a black terminal ring (5 dorsals long). Ventrally this species is black and white or black and yellowish white.

There are 1 + 1 temporals, 232 ventrals, and 31 subcaudals. These meristics are based on the holotype, a female. Other features of lepidosis are typical of the genus *Micrurus*.

SIMILAR SPECIES The most similar sympatric coral snake is *M. steindachneri*, which differs from *M. petersi* by having a dark snout and 22–42 black body rings. *Micrurus annellatus* is often bicolored and may be sympatric with *M. petersi*, however, it possesses a white or orange parietal ring while *M. petersi* has a black head cap. *Micrurus mipartitus* has a red-to-orange parietal ring and a black-and-red tail. *Micrurus langsdorffi* has 30–91 or more black (brown, or yellow) body rings and red rings crossing the venter. See the discussion of false coral snake in Mimics of Venomous Snakes.

REFERENCES Miyata, 1982; Roze, 1967, 1983.

### *Micrurus proximans* Smith and Chrapliwy
(Map 30)

LOCAL NAMES Coral, coralillo.

ENGLISH NAME Nayarit coral snake.

DISTRIBUTION This species is found along the Pacific Coast of Nayarit, Mexico (Map 30). It is known only from elevations of less than 150 m.

HABITAT Tropical deciduous forest and thorn forest.

DESCRIPTION A medium-sized coral snake, *M. proximans* reaches a total length of over 800 mm.

The pattern consists of black, yellow, and red rings. The 18–22 black rings are not disposed in triads. Black

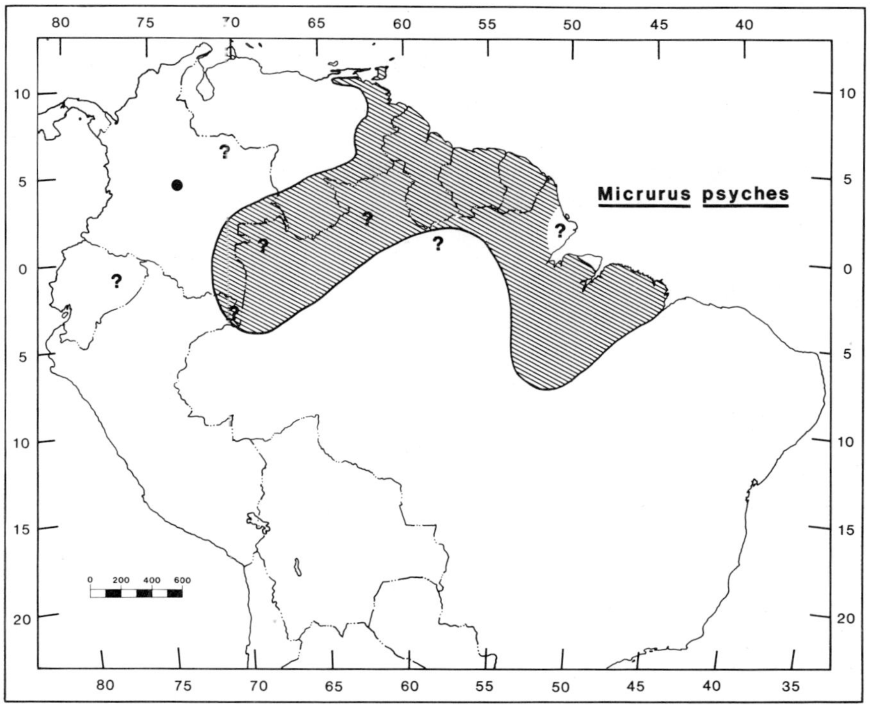


**Map 31.** Distribution of *Micrurus psyches* in northwestern South America. The presence of this species in eastern Amapá, Brazil, has not been confirmed and its distribution in northern Brazil is unknown. The dot in Colombia represents a questionable allocation (see *M. psyches medemi* in species account Remarks). Question marks represent possible areas of occurrence.

rings are 2½–3 middorsals and usually 1–2 ventrals long, although in females many rings may be incomplete ventrally. There are 4–6 black rings and no red rings on the tail. The black nuchal ring involves the posterior tips of the parietals and extends posteriorly 4–5 scale lengths on the nape. The pale parietal ring is short dorsally, not involving the anterior tips of the parietals; it is longer laterally, involving part or all of the supralabials 4–7; and it extends at the margin of the lip to below the middle of the eye. The yellow rings are ½–1 scales long and incomplete ventrally. Most of the dorsal red scales are tipped with black; red rings are 6–9 dorsals in length. The black head cap is variable and may or may not reach the lips; therefore, the snout may be entirely black or the supralabials may be pale.

Supra-anal keels are present in males. There are 1 + 1 or 1 + 2 temporals, 205–237 ventrals, and 36–40 subcaudals. Other features of lepidosis are characteristic of the genus *Micrurus*.

SIMILAR SPECIES *Micrurus distans* usually may be distinguished from *M. proximans* by its longer black nuchal ring that extends 6–8 dorsal scale lengths and by its longer yellow body rings 1–2 dorsals in length.

REMARKS This rare snake is known from only a few specimens.

REFERENCES Golay, 1985; Roze, 1967, 1983; H. M. Smith and Chrapliwy, 1958; H. M. Smith and Taylor, 1966; Zweifel, 1959b.

### *Micrurus psyches* (Daudin)

(Figs. 92–95; Map 31)

LOCAL NAMES Coral. Brazil: cobra-coral. Colombia: culebra de corbata (Andes of Meta). Suriname: kraalslang, krarasneke. Trinidad: common coral snake, corail, coral snake (male), male coral, serpent-corail (femále), small coral. Venezuela: coral, coral morada (*M. p. psyches*).

ENGLISH NAME Carib coral snake.

DISTRIBUTION This species occurs in northern South America from east central Colombia through southern and eastern Venezuela, Trinidad, the Guianas, and Brazil in the states of Pará and Maranhão (Map 31). Its range in Brazil is likely to be more extensive, at least including Roraima and Amapá. Records of its occurrence in extreme southern Colombia and the single record for Ecuador need verification. Records from the islands of Martinique, St. Thomas, and St. Vincent are not considered to be valid. See Remarks for the distributions of subspecies. Its vertical distribution is not known but this is primarily a lowland form; we have taken *M. p. medemi* at 500 m in Colombia (see Remarks), but *M. p. psyches* has been taken at 1,700 m on Mt. Roraima, Venezuela.

HABITAT Lower montane wet forest and lowland rainforest.

DESCRIPTION *Micrurus psyches* includes some subspecies that average 250–500 mm in overall length and others that may reach 910 mm.

It may be bicolored, tricolored, or uniform black dorsally (see Remarks). When tricolored, triads are not present in the pattern. Normally the head is black, including all supracephalic scales. A white or yellow occipital band or ring is usually present (but see *M. p. donosoi* and *M. p. paraensis*); it may be complete, bordering the parietals; incomplete, broken at the parietal tips; or reduced to the temporals. It is sometimes absent (see Remarks) or present only ventrally, and it frequently encroaches upon the parietal edges. Beneath the head, the occipital ring may extend anteriorly and involve one to several pairs of infralabials, which may or may not be spotted with black. Alternatively, it may involve only the chinshields. Red pigment usually is not present on the head. The black nuchal ring is 4–7 middorsals in length and may or may not be connected to the black head cap at the parietal tips (normally, it is). The nuchal ring is bordered posteriorly by a white or yellow ring which may appear as an isolated series of specks or may cover ½–2 middorsals. *Micrurus psyches* as recognized currently includes a confusing array of colors and patterns among its subspecies (see Remarks). In general, red pigment is lacking on the tail and there is a tendency toward melanism in at least three races (see Remarks).

Supra-anal keels are absent. There are usually 1 + 1 temporals but there may be 1 + 2 or 0 + 1. There are 179–231 ventrals (most often 190–210) and 29–52 mostly divided subcaudals. For details on pattern and scutellation see subspecies discussed under Remarks. Other features of lepidosis are typical of the genus *Micrurus*.

SIMILAR SPECIES In eastern Colombia *M. psyches* is essentially a bicolored snake. The race *M. p. medemi* is distinctive in that one to several black caudal rings are reduced to blotches that partially divide the yellow caudal rings. *Micrurus psyches* (both the nominate form and *M. p. medemi*) may be distinguished from *M. mipartitus* by its lack of red pigment on the head and tail (present in *M. mipartitus*), and from *M. narduccii*, *M. collaris*, and *M. karlschmidti* by the presence of complete rings on the body (partial or incomplete in *M. narduccii*). In Venezuela, *M. p. circinalis* may be confused most easily with *M. dumerilii*. *Micrurus p. circinalis* differs from *M. dumerilii* in that adult males lack supra-anal keels, possess narrower red rings, and have heterogeneous temporals (see Remarks). *Micrurus p. psyches*, a bicolored race, is not known to be sympatric with any other bicolored, ringed *Micrurus* species throughout its range in Venezuela and the Guianas. On Trinidad, *M. p. circinalis* has one sympatric congener, *M. lemniscatus*, which may be distinguished easily by its triad pattern and red parietals. *Micrurus averyi* usually possesses red pigment on the head and exceptionally long red body rings, and usually lacks all trace of black stippling in the red rings. *Micrurus langsdorffi ornatissimus*, possibly sympatric with *M. psyches*, possesses a distinctive pattern of spots on the dorsum of the head. *Micrurus p. donosoi* is distinctive in that it lacks rings (being black dorsally) and has red ventral bands with heavy concentrations of black pigment. See also the discussion of false coral snakes in Mimics of Venomous Snakes.

REMARKS Six races of *M. psyches* are currently recognized. *Micrurus p. psyches* (Fig. 92) is said to occur from east central (and possibly southern) Colombia through southern and eastern Venezuela and across the Guianas. Based on our field experience, with the exception of *M. p. remotus*, we doubt the presence of this species in Colombia. *Micrurus p. psyches* appears bicolored, with white or yellow rings alternating with black or blue-black rings (22–29 in males; 27–41 in females); the red rings are usually completely obfuscated by black pigment. There are 185–226 ventrals (185–211 in males; 203–226 in females) and 30–50 subcaudals.

*Micrurus p. circinalis* (Fig. 93) is found in northeastern Venezuela, adjacent Guyana, and Trinidad (including Gaspareé Island). This is a tricolored race with 21–35 black body rings (2–4 middorsals in length) plus 5–12 more on the tail. White rings are short, often less than 1 middorsal in length, and usually intense, although there is a tendency toward melanism and red rings are heavily stippled. The temporals are heterogeneous, with the anterior temporal often reduced or absent. There are 178–210 ventrals (one report of 231; 178–193 in males; 192–210 in females), and 29–50 subcaudals (40–50 in males; 29–35 in females).

*Micrurus p. donosoi* is known only from three specimens collected north of São Felix, upper Rio Xingu, southern Pará, Brazil. This race lacks rings dorsally, being entirely black. The temporal region is white or yellow, and this pigment extends across the venter of the head, projecting anteriorly onto the first 1–2 pairs of infralabials and posteriorly such that the black nuchal band is concave anteriorly. There are 16–18 black bands on the venter, separated by red interspaces that are heavily pigmented with black, and 7–11 black bands on the venter of the tail. There are 192–193 ventrals and 42–50 subcaudals. Different authors consider this to be either a full species or conspecific with *M. p. paraensis*.

*Micrurus p. medemi* (Fig. 94) is known only from Villavicencio, Departamento de Meta, Colombia. This is a tricolored race with the red rings heavily melanic dorsally such that specimens appear to be bicolored. There are 15–25 black body rings (15–22 in males; 22–25 in females) plus 5–9 on the tail. The black rings are 4–5 middorsals long and are bordered by yellow rings 1½ middorsals long that are somewhat expanded laterally. Melanized red rings are up to 10 middorsals long. The occipital marking is usually complete around the parietals in this subspecies. All yellow scales are tinged with black. This race is distinctive in that one or more of the yellow caudal rings contain diamond-shaped black blotches dorsally, beginning above the cloaca. A single report of 35 black body rings for this subspecies probably includes melanized red rings. There are 193–218 ventrals (193–210 in males; 211–218 in females) and 28–50 subcaudals (45–50 in males; 28–33 in females).

*Micrurus p. paraensis* (Fig. 95) occurs in northern, eastern, and southern Pará and western Maranhão, Brazil. Two specimens (UTA R-15674-75) are known from southern Suriname. This is a tricolored race with 11–20 black body rings plus 3–14 more on the tail. The black rings are about 3 middorsals long, bordered by broken white rings ½ middorsal long, and separated by red rings 7–10 or more middorsals long. The red rings tend to be immaculate dorsally but may contain black pigment on the venter. White temporal markings may reach the parietals in typical *M. psyches* fashion or they may be reduced or absent. There are 188–213 ventrals (188–200 in males; 194–213 in females) and 30–52 subcaudals (45–52 in males; 30–47 in females). This is considered to be a full species by some authors.

*Micrurus p. remotus* is known from Cerro de la Neblina, Amazonas, Venezuela, and the distribution of this subspecies includes the adjacent uplands of Venezuela and Amazonas state, Brazil, and extends into eastern Colombia. The pattern is tricolored with 25–34 black body rings plus 7–11 more on the tail. The black rings are 2–3 dorsals long and separated by red rings containing black-tipped scales. The yellowish white rings are interrupted, irregular, and ½ middorsal in length. The temporals and posteriormost supralabials are of a yellowish cast with considerable black pigment. There are 202–221 ventrals (202–203 in males; 214–221 in females) and 32–49 subcaudals (42–49 in males; 32–34 in females).

Much confusion surrounds *M. psyches*, owing probably to the inclusion of more than one species among its races. The peculiar distribution of *M. p. medemi* suggests an Andean affinity, perhaps with *M. steindachneri* rather than *M. psyches*. Records of *M. p. psyches* in the llanos of Colombia are questionable, especially given the distribution of this race in adjacent Venezuela. In southern Colombia, *M. langsdorffi ornatissimus* often is bicolored, and preserved specimens could be misidentified as *M. psyches*, thus causing the latter to be recorded from that region. Tricolored races in northeastern South America bear strong resemblance to *M. averyi* and *M. corallinus*. *Micrurus p. circinalis* is difficult to distinguish from sympatric races of *M. dumerilii*.

REFERENCES Abuys, 1987a, 1987b; Amaral, 1925b (as *M. corallinus*, in part), 1931a; W. Beebe, 1946; Boos, 1975, 1984a, 1984b; Boos and Quesnel, 1968; Brongersma, 1967; Chippaux, 1987; Cope, 1876b; Cunha and Nascimento, 1973, 1978, 1982a; Daniel, 1949; Daudin, 1803; Duellman, 1979; Duméril et al., 1854; Dunn, 1944a; Emsley, 1977; Gasc and Rodrigues, 1980; Hoge and Lancini, 1962; Hoge and Romano-Hoge, 1981b; Hoge et al., 1976; Hoge, Cordeiro, and Romano, 1977; Jan, 1858; Jan and Sordelli, 1870–1881; Lancini, 1970, 1979; Marcuzzi, 1950; Medem, 1969; Milá de la Roca, 1932; Mole, 1914, 1924; Moonen et al., 1978; P. Müller, 1973; Nascimento et al., 1987; Nicéforo-María, 1933, 1942; Parker, 1935; Quelch, 1898; Rivero-Blanco and Dixon, 1979; Roux-Esteve, 1983; Roze, 1955, 1966a, 1967, 1970a, 1983, 1987; Sandner-Montilla, 1985b; Schmidt, 1936a, 1955, 1957a; Vellard, 1941; Vetencourt Finol., 1960; Wehekind, 1960.

### ***Micrurus putumayensis*** **Lancini**

(Fig. 96; Map 32)

LOCAL NAMES Coral. Brazil: boicoral, cobra coral. Peru: naca-naca.

ENGLISH NAME Putumayo coral snake.

DISTRIBUTION The northwest Amazon Basin in northeastern Peru, northwestern Brazil, and southeastern Colombia (Map 32). The vertical distribution is from near sea level to 100 m or more.

HABITAT Tropical rainforest in primary or slightly open, mature secondary forest situations.

DESCRIPTION *Micrurus putumayensis* is a medium-sized coral snake with a maximum overall length of 805 mm but generally averages 600–700 mm.

This species is apparently bicolored, and there is some confusion as to whether the pale rings are yellow or red. Based upon reliable information for nine Peruvian specimens, we feel it most likely that *M. putumayensis* is a black and yellow ringed species. A black cap extends from the tip of the snout posteriorly, covering the parietals, postoculars, fourth supralabials, and most of the venter of the head. The black cap is bordered by a yellow ring that traverses the occipital-nuchal region and is heavily pigmented with black. The remaining head scales are black except for 3–4 of the posteriormost labials and the gulars, which are yellow with numerous streaks and spots of black pigment. There are 7–14 black body rings and 2–3 more on the tail. The black rings are 7–19 dorsals in length, occasionally fused or vestigial, and in the form of an ovoid blotch. The yellow rings are 4–13 scales long, usually shorter than the adjacent black rings, and heavily suffused dorsally and sometimes ventrally with black pigment. The borders between the yellow and black rings are ill defined, but the yellow rings are always clearly visible ventrally. All yellow dorsals are tipped with black and may even be entirely black such that rings might not be apparent dorsally. Occasionally, some of the ventrals in the yellow zones show a very slight orange or reddish suffusion, and they may have black borders. The last body ring is yellow and the tail tip is black.

There are 1 + 1 temporals (one specimen has been reported with 1 + 2), 192–226 ventrals, and 32–51 subcaudals. Other features of lepidosis are typical of the genus *Micrurus*.

SIMILAR SPECIES Other bicolored coral snakes with which *M. putumayensis* might be sympatric are *M. karlschmidti*, *M. langsdorffi*, and *M. narduccii*. All three of these species lack the long yellow rings of *M. putumayensis*, especially ventrally. Bicolored specimens of *M. langsdorffi* have well-defined narrow white rings, visible dorsally, while *M. narduccii* and *M. karlschmidti* either lack complete rings or have only a few. The latter two species have orange-to-red rings on the head and some part of the tail. Other species that bear a superficial resemblance to *M. putumayensis* are *M. hemprichii* and *M. spixii*. *Micrurus hemprichii* has a tricolored pattern (although the black rings are very long) and an undivided anal plate. *Micrurus spixii* is also tricolored, although the red rings are often heavily melanized. *Micrurus spixii* lacks the black snout and head cap characteristic of *M. putumayensis*.

REMARKS The species *Micrurus annellatus*, *M. psyches*, and *M. margaritiferus* also could be sympatric

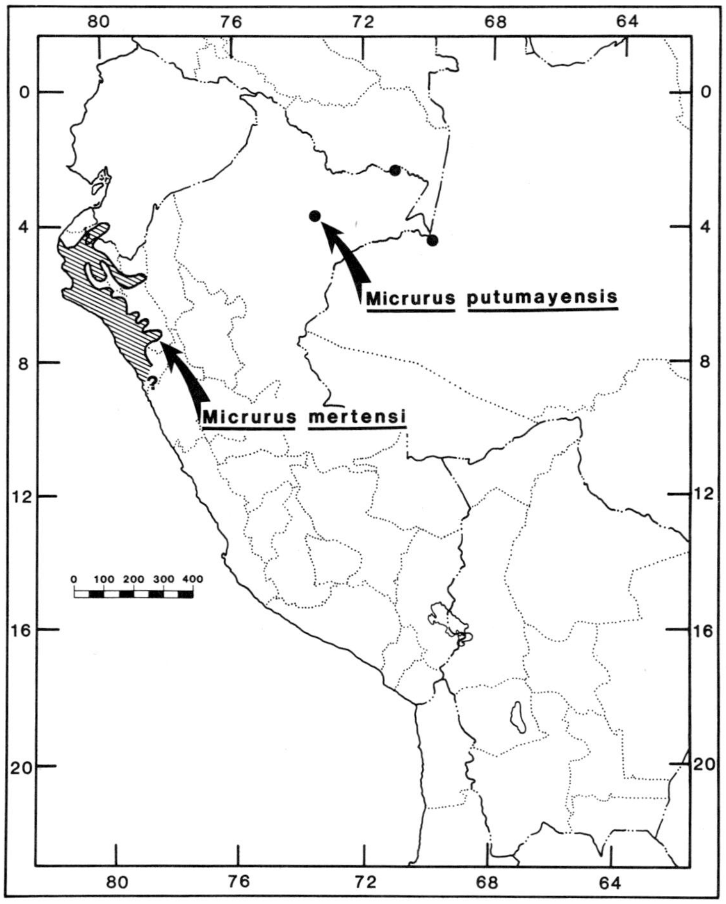


**Map 32.** Distributions of *Micrurus mertensi* (*diagonal lines*) and *M. putumayensis* (*dots*) in western South America. The range of *M. mertensi* probably extends farther south than is shown. Question mark represents possible area of occurrence of *M. mertensi*.

with *M. putumayensis*; see their respective accounts for their characteristics.

REFERENCES Carrillo de Espinoza, 1983; Dixon and Soini, 1986; Lancini, 1962a, 1962b; Lema, 1972; Medem, 1969; Meneses, 1974a; Roze, 1967, 1983; Soini, 1973, 1974a.

### *Micrurus ruatanus* (Günther)

(Map 33)

LOCAL NAMES Coral, coralillo.

ENGLISH NAME Roatán coral snake.

DISTRIBUTION This species is from the Isla de Roatán in the Departamento de Islas de Bahía of Honduras (Map 33). Isla de Roatán is the largest of the Islas de Bahía, about 48 km long and 5.2 km at its greatest width. *Micrurus ruatanus* has been found at low elevations on both the north and south sides of the island; the highest point on the island, Picacho Hill, is only 235 m.

HABITAT Tropical moist forest.

DESCRIPTION This relatively small coral snake reaches a maximum total length of 620 mm.

It is bicolored black and dark red. The snout is black and the black pigment covers the mental, the first 3 infralabials, the rostral, internasals, prefrontals, supralabials 1–3, and the anterior portions of the frontal, supraoculars, and supralabial 4. The parietal ring, which covers the rest of the head, is dark red. The black nuchal ring begins *posterior* to the parietal tips and is 3–5 middorsals long. The body is patterned with dark red and black rings. There are 33–45 black body rings that tend to alternate, albeit irregularly, in length; longer rings about 3 middorsals long are generally followed by shorter rings about 1–2 middorsals long that are often incomplete or broken laterally. This alternation of long and short rings tends to be more pronounced on the posterior portion of the body.

Supra-anal keels are present in adult males and there are 1 + 1 temporals, 183–204 ventrals, and 34–46 mostly divided subcaudals (in males 5–12 may be undivided). Other features of lepidosis are typical of the genus *Micrurus*.

SIMILAR SPECIES No other coral snake or other brightly ringed species is known from the Islas de Bahía. *Micrurus ruatanus* is the only dangerously venomous snake known to inhabit these islands.

On the adjacent mainland on Honduras, *M. nigrocinctus* differs from *M. ruatanus* in having (1) fewer black body rings (11–29); (2) more ventrals in each sex (190–208 vs. 183–185 in males, and 206–224 vs. 193–204 and females); (3) no alternating long and short black body rings; and (4) a greater overall length, commonly over 700 mm. *Micrurus diastema* differs in that it (1) often has a tricolored pattern of red, yellow, and black

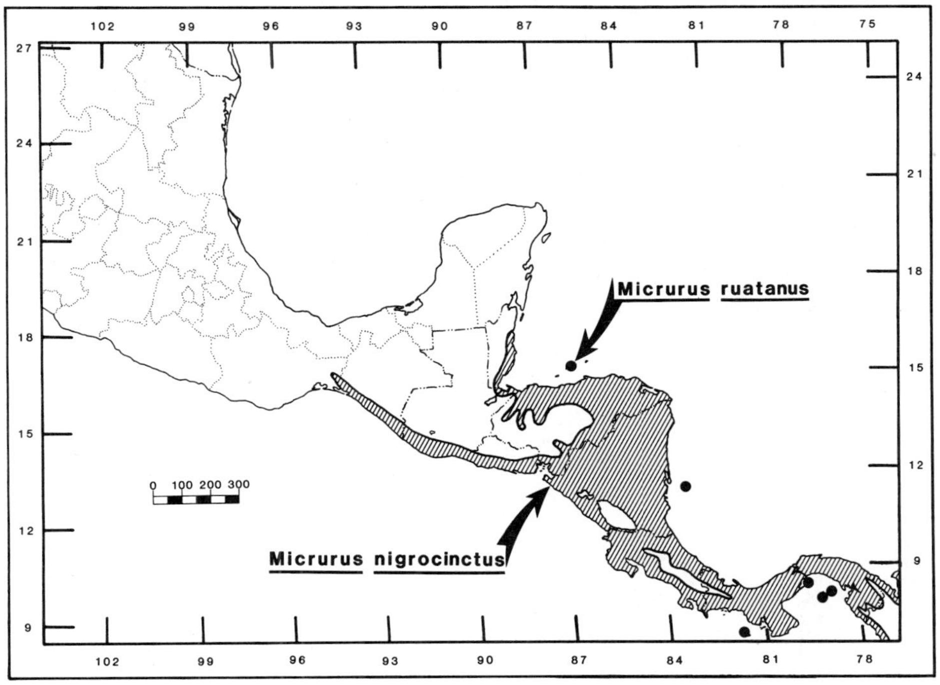


**Map 33.** Distributions of *Micrurus nigrocinctus* and *M. ruatanus* in Middle America. *Micrurus ruatanus* is restricted to the Isla de Roatán off the coast of Honduras; all other island records are for *M. nigrocinctus* and include Isla del Maíz Grande (Great Corn Island) off the Caribbean Coast of Nicaragua and the islands of Coiba, Taboga, San José, and San Miguel off the Pacific Coast of Panama. The distribution of *M. nigrocinctus* in Colombia is not extensive and is not mapped.

rings; (2) has a pale tip of the snout including the rostral; and (3) lacks supra-anal keels in males.

REMARKS *Micrurus ruatanus* has sometimes been considered a subspecies of *M. nigrocinctus*, and there is little question that the isolated population on Roatán is closely related to, if not conspecific with, *M. nigrocinctus*.

It has been reported that inhabitants of the Isla de Roatán do not regard this snake as venomous.

REFERENCES Barbour, 1928; Dunn, 1940a; Günther, 1885–1902; Meyer, 1969; Roze, 1967, 1983; Schmidt, 1933a; Wilson, 1983; Wilson and Hahn, 1973; Wilson and Meyer, 1985.

## *Micrurus sangilensis* Nicéforo-María

(Map 34)

LOCAL NAME Coral.

ENGLISH NAME Santander coral snake.

DISTRIBUTION Colombia. This species is known from three sites in the Departamento de Santander, and another in the adjacent Departamento de Cundinamarca of Colombia (Map 34). All localities are situated between the Cordilleras Central and Oriental of the Andes along the Río Suárez and Río Lebrija drainages; both are part of the Río Magdalena Basin. The vertical distribution is from 1,018 to 1,737 m.

HABITAT Dry tropical forest, lower montane dry forest, and lower montane humid forest.

DESCRIPTION The only published information on the size of this species is for the holotype, which measures 545 mm in total length.

This species is tricolored with rings of red, black, and yellow that form a pattern of 17–22 triads on the body. There are 5–10 black rings on the tail, separated by yellow rings that are often suffused with black. The red rings separating the triads are stippled with black. The head is black from the snout to the posterior edge of the parietals. A yellow crescent-shaped band covers the posterior 3–4 supralabials and the temporals, and borders the parietals in their entirety. Ventrally the head is black with the throat and posterior infralabials yellow, with black spots or lines. The triads are composed of well-defined black rings in each center (3–4 dorsals in length), bordered by narrow yellow and black rings up to 1–2 scales in length. The red rings (4–10 middorsals in length) separating the triads are longest anteriorly, becoming approximately equal in size to the black rings posteriorly. The long black nuchal ring (4–6 middorsal scale lengths) constitutes the middle ring of the first body triad.

Supra-anal keels are absent and there are 1 + 1 or 1 + 2 temporals, 190–217 ventrals, and 33–53 subcaudals. Other features of lepidosis are typical of the genus *Micrurus*.

SIMILAR SPECIES The only tricolored coral snakes sympatric with *M. sangilensis* are *M. dissoleucus* and *M. dumerilii*. *Micrurus sangilensis* may be distinguished from *M. dissoleucus* by the presence of two black rings in the first body triad (only one in *M. dissoleucus*). *Micrurus dumerilii* has fewer than 14 triads on the body and supra-anal keels are present in males, whereas *M. sangilensis* has 17–22 triads and no supra-anal keels. See also the discussion of false coral snake in Mimics of Venomous Snakes.

REMARKS This species has often been considered to be a race of *M. bocourti*, to which it is very similar.

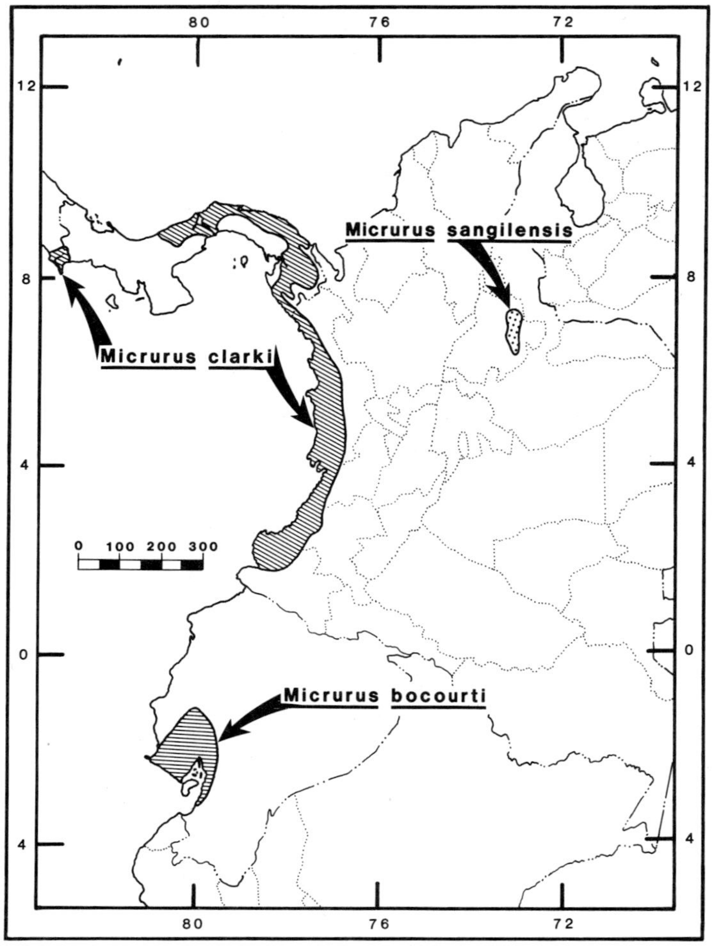


**Map 34.** Distributions of *Micrurus bocourti* (*horizontal lines*), *M. clarki* (*diagonal lines*), and *M. sangilensis* (*stipples*) in lower Central America and northwestern South America.

However, a large hiatus in their respective distributions has remained unresolved.

REFERENCES Nicéforo-María, 1942; Pérez-Santos and Moreno, 1986; Roze, 1967, 1983; Schmidt, 1955.

### *Micrurus spixii* Wagler

(Figs. 97–101; Map 35)

LOCAL NAMES Coral. Bolivia: coral venenosa. Brazil: chumbéguaça, cobra-coral. Colombia: acavai (Guahibo tribe), huayamacaicha (Cuiva tribe). Peru: nacanaca. Venezuela: coral.

ENGLISH NAME Amazonian coral snake.

DISTRIBUTION The Amazon and Orinoco basins. Four races of this species are currently recognized (see Remarks) and their collective ranges include the Amazon River Basin from western Maranhão, northern Goiás, and Ilha do Marajó, Pará through Amazonas state in Brazil; southern Venezuela (Territorio de Amazonas); Colombia east of the Andes as far north as Meta and Vichada; eastern Ecuador; eastern Peru; western Brazil (in Rondônia, Mato Grosso, and probably Acre); and northern and central Bolivia (Map 35). The distribution of this species in Brazil should prove to be more extensive than currently known, and it may occur in western Guyana, southern Suriname, and southeastern French Guiana. Its vertical distribution is to at least 1,200 m.

HABITAT *Micrurus spixii* is primarily a denizen of the forest floor in primary tropical rainforest situations. However, it also occurs in secondary areas, around human habitations, and in savanna/gallery forest associations in the llanos of eastern Colombia. Like most coral snakes, it tends to frequent humid areas in riparian situations.

DESCRIPTION This is a large, heavy-bodied species, averaging 800–1,100 mm in overall length but reaching a maximum of 1,602 mm. It is rivaled in size by only one congener, *M. surinamensis*.

*Micrurus spixii* is a tricolored snake with a pattern consisting of 4–9 (rarely 10) body triads; the first triad is usually incomplete, being represented by only 2 rings. The single caudal triad also may be incomplete; the caudal configuration depends on whether the last body triad straddles the base of the tail, a frequent occurrence in *M. spixii*. The dorsum of the head ranges from black (*M. s. spixii*), to black with light gray spots (*M. s. martiusi*), to tricolored (*M. s. obscurus* and *M. s. princeps*). Laterally, the snout and first 2–3 pairs of supralabials are generally dirty white with considerable scattered black pigment; this white color extends dorsally onto the internasals, prefrontals, and anterior edges of the supraoculars and frontal as follows: not at all or only as

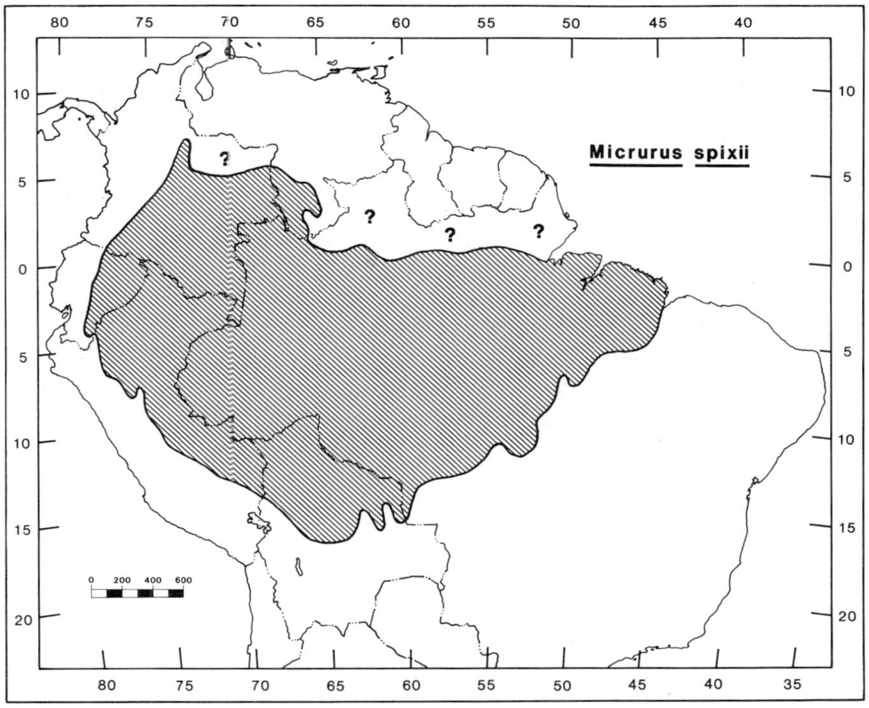


**Map 35.** Distribution of *Micrurus spixii* in Amazonian South America. The distribution of this species may be more extensive in northern Brazil and Colombia than is shown. Question marks represent possible areas of occurrence.

white highlights (*M. s. spixii*); as irregular spotting and white highlights (*M. s. martiusi*); as a band with symmetrical black spotting (*M. s. obscurus*); or as a band with faint black spots or stipples (*M. s. princeps*). Generally the supraoculars and frontal are black medially, encroached upon anteriorly by white and (in *M. s. obscurus* and *M. s. princeps*) posteriorly by red. The black pigment extends laterally through the eye and adjacent third and fourth supralabials, although this may be encroached upon by white or red.

A red parietal ring extends from the posterior portion of the frontal and supraoculars nearly to the posterior parietal tips and laterally from the postoculars to the temporals and adjacent 5–7 supralabials. The extent of this red color is highly modified by black or brownish pigment laterally. In the subspecies *M. s. spixii* and *M. s. martiusi* the red parietal ring is obscured completely by the black nuchal ring that covers the parietals and posterior temporals and first few rows of dorsals. In *M. s. obscurus*, the red parietal ring is generally well developed but usually contains anterior extensions of black pigment from the nuchal ring onto the parietal scales, which may be large or reduced, irregular or symmetrical. The black nuchal ring varies in condition: it may be absent; vestigial (along the posterior parietal region); confined to the parietals; or coalesced with the median black ring of the first body triad, which tends to have an anterior projection dorsally. Accordingly, the first body triad may be complete with normal black rings; complete with the first black ring vestigial; lacking the first black ring; or lacking both the first black ring and the first yellow ring. The black triad rings (aside from the above) are subequal or the median black rings may be slightly longer. They are separated by white or yellow rings which are generally two to three times longer (5–11 middorsals or more) than the black rings. These white rings equal or exceed even the red rings in length. The red rings are 3–16 or more middorsals in length and each scale is edged in black or bears black apical stippling.

Ventrally, the head is red with scattered black pigment, primarily on the anterior infralabials. There is sometimes white pigment on these infralabials. The yellow rings contain considerable black pigment ventrally, usually concentrated along the distal edges of the scales. There is occasionally some black ventral speckling on the red rings; otherwise the ventral colors are immaculate. Pattern anomalies include fusion of triads (quinquads) and deficiencies of black rings. Generally, the last body ring is the posterior black ring of the last complete triad or the red ring that follows it. The black supra-anal ring is frequently incomplete ventrally and may be greatly reduced.

There are 1 + 1 (occasionally 1 + 2) temporals, 200–229 ventrals (there is an unsubstantiated report of 275), and 15–24 subcaudals (one report of 29), several of which are usually entire. Supra-anal keels are absent. Other features of lepidosis are typical of the genus *Micrurus*.

SIMILAR SPECIES There are six species of tricolored and triad-patterned coral snakes known to be sympatric with *M. spixii* in some part of its range. *Micrurus filiformis* possesses a black snout, red parietal tips, 262–333 ventrals, 30–45 subcaudals, 11–20 body triads, and a very slender body build. *Micrurus frontalis* may be sympatric in Bolivia, but in this species the parietals are normally black and the first body triad is usually complete and well defined. *Micrurus frontifasciatus* possesses red parietal tips, white infralabials, and 31 subcaudals. *Micrurus hemprichii* has a black snout, 156–191 ventrals, 23–34 subcaudals, and an undivided anal plate. *Micrurus isozonus* is sympatric with *M. spixii obscurus* and extremely similar in size and appearance.

However, it may be distinguished from *M. s. obscurus* by its higher number of subcaudals (24–32 vs. 15–24) and greater number of body triads (8–13 vs. 4–7 or, rarely, 8–9). It is problematical that a few specimens of *M. s. obscurus* are known with 8–9 body triads. Generally, *M. isozonus* has a slightly more slender body build and inhabits savannah and seasonally dry forest. *Micrurus s. obscurus* also occurs sporadically in these areas but is primarily a denizen of humid tropical rainforest. The tendency for the first 1 or 2 black rings of the first body triad to extend in an anterior middorsal direction is evident in both species in eastern Colombia, but to a much greater degree in *M. spixii*. The white rings are usually not quite so elongated in *M. isozonus* as in sympatric *M. spixii*. *Micrurus lemniscatus* possesses a black snout, red parietal tips, 210–268 ventrals, 25–43 subcaudals, 7–17 body triads, and a moderately slender body build. *Micrurus surinamensis* has a red head with black scale outlines and only the fourth supralabial is in contact with the eye (third and fourth in all other coral snakes). See also the discussion of false coral snakes in Mimics of Venomous Snakes.

REMARKS Four subspecies are currently recognized. *Micrurus s. spixii* (Fig. 97), from the middle Amazon Basin of Brazil, has 4–7 body triads, lacks the elongated neck mark, and the first triad ring is often vestigial. *Micrurus s. martiusi* (Fig. 98), from eastern Brazil in Pará, Mato Grosso, and Goiás (the lower Rio Amazonas region), has 5–9 (rarely 10) body triads, the first triad ring is sometimes present, and the elongated neck mark is absent. *Micrurus s. obscurus* (Figs. 99–101) is from northwestern Brazil, southern Venezuela, eastern Colombia, eastern Ecuador, eastern Peru, and northern Bolivia. It possesses 4–7 body triads (up to 8–9 in the Colombian llanos); the first triad ring is variable (present, absent, or vestigial); and the median black ring of the first triad usually has a dorsal anterior extension. *Micrurus s. princeps*, from northwest and central Bolivia, has 6–8 body triads, the first triad ring is usually present, the parietal scales are red and usually lack darker markings, and the red rings are twice as long as the yellow rings.

This species, perhaps the best known of South American coral snakes, is still poorly understood. Zones of intergradation among the geographic races have yet to be established and variation is scarcely documented. Specimens of *M. s. obscurus* from the Colombian llanos bear remarkable similarity to *M. isozonus* and diverge from the norm in the number of body triads, condition of the median black ring of the first triad (minimal elongation), and consistent presence of the first black triad (nuchal) ring. As with most coral snakes, the temperament of *M. spixii* is uncertain. We have observed docile as well as highly irritable specimens. Owing to its great size, this species is capable of delivering a bite through moderate clothing.

REFERENCES Amaral, 1925b, 1930b, 1948b, 1978; Azevedo, 1962a; Barbour and Noble, 1920; Boulenger, 1905; Carrillo de Espinoza, 1983; Cendrero et al., 1972; Chippaux, 1987; Cunha and Nascimento, 1973, 1978, 1982a; Cunha et al., 1985; Daniel, 1949; Dixon and Soini, 1986; Duellman, 1978; Dunn, 1944a; Gray, 1829; Griffin, 1916; Hoge and Lancini, 1962; Hoge and Romano, 1973; Hoge and Romano-Hoge, 1981b; Hoge et al., 1973; Hoogmoed and Gruber, 1983; Jan, 1859a, 1859b; Jan and Sordelli, 1870–1881; Kempff-Mercado, 1975; Lancini, 1970, 1979; Machado, 1945a; Medem, 1969; Meneses, 1974a; Milá de la Roca, 1932; Miyata, 1982; L. Müller, 1926; P. Müller, 1971; Nicéforo-María, 1942; Orcés, 1943, 1948; J. A. Peters, 1960a; Prado, 1945; Prado and Hoge, 1948; Roux-Esteve, 1983; Roze, 1954, 1955, 1957, 1966a, 1967, 1983; Sandner-Montilla, 1975, 1985b; Santos, 1981; Schmidt, 1936a, 1953b, 1955; Schmidt and Walker, 1943a; Silva Haad and Rodríguez R., 1985; Soini, 1974b; Vellard, 1941; Vetencourt Finol., 1960; Wagler, 1824.

### *Micrurus spurrelli* (Boulenger)

(Map 36)

LOCAL NAME Coral.

ENGLISH NAME Colombian coral snake.

DISTRIBUTION This species is known reliably only from the region of Peña Lisa, Río Condotó drainage, Chocó, Colombia (Map 36 see Remarks). The region is 100 m in elevation.

HABITAT Tropical rainforest.

DESCRIPTION *Micrurus spurrelli* is known only from three specimens. All are small, measuring 230–270 mm in length.

This species has a bicolored body pattern with black and white rings running the entire length except for the tail, which is black and red. The head is black anteriorly and has either a white prefrontal band that is complete or a white middorsal line that extends from the parietals forward to the tip of the snout. This line, when present, may be in contact with the second white ring, which passes across the distal portion of the parietals, the posterior temporals, and the posterior 1–2 supralabials. The anterior border of the white parietal ring is rather sinuous in outline. The remainder of the dorsum of the head is black. Ventrally the head is white except for infralabials 3–6 or 7, which are black. There is scattered black pigment along the gular sutures. It is not known for certain if the pale color on the head of living *M. spurrelli* is white; it may be red. The first black nuchal ring passes posterior to the white parietal ring and extends for 6 dorsals. If complete ventrally, it is narrowed markedly due to a posterior extension of the white parietal ring and an anterior extension of the first white body ring. There are 52 black body rings, which expand ventrally to 2–3 ventrals long, with white intervening rings 2 (rarely 3) ventrals in length. In the holotype this condition is reversed, with the white rings being the larger ventrally. Nearly all pale rings are spotted dorsally with black pigment but they are usually immaculate ventrally. The tail has 7 black rings, which alternate with red rings that are spotted with black pigment. Viewed dorsally the white body rings are shorter than the intervening black rings.

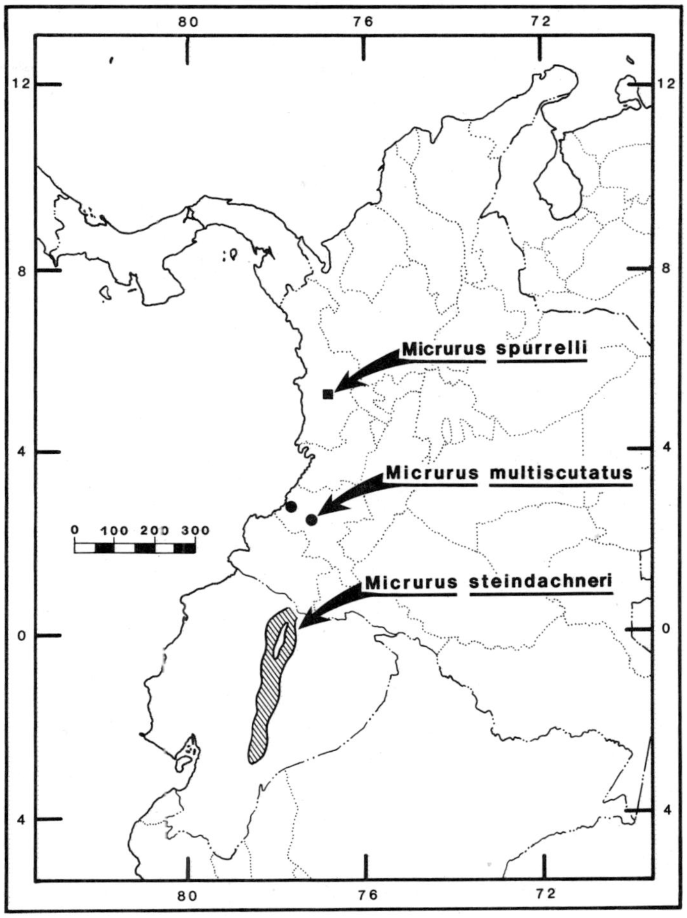


**Map 36.** Distributions of *Micrurus multiscutatus* (dots), *M. spurrelli* (square) and *M. steindachneri* (diagonal lines) in northwestern South America. *Micrurus steindachneri* probably ranges into Colombia, and perhaps into extreme northern Peru.

There are 1 + 1 temporals, 232–244 ventrals, and 36–37 subcaudals. Other features of lepidosis are typical of the genus *Micrurus*.

SIMILAR SPECIES *Micrurus spurrelli* is quite similar in pattern to *M. mipartitus*. They can be distinguished largely on the basis of the head pattern, which in *M. mipartitus* involves a red or orange parietal ring passing just posterior to the eyes and preceded by a uniformly black snout. In *M. spurrelli* there is a prefrontal white (red?) band that may or may not be complete middorsally but is present in some form. All other coral snakes in the range of *M. spurrelli* have patterns that include broad red rings on the body. See Mimics of Venomous Snakes for a discussion of false coral snakes.

REMARKS There is much confusion surrounding this species and the similar species *M. mipartitus*. The stated range for *M. spurrelli* includes the Peña Lisa region, Chocó, and the region around Villavicencio, Meta (stated erroneously to be Cundinamarca). On purely zoogeographic grounds we question such a distribution. Moreover, the locality data for the specimen purportedly from Villavicencio were never considered to be reliable. We have had extensive experience with snakes from the Villavicencio region and know of nothing similar to *M. spurrelli* in that area with the exception of *M. mipartitus anomalus*. We therefore reject the proposed distribution for *M. spurrelli* and consider it confined to the western lowlands of Colombia.

Owing to a paucity of material there is uncertainty as to the actual color of the pale dorsal rings in this species. The holotype was described by Boulenger as black and white with a black and red tail. It seems likely that this approximates the color in life; if not, there should have been detectable traces of red elsewhere.

REFERENCES Amaral, 1930a; Boulenger, 1914; Nicéforo-María, 1942; Roze, 1967, 1983; Schmidt, 1955.

### *Micrurus steindachneri* (Werner)

(Figs. 102, 103; Map 36)

LOCAL NAME Coral.

ENGLISH NAME Steindachner's coral snake.

DISTRIBUTION Ecuador. This species is found along the eastern slopes of the Andes from the headwaters of the Río Santiago north into the province of Napo around the headwaters of the Río Coca (see Map 36). Suitable habitat exists for a considerable distance to the north and its occurrence in Colombia would not be surprising. To the south its distribution is probably only as far as the upper Río Marañón (Huancabamba Depression; see Remarks), possibly including extreme northern Peru. Its vertical distribution is to at least 1,800 m and probably considerably higher.

HABITAT Lower montane wet forest and cloud forest.

DESCRIPTION *Micrurus steindachneri* has been reported to reach 860 mm in overall length.

This coral snake is tricolored, although the yellow rings are greatly reduced and the red rings may be melanistic dorsally. The pattern does not include triads; black rings number 22–42 on the body and 4–12 on the tail. The snout and top of the head are black, including the eyes, part of the anterior temporals, the first 3–4 supralabials, and the parietals. The posterior 2–3 supralabials are brownish yellow, usually with black pigment along the sutures. The temporals are colored similarly but may be suffused with red or spotted with black, and they may encroach upon the edges of the parietals. The brownish yellow color is carried onto the venter of the head, where it crosses the posterior 3–4 infralabials and extends onto the chinshields, which also bear black smudges. The mental and first 3 infralabials are black. The black nuchal ring covers 3–5 dorsals and is in contact with the parietal tips. Ventrally it projects anteriorly, bordering the infralabials and posterior chinshields. The black body rings are 3–7 middorsals in length. Yellow rings are ½–2 middorsals long and the scales are black apically. Yellow rings are sometimes expanded along the paraventrals. Red rings are 2–5 middorsals long and heavily suffused with black (see Remarks); they may or may not extend onto the ventrals (see Remarks). The red rings are often obscured on the tail and the black rings may fuse dorsally such that the tail is entirely black.

There are 1 + 1 temporals, 200–234 ventrals, and 29–49 subcaudals, mostly divided. Supra-anal keels are absent. Other features of lepidosis are typical of the genus *Micrurus*.

SIMILAR SPECIES The only tricolored coral snakes that lack a triad pattern and are sympatric with *M. steindachneri* are *M. langsdorffi*, which possesses pale supracephalic spots and often lacks black body rings, and *M. petersi*, which has a pale snout and 21 black body rings.

REMARKS Two subspecies of *M. steindachneri* are recognized: *Micrurus s. steindachneri* occurs along the upper Río Santiago watershed on the eastern versant of the Andes in southern Ecuador (Macas-Méndez region). In this subspecies the red rings are black dorsally and stippled laterally, and the yellow rings are barely noticeable, being only ½–1 middorsals long. Males possess 200–208 ventrals; females have 35–36 subcaudals and 38–42 black body rings. *Micrurus s. orcesi* (Figs. 102, 103) occurs on the eastern versant of the Andes in northern Ecuador (Napo and Pastaza provinces). The coloration of this subspecies is similar to the nominate form, although the yellow rings may be somewhat more pronounced. Males possess 214–216 ventrals; females have 29–33 subcaudals and 30–37 black body rings. This subspecies has been cited as occurring in Chimbo, Peru, but it is likely that the data refer to the Río Chambo or possibly Puente del Chimbo, which are both in Ecuador.

It is possible that *M. steindachneri* lacks red pigment on the venter. The only freshly collected specimen of which we are aware (Fig. 103) bears slight traces of red on the underside. Whether this is peculiar to individuals, populations, or the species is unknown, but this characteristic would be difficult to discern in preserved specimens such as those utilized in the original description of *M. s. orcesi*.

Our knowledge of *M. steindachneri* is hampered by a lack of material. Variation within the species is inadequately documented and its relationship with *M. psyches medemi* merits further study.

*Micrurus steindachneri* is known to have a tail display.

REFERENCES Duellman, 1979; Greene and McDiarmid, 1981; Miyata, 1982; Roze, 1967, 1983; Tiedemann and Haupl, 1980; Werner, 1901a, 1927.

## *Micrurus stewarti* Barbour and Amaral

(Map 37)

LOCAL NAMES Coral, coralilla, gargantilla.

ENGLISH NAME Panamanian coral snake.

DISTRIBUTION Panama. This species is known only from El Valle de Antón and Cerro Bruja and associated uplands (Sabanita). These localities lie in highlands of moderate elevations that flank either side of the Panama Canal (Map 37). The vertical distribution is from about 100 to 1,200 m.

HABITAT Subtropical wet forest and lower montane wet forest.

DESCRIPTION *Micrurus stewarti* is a small coral snake: males are known to reach 595 mm in total length and females 666 mm.

This species is bicolored red and black. The snout is black to the level of the eye and involves parts of the frontal, supraoculars, and third or fourth supralabial. The pale parietal ring is red and includes the postoculars; the infracephalic scales are red except for dark mottling on the chin. The black nuchal ring begins behind the parietals and is long, involving 10–15 ventrals. There is a highly irregular alternation of black rings on the body, a relatively long one followed by a shorter one, and these are separated from each other by a still shorter red ring with black-tipped scales. There is a total of 13–21 black body rings that, exclusive of the black nuchal ring, involve 3–14 ventrals. The red rings on the body involve 4–5 ventrals. A red ring lies over the vent region and may involve a single subcaudal or may be incomplete and involve no subcaudals. There are 2–5 black tail rings and 2 or 3 red tail rings. The first black tail ring is longer than the rest and involves 10–18 subcaudals.

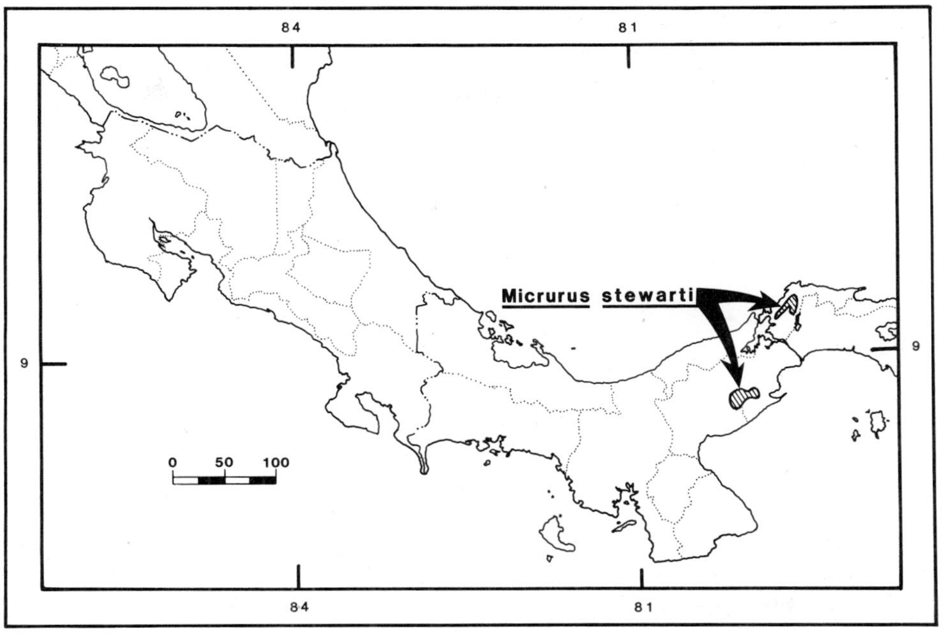


**Map 37.** Distribution of *Micrurus stewarti* in central Panama.

Supra-anal keels are present in males and weakly developed in females. There are 1 + 1 or 1 + 2 temporals, 197–223 ventrals, and 40–55 subcaudals, a few of which may be undivided proximally. Other features of lepidosis are typical of the genus *Micrurus*.

SIMILAR SPECIES Other lower Central American coral snakes include *M. ancoralis* and *M. dissoleucus*, which are easily distinguished from *M. stewarti* by having black body rings disposed in triads. *Micrurus clarki* and *M. nigrocinctus* are unlike *M. stewarti* in that they are tricolored species having black, yellow, and red rings on the body. The red rings of adult *M. alleni* from the Pacicic versant of southeastern Costa Rica and southwestern Panama may be obfuscated with black, and thus some specimens have a bicolored pattern of black and *yellow* dorsally; however, red is still present on the venters of these snakes.

*Micrurus stewarti* is most likely to be confused with the several other species of bicolored coral snakes found in Panama. *Micrurus multifasciatus* possesses a higher number (40–65) of black body rings that tend to be shorter (4–6 middorsal scale lengths), including the black nuchal ring (5–8 middorsal scale lengths). This species may be sympatric with *M. stewarti* although it is generally found at lower elevations. *Micrurus mipartitus* likewise sometimes may be distinguished from *M. stewarti* by its high number (34–80) of relatively short black body rings. *Micrurus multifasciatus* differs from *M. stewarti* in its high number of ventrals (a minimum of 233 in *M. multifasciatus* as opposed to a maximum of 223 in *M. stewarti*), and both *M. multifasciatus* and *M. mipartitus* differ from *M. stewarti* in their low number of subcaudals (maximum of 33 and 35 in *M. multifasciatus* and *M. mipartitus*, respectively, as opposed to a minimum of 40 in *M. stewarti*).

Some *Pliocercus euryzonus* (Fig. 517) from Panama have almost identical body coloration with *M. stewarti*. Other harmless bicolored snakes from Panama include members of the genera *Lampropeltis* (some adults, Fig. 493), *Liophis* (Fig. 499), and *Oxyrhopus* (Figs. 505, 506). See Mimics of Venomous Snakes for a discussion of false coral snakes.

REMARKS *Micrurus schmidti* (Dunn, 1940) is a junior synonym of *M. stewarti*. There is one report of this snake being bicolored yellow and black, but this may describe a preserved specimen.

REFERENCES Barbour and Amaral, 1928; H. C. Clark, 1942; Dunn, 1940a; Dunn and Bailey, 1939; Evans, 1947; Greene and McDiarmid, 1981; Grocott and Sadler, 1958; Roze, 1967, 1983; Savage and Vial, 1974; Schmidt, 1933b.

### *Micrurus stuarti* Roze

(Map 38)

LOCAL NAMES Coral, coralillo.

ENGLISH NAME Stuart's coral snake.

DISTRIBUTION This species occupies moderate and probably intermediate elevations of the Pacific versant in southwestern Guatemala from the Departamento de San Marcos to at least the Departmento de Suchitepéquez (Map 38; see Remarks). The only specimen bearing elevational data was collected at 1,345 m.

HABITAT Subtropical wet forest and lower montane wet forest.

DESCRIPTION A small coral snake, *M. stuarti* is known to reach a total length of about 600 mm.

This tricolored species is black, yellow, and red. The snout is black, and the black pigment extends posteri-

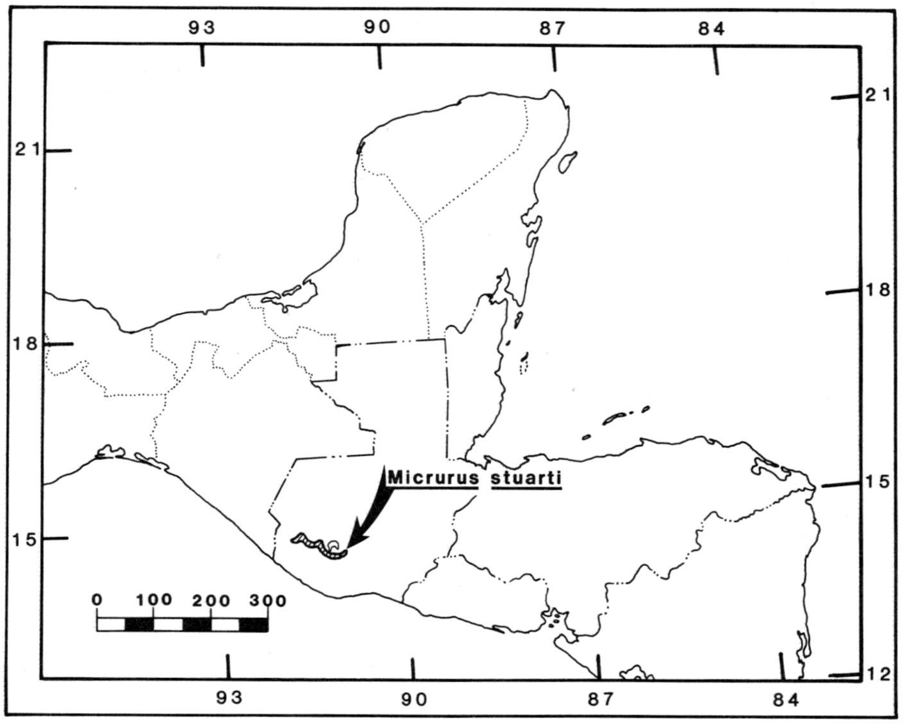


**Map 38.** Distribution of *Micrurus stuarti* along the Pacific versant of southern Guatemala.

orly to cover most of the supraoculars (often reaching the suture between the supraoculars and parietals), three-fourths of the frontal, anterior portions of the postoculars, and supralabials 1–4. The pale parietal ring is dark brown (at least in preservative). Most of the infracephalic scales are black or heavily mottled in black. The black nuchal ring involves the posterior tips of the parietals and extends about 8–9 middorsal scale lengths. There are 13–19 black body rings which, exclusive of the black nuchal ring, are 4 middorsals and 3–4 ventrals long. These are bordered by narrow yellow rings that are up to 1 middorsal long. The red body rings are three or more times longer than the black body rings, and the red dorsals have large distinct black spots on their tips, and occasionally several spots coalesce to form a larger black blotch. The red ventrals are generally immaculate. There are 3 or 4 black rings on the tail, exclusive of the black tips, which are more than twice as long as the brown (in preservative) rings separating them. Many of the scales in the brown tail rings are partially marked with black, especially their posterior tips.

Supra-anal keels are poorly developed in males. There are 1 + 2 temporals, 210–231 ventrals, and 37–48 subcaudals. Other features of lepidosis are typical of the genus *Micrurus*.

SIMILAR SPECIES The only other coral snakes occurring in the Pacific drainages of Guatemala are *M. browni*, *M. latifasciatus*, and *M. nigrocinctus*. *Micrurus browni* (in Guatemala) may be distinguished from *M. stuarti* by generally having more black body rings (19–27) and more black tail rings (6–7); although the red dorsals are black tipped, this species generally does not have irregular large black blotches involving several scales, as is characteristic of *M. stuarti*. *Micrurus latifasciatus* possesses particularly long rings (17–26 ventrals in length), a low number of black body rings (6–9), and a black nuchal ring that does not involve the posterior tips of the parietals. *Micrurus nigrocinctus* (from the Pacific versant of Guatemala) has a higher number of black body rings (more than 10), the red dorsals are generally immaculate but may have tiny black spots, and there are fewer ventrals in both sexes (193–206 vs. 210–214 in males; and 210–219 vs. 224–231 in females).

REMARKS This species is known from very few specimens and has been reported from only two localities in Guatemala: Finca La Paz in the Departamento de San Marcos and Finca El Naranjo in the Departamento de Suchitepéquez. Both of these localities, separated by some 65 km, are located on the piedmont of the Pacific versant and, in view of the seemingly continuous suitable habitat between them, there is no reason to assume that this species has a broken distribution in southwestern Guatemala. This snake possibly ranges along the Pacific piedmont into Chiapas, Mexico, and eastward to the Volcán de Agua, Departamento de Escuintla, in central Guatemala.

REFERENCES Golay, 1985; Roze, 1967, 1983.

### *Micrurus surinamensis* (Cuvier)

(Figs. 104, 105; Map 39)

LOCAL NAMES Coral, coralillo. Bolivia: coral venenosa. Brazil: boichumbéguaçu, cobra-coral. Colombia: coral de agua. Ecuador: culebra del agua. Guyana: himeralli. Peru: naca-naca. Suriname: koraalslang, kraalslang, krarasneke. Venezuela: coral.

ENGLISH NAME Aquatic coral snake.

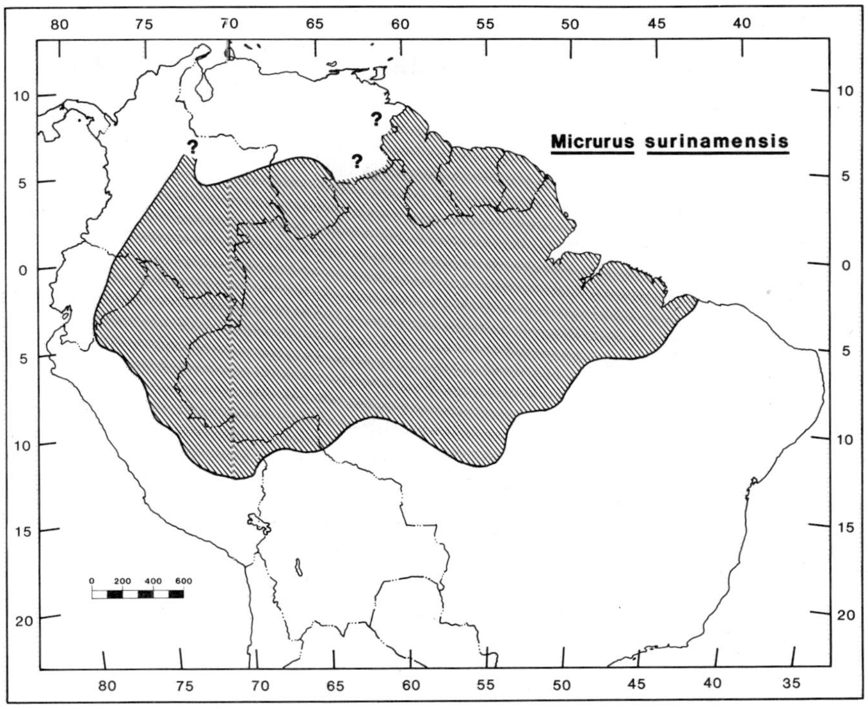


**Map 39.** Distribution of *Micrurus surinamensis* in Amazonian South America. The northern extent of this species' range in Venezuela and Colombia is poorly known.

DISTRIBUTION The Orinocoan and Amazonian drainages of Colombia; Amazonian drainages of Ecuador, Peru, and Bolivia; the entire Amazon Basin of Brazil from northern Mato Grosso and Maranhão northward including Rondônia, Acre, Amazonas state, Roraima, Pará, and Amapá; the Guianas; and southern Venezuela (Map 39; see Remarks). The vertical distribution is to at least 576 m.

HABITAT Lower montane wet forest and tropical rainforest along streams, rivers, or other bodies of water. We have observed this species in nature swimming and in captivity submerged for prolonged periods of time.

DESCRIPTION This is one of the largest species of coral snake, averaging 800–1,000 mm in overall length. The largest museum specimen known measures 1,262 mm, although there is an unverified report of a Colombian specimen 1,800 mm long and another of similar size in Guyana. If these reports are correct, *M. surinamensis* is the largest known species of coral snake. In addition to its length, this species is also robust, being perhaps the heaviest of the coral snakes.

*Micrurus surinamensis* is a tricolored coral snake with red rings separating a pattern of 5–8⅔ black body triads with an additional ½–⅔ + 1 on the tail. The penultimate triad straddles the cloaca, resulting in a fractional body and tail count. The head is red dorsally from the tip of the snout to the posterior portion of the parietals. The posterior sutures of all dorsal cephalic scales are bordered in black, sometimes heavily. A short black band (sometimes complete ventrally) passes across the posterior tips of the parietals and a portion of the posterior temporals, expanding anteriorly on the infralabials such that the last 2 are black. This black band or ring is the first ring of the first body triad. It is followed by a cream-to-yellow ring that expands anteriorly on the venter to include almost the entire gular region except the infralabials and anterior edges of the first pair of chinshields, which are red. The median black ring of each triad is the largest and may be three or more times longer than the outer black rings. The cream (or yellow) rings are shorter middorsally than the outer black triad rings but they expand laterally and ventrally, sometimes to over twice their middorsal length. The intervening red rings range from approximately equal in length to the median black triad rings to as long as 20 or more middorsals, and they invariably contain black pigment. This pigment may be evenly distributed as apical stippling or it may appear as irregularly scattered spots. The cream (or yellow) rings may have black apical stippling or they may be immaculate. This varies considerably and we have seen both extremes in individuals from the same population. Ventrally the cream rings tend to be immaculate, while the red rings usually contain some black pigment which often appears as a black blotch.

*Micrurus surinamensis* is a unique coral snake with some distinctive features worth mentioning. The snout is slightly compressed dorsoventrally and swollen posteriorly. The eyes and nostrils are situated more dorsally than in other coral snakes, and the orbit of the eye is in contact with only 1 supralabial, the fourth. In all other coral snakes both the third and fourth supralabials are in contact with the orbit. The frontal scale is laterally compressed in this species, with its posterior margin scarcely wider than the adjacent supraoculars. Although coral snakes lack a loreal scale, some specimens of *M. surinamensis* from Guyana and Suriname have a vertical division in the preocular such that a loreal appears to exist between the preocular and nasal scales. In very large males 1–3 supra-anal scales may be keeled.

There are 1 + 1 or 1 + 2 (rarely 1 + 3 or 2 + 2) very

large temporals, 160–215 ventrals, and 27–40 subcaudals, mostly divided. Dorsals on the anterior of the body are in 17–19 rows. Other features of lepidosis are typical of the genus *Micrurus*.

SIMILAR SPECIES *Micrurus surinamensis* is one of the most unmistakable coral snakes. The red cephalic scales with black borders plus the single (fourth) supralabial in contact with the eye are features unique in this genus or not found among sympatric congeners. See Mimics of Venomous Snakes for a discussion of false coral snakes.

REMARKS Two races are recognized: *M. s. surinamensis* (Fig. 104), with 160–187 ventrals and 27–38 subcaudals; and *M. s. nattereri* (Fig. 105), with 180–215 ventrals and 37–40 subcaudals. *Micrurus s. nattereri* is restricted to the upper reaches of the Río Orinoco and Río Negro systems in southern Venezuela, northwest Brazil, and eastern Colombia. There is a report of its occurrence in the state of Apure, Venezuela. Its presence in eastern Colombia is confirmed only for the Río Vaupés system, a major tributary of the Río Negro (Fig. 105). Along the eastern versant of the Andes in Colombia, *M. s. surinamensis* is found at least as far north as Medina, Cundinamarca.

REFERENCES Abuys, 1987b; Amaral, 1925b, 1930b, 1932, 1948a, 1948b, 1974, 1978; Brongersma, 1967; Carrillo de Espinoza, 1983; Cendrero et al., 1972; Chippaux, 1987; Cope, 1860c, 1876b; Cunha and Nascimento, 1973, 1978, 1982a; Daniel, 1949; Dixon and Soini, 1986; Duellman, 1978; Dunn, 1944a; Gasc and Rodrigues, 1980; Greene, 1973; Gutiérrez et al., 1988; Hoge, 1958, 1967; Hoge and Lancini, 1960, 1962; Hoge and Romano, 1973; Hoge et al., 1973; Hoogmoed, 1979; Kempff-Mercado, 1975; Lancini, 1970, 1979; Machado, 1945a; Medem, 1969; Meneses, 1974a; Milá de la Roca, 1932; Miyata, 1982; Moonen et al., 1978; Nicéforo-María, 1942; Orcés, 1943, 1948; Parker, 1935; J. A. Peters, 1960a; Prado, 1945; Quelch, 1898; Roux-Esteve, 1983; Roze, 1955, 1966a, 1967, 1983; Sandner-Montilla, 1985b; Santos, 1981; Schmidt, 1936a, 1952, 1955; Schmidt and Walker, 1943a; Silva Haad and Rodríguez R., 1985; Soini, 1974b; Vellard, 1941; Vetencourt Finol., 1960.

### *Micrurus tschudii* (Jan)

(Figs. 106, 107; Map 40)

LOCAL NAMES Coral. Peru: coralillo, naca-naca, serpiente de coral, víbora de coral.

ENGLISH NAME Desert coral snake.

DISTRIBUTION The semi-arid Pacific coast of South America, from southern Ecuador (north of the Catamayo Valley) south throughout the Peruvian west coast and possibly south into northwestern Bolivia (Map 40; see Remarks). The vertical distribution is from near sea level to at least 1,450 m.

HABITAT Tropical deciduous forest, dry tropical forest, and thornscrub. This species is most likely to be encountered in riparian situations.

DESCRIPTION *Micrurus tschudii* is a small species of coral snake, averaging 200–250 mm but attaining as much as 880 mm in overall length (see Remarks).

This is a tricolored coral snake with a pattern consisting of 10–22 black body triads plus 1–2⅓ triads on the tail. In general the median black ring of each triad is longest, although the black rings may be subequal. The snout is black, and this usually includes the first 4–5 supralabials, anterior part of the frontal, anterior part of the supraoculars, anterior temporals, and eyes. In some specimens the internasal area is white and there may be a white spot on the rostral. A red-orange parietal ring includes the rest of the frontal, which may be black edged, the anterior portion of the parietals, the posterior temporals, and sometimes the anterior temporal. The black nuchal ring crosses the posterior tips of the parietals or as much as the posterior halves of these scales. In some specimens the nuchal ring is united along the supralabials with the black snout, thus reducing the red parietal ring to a spot or blotch. The venter of the head is cream or yellow, although the subspecies *M. t. tschudii* tends to have black pigment on the infralabials and anterior chin shields. The black nuchal ring is usually incomplete ventrally on specimens of *M. t. olssoni*, being interrupted by a narrow line of yellow pigment.

The red body rings in this species tend to be irregular in length and frequently are shorter than the black triad rings, such that the triads are the dominant element in the pattern. The borders of the yellow rings are jagged, tending to follow scale outlines. There are fused triads (quinquads) frequently, and there may be lateral or ventral fusion of black rings. In some cases red rings may be reduced to a blotch or spot on the dorsum. Some spotting or stippling with black is usually present on red rings and yellow rings, although in many specimens the yellow rings are immaculate. There is little black stippling on the venter but this varies. The white (or yellow) rings are generally 2 middorsals in length, while the black rings are 4–5 middorsals in length. Red rings vary from 2 to 4 middorsals in length. Generally, the last body ring is the last black ring of a triad.

There are 1 + 1 temporals, 188–232 ventrals, and 25–29 subcaudals. Other features of lepidosis are typical of the genus *Micrurus*.

SIMILAR SPECIES *Micrurus tschudii* is sympatric with two congeners, *M. bocourti* and *M. mertensi*. In *M. bocourti* the first body triad is represented by only 2 black rings (3 in *M. tschudii*). Moreover, the tail of *M. bocourti* is bicolored (tricolored in *M. tschudii*) and *M. bocourti* has a greater number of subcaudals (32–50 vs. 25–29). *Micrurus mertensi* lacks triads, has a black parietal cap, and 31 or more subcaudals. *Micrurus mertensi* may be a larger species than *M. tschudii*; it reaches at least 880 mm and is stated to approach 1 m in overall length. See also the discussion of false coral snakes in Mimics of Venomous Snakes.

REMARKS Two subspecies are recognized. *Micrurus t. tschudii* (Fig. 106) ranges from the Departamento de La Libertad, Peru, south to the Rímac Valley, possibly

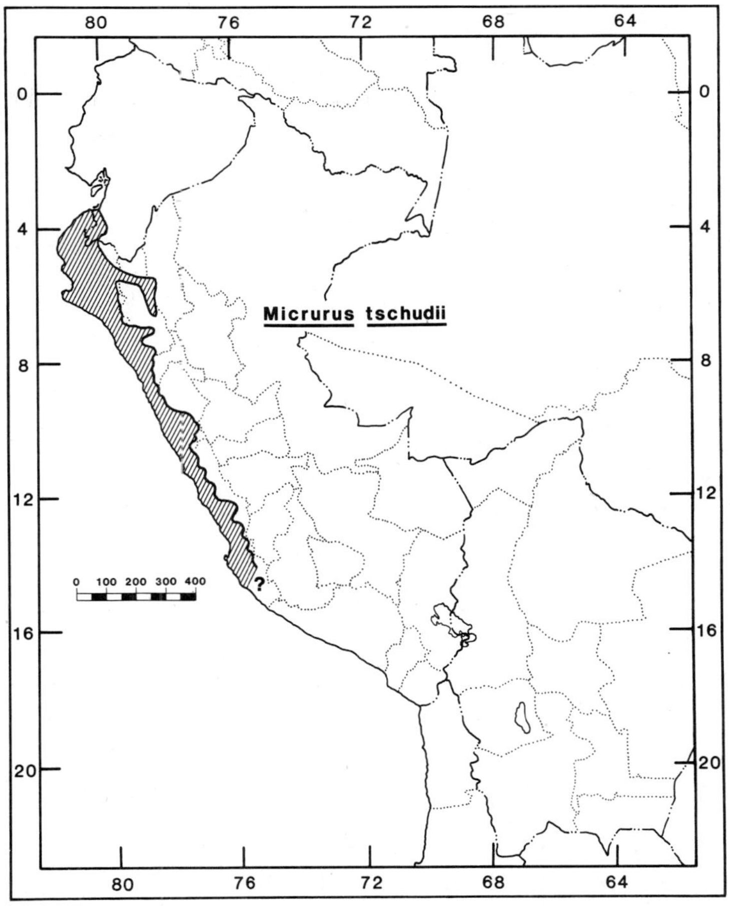


**Map 40.** Distribution of *Micrurus tschudii* in southern Ecuador and Peru; the southern extent of its distribution may be more extensive than is shown.

extending into northwest Bolivia. This subspecies has 200–232 ventrals, 12–22 triads, a complete nuchal ring, and black pigment present on the yellow rings, infralabials, and anterior chinshields. *Micrurus t. olssoni* (Fig. 107) ranges from the Catamayo Valley of Ecuador southward to the Departamento de Piura, Peru, possibly intergrading with *M. t. tschudii* in the Departamento de La Libertad. This subspecies has 188–213 ventrals, 10–14 triads, and usually an incomplete nuchal ring; black pigment is usually absent on the yellow rings, infralabials, and anterior chinshields. *Micrurus t. olssoni* reportedly reaches a larger size than the nominate form (700–880 mm vs. 600–700 mm).

*Micrurus tschudii* appears to be especially diurnal and it has been encountered climbing trees. The postulated occurrence of *M. tschudii* in Bolivia is difficult to explain, as the Andes constitute a formidable barrier to dispersal in this region. *Micrurus peruvianus* is similar in some respects to *M. tschudii* but is separated from it distributionally by the Andes Mountains.

REFERENCES Amaral, 1925b; Carrillo de Espinoza, 1977, 1983; Cope, 1876b, 1877; Greene and McDiarmid, 1981; Jan, 1858; Kempff-Mercado, 1975; Meneses, 1974a, 1974b; Miyata, 1982; Orcés, 1948; Parker, 1938; J. A. Peters, 1960a; Roze, 1967, 1983; Schmidt, 1936a; Schmidt and Schmidt, 1925; Schmidt and Walker, 1943b.

# Sonoran Coral Snake

## Genus *Micruroides* Schmidt, 1928

The genus *Micruroides* (family Elapidae) contains one species, *M. euryxanthus*, which is restricted to northwestern Mexico and the southwestern United States. Three subspecies are recognized on the basis of pattern and lepidosis. The adult length generally does not exceed 500 mm.

A typical complement of head scales is present: 2 internasals, 2 prefrontals, 2 supraoculars, 1 frontal, and 2 parietals. One preocular, 2 postoculars, 7 supralabials, 7 infralabials, and 1 + 2 temporals are usually present; the loreal is absent. The chinshields characteristically are reduced, with the median suture between the enlarged first pair of infralabials longer than that of the single pair of chinshields. There are 15 smooth dorsal scale rows throughout most of the length of the body except for just behind the head, where there are usually 17. The color pattern on the body consists of alternating red and black rings that are separated by shorter yellow or white rings. For additional features of lepidosis and pattern see the following *M. euryxanthus* account.

The maxillary bones are relatively elongated and anteriorly their dentition consists of paired immoveable hollow fangs on each bone followed by 1 or 2 small solid teeth on the posterior end, which terminate at about the level of the suture between supralabials 4 and 5.

The hemipenes extend for about 7 subcaudals and are bifurcated with branches of the sulcus spermaticus extending onto each lobe. A naked fold or furrow that is parallel to the sulcus spermaticus extends the length of the base. Proximally the organs are essentially naked except for a few scattered spinules. About the distal two-thirds of the organs are covered with spines, except for the zone flanking the sulcus from the basal perimeter of the spines to the crotch. The size of the spines gradually diminishes toward the apex of each lobe; the apex terminates in a minute papilla-like projection.

Bites by *Micruroides* produce primarily local effects, and no fatalities are known to have occurred. A report of four cases noted that there was moderate pain, paresthesia, numbness, and incoordination of the bitten extremity with systemic symptoms of nausea and drowsiness. Generalized muscular paralysis was not a problem.

### *Micruroides euryxanthus* (Kennicott)

(Figs. 11, 12, 108, 109; Map 41)

LOCAL NAMES Coralillo, coralillo de Sonora.

ENGLISH NAME Sonoran coral snake.

DISTRIBUTION This species occurs from central Arizona to southwestern New Mexico southward into Mexico. In northern Mexico it ranges from extreme northwestern Chihuahua to about Sonoita, Sonora, thence southward through most of the state of Sonora to about Mazatlán, Sinaloa, extending up river valleys into southwestern Chihuahua and probably northwestern Durango (Map 41). The species is also known from Isla Tiburón in the Gulf of California. No specimens have been taken from northern Sinaloa, but this hiatus in distribution may be an artifact of collecting. The vertical distribution is from near sea level to about 1,800 m.

HABITAT Desert, mesquite-grassland, tropical deciduous forest, thorn forest, and lower pine-oak forest.

DESCRIPTION *Micruroides euryxanthus* is a small, slender coral snake that is commonly about 400 mm in overall length and rarely reaches 550 mm.

The snout is black with the black pigment extending posteriorly behind the eyes to include all of the supralabials, the tertiary temporals, and most or all of the parietals. On the lower jaw all of the infralabials are darkly pigmented; the chinshields and gulars are paler but often suffused with black or brown. A broad *yellow* or *white* nuchal ring 1½–6 scales long immediately follows the black on the head. The nuchal ring generally encroaches on the posterior tips of the parietals in specimens from the northern portion of the range; specimens from Sinaloa have entirely black parietals. Following the pale nuchal rings the body possesses a series of rings disposed in a red-yellow-black-yellow-red sequence. There are 11–13 black rings on the body. The scales of the red rings tend to be virtually unmarked with black pigment. There is a considerable variation among populations in the length of the red rings. Generally, snakes from the northern half of Sonora possess red rings about 4–9 middorsals long with a total of 42–93 red scales in the vertebral row of the body; snakes further south have red rings about 9–13 dorsals long and a total of 93–113 red scales in the vertebral row of the body. The yellow body rings vary from about 3–4 dorsals long in specimens from the north to less than 1 scale length in snakes from the extreme southern portion of the range. The tail has 1 or 2 black rings separated by yellow or white rings. The dorsals are smooth and usually disposed in 17 longitudinal rows immediately behind the head; this number is reduced to 15 by the level of the 10th ventral and remains constant throughout the rest of the body to the vent. The anal plate is divided.

There are 205–245 ventrals and 19–31 subcaudals,

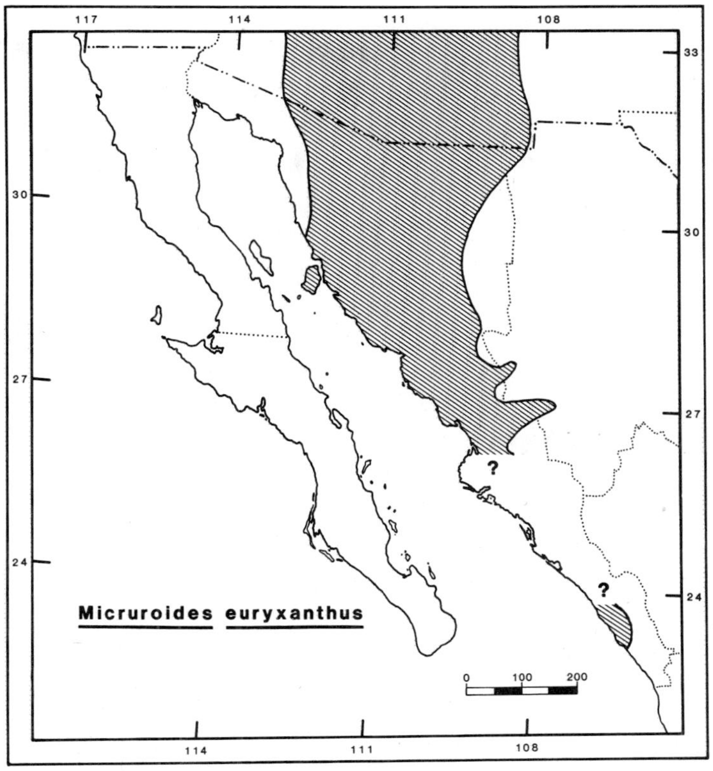


**Map 41.** Distribution of *Micruroides euryxanthus* in northwestern Mexico and the adjacent United States. No records are available for much of Sinaloa; whether this hiatus is real or an artifact of collecting is unknown. The species occurs on Isla Tiburón in the Gulf of California.

many of which may be undivided. For other features of lepidosis see the generic account for *Micruroides*.

SIMILAR SPECIES Two coral snakes of the genus *Micrurus* occur along the northern portion of the west coast of Mexico: *M. distans* and *M. proximans*. Both of these are distinguished easily from *Micruroides euryanthus* by having a pale parietal ring followed by a black ring, 2 rather than 1 pair of chinshields, 15 rather than 17 dorsal scale rows immediately behind the head, and 1 + 1 rather than 1 + 2 temporals. Some harmless genera that superficially resemble *Micruroides* are *Chilomeniscus* (Fig. 463), *Chionactis* (Figs. 464, 465), and *Rhinocheilus* (Figs. 520, 521), but these have pale rather than black snouts and bands that do not encircle the body ventrally. Members of the genus *Lampropeltis* (Figs. 497, 498) possess a loreal and brightly colored rings; however, the sequence of color is different than that of *Micruroides*, with alternating red and yellow markings separated by yellow or white rings.

REMARKS In Arizona this species is reported to be most common in river bottoms and arroyos. This is a secretive snake that appears on the surface generally at dusk or after dark; infrequently, it is found abroad during daylight on overcast days or after rains. When molested, this species attempts to escape or, similar to most coral snakes of the genus *Micrurus*, will display its tail. It may also bite, and fart loudly for its size, if agitated.

Three subspecies are recognized, two of which are restricted to Mexico: *M. e. euryxanthus* (Fig. 108) is found in the southwestern United States, in extreme northwestern Chihuahua, about the northern third of Sonora, and on Isla Tiburón; *M. e. australis* (Fig. 109) occurs in the southern two-thirds of Sonora and northern Sinaloa; and *M. e. neglectus* is known only from the vicinity of Mazatlán, Sinaloa.

REFERENCES Bogert and Oliver, 1945; Cendrero et al., 1972; Cliff, 1954; Cohen and Seligmann, 1967; Cope, 1861, 1879, 1887, 1892, 1896; Coues, 1875; Cuesta Terron, 1932; Duellman, 1957; Echternacht, 1973; Garman, 1884a; Gates, 1956a, 1957; Gehlbach, 1972; Gloyd, 1937; Greene, 1973; Greene and McDiarmid, 1981; Hahn and May, 1972; Hardy and McDiarmid, 1969; Hensley, 1950; Kennicott, 1860; Klemmer, 1963; Lowe, 1948, 1955, 1964; Lowe et al., 1986; Martín del Campo, 1935; Mocquard, 1908–1909; R. W. Murphy, 1983b; R. W. Murphy and Ottley, 1984; Nickerson and Mays, 1970; Ortenburger and Ortenburger, 1927; Romer, 1956; Roze, 1967, 1974, 1983; Russell, 1967; Ruthven, 1907; Schmidt, 1928a, 1937; Shaw, 1971; H. M. Smith and Taylor, 1945, 1966; Soulé and Sloan, 1966; Stebbins, 1985; Stejneger, 1895, 1902; Stejneger and Barbour, 1943; Stevan and Seligmann, 1970; Tanner, 1985; Van Denburgh, 1924; Vitt and Hulse, 1973; Webb, 1984; Woodin, 1953; Zweifel and Norris, 1955.

# Pelagic Sea Snake

## Genus *Pelamis* Daudin, 1803

The genus *Pelamis* (family Elapidae) contains a single species, *P. platurus*, which is the most widely ranging venomous snake. Among sea snakes, the color pattern of the genus *Pelamis* is unique, being composed of broad longitudinal stripes rather than some combination of transverse bands or rings.

Other obvious characteristics of the genus include enlarged, regular headshields; small, juxtaposed scales on the body; small, divided ventrals which are scarcely larger than the dorsals; and the absence of a mental groove. *Pelamis platurus*, like other sea snakes, is marine, but it has considerable tolerance to low salinities and often frequents inshore regions.

Although reports exist that bites by *Pelamis* have resulted in death, no reference or source of information was cited. In one recent report no sea snake bites were reported to be known from Costa Rica, but the venom of this species was noted to be relatively toxic to mice. It has been suggested that it is unlikely an adult *Pelamis* snake could kill an adult human; this conclusion was based on an experiment in which 10 mg of venom was required to kill a 60-kg sheep, and the average yield of venom in an adult *Pelamis* was found to be only 0.87 mg. Nevertheless, *Pelamis* has been implicated in human fatalities in Panama, Colombia, and Costa Rica.

### *Pelamis platurus* (Linnaeus)

(Figs. 110–112)

LOCAL NAMES Culebra del Mar, serpiente pelágica, serpiente del mar, serpiente marina. Guatemala: cantil listada, zapatilla. Nicaragua: serpiente de mar listada. Peru: víbora marina.

ENGLISH NAME Pelagic sea snake.

DISTRIBUTION This species occurs in tropical and subtropical seas of the Indo-Australian region and from the east coast of Africa through the Indian and Pacific oceans to the Western Hemisphere, where it is found along the Pacific Coast of the Americas, from the Gulf of California south to Ecuador (including the Galapagos Islands) and northern Peru. Isolated specimens have been collected as far north as San Clemente, California, and as far south as Isla de Pascua (Easter Island), Chile; there are two questionable records from the Caribbean. In Panama, these snakes frequently wash up along the shore of the causeway leading to the islands of Naos, Culebra, Venado, and Flamenco, and they are common along the beach of San José in the Islas de las Perlas.

HABITAT A thoroughly pelagic sea dweller, this species is often encountered in large numbers floating among flotsam at the surface of slicks where sea currents come together and in shallow offshore waters with temperatures above 20°C. *Pelamis platurus* is particularly abundant during the dry season off the coast of Costa Rica.

DESCRIPTION This medium-sized, relatively slender sea snake has a maximum recorded length of 1,130 mm, but it seldom exceeds 750 mm in total length in eastern Pacific waters. The tail is flattened and oarlike.

The color pattern is highly variable but basically involves a black or brown dorsum contrasting with a yellow, cream, or paler brown venter. The pattern tends to be of broad stripes but variations include additional spotting, wavy stripes, or bars. The dorsal color is differentiated sharply from the venter, and the two colors usually meet in a continuous line along the sides of the body. The pattern on the tail is an especially variable reticulation of black or brown and yellow. Rarely, specimens may show this tail pattern throughout the body, or lack all dark markings.

The head is elongated, narrow, and compressed; there are enlarged shields on top of the head (one between the supraoculars). There are no internasals, the nasals making contact on the dorsal surface of the snout. Each nasal contains a valved nostril. There are 7–11 supralabials, 11–13 infralabials, 44–67 midbody dorsal scale rows, 260–465 ventrals (scarcely larger than adjacent scales; usually divided by a midventral groove), and 39–66 subcaudals (although some authors state that these cannot be differentiated). The dorsals are small, juxtaposed, and hexagonal or quadrangular in shape.

SIMILAR SPECIES The only other venomous snakes that occupy a marine habitat are species that have not been recorded reliably from the Western Hemisphere. In contrast to the broad stripes typical of the *Pelamis* color pattern, other species of sea snakes tend to be ringed or banded. All eels have smooth skin with a mucous covering; they also have gills.

REMARKS *Pelamis platurus* is normally quite inoffensive, but when restrained or when stranded on the beach it will bite to defend itself. Sea snake venom is highly toxic, so any bite should be treated as a serious matter. Caution should be exercised while swimming and when dealing with specimens found trapped in nets or stranded on the beach.

REFERENCES Acosta-Solís, 1944; Alvarez del Toro, 1983; Ambrose, 1956; Ayerbe, 1979; Barbour, 1906; Bogert and Oliver, 1945; Bolaños, 1982, 1983, 1984; Bolaños et al., 1974; Carrillo de Espinoza, 1970, 1983; Casas-Andreu, 1981; Cendrero et al., 1972; H. C. Clark, 1942; Cochran, 1946; Cogger, 1983; Cope, 1859, 1868, 1876a; Cruz et al., 1979; Curran and Kauffeld, 1937; Daniel, 1949; Donoso-Barros, 1966; Duellman, 1961; Duke, 1967; Dunn, 1944a; Dunson, 1975; Elton, 1948; Garman, 1884a, 1892a, 1892b; 1908; Girard, 1858; Gray, 1829; Grocott and Sadler, 1958; Gutiérrez and Bolaños, 1980; Halstead, 1970; Hardy and McDiarmid, 1969; Heatwole, 1987; Hecht et al., 1974; Hidalgo, 1980; Hoge and Romano, 1971a; Klawe, 1964; Kropach, 1971a, 1971b, 1972, 1975; Mao and Chen, 1980; Marinkelle, 1966; Martín del Campo, 1935, 1950; Medem, 1969, 1979; Mocquard, 1908–1909; C. W. Myers, 1972; G. S. Myers, 1945; Nicéforo-María, 1942; Ocaranza, 1930; Ochoterena, 1934; Orcés, 1942, 1943, 1948; Parker, 1926; Patzelt, 1979; J. A. Peters, 1960a; Peterson and Smith, 1974; Pickwell and Culotta, 1980; Pickwell et al., 1983; Ravenau de Lussan, 1690; Reynolds and Pickwell, 1984; Rodas, 1938; Sanborn and Loomis, 1976; Schmidt, 1922, 1933b; Scott, 1969; Shuntov, 1963, 1971; H. M. Smith, 1958; H. M. Smith and Mittleman, 1943; H. M. Smith and Taylor, 1945; M. Smith, 1926; Stebbins, 1985; Stejneger and Barbour, 1943; Stuart, 1963; Swaroop and Grab, 1954; E. H. Taylor, 1951, 1953a; R. T. Taylor et al., 1974; Trejos, 1937; Tu, 1976; Villa, 1984; Voris, 1983; Wilson and Meyer, 1985; Wilson et al., 1978; Zweifel, 1960.

# Cantil and Copperhead

## Genus *Agkistrodon* Beauvois, 1799

Three species of *Agkistrodon* (family Viperidae) inhabit North America. *Agkistrodon piscivorus* is extralimital to our consideration and *A. contortrix* barely ranges into extreme north-central Mexico. However, *A. bilineatus* occurs in the north from Tamaulipas and Sonora, Mexico, southward to northwestern Costa Rica. The range of *A. bilineatus* is more-or-less continuous along the Pacific drainage, but fragmented into several populations on the Atlantic side in Mexico and Guatemala (see Map 42). Although a few reports exist for *A. piscivorus* near the U.S.-Mexican border, no recent records exist for this species from within about 120 km of the Río Grande and it is probably extralimital to Mexico. Members of this genus are semiaquatic to terrestrial and are found most frequently in the vicinity of water. However, both *A. bilineatus* and *A. contortrix* have been taken in xeric habitats far from permanent streams or ponds.

The following discussion of variation in the genus *Agkistrodon* refers to *A. contortrix* and *A. bilineatus* only. The canthus rostralis is prominent and the scales on the crown of the head are usually large and platelike; in *A. contortrix* there are generally 9 large symmetrical plates, but in *A. bilineatus* the plates are often irregularly fragmented. The pupil of the eye is vertically elliptical and there are 7 or 8 (usually 8) supralabials, 9–12 infralabials, 21–23 (usually 23) midbody dorsal scale rows, 129–153 ventrals, and 46–68 subcaudals, some or most of which may be divided. The middorsal body scales are keeled and the anal plate is undivided. For a description of color and pattern for members of this genus see the appropriate species accounts.

The inverted hemipenes extend the length of 7–9 subcaudals and are divided with a bifurcated sulcus spermaticus that extends to the apices. The lobes are subcylindrical in *A. contortrix* and may be somewhat attenuated in *A. bilineatus*. The proximal portion of each lobe bears 12–16 large spines in *A. contortrix* and 25–32 in *A. bilineatus*. In *A. contortrix* these spines are located on the sulcate, lateral, and asulcate surfaces, but not in the mesial area; in *A. bilineatus* the spines encircle the proximal portion of each lobe. Calyces with micro-ornamentation of soft spinules cover the distal portions of the lobes; in *A. bilineatus* these cover the distal two-thirds of the lobes; in *A. contortrix* the calyces extend medially almost to the crotch and laterally cover the distal four-fifths of the lobes. The basal portion of the organ is virtually naked in both species.

### *Agkistrodon bilineatus* Günther

(Figs. 113–118; Map 42)

LOCAL NAMES Cantil (Pacific Coast from Mexico to Costa Rica, Río Grijalva Depression of Chiapas, Mexico, víbora castellana (Pacific coast from Guatemala to Nicaragua). Guatemala: barba amarilla (Río Chixoy; this is the same name given to *Bothrops asper* through much of its range), cantil de agua (Departamento de Escuintla). Mexico: cumcóatl (Náhuatl); metapil (Tamaulipas); pichicuate (Jalisco, Nayarit, Sinaloa, Sonora); víbora de freno (southeastern Mexico); víbora enjaquimada (Río Grijalva Depression); volpochh (Yucatán Peninsula; this Mayan name has been variously spelled "wolpoch" or "vol-poch"); zolcóatl, zolcuate (west coast); Nicaragua: castellana de Jáquima.

ENGLISH NAME Cantil.

DISTRIBUTION *Agkistrodon bilineatus* is found at low to moderate elevations along the Pacific Coast and foothills from southern Sonora, Mexico, southward through Guatemala, El Salvador, and Nicaragua, to northwestern Costa Rica; its range includes parts of the Río de las Balsas Depression, the Isla María Madre (and perhaps other islands) in the Islas de Tres Marías, Mexico, and the Isla de Zacate Grande in the Gulf of Fonseca, Honduras. At least four widely disjunct populations occur in Atlantic drainages: in Tamaulipas, Nuevo León, and possibly northern Veracruz; in the Yucatán Peninsula, including the states of Campeche, Yucatán, and Quintana Roo, Mexico, and northern Belize; in the middle Río Grijalva Valley of Chiapas; and in the Río Chixoy (Negro) Valley in central Guatemala (Map 42). The vertical distribution is from near sea level to about 1,500 m.

HABITAT Throughout its range the species occurs in seasonally dry forest. Over most of its range it inhabits tropical deciduous forest (tropical dry forest), thorn forest (tropical scrub forest), and savanna. In northeastern Mexico it ranges into mesquite-grassland and in the southern part of the Yucatán Peninsula it occurs in what has been described as rainforest—however, this region experiences a relatively harsh dry season.

DESCRIPTION This is a heavy-bodied snake with a relatively long slender tail. Adults commonly exceed 800 mm in total length and some specimens may reach 1,380 mm. This species possesses longer fangs than any

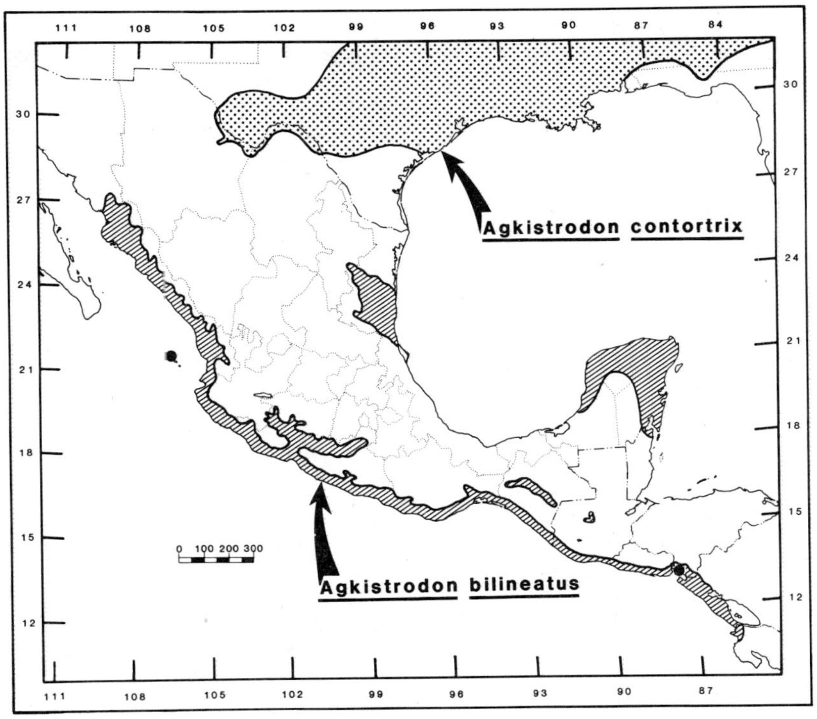


**Map 42.** Distribution of members of the genus *Agkistrodon* occurring in Mexico and Central America. *Agkistrodon contortrix* (*stipples*) barely ranges into northern Coahuila and Chihuahua, whereas *A. bilineatus* (*diagonal lines*) has an extensive, but disjunct, range throughout much of the region. Dots represent island records for *A. bilineatus*: Isla María Madre in the Islas Marías off the west coast of Mexico and the Isla de Zacate Grande in the Gulf of Fonseca, Honduras.

of its North American congeners, and its fangs are also relatively longer in relation to its head and body.

A pair of pale stripes is present on each side of the head. The upper stripe extends from the rostral across the canthus, including the lateral margins of the internasals, prefrontals, and supraoculars; and then from the upper postocular across the temporals to a point above the angle of the jaws; then it arches downward to merge with the lower lateral head stripe. The lower stripe extends from the prenasal across the supralabials to the rictus and thence posteriorly to a point above the jaw articulation. This pale stripe usually is bordered below by dark pigment (orange, brown, and/or gray), or it may extend to the lip margin, especially posteriorly. Either the upper or lower lateral facial stripes may be interrupted on the back of the head. A broad vertical pale stripe is present on the rostral and mental. The venter of the head is reddish brown to orange, often heavily peppered with black, and has well-defined yellow spots on the infralabials and gulars. A pale line usually is present that runs diagonally across the fifth infralabial and continues onto 1 or more adjacent gulars. The ground color is dark gray to almost black, dark gray brown, or dark reddish brown. A series of crossbands is outlined irregularly with diagonal series of white, cream, or yellow flecks. The crossbands are usually paler than the ground color and in populations from northeastern Mexico they may be bright orange laterally. However, the color intervening between the series of pale flecks may be the same as the rest of the dorsum, especially in large adults from the Pacific Coast of Mexico and Guatemala. The venter is gray, grayish brown, or reddish brown (paler along the middle of the belly) with irregular pale markings, especially laterally. Dark chestnut brown ventrolateral spots are present.

The distal half of the tail is usually pale gray or greenish gray. The tongue is orange, red, or orangish pink with yellowish tips. The lower portion of the iris is orange, hazel, or brown; the upper half is paler. Juveniles most frequently have a reddish brown ground color but also may have an orange, pale gray, or pale brown dorsum. The distal portion of the tails of juvenile snakes is bright yellow.

There are generally 9 large symmetrical head plates, but these may be irregular in some specimens: the frontal may be fragmented, the prefrontals may be separated by an elongated median scale, and the parietals may be subdivided irregularly into smaller scales for a total of up to 15 or more scales on the dorsum of the head. There are 8 supralabials, 10–12 infralabials, 23 (rarely 21) midbody dorsal scale rows; 129–144 ventrals, and 46–68 subcaudals, 4–38 of which may be undivided.

SIMILAR SPECIES *Agkistrodon bilineatus* is distinguished easily from all other snakes in Middle America by the following combination of characteristics: large head plates, a loreal pit, a pair of distinctive pale stripes on each side of the head, and no rattle.

REMARKS Currently, four subspecies are recognized: *A. b. taylori* (Fig. 117) in northeastern Mexico; *A. b. bilineatus* (Fig. 113) along the Pacific Coast of Mexico, Guatemala, and El Salvador, and in the Río Grijalva Valley of Chiapas, Mexico; *A. b. russeolus* (Fig. 116) on the Yucatán Peninsula; and *A. b. howardgloydi* (Figs. 114, 115) along the Pacific Coast of Honduras, Nicaragua, and Costa Rica. The status of the Río Chixoy, Guatemala, population (Fig. 118) as well as the interspecific relationships of the genus *Agkistrodon* are currently under study by several investigators.

Bites from this species have caused human fatalities, in a few cases in a matter of hours. However, envenomation by *A. bilineatus* has not been reported in detail. Necrotic effects of its venom are said to be extensive. In one report, one of six cases required amputation. This species can be quite aggressive when provoked, thrashing its tail back and forth and lunging repeatedly at antagonists.

REFERENCES Allen, 1949; Alvarez del Toro, 1972, 1983; Barrera, 1963; Bogert and Oliver, 1945; Bolaños, 1982, 1983, 1984; Bolaños and Montero, 1970; Boulenger, 1896; Burger and Robertson, 1951; Caballero y Caballero, 1954; Campbell and Vannini, 1988; Casas-Andreu, 1981; Cendrero et al., 1972; Conant, 1982, 1984; Cope, 1865, 1887; Cruz et al., 1979; Cuesta Terron, 1921b, 1930a; Davis and Smith, 1953; Ditmars, 1930, 1937; Dixon et al., 1962; Duellman, 1954, 1958, 1961, 1965a, 1965b; Dugès, 1889, 1896; Ernst, 1965; Gadow, 1905; Gaige, 1936; Garman, 1884a; George, 1930a; Gloyd, 1956, 1972; Gloyd and Conant, 1943; Groombridge, 1986; Günther, 1863, 1895–1902; Hardy and McDiarmid, 1969; Henderson, 1978; Henderson and Hoevers, 1975; Hoevers and Henderson, 1974; Lee, 1980; Loveridge, 1928a; Martin, 1958; Martín del Campo, 1935, 1937a, 1938b, 1950, 1953, 1984; Mertens, 1952a, 1952b; Mocquard, 1908–1909; P. Müller, 1973; Noguchi, 1909; Ocaranza, 1930; Ochoterena, 1934; Oliver, 1937; Prado, 1945; Rodas, 1938; Rosado-López and Laviada-Arrigunada, 1977; Schmidt, 1941; Schmidt and Andrews, 1936; Schmidt and Owens, 1944; Schmidt and Shannon, 1947; H. M. Smith, 1939, 1970; H. M. Smith and Grant, 1958; H. M. Smith and Taylor, 1945, 1966; P. W. Smith and Darling, 1952; Stejneger, 1899; Stuart, 1963; Sumichrast, 1873, 1880, 1881–1882, 1882; E. H. Taylor, 1938b, 1940; R. T. Taylor et al., 1974; Van Denburgh and Slevin, 1914; Velasco, 1895; Villa, 1962, 1984; Webb, 1984; Werner, 1922; Wilson and Meyer, 1985; Zweifel, 1959a, 1960.

## *Agkistrodon contortrix* (Linnaeus)

(Figs. 119, 120; Map 42)

LOCAL NAMES Unknown for Mexico.

ENGLISH NAME Copperhead.

DISTRIBUTION The United States and Mexico. *Agkistrodon contortrix* has been recorded from Chihuahua and Coahuila, Mexico, on the basis of a few specimens and reliable sightings. Most of the region in Mexico where the species might be expected to occur has been poorly collected. Map 42 delineates the predicted range for the species in Mexico based on its known range in the adjacent United States, on specimens and sight records, and on ecological factors. As presented here, its range in Mexico extends along the banks of the Río Bravo del Norte (Rio Grande) and associated canyons from extreme northeastern Chihuahua through northern Coahuila from the Sierra del Carmen to about Piedras Negras. Its vertical distribution in west Texas is from about 300 to over 1,500 m.

HABITAT This species can be found in desert (within its Latin American range); it is most often in the vicinity of permanent or semipermanent water, but sometimes also inhabits dry arroyos.

DESCRIPTION This is a stout-bodied species, with adults of Mexican populations usually attaining 450–650 mm in total length and rarely exceeding 800 mm.

A distinctive black spot is present on the posterior portion of each parietal. A thin white line extends from the posterior edge of the eye to the rictus and along the infralabials (Fig. 120). The dorsal pattern consists of a series of alternating pale and dark crossbands; some of these may not be continuous across the middorsum and may be arranged as separate lateral bars. The ground color of the central portion of the 13–19 dark brown-edged crossbands is sandy to chestnut brown, cinnamon-bay, or pale chocolate brown. Often the darker midbody crossbands are marked by a pair of round dark lateral spots. The dorsal ground color is pale grayish yellow, pale hazel-brown, yellowish buff, or tan. The venter is mottled heavily with dark mahogany to black blotches interspersed with pale intrusions from the dorsal ground color. The tail is greenish gray with paler crossbands or lateral bars. The iris is yellow to copper colored. Juveniles are marked similarly to adults, but tend to be paler and have yellowish or greenish pigment on the tail tip.

There are generally 9 large symmetrical head plates, 7–8 (mode 8) supralabials, 9–10 (mode 10) infralabials, 21–23 (usually 23) midbody dorsal scale rows, 147–153 ventrals, and 52–60 subcaudals, most of the proximal ones undivided (the distal 15–33 may be divided).

SIMILAR SPECIES No dangerously venomous snakes are likely to be confused with this species within its range in Mexico. *Trimorphodon biscutatus*, a slender opisthoglyphous snake, has dorsal crossbands, but these are dark brown and become narrowly tapered ventrolaterally, and the ventrals are mostly pale with light brown mottling. Two harmless species of water snakes, *Nerodia erythrogaster* and *N. rhombifer*, occur within the range of *A. contortrix*; these snakes are thick-bodied with a large head and will bite readily if provoked. *Nerodia erythrogaster* has an unmarked yellow belly and large blotches or short pale crossbars on the middorsum; *N. rhombifer* has a yellow belly marked with dark round or crescent-shaped spots and a dorsal pattern of chainlike markings. Both species of water snakes have a round pupil and usually a divided anal plate.

REMARKS Five subspecies of *A. contortrix* have been described. Of these, four are extralimital to Latin America; only *A. c. pictigaster*, the trans-Pecos copperhead, ranges into northern Mexico.

*Agkistrodon contortrix* may be found considerable distances from permanent water in areas of desert shrub, but it is most common in wooded regions containing rocky canyons, springs, or streams. It is active generally only after dark.

Envenomation by this species produces severe local pain, edema and erythema, in addition to nausea, vomiting, and occasionally hypotension (shock). In general, signs and symptoms are milder than with *A. bilineatus* and *A. piscivorus*, being "severe" in only 11%

of the cases in one large series of snakebites reported. Although the majority of cases may not necessitate antivenom therapy, serious envenomation has been reported with severe swelling, hypotension, and thrombocytopenia in one case and vascular insufficiency to a lower extremity in another (although use of cryotherapy may have contributed to the problem). Deaths are unusual following *A. contortrix* envenomation, but they do occur. The fatality rate has been estimated to be 0.01% for snakebite from this species.

REFERENCES Axtell, 1959; Baird, 1859; Brown, 1903a; Conant, 1975; Cope, 1860c; Engelhardt, 1932; Fitch, 1960; Flury, 1949; Gehlbach, 1956; Gloyd and Conant, 1943; Groombridge, 1986; Jameson and Flury, 1949; Krochmal and Anderson, 1976; Martín del Campo, 1935, 1950; Milstead, 1960a, 1960b; Milstead et al., 1950; Minton, 1959; Minton and Minton, 1980; Mocquard, 1908–1909; Parrish and Carr, 1967; Raun and Gehlbach, 1972; Santiago, 1979; Schmidt and Smith, 1944; Seifert, 1972; H. M. Smith and Buechner, 1947; H. M. Smith and Taylor, 1945; Stejneger, 1895; Stejneger and Barbour, 1943; Strecker, 1928; Strecker and Johnson, 1935; Tennant, 1984; Werler, 1967; Wright and Wright, 1957.

# Palm-Pitvipers

## Genus *Bothriechis* Peters, 1859

The genus *Bothriechis* (family Viperidae) comprises seven species of relatively slender arboreal pitvipers. Members of this genus commonly reach a total length of 600–800 mm, and *B. aurifer*, *B. bicolor*, and *B. lateralis* are known to reach 1 m or more. Arboreal adaptations include a ground color that is generally some shade of green (for an exception, see the description of *B. schlegelii*), with or without dark or pale markings, and a prehensile tail that is usually at least 15% of the overall length.

Some of the more obvious characteristics of the genus include a sharply defined canthus rostralis, an unelevated snout, and a rostral that is broader than it is high. The pupil of the eye is vertically elliptical. The scales on the crown of the head are extremely variable; the number of intersupraoculars ranges from 1 (some *B. aurifer*) to 10 (some *B. schlegelii*). There are generally 9–11 supralabials (except in *B. schlegelii*, which commonly has 8), 9–13 infralabials (except in *B. nigroviridis* and *B. schlegelii*, which may have fewer), 19–25 midbody dorsal scale rows, 137–175 ventrals, and 42–72 undivided subcaudals. A summary of the variations found in selected scale characteristics for members of this genus is presented in Table 28.

The inverted hemipenes in *Bothriechis* extend the length of 6–9 subcaudals and are bifurcated with a divided sulcus spermaticus. Each lobe is usually subcylindrical or, rarely, tapered. The proximal portion of the hemipenes bears large spines, with minor interspecific variation in number. Most species have 16–24 enlarged spines; however, *B. lateralis* possesses only 10–12. Distally the organ is capitate with papillate calyces. *Bothriechis nigroviridis* and *B. schlegelii* have enlarged mesial spines flanking the crotch as do many species of *Bothrops*.

Six of the seven species within this genus are confined to montane regions lying between the Isthmus of Tehuantepec, Mexico, and central Panama; *B. schlegelii* ranges from southern Mexico to central Ecuador in moist lowlands and foothills.

Bites result primarily in pain, swelling bleb formation, ecchymosis, and occasionally necrosis. Morbidity is generally less than with bites by *Bothrops* species, and mortality is unusual. Bites to hands, fingers, and occasionally the face are more common owing to the snakes' arboreal habits. Necrosis of a digit with contracture or amputation is the most common serious result. However, a fatal bite delivered to the tongue by *B. schlegelii* has been reported.

Members of this genus are referred to as palm-pitvipers in allusion to the habit of some species of coiling in low vegetation that includes small palms. See Mimics of Venomous Snakes for a discussion of harmless snakes with appearances similar to palm-pitvipers.

### ***Bothriechis aurifer*** **(Salvin)**

(Figs. 121, 122; Map 44)

LOCAL NAMES Guatemala: cantil loro, cantil verde, gushnayera, ic bolay, tamagás verde, víbora del árbol, víbora verde. Mexico: nauyaca manchada, nauyaca verdinegra.

ENGLISH NAME Yellow-blotched palm-pitviper.

DISTRIBUTION Disjunct in highland regions: moderate and intermediate elevations of extreme west-central Chiapas, Mexico (vicinity of Lagunas de Montebello, higher tributaries of the Río Lacantum); the Atlantic drainages of the Sierra de los Cuchumatanes, Sierra de Chuacús, and Sierra de las Minas in Guatemala. The vertical distribution is generally from 1,200 to 2,300 m, but a few specimens have been reported from lower elevations on the north face of the Sierra de las Minas (see Map 44).

HABITAT This species is most abundant in lower montane rainforest (cloud forest), but it enters subtropical wet forest (pine-oak forest) along mesic ravines.

DESCRIPTION A relatively slender, green, prehensile-tailed pitviper, *B. aurifer* occasionally exceeds 1 m in total length (UTA R-13616, 1,010 mm), but is usually less than 700 mm.

The dorsum usually has black-bordered yellow blotches with an irregular, often broken, black dorsal stripe intervening between the blotches (Fig. 121). The venter frequently is paler than the dorsum and is yellowish green. The iris is most commonly yellowish green (occasionally bronze) with black specks or reticulations. Juveniles have a pale lime green ground color and a yellow or chartreuse tail tip. Over 90% of known specimens possess some dark dorsal pattern, but specimens may be encountered that have a uniformly green dorsum and lack dark postocular stripes.

This species has 1–5 intersupraoculars, 8–12 supralabials, 9–13 infralabials, 18–21 (mode 19) midbody dorsal scale rows, 150–166 ventrals, and 44–66 mostly undivided subcaudals.

**Table 28**
Variation of selected scale characteristics in members of the genus *Bothriechis*

| *Species* | *Intersupraoculars* | *Supralabials* | *Infralabials* | *Ventrals* | *Subcaudals* | *Midbody dorsal scale rows (mode)* |
|---|---|---|---|---|---|---|
| *B. aurifer* | 1–5 | 8–12 | 9–13 | 150–166 | 44–66 | 18–21 (19) |
| *B. bicolor* | 7–11 | 9–12 | 10–13 | 160–175 | 58–72 | 21 |
| *B. lateralis* | 4–10 | 8–11 | 10–13 | 157–171 | 54–70 | 21–23 (23) |
| *B. marchi* | 3–7 | 9–12 | 10–13 | 156–174 | 55–69 | 19–21 (19) |
| *B. nigroviridis* | 4–8 | 8–11 | 8–12 | 139–158 | 47–58 | 17–21 (19) |
| *B. rowleyi* | 3–5 | 9–10 | 9–12 | 154–163 | 53–66 | 19 |
| *B. schlegelii* | 5–10 | 7–10 | 8–12 | 137–169 | 42–64 | 21–25 (23) |

*Note.* For additional information refer to individual species accounts.

SIMILAR SPECIES The only other venomous snakes with which this species may be confused are *B. bicolor* and possibly *B. schlegelii*. *Bothriechis aurifer* may be distinguished from *B. bicolor* and *B. schlegelii* by the presence of enlarged, irregularly arranged dorsal head scales that are often somewhat flattened (rather than small, keeled scales). *Bothriechis bicolor* lacks postocular stripes and a dorsal pattern, and *B. schlegelii* in Guatemala and southern Mexico possesses orange or red ventrolateral blotches, a checkered or mottled venter, and raised spinelike superciliaries. Members of the relatively harmless genera *Drymobius* (Fig. 539), *Leptophis* (Fig. 541), and *Oxybelis* (Fig. 543) also may be green, but are distinguished easily from *B. aurifer* by the presence of 9 large head plates, divided subcaudals, and the absence of a facial pit.

REMARKS Although this is an arboreal species, it is encountered frequently on the ground or in low vegetation (up to 1.5 m). It appears to be most active by day. This species has a limited distribution, but may be not uncommon within virgin forest. This snake is known to have caused fatalities in Guatemala.

REFERENCES Alvarez del Toro, 1983; Bogert, 1968; Bolaños, 1982; Boulenger, 1896; Campbell, 1982b; Cope, 1887; Günther, 1895–1902; Martín del Campo, 1938a, 1950; Mocquard, 1908–1909; F. Müller, 1878; P. Müller, 1973; Rodas, 1938; Salvin, 1860; Slevin, 1939; H. M. Smith, 1941a; H. M. Smith and Moll, 1969; H. M. Smith and Taylor, 1945; Stuart, 1943, 1948, 1950, 1963; Werner, 1896, 1922.

## *Bothriechis bicolor* (Bocourt)

(Figs. 123, 124; Map 46)

LOCAL NAMES Guatemala: gushnayera, víbora romana (Suchitepéquez), víbora verde. Mexico: nauyaca bicolor , nauyaca verde.

ENGLISH NAME Guatemalan palm-pitviper.

DISTRIBUTION *Bothriechis bicolor* occupies moderate and intermediate elevations along the Pacific versant of the southern Volcanic Cordillera of Guatemala from the Volcán de Agua westward to Cerro Ovando in southeastern Chiapas, Mexico. It has also been taken from several localities in Honduras, including the Sierra de Merendón and the Cerro Santa Bárbara (see Map 46). It may occur locally in small portions of southeastern Guatemala and adjacent El Salvador. The vertical distribution is from 500 to 2,000 m; this species is now rare in lower portions of its range owing to habitat destruction.

HABITAT Lower montane wet forest and lower montane moist forest.

DESCRIPTION This relatively slender, green, prehensile-tailed pitviper may reach 1 m in total length, but is generally 600–700 mm.

The top of the head is uniformly green and a black postocular stripe is absent. The dorsum is green or bluish green and is usually without any pattern, but occasional specimens from Mexico and Honduras may possess dorsal black markings in the form of dots or flecks and/or blue blotches. The interstitial skin and borders of some scales are often blue. The venter is somewhat paler than the dorsum and is generally a uniform yellowish green. The iris is green with black reticulations and the tip of the tail may be black or gray, especially in smaller specimens. Juveniles tend to be paler than adults and are generally yellow-green, but rarely they may be brown.

This species has 7–11 intersupraoculars, 9–12 supralabials, 10–13 infralabials, 21 midbody dorsal scale rows, 160–175 ventrals, and 58–72 undivided subcaudals.

SIMILAR SPECIES *Bothriechis bicolor* may be distinguished from *B. aurifer*, *B. marchi*, and *B. rowleyi* by having numerous small keeled intersupraoculars. It differs from *B. schlegelii* in lacking raised spinelike superciliaries, any ventral pattern, and ventrolateral blotches.

Other green snakes that occur within the range of *B. bicolor* but are relatively harmless colubrids include *Drymobius chloroticus* (Fig. 539), *Leptophis ahaetulla* (Fig. 541), and *Oxybelis fulgidus* (Fig. 543).

REMARKS The habits of this snake remain virtually unknown. We infrequently have observed it active by day. Specimens have been encountered coiled in low streamside vegetation and in coffee trees. One of its local names in Guatemala, gushnayera, is derived from its purported habit of commonly being found coiled in the *gushnay* plant (family Araceae). *Bothriechis ornatus* appears to be a junior synonym of *B. bicolor*. The venom of *B. bicolor* has never been examined.

REFERENCES Alvarez del Toro, 1983; Bocourt, 1868; Bogert, 1968; Bolaños, 1982, 1983; Boulenger, 1896; Campbell, 1982b; Cope, 1887; Greene, 1972; Günther, 1895–1902; Juliá-Zertuche and Varela-J., 1978; Martín del Campo, 1950; Meyer, 1969; Meyer and Wilson, 1971; Mocquard, 1908–1909; F. Müller, 1878; Noguchi, 1909; H. M. Smith, 1941a; H. M. Smith and Moll, 1969; H. M. Smith and Taylor, 1945; Stuart, 1963; Werner, 1896, 1922; Wilson, 1983; Wilson and Meyer, 1985.

### *Bothriechis lateralis* Peters

(Figs. 125–128; Map 43)

LOCAL NAMES Costa Rica and Panama: lora. Nicaragua: chocoya, lora.

ENGLISH NAME Side-striped palm-pitviper.

DISTRIBUTION Moderate and intermediate elevations from the Cordillera de Tilarán in Costa Rica, across the Cordillera Central and Cordillera de Talamanca to the provinces of Chiriquí and Veraguas, Panama (Map 43). The vertical distribution ranges from 850 to 1,980 m.

HABITAT Lower montane moist and wet forests, and rainforest.

DESCRIPTION This relatively slender, green, prehensile-tailed pitviper may exceed 1,000 mm in total length, but is generally less than 700 mm.

The dorsum of the head is uniformly green, but a blue or blue-gray postocular stripe may be present; if so, it is weakly defined, especially in large adults. The dorsum is emerald or bluish green, usually with alternating or opposite paravertebral vertical bars. The venter is uniformly yellowish green, bordered by paraventral stripes that involve the lower portion of the paraventral scale row and the extreme lateral portions of the ventrals. The iris is yellow. Typically, a juvenile is brown, with dark brown head markings, postocular stripes, and paravertebral markings; a bronze iris; and a yellow or chartreuse tail tip.

There are 4–10 intersupraoculars, 8–11 supralabials, 10–13 infralabials, 21–23 (mode 23) midbody dorsal scale rows, 157–171 ventrals, and 54–70 subcaudals.

SIMILAR SPECIES In *Bothriechis marchi* pale paraventral markings and postocular stripes are absent, there are usually 19 midbody dorsal scale rows (rather than 21–23), and juveniles have a black tail tip. *Bothriechis nigroviridis* differs from *B. lateralis* by having the green ground color strongly mottled or speckled with black; pale green, black-edged dorsal blotches; a venter mottled with black; the top of the head with black markings, including well-defined postocular stripes and often parietal stripes; an essentially black iris; an absence of yellow paravertebral bars; usually fewer than 158 ventrals; and a black tail tip in juveniles. *Bothriechis schlegelii* differs from *B. lateralis* in possessing raised spinelike superciliaries and usually having parietal and occipital blotches, well-defined postocular stripes, and a venter that is distinctly mottled, stippled, or blotched (for variation in color pattern, see the species account and Figs. 138–146).

REMARKS This species frequently is found coiled in vegetation along or over watercourses. It appears to be most abundant between 1,200 and 1,800 m.

REFERENCES Amaral, 1927c; Bogert, 1968; Bolaños, 1971, 1982, 1983, 1984; Boulenger, 1896; Campbell, 1982b; Cendrero et al., 1972; H. C. Clark, 1942; Cope, 1876a, 1887; Duke, 1967; Dunn, 1940a, 1947; Elton, 1948; Grocott and Sadler, 1958; Groombridge, 1986; Günther, 1895–1902; Gutiérrez et al., 1979; Mocquard, 1908–1909; C. W. Myers, 1969; Nemuras, 1967; Noguchi, 1909; W. C. H. Peters, 1863; Picado, 1930, 1931; Savage, 1980; Scott, 1969; E. H. Taylor, 1951, 1954; R. T. Taylor et al., 1974; Timmerman and Hayes, 1981; Trejos, 1937; R. W. Van Devender, 1980; Villa, 1962, 1984; Walters, 1953; Werner, 1922.

### *Bothriechis marchi* (Barbour and Loveridge)

(Figs. 129–131; Map 44)

LOCAL NAMES Honduras: tamagá verde. Nicaragua: chocoya, lora, víbora de las palmas.

ENGLISH NAME March's palm-pitviper.

DISTRIBUTION *Bothriechis marchi* frequents low, moderate, and intermediate elevations of the Atlantic drainage of Honduras. It is known from the Sierra de Omoa, Sierra de Espíritu Santo, Cerro Santa Bárbara, Sierra de Nombre de Dios, and the Sierra de Sulaco. The Sierra de Espíritu Santo lies on the Guatemalan-Honduran border and it is probable that this species occurs in Guatemala in the mesic forests that flank the lower Río Motagua Valley to the south. This species probably also occurs in eastern Honduras in some of the higher, relatively unexplored ranges such as the Sierra de Agalta, and apparently occurs as far south as the Cordillera de Isabelia in Nicaragua (Map 44). Its vertical distribution is from about 500 to over 1,500 m. A few specimens have been reported from near sea level; we suspect that these either represent localized populations or, more likely, bear erroneous locality data.

HABITAT Rainforest, lower montane wet forest, and cloud forest.

DESCRIPTION A relatively slender, green, arboreal, and prehensile-tailed pitviper, this snake frequently exceeds 800 mm in total length; the longest known specimen measures 968 mm.

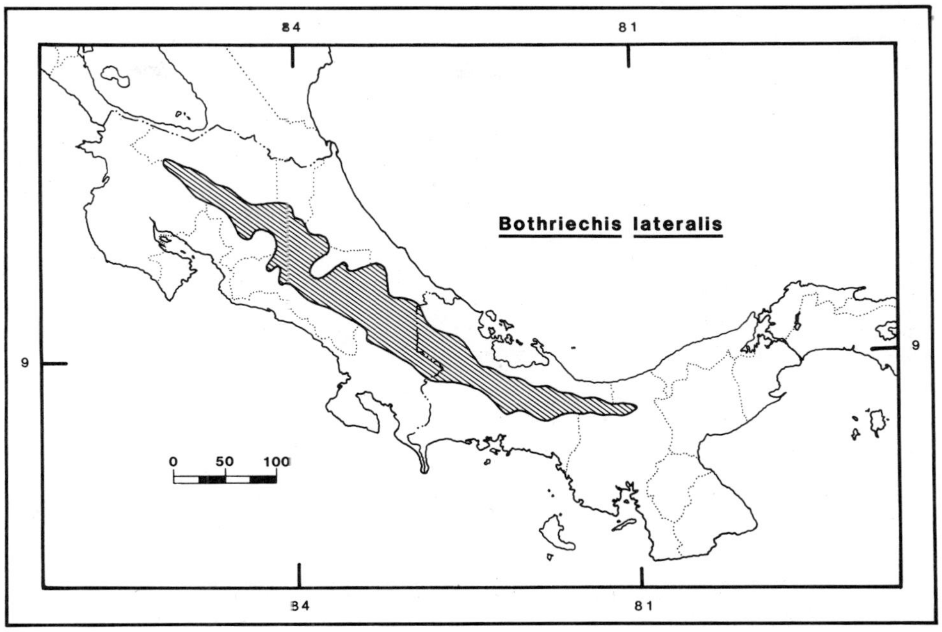


**Map 43.** Distribution of *Bothriechis lateralis* in Costa Rica and Panama.

The head and dorsum of adults are essentially uniformly green, blue-green, or yellowish green, although a few specimens possess dorsals outlined in black, and others have irregular blue or yellowish green mottling on dorsals. There is no postocular stripe, or, if present, it is faintly indicated and blue-green. The venter is uniformly yellow, yellowish green, or blue-green. The iris is yellow to yellowish green.

Juveniles may have either a yellowish green (Fig. 130) or pale brown dorsum (Fig. 131) with blue or dark brown head markings, postocular stripes, and paravertebral blotches; the iris is bronze and the tip of the tail is dark green or black.

There are 3–7 intersupraoculars, 9–12 (mode 10) supralabials, 10–13 (generally 11 or 12) infralabials, 19–21 (mode 19) midbody dorsal scale rows, 156–174 ventrals, and 55–69 subcaudals.

SIMILAR SPECIES *Bothriechis bicolor* is generally similar to *B. marchi* but differs in having a green iris (rather than yellow or greenish yellow), more numerous intersupraoculars that are distinctly keeled (rather than smooth), and 21 midbody dorsal scale rows (rather than usually 19). *Bothriechis aurifer*, *B. lateralis*, and most *B. schlegelii* specimens differ from *B. marchi* in possessing, respectively, a distinctive pattern of black-and-yellow dorsal markings, yellow paraventral stripes, and alternating yellow and reddish brown blotches on the

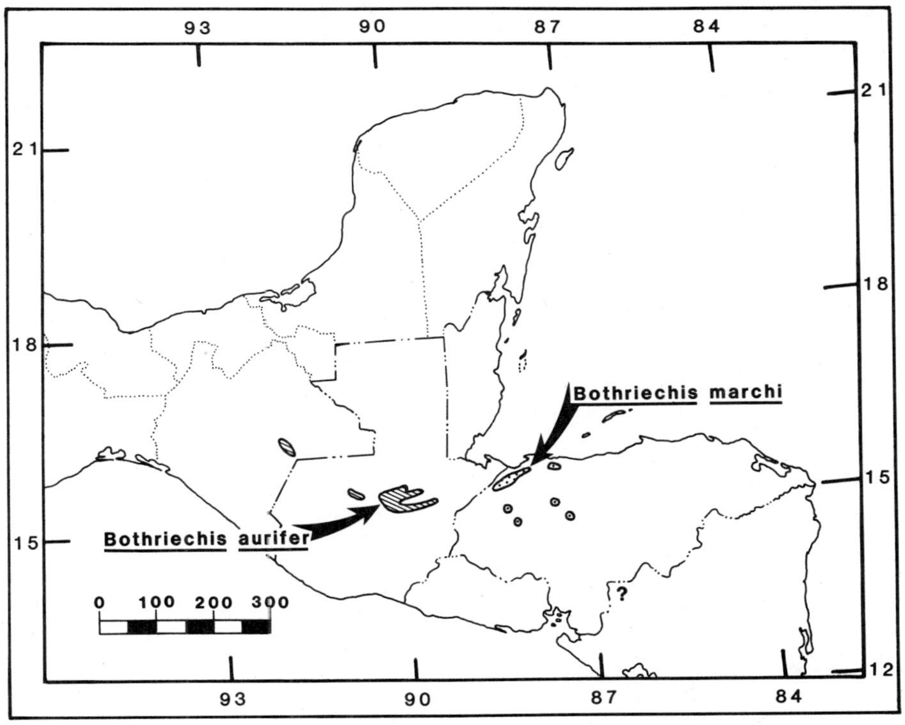


**Map 44.** Distributions of *Bothriechis aurifer* (*diagonal lines*) and *B. marchi* (*stipples*) in Nuclear Central America.

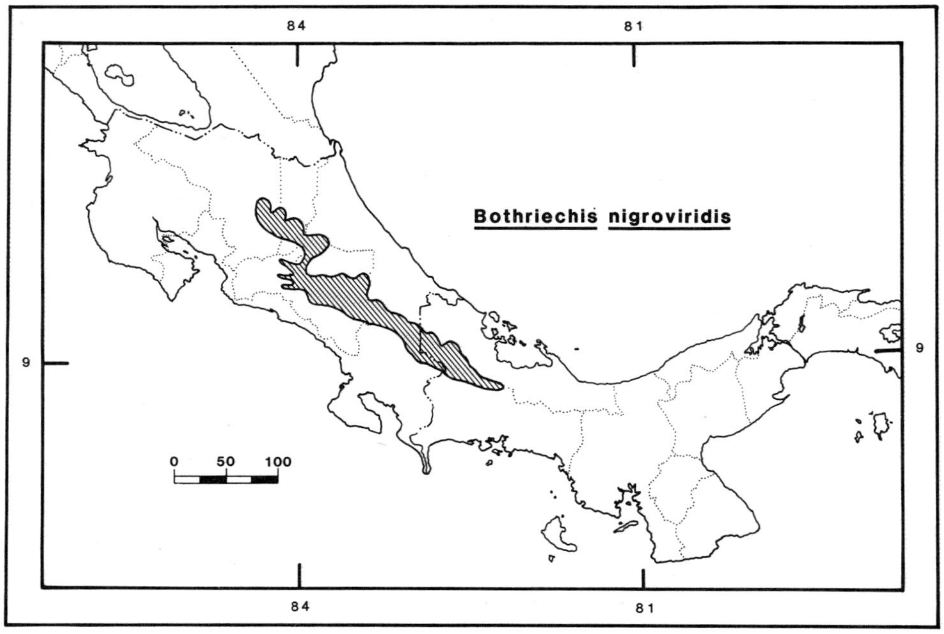


**Map 45.** Distribution of *Bothriechis nigroviridis* in Costa Rica and Panama.

lower dorsals that extend onto the ventrals. *Bothriechis lateralis* and *B. schlegelii* usually have 23 midbody dorsal scale rows (rather than 19).

REMARKS The local name *tamagá verde* is applied widely in Honduras to many kinds of green snakes, most of which are not dangerous, including members of the genera *Drymobius* (Fig. 539), *Leptophis* (Fig. 541), and *Oxybelis* (Fig. 543).

Three fatalities have been reported in Honduras from bites by this snake. A patient who recovered had symptoms that included severe swelling, intense pain, difficulty in breathing, dizziness, and exhaustion.

REFERENCES Barbour and Loveridge, 1929b; Campbell, 1982b; P. J. Clark and Inger, 1942; George, 1930b; March, 1929b; Meyer, 1969; Rokosky, 1942; Villa, 1962, 1984; Wilson and Meyer, 1985.

### *Bothriechis nigroviridis* Peters

(Figs. 132, 133; Map 45)

LOCAL NAMES Costa Rica: víbora de árbol.

ENGLISH NAME Black-speckled palm-pitviper.

DISTRIBUTION This species occurs at intermediate and high elevations from the Cordillera Central in southeastern province of Alajuela, Costa Rica, southeastward through the Cordillera de Talamanca to the province of Chiriquí, Panama (Map 45). It inhabits both the Atlantic and Pacific drainages. Its vertical distribution is from 1,150 to over 2,400 m.

HABITAT Lower montane wet forest, cloud forest, and high montane forest.

DESCRIPTION *Bothriechis nigroviridis* is a relatively slender, green, prehensile-tailed pitviper. Although it may exceed 800 mm in total length, it is more commonly less than 600 mm.

The top of the head is heavily mottled with black, and black parietal stripes often are present. A well-defined black postocular stripe extends from behind the eye to the angle of the jaw. The dorsum is generally emerald green (rarely yellowish green) and strongly mottled with black. Pale green, black-edged dorsal blotches may be present. The venter is yellowish green and lightly mottled with black. The iris is so heavily stippled as to appear black. Juveniles possess a similar pattern to that of adults, but may be slightly paler and have a black tail tip.

There are 4–8 intersupraoculars, 8–11 supralabials (usually 9 or 10), 8–12 infralabials (generally 10), 17–21 (mode 19) midbody dorsal scale rows, 139–158 ventrals, and 47–58 subcaudals (there is a single record of 62 subcaudals).

SIMILAR SPECIES *Bothriechis lateralis* may be distinguished from this species by possessing a distinct yellow ventrolateral stripe, a yellow iris, a green ground color that is not strongly suffused with black, yellow paravertebral vertical bars, a yellow (rather than black) tail tip in juveniles, the absence of a black postocular stripe, usually a greater number of ventrals (157 or more) and subcaudals (54 or more), and usually more midbody dorsal scale rows (mode 23). *Bothriechis schlegelii* differs from *B. nigroviridis* in having distinctly raised superciliary scales forming eyelashes and usually 23 middorsal scale rows and usually 8 (rather than 9 or 10) supralabials. The yellow (oropel) phase of *B. schlegelii* cannot be confused easily with any other snake owing to its remarkable coloration. Patterned *B. schlegelii* differ from *B. nigroviridis* in usually having reddish brown dorsal blotches, a reddish brown postocular stripe (rather than black), a venter that is distinctly speckled or mottled with reddish brown and yellow, and juveniles with a yellow tail tip (rather than black).

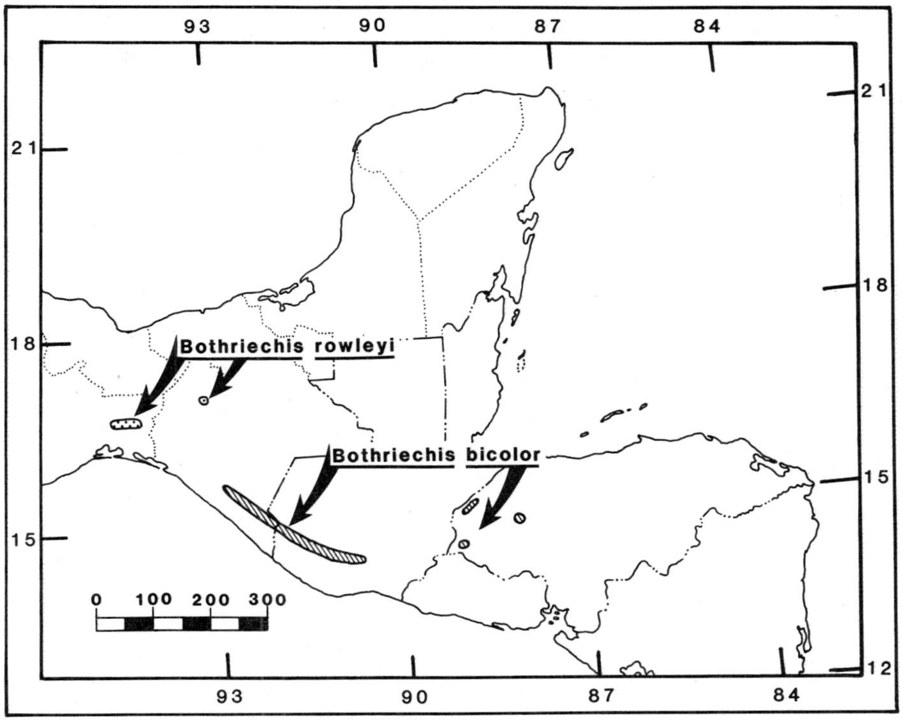


**Map 46.** Distributions of *Bothriechis bicolor* (*diagonal lines*) and *B. rowleyi* (*stipples*) in Nuclear Central America.

REMARKS This species has a limited range and is relatively rare. It appears to be most common in undisturbed habitat. This species has been implicated in human fatalities, and bites from *B. nigroviridis* are reported to cause intense pain, nausea, and asphyxia.


REFERENCES Bolaños, 1971, 1982, 1983, 1984; Boulenger, 1896; Campbell, 1982b; H. C. Clark, 1942; Cope, 1876a; Duke, 1967; Dunn, 1940a, 1947, 1951; Elton, 1948; Grocott and Sadler, 1958; Groombridge, 1986; Günther, 1895–1902; Gutiérrez et al., 1979; Mocquard, 1908–1909; P. Müller, 1973; C. W. Myers, 1969; Nemuras, 1967; Noguchi, 1909; Picado, 1930, 1931; Savage, 1980; Scott, 1969; E. H. Taylor, 1951, 1954; R. T. Taylor et al., 1974; Timmerman and Hayes, 1981; Trejos, 1937; R. W. Van Devender, 1980; Villa, 1984; Walters, 1953; Werner, 1922; Wettstein, 1934; Wilson, 1983.


## *Bothriechis rowleyi* (Bogert)

(Figs. 134–137; Map 46)

LOCAL NAMES Víbora de árbol, víbora verde.

ENGLISH NAME Rowley's palm-pitviper.

DISTRIBUTION *Bothriechis rowleyi* inhabits intermediate elevations of extreme southeastern Oaxaca, Mexico; these highlands include Cerro Baúl, Cerro Azul, and Cerro Atravesado. A single specimen known from the Selva Negra of the northern Chiapan highlands appears to be this species. Most of the range is on the Atlantic drainage, but the species also occurs sporadically on the Pacific versant (Map 46). Its vertical distribution is from 1,500 to 1,830 m.

HABITAT Cloud forest and mesic ravines in pine-oak forest.

DESCRIPTION This relatively slender, green, prehensile-tailed pitviper reaches at least 973 mm in total length (UTA R-22243).

This is essentially an all green snake. The dorsum is emerald green with blue interstitial skin; often blue blotches or rarely black and yellow markings are present (Figs. 134, 135, 137). The venter is uniformly yellowish green. The postocular stripe is absent. The iris is yellow. Juveniles are pale yellowish green with brown or purple dorsal blotches and a black tail tip (Fig. 136).

Characteristically there are 3–5 intersupraoculars, 9–10 supralabials, 9–12 infralabials, 19 midbody dorsal scale rows, 154–163 ventrals, and 53–66 undivided subcaudals.

SIMILAR SPECIES The only other species in Mexico with which this species may be easily confused are *B. bicolor*, which possesses more intersupraoculars (7–11), more midbody dorsal scale rows (21), and a green iris (rather than yellow); and *B. aurifer*, which usually has distinctive black-and-yellow dorsal markings, a well-defined black postocular stripe, a bronze or yellowish green iris, and a yellow tail tip in juveniles (rather than black).

REMARKS Almost all specimens of this snake have been collected in association with palm thickets on the moist, shaded slopes bordering ravines.

The venom of this rare snake has never been analyzed, but its bite is reported to be dangerous by persons living within its range.

We consider *Bothrops nigroviridis macdougalli* a synonym of *Bothriechis rowleyi*.


REFERENCES Bogert, 1968; Campbell, 1982b; Lynch and Smith, 1965, 1966; MacDougall, 1971; H. M. Smith and Moll, 1969.

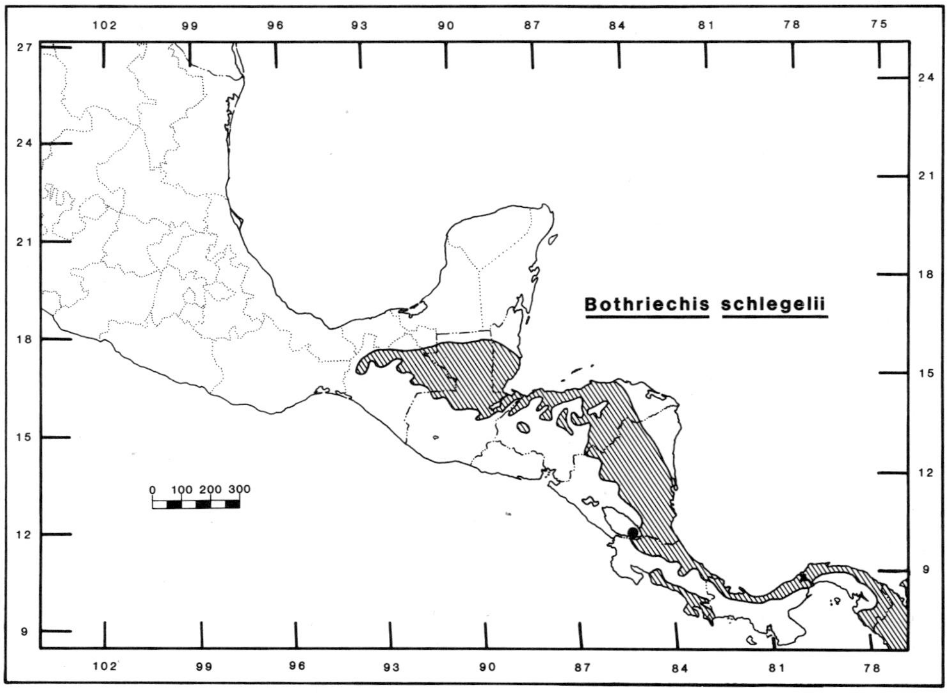


**Map 47.** Distribution of *Bothriechis schlegelii* in Mexico and Central America. The dot represents a record for an island in the Islas de Solentiname in Lake Nicaragua. For the continuation of this species' range into lower Central America and South America see Map 48.

## *Bothriechis schlegelii* (Berthold)

(Figs. 138–146; Maps 47, 48)

LOCAL NAMES Belize: green tommygoff. Colombia: birri, bocaracá, colgadora, flecha, jerga, manzanilla, mortiñera, muerde-hojas, pató (Urrao, Antioquia), patoco de pestaña, patuta, pauta víbora, pestañosa, piri, tiro, toboba de pestaña, veinticuatro, víbora, víbora cabeza de candado, víbora de tierra fría (Antioquia), víbora granadilla, víbora grano de oro, yaruma (Chocó). Costa Rica, Nicaragua, and Panama: bocaracá, culebra de cachitos, oropel, sleeping gough, terciopelo de pestaña. Ecuador: cordoncillo amarillo, cushuli, lora, papagayo, sura. Guatemala: chaj bolay, víbora del árbol. Mexico: nauyaca cornuda, nauyaca de pestañas. Venezuela: colgadora, mapanaré, mapanaré cejuda, mapanaré mariposa, pestañosa, víbora.

ENGLISH NAME Eyelash palm-pitviper.

DISTRIBUTION This species occupies low and moderate elevations of the Atlantic versant from northern Chiapas, Mexico, through southern Belize, northern Guatemala, Honduras, Nicaragua, and Costa Rica; and Panama (Map 47) into South America, where it ranges into western Venezuela and western Ecuador. In parts of Costa Rica, Panama, and northwestern South America, *B. schlegelii* occurs on the Pacific versant and coast (Map 48). There appears to be clinal variation in the upper vertical distributional limit of this species, with populations inhabiting higher elevations in the southern part of its range. In Mexico and Guatemala its vertical distribution is from near sea level to about 1,000 m, in Costa Rica from near sea level to about 1,500 m, and in Colombia from near sea level to at least 2,640 m.

HABITAT Tropical moist forest, wet subtropical forest (cloud forest), and montane wet forest.

DESCRIPTION This relatively slender, prehensile-tailed pitviper reaches a maximum overall length in excess of 800 mm, but is more commonly less than 600 mm.

In most populations the supraciliaries are raised into spinelike processes, but this is an extraordinarily variable species not only in scalation, but also in color and pattern. Members of a single population may exhibit several distinct color phases. The majority of specimens have a green, olive-green, or gray-green ground color finely suffused with black (Figs. 138, 139). There are distinct tan, brown, auburn, or rust-colored markings on the head, including paired parietal and occipital blotches and postocular stripes. The dorsum has a broken zig-zag stripe of similar color to the head markings that extends onto the tail. Additionally, there may be beige, yellow, or pink paravertebral markings on the body and tail arranged either opposite or alternate to one another. Small dark spots involving only 1 or 2 scales are present laterally. The gular region and anterior ventrals are immaculate or lightly pigmented. Distinctive alternating yellow and auburn ventrolateral blotches involving the first 2 scale rows and the lateral one-third of the ventrals extend the length of the body. The venter usually has an irregular arrangement of pale yellow spots owing to the irregular dense stippling. Laterally, the subcaudals are auburn or rust colored and the proximal portion of the tail often has a black-bordered midventral yellow stripe.

Specimens from Colombia and Venezuela resemble those described above, but frequently are much darker and possess dense black mottling (Fig. 142). Snakes from Ecuador frequently possess an uninterrupted ventrolateral white or yellow stripe on their bodies, which involves the first 2 scale rows (instead of alternating pale and dark blotches); the paravertebral blotches are arranged opposite one another and extend farther down

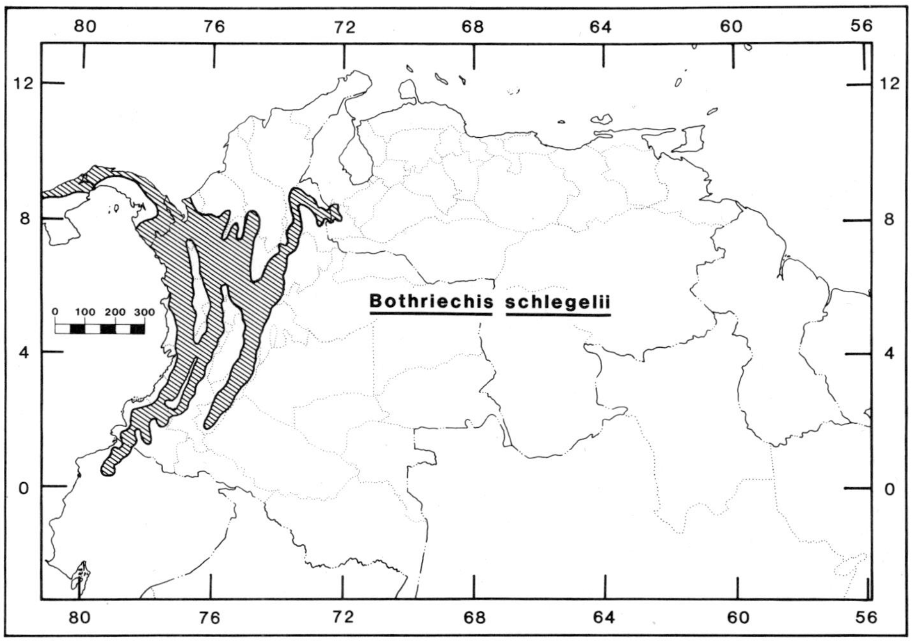


**Map 48.** Distribution of *Bothriechis schlegelii* in lower Central America and northwestern South America.

the side of the body (Fig. 146). The ventrals of Ecuadorian snakes are yellow and/or reddish brown with black stippling confined laterally.

The yellow phase or oropel is known from Honduras, Nicaragua, Costa Rica, and western Panama (Figs. 140, 141). These snakes have a bright golden yellow ground color, both dorsally and ventrally, which often is devoid of any distinct dorsal pattern, or there may be black flecks or dots scattered over the dorsum in varying degrees. Other specimens may have faint rust-colored zigzag patterns and postocular stripes. Rather uniformly colored salmon, dark golden, and rust-colored specimens are also known from various parts of the range, but they are not as common as the oropel phase. The iris is usually similar to the ground color.

The more salient features of scalation include 5–10 intersupraoculars, 7–10 supralabials, 8–12 infralabials, 21–25 (mode 23) midbody dorsal scale rows, 137–169 ventrals, and 42–64 mostly undivided subcaudals. The number of ventrals and subcaudals is clinal, with a lower number occurring in the southern portion of the range. The size of superciliaries tends to be reduced in Ecuadorian and some Colombian snakes (Figs. 145, 146).

SIMILAR SPECIES *Bothriechis schlegelii* may be distinguished from its congeners by its possession of raised superciliaries between the supraocular and the eye; in all but the uniformly colored yellow, salmon, and rust-colored snakes, the heavily pigmented or patterned venter is also distinctive. *Bothriopsis albocarinata*, *B. alticola*, and *B. bilineata* all have a green dorsum, but each may be distinguished easily from *B. schlegelii* on the basis of distribution and having divided subcaudals.

REMARKS This widespread snake is abundant in most parts of its range, but appears to be uncommon in Guatemala and southern Mexico.

*Bothrops supraciliaris* is a junior synonym of *B. schlegelii*.

REFERENCES Acosta-Solís, 1944; Alvarez del Toro, 1983; Amaral, 1925b, 1927c, 1927d, 1931b, 1937b; Antonio, 1980; Ayerbe et al., 1977, 1979; Bates, 1928; Berthold, 1846; Blanchard, 1889; Bolaños, 1971, 1982, 1983, 1984; Boulenger, 1896, 1898b; Brattstrom and Howell, 1954; Cendrero et al., 1972; Campbell, 1982b; H. C. Clark, 1925, 1942; Cope, 1860c, 1868, 1874, 1876a, 1887; Cuesta Terron, 1930a; Daniel, 1949, 1959; Despax, 1911; Ditmars, 1930; Duellman, 1963, 1979; Duke, 1967; Dunn, 1942, 1944a, 1944b, 1949; Dunn and Bailey, 1939; Dunn and Emlen, 1932; Dunn and Stuart, 1951; Eichelbaum, 1927; Elton, 1948; Gaige et al., 1937; García, 1896; Garman, 1884a; George, 1930b; Grocott and Sadler, 1958; Groombridge, 1986; Gutiérrez et al., 1979; Henderson and Hoevers, 1975; Heyer, 1967; Hoge and Lancini, 1962; Jan, 1859a; Klemmer, 1963; Lancini, 1970, 1979; Lee, 1980; Martín del Campo, 1935, 1950; Meyer, 1969; Mocquard, 1908–1909; P. Müller, 1973; C. W. Myers and Rand, 1969; Neill, 1960; Nemuras, 1967; Nicéforo-María, 1929b, 1930a, 1942; Noguchi, 1909; Orcés, 1942, 1943, 1948; Patzelt, 1979; Pérez-Santos, 1986a; Pérez-Santos and Moreno, 1986; J. A. Peters, 1960a; Picado, 1930, 1931; Pifano et al., 1950; Posada-Arango, 1889a, 1889b; Rendahl and Vestergren, 1940; Saavedra R. et al., 1975; Savage, 1980; Schmidt, 1933b, 1941; Scott, 1969; Seifert, 1983; H. M. Smith and Taylor, 1945; Steindachner, 1870; Stuart, 1963; E. H. Taylor, 1951, 1954; R. T. Taylor et al., 1974; Timmerman and Hayes, 1981; Trejos, 1937; Troschel, 1860; Vetencourt Finol., 1960; Villa, 1962, 1984; Werman, 1984a, 1984c; Werner, 1922; Wilson, 1983; Wilson and Meyer, 1985; Wettstein, 1934.

# Forest-Pitvipers

## Genus *Bothriopsis* Peters, 1861

The genus *Bothriopsis* (family Viperidae) includes eight species of small to large (sometimes exceeding 1,500 mm), moderately slender pitvipers, most of which show arboreal adaptations. These include a long prehensile tail and a cryptic color pattern that usually contains a considerable amount of green, with or without dark or pale markings.

Some of the more obvious characteristics of the genus are a normal snout with a well-defined canthus rostralis and a rostral that is either about as high as or higher than it is broad. The pupil of the eye is vertically elliptical. The scales on the crown of the head generally number from 5 to 9 (except in *B. medusa*, which has fewer). There are 6–9 supralabials, 8–12 infralabials, 19–29 midbody dorsal scale rows, 153–254 ventrals, and 41–91 subcaudals (most of which are usually divided, but this may vary considerably). A summary of the variations in these characteristics found among the members of this genus is given in Table 29.

The everted hemipenes of *B. bilineata* and *B. taeniata* extend 6–8 subcaudals; the organ is divided, with the sulcus spermaticus bifurcating at the level of subcaudals 1–2 and extending to the apices of each lobe. There are 30–40 large hooks on the basal part of the organ and proximal portions of the lobes; the size of the hooks diminishes distally. A number of moderate-sized hooks are present in the upper mesial area; the crotch is naked or has a few small spines. Each lobe is attenuated, and the distal half is calyculate. Micro-ornamentation of proximal calyces is spinulate; distal calyces are smooth.

Six of the eight species within this genus are confined to montane regions of Venezuela, Colombia, Panama, Ecuador, Peru, and Bolivia. *Bothriopsis bilineata* and *B. taeniata* have a similar distribution, but both species are absent from Panama and the Venezuelan Andes, and they occur in lowland regions throughout the Amazon Basin, including Brazil and the Guianas.

Members of this genus are referred to as forest-pitvipers because all *Bothriopsis* species appear to be confined to forests. See Mimics of Venomous Snakes for a discussion of harmless snakes with appearances similar to forest-pitvipers.

### ***Bothriopsis albocarinata*** **(Shreve)**

(Figs. 147, 148; Map 49)

LOCAL NAMES Loro mashaco, macanchillo, ysipi (validity of these names requires confirmation).

ENGLISH NAME Ecuadorian forest-pitviper.

DISTRIBUTION This species is known only from the eastern versant of the Andes of Ecuador in the provinces of Napo and Pastaza (Map 49). It has been collected near the headwaters of the Río Bobonaza and the Río Arajuno, and also from the Río Pastaza. *Bothriopsis albocarinata* is primarily an inhabitant of the high Andes and has a vertical distribution of 500 to over 3,000 m.

HABITAT The few recorded collecting localities are situated in cloud forest or upper rainforest.

DESCRIPTION *Bothriopsis albocarinata* is a moderately slender, small arboreal pitviper that reaches at least 659 mm in total length.

The dorsal ground color is dark to medium green and tends to become more obscure anteriorly. A black postocular stripe terminates at the rictus, and a parallel black stripe of about the same length extends from above the supraoculars to the angle of the jaws. The labials tend to be very dark green with no mottling. The dorsal pattern consists of a series of as many as 29 dark bands; those on the anterior portion of the body usually coalesce with one another. In some specimens, these bands have faint pale margins and they may have paler interspaces due to yellow pigment on the keels of the dorsals, but the amount of yellow pigment is highly variable and may be present on all dorsals or be entirely absent. Ventrally, the color is yellow with black mottling that usually increases posteriorly to such a degree that the tail is uniformly dark. The chin region is usually pale, with the exception of the infralabials. The tail tip is sometimes paler than the adjacent portion, and it has a rounded terminal spine.

This species has 5–6 intersupraoculars, 7–9 (usually 7) supralabials (the second fused with the prelacunal), 8–10 infralabials, 19–21 (usually 21) midbody dorsal scale rows, 167–181 ventrals, and 53–64 subcaudals (usually some of the distal ones are divided, but the number of divided subcaudals varies considerably).

SIMILAR SPECIES Other species of *Bothriopsis* that have distributions overlapping that of *B. albocarinata* are *B. bilineata* and *B. taeniata*. In *B. bilineata* there are 23–35 midbody dorsal scale rows, a distinct white or yellow ventrolateral line, and a pale green dorsum with no crossbands. *Bothriopsis taeniata* has 25–29 midbody dorsal scale rows, 203–254 ventrals, and cream-colored

**Table 29**

Variation of selected scale characteristics in members of the genus *Bothriopsis*

| *Species* | *Intersupraoculars* | *Supralabials* | *Infralabials* | *Ventrals* | *Subcaudals* | *Midbody dorsal scale rows (mode)* |
|---|---|---|---|---|---|---|
| *B. albocarinata* | 5–6 | 7–9 | 8–10 | 167–181 | 53–64 | 19–21 (21) |
| *B. alticola* | 5 | 7 | — | 178 | 63+ | 19 |
| *B. bilineata* | 5–9 | 7–9 | 8–12 | 192–220 | 55–76 | 23–35 (27) |
| *B. medusa* | 1–6 | 6–9 | 8–10 | 153–168 | 46–62 | 20–21 |
| *B. oligolepis* | 5–7 | 7–8 | 10–11 | 178–192 | 41–63 | 23–25 |
| *B. peruviana* | 7–8 | 7–8 | 9–10 | 188–196 | 53–66 | 23 |
| *B. punctata* | 6–9 | 7–9 | 10–12 | 195–207 | 70–95 | 25–29 (27) |
| *B. taeniata* | 5–9 | 6–8 | 9–12 | 203–254 | 66–91 | 25–29 (27) |

*Note.* For additional information refer to individual species accounts.

ventrolateral spots. *Bothriopsis alticola* is not readily distinguishable from *B. albocarinata* (see Remarks for *B. alticola*). Species of the genus *Bothrops* found in the area include *B. atrox*, *B. lojanus*, and *B. microphthalmus*. *Bothrops atrox* has 23 or more midbody dorsal scale rows and is not green. *Bothrops lojanus*, which occurs on the western versant of the Andes, has fewer than 155 ventrals and fewer than 50 subcaudals. *Bothrops microphthalmus* has the second supralabial separated from the prelacunal, 137–173 ventrals, and 49–56 ventrals. The lower elevational limits for *Bothriopsis albocarinata* are not known reliably (see also the species accounts for *Bothrops brazili* and *Porthidium hyoprora*). See the description of *Bothriopsis alticola* for comments as to its status.

REMARKS The habits of this snake remain virtually unknown and few specimens exist in museum collections.

REFERENCES Carrillo de Espinoza, 1983; Duellman, 1979; Klemmer, 1963; Meneses, 1974a, 1974b; Parker, 1934; J. A. Peters, 1955, 1960a; J. A. Peters and Orejas-Miranda, 1970; Shreve, 1934; Touzet, 1983.

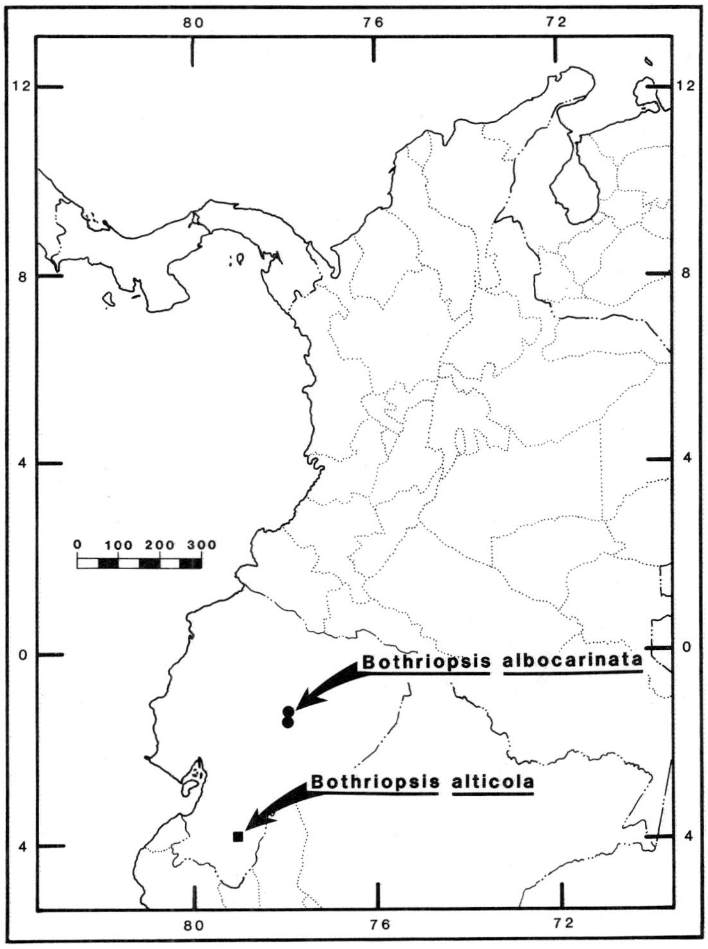


**Map 49.** Distributions of *Bothriopsis albocarinata* (dots) and *B. alticola* (square) in Ecuador.

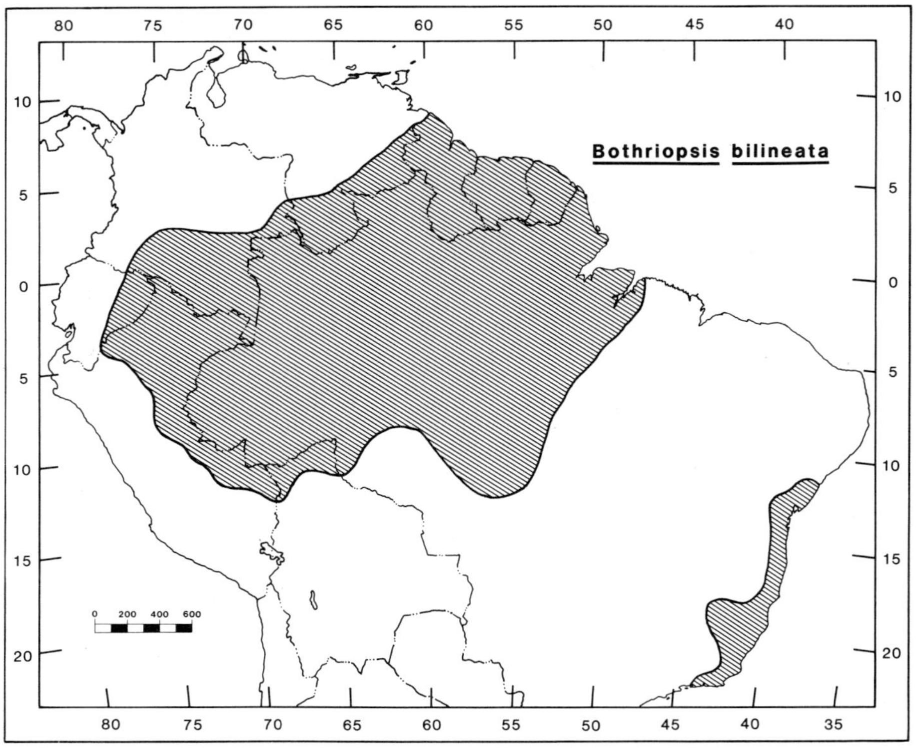


**Map 50.** Distribution of *Bothriopsis bilineata* in Amazonian South America and the coastal forest of Brazil.

### *Bothriopsis alticola* (Parker)

(Map 49)

LOCAL NAMES Loro mashaco, macanchillo, ysipi (exact usage of these names requires confirmation).

ENGLISH NAME Andean forest-pitviper.

DISTRIBUTION Ecuador. Known only from the type locality, 5 km east of Loja, province of Loja (see Map 49). The type locality is at about 2,800 m.

HABITAT Upper montane temperate forest. The Loja region is semi-arid, so *B. alticola* presumably occupies riparian situations.

DESCRIPTION This species is known only from the holotype, which measures 659 mm (tail incomplete) in length. *Bothriopsis alticola* is presumably an arboreal species.

The dorsum is greenish yellow with a series of transverse black spots that coalesce anteriorly and posteriorly but are distinct at midbody. A black postorbital stripe extends from behind the eye to the rictus, and a parallel black stripe begins posterior to the supraoculars. The dorsal spots are pale edged and appear to have pale centers owing to yellow pigment on the keel of each scale. Indistinct areas of dark pigment and yellow keels exist in the interspaces between the dorsal markings. The venter is yellow with black pigment increasing posteriorly. The distal fifth of the tail is pale (cream or perhaps pink).

There are 5 keeled intersupraoculars; 7 supralabials, the second integrated with the prelacunal; 19 midbody dorsal scale rows; 178 ventrals; and more than 62 subcaudals (tail incomplete), the first 20 of which are single and the remainder divided. The tail is prehensile.

SIMILAR SPECIES *Bothriopsis alticola* may be distinguished from all sympatric pitvipers by the following combination of characters: 19 midbody dorsal scale rows; second supralabial integrated with prelacunal; a green dorsum; and a prehensile tail. *Bothriopsis albocarinata* (see Remarks in that species account) is not readily distinguishable from *B. alticola*.

REMARKS During the same year that Parker (1934) described *B. alticola* from the Loja vicinity, Shreve (1934) described *B. albocarinata* from the "Río Pastaza, between Canelos and the Río Marañón." The two taxa overlap in virtually every scale characteristic and detail of pattern, and we suspect strongly that only a single species is represented.

REFERENCES Duellman, 1979; Klemmer, 1963; P. Müller, 1973; Orcés, 1948; Parker, 1934, 1938; J. A. Peters, 1955, 1960a; J. A. Peters and Orejas-Miranda, 1970; Shreve, 1934; Touzet, 1983.

### *Bothriopsis bilineata* (Wied)

(Figs. 149–151; Map 50)

LOCAL NAMES Bolivia: víbora loro. Brazil: cobra papagaio, cobra verde, jararaca-pinto-de-ouro, jararaca verde, mboi-hobú, ouriçana patioba, paraamboia, parauá-boi, surucucú de patioba, surucucú de pindoba, surucucú patioba boiubú. Colombia: lora. Ecuador: orito machácuy. Peru: loro machaco. Suriname: papegaaislang, popokaisneki. Venezuela: mapanare rayada, mapanare verde.

ENGLISH NAME Two-striped forest-pitviper.

DISTRIBUTION Amazonian Colombia, Ecuador, Peru, Bolivia, and Brazil; also the equatorial forests of Venezuela, the Guianas, and an isolated population in the Atlantic forests from the state of Bahía to the state of Río de Janeiro, Brazil (Map 50). The vertical distribution probably does not exceed 1,000 m.

HABITAT This species is most abundant in lowland rain forest, especially in close association with waterways.

DESCRIPTION A relatively slender, green, prehensile-tailed pitviper, *B. bilineata* occasionally reaches 1 m in total length, but is generally less than 700 mm.

The head is green with small black spots scattered throughout or, alternatively, green with isolated tan or reddish brown spots that are black bordered. A weakly defined postocular stripe that terminates at the angle of the mouth is sometimes present. The iris is pale green, and the labials are yellow green. The tongue is pinkish gray with dark gray tips. The dorsum is pale green, either lightly speckled with black or with a series of tan or reddish brown spots (usually paired) down the back (see Remarks). A creamy yellow line borders the ventrals on each side for the length of the snake. The ventrals are yellow with a green tinge on the edges. The distal portion of the tail is pink, bordered by yellow (one individual has been reported with a whitish yellow tail tip).

This species has 5–9 intersupraoculars, 7–9 supralabials, 8–12 infralabials, 23–35 midbody dorsal scale rows (see Remarks), 192–220 ventrals, and 55–76 (mostly divided) subcaudals.

SIMILAR SPECIES There is one other prehensile-tailed pitviper in South America that sometimes has a white or yellow line along the first row of dorsal scales, namely, *Bothriechis schlegelii*. This species may be distinguished from *Bothriopsis bilineata* by having undivided subcaudals and, usually, raised spinelike superciliaries. *Bothriechis schlegelii* has never been recorded reliably from the Amazonian slopes of the Andes and probably is nowhere sympatric with *B. bilineata*. In Ecuador, Peru, and Bolivia, there are four other "green" pitvipers: *Bothriopsis albocarinata*, *B. alticola*, *B. peruviana*, and *B. oligolepis*. However, all of these lack paraventral stripes and all have distinctive blotches on the dorsum. *Bothriopsis peruviana* sometimes has a series of large yellowish ventrolateral spots, but not stripes. *Bothriopsis taeniata* often appears green overall and has a ventrolateral row of spots (no stripes) along the first and second row of dorsals and the outer edges of the ventrals. Moreover, it has a distinctive and complex dorsal pattern. The only other slow-moving green arboreal snake with which *B. bilineata* might be confused is the nonvenomous emerald tree boa, *Corallus canina* (Fig. 538), which has smooth scales, sensory pits in the labials rather than a large loreal pit, and a red ground color in individuals less than 500 mm in total length.

REMARKS This is an arboreal species, most frequently encountered in shrubs, trees, and vines 1 m or more above the ground.

In a study of 93 cases of pitviper envenomation near Leticia, Colombia, 14 were by *B. bilineata*. The incidence of finger bites was high compared to *Bothrops atrox*, and one involved the face. Other results were not detailed. Published allegations of extreme toxicity for this species require substantiation.

Two subspecies of this snake are recognized: *Bothriopsis b. bilineata*, from the equatorial forests of Venezuela, the Guianas, and Brazil (including the Atlantic slopes), possesses vertical dark bars on the supralabials and tan or reddish brown spots with black specks on a green dorsum; *B. b. smaragdina*, from Amazonian Colombia, southern Venezuela, northern and western Brazil, Ecuador, Peru, and Bolivia, lacks dark vertical bars on the supralabials and has a green dorsum finely peppered with black. Specimens reported from Pará, Brazil, tend to have more middorsal scale rows (greater than 30) than other populations.

REFERENCES Amaral, 1926d, 1930b, 1930c, 1931c, 1938, 1978; Angel, 1983; Ayerbe, 1979; Boulenger, 1896; Brongersma, 1967; Campbell, 1973; Carrillo de Espinoza, 1970, 1983; Chippaux, 1987; Cope, 1870; Cunha, 1967; Cunha and Nascimento, 1975b, 1978; Cunha et al., 1985; Daniel, 1949; Dixon, 1979; Dixon and Soini, 1986; Duellman, 1978; Dunn, 1944a; Fonseca, 1949; Gasc and Rodrigues, 1980; Gliesch, 1925; Greene and Campbell, 1972; Groombridge, 1986; Günther, 1861; Hoge, 1964, 1966, 1967; Hoge and Lancini, 1962; Hoge and Romano, 1973; Hoge and Romano-Hoge, 1981a, 1981b; Hoogmoed, 1979, 1983; Kempff-Mercado, 1975; Lancini, 1970, 1979; Machado, 1945b; Medem, 1969; Meneses, 1974a, 1974b; Moonen, 1982; Moonen et al., 1978; P. Müller, 1971, 1973; Nahas et al., 1979; Nicéforo-María, 1942; Noguchi, 1909; Orcés, 1942, 1943, 1948; Orton, 1876; Parker, 1935; J. A. Peters, 1960a; J. A. Peters and Orejas-Miranda, 1970; Prado, 1945; Renjifo, 1979; Roze, 1966a, 1970a; Schulte, 1988; Silva Haad, 1982a, 1982b; Soini, 1974b; Tinoco, 1978; Touzet, 1983; Vetencourt Finol., 1960; Werner, 1922.

### *Bothriopsis medusa* (Sternfeld)

(Fig. 152; Map 51)

LOCAL NAMES mapanare tigrito, tigra mariposa, tigra veinticuatro, viejita.

ENGLISH NAME Venezuelan forest-pitviper.

DISTRIBUTION This species is endemic to the central range of the Cordillera de la Costa from Caracas to Valencia, Venezuela (Map 51). Its vertical distribution is from about 1,400 to over 2,000 m (there is an unverified report from 2,800 m).

HABITAT Lower montane wet forest and cloud forest, including areas of considerable cold.

DESCRIPTION *Bothriopsis medusa* is a moderately slender, apparently terrestrial pitviper. Overall lengths of adults commonly fall between 500 and 700 mm. The maximum size reported is 800 mm.

The overall ground color is tan, yellowish brown, gray, or olive. A dark postocular stripe stretches from the eye to the angle of the jaw, often coalescing with the first lateral body blotch, which is horizontally elongated; the postocular stripe is delimited dorsally by a pale narrow border. The pattern consists of a series of

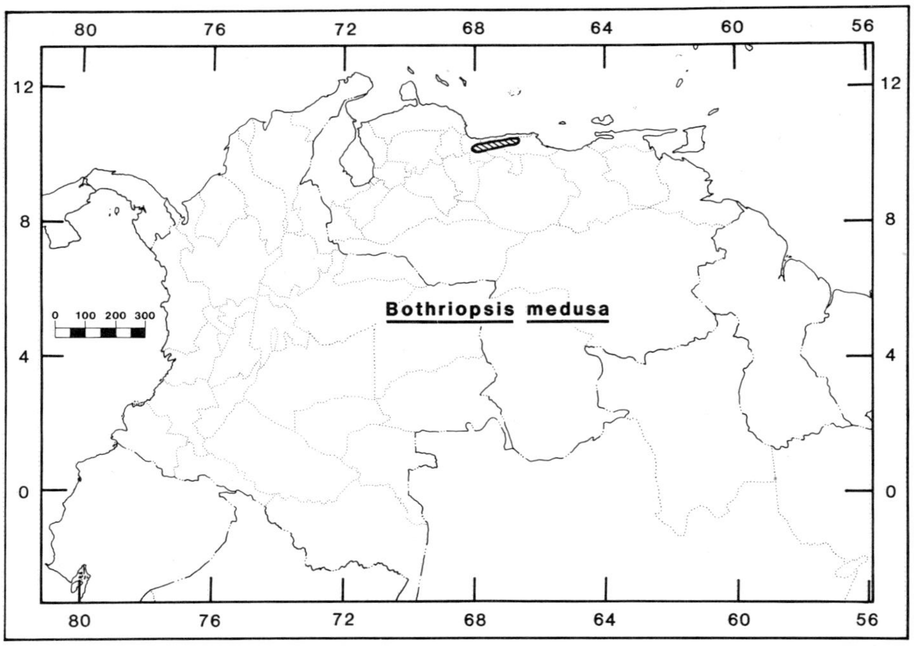


**Map 51.** Distribution of *Bothriopsis medusa* in the Cordillera de la Costa of northern Venezuela.

wide, irregular transverse bands that are dark brown with pale centers (reported to be more distinct in males). These bands are weakly subdivided laterally and are separated from one another by narrow pale interspaces. The contrast in some specimens is so poor that they may appear unicolored dorsally. The venter is yellow with numerous small blotches and specks of dark pigment.

The canthals, internasals, and rostral are distinctly raised into a canthal ridge. There are 1–6 intersupraoculars, 6–9 (usually 7) supralabials, 8–10 infralabials, 20 or 21 midbody dorsal scale rows, 153–168 ventrals, and 46–62 subcaudals (most of which are undivided).

SIMILAR SPECIES Throughout its range it is likely to be confused only with *Bothrops asper* or *Bothrops venezuelensis*. *Bothriopsis medusa* may be distinguished from both of these species by its lower number of ventrals (153–168 as opposed to usually more than 180). Two other members of the genus *Bothriopsis* occur in Venezuela—*B. bilineata* and *B. taeniata*—but *B. medusa* may be distinguished by its lower number of ventrals (153–168 as opposed to more than 190) and its markedly different distribution. Similar-appearing nonvenomous species include *Boa constrictor* (Fig. 547) and *Xenodon rabdocephalus* (Fig. 565).

REMARKS According to earlier accounts, *B. medusa* was not a rare snake; apparently, it occurred within the city limits of Caracas until recently. Nonetheless, it is very poorly known today, and published information is scant. It is now considered to be very rare, its low numbers perhaps owing to alteration of habitat. The venom is said to have a mild effect on humans.

*Bothrops eneydae*, described by Sandner-Montilla in 1976, strongly resembles *Bothriopsis medusa*. However, the status of *Bothrops eneydae* remains unresolved owing to insufficient data. We suspect that *Bothrops eneydae* will prove to be a junior synonym of *Bothriopsis medusa*.

REFERENCES Duellman, 1979; García-López and Sandner-Montilla, 1962; Hoge and Lancini, 1962; Lancini, 1970, 1979; Marcuzzi, 1950; Milá de la Roca, 1932; P. Müller, 1973; Pifano C. and Romer, 1949a; Roze, 1952, 1966a, 1970a; Sandner-Montilla, 1975, 1976, 1985a; Sternfeld, 1920; Vellard, 1941; Vetencourt Finol., 1960; Werner, 1922.

## *Bothriopsis oligolepis* (Werner)

(Figs. 153, 154; Map 52)

LOCAL NAMES Bolivia: yoperojobobo venenosa. Peru: jergón negro, lamón, loro machaco (?).

ENGLISH NAME Inca forest-pitviper.

DISTRIBUTION *Bothriopsis oligolepis* is known from the eastern versant of the Andes in Peru and Bolivia; there are several records from the Cordillera Central of Peru (Map 52). The vertical distribution is presumably from 1,000 to over 2,000 m above sea level.

HABITAT Cloud forest.

DESCRIPTION This moderately stocky, prehensile-tailed, medium-sized pitviper may exceed 1 m in length.

The dorsal surface of the head is primarily black, with pale green highlights on the canthals and supraoculars, and in the temporal region above the black postocular stripe. The labials and snout are green with black speckling. The iris is black with faint paler smudges. The dorsum is bright green, very heavily blotched and speckled with black, with 32–40 ill-defined black blotches that may or may not meet middorsally to form crossbands. These bands are bordered by bright green scales that are heavily speckled with black. Areas between the black bands are suffused with black, forming a secondary series of bands. The tail pattern is more condensed than that of the body, and the tail may have a yellow tip. Ventrally the chin is creamy yellow with black-and-

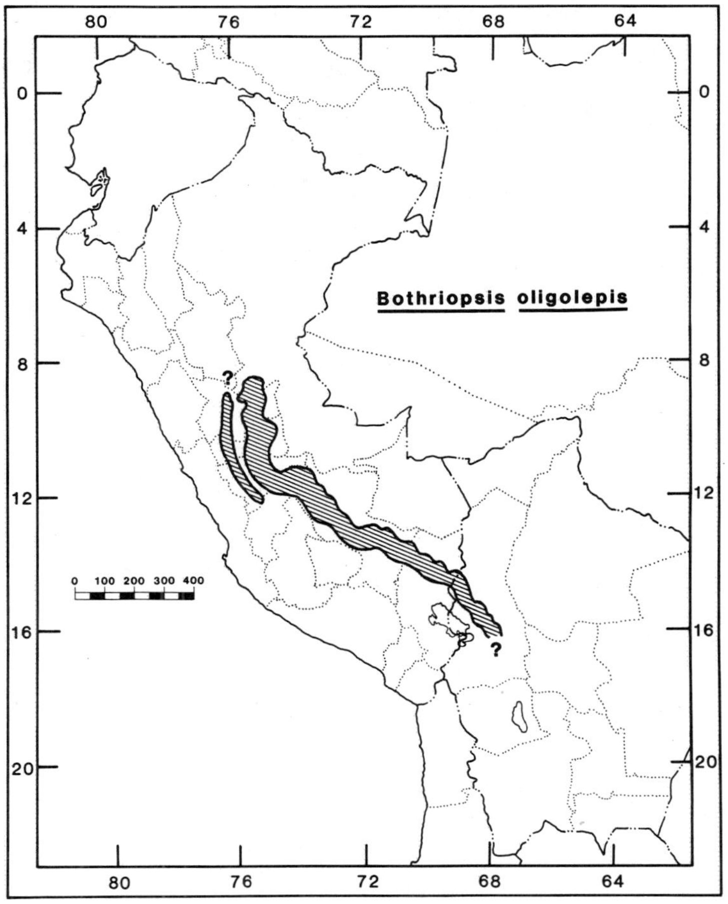


**Map 52.** Distribution of *Bothriopsis oligolepis* in Peru; the southern extent of its range in Bolivia is not known.

green speckling on the labials; the rest of the venter is creamy yellow with increasing black-and-green speckling posteriorly. The underside of the tail is similar to the ventrals, but paler toward the tip.

This species has 5–7 intersupraoculars, 7 or 8 supralabials, 10 or 11 infralabials, 23–25 midbody dorsal scale rows, 178–192 ventrals, and 41–63 subcaudals (mostly divided).

SIMILAR SPECIES *Bothriopsis oligolepis* may be distinguished from *B. bilineata* and *B. peruviana* by its high number of dark dorsal bands. It may be distinguished from *B. taeniata* by its lack of ventrolateral white spots and a lower number of dorsal scale rows. *Bothriopsis oligolepis* may further be distinguished from all of these species by its bluntly rounded snout.

REMARKS This is an extremely rare snake about which virtually nothing is known.

REFERENCES Amaral, 1926b, 1930a; Boulenger, 1912; Carrillo de Espinoza, 1983; Duellman, 1979; Dunn, 1946; Griffin, 1916; Meneses, 1974a, 1974b; Pifano C. and Romer, 1949a; Werner, 1901b, 1922.

## *Bothriopsis peruviana* (Boulenger)

(Figs. 155, 156; Map 53)

LOCAL NAMES Jergón, jergón negro (?), loro mashaco (?).

ENGLISH NAME Peruvian forest-pitviper.

DISTRIBUTION This species is currently known only from the Cordillera de Carabaya in southeastern Peru (northern Puno). It very likely occurs in the Cerros de Bala region of the Departamento de La Paz, Bolivia (Map 53). Its northwestern limits in Peru are unknown. Scant collecting records indicate *B. peruviana* to be a montane form, but its vertical distribution has not been established.

HABITAT Presumably wet montane forest.

DESCRIPTION A moderately slender, prehensile-tailed arboreal pitviper, *B. peruviana* reaches a length of at least 986 mm.

The ground color of the head and dorsum ranges from green to grayish green. The top of the head usually is crossed by a black band that curves back toward the rictus at either end. A well-defined black postorbital stripe terminates at the angle of the mouth and usually does not involve the supralabials. A black chevron, broken middorsally, forms a pair of blotches in the occipital region. These blotches sometimes are joined with a pair of dark spots on the dorsum of the neck, thus forming a pair of sinuous blotches that span the head-neck region. The iris is silvery green. The body pattern consists of a series of pairs of poorly defined yellowish white crossbands that are weakly bordered in black. This pattern tends to partially break up or fade anteriorly, thus resulting in spots of both colors. Sometimes a series of large

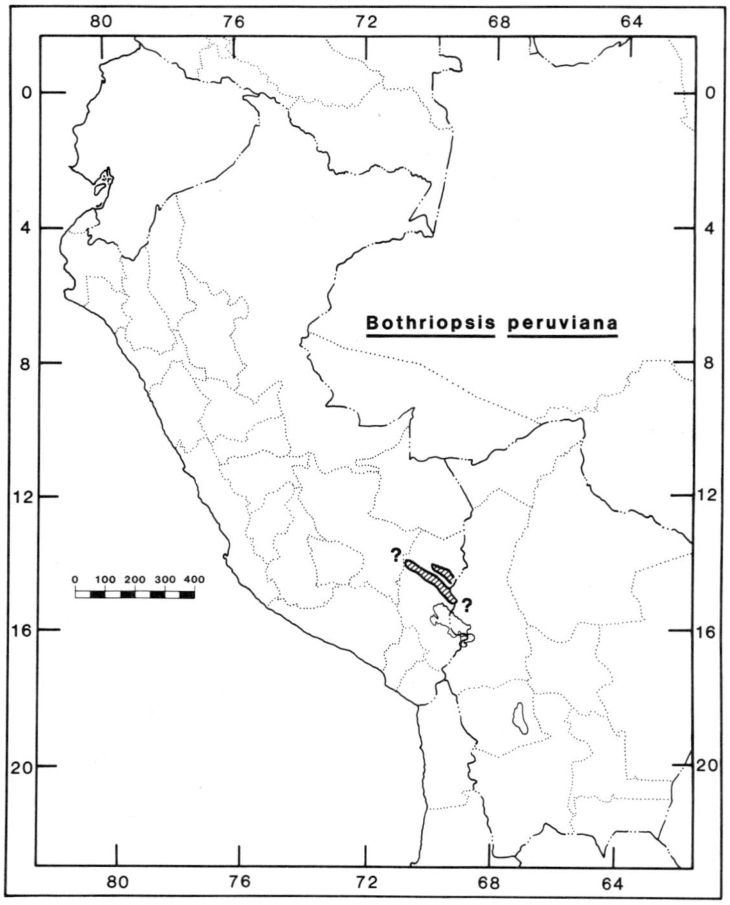


**Map 53.** Distribution of *Bothriopsis peruviana* in southeastern Peru; this species almost certainly occurs in Bolivia as well.

yellowish ventrolateral spots is present. The venter is yellow with pale green mottling. A black-edged, yellow streak occurs along either side of the tail. The distal third to half of the tail is pink with dark mottling.

There usually are 7 or 8 intersupraoculars, 7 or 8 supralabials (second integrated with the prelacunal), 9 or 10 infralabials, 23 midbody dorsal scale rows, 188–196 ventrals, and 53–66 subcaudals (mostly divided).

SIMILAR SPECIES Three members of the genus *Bothriopsis* might be found within the range of *B. peruviana*: *B. bilineata*, *B. oligolepis*, and *B. taeniata*. *Bothriopsis bilineata* has a distinct cream-colored ventrolateral stripe and a largely uniform dorsum, whereas *B. peruviana* lacks the stripe and has a banded dorsum. *Bothriopsis oligolepis* has 32–40 *black* crossbands dorsally, and a bluntly rounded snout, while *B. peruviana* has fewer than 20 *pale* crossbands and an obtusely acuminate snout. *Bothriopsis taeniata* has predominantly undivided subcaudals, a dorsal pattern that includes 30–40 black bands, a brightly speckled iris, and a long lance-shaped head, all unlike *B. peruviana*. *Bothrops atrox* has a variable dorsal coloration, but it is never green, and *Bothrops microphthalmus*, also a brown or gray species, has the second supralabial entirely separated from the prelacunal, which borders the loreal pit.

REMARKS This species is rare in collections. Nothing regarding its habits or habitat has been reported.

REFERENCES Amaral, 1930c; Boulenger, 1903; Carrillo de Espinoza, 1983; Meneses, 1974a, 1974b; J. A. Peters and Orejas-Miranda, 1970; Pifano C. and Romer, 1949a; Werner, 1922, 1927.

### *Bothriopsis punctata* (García)

(Figs. 157; Map 54)

LOCAL NAMES Colombia: cuatronarices, dormilona, flecha, mapanaré rabiseca, pelo de gato (Cauca and Nariño), rabiseca, rabo de chucha.

ENGLISH NAME Chocoan forest-pitviper.

DISTRIBUTION This species occupies the Pacific foothills and coastal plain from eastern Panama through western Colombia to northwestern Ecuador (Map 54). It is absent in the inter-Andean valleys and east of the Andes. In the Cordillera Occidental of Colombia, this species has been reported up to an elevation of 2,300 m, and we are aware of a specimen (Fig. 54) from near Urrao, Antioquia, Colombia, at 1,885 m.

HABITAT Subtropical moist and wet forests, tropical moist and wet forests, and montane wet forest.

DESCRIPTION This large, semiarboreal forest-pitviper commonly exceeds 1 m in overall length and may exceed 1,500 mm.

The top of the head is tan and symmetrically patterned

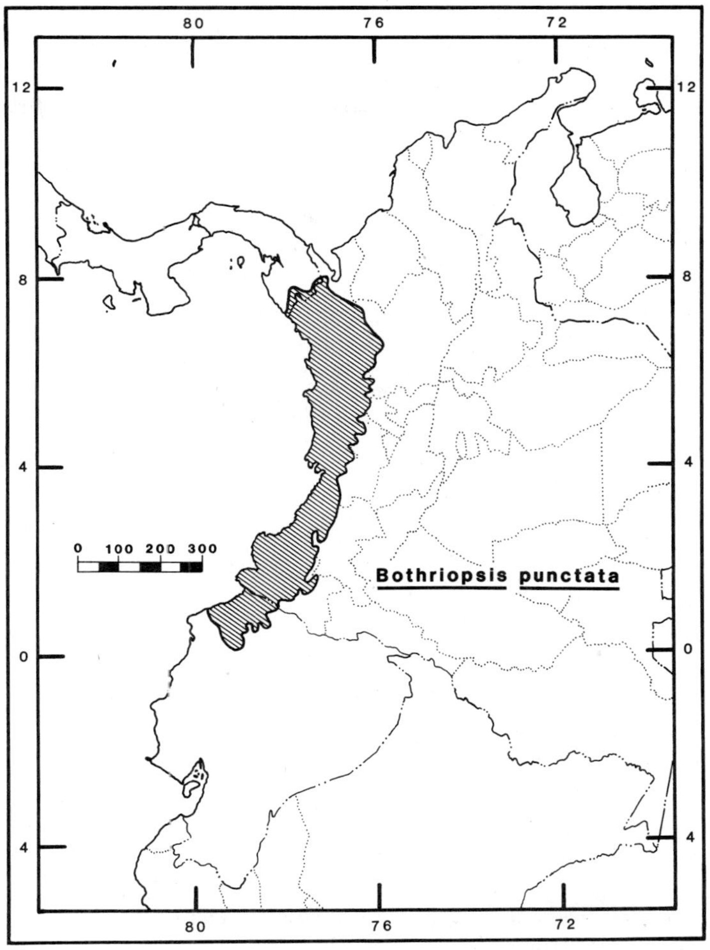


**Map 54.** Distribution of *Bothriopsis punctata* in extreme eastern Panama and northwestern South America.

with dark brown markings that extend from the prefrontal region to the occiput. A broad, dark brown postorbital stripe extends from the eye to the rictus and involves the upper portions of the posteriormost 2 or 3 supralabials. The postorbital stripe is darkest along its outer edges and is narrowly pale edged above and below. Supralabials are tan, sometimes with a narrow, dark brown vertical bar under the pit. Infralabials and gulars are pale tan to cream. The ground color is pale brown to greenish tan, with 16–22 pairs of darker brown, pale-edged paravertebral blotches, some of which are fused dorsally. These blotches are offset with lateral blotches, creating a semibanded appearance. A third series of dark ventrolateral blotches alternates with paler spots and extends onto the ventral scales. The venter is cream to pale tan with brown spots. The distal portion of the tail (often as much as one-half) is uniformly pale both dorsally and ventrally. The iris is bronze with darker reticulations, becoming paler along the periphery. Juveniles resemble adults in color and pattern.

There are 6–9 intersupraoculars; 7–9 supralabials, the second integrated with the prelacunal; 10–12 infralabials; 25–29 midbody dorsal scale rows; 195–207 ventrals; and 70–95 paired subcaudals, terminating in a long rounded tail spine that may turn up slightly at the tip.

SIMILAR SPECIES *Bothrops asper*, a highly variable species, may resemble *Bothriopsis punctata*, with which it is sympatric. *Bothriopsis punctata* differs from *Bothrops asper* by usually having a higher number of subcaudals 70–95 vs. 48–81), a prehensile tail that is pale distally in adults, rounded (rather than X-shaped) dorsal blotches, and an ornate pattern (rather than being uniformly brown) on top of the head. *Bothriopsis punctata* may be distinguished from *Bothrops microphthalmus*, *Bothrops pulcher*, and *Porthidium nasutum* by its higher number of ventral scales (more than 177). *Bothriopsis punctata* may be distinguished further from *Bothrops microphthalmus* by the condition of the second supralabial, which is fused with the prelacunal to form the anterior border of the loreal pit (i.e., a lacunolabial) in *Bothriopsis punctata*, but is not fused with the prelacunal in *Bothrops microphthalmus*. The arboreal pitviper *Bothriechis schlegelii* has supraciliaries with spinelike processes and undivided subcaudal scales. *Lachesis muta* has finely divided posterior subcaudals (2–4 per row, Fig. 316), conical keels on the dorsals, an immaculate venter, and a much lower subcaudal count (fewer than 50) than *Bothriopsis punctata*. The long lance-shaped head and exceptionally long fangs of *B. punctata* are also distinctive characteristics. See also the comments about *Xenodon* (Figs. 565–567), *Leptodeira* sp. (Fig. 557), and *Drymobius* in Mimics of Venomous Snakes.

REMARKS *Bothriopsis punctata* appears to be common nowhere. Its body shape and great tail length lead us to believe that it may be highly arboreal. Particular caution should be exercised when moving through dense secondary growth in forested foothill situations. We know of no recorded instance of snakebite from this species; however, its size alone would seem to render it potentially capable of delivering a fatal bite.

REFERENCES Acosta-Solís, 1944; Amaral, 1923, 1925b, 1927d, 1930a, 1930b, 1931b; Ayerbe, 1979; Bolaños, 1982, 1983; Blanchard, 1889; Daniel, 1949; Dunn, 1944a; Dunn and Bailey, 1939; García, 1896; Grocott and Sadler, 1958; Groombridge, 1986; P. Müller, 1973; Nicéforo-María, 1929a, 1939, 1942; Orcés, 1942, 1943, 1948; Peracca, 1910; Pérez-Santos and Moreno, 1986; J. A. Peters, 1960a; Posada-Arango, 1889a, 1889b; Rendahl and Vestergren, 1940; Renjifo, 1979; Saavedra R. et al., 1975; Schmidt, 1933b; Werner, 1922.

### *Bothriopsis taeniata* (Wagler)

(Figs. 158–162; Map 55)

LOCAL NAMES Brazil: jararaca-amarela, jararaca cinca (Amazonas), jararaca cinzenta, jararaca-tigrina. Colombia: cuatro narices, macabrel, macaurel, rabo de ratón. Peru: jergón de árbol; jergón arborícola; Marashar, nashipkit (Aguaruna names). Suriname: boomowroe-koekoe. Venezuela: mapanaré, mapanaré liquenosa.

ENGLISH NAME Speckled forest-pitviper.

DISTRIBUTION South America east of the Andes including equatorial forests of Colombia, Venezuela, the Guianas, Brazil, Ecuador, Peru, and Bolivia (Map 55). The vertical distribution is from sea level to at least 1,900 m.

HABITAT Lowland and foothill rainforests and moist tropical forest.

DESCRIPTION This relatively slender, prehensile-tailed pitviper may reach a length in excess of 1,500 mm, although it is usually less than 900 mm.

The pattern is exceedingly complex and the overall color variable from lavender gray to yellow green. The head is the same shade as the rest of the ground color, but with several black blotches on top and profuse black-and-yellow speckling overall. A black postocular stripe terminates at the angle of the mouth. The iris is speckled black and yellow. The chin is pale yellow, the dark speckling around the labials becoming heavier posteriorly such that the entire underside becomes predominantly maroon-brown with the yellow ground color showing through as specks. Dorsally the pattern consists of 30–40 black bands that are speckled throughout, often fail to meet middorsally, and may be divided on the sides so as to appear to be divided into four parts. There are areas of concentrated black-and-yellow speckling midway between the dorsal bands. A series of 50–90 white or yellow spots is situated at the juncture of the dorsals and ventrals; each spot covers 1–2 dorsals and part of the adjacent 1–2 ventrals with an interspace of 1–4 ventrals between them. The distal third to half of the tail is often pink in color and the tongue is black.

This species has 5–9 intersupraoculars, 6–8 supralabials (the second fused with the prelacunal), 9–12 infralabials, 25–29 midbody dorsal scale rows, 203–254 ventrals, and 66–91 subcaudals (mostly single).

SIMILAR SPECIES *Bothriopsis taeniata* may be distinguished from all other members of its genus by its predominantly single subcaudals and row of bold white spots at the juncture of the dorsals and ventrals. *Bothriopsis taeniata* has more ventrals (203–254) than any of its congeners except *B. bilineata*, from which it is distinguished easily on the basis of color and pattern. The brightly speckled iris, long lance-shaped head, and exceptionally long fangs of *B. taeniata* are additional distinctive characteristics. Aside from members of the genus *Bothriopsis*, there are no other prehensile-tailed pitvipers within the range of *B. taeniata*.

REMARKS The species evidently undergoes considerable ontogenetic change in color. A litter of juveniles from Suriname (UTA R-15408-14) were soft gray dorsally with darker gray blotches. The anterior and posterior edges of the dorsal blotches were edged with white. The posterior third of the tail varied from yellow to pink. The canthal region and postorbital stripe were very dark rich red brown. The iris was gold, paler dorsally, and red along the ventral half (in conjunction with the postorbital stripe). This is an arboreal species, usually encountered in primary forest or forest-edge situations, in vines and low vegetation. It appears to be common nowhere, and owing to its cryptic coloration, it is very difficult to see. Bites from *B. taeniata* have not been reported, but its size, venom characteristics, and fang length warrant caution. This species has long been known as *Bothrops castelnaudi*, but this name recently has been shown both by Cunha and Nascimento (1978) and by Hoogmoed and Gruber (1983) to be a junior synonym of what here is called *Bothriopsis taeniata*. The species occupies a large area of South America and future studies presumably will delineate geographic races. The subspecies *B. t. lichenosa* is known from a single Venezuelan specimen that differs from typical *B. t. taeniata* in having a lower number of ventrals and subcaudals.

REFERENCES Amaral, 1930b, 1930c, 1937b, 1938, 1948a; Ayerbe, 1979; Blanchard, 1889; Boulenger, 1896; Carrillo de Espinoza, 1983; Chippaux, 1987; Cope, 1860c; Cunha and Nascimento, 1972, 1975a, 1975b, 1978, 1982a; Cunha et al., 1985; Daniel, 1949; Duellman, 1978; Dunn, 1944a; Fonseca, 1949; Fugler and Walls, 1978; Groombridge, 1986; Hoge and Lancini, 1962; Hoge and Romano-Hoge, 1981a, 1981b; Hoogmoed and Gruber, 1983; Jan, 1859a; Lancini, 1970, 1978, 1979; Machado, 1945b; Medem, 1969; Meneses, 1974a, 1974b; Moonen, 1982; P. Müller, 1973; Nahas et al., 1979; Nicéforo-María, 1939, 1942; Noguchi, 1909; Orcés, 1942, 1943, 1948; Parker, 1934, 1938; Pérez-Santos and Moreno, 1986; J. A. Peters, 1960a; Pifano C. and Romer, 1949a; Prado, 1945; Roze, 1958c, 1966a, 1970a; Sandner-Montilla, 1978; Shreve, 1947b; Silva Haad, 1982b; Soini, 1974b; Vetencourt Finol., 1960; Wagler, 1824; Werner, 1922.

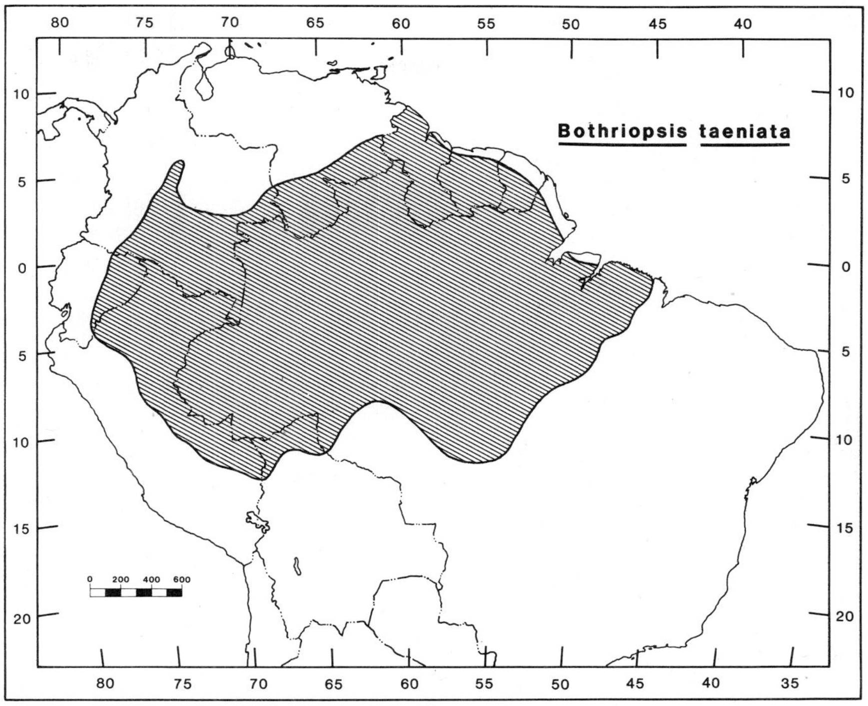


**Map 55.** Distribution of *Bothriopsis taeniata* in Amazonian South America.

# Lanceheads

## Genus *Bothrops* Wagler, 1824

The genus *Bothrops* (family Viperidae) contains 31 species; members of this group are called lanceheads owing to the distinctive head shape seen in most species. The genus is distributed primarily in South America, with one species, *B. asper*, ranging through Central America and into northern Mexico. Three insular endemic species are recognized: *B. caribbaeus* on Saint Lucia, *B. insularis* on Ilha Queimada Grande off the coast of Brazil, and *B. lanceolatus* on Martinique; *Bothrops asper* occurs on the island of Trinidad as well as the South American mainland. These are terrestrial snakes, although all can climb (and some do so frequently). Some species are small, seldom exceeding 500–700 mm in total length, while others may reach 2.5 m or more.

Most members of the genus *Bothrops* possess a sharply defined canthus rostralis and an unelevated snout; exceptions are *B. lojanus* and *B. microphthalmus*, which have a slightly upturned snout, and *B. ammodytoides*, which has a nasal appendage. The scales on the crown of the head are extremely variable: the number of intersupraoculars ranges from 2 (some *B. pulcher*) to 14 (some *B. cotiara* and some *B. venezuelensis*). There are generally 7–9 supralabials (*B. cotiara* and *B. roedingeri* possess 11 or more), 9–11 infralabials, 21–29 midbody dorsal scale rows, 139–240 ventrals, and 30–86 subcaudals, usually divided. A summary of the variations found in selected scale characteristics for members of this genus is presented in Table 30.

The everted hemipenes are 8–11 subcaudals long in most species of *Bothrops*. The organ is divided deeply, and in most species the sulcus spermaticus bifurcates at the level of subcaudals 1–3; the organ itself is divided at the level of subcaudals 2–4. The sulcus extends to the apex of each lobe. The base of the organ in *B. alternatus* and related species is exceptionally long and the organ divides at the level of subcaudal 7 or 8. The lobes may be subcylindrical (*B. atrox*, *B. alternatus*), moderately attenuated (*B. asper*, *B. neuwiedi*), or strongly attenuated (*B. brazili*). Spines tend to be confined mostly to the proximal one-half to two-thirds of the lobes, but may extend down below the level of the crotch onto the base in the shoulder region. Spines are well developed in the upper mesial region and are usually situated a little more distally than spines on the opposite side of the lobes. Most species have from 50 to 70 medium to large spines on *each* lobe; a few species, such as *B. alternatus* and *B. neuwiedi*, have fewer (35–40 and 28–35, respectively). The asulcate side of the base is mostly naked; the sulcate side and lower crotch area often possess small spinules. The distal one-third to one-half of the lobes possess calyces. The micro-ornamentation of these calyces is usually papillate, but some species bear calyces with sharply projecting papillae that approach a spinulate condition (*B. atrox*); other species may have smooth or scalloped ridges, at least distally (*B. alternatus* and *B. brazili*, respectively). *Bothrops alternatus* has a deep, well-formed, naked basal groove on the lateral side of the organ.

Lanceheads are primarily denizens of the lowlands usually found at elevations of 1,500 m or less. However, many species are markedly eurytopic, occurring from xeric regions near sea level to cloud forests at 2,500 m or more. *Bothrops andianus* has been found as high as 3,300 m above sea level and several other species closely approach this elevation. Members of this genus occupy a wide range of habitats and some have become important causes of human envenomation owing to the abundance of these snakes in cultivated regions.

Many of the species of large lanceheads from the lowlands of the Amazon Basin northward (through Central America) are superficially quite similar to one another in appearance. This resemblance has caused much confusion, especially in distinguishing between *B. asper* and *B. atrox*. Typically, the ground color is some hue of brown or gray with a series of dark, paravertebral, subtrapezoidal to subtriangular markings that are pale bordered to some degree. Several of the species occurring in southern South America are marked more ornately, with boldly contrasting patterns and extensive facial striping. Some species (*B. ammodytoides*, *B. pictus*, *B. roedingeri*) tend to be tan with a pattern of middorsal blotches or spots.

The species *B. eneydae* Sandner-Montilla (1976) cannot be distinguished on the basis of the description; pending the availability of specimens we prefer to leave this taxon unallocated (but see Remarks for *Bothriopsis medusa*). The description and accompanying illustrations of *Bothrops isabelae* (Sandner-Montilla, 1979b) conform completely with *B. asper* and we regard it as such. Published allegations of the occurrence of *B. lanceolatus* on the South American mainland are without foundation.

Snakes of the genus *Bothrops* are responsible for more human morbidity in the New World than any other group of venomous snakes; the most important species are *B. asper* in Central America and *B. atrox* and *B. jararaca* in South America. Mortality without treatment is about 7%, but with treatment it is reduced to 0.5–3%.

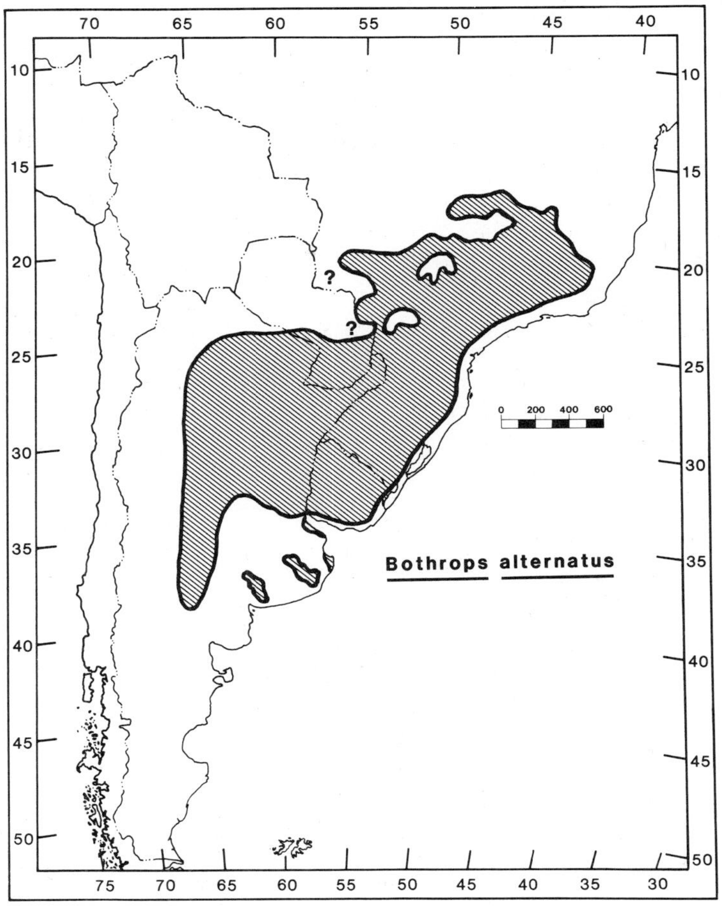


**Map 56.** Distribution of *Bothrops alternatus* in southern South America. Several disjunct populations occur in the province of Buenos Aires. Question marks represent possible areas of occurrence.

Signs and symptoms have been reported as follows: local pain, nausea, vomiting, sweating, headache, massive extremity swelling, hemorrhagic blebs, ecchymosis, erythemia, hypotension, tachycardia, coagulopathy with hypofibrinogenemia and thrombocytopenia, hematemesis, melena, hematuria, intracerebral hemorrhage, renal failure secondary to hypotension or bilateral cortical necrosis. Death most commonly results from hypotension secondary to hypovolemia, renal failure, or intracranial hemorrhage.

### *Bothrops alternatus* Duméril, Bibron, and Duméril

(Figs. 179–180; Map 56)

LOCAL NAMES Argentina: kiririóg-aká-kurussú, yarará (Guaraní dialect); mboí cuatía; víbora de la cruz; yarará grande. Brazil: boicoatiara, boicotiara (Tupi dialect); coatiara, cotiara (southern portion of country); cruzeira; cruzeiro; jararaca de agosto (Lagoa dos Patos region, Rio Grande do Sul); jararaca rabo-de-porco (Rio Grande do Sul); urutú. Paraguay: ('m) bói-cuatiá, ('m) bói-kwatiara (Gí dialect); yarará acácusú (Guaraní dialect). Uruguay: crucera, de la cruz, víbora de la cruz, yarará.

ENGLISH NAME Urutu.

DISTRIBUTION Brazil, Paraguay, Uruguay, and Argentina. In Brazil this species occurs from the broadleaf forests of Minas Gerais, and possibly southern Goiás, south through inland regions of São Paulo, Paraná, and Santa Catarina into Rio Grande do Sul. It also is found in Mato Grosso along the Rio Paraná and in the extreme south-central part of the state. *Bothrops alternatus* is found throughout Uruguay, in southern Paraguay, and northern and central Argentina from Misiones and Tucumán south to Río Negro, with disjunct populations in central and eastern Buenos Aires. In the Argentinian province of Buenos Aires it is known to occupy two isolated mountain ranges (Map 56). Its vertical distribution is from near sea level to about 700 m.

HABITAT By most accounts, this species is an inhabitant of low-lying swampy areas, riparian situations, marshes, and other humid habitats. It is found in tropical, semitropical, and temperate deciduous forests and is said to be common on sugar cane plantations. In Argentina, *Bothrops alternatus* occupies open fields and rocky areas in the Sierra de Achiras, Córdoba, and the Sierra de la Ventana, Buenos Aires. It is possible that this species occurs in a variety of habitats depending on latitude, but it appears to be absent from xerophytic situations.

DESCRIPTION *Bothrops alternatus* is a large, heavy-bodied terrestrial lancehead reportedly exceeding 2 m in length but with a verified maximum of 1,690 mm. Average size is closer to 1,000 mm.

This species is exceedingly variable in form, and it

**Table 30**

Variation of selected features in members of the genus *Bothrops*

| Species | Dorsal pattern | Ventral pattern | Top of head | Postorbital stripe | Intersupra-oculars | Supra-labials | Lacuno-labials | Midbody dorsal scale rows | Ventrals | Subcaudals |
|---|---|---|---|---|---|---|---|---|---|---|
| *B. alternatus* | Brown, tan, or gray, with 24 or more darker markings laterally that meet or alternate middorsally and are pale edged. Paraventral spots alternate with this and interspaces are spotted. | A dark stripe from neck to tail tip, broader posteriorly and sometimes obscuring entire venter. Dark spots on outer edges of ventrals. | Ornate, with tan-to-white transverse and longitudinal markings; a pale bar or spot between supraoculars. | Present | 8–13 | 8–10 | Absent | 24–37 (27–33) | 155–190 | 30–53 |
| *B. amodytoides* | Tan or gray, palest medially, with 30 or more dark brown rounded vertebral blotches. These may be split, may alternate or be opposite each other, and may form a zig-zag stripe. Laterally, there are 3 series of weak, alternating blotches. | White color with black speckles scattered throughout, especially laterally. | Tan with dark brown symmetrical, elongated, markings. | Present | 7–11 | 8–11 | Present or absent | 23–25 | 147–160 | 30–41 |
| *B. andianus* | Olive-gray to brown, with 18–24 dark pale-edged triangles laterally, mostly meeting middorsally. | Cream-to-yellow color, mottled heavily with dark gray or black; sometimes with a median yellow streak anteriorly. Gray and white spots along outer edges of ventrals. | Darker than rest of dorsum; generally unmarked. | Present | 3–8 | 7 | Present | 21–25 | 157–177 | 49–58 |
| *B. asper* | Tan, brown, olive, gray, grayish brown, pink or nearly black, with 18–25 dark, pale-edged triangles laterally with apices alternating or opposite each other middorsally. Dark paravertebral blotches in interspaces. | Yellow, cream, or whitish gray, with darker mottling that increases posteriorly. Dark gray ventrolateral spots on alternate scales. | Unmarked, or with vague occipital blotches or streaks. | Present | 5–11 (6–9) | 7–8 (7) | Present | 23–33 (25–29) | 161–240 | 46–81 |
| *B. atrox* | Olive, brown, tan, gray, yellow, or rust, with rectangular or trapezoidal pale-bordered blotches laterally that alternate or are opposite each other middorsally. Interspaces immaculate or spotted; pattern often diffuse. | White, cream, or yellowish gray with dark spots increasing posteriorly; dark paraventral spots on alternate scales. | Unmarked, or with vague occipital blotches or streaks. | Present | 3–11 (5–9) | 6–9 (7) | Present | 23–29 (23–25) | 169–212 | 47–86 (<75) |
| *B. barnetti* | Medium brown to straw colored with 17–24 brown, pale-edged triangular or trapezoidal blotches that alternate or meet middorsally. Interspaces have diffuse brown spots; a series of small brown paraventral spots also present. | Immaculate white with dark speckling on outer edges of ventrals. | Dark brown with no markings visible or with a wavy dark brown V-shaped mark with its apex on the intercanthals. | Present | 5–8 | 7–9 | Present | 23–25 | 172–184 | 40–47 |
| *B. brazili* | Pinkish tan to pale gray, with 9–18 dark gray bands or triangular C's with black borders. Vertebral region often tinged with rust color. | Uniform yellow or pinkish cream with slightly darker mottling. Outer edges of alternate ventrals have single gray splotches. | Usually unmarked pinkish gray to pinkish tan. | Absent or faint | 3–10 (5–6) | 7–9 | Present | 23–29 (25–27) | 151–202 | 42–68 |
| *B. caribbaeus* | Gray, gray-brown, yellow, red, or chocolate with square to trapezoidal lateral markings, alternating or opposite each other middorsally, sometimes bordered by pale scales and ventrally by 2 dark basal spots. Pattern often reduced or faded. | Unmarked yellow. | Unpatterned. | Present | 4–6 | 7–8 (7) | Present | 25–29 | 196–213 | 64–72 |
| *B. cotiara* | Tan to pale olive-brown with 14–17 trapezoidal markings on the neck and body; these are brown with black borders, are paravertebral, and alternate or are opposite each other. There are lateral triangular marks and scattered spots. | Cream, powdered with black in the gular region, becoming entirely black with olive-green spots laterally and on some sutures. | With a pale-edged dark brown spear-shaped marking that bifurcates posteriorly. | Present | 10–14 | 8–9 | Usually absent | 25–29 (27) | 151–173 | 34–52 |

|  |  |  |  |  |  |  |  |  |  |  |
|---|---|---|---|---|---|---|---|---|---|---|
| *B. erythromelas* | Brown to reddish brown, with brown-to-black triangular markings that alternate or are opposite each other middorsally. Usually, a paraventral series of spots; interspaces spotted. | Yellowish tan with diffuse gray ventrolateral blotches. | Sometimes with a dark spot on intercanthals and intersupraoculars and usually a pair of elongated nuchal blotches; sometimes patternless. | Present | 5–6 | 7–8 | Absent | 19–21 | 139–158 | 32–42 |
| *B. fonsecai* | Tan to medium brown, with 17–19 black trapezoidal blotches paravertebrally; these may alternate or be opposite each other and they are edged in yellowish tan. There is a series of lateral, often fused blotches and a series of black paraventral spots. Interspaces contain scattered dark spots. | Dark gray to black, with white pigment most prevalent anteriorly and along the lateral edges of alternate scales. Venter of the tail is black. | A dark brown or black blotch in the form of a spearpoint that bifurcates posteriorly. A tan bar or pair of spots in the intersupraocular region. Entire supracephalic blotch bordered by yellowish tan. | Present | 8–10 | 8–10 | Absent | 26–28 | 165–179 | 39–57 |
| *B. iglesiasi* | Brown dorsally with about 21 long dark bands on the body and about 6 on the tail. These bands have irregular borders and may be divided and juxtaposed middorsally. The ground color pales somewhat adjacent to the bands. | Yellow with extensive dark brown spotting that sometimes is concentrated toward the lateral edges of the ventrals. | White markings on supraoculars, internasals, and canthals and a white blotch on the occiput. | Present | ca. 5 | 8–9 | Absent | 21–25 (23) | 160–170 | 35–43 |
| *B. insularis* | Pale yellowish brown with broad or narrow triangular or quadrangular blotches that alternate or meet (forming bands). The blotches may be absent, faint, or broken middorsally into spots. | Uniform pale yellow or cream, sometimes with brown markings along edges of ventrals. | Unmarked. | Usually absent | 5–9 (7) | 8–9 | Present or absent | 23–29 (25) | 171–195 | 48–65 |
| *B. itapetiningae* | Light or dark brown, with red, pink, or orange overtones; with a series of narrow transverse oval blotches, narrowly separated middorsally and dorsolaterally, sometimes pale edged, and situated opposite each other or alternate. Diffuse blotches in interspaces; dark paraventral spots. | White with brown specks scattered irregularly over the anterior third and coalescing posteriorly to form darker blotches. Pink pigment often present. White and brown usually alternate in the paraventral area. | Usually with a dark spot on the intercanthals or anterior intersupraoculars; a wavy dark stripe, sometimes interrupted, on each side of head. Stripe may be broken into 3 pairs of markings, all pale edged. | Present | 5–9 | 8 | Absent | 25–27 | 144–160 | 26–38 |
| *B. jararaca* | Tan, brown, gray, yellow, olive, or nearly maroon with a series of dark brown, pale-edged trapezoidal or subtriangular lateral markings that are opposite each other or alternate middorsally. There are paler areas within the dark markings and many times pattern anomalies are present. | Pale green to yellowish white with irregular blotching or powdering of gray pigment; sometimes uniformly gray. | Unicolored or with diffuse dark markings on the occiput. | Present | 5–12 | 6–10 (8–9) | Present | 20–27 (23–25) | 170–216 | 44–71 |
| *B. jararacussu* | Pale gray, tan, yellow, brown, pink, or black. Dorsal pattern extremely variable but usually involves a series of bold lateral triangular or C-shaped markings that approach the middorsum and may alternate or be opposite each other. Interspaces with blotches or ocelli. Lateral markings broadly pale edged. Pattern sometimes reduced. | Cream to yellow with some black spotting, especially at lateral edges of ventrals. | Dark brown or black and unmarked dorsally. | Present | 4–8 | 8 | Present | 23–29 (23–27) | 166–186 | 44–66 |
| *B. lanceolatus* | Gray, brown, or yellowish tan with pale-bordered paravertebral dark markings that may be reduced to spots, obscured, or absent. Darker basal spots sometimes present laterally. Components may fuse to form bands. | Nearly immaculate white or yellow, sometimes with a scattering of gray pigment or with faint paraventral spots. | Unmarked. | Present or absent | 5–11 | 7–8 | Present | 29–33 | 208–240 | 55–72 |
| *B. leucurus* | Reddish brown to tan with 18–21 transverse, rectangular or trapezoidal markings that may unite to form bands or be separated middorsally. These markings may be black to brown, and may be paler medially and sometimes have black-and-white borders. Interspaces are often spotted, as is the paraventral region. | Dark brown with paler spots beneath head, becoming yellow or white beneath body with dark pigment concentrated laterally and irregular spotting medially. Venter sometimes immaculate. | Usually with some irregular dark spots on snout and occiput, to form transverse markings that extend onto the nape. Pattern may be obscured by dark pigment. | Present | 7 | 7–8 | Present | 24–31 | 195–225 | 63–75 |

**Table 30—*continued***

| *Species* | *Dorsal pattern* | *Ventral pattern* | *Top of head* | *Postorbital stripe* | *Intersupra-oculars* | *Supra-labials* | *Lacuno-labials* | *Midbody dorsal scale rows* | *Ventrals* | *Subcaudals* |
|---|---|---|---|---|---|---|---|---|---|---|
| *B. lojanus* | Tan to medium brown with a dark brown zig-zag stripe middorsally that breaks up into spots posteriorly. Up to 48 small brown blotches laterally parallel the middorsal pattern. Paraventral region with alternate pale and dark spots. | Yellow mottled with pale to dark brown, darker posteriorly. Venter of tail salmon to brick red. | Usually with some elongated, symmetrically arranged dark brown markings beginning anterior to supraoculars and extending to temporal region. Head pattern often diffuse. | Present | 3–5 (5) | 7–8 | Usually present | 21–23 (23) | 144–155 | 37–46 |
| *B. marajoensis* | Olive-brown, usually darker middorsally, with 19–21 brown-to-black, tan-bordered markings that are triangular to trapezoidal in shape. Interspaces with ill-defined brown spots, some pale edged. Tail black; black paraventral spots. | Cream to yellow, checkered heavily with black and most concentrated along the outer edges of ventrals. | Basically unmarked but darker than dorsum. | Present | 5+ | 7–8 | Present | 25 | 176–194 | 60 |
| *B. microphthalmus* | Brown to straw-colored to gray with 18–21 lateral trapezoidal to nearly triangular markings, usually with paler centers. Dorsal markings alternate or meet (forming bands) middorsally. The pale centers are often dark medially. The entire pattern may be obscured by the ground color. | Gulars and infralabials immaculate yellow to mostly dark with pale spots. Belly mottled heavily with brown pigment, especially laterally and increasing posteriorly. | Usually unmarked. | Present | 4–8 | 7–8 | Absent | 21–25 | 137–173 | 44–56 |
| *B. moojeni* | Tan, grayish brown, or olive-gray, with 18–21 gray-to-black trapezoidal markings usually slightly juxtaposed middorsally. Tail with 4–7 diffuse gray-to-brown crossbands. Dorsal markings are pale edged. Interspaces may have darker spots. A pair of sinuous pale lines often visible on neck. | Usually white with a few dark dots widely scattered throughout. | Patternless but usually darker than rest of body. | Present | 9–10 | 7 | Present | 23–29 | 179–210 | 44–70 |
| *B. neuwiedi* | Tan, reddish or yellowish brown, brown, gray, pinkish gray, or olive with dorsolateral blotches that alternate or are opposite each other middorsally. These markings vary greatly in size and number according to subspecies. There are 2 dark spots at the base of each dorsal blotch; the latter are usually pale bordered. Interspaces usually with diffuse spots. Highly variable. | White with gray specks scattered throughout, sometimes fusing to form transverse markings along the sutures of the ventrals. | Usually with some dark spots in a symmetrical pattern, including a spot on the snout, a pair near the supraoculars, and one or more pairs in the temporal region. | Present | 6–9 | 7–10 (8–9) | Absent | 21–29 | 163–190 | 37–54 |
| *B. pictus* | Pale gray to tan with a row of brown ovoid or square blotches that are often split middorsally, slightly juxtaposed, and fused to form a zig-zag "stripe." Blotches are often irregular and bordered with white and/or black. A smaller lateral series of blotches is colored identically to the dorsal blotches. Interspaces contain diffuse dark markings. Dark brown spots in paraventral region. | Cream to white with diffuse darker specks throughout. | Ornate, with a symmetrical pattern usually including a transverse band above the supralabials followed by 2 pairs of oblique stripes in the temporal region. One or 2 spots are found on the middorsum of the head. | Present | 5–7 | 8–12 | Present or absent | 21–25 (21–23) | 152–173 | 40–52 |
| *B. pirajai* | Brownish yellow to yellowish gray with 15–18 or more dark dorsal markings that are quadrangular to triangular, alternate or are opposite each other, and sometimes are connected middorsally via a wavy black stripe. Dorsal markings have pale centers or ocelli laterally. Interspaces immaculate, spotted, or blotched. | Yellow, slightly to profusely speckled with dark pigment. | Yellowish gray to grayish black; usually unmarked or with pale temporal stripe. | Present | 5–7 | 8–9 | Present | 25–27 | 155–167 | 43–52 |

| | | | | | | | | | | |
|---|---|---|---|---|---|---|---|---|---|---|
| *B. pradoi* | Grayish brown with about 15 trapezoidal markings on each side that alternate or are opposite each other at middorsum. Each marking has a pair of basal blotches. Pale transverse zones border all markings. Interspaces with diffuse spots. Paraventral region with dark brown spots. | Heavily spotted with dark gray-brown pigment. | Unmarked, but sometimes more pigmented than dorsum. | Present | 10 | 7 | Present | 23–25 | 191–207 | 56–70 |
| *B. pulcher* | Nearly uniform brown with broad, diffuse bands occasionally visible, especially posteriorly. The bands are faintly bordered with paler brown. | Pale tan, often with a reddish cast posteriorly, and with small dark blotches on the outer edges of the ventrals. | Unpatterned. | Usually not visible | 2–7 | 7 | Present | 21–25 (23) | 139–174 | 44–64 |
| *B. roedingeri* | Pale gray-brown with a series of dorsal spots bordered with some black and white pigment and partially to completely divided medially. These are slightly juxtaposed and may form transverse bands in the neck, lower body, and tail region. Laterally there is a row of smaller dark spots, and there are small dark spots on the paraventrals. | Immaculate white except in the gular region which has some dark spots. | Ornate with dark spots anterior to the supraoculars and on the supraoculars, and with oblique occipital stripes. The pattern is symmetrical and occasionally fused. | Present | 6–7 | 11–12 | Present or absent | 23–25 | 179–185 | 43–48 |
| *B. sanctaecrucis* | Tan to pale gray (darkest middorsally) with 18–21 triangular to trapezoidal, white-bordered blotches that alternate or are opposite each other. Dark brown paraventral blotches border bases of dorsal blotches. Interspaces with ill-defined dark markings. | Unmarked white or yellow with some dark pigment on outer edges of ventrals and on subcaudals. | Unmarked or with faint, pale occipital stripes forming a V with apex on the intercanthals. | Usually absent | 6–9 | 8 | Present | 25 | 177–182 | 56–57 |
| *B. venezuelensis* | Yellowish tan, brown, gray, or olive, sometimes with a reddish or pinkish cast, with a highly variable pattern consisting of lateral trapezoidal dark-edged blotches that alternate or are opposite each other middorsally and may be broken into clusters of spots or rectangles. Interspaces contain black pigment and there are dark paraventral spots. | Tan to yellowish white with extensive black pigment, especially along the sides. | Unmarked or with diffuse darker mottling bordered on each side by a broad, diffuse pale temporal stripe. | Present | 8–14 (5–6) | 6–9 | Usually present | 19–27 (23–25) | 179–219 | 48–73 |
| *B. xanthogrammus* | Dark olive with a yellow zig-zag stripe from head to tail on each side of the body, forming V's with apices opposite or somewhat juxtaposed middorsally. | Black, paler medially, with yellow ventrolateral spots. | Black, with a lateral yellow stripe bordering the periphery of the entire head. | Present | 9–10 | 7 | Present | 27 | 196 | 54 |

*Note.* For additional information refer to individual species accounts.

bears a complex pattern. The dorsal ground color may be brown, tan, or gray, sometimes with an olive cast. The dorsum of the head is chocolate brown to nearly black with a variety of tan-to-white transverse and longitudinal markings. Usually, a transverse bar connects the supraoculars, although this may be broken or reduced to a spot. A longitudinal marking of the same pale shade approaches this intersupraocular bar from the occipital region, and at times the two are united. The longitudinal head marking may be stripelike, bear lateral processes, bifurcate posteriorly toward the angle of the jaws, or exist in combinations or interrupted versions of the above. Generally, the dorsal surfaces of the canthals are pale, especially toward the tip of the snout. Laterally, a broad, medium-brown, dark-edged band covers the subocular region and continues posteriorly to the rictus, usually crossing some of the supralabials and infralabials. Sometimes this band projects anteriorly to the region of the loreal pit; also, it may undulate posteriorly. A bright cream stripe borders this band dorsally, extending from the postorbital region to the rictus. The supralabials are white and form a ventral border to the facial band. A narrow white vertical marking extends from the supralabials to the preoculars.

The head is cream ventrally with two distinct dark brown stripes extending from below the angle of the jaw anteriorly and converging on the mentals and rostral. These stripes are inferior to the infralabials and sometimes embrace a brown blotch on the chinshields. The iris is olive to bronze, much the same shade as the facial band. The tongue is reddish black. On the body, a series of 24–27 (or more) chocolate brown to black markings covers each side, and these either meet or alternate middorsally. These markings are boldly bordered in cream or white. Each marking is expanded laterally and invaded from below by the paler ground color, which may be cross shaped, may enclose a darker blotch, or may extend laterally such that it divides its dorsal marking into three parts. Frequently, the effect is that the larger marking has the C shape of a telephone receiver; rarely, the dorsal markings are in the form of ocelli. The interspaces throughout this pattern are dotted irregularly with oval dark brown blotches. An additional series of dark-edged brown spots spans the paraventral region and overlaps onto the ventrals. On the tail the pattern coalesces into a zig-zag configuration. In some individuals the pattern is so concentrated that little or no difference exists between the color of the markings and the interspaces; in others, the markings are more broadly spaced. Ventrally a dark brown to black stripe runs from the neck to the tail tip, usually expanding posteriorly and on rare occasions covering most of the venter.

There are 8–13 intersupraoculars, strongly keeled; 8–10 supralabials, none in contact with the prelacunal; 12–14 infralabials; 24–37 (usually 27–33) midbody dorsal scale rows; 155–190 (usually 168–178) ventrals; and 30–53 (usually 33–47) divided subcaudals.

SIMILAR SPECIES Of the lanceheads in which the supralabials are not integrated with the prelacunal, there are five species sympatric with *B. alternatus*, and one whose southern distribution approaches its range. *Bothrops ammodytoides* differs in color (tan), pattern, and in possessing an upturned snout; *B. cotiara* differs in habitat preference, number of infralabials, ventral coloration, and head pattern. *Bothrops erythromelas*, of doubtful sympatry, possesses 19–21 midbody dorsal scale rows (vs. 24–37). *Bothrops fonsecai* differs in head pattern, ventral coloration, and the shape of the postorbital stripe (tends to hook downward at the rictus), but overall is very similar to *B. alternatus*. *Bothrops itapetiningae* has only 10 infralabials, a lower range of ventrals and subcaudals, and a distinctly different pattern; it is not known to exceed 500 mm in total length. *Bothrops neuwiedi* possesses 21–29 dorsal scale rows (vs. 24–37) and 6–9 intersupraoculars (vs. 8–13), and it differs in head markings and body pattern; this species is extremely variable in coloration and pattern.

REMARKS *Bothrops alternatus* is an important cause of venomous snakebite throughout its range. Although seldom fatal, its bite often results in severe local damage. There is a report of a striped specimen from Uruguay.

REFERENCES Abalos, 1961, 1977; Abalos and Bucher, 1970; Abalos and Mischis, 1975; Abalos and Pirosky, 1963; Abalos et al. 1964; Achával, 1976, 1979; Achával et al., 1976, 1978; Amaral, 1925a, 1926d, 1930b, 1931c, 1934b, 1938, 1974, 1978; Barrio, 1961b; Barrio and Miranda, 1967b; Bertoni, 1914, 1939; Boulenger, 1896; Canese, 1966; Cei, 1987; Cendrero et al., 1972; Cope, 1860c; Devincenzi, 1925; Ditmars, 1930; Fernández Barrán and Freiberg, 1951; Fonseca, 1949; Freiberg, 1968, 1984; Gallardo, 1977; Gatti, 1955; Gliesch, 1925, 1931; Groombridge, 1986; Hoge, 1953b, 1953e; Hoge and Belluomini, 1959, 1964; Hoge and Romano, 1973; Hoge and Romano-Hoge, 1981b; Klappenbach and Orejas-Miranda, 1969; Klemmer, 1963; Lacerda, 1884; Laurent and Teran, 1981; Lema, 1960b, 1971a, 1971b; Lema and Fabián-Beurmann, 1977; Lema et al., 1980; Machado, 1945b; Magalhães, 1925; Melgarejo et al., 1980; Migone, 1929; Miranda et al., 1983; L. Müller, 1927; P. Müller, 1971, 1973; J. A. Peters and Orejas-Miranda, 1970; Prado, 1945; Schouten, 1931, 1937; Tada and Villa, 1975; Talbot, n.d.; Vanzolini and Ferreira Brandão, 1946; Vaz-Ferreira and Sierra de Soriano, 1960; Werner, 1922.

### ***Bothrops ammodytoides*** **Leybold**

(Figs. 173, 174, 181; Map 57)

LOCAL NAMES Cenicienta (see Remarks), yarará ñata.

ENGLISH NAME Patagonian lancehead.

DISTRIBUTION Argentina. *Bothrops ammodytoides* occurs along the eastern versant of the Andes from the province of Tucumán south into southern Santa Cruz (Patagonia). In eastern Argentina, it is found as far north as southern and southeastern Buenos Aires, Córdoba, and San Luis. It is the most southerly distributed of snakes. The vertical distribution is from sea level to at least 2,000 m.

HABITAT This species inhabits temperate to subtropical savannas and steppes, primarily in sandy, rocky

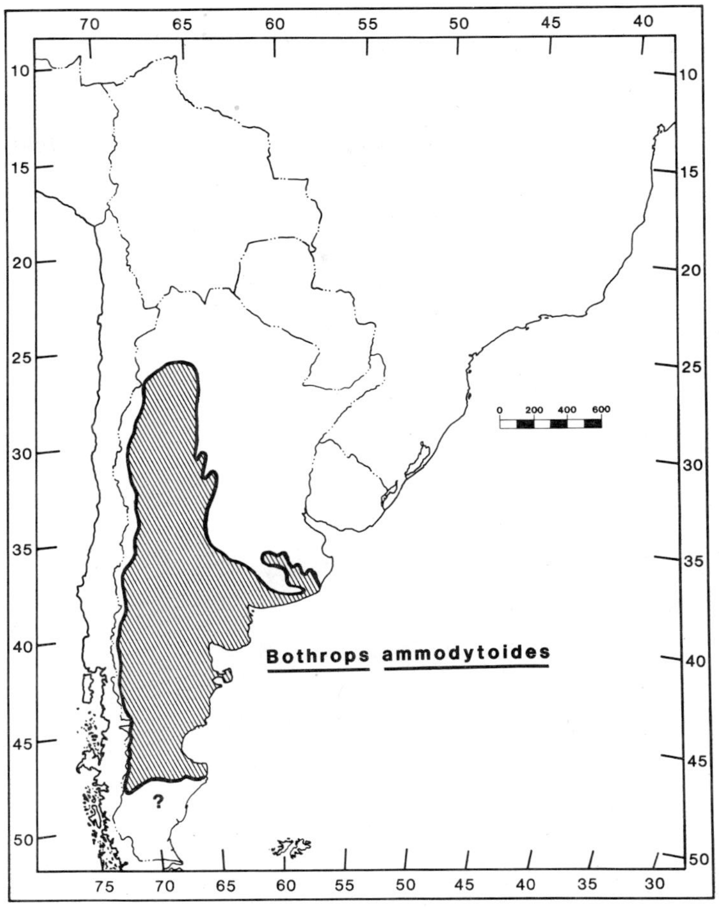


**Map 57.** Distribution of *Bothrops ammodytoides* in Argentina. The species occurs farther south than any other snake. The southern limits of its distribution have not been clearly established.

areas including coastal dunes, steep river banks, and salt flats; arid regions are preferred. At its upper distributional limits, *B. ammodytoides* might range into temperate broadleaf evergreen forest. There are reports that *B. ammodytoides* frequently occupies the rocky tunnels of the plains viscacha (*Lagostomus maximus*: Chinchillidae) in the Argentine Pampas.

DESCRIPTION *Bothrops ammodytoides* is a stocky, terrestrial lancehead averaging 450–750 mm in total length but reaching nearly 1,000 mm (see Remarks).

The dorsum of the head is gray to yellowish tan, with extensive dark brown markings on top of the snout, in the intercanthal region, on and between the supraoculars, and in the temporal and occipital regions. These markings tend to be arranged symmetrically, and form curved elongated blotches on the occiput. A broad, dark brown postorbital stripe extends from behind and under the eye to the angle of the jaw, encroaching upon the posteriormost 4–5 supralabials; it is evident especially along the labial sutures. A brown spot may be present on supralabials 3–5, otherwise the canthal region is white, with or without fine gray peppering. The infralabials are white with brown spots along the scale sutures. The tongue is black. The iris is dark brown, with paler brown flecks and a silver border at the pupil. The dorsum of the body is tan or gray, being palest on about 7 middorsal scale rows throughout the length of the body. There are about 30–32 dark brown, rounded vertebral blotches plus 3–5 more on the tail. Anteriorly, these blotches tend to be split middorsally and may alternate or be slightly juxtaposed. Frequently, these blotches will be linked together, forming an undulating or zig-zag stripe along portions of the dorsum. The sides are marked by three series of poorly defined alternating blotches or spots, usually brown or dark gray in color.

The paraventral scales and the lateral edges of the ventrals are tinged heavily with dark gray or black pigment. Many of the keels, especially laterally, are tan, giving a diffuse appearance to the pattern. The tail, which is short and extremely thickened, is of a darker and grayer shade than the rest of the dorsum; the blotches cover the dorsum and sides of the tail and give a banded effect. The venter is white, with black speckling scattered throughout, especially laterally.

There are 7–11 intersupraoculars; 8–11 supralabials, the second may or may not be integrated with the prelacunal (see Remarks); 11 or 12 infralabials; 23–25 midbody dorsal scale rows; 147–160 ventrals; and 30–41 divided subcaudals. There is an unverified report of 51 subcaudals for this species. The rostral is vertically elongated in such a way that the snout is upturned, similar to that of the hognosed pitvipers of the genus *Porthidium*.

SIMILAR SPECIES Five other pitviper species occur in Argentina. Of these, *B. cotiara*, *B. jararaca*, and *B. jararacussu* are not sympatric with *B. ammodytoides*. *Bothrops alternatus* is a large species, distinctly patterned, with a normal snout, and generally possessing a

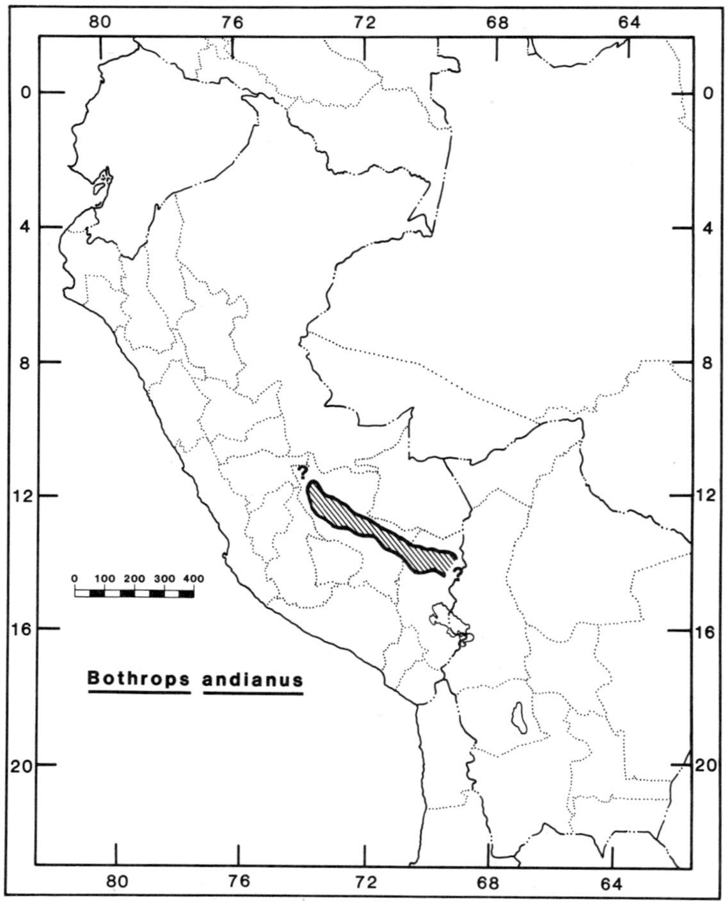


**Map 58.** Distribution of *Bothrops andianus* in Peru; this species may range into Bolivia.

higher number of ventrals and intersupraoculars. *Bothrops neuwiedi*, a highly variable species, has a normal snout and a higher number of ventrals (168 or more vs. 147–160) and subcaudals (41 or more vs. 30–41).

REMARKS The type locality of *B. ammodytoides* has traditionally been referred to as "northern Argentina"; more specifically, it should be indicated as the province of Mendoza. The vernacular name *cenicienta* was included by Leybold (1873) in his description; purportedly, the local people used this term because of the similarity of a coiled *B. ammodytoides* to a pile of ashes.

The condition of the second supralabial and prelacunal requires clarification. The two scales are stated to be discrete in this species, but published illustrations indicate that this may be a variable characteristic, and in at least some populations the prelacunal is adjacent to the *third* supralabial. In the region of Valcheta (Patagonia) a population exists of unusually large *B. ammodytoides*. This species has an irritable temperament and might be capable of causing human fatalities.

REFERENCES Abalos, 1977; Abalos and Mischis, 1975; Abalos and Pirosky, 1963; Barrio, 1961b; Boulenger, 1896; Cei, 1975, 1979, 1987; Cendrero et al., 1972; Doello-Jurado, 1916; Fernández Barrán and Freiberg, 1951; Freiberg, 1968, 1984; Gallardo, 1977; Garman, 1881; Hoge and Romano-Hoge, 1981a; Koslowsky, 1895; Laurent and Teran, 1981; Leybold, 1873; Miranda et al., 1983; F. Müller, 1885; P. Müller, 1973; Noguchi, 1909; J. A. Peters and Orejas-Miranda, 1970; Tada and Villa, 1975; Werner, 1922.

### *Bothrops andianus* Amaral

(Figs. 182, 183; Map 58)

LOCAL NAMES Jergón, jergona, terciopelo.

ENGLISH NAME Andean lancehead.

DISTRIBUTION Peru. This species is known only from the Departamento de Cuzco and Departamento de Puno. The majority of specimens have been collected at the type locality, Machupicchu (eastern Andes-Río Urubamba) and along the Río Cosireni (Map 58). The vertical distribution is from 1,800 to about 3,300 m.

HABITAT *Bothrops andianus* frequents montane and lower montane wet forests. It is an inhabitant of the Peruvian *selva alta*, probably never descending below the foothill region (*ceja de la montaña*).

DESCRIPTION *Bothrops andianus* is a terrestrial lancehead, recorded to range in length from 464 to 700 mm.

Dorsally the ground color is olive-gray to brown, sometimes darker anteriorly. The canthus and supralabials are paler brown. A well-defined dark chocolate brown postorbital stripe passes from the posterior edge of the eye to the angle of the jaw and sometimes beyond, encompassing upper portions of the 2 or 3 posteriormost supralabials. This stripe is bordered ventrally by a thin

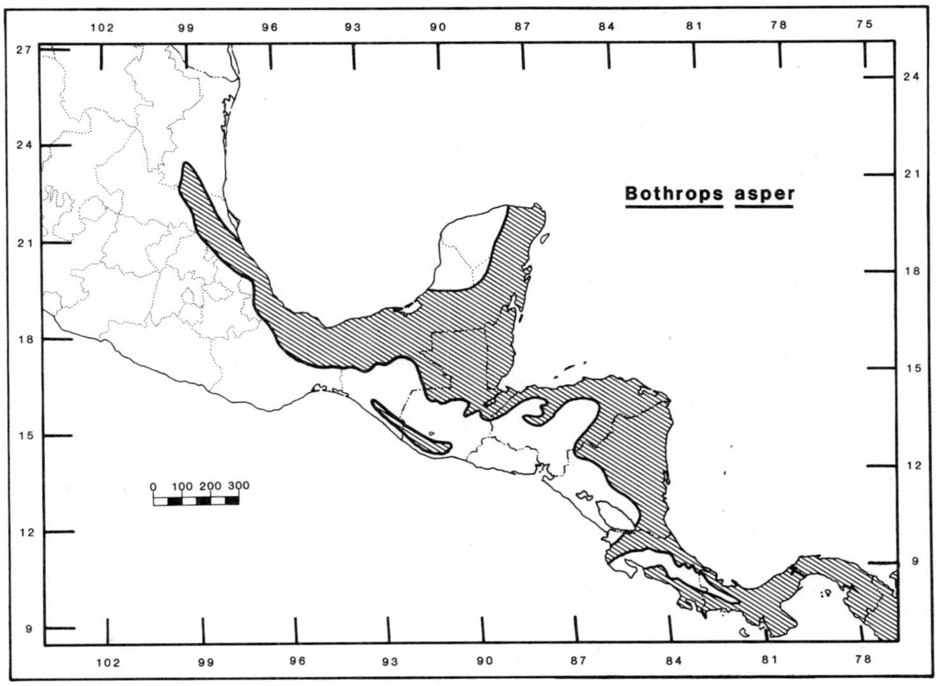


**Map 59.** Distribution of *Bothrops asper* in Mexico and Central America. For the continuation of this species' range into South America consult Map 60.

white line that contrasts sharply with the postorbital stripe. The iris is colored similarly to the supralabials. The ventral side of the head is cream to yellow in hue, usually mottled or speckled with dark brown or black. The gular region tends to be especially dark in juveniles. The infralabials have pale spots in their centers. The tongue is dark pinkish brown. The dorsal pattern consists of a series of 18–24 dark, pale-edged triangles that run along the sides of the body. Their apices are often rounded and usually are opposite one another middorsally, although some may alternate. Each triangle is invaded extensively from the ventral side by the paler ground color such that a series of ill-defined spots appears along the third and fourth rows of dorsals. The basal centers of the triangles often bear suffusions of dark pigment. The dorsal pattern is continuous onto the tail. The distal subcaudals are pale. The venter is cream to yellow, mottled heavily with dark gray, brown, or black, which sometimes creates a medial yellow streak anteriorly. On the lateral edges of the ventrals, the dark pigment alternates with white, occasionally including the paraventrals.

The rostral is as high or higher than wide and truncated dorsally. There are 3–8 intersupraoculars (the medial scales are sometimes enlarged), 7 supralabials (the second is fused with the prelacunal to form a lacunolabial), 8–11 infralabials, 21–25 midbody dorsal scale rows, 157–177 ventrals, and 49–58 divided subcaudals.

SIMILAR SPECIES The following characteristics distinguish *B. andianus* from similar sympatric or nearly sympatric pitvipers: The second supralabial is in contact with the loreal pit, whereas it is separated in *B. microphthalmus*. *Bothrops andianus* lacks a prehensile tail (present in sympatric members of the genus *Bothriopsis*) and possesses divided subcaudals (they are mostly single in *Porthidium* and finely subdivided distally in *Lachesis*). See also the discussion of false pitvipers in Mimics of Venomous Snakes.

REMARKS This is another species patterned somewhat similarly to *B. atrox*.

REFERENCES Amaral, 1923; Barbour, 1913; Barbour and Noble, 1920 (as *B. pictus*); Carrillo de Espinoza, 1983; Duellman, 1979; Hoge and Romano-Hoge, 1981a; Meneses, 1974a, 1974b.

### *Bothrops asper* (Garman)

(Figs. 175, 176, 184–192; Maps 59, 60)

LOCAL NAMES Belize: yellow-jaw tommygoff. Colombia: barba amarilla (coast); boquidorá, boquidorada (Caribbean coast); cuatronarices; equis; equis negra; equis rabo de chucha (Isla Gorgona, Cauca); gata; macabrel; macaurel; mapaná; mapaná de uña; mapaná equis; mapaná prieta; mapaná rabo blanco; mapaná tigre (Chocó); mapaná rabo seco; montuno; pelo de gato (Cauca); pudridora; rabiamarilla; rabiseca; rabo de ratón; tama (Emberá Indians, Chocó); taya, taya equis (Cundinamarca, Tolima, Valle de Cauca); uña de gato. Costa Rica: terciopelo, toboba rabo amarillo; toboba tiznada (Pacific versant). Ecuador: equis (coast). Guatemala: barba amarilla; cantil boca dorada (south coast); cantil devanador (Atlantic versant). Honduras: barba amarilla. Mexico: ahueyactli, barba amarilla, cola blanca, cuatro narices, nauhyacacóatl, nauyaca, nauyaca cola de hueso, nauyaca real, nauyaque, palanca, palanca loca, palanca lora, palancacoate, palancacóatl, palancacuate, rabo de hueso, tepocho, tepotzo, víbora sorda, xochinauyaque. Nicaragua: barba amarilla, terciopelo. Panama: barba amarilla, equis, terciopelo; krundíbi (Guaymí Indian

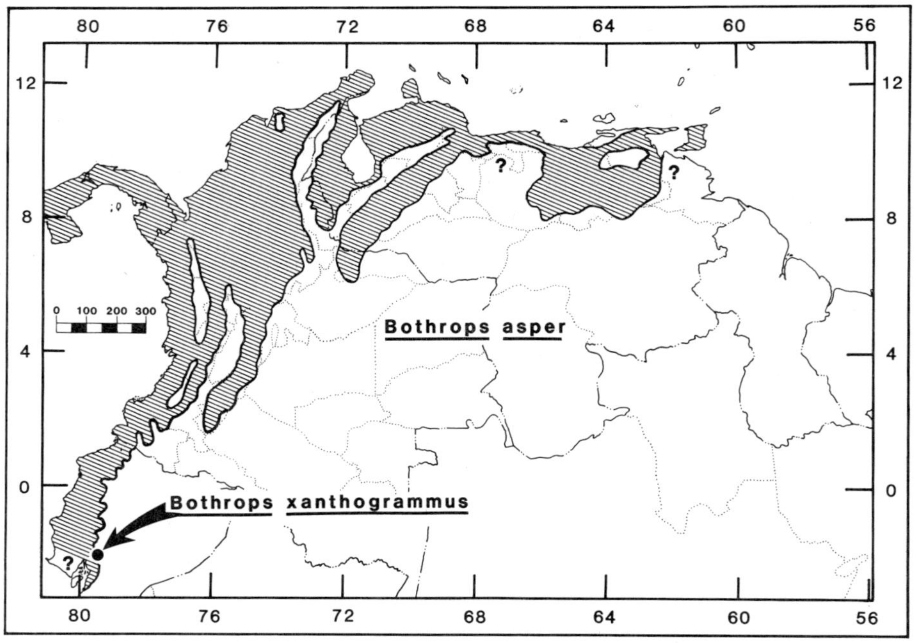


**Map 60.** Distribution of *Bothrops asper* in lower Central America and northern South America, including Trinidad, and of *Bothrops xanthogrammus* (*dot*), known only from the type locality in Ecuador. Question marks represent possible areas of occurrence of *B. asper*.

name, Bocas del Toro). Trinidad: fer-de-lance; mapepire balsain (also spelled: balsin, balcin, valsin, barcin); rabo frito (juveniles). Venezuela: guayacán (Zulia); macagua, macaurel (central coast); mapanaré (Andes); terciopelo (west); cachete de puinca, changuanga, chigdu, cuaima carbón, cuatronariz, deroya, doroya; juba-vitu (Indigenous tribal name), macao, mapanaré terciopelo, rabo-amarillo, sapamanare, talla equis, tigra, tukeka.

ENGLISH NAME Terciopelo.

DISTRIBUTION In Middle America, this species is found on the Atlantic versant of Mexico from south-central Tamaulipas southward through the southern and eastern portion of the Yucatán Peninsula, northern Guatemala and Honduras, and the Atlantic lowlands of Nicaragua, Costa Rica, and Panama. A disjunct population occurs on the Pacific versant of Chiapas and Guatemala. It is not improbable that a single record for Atoyac in the Pacific lowlands of Guerrero, Mexico, is accurate, but no further material has been forthcoming from this region. It is also possible that this record refers to Atoyac, Veracruz. This species crosses over to the Pacific in northwestern Costa Rica and is widespread in lower portions of the Pacific drainages of south-central and southeastern Costa Rica. In Panama, *B. asper* apparently occurs throughout most of the country, exclusive of the highlands (Map 59).

The mainland South American distribution includes the Pacific versant of the Colombian and Ecuadorian Andes and the adjacent coastal lowlands. The southernmost extension along the west coast of South America appears to be delimited by the semi-arid region south of Guayas, Ecuador; there are no records of *B. asper* from northern coastal Peru. This species is known from the Isla de Gorgona (and probably occurs on Gorgonilla) off the Colombian Pacific Coast. It is distributed across the Caribbean coastal plain and throughout the inter-Andean valleys of Colombia, thence eastward across northern and central Venezuela north of the Río Orinoco, as far as the Delta Amacuro region. *Bothrops asper* also appears to be the species of lancehead occurring on Trinidad, but the situation there is complicated owing to its proximity to the Orinoco Delta, a region where *B. asper* and *B. atrox* may be sympatric (see Remarks). Reports of a *Bothrops* species from Tobago are probably erroneous; however, if substantiated, they may be referable to *B. asper*. Throughout its South American range, this species occurs mostly west and north of the Andes (Map 60). An exception to this is in Venezuela, where *B. asper* has populations along the southern and southeastern versant of the Cordillera de Mérida and the Cordillera de la Costa. Such a distribution is understandable owing to the presence of the San Cristóbal Depression and the Barquisimeto Depression, two regions of sufficiently low elevation that passage of lowland species across the mountains is feasible. We are aware of specimens (Fig. 190) from northwestern Arauca, Colombia, but *B. asper* appears not to have dispersed southward; *B. atrox* is known from the remainder of the eastern versant of the Colombian Andes (see Remarks). The situation at the eastern extreme of the range is unclear, but the rainforests west of the Orinoco Delta seem to be the limiting factor.

*Bothrops asper* is primarily a lowland form; in Mexico and Central America it ranges from about sea level up to a maximum of 1,200–1,300 m. It apparently ranges considerably higher in parts of South America: the vertical distribution is to at least 2,640 m in Colombia, and in Venezuela it has been recorded up to 2,500 m above sea level.

HABITAT *Bothrops asper* may be found in a variety of habitats throughout its range, but it is principally a species of tropical rainforest and tropical evergreen forest. It occurs in some dry regions covered with tropical deciduous forest, thorn forest, or pine savanna, but it is less common in these forests than in humid regions and appears to be restricted to the proximity of rivers or other bodies of water. In Mexico, Guatemala, and Venezuela, this species has been taken in cloud forests. On Trinidad, the preferred habitat includes forested uplands.

DESCRIPTION *Bothrops asper* is a large, moderately slender, terrestrial lancehead (see Remarks) that averages 1,200–1,800 mm as an adult, but may reach a total length in excess of 2,500 mm. We are aware of reports of lengths up to 3,050 mm for this species in South America, but these claims may be fanciful. Juveniles and young adults are slender, but large specimens may attain considerable girth.

*Bothrops asper* is highly variable in both color and pattern, and the dorsal ground color may be tan, brown, olive, gray, grayish brown, pink, or nearly black. The dorsum of the head usually is unmarked, although some ill-defined blotches or streaks may be present in the occipital region. The labials and canthal region normally are unmarked or only diffusely pigmented, and usually are pale yellow in color. A dark brown postorbital stripe extends from behind the eye to the angle of the mouth and may encroach upon the posteriormost 1–2 (rarely 3) supralabials; alternatively, this stripe may be exceedingly narrow and not in contact with any supralabials. Usually a diffuse pale stripe, some 2–3 scales wide, borders the postocular stripe dorsally, although in some specimens this pale stripe is lacking. The underside of the head is usually immaculate pale yellow. The dorsal body pattern consists of a series of 18–25 pale-edged dark brown to blackish triangles on each side with their wide bases directed ventrally and their apices either opposite or juxtaposed at the vertebral line. These triangles are invaded centrally by paler ground color, usually ash gray; this color may extend laterally and divide each triangle, leaving a pair of basal spots. Frequently, the pale borders to the triangles are broad and prominent such that the predominant pattern appears to be zig-zag yellow or beige striping. When the triangular markings are opposite, the effect when viewed dorsally is of a series of X's, an appearance which undoubtedly spawned the vernacular name *equis*. The pale borders tend to be expanded on the lower sides and often meet, isolating the darker ground color in the interspaces between the triangles. Darker oval paravertebral blotches may be present in these interspaces. In some specimens the bold borders are absent, and instead the triangular markings are narrowly edged with white.

The dorsal pattern becomes concentrated on the tail, which may be dark gray to black, with paler transverse bars. In juvenile males the tail tip is yellow to pinkish orange; local names such as *cola de hueso*, *rabo de hueso*, and *cola blanca* allude to this coloration. The venter, including the infracephalic scales, is cream, whitish gray, or, most frequently, yellow (thus, the origin of the widespread use of the name *barba amarilla*) with varying amounts of gray-to-black mottling on the ventrals that increases posteriorly. A series of dark gray ventrolateral spots on alternate scales runs the length of the body.

There are 1 or 2 interoculabials and a single loreal per side. There are 5–11 (usually 6–9) keeled intersupraoculars; 7 or 8 (usually 7) supralabials, the second fused with the prelacunal; 8–12 (usually 10 or 11) infralabials; 23–33 (usually 25–29) midbody dorsal scale rows; 161–240 (usually 185–220) ventrals; and 46–81 (usually 56–70) divided subcaudals.

SIMILAR SPECIES *Bothrops asper* is the only member of the genus ranging north of Colombia on the mainland and is easily distinguished from other Middle American pitvipers by a *combination* of a lacunolabial and divided subcaudals.

In South America the situation becomes a bit more confusing. Four sympatric pitvipers have a normal snout, a lacunolabial, and divided subcaudals: *Bothriopsis medusa*, which possesses fewer ventrals and usually single subcaudals (but they may be divided), and is probably found at higher elevations than *B. asper*; *Bothriopsis punctata*, which possesses a distinct pattern on top of the head and has 70–95 subcaudals; *Bothrops lojanus*, which is of doubtful sympatry, being a high-elevation species, usually has smooth intersupraoculars and possesses fewer ventrals and subcaudals; and *Bothrops pulcher*, which possesses fewer ventrals and fewer intersupraoculars. *Bothrops venezuelensis* is a distinctive species but nevertheless overlaps with *B. asper* in virtually every aspect of scutellation. *Bothrops venezuelensis* differs from *B. asper* in head shape (slightly rounded vs. slightly pointed), nature of the postorbital stripe, color of the canthus and dorsum, and pattern. See the *B. venezuelensis* species account for further details. *Bothrops xanthogrammus*, quite possibly a synonym of *B. asper*, may be distinguished from the latter solely on the basis of its smooth intersupraoculars. See the *B. xanthogrammus* species account for a discussion of its distinctiveness.

The zone of sympatry between *B. atrox* and *B. asper* has not been well established, but both species appear to occur in the region around the southern Mérida Andes and around the Orinoco Delta. Records for *Bothrops* from the Venezuelan llanos are curiously lacking; *B. atrox* is abundant throughout the llanos of Colombia. These two species not only overlap in scale characteristics, they also have somewhat similar patterns. In general, *B. atrox* is smaller (average maximum length about 1,200 mm.), has a broader postocular stripe (which usually encroaches upon at least the 3 posterior supralabials), smaller supralabials, and a lower canthus, tends to be banded or spotted dorsally, and may have a darker venter. Generally, the edges of the dorsal markings tend to be more vertically aligned than diagonally, as in *B. asper*. The keels of the middorsals of both species do not extend to the distal edge of the scale. However, *B. asper* differs from *B. atrox* in having longer keels that extend forward on the cephalic portion of the scales to a point about even with the distal tip of the anterior contiguous scale; in *B. atrox* the keel usually stops well short of this point. There are notable behavioral differences, although it is obvious that such measures are of minimal use in the field (see Remarks). The canthus of *B. atrox* tends to be more heavily pigmented than that of *B. asper*, although this varies individually and ontogenetically.

REMARKS The status and relationship of *B. asper* and *B. atrox* to each other are poorly known and controversial. This confusion, in part, is due to the fact that most systematic treatises have lumped together populations representing two or more species (usually as *B. atrox*), thus preventing the discovery of characteristics that might serve to separate the two. We think that the distributional relationships set forth here will point toward productive areas for investigation, which we hope will reduce the taxonomic mystery. Two localities of particular interest are the northwestern Arauca region in Colombia and adjacent Venezuela, where we have observed specimens referable to *B. asper* (Fig. 190) and to *B. atrox* (Fig. 194) in close proximity to one another. The status of specimens from the region around the Orinoco Delta is less clear, but *B. asper* may reach its eastern terminus there—material from extreme eastern Venezuela and the adjacent Guianas is clearly referable to *B. atrox*.

*Bothrops asper* is an adaptable species, occupying a variety of habitats; young specimens are often semiarboreal, and we have occasionally encountered adults in bushes and low trees. In marked contrast to the majority of *B. atrox* with which we have dealt, *B. asper* is excitable and unpredictable when molested. Specimens can (and often do) move very rapidly, reversing directions abruptly, and defending themselves vigorously. An adult *B. asper*, if cornered and fully aroused, is a redoubtable adversary and must be regarded as extremely dangerous.

*Bothrops asper* is active after dark; when found by day, it is almost always inactive. In many lowland regions of the Neotropics, this is the most commonly encountered snake.

Scale counts included in this account represent those deemed applicable to populations of *B. asper*; published data representing Amazonian populations or composites were omitted. A careful assessment of variation, with special regard to locality, is needed. The species *B. isabelae*, which is not distinguishable as originally described, may represent either *B. asper* or *B. atrox*, although it most resembles *B. asper*.

REFERENCES Acosta-Solís, 1944; Alemán G., 1953; Alvarez del Toro, 1983; Amaral, 1925a, 1925b, 1927c, 1927d, 1928, 1937b, 1955a; Angel, 1983; Atkinson, 1907; Axtell and Wasserman, 1953; Ayerbe, 1979; Ayerbe et al., 1977; Barbour, 1905, 1916; Barbour and Loveridge, 1929a; Bates, 1928; Bolaños, 1971, 1982, 1983, 1984; Boos, 1975, 1984b; Boos and Quesnel, 1968; Booth, 1959; Boulenger, 1896, 1898b; Brattstrom and Howell, 1954; Breder, 1946; Burger and Smith, 1950; H. C. Clark, 1925, 1942, 1951; Cooper, 1972; Cope, 1861, 1865, 1874, 1876a, 1879, 1885a, 1885b, 1886, 1887; Cuesta Terron, 1921b, 1930a; Daniel, 1949; Despax, 1911; Ditmars, 1928b, 1930, 1937; Duellman, 1963, 1965a; Dugand, 1975; Dugès, 1894, 1896; Duke, 1967; Dunn, 1933, 1944a, 1944b, 1949, 1951; Dunn and Bailey, 1939; Dunn and Emlen, 1932; Eichelbaum, 1927; Elton, 1948; Emsley, 1977; Ferrari-Perez, 1886; Flores Villela et al., 1987; Gadow, 1905; Gaige et al., 1937; García, 1896; García López and Sandner-Montilla, 1962; Garman, 1884a; George, 1930a, 1930b; Greene, 1986; Grocott and Sadler, 1958; Groombridge, 1986; Günther, 1885–1902; Gutiérrez et al., 1979, 1980; Hall and Dalquest, 1963; Hallowell, 1845; Hatt, 1930; Henderson and Hoevers, 1975; Heyer, 1967; Hirth, 1964; Hoge, 1966; Hoge and Lancini, 1962; Hoge and Romano, 1973; Hoge and Romano-Hoge, 1981a; Johnson and Dixon, 1984; Lancini, 1970, 1979; Lee, 1980; Lynch and Smith, 1965; Macphail, 1929; Malkin, 1956; March, 1928a; Marcuzzi, 1950; Martin, 1955a, 1955b, 1958; Martín del Campo, 1935, 1937a, 1938a, 1950, 1984; McCoy, 1971; Medem, 1969, 1979; Meyer, 1969; Milá de la Roca, 1932; Minton and Minton, 1980; Mocquard, 1908–1909; Mole, 1914, 1924; Moreno, 1873; P. Müller, 1973; C. W. Myers and Rand, 1969; Neill, 1960, 1965; Neill and Allen, 1959a, 1960, 1962; Nemuras, 1967; Nicéforo-María, 1929b, 1930c, 1942; Nickerson et al., 1978; Nutter, 1927; Ocaranza, 1930; Ochoterena, 1934; Orcés, 1942, 1943, 1948; Parker, 1926; Patzelt, 1979; Pawley, 1969; Pérez-Higadera [*sic*] et al., 1987; Pérez-Higareda, 1978; Pérez-Santos, 1986a, 1986b; Pérez-Santos and Moreno, 1986; J. A. Peters, 1953, 1960a; J. A. Peters and Orejas-Miranda, 1970; W. C. H. Peters, 1861; Picado T., 1931; Procter, 1918; Ramírez-Bautista et al., 1981; Reddell and Mitchell, 1971; Rendahl and Vestergren, 1940; Renjifo, 1979; Rodas, 1938; Rohl, 1949; Roze, 1958a, 1959, 1966a, 1970a; Ruthven, 1912, 1922; Saavedra R. et al., 1975; Sandner-Montilla, 1975, 1979a, 1979b, 1981; Schmidt, 1941; Schmidt and Andrews, 1936; Scott, 1969, 1983a; Sexton and Heatwole, 1965; Shannon and Smith, 1950; Shreve, 1947a; H. M. Smith, 1938, 1941a, 1943, 1944b, 1947b, 1960b, 1970; H. M. Smith and Taylor, 1945; Stuart, 1934, 1935, 1937, 1948, 1950, 1958, 1963; Sumichrast, 1864a, 1864b, 1870, 1873, 1882; Swanson, 1945; E. H. Taylor, 1949, 1950, 1951, 1952, 1954; R. T. Taylor et al., 1974; Test et al., 1966; Timmerman and Hayes, 1981; Tinoco, 1978; Trejos, 1937; Touzet, 1983; Vellard, 1941; Vetencourt Finol., 1960; Villa, 1962, 1984; Webb and Fugler, 1957; Wehekind, 1960; Wilson, 1983; Wilson and Meyer, 1985.

## ***Bothrops atrox* (Linnaeus)**

(Figs. 177, 178, 199; Map 61)

LOCAL NAMES Bolivia: yoperojobobo venenosa. Brazil: acuambóia, caissaca (northeast), cambéua, combóia, cuambóia, jararaca (north and central), jararaca do norte, jararaca-do-rabo-branco, jararaca grão de arroz. Colombia: ala (Cubeo name), bula; cuatronarices; mapaná; mata caballo; pudridora; putrificador; taya; taya equis; térotero (juveniles); cacutali, macubuleru (Guahibo tribal names). Ecuador: equis, pitalala, shishi (juveniles). Guyana: labarriayre. Peru: cascabel (juveniles); jergón; jergona; machacú, marashar, nashipkit (Aguaruna names). Suriname: bergimaka, labaria, lanspuntslang, rasper, owroekoekoe, petjake. Venezuela: cuaima parda, juba-vitu (tribal name), karahirima (Yanoáma name), mapanaré, mapanaré guayanesa, rabo amarillo, rabo de candela, sororaima (Macuschí name), terciopelo.

ENGLISH NAME Common lancehead.

DISTRIBUTION This species inhabits all countries of South America exclusive of Chile, Paraguay (see Remarks), Uruguay, and Argentina. In Colombia, *B. atrox* is found east of the Andes; it occurs south of the Río Orinoco in southern and eastern Venezuela (see Remarks); throughout the Guianas; in Amazonian Brazil south into Pará, Maranhão (see Remarks), and Rondônia; in northeastern Bolivia and eastern Peru (east of the Andes) from the Departamento de Santa Cruz de la Sier-

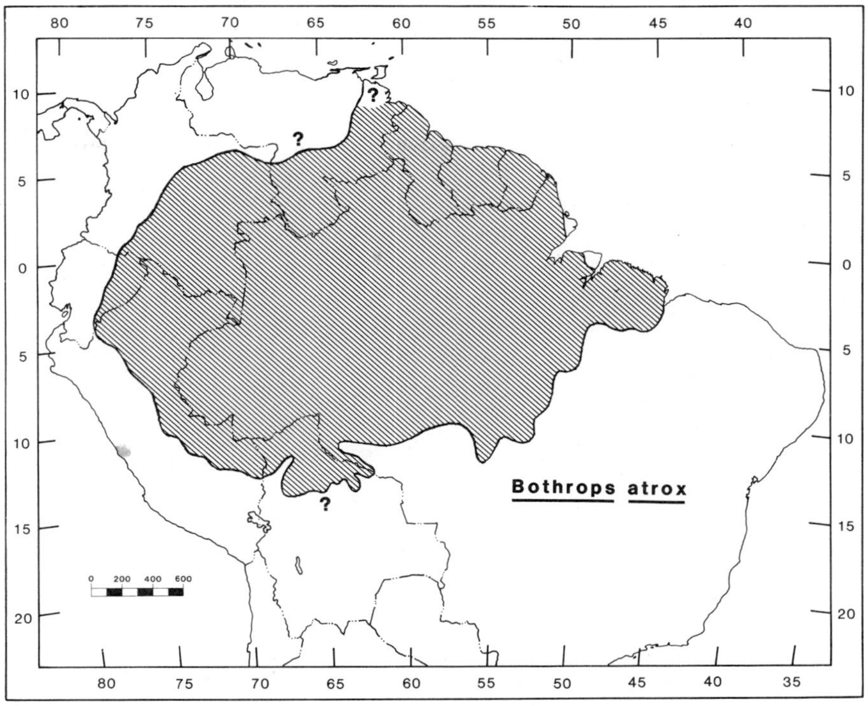


**Map 61.** Distribution of *Bothrops atrox* in northern South America. Question marks represent possible areas of occurrence.

ra (Bolivia) north to the Departamento de Loreto (Peru); and throughout Ecuador east of the Andes (Map 61). Its vertical distribution is to at least 1,200 m in Ecuador; in Suriname it has been recorded at 600 m elevation. The vertical distribution of *B. atrox* along the eastern versant of the Andes in Colombia, Peru, and Bolivia is unknown, but the species may be replaced by other species of lanceheads at elevations above about 1,500 m. There is a questionable record of 2,500 m in Colombia. This species has been taken at 1,280 m in the Gran Sabana, Bolívar, Venezuela.

HABITAT *Bothrops atrox* occupies a variety of habitats, including lower montane wet forest, savanna/gallery forest, tropical deciduous forest, and rainforest. Generally, this species prefers damp locales; it is found in close association with creeks, lakes, or river concourses. However, *B. atrox* is also encountered frequently in cultivated areas, moist fields, and around human habitations, including weedy lots in urban areas.

DESCRIPTION *Bothrops atrox* is a moderately heavy-bodied, terrestrial (see Remarks) lancehead that averages about 750–1,000 mm in total length. Reports of maximum size attained by this species are unclear because of the traditional confusion with *B. asper* (see Remarks). It is safe to state that 1,500 mm represents a very large specimen of *B. atrox* and that 2,000 mm is probably the maximum length.

The dorsal color and pattern are extremely variable, and the snake may be an overall olive, brown, tan, gray, yellow, or (rarely) rusty hue. The dorsum of the head tends to be the same or a slightly darker hue than the dorsal ground color; the head is generally unmarked although there may be some diffuse darker areas in the occipital region. A moderately wide, dark brown postorbital stripe passes posteriorly from behind the eye to the angle of the mouth, where it is usually curved downward. This stripe normally occupies the upper portions of the three posteriormost supralabials, and often completely covers the ultimate supralabial. In some specimens, the postorbital stripe may be narrowly bordered dorsally and/or ventrally by white, although the pale coloration is never pronounced. In other (especially Guianan) specimens the sides of the head are uniformly dusky, occluding the postorbital stripe. The pigment on top of the head usually is paler just above the postorbital stripe. The canthal region is variable in color but usually bears some peppering or clouding of dark pigment; this tends to fade with age, so that juveniles may have dark supralabials, while in old adults they may be tan to yellow. In many specimens, the sutures between the second, third, fourth, and fifth supralabials are bordered with dark pigment; this is especially pronounced between the third and fourth supralabials, and it is most conspicuous overall in juvenile or young specimens.

The venter of the head varies from cream to yellow to yellowish gray, with or without darker mottling. Again, the latter tends to be more prevalent in juveniles; in some specimens a dark stripe divides the jaw longitudinally before fading in the neck region. The iris is gold with varying amounts of dark reticulations. The tongue is black. The body pattern is highly variable, both in configuration and in degree of contrast. In some specimens, the pattern is prominent and well differentiated from the ground color, while in others, it may be reduced to a few spots or nearly absent. In general, the pattern consists of a series of rectangular or trapezoidal blotches extending from the junction of the ventrals dorsally to the midline. These blotches may or may not alternate with the series on the opposite side, and they frequently form bands crossing the entire dorsum. Diffuse (occasionally prominent) pale borders offset each blotch, and gray or tan pigment invades the basal portion of each blotch, sometimes subdividing it basally into a pair of ventrolateral spots.

In some specimens, the dorsal markings are conspicuously darker than the intervening ground color, while in others there is little difference and the pattern is only discernible because of the pale borders. The interspaces are faintly to heavily blotched or spotted; alternatively, they may be immaculate. The dorsal ground color may be somewhat paler on the sides and is sometimes suffused with yellow or rust in the paraventral region. The pattern fades posteriorly, and the tail may be unmarked; in juveniles, the tail tip is frequently a yellow or pink color (see Remarks). The ventral side of this species may be white, cream, or yellowish gray, with gray-to-black spots or blotches that increase posteriorly but may fade under the tail. Generally, these dark markings are most conspicuous ventrolaterally, where they form a series of paraventral spots, starkly alternating with the pale ventral ground color. These spots are visible when the species is viewed dorsally, and they often constitute the most conspicuous element in the overall pattern. The anterior portion of the venter tends to be dark in juveniles, and the markings are often white and black. The venter fades in older specimens, tending to become yellow and gray, and anterior dark markings may be entirely lacking.

There are 3–11 (usually 5–9) keeled intersupraoculars; 6–9 (normally 7) supralabials, the second fused with the prelacunal; 7–13 (usually 9–11) infralabials; 23–29 (usually 23–25) midbody dorsal scale rows (see Remarks); 169–212 ventrals (see Remarks); and 47–86 (usually not over 75) divided subcaudals.

SIMILAR SPECIES Throughout its range, *B. atrox* is or may be sympatric with five species of terrestrial lanceheads that share with it the characteristic of having the second supralabial fused with the prelacunal.

*Bothrops andianus* possesses fewer dorsals at midbody (21–25 vs. 23–29), fewer ventrals (157–177 vs. 169 or more), and a generally lower number of intersupraoculars and subcaudals.

*Bothrops asper* is possibly sympatric in Arauca, Colombia, and Guanare, Venezuela, and perhaps also in Delta Amacuro, Venezuela (see Remarks). *Bothrops asper* overlaps *B. atrox* in most scale characteristics, although it appears to have a wider range of variation and may prove to possess a higher average number of dorsals and ventrals. The canthus is higher in *B. asper* and the postorbital stripe tends to be narrower, usually encroaching upon only the last 2 supralabials. Although the canthal region may become somewhat paler in old adults of *B. atrox*, it tends to be pale through life in *B. asper*. The dorsal pattern of *B. asper* frequently involves more boldly contrasting elements and broader pale borders than that of *B. atrox*. *Bothrops asper* is a larger species, with reports of individuals approaching or possibly exceeding 3 m. For further information see the *B. asper* species account.

*Bothrops brazili* possesses more supralabials (usually 8 or 9 vs. 7 or, rarely, 8), and tends to lack a well-defined postorbital stripe. This species is also quite distinct from *B. atrox* in pattern and coloration. The head is relatively larger, the canthus seems to be higher, and the postorbital stripe is faint or absent in *B. brazili*. Most specimens possess a pinkish copper eye color and a brown or pink tongue (gold iris and black tongue in *B. atrox*).

*Bothrops marajoensis* is extremely similar to *B. atrox* (see Remarks), but apparently differs in that it lacks all markings on the supralabials, has paravertebral blotches that are consistently alternately arranged (rather than opposite each other) on either side of the midline, and has a long low keel (rather than a short high keel) on each dorsal. The latter feature is particularly tenuous in that numerous populations of *B. atrox* also possess long low keels.

*Bothrops moojeni* possesses a narrow postorbital stripe, pale supralabials, and an unmarked gular region. The venter of sympatric *B. moojeni* (in Maranhão, Brazil) tends to be unmarked. Most *B. moojeni* possess a pair of undulating elongated markings on the neck. The dorsal pattern is more conspicuously contrasting than that of sympatric *B. atrox*.

REMARKS The relationship between *B. atrox* and *B. asper* has been confused in the literature. Both species are wide ranging, highly variable, and exhibit pattern and scutellation sufficiently generalized so as to make differentiation a difficult task. The majority of reports have represented composite series of these two species with regard to everything from vernacular names to scutellation. We have included under this account only information definitely attributable to *B. atrox*. A careful compilation of data from populations of known provenance will undoubtedly alter the ranges of variation we have included.

The southern distributional limits for *B. atrox* are unclear, owing in part to the lack of information from eastern Bolivia and northern Paraguay, and to the uncertain status of *B. moojeni* and *B. sanctaecrucis*. For the present, we prefer to regard reports of *B. atrox* from northern Argentina as representing *B. moojeni*. At the mouth of the Amazon River, in Pará and Maranhão, the situation again becomes confusing due to the presence of the poorly differentiated *B. marajoensis*. To the north, in Venezuela, another interesting situation arises. Reports of *Bothrops* from the Venezuelan llanos are curiously lacking, yet we have found *B. atrox* to be abundant in the llanos of eastern Colombia. *Bothrops asper* occurs on the southern side of the Venezuelan Andes and is possibly sympatric with *B. atrox* in northwestern Arauca (Colombia) and adjacent Guanare (Venezuela). We are aware of specimens referable to each species from localities a scant 90 km apart (see Figs. 190 and 194). *Bothrops asper* apparently reaches its eastern limits in the area of the Orinoco Delta in eastern Venezuela. Information on possible sympatry with *B. atrox* in this region is lacking.

Although *B. atrox* is primarily a terrestrial species, juveniles and even large adults will frequently climb, and we have observed specimens at night as much as 4 m above the ground. In the llanos of Colombia, this species is sometimes found among the stem bases of the moriche palm (*Mauritia flexuosa*) high above the ground in an otherwise smooth-trunked tree.

In northeastern Peru, juvenile *B. atrox* are referred to frequently as *cascabel*, a name used normally for rattlesnakes but apparently here applied with reference to the pale tail tip. We have observed juveniles of *B. atrox* without the pale tail coloration and are uncertain whether the presence or absence is always gender related, as has been postulated.

The ranges for the numbers of dorsals and ventrals included in this account are lower than those reported elsewhere for *B. atrox*, and it is possible that other reports are correct. We have opted for a more conservative stance owing to the frequent inclusion of *B. asper* in discussions of *B. atrox*. The species *B. isabelae*, which is not distinguishable as originally described, may be referable to *B. asper* or *B. atrox*.

*Bothrops atrox* is a notorious cause of snakebite envenomation in humans. Its propensity for living near humans coupled with its potent venom combine to make it one of the most medically important snakes in the Neotropics.

REFERENCES Abalos and Mischis, 1975; Acosta-Solís, 1944; Amaral, 1925a, 1925b, 1926b, 1926d, 1930b, 1931c, 1937b, 1938, 1948a, 1948b, 1955a, 1974, 1978; Angel, 1983; Appun, 1961; Boos and Quesnel, 1968; Boulenger, 1896; Brongersma, 1967; A. E. Brown, 1893; Burger and Smith, 1950; Carrillo de Espinoza, 1970, 1983; Cendrero et al., 1972; Chippaux, 1987; Cope, 1860c; Cunha and Nascimento, 1975b, 1978, 1982a; Cunha et al., 1985; Daniel, 1949; Dixon and Soini, 1986; Duellman, 1978; Dunn, 1944a; Fonseca, 1949; Fugler and Walls, 1978; Fukada, 1964; García López and Sandner-Montilla, 1962; Gasc and Rodrigues, 1980; Goldman, 1979; Gomes, 1918a; Gray, 1829; Groombridge, 1986; Hagmann, 1909; Henderson et al., 1976; Hoge, 1953a, 1953b, 1966, 1967; Hoge and Lancini, 1962; Hoge and Romano-Hoge, 1981a, 1981b; Hoge, Romano, and Cordeiro, 1977; Hoge, Santos, et al., 1973; Hoogmoed and Gruber, 1983; Jan, 1859b; Johnson and Dixon, 1984; Kaiser and Michl, 1971; Kempff-Mercado, 1975; Koslowsky, 1898; Lacerda, 1884; Lancini, 1970, 1979; Lema, 1960b; Lescure and Gasc, 1986; Linnaeus, 1758; Machado, 1945b; Marcuzzi, 1950; Marinkelle, 1966; Medem, 1969; Meneses, 1974a, 1974b; Milá de la Roca, 1932; Minton et al., 1968; Mocquard, 1908–1909; Moonen, 1982; Moonen et al., 1978; P. Müller, 1971; Nicéforo-María, 1930b, 1933, 1942; Noguchi, 1909; Orcés, 1942, 1943, 1948; Orton, 1876; Parker, 1935; Patzelt, 1979; Pérez-Santos and Moreno, 1986; J. A. Peters, 1960a; J. A. Peters and Orejas-Miranda, 1970; Prado, 1945; Procter, 1918; Quelch, 1898; Rendahl, 1937; Renjifo, 1979; Roze, 1958b, 1966a, 1970a; Sandner-Montilla, 1975, 1979a, 1979b; Schmidt and Walker, 1943a; Shreve, 1947b; Silva Haad, 1982; Soini, 1974b; Touzet, 1983; Vellard, 1941, 1946; Vetencourt Finol., 1960; Wagler, 1824.

## *Bothrops barnetti* Parker

(Fig. 200; Map 77)

LOCAL NAMES Peru: cascabel, macanche, sancarranca.

ENGLISH NAME Barnett's lancehead.

DISTRIBUTION Peru. At present this species is known from two areas on the Pacific Coast: between Lobitos and Talara (Piura), and the Río Moche (La Libertad) (Map 77). It conceivably could extend northward into Tumbes and via the Catamayo Valley into adjacent southwestern Ecuador. Its southern distributional limits are unknown. Vertical distribution is also unknown; recorded localities are near sea level.

HABITAT Arid desert scrub. The collection data available suggest this species may be found in riparian situations within its habitat.

DESCRIPTION *Bothrops barnetti* is a stout, terrestrial lancehead with recorded lengths of 573–795 mm.

The dorsum of the head and body vary from medium brown to pale gray to straw color, becoming paler laterally. The top of the head bears a wavy dark brown V-shaped mark with its apex on the intercanthals. This supracephalic marking may be fragmented into a discrete series of markings on the intercanthals, posterodorsal to the eyes, and across the occiput to the neck. These markings are edged in paler brown to white, especially evident in the temporal region. A broad dark brown postorbital stripe crosses the posteriormost 4 supralabials. A pale brown spot crosses the supralabials from below the eye to the mouth and another from the loreal pit to the mouth. Otherwise the sides of the head are cream. The iris is medium brown like the dorsal ground color. The supraoculars may be darker than the dorsum of the head or, alternatively, the dorsum of the head may be dark brown, nearly obscuring all markings. The body is marked with 17–24 pairs of pale-bordered, dark brown, trapezoidal or triangular blotches which alternate or meet middorsally, in the latter case giving a bow-tie appearance. The bases of these blotches are invaded by the paler lateral ground color, producing a pair of rounded brown spots sometimes with a smaller spot between them. The brown interspaces usually also contain poorly defined spots, with a dorsolateral spot between succeeding triangular blotches. A series of small brown spots occupies the paraventrals and speckling is present on adjacent lateral edges of the ventral scales, which are otherwise immaculate white. The dorsal pattern becomes more concentrated on the tail, appearing as a series of alternating bands or rings of brown and white or as a zig-zag brown stripe. Usually 7–10 brown bands occur on the tail.

There are 5–8 keeled intersupraoculars, 7–9 supralabials (the second is in contact with, or is fused with, the prelacunal), 10 or 11 infralabials, 23–25 midbody dorsal scale rows, 172–184 ventrals, and 40–47 divided subcaudals plus a long terminal spine.

SIMILAR SPECIES The only lancehead known to be sympatric with *B. barnetti* is *B. pictus*, which has fewer ventrals (152–173 vs. 172–182) and a considerably different pattern than *B. barnetti*. However, *B. pictus* is extremely variable and if, as we suspect, it proves to be conspecific with *B. roedingeri*, the range of ventrals would encompass that of *B. barnetti*. Conversely, *B. roedingeri*, if valid, could be sympatric with *B. barnetti*, but the ranges of both are insufficiently known at present. *Bothrops pictus* lacks the alternating or opposite triangular to trapezoidal dorsal blotches characteristic of *B. barnetti*. See the species accounts for *B. pictus* and *B. roedingeri* for further information.

REMARKS This species appears to be rare in collections, and nothing is known of its habits.

REFERENCES Carrillo de Espinoza, 1983; Hoge, 1966; Meneses, 1974a, 1974b; P. Müller, 1973; Parker, 1938; Schmidt and Walker, 1943b.

### *Bothrops brazili* Hoge

(Figs. 201–205; Map 62)

LOCAL NAMES Brazil: jararaca vermelha, jararacusu, surucucu vermelha (falsa). Colombia: rabo de ratón. Guyana: kalakunaro. Peru: jergón. Suriname: bergi-owroekoekoe, boesi-owroekoekoe, labaria, morabana. Venezuela: mapanaré, mapanaré de amazonas.

ENGLISH NAME Brazil's lancehead.

DISTRIBUTION This species frequents equatorial forests of Bolivia, Peru, Ecuador, Colombia, Venezuela, Guyana, Suriname, French Guiana, and Brazil in the states of Pará, Amazonas, and the northern Mato Grosso. In the Andean countries, it is found exclusively to the east of the mountains in the Amazon watershed. It has not been reported previously from Ecuador, but Charles Myers of the American Museum of Natural History has informed us of specimens in that collection from eastern Ecuador (Map 62). Its vertical distribution is unknown, but we have collected specimens at 300 m in southeastern Colombia, and it has been recorded from 460 m in Suriname. It probably exists on the higher tepuis in Guyanan Amazonia but would be unlikely to occur above 1,000 m.

HABITAT *Bothrops brazili* has been recorded only from elevated primary forest situations in lowland equatorial South America in the Amazon Basin. It appears to be restricted to humid leaf litter habitat.

DESCRIPTION *Bothrops brazili* is a stout, terrestrial lancehead. Adults commonly are between 700 and 900 mm in overall length and may attain lengths of at least 1,400 mm.

The dorsum of the head is pinkish tan to pinkish gray, usually uniform. Occasionally a pale brown, poorly defined postocular stripe, bordered below by a dark brown line, is visible from the eye to the angle of the mouth, but in most specimens this is lacking. The rostral and inferior edges of the supralabials are paler than the rest of the head. A lateral series of 9–18 dark ash gray bands or triangular C's, alternating or opposite each other, cross the dorsum of the body. The dorsal ground color is similar to that of the head but usually darker. It appears that specimens from the northern portion of the range more frequently have a pattern of rectangular or slightly triangular crossbands, while specimens from Peru and Brazil (south of the Amazon) southward usually have a pattern consisting of triangular C's. The transverse markings are bordered irregularly in sooty black. The vertebral region often has a rusty tinge. The dorsum of the tail is similar to that of the body but may be predominantly black. The venter is usually a uniform yellow or pinkish cream, with slightly darker mottlings. Conspicuous gray splotches are present at the juncture of the ventrals and dorsals, roughly on alternate ventrals. The first row of dorsals is usually the color of the ventrals. The iris is coppery gold to pinkish copper. The tongue is brown with pink flecks.

There are 3–10 (usually 5–6) intersupraoculars; 7–9 supralabials, the second integrated with the prelacunal; 10–12 infralabials; 23–29 (usually 25–27) midbody dorsal scale rows; 151–202 ventrals (usually fewer than 190; see Remarks); and 42–68 subcaudals, usually in pairs.

SIMILAR SPECIES The fact that most specimens of *B. brazili* lack a postocular stripe serves to distinguish it from virtually all sympatric pitviper species. Superficially, perhaps the most similar species is *Porthidium hyoprora*, which has a nasal appendage, the second supralabial discrete from the prelacunal, single subcaudals, and a lower ventral count than *B. brazili*. *Bothrops atrox* has a distinctive postorbital stripe and usually more than 180 ventrals, while *B. brazili* normally lacks the bold postorbital stripe and usually has fewer than 180 ventrals. *Bothrops sanctaecrucis* possesses fewer infralabials and a higher average number of ventrals. Forest pitvipers (genus *Bothriopsis*) have distinctive color patterns and prehensile tails. *Lachesis muta* has rugose scales with conical keels, finely divided posterior subcaudals, a distinct postorbital stripe, and a different dorsal pattern.

REMARKS Populations of *B. brazili* appear to exhibit variation in pattern and scutellation; further analysis will probably result in some partitioning of the species. There is evidence that adult female *B. brazili* may be much larger than males. Individuals in a series of three specimens reported from Carajás, Pará, Brazil, represent the highest ventral (202) and subcaudal (68) counts known for the species. It has been suggested that the relative scarcity of *B. brazili* throughout its range is due to its preference for strictly primary forest habitat and to competition from *B. atrox*, which can adapt more readily to altered environments. While bites from the uncommon *B. brazili* have not been recorded, we have found that it is greatly feared by Indians in southeastern Colombia. Much confusion has surrounded the recognition of this species, owing largely to Amaral's (1923) description of *B. neglecta*. The type series for *B. neglecta* included the holotype, referable to *B. pirajai*, and a paratype described by Hoge 31 years later (1954) as *B. brazili*.

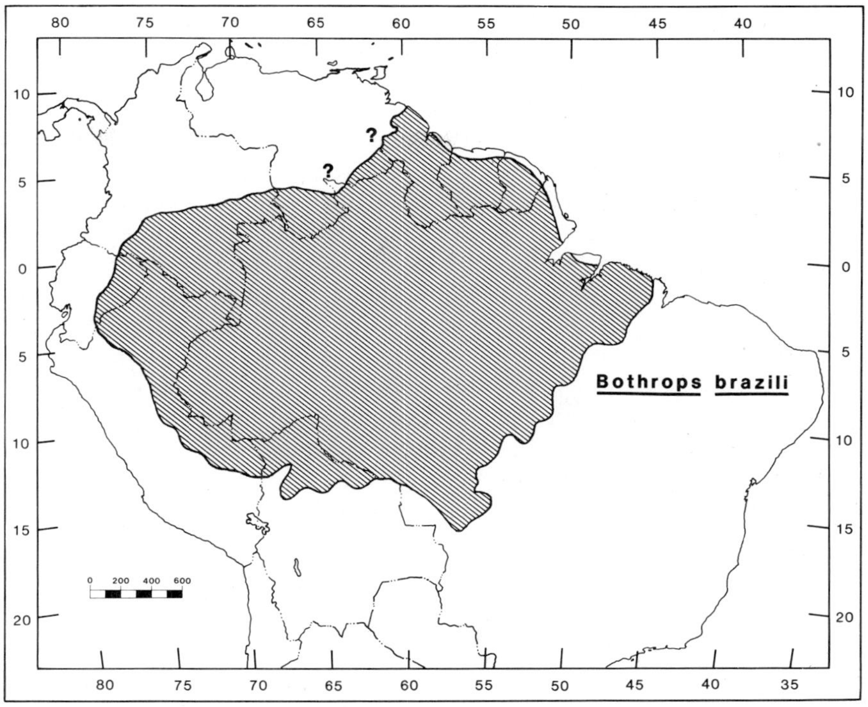


**Map 62.** Distribution of *Bothrops brazili* in northern South America. Question marks represent possible areas of occurrence.

REFERENCES Amaral, 1923, 1926a, 1930b, 1938, 1955b, 1978; Ayerbe, 1979; Brongersma, 1967; Carrillo de Espinoza, 1983; Chippaux, 1987; Cunha and Nascimento, 1975b, 1978, 1982a; Cunha et al., 1985; Daniel, 1949; Dixon and Soini, 1986; Duke, 1967; Dunn, 1937, 1944a; Fonseca, 1949; Gasc and Rodrigues, 1980; Groombridge, 1986; Hoge, 1954, 1964, 1966, 1967; Hoge and Lancini, 1962; Hoge and Romano, 1973; Hoge and Romano-Hoge, 1981a, 1981b; Hoge et al., 1973; Kempff-Mercado, 1975; Lancini, 1970; Medem, 1969; P. Müller, 1973; Nicéforo-María, 1939, 1942; Parker, 1935; J. A. Peters and Orejas-Miranda, 1970; Prado, 1945; Renjifo, 1979; Roze, 1954, 1957; Silva Haad, 1982b; Soini, 1974b; Vetencourt Finol., 1960.

## *Bothrops caribbaeus* (Garman)

(Figs. 206–297; Map 68)

LOCAL NAMES Fer-de-lance (see Remarks), rat-tail (see Remarks), serpent, St. Lucia serpent, St. Lucia viper.

ENGLISH NAME Saint Lucia lancehead.

DISTRIBUTION Saint Lucia Island, Lesser Antilles. On the west coast this species is found from near Castries south to Canaries; on the east coast it occurs from Marquis south to Micoud (see Map 68). *Bothrops caribbaeus* is not found in the arid northern extreme of the island; it also is absent from the southern and central highlands and from the south coast. The vertical distribution is to about 200 m.

HABITAT This species frequents lowland tropical forest, including some coastal plain regions of low humidity. It is said to be locally abundant in cocoa plantations and beneath piles of coconut husks.

DESCRIPTION *Bothrops caribbaeus* is a large, semiarboreal lancehead averaging about 1,000 mm but reaching over 2,000 mm in total length.

The dorsal ground color varies and may be gray, gray-brown, yellow, or even red; gray is seen most frequently. The ground color usually intensifies middorsally. The dorsum of the head is unpatterned or faintly patterned and may be the same shade as the dorsum of the body or darker, sometimes being nearly black. A dull, dark brown to black postorbital stripe passes from behind the eye toward the angle of the jaw; in some specimens it may be in contact with the upper portion of the sixth and/or seventh supralabials, while in others the stripe does not involve these scales. The postorbital stripe usually terminates just dorsal to the angle of the jaw, but in some specimens it appears to fuse with the neck pattern owing to the presence of dark pigment in the occipital region; it never involves infralabials. The postorbital stripe is bordered dorsally by a cream, tan, or yellow stripe, the color matching the shade of the canthus and supralabials, which are unpatterned but may bear some rust-colored pigment. The underside of the head is cream or yellow, without other markings. The iris is pale gray to slightly copper colored, with darker reticulations.

The markings on the dorsum of the body vary from slate gray to chocolate to rust-red, and are situated on pale gray, brown, or yellow ground colors, respectively. The pattern consists of a series of square to trapezoidal dorsolateral markings that alternate or meet middorsally, bordered slightly or not at all by pale scales; they are bordered ventrally by two dark basal spots. In the majority of specimens, these markings are reduced or faded such that they are visible laterally only at the basal spots and middorsally as poorly defined rectangles or squares. A tendency toward darkening of the ground color middorsally results in an irregular, undulating or zig-zag stripe that connects the dorsal markings in many specimens. When this occurs, the pattern is most readily discernible along the anterior third of the specimen. The tail is gray to pink, with irregular pale markings. It is said that male specimens of *B. caribbaeus* tend to be darker than females and may have an olive tint overall. There may be an ontogenetic tendency toward pattern loss, especially laterally. The venter is yellow and unmarked. There are purportedly two tail color morphs (pink and yellow?) in juveniles.

There are 4–6 keeled intersupraoculars; 7 or 8 (usually 7) supralabials, the second integrated with the prelacunal; 9–11 infralabials; 25–29 midbody dorsal scale rows; 196–213 ventrals; and 64–72 divided subcaudals.

SIMILAR SPECIES Within its range, *B. caribbaeus* is the only venomous reptile. *Boa constrictor* (Fig. 547) is patterned differently and lacks a loreal pit.

REMARKS The vernacular name *fer-de-lance* has enjoyed widespread and indiscriminate usage for any large, terrestrial lancehead and, as such, is important; see the *B. lanceolatus* species account for further discussion. The name *rat-tail* was utilized by Gray (1842), with the implication that it represented a local vernacular term; its validity is questionable. There is some taxonomic confusion regarding the validity of the name *B. caribbaeus* (Garman), and it is possible that this taxon was described previously by Gray. Deaths have been recorded from the bite of this species.

REFERENCES Amaral, 1925b, 1955a; Cendrero et al., 1972 (as *B. atrox*); Dowling, 1965; Garman, 1887b; Gosner, 1987; Gray, 1842; Groombridge, 1986; Hadley and Gans, 1972; Hoge, 1966; Hoge and Romano-Hoge, 1981a; Lazell, 1964; Long, 1974; Minton et al. 1968; P. Müller, 1973; Procter, 1918; Schwartz and Henderson, 1985; Schwartz and Thomas, 1975; Tyler, 1849; Underwood, 1962; Werner, 1927.

## *Bothrops cotiara* (Gomes)

(Figs. 208, 209; Map 69)

LOCAL NAMES Argentina: cotiara, yarará de vientre negro, yarará negra. Brazil: boicoatiara (Tupi); boicotiara (Tupi dialect, São Paulo and Paraná); coatiara, cotiara (Tupi dialect); jararaca-de barriga-preta (central Santa Catarina); jararaca preta; kwatiara, ('m) bói-kwatiara (Guaraní dialect).

ENGLISH NAME Cotiara.

DISTRIBUTION Argentina and Brazil. Southeastern São Paulo, Paraná, Santa Catarina, and Rio Grande do Sul, in Brazil, extending into Argentina in Misiones (see Map 69; see Remarks). The vertical distribution is to at least 1,800 m.

HABITAT Humid, temperate *Araucaria* forest and associated savanna.

DESCRIPTION *Bothrops cotiara* is a heavy-bodied, terrestrial lancehead averaging 700–800 mm but reaching at least 1,000 mm in overall length.

The dorsal ground color is tan to pale olive-brown on the head and body. The dorsum of the head bears a prominent, dark brown spear-shaped marking that is dark, pale edged, and bifurcates posteriorly. The invading ground color often assumes the shape of a second spear; in some cases it is nearly broken into isolated spots. A broad brown postorbital stripe edged in black runs from behind the eye to the angle of the jaw and does not turn downward. An additional black-edged brown spot is usually present beneath the eye, between the third and fourth supralabials. Otherwise, the labials are beige to cream. The gular region and infralabials are the same, with increasing suffusion of dark pigment. The iris is dark brown, becoming paler adjacent to the pupil. There are 14–17 trapezoidal markings on the neck and body; these are brown with black borders and are situated paravertebrally, alternating or opposite each other. When opposite, the markings may contact one another, giving a bow-tie effect. Laterally, triangular blotches, colored identically to the paravertebral markings, are situated adjacent to each basal corner such that 2 are associated with each trapezoid. Smaller, irregular blotches are scattered throughout the intervening spaces; most are colored similarly to those of the principal pattern. The dark markings intensify on the tail and become indiscernible. A series of dark brown or black paraventral spots occupies the first 1–2 dorsal scale rows. In many specimens, the overall dorsal pattern is accentuated by the presence of narrow pale edging on all spots and blotches. The dorsal pattern may be prominent, complex, and ornate, or simple and greatly reduced (see Remarks). The venter is cream, is powdered with black in the gular region, and quickly becomes entirely black with olive green spots laterally and olive green on some sutures. The tail is colored similarly, with pale areas concentrated along the midline.

There are 10–14 keeled intersupraoculars; 8 or 9 supralabials, the second usually not fused with the prelacunal (see Remarks); 9–12 infralabials; 25–29 (usually 27) midbody dorsal scale rows; 151–173 ventrals; and 34–52 divided subcaudals. There is a report of 74 subcaudals, but this requires confirmation.

SIMILAR SPECIES The range of *B. cotiara* approaches closely or overlaps that of seven other lanceheads, although its specialized habitat probably serves to separate it ecologically from most of them. *Bothrops alternatus* possesses a pale venter and a more intricate pattern on the dorsum of the head and body. *Bothrops fonsecai* is extremely similar to *B. cotiara*, but possesses more black pigment on the infracephalic scales and has a hooklike configuration to the posterior portion of the postorbital stripe. The elements of the primary dorsal pattern tend to be fused in *B. fonsecai* and discrete in *B. cotiara*. *Bothrops fonsecai* also possesses fewer intersupraoculars. *Bothrops itapetiningae* has more pale areas on the venter and 26–38 subcaudals (vs. 34–52). The pattern of *B. itapetiningae* is distinctive and its

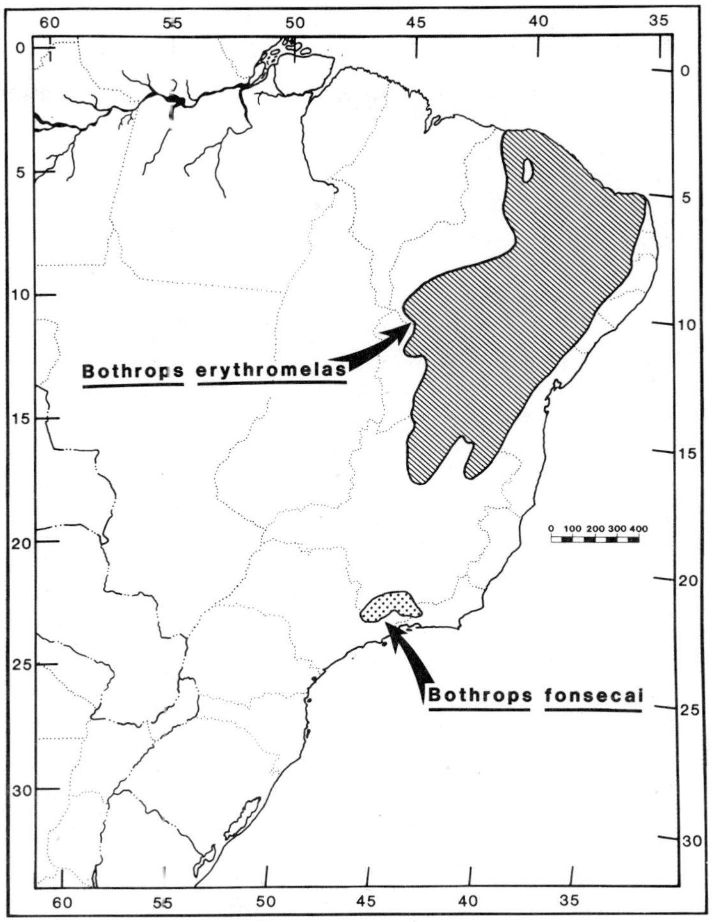


**Map 63.** Distributions of *Bothrops erythromelas* (*diagonal lines*) and *B. fonsecai* (*stipples*) in Brazil.

head markings are greatly reduced in comparison with *B. cotiara*. *Bothrops neuwiedi* has a paler venter and fewer intersupraoculars than *B. cotiara*. All other sympatric lanceheads have a second supralabial that is fused with the prelacunal (forming a lacunolabial) and lack the distinctive spear-shaped head marking.

REMARKS Reports of the occurrence of *B. cotiara* in southeastern Minas Gerais and Rio de Janeiro are probably based on *B. fonsecai*. Pattern anomalies, primarily fusion of the elements into a stripe, have been reported for this species. There also is variation in the fusion or nonfusion of the second supralabial and the prelacunal.

REFERENCES Abalos, 1977; Abalos and Mischis, 1975; Abalos and Pirosky, 1963; Amaral, 1925a, 1926d, 1930b, 1931c, 1938, 1974, 1978; Fernández Barrán and Freiberg, 1951; Fonseca, 1949; Freiberg, 1968, 1984; Gliesch, 1925; Gomes, 1913; Groombridge, 1986; Hoge and Belluomini, 1959, 1964; Lema, 1960a, 1960b, 1971a, 1971b; Lema et al., 1980; Machado, 1945b; P. Müller, 1971, 1973; J. A. Peters and Orejas-Miranda, 1970; Prado, 1945.

### *Bothrops erythromelas* Amaral

(Fig. 210; Map 63)

LOCAL NAMES Jararaca, jararaca da secca, jararacussú.

ENGLISH NAME Caatinga lancehead.

DISTRIBUTION Northeast portion of Brazil in the states of Alagoas, Bahia, Ceará, extreme eastern Maranhão, Minas Gerais, Paraíba, Pernambuco, Piauí, Rio Grande do Norte, and Sergipe (Map 63). The vertical distribution probably does not exceed 2,000 m.

HABITAT This species frequents xeric and semi-arid thorn forest, dry tropical deciduous forest, and open rocky areas. It is said to frequent elevated sandy, rocky zones and to live beneath mats of terrestrial bromeliads (macambira, *Bromelia laciniosa*). It has also been reported from along river margins.

DESCRIPTION *Bothrops erythromelas* is a slender, terrestrial lancehead that averages 400–500 mm in total length with a reported maximum of 793 mm.

The head is brown to reddish brown dorsally, with a variable pattern of darker markings. Sometimes a dark spot is present on the intercanthals and intersupraoculars, and usually a pair of elongated blotches occurs on the neck and occipital region. The canthus is short and tan to dark brown, often darker than the dorsum of the head. A white-bordered, reddish brown postorbital stripe extends from the eye to the angle of the jaw; in some specimens the postorbital stripe may be obscure. The supralabials beneath the eyes usually are paler in color than the canthus and may be white along their lower edges. The eyes are rather large and may have a dark tan mark below them. The dorsum of the body is brown to reddish brown; a series of dark brown or black, roughly triangular markings, narrowly edged in black and white or tan, alternate or meet middorsally. When opposite, these markings fuse to form a band. Each triangular marking contains a rounded blotch, which is sometimes expanded, separating the basal portion of the triangular markings into a separate series of spots. The areas of intervening ground color between the triangular markings often bear single pale-edged dark blotches. The venter is yellowish tan with ill-defined dark blotches on the sides of the ventrals extending onto the first two rows of dorsals. The remainder of the venter is finely speckled with brown. The iris is pale grayish gold.

There are 5 or 6 (often smooth) intersupraoculars, 7 or 8 supralabials (second discrete from the prelacunal), 9–11 infralabials, 19–21 midbody dorsal scale rows, 139–158 ventrals, and 32–42 divided subcaudals.

SIMILAR SPECIES The ranges of numerous lanceheads closely approach that of *B. erythromelas*, however sympatry is doubtful because of the restricted habitat for *B. erythromelas*. The following species are or may be sympatric with *B. erythromelas*: *B. iglesiasi* has 21–25 midbody dorsals (vs. 19–21) and 160–170 ventrals (vs. 144–158); *B. jararaca*, *B. leucurus*, and *B. pirajai* usually have the second supralabial fused with the prelacunal; and *B. neuwiedi* possesses 163 or more ventrals (vs. 144–158) and 37–53 subcaudals (vs. 32–42).

REMARKS The habits of this species are unknown. There are reports of *B. erythromelas* having 21–17 rows of dorsals, but we suspect this is a printing error. Experimental work has shown the venom of this species is white in color and lacks thrombinlike activity owing to a fibrinogenolytic effect.

REFERENCES Amaral, 1923, 1926a, 1930a, 1930b, 1938, 1978; Cendrero et al., 1972; Cordeiro and Hoge, 1974; Fonseca, 1949; Hoge, 1966; Hoge and Romano, 1973; Hoge and Romano-Hoge, 1981b; Ihering, 1911; Lema, 1983; Machado, 1945b; P. Müller, 1973; Nahas et al., 1979; Prado, 1945; Vanzolini et al., 1980; Vellard, 1943.

## *Bothrops fonsecai* Hoge and Belluomini

(Figs. 211–213; Map 63)

LOCAL NAMES Cotiara, jararaca.

ENGLISH NAME Fonseca's lancehead.

DISTRIBUTION Brazil, in northeastern São Paulo, southern Rio de Janeiro, and extreme southern Minas Gerais (see Map 63). The vertical distribution probably does not exceed 1,800 m.

HABITAT Well-drained areas of the Atlantic forest in zones dominated by *Araucaria*, *Podocarpus*, and other trees.

DESCRIPTION *Bothrops fonsecai* is a heavy-bodied, terrestrial lancehead; the only reported length is for the holotype, an adult male that measured 872 mm.

The dorsal color is tan to medium brown. Most of the top of the head is covered by a dark brown to black blotch in the form of an arrowhead invaded posteriorly by the ground color such that the blotch bifurcates on the neck. Usually two yellowish tan spots (which sometimes fuse into an oblong blotch) are located in the intersupraocular region or slightly posterior. The entire supracephalic blotch is bordered with yellowish tan; this color separates the postorbital stripe, which is broad, very dark, and infringes upon the posterior 4–5 supralabials before curving ventrally at the angle of the jaw. The remainder of the canthus is tan to medium brown. The supralabials are white and are nearly immaculate, except where encroached upon by the postocular stripe; occasionally a black spot is present below the loreal pit and/or below the eye. The iris is dark brown, nearly black. On the ventral side, the infralabials are black with some white spots. Much of the underside of the jaw is white with black speckling, and black pigment sometimes is complete across the neck below the angle of the jaw.

On the dorsum of the body, there are 17–19 black trapezoidal blotches on either side of the middorsal line; these blotches alternate or are opposite each other and are prominently edged in yellowish tan. A lateral series of paired smaller blotches, equally prominently colored, is situated below each dorsal blotch. These lateral blotches may be separate, fused to form bow ties, or each fused to a corner of a dorsal blotch, giving the C-shaped appearance of a telephone receiver. Smaller, poorly defined black spots (some pale edged) are scattered middorsally and in the interspaces between the dorsal blotches and lateral blotches. Another series of prominent black blotches occupies the paraventrals and ventrals; the intervening paraventrals are white to tan. The dorsal pattern concentrates on the tail, which bears 5–9 pale-edged black blotches. The venter is dark gray to black, with white pigment most prevalent anteriorly and along the lateral edges of alternate scales. The venter of the tail is black. This is a brightly patterned species of ornate aspect.

There are 8–10 keeled intersupraoculars; 8–10 supralabials, none integrated with the prelacunal; 9 infralabials, 26–28 midbody dorsal scale rows; 165–179 ventrals, and 39–57 divided subcaudals.

SIMILAR SPECIES Of the pitvipers whose ranges overlap or closely approach that of *B. fonsecai*, five share with it the characteristic of having the second supralabial discrete from the prelacunal. *Bothrops alternatus* is extremely similar in pattern but may be distinguished by its striped venter, longitudinal pale stripes on the head, and the postorbital stripe that tends to be straight rather than curved downard at the rictus. *Bothrops cotiara* also is quite similar to *B. fonsecai* but has a paler ground color, a more reduced pattern, a straight postorbital stripe, a pale anterior venter, a comparatively pale gular region, and 10–14 intersupraoculars. *Bothrops erythromelas* has a restricted habitat and is unlikely to be sympatric with *B. fonsecai*; it has a large gold-to-yellow eye, and a ground color, adult size, and pattern at complete variance with *B. fonsecai*. *Bothrops*

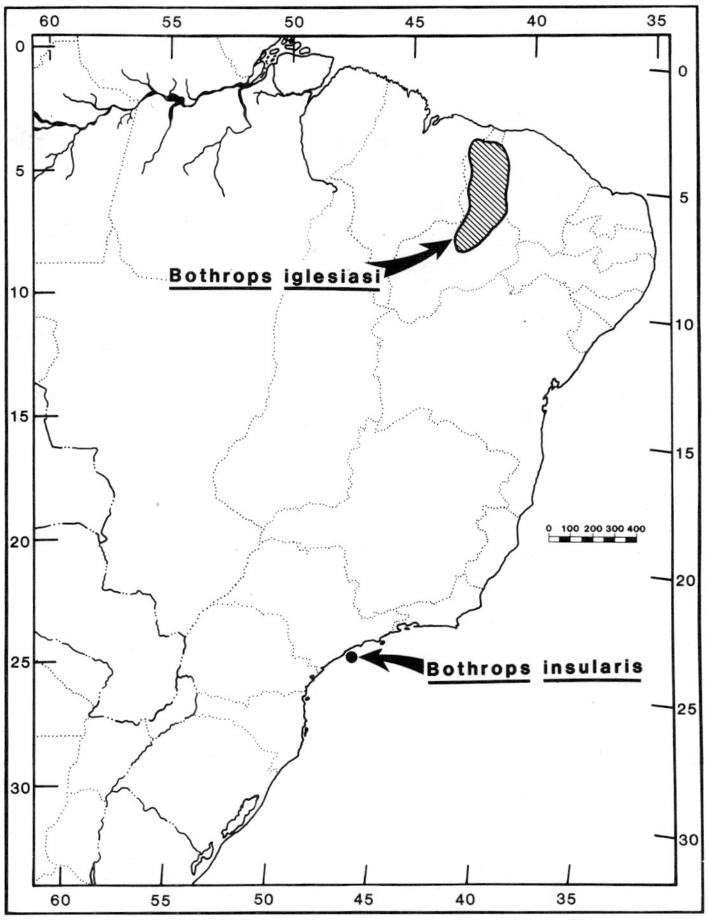


**Map 64.** Distributions of *Bothrops iglesiasi* (*diagonal lines*) and *B. insularis* (*dot*), the latter restricted to Ilha Queimada Grande off the coast of the state of São Paulo, Brazil.

*itapetiningae* has a distinctive pattern and fewer subcaudals (26–38 vs. 39–57). *Bothrops neuwiedi* is quite variable, but its pattern never closely approaches that of *B. fonsecai.* Moreover, *B. neuwiedi* has a paler venter and a less prominent postorbital stripe than *B. fonsecai.*

REMARKS Owing to its similarity to *B. alternatus*, some authors consider *B. fonsecai* to be a subspecies of the former.

REFERENCES Amaral, 1978; Groombridge, 1986; Hoge, 1966; Hoge and Belluomini, 1959, 1964; Lema, 1960b; J. A. Peters and Orejas-Miranda, 1970.

### *Bothrops iglesiasi* Amaral

(Map 64)

LOCAL NAME Jararaquinha.

ENGLISH NAME Sertão lancehead.

DISTRIBUTION Brazil. *Bothrops iglesiasi* is known only from the inland regions of the state of Piauí (Map 64). The only specific locality reported is that of the type series collected at Fazenda Grande on the "right bank" of the Rio Gurguéia. This was amended by Amaral (1926a) to the town of Regeneracão. The vertical distribution for this species probably does not exceed 300 m.

HABITAT *Bothrops iglesiasi* is said to inhabit dry to semi-arid rocky regions.

DESCRIPTION This slender terrestrial lancehead averages 400–500 mm in total length, but reaches at least 660 mm.

The following information has been extracted from the type description and a few published illustrations. The overall color is brown dorsally, including the head. The dorsum of the head bears white markings on the supraoculars, internasals, and canthal region, and there is a white blotch on the occiput. The sides of the head are dark, and there appears to be an indistinct brown postorbital stripe that runs posteriorly to the angle of the jaw, although this may be absent. There is extensive mottling on the labials. The dorsal pattern consists of a series of about 21 long dark bands on the body with about 6 more on the tail. These bands have irregular borders and may be divided and juxtaposed middorsally. The ground color is somewhat paler adjacent to the bands. The underside of the head and body are yellow, with extensive dark brown spotting. In some specimens this spotting assumes a regular pattern and tends to be most concentrated toward the outer edges of the ventrals.

There appear to be 4 or 5 keeled intersupraoculars, 8 or 9 supralabials (the second not fused with the prelacunal and the fourth being tallest), 9–13 infralabials, 21–25 (usually 23) midbody dorsal scale rows, 160–170 ventrals, and 35–43 subcaudals (most are divided).

SIMILAR SPECIES There are only two sympatric species of lanceheads with which *B. iglesiasi* might be confused: *Bothrops erythromelas* has a lower number of ventrals (139–158 vs. 160–170) and a lower number of midbody dorsal scale rows (19–21 vs. 21–25). *Bothrops neuwiedi* has a dorsal pattern of large pale-edged black spots in a single or double series with smaller lateral series, suboculars that are separated from the supralabials by a series of 2 or 3 rows of scales (1 in *B. iglesiasi*), the third and the fourth supralabials extended vertically (only the fourth in *B. iglesiasi*), and a higher number of ventrals (166–187 vs. 160–170) and subcaudals (40–53 vs. 35–43). See also the species accounts for *Lachesis* and *Crotalus*, and the discussion of false pitvipers in Mimics of Venomous Snakes.

REMARKS This species is stated to be quite common at the type locality, yet it remains poorly known and inadequately described.

REFERENCES Amaral, 1923, 1926a, 1930b, 1938, 1978; Fonseca, 1949; Hoge, 1966; Hoge and Romano, 1973; Hoge and Romano-Hoge, 1981b; Machado, 1945b; Prado, 1945.

### *Bothrops insularis* (Amaral)

(Figs. 214, 215; Map 64)

LOCAL NAME Jararaca ilhoa.

ENGLISH NAME Golden lancehead.

DISTRIBUTION Brazil. This species is endemic to the Ilha Queimada Grande (state of São Paulo), an island situated 64 km southwest of Bahia de Santos near Peruíbe (see Map 64). The vertical distribution extends to 200 m above sea level.

HABITAT The island is rocky, with scrubby forest and shrubs throughout. There is little precipitation and no pronounced change of seasons (see Remarks).

DESCRIPTION *Bothrops insularis* is a somewhat slender, semi-arboreal lancehead that averages 700 mm in overall length but may reach 1,000 mm.

The dorsum of the head and body are pale yellowish brown. Most specimens lack a well-defined postorbital stripe; if present, it is delineated by a paler stripe just dorsal to it. The eyes, labials, and underside of the head are the same color as the dorsum. The dorsal pattern consists of blotches that may be triangular or quadrangular in shape, broad or narrow, and alternating or opposite each other. When opposite, a banded pattern is created. Some specimens are patterned only faintly or not at all. The blotches may be broken middorsally, forming scattered spots, especially posteriorly. The venter is uniformly pale yellow or cream; some specimens have pale brown markings along the edges of the ventrals. Juveniles are yellowish pink or brownish pink dorsally, with faint blotches; the venter is the same as in adults.

There are 5–9 (usually 7) keeled intersupraoculars, 8 or 9 supralabials (the second is usually fused with the prelacunal), 11 infralabials (there is an unverified report of 8 or 9), 23–29 (mode 25) midbody dorsal scale rows, 171–195 ventrals, and 48–65 subcaudals (most are divided).

SIMILAR SPECIES *Bothrops insularis* is known only from its island habitat, where there are no sympatric venomous snakes.

REMARKS *Bothrops insularis* may be either arboreal or terrestrial. There is a high population density of this species on Ilha Queimada Grande. Indications are that this species possesses exceptionally toxic venom. This is one of the few species of snakes in which the presence of an intersex has been demonstrated.

REFERENCES Amaral, 1921b, 1922, 1930b, 1938, 1978; Cendrero et al., 1972; Ditmars, 1930; Fonseca, 1949; Gliesch, 1925; Hoge, 1950, 1966; Hoge et al., 1960; Hoge and Romano, 1973; Hoge and Romano-Hoge, 1981b; Klemmer, 1963; Machado, 1945b; Mertens, 1966; Neill, 1957; Prado, 1945; Schreiber et al., 1958.

### *Bothrops itapetiningae* (Boulenger)

(Figs. 216; Map 65)

LOCAL NAMES Boipeva, cotiarinha, furta-cor, jararaca do campo, pequena cotiara.

ENGLISH NAME São Paulo lancehead.

DISTRIBUTION *Bothrops itapetiningae* is found in south-central and southern Brazil from the states of Minas Gerais and southern Goiás south through southern Mato Grosso, São Paulo, and the Paraná Plateau (Map 65). There are two records from Rio Grande do Sul that, if valid, establish the occurrence of *B. itapetiningae* in Santa Catarina as well. At its southeastern extreme, the range of this species reaches the Paraguay border. Its vertical distribution probably does not exceed 1,500 m.

HABITAT This species is said to inhabit open fields and bushy areas.

DESCRIPTION *Bothrops itapetiningae* is a stocky terrestrial lancehead averaging 300–400 mm in total length, and apparently not exceeding 500 mm. If the reported size is representative, this is the smallest species of pitviper known in Brazil.

The dorsum of the head and body may be pale or dark brown with red, pink, or orange overtones. The sides of the snout are white to very pale tan. There is a broad pale brown to dark reddish brown postorbital stripe from the eye to the angle of the jaw that covers several of the posterior supralabials and infralabials. A rounded dark spot usually is present on the intercanthals or anterior intersupraoculars. On each side of the top of the head a wavy dark stripe, sometimes interrupted, extends from the intersupraocular region to the occiput. This dark stripe may be broken into a series of three paired markings: the first, a pair of spots on the intersupraoculars, followed by two pairs of oblique stripes covering the

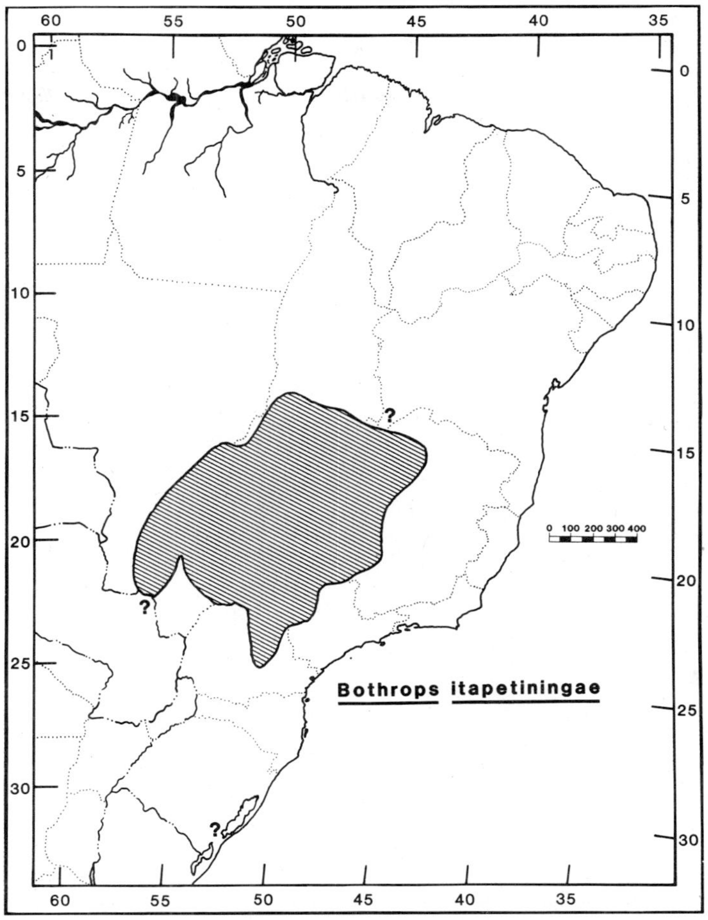


**Map 65.** Distribution of *Bothrops itapetiningae* in Brazil. Question marks represent possible areas of occurrence.

occipital region and nape. These markings, like the dorsal body markings, are usually edged in white. The remainder of the supralabials and the underside of the head are mostly white, with scattered brown speckling sometimes present.

The dorsal pattern consists of a series of narrow, transversely oval blotches, narrowly separated middorsally and dorsolaterally, situated alternately or opposite one another along the middorsal line. These blotches are dark brown brightly edged in white. The dorsolateral separation is sometimes sufficiently wide so as to create a second series of markings consisting of the basal portions of the dorsal blotches. The ground color intervening between the oval blotches usually contains a series of diffuse dark brown spots, one between each oval. The paraventrals contain a series of small dark spots that may extend onto the ventrals. The tail tip is black and brown to white. The venter is white with brown specks scattered irregularly over the anterior third, coalescing posteriorly to form progressively darker blotches that contrast strongly with the white ventral color, especially in the paraventral region. The lower sides may show more pink pigment than the rest of the dorsum. The iris is gold and the lower portion is suffused with brown.

There are 5–9 keeled intersupraoculars, 8 supralabials (none in contact with the prelacunal; the third and fourth are largest), 10 infralabials, 25–27 midbody dorsal scale rows, 144–160 ventrals, and 26–38 divided subcaudals (usually 33 or fewer).

SIMILAR SPECIES The ranges of several species of lancehead closely approach or overlap that of *B. itapetiningae*. *Bothrops alternatus* possesses 24–37 midbody dorsal scale rows (vs. 25–27), 155–190 ventrals (vs. 144–160), and 30–53 subcaudals (vs. 26–38); see the species account for an explanation of the head markings. *Bothrops cotiara* has 151–173 ventrals (vs. 144–160), 34–52 subcaudals (vs. 26–38), and a black venter with paler markings and a distinctive pattern on the head. *Bothrops fonsecai* possesses 26–28 midbody dorsal scale rows (vs. 25–27), 165–179 ventrals (vs. 144–160), 39–57 subcaudals (vs. 26–38), a black venter with paler markings, and a distinctive hook-shaped postocular stripe. In *B. jararaca*, *B. jararacussu*, and *B. moojeni*, the anterior border of the loreal pit is formed by the lacunolabial (the second supralabial and prelacunal are discrete in *B. itapetiningae*). *Bothrops neuwiedi* possesses 163 or more ventrals (vs. 144–160) and 40 or more subcaudals (vs. 26–38).

REMARKS This species shows affinities with *B. erythromelas*, found to the north, and *B. ammodytoides*, found to the south in Argentina. Its venom, along with that of *B. erythromelas*, is said to be white.

REFERENCES Amaral, 1923, 1930a, 1930b, 1938, 1978; Boulenger, 1907; Cendrero et al., 1972; Ditmars, 1930; Fonseca, 1949; Gliesch, 1925; Hoge and Romano-Hoge, 1981b; Klemmer, 1963; Lema, 1962, 1971a; Machado, 1945b; Magalhães, 1925; Prado, 1945; Vellard, 1943, 1946; Werner, 1922.

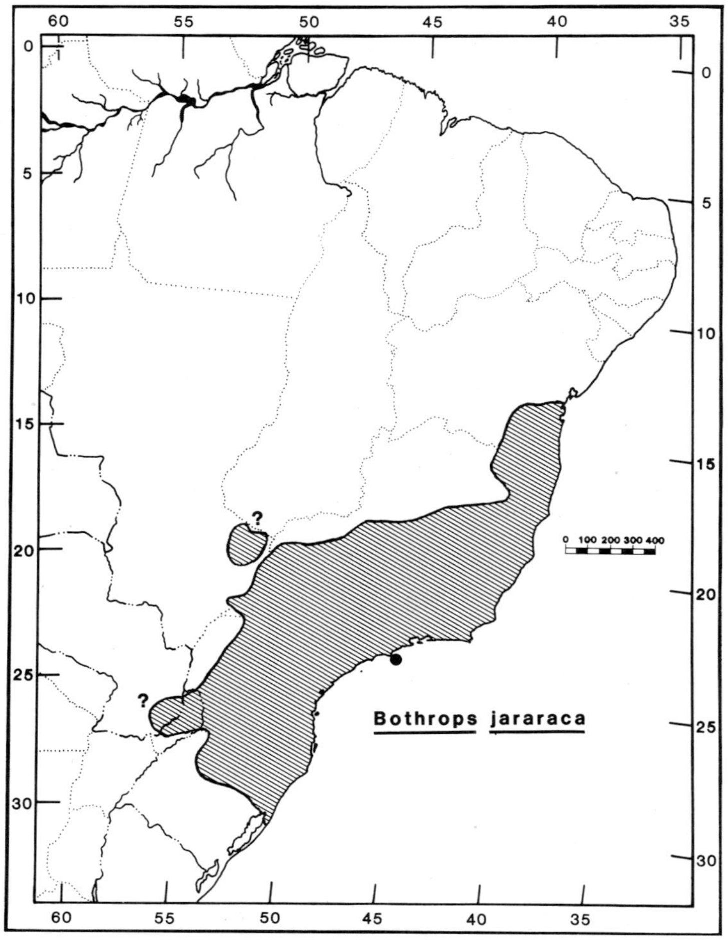


**Map 66.** Distribution of *Bothrops jararaca* in southeastern South America. The dot represents Ilha de São Sebastião. Question marks represent possible areas of occurrence.

## *Bothrops jararaca* (Wied)

(Figs. 217–219; Map 66)

LOCAL NAMES Argentina: yararaca, yararaca perezosa. Brazil: caissaca, jaraca, jaracá, jararaca, jararaca da matta virgem, jararaca do campo, jararaca do cerrado, jararaca dormideira, jararaca preguiçosa. Paraguay: yarará.

ENGLISH NAME Jararaca.

DISTRIBUTION Brazil, Paraguay, and Argentina. In Brazil, *B. jararaca* is found in southern Bahia, Espírito Santo, Rio de Janeiro, Minas Gerais, São Paulo, Paraná, Santa Catarina (including the Ilha de São Sebastião), and Rio Grande do Sul; it extends westward into extreme eastern Mato Grosso and possibly southern Goiás. The species occurs also in northern Argentina (Misiones) and in northeastern Paraguay (Map 66). The vertical distribution is unreported, but this species is most frequently encountered at low to intermediate elevations.

HABITAT *Bothrops jararaca* occupies a diversity of habitats: tropical deciduous (broadleaf) forests and savanna as well as semitropical upland forests. It is said to prefer open regions (such as cultivated areas) in close proximity to vegetation cover.

DESCRIPTION A slender, terrestrial lancehead, *B. jararaca* may be as long as 1,600 mm, although the average length is considerably less.

The color and pattern of this species are extremely variable, the pattern being subject to many anomalies. The dorsal ground color may be tan, brown, gray, yellow, olive, or nearly maroon; it is usually somewhat darker on the head and the anterior and posterior portions of the body. The dorsum of the head often bears diffuse dark markings on the occipital area, but these may be absent or obscured by darker pigment. A prominent, dark brown postorbital stripe extends from behind the eye to the angle of the jaw, usually encroaching upon the posterior three supralabials. This stripe is bordered dorsally by a distinct pale zone. The canthal region and supralabials are otherwise unmarked, although some specimens may bear a dark spot between the third and fourth supralabials. The iris is gold to greenish gold with slight darker reticulations.

The dorsal pattern consists of a series of pale-edged, dark brown trapezoidal or subtriangular markings on either side of the body, their apices on the vertebral line. These markings may either be opposite each other, or partially to completely juxtaposed; an individual will usually have all three variations. The pale borders of the brown markings are usually diffuse, but broad, and the dorsal markings are invaded heavily by the paler ground color basally. The configuration of each dorsal marking is subject to considerable, and often extreme, variation, with elongations, fusions, and fragmentations occurring. In some specimens, the middorsal region is unmarked, with the dorsal pattern reduced to a pair of undulating dorsolateral stripes. The interspaces tend to have irregular, diffuse mottling, especially on the posterior third of the body. In many specimens, the basal invasions of ground color into the dorsal blotches may have distinct shapes with well-defined edges, creating a C-shaped image resembling the outline of a telephone receiver. The overall pattern becomes more concentrated on the tail, usually appearing as irregular pale gray markings on a dark ground color. The venter is pale greenish to yellowish white with irregular blotching or a powdering of gray pigment; alternatively, it may be uniformly gray.

There are 5–12 weakly keeled intersupraoculars; 7–9 supralabials (usually 8; one record each for 6 and 10 exists), the second integrated with the prelacunal; 9–13 (usually 10–12) infralabials; 20–27 (usually 23–25) midbody dorsal scale rows; 170–216 (rarely as many as 218) ventrals; and 51–71 subcaudals, most are divided (single records for 35 and 44 exist).

SIMILAR SPECIES There are five species of lancehead known to be at least partially sympatric with *B. jararaca* that share a similar pattern and have the second supralabial fused with the prelacunal (forming a lacunolabial). *Bothrops jararacussu* is a larger, heavier species with a distinctive dorsal pattern including bold cream or yellow markings. The outer internasals are in contact with each other medially (separated in *B. jararaca*). Although there is overlap, *B. jararacussu* generally has fewer intersupraoculars (4–8) and fewer ventrals (166–186) than *B. jararaca*. *Bothrops leucurus* has a distinctly marked head and a dorsal pattern that may be more angular and complex than most *B. jararaca* specimens. *Bothrops moojeni* is a heavier species that usually has 7 supralabials (usually 8 in *B. jararaca*), a pale venter (Brazilian populations), a higher and paler canthus, a narrower postorbital stripe that usually only encroaches upon the 2 posteriormost supralabials, and a distinctive but poorly defined pair of sinuous nape markings. *Bothrops pirajai* is a heavier species that usually has 7 supralabials, 155–164 ventrals, and 43–53 subcaudals. *Bothrops pradoi* possesses a pattern that includes numerous irregular dark spots and blotches in the interspaces within the primary system of dorsal markings. There are 7 supralabials, a slightly raised canthus, and considerable dark spotting on the labials.

REMARKS *Bothrops jararaca* is an important cause of snakebite and is abundant in many parts of its range.

REFERENCES Abalos, 1977; Abalos and Mischis, 1975; Abalos and Pirosky, 1963; Amaral, 1925a, 1925b, 1926b, 1926d, 1931c, 1974, 1978; Bertoni, 1939; Brazil, 1914; A. E. Brown, 1893; Canese, 1966; Cendrero et al., 1972; Fernández Barrán and Freiberg, 1951; Fonseca, 1949; Freiberg, 1968, 1984; Gatti, 1955; Gliesch, 1925; Groombridge, 1986; Hoge, 1953e, 1966; Hoge and Romano-Hoge, 1981a, 1981b; Hoge, Belluomini, and Fernandes, 1977; Hoogmoed and Gruber, 1983; Jan, 1859b; Jan and Sordelli, 1870–1881; Johnson, 1952; Kaiser and Michl, 1971; Lacerda, 1884; Lema, 1960b, 1971b; Lema et al., 1980; Machado, 1945b, 1945c; Minton et al., 1968; P. Müller, 1968, 1969a, 1971; J. A. Peters and Orejas-Miranda, 1970; Prado, 1945; Procter, 1918; Santos, 1981; Sazima, 1987; Talbot, n.d.; Vanzolini, 1946, 1948; Wagler, 1824.

## ***Bothrops jararacussu* Lacerda**

(Figs. 220, 221; Map 67)

LOCAL NAMES Argentina: kiririóg-saiyú, surucucú apeté (Guaraní dialect), yarará-cussú, yarará dorada, yarará-guasú. Bolivia: yope pintada, yoperojobobo venenosa. Brazil: cabeça de sapo, patrona (Bahia and vicinity); jararacuçú; jararacuçú malha de sapo; jararacuçú tapete; jararacuçú verdadeiro; surucucú dourado (Rio de Janeiro and southeastern Minas Gerais); surucucú tapete; urutú amarelo; urutú dourado; urutú estrela; urutú preto. Paraguay: yarará-guasú, yarará-guazú.

ENGLISH NAME Jararacussu.

DISTRIBUTION Brazil, Paraguay, southern Bolivia, and northeast Argentina. In Brazil, *B. jararacussu* occurs from extreme southern Bahia westward across southern Minas Gerais into Mato Grosso and thence southward, including Espírito Santo, Rio de Janeiro, São Paulo, Paraná, Santa Catarina, and northwest Rio Grande do Sul. The range extends into northeast Argentina in Misiones, across Paraguay, and into southern Bolivia in the Río Pilcomayo drainage (Map 67; see Remarks). Primarily a lowland species, it does occur in highlands in suitable habitat. The vertical distribution extends from near sea level to about 600–700 m.

HABITAT *Bothrops jararacussu* is found in tropical rainforest, tropical semideciduous forest, broadleaf evergreen forest, and *paraná* pine forest in swampy, low-lying areas and along river margins.

DESCRIPTION A large, heavy-bodied lancehead, *B. jararacussu* averages 1 m or more, but reaches at least 2,200 mm in total length.

The dorsal ground color varies from pale gray or pink to tan, yellow, brown, or black. The top of the head is usually dark brown to sooty black. The head is large and a dark brown or black postorbital stripe runs from the eye to the angle of the jaw, covering portions of the sixth through the eighth supralabials. This stripe is bordered dorsally by a thin yellow, beige, or gray stripe that extends onto the neck, where the postorbital stripe unites with the body pattern. The canthal region and supralabials may be pale gray, tan, or yellow, and unmarked, or black pigment may be present, especially along sutures. The infralabials and gular region usually are immaculate yellow or cream. The iris is gold, with dark red highlights around the pupil.

The dorsal body pattern is extremely variable but usually involves a series of bold lateral triangular or C-shaped markings that approach the middorsum and may alternate or be opposite one another. The inter-

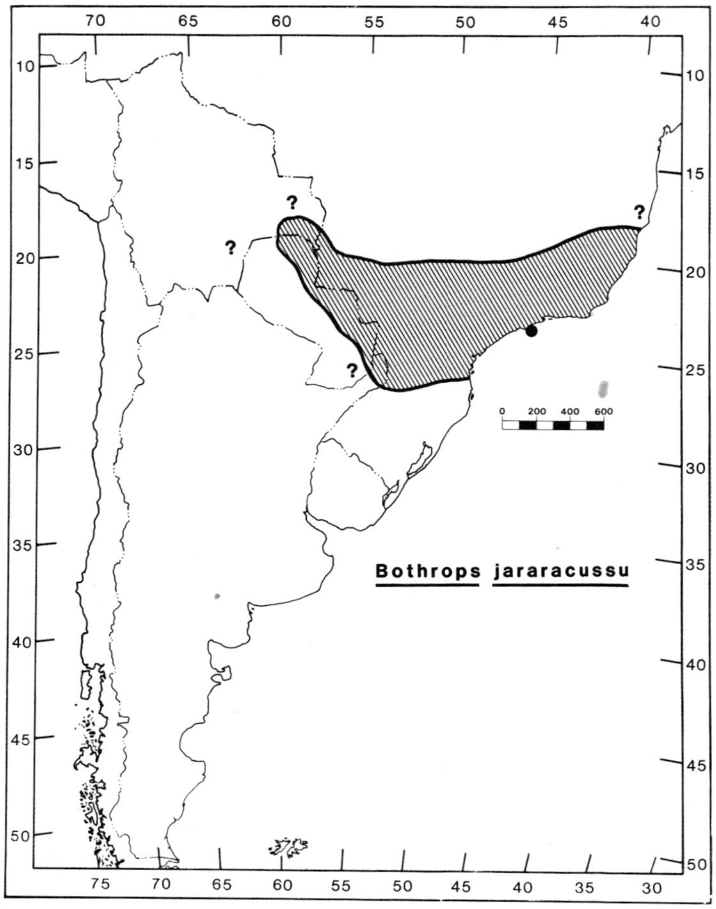


**Map 67.** Distribution of *Bothrops jararacussu* in southeastern South America. The dot represents Ilha de São Sebastião. Question marks represent possible areas of occurrence.

spaces usually bear small diffuse blotches or ocelli, often clustered in pairs middorsally. The lateral markings are edged broadly with pale tan, gray, or yellow, such that this shade actually obscures the dark ground color, often reducing it to an undulating middorsal stripe. In other specimens, the pattern is reduced and the pale edging not nearly so well defined. Still others may show a coalescence of dark pigment such that all elements of the pattern fuse and form an asymmetrical design. There is evidence that an ontogenetic increase in melanism exists in *B. jararacussu*; if true, then much of the variation reported might be explained. Old adults not infrequently are melanized heavily, although an occasional specimen will be predominantly yellow overall. The tail is usually black dorsally. The venter is cream to yellow with some black spotting, especially toward the paraventrals. In most individuals, the collective effect of the pattern is one of ornate contrast; many specimens tend to be dark velvety black and bright creamy yellow. However, the pattern and colors may be muted.

There are 4–8 keeled intersupraoculars; 8 supralabials, the second integrated with the prelacunal; 9–11 infralabials; 23–29 midbody dorsal scale rows (usually 23–27); 166–186 ventrals; and 44–66 subcaudals, most are divided (there is one report of 29 subcaudals in this species).

SIMILAR SPECIES *Bothrops jararacussu* is or may be sympatric with at least 17 species of pitviper. The following combination of characteristics distinguishes it from most: a snout normal in shape, a distinct postorbital stripe, the second supralabial fused with the prelacunal to form a lacunolabial, no rattle, all or most subcaudals divided, and the tail not prehensile. *Lachesis muta* has finely divided subcaudals distally. *Bothrops jararaca* has outer internasals that are separated from each other by 1 or more scales (in contact in *B. jararacussu*) and a distinctive pattern not involving bold, contrasting colors. Although there is overlap, *B. jararaca* tends to have more (5–12) intersupraoculars and ventrals (170–216); also it lacks the broad, triangular head shape of *B. jararacussu*. *Bothrops leucurus* possesses 195–225 ventrals and has a distinctive series of dark markings on the dorsum of the head (lacking in *B. jararacussu*). *Bothrops moojeni* has 9 or 10 intersupraoculars, usually a nearly immaculate venter, and a narrow postorbital stripe. *Bothrops pirajai* has fewer ventrals (155–167 vs. 170–186), although its pattern is quite similar to that of *B. jararacussu*. *Bothrops pradoi* has a greater number of intersupraoculars (10 or more vs. 4–8) and ventrals (191–207 vs. 170–186). *Bothrops sanctaecrucis* lacks a well-defined postorbital stripe, has an indistinct dorsal pattern, and has a venter that is essentially immaculate (see Remarks for *B. atrox*).

REMARKS The stated occurrence of *B. jararacussu* in the Río Pilcomayo drainage of southern Bolivia is puzzling. Specimens have not been reported from the adjacent Paraguayan Chaco; rather they tend to occur to the

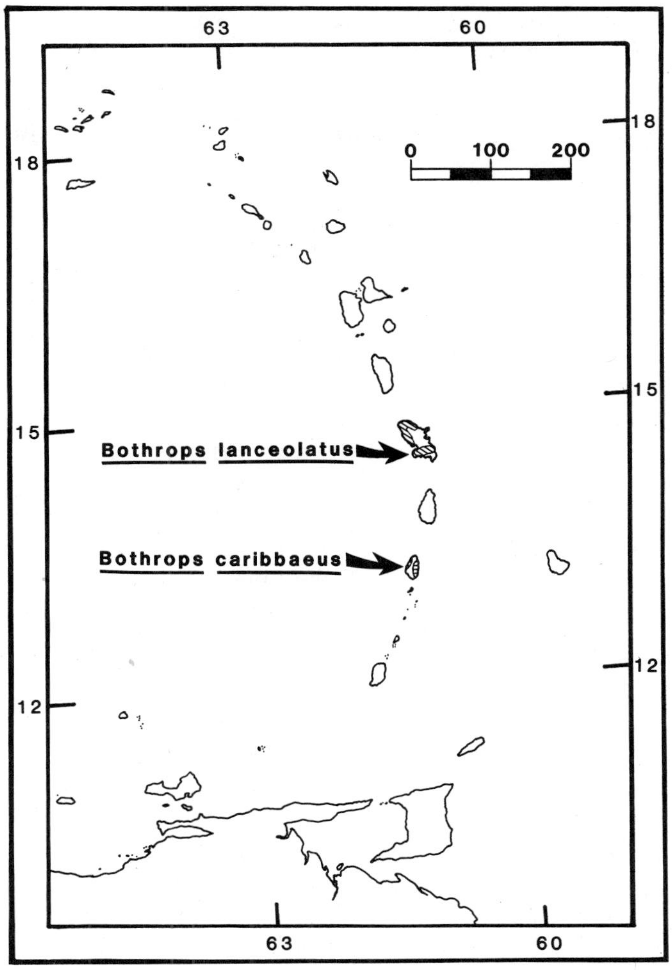


**Map 68.** Distributions of *Bothrops caribbaeus* (*horizontal lines*) and *B. lanceolatus* (*diagonal lines*) on the islands of Saint Lucia and Martinique, respectively, Lesser Antilles.

north along the Río Paraguay. It thus seems more likely that *B. jararacussu* would exist in the southeastern Departamento de Santa Cruz (as indicated on Map 67), although an isolated population may eventually be encountered along the upper Río Pilcomayo in Chuquisaca or Tarija.

Like many of the large, terrestrial lanceheads, *B. jararacussu* lacks distinctive scutellation; however, the dorsal pattern serves to distinguish it from its congeners. *Bothrops jararacussu* has an exceptionally large capacity for venom and is an important source of snakebite.

REFERENCES Abalos, 1977; Abalos and Mischis, 1975; Abalos and Pirosky, 1963; Amaral, 1925a, 1925b, 1926d, 1930b, 1931c, 1938, 1974, 1978; Bertoni, 1914, 1939; Brazil, 1914; Canese, 1966; Cendrero et al., 1972; Ditmars, 1937; Fernández Barrán and Freiberg, 1951; Fonseca, 1949; Freiberg, 1968, 1984; Gatti, 1955; Gliesch, 1925; Groombridge, 1986; Hoge, 1966; Hoge and Romano, 1973; Hoge and Romano-Hoge, 1981a, 1981b; Ihering, 1911; Kaiser and Michl, 1971; Kempff-Mercado, 1975; Lacerda, 1884; Lema, 1960b; Lema and Leitão de Araujo, 1980; Machado, 1945b; Migone, 1929; L. Müller, 1927; P. Müller, 1968, 1969a; J. A. Peters and Orejas-Miranda, 1970; Prado, 1945; Procter, 1918; Santos, 1981; Schouten, 1937; Talbot, n.d.

### *Bothrops lanceolatus* (Lacépède)

(Figs. 222–225; Map 68)

LOCAL NAMES Fer-de-lance (see Remarks), le serpent, le trigonocephale, serpent, serpent croissant (females), serpent jaune (males and juveniles), serpent rouge (males and juveniles), vipére jaune.

ENGLISH NAME Martinique lancehead.

DISTRIBUTION The island of Martinique, West Indies. The distribution seems to be disjunct, with two isolated populations confined to humid upland regions in the northern and southern portions of the island. The northern population ranges over roughly one-third of Martinique from above Fort-de-France northward to the Montagne Pelée Massif and in wetter portions of the northern windward coast. The southern population ranges from the region of Morne Serpent and Morne Vauclin southwestwardly into the hilly region between Les Trois-Ilets and Les Anses-d'Arlets (Map 68). The vertical distribution ranges to about 1,300 m.

HABITAT *Bothrops lanceolatus* is an inhabitant of tropical moist forest and tropical wet forest, primarily in upland regions. It also occupies rocky hillsides and tends to be arboreal, having been found as high as 20 m above ground.

DESCRIPTION *Bothrops lanceolatus* is a large, semiarboreal lancehead that averages 1,500 mm or more in length and can attain a size in excess of 2,000 mm. There is an unofficial record of 2,980 mm for this species; if true, it surely represents an extreme case.

The dorsal ground color varies from gray to brown to yellowish tan. The dorsum of the head is usually the same color as the body, although it may be somewhat darker; in particularly obscure specimens it may be nearly black. A shiny, dark brown to black postorbital stripe extends from behind the eye to the angle of the jaw and thence downward, sometimes merging with the neck pattern. This stripe covers portions of the posteriormost 3 or 4 supralabials and a portion of the last infralabial. The postorbital stripe is not invariably present; some specimens tend to be yellow overall (Fig. 224) and may lack a facial stripe or have it poorly defined. The canthus and supralabials are unpatterned but may show a dusting of pink and/or dark speckles overall or below the eye. The postorbital stripe (when present) is bordered above by a narrow pale stripe. The iris is pale grayish tan with dark speckling; in some specimens it is uniformly yellowish tan. The dorsal pattern also is variable; some specimens lack all traces of dark marking, while others are so obscure the markings are difficult to discern. A series of paravertebral dark markings is invaded by the paler ground color such that only the peripheral dark pigment remains, giving each a configuration reminiscent of a horseshoe. These markings are bordered anteriorly and posteriorly by paler pigment and the middorsal pattern frequently is obscured, leaving a disjunct series of poorly defined pale spots and a lateral series of dark spots (representing the basal corners of each marking). In specimens lacking a middorsal darkening, the pattern may appear banded; others may lack the lateral component. The venter is nearly immaculate; there may be a scattering of gray or some weakly defined paraventral spots. The distal portion of the tail is pink in juveniles.

There are 5–11 keeled intersupraoculars; 7–8 supralabials, the second integrated with the prelacunal; 9–11 infralabials; 29–33 midbody dorsal scale rows; 208–240 ventrals; and 55–72 subcaudals, all or most of which are paired.

SIMILAR SPECIES No other venomous snakes inhabit the island of Martinique; the two other species of snakes on the island bear no resemblance to *B. lanceolatus*.

REMARKS The popular name *fer-de-lance* has been applied most often to mainland forms such as *B. asper* and *B. atrox*, and it has become moderately entrenched in the English language. Apparently, the term was coined by Lacépède when he described *B. lanceolatus*, as he allegedly disliked the vernacular name *vipére jaune*. Thus, while *fer-de-lance* applies strictly to the Martinique species, it has no vernacular value and has never been used on the island.

Deaths have been recorded from the bite of *B. lanceolatus*. An early reference to the alleged occurrence of *B. lanceolatus* on the island of Petit Martinique (Grenadines) has been interpreted as due to disagreement about vernacular names. But because there are no snakes extant on that island, the matter of whether *B. lanceolatus* or some other lancehead (or harmless species) existed there in the recent past remains unresolved. *Bothrops lanceolatus* has been cited as occurring on the South American mainland; these reports apparently were based on specimens of *B. asper*, *B. atrox*, or *B. moojeni*.

REFERENCES Amaral, 1921a, 1925a, 1925b, 1955a; Barbour, 1914; Boulenger, 1896; A. E. Brown, 1893; Dowling, 1965; Gosner, 1987; Groombridge, 1986; Hoge, 1953d, 1966; Hoge and Romano-Hoge, 1981a; Lalung, 1934; Lazell, 1964; Minton et al., 1968; P. Müller, 1973; Noguchi, 1909; Procter, 1918; Sandner-Montilla, 1979a, 1981; Schwartz and Henderson, 1985; Schwartz and Thomas, 1975; Underwood, 1962; Vellard, 1946; Werner, 1927.

### *Bothrops leucurus* Wagler

(Fig. 226; Map 71)

LOCAL NAME Jararaca.

ENGLISH NAME White-tailed lancehead.

DISTRIBUTION Brazil. This species is known only from the region of Salvador in Bahia (see Map 71). There is an unsubstantiated record from Sergipe. The vertical distribution ranges from near sea level to about 300–400 m.

HABITAT The habitat is inadequately reported, but *B. leucurus* allegedly inhabits Atlantic forest remnants in valleys. It is also found in regions of agricultural activity where deforestation has taken place.

DESCRIPTION *Bothrops leucurus* is a slender, terrestrial lancehead with a reported maximum length of 1,117 mm (see Remarks).

The dorsal ground color varies from reddish brown to tan, possibly darker on the head. A dark postorbital stripe extends from behind the eye to the corner of the mouth, although the canthus may be suffused with dark pigment such that this stripe is not visible (see Remarks). The dorsum of the head usually bears some irregular dark spots, and these may be present on both the snout and occiput, occasionally fusing to form transverse markings. The postorbital stripe is bordered dorsally by a paler zone which, in turn, is bordered broadly in black. A pair of curved dark markings on the posterior occiput may extend onto the neck. The dorsal pattern consists of 18–21 transverse rectangular or trapezoidal markings that may be united to form bands or that may be separated along the midline and slightly juxtaposed. These markings may be paler medially and bordered in black and white, or they may be predominantly black. The intervening spaces may be unmarked, or they may contain irregular black spots and blotches. The transverse dorsal markings are bordered basally by two black spots that collectively form a series along each side. The underside of the head is dark brown with lighter spots; beneath the body, the dark pigment is concentrated laterally with irregular mottling medially. In some individuals, the venter may be uniformly yellow or white. The tip of the tail is white, at least in juveniles.

There are usually 7 intersupraoculars; 7–8 supralabials, the second integrated with the prelacunal; 24–31 midbody dorsal scale rows; 195–225 ventrals; and 63–75 divided subcaudals (see Remarks).

SIMILAR SPECIES *Bothrops leucurus* is sympatric with four species of lancehead that share the characteristic of having a lacunolabial (second supralabial fused with the prelacunal). *Bothrops jararaca* possesses 5–12 intersupraoculars, a pattern not usually involving dark markings on top of the head, and a body pattern somewhat different from that of *B. leucurus*. *Bothrops jararacussu* is larger and heavier bodied than *B. leucurus*, and differs from it in pattern and in possessing 166–186 ventrals. *Bothrops pirajai* is a lancehead of heavy build that possesses 155–167 ventrals. *Bothrops pradoi* differs from *B. leucurus* in possessing darkly spotted labials and 10 intersupraoculars.

REMARKS *Bothrops leucurus* is poorly known. It has been considered by some to be conspecific with *B. megaera* Wagler, of which its name is a senior synonym. We have seen no compelling evidence that this is correct, but the above account is nonetheless a composite that includes the description of *B. megaera*. The holotype of *B. megaera* had an incomplete tail; aside from this, data on its lepidosis are included in this account. The holotype of *B. megaera* is lost, but it represented the maximum known size for the species, 1,117 mm. Wagler (1824) based his description of *B. leucurus* upon juveniles (thus, probably the reference to white tails). Substantive pattern differences (immaculate venter, uniform dorsal bands, shaded postorbital region) exist between the descriptions of these two taxa, and their relationship is worthy of closer investigation—especially since other poorly known species such as *B. pirajai* and *B. pradoi* are found in Bahía (there is a paucity of specimens or studies emanating from that region).

REFERENCES Boulenger, 1896; Hoge, 1966; Hoge and Romano, 1973; Hoge and Romano-Hoge, 1981b; Hoogmoed and Gruber, 1983; Johnson and Dixon, 1984; P. Müller, 1973; Wagler, 1824.

### *Bothrops lojanus* Parker

(Fig. 227; Map 78)

LOCAL NAMES Macanchi, macaucho, tigre, ysipi (?).

ENGLISH NAME Lojan lancehead.

DISTRIBUTION Ecuador. This species is known only from the provinces of Loja and Zamora-Chinchipe. Although most specimens collected have been from the vicinity of the city of Loja, the species has also been collected near Saraguro (see Map 78). The vertical distribution ranges from 2,100 to 2,250 m.

HABITAT *Bothrops lojanus* is an inhabitant of arid temperate regions, primarily in montane dry forest.

DESCRIPTION *Bothrops lojanus* is a moderately stocky terrestrial lancehead that averages 400–500 mm in length, but can reach as much as 610 mm.

The dorsum of the head and body is tan to medium brown. The top of the head usually bears some elongated, symmetrically arranged dark brown markings beginning just anterior to the intersupraoculars and extending posteriorly over the temporal region. These may be poorly defined. A prominent, dark brown postorbital stripe crosses the posteriormost 2–3 supralabials and extends to the angle of the jaw, where it sometimes is fused with the first lateral blotch. The postorbital stripe is edged ventrally in white. The supralabials are somewhat paler than the rest of the head and may contain some white flecks and dark peppering. The iris is dark brown (a continuation of the postorbital stripe) fading to light brown dorsally. The underside of the head is tan and sometimes heavily mottled with white, a continuation of the supralabial pattern. Middorsally, the body bears a dark brown zig-zag stripe that tends to become fragmented posteriorly into a series of black-edged dark brown blotches. Laterally, small, indistinct brown blotches (up to 48) parallel the middorsal pattern. The paraventrals and adjacent edges of the ventrals are alternately white and dark brown, creating a spotted effect. The venter is yellow, mottled or flecked with pale to dark brown, becoming increasingly darker posteriorly. The subcaudals are usually salmon to brick red, at least distally. The tail has a ventrolateral pale stripe for most of its length, and pale vertical bars extend up on the sides and may coalesce middorsally.

There are 3–5 (usually 5) smooth or faintly keeled intersupraoculars, sometimes with a large median scale; 7–8 supralabials (the second usually fused with the prelacunal); 8–10 infralabials; 21–23 (usually 23) midbody dorsal scale rows; 144–155 ventrals; and 37–46 subcaudals (most are divided).

SIMILAR SPECIES *Bothrops lojanus* may be distinguished from Ecuadorian *Bothriechis*, *Bothriopsis*, and *Porthidium* species by its divided subcaudals and/or low number of ventrals (155 or fewer). Other similar pitvipers from the Ecuadorian region include *B. microphthalmus*, which has the prelacunal discrete from the second supralabial; *B. pulcher*, which has a banded or unicolor dorsum and a poorly defined postocular stripe or none; and *B. brazili*, an Amazonian species that usually lacks a postocular stripe and has 151–202 ventrals. See also the species accounts for *B. asper* and *B. xanthogrammus*.

REMARKS The correct application of the vernacular name *ysipi* requires confirmation.

REFERENCES Duellman, 1979; Groombridge, 1986; Hoge and Romano-Hoge, 1981a; Orcés, 1948; Parker, 1930, 1932, 1934, 1938; J. A. Peters, 1955, 1960a; J. A. Peters and Orejas-Miranda, 1970; Touzet, 1983.

### *Bothrops marajoensis* Hoge

(Fig. 228; Map 69)

LOCAL NAME Jararaca.

ENGLISH NAME Marajó lancehead.

DISTRIBUTION Brazil. *Bothrops marajoensis* is found in Amapá, on the Ilha Marajó, state of Pará (Map

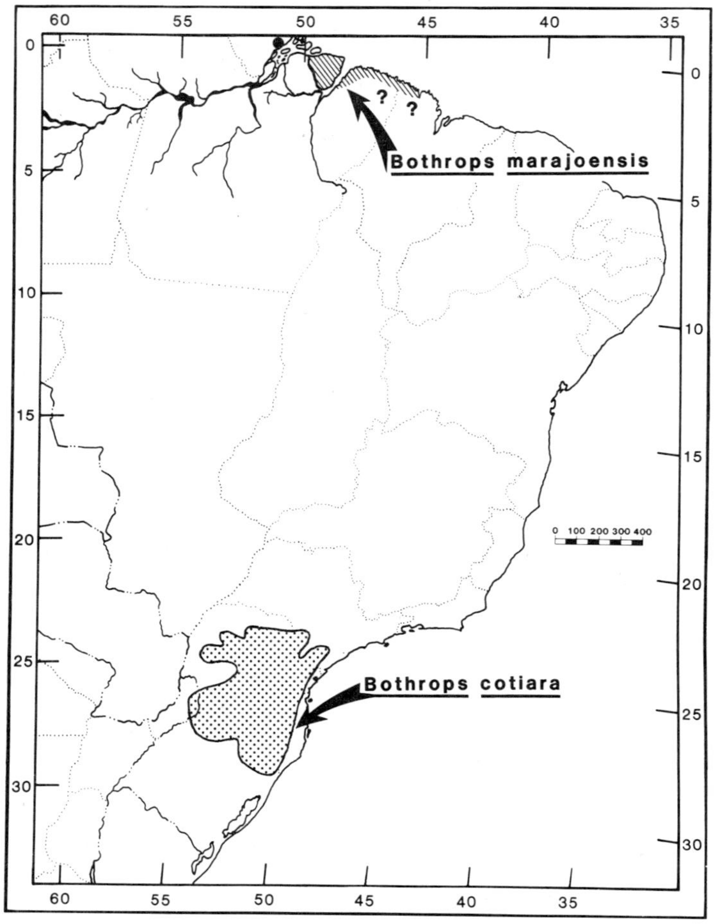


**Map 69.** Distributions of *Bothrops cotiara* (*stipples*) and *B. marajoensis* (*diagonal lines*) in eastern South America. The distribution of *B. marajoensis* in the southeastern portion of its range is poorly known. The dot represents a record for *B. marajoensis* in Macapá, Amapá, Brazil. Question marks represent possible areas of occurrence.

69), and possibly southward along the coast of mainland Pará and questionably into equatorial regions of the state of Maranhão (see Remarks). The stated distribution comprises coastal lowlands in the Amazon Delta, not much above sea level.

HABITAT This species is said to inhabit lowland savannah on Ilha Marajó, where it occurs on the mainland; it may be restricted to savannas, but data are lacking (see Remarks).

DESCRIPTION *Bothrops marajoensis* is a terrestrial lancehead of medium build that reaches an overall length of about 1,500 mm.

The dorsum of the head and body is olive-brown, usually darker middorsally and on the head. A prominent dark brown postorbital stripe partially covers the posteriormost 2–3 supralabials, extending beyond them and sometimes curving downward at the angle of the jaw. The postorbital stripe is bordered dorsally by an olive-tan occipital stripe about 3 scales in width. The canthus and labials are olive-tan and unmarked except for an occasional dark brown spot. The iris is bronze, becoming paler peripherally. There are 19–21 brown-to-black dorsal markings on the body, triangular to trapezoidal in shape and formed by 4 spots, the upper 2 fused and the lower 2 separated from each other and from the upper 2. These markings tend to alternate middorsally rather than to form bands. Laterally, the areas contained within these markings may be paler than the dorsal ground color. The dorsal markings are bordered distinctly with tan, which covers ½–2 dorsals. The interspaces are occupied middorsally by ill-defined brown spots, some of which are pale edged. On the tail, the pattern becomes concentrated such that the tail may appear black; alternatively, 4–5 dark bands may be present. The venter is cream to yellow, checkered heavily with black (including the tail). Laterally, the black pigment forms a series of spots that encroach upon the paraventrals. The tail tip is pale ventrally.

There are 5 or more keeled intersupraoculars (the supraoculars are rather narrow); 7–8 supralabials, the second integrated with the prelacunal; 8–9 infralabials; 25 midbody dorsal scale rows; 176–194 ventrals; and 60 paired subcaudals.

SIMILAR SPECIES Depending on the southern extent of the range of *B. marajoensis*, there are 5–9 potentially sympatric pitvipers. Of these, only 4 are likely to be confused with *B. marajoensis*. The forest-pitvipers *Bothriopsis bilineata* and *Bothriopsis taeniata* have patterns and pigments at variance with *Bothrops marajoensis* and possess 192 or more ventrals. *Bothrops brazili* lacks a well-defined postorbital stripe and has a dissimilar pattern. *Bothrops atrox* overlaps *B. marajoensis* in characteristics of scutellation, but apparently differs somewhat in pattern by having spotted supralabials, a tendency to form transverse bands dorsally, and a short, raised keel on each dorsal (the keel is long and low in *B. marajoensis*). There may also be habitat differ-

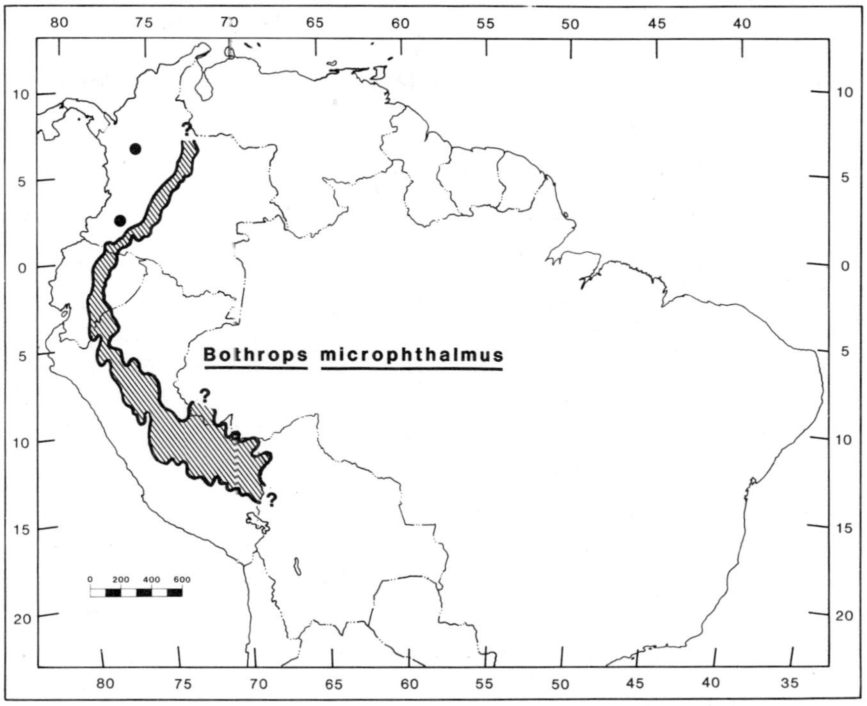


**Map 70.** Distribution of *Bothrops microphthalmus* in northwestern South America. The dots represent isolated records for the subspecies *B. m. colombianus*. Question marks represent possible areas of occurrence.

ences. See also the species accounts for *B. erythromelas*, *B. moojeni*, and *B. neuwiedi*.

REMARKS *Bothrops marajoensis* is a problematic species. Its distribution has been stated variously (even in the same publication) to be restricted to Ilha Marajó and to include the mainland of Pará and Maranhão. Its distinction from *B. atrox* is tenuous at best. Recent works on eastern Pará have cited only the latter species as occurring there. The occurrence of *B. marajoensis* in Amapá (Fig. 228) has not been reported previously and may indicate a more extensive distribution north of Ilha Marajó. The condition of the dorsal keels may be variable. In the absence of more compelling data, we tentatively regard *B. marajoensis* as distinct.

REFERENCES Cunha and Nascimento, 1978; Hagmann, 1909; Hoge, 1966; Hoge and Romano, 1973; Hoge and Romano-Hoge, 1981a, 1981b; P. Müller, 1969b, 1971, 1973; J. A. Peters and Orejas-Miranda, 1970.

## *Bothrops microphthalmus* Cope

(Figs. 229, 230; Map 70)

LOCAL NAMES Bolivia: yoperojobobo. Brazil: jararaca (?). Colombia: equis colorada (Cordillera Occidental), mapaná (Cordillera Oriental), talla, taya. Ecuador: hoja podrida. Peru: equis, jergón, jergón pudridora, jergón shushupe.

ENGLISH NAME Small-eyed lancehead.

DISTRIBUTION Amazonian slopes of the Andes in Colombia, Ecuador, and Peru. This species is known from a single specimen in Bolivia and a questionable record from Brazil. Another population exists on the Pacific slopes of the Andes in southwest Colombia (Map 70; see Remarks). The vertical distribution extends to at least 2,350 m and probably much higher.

HABITAT Lower montane wet forest and cloud forest.

DESCRIPTIONS *Bothrops microphthalmus* is a terrestrial, slightly heavy-bodied lancehead that reaches an overall length of at least 1,360 mm (see Remarks) but averages 400–700 mm.

This species is variably colored, with the dorsum of the head and body ranging from brown to straw colored to gray. Adults tend to become more melanized with age; juveniles may be quite pale in color. The dorsum of the head usually lacks distinct markings. The sides of the head are usually paler than the ground color or they may be yellow, with or without profuse fine speckling on the labials. A dark brown postorbital stripe, pale edged above, extends from the eye to the angle of the jaw. The iris is grayish gold to brownish gold with speckling throughout and a tendency toward paleness dorsally and along the circumference. The pupil is edged narrowly in gold. The dorsal pattern consists of about 18–21 irregular transverse markings, usually with paler centers, that are opposite one another or juxtaposed middorsally. These markings are usually most prominent posteriorly, although they may be obscured by dark ground color. Laterally viewed, they may be trapezoidal to nearly triangular in shape. The usually paler interspaces may show some darkening middorsally, the palest scales being those bordering bands. The pattern sometimes is fused on the tail to form a partial stripe. The distal portion of the tail is salmon ventrally and, in juveniles, dorsally as well. Ventrally the gulars and infralabials vary from being yellow and unmarked to mostly dark with a few pale spots. The belly usually is mottled heavily with dark brown pigment, especially on the lateral edges of the ventrals; the pigmentation increases posteriorly, the belly becoming black toward the tail. In this species, the anterior portion of the snout is very slightly upturned, and the eyes are relatively smaller than those of similar lanceheads.

There are 4–8 keeled intersupraoculars; 7 or 8 supralabials, the second discrete from the prelacunal; 9–11 infralabials; 21–25 midbody dorsal scale rows (see Remarks); 137–173 ventrals (see Remarks); and 44–56 divided subcaudals.

SIMILAR SPECIES *Bothrops microphthalmus* is distinguishable from all sympatric congeners by the following combination of characteristics: a prelacunal discrete from the second supralabial, fewer than 180 ventrals, and most subcaudals divided. See the species accounts for *B. asper*, *B. atrox*, *B. brazili*, *B. lojanus*, *B. neuwiedi*, *B. pulcher*, *Porthidium hyoprora*, and *P. nasutum*.

REMARKS *Bothrops microphthalmus* has not been studied adequately, and it may represent a composite of more than one species. The enigmatic *B. m. colombianus* was described from the Pacific slopes of the Cordillera Occidental of the Colombian Andes. It is known only from the type locality (La Costa, Cauca; elevation 800 m) and from the vicinity of Yarumal, Antioquia; it is distinguished from the nominate race on the basis of having a higher number of midbody dorsal scale rows (25 vs. 21–23), a higher number of ventrals (166–173), and a different coloration. There is an unverified report from Andagoya, Chocó. The two specimens on which the description was based are the largest yet recorded for the species (1,295 and 1,360 mm); the nominate race is not known to exceed 941 mm. The color description provided for the type series is inadequate and does not sharply distinguish this unique population. An additional specimen is reported to have tubercular keels on the dorsals, a small black spot on the supralabials and infralabials below the eye, and an essentially pale venter with prominent black paraventral blotches. The nominate race, *B. m. microphthalmus* (Figs. 229, 230), occupies the remainder of the species' range and apparently occurs in Colombia, where it has been recorded along the eastern versant of the Andes in Boyacá, Casanare, and Cundinamarca. Specimens from Casanare have a ventral count as high as 168, but possess the typical complement of middorsals (23).

REFERENCES Amaral, 1930a; Ayerbe, 1979; Boulenger, 1896, 1912; Carrillo de Espinoza, 1983; Cope, 1876b, 1879; Groombridge, 1986; Hoge and Romano-Hoge, 1981a; Kempff-Mercado, 1975; Meneses, 1974a, 1974b; P. Müller, 1973; Nicéforo-María, 1964, 1975; Noguchi, 1909; Orcés, 1942, 1943, 1948; Pérez-Santos and Moreno, 1986; J. A. Peters, 1960a; J. A. Peters and Orejas-Miranda, 1970; Prado and Hoge, 1948; Rendahl and Vestergren, 1940; Renjifo, 1979; Schmidt and Walker, 1943a; Soini, 1974b.

## *Bothrops moojeni* Hoge

(Figs. 231, 232; Map 71)

LOCAL NAME Caissaca.

ENGLISH NAME Brazilian lancehead.

DISTRIBUTION Brazil and Paraguay. This species is known in Brazil from the Federal District and the states of Piauí, Paraná, São Paulo, Mato Grosso, Mato Grosso do Sul, Minas Gerais, Goiás, and Maranhão (see Remarks). In Paraguay, this species has been found in the northeast (Map 71; see Remarks). The vertical distribution ranges from the lowlands to at least 1,500 m.

HABITAT Semi-arid (or seasonally dry) tropical savannahs.

DESCRIPTION *Bothrops moojeni* is a large terrestrial lancehead with a maximum total length of at least 1,680 mm.

The dorsal color varies and may be tan, grayish brown, or olive-gray. The dorsum of the head is patternless and usually darker than that of the body. A dark gray to brown postorbital stripe extends from behind the eye to the angle of the jaw, usually covering portions of the two posteriormost supralabials. This stripe may be broad or narrow; it is bordered dorsally by a pale gray to tan occipital stripe that extends from behind the supraoculars to the sides of the neck. The canthus and labials are immaculate and of the same pale color as the occipital stripe. The iris is pale and matches the canthus in color. The tongue is dark gray to grayish pink. The dorsal pattern on the body consists of 18–21 dark gray to black trapezoidal markings, either opposite each other or (usually) slightly juxtaposed middorsally; on the tail there are 4–7 poorly defined gray-to-brown crossbands. There are usually 2 pale stripes, slightly undulating, on the neck. The dorsal markings are edged in tan or pale gray, which extends laterally to the venter and embraces a series of black spots located in pairs opposite the bases of the dorsal markings. The dark interspaces are somewhat diamond shaped and may contain ill-defined darker spots. The gular region and venter are nearly immaculate white with scattered, poorly defined gray dots. Juveniles have a pale tail tip.

There are 9 or 10 keeled intersupraoculars; 7 supralabials, the second fused with the prelacunal (forming a lacunolabial); 8–11 infralabials; 23–29 midbody dorsals; 179–210 ventrals; and 44–70 paired subcaudals. There is a questionable report of 33 midbody dorsal scale rows for this species.

SIMILAR SPECIES *Bothrops moojeni* is or may be sympatric with at least 14 species of pitvipers. The following combination of characteristics distinguish it from most: divided subcaudals, a distinct postorbital stripe, the second supralabial integrated with the prelacunal, no rattle, and a nearly immaculate venter. *Bothriopsis bilineata* has a green dorsum and a cream ven-

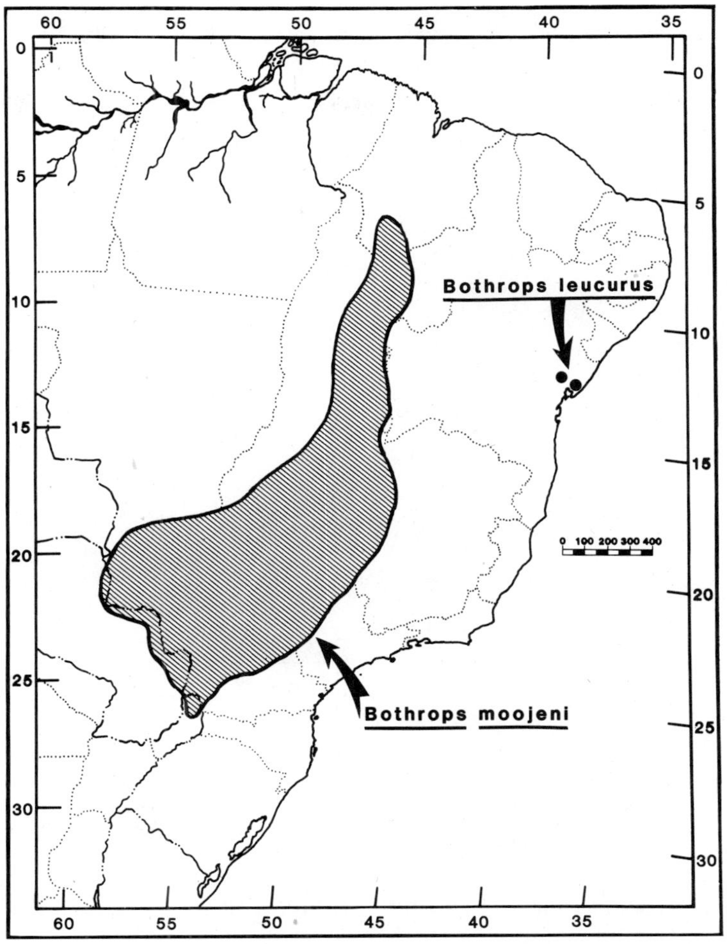


**Map 71.** Distributions of *Bothrops leucurus* (*dots*) and *B. moojeni* (*diagonal lines*) in eastern South America. Square represents a report from near Poconé, Matto Grosso, Brazil.

trolateral stripe. *Bothrops alternatus*, *B. cotiara*, and *B. fonsecai* possess distinctive markings on the dorsum of the head. *Bothrops jararacussu* possesses 8 or fewer intersupraoculars (vs. 9 or 10 in *B. moojeni*) and a pattern different from that of *B. moojeni*. *Bothrops jararaca* and *B. atrox* possess venters containing dark spots, and the latter species has a broader postorbital stripe and dark pigment on the supralabials (sympatric populations) and in the gular region.

REMARKS *Bothrops moojeni* is yet another of the terrestrial lanceheads with pattern and scale variability that overlaps considerably with that of other species. The relationship between *B. moojeni* and *B. atrox* needs elucidating. It is possible that *B. moojeni* simply represents the southernmost population of *B. atrox*. Specimens collected recently from eastern Paraguay (Fig. 232) seem referable to *B. moojeni*, but show considerable variation with regard to pigmentation on the venter. This species may occur in Misiones, Argentina, and western Santa Catarina, Brazil, but reports thus far are unsubstantiated. It seems certain that *B. moojeni* will be found in the Pantanal of southeastern Departamento de Santa Cruz, Bolivia, as it is abundant a short distance to the south along the Río Paraguay. Recently a specimen was collected near Poconé, Mato Grosso, Brazil, and we suspect that *B. moojeni* occurs throughout the Pantanal. *Bothrops sanctaecrucis*, found to the west in El Beni and Santa Cruz, bears a strong resemblance to *B. moojeni*.

REFERENCES Abalos and Mischis, 1975; Bertoni, 1914; Cendrero et al., 1972; Fernández Barrán and Freiberg, 1951; Fonseca, 1949; Groombridge, 1986; Hoge, 1966; Hoge and Romano, 1973; Hoge and Romano-Hoge, 1981a, 1981b; Hoge et al., 1975, 1981; Johnson and Dixon, 1984; Leloup, 1975; Machado, 1945b; Maclean, 1968; McDiarmid and Foster, 1987; P. Müller, 1973; J. A. Peters and Orejas-Miranda, 1970; Schouten, 1931.

### *Bothrops neuwiedi* Wagler

(Figs. 233–237; Maps 72, 73)

LOCAL NAMES Argentina: crucera, kiririog, piña machajuay, víbora de la cruz, víbora de rabo blanco (La Rioja), yara, yarará, yarará chica, yarará de cola blanca, yarará-í, yararaquiña. Bolivia: yoperojobobo. Brazil: boca de sapo, bocuda (Mato Grosso); jararaca; jararaca cruzeira, jararaca pintada (Rio Grande do Sul); jararaca do rabo branco (São Paulo to extreme southern Brazil); jararaquinha; rabo de osso (Goiás); tira peia (northeastern Brazil); urutú. Paraguay: kyryry'o. Uruguay: víbora de la cruz, yarará.

ENGLISH NAME Neuwied's lancehead.

DISTRIBUTION Brazil, Paraguay, Bolivia, Uruguay, and Argentina (Maps 72, 73). In Brazil, this species is

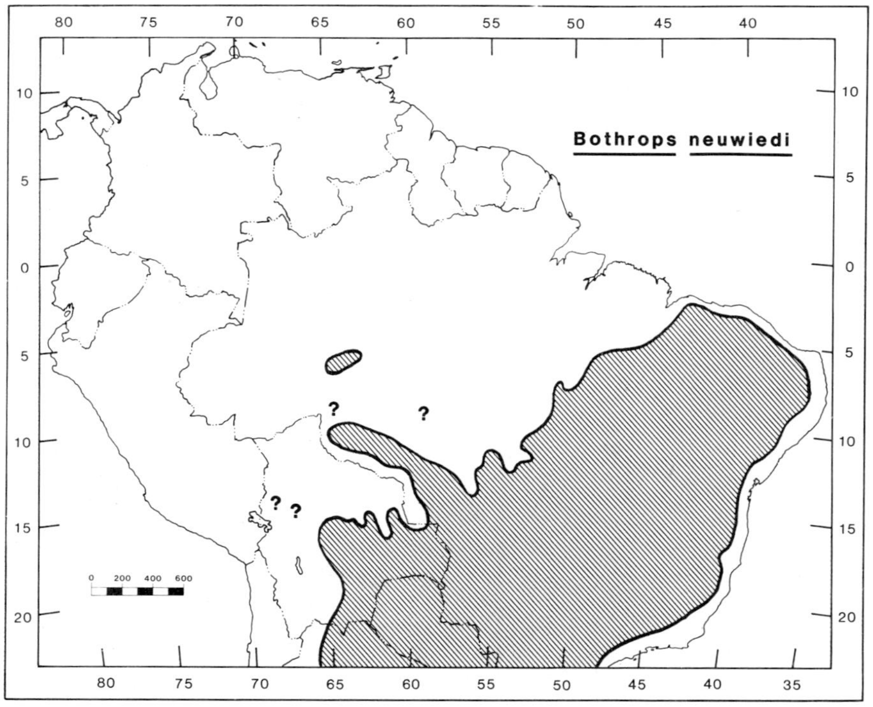


**Map 72.** Distribution of *Bothrops neuwiedi* in the northern portion of its extensive range in South America. The southern distribution of this species is shown in map 73. Question marks represent possible areas of occurrence.

found throughout the sub-Amazonian region from southern Maranhão, Piauí, and Ceará, west through Goiás, Mato Grosso, and Rondônia, and including all the southern states except Santa Catarina (Map 72; see Remarks). There is one isolated population in Amazonas, Brazil. In Bolivia, *B. neuwiedi* is known from the Departamento de Santa Cruz and the Departamento de Cochabamba, thence eastward across southern Paraguay (see Remarks), the Argentine Chaco, Uruguay, and southward into the Argentine pampas as far south as the Departamento de La Pampa, Departamento de San Luis, and Departamento de Santa Fe (Map 73; see Remarks for distributions of subspecies). The vertical distribution ranges from near sea level to over 600 m.

HABITAT This species frequents savanna, thorn scrub, tropical and semitropical deciduous forest, and temperate forest. The habitat is variable (see Remarks) but usually involves dry or semi-arid rocky regions. There are races, however, that occupy humid or even marshy regions.

DESCRIPTION *Bothrops neuwiedi* is a generally terrestrial (see Remarks) lancehead of medium build that averages 600–700 mm in total length but may reach 1,150 mm.

The dorsal ground color of the head and body is variable and may be tan, reddish or yellowish brown, brown, gray, pinkish gray, or olive (see Remarks for a discussion of subspecies and their differences). The top of the head almost always bears some dark spots or blotches, arranged more-or-less symmetrically. These may include a blotch on the snout (between the canthals), a pair of spots or blotches near the supraoculars, and one or more pairs of blotches in the occipital-temporal region. In most specimens, the posteriormost pair of supracephalic blotches are elongated onto the neck in a stripelike fashion. This elongation may occur with other head markings as well. The dark spots or blotches are sometimes prominently edged in white; alternatively, they may be ill defined. A dark brown postorbital stripe runs from behind the eye to the angle of the jaw, sometimes curving slightly downward at its terminus. This stripe may be pale edged ventrally; alternatively, it may be obscured by dark facial pigment. The canthus may be pale tan and unmarked to dark gray with darker spots. The labials vary from unmarked to prominently spotted with black and white. The iris may be bronze or bright gold, and the tongue is dark pinkish gray.

The body pattern consists of a series of dorsolateral blotches that may be trapezoidal, triangular, or subtriangular in shape and that alternate or are opposite one another middorsally. These markings may be few and large or many and reduced (see Remarks), and they usually are pale edged. The middorsal interspaces usually are marked with diffuse spots or blotches, and these may be paired. The primary blotches have the apices situated middorsally; each basal vertex is bordered by an oval or round blotch, such that 2 accompany each base, and these tend to form a lateral series of blotches. A series of gray, brown, or orange paraventral spots may be present, and the interspaces often are russet in color. The entire pattern is variable, even within populations, and the markings may be fragmented, reduced, fused, prominently contrasting, and so on. In some specimens, the dorsal blotches may be suffused with pale tan or gray or invaded by the ground color. The tail tip is white in juveniles. The venter is white with a profusion of gray specks scattered throughout; these may fuse to form transverse markings along the scale sutures, especially laterally.

There are 6–9 keeled intersupraoculars (see Remarks); 8 or 9 supralabials (rarely 7 or 10), the second not integrated with the prelacunal (see Remarks); 9–13 (usually

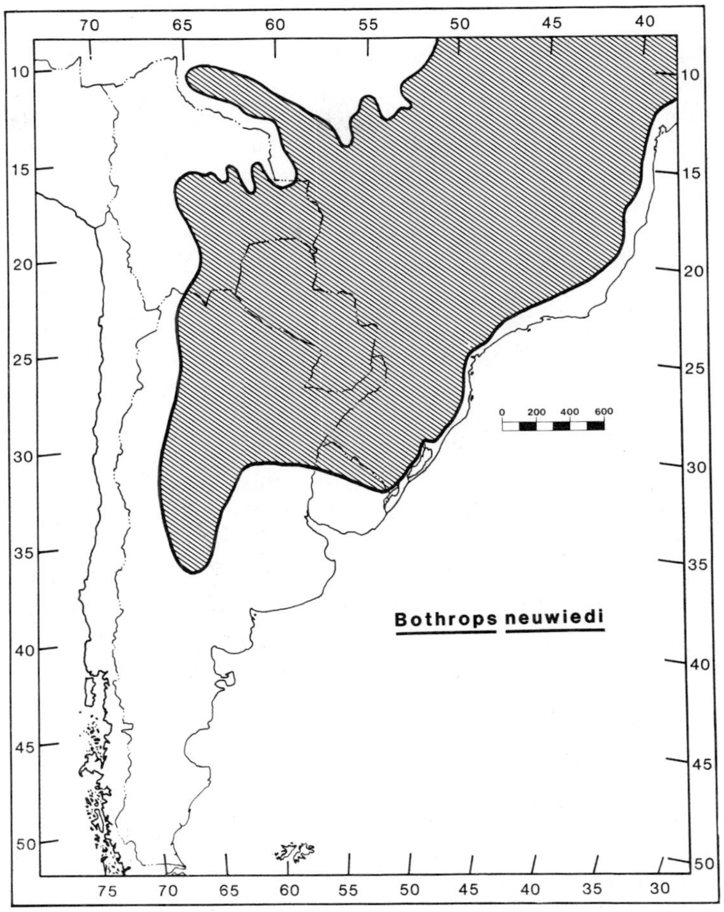


**Map 73.** Distribution of *Bothrops neuwiedi* in the southern portion of its range in South America.

10 or 11) infralabials; 21–29 (usually 23–27) midbody dorsal scale rows; 163–190 ventrals; and 37–54 divided subcaudals (there is a record of 25 subcaudals, perhaps an error).

SIMILAR SPECIES *Bothrops neuwiedi* shares parts of its vast range with many other pitviper species, six of which have the prelacunal discrete from the second supralabial and thus cannot be distinguished from *B. neuwiedi* on the basis of that characteristic alone. *Bothrops alternatus* has 8–13 intersupraoculars (vs. 6–9), usually 27–33 midbody dorsal scale rows (vs. 21–29), and a distinctive pattern. *Bothrops cotiara* possesses 10–14 intersupraoculars (vs. 6–9) and a dark venter. *Bothrops erythromelas* has 19–21 midbody dorsal scale rows, 139–158 ventrals, and 32–42 subcaudals (all lower counts than *B. neuwiedi*). *Bothrops fonsecai* possesses 8–10 intersupraoculars, a mostly black venter, and a distinctive dorsal pattern that includes a bold postorbital stripe. *Bothrops iglesiasi* has one row (vs. 2 or 3) of suboculars between the eye and supralabials and a dorsal pattern unlike that of *B. neuwiedi*. *Bothrops itapetiningae* possesses 144–160 ventrals and 26–38 subcaudals (fewer than *B. neuwiedi*). *Bothrops ammodytoides*, which is variable with regard to the prelacunal condition, has an upturned snout.

REMARKS Our knowledge of the distribution of *B. neuwiedi*, like that of most Latin American venomous snakes, will expand as additional material becomes available. It would not be surprising to encounter this species farther north in the Serra dos Parecis and Serra da Cachimbo, Brazil; the species also should occur in Santa Catarina, Brazil. Other areas it possibly inhabits include those outside its currently known range in Brazil (Caatinga and surrounding region), eastern Bolivia, and western Paraguay, where *B. neuwiedi* is apparently widespread but poorly documented. Its range in Bolivia could conceivably extend northward into southern Peru.

One report cites 11–14 intersupraoculars for *B. neuwiedi*; this number seems unlikely to us. The condition of the prelacunal, reported consistently as discrete from the supralabials, may be subject to variation. We have examined specimens in which the suture is barely discernible.

Twelve subspecies of *B. neuwiedi* are currently recognized. These races are distinguished largely on the basis of pattern and color, and published information is sparse for many of them.

*Bothrops n. neuwiedi* is yellowish brown dorsally with dark brown, yellow-bordered quadrangular blotches along the vertebral line and a series of smaller, rounded blotches laterally. The quadrangular blotches are the result of fused trapezoidal dorsolateral markings. The top of the head has a pair of dark narrowly elongated blotches from behind the eyes to the nape. The venter is yellow, with dark edging along the sutures. There are 8 supralabials, 166–175 ventrals, and 42–47 subcaudals. This race is known from Bahia, Brazil, in low humid locales south of the Rio Paraguaçu; there is a perplexing record of an isolated population in western Amazonas, Brazil.

*Bothrops n. bolivianus* (Fig. 233) is tan to reddish brown dorsally with a series of darker brown triangular markings having apices that are either opposite each other or alternate along the vertebral line. The base of each of these markings offsets a pair of rounded, dark brown spots. The top of the head sometimes bears a dark transverse intercanthal band, another between the supraoculars, and two pairs of oblique, elongated markings on the occiput and nape. In some specimens, especially adults, the pattern is obscure. The venter is white to yellowish white with darker specks, especially laterally. This race is known from the departamento de Beni, the Departamento de Santa Cruz, the Departamento de Cochabama, and the departamento de Tarija, Bolivia, eastward into western Mato Grosso, Brazil.

*Bothrops n. diporus* (Fig. 234) is reddish brown to gray-brown dorsally with fused, subtriangular dorsolateral markings that create a series of transverse bow-tie–shaped blotches. A stripe of paler ground color on each side separates these blotches from rounded basal pairs of spots. The dorsum of the head bears symmetrically arranged spots that usually combine to leave a pale cross-shaped space. However, the head markings are highly variable and may be fused or fragmented. The venter is white with dark pigment concentrated along the sutures. There are 7 intersupraoculars, 8–10 supralabials, 10–13 infralabials, 23–27 midbody dorsal scale rows, 172–190 ventrals, and 37–50 subcaudals. This race is found in southern and eastern Paraguay, extending slightly into Brazil in the Mato Grosso do Sul and Paraná regions, and southward throughout Argentina as far south as La Pampa, San Luis, Mendoza, and Santa Fe.

*Bothrops n. goyazensis* is grayish olive dorsally with rounded, quadrangular or slightly triangular paravertebral markings and pairs of round spots bordering each base. All paravertebral markings are dark brown with pale borders. The top of the head has a dark intercanthal spot, a pair of dark spots behind the supraoculars, a pair of round or crescent-shaped supratemporal markings, and a pair of occipital blotches with stripelike posterior extensions onto the neck. The postorbital stripe is narrowly bordered in white. The venter is yellowish white with dark pigment along the scale sutures. There are 8 or 9 supralabials, 9 infralabials, 23 midbody dorsal scale rows, 168–180 ventrals, and 40–49 subcaudals. This race occurs in elevated, dry, cool regions in Goiás, Brazil.

*Bothrops n. lutzi* is pale greenish gray dorsally, with a series of irregular, dark brown vertebral markings and scattered spots on the sides. The dorsum of the head usually bears 5 spots as follows: 1 on the snout between the canthals, 1 posterior to each supraocular, and a pair in the occipital region. Additionally, there may be a pair of elongated supratemporal markings and elongated, irregular nape blotches. The venter is yellowish white with irregular dark brown spotting. There are 5 intersupraoculars, 8 or 9 supralabials, 23 midbody dorsal scale rows, 164–180 ventrals, and 40–46 subcaudals. This race occupies dry, warm regions from about 300 to 500 m above sea level in northern Bahia, Brazil. It is reported from the area around Serra de Monte Santo, Jaguarary, Itiuba, and along the Rio São Francisco.

*Bothrops n. mattogrossensis* is brown dorsally with the dark brown paravertebral markings invaded heavily by the ground color such that they appear as small rounded or slightly squarish blotches, often of irregular shape. The lateral spots are spaced widely, and all dorsal markings are edged weakly with pale pigment. There are gray-black paraventral spots, and many of the paraventral scales are tinged with orange. The dorsum of the head bears a spot between the canthals and four pairs of spots on the occiput posterior to the supraoculars; these spots are irregular in shape and may be fused. The spots tend to become crescentic in the nuchal region. The venter is yellow with diffuse, irregular brown spots. There are 8 or 9 supralabials, 170–178 ventrals, and 42–50 subcaudals. This race occupies low-lying, humid regions in Mato Grosso do Sul, Brazil. Unlike other races, this taxon is said to be at least partially arboreal.

*Bothrops n. meridionalis* is chocolate brown dorsally, becoming paler on the sides, with black paravertebral markings that are bordered with white. These markings are interspersed with subtriangular blotches that are alternate or opposite; the latter are blackish brown and bordered with white. The paraventral region has dark gold spots and the venter is profusely marked with black spots, the larger being situated laterally. The dorsum of the head contains a prefrontal rounded blotch and 2 longitudinal blotches in the occipitonuchal region. All dorsal head markings are black with white borders. There are 8 or 9 supralabials, 22–25 midbody dorsal scale rows, 166–173 ventrals, and 39–48 subcaudals. This race, which includes *B. n. fluminensis*, is restricted to the states of Rio de Janeiro and Espírito Santo, Brazil.

*Bothrops n. paranaensis* is olive-brown dorsally with quadrangular, vertebral blotches and rounded irregular spots in the interspaces. The lateral spots are somewhat flattened and squarish. All dorsal markings are pale edged. The dorsum of the head bears 5 to 8 elongated, dark brown or black markings, usually in pairs and with the posteriormost having stripelike extensions onto the neck. The venter is white or yellow with dark blotches. There are 8 or 9 supralabials, 25 midbody dorsal scale rows, 168–179 ventrals, and 40–49 subcaudals. This race inhabits elevated, dry temperate areas in Paraná, Brazil, and possibly adjacent Misiones, Argentina.

*Bothrops n. pauloensis* (Fig. 235) is reddish tan dorsally with widely spaced blackish brown vertebral blotches that are either shaped like bowties or are fragmented and irregular. Interspaces are occupied by rounded spots and a series of spots exists on each side. The paraventral region is often suffused with reddish pigment. All dorsal markings are edged variably with cream or tan. The top of the head usually bears an interocular spot, followed by two pairs of occipital spots; the posterior pair of spots are elongated. The canthal region may be gray, obscuring the postorbital stripe. The iris is bright gold. The venter is cream colored, with scattered gray spots. There are 8 or 9 supralabials, 171–187 ventrals, and 40–53 subcaudals. This distinctive race occupies humid, cool regions from about 200 to 500 m above sea level in southern São Paulo, Brazil.

*Bothrops n. piauhyensis* is reddish to yellowish tan dorsally with brown irregular or squarish vertebral blotches that are peripherally black with white margins. Interspaces are occupied by rounded spots, often poorly defined, and a series of lateral spots is present. The paraventral region may be somewhat suffused with darker pigment. The top of the head bears a frontal blotch, a horseshoe-shaped mark in the intersupraocular region, and two pairs of markings in the temporal and occipital region. The occipital markings may be fused with the elongated neck markings. The venter is yellowish brown dotted with black and brown pigment. There are 8 supralabials, 163–170 ventrals, and 43–48 subcaudals. This race occurs in xerophytic to subxerophytic areas in Piauí, Pernambuco, Ceará, and southern Maranhão, Brazil.

*Bothrops n. pubescens* (Fig. 236) is chocolate brown to maroon dorsally with numerous dark brown or blackish vertebral blotches bordered with white pigment that may be trapezoidal, subtriangular, or nearly square in shape. These blotches are often divided middorsally and may be slightly juxtaposed or opposite each other. The interspaces are occupied by irregular, pale-edged dark spots; a similarly marked series exists laterally, disposed in pairs adjacent to each dorsal marking. The paraventrals often contain reddish pigment. The dorsum of the head bears dark frontal and intersupraocular markings that are often partially fused. The frontal marking may be absent, and the head marking(s) may have lateral extensions to the postorbital stripes and/or posterior extensions to the nape. The postorbital stripe often is suffused with black and the labials are spotted with black and white, although this may be indistinct. The iris is brownish gray and the pupil is ringed narrowly in gold. The venter is pinkish white with irregular dark markings, concentrated primarily along the scale sutures. The venter of the head is peppered with dark pigment. Young specimens are said to have white tail tips. There are 7 intersupraoculars, 7–9 (usually 8) supralabials, 10–12 (usually 11) infralabials, 23–29 (usually 25) midbody dorsal scale rows, 169–185 ventrals, and 40–51 subcaudals. The holotype was reported to have only 25 subcaudals. This race is known from Rio Grande do Sul, Brazil, and from Uruguay. In Brazil it is said to frequent low, humid, and cold places, while in Uruguay it is said to inhabit rocky ridges and rockpiles.

*Bothrops n. urutu* (Fig. 237) is tan or brown dorsally, with numerous pale-edged dark brown triangular markings with apices directed vertebrally. These may alternate, but they tend to be opposite one another, fusing to form bow ties. The interspaces are usually occupied by two pale-bordered dark spots with numerous ill-defined blotches and spots throughout. A pair of dark, pale-edged lateral spots is situated adjacent to the base of each dorsal triangle. The dorsum of the head bears a frontal marking and 2–4 elongated occipital markings. Elongated blotches occur on the nape, and the postorbital stripe is bordered in white. The venter is yellow blotched irregularly with dark pigment. There are 8 or 9 supralabials, 166–182 ventrals, and 40–51 subcaudals. This race occupies elevated, humid, cool localities in south-central Minas Gerais and northern São Paulo, Brazil.

*Bothrops neuwiedi* is an important cause of snakebite in southern South America. Its races need to be defined more precisely. As currently recognized, several of the subspecies appear to be quite similar to one another (especially *B. n. paranaensis* and *B. n. pubescens*); moreover, the distinction between *B. n. piauhyensis* and *B. iglesiasi* needs clarification.

REFERENCES Abalos, 1977; Abalos and Baez, 1963; Abalos et al., 1964; Abalos and Bucher, 1970; Abalos and Mischis, 1975; Abalos and Pirosky, 1963; Achával, 1976; Achával et al., 1976, 1978; Amaral, 1925a, 1925b, 1926d, 1927a, 1930b, 1930d, 1931c, 1933, 1938, 1978; Bertoni, 1914, 1939; Boulenger, 1896, 1898a; Canese, 1966; Cei, 1987; Cendrero et al., 1972; Cope, 1862, 1870; Fernández Barrán and Freiberg, 1951; Fonseca, 1949; Freiberg, 1968, 1982; Gallardo, 1977, 1979; Gatti, 1955; Gliesch, 1925; Griffin, 1916; Groombridge, 1986; Hoge, 1953a, 1959, 1966; Hoge and Romano, 1973; Hoge and Romano-Hoge, 1981a, 1981b; Hoogmoed and Gruber, 1983; Jan, 1859b; Kaiser and Michl, 1971; Kempff-Mercado, 1975; Klappenbach and Orejas-Miranda, 1969; Koslowsky, 1898; Lacerda, 1884; Laurent and Teran, 1981; Lema, 1960b, 1971a, 1971b, 1983; Lema and Fabián-Beurmann, 1977; Lema et al., 1980; Lönnberg, 1902; Machado, 1945b; Magalhães, 1925; Melgarejo, 1977; Mertens, 1929; Miranda Ribeiro, 1915; F. Müller, 1885; L. Müller, 1927; P. Müller, 1971; Noguchi, 1909; Peracca, 1897; Prado, 1945; Schouten, 1931, 1937; Tada and Villa, 1975; Talbot, n.d.; Vanzolini, 1948; Vanzolini et al., 1980; Vaz-Ferreira and Sierra de Soriano, 1960; Wagler, 1824; Werner, 1922.

### *Bothrops pictus* (Tschudi)

(Figs. 238–240; Map 74)

LOCAL NAMES Jergona, jergón de la costa, macanche, miuamaru, sancarranca, víbora.

ENGLISH NAME Desert lancehead.

DISTRIBUTION Peru, on the lower western slopes of the Andes and throughout the coastal plain from the Departamento de La Libertad south into the Departamento de Arequipa (Map 74). Two specimens were reported from the Río Cosireni (Departamento de Cuzco) by Barbour and Noble, but these are *B. andianus*. The vertical distribution reaches at least 2,300 m above sea level.

HABITAT Arid to semi-arid foothills, river valleys and lower Andean slopes, and dry rocky regions dotted with scrubby leguminous trees.

DESCRIPTION *Bothrops pictus* is a variably patterned, stocky terrestrial lancehead averaging 400–650 mm in total length but reaching as much as 1,000 mm (see Remarks).

The dorsum of the head and body is pale gray to tan, usually uniform. A wide brown to dark brown postorbital stripe crosses the posteriormost 3–4 pairs of supral-

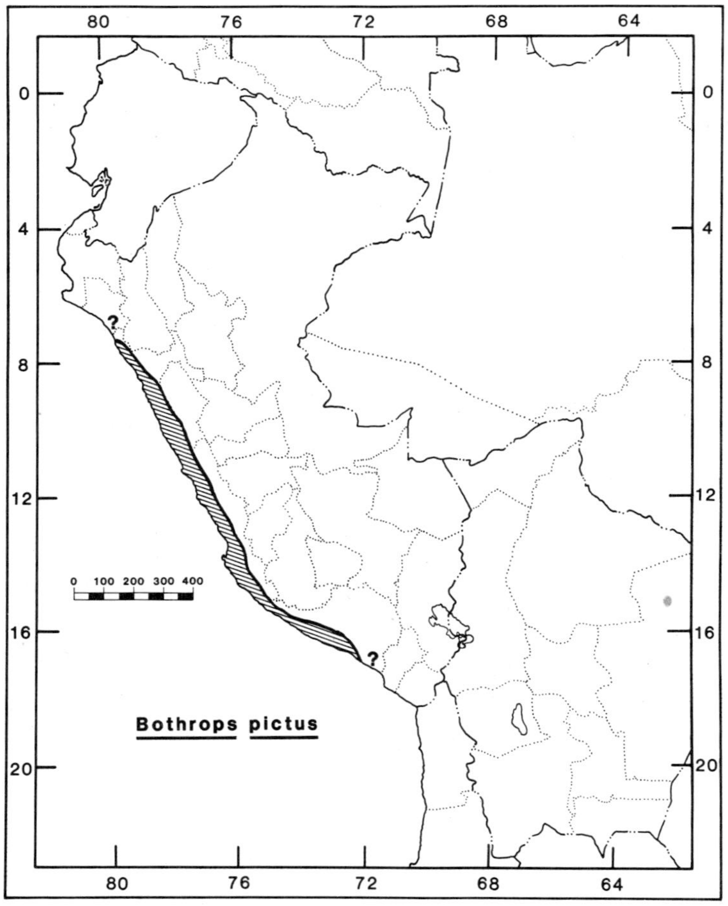


**Map 74.** Distribution of *Bothrops pictus* along the west coast of Peru. The distributional limits for this species are not well known.

bials and continues onto the underside of the head near the first ventral. A brown blotch is situated below the eye and covers the adjacent fourth and fifth supralabials. One or two ill-defined spots occupy the posterior intercanthals; these spots sometimes are fused to form a transverse band just anterior to the supraoculars. There is a symmetrical but variable pattern on the dorsum of the head; it generally consists of a transverse band or one or two spots on the posterior portion of the supralabials. The head pattern is followed by or attached to an oblique pair of stripes directed posteriorly over the temporal region. These stripes in turn are succeeded by a larger pair of oblique stripes (sometimes fused) oriented posteriorly and terminating in the vicinity of the angle of the jaw. One or two spots are usually situated between the two pairs of oblique stripes. The entire cephalic pattern may be diffuse or may be subdivided into spots and blotches. The first one or two pairs of supralabials occasionally contain some dark pigment. Ventrally, the anterior infralabials may be suffused with dark specks of pigment, and there are usually one or two dark brown spots nearly opposite the dark brown subocular spot. The remainder of the throat region contains scattered dark specks.

The dorsum of the body consists of a row of brown ovoid or square blotches that are often split middorsally, slightly juxtaposed, and fused to form a zig-zag stripe over portions of the body. The borders of these blotches are irregular and often highlighted by slight traces of black and white pigment. A smaller lateral series of spots are colored identically to the middorsal blotches and the interspaces often contain diffuse concentrations of brown pigment that appear to create a tertiary series of blotches. The paraventral region is delineated by a series of dark brown spots extending onto the outer edges of the ventrals. The tail is nearly all dark brown or black due to encroachment by the middorsal markings. In juvenile specimens, the posterior portion of the tail is white. The venter is cream to white with diffuse darker specks throughout. The iris is gray, approximating the postorbital stripe in color. The tongue is black.

There are 5–7 (possibly unkeeled) intersupraoculars; 8–12 supralabials, with the second, third, or none integrated with the loreal pit; 9–13 infralabials; 21–25 (usually 21–23) midbody dorsal scale rows; 152–173 ventrals; and 40–52 divided subcaudals (Jan [1863] illustrated a specimen with 36 subcaudals; see Remarks).

SIMILAR SPECIES The only sympatric venomous snakes with which *B. pictus* is likely to be confused are *B. roedingeri* and *B. barnetti*. The former species is virtually indistinguishable from *B. pictus* (see Remarks for *B. roedingeri*) except by the ventral count (179–185 in *B. roedingeri* vs. 152–173 in *B. pictus*). *Bothrops barnetti* may be distinguished on the basis of its higher ventral count (172–184) and different pattern.

REMARKS *Bothrops pictus* exhibits considerable variation in dorsal ground color (pinkish tan to gray), pattern color (medium brown to dark gray), and pattern

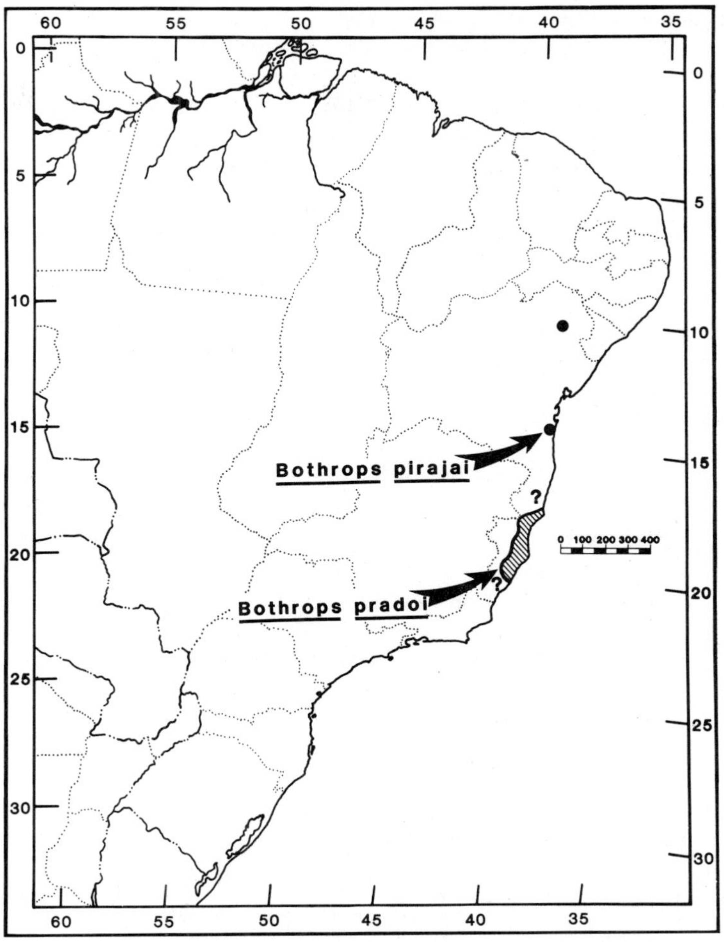


**Map 75.** Distributions of *Bothrops pirajai* (*dots*) and *B. pradoi* (*diagonal lines*) in eastern Brazil. The distributions of these species may be more extensive than are shown.

configuration (discrete blotches to a zig-zag middorsal stripe). See the species account for *B. roedingeri* for further comments. This species was described by Tschudi (1845) as having 74 subcaudals, which apparently was an error since the adult lectotype has recently been shown to have only 43 subcaudals. The reported variation in ventrals probably includes some errors also; we are unaware of specimens with fewer than 167 ventrals.

This is a dangerously venomous species that has caused death in humans.

REFERENCES Amaral, 1925a; Barbour and Noble, 1920; Boulenger, 1896; Carrillo de Espinoza, 1970, 1977, 1983; Cope, 1877; Duellman, 1979; Groombridge, 1986; Jan, 1863; Luján Medina, 1973; Meneses, 1974a, 1974b; Mertens, 1942; Noguchi, 1909; Pefaur et al., 1978; Pesce and Lumbreras, 1965; Pifano C. and Romer, 1949a; Prado and Hoge, 1948; Schätti, 1986; Schmidt and Walker, 1943a, 1943b; Tschudi, 1845; Werner, 1901b, 1922.

### *Bothrops pirajai* Amaral

(Map 75)

LOCAL NAME Jararacuçu.

ENGLISH NAME Piraja's lancehead.

DISTRIBUTION Brazil. This species is found in central and southern Bahia (in the Ilhéus-Itabuna region); it has been taken at Monte Santo, between Rio Itapicuru and Rio São Francisco (Bahia) (Map 75). It is said also to occur in northeastern Minas Gerais. The vertical distribution is unknown.

HABITAT The only reported information is that *B. pirajai* inhabits "cocoa groves" (cacao?). Presumably it is found in Atlantic lowland wet forest and lower montane wet forest.

DESCRIPTION *Bothrops pirajai* is a stocky terrestrial lancehead with a maximum recorded length of 1,130 mm.

The dorsum of the head is yellowish gray to black and is said to be unmarked; however, a published illustration of a specimen depicts a prominent black postocular stripe that crosses the 3 posteriormost supralabials and is bordered above by a narrow pale gray stripe. A black blotch may be present behind each eye on the dorsum of the head. The sides of the head and labials are pale grayish white with dark scale sutures. The iris is gold. The body is brownish yellow to yellowish gray dorsally with 15–19 or more black to brownish black dorsal markings that may be shaped like an inverted Y or slightly quadrangular. These markings may alternate or be opposite one another, and they may be interconnected via a wavy black middorsal stripe. Laterally these markings contain pale gray scales that sometimes enclose an ill-defined black spot. The long interspaces separating the dark dorsal markings may be immaculate, they may contain scattered black scales, or black pigment may coalesce to form an ill-defined alternating series of black blotches. The dorsal pattern tends to become concentrated posteriorly such that the tail is nearly uniformly black. The venter is yellow and slightly to profusely speckled with brown or brownish black. The sides of the ventrals are marked black spots or blotches that usually involve the paraventrals.

There are 5–7 intersupraoculars; 8 or 9 supralabials, the second integrated with the prelacunal; 10–12 infralabials; 25–27 midbody dorsal scale rows; 155–167 ventrals; and 43–52 subcaudals, usually in pairs (the holotype has 31 but evidently is missing part of the tail).

SIMILAR SPECIES A number of pitvipers have ranges that closely approach that of *B. pirajai*, although microsympatry is doubtful in many cases owing to habitat specializations. Five species have the second supralabial fused with the prelacunal (as in *B. pirajai*): *B. jararaca* possesses 170 or more ventrals and 44 or more subcaudals; *B. jararacussu*, in Brazil, possesses 170 or more ventrals; *B. leucurus* has 195 or more ventrals; *B. pradoi* possesses 191 or more ventrals; and *Bothriopsis bilineata* is green dorsally and has 192 or more ventrals.

REMARKS A poorly known and apparently uncommon species, *B. pirajai* is extremely similar in appearance to some specimens of *B. brazili*, a possibly closely related Amazonian form. It also bears a strong resemblance to *B. jararacussu*. See the *B. brazili* species account for an explanation of the nomenclatorial history.

REFERENCES Amaral, 1923, 1926a, 1938, 1978; Cendrero et al., 1972; Fonseca, 1949; Hoge, 1966; Hoge and Romano, 1973; Hoge and Romano-Hoge, 1981b; Machado, 1945b; P. Müller, 1973; J. A. Peters and Orejas-Miranda, 1970; Prado, 1945.

## *Bothrops pradoi* (Hoge)

(Fig. 241; Map 75)

LOCAL NAMES Jararaca, preguiçosa (vicinity of Aracruz, Espírito Santo)

ENGLISH NAME Prado's lancehead.

DISTRIBUTION Brazil. This species occurs in Espírito Santo and southern Bahia (see Map 75). The vertical distribution ranges from the lowlands up to about 300 m above sea level.

HABITAT Published information is lacking. Presumably this species occurs in the Atlantic rainforest and tropical deciduous forest. It is also said to occur in deforested agricultural areas, especially in humid, rocky valleys.

DESCRIPTION *Bothrops pradoi* is a slender terrestrial lancehead that averages 600–900 mm in length with a recorded maximum of 1,150 mm.

The dorsal coloration is grayish brown, sometimes more darkly pigmented on the dorsum of the head. The canthals and supraoculars are diffusely marked with tan or pale grayish brown; this color continues posteriorly as a well-defined occipital stripe about 3 scales wide that sometimes contains a narrow stripe of darker pigment in its center. The mental region contains dark pigment. A prominent dark brown postorbital stripe runs from the eye to the angle of the jaw before curving slightly downward; it usually encroaches upon the upper portions of the 3 posteriormost supralabials and the ultimate infralabial. A series of large dark brown spots occurs on the sutures between the second, third, fourth, and fifth supralabials; these markings may be absent or faint in some specimens. An additional series sometimes is present on the infralabials, and these may alternate with or be opposite the supralabial spots. In some specimens the paler interspaces on the labials bear ill-defined brown markings, creating a mottled effect. There is often a brown spot at the nostril, making it seem large and pronounced; this characteristic may be restricted to males. Some specimens bear only diffuse facial markings. The dorsum of the head is somewhat ornate, with symmetrically arranged blotches that may include an intercanthal blotch, a pair of supratemporal blotches, and a pair of nuchal blotches. The iris is gold and the tongue is dark gray.

The body pattern consists of about 15–19 trapezoidal dark brown markings on each side that alternate or are opposite each other at middorsum. On the neck there is a pair of undulating pale streaks flanked by black. A pair of irregular dark markings exists below each of the trapezoidal marks. A distinct pale border forms a transverse line at the margins of both the trapezoidal and the basal markings, sometimes giving the appearance of continuous bands. Irregular diffuse blotches occupy the interspaces between these markings and some may be pale margined, although never as distinctly as the principal pattern. A series of dark brown paraventral spots occupies the first 1 or 2 dorsals and a portion of the adjoining ventral. The venter is heavily spotted with dark gray-brown pigment. Some specimens lack most traces of a pattern and others may be heavily melanized. The tips of the tails of juveniles are pink.

There are 10 small keeled intersupraoculars (see Remarks); 7 supralabials, the second integrated with the prelacunal; 9 or 10 infralabials; 23–25 midbody dorsal scale rows; 191–207 ventrals; and 56–70 subcaudals, all or most of which are divided. In addition, the canthal region is raised slightly.

SIMILAR SPECIES Four other *Bothrops* species have the second supralabial fused with the prelacunal and geographic ranges closely approaching or overlapping that of *B. pradoi*: *B. jararaca*, which has a paler venter, 8 or 9 supralabials, a more reduced *canthus*, and a different dorsal pattern; *B. jararacussu*, which has a heavier body build, a paler venter, 8 supralabials, and a lower number of ventrals (166–186 vs. 191–207); *B. leucurus*, which has a paler venter, unmarked supralabials, more triangular (rather than trapezoidal) dorsal

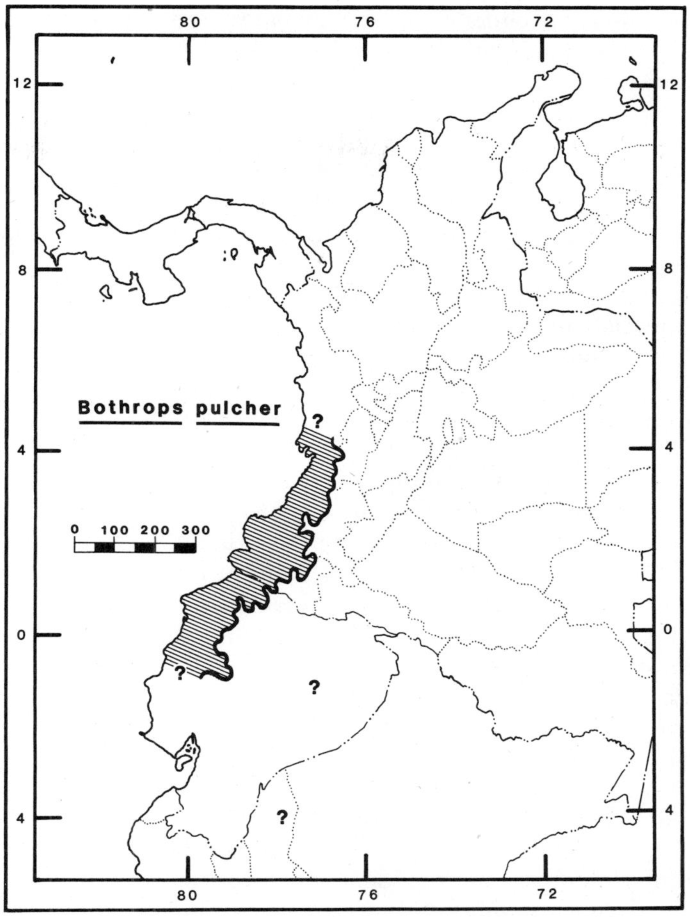


**Map 76.** Distribution of *Bothrops pulcher* in northwestern South America. The distribution of this species is poorly known and may extend north and south of the area indicated; isolated records from the eastern side of the Andes, if accurate, are a biogeographic enigma.

markings that are boldly edged with pale borders (see Remarks and *B. leucurus* species account), and appears to have about 7 intersupraoculars; and *B. pirajai*, which possesses a heavier body build, 155–164 ventrals, 43–53 subcaudals, and a pale venter.

REMARKS *Bothrops pradoi* has been discussed only minimally in the literature, and mostly by its original describer. The description includes the comment that the species possesses 10 intersupraoculars but illustrations included in subsequent articles depict only 4 or 5. The relationship of this species with *B. leucurus*, and the possible role of sexual dimorphism in the latter, merit scrutiny.

REFERENCES Amaral, 1955b; Biasi et al., 1977a, 1977b; Freiberg, 1982; Groombridge, 1986; Hoge, 1948a, 1966; Hoge and Romano, 1973; Hoge and Romano-Hoge, 1981b; P. Müller, 1973.

### *Bothrops pulcher* (Peters)

(Fig. 242; Map 76)

LOCAL NAMES Unknown.

ENGLISH NAME Dusky lancehead.

DISTRIBUTION This species has been recorded from Amazonian Ecuador and Peru as well as the Pacific lowlands of Colombia (Map 76). The type locality, Quito, is clearly not the habitat of *B. pulcher* and it seems certain the type specimen was from elsewhere in Ecuador. We feel that the stated distribution—on both sides of the Andes—is unlikely and remains to be clarified. For the present, we regard *B. pulcher* as occurring in the Pacific lowlands of Colombia and northwest Ecuador, and on the western slopes of the Andes in Ecuador at least as far south as Cotopaxi. In Colombia its presence is confirmed only for the Departamento Valle del Cauca; there is an unconfirmed record from the Departamento del Chocó. Records from Peru seem to be based on hearsay. From published locality records it is not possible to ascertain whether *B. pulcher* might be restricted to intermediate and high elevations; if so, then its curious absence from most collections would be understandable. Its vertical distribution extends from the lowlands to at least 2,500 m (in Ecuador).

HABITAT Tropical moist and wet forests. The few specimens with adequate collecting data were taken in forested situations in close proximity to rivers.

DESCRIPTION A moderately stout, medium-sized lancehead, *B. pulcher* may attain a length of 753 mm.

The overall pattern consists of bands, although in the majority of specimens these may be only partially visible, with the dorsum appearing uniform brown. The bands seem to be most pronounced posteriorly, and they are vaguely bordered with paler brown. A pale line extends from the eye to the corner of the mouth and down to the ventrals; this line borders a darker brown postocular stripe that often blends with the dorsal ground color. Dark-bordered white spots occur on the chinshields and infralabials. In some specimens, the sides of the head are pale, revealing a white-edged brown spot on the supralabials below the eye and two more on the infralabials. The venter is pale tan to red with small dark blotches on the outer edges of the ventrals. The dorsal keels tend to be tubercular.

There are 2–7 (usually 4 or fewer) keeled intersupraoculars, 7 supralabials, with the second fused with the prelacunal, 8–10 infralabials, 21–25 (usually 23) midbody dorsal scale rows, 139–174 ventrals, and 44–64 divided subcaudals (see Remarks).

SIMILAR SPECIES Where *B. pulcher* is known to occur, it is or may be sympatric with the following pitvipers: *Bothriechis schlegelii*, *Bothriopsis albocarinata*, *Bothriopsis alticola*, *Bothriopsis punctata*, *Bothrops asper*, *Bothrops lojanus*, *Bothrops microphthalmus*, *Lachesis muta*, and *Porthidium nasutum*. Unlike *Bothrops pulcher*, *Bothriechis schlegelii* has spinelike superciliaries and undivided caudals. *Bothriopsis albocarinata* and *B. alticola* are green arboreal pitvipers. *Bothriopsis punctata* has a well-defined postocular stripe, an ornate head pattern, a pale tail tip, and a much higher average number of subcaudals (85) than *Bothrops pulcher*. *Bothrops asper* has a well-defined pattern consisting of X-shaped dorsal blotches, a well-defined postocular stripe, a higher average number of ventrals (196 vs. 146), and a higher average number of subcaudals (66 vs. 50). *Bothrops lojanus* differs from *B. pulcher* in pattern and in possessing a well-defined postorbital stripe. The prelacunal is discrete from the second supralabial in *Bothrops microphthalmus* but they are integrated in *B. pulcher*; furthermore, *B. microphthalmus* is an upland form, whereas *B. pulcher* is found primarily in the lowlands and at intermediate elevations. *Lachesis muta* differs from *B. pulcher* in having finely divided subcaudals (2–4 per row posteriorly), conical keels on the dorsals, and a higher average number of ventrals (216 vs. 146) and dorsal scale rows (39 vs. 23). *Porthidium nasutum* differs from *B. pulcher* in having a sharply upturned snout, a well-defined postorbital stripe, and a dorsal pattern consisting of rectangular blotches, usually with a middorsal white stripe. See also the discussion of false pitvipers in Mimics of Venomous Snakes.

REMARKS This species is poorly represented in museum collections, and nothing has been published regarding its habits. It appears that Colombian specimens have a lower number of ventrals and subcaudals than those from Ecuador. Clearly, further study is needed. There are no reports of human envenomation by this species.

REFERENCES Ayerbe, 1979; Boulenger, 1896; Carrillo de Espinoza, 1983; Despax, 1911; Groombridge, 1986; Meneses, 1974b; Noguchi, 1909; Orcés, 1943, 1948; J. A. Peters, 1955, 1960a; J. A. Peters and Orejas-Miranda, 1970; W. C. H. Peters, 1863; Renjifo, 1979.

## ***Bothrops roedingeri*** **Mertens**

(Map 77)

LOCAL NAME Víbora.

ENGLISH NAME Roedinger's lancehead.

DISTRIBUTION Peru. This species is known reliably only from the type locality, Hacienda Huayuri, vicinity of Nazca, Departamento de Ica, Peru (Map 77). It has been reported from (and doubtless occurs in) the adjacent Departamento de Arequipa, but voucher specimens are lacking. Vertical distribution probably ranges from 900 to 2,000 m.

HABITAT Coastal and foothill desert.

DESCRIPTION The only reported sizes are for the type series, two juveniles that measured 269 and 328 mm. This is a terrestrial species with a short nonprehensile tail.

The dorsal ground color is basically pale gray-brown. The dorsum of the head is marked with two ill-defined dark brown spots in a transverse row just anterior to the intersupraoculars. Two brown-gray stripes extend obliquely from the occipital region onto the neck; anteriorly these embrace a pair of dark dots that extend to the supraoculars. The oblique stripes may fuse to form a trapeze-shaped marking. The area between the fourth and fifth supralabials bears a dark transverse marking; another runs obliquely from the postorbital region to the corner of the mouth. The dorsum is marked with a series of poorly defined spots that contain some black and white pigment along the borders. These spots are partially to completely divided middorsally and are slightly juxtaposed; they may fuse to form transverse stripes in the neck, lower body, and tail region. There is a lateral row of smaller dark spots that are also poorly defined. A row of small dark spots on the paraventrals encroaches upon the outer edges of the ventrals. Two dark spots occur on the underside of the head in the lower lip region; an additional pair may or may not be present on the throat. When both pairs are present, they are at right angles to one another. Otherwise, the venter is immaculate white.

There are 6 or 7 intersupraoculars (supraoculars are large and smooth); 11 or 12 supralabials (the third is integrated with the prelacunal in the holotype and is discrete from it in the paratype); 13 or 14 infralabials; 23–25 midbody dorsal scale rows, each with a prominent keel throughout its length; 179–185 ventrals; and 43–48 divided subcaudals.

SIMILAR SPECIES Of the sympatric venomous snakes, *B. roedingeri* is likely to be confused only with *B. pictus*, which is similar in most features (see Remarks). Perhaps the only differing characteristic is the number of ventrals (152–173 in *B. pictus* vs. 179–185 in *B. roedingeri*). See also the species account for *B. barnetti*.

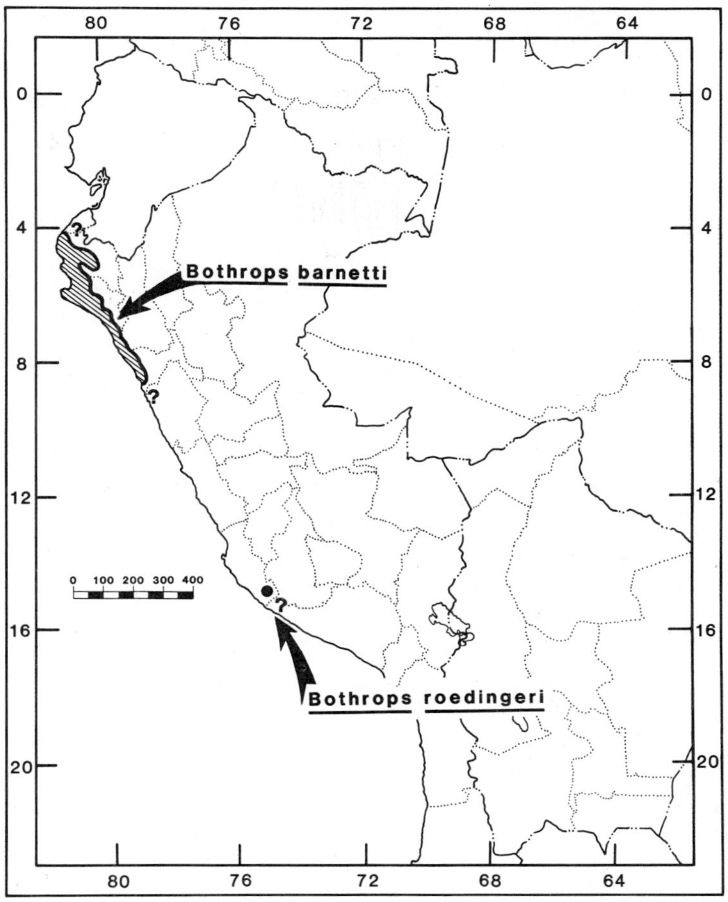


**Map 77.** Distributions of *Bothrops barnetti* (*diagonal lines*) and *B. roedingeri* (*dot*) in western Peru. The distributions of these species may be more extensive than are shown.

REMARKS In describing *B. roedingeri*, Mertens (1942) stated that it is "closest to *B. ammodytoides*." The resemblance may be superficial, as both species have patterns typical of desert pitvipers. Mertens also made no mention of *B. pictus*, a sympatric and extremely similar (if not identical) congener; it is possible he was unaware of the existence of *B. pictus*. Based on published information, the two species overlap in almost every feature. Thus, the possibilities are that *B. roedingeri* is synonymous with *B. pictus*; that the two are so similar that mixed series have been reported as *B. pictus*; or that *B. roedingeri* represents a race of *B. pictus*, a species known to be highly variable. Information on variation in *B. pictus* from throughout its range is lacking; it is possible that it will be found to overlap with *B. roedingeri* in ventral count. We suspect strongly that *B. roedingeri* Mertens is a junior synonym of *B. pictus* (Tschudi), but we have chosen to retain specific status for *B. roedingeri* pending the outcome of studies in progress.

REFERENCES Carrillo de Espinoza, 1983; Meneses, 1974a, 1974b; Mertens, 1942; P. Müller, 1973; Pefaur et al., 1978.

### *Bothrops sanctaecrucis* Hoge

(Map 78)

LOCAL NAMES Yoperojobobo pintada (?), yoperojobobo venenosa.

ENGLISH NAME Bolivian lancehead.

DISTRIBUTION Bolivia. This species is known only from the upper Río Beni region (Río Sécure), Departamento de El Beni, and from the vicinity of Ichilo, (upper Río Mamoré), Departamento de Santa Cruz (Map 78). The vertical distribution is from the lowlands to at least 450 m.

HABITAT Lower montane wet forest and possibly rainforest.

DESCRIPTION *Bothrops sanctaecrucis* is a terrestrial lancehead of medium build. There are no reports of the total length attained by this species, but a female paratype (UTA R-18689) is 665 mm in total length. The head size of the holotype (44 mm) indicates a snake about 1 m in length.

Dorsally, the head and body are tan to pale gray, the pigment tending to be darkest middorsally. The top of the head may be unmarked or have faint pale occipital stripes that merge to form a V with its apex on the intercanthals. Usually there is no postorbital stripe, although the upper edges of the posterior supralabials may be slightly darker, forming a faint stripe. The labials and gular region are unmarked. The eye is large and the iris is pale gold. About 18–21 triangular to trapezoidal brown blotches mark the body; these are opposite each other or slightly juxtaposed and are prominently bor-

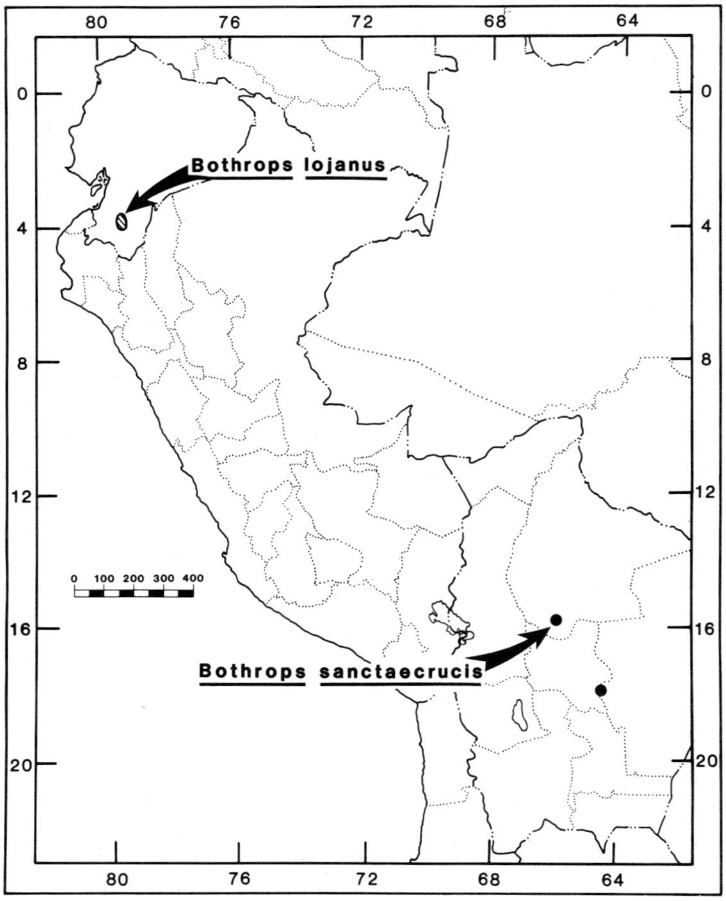


**Map 78.** Distributions of *Bothrops lojanus* (*diagonal lines*) and *B. sanctaecrucis* (*dots*) in western South America.

dered with white. Laterally, a series of dark brown paraventral blotches borders the bases of the dorsal blotches. A secondary series of ill-defined dark markings occupies the interspaces between the body blotches. The pattern is more condensed toward the tail, often creating a zig-zag stripe. The venter is essentially immaculate white or yellow except for some dark outer edges of ventrals and grayish pigment on the subcaudals.

There are 6–9 intersupraoculars; 8 supralabials, the second integrated with the prelacunal; 9 or 10 infralabials; 25 midbody dorsal scale rows; 177–182 ventrals; and 56 or 57 divided subcaudals.

SIMILAR SPECIES All pitvipers possibly sympatric with *B. sanctaecrucis* have well-defined postorbital stripes with the exception of *B. brazili*, which possesses 8 or 9 supralabials, 10–12 infralabials, and a dorsal pattern distinct from that of *B. sanctaecrucis*. Although *B. brazili* may have up to 202 ventrals, most individuals possess fewer than 180. *Bothrops microphthalmus*, *B. neuwiedi*, and *Porthidium hyoprora* all have the prelacunal discrete from the second supralabial. *Bothrops atrox*, *B. jararacussu*, and *Bothriopsis taeniata* have well-defined postorbital stripes and distinctive dorsal patterns, and lack and an immaculate venter. See also the species account for *Bothrops andianus*.

REMARKS This species remains an enigma; there are few literature references to it, and, in spite of a large type series, variation is unreported.

REFERENCES Groombridge, 1986; Hoge, 1966; Hoge and Romano-Hoge, 1981b; Kempff-Mercado, 1975; J. A. Peters and Orejas-Miranda, 1970.

### *Bothrops venezuelensis* Sandner-Montilla

(Figs. 243–246; Map 79)

LOCAL NAMES Barriga morada, cuatro narices, rabo candela, terciopelo, tigra mariposa.

ENGLISH NAME Venezuelan lancehead.

DISTRIBUTION Venezuela. This species is found in the central range of the Cordillera de la Costa, including the states of Carabobo, Aragua, the Federal District, and Miranda. It occurs elsewhere in the Venezuelan Andes in Mérida, Trujillo, Lara, Falcón, Yaracuy, and Sucre (see Remarks). A specimen (KU 133536) exists from Cerro Azul, Sucre, a locality near the tip of the Paria Peninsula at 600 m elevation (Map 79). Primarily an upland species, it is usually encountered between 1,000 and 2,200 m in elevation. There are reports of its occurrence at 2,800 m above sea level.

HABITAT Lower montane wet forest and cloud forest, including temperate areas where cold weather conditions occur.

DESCRIPTION *Bothrops venezuelensis* is a large, primarily terrestrial lancehead reaching an overall length of at least 1,520 mm but averaging about 1,000 mm.

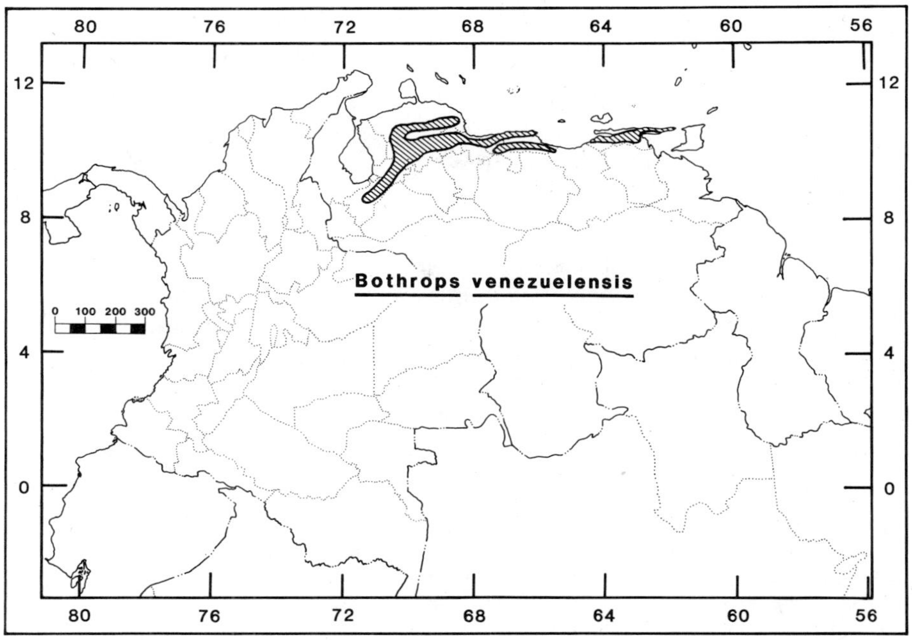


**Map 79.** Distribution of *Bothrops venezuelensis* in northern Venezuela.

The dorsal ground color is variable and may be yellowish tan, brown, gray, or olive; some specimens are a shade of red or pink overall. Many specimens show much countershading, making discernment of the ground color difficult. The dorsum of the head may be unmarked (colored like the body), or it may bear diffuse darker mottling bordered on either side by a single, broad, pale, ill-defined temporal stripe that includes the supraocular. The temporal stripes, in turn, are bordered on the side of the head by prominent, dark brown or black postorbital stripes that are narrowly edged in white (especially below). The postorbital stripes extend from behind the eyes across portions of the fifth and sixth and usually all of the seventh supralabials before hooking downward at the angle of the jaw and covering part of the posteriormost infralabial on either side. The supralabials and canthal region are suffused heavily with dark speckling, sometimes intensifying into vague blotches along the supralabial sutures. Some specimens show a yellow or pink suffusion, especially along the lower portions of the supralabials. Ventrally, the gular region is pale cream or tan with gray speckling that often tends to concentrate along the sutures between scales. The iris is coppery pink with scattered darker speckling. The tongue is black.

The dorsal pattern is variable and often complex. At its simplest it can consist of a series of black-edged brown trapezoidal markings that are situated paravertebrally and tend to be opposite each other or slightly juxtaposed; the overall effect is of bands. These bands are offset by diffuse gray zones and the basal area of each brown trapezoid is suffused with the dorsal ground color. In some specimens, all markings are further highlighted with narrow white borders. At its most complex, the pattern involves the reduction of the dark bands into four triangular spots that point inward and are situated paravertebrally. These may fuse, leaving two elongated rectangles running parallel with the spine. The diffuse gray zones remain associated with the dark dorsal markings, and the interspaces usually are suffused with black pigment. A series of dark brown to black paraventral spots is situated roughly opposite the paravertebral markings. The overall effect is disruptive, presumably rendering the animal rather difficult to discern in leaf litter. Toward the tail, the pattern coalesces into a nearly uniform black color with a few transverse cream bars. In juvenile specimens the distal portion of the tail is pink. The venter is tan to yellowish white and is pigmented heavily with black, which tends to concentrate as alternating spots at the juncture of the first dorsal row. In some specimens, dark pigment predominates, obscuring even the dorsal pattern.

There are reportedly 8–14 intersupraoculars, although the specimens we have examined have 5 or 6 keeled intersupraoculars (see Remarks); 6–9 supralabials, the second usually integrated with the prelacunal; 9–13 infralabials; 19–27 (usually 23–25) midbody dorsal scale rows; 179–219 ventrals; and 48–73 subcaudals, most of which are divided.

SIMILAR SPECIES *Bothrops venezuelensis* might be confused with three venomous snake species. *Bothrops asper* cannot be distinguished readily from *B. venezuelensis* on the basis of scale characteristics, although the two are quite dissimilar. *Bothrops asper* has a pointed snout (obtusely rounded in *B. venezuelensis*), a narrow postorbital stripe that lacks pale edges and usually is not in contact with the sixth supralabial or the posteriormost infralabials, and a venter that tends to be predominantly pale. The canthal region and labials are usually uniformly yellow in *B. asper* (stippled in *B. venezuelensis*) and the dorsal pattern consists of prominently edged triangular markings (pattern is different in *B. venezuelensis*). Juvenile *B. asper* have either a normal-colored or bright yellow tail tip, while juvenile *B. vene-*

zuelensis have a reddish pink tail tip. *Bothriopsis medusa* has 6 or fewer intersupraoculars (vs. 5 or more), 153–168 ventrals (vs. 179–219), and mostly undivided subcaudals. *Porthidium lansbergii* has an upturned snout, 139–161 ventrals (vs. 179–219), and 27–41 undivided subcaudals. See also the species account for *Bothrops atrox*.

REMARKS A report of a specimen of *B. venezuelensis* with 18 intersupraoculars requires confirmation. Because some of the literature about the distribution of *B. venezuelensis* is conflicting, we have included only those states reliably reported to contain it. The names *B. pifanoi* and *B. venezuelae*, still seen in the recent literature, are junior synonyms of *B. venezuelensis*.

REFERENCES Cendrero et al., 1972; García López and Sandner-Montilla, 1962; Hoge and Romano-Hoge, 1981a; Lancini, 1970, 1979; Milá de la Roca, 1935; J. A. Peters, 1968; J. A. Peters and Orejas-Miranda, 1970; Roze, 1970a; Sandner-Montilla, 1952, 1961, 1966, 1975, 1983; Sandner-Montilla and Romer, 1961; Sexton, 1958; Sexton and Heatwole, 1965; Test et al., 1966.

### *Bothrops xanthogrammus* (Cope)

(Figs. 247, 248; Map 60)

LOCAL NAMES Unknown.

ENGLISH NAME Cope's lancehead.

DISTRIBUTION Ecuador and possibly Colombia (see Remarks). This species has been recorded reliably only from the type locality, Pallatanga, Chimborazo, Ecuador. The site is on the upper Río Coco, Pacific slope of the Andes (see Map 60). The elevation is about 1,500 m.

HABITAT Lower montane forest that is seasonally dry.

DESCRIPTION *Bothrops xanthogrammus* is a large, terrestrial lancehead; the only size on record is that of the holotype, which measured 1,542 mm.

The dorsum of the head is black, bordered laterally by a yellow stripe that crosses the canthal, supraocular, and temporal regions. Beneath this is a black postorbital stripe that runs from behind the eye to the angle of the jaw. The canthal region, labials, and underside of the head are bright yellow. The type description is of a snake having a very dark olive dorsum, with a yellow zig-zag line from head to tail on each side of the body, forming V's with apices opposite or somewhat juxtaposed middorsally. The yellow temporal stripes unite with the zig-zag body stripes at the neck to form a V-shaped marking. The venter is black, paler medially, and tends to be marked with yellow ventrolateral spots.

There are 9 or 10 smooth intersupraoculars (see Remarks); 7 supralabials, the second integrated with the prelacunal; 11 infralabials; 27 midbody dorsal scale rows; 196 ventrals; and 54 divided subcaudals.

SIMILAR SPECIES With the exception of the supracephalic scales, which are smooth, *B. xanthogrammus* lacks distinctive scutellation (see Remarks). The only possibly sympatric pitviper that normally shares the characteristic of smooth supracephalic scales is *B. lojanus*. It differs from *B. xanthogrammus* in having 23 or fewer dorsals (vs. 27) and 155 or fewer ventrals (vs. 196).

REMARKS The holotype of *B. xanthogrammus* consists of a skull and stuffed body; thus, the purported condition of the head scales cannot be verified. While smooth supracephalic scales do not constitute a normal condition for large, terrestrial *Bothrops* species, this feature may appear adventitiously. In such cases, the scales usually are imbricate and rugose, despite the absence of keels.

Although this species has been cited as occurring in Colombia and Venezuela, there are no specimens in collections, and it seems that these range extensions require the synonymizing of *B. quadriscutatus* Posada-Arango with *B. xanthogrammus*. While both forms may represent the same taxon, there are unresolved questions.

The type locality for *B. xanthogrammus*, as well as aspects of its scutellation and pattern, lead us to suspect strongly that it actually is a specimen of the ubiquitous and variable *B. asper* (Fig. 187). Pending the outcome of our studies, we have chosen to retain specific status for *B. xanthogrammus*.

REFERENCES Acosta-Solís, 1944; Amaral, 1930c, 1931b; Ayerbe, 1979; Blanchard, 1889; Boulenger, 1896; Cope, 1868; Daniel, 1949; Duellman, 1979; Dunn, 1944a; Milá de la Roca, 1932; P. Müller, 1973; Nicéforo-María, 1942; Noguchi, 1909; Orcés, 1942, 1943, 1948; J. A. Peters, 1955, 1960a; Posada-Arango, 1889a, 1889b; Quintini N., 1927, 1936; Roze, 1966a; Vellard, 1941; Werner, 1922.

Fig. 3. *Heloderma horridum horridum*, female, 662 mm TL; Mexico. Photo by John H. Tashjian at the Fort Worth Zoo.

Fig. 4. *Heloderma horridum horridum*, female, 620 mm TL (UTA R-18694); Continental Divide near Rizo de Oro, Chiapas, Mexico. Photo by Joseph T. Collins, courtesy of Darrel Frost.

Fig. 5. *Heloderma horridum alvarezi*, male, 695 mm TL; Río Grijalva Valley, near Tuxtla Gutiérrez, Chiapas, Mexico. Photo by John H. Tashjian at the Fort Worth Zoo.

Fig. 6. *Heloderma horridum alvarezi*, female, 690 mm TL; Río Grijalva Valley, near Tuxtla Gutiérrez, Chiapas, Mexico. Photo by John H. Tashjian at the Fort Worth Zoo.

Fig. 7. *Heloderma horridum exasperatum*, male, 610 mm TL; Mexico. Photo by John H. Tashjian at the Fort Worth Zoo.

Fig. 8. *Heloderma horridum charlesbogerti*, male, 680 mm TL (UTA R-15002); vicinity of Bejuco, about 12 km south-southeast of Gualán, Departamento de Zacapa, Guatemala, about 600 m elevation. Specimen courtesy of Jay P. Vannini.

Fig. 9. *Heloderma suspectum suspectum*, male, 394 mm TL (UTA–Live Collection); near Hermosillo, Sonora, Mexico.

Fig. 10. *Heloderma suspectum suspectum*, same as Fig. 9, dorsolateral aspect of head.

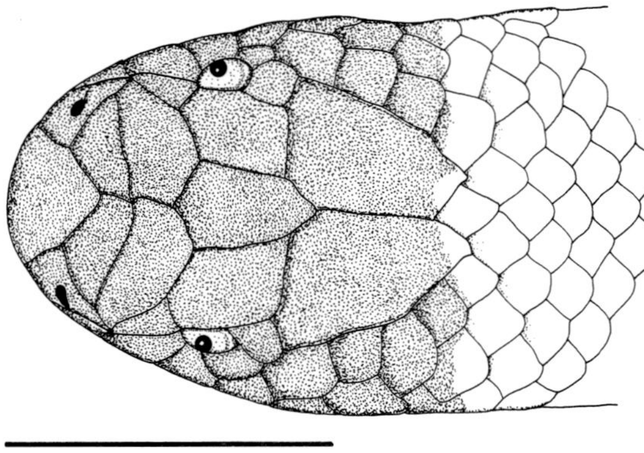

*Fig. 11.* Dorsal view of head of *Micruroides euryxanthus euryxanthus*, male, 420 mm TL (UTA R-16660); Catalina Mountains (foothills), Hardy Road, 0.2 km west of the junction with Oracle Road, Pima, Arizona, USA. Line represents 5 mm. Drawing by Clay M. Garrett.

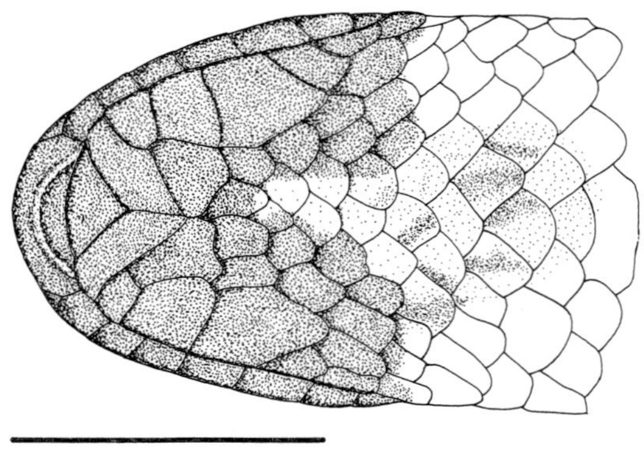

*Fig. 12.* Ventral view of head of *Micruroides euryxanthus euryxanthus*, same as Fig. 11. Drawing by Clay M. Garrett.

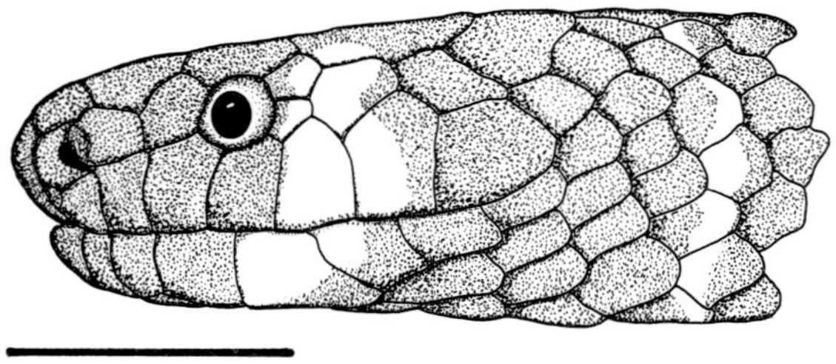

*Fig. 13.* Lateral view of head of *Micrurus elegans veraepacis*, female, 434 mm TL (UTA R-7717); 2.0 km east, 2.3 km south of Purulhá, Baja Verapaz, Guatemala, 1,524 m elevation. The pale head ring is short and incomplete dorsally in this species. This individual has 1 + 1 temporals on each side. Line represents 5 mm. Drawing by Clay M. Garrett.

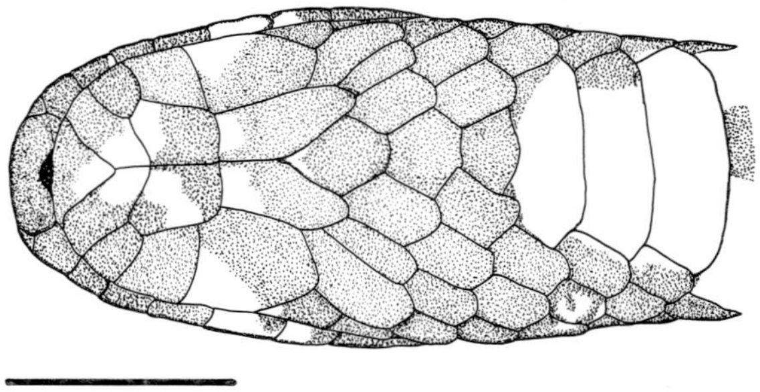

*Fig. 14.* Ventral view of head of *Micrurus elegans veraepacis*, same as Fig. 13. In most species of coral snakes, the first pair of infralabials are in contact with each other along the midline behind the mental, thus separating the mental from the chinshields. This specimen is drawn slightly turned to the right along its longitudinal axis. Line represents 5 mm. Drawing by Clay M. Garrett.

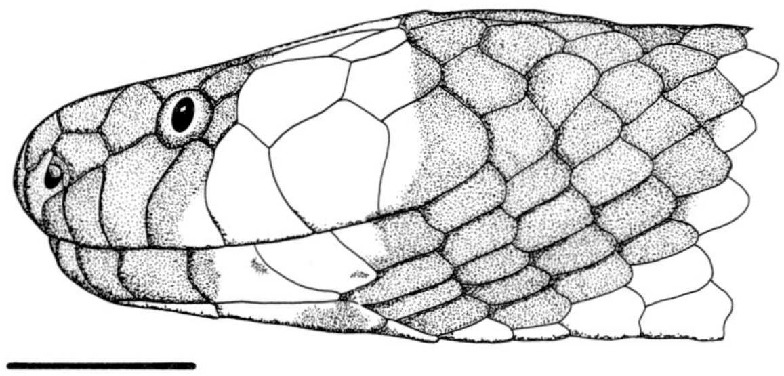

*Fig. 15.* Lateral view of head of *Micrurus browni browni*, male, 628 mm TL (UTA R-6633); Cerro Baúl, Oaxaca, Mexico. This species usually has 1 + 2 temporals per side and, as is typical for most coral snakes, the third and fourth supralabials are in contact with the orbit. Line represents 5 mm. Drawing by Clay M. Garrett.

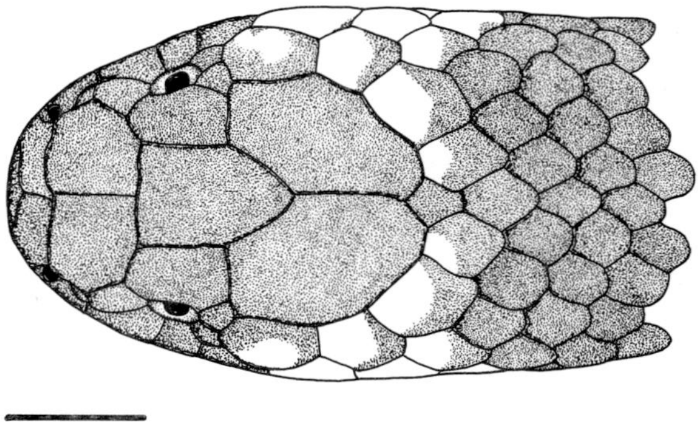

*Fig. 16.* Dorsal view of head of *Micrurus hemprichii ortoni*, male, 810 mm TL (UTA R-9683); Wacará, Vaupés, Colombia, 182 m elevation. Coral snakes possess a typical complement of 9 large head plates, including 2 internasals, 2 prefrontals, 2 supraoculars, a frontal, and 2 parietals. The frontal is usually wider than either supraocular (but see Fig. 18). Line represents 5 mm. Drawing by Clay M. Garrett.

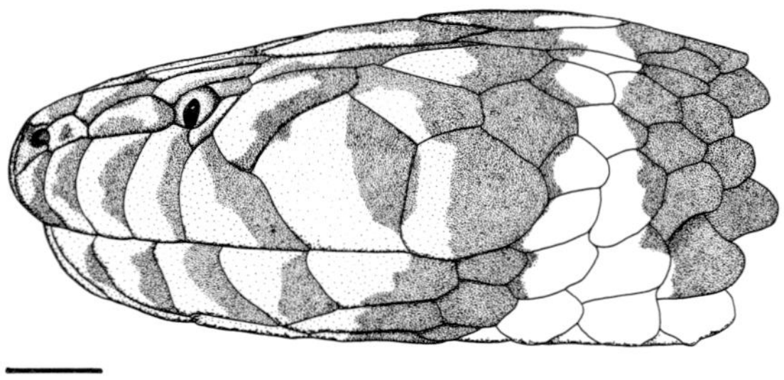

*Fig. 17.* Lateral view of head of *Micrurus surinamensis surinamensis*, female, 1,190 mm TL (UTA R-15679); Tepoe, district of Sipaliwini, Suriname. Unlike other coral snakes, in this species usually only the fourth supralabial is in contact with the orbit (compare with Figs. 13 and 15). Line represents 5 mm. Drawing by Clay M. Garrett.

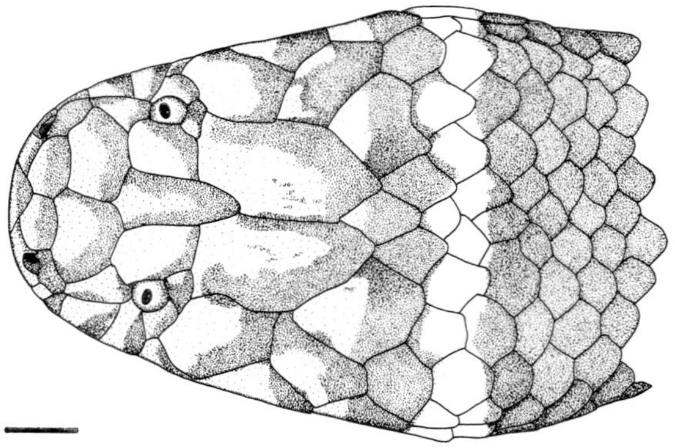

*Fig. 18.* Dorsal view of head of *Micrurus surinamensis surinamensis*, same as Fig. 17. The frontal is unusually narrow in this species, narrower than either supraocular, and many of the head scales are red bordered with black. Line represents 5 mm. Drawing by Clay M. Garrett.

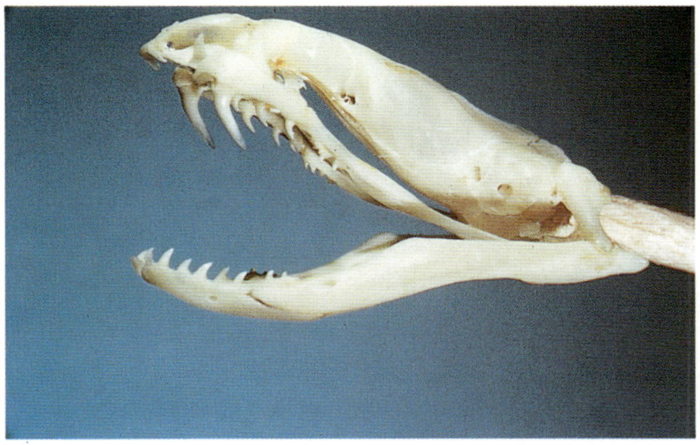

*Fig. 19.* The skull of a coral snake, genus *Micrurus*, exhibiting a proteroglyphous condition whereby the fangs are affixed to a relatively immobile maxillary bone and thus are permanently erect. The skull illustrated is of *Micrurus elegans*, female, 822 mm TL (UTA R-7072); Cerro Verde, Baja Verapaz, Guatemala, 1,700 m elevation. The skull is 17 mm in length from the front face of the premaxilla to the occipital condyle, and the fangs are about 2.5 mm in length.

*Fig. 20. Micrurus alleni*, adult; Tronadora, Guanacaste, Costa Rica. Note shape of black head cap. Photo by R. Wayne Van Devender.

*Fig. 21. Micrurus ancoralis ancoralis*, male, 777 mm TL (RWM 12923-at USNM); 12.6 km north by road of Santa Rosa, El Oro, Ecuador. In coral snakes, pattern anomalies may result in quinquads or other atypical sequences. Photo by Roy W. McDiarmid.

*Fig. 22. Micrurus ancoralis ancoralis*, same as Fig. 21, ventral aspect.

*Fig. 23. Micrurus ancoralis jani;* Pantanos, Campamento Ingeominas (Río Amparradó), Antioquia, Colombia, approximately 1,800 m elevation. The oblique first white ring is characteristic. Photo by Juan M. Renjifo, courtesy of the Instituto Nacional de Salud, Bogotá, Colombia.

*Fig. 24. Micrurus annellatus annellatus* approximately 65 km east-northeast of Pucallpa, Ucayali, Peru. Photo by Peter P. Marra.

*Fig. 25. Micrurus annellatus balzani*, female, 600 mm TL (USNM 247702); Explorer's Inn, Tambopata Reserve, 30-km straight-line distance south-southwest of Puerto Maldonado, Río Tambopata, Madre de Dios, Peru. The short pale parietal ring is characteristic. Photo by Roy W. McDiarmid.

*Fig. 26. Micrurus averyi*, female, 366 mm TL (MZUSP 8448); "INPA-WWF Reserves," vicinity of Manaus, Amazonas, Brazil, 120 m elevation. Photo by Barbara Zimmerman.

Fig. 27. *Micrurus bernadi*, male, 505 mm TL (UMMZ 85967); Necaxa, Puebla, Mexico. Preserved specimen. Photo by Harry W. Greene.

Fig. 28. *Micrurus bernadi*, same as Fig. 27, ventral aspect.

Fig. 29. *Micrurus browni browni*, female, approximately 400 mm TL; vicinity of Tuxtla Gutiérrez, Chiapas, Mexico, about 1,000 m elevation. Photo by David M. Dennis.

Fig. 30. *Micrurus clarki*, male, 605 mm TL (KU 112527); Camp Sasardí, San Blas, Panama, 12 m elevation. Photo by Charles W. Myers, American Museum of Natural History.

Fig. 31. *Micrurus collaris* (RMNH); Brownsberg, Brokopondo, Suriname. Preserved specimen. Photo by Marinus S. Hoogmoed.

Fig. 32. *Micrurus collaris*, same as Fig. 31, ventral aspect.

Fig. 33. *Micrurus corallinus*, male; Itaipuaçu, Maricá, Rio de Janeiro, Brazil. Photo by Anibal Melgarejo.

Fig. 34. *Micrurus corallinus*; Ubatuba, São Paulo, Brazil. Photo by Janis A. Roze.

Fig. 35. *Micrurus decoratus*; Nova Friburgo, Rio de Janeiro, Brazil. Photo by Anibal Melgarejo.

Fig. 36. *Micrurus diastema* subsp.; Sierra de los Tuxtlas, Veracruz, Mexico. Two subspecies, *M. d. diastema* and *M. d. sapperi*, intergrade in this region. Photo by Richard C. Vogt.

Fig. 37. *Micrurus diastema sapperi*, male, 274 mm TL (CM 112110); 4 km east of Chial, Cayo, Belize. Photo by Paul Freed, courtesy of the Carnegie Museum, Pittsburgh.

Fig. 38. *Micrurus diastema alienus*, 356 mm TL (TLBrown 16707). Cobá, Quintana Roo, Mexico. Photo by T. L. Brown, courtesy of Charles M. Bogert.

Fig. 39. *Micrurus diastema aglaeope*, female, 622 mm TL (UTA R-14125). On mainland opposite Hog Island, Departamento de Atlántida, Honduras.

Fig. 40. *Micrurus dissoleucus dissoleucus*. Cúcuta, Norte de Santander, Colombia. Photo by Juan M. Renjifo, courtesy of the Instituto Nacional de Salud, Bogotá.

Fig. 41. *Micrurus distans distans*, male, 777 mm TL (UTA R-14471); 8 km west of Alamos on Navojoa Road, Sonora, Mexico. Photo by David G. Barker at the Dallas Zoo.

Fig. 42. *Micrurus dumerilii* subsp.; Colonia Arturo Vargas, Ciudad Perdida, La Frontera, Sierra Nevada de Santa Marta, Magdalena, Colombia. Unlike this individual, many specimens from northern Colombia possess triads. Photo by Juan M. Renjifo, courtesy of the Instituto Nacional de Salud, Bogotá.

Fig. 43. *Micrurus dumerilii transandinus;* El Cedro (Río Juradó), Chocó, Colombia. Photo by Juan M. Renjifo, courtesy of the Instituto Nacional de Salud, Bogotá.

Fig. 44. *Micrurus dumerilii transandinus* (JDL 13774); Río Calima, Valle del Cauca, Colombia. Black pigment tends to form weak accessory rings on this specimen. Photo by Juan M. Renjifo.

Fig. 45. *Micrurus elegans veraepacis*, female, 437 mm TL (UTA R-7717); 2.0 km east, 2.3 km south of Purulhá, Baja Verapaz, Guatemala, 1,524 m elevation. The triads in this species are unusual in being so narrowly separated by pale pigment. This is one of two species of coral snakes north of Panama that has triads.

Fig. 46. *Micrurus ephippifer*; El Águila, Oaxaca, Mexico. Photo by Charles M. Bogert.

Fig. 47. *Micrurus ephippifer*, male, 718 mm TL (LACM 114162); 31 km northwest of El Camarón on Highway 190, Oaxaca, Mexico. Note extensive melanization of dorsal portion of red body rings. Photo by Roy W. McDiarmid.

Fig. 48. *Micrurus ephippifer*, same as Fig. 47, ventral aspect.

Fig. 49. *Micrurus filiformis;* Apiay (Villavicencio), Meta, Colombia, 360 m elevation. Photo by Juan M. Renjifo, courtesy of the Instituto Nacional de Salud, Bogotá.

Fig. 50. *Micrurus frontalis frontalis*, female, 635 mm TL (ZUEC 078); Altinópolis, São Paulo, Brazil. Photo by Ivan Sazima.

Fig. 51. *Micrurus frontalis frontalis;* Areguá, Central, Paraguay. Photo by Lawrence E. Naylor.

Fig. 52. *Micrurus frontalis altirostris;* Dos de Mayo, Misiones, Argentina. Photo by diTada-Martori, courtesy of the Departamento de Ciéncias Naturales, Universidad Nacional de Río Cuarto, Córdoba.

Fig. 53. *Micrurus frontalis altirostris;* Sierra de Mahoma, San José, Uruguay. Photo by Anibal Melgarejo.

Fig. 54. *Micrurus frontalis* subsp.; note the defensive tail display. Photo by Marcos A. Freiberg.

Fig. 55. *Micrurus frontifasciatus,* approximately 200 mm TL; Aiquiles, Cochabamba, Bolivia, 2,150 m elevation. Photo by Ken Preston-Mafham.

Fig. 56. *Micrurus fulvius microgalbineus;* Río Frio, near Gómez Farías, Tamaulipas, Mexico. Photo by Ernest A. Liner.

Fig. 57. *Micrurus fulvius tener,* female, 560 mm TL (UTA R-18012); vicinity of Los Angeles, 8 km east of intersection of State Highway 97 and FM 469, La Salle, Texas, USA.

Fig. 58. *Micrurus hemprichii hemprichii,* male, approximately 350 mm TL; Kwamalasemutu, district of Sipaliwini, Suriname. Photo by John deBruin.

Fig. 59. *Micrurus hemprichii ortoni*, male, 615 mm TL (RWM 10514-at USNM); vicinity of Huampami (Río Cenepa), Amazonas, Peru, 210 m elevation. Photo by Roy W. McDiarmid.

Fig. 60. *Micrurus hippocrepis*; El Estor, Izabal, Guatemala. Photo by Ricardo Mata, courtesy of Jay P. Vannini.

Fig. 61. *Micrurus hippocrepis*, female, 390 mm TL (KU 191138); 5.1 km west-southwest of Puerto Santo Tomás (Montañas del Mico), Izabal, Guatemala, 152 m elevation. Incomplete black rings are common in this species (see Fig. 514).

Fig. 62. *Micrurus ibiboboca*, male, 898 mm TL (ZUEC 027); Fazenda São Joaquim, Serrinha, Bahia, Brazil. Photo by Ivan Sazima.

Fig. 63. *Micrurus isozonus*; Aragua, Venezuela. Photo by Scott J. Maness, courtesy of John E. Simmons.

Fig. 64. *Micrurus langsdorffi langsdorffi*; Río Comeña, tributary of the Río Pirá-Paraná, Vaupés, Colombia. Preserved specimen photographed at the Instituto Nacional de Salud, Bogotá.

Fig. 65. *Micrurus laticollaris maculirostris*, adult (DMNH 4869); 33.1 km east of Manzanillo on Mexico Highway 200, Colima, Mexico. Photo by Terry L. Hibbitts.

Fig. 66. *Micrurus latifasciatus*, female (UTA R-21806); Finca El Faro, Quezaltenango, about 4 km north of El Palmar, Guatemala, 875 m elevation.

Fig. 67. *Micrurus lemniscatus carvalhoi*, male, approximately 700 mm TL; Bela Vista, Rio Claro, São Paulo, Brazil. Photo by Ivan Sazima, courtesy of Augusto Shinya Abe.

Fig. 68. *Micrurus lemniscatus diutius*; Arima Valley, Trinidad. Photo by John C. Murphy.

Fig. 69. *Micrurus lemniscatus diutius*, same as Fig. 68. The small eye and absence of a loreal are typical of the genus. Photo by J. C. Murphy.

Fig. 70. *Micrurus lemniscatus helleri*; La Chorrera (Río Igará-Paraná), Amazonas, Colombia. The short white body rings are not typical of northern Colombian populations of this species (see Fig. 71). Photo by Juan Manuel Renjifo, the Instituto Nacional de Salud, Bogotá.

Fig. 71. *Micrurus lemniscatus helleri*; Medina, Cundinamarca, Colombia, 576 m elevation. Photo by Juan M. Renjifo, courtesy of the Instituto Nacional de Salud, Bogotá.

Fig. 72. *Micrurus limbatus*; Sierra de los Tuxtlas, Veracruz, Mexico. This species may possess a pattern of black dorsal blotches or rings (see Fig. 73). Photo by Richard C. Vogt.

Fig. 73. *Micrurus limbatus*; Volcán Santa Marta, Sierra de los Tuxtlas, Veracruz, Mexico. Photo by Richard C. Vogt.

Fig. 74. *Micrurus margaritiferus*, male, [illegible]46 mm TL (RWM 11170-at USNM); near Pais (Río Cenepa), Amazonas, Peru. Photo by Roy W. McDiarmid.

Fig. 75. *Micrurus margaritiferus*, same as Fig. 74, ventral aspect. Photo by Roy W. McDiarmid.

Fig. 76. *Micrurus margaritiferus*, female, 773 mm TL (RWM 10370-at USNM); near San Antonio (Río Cenepa), Amazonas, Peru. Ventral aspect. Photo by Roy W. McDiarmid.

Fig. 77. *Micrurus mipartitus mipartitus*; near Urrao, Antioquia, Colombia. The orange cephalic pigment is unusually extensive on this specimen. Photo by Juan M. Renjifo, courtesy of the Instituto Nacional de Salud, Bogotá.

Fig. 78. *Micrurus mipartitus anomalus*, 283 mm TL (WWL 1135); Bella Vista, Cundinamarca, Colombia.

Fig. 79. *Micrurus mipartitus decussatus*; Uribe, Tambo, Cauca, Colombia. Photo by Juan M. Renjifo, courtesy of the Instituto Nacional de Salud, Bogotá.

Fig. 80. *Micrurus mipartitus semipartitus*, female, 484 mm TL (TCWC 58951); Highway 12 at the Río Santa Cruz, 42.6 km north of Altagracia, Miranda, Venezuela, 350 m elevation. Photo by James R. Dixon.

Fig. 81. *Micrurus multifasciatus hertwigi*; Costa Rica. Photo by Roy W. McDiarmid.

Fig. 82. *Micrurus multiscutatus*, female, 615 mm TL (AMNH 109781); Quebrada Guanguí, 0.5 km above Río Patia (upper Río Saija drainage), Cauca, Colombia, 100–200 m elevation. Photo by Charles W. Myers, American Museum of Natural History.

Fig. 83. *Micrurus narduccii*, female, 553 mm TL (RWM 15962-at USNM); vicinity of Galilea (Río Santiago), Amazonas, Peru. Photo by Roy W. McDiarmid.

Fig. 84. *Micrurus narduccii*, same as Fig. 83, ventral aspect. Photo by Roy W. McDiarmid.

Fig. 85. *Micrurus nigrocinctus nigrocinctus*, male, 580 mm TL (UTA R-14470); Finca La Pacifica, Guanacaste, Costa Rica. The yellow rings of individuals in some populations may be present, absent, or present only on part of the body (see Fig. 88). Photo by Edmund D. Brodie, Jr.

Fig. 86. *Micrurus nigrocinctus nigrocinctus*, same as Fig. 85, ventral aspect. Photo by Edmund D. Brodie, Jr.

Fig. 87. *Micrurus nigrocinctus divaricatus*, male, 572 mm TL (UTA R-14124); on mainland opposite Hog Island, Departamento de Atlántida, Honduras. The comment on Fig. 85 about yellow rings also applies to this subspecies (see Fig. 88).

Fig. 88. *Micrurus nigrocinctus divaricatus*, female, 1,095 mm TL (UTA R-15786); on mainland opposite Hog Island, Departamento de Atlántida, Honduras. The comment on Fig. 85 about yellow rings also applies to this subspecies (see Fig. 87)

Fig. 89. *Micrurus nigrocinctus mosquitensis*, female, 429 mm TL (UTA R-12919); Pavones de Turrialba, Cartago, Costa Rica, 600 m elevation.

Fig. 90. *Micrurus nigrocinctus zunilensis*; near Sonsonate, Sonsonate, El Salvador. Photo by Lawrence E. Naylor.

Fig. 91. *Micrurus peruvianus*, male, 356 mm TL (LACM 49433); 0.5 km east of Bellavista, Cajamarca, Peru, 526 m elevation. Photo by James R. Dixon.

Fig. 92. *Micrurus psyches psyches*, male, 480 mm TL (RMNH 15079); Mapane Creek, district of Suriname, Suriname. Preserved specimen. Photo by Marinus S. Hoogmoed, courtesy of the Rijksmuseum van Natuurlijke Historie, Leiden.

Fig. 93. *Micrurus psyches circinalis*; Trinidad. Photo by Hans Boos.

Fig. 94. *Micrurus psyches medemi*; Villavicencio, Meta, Colombia, 467 m elevation. Photo by Juan M. Renjifo, courtesy of the Instituto Nacional de Salud, Bogotá.

Fig. 95. *Micrurus psyches* cf. *paraensis*, female, 615 mm TL (UTA R-15674); Kwamalasemutu, district of Sipaliwini, Suriname. Photo by John deBruin.

Fig. 96. *Micrurus putumayensis*, female, 804 mm TL (TCWC 47619); Centro Unión, Loreto, Peru. Ventral aspect. Photo by James R. Dixon.

Fig. 97. *Micrurus spixii spixii*, male, 962 mm TL (LJV 0677); Mina 14 do Abril, Mineração (Santa Barbara), Rondônia, Brazil. Photo by Laurie J. Vitt.

Fig. 98. *Micrurus spixii martiusi*, male, 890 mm TL (USNM 267833); 65.5 km southwest of Itaituba, Parque Nacional da Amazônia (Rio Tapajós), Pará, Brazil. Photo by Gail A. Stone.

Fig. 99. *Micrurus spixii obscurus*, female, 827 mm TL (WWL 940); Finca La Libertad, near Villavicencio, Meta, Colombia, 310 m elevation.

Fig. 100. *Micrurus spixii obscurus*, same as Fig. 99, lateral aspect of the head. Note the absence of a loreal.

Fig. 101. *Micrurus spixii obscurus*, male, 1,1[illegible]3 mm TL (RWM 10469-at USNM); Paagat II, lower Alto Cenepa, Amazonas, Peru. Ventral aspect. Photo by Roy W. McDiarmid.

Fig. 102. *Micrurus steindachneri orcesi*, female, 770 mm TL (MCZ 156960); 14.7 km northeast of Río Salado, Napo, Ecuador, 1,310 m elevation. Photo by Roy W. McDiarmid.

Fig. 103. *Micrurus steindachneri orcesi*, same as Fig. 102, ventral aspect. Photo by Roy W. McDiarmid.

Fig. 104. *Micrurus surinamensis surinamensis*; Finca El Acuario, 14 km south of Villavicencio, Meta, Colombia, 450 m elevation. The dorsoventral flattening of the body and the curling and raising of the tail are a characteristic defensive posture. Photo by Juan M. Renjifo, courtesy of the Instituto Nacional de Salud, Bogotá.

Fig. 105. *Micrurus surinamensis nattereri*, female, 271 mm TL (WWL 935); Pamopetá (Caño Tí), Vaupés, Colombia, 213 m elevation.

Fig. 106. *Micrurus tschudii tschudii*; Valle del Chillón, north of Lima, Peru. Photo by Janis A. Roze.

*Fig. 107. Micrurus tschudii olssoni,* male, 480 mm TL (MCZ 161219); near Petro Peru oil well #5900, near Miramar, Talara, Alta Piura, Peru. Photo by Julius Boos.

*Fig. 108. Micruroides euryxanthus euryxanthus;* 0.2 km east of Portal, Cochise, Arizona, USA. Photo by David L. Hardy.

*Fig. 109. Micruroides euryxanthus australis;* 16–22 km north of Hermosillo on Mexican Highway 15, Sonora, Mexico. The raised, curled tail is a defensive posture. Photo by Robert W. Hansen.

*Fig. 110. Pelamis platurus,* male, 417 mm TL; Pacific Ocean, Gulf of Chiriquí, Panama. The tail is strongly compressed laterally in sea snakes, an adaptation for swimming. This is a typically patterned specimen, but this species is highly variable (see Figs. 111, 112). Photo by Paul Freed at the Houston Zoo.

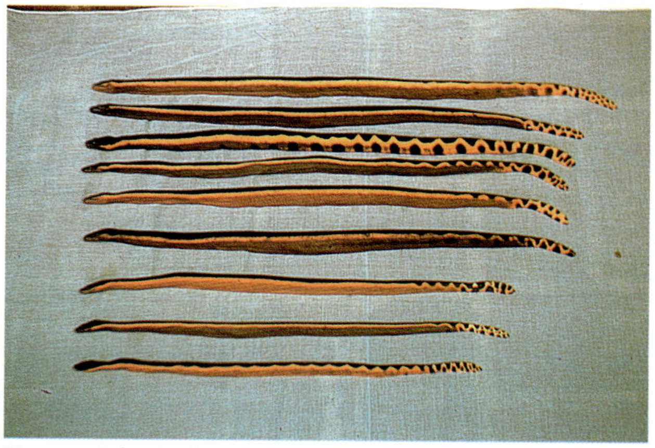

*Fig. 111. Pelamis platurus;* Pacific Ocean, off west coast of Mexico. Considerable pattern and color variation are found in this species. Photo by William A. Dunson.

*Fig. 112. Pelamis platurus.* Gulf of Dulce, Costa Rica. A totally xanthic specimen. Photo by William A. Dunson.

*Fig. 113. Agkistrodon bilineatus bilineatus,* female, large adult; vicinity of Taxisco, Santa Rosa, Guatemala. Photo by John H. Tashjian at the San Antonio Zoo.

*Fig. 114. Agkistrodon bilineatus howardgloydi,* holotype, male, 746 mm TL (AMNH 125525); 0.8 km north of Mirador el Cañón del Tigre, Parque Nacional Santa Rosa, Guanacaste, Costa Rica. Photo by Louis Porras.

Fig. 115. *Agkistrodon bilineatus howardgloydi*, same as Fig. 114. Photo by David L. Hardy.

Fig. 116. *Agkistrodon bilineatus russeolus*, holotype, male, 850 mm TL (KU 70905); 11.7 km north of Pisté, Yucatán, Mexico. Photo by J. B. Tulecke, courtesy of the University of Kansas.

Fig. 117. *Agkistrodon bilineatus taylori*; vicinity of Sota La Marina, Tamaulipas, Mexico. Photo by David G. Barker at the Dallas Zoo.

Fig. 118. *Agkistrodon bilineatus* subsp., male, 850 mm TL (UTA R-6359); 15 km (air line) west-southwest of San Cristóbal Verapaz, Alta Verapaz, Guatemala.

Fig. 119. *Agkistrodon contortrix pictigaster*, female, 688 mm TL (TCWC 64446); along the Río Grande del Norte (Rio Grande), approximately 0.8 km upstream from the mouth of Fresno Creek, Chihuahua, Mexico. Specimen courtesy of Rick J. Green.

Fig. 120. *Agkistrodon contortrix pictigaster*, female, large adult (UTA–Live Collection); Pumpville Road north of Comstock, Val Verde, Texas, USA.

Fig. 121. *Bothriechis aurifer*, female (UTA); Cerro Verde, Baja Verapaz, Guatemala, 1,500 m elevation.

Fig. 122. *Bothriechis aurifer* (UTA); near La Unión Barrios, Baja Verapaz, Guatemala, 1,500 m elevation. Photo by David G. Barker at the Dallas Zoo.

Fig. 123. *Bothriechis bicolor*, male, approximately 600 mm TL (UTA–Live Collection); south slope of Volcán de Agua, Finca Rosario Vista Hermosa, Escuintla, Guatemala, approximately 1,200 m elevation. Individuals occasionally have an irregular pattern of black speckling.

Fig. 124. *Bothriechis bicolor*, female, 909 mm TL (UTA R-18365); south slope of Volcán de Agua, Finca Rosario Vista Hermosa, Escuintla, Guatemala, approximately 1,300 m elevation. The loreal pit is clearly evident.

Fig. 125. *Bothriechis lateralis;* Costa Rica. Photo by John H. Tashjian at the Dallas Zoo.

Fig. 126. *Bothriechis lateralis*, female, approximately 600 mm TL; near San José, Costa Rica.

Fig. 127. *Bothriechis lateralis*, age 21 days; Costa Rica. The tan ground color and pale tail tip are typical of neonates.

Fig. 128. *Bothriechis lateralis*, the same specimen as in Fig. 127 at 40 weeks of age.

Fig. 129. *Bothriechis marchi;* north of San Pedro Sula, Cortés, Honduras. Photo by John H. Tashjian.

Fig. 130. *Bothriechis marchi*, neonate; Honduras. This species may be green or brown (see Fig. 131) at birth. Specimen courtesy of the Houston Zoo.

*Fig. 131. Bothriechis marchi*, neonate; Honduras. This species may be brown or green (see Fig. 130) at birth. Specimen courtesy of the Houston Zoo.

*Fig. 132. Bothriechis nigroviridis*, adult near San Isidro del General, San José, Costa Rica. Photo by John H. Tashjian at the Dallas Zoo.

*Fig. 133. Bothriechis nigroviridis*; San Gerardo, San José, Costa Rica. The loreal pit is clearly evident. Photo by R. Wayne Van Devender.

*Fig. 134. Bothriechis rowleyi*, male, 96[illegible] mm TL (UTA R-23954); Cerro Baúl, Oaxaca, Mexico, 1,600 m elevation. Photo by David G. Barker at the Dallas Zoo.

*Fig. 135. Bothriechis rowleyi*, male, adult (UTA–Live Collection); Cerro Baúl, Oaxaca, Mexico. Photo by R. Wayne Van Devender at the Dallas Zoo.

*Fig. 136. Bothriechis rowleyi*, female, age [illegible] days. Female parent from Cerro Baúl, Oaxaca, Mexico. Photo by Paul Freed at the Houston Zoo.

*Fig. 137. Bothriechis rowleyi*, the same specimen as in Fig. 136 at approximately 56 days.

*Fig. 138. Bothriechis schlegelii*, female, 6[illegible]5 mm TL (KU 187441); 12.6 km by road west of Puerto Santo Tomás (Montañas del Mico), Izabal, Guatemala, 774 m elevation. Photographed in situ; mouth is agape in typical defensive posture. The color pattern of this specimen is that most frequently found in snakes from the northern portion of the range.

Fig. 139. *Bothriechis schlegelii;* Limón Province, Costa Rica. Photo by Saul Friess.

Fig. 140. *Bothriechis schlegelii*, female; Limón Province, Costa Rica. Uniformly yellow specimens are commonly referred to as "oropel." Photo by George Grall.

Fig. 141. *Bothriechis schlegelii;* Costa Rica. The spinelike superciliaries and loreal pit are clearly evident. Photo by John H. Tashjian at the San Antonio Zoo.

Fig. 142. *Bothriechis schlegelii;* Pantanos, Campamento Ingeominas (Río Amparradó), Antioquia, Colombia, approximately 1,800 m elevation. Photo by Juan M. Renjifo, courtesy of the Instituto Nacional de Salud, Bogotá.

Fig. 143. *Bothriechis schlegelii*, 479 mm TL; Topacio (vicinity of Pance), Municipio de Cali, Valle del Cauca, Colombia, 1,650 m elevation. Photo by Dennis M. Harris.

Fig. 144. *Bothriechis schlegelii*, female, approximately 550 mm TL; El Parque Nacional Natural La Cueva de los Guácharos, Huila, Colombia, 2,000 m elevation.

Fig. 145. *Bothriechis schlegelii*, male, 486 mm TL (KU 179509); Tandapi, Pichincha, Ecuador. Photo by John D. Lynch.

Fig. 146. *Bothriechis schlegelii*, female, 584 mm TL (MCZ 156886); 2 km north and 1 km east of Santo Domingo de los Colorados, Pichincha, Ecuador, 570 m elevation. In this specimen the characteristic white paraventral spots have fused, forming a stripe. The superciliaries are raised only slightly, as is typical of southern populations. Photo by Ken Miyata, courtesy of the Museum of Comparative Zoology, Harvard University.

Fig. 147. *Bothriopsis albocarinata*, specimen on left is a female, 419 mm TL (KU 121347), specimen on right is a male, 441 mm TL (KU 121348); Río Negro, Tungurahua, Ecuador, elevation 1,260 m. Preserved specimens. Photo by John E. Simmons, courtesy of the Museum of Natural History, University of Kansas.

Fig. 148. *Bothriopsis albocarinata*, same as Fig. 147, ventral aspect. Photo by John E. Simmons, courtesy of the Museum of Natural History, University of Kansas.

Fig. 149. *Bothriopsis bilineata bilineata*, male, approximately 400 mm TL; vicinity of Sipaliwini, district of Sipaliwini, Suriname. The darkly pigmented tail and the white paraventral stripe are typical of this species. Photo by John H. Tashjian at the Dallas Zoo.

Fig. 150. *Bothriopsis bilineata bilineata*, same as Fig. 149. The loreal pit is clearly evident. Photo by David G. Barker at the Dallas Zoo.

Fig. 151. *Bothriopsis bilineata smaragdina*, female, 933 mm TL (UTA R-22581); Ecuador. Specimen courtesy of the Dallas Zoo.

Fig. 152. *Bothriopsis medusa*; Venezuela. Photo by Fernando Sandner-Montilla.

Fig. 153. *Bothriopsis oligolepis*, female, 941 mm TL (LSU 41037); Santa Cruz, about 9 km south-southeast of Oxapampa, Pasco, Peru, 2,050 m elevation. Recently killed specimen. Photo by Thomas S. Schulenberg, courtesy of the Louisiana State University Museum of Zoology.

Fig. 154. *Bothriopsis oligolepis*, same as Fig. 153. Photo by Thomas S. Schulenberg, courtesy of the Louisiana State University Museum of Zoology.

*Fig. 155. Bothriopsis peruviana;* Peru. Photo by Janis A. Roze.

*Fig. 156. Bothriopsis peruviana;* Peru. Specimen courtesy of the Departamento de Animales Venenosos del Instituto de Salud Pública, Lima.

*Fig. 157. Bothriopsis punctata;* Pantanos, Campamento Ingeominas (Río Amparradó), Antioquia, Colombia, approximately 1,800 m elevation. Photo by Juan M. Renjifo, courtesy of the Instituto Nacional de Salud, Bogotá.

*Fig. 158. Bothriopsis taeniata taeniata,* male, approximately 1,000 mm TL; Kwamalasemutu, district of Sipaliwini, Suriname. Photo by John H. Tashjian at the Dallas Zoo.

*Fig. 159. Bothriopsis taeniata taeniata,* female, approximately 500 mm TL; Kwamalasemutu, district of Sipaliwini, Suriname. Photo by John H. Tashjian at the Dallas Zoo.

*Fig. 160. Bothriopsis taeniata taeniata,* female, 1,165 mm TL (WWL 962); Alto Río Guayuriba, 18 km south of Villavicencio, Meta, Colombia, 480 m elevation.

*Fig. 161. Bothriopsis taeniata taeniata,* male, approximately 950 mm TL; Sinop, Mato Grosso, Brazil. Photo by Ivan Sazima, courtesy of the Instituto Butantan, São Paulo.

*Fig. 162. Bothriopsis taeniata taeniata,* same as Fig. 160. The loreal pit is clearly evident.

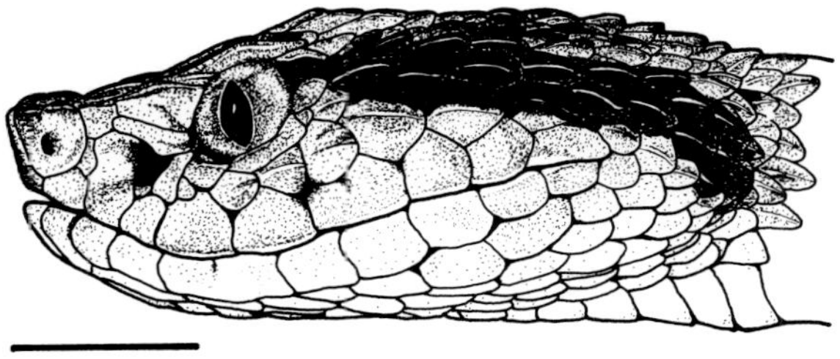

Fig. 163. Lateral view of head of *Bothriechis aurifer*, female, 390 mm TL (UTA R-7040); Cerro Quisís, Hacienda Vieja, Baja Verapaz, Guatemala, 1,700 m elevation. Line represents 5 mm. Drawing by Ty M. Kubin.

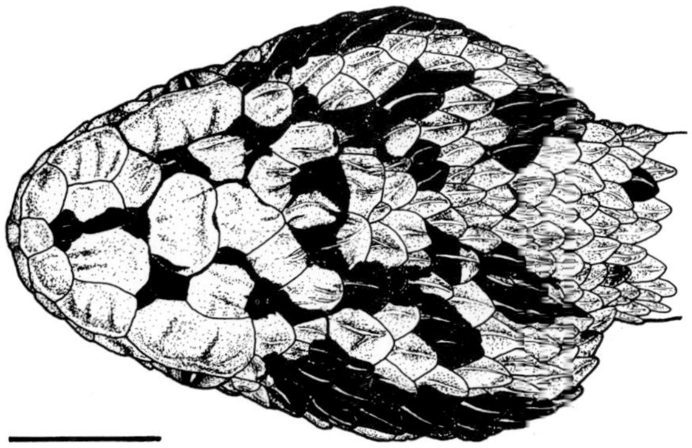

Fig. 164. Dorsal view of head of *Bothriechis aurifer*, same as Fig. 163. This species and several of its congeners have relatively large, unkeeled, irregularly arranged scales on the top of the head. Drawing by Ty M. Kubin.

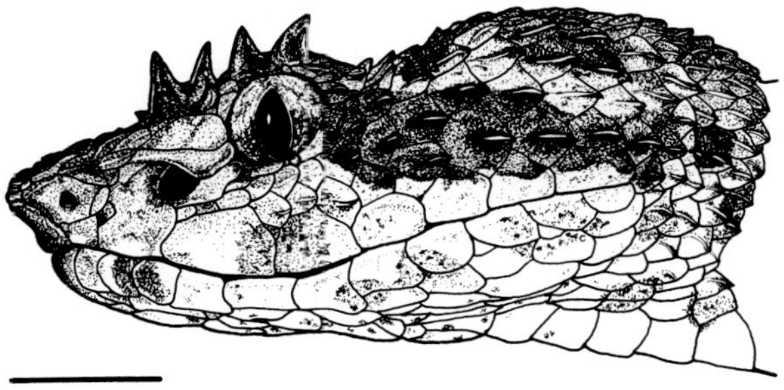

Fig. 165. Lateral view of head of *Bothriechis schlegelii*, male, 585 mm TL (UTA R-12957); Los Amates, Aldea Vista Hermosa, Izabal, Guatemala, 550 m elevation. There are usually fewer supralabials in this species than in other species of *Bothriechis*. Line represents 5 mm. Drawing by Ty M. Kubin.

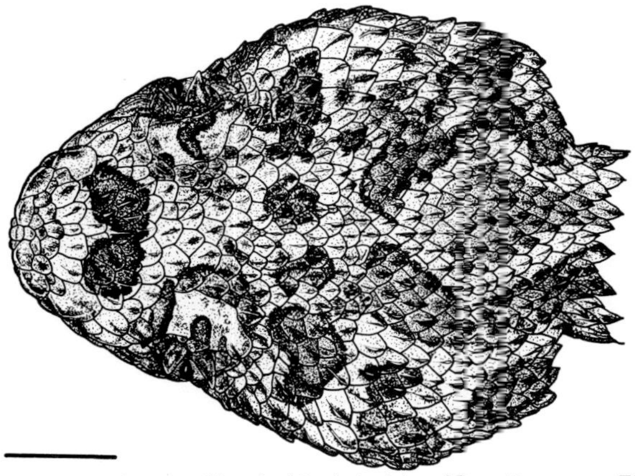

Fig. 166. Dorsal view of head of *Bothriechis schlegelii*, same as Fig. 165. Drawing by Ty M. Kubin.

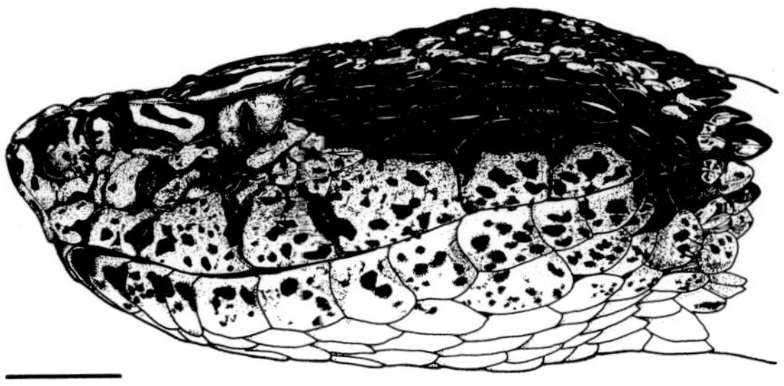

Fig. 167. Lateral view of head of *Bothriopsis oligolepis*, female, 941 mm TL (LSUMZ 41037); Santa Cruz, about 9 km south-southeast of Oxapampa, Pasco, Peru, 2,050 m elevation. Line represents 5 mm. Drawing by Ty M. Kubin.

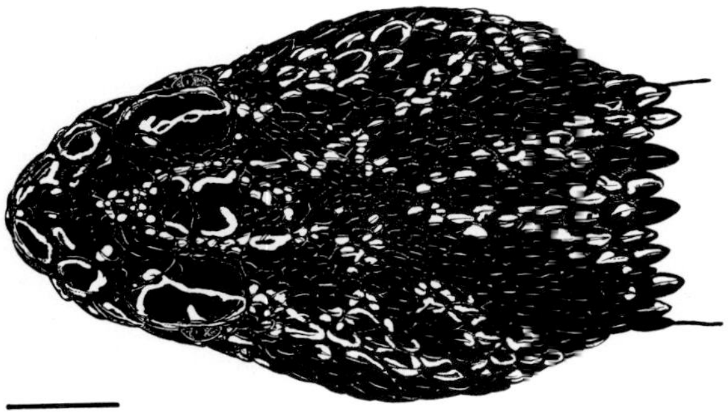

Fig. 168. Dorsal view of head of *Bothriopsis oligolepis*, same as Fig. 167. Drawing by Ty M. Kubin.

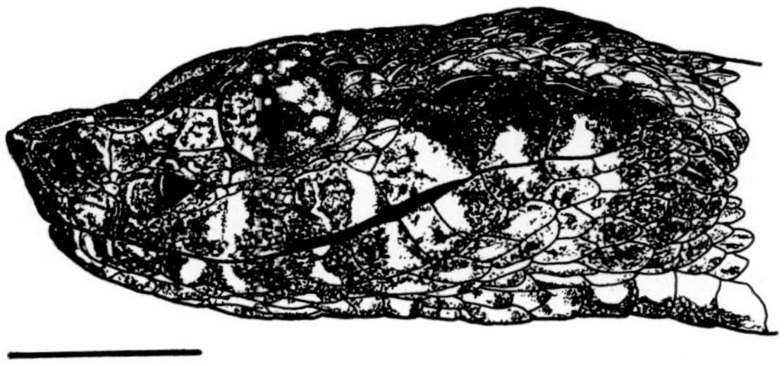

Fig. 169. Lateral view of head of *Bothriopsis taeniata taeniata*, female, 429 mm TL (UTA R-10501); Sipaliwini, district of Sipaliwini, Suriname. Line represents 5 mm. Drawing by Ty M. Kubin.

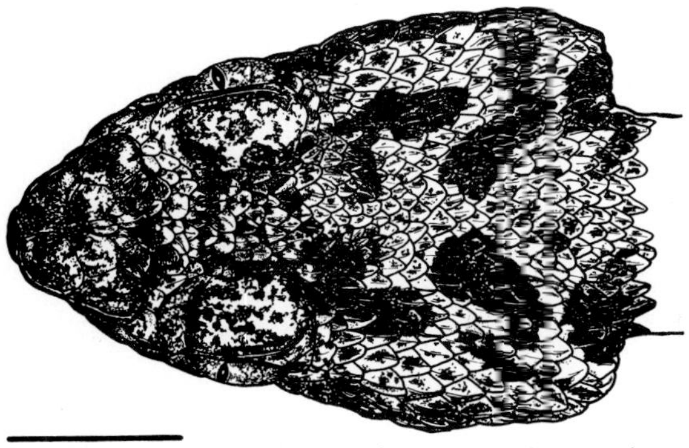

Fig. 170. Dorsal view of head of *Bothriopsis taeniata taeniata*, same as Fig. 169. Drawing by Ty M. Kubin.

*Fig. 171.* Lateral view of head of *Bothrops alternatus*, male 745 mm TL (UTA R-5602); near Asunción, Paraguay. Note the second supralabial and prelacunal are discrete from one another (not fused into a single scale as in Figs. 175 and 177). Line represents 5 mm. Drawing by Clay M. Garrett.

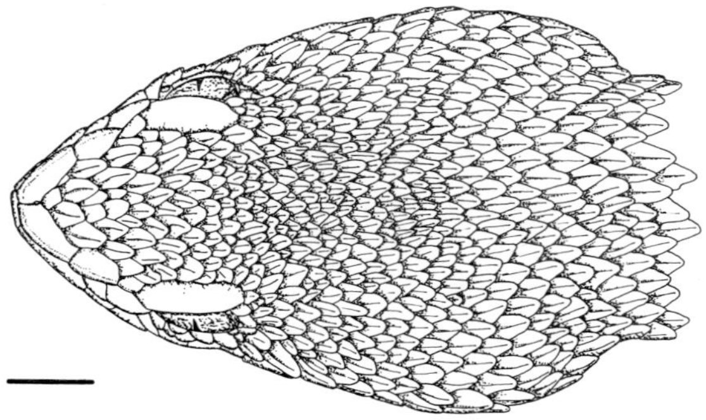

*Fig. 172.* Dorsal view of head of *Bothrops alternatus*, same as Fig. 171. The supraoculars are relatively narrow in this species. Drawing by Clay M. Garrett.

*Fig. 173.* Lateral view of head of *Bothrops ammodytoides*, female, 574 mm TL (UTA R-16334); Unión, San Luis, Argentina. The second supralabial and prelacunal are fused into a single scale, the lacunolabial. Line represents 5 mm. Drawing by Clay M. Garrett.

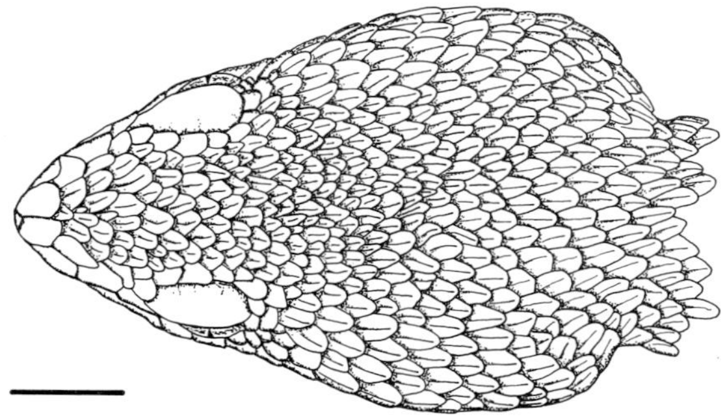

*Fig. 174.* Dorsal view of head of *Bothrops ammodytoides*, same as Fig. 173. Drawing by Clay M. Garrett.

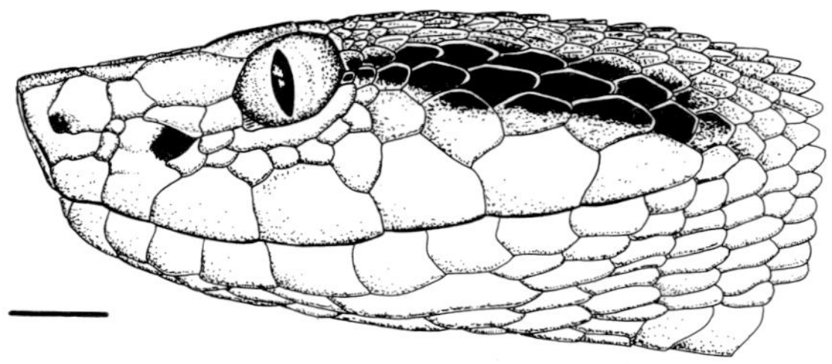

*Fig. 175.* Lateral view of head of *Bothrops asper*, female, 1,141 mm TL (UTA R-15651); Las Dantas, El Estor, Izabal, Guatemala, 50 m elevation. The last 1–2 supralabials may enter the dark postocular stripe. Line represents 5 mm. Drawing by Clay M. Garrett.

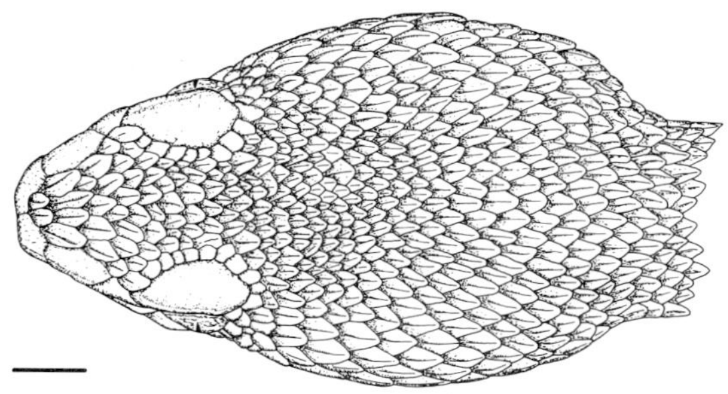

*Fig. 176.* Dorsal view of head of *Bothrops asper*, same as Fig. 175. Drawing by Clay M. Garrett.

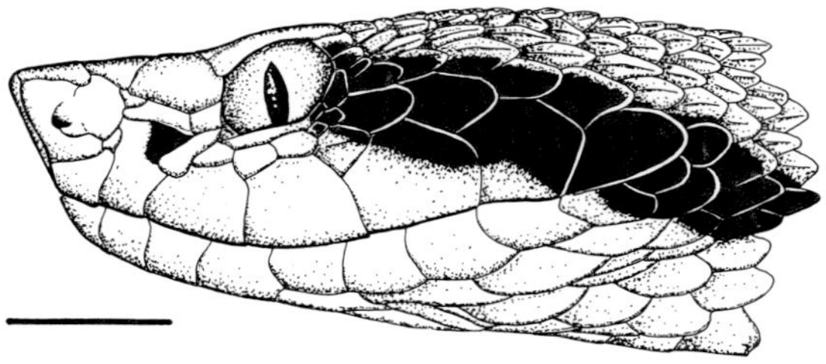

*Fig. 177.* Lateral view of head of *Bothrops atrox*, male, 545 mm TL (UTA R-3771); Lomalinda, Meta, Colombia, elevation 200 m. The posteriormost 3 supralabials usually enter the dark postocular stripe. Note the second supralabial is fused with the prelacunal, forming a lacunolabial—a condition found in many Neotropical pitvipers. Line represents 5 mm. Drawing by Clay M. Garrett.

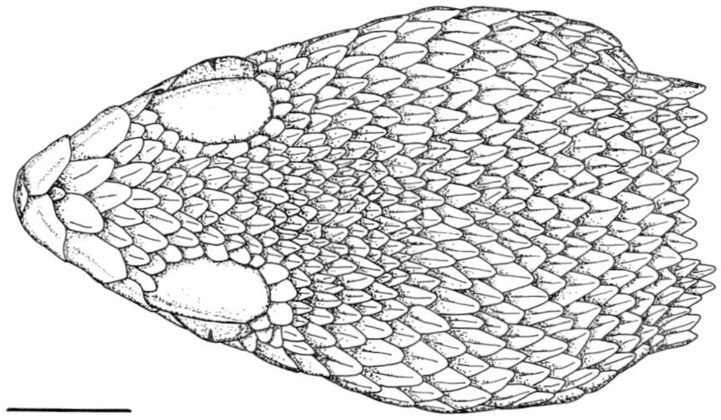

*Fig. 178.* Dorsal view of head of *Bothrops atrox*, same as Fig. 177. Drawing by Clay M. Garrett.

Fig. 179. *Bothrops alternatus*; Monte Alto, Minas Gerais, Brazil. Photo by Ivan Sazima, courtesy of the Instituto Butantan, São Paulo.

Fig. 180. *Bothrops alternatus*; El Parque Nacional Ybycui, Paraguarí, Paraguay. Photo by Lawrence E. Naylor.

Fig. 181. *Bothrops ammodytoides*; Departamento de Buenos Aires, Argentina. Photo by John H. Tashjian at the California Polytechnic University at Pomona.

Fig. 182. *Bothrops andianus*, male, 392 mm TL (USNM 267837); Río Macusani Valley, 4 km north-northeast (air line) of Ollachea, Puno, Peru, elevation 2,380 m. Photo by John E. Cadel.

Fig. 183. *Bothrops andianus*, specimen above is male, 176 mm TL (USNM 267839), specimen below is female, 187 mm TL (USNM 267838); Río Macusani Valley, 4 km north-northeast of Ollachea, Puno, Peru, 2,380 m elevation. Photo by John E. Cadel.

Fig. 184. *Bothrops asper*, female, approximately 200 mm TL (UTA R-22580); 12.3 km northwest of Sontecomapan, Veracruz, Mexico. This specimen was collected on 16 March 1973 and was photographed shortly thereafter. It died in December 1987 and had grown to 1,963 mm in total length.

Fig. 185. *Bothrops asper*, female, 465 mm TL (UTA R-17031); between Tulum and Cobá at kilometer 14, Quintana Roo, Mexico.

Fig. 186. *Bothrops asper*; Estación Biológica La Selva, Heredia, Costa Rica. Photo by David L. Hardy.

Fig. 187. *Bothrops asper;* vicinity of Bolívar, Cauca, Colombia. The ornate head pattern is common on specimens from the southern portion of the range (see *B. xanthogrammus* species account). Photo by Juan M. Renjifo, courtesy of the Instituto Nacional de Salud, Bogotá.

Fig. 188. *Bothrops asper;* Armero, Tolima, Colombia. Photo by Juan M. Renjifo, courtesy of the Instituto Nacional de Salud, Bogotá.

Fig. 189. *Bothrops asper;* Chiriguaná, El Cesar, Colombia. Photo by Juan M. Renjifo, courtesy of the Instituto Nacional de Salud, Bogotá.

Fig. 190. *Bothrops asper;* Saravena, Arauca, Colombia. The iris is opaque due to the shedding cycle. This specimen is representative of the population found east of the Andes in Colombia and Venezuela (see Fig. 194). Photo by Juan M. Renjifo, courtesy of the Instituto Nacional de Salud, Bogotá.

Fig. 191. *Bothrops asper;* Los Teques, Miranda, Venezuela. Photo by Robert Godshalk.

Fig. 192. *Bothrops* cf. *asper;* El Tucuche, Trinidad. Photo by John C. Murphy.

Fig. 193. *Bothrops atrox,* female, 1,500 mm TL (WWL 455); El Alto de Menegua, near Puerto López, Meta, Colombia, 225 m elevation.

Fig. 194. *Bothrops atrox;* Puerto Rondón, Arauca, Colombia, 150 m elevation. This population ranges to within about 100 km east of a population of *B. asper* (see Fig. 190). Photo by Juan M. Renjifo, courtesy of the Instituto Nacional de Salud, Bogotá.

*Fig. 195. Bothrops atrox;* Guyana. Photo by John H. Tashjian.

*Fig. 196. Bothrops atrox,* juvenile; Suriname. Photo by Marinus S. Hoogmoed, courtesy of the Rijksmuseum van Natuurlijke Historie, Leiden.

*Fig. 197. Bothrops atrox,* male, approximately 400 mm TL (UTA R-9832); vicinity of Iquitos, Loreto, Peru.

*Fig. 198. Bothrops atrox,* female, 774 mm TL (USNM 247704); Explorer's Inn, Tambopata Reserve, 30-km straight-line distance south-southwest of Puerto Maldonado, Río Tambopata, Madre de Dios, Peru. Photo by Roy W. McDiarmid.

*Fig. 199. Bothrops atrox,* same as Fig. 198. Photo by Roy W. McDiarmid.

*Fig. 200. Bothrops barnetti;* vicinity of Olmos, Lambayeque, Peru. Photo by Harry W. Greene, courtesy of the Museo Javier Prado, Lima.

*Fig. 201. Bothrops brazili,* juvenile; Araracuara, Caquetá, Colombia. Photo by Juan M. Renjifo, courtesy of the Instituto Nacional de Salud, Bogotá.

*Fig. 202. Bothrops brazili,* female, 1,400 mm TL (RWM 10790-at USNM); south of Aintami, vicinity of Huampami (Río Cenepa), Amazonas, Peru, 210 m elevation. Photo by Roy W. McDiarmid.

*Fig. 203. Bothrops brazili*, female, approximately 840 mm TL (UTA–Live Collection); vicinity of Apoera, district of Sipaliwini, Suriname. Typically, the postorbital stripe is absent or reduced in this species. The loreal pit is clearly evident. Specimen courtesy of the Dallas Zoo.

*Fig. 204. Bothrops brazili;* Cáceres, Mato Grosso, Brazil. Photo by Ivan Sazima, courtesy of the Instituto Butantan, São Paulo.

*Fig. 205. Bothrops brazili*, male, approximately 670 mm TL (UTA–Live Collection); vicinity of Apoera, district of Sipaliwini, Suriname. Note the pale iris and ill-defined postocular stripe. Specimen courtesy of the Dallas Zoo.

*Fig. 206. Bothrops caribbaeus;* Anse Gallet, Saint Lucia, West Indies. Photo by Hans Boos.

*Fig. 207. Bothrops caribbaeus;* Dennery, Saint Lucia, West Indies. This specimen is coiled in a coconut husk, a favorite resting place. Photo by Hans Boos.

*Fig. 208. Bothrops cotiara;* Pôrto União, Santa Catarina, Brazil. Photo by Ivan Sazima, courtesy of the Instituto Butantan, São Paulo.

*Fig. 209. Bothrops cotiara*, male, 730 mm TL; Videira, Santa Catarina, Brazil. Photo by Ivan Sazima, courtesy of the Instituto Butantan, São Paulo.

*Fig. 210. Bothrops erythromelas*, female, 512 mm TL (ZUEC 609); Glória, Bahia, Brazil. Photo by Ivan Sazima.

*Fig. 211. Bothrops fonsecai*, male; Serra da Bocaina, Bananal, São Paulo, Brazil. Photo by Ivan Sazima, courtesy of the Instituto Butantan, São Paulo.

*Fig. 212. Bothrops fonsecai*, female, approximately 700 mm TL; Campos do Jordão, São Paulo, Brazil. Photo by Ivan Sazima, courtesy of the Instituto Butantan, São Paulo.

*Fig. 213. Bothrops fonsecai*, female; Macaé de Cima, Nova Friburgo, Rio de Janeiro, Brazil. Photo by Anibal Melgarejo.

*Fig. 214. Bothrops insularis;* Ilha Queimada Grande, São Paulo, Brazil. Photo by Ivan Sazima, courtesy of the Instituto Butantan, São Paulo.

*Fig. 215. Bothrops insularis*, adult; Ilha Queimada Grande, São Paulo, Brazil. Specimen photographed in the field. Photo by Sherman A. Minton.

*Fig. 216. Bothrops itapetiningae*, female; Itirapina, São Paulo, Brazil. Photo by Ivan Sazima, courtesy of the Instituto Butantan, São Paulo.

*Fig. 217. Bothrops jararaca*, female, 1,150 mm TL (ZUEC 612); Fazenda Santa Genebra, Campinas, São Paulo, Brazil. Photo by Ivan Sazima.

*Fig. 218. Bothrops jararaca*, female, 384 mm TL (SG/013); Fazenda Santa Genebra, Campinas, São Paulo, Brazil. Photo by Ivan Sazima.

Fig. 219. *Bothrops jararaca;* Brazil. Photo by David G. Barker at the Gladys Porter Zoo.

Fig. 220. *Bothrops jararacussu;* Santa Teresa, Espírito Santo, Brazil. Photo by Ivan Sazima, courtesy of the Instituto Butantan, São Paulo.

Fig. 221. *Bothrops jararacussu,* subadult female; São Paulo, Brazil. Photo by Ivan Sazima, courtesy of Augusto Shinya Abe.

Fig. 222. *Bothrops lanceolatus;* Martinique, West Indies. Photo by John H. Tashjian, courtesy of the Bronx Zoo.

Fig. 223. *Bothrops lanceolatus,* juvenile; Martinique, West Indies. Photo by Hans Boos.

Fig. 224. *Bothrops lanceolatus;* Martinique, West Indies. Photo by Hans Boos.

Fig. 225. *Bothrops lanceolatus,* juvenile; Martinique, West Indies. Photo by Hans Boos.

Fig. 226. *Bothrops leucurus,* female; Feira de Santana, Bahia, Brazil. Specimens referable to this species and to *B. pradoi* (Fig. 241) may be indistinguishable from one another. Photo by Ivan Sazima, courtesy of the Instituto Butantan, São Paulo.

Fig. 227. *Bothrops lojanus*, female, 455 mm TL (KU 135213); Saraguro, Loja, Ecuador, elevation 2,500 m. Photo by Thomas H. Fritts, courtesy of the Museum of Natural History, University of Kansas.

Fig. 228. *Bothrops marajoensis*, female, approximately 1,500 mm TL; Macapá, Amapá, Brazil. Photo by Ivan Sazima, courtesy of the Instituto Butantan, São Paulo.

Fig. 229. *Bothrops microphthalmus microphthalmus;* Gutiérrez, Cundinamarca, Colombia, 2,350 m elevation. Photo by Juan M. Renjifo, courtesy of the Instituto Nacional de Salud, Bogotá.

Fig. 230. *Bothrops microphthalmus microphthalmus;* Corinto, Boyacá, Colombia, approximately 2,300 m elevation. Photo by Juan M. Renjifo, courtesy of the Instituto Nacional de Salud, Bogotá.

Fig. 231. *Bothrops moojeni;* Casa Branca, São Paulo, Brazil. Photo by Ivan Sazima, courtesy of the Instituto Butantan, São Paulo.

Fig. 232. *Bothrops moojeni;* El Parque Cerro Cora, Amambay, Paraguay. Photo by Lawrence E. Naylor.

Fig. 233. *Bothrops neuwiedi bolivianus*, 675 mm TL; Serranía Huanchaca, Santa Cruz, Bolivia. Photo by Paolo Bettella.

Fig. 234. *Bothrops neuwiedi diporus*, female; Carazinho, Rio Grande do Sul, Brazil. Photo by Ivan Sazima, courtesy of the Instituto Butantan, São Paulo.

Fig. 235. *Bothrops neuwiedi pauloensis;* Ribeirão Prêto, São Paulo, Brazil. Photo by Ivan Sazima, courtesy of the Instituto Butantan, São Paulo.

Fig. 236. *Bothrops neuwiedi pubescens,* female; Sierra de Animas, Maldonado, Uruguay. Photo by Anibal Melgarejo.

Fig. 237. *Bothrops neuwiedi urutu,* male, 730 mm TL (ZUEC 0524); Serra do Cipó, Santana do Riacho, Minas Gerais, Brazil. Photo by Ivan Sazima.

Fig. 238. *Bothrops pictus;* Peru. Photo by Janis A. Roze.

Fig. 239. *Bothrops pictus,* juvenile; vicinity of Lima, Lima, Peru.

Fig. 240. *Bothrops* cf. *pictus;* Peru. Note the unusual expansion of the dark dorsal pattern. Photo by Janis A. Roze.

Fig. 241. *Bothrops pradoi,* male; Nova Venécia, Espírito Santo, Brazil. The dark spot on the nostril may be characteristic of males of this species. Photo by Ivan Sazima, courtesy Instituto Butantan, São Paulo.

Fig. 242. *Bothrops pulcher,* male, approximately 400 mm TL (Naturhistorisches Museum–Basel), Las Pampas, Cotopaxi, Ecuador, approximately 2,500 m elevation. Preserved specimen.

Fig. 243. *Bothrops venezuelensis*; El Parque Nacional Henri Pittier, Aragua, Venezuela. Photo by Robert Godshalk.

Fig. 244. *Bothrops venezuelensis;* El Parque Nacional Henri Pittier, Aragua, Venezuela. Photo by Robert Godshalk

Fig. 245. *Bothrops venezuelensis*, same as Fig. 244. Note variation in dorsal body pattern. Photo by Robert Godshalk.

Fig. 246. *Bothrops venezuelensis;* El Parque Nacional Rancho Grande, Aragua, Venezuela. Photo by R. D. Bartlett.

Fig. 247. *Bothrops xanthogrammus*, holotype, probably a male, reported to be 1,542 mm TL in original description (ANSP 9978); Pallatanga, Chimborazo, Ecuador. This site lies at an elevation of 1,500 m on the Pacific slopes of the Andes. The headless, stuffed skin illustrated is the holotype of this species, which may be conspecific with *B. asper*.

Fig. 248. *Bothrops xanthogrammus*, same as Fig. 247, ventral aspect.

Fig. 249. *Lachesis muta muta*, female, adult (UTA–Live Collection); Tepoe, district of Sipaliwini, Suriname.

Fig. 250. *Lachesis muta melanocephala*, female, 1,808 mm TL (UTA R-7417); Osa Peninsula, Puntarenas, Costa Rica. Photo by John H. Tashjian at the Fort Worth Zoo.

*Fig. 251. Lachesis muta rhombeata*, approximately 400 mm TL; Recife, Pernambuco, Brazil. Photo by Ivan Sazima, courtesy of the Instituto Butantan, São Paulo.

*Fig. 252. Lachesis muta stenophrys*, male, approximately 1,100 TL (UTA–Live Collection); vicinity of Linda Vista de Siquirres, Limón, Costa Rica, 500 m elevation.

*Fig. 253. Lachesis muta stenophrys;* Costa Rica. This skull is representative of the solenoglyphous condition, whereby the fangs are attached to a maxillary bone capable of considerable rotation. The fangs may be erected during a strike or bite, but when at rest they are folded back in the mouth. Photo by R. Wayne Van Devender.

*Fig. 254. Ophryacus undulatus*, female, approximately 550 mm TL (UTA); near Omilteme, Guerrero, Mexico, 2,134 m elevation.

*Fig. 255. Ophryacus undulatus*, male, approximately 600 mm TL (UTA); near Omilteme, Guerrero, Mexico, 1,980 m elevation. Photo by R. Wayne Van Devender at the Dallas Zoo.

*Fig. 256. Ophryacus undulatus*, juvenile (UTA–Live Collection); parents from near Omilteme, Guerrero, Mexico, approximately 2,000 m elevation.

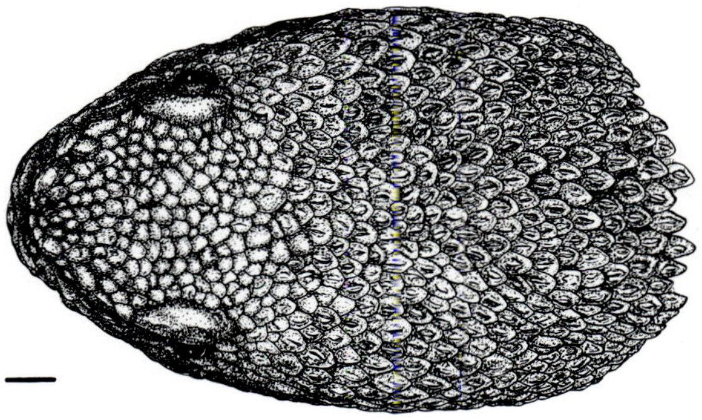

Fig. 257. Dorsal view of head of *Lachesis muta stenophrys*, female, 1,425 mm TL (UTA R-15415); near Pavones de Turrialba, Cartago, Costa Rica, 500 m elevation. Line represents 5 mm. Drawing by Ty M. Kubin.

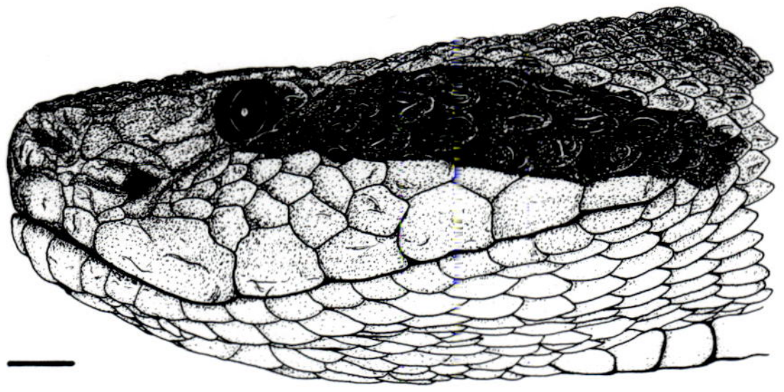

Fig. 258. Lateral view of head of *Lachesis muta stenophrys*, female, 1,550 mm TL (UTA R-12945); about 1.0 km south of Siquirres-Limón Highway in Río Pacuare Valley, Limón, Costa Rica, 200 m elevation. Line represents 5 mm. Drawing by Ty M. Kubin.

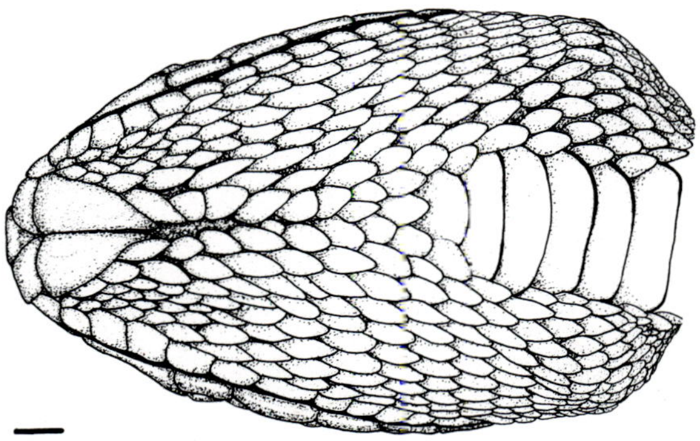

Fig. 259. Ventral view of head of *Lachesis muta stenophrys*, same as Fig. 257. Drawing by Ty M. Kubin.

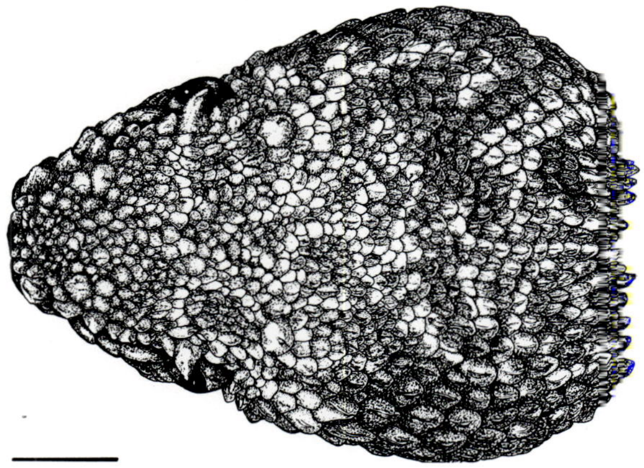

Fig. 260. Dorsal view of head of *Ophryacus undulatus*, male, 607 mm TL (UTA R-4108); 5.1 km east of Omilteme, Guerrero, México, 1,980 m elevation. Line represents 5 mm. Drawing by Ty M. Kubin.

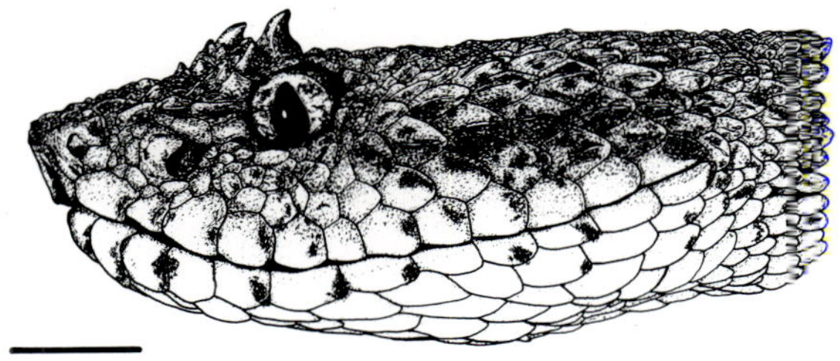

Fig. 261. Lateral view of head of *Ophryacus undulatus*, same as Fig. 260. Drawing by Ty M. Kubin.

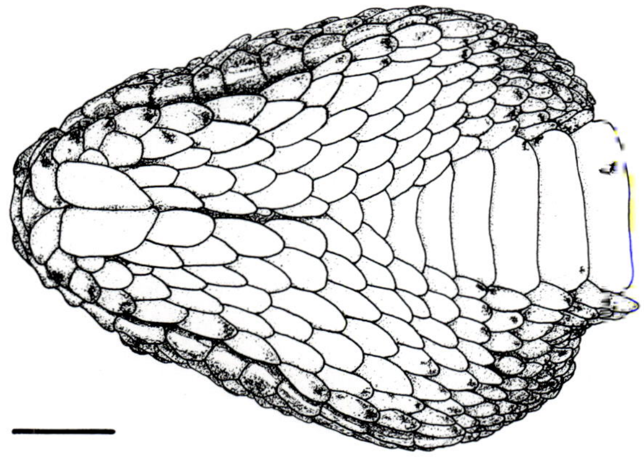

Fig. 262. Ventral view of head of *Ophryacus undulatus*, same as Fig. 260. Drawing by Ty M. Kubin.

*Fig. 263.* *Porthidium barbouri*, male, 542 mm TL (UTA R-15558); 2.5 km southwest of Omilteme, Guerrero, Mexico, 2,490 m elevation. Photo by John H. Tashjian at the Dallas Zoo.

*Fig. 264.* *Porthidium barbouri*, male, 542 mm TL (UTA R-15558); 2.5 km southwest of Omilteme, Guerrero, Mexico, 2,490 m elevation.

*Fig. 265.* *Porthidium barbouri*, male, 434 mm TL (UTA R-4450); 0.8 km north of Puerto del Gallo, Guerrero, Mexico, 2,896 m elevation.

*Fig. 266.* *Porthidium barbouri*, female, 154 mm TL (UTA R-6238); parents from near Omilteme, Guerrero, Mexico.

*Fig. 267.* *Porthidium dunni*, male, 530 mm TL (UTA R-17905); Cerro Quiengola, Paso Alicia, Oaxaca, Mexico. Photo by David J. Barker at the Dallas Zoo.

*Fig. 268.* *Porthidium dunni*, male, 264 mm TL (UTA R-12553); 10.1 km southwest of Rizo de Oro (Chiapas), Oaxaca, Mexico, 652 m elevation.

*Fig. 269.* *Porthidium godmani*, male, 615 mm TL (UTA R-14535); Cerro Verde, Baja Verapaz, Guatemala, 1,829 m elevation.

*Fig. 270.* *Porthidium godmani*, same as Fig. 269, ventral aspect.

Fig. 271. *Porthidium godmani;* Santa María de Dota, Costa Rica. Some specimens have a reddish cast to the dorsal ground color. Photo by Saul Friess, courtesy of Louis Porras.

Fig. 272. *Porthidium hespere,* female, holotype, 579 mm TL (UTA R-4443); 12 km (air line) northeast of Tecomán, Municipio de Ixlahuacán, Colima, Mexico, 300 m elevation.

Fig. 273. *Porthidium hyoprora;* La Chorrera, Amazonas, Colombia. Photo by Juan M. Renjifo, courtesy of the Instituto Nacional de Salud, Bogotá.

Fig. 274. *Porthidium lansbergii lansbergii;* Colombia. Photo by Juan M. Renjifo, courtesy of the Instituto Nacional de Salud, Bogotá.

Fig. 275. *Porthidium lansbergii lansbergii;* Los Cerezos (Uribia), La Guajira, Colombia. Photo by Juan M. Renjifo, courtesy of the Instituto Nacional de Salud, Bogotá.

Fig. 276. *Porthidium lansbergii rozei;* Parque Nacional Terepaima. Sierra de Portuguesa, Lara, Venezuela, 500 m elevation. Photo by Enrique Yústiz.

Fig. 277. *Porthidium melanurum,* female, 575 mm TL (UTA R-13032); El Tejocote, Oaxaca, Mexico 2,134 m elevation. Photo by John H. Tashjian at the Dallas Zoo.

Fig. 278. *Porthidium melanurum,* male, 302 mm TL (UTA R-12556); 8.0 km west-northwest of Acatepec (Sierra Acatepec), Puebla, Mexico, 2,100 m elevation.

Fig. 279. *Porthidium melanurum*, male, 466 mm TL (UTA R-12559); 8.0 km west-northwest of Acatepec (Sierra Acatepec), Puebla, Mexico, 2,100 m elevation.

Fig. 280. *Porthidium melanurum*, same as Fig. 279, ventral aspect of the head.

Fig. 281. *Porthidium nasutum*, female, 450 mm TL (UTA R-15292); Costa Rica.

Fig. 282. *Porthidium nasutum*, male, 380 mm TL (UTA R-18690); Pavones de Turrialba, Cartago, Costa Rica.

Fig. 283. *Porthidium nasutum*, female, 555 mm TL (CRE 6391); Rincón de Osa, Puntarenas, Costa Rica, 20–40 m elevation. Photo by Dennis R. Paulson.

Fig. 284. *Porthidium nasutum*; Caracolí, Antioquia, Colombia. Photo by Juan Manuel Renjifo, courtesy of the Instituto Nacional de Salud, Bogotá.

Fig. 285. *Porthidium nasutum*; Ecuador. Photo by Saul Friess, courtesy of Louis Porras.

Fig. 286. *Porthidium nummifer nummifer*, approximately 600 mm TL; Veracruz, Mexico. Photo by R. Wayne Van Devender.

*Fig. 287.* *Porthidium nummifer mexicanum*, female, 839 mm TL (UTA R-12943); Pavones de Turrialba, Cartago, Costa Rica, 500 m elevation. The gape is a defensive response.

*Fig. 288.* *Porthidium nummifer occiduum*, female, 623 mm TL (UTA R-12605); 19 km northwest of Rizo de Oro (Cerro Baúl), Oaxaca, Mexico, 1,524 m elevation.

*Fig. 289.* *Porthidium nummifer occiduum*, adult; south slope of Volcán de Agua, Finca Rosario Vista Hermosa, Escuintla, Guatemala. Photo by John H. Tashjian at the Dallas Zoo.

*Fig. 290.* *Porthidium olmec*, female, 520 mm TL (UTA R-18691); Volcán Santa Marta (Sierra de los Tuxtlas), Veracruz, Mexico. Specimen courtesy of John E. Werler.

*Fig. 291.* *Porthidium olmec*, male, approximately 500 mm TL (UTA–Live Collection); Volcán Santa Marta (Sierra de Los tuxtlas), Veracruz, Mexico. The gape is a defensive response. Photo by John H. Tashjian, courtesy of John E. Werler.

*Fig. 292.* *Porthidium ophryomegas*; near San Pedro Sula, Honduras. Photo by John H. Tashjian.

*Fig. 293.* *Porthidium picadoi*, male, adult (UTA–Live Collection); Alto La Palma (south of Limón, inland from Cahuita), Limón, Costa Rica.

*Fig. 294.* *Porthidium picadoi*, same as Fig. 293. The supraoculars in this taxon tend to be long and narrow.

Fig. 295. *Porthidium tzotzilorum*, holotype, male, 386 mm TL (UTA R-9491); 10.9 km east-southeast of San Cristóbal de las Casas, Chiapas, Mexico, 2,300 m elevation.

Fig. 296. *Porthidium tzotzilorum*; Município de Teopisca, Chiapas, Mexico. Photo by John H. Tashjian, courtesy of Joseph Copp.

Fig. 297. *Porthidium tzotzilorum*, male, 313 mm TL (UTA R-4529); 12.8 km east-southeast of Teopisca, Chiapas, Mexico, 2,134 m elevation. Photo by John H. Tashjian.

Fig. 298. *Porthidium yucatanicum*, male, 550 mm TL (UTA R-16960); 19 km east of Cayal on Mexican Highway 261, Campeche, Mexico.

Fig. 299. *Porthidium yucatanicum*; 4.8 km northeast of Carrillo Puerto, Quintana Roo, Mexico. Photo by John H. Tashjian at the California Academy of Sciences, San Francisco.

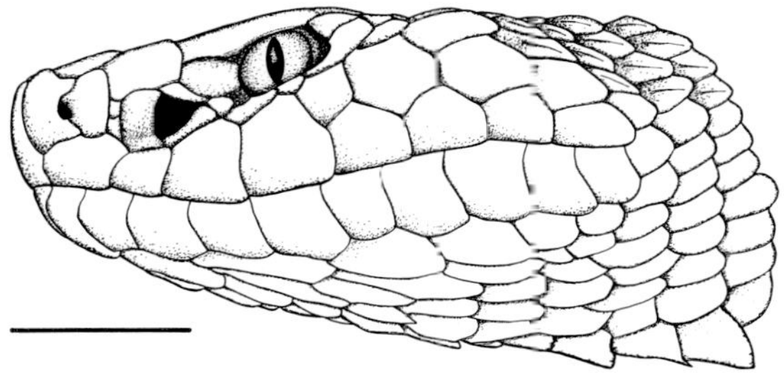

*Fig. 300.* Lateral view of head of *Porthidium barbouri*, male, 434 mm TL (UTA R-4450); 0.8 km north of Puerto del Gallo, Guerrero, Mexico, 2,896 m elevation. Line represents 5 mm. Drawing by Clay M. Garrett.

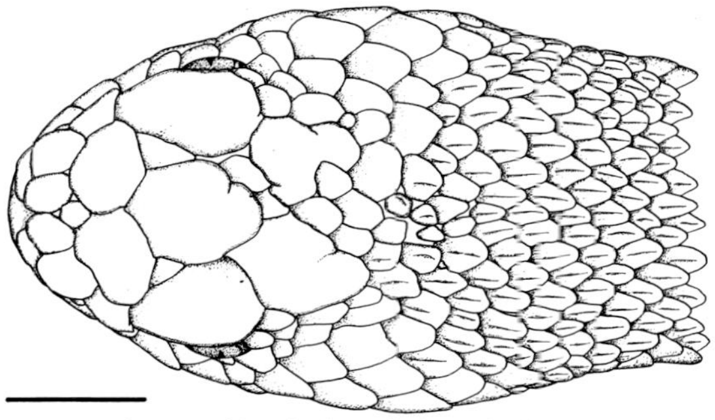

*Fig. 301.* Dorsal view of head of *Porthidium barbouri*, same as Fig. 300. The supracephalic scales of this species are usually large and often highly irregular in shape. Drawing by Clay M. Garrett.

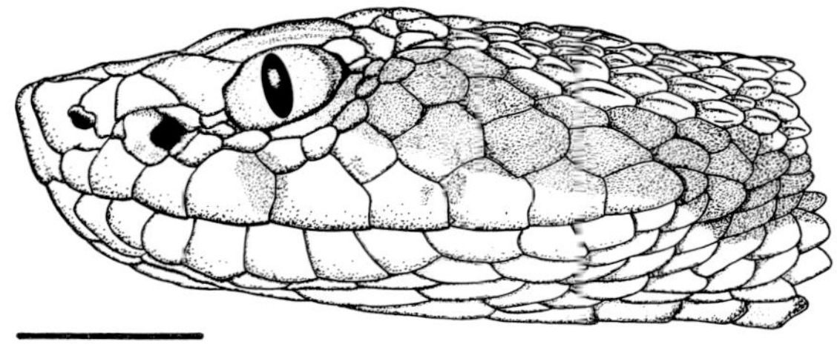

*Fig. 302.* Lateral view of head of *Porthidium godmani*, male, 327 mm TL (UTA R-7066); Cerro Quisís, Baja Verapaz, Guatemala, 1,830 m elevation. Line represents 5 mm. Drawing by Clay M. Garrett.

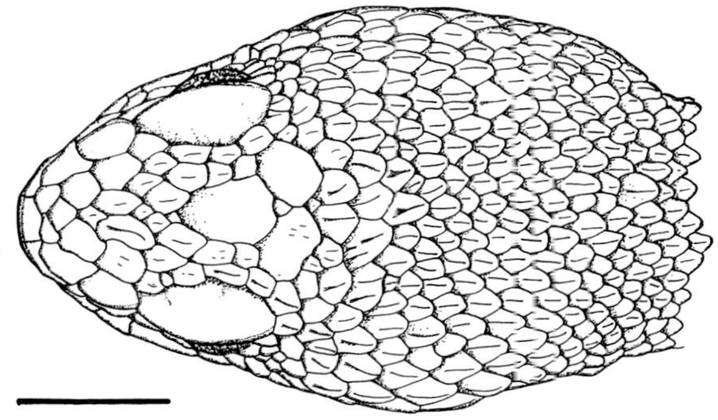

*Fig. 303.* Dorsal view of head of *Porthidium godmani*, same as Fig. 302. The supracephalic scales of this species are highly variable in size and shape. Drawing by Clay M. Garrett.

*Fig. 304.* Lateral view of head of *Porthidium nummifer occiduum*, male, 597 mm TL (UTA R-12785); south slope of Volcán de Agua, Finca Rosario Vista Hermosa, Escuintla, Guatemala, 1,372 m elevation. In some specimens, particularly those from southern populations, 1–4 nasorostrals intervene between the rostral and prenasal. The individual illustrated is typical of members of the population inhabiting the Pacific versant of Guatemala, in which nasorostrals are absent. Line represents 5 mm. Drawing by Clay M. Garrett.

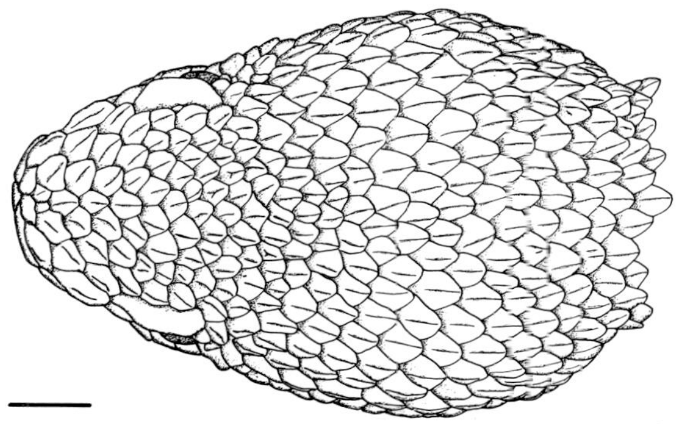

*Fig. 305.* Dorsal view of head of *Porthidium nummifer occiduum*, same as Fig. 304. The supraoculars in this species are long and narrow or completely divided into smaller scales; intersupraoculars are relatively numerous and the supracephalic scales are strongly keeled. Drawing by Clay M. Garrett.

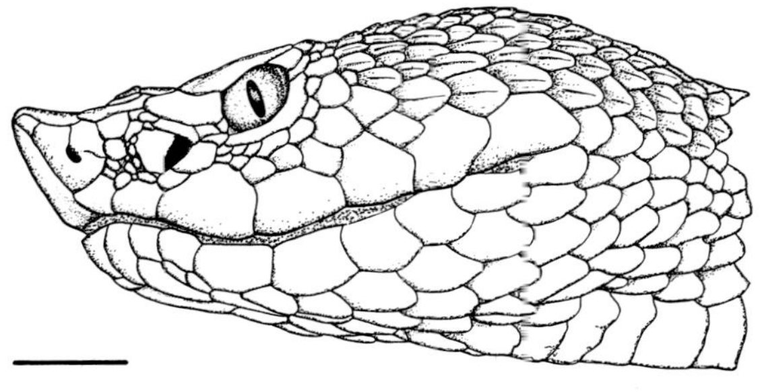

*Fig. 306.* Lateral view of head of *Porthidium hyoprora*, male, 453 mm TL (MVZ 175374); Quebrada Caterpiza, Río Santiago, Amazonas, Peru. This species characteristically has at least one upper nasorostral and numerous small prefoveals. Line represents 5 mm. Drawing by Clay M. Garrett.

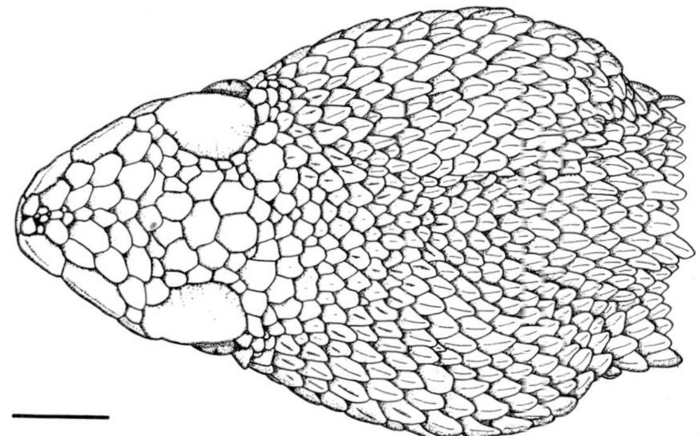

*Fig. 307.* Dorsal view of head of *Porthidium hyoprora*, same as Fig. 306. The outer internasals are usually separated from each other by 2 or more scales. Drawing by Clay M. Garrett.

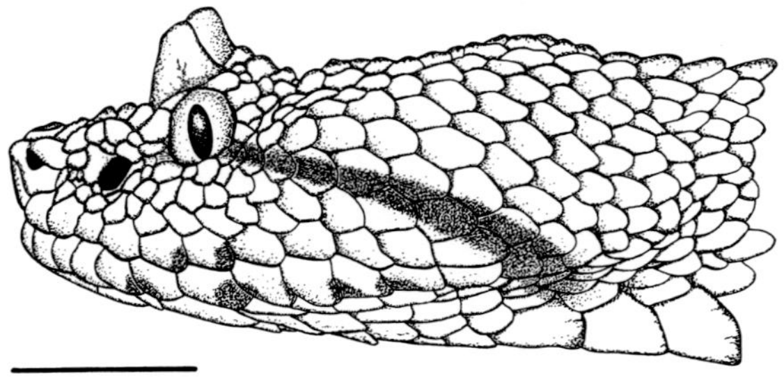

*Fig. 308.* Lateral view of head of *Porthidium melanurum*, male, 345 mm TL (UTA R-12557); Sierra Acatepec, 8.0 km south-southwest of Acatepec, Puebla, Mexico, 2,100 m elevation. Finely divided cephalic scalation and raised supraocular horns characterize this species. Line represents 5 mm. Drawing by Clay M. Garrett.

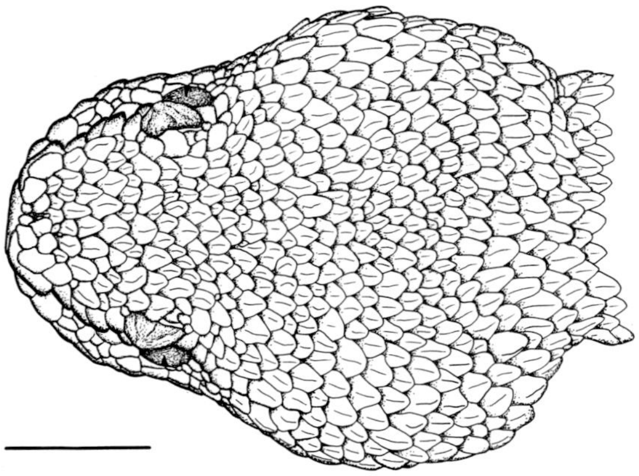

*Fig. 309.* Dorsal view of head of *Porthidium melanurum*, same as Fig. 308. Drawing by Clay M. Garrett.

*Fig. 310.* Lateral view of head of *Porthidium ophryomegas*, male, 441 mm TL (UTA R-7722); vicinity of Juigalpa, Chontales, Nicaragua. The canthus is sharp in this species, but the snout is not upturned. Line represents 5 mm. Drawing by Clay M. Garrett.

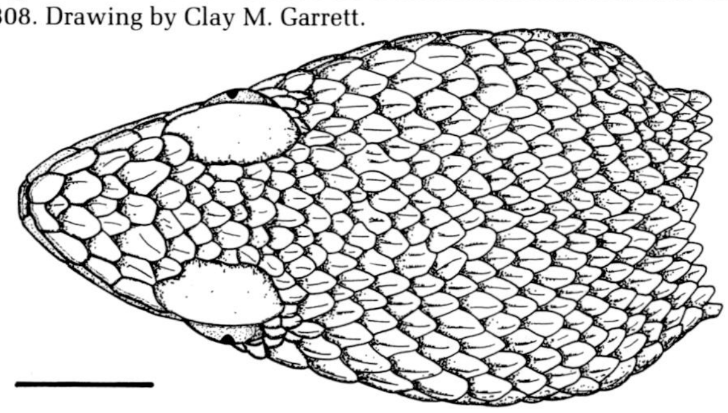

*Fig. 311.* Dorsal view of head of *Porthidium ophryomegas*, same as Fig. 310. Unlike most other hognosed vipers, this species has 2 canthals per side, a reflection of the long lance-shaped head. Drawing by Clay M. Garrett.

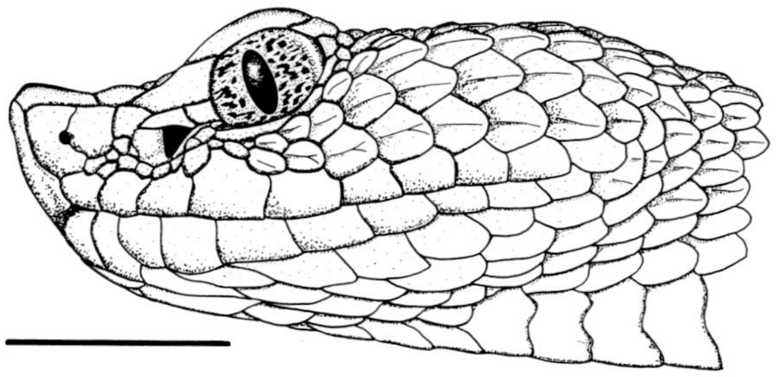

*Fig. 312.* Lateral view of head of *Porthidium dunni*, male, 273 mm TL (UTA R-12553); 10.1 km southwest of Rizo de Oro, Oaxaca, Mexico, 652 m elevation. Many of the hognosed pitvipers have strongly upturned snouts. In this species, the middle preocular is usually divided vertically and the prelacunal is not fused with the second supralabial (a characteristic of hognosed pitvipers in general). Line represents 5 mm. Drawing by Clay M. Garrett.

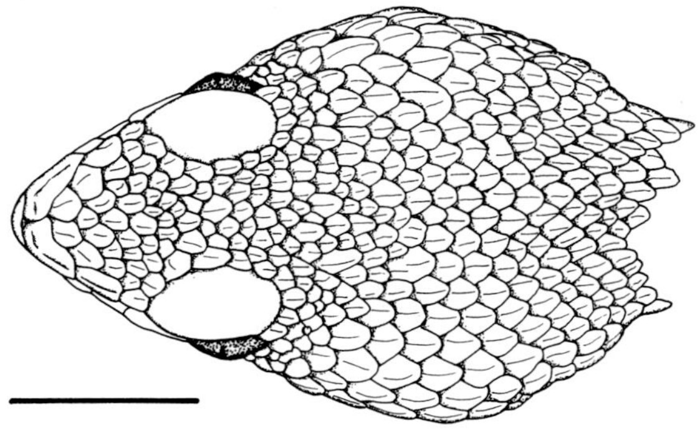

*Fig. 313.* Dorsal view of head of *Porthidium dunni*, same as Fig. 312. In this species there are 2 large intercanthals or 2 large scales plus several small ones. Drawing by Clay M. Garrett.

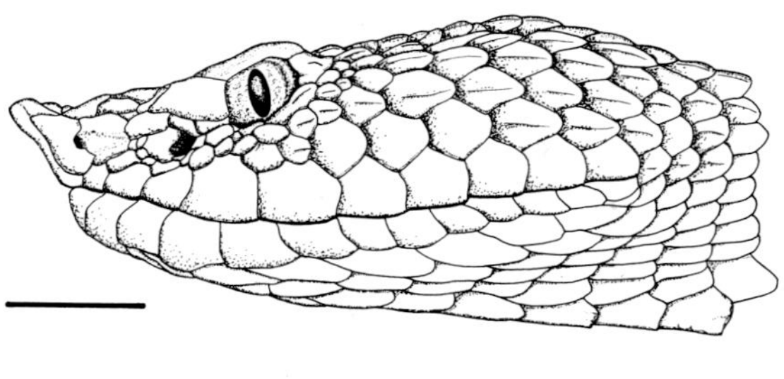

*Fig. 314.* Lateral view of head of *Porthidium nasutum*, female, 403 mm TL (UTA R-16100); near Las Cañas, Izabal, Guatemala. This species has a snout upturned to a greater degree than other hognosed pitvipers, although several other species, including *P. lansbergii*, have greatly protruding snouts. Line represents 5 mm. Drawing by Clay M. Garrett.

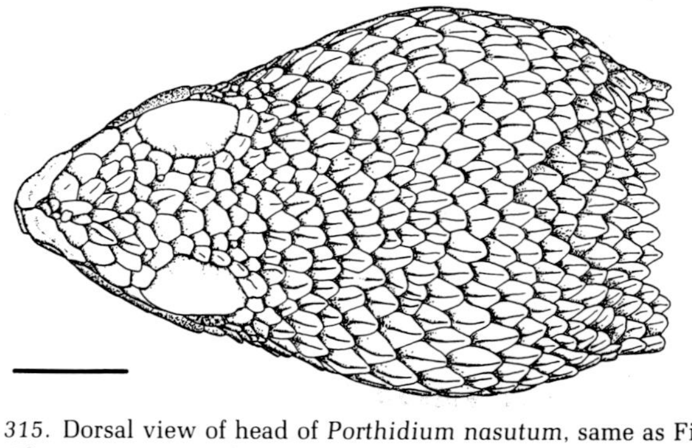

*Fig. 315.* Dorsal view of head of *Porthidium nasutum*, same as Fig. 314. The outer internasals are usually in contact with each other or separated by no more than a single scale. Drawing by Clay M. Garrett.

*Fig. 316.* Three types of subcaudal arrangements found in pitvipers: (*top*) subcaudals mostly paired (divided), typical of most members of the genera *Bothrops, Bothriopsis,* and *Ophryacus;* (*center*) subcaudals paired on most of the tail except distally, where they become more finely divided, an arrangement found only in the genus *Lachesis;* (*bottom*) subcaudals mostly single (undivided), typical of the genera *Agkistrodon, Bothriechis, Porthidium, Crotalus,* and *Sistrurus.*

*Fig. 317. Crotalus atrox,* female, 540 mm TL (UTA R-12566); 7.1 km south of Venados, Hidalgo, Mexico, 1,640 m elevation.

*Fig. 318. Crotalus atrox;* Isla San Pedro Mártir, Baja California Norte, Mexico. Photo by John H. Tashjian at the California Academy of Sciences, San Francisco.

*Fig. 319. Crotalus basiliscus;* Colima, Mexico. Photo by Ed Cassano, courtesy of Louis Porras.

*Fig. 320. Crotalus basiliscus;* Colima, Mexico. Photo by Ed Cassano, courtesy of Louis Porras.

*Fig. 321. Crotalus basiliscus;* Bahía de San Carlos, 16 km northwest of Guaymas, Sonora, Mexico. Photo by John H. Tashjian.

*Fig. 322. Crotalus* cf. *basiliscus;* Alamos, Sonora, Mexico. Photo by John H. Tashjian at the Dallas Zoo.

*Fig. 323. Crotalus* cf. *basiliscus;* Alamos, Sonora, Mexico. Photo by John H. Tashjian at the California Academy of Sciences.

Fig. 324. *Crotalus catalinensis;* Isla de Santa Catalina, Baja California Sur, Mexico. Photo by Louis Porras.

Fig. 325. *Crotalus catalinensis,* same as Fig. 324. View of tail and vestigial rattle. The rattles characteristically are shed in this species and *C. ruber lorenzoensis.* Photo by Louis Porras.

Fig. 326. *Crotalus cerastes cercobombus;* southwest of Red Rock, Pinal County, Arizona, USA. Photo by John H. Tashjian.

Fig. 327. *Crotalus cerastes laterorepens;* 8 km south of San Luis, Sonora, Mexico. Photo by John H. Tashjian at the California Academy of Sciences, San Francisco.

Fig. 328. *Crotalus durissus durissus;* near Managua, Managua, Nicaragua. Photo by John H. Tashjian.

Fig. 329. *Crotalus durissus durissus,* male, 381 mm TL (UTA R-12567); 7.4 km northeast of Tapanatepec, Oaxaca, Mexico, 305 m elevation.

Fig. 330. *Crotalus durissus cascavella,* female, 1,170 mm TL (ZUEC 610); Glória, Bahia, Brazil. Photo by Ivan Sazima.

Fig. 331. *Crotalus durissus collilineatus;* Rio Verde, Goiás, Brazil. Photo by Ivan Sazima, courtesy of Augusto Shinya Abe.

Fig. 332. *Crotalus durissus culminatus*; Michoacán, Mexico. Photo by Louis Porras.

Fig. 333. *Crotalus durissus cumanensis*; vicinity of Barranquilla, Atlántico, Colombia. Photo by John H. Tashjian.

Fig. 334. *Crotalus durissus cumanensis*, female, adult; Puerto Borracho (Río Tomo), Vichada, Colombia.

Fig. 335. *Crotalus durissus dryinas*, male, approximately 650 mm TL (UTA–Live Collection); Guyana. Photo by Louis Porras.

Fig. 336. *Crotalus durissus dryinas*, [illegible]41 mm TL (RMNH 23512); Matapica Creek, coastal Suriname. Photo by A. Abuys.

Fig. 337. *Crotalus durissus ruruima*; Parupa, Bolívar, Venezuela, 1,210 m elevation. Photo by William E. Duellman, courtesy of the Museum of Natural History, University of Kansas, Lawrence.

Fig. 338. *Crotalus durissus* subsp.; Sipaliwini Savanna, district of Sipaliwini, Suriname. Photo by Joep M. Moonen.

Fig. 339. *Crotalus durissus terrificus*; Rio Claro, São Paulo, Brazil. Photo by Ivan Sazima, courtesy of Augusto Shinya Abe.

Fig. 340. *Crotalus durissus terrificus;* Parque Nacional Cerro Corá, Amambay, Paraguay. Photo by Norman J. Scott, Jr.

Fig. 341. *Crotalus durissus totonacus;* coastal Tamaulipas, Mexico. Photo by Louis Porras.

Fig. 342. *Crotalus durissus trigonicus;* Rupununi Savanna, Guyana. Photo by Hans Boos.

Fig. 343. *Crotalus durissus tzabcan.* Yucatán Peninsula, Mexico. Photo by Louis Porras.

Fig. 344. *Crotalus durissus unicolor;* Aruba Island. Photo by John H. Tashjian at the Houston Zoo.

Fig. 345. *Crotalus durissus unicolor,* female, adult; Aruba Island. Photo by David G. Barker at the Dallas Zoo.

Fig. 346. *Crotalus durissus vegrandis;* Sabanas de Maturín, Monagas, Venezuela. Photo by Louis Porras.

Fig. 347. *Crotalus enyo enyo;* Puerto Escondido, Baja California Sur, Mexico. Photo by John H. Tashjian at the San Diego Zoo.

Fig. 348. *Crotalus enyo cerralvensis;* Isla Cerralvo, Baja California Sur, Mexico. Photo by John H. Tashjian at the California Academy of Sciences, San Francisco.

Fig. 349. *Crotalus enyo furvus,* male El Rosario, Baja California Norte, Mexico. Photo by David G. Barker at the Dallas Zoo.

Fig. 350. *Crotalus exsul;* Isla Cedros, Baja California Norte, Mexico. Photo by John H. Tashjian.

Fig. 351. *Crotalus exsul;* Isla Cedros, Baja California Norte, Mexico. Photo by Louis Porras.

Fig. 352. *Crotalus intermedius intermedius;* north of Perote, Veracruz, Mexico. Photo by John H. Tashjian.

Fig. 353. *Crotalus intermedius intermedius* (KU); vicinity of Cacaloapan, Puebla, Mexico. Photo by John H. Tashjian at the Dallas Zoo.

Fig. 354. *Crotalus intermedius gloydi,* female, 428 mm TL (UTA R-12569); El Tejocote, Oaxaca, Mexico, 2,377 m elevation.

Fig. 355. *Crotalus intermedius omiltemanus,* female, 538 mm TL (UTA R-6245); 1.6 km east of Omilteme, Guerrero, Mexico, approximately 2,000 m elevation.

*Fig. 356. Crotalus lannomi,* holotype, female, 638 mm TL (BYU 23800); 2.9 km west of Paso Los Mazos (vicinity of Autlán), or 35.2 km west by road from the Río Tuxcacuesco, a branch of the Río Armería, on Mexican Highway No. 80, Jalisco, Mexico. Preserved specimen. Photo by John H. Tashjian at Brigham Young University, Provo, Utah.

*Fig. 357. Crotalus lepidus lepidus;* near Del Rio, Val Verde County, Texas, USA. Photo by John H. Tashjian at the California Academy of Sciences, San Francisco.

*Fig. 358. Crotalus lepidus klauberi,* male, aproximately 550 mm TL; Arroyo Mesteño (Sierra del Nido), Chihuahua, Mexico. Photo by David G. Barker at the Dallas Zoo.

*Fig. 359. Crotalus lepidus klauberi,* female, approximately 450 mm TL; Arroyo Mesteño (Sierra del Nido), Chihuahua, Mexico.

*Fig. 360. Crotalus lepidus klauberi;* vicinity of Coyotes, Durango, Mexico. Photo by Louis Porras.

*Fig. 361. Crotalus lepidus klauberi;* north of Coyotes (Banderas de Águila), Durango, Mexico, 2,440 m elevation. Photo by Louis Porras.

*Fig. 362. Crotalus lepidus klauberi,* male, approximately 300 mm TL (UTA–Live Collection); 2 km above "Cascada," near Río Basaseachic, Chihuahua, Mexico. Photo by David G. Barker.

*Fig. 363. Crotalus lepidus klauberi;* 14.4 km west of Valparaíso, Zacatecas, Mexico, 2,260 m elevation. Photo by Ed Cassano, courtesy of Louis Porras.

*Fig. 364. Crotalus lepidus maculosus;* west of La Ciudad, Durango, Mexico. Photo by John H. Tashjian, courtesy of Charles Radcliffe.

*Fig. 365. Crotalus lepidus maculosus;* El Carrizo, Sinaloa, Mexico. Photo by Louis Porras.

*Fig. 366. Crotalus lepidus maculosus* (RWM 1780 at LACM); vicinity of the Sinaloa-Durango border, 7.6 km east of Santa Rita along Mexican Highway No. 40, Mexico. Photo by Roy W. McDiarmid.

*Fig. 367. Crotalus lepidus morulus;* Rancho Viejo (Gómez Farías), Tamaulipas, Mexico. Photo by Louis Porras.

*Fig. 368. Crotalus lepidus morulus.* Rancho del Cielo, Tamaulipas, Mexico. Photo by John H. Tashjian at the Gladys Porter Zoo, Brownsville, Texas, USA.

*Fig. 369. Crotalus lepidus morulus,* female, adult; 17.1 km east of San Antonio de las Alazanas, Coahuila, Mexico, 2,682 m elevation. Photo by David G. Barker at the Dallas Zoo.

*Fig. 370. Crotalus lepidus morulus,* male, adult; 17.1 km east of San Antonio de las Alazanas, Coahuila, Mexico, 2,682 m elevation. Photo by David G. Barker at the Dallas Zoo.

*Fig. 371. Crotalus mitchellii mitchellii;* Bahía de Los Angeles, Baja California Norte, Mexico. Photo by Louis Porras.

Fig. 372. *Crotalus mitchellii mitchellii*; Isla Monserrate, Baja California Sur, Mexico. Photo by John H. Tashjian.

Fig. 373. *Crotalus mitchellii mitchellii*; south of La Paz, Baja California Sur, Mexico. Photo by John H. Tashjian at the Dallas Zoo.

Fig. 374. *Crotalus mitchellii angelensis*; Isla Angel de la Guarda, Baja California Norte, Mexico. Photo by John H. Tashjian at the California Academy of Sciences, San Francisco.

Fig. 375. *Crotalus mitchellii angelensis*, 1,400 mm TL; Isla Angel de la Guarda, Baja California Norte, Mexico. Photo by John H. Tashjian.

Fig. 376. *Crotalus mitchellii muertensis*; Isla El Muerto, Baja California Norte, Mexico. Photo by John H. Tashjian.

Fig. 377. *Crotalus mitchellii pyrrhus*; 19.2 km north of Palm Springs, Riverside County, California, USA. Photo by John H. Tashjian.

Fig. 378. *Crotalus mitchellii pyrrhus*. Snow Creek Canyon, Riverside County, California, USA. Photo by John H. Tashjian.

Fig. 379. *Crotalus mitchellii pyrrhus*; San Marcos, San Diego County, California, USA. Photo by John H. Tashjian.

*Fig. 380. Crotalus molossus molossus;* Coahuila, Mexico. Photo by Louis Porras.

*Fig. 381. Crotalus molossus molossus,* male; Sierra del Nido, Chihuahua, Mexico. Photo by Ed Cassano, courtesy of Roy W. McDiarmid.

*Fig. 382. Crotalus molossus molossus;* between Navojoa and Alamos, Sonora, Mexico. Specimens from the northern portion of the range retain the tail rings in adults and are not readily distinguishable from *C. basiliscus.* Photo by John H. Tashjian.

*Fig. 383. Crotalus* cf. *molossus;* El Carrizo, Sinaloa, Mexico. Photo by Louis Porras.

*Fig. 384. Crotalus molossus molossus;* Isla Tiburón, Sonora, Mexico. Photo by John H. Tashjian.

*Fig. 385. Crotalus molossus estebanensis;* Isla San Esteban, Sonora, Mexico. Photo by Louis Porras.

*Fig. 386. Crotalus molossus nigrescens;* Coyotes, Durango, Mexico. Photo by Ed Cassano, courtesy of Louis Porras.

*Fig. 387. Crotalus molossus nigrescens,* male, 980 mm TL (KU 40363); Hacienda de Atotonilco, 19.2 km southeast of Yerbanis, Durango, Mexico, 6,680 m elevation. Photo by John H. Tashjian at the University of Texas at El Paso.

*Fig. 388. Crotalus molossus nigrescens;* 17.6 km west of Durango, Durango, Mexico. Photo by John H. Tashjian.

*Fig. 389. Crotalus molossus nigrescens;* 16 km north of Uruapan, Michoacán, Mexico. Photo by John H. Tashjian.

*Fig. 390. Crotalus molossus oaxacus,* male, 1,182 mm TL (UTA R-12574); 5.6 km south-southwest of Zapotitlán Salinas, Puebla, Mexico, 1,524 m elevation. Snakes from this population, similar to specimens in the extreme northern portion of the range, may retain the banded or ringed tail pattern into adulthood.

*Fig. 391. Crotalus molossus oaxacus,* female; El Tejocote, Oaxaca, Mexico, 2,300 m elevation. Photo by John H. Tashjian at the Dallas Zoo.

*Fig. 392. Crotalus polystictus;* Rancho San Francisco, 2.5 km northwest of Tapalpa, Jalisco, Mexico, 2,134 m elevation. Photo by John H. Tashjian.

*Fig. 393. Crotalus polystictus,* same as Fig. 392. Photo by Ed Cassano, courtesy of Roy W. McDiarmid.

*Fig. 394. Crotalus pricei pricei,* female; vicinity of Coyotes, Durango, Mexico. Photo by Ed Cassano, courtesy of Louis Porras.

*Fig. 395. Crotalus pricei pricei;* Llano Grande, Durango, Mexico. Photo by John H. Tashjian at the Fort Worth Zoo.

Fig. 396. *Crotalus pricei pricei*, adult female; west of La Ciudad, Durango, Mexico. Photo by John H. Tashjian at the Dallas Zoo.

Fig. 397. *Crotalus pricei pricei*, male, 492 mm TL (UTA R-6251); Los Bancos, west of La Ciudad, Durango, Mexico. Photo by John H. Tashjian at the Dallas Zoo.

Fig. 398. *Crotalus pricei miquihuanus;* Cerro Potosí, Nuevo León, Mexico. Photo by John H. Tashjian.

Fig. 399. *Crotalus pricei* subsp., male, adult; vicinity of La Congoja, Municipio de San José de Gracia, Aguascalientes, Mexico, 2,758 m elevation. Photo by David G. Barker, courtesy of David Lazcano.

Fig. 400. *Crotalus pusillus*, adult; north of Dos Aguas, Michoacán, Mexico. Photo by R. Wayne Van Devender at the Dallas Zoo.

Fig. 401. *Crotalus pusillus;* vicinity of Dos Aguas, Michoacán, Mexico. Photo by John H. Tashjian.

Fig. 402. *Crotalus ruber ruber;* Isla Danzante, Baja California Sur, Mexico. Photo by John H. Tashjian at the California Academy of Sciences, San Francisco.

Fig. 403. *Crotalus ruber ruber;* Isla Angel de la Guarda, Baja California Norte, Mexico. Photo by John H. Tashjian.

Fig. 404. *Crotalus ruber lucasensis;* Bahía de Los Angeles, Baja California Norte, Mexico. Photo by Louis Porras.

Fig. 405. *Crotalus ruber lorenzoensis;* Isla San Lorenzo Sur, Baja California Norte, Mexico. Photo by John H. Tashjian at the San Diego Zoo.

Fig. 406. *Crotalus ruber lorenzoensis;* Isla San Lorenzo Sur, Baja California Norte, Mexico. Photo by John H. Tashjian at the Arizona-Sonora Desert Museum, Tucson.

Fig. 407. *Crotalus scutulatus scutulatus;* Cuencamé, Durango, Mexico. Photo by Ed Cassano, courtesy of Louis Porras.

Fig. 408. *Crotalus scutulatus scutulatus*, adult (MSUM); Hacienda de Atotonilco, 19.2 km southeast of Yerbanis, Durango, Mexico. Photo by John H. Tashjian at the University of Texas at El Paso.

Fig. 409. *Crotalus scutulatus salvini;* El Limón Totalco, Veracruz, Mexico. Photo by James R. McCranie.

Fig. 410. *Crotalus stejnegeri*, male, 592 mm TL (UTA R-10499); Plomosas, Sinaloa, Mexico, 1,067 m elevation. Photo by R. Wayne Van Devender at the Dallas Zoo.

Fig. 411. *Crotalus tigris;* Pima County, Arizona, USA. Photo by Louis Porras.

Fig. 412. *Crotalus tigris;* Isla Tiburón, Sonora, Mexico. Photo by Norman J. Scott, Jr.

Fig. 413. *Crotalus tortugensis*, female; Isla Tortuga, Baja California Sur, Mexico. Photo by David G. Barker at the Dallas Zoo.

Fig. 414. *Crotalus tortugensis;* Isla Tortuga, Baja California Sur, Mexico. Photo by John H. Tashjian at the San Diego Zoo.

Fig. 415. *Crotalus transversus*, female, 434 mm TL (UCM 51423); near Lagunas de Zempoala, Morelos, Mexico, 2,987 m elevation. Photo by John H. Tashjian, courtesy of Charles Radcliffe.

Fig. 416. *Crotalus triseriatus triseriatus;* near Lagunas de Zempoala, Morelos, Mexico. Photo by Joseph T. Collins, courtesy of the Dallas Zoo.

Fig. 417. *Crotalus triseriatus triseriatus*, female, 448 mm TL (UTA R-12603); environs of Huitzilac, Morelos, Mexico, 2,743 m elevation.

Fig. 418. *Crotalus triseriatus armstrongi*, holotype, male, 484 mm TL (UTA R-6258); Rancho San Francisco, 2.4 km northwest of Tapalpa, Jalisco, Mexico, 2,103 m elevation.

Fig. 419. *Crotalus triseriatus armstrongi*, female; Rancho San Francisco, 2.4 km northwest of Tapalpa, Jalisco, Mexico, approximately 2,100 m elevation. Photo by John H. Tashjian at the Dallas Zoo.

*Fig. 420. Crotalus triseriatus armstrongi*, male; Rancho San Francisco, 2.4 km northwest of Tapalpa, Jalisco, Mexico, approximately 2,100 m elevation. Photo by John H. Tashjian.

*Fig. 421. Crotalus triseriatus armstrongi*, female, 425 mm TL (UTA R-12591); Rancho San Francisco, 2.4 km northwest of Tapalpa, Jalisco, Mexico, 2,134 m elevation.

*Fig. 422. Crotalus triseriatus aquilus*, male, adult; La Estanzuela, Hidalgo, Mexico, approximately 3,000 m elevation. Photo by Louis Porras at the Dallas Zoo.

*Fig. 423. Crotalus triseriatus aquilus*; vicinity of Jacala, Hidalgo, Mexico. Photo by John H. Tashjian.

*Fig. 424. Crotalus triseriatus aquilus*; Los Marmoles, 8.4 km southwest of Durango, Hidalgo, Mexico, approximately 2,300 m elevation. Photo by John H. Tashjian at the Dallas Zoo.

*Fig. 425. Crotalus triseriatus aquilus*; El Valle de los Fantasmas, San Luis Potosí, Mexico. Photo by Louis Porras at the Dallas Zoo.

*Fig. 426. Crotalus triseriatus aquilus*; Álvarez, San Luis Potosí, Mexico. Photo by Louis Porras.

*Fig. 427. Crotalus triseriatus aquilus*, female, 420 mm TL (UTA R-12593); Los Marmoles, 8.4 km southwest of Durango, Hidalgo, Mexico, 2,298 m elevation.

Fig. 428. *Crotalus viridis viridis;* 16 km south of Animas, Hidalgo, New Mexico, USA. Photo by John H. Tashjian.

Fig. 429. *Crotalus viridis caliginus,* male, 703 mm TL (UTA R-6945); north end of Isla Coronado del Sur, Baja California Norte, Mexico. Photo by John H. Tashjian at the Dallas Zoo.

Fig. 430. *Crotalus viridis helleri;* 24 km south of El Arco, Baja California Sur, Mexico. Photo by Louis Porras.

Fig. 431. *Crotalus willardi willardi;* Santa Rita Mountains, Pima County, Arizona, USA. Photo by Louis Porras.

Fig. 432. *Crotalus willardi amabilis,* male; Arroyo Mesteño (Sierra del Nido), Chihuahua, Mexico, approximately 2,300 m elevation. Photo by David G. Barker.

Fig. 433. *Crotalus willardi meridionalis;* Banderas de Águila (north of Coyotes), Durango, Mexico, 2,440 m elevation. Photo by Ed Cassano, courtesy of Louis Porras.

Fig. 434. *Crotalus willardi meridionalis,* same as Fig. 433. Photo by Saul Friess, courtesy of Louis Porras.

Fig. 435. *Crotalus willardi obscurus,* female, 486 mm TL (UTA R-17850); Sierra San Luis, canyon just north of Cañón Diablo, Sonora, Mexico, approximately 1,950 m elevation. Photo by David G. Barker.

Fig. 436. *Crotalus willardi silus*, male, 670 mm TL (UTA R-17850); Sierra La Púrica, Sonora, Mexico. Photo by David G. Barker at the Dallas Zoo.

Fig. 437. *Sistrurus catenatus edwardsi*; near La Escondida, 16 km west of Aramberri, Nuevo León, Mexico. Photo by John H. Tashjian.

Fig. 438. *Sistrurus catenatus edwardsi*; 16 km south of Cuatro Ciénegas, Coahuila, Mexico. Photo by George Grall.

Fig. 439. *Sistrurus ravus ravus*, female, 555 mm TL (UTA R-12636); environs of Huitzilac, Morelos, Mexico, 2,743 m elevation. Note the large head plates, typical of the genus.

Fig. 440. *Sistrurus ravus ravus*, male, 216 mm TL (UTA R-12615); 5.1 km south-southwest of Zapotitlán Salinas, Puebla, Mexico, 1,494 m elevation. The single rattle segment or button is typical of juvenile rattlesnakes after they have shed their skins one time.

Fig. 441. *Sistrurus ravus brunneus*, male, 663 mm TL (UTA R-12613); 12.4 km west of Totontepec (Sierra Mixe), Oaxaca, Mexico, 2,524 m elevation.

Fig. 442. *Sistrurus ravus exiguus*, paratype, male, 601 mm TL (UTA R-7221); 1.0 km east of Omilteme, Guerrero, Mexico, 1,980 m elevation. Photo by David G. Barker at the Dallas Zoo.

Fig. 443. *Sistrurus ravus exiguus*, paratype, male, 574 mm TL (UTA R-5663); Ejido San Vicente (east of Jazmín), Guerrero, Mexico.

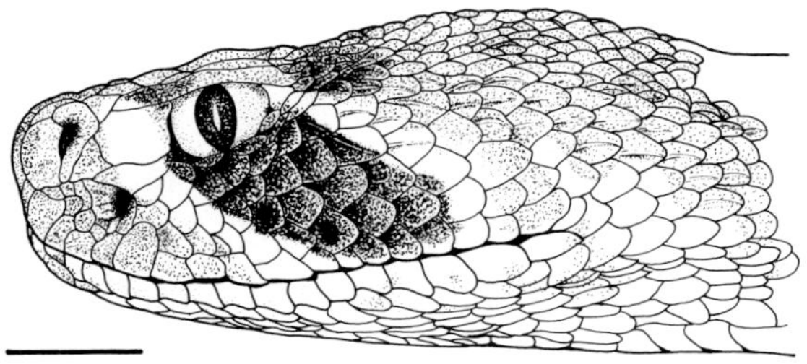

*Fig. 444.* Lateral view of head of *Crotalus atrox*, female, 545 mm TL (UTA R-12566); 7.1 km south of Venados, Hidalgo, Mexico, 1,640 m elevation. In this species the interoculabial series is complete, the anterior subocular is separated from the supralabial series by 1 or more rows of scales, and the upper preocular is usually in contact with the postnasal (or such contact is prevented by an upper loreal). Notice the pale stripe behind the eye extends to slightly in front of the rictus. Line represents 5 mm. Drawing by Ty M. Kubin.

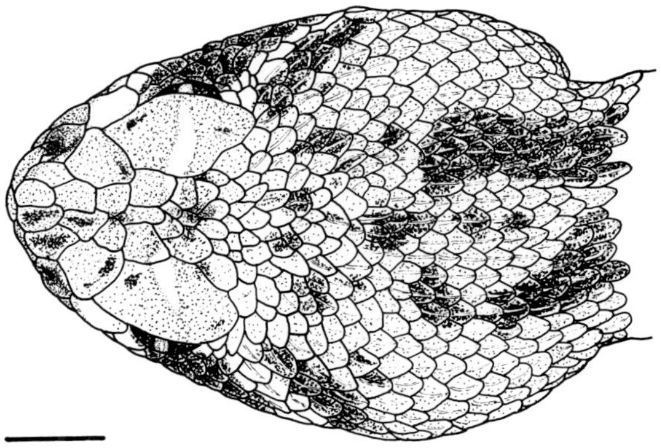

*Fig. 445.* Dorsal view of head of *Crotalus atrox*, same as Fig. 444. Drawing by Ty M. Kubin.

*Fig. 446.* Lateral view of head of *Crotalus durissus durissus*, male, 385 mm TL (UTA R-12567); 7.4 km northeast of Tehuantepec, Oaxaca, Mexico, 305 m elevation. Line represents 5 mm. Drawing by Ty M. Kubin.

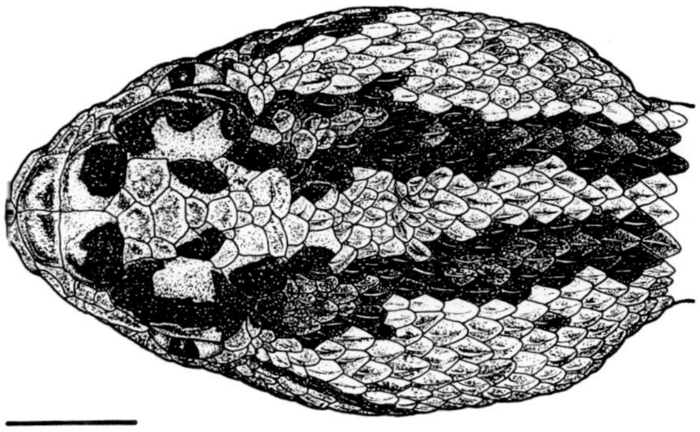

*Fig. 447.* Dorsal view of head of *Crotalus durissus*, same as Fig. 446. Note the large, flat pair of internasals and prefrontals; this scale arrangement on the snout is also characteristic of other species of rattlesnakes, including *C. basiliscus* and *C. molossus*. Drawing by Ty M. Kubin.

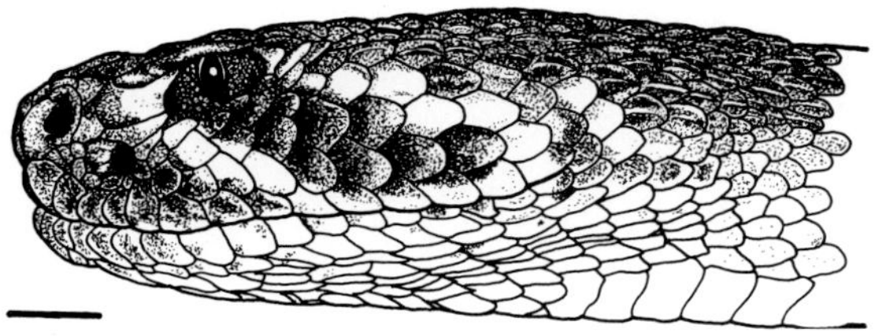

*Fig. 448.* Lateral view of head of *Crotalus scutulatus scutulatus*, male, 1,005 mm TL (UTA R-17932); 10 km southeast of Nuevo Casas Grandes on Highway 10, Chihuahua, Mexico. The pale stripe behind the eye usually extends to about the rictus. Line represents 5 mm. Drawing by Ty M. Kubin.

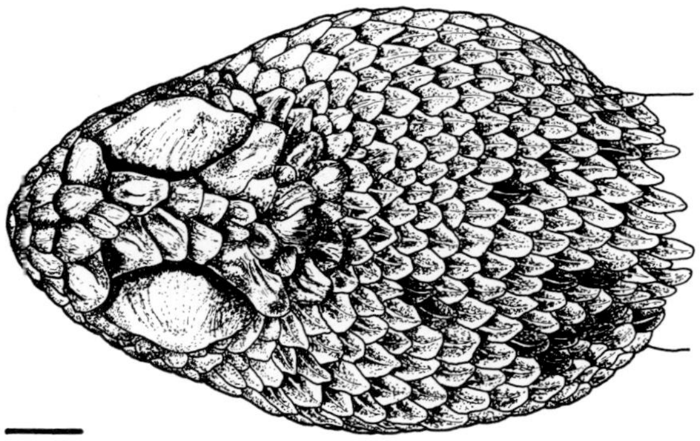

*Fig. 449.* Dorsal view of head of *Crotalus scutulatus scutulatus*, same as Fig. 448. The supracephalic scales in this species are usually relatively large and possess numerous striations. Drawing by Ty M. Kubin.

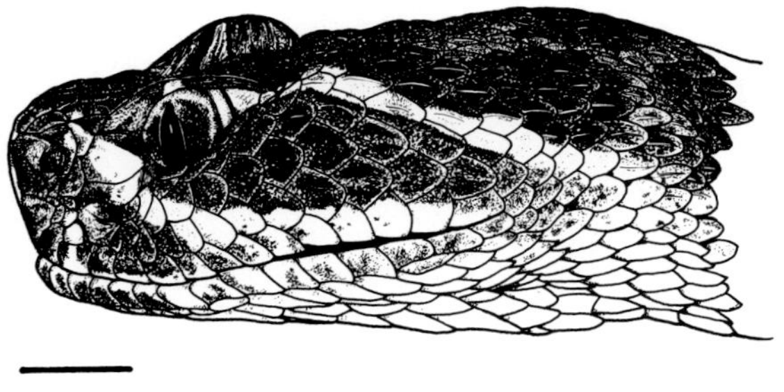

*Fig. 450.* Lateral view of head of *Crotalus viridis viridis*, female, 775 mm TL (UTA R-18255); U.S. Highway 56 between Clayton and Springer, Union, New Mexico, USA. The pale stripe behind the eye usually extends posteriorly well above the rictus. Line represents 5 mm. Drawing by Ty M. Kubin.

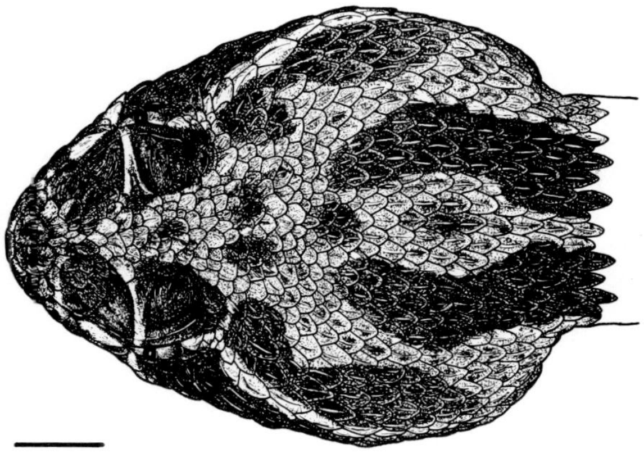

*Fig. 451.* Dorsal view of head of *Crotalus viridis viridis*, same as Fig. 450. Characteristically, 4 internasals are present (an additional tiny median scale is present in this specimen). Drawing by Ty M. Kubin.

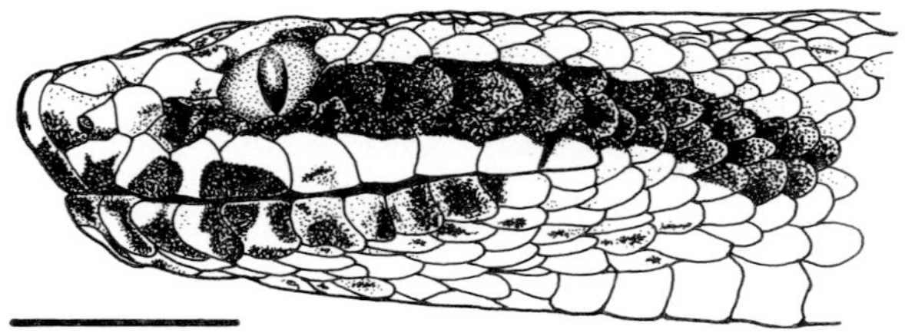

*Fig. 452.* Lateral view of head of *Crotalus intermedius gloydi*, male, 346 mm TL (UTA R-14214); Sierra Aloapaneca, 1.0 km west of La Cumbre, Oaxaca, Mexico, 2,719 m elevation. The interoculabial series is incomplete and the anterior subocular is in contact with the supralabial series. This species characteristically possesses no prefoveals. Line represents 5 mm. Drawing by Ty M. Kubin.

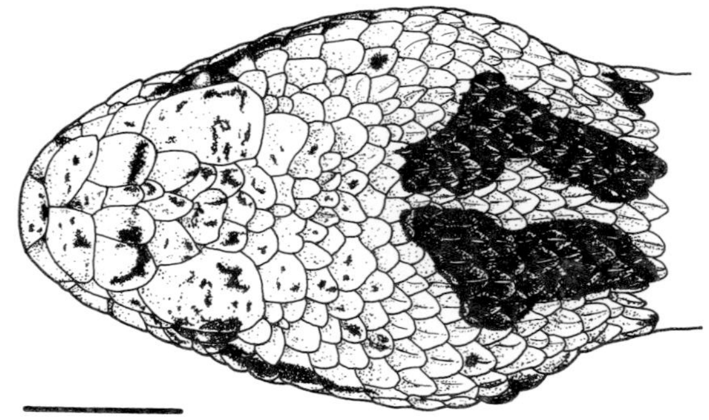

*Fig. 453.* Dorsal view of head of *Crotalus intermedius gloydi*, same as Fig. 452. Drawing by Ty M. Kubin.

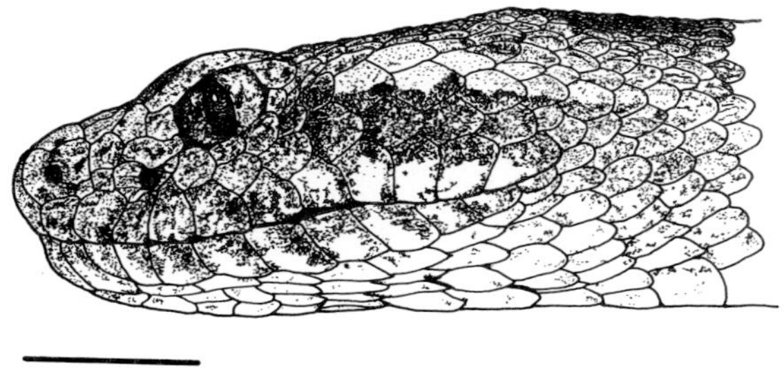

*Fig. 454.* Lateral view of head of *Crotalus lepidus klauberi*, male, 419 mm TL (UTA R-17833); Sierra San Luis, Cañón Diablo, Sonora, Mexico, 1,950 m elevation. The upper preocular is divided vertically; the anterior portion of this scale is higher than the posterior and extends over the edge of the canthus in front of the supraocular. Line represents 5 mm. Drawing by Ty M. Kubin.

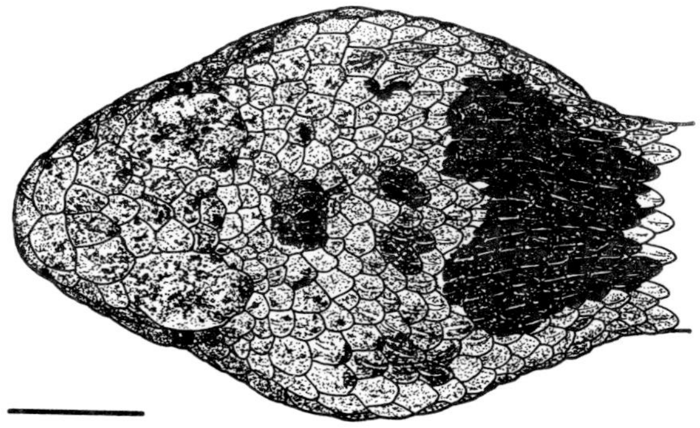

*Fig. 455.* Dorsal view of head of *Crotalus lepidus klauberi*, same as Fig. 454. Drawing by Ty M. Kubin.

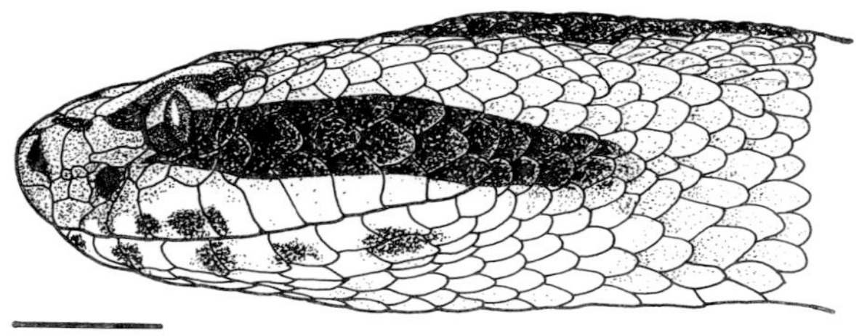

*Fig. 456.* Lateral view of head of *Crotalus triseriatus triseriatus*, male, 407 mm TL (UTA R-12600); near Huitzilac, Morelos, Mexico, 2,743 m elevation. The canthals are separated from each other by several scales. Line represents 5 mm. Drawing by Ty M. Kubin.

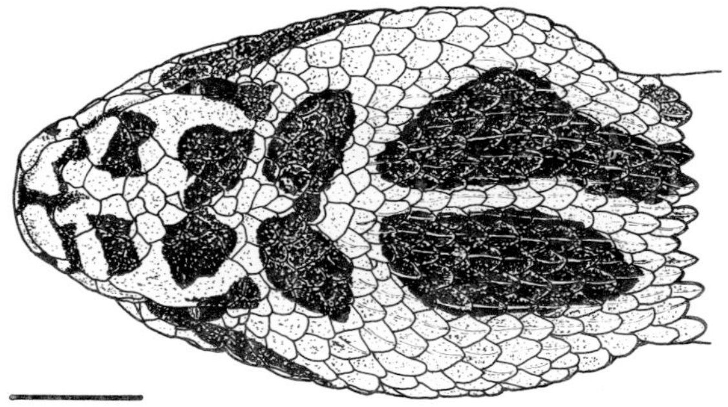

*Fig. 457.* Dorsal view of head of *Crotalus triseriatus triseriatus*, same as Fig. 456. Drawing by Ty M. Kubin.

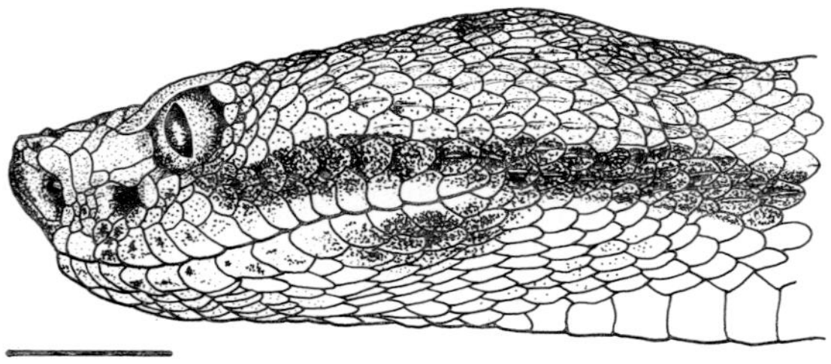

*Fig. 458.* Lateral view of head of *Crotalus willardi obscurus*, male, 451 mm TL (UTA R-17903); Sierra San Luis, canyon north of Cañón Diablo, Sonora, Mexico, 1,950 m elevation. Some members of this subspecies lack distinctive pale facial markings (see Figs. 431–434, 436). Line represents 5 mm. Drawing by Ty M. Kubin.

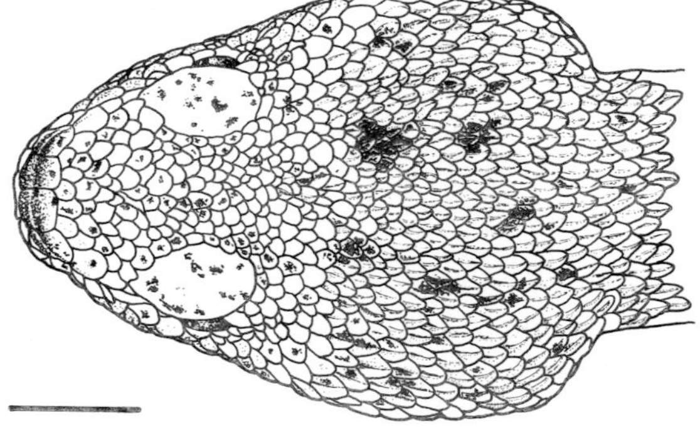

*Fig. 459.* Dorsal view of head of *Crotalus willardi obscurus*, same as Fig. 458. Drawing by Ty M. Kubin.

Fig. 460. *Anilius scytale scytale*, female, 1,054 mm TL (WWL 861); near Villavicencio, Meta, Colombia, 450 m elevation.

Fig. 461. *Apostolepis assimilis*, female, 477 mm TL (ZUEC 525); Arujá, São Paulo, Brazil. Photo by Ivan Sazima.

Fig. 462. *Atractus elaps*; near Villavicencio, Meta, Colombia, 450 m elevation. Photo by Juan M. Renjifo, courtesy of the Instituto Nacional de Salud, Bogotá.

Fig. 463. *Chilomeniscus cinctus*; Pinal County, Arizona, USA. Photo by Joseph T. Collins.

Fig. 464. *Chionactis occipitalis annulata*; Sonora, Mexico. Photo by Joseph T. Collins.

Fig 465. *Chionactis palarostris*; Organ Pipe National Monument, Pima County, Arizona, USA. Photo by R. Wayne Van Devender.

Fig. 466. *Clelia clelia clelia*, male, hatchling, 365 mm TL (UTA R-19708); Finca Semuc (Sierra de Santa Cruz), Izabal, Guatemala.

Fig. 467. *Dipsas bicolor*, female, 586 mm TL (UTA R-12899); Pavones de Turrialba, Costa Rica, 600 m elevation.

Fig. 468. *Dipsas catesbyi*, female, 553 mm TL (USNM 247695); Explorer's Inn, Tambopata Reserve, 30-km straight-line distance south-southwest of Puerto Maldonado, Río Tambopata, Madre de Dios, Peru. Photo by Roy W. McDiarmid.

Fig. 469. *Elaphe flavirufa*, female, 525 mm TL (UTA R-20796); El Moro, Izabal, Guatemala.

Fig. 470. *Elapomorphus tricolor*; Córdoba, Argentina. Photo by di-Tada-Martori, courtesy of the Departamento de Ciencias Naturales, Universidad Nacional de Río Cuarto.

Fig. 471. *Erythrolamprus aesculapii aesculapii*; Araracuara, Caquetá, Colombia. Compare with *Micrurus hemprichii ortoni* (Fig. 59). Note the tail display, typical of *Micrurus*. Photo by Juan M. Renjifo, courtesy of the Instituto Nacional de Salud, Bogotá.

Fig. 472. *Erythrolamprus aesculapii aesculapii*, female, 901 mm TL (RWM 13396-at USNM); Explorer's Inn, Tambopata Reserve, 30-km straight-line distance south-southwest of Puerto Maldonado, Río Tambopata, Madre de Dios, Peru. Compare with *Micrurus spixii obscurus* (Fig. 99). Photo by Roy W. McDiarmid.

Fig. 473. *Erythrolamprus aesculapii aesculapii*, female, 897 mm TL (UTA R-15792); Tepoe, district of Sipaliwini, Suriname. Compare with *Micrurus lemniscatus diutius* (Fig. 68).

Fig. 474. *Erythrolamprus aesculapii aesculapii*, female, 995 mm TL (UTA R-15793); Tepoe, district of Sipaliwini, Suriname.

Fig. 475. *Erythrolamprus aesculapii venustissimus*; São Paulo, Brazil. Compare with *Micrurus corallinus* (Figs. 33, 34). Photo by John E. Cadle.

Fig. 476. *Erythrolamprus aesculapii* cf. *venustissimus;* El Parque Nacional Ybycuí, Paraguarí, Paraguay. Photo by Lawrence E. Naylor.

Fig. 477. *Erythrolamprus bauperthuisii,* male, 490 mm TL (MVZ 176250); Santa Elena Road, 23.1 km south of turnoff to Kavanayen, Bolívar, Venezuela. It has recently been suggested that this taxon is conspecific with *E. aesculapii.* Photo by John E. Cadle.

Fig. 478. *Erythrolamprus bizona;* Costa Rica. Photo by Ed Cassano, courtesy of Louis Porras.

Fig. 479. *Erythrolamprus guentheri,* female, 558 mm TL (RWM 11234-at USNM); vicinity of San Antonio (Río Cenepa), Amazonas, Peru, 210 m elevation. Compare with *Micrurus langsdorffi langsdorffi* (Fig. 54) and *Micrurus steindachneri orcesi* (Fig. 102). Photo by Roy W. McDiarmid.

Fig. 480. *Erythrolamprus guentheri,* male, 600 mm TL (RWM 11473-at USNM); vicinity of Tujushik entse (between Huampami and Chavez Valdivia), Río Cenepa, Amazonas, Peru, 210 m elevation. Compare with *Micrurus margaritiferus* (Figs. 74–76). Photo by Roy W. McDiarmid.

Fig. 481. *Erythrolamprus mimus micrurus,* juvenile; Estación Biológica La Selva, Heredia, Costa Rica, 500 m elevation. Photo by David L. Hardy.

Fig. 482. *Erythrolamprus pseudocorallus,* juvenile (CVULA IV-2819); vicinity of La Azulita, Mérida, Venezuela. Compare with *Micrurus dissoleucus dissoleucus* (Fig. 40) and *Micrurus dumerilii* subsp. (Fig. 42). Photo by Pascual Soriano, courtesy of Enrique La Marca.

Fig. 483. *Geophis cancellatus,* female, 547 mm TL (UTA R-12319); Colonia Rodulfo Figueroa (Cerro Baúl), Oaxaca, Mexico, 1,524 m elevation.

*Fig. 484. Geophis duellmani*, male, 192 mm TL (UTA R-12333); 6.8 km south of Vista Hermosa (north slope of the Sierra de Juárez), Oaxaca, Mexico, 1661 m elevation.

*Fig. 485. Geophis semidoliatus*, female, 314 mm TL (UTA R-19910); Parque Moctezuma, Barranca de San Miguel, Cuautlalpan, Veracruz, Mexico.

*Fig. 486. Gyalopion quadrangulare;* Carretera Estatal (State Highway) 23, Sinaloa, Mexico. Photo by R. Wayne Van Devender.

*Fig. 487. Hydrodynastes bicinctus*, male, approximately 1,500 mm TL; El Tapón, Caño La Hormiga, Vichada, Colombia.

*Fig. 488. Hydrops triangularis venezuelensis*, female, 515 mm TL (WWL 1336); Finca El Acuario, Vereda Las Mercedes, Meta, Colombia, 450 m elevation.

*Fig. 489. Lampropeltis mexicana greeri;* vicinity of Coyotes, Durango, Mexico. Photo by Ed Cassano, courtesy of Louis Porras.

*Fig. 490. Lampropeltis triangulum andesiana*, male, 1,448 mm TL; El Alto del Oso, vicinity of El Parque Nacional Natural La Cueva de los Guácharos, Huila, Colombia, 2,000 m elevation. Photo by John H. Tashjian at the Dallas Zoo.

*Fig. 491. Lampropeltis triangulum arcifera*, male, 890 mm TL (UTA R-12345); 2.4 km northwest of Tapalpa, Jalisco, Mexico, approximately 2,134 m elevation.

Fig. 492. *Lampropeltis triangulum campbelli*, male, 726 mm TL (UTA R-12344); 5.6 km south-southwest of Zapotitlán Salinas, Puebla, Mexico, 1,524 m elevation.

Fig. 493. *Lampropeltis triangulum hondurensis*, male, adult; Honduras. Compare with *Micrurus nigrocinctus divaricatus* (Fig. 88). Photo by David G. Barker at the Dallas Zoo.

Fig. 494. *Lampropeltis triangulum micropholis;* Nabugá, Chocó, Colombia. Photo by Juan M. Renjifo, courtesy of the Instituto Nacional de Salud, Bogotá.

Fig. 495. *Lampropeltis triangulum oligozona*, juvenile male (UTA–Love Collection); Finca Media Monte, between Palín and Escuintla, Escuintla, Guatemala, 610 m elevation.

Fig. 496. *Lampropeltis triangulum polyzona*, male, 1,280 mm TL (UTA R-12340); Blue Creek Village, vicinity of Slattery Field Station, Toledo, Belize.

Fig. 497. *Lampropeltis triangulum sinaloae*, male, adult; Pacific slopes, Sinaloa, Mexico. Photo by David G. Barker at the Dallas Zoo.

Fig. 498. *Lampropeltis pyromelana knoblocki*, female, 765 mm TL (UTA R-17828); Cascada de Basaseachic, above falls, near Río Durazno, Chihuahua, Mexico. Photo by David G. Barker.

Fig. 499. *Liophis epinephalus* subsp; Panama. Dorsoventral flattening is a common behavior among the false coral snakes. In this species, this posture causes the red rings on the anterior of the body to become more apparent. Photo by R. Wayne Van Devender.

Fig. 500. *Lystrophis semicinctus*, male, 469 mm TL (UTA R-19707); vicinity of Santa Cruz de la Sierra, Santa Cruz, Bolivia.

Fig. 501. *Ninia sebae sebae* (KU 191037); 1.0 km south-southeast of Matanzas, Baja Verapaz, Guatemala, approximately 1,500 m elevation. This species is highly variable in pattern, sometimes appearing to be ringed.

Fig. 502. *Oxyrhopus* cf. *occipitalis*, female, 755 mm TL (UTA R-16385); Tepoe, district of Sipaliwini, Suriname. This species may be a composite, including *O. formosus*.

Fig. 503. *Oxyrhopus leucomelas*, female, 272 mm TL (WWL 900); Vereda de Portachuelo, vicinity of Manzanares, Meta, Colombia, 1,660 m elevation.

Fig. 504. *Oxyrhopus melanogenys*, male, 558 mm TL (RWM 11249-at USNM); vicinity of San Antonio (Río Cenepa), Amazonas, Peru, 210 m elevation. Compare with *Micrurus hemprichii ortoni* (Fig. 59). Photo by Roy W. McDiarmid.

Fig. 505. *Oxyrhopus petola*, male, 447 mm TL (RWM 11989-at USNM); Río Palenque Science Center, Pichincha, Ecuador. Ontogenetic color change in this species usually involves a gradual posterior to anterior suffusion of white bands with red pigment. Photo by Roy W. McDiarmid.

Fig. 506. *Oxyrhopus petola*, male, 938 mm TL (RWM 13084-at USNM); 1 km south of Patricia Pilar, vicinity of the Río Palenque Science Center, Pichincha, Ecuador. Photo by Roy W. McDiarmid.

Fig. 507. *Oxyrhopus rhombifer inaequifasciatus*; Paraguay.

Fig. 508. *Oxyrhopus venezuelensis;* El Parque Nacional Henri Pittier, Aragua, Venezuela. Compare with *Micrurus dumerilii transandinus* (Fig. 43). Photo by Robert Godshalk.

Fig. 509. *Phyllorhynchus browni browni;* 20 km north of Mazatlán, Sinaloa, Mexico. Photo by Ed Cassano, courtesy of Louis Porras.

Fig. 510. *Pliocercus elapoides celatus*, male, 465 mm TL (TCWC 48196); El Salto Falls, San Luis Potosí, Mexico. Compare with *Micrurus fulvius microgalbineus* (Fig. 56). Photo by James R. Dixon.

Fig. 511. *Pliocercus elapoides salvinii*, female, 550 mm TL (UTA R-3159); 9.0 km east-southeast of Tebanca, Sierra de los Tuxtlas, Veracruz, Mexico. Compare with *Micrurus limbatus* (Fig. 73). Photo by William F. Pyburn.

Fig. 512. *Pliocercus elapoides diastemus*, female, 341 mm TL (UTA R-5774); 19 km northwest of Rizo de Oro (Cerro Baúl), Oaxaca, Mexico. The tail is incomplete in this specimen. Compare with *Micrurus browni browni* (Fig. 29).

Fig. 513. *Pliocercus elapoides salvinii*, female, 420 mm TL (KU 187344); San José El Espinero (southeastern side of Cerro Verde), Baja Verapaz, Guatemala, 1,400 m elevation.

Fig. 514. *Pliocercus elapoides laticollaris*, female, 270 mm TL (UTA R-16033); 7.2 km west-southwest of Puerto Santo Tomás (Montañas del Mico), Izabal, Guatemala, 300 m elevation. The tail is incomplete in this specimen, a common occurrence in this long-tailed species. Compare with *Micrurus hippocrepis* (Fig. 61).

Fig. 515. *Pliocercus elapoides laticollaris*, male, 330 mm TL (KU 187343); 12.6 km by road west of Puerto Santo Tomás (Montañas del Mico), Izabal, Guatemala, 774 m elevation. Compare with *Micrurus hippocrepis* (Fig. 60).

Fig. 516. *Pliocerus elapoides* subsp.; Honduras. Compare with *Micrurus diastema aglaeope* (Fig. 39). Photo by Louis Porras.

Fig. 517. *Pliocercus euryzonus;* Estación Biológica La Selva, Heredia, Costa Rica. Compare with *Micrurus multifasciatus hertwigi* (Fig. 81). Photo by David L. Hardy.

Fig. 518. *Pseudoboa neuwiedi*, female, 870 mm TL (UTA R-19722); Lomalinda, Meta, Colombia, 220 m elevation.

Fig. 519. *Rhinobothryum bovalli* female, 1,450 mm TL (UTA R-9419); Costa Rica. Compare with *Micrurus alleni* (Fig. 20) and *Micrurus nigrocinctus mosquitensis* (Fig. 89). Photo by John H. Tashjian.

Fig. 520. *Rhinocheilus lecontei antoni;* Carretera Estatal (State Highway) 23, Sinaloa, Mexico. Photo by R. Wayne Van Devender.

Fig. 521. *Rhinocheilus lecontei lecontei*, female, 798 mm TL (UTA R-16610); 13.4 km west-northwest of junction of State Highway 16 and FM 624, on FM 624, McMullen, Texas, USA. Photo by David G. Barker.

Fig. 522. *Scaphiodontophis annulatus*, male, 720 mm TL (KU 191073); 5.1 km west-southwest of Puerto Santo Tomás (Montañas del Mico), Izabal, Guatemala, approximately 150 m elevation.

Fig. 523. *Scaphiodontophis annulatus*, male, 620 mm TL (UTA R-16201); Nuevo Progreso, San Marcos, Guatemala.

Fig. 524. *Scaphiodontophis annulatus*; Puntarenas, Costa Rica. Compare with *Micrurus alleni* (Fig. 20) and *Micrurus nigrocinctus mosquitensis* (Fig. 89). Photo by R. Wayne Van Devender.

Fig. 525. *Scaphiodontophis annulatus*; vicinity of Limón, Limón, Costa Rica. Compare with *Micrurus nigrocinctus mosquitensis* (Fig. 89). Photo by Roy W. McDiarmid.

Fig. 526. *Scolecophis atrocinctus*; Bosque El Imposible, Santa Ana, El Salvador. Photo by Lawrence E. Naylor.

Fig. 527. *Sibon anthracops*, male, 433 mm TL (UTA R-5552); Palencia, Guatemala, Guatemala.

Fig. 528. *Sibon sartorii*, juvenile; Honduras. Photo by Louis Porras.

Fig. 529. *Sibon sartorii*, adult; Yucatán Peninsula, Mexico. Photo by Ed Cassano, courtesy of Louis Porras.

Fig. 530. *Simophis rhinostoma*, male, 306 mm TL (ZUEC); Fazenda Santa Genebra, Campinas, São Paulo, Brazil. Compare with *Micrurus frontalis* (Figs. 50–52). Photo by Ivan Sazima.

Fig. 531. *Sonora semiannulata*, male 267 mm TL (UTA R-5712); 17.6 km west of Paila, Coahuila, Mexico.

Fig. 532. *Stenorrhina freminvillei;* Yucatán Peninsula, Mexico. Individuals of *Micrurus diastema* from the Yucatán Peninsula often are mostly red, lacking most or all of the black body rings. Photo by Ed Cassano, courtesy of Louis Porras.

Fig. 533. *Tantilla annulata;* Comadre, Limón, Costa Rica. Photo by R. Wayne Van Devender.

Fig. 534. *Tripanurgos compressus,* female, 1,188 mm TL (UTA R-18407); Suriname.

Fig. 535. *Chironius monticola,* male, 1,298 mm TL (USNM-FS 066645); Vereda de Portachuelo, vicinity of Manzanares, Meta, Colombia, 1,640 m elevation.

Fig. 536. *Chironius multiventris,* female, 1,305 mm TL (UTA R-15761); Tepoe, district of Sipaliwini, Suriname.

Fig. 537. *Chironius scurrulus,* female, 800 mm TL (UTA R-15745); Tepoe, district of Sipaliwini, Suriname. This species undergoes an ontogenetic color change; adults usually become a reddish color overall.

Fig. 538. *Corallus caninus,* female, 540 mm TL; Suriname. This species is usually reddish brown as a juvenile. Specimen courtesy of the Dallas Zoo.

Fig. 539. *Drymobius chloroticus,* male, 997 mm TL (UTA R-12277); 19 km southwest of Rizo de Oro (Cerro Baúl), Oaxaca, Mexico.

Fig. 540. *Leptophis ahaetulla ahaetulla*, male, 1,075 mm TL (UTA R-15864); Tepoe, district of Sipaliwini, Suriname. Compare with *Bothriopsis bilineata bilineata* (Fig. 149).

Fig. 541. *Leptophis ahaetulla praestans*, male, 1,[illegible]86 mm TL (UTA R-12685); vicinity of Slattery Field Station, Blue Creek Village, Toledo, Belize.

Fig. 542. *Liophis typhlus*, male, 537 mm TL (WWL 977); Pamopetá, Caño Tí, Vaupés, Colombia, 213 m elevation.

Fig. 543. *Oxybelis fulgidus*, female, 1,83[illegible] mm TL (UTA R-19911); 5.1 km west-southwest of Puerto Santo Tomás, Montañas del Mico, Izabal, Guatemala, 150 m elevation. The bite of this species has been known to cause local pain and swelling.

Fig. 544. *Philodryas olfersi*; São Paulo, Brazil. The bite of this species has been known to cause local pain and swelling. Photo by John E. Cadle.

Fig. 545. *Philodryas viridissimus viridissimus*, female, 1,458 mm TL (UTA R-22246); Tepoe, district of Sipaliwini, Suriname. The bite of this species is now known to cause swelling, discoloration, and local pain (see Fig. 546).

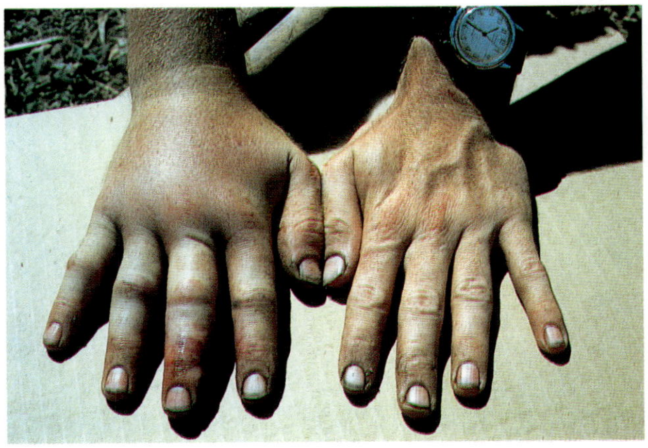

Fig. 546. Local envenomation. Effects of a *Philodryas viridissimus* bite. Specimen is a female, 1,001 mm TL (MVZ 163308); vicinity of Huampami, Río Cenepa, Amazonas, Peru, 210 m elevation. Photo by John E. Cadle.

Fig. 547. *Boa constrictor imperator*, female, adult (KU 190885); 13.3 km west-southwest of Puerto Santo Tomás (Montañas del Mico), Izabal, Guatemala, 945 m elevation.

Fig. 548. *Chironius fuscus*, female, 1,137 mm TL (WWL 901); Finca Las Orquidias, La Reforma, Meta, Colombia, 615 m elevation.

Fig. 549. *Conophis lineatus*, female, 654 mm TL (UTA R-15769); on mainland opposite Hog Island, Atlántida, Honduras. The bite of this species frequently results in swelling, discoloration, and pain.

Fig. 550. *Corallus annulatus;* Estación Biológica La Selva, Heredia, Costa Rica. Photo by David L. Hardy.

Fig. 551. *Corallus enydris enydris;* Suriname.

Fig. 552. *Cryophis hallbergi*, male, 614 mm TL (UTA R-12271); 4.8 km south of Vista Hermosa (north slope of the Sierra de Juárez), Oaxaca, Mexico, 1,622 m elevation.

Fig. 553. *Dipsas variegata;* Parque Nacional Henri Pittier, Aragua, Venezuela. Photo by Robert Godshalk.

Fig. 554. *Dipsas variegata*, female, 650 mm TL (UTA R-15772); Tepoe, district of Sipaliwini, Suriname.

Fig. 555. *Epicrates cenchria alvarezi*, female, approximately 1,000 mm TL (UTA–Live Collection); Santiago del Estero region, Argentina. Compare with *Bothrops neuwiedi diporus* (Fig. 234).

Fig. 556. *Heterodon nasicus kennerlyi*, male, 205 mm TL; Gómez Palacio, Durango, Mexico. Compare with *Sistrurus catenatus edwardsi* (Figs. 437, 438). The bite of this species has been reported to cause pain and swelling.

Fig. 557. *Leptodeira annulata ashmeadi*, male, 312 mm TL (USNM-FS 066653); Finca El Buque, Villavicencio, Meta, Colombia, 490 m elevation. The bite of this species can cause local pain and swelling.

Fig. 558. *Leptodeira septentrionalis septentrionalis*, female, 510 mm TL (UTA R-12355); 34.4 km northeast of Lolotla, Hidalgo, Mexico, 1,384 m elevation.

Fig. 559. *Leptodeira septentrionalis polysticta*, female, 732 mm TL (UTA R-16869); Honduras.

Fig. 560. *Lystrophis dorbignyi*; La Posta, Córdoba, Argentina. Compare with *Bothrops alternatus* (Figs. 179, 180) and *Bothrops neuwiedi diporus* (Fig. 234). Photo by diTada-Martori, Departamento de Ciencias Naturales, Universidad Nacional de Río Cuarto, Córdoba, Argentina.

Fig. 561. *Thamnodynastes* sp., female, adult (WWL 3062); Uribia, La Guajira, Colombia.

Fig. 562. *Trimorphodon tau*, male, 318 mm TL (UTA R-12536); 5.6 km south-southwest of Zapotitlán Salinas, Puebla, Mexico, 1,524 m elevation.

Fig. 563. *Xenodon rabdocephalus*; Estación Biológica La Selva, Heredia, Costa Rica. Compare with *Bothrops asper* (Fig. 186). Photo by David L. Hardy.

Fig. 564. *Xenodon rabdocephalus*, adult (CRE 2987); Finca La Reforma, San Rafael de Ojo de Agua, San José, Costa Rica, 850 m elevation. Compare with *Porthidium picadoi* (Fig. 293). Photo by Roy W. McDiarmid.

Fig. 565. *Xenodon rabdocephalus*, female, 885 mm TL (WWL 848); Finca Las Orquidias, La Reforma, Meta, Colombia, 760 m elevation. Compare with *Bothrops atrox* (Fig. 193).

Fig. 566. *Xenodon severus*, juvenile, 225 mm TL (RWM 10337-at USNM); Chavez Valdivia, at junction of the Río Cenepa and Río Comaina, Río Cenepa, Amazonas, Peru. Photo by Roy W. McDiarmid.

Fig. 567. *Xenodon severus*, female, approximately 1,000 mm TL; Finca El Buque, Villavicencio, Meta, Colombia, 490 m elevation.

Fig. 568. *Waglerophis merremi*; El Parque Nacional Ybycuí, Paraguarí, Paraguay. Compare with *Bothrops neuwiedi bolivianus* (Fig. 233). Photo by Lawrence E. Naylor.

# Topographic and Vegetation Maps of Latin America

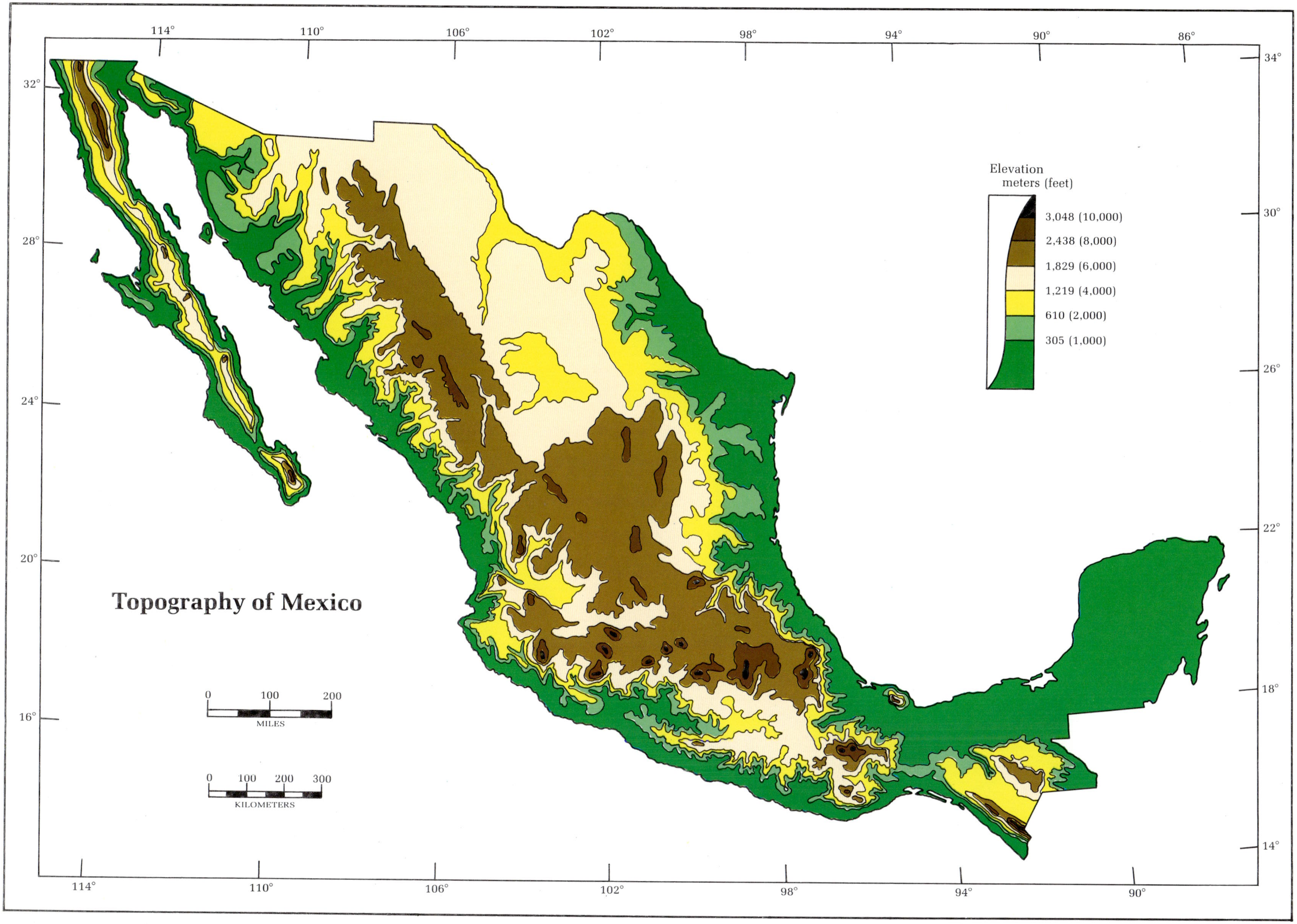
Topography of Mexico
Elevation
meters (feet)
3,048 (10,000)
2,438 (8,000)
1,829 (6,000)
1,219 (4,000)
610 (2,000)
305 (1,000)
0
100
200
MILES
0
100
200
300
KILOMETERS
114°
110°
106°
102°
98°
94°
90°
86°
34°
32°
30°
28°
26°
24°
22°
20°
18°
16°
14°

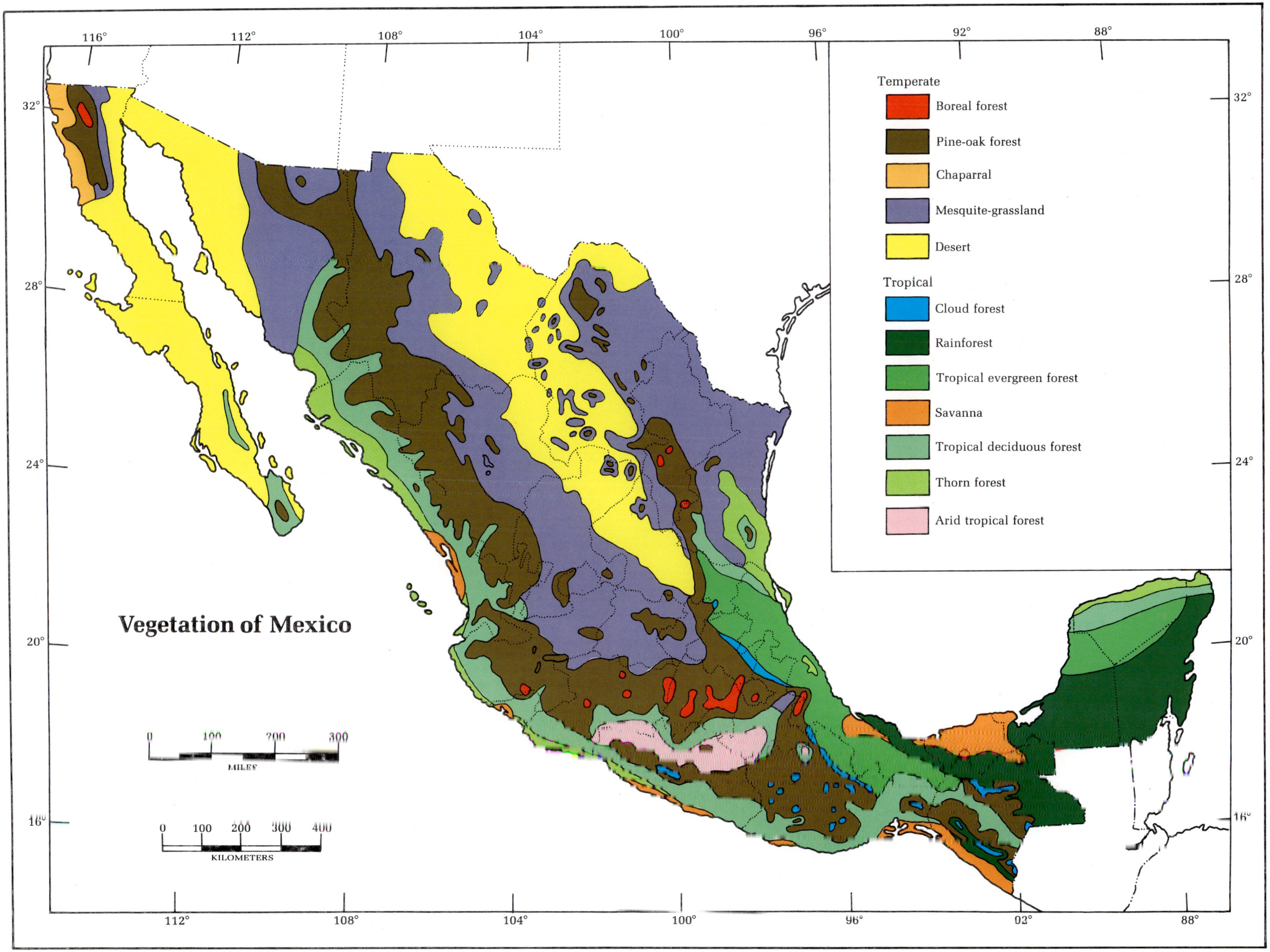
Vegetation of Mexico
Temperate
Boreal forest
Pine-oak forest
Chaparral
Mesquite-grassland
Desert
Tropical
Cloud forest
Rainforest
Tropical evergreen forest
Savanna
Tropical deciduous forest
Thorn forest
Arid tropical forest
0
100
200
300
MILES
0
100
200
300
400
KILOMETERS
116°
112°
108°
104°
100°
96°
92°
88°
32°
28°
24°
20°
16°

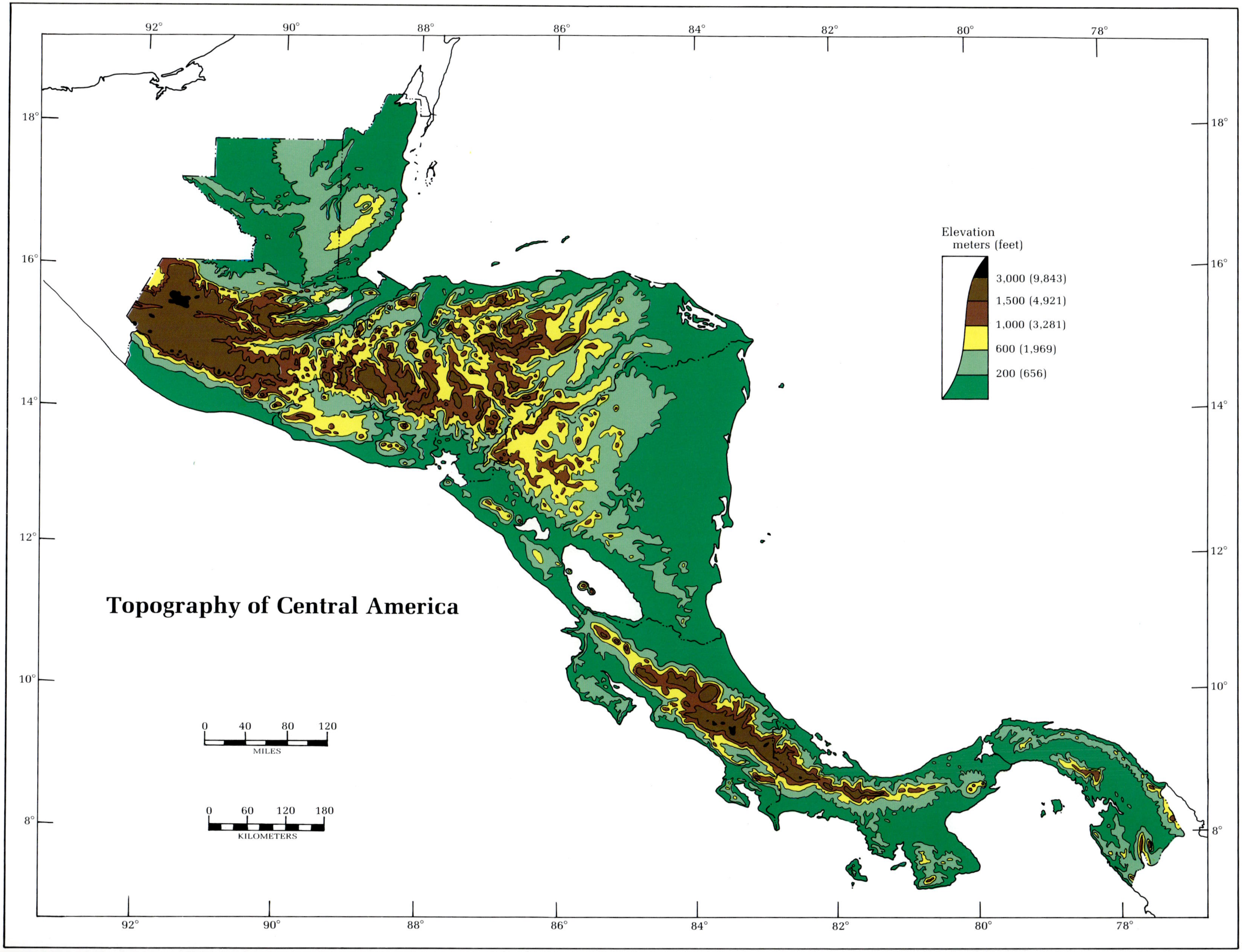
Topography of Central America
Elevation
meters (feet)
3,000 (9,843)
1,500 (4,921)
1,000 (3,281)
600 (1,969)
200 (656)
0
40
80
120
MILES
0
60
120
180
KILOMETERS
92°
90°
88°
86°
84°
82°
80°
78°
18°
16°
14°
12°
10°
8°

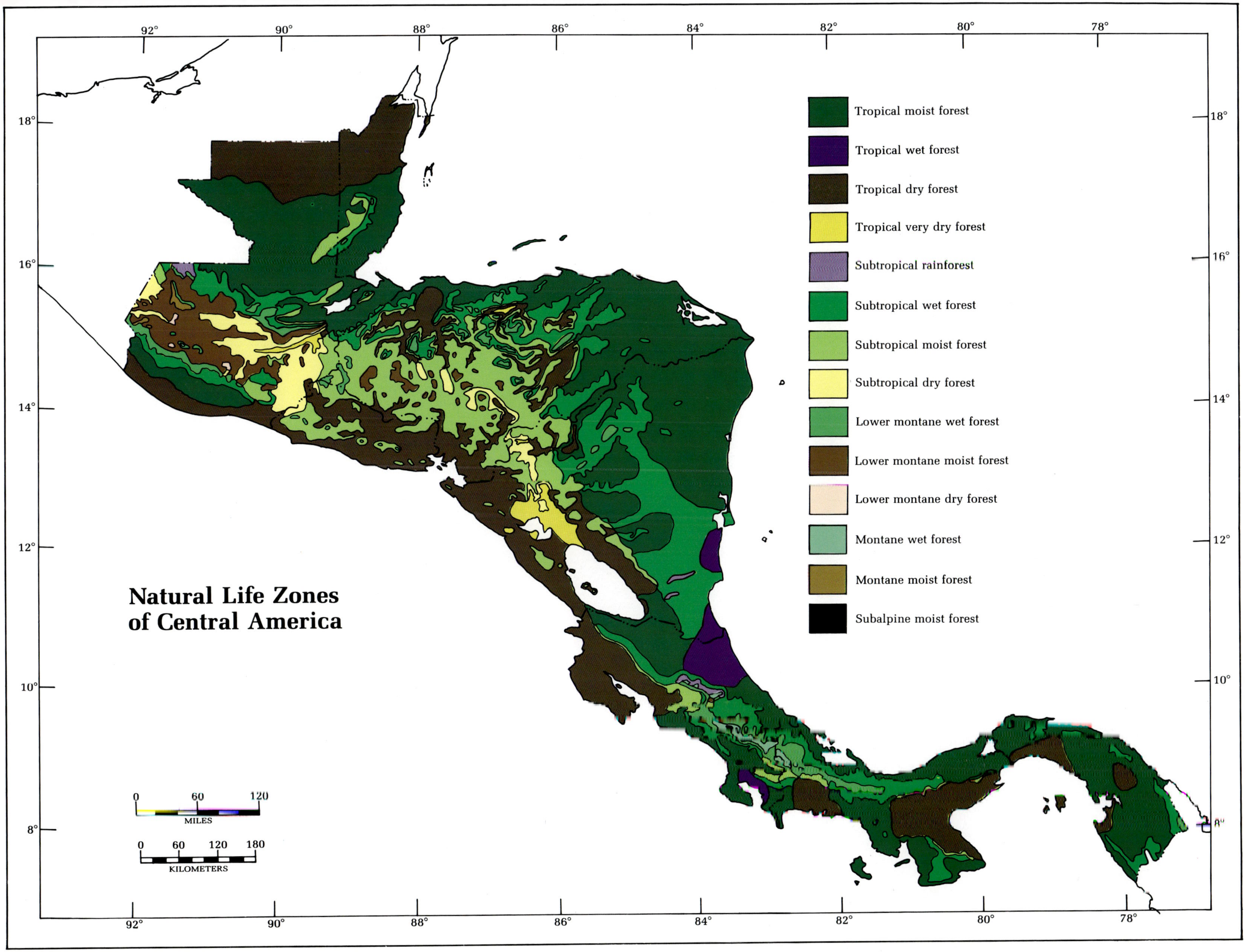

Natural Life Zones of Central America
Tropical moist forest
Tropical wet forest
Tropical dry forest
Tropical very dry forest
Subtropical rainforest
Subtropical wet forest
Subtropical moist forest
Subtropical dry forest
Lower montane wet forest
Lower montane moist forest
Lower montane dry forest
Montane wet forest
Montane moist forest
Subalpine moist forest
0 60 120
MILES
0 60 120 180
KILOMETERS
92° 90° 88° 86° 84° 82° 80° 78°
18° 16° 14° 12° 10° 8°

# Topography of South America

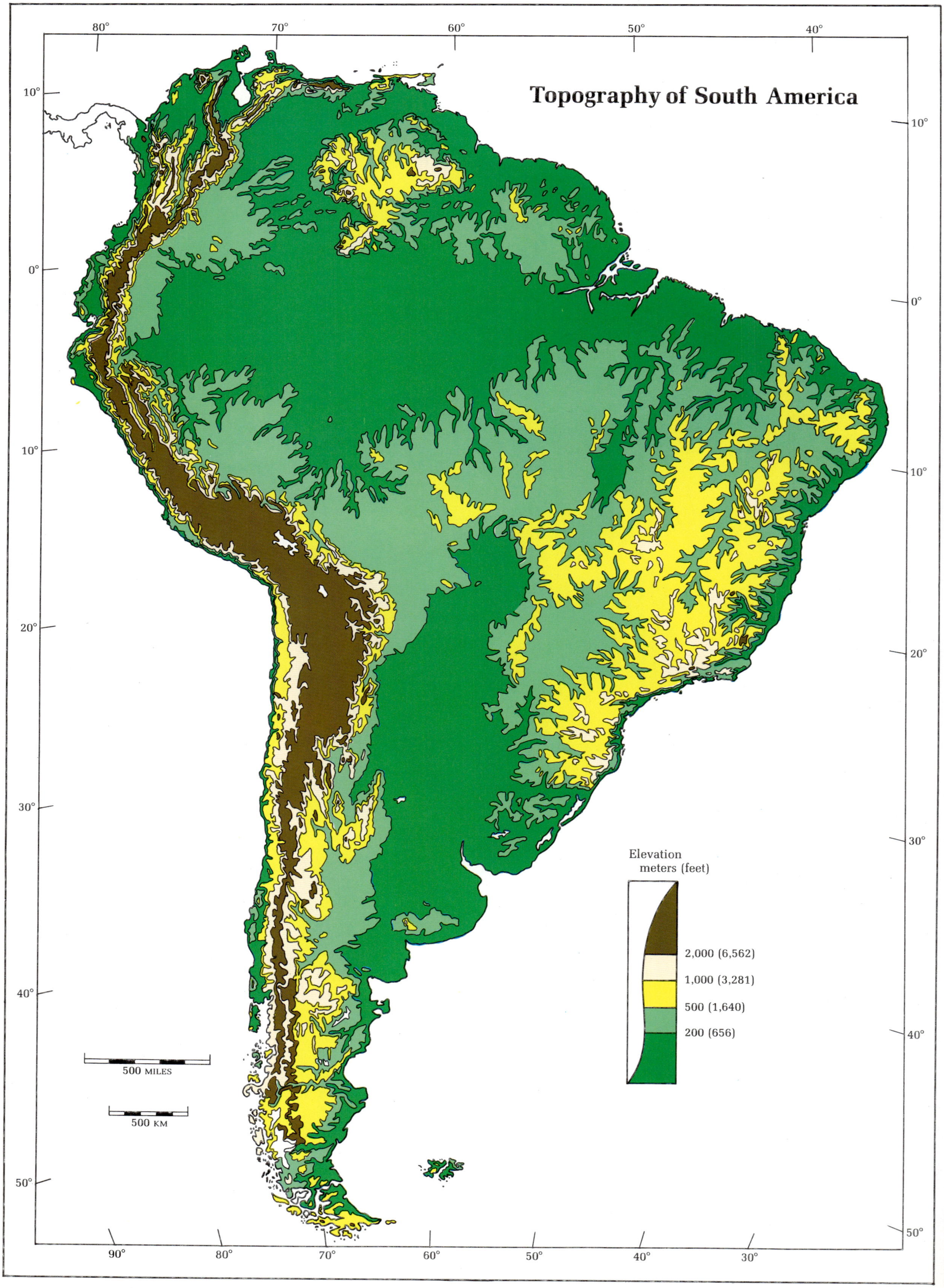

# Vegetation and Edaphic Zones of South America

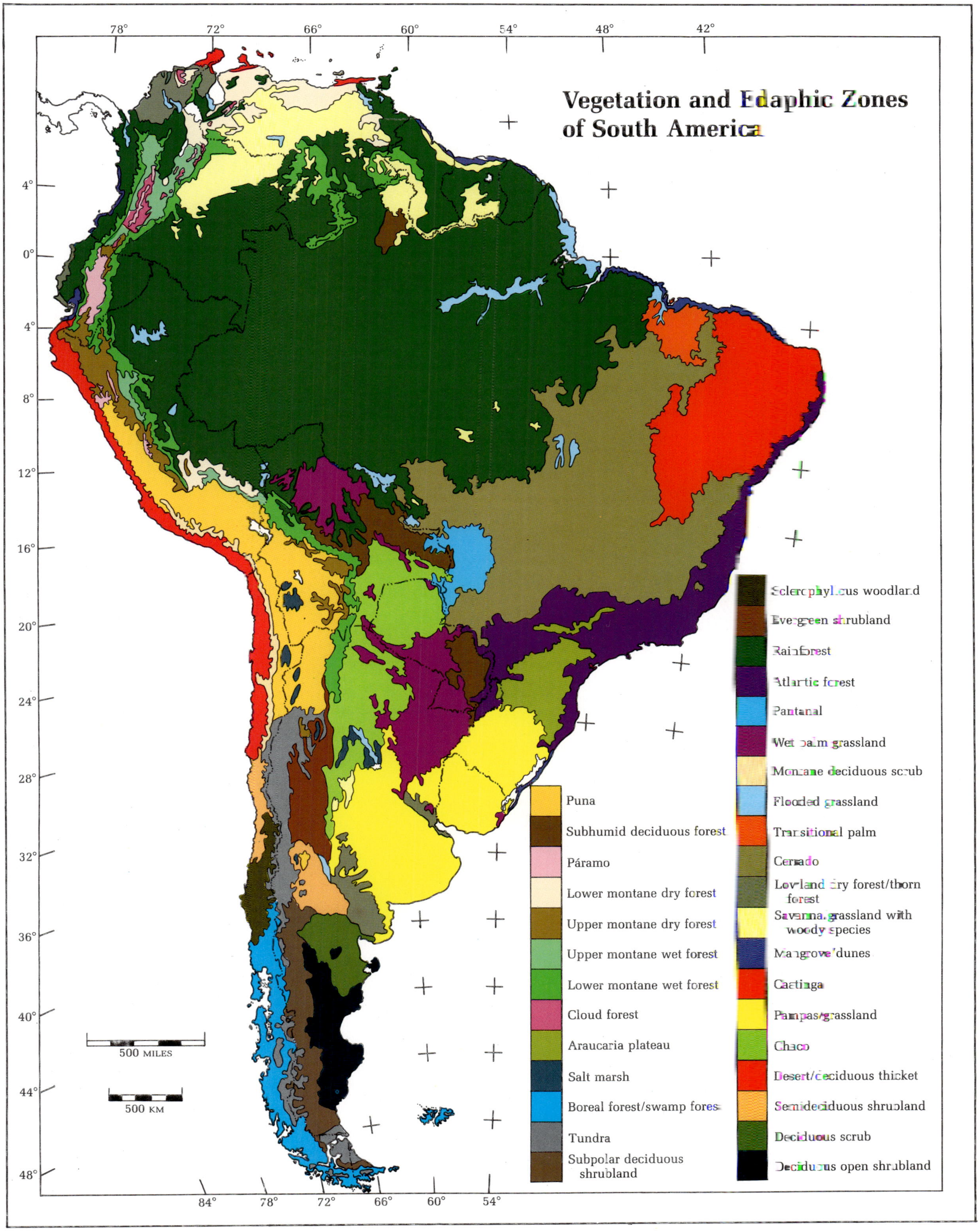

# Bushmaster

## Genus *Lachesis* Daudin, 1803

The genus *Lachesis* (family Viperidae) contains a single species, *L. muta*, which is disjunctly distributed in parts of lower Central America and northern South America. This gigantic snake is the largest species of New World venomous snakes and is the longest viper in the world. It is unique among New World vipers in that it lays eggs rather than giving birth to live young.

The rostral is roughly triangular and it is generally broader than high. There are 3/3 preoculars; the upper is the largest and the middle and lower extend forward to form the upper and lower border, respectively, of the pit. The second supralabial is fused with the prelacunal, which forms the anterior border of the pit. Three or 4 interoculabials are located between the suboculars and supralabials. The supraoculars are large and elongated. The internasals generally are not in contact with each other, and there are 2 or 3 canthals on each side. The canthus rostralis is rounded. The dorsals are broad with rounded apices and lack apical pits. The middorsals possess prominent knoblike keels, especially in large adults; the height of the keels diminishes laterally and the first 3–5 dorsal scale rows may be smooth. The free apical portions of the dorsals are meager and may or may not extend as far as the interstitial epidermal fold at the cranial end of the following scale. The tail spine is laterally compressed, straight and spinelike, and extends a length equal to the preceding 4–6 subcaudals.

The eye is relatively small with a vertically elliptical pupil that is usually not readily apparent because of the overall darkness of the eye. When the fangs are at rest they extend to the level of the fifth supralabial.

The hemipenes extend about 9 subcaudals and are divided for about two-thirds of their length. The sulcus spermaticus bifurcates at the level of subcaudals 2 or 3 and extends to the apex of each lobe. The base of the organ is naked except for a few spinules just before the proximal portions of the lobes. Laterally, on both sides of the organ, naked furrows extend from the base to the proximal portions of the lobes. The lobes are attenuated and the proximal ⅔–¾ of each is covered with 65–80 moderate-sized spines that are more numerous in the mesial area. The distal ¼–⅓ of the lobes bears calyces with smooth ridges. For other details of color pattern, lepidosis, habitat, and distribution see the following account of *L. muta*.

A total of 25 cases of human envenomation by *Lachesis* has been reported. In a Costa Rican study, 3 of 4 reported cases of bites by *L. m. stenophrys* were fatal; the fourth victim sustained a severe upper extremity contracture. All were treated in medical facilities and given antivenom. Death occurred on the third to fifth day and resulted from shock secondary to massive swelling, suppuration of tissues, and overwhelming infection. Major organ hemorrhage was not a problem. In 1985 another envenomation by this subspecies occurred in Costa Rica and proved fatal despite hospital treatment and antivenom administration.

Two cases of envenomation by *L. m. muta* have been reported in detail from Leticia, Colombia; they were characterized by pain, marked swelling of the extremity, early hypotension (shock), bradycardia, and abdominal cramps with diarrhea. Both victims were treated with Instituto Butantan antivenom (*Bothrops-Crotalus*), and recovery was uneventful.

No information was given on the other 18 bites in Brazil, except that 1 was fatal, giving an overall incidence of fatality of 20% (80% in Costa Rica). Thus, although envenomation appears to be infrequent, it should be treated as potentially severe and life-threatening based on available clinical data.

### *Lachesis muta* (Linnaeus)

(Figs. 249–253, 257–259; Maps 80, 81)

LOCAL NAMES Bolivia: cascabel púa, diamante, pucarara. Brazil: surucucú (Amazon Basin), surucucú de fogo (northeast), surucucú pico de jaca (Pará-Bahia), surucucutinga, surucútinga (central region). Colombia: abáacua, a'tami (Guahibo tribal names), cuaima (Vichada); culebra sibucáno; diamante; macaurel; mapaná rayo; mapanaré (Arauca); martiguaja; montuno; pudridora; rieca (llanos); sunguseró (Desana); surucucú; verrugosa, verrugosa del Chocó (western lowlands). Costa Rica, Nicaragua, and Panama: cascabela muda, mapaná, matabuey, plato y negro (southeastern Costa Rica), verrugosa. Ecuador: guacama, shushupe, verrugosa. French Guiana: maitre de la brousse. Guyana: couanacouche (Indian name). Nicaragua: matabuey, mazacuata (this name also refers to *Boa constrictor* in northern Central America), toboa real. Panama: íja (Guaymí Indian name, Bocas del Toro). Peru: shuchupe, shushupe. Suriname: bosmeester, kapasisneki, makasneki, makkaslang. Trinidad: mapepire gallé, mapepire z'ananna, pineapple mapepire. Venezuela: boba, concha piña, cresta del gallo, cuaima, cuaima concha de piña, cuaima gallo, daya, guayma, juba-vitu (Indian name), macagua, mapanaré verrugosa, pararaipú (Indian name).

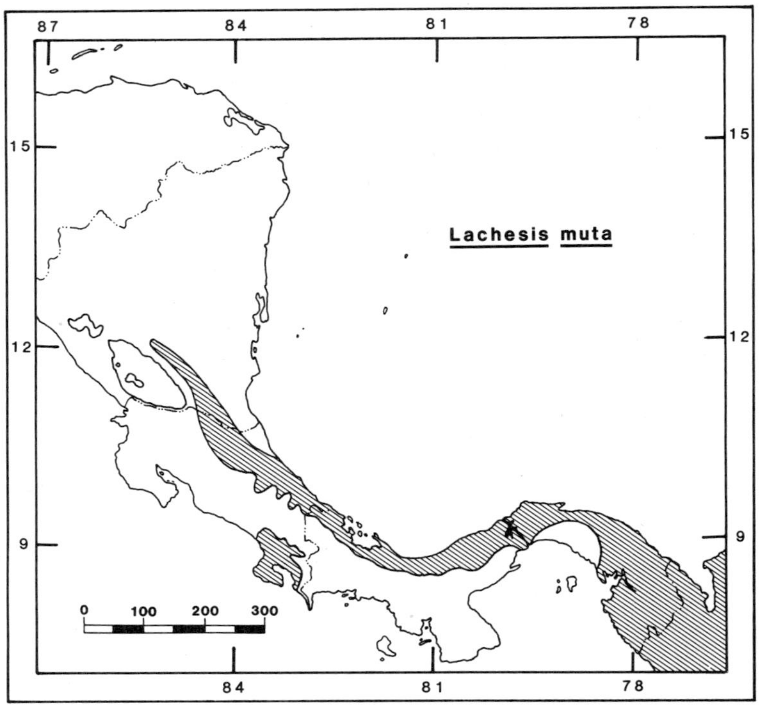


**Map 80.** Distribution of *Lachesis muta* in the northern portion of its range in lower Central America. This species' range in Nicaragua is mapped on the basis of several specimens bearing questionable locality data. For the continuation of the distribution of this species into South America consult Map 81.

ENGLISH NAME Bushmaster.

DISTRIBUTION Central and South America. There appear to be four disjunct populations of this species (Maps 80, 81): (1) One population occurs in the Atlantic lowlands from southern Nicaragua through Costa Rica and Panama to northwestern Colombia, including the Pacific lowlands of central Panama, Colombia, and Ecuador (south to the upper Río Daule) and the Caribbean coast of northwest Colombia north to Sucre and east to the Río Cauca Valley (into Antioquia) and along the Río Magdalena Valley (into Caldas and possibly Tolima). (2) The Pacific lowlands of southeastern Costa Rica are inhabited by another. (3) Yet another exists east of the Andes in Colombia from the upper Río Meta and Río Vichada southward throughout the equatorial forests of Colombia, southern and eastern Venezuela, Trinidad (especially in Diego Martin and Arima districts), Guyana, Suriname, French Guiana, northern Brazil, eastern Ecuador, eastern Peru, and northeastern Bolivia. (4) An isolated population in the Atlantic forest of Brazil (see Remarks) ranges from southern Rio Grande do Norte or Paraíba south to Rio de Janeiro (Map 81). The vertical distribution of this species is from near sea level to about 1,000 m in Central America; in northern South America it ranges to at least 1,800 m.

HABITAT This snake occurs in tropical rainforests and lower montane wet forests that receive more than 2,000 mm, and usually more than 4,000 mm, of rainfall per annum. In a few regions (Nicaragua and llanos of Colombia) it apparently enters tropical dry forests (or seasonally dry forests) in riparian situations. *Lachesis* is an inhabitant of primary forest, often living near large buttressed trees (*Ceiba*, *Swietenia*, etc.) or adjacent to fallen trees. Upon occasion it may be encountered in secondary forest situations but in areas recently cleared or adjacent to virgin forest.

DESCRIPTION This terrestrial snake is the longest of all vipers, commonly exceeding 2,000 mm in total length, with exceptional specimens reportedly reaching or exceeding 3,600 mm. There is an unsubstantiated report of a specimen 4,267 mm in total length.

A prominent ridge is present middorsally, especially on the anterior portion of the body. The head is broadly rounded with an unelevated snout. The dorsum of the head may be tan, brown, or black; if pale, there are often a few small-to-large, brown-to-black spots. A dark postocular stripe extends at least to the rictus and often to below the angle of the jaw. Except for snakes from Pacific Costa Rica, in which the postocular stripe merges with the black dorsum of the head, the postocular stripe is separated dorsally from the dark markings and darker ground color of the head by a thin pale stripe one to several scales wide. The supralabials are usually immaculate and the infracephalic scales are cream, yellow, or pinkish without dark markings. The ground color is reddish brown, yellowish tan, or pinkish tan. There are 20–37 dark brown or black middorsal diamond-shaped blotches (forming triangles laterally) on the dorsum. The lateral corners of the body blotches are extended into vertical bars that generally extend to scale rows 2 or 3, but may extend to the outer side of the ventrals. The dark dorsal markings are often narrowly bordered by yellow or cream. The center of each lateral triangular portion of the dorsal blotches is frequently pale and of about the same hue as the ground color. The tail has 4–7 black blotches that extend to the outer edges of the subcaudals. The venter is white or ivory and the subcaudals are mostly pale with dark mottling. The iris is red-brown

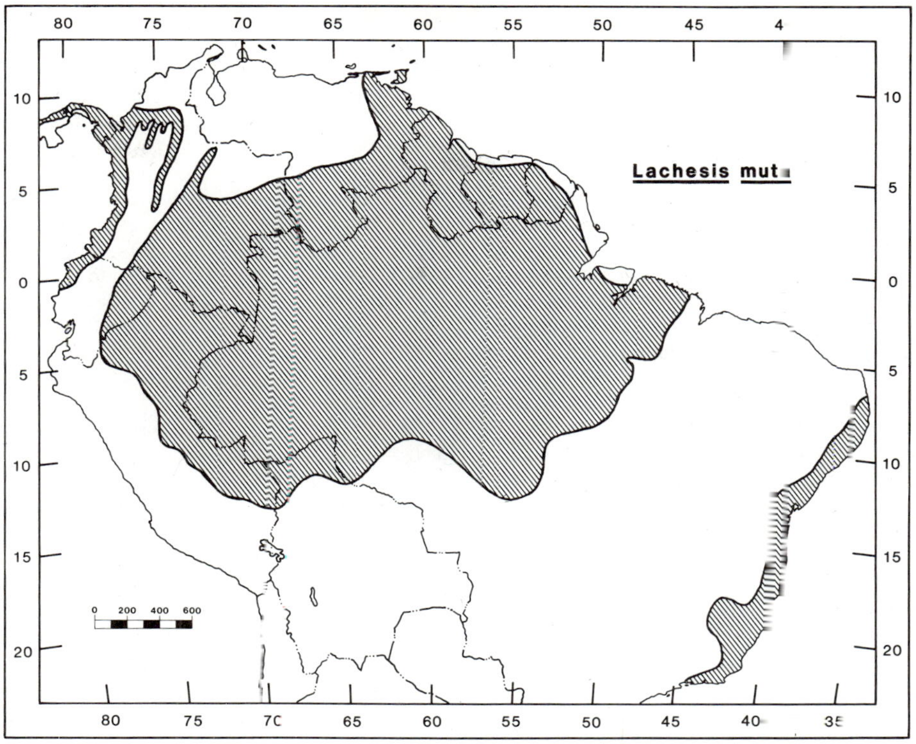


**Map 81.** Distribution of *Lachesis muta* in the southern portion of its range in northern South America. This species occurs on Trinidad and along the coastal forest of Brazil.

and may be bright and distinct or heavily pigmented and obscure. The tongue is black.

The supracephalic scales are smooth or obtusely keeled and there are 9–15 intersupraoculars. There are 8–10 (usually 9 or 10) supralabials (the second is fused with the prelacunal), 12–17 (usually 13 or 14) infralabials, 31–39 dorsal scale rows at midbody (one report of 27), 200–247 ventrals, and 43–56 subcaudals. A few of the proximal subcaudals may be entire, but most are divided (paired), and the distal 13–18 are finely divided into 4 or 5 rows of small spinelike scales (Fig. 316).

SIMILAR SPECIES Even cursory examination of *L. muta* should readily distinguish this species from other snakes occurring within its wide range. Owing to their strongly keeled dorsals, the species perhaps most frequently confused with *L. muta* are *Porthidium nummifer* and *P. picadoi* of Costa Rica and Panama; however, both of these are proportionately stouter than *L. muta*, and they possess fewer midbody dorsal scale rows (31 or fewer), ventrals (155 or fewer), and subcaudals (40 or fewer, none of which are finely divided distally), and have venters that are darkly mottled.

Some members of the genus *Bothrops*, such as *B. asper*, *B. atrox*, and *B. brazili*, attain respectable lengths, but they may be distinguished from *L. muta* on the basis of head shape and many features of lepidosis and color pattern (see individual species accounts).

REMARKS Four subspecies have been described for *L. muta*: *L. m. stenophrys* (Figs. 252, 253, 257–59) from the Atlantic lowlands of Costa Rica and Panama, crossing over to the Pacific in central Panama; *L. m. melanocephala* (Fig. 250) from the Pacific lowlands of southeastern Costa Rica; *L. m. muta* (Fig. 249) from the equatorial forests of Colombia, Venezuela, Trinidad, Guyana, Suriname, French Guiana, Brazil, Ecuador, Peru, and Bolivia; and *L. m. rhombeata* (Fig. 251) from the Atlantic forests of east-central Brazil (erroneously reported from Bolivia).

The status of snakes from eastern Panama, Pacific Colombia and Ecuador, and the inter-Andean valleys of Colombia has never been determined satisfactorily. Although some records refer to snakes from these regions as *L. m. muta*, we suspect on geographic grounds that their affinities are with *L. m. stenophrys*.

A few of the characteristics defining these subspecies are as follows: relatively fewer ventrals in males and females of *L. m. stenophrys*; small dark spots on the head and a narrow postocular stripe in *L. m. muta*; and large dark spots on the head and a broad postocular stripe in *L. m. rhombeata*. The population of Pacific Costa Rica (*L. m. melanocephala*) has a black ground color on the dorsum of the head that extends laterally to merge with the dark postocular stripe.

These snakes are crepuscular and nocturnal. It is our experience that the aggressiveness of this species has been exaggerated greatly. Most *Lachesis* specimens we have encountered in the field, or have reliable reports of, have been rather unaggressive. However, specimens found active after dark may be quick to strike and display a formidable defense posture, including neck inflation and audible tail vibration. Snakes from the Pacific lowlands of Costa Rica are atypical in usually being highly aggressive anytime they are disturbed.

REFERENCES Abalos, 1977; Acosta-Solís, 1944; Amaral, 1925b, 1925c, 1926d, 1927c, 1930b, 1930c, 1938, 1948a, 1974, 1978; Andersson, 1899; Angel, 1983; Ayerbe, 1979; Bancroft, 1769; Barbour, 1930; Bates, 1928; W. Beebe, 1946; Bellairs, 1969; Bolaños, 1971, 1982, 1983, 1984; Bolaños et al., 1978, 1982; Boos, 1975, 1984b; Boos and Quesnel, 1968; Boulenger, 1896; Brattstrom, 1964; Brongersma, 1967; Burger, 1971; Carrillo de Espinoza, 1970, 1983; Cendrero et al., 1972; Chippaux, 1987; H. C. Clark, 1942, 1951; Cope, 1860c; 1875, 1876a, 1887; Cordeiro and Hoge, 1974; Cunha and Nascimento, 1975b, 1978, 1982a; Cunha et al., 1985; D'Alessandro, 1972; Daniel, 1949; Ditmars, 1937; Dixon and Soini, 1986; Duellman, 1978; Duke, 1967; Dunn, 1944a, 1949; Dunn and Bailey, 1939; Eichelbaum, 1927; Elton, 1948; Emsley, 1977; Fonseca, 1949; Fountain, 1902; García, 1896; García-López and Sandner-Montilla, 1962; Garman, 1884a; Gasc and Rodrigues, 1980; Gliesch, 1925; Gray, 1829; Greene, 1986; Greene and Santana, 1983; Grocott and Sadler, 1958; Groombridge, 1986; Gumilla, 1741; Günther, 1861, 1895–1902; Gutiérrez et al., 1979; Hagmann, 1909; Higgins, 1870; Hoge, 1966, 1967; Hoge and Lancini, 1962; Hoge and Romano, 1973; Hoge and Romano-Hoge, 1981a, 1981b; Holdridge, 1964; Hoogmoed, 1979, 1983; Hoogmoed and Gruber, 1983; Ihering, 1911; Jan, 1859a, 1859b; Jan and Sordelli, 1870–1881; Kaiser and Michl, 1971; Kempff-Mercado, 1975; Klemmer, 1963; Lacerda, 1884; Lancini, 1970, 1979; Lancini V., 1983; Machado, 1945b; Martínez and Bolaños, 1982; Medem, 1969; Meneses, 1974a, 1974b; Milá de la Roca, 1932; Minton et al., 1968; Mocquard, 1908–1909; Mole, 1914, 1924; Moonen, 1982; Moonen et al., 1978; L. Müller, 1927; P. Müller, 1968, 1969a, 1969b, 1971, 1973; Nemuras, 1967; Nicéforo-María, 1929b, 1930b, 1933, 1942; Noguchi, 1909; Orcés, 1942, 1943, 1948; Orton, 1876; Parker, 1935; Patzelt, 1979; J. A. Peters, 1960a; J. A. Peters and Orejas-Miranda, 1970; Picado T., 1931; Prado, 1945; Quelch, 1898; Reichel-Dolmatoff, 1968; Roge [*sic*] and Romano, 1977; Rohl, 1949; Roze, 1966a; Sandner-Montilla, 1975, 1985a; Schmidt, 1957b; Scott, 1969; Soini, 1974b; Solórzano and Cerdas, 1986; Swanson, 1945; E. H. Taylor, 1951; R. T. Taylor, et al., 1974; Trejos, 1937; Van Bourgondien and Bothner, 1969; Vellard, 1941, 1949; Verteuil, 1884; Vetencourt Finol., 1960; Vial and Jimenez-Porras, 1967; Villa, 1962, 1971, 1984; Wagler, 1824; Wehekind, 1960; Werner, 1922.

# Mexican Horned Pitviper

## Genus *Ophryacus* Cope, 1887

The genus *Ophryacus* (family Viperidae) contains a single species, *O. undulatus*, which is distributed disjunctly in the highlands of east-central and southern Mexico west of the Isthmus of Tehuantepec.

The rostral is broader than high and there are 3 preoculars (middle vertically divided), and generally about 3 suboculars and 4 postoculars. A single scale above the eye forms a long slender spine or, less frequently, a flattened horn. Many of the canthals and the internasals are also raised into short spines. The scales in the supraocular region, as well as the crown, are small and keeled. The second supralabial is separated from the prelacunal by small subfoveals. The middorsals at midbody are relatively broad and obtusely rounded. The keel generally extends to the tip of the scale or nearly so and apical pits are not apparent. The free portion of the apex of a dorsal is moderate in extent and does not greatly overlap the contiguous scale; the interstitial epidermal fold at the cranial end of the scale is well developed. The tail spine is straight and is as long as the preceding 2–3 subcaudals; it is pointed or obtusely rounded with 2 dorsal capping scales. The pupil is vertically elliptical. The fang extends to the level of the seventh supralabial.

The hemipenes are divided and extend 10 or 11 subcaudals. The organs bifurcate at subcaudal 4 or 5; the sulcus spermaticus bifurcates at subcaudal 1 or 2 and extends to the apices. Each lobe is subcylindrical and tapers slightly toward the apex. There are 4 or 5 basal spines and about 45–50 large spines on the proximal half of each lobe, with the highest number of spines in the mesial region. The size of these spines decreases distally—except in the mesial region, where spines tend to get larger distally and extend further toward the apices. The distal half of the lobes are calyculate with spinulate micro-ornamentation.

For other details of color, pattern, lepidosis, habitat, and distribution of *O. undulatus* see the following account.

The clinical effects of the venom of *Ophryacus* are unknown.

### *Ophryacus undulatus* (Jan)

(Figs. 254–256, 260–262; Map 82)

LOCAL NAMES Cuernillos, mazacóatl (Náhuatl), Nauyaca, torito, víbora cornuda, víbora de cachitos (same name that is used for *Porthidium melanurum* in some regions), víbora de cuernecitos.

ENGLISH NAME Mexican horned pitviper.

DISTRIBUTION Mexico. This species is found at intermediate elevations in mountains of the southern portions of the Sierra Madre Oriental, Mesa del Sur, and Sierra Madre del Sur (Map 82). Its vertical distribution is from about 1,800 to 2,800 m.

HABITAT Pine-oak and cloud forests.

DESCRIPTION This species is a moderately stout, semiarboreal pitviper that commonly reaches an overall length of between 550 and 700 mm.

The ground color of adults is pale to dark gray or yellowish to brownish green. Most specimens have a suffusion of yellow, orange, pink, or green within the ground color. We have seen a few specimens from cloud forest near Orizaba, Veracruz, that had a particularly bright leaf green ground color. Generally the dorsals are heavily spotted with small black flecks. Although patternless specimens are known, especially from central Oaxaca, and some specimens become dark with age so as to obscure the pattern, some evidence of dorsal pattern is usually present. In paler specimens dark markings, including paired occipital blotches, are present on the dorsum of the head. The dorsal pattern consists of a series of dark blotches, most of which are confluent, forming an undulant or zig-zag stripe. Laterally a series of 30–40 small dark blotches may offset each dorsal blotch, but most frequently they are absent. Ventral to the dark lateral blotches there may be a series of small pale blotches on scale rows 1 and 2 (sometimes also 3). A dark postocular stripe is not usually present. The mental and infralabials usually have a few black flecks; gulars and anterior ventrals are white or yellowish and almost immaculate, except for a few widely dispersed black flecks that tend to be mostly on the outside lateral margins of the scales. Posteriorly the ventrals become darker, with a heavier concentration of black flecking. The subcaudals are dark gray with black flecks or mottling.

Juveniles tend to be paler than adults, and they tend to have well-defined markings. The ground color is greenish gray to brownish gray. The dorsum of the head has irregularly shaped but symmetrically arranged dark blotches, including a pair above the eyes with extensions to the tips of the supraocular spines, a large pair

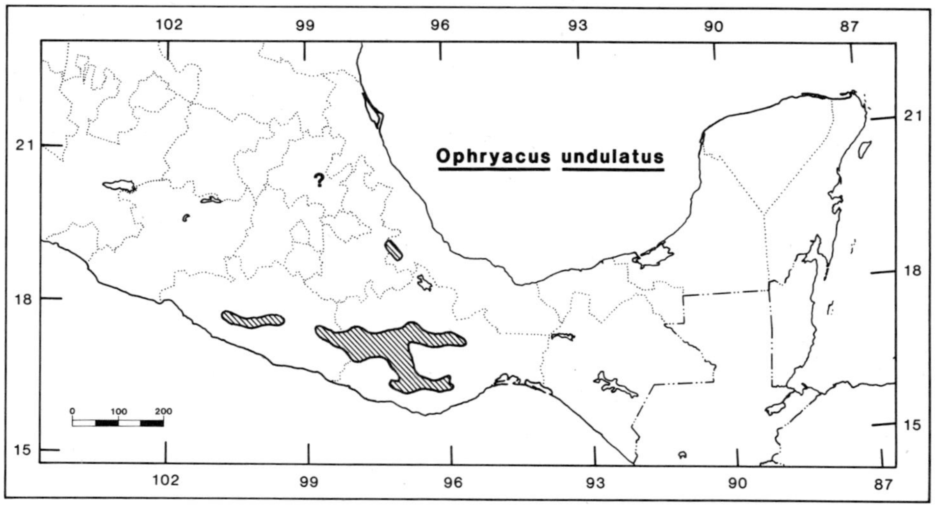


**Map 82.** Distribution of *Ophryacus undulatus* in central and southern Mexico. The question mark represents an old locality record for Actopan, Hidalgo, which probably is in error. Another old record for Actopan, Veracruz is not indicated, as this locality is almost certainly at too low an elevation for this species.

over the occipital region, a pair of small rounded spots over the parietal region, and a hook-shaped pair on the nape. The side of the head from the tip of the snout to the rictus is dark brown. A few supralabials often have diffuse orange or pink markings. An undulating middorsal brown stripe extends onto the tail. The venter of the head is orange-tan with a gray suffusion on the infralabials. The venter is a uniform reddish gray with a very light paler speckling. The subcaudals are somewhat darker than the ventrals. The iris is gray with profuse darker reticulations. The tongue is gray with darker speckling.

This species has 12–18 intersupraoculars (the number of scales between the elongated supraocular spines); 10 (the type of *B. sphenophrys*) and 20 have been recorded from single specimens. There are 10–13 supralabials, (none in contact with the prelacunal), 11–14 infralabials, 21 middorsal scale rows, 157–171 ventrals, and 37–57 subcaudals (most or all divided).

SIMILAR SPECIES The only other species of pitvipers in Mexico possessing supraocular spines or horns are *Bothriechis schlegelii* and *Porthidium melanurum*. *Ophryacus undulatus* may be distinguished from both of these by the presence of divided or paired subcaudals. Furthermore, *B. schlegelii* has a large flat supraocular and fewer than 10 intersupraoculars. The only other Mexican species of pitviper having paired subcaudals is *Bothrops asper*, which has a lacunolabial, fewer than 10 intersupraoculars, a large supraocular that does not form into a spine, and a brown ground color with X-shaped markings.

REMARKS We tentatively regard *Bothrops sphenophrys* as a junior synonym of *O. undulatus* and have included data for the single known specimen of *B. sphenophrys* in the above description. Recent collecting in the mountains of Oaxaca has revealed the presence of snakes clearly referable to *O. undulatus* near the type locality of *B. sphenophrys* and has provided additional material that has increased our understanding of the variation present in *O. undulatus*. Most of the characteristics distinguishing *B. sphenophrys* from *O. undulatus* have proved to fall within the normal range of variation for populations of *O. undulatus* from central Oaxaca and Guerrero. For example, the conspicuous supraocular horn, which is generally slender, elongated, and more-or-less cylindrical in *O. undulatus*, may occasionally be flat and wedge-shaped (as described in *B. sphenophrys*), particularly in juveniles. However, at least two features of the holotype of *B. sphenophrys*, the numbers of intersupraoculars (10) and subcaudals (57), differ slightly from the range of variation known for the sample of *O. undulatus* at hand (12–18 and 37–52, respectively).

We refer to this snake as being semiarboreal. This species is found most frequently on the ground and often takes refuge under rocks or logs. However, in densely wooded situations, particularly along the edges of cloud forests or in ravines, this snake readily climbs and we have taken it coiled in vegetation 3–4 m above the ground. We have observed this snake active only by day.

Several locality records for *O. undulatus* are suspect. Specimens recorded from Oaxaca, Oaxaca, almost certainly come from the surrounding mountains, which are covered by pine-oak forest, and not the Valley of Oaxaca which is more xeric. Even more problematical is a snake reported from Actopan, Hidalgo, which represents the only specimen known from the region; the vegetation of this locality is tropical arid scrub. This specimen may have been collected in the mountains to the east of Actopan, which appear to contain suitable habitat. Alternatively, the specimen may have come from the vicinity of Actopan, Veracruz, but this locality is at a much lower elevation than *O. undulatus* is known to inhabit.

REFERENCES Altini, 1942; Boulenger, 1896; Burger, 1971; Cope, 1865, 1887; Cuesta Terron, 1921b, 1930a; Davis and Dixon, 1959; Ferrari-Perez, 1886; Gadow, 1905; Garman, 1884a; Groombridge, 1986; Günther, 1895–1902; Jan, 1859a, 1863; Lynch and Smith, 1966; Martín del Campo, 1935, 1937a, 1950; Mocquard, 1908–1909; P. Müller, 1973; Muñoz Alonso, 1988; Noguchi, 1909; Ocaranza, 1930; H. M. Smith, 1941a, 1960a; H. M. Smith and Taylor, 1945, 1950b, 1966; Sumichrast, 1864a, 1870, 1873, 1882; E. H. Taylor, 1943.

# Hognosed and Montane Pitvipers

## Genus *Porthidium* Cope, 1871

The genus *Porthidium* (family Viperidae) is composed of 14 species of terrestrial pitvipers. Members of this genus have bodies that range from relatively slender (*P. ophryomegas*) to exceedingly stout (*P. nummifer, P. olmec, P. picadoi*), and the overall length of adults ranges from about 450 mm (*P. barbouri, P. tzotzilorum*) to over 1 m (*P. picadoi*). The color pattern of the montane pitvipers (*P. barbouri, P. godmani, P. melanurum, P. nummifer, P. olmec, P. picadoi, P. tzotzilorum*) consists of a series of dark dorsal blotches, often coalescing to form a zig-zag stripe, on a tan, brown, gray, or orange background. The hognosed pitvipers (*P. dunni, P. hespere, P. hyoprora, P. lansbergii, P. nasutum, P. ophryomegas, P. yucatanicum*) possess dark square, rectangular, or triangular paravertebral blotches that are arranged alternately or opposite each other and usually are separated by a narrow pale vertebral stripe; the ground color is most frequently brown or gray.

The canthus rostralis is sharply defined in all members of this group. In montane pitvipers the rostral is broader than high, whereas in hognosed pitvipers the rostral is higher than broad. The tip of the snout in hognosed pitvipers may be unelevated (*P. hespere, P. lansbergii, P. ophryomegas*), moderately elevated (*P. dunni, P. hyoprora, P. yucatanicum*), or greatly elevated (*P. nasutum*). The scales on the crown of the head may be large and platelike (*P. barbouri*), moderately enlarged with variable keeling (*P. godmani, P. tzotzilorum*), or small, imbricate, and usually keeled. There may be only 1 intersupraocular in some specimens of *P. barbouri*, but most species have 3–7, except for *P. melanurum, P. nummifer, P. olmec* and *P. picadoi*, which have more. The great amount of variation among members of this group is further exemplified by some of the other meristic features: there are 7–14 supralabials, 8–14 infralabials, 17–31 midbody dorsal scale rows, 103–174 ventrals, and 22–64 subcaudals. A summary of the variations found in selected scale characteristics among members of this genus is presented in Table 31.

The hemipenes of *Porthidium* are divided; the sulcus spermaticus bifurcates at the level of subcaudals 1–4 and extends to each apex. The everted hemipenes extend to the level of subcaudal 6–12. The lobes may be subcylindrical or attenuated. In *P. barbouri, P. godmani,* and *P. tzotzilorum* 12–40 large spines appear on the proximal third of each lobe; the remainder of the lobe is covered by calyces that possess either spinulate or papillate micro-ornamentation. The base of the organ below the level of the crotch is mostly naked, except for a few small spines that tend to be concentrated on the lateral surfaces. Each of the hemipenes of *P. melanurum* bears 18–23 large spines (including the large basal hooks) on the proximal portion of each lobe and contiguous part of the base; these spines are most numerous in the mesial area just above the crotch. Spinulate calyces extend laterally down each lobe to the level of the crotch; in the mesial area spines cover ¼–⅓ of the proximal part of each lobe. In *P. nummifer* the hemipenes are long and slender with the proximal two-thirds of each lobe bearing 35–50 medium-sized spines; the remainder of each lobe is covered by high-ridged calyces that have scalloped to spinulate micro-ornamentation. Most of the base is naked except for a few small spines laterally or on the sulcate side

Hemipenes from the two species of hognosed pitviper that we have examined (*P. nasutum* and *P. yucatanicum*) possess especially distinctive ornamentation. In these snakes 35–65 small-to-large spines (including 2–6 large basal hooks) cover the proximal ¾–⅘ of each lobe and adjacent base. the crotch and proximal portion of the mesial area are characteristically naked. In *P. nasutum* the distal one-fifth of each lobe is covered by a series of spinulate ridges arranged in more-or-less concentric circles. The apex terminates in a large soft papilla, the asulcate side of which is deeply emarginate. The distal one-fourth to one-fifth of each lobe in *P. yucatanicum* is covered by ridges with long soft spines. A small naked apical disc is present, in the center of which is a soft papilla. The sulcus spermaticus extends into the papillae in both *P. nasutum* and *P. yucatanicum*.

This genus is confined largely to Mexico and Central America. *Porthidium nummifer* extends northward along the Atlantic foothills of Mexico to San Luis Potosí, and on the west coast *P. hespere* occurs in Colima. Two species, *P. lansbergii* and *P. nasutum*, range into northern South America, and *P. hyoprora* is restricted to the Amazon Basin.

Several distinct lineages are evident within this genus. The montane pitvipers occur mostly at elevations exceeding 1,500 m, although one component of this group (*P. nummifer, P. olmec,* and *P. picadoi*) descends into hilly lowland regions. The hognosed pitvipers are restricted mostly to elevations below 1,000 m, and most species inhabit regions that are seasonably xeric. In Middle America only *P. lansbergii* and *P. nasutum* live in wet lowland rainforest; in South America *P. hyoprora* and *P. nasutum* are restricted to this type of forest.

**Table 31**
Variation of selected scale characteristics in members of the genus *Porthidium*

| Species | Intersupraoculars | Supralabials | Infralabials | Ventrals | Subcaudals | Midbody dorsal scale rows (mode) |
|---|---|---|---|---|---|---|
| *P. barbouri* | 1–4 | 7–10 | 8–11 | 130–145 | 26–32 | 17–19 (17) |
| *P. dunni* | 4–6 | 9–11 | 10–12 | 141–158 | 30–41 | 21–23 (23) |
| *P. godmani* | 3–7 | 7–10 | 8–11 | 130–148 | 22–36 | 21 |
| *P. hespere* | 5 | 10 | 11–12 | 156 | 30 | 23 |
| *P. hyoprora* | 4–9 | 7–8 | 9–11 | 124–141 | 38–57 | 21–25 (23) |
| *P. lansbergii* | 5–7 | 8–10 | 8–13 | 139–161 | 27–41 | 23–25 (25) |
| *P. melanurum* | 9–13 | 10–14 | 9–12 | 142–149 | 36–42 | 21 |
| *P. nasutum* | 3–7 | 8–11 | 10–13 | 123–145 | 24–41 | 21–27 (23) |
| *P. nummifer* | 7–12 | 9–12 | 10–14 | 114–135 | 22–39 | 23–31 |
| *P. olmec* | 8–9 | 10–12 | 11–13 | 103–115 | 25–33 | 23 |
| *P. ophryomegas* | 5–6 | 8–10 | 10–13 | 156–174 | 32–64 | 23–27 (25) |
| *P. picadoi* | 7–11 | 9–10 | 9–13 | 141–155 | 31–40 | 25–29 (25) |
| *P. tzotzilorum* | 3 | 9–11 | 9–12 | 120–134 | 23–36 | 19–23 (21) |
| *P. yucatanicum* | 3–7 | 9–11 | 10–14 | 141–155 | 31–43 | 23–27 (25) |

*Note.* For additional information refer to individual species accounts.

In Costa Rica, 10–15% of snakebites are inflicted by the smaller species of this genus. Low venom yield (about 15 mg) due to small size probably accounts for only mild to moderate severity from envenomation, and necrosis is the most important clinical effect in some cases when digits are involved. *Porthidium nummifer* and *P. picadoi* are larger and produce more venom (50–60 mg) but inflict only about 1% of reported bites in Costa Rica. Apparently, only in rare instances are members of this genus capable of delivering a fatal bite (but see Remarks for *P. nasutum*).

### *Porthidium barbouri* (Dunn)

(Figs. 263–266, 300, 301; Map 85)

LOCAL NAMES Nauyaca, víbora colorada, víbora sorda.

ENGLISH NAME Barbour's montane pitviper.

DISTRIBUTION Intermediate and high elevations of the Sierra Madre del Sur in Guerrero, Mexico (see Map 85). The vertical distribution ranges from 2,390 to 3,300 m.

HABITAT Pine-oak and cloud forests.

DESCRIPTION This moderately stout, terrestrial pitviper may reach 510 mm in total length, but adults are generally between 300 and 400 mm.

The ground color is reddish brown with a dark brown, often ill-defined dorsal zig-zag stripe that is bordered narrowly with black. From 25 to 28 dark brown lateral body blotches are rounded above and extend to the ventrals. The pattern may become obscure overall with age. A dark brown postocular stripe is present and the supralabials are pink or yellow with fine brown stippling. The first lateral body blotch is elongated and may extend posteriorly. The juveniles possess a pale brown to greenish brown ground color, a pattern that is more distinct than in adults, and a tail that is chartreuse distally.

The number and arrangement of the scales on top of the head appear to be more variable than those reported for any other snake. Some specimens have a pattern slightly similar to that of *Agkistrodon* (cantil) or *Sistrurus* (Mexican pygmy rattlesnake), but have 11 rather than 9 scales with the inclusion of a pair of canthals. The dorsal head scales in other specimens are extremely fragmented. There are 1–4 intersupraoculars; 7–10 (generally 8 or 9) supralabials; 8–11 (mode 9) infralabials; 17–19 (mode 17) midbody dorsal scale rows; 130–145 ventrals; and 26–32 subcaudals (undivided).

SIMILAR SPECIES There are no snakes in Guerrero, Mexico, with which this snake may be easily confused. *Ophryacus undulatus* occurs sympatrically with *P. barbouri* but differs by having raised hornlike scales over the eyes and divided subcaudals. The race of *Sistrurus ravus* inhabiting the region often may have a similar reddish brown ground color, but is distinguished easily by the presence of a rattle and the absence of canthals.

REMARKS This is an alert, diurnal species that has been found crawling or sunning along the edges of clearings or in patches of sunlight within the forest. When disturbed it is generally quick to retreat.

REFERENCES Campbell, 1977, 1985, 1989; Davis and Dixon, 1959; Dunn, 1919; Martín del Campo, 1935, 1937a, 1950; Muñoz Alonso, 1988; Shreve, 1938; H. M. Smith, 1941a; H. M. Smith and Taylor, 1945, 1950b; E. H. Taylor, 1943; Werner, 1922.

### *Porthidium dunni* (Hartweg and Oliver)

(Figs. 267, 268, 312, 313; Map 91)

LOCAL NAMES Chatilla, víbora chata (Oaxaca).

ENGLISH NAME Dunn's hognosed pitviper.

DISTRIBUTION Low elevations of the Pacific foothills and coastal plain from about southwestern Oaxaca to extreme western Chiapas, Mexico (see Remarks and

Map 91). The vertical distribution ranges from near sea level to a little over 500 m.

HABITAT This species frequents tropical deciduous forest. In the Pacific coastal lowlands it inhabits a semiarid region characterized by thorny, relatively short trees usually not exceeding 3 m in height. In some areas higher in the Pacific foothills the trees may be more than twice as tall. Throughout most of the region the vegetation forms an almost impenetrable tangle. The rainy season extends from June to October, with June and July being the wettest months. The amount of annual precipitation may vary considerably over short distances in this region. For example, the mean annual rainfall at Salina Cruz on the Pacific Ocean is 1,040 mm, whereas Tehuantepec, only 15 km inland, receives 440 mm. Fluctuations of mean monthly temperatures throughout the range of *P. dunni* amount to only a few degrees; mean annual temperatures tend to be warm, with recordings of 25–27°C.

DESCRIPTION *Porthidium dunni* is a moderately stout, terrestrial pitviper. Overall lengths of adults commonly fall between 300 and 400 mm. The largest specimen known measures 542 mm.

The dorsum of the head is pale gray or brown, often with fine brown stippling. Ventrally the side of the head is dark from the lower posterior margin of the eye to just above the angle of the jaw; above this a pale postocular band extends to the posterior temporal region. A pale vertebral line extends from the nape to the tail, with 14–23 dark brown blotches on each side arranged alternately or opposite each other. The ground color intervenes ventrally to bisect each blotch into two partially divided components. Blotches often are connected to form a dorsal zig-zag stripe. The ground color may be gray, tan, or pale orangish brown. Two series of rounded gray lateral blotches are present; one series involves scale rows 2–5 and the other is located on the lateral margins of the ventrals and scale rows 1 and 2. The amount of dark pigmentation is highly variable. Most specimens have a heavy concentration of black or brown stippling on the mental and infralabials that is broken by about three yellow or cream-colored spots; the ventrals are white and become more heavily pigmented posteriorly. The subcaudals tend to have dense stippling or mottling, especially laterally.

There are 4–6 (usually 4 or 5) intersupraoculars, 9–11 (mode 10) supralabials, 10–12 (usually 10 or 11) infralabials, 21–23 (usually 23) midbody dorsal scale rows, 141–158 ventrals, and 30–41 undivided subcaudals.

SIMILAR SPECIES *Porthidium dunni* is a member of the hognosed pitviper group. It may be distinguished from *P. hespere* by having 19 rather than 17 dorsal scale rows just anterior to the vent, a middle preocular that reaches the orbit and is divided vertically, 2 or occasionally 3 intercanthals rather than 4, and more strongly elevated internasals. *Porthidium dunni* differs from *P. yucatanicum* in having 19 rather than 21 dorsal scale rows posteriorly, the lateral surfaces of the head mostly dark rather than pale with light speckling, internasals that are more strongly elevated, and a ground color that is more strongly suffused with small black flecks. *Porthidium nasutum*, besides occurring in a markedly different habitat, has a rostral considerably higher than broad, thus dramatically elevating the canthus rostralis (Fig. 312). See also the discussion of *Boa constrictor* (Fig. 547) in Mimics of Venomous Snakes.

REMARKS This species has been recorded previously from the state of Chiapas only once. Two specimens in the collection at The University of Texas at Arlington serve to further document its presence there: UTA R-12553 from near the Oaxaca-Chiapas border and UTA R-8356 from a few kilometers within Chiapas were both taken from the Pan American Highway (Mexican Highway 190). Inasmuch as suitable habitat extends farther into western Chiapas, there is little doubt that the species ranges even farther to the east than we report here.

REFERENCES Amaral, 1927b, 1944a; Bocourt, 1876; Campbell, 1976; Chrapliwy and Fugler, 1955; Hartweg and Oliver, 1938, 1940; Johnson, 1974; Lynch and Smith, 1966; Martín del Campo, 1935, 1937a, 1950; H. M. Smith, 1941a; H. M. Smith and Taylor, 1945, 1950b; Sumichrast, 1873, 1880, 1881–1882, 1882; Werler and Smith, 1952; Woodbury and Woodbury, 1944.

## *Porthidium godmani* (Günther)

(Figs. 269–271, 302, 303; Map 85)

LOCAL NAMES Costa Rica: toboba de altura. Guatemala: sheta, tamagás. Mexico: nauyaca del frío (Chiapas). Nicaragua: toboa oscura, toboíta.

ENGLISH NAME Godman's montane pitviper.

DISTRIBUTION The distribution of this species is disjunct; it occurs in both Nuclear and Isthmian Central America at intermediate and high elevations. The range of this species extends from the northwestern portion of the Sierra Madre de Chiapas in southeastern Oaxaca, Mexico, across portions of Guatemala, Honduras, and El Salvador into northwestern Nicaragua, and from the Cordillera Central in north-central Costa Rica to the southeastern portion of the Cordillera de Talamanca in northwest province of Chiriquí, Panama (see Map 85). The vertical distribution ranges from about 1,600 to 3,200 m.

HABITAT Lower montane wet forest and cloud forest; lower montane dry forest, largely pine-oak; and high montane forest and meadow.

DESCRIPTION This moderately stout, terrestrial pitviper occasionally exceeds 750 mm in total length but is more frequently between 400 and 600 mm.

The color and pattern of this species are highly variable. The ground color of the dorsum may be brown, reddish brown, grayish brown, or orange. Dark brown dorsal blotches often merge to form a distinctive zig-zag dorsal stripe. About 20–33 dark lateral blotches are present, of which the anteriormost may be elongated and extend 10–20 scale lengths down the neck. A dark brown postocular stripe is invariably present. Typically, the supralabials, infralabials, gular area, and anterior ventrals are pale yellow or orange with little or no mottling. The ventrals become progressively darker posteriorly and may be entirely gray or black, as are the proximal subcaudals; the distal subcaudals are pale in specimens from Nuclear Central America and usually dark in those from Isthmian Central America. The iris may be various shades of brown or gray. Juveniles are relatively similar to adults but may have a paler ground color (and therefore a sharper contrast in pattern) and a pale yellow tail.

There are 3–7 intersupraoculars, 7–10 supralabials (mode 8), 8–11 infralabials (mode 9), 21 midbody dorsal scale rows, 130–148 ventrals, and 22–36 undivided subcaudals.

SIMILAR SPECIES *Porthidium godmani* is widespread, but restricted to the uplands. Over much of its range it is not sympatric with other terrestrial vipers. The only other snakes occurring in highland regions with which it might possibly be confused are *P. nummifer* and *P. tzotzilorum*. *Porthidium tzotzilorum* has smaller lateral blotches, involving only 2–3 scales (rather than 5–7); a postorbital stripe that is distinctly pale bordered above as well as below; and generally fewer ventrals. *Porthidium nummifer* is an extremely stout snake with 7–12 intersupraoculars, 23–27 midbody dorsal scale rows, and generally fewer ventrals.

The hognosed pitvipers, *P. dunni*, *P. nasutum*, and *P. ophryomegas*, rarely occur above 900 m and have a sharper canthus and generally a strongly elevated snout, the rostral higher than wide, 23–31 midbody dorsal scale rows, and a pattern that consists of paired blotches often bisected by a thin pale vertebral line.

REMARKS This snake is abundant within its range. It is mostly diurnal and frequently is seen crawling or coiled along forest paths. The venom of this snake is not especially dangerous, and no fatalities have been reported. Three Guatemalan cases treated by Stadelman (1940), two in young children, involved fever and considerable swelling. Three additional cases in Guatemala City were mild and did not require hospitalization. The specific epithet *godmanni*, which is still used by some authors, was invalidated by Cope (1871).

REFERENCES Altini, 1942; Alvarez del Toro, 1983; Barbour and Loveridge, 1929a; Bogert, 1968; Bolaños, 1982, 1983, 1984; Boulenger, 1896; Campbell, 1977, 1982b, 1985; H. C. Clark, 1942, 1951; Cope, 1871, 1887; Ditmars, 1930, 1937; Duke, 1967; Dunn, 1940a, 1947; Dunn and Emlen, 1932; Elton, 1948; Fischer, 1880; Grocott and Sadler, 1958; Groombridge, 1986; Günther, 1863, 1895–1902; Gutiérrez et al., 1979; Hahn, 1971; Lynch and Smith, 1965; Martín del Campo, 1935, 1937a, 1938a, 1950; Mertens, 1952b; Meyer, 1969; Mocquard, 1908–1909; Nemuras, 1967; Noguchi, 1909; Schmidt, 1928b; Scott, 1969; H. M. Smith, 1941a; H. M. Smith and Taylor, 1945; Stadelman, 1940; Stuart, 1943, 1948, 1950, 1951, 1954b, 1963; E. H. Taylor, 1951; R. T. Taylor et al., 1974; Uzzell and Starrett, 1958; Villa, 1962, 1984; Werner, 1922; Wilson, 1983; Wilson and Meyer, 1985.

## *Porthidium hespere* (Campbell)

(Fig. 272; Map 91)

LOCAL NAME Colmillo de puerco (Colima).

ENGLISH NAME Western hognosed pitviper.

DISTRIBUTION Mexico. This species is known definitely only from the type locality, 19.2 air-line km northeast of Tecomán, Municipio de Ixlahuacán, Colima (see Map 91). This locality lies between the Río Armeria and Río Salado at an elevation of about 300 m. It is possible that this species ranges into the arid Tepalcatepec Valley in Michoacán and into the southeastern arm of Jalisco that separates Michoacán from Colima.

HABITAT This species inhabits tropical deciduous forest. The forest in this region is low, generally not exceeding 10 m. A harsh dry season extends from November to May. Total annual precipitation is 600–800 mm.

DESCRIPTION *Porthidium hespere* remains known from a single specimen discovered in 1973. This snake is a moderately stout, terrestrial pitviper that has an overall length of 579 mm.

The dorsum of the head is unmarked and pink in coloration. A brownish gray postocular stripe extends from behind the eye across the posterior angle of the jaw. A narrow golden brown vertebral line extends from the nape to the tail. On either side of the vertebral line are 17 greenish brown body blotches that are arranged alternately or opposite each other. These blotches are disposed in paired components with a pale gray ground color bisecting them; a buff or orange ground color is present between blotches, giving a banded appearance that is more distinct posteriorly. The dorsal blotches are connected to form a zig-zag pattern over most of the dorsum. Each element of the dorsal blotches is offset laterally by a small round gray blotch. The gular region is white with a few black flecks. Brownish green mottling is present on the mental and infralabials 1, 5, 6, 9, and 10. Anteriorly, the venter is pale pink, grading to salmon posteriorly. Numerous small dark blotches mottle the venter, especially laterally. The venter of the tail is yellow with dense black stippling on the lateral borders of the subcaudals.

There are 5 intersupraoculars, 10 supralabials, 11 or 12 infralabials, 23 midbody dorsal scale rows, 156 ventrals, and 30 undivided subcaudals.

SIMILAR SPECIES The other species of hognosed pitvipers in Mexico are *P. dunni*, *P. nasutum*, and *P. yucatanicum*. *Porthidium hespere* most closely resembles *P. dunni* and *P. yucatanicum*, and it may be distinguished from these species by having 17 rather than 19 or more dorsal scale rows just anterior to the vent, a middle preocular that is excluded from the orbit and not divided vertically, 4 rather than 2 or 3 intercanthals, and internasals that are moderately rather than strongly elevated. In Mexico *P. nasutum* occurs only in mesic forest

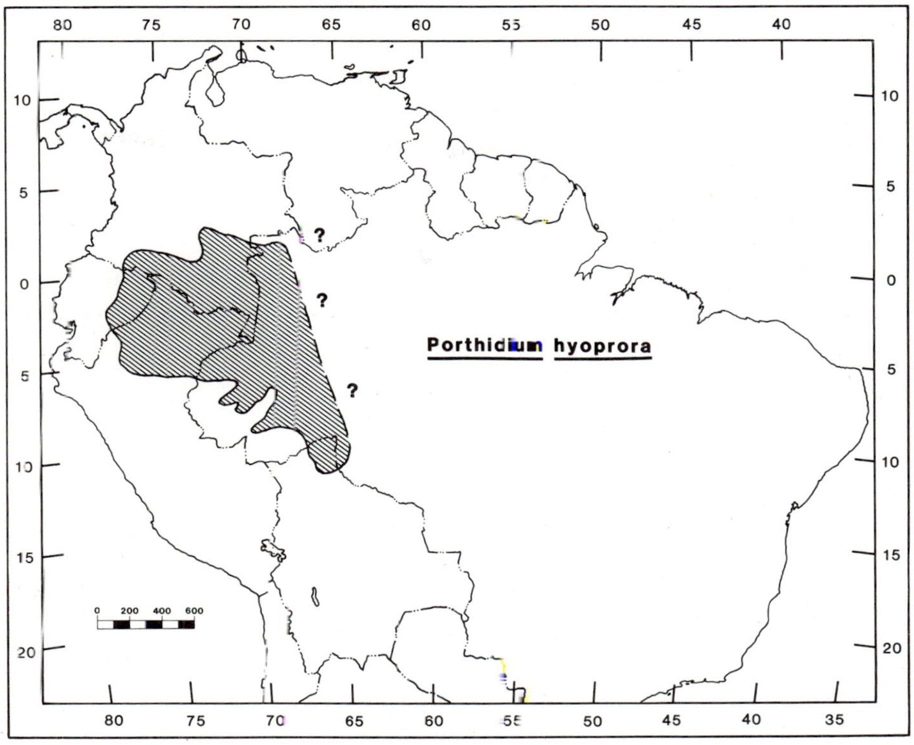


**Map 83.** Distribution of *Porthidium hyoprora* in northwestern South America. How far east this species occurs in the Amazon Basin is open to speculation.

habitats of the Atlantic drainages in the southeastern portion of the country and may be distinguished from *P. hespere* by having a rostral that is about two times higher than wide; in *P. hespere*, the rostral is less than one and one-half times higher than wide and the canthus rostralis is not as strongly curved upward. Because of the large head and stout body, it is possible that small specimens of *Boa constrictor* (Fig. 547) may be mistaken for *P. hespere*. Many features will distinguish *Boa constrictor*, including more than 50 midbody dorsal scale rows, a dorsal pattern of square or rectangular blotches without a pale vertebral line, the presence of anal spurs, and the absence of loreal pits.

REMARKS Despite the apparently restricted habitat of *P. hespere* and the paucity of specimens, this species may be locally abundant, as are other members of the hognosed pitviper group. It is probable that the species is active only by night during or immediately following the brief rainy periods experienced in the region from June to October. The only known specimen of *P. hespere* was misidentified as *Boa constrictor* by a resident of the area. He was subsequently bitten on the right index finger and envenomated. Symptoms included severe pain and swelling and the bite resulted in permanent stiffness of the finger.

REFERENCES Campbell, 1976.

## *Porthidium hyoprora* (Amaral)

(Figs. 273, 306, 307; Map 83)

LOCAL NAMES Bolivia: yoperojobobo. Colombia: equis sapa, jergón. Ecuador: hocico de puerco, namacunchi, ushuculi. Peru: jergón, jergón-shuchupe.

ENGLISH NAME Amazonian hognosed pitviper.

DISTRIBUTION This species occupies low elevations in equatorial forests of the Amazon Basin in Colombia, eastern Ecuador, Peru, Bolivia, and western Brazil in Amazonas and Rondônia (Map 83). It is known from as far north as the Río Tiquié in southeastern Colombia and is likely to occur in southern Venezuela (there is one unsubstantiated report) and perhaps in the southern Guianan region. The known vertical distribution extends from near sea level to at least 1,000 m.

HABITAT Rainforest or very humid tropical forest, usually near water, in leaf litter of elevated ground.

DESCRIPTION *Porthidium hyoprora* is a moderately stout, terrestrial pitviper. The overall length of adults commonly falls between 400 and 500 mm, but the species attains a length of at least 785 mm.

The dorsum of the head is dark reddish brown or grayish brown, sometimes with a coppery tinge. The sides of the head, including the supralabials, are a uniform dark brown. A narrow, poorly defined, pale brown postocular stripe, 3 scales wide, extends to the rictus. The dorsum is reddish brown to yellowish brown with 14–19 dark reddish brown trapezoidal or occasionally rectangular blotches, alternating or joined middorsally, on either side of the body. These blotches are irregularly outlined with yellowish white, extend laterally to scale row 4, and have small darker brown spots (becoming more obscure posteriorly) along their bases. The pale interspaces may be wider or narrower than the blotches. White highlights along the first row of dorsals occasionally coalesce to form a poorly developed ventrolateral stripe, especially in the neck region. In juveniles a red vertebral line is weakly defined and the dorsal blotches lack the pale border. The gulars, mental, and infralabials vary from grayish brown peppered with tan to dirty cream. The ventrals are grayish brown medially, becoming paler laterally, with or without alternating dark brown spots. In some specimens the venter is cream colored with faint scattered dusky brown markings. In juveniles the venter is dark with a paler midventral area. The iris is the same dark brown as the side of the head; the upper portion of the iris is pale brown, matching the postorbital stripe.

There are 4–9 intersupraoculars; 7 or 8 supralabials, the second not fused with the prelacunal; 9–11 infralabials; 21–25 (usually 23) midbody dorsal scale rows; 124–141 ventrals; and 38–57 subcaudals, all or most of which are single.

SIMILAR SPECIES Throughout its range, *P. hyoprora* is sympatric with a number of pitviper species. It is the only member of the hognosed pitviper group known to occur in the Amazon Basin, and its distinctive upturned snout serves to distinguish it at once. *Porthidium hyoprora* may be further distinguished from members of the genus *Bothriopsis* by its color pattern, its shorter nonprehensile tail, and the separation of the prelacunal from the second supralabial. *Bothrops microphthalmus* has a normal, though somewhat upturned, snout, a grayish brown dorsum, paired subcaudals, and a higher average ventral count than *P. hyoprora*. Additionally, the vertical distribution of *B. microphthalmus* makes it unlikely that it coexists with *P. hyoprora*. *Bothrops atrox* has a normal snout, a higher number of ventrals, paired subcaudals, a second supralabial that is fused with the prelacunal and forms the anterior margin of the loreal pit, and a dorsal pattern consisting of square blotches (usually trapezoidal in *P. hyoprora*). *Bothrops sanctaecrucis* has a dorsal pattern of triangular blotches, the second supralabial fused with the prelacunal, a normal snout, a higher number of ventrals, and an unmarked venter. *Lachesis muta* has finely divided distal subcaudals (2–4 to a row posteriorly), a contrasting dorsal pattern, conical keels on the dorsals, 9–15 intersupraoculars, and an unmarked venter. Perhaps the most similar species is *Bothrops brazili*, which has a normal snout, the second supralabial fused with the prelacunal, a higher ventral count, and mostly paired subcaudals.

REMARKS *Porthidium hyoprora* has been taken only from forest floor situations, near water, in primary or mature secondary rainforest. It appears to be common nowhere. When molested, adults tend to thrash to and fro, changing the position of the body and the orientation of the head. They are reluctant to strike, however. The species *Bothrops* (or *Porthidium*) *pessoai*, described by Prado (1939) from Amazonas, Brazil, clearly is based on a specimen of *P. hyoprora*, as indicated by Amaral (1944b).

REFERENCES Amaral, 1935, 1937a, 1944b, 1955c, 1978; Carrillo de Espinoza, 1983; Cope, 1868; Daniel, 1949; Dixon and Soini, 1986; Dunn, 1944a; Fonseca, 1949; Hoge, 1948b, 1953c; Kempff-Mercado, 1975; Machado, 1945b; Meneses, 1974a, 1974b; P. Müller, 1973; Neill, 1966; Nicéforo-María, 1938, 1942; Orcés, 1943, 1948; Pérez-Santos and Moreno, 1986; J. A. Peters, 1960a; J. A. Peters and Orejas-Miranda, 1970; Pifano C. and Romer, 1949b; Prado, 1939, 1945; Renjifo, 1979; Sandner-Montilla, 1985a; Silva Haad, 1982b; Soini, 1974b.

## *Porthidium lansbergii* (Schlegel)

(Figs. 274–276; Map 84)

LOCAL NAMES Colombia: mapaná, mapaná barriga del moncholo, panoco, patoco, patoco saltón, patoquilla veinticuatro, saltona, trabichuri (Emberá tribe), veinticuatro. Panama: patoco, tamagás. Venezuela: daya, deroya (Zulia), macagua amarilla, mapanaré del monte (Isla de Margarita), mapanaré rabo frito, matacaballo, morona, petaca, rabo amarillo, rabo de candela, saltona, sapa, sapa (Trujillo), sapamanare, talla equis.

ENGLISH NAME Lansberg's hognosed pitviper.

DISTRIBUTION This species occupies xeric coastal lowlands of central Panama on the Pacific versant and humid coastal forest on both coasts in eastern Panama. In Colombia it is found on the arid to semi-arid coastal plain from the Río Uré and Río Sinú (Córdoba) in the west, eastward through northern and central Venezuela. In Colombia, *P. lansbergii* is also found in the Río Magdalena Valley as far south as Honda (Tolima). Although records do not exist, the species probably occurs in the Colombian Chocó and in Antioquia on the Caribbean Coast (Map 84). In Venezuela, *P. lansbergii* occupies both the coastal plain and interior valleys of the Cordillera de la Costa, and is found on Isla de Margarita and the Paria Peninsula. The vertical distribution of this species extends to at least 1,270 m.

HABITAT *Porthidium lansbergii* has long been considered an inhabitant of lowland regions, inhabiting arid and semi-arid belts of thorn forest and dry tropical forest. However, it apparently occurs also in humid coastal and foothill forests in eastern Panama, at an elevation approaching 1,000 m in the Pirre Range of the Darién uplands.

DESCRIPTION *Porthidium lansbergii* is a moderately slender, terrestrial pitviper. The maximum recorded length is 900 mm but it is usually 300–500 mm.

The dorsum of the head is typically tan to brown, sometimes with a darker parietal region. The canthus rostralis may be the same shade or darker, occasionally black. The labials are sometimes mottled with white or may be the same shade as the canthus. A tan postorbital stripe is usually present, which extends to the angle of the jaw. A narrow white, yellow, or tan vertebral line extends from just behind the head to the tail in most specimens. A series of 16–25 dark brown quadrangular blotches, sometimes juxtaposed on the middorsum,

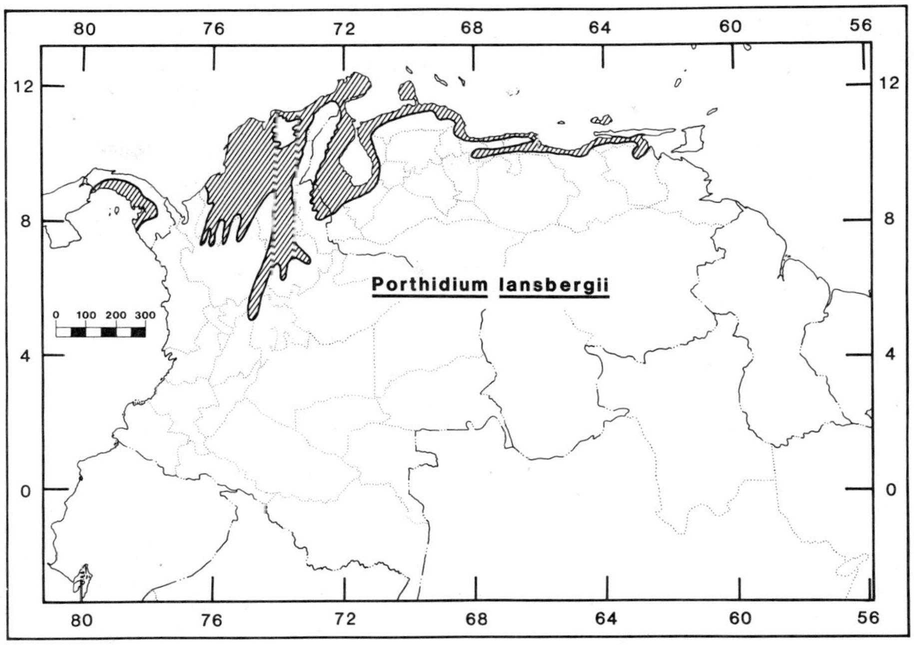


**Map 84.** Distribution of *Porthidium lansbergii* in Panama and northern South America. This species occurs on the Isla de Margarita off the coast of Venezuela.

constitutes the dorsal pattern. In populations along the eastern extreme of the range these blotches are wider than their interspaces. Narrow, dark paraventral extensions usually are present, and these become suffuse on the lateral portions of the ventral scales. *Porthidium lansbergii* exhibits much individual variation, and pale specimens with a pattern that is reduced or even absent are not uncommon. We have observed specimens of a uniformly bright orange color from northern Colombia; the color obscured all cephalic, dorsal, and ventral markings—even the eyes were orange. In typically patterned individuals, the distal portion of the tail may be of a paler color; this is especially so in eastern populations. The venter is usually tan to white with darker mottling that is sometimes restricted to the lateral portions of the ventrals. The infralabials and gular region are often suffused with the supracephalic or canthal coloration. The iris may be brown with paler reticulations, but this varies with color pattern. The tongue is black.

There are 5–7 intersupraoculars, 8–10 supralabials (usually 9), 8–13 infralabials, 23–25 midbody dorsal scale rows (usually 25), 139–161 ventrals, and 27–41 undivided subcaudals.

SIMILAR SPECIES Three other hognosed pitvipers inhabit countries in which *P. lansbergii* is found: *P. hyoprora*, *P. nasutum*, and *P. ophryomegas*. *Porthidium hyoprora* has fewer supralabials (7 or 8 vs. 9 or 10), fewer ventrals (124–141 vs. 139–161), more subcaudals (38–57 vs. 27–41), and is an Amazon Basin inhabitant. *Porthidium nasutum* has fewer ventrals (123–145 vs. 139–161) and a more pronounced nasal appendage; it tends to inhabit more mesic regions, although some areas in Panama and western Colombia may be exceptions to this generalization. *Porthidium ophryomegas* has 2 canthals on each side of the head (1 in *P. lansbergii*), more ventrals (156–174 vs. 139–161), more subcaudals (32–64 vs. 27–41), and a normal snout (upturned in *P. lansbergii*). *Porthidium ophryomegas* probably is not sympatric with *P. lansbergii*; Panama may represent the southern and northern limits of their respective ranges. See also the comments on *Boa constrictor* (Fig. 547) and species of *Leptodeira* (Fig. 557) in Mimics of Venomous Snakes.

REMARKS Two races of *Porthidium lansbergii* are currently recognized. The nominate form, *P. l. lansbergii*, occurs from central Panama to western Venezuela, where it is replaced by *P. l. rozei*—which occupies the remaining portion of species' range. The latter form is distinguished primarily by having fewer ventrals, a pale tan ground color (this varies), and dorsal blotches that are normally wider than their interspaces. *Porthidium lansbergii* has had a confused taxonomic history largely because similar species of *Porthidium* in Central America were incorrectly identified as being conspecific with it. This species frequently is encountered crossing roads at night, and it is most active during the wet season. It is a relatively lethargic snake, generally coiling tightly when confronted.

REFERENCES Alemán G., 1953; Amaral, 1925b, 1927b, 1928, 1929e, 1931a, 1931b, 1937a, 1944a; Angel, 1983; Ayerbe, 1979; Bates, 1928; Bocourt, 1876; Bolaños, 1982, 1983; Boulenger, 1896; Campbell, 1976; Clark, 1942; Daniel, 1949; Dugand, 1975; Duke, 1967; Dunn, 1928, 1940b, 1944a, 1949; Dunn and Bailey, 1939; Elton, 1948; Grocott and Sadler, 1958; Groombridge, 1986; Hoge, 1966; Hoge and Lancini, 1962; Hoge and Romano-Hoge, 1981a; Lancini, 1962d, 1970, 1979; Loveridge, 1928b; Medem, 1969; Milá de la Roca, 1932; Mocquard, 1908–1909; P. Müller, 1973; Nemuras, 1967; Nicéforo-María, 1930c, 1938, 1942; Noguchi, 1909; Pérez-Santos, 1986a, 1986b; Pérez-Santos and Moreno, 1986; J. A. Peters, 1968; J. A. Peters and Orejas-Miranda, 1970; Pifano C. and Romer, 1949b; Prado, 1939; Quintini, 1936; Renjifo, 1979; Rivero-Blanco and Dixon, 1979; Roze, 1964, 1966a, 1970a; Ruthven, 1922; Sandner-Montilla, 1975; Swanson, 1945; Tinoco, 1978; Trejos, 1937; Vellard, 1941; Vetencourt Finol., 1960; Werner, 1922; Wilson and Meyer, 1985.

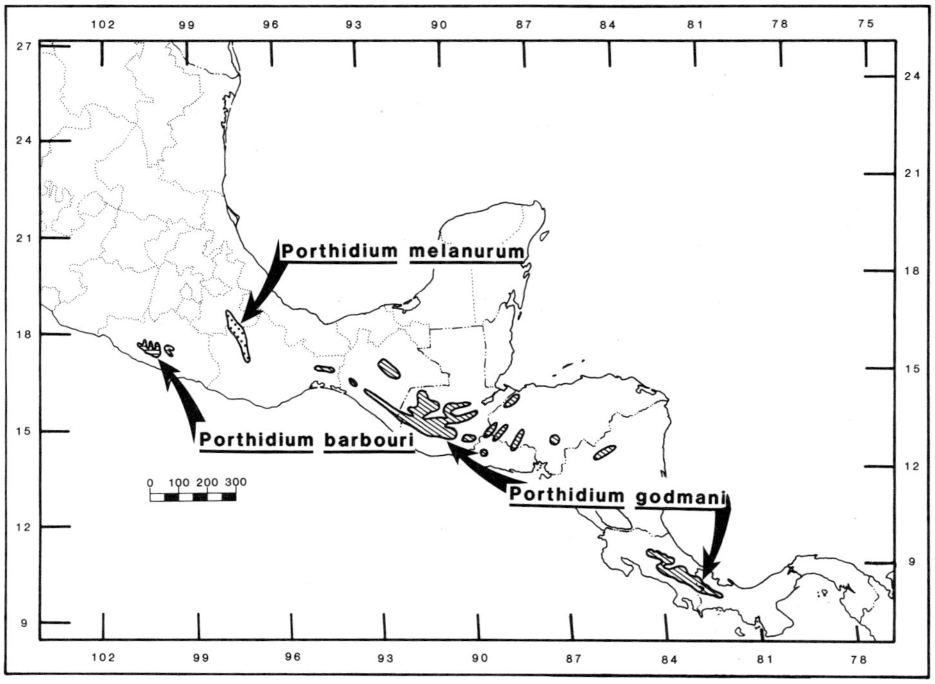


**Map 85.** Distributions of *Porthidium barbouri (horizontal lines), P. godmani (diagonal lines),* and *P. melanurum (stipples)* in southern Mexico and Central America. *Porthidium godmani* occurs as a series of disjunct highland populations and is one of the few species of snakes to inhabit the higher elevations on either side of the Nicaraguan Depression.

### *Porthidium melanurum* (Müller)

(Figs. 277–280, 308, 309; Map 85)

LOCAL NAMES Cornuzuelo, necascuatl, torito (Puebla); víbora de cachitos (Oaxaca).

ENGLISH NAME Black-tailed montane pitviper.

DISTRIBUTION Mexico. This species occupies intermediate elevations from southern Puebla to central Oaxaca. Most of its range falls within the Atlantic drainage; however, in the south it crosses the Continental Divide and includes some of the upper tributaries of the Río Atoyac (Map 85). The vertical distribution of this snake ranges from about 1,600 to 2,400 m.

HABITAT This snake inhabits high arid tropical scrub and tropical deciduous forest in the north and pine-oak forest in the south. Much of the area it inhabits has been overgrazed, cleared, or greatly eroded because of agricultural development. In the more xeric portions of its range, we have taken *P. melanurum* from beneath agaves or from clumps of cacti; to the south, we most frequently have encountered this snake under pine logs.

DESCRIPTION This moderately stout, terrestrial pitviper commonly reaches lengths of between 375 and 500 mm, but specimens may occasionally exceed 550 mm.

The ground color of the head and dorsum ranges from pale ash gray to orangish brown. The top of the head generally has indistinct dark markings that may extend posteriorly to merge with the first dorsal blotch. A dark postocular stripe extends from the lower posterior margin of the eye to the angle of the jaw or beyond. The dark gray to dark brown dorsal blotches are interconnected to form a zig-zag stripe that is offset laterally by 30–46 round blotches. The first lateral blotch is horizontally elongated and may extend for as much as one-third of the body length. The infralabials are strongly marked with dark brown to black spots (Fig. 280), and the ventrals are heavily flecked with gray or brown laterally, less so midventrally. The subcaudals may be flecked uniformly with dark pigment or may be paler midventrally. The coloration of the tail is one of the most conspicuous features of this species. Dorsally the tail tends to be charcoal gray to almost black; ventrolaterally a narrow white or yellow line extends from the vent to the distal portion of the tail, which is marked by a series of yellow or white flecks that are often arrayed in 2–5 incomplete vertical bars. The lateral tail stripe involves scale rows 1 and 2 proximally, and only the parasubcaudal row distally. A distinct narrow, pale band extends around the body just posterior to the anal plate; this band most frequently is broken middorsally.

There are 9–13 intersupraoculars, 10–14 supralabials (usually 10 or 11), 9–12 infralabials (usually 11), 21 midbody dorsal scale rows, 142–149 ventrals, and 36–42 undivided subcaudals.

SIMILAR SPECIES This is a distinctive species that is unlikely to be confused with any other snake in Mexico, except perhaps for two species that are similar in having scales above the eyes that are raised into hornlike or spinelike processes. *Ophryacus undulatus* can be distinguished from *P. melanurum* by the presence of divided (paired) rather than undivided subcaudals, by a supraocular process that is generally (but not always) spinelike rather than somewhat flat and rounded, by gulars and anterior ventrals that tend to be pale with little if any stippling, and by the absence of a pale lateral stripe on the tail. *Bothriechis schlegelii* is an arboreal species with a prehensile tail. This species inhabits mesic lowland forests in the southeastern portion of the

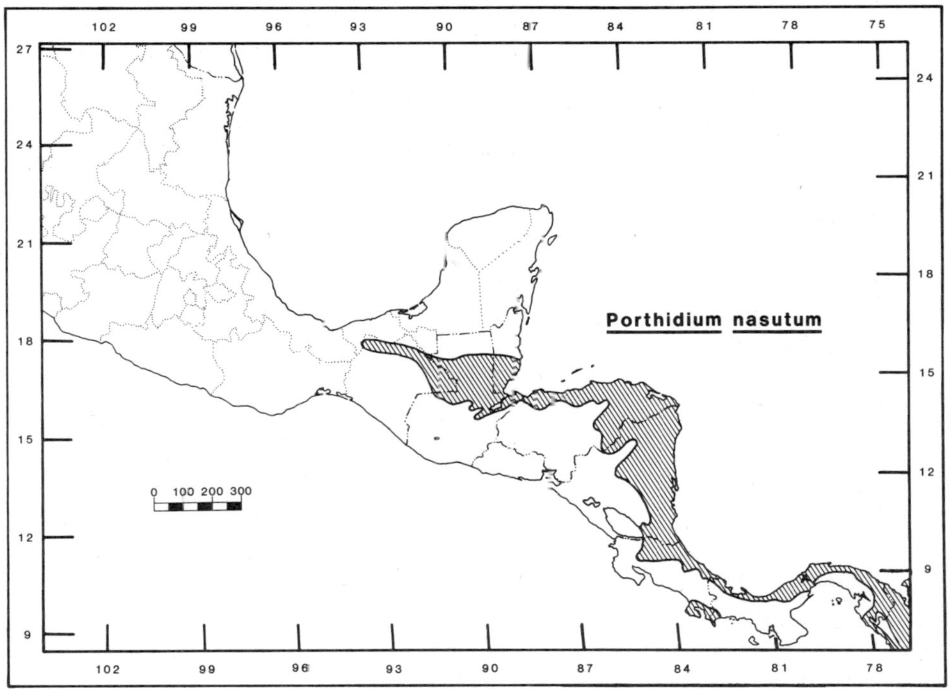


**Map 86.** Distribution of *Porthidium nasutum* in the northern portion of its range in Middle America. For the distribution of this species in South America consult Map 87.

country. Mexican specimens have at least 2 or 3 scales on each side raised into small spinelike processes; have a large, flat supraocular; and tend to have fewer supralabials and more numerous midbody scale rows, ventrals, and subcaudals than *P. melanurum*.

The two most conspicuous features of scalation that serve to distinguish this species from most other Mexican pitvipers are scales that are raised into a single soft hornlike process over the eyes, and a tail spine that is long, pointed, and curved upward.

REMARKS Evening temperatures are cool throughout the range of this snake and we have not found it active after dark. We have encountered it during the early morning or late afternoon coiled near agaves or in the shade of small bushes.

REFERENCES Campbell and Armstrong, 1979; Martín del Campo, 1935, 1937a, 1950; L. Müller, 1923; H. M. Smith, 1940, 1941a; H. M. Smith and Taylor, 1945, 1950b.

## *Porthidium nasutum* (Bocourt)

(Figs. 281–285, 314, 315; Maps 86, 87)

LOCAL NAMES Belize: tommygoff. Colombia: cabeza de candado, cachetona (Chocó), equis-veinticuatro, hilván, patoquilla real, veinticuatro, víbora pajonera. Costa Rica and Panama: tamagá. Ecuador: víbora. Guatemala: chalpate (Petén). Mexico: nauyaca chatilla. Nicaragua: aspid, chatilla.

ENGLISH NAME Rainforest hognosed pitviper.

DISTRIBUTION This species is found at low and moderate elevations of the Atlantic drainage from northwestern Chiapas (and possibly southern Tabasco and eastern Veracruz), Mexico, eastward through northern Guatemala and the Caribbean lowlands of Central America to Panama and northern Colombia. It occurs locally on Pacific drainages of Costa Rica and Panama, and thence southward on the Pacific Coast to Ecuador (Maps 86, 87). Its vertical distribution throughout most of its range extends from near sea level to about 900 m; in Colombia there is a record at 1,880 m.

HABITAT Lowland rainforest and lower montane wet forest.

DESCRIPTION This moderately stout, terrestrial pitviper rarely exceeds 600 mm in total length, and is generally less than 400 mm.

The ground color is tan, brown, reddish brown, yellowish brown, grayish brown, or gray. In juveniles and some adults a pale vertebral line is present; on either side of this line are 15–23 triangular or rectangular blotches arranged either alternately or opposite each other. In some larger specimens, the dorsal blotches and vertebral line may be somewhat faded, especially posteriorly. The venter is mottled heavily with brown. The iris is generally dark brown. Juveniles possess a somewhat paler ground color than adults and a more vivid pattern.

There are 3–7 intersupraoculars, 8–11 (generally 9 or 10) supralabials, 10–13 (generally 11 or 12) infralabials, 21–27 (mode 23) midbody dorsal scale rows, 123–145 ventrals, and 24–41 undivided subcaudals.

SIMILAR SPECIES Most of the other species of hognosed pitvipers found in countries inhabited by *P. nasutum* occur in drier habitats; the exceptions are *P. lansbergii* in eastern Panama and *P. hyoprora*, an Amazon Basin resident not sympatric with *P. nasutum*. *Por-*

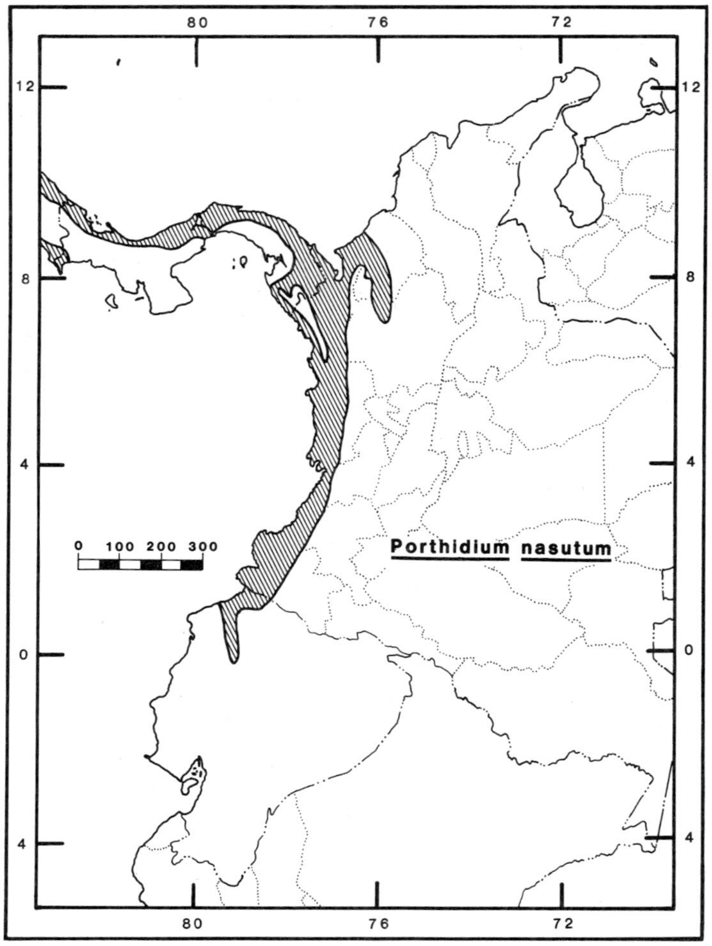


**Map 87.** Distribution of *Porthidium nasutum* in the southern portion of its range in lower Central America and northwestern South America.

*thidium nasutum* differs from all other hognosed pitvipers in the degree to which the tip of the snout is upturned; the rostral is about one and one-half (or more) times higher than broad. *Porthidium ophryomegas* differs from *P. nasutum* in having more ventrals (156–174 vs. 123–145), more dark dorsal body blotches (24–40 vs. 16–23), and usually more midbody dorsal scales (mode 25 vs. mode 23). *Porthidium dunni*, *P. lansbergii*, and *P. yucatanicum* usually have more ventrals than *P. nasutum* (141–158, 139–161, and 141–155 vs. 123–145, respectively), and *P. lansbergii* and *P. yucatanicum* most frequently have 25 rather than 23 midbody dorsal scale rows.

Other species of terrestrial pitvipers that may be sympatric with *P. nasutum* throughout much of its range include *Bothrops asper* and *P. nummifer*. *Bothrops asper* has more ventrals, subcaudals, and midbody dorsal scale rows, a second supralabial that is fused with the prelacunal, divided (paired) subcaudals, a rostral that is less than one and one-half times higher than broad, and a pattern consisting of triangles laterally without a pale vertebral line. *Porthidium nummifer* is a much stouter snake that possesses a rostral that is broader than high, 7 or more intersupraoculars, and a pattern of dark middorsal blotches that are not bisected by a narrow pale vertebral line. The keels of middorsals in *P. nummifer*, especially large adults, tend to be knoblike. See also the comments about *Boa constrictor* (Fig. 547) and *Leptodeira* sp. (Fig. 557) in Mimics of Venomous Snakes.

REMARKS This species may be active either by day or at night. Owing to its coloration and small size it is often almost imperceptible on the forest floor. It frequently is found coiled in patchy sunlight in leaf litter. Although this species is terrestrial, it occasionally may climb into low bushes and shrubs. This snake generally is not considered capable of delivering a fatal bite, but a few human fatalities have been reported.

REFERENCES Acosta-Solís, 1944; Alvarez del Toro, 1983; Amaral, 1925a, 1927b, 1927d, 1929a, 1929e, 1931a, 1931b, 1935, 1937a, 1944a; Barbour and Brooks, 1923; Barbour and Loveridge, 1929b; Bocourt, 1868, 1876; Bolaños, 1971, 1982, 1983, 1984; Boulenger, 1896, 1898b; Campbell, 1976; Cendrero et al., 1972; H. C. Clark, 1925, 1942; Cope, 1871, 1876a, 1879, 1887; Daniel, 1949; Ditmars, 1930, 1937; Duellman, 1963; Duke, 1967; Dunn, 1933, 1940b, 1944a, 1949; Dunn and Bailey, 1939; Dunn and Emlen, 1932; Elton, 1948; García, 1896; George, 1930b; Grocott and Sadler, 1958; Groombridge, 1986; Günther, 1895–1902; Gutiérrez et al., 1979; Henderson and Hoevers, 1975; Heyer, 1967; Lee, 1980; Loveridge, 1928b; Martín del Campo, 1950; McCranie and Porras, 1978; Medem, 1969; Meyer, 1969; Minton and Minton, 1980; Mocquard, 1908–1909; P. Müller, 1973; Neill, 1965; Nemuras, 1967; Nicéforo-María, 1938, 1942; Orcés, 1942, 1943, 1948; Patzelt, 1979; Pérez-Santos, 1986a; Pérez-Santos and Moreno, 1986; J. A. Peters, 1960a; Picado T., 1931, 1936; Pifano C. and Romer, 1949b; Porras et al., 1981; Posada-Arango, 1889a, 1889b; Prado, 1939; Rendahl and Vestergren, 1940, 1941; Rodas, 1938; Schmidt, 1933b, 1941; Scott, 1969; H. M. Smith, 1941a, 1943; H. M. Smith and Taylor, 1945; Stuart, 1950, 1958, 1963; E. H. Taylor, 1951, 1954; R. T. Taylor et al., 1974; Trejos, 1937; Vetencourt Finol., 1960; Villa, 1962, 1984; Werner, 1922; Wettstein, 1934; Wilson, 1983; Wilson and McCranie, 1984; Wilson and Meyer, 1985.

### *Porthidium nummifer* (Rüppell)

(Figs. 286–289, 304, 305; Map 90)

LOCAL NAMES Mano de piedra. Belize: jumping tommygoff. Costa Rica, Honduras, and Nicaragua: timbo, patoca. Guatemala: cantil sapo (southern); chinchintor (northern), tamagás; mococh (northern El Quiché); sulcuat (Quezaltenango). Mexico: mano de metate (Oaxaca and southern Veracruz); mano de metate, nauyaca, saltadora (Chiapas); metapilcoate, metapilcuate (corruptions from Náhuatl); metlapilocóatl (Náhuatl); tepocho, tepotzo, tepoxo (Orizaba region); víbora sorda. Nicaragua: cabeza de sapo.

ENGLISH NAME Jumping pitviper.

DISTRIBUTION Low, moderate, and intermediate elevations of the Atlantic drainage from San Luis Potosí, Mexico, to the Canal Zone of Panama; on the Pacific from southeastern Oaxaca, Mexico, through Chiapas and Guatemala to El Salvador, and in Costa Rica and Panama (see Map 90). The vertical distribution ranges from about 40 to 1,600 m.

HABITAT Mesic forests, including tropical rainforest (tropical moist and wet forests) and lower cloud forest (subtropical wet forest).

DESCRIPTION This is an exceedingly stout, terrestrial pitviper. Adults commonly are 400–600 mm in overall length and may attain lengths of over 800 mm. Specimens from the northern versant of Nuclear Central America and Costa Rica appear to reach the greatest lengths, whereas those from the Pacific versant of Nuclear Central America are relatively small.

The dorsum of the head is pale to dark brown, with or without darker markings. A dark brown postocular stripe extends from behind the eye to the angle of the jaw. In snakes from the northern part of the range the postocular stripe generally is lower on the side of the head and may involve the uppermost portions of the last 2–3 supralabials as well as 2–4 lower temporals; in the south, the postocular stripe tends to be situated higher or is arched, excluding the supralabials and involving 0–3 lower temporals. The posterior extent of the postocular stripe is variable, but it frequently continues well posterior to the angle of the jaw to a point over the mandibular articulation. A pair of dark brown nape blotches frequently is fused posteriorly. A series of about 15–20 dark brown rhomboidal dorsal blotches extends onto the tail. Some dorsal blotches may be fused with one another to form a partial zig-zag stripe. Snakes from the Atlantic versant of Chiapas, Mexico, to Nicaragua, and from Costa Rica and Panama, tend to have lateral blotches that coalesce with the dorsal blotches; whereas the lateral blotches in snakes from the Pacific versant of southeastern Oaxaca and Chiapas, Mexico, Guatemala, and El Salvador frequently are separate from the dorsal blotches. The ground color is generally brown or grayish brown, although snakes from southeastern Oaxaca and the Pacific versant of Guatemala may be pinkish brown, reddish brown, or purplish brown. Snakes frequently become darker with age and may become totally melanistic in some parts of the range. The venter ranges from almost immaculate to heavily mottled with brown, but small ventrolateral blotches are almost invariably present. The subcaudals are mostly dark except for a few pale markings or a proximal irregular, pale midventral stripe.

There are 7–12 intersupraoculars and the supraoculars are frequently fragmented into numerous small keeled scales (Fig. 305); when present the supraoculars are long and narrow. There are 9–12 (usually 10 or 11) supralabials, 10–14 (usually 11 or 12) infralabials, 23–31 midbody dorsal scale rows (modes vary among populations of this wide-ranging species), 114–135 ventrals (the lower numbers characteristic of northern populations), and 22–39 undivided subcaudals (northern populations have fewer than southern populations). This species has an extremely rugose appearance owing to the prominent high keeling of the dorsals. This keeling is best developed on the vertebral and paravertebral scale rows of larger specimens. Small scales, termed nasorostrals, often are present between the rostral and nasal. A series of 2–4 nasorostrals intervenes to completely preclude rostral-nasal contact in southern populations. Snakes from the northern part of the range may have 0–2 nasorostrals, and the rostral and nasal usually make at least partial contact.

SIMILAR SPECIES *Porthidium nummifer* is a distinctive snake that is rarely confused with most other pitvipers. Two species occurring in lower Central America, *P. picadoi* and *Lachesis muta*, superficially resemble *P. nummifer* in having strongly keeled dorsals. *Porthidium picadoi* possesses more ventrals (141–155 vs. 114–135) than *P. nummifer*, the middle preocular is in contact with the orbit (excluded in *P. nummifer* by upper preocular), a single row of anterior subfoveals separates the prelacunal from the anterior supralabials (2 or 3 rows in *P. nummifer*), and no nasorostrals are present to separate (at least partially) the rostral from the prenasals (2–4 nasorostrals intervene to preclude rostral-prenasal contact in *P. nummifer* from Costa Rica and Panama). Furthermore, in *P. picadoi* the supraoculars are long and narrow (often subdivided into numerous keeled scales in Costa Rican specimens of *P. nummifer*) and the lateral blotches are distinctly separated from the dorsal blotches (often coalesced in *P. nummifer*). *Lachesis muta* may be distinguished from *P. nummifer* by the finely divided posterior subcaudals (Fig. 316), the immaculate venter, and the greater number of ventrals, subcaudals, and midbody dorsal scale rows; this species also attains a length of over 2 m. *Porthidium olmec* of southern Veracruz, Mexico, is morphologically similar to *P. nummifer*, to which it is obviously closely related (see Similar Species and Remarks for *P. olmec*). See also the species accounts for *Bothrops asper* and *Porthidium nasutum*, and the discussion of *Boa constrictor* (Fig. 547) in Mimics of Venomous Snakes.

REMARKS This snake's common name is derived from its purported ability to launch itself great distances when striking; reportedly it can strike over distances equal to or greater than its body length. These claims are greatly exaggerated and in actuality this species can strike only a little over one-half of its length. Some specimens will display a rather dramatic open-mouth threat when provoked (Fig. 287). This nocturnal species is usually slow moving and nonaggressive, and possesses relatively short fangs. Individuals generally are encountered coiled on the forest floor, but there is a report of a specimen taken from a tree cavity 3 m above the ground. Despite the impressive size attained by this species, its venom may not be as potent as that of most other species of pitvipers. Several victims of snakebite in Guatemala and Honduras suffered only localized pain and swelling, were discharged from the hospital in several days, and suffered no permanent damage.

This species has had a confused taxonomic history and the relationships of the various populations are still not well understood. Currently, three subspecies are recognized: *P. n. nummifer* (Fig. 286) of the Atlantic versant from San Luis Potosí to central Oaxaca, Mexico; *P. n. mexicanum* (Fig. 287) of the Caribbean drainage from Chiapas, Mexico, to central Panama; and *P. n. occiduum* (Figs. 288, 289) of the Pacific slopes of Chiapas, Guatemala, and El Salvador, and both the Pacific and Atlantic slopes in extreme southeastern Oaxaca. *Porthidium olmec* and *P. picadoi* are closely related.

REFERENCES Alvarez del Toro, 1972, 1983; Barbour and Loveridge, 1929b; Bocourt, 1876; Bolaños, 1971, 1982, 1983, 1984; Booth, 1959; Boulenger, 1896; Burger, 1950; Cendrero et al., 1972; H. C. Clark, 1942; Cope, 1861, 1865, 1876a, 1887; Cuesta Terron, 1930a; Dugès, 1896; Duke, 1967; Dunn, 1939; Dunn and Bailey, 1939; Dunn and Emlen, 1932; Elton, 1948; Fischer, 1880; Garman, 1884a; George, 1930a, 1930b; Greene, 1972; Grocott and Sadler, 1958; Groombridge, 1986; Günther, 1895–1902; Gutiérrez et al., 1979; Henderson and Hoevers, 1975; Hoge and Romano-Hoge, 1981a; Jan, 1859a; Jiménez-Porras, 1964, 1967; Kaiser and Michl, 1971; Lee, 1980; March, 1929a; Martín del Campo, 1935, 1937a, 1938a, 1950, 1984; Mertens, 1952b; Meyer, 1969; Mocquard, 1908–1909; Neill, 1960, 1965; Neill and Allen, 1960; Ocaranza, 1930; Pérez-Higareda et al., 1985; W. C. H. Peters, 1861; Picado T., 1931; Ramírez-Bautista et al., 1981; Rodas, 1938; Rokosky, 1941; Rüppell, 1845; Savage, 1980; Schmidt, 1941; Scott, 1969; Shannon, 1951; H. M. Smith, 1941a; H. M. Smith and Taylor, 1945, 1966; Stuart, 1935, 1948, 1950, 1963; Sumichrast, 1864a, 1870, 1873, 1882; Tanner, 1957; E. H. Taylor 1949, 1951, 1954; R. T. Taylor et al., 1974; Trejos, 1937; Villa, 1962, 1984; Werman, 1984b; Werner, 1922; Wilson, 1983; Wilson and Meyer, 1985.

### *Porthidium olmec* Pérez-Higareda, Smith, and Juliá-Zertuche

(Figs. 290, 291; Map 90)

LOCAL NAME Mano de piedra.

ENGLISH NAME Olmecan pitviper.

DISTRIBUTION This species occurs at low to moderate elevations of the Sierra de los Tuxtlas in southern Veracruz, Mexico (see Map 90). It is known from elevations of 530–1,100 m, but probably ranges to the summits of the higher peaks and crests in the region, several of which exceed 1,500 m.

HABITAT Upper rainforest (lower montane wet forest) and cloud forest.

DESCRIPTION This is an extremely stout, terrestrial pitviper; males are known to reach a total length of 500 mm, and females 770 mm.

The dorsal ground color between the dorsal blotches is red, reddish gray, or orangish tan, becoming pink to pinkish gray on the sides. A dark brown postocular stripe extends diagonally from the lower posterior edge of the eye over the rictus to the posterior ventrolateral surface of the head; the postocular stripe may touch the posterior portion of the last supraocular. A pair of elongated, dark brown nuchal blotches are often fused posteriorly, followed by 19–23 dark brown rhomboidal or diamond-shaped dorsal blotches.

The dorsal blotches are sometimes bordered narrowly by white or pale yellow and, in about one-half of the known specimens, they may be fused anteriorly to form a sinuous or zig-zag band; in other specimens the dorsal blotches are separated from each other. A series of 19–23 vertically elongated chestnut brown to black lateral blotches are opposite the dorsal blotches and usually coalesce with them or are separated by 1 scale. The lateral blotches sometimes are highlighted by a narrow white or yellow border. The top of the head varies from orangish tan to dark gray. Some specimens have small, rounded, reddish brown spots below the eye and/or on the lower jaw. The underside of the head is white, yellow, or creamy tan, often with dense brown or black peppering on the mental, anterior infralabials, and anterior portion of the chinshields. The belly is white or cream with irregular brown mottling that becomes darker posteriorly. A series of irregular cinnamon blotches that contain black speckling is present on each side, covering the edges of 2–4 ventrals and dorsal scale rows 1–2. This series of ventrolateral blotches alternates with the dark lateral blotches. In large adults the tail tip is charcoal gray and the subcaudals are dark gray to black; in juveniles the distal portion of the tail is yellow. The iris is gray or copper-colored with fine black specks. The tongue is red with gray splotches on the anterior stem and tips.

The rostral is triangular and almost always separated from the prenasals by 3/3 nasorostrals. The supracephalic scales are small and strongly keeled. There are 4 internasals and 2/2 canthals with raised borders. Two small scales intervene on each side between the posteriormost canthal and supraoculars. The supraoculars are either very narrow and elongated or fragmented into small scales of about the same size as the surrounding supracephalic scales; there are 8 or 9 scales between the supraoculars. A single loreal is present on each side. There are generally 3/3 preoculars; the upper is the largest, the middle is separate from the supralacunal, and the lower is reduced and may be broken into several tiny scales. The subocular is most frequently a single elongated, crescent-shaped scale and there are 2 or 3 interoculabials. Ten to 12 (mode 11) supralabials and 11–13 (usually either 12 or 13) infralabials are present. The chinshields are separated from the first of 2 or 3 preventrals by 3 or 4 pairs of gulars. There are 28 (sometimes 27) anterior, 23 midbody, and 19 posterior dorsal scale rows; 103–115 ventrals; and 25–33 undivided subcaudals. Each dorsal possesses a keel that reaches the scale tip and is weakly knobbed.

SIMILAR SPECIES Few snakes in the area may be confused with this robust pitviper. *Bothrops asper* is more slender, it has more ventrals and subcaudals, the subcaudals are divided, the supraocular is well developed, the second supralabial is fused with the prelacunal, and the pattern does not consist of dark brown middorsal blotches. *Boa constrictor* (Fig. 547) lacks the large loreal pits characteristic of pitvipers; has more numerous midbody dorsal scale rows, ventrals, and subcaudals; and possesses anal spurs. Other snakes occurring in the Sierra de los Tuxtlas that may be mistaken as dangerously venomous are *Leptodeira* (Fig. 559) and *Xenodon* (Figs. 563, 564).

The geographic range of *P. nummifer* closely approaches that of *P. olmec* in the highlands of northern Oaxaca (see Map 90); these species obviously are related, but Oaxacan specimens of *P. nummifer* differ from *P. olmec* in having usually 2 or fewer nasorostrals, more than 115 ventrals, usually 25 anterior dorsal scale rows, and most lateral body blotches separated from the dorsal blotches by 1 or 2 scales.

REMARKS The status of *P. olmec* is uncertain. Although it is allopatric and distinguishable from populations of *P. nummifer*, it is possible that it should be recognized as a subspecies of the latter.

In captivity *P. olmec* is shy and tends to lower and hide the head upon initial contact; if greatly irritated, it will raise the head and vibrate the tail.

REFERENCES Andrle, 1964; Burger, 1950; Flores Villela et al., 1987; Pérez-Higadera [*sic*] et al., 1987; Pérez-Higareda, 1978; Pérez-Higareda et al., 1985.

## *Porthidium ophryomegas* (Bocourt)

(Figs. 292, 310, 311; Map 88)

LOCAL NAMES Costa Rica: toboba chinga. El Salvador and Nicaragua: corníz, tamagás. Guatemala: víbora castellana (Motagua Valley).

ENGLISH NAME Slender hognosed pitviper.

DISTRIBUTION South-central Guatemala possibly to eastern Panama at low and moderate elevations of the Pacific drainage; on the Atlantic, in portions of several dry rainshadow valleys in Guatemala and Honduras including the Río Motagua, Río Ulúa, Río Aguán, and Río Patuca (Map 88). The vertical distribution extends from near sea level to about 1,000 m.

HABITAT This species frequents seasonally dry forests including tropical dry and arid forests, subtropical dry forest, and the drier portions of tropical moist forests. There have been reports of this species from more mesic habitats as well, but its distribution in habitats such as subtropical wet and moist forests is extremely restricted at best and we suspect that some of these reports are based on specimens with incorrect locality data or misidentifications.

DESCRIPTION This relatively slender hognosed pitviper commonly reaches 400–500 mm in total length; an exceptional specimen measures 770 mm overall (UTA R-15293).

The dorsum of the head is tan, gray, or brown. In paler specimens small dark brown spots are present on top of the head, often arranged in pairs on the prefrontal, frontal, and parietal regions. A pair of dark brown nape blotches in the occipital region extend posteriorly; these blotches often coalesce with each other or with the first paravertebral body blotches. A dark brown postocular stripe extends from behind the eye to the angle of the jaw and curves downward to involve most of the supralabials behind the posterior edge of the eye. The postocular stripe is pale bordered below with a white-to-yellow marking extending from below the eye downward to the mouthline and thence posteriorly 3–5 supralabials along the lip margin. Paler snakes tend to have a pale line bordering the postocular stripe above. Distinct dark spots generally are present below the loreal pit and below the eye.

A narrow white, yellow, or rust-brown vertebral line extends from just behind the head onto the tail. A series of 24–40 rectangular dark brown to almost black dorsal blotches are arranged opposite one another or alternate on either side of the vertebral line. These blotches may have a narrow white border that extends more-or-less perpendicularly from the vertebral line. As in all members of the hognosed pitviper group, most of the dorsal blotches are composed of paired components, with the ground color partially bisecting each blotch from the ventral side. The ground color is tan, brown, gray, or grayish brown, usually becoming paler paravertebrally between blotches. Some large specimens become so dark that the body pattern is practially obscured. Dark round lateral blotches offset each of the dorsal blotches, and a series of irregular ventrolateral blotches coalesces with the ventral pigmentation. The venter of most specimens is mottled heavily with gray or dark brown. The infralabials and gulars in particular tend to be dark, with strikingly contrasting white or yellow bars or spots. The ventrals are pale with strong mottling, particularly along the anterior portion of each scale, and blotches frequently connect the brown pigment of one ventral with that of another. The proximal one-half to two-thirds of the tail is densely mottled, but distally the tail becomes mostly pale with diffuse brown speckling.

There are 5 or 6 intersupraoculars, 8–10 supralabials (usually 9 or 10), 10–13 infralabials (usually 11 or 12), 23–27 (mode 25) midbody dorsal scale rows, 156–174 ventrals, and 32–64 undivided subcaudals.

SIMILAR SPECIES Two other hognosed pitvipers may inhabit countries in which *P. ophryomegas* is found: *P. lansbergii* and *P. nasutum*. These species may be distinguished from *P. ophryomegas* by the presence of a single canthal (Fig. 315) on each side (2 on each

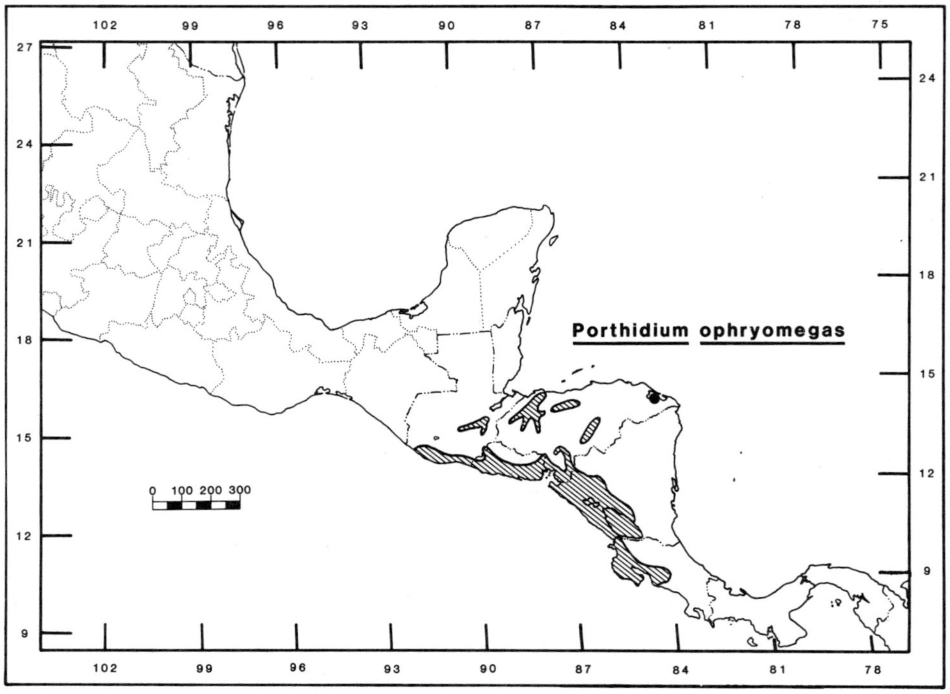


**Map 88.** Distribution of *Porthidium ophryomegas* in Central America. This species occurs mainly along the west coast, but also in some of the drier rainshadow valleys of the Atlantic drainage. Reports of specimens from Panama may not be valid.

side in *P. ophryomegas*; see Fig. 311), fewer ventrals (123–145 in *P. nasutum*, 139–161 in *P. lansbergii*, and 156–174 in *P. ophryomegas*), and an upturned snout (strongly elevated in *P. nasutum*, only slightly so in *P. lansbergii*). Furthermore, *P. nasutum* (see Map 87) occurs in more mesic habitats than *P. ophryomegas* (Map 88), and *P. lansbergii* reaches the northern (and western) terminus of its range in eastern Panama (see Map 84). Other species of pitvipers occurring within or near the range of *P. ophryomegas* lack the pale vertebral line. *Boa constrictor* (Fig. 547) has more numerous dorsal scale rows, lacks a loreal pit, and attains a greater size.

REMARKS This species has been encountered most frequently crossing roads at night. It is most active during the wet season. This is an alert snake that is quick to strike. There are no reported deaths from bites by this species.

REFERENCES Amaral, 1927b, 1929e, 1937a; Barbour and Loveridge, 1929b; Bolaños, 1982, 1983, 1984; Campbell, 1976; Cope, 1861, 1887; Ditmars, 1930; Dunn, 1928; Groombridge, 1986; Günther, 1895–1902; Heyer, 1967; Mertens, 1952b; Meyer, 1969; Mocquard, 1908–1909; P. Müller, 1973; Picado T., 1931, 1936; Pifano C. and Romer, 1949b; Rodas, 1938; Scott, 1969; Stuart, 1963; E. H. Taylor, 1951, 1954; R. T. Taylor et al., 1974; Villa, 1962, 1984; Werner, 1922; Wettstein, 1934; Wilson, 1983; Wilson and Meyer, 1985.

### *Porthidium picadoi* (Dunn)

(Figs. 293, 294; Map 89)

LOCAL NAMES Costa Rica: mano de piedra, patoca, timbó (these names also apply to *P. nummifer* in parts of its range).

ENGLISH NAME Picado's pitviper.

DISTRIBUTION This species occurs at low and moderate elevations in Costa Rica and western Panama, including the Cordillera de Tilarán, Cordillera Central, and Cordillera de Talamanca (Map 89). It appears to be restricted to the Atlantic drainage except in the Cordillera de Tilarán and the mountains surrounding the Valle Central, in which San José is located. In Panama it is known only from the extreme northwestern portion of the country in the provinces of Bocas del Toro and Chiriquí. The vertical distribution ranges from about 50 to a little over 1,500 m.

HABITAT Subtropical moist and wet forests, tropical moist and wet forests, and montane wet forest.

DESCRIPTION This is an extremely thick-bodied snake, although not quite as stout as its close relative, *P. nummifer*. *Porthidium picadoi* commonly reaches 750 mm in overall length and may exceed 1 m: a specimen (UTA R-15617) in the herpetological collection of the University of Texas at Arlington measured 1,078 mm in total length before preservation.

The top of the head is dark brown or auburn with or without irregular darker brown markings. A broad dark brown postorbital stripe extends from behind the eye over and well beyond the angle of the jaw, and involves the upper portions of the posteriormost 2–3 supralabials. The postorbital stripe is narrowly outlined in black and bordered with pale yellow above and below. The side of the head below the postorbital stripe is pale yellow with heavy brown or gray speckling. A dark spot generally is present below the eye and a smaller spot is situated below the loreal pit. The infralabials are white

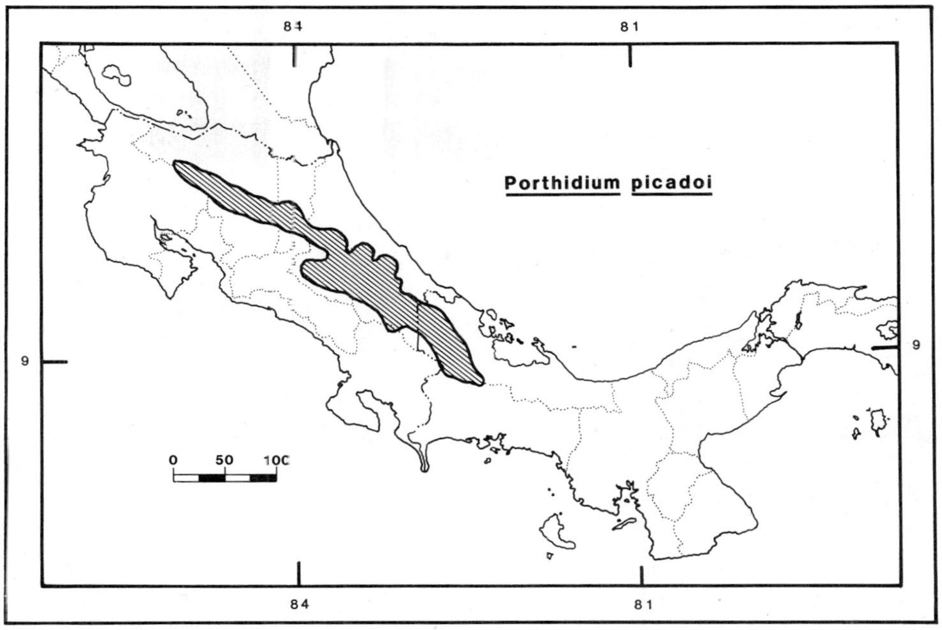


Map 89. Distribution of *Porthidium picadoi* in Costa Rica and Panama.

with 2–4 dark brown blotches along the lower jaw. The ground color is medium to chestnut brown with pale reddish brown contiguous with the dark dorsal blotches. Yellow markings intervene to distinctly separate most lateral blotches from dorsal blotches, especially anteriorly. The usual 25–30 dorsal blotches often are connected anteriorly to form a zig-zag pattern. Dark brown markings are evident on the tail of smaller specimens, but in large adults the tail may be uniformly dark brown. The venter is white to yellow with an irregular brown checkerboard pattern that becomes more intense posteriorly. The subcaudals are uniformly dark brown, gray, or black. The iris is dark brown to almost black. Juveniles are relatively similar to adults but tend to have a paler ground color, which produces a more distinctly contrasting pattern.

There are 7–11 intersupraoculars (the supraoculars are long and narrow), 9 or 10 supralabials, 9–13 infralabials, 25–29 midbody dorsal scale rows, 141–155 ventrals, and 31–40 undivided subcaudals.

SIMILAR SPECIES *Porthidium nummifer* is quite similar superficially to *P. picadoi*, and these species may be sympatric in some areas. *Porthidium picadoi* is distinguished most easily from sympatric *P. nummifer* (characteristics of *P. nummifer* within parentheses) by having 141–155 ventrals (121–135), no nasorostrals separating the prenasals from the rostral (present in Costa Rican specimens), 1 row of anterior subfoveals separating the prelacunal from anterior supralabials (2 or 3 rows), the middle preocular in contact with the orbit (excluded from the orbit by the upper preocular), long and narrow supraoculars (most frequently subdivided into numerous keeled scales in Costa Rican specimens), lateral blotches distinctly separated from dorsal blotches (often coalesced), and a general ground color of reddish brown or chestnut brown (deep coffee brown). Because of the rugosity of the dorsals and vaguely similar patterns and coloration, it is possible for *P. picadoi* to be confused with *Lachesis muta*. However, *L. muta* is a proportionately more slender species that reaches a much greater length, has finely divided posterior subcaudals (Fig. 316), and possesses an immaculate venter (see the genus account for other distinctive features of *Lachesis*).

REMARKS This species occupies a diverse number of habitats over a considerable elevational range (see Distribution and Habitat), but seems to be common nowhere. Snakes encountered in the field or recently captured are occasionally pugnacious, but this species generally is calm and slow moving unless provoked. We have observed *P. picadoi* to gape when threatened. The few specimens for which there are adequate collecting data were taken from or near primary forest coiled in leaf litter at the base of large trees with buttressed roots or in shallow depressions in the ground.

REFERENCES Bolaños, 1982, 1983, 1984; Dunn, 1939; Gutiérrez et al., 1979; Heyer, 1967; Jiménez-Porras, 1967; Savage, 1980; Scott, 1969; E. H. Taylor, 1951, 1954; R. T. Taylor et al., 1974; Werman, 1984b.

## *Porthidium tzotzilorum* (Campbell)

(Figs. 295–297; Map 90)

LOCAL NAMES Nauyaca del Frío, víbora.

ENGLISH NAME Tzotzil montane pitviper.

DISTRIBUTION Intermediate elevations on the relatively flat tableland of the Meseta Central of Chiapas, Mexico (Map 90). The vertical distribution ranges from 2,050 to 2,500 m.

HABITAT Humid pine-oak forest.

DESCRIPTION This moderately stout, terrestrial pitviper probably does not exceed 500 mm in total length.

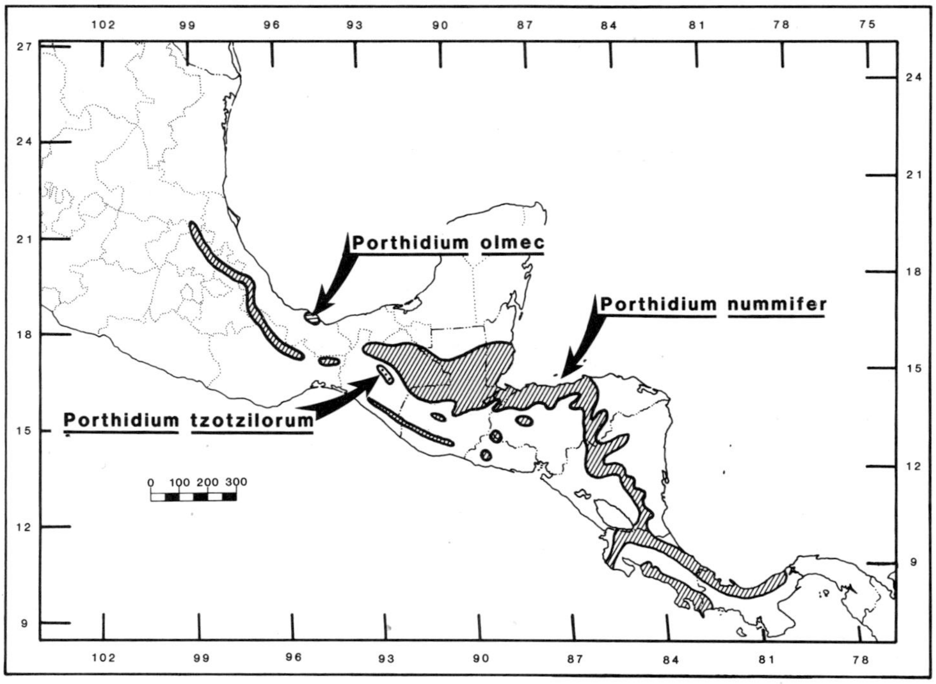


**Map 90.** Distributions of *Porthidium nummifer* (*diagonal lines*), *P. olmec* (*horizontal lines*), and *P. tzotzilorum* (*stipples*) in Mexico and Central America.

The ground color may be either dark grayish brown or rust. The 29–49 (mean 40) distinctive small lateral body blotches occupy 2–3 scales. The first lateral body blotch is highly variable and may extend up to 10 scale lengths. The dark brown anterior dorsal blotches are often fused to form a zig-zag stripe. The infralabials and gular area generally are mottled heavily and the ventrals often tend to become darker posteriorly. A dark postocular stripe extends from behind the eye to the angle of the jaw and is pale bordered above and below. The distal one-half to two-thirds of the subcaudals are pale.

The median scale in the frontal region is large and there are generally 3 intersupraoculars, 9–11 (mode 9) supralabials, 9–12 (mode 11) infralabials, 19–23 (mode 21) midbody dorsal scale rows, 120–134 ventrals, and 23–36 undivided subcaudals.

SIMILAR SPECIES The only other species of pitviper with which *P. tzotzilorum* may be sympatric is *P. godmani*, which can be distinguished most easily from *P. tzotzilorum* by the presence of relatively large lateral blotches that involve 5–7 scales and a postocular stripe that is distinctly pale bordered below, but not above. Hognosed pitvipers that inhabit Chiapas, Mexico, *P. nasutum* and *P. dunni*, occur at much lower elevations, generally less than 900 m, and possess a sharp canthus and elevated snout, a rostral that is higher than wide, 23 midbody dorsal scale rows, and a pattern that consists of paired blotches bisected by a narrow vertebral stripe.

REMARKS This species occurs in seasonally dry forest consisting predominantly of tall pines and/or epiphyte-laden oaks. *Porthidium tzotzilorum* appears to be secretive and is encountered most frequently under logs and rocks.

REFERENCES Alvarez del Toro, 1972, 1983, (in part, discussed under *P. godmani*); Campbell, 1985.

## *Porthidium yucatanicum* (Smith)

(Figs. 298, 299; Map 91)

LOCAL NAMES Chac-can (Mayan name), víbora.

ENGLISH NAME Yucatán hognosed pitviper.

DISTRIBUTION Mexico; the northern half of the Yucatán Peninsula (Map 91; see regional account for Belize). The vertical distribution ranges from a few meters above sea level to about 250 m.

HABITAT This species inhabits tropical deciduous forest and thorn forest in a region that is composed of porous limestone covered by a scrubby xerophytic vegetation. It has been suggested that most of this region represents a subclimax formation resulting from centuries of the slash-and-burn agriculture practiced by the Mayan Indians.

DESCRIPTION This is a moderately stout, terrestrial hognosed pitviper. The overall length of adults is most frequently between 350 and 450 mm, although specimens may exceed 550 mm.

The dorsum of the head is grayish brown to pale orangish brown with fine black speckling and with or without irregular dark markings. In some specimens the lateral surface of the head, mental, infralabials, and gular region is pale tan to pink with light brown speckling; in other specimens these areas are grayish brown with dense brown-to-black stippling. All specimens have 3 or 4 pale yellow or white spots or bars on the infralabials and gulars. A pale postocular stripe extending from the lower posterior portion of the orbit to above the angle of the jaw is evident in darker specimens. A pale yellow-to-orange vertebral line extends from the nape to the tail on each side of which are 13–21 dark brown rectangular

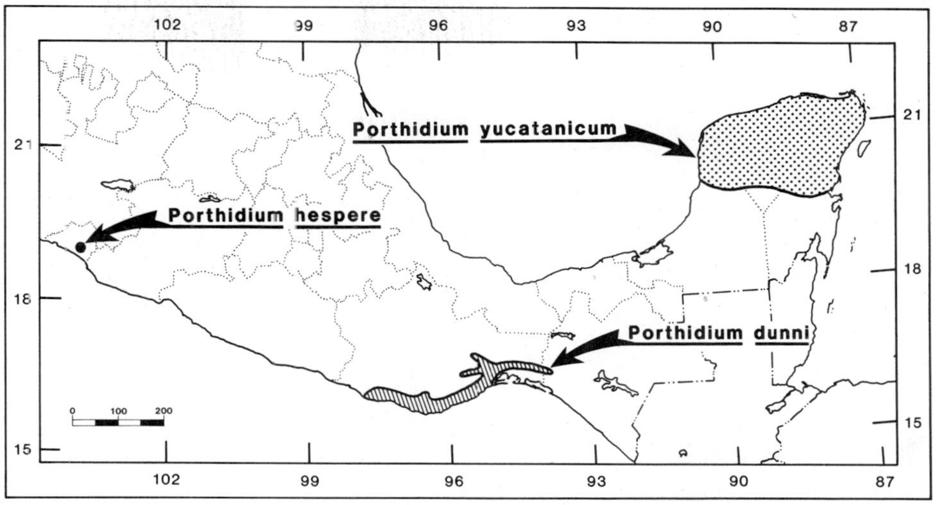


**Map 91.** Distributions of *Porthidium dunni* (*diagonal lines*), *P. hespere* (*dot*), and *P. yucatanicum* (*stipples*) in Mexico.

blotches that have margins more-or-less perpendicular to the long axis of the body. These blotches are darker toward their lateral margins and are bisected ventrally by the ground coloration, which may be reddish brown, tan, gray, or grayish brown. Darker specimens often have an alternating ground color of reddish brown between the body blotches and gray or grayish brown between the bisected portions of individual blotches. Blotches may be arranged alternately, but more frequently are situated opposite one another, which gives the snakes a banded appearance. Staggered blotches are present on the sides of the body; one series of dark lateral blotches offsets each component of the dorsal blotches and another series of pale gray blotches is present ventrolaterally. The venter is white or yellowish tan with varying amounts of diffuse brown flecking. In small specimens and young adults the distal half of the tail is yellow, but this coloration is replaced by dark pigmentation in large adults. The iris is pale gray to tan with fine black flecking. The tongue is dark grayish pink.

There are 3–7 (usually 4 or 5) intersupraoculars, 9–11 (usually 9 or 10) supralabials, 10–14 (usually 11 or 12) infralabials, 25 (rarely 23 or 27) midbody dorsal scale rows, 141–155 ventrals, and 31–43 undivided subcaudals.

SIMILAR SPECIES *Porthidium yucatanicum* is one of four members of the hognosed pitviper group occurring in Mexico. It is geographically remote from *P. hespere* and *P. dunni*, and may be distinguished from these species by the presence of generally 25 dorsal scale rows at midbody (both *P. hespere* and *P. dunni* have 23 or fewer), and 21 dorsal scale rows just anterior to the vent (*P. hespere* has 17, *P. dunni* almost invariably has 19). The most geographically proximate species of hognosed pitviper to *P. yucatanicum* is *P. nasutum*, which occurs in more mesic habitats in the southern portion of the Yucatán Peninsula. *Porthidium nasutum* may be distinguished from *P. yucatanicum* by having a more elevated snout and, correspondingly, a rostral that is about one and one-half times higher than broad, and by usually possessing a lower number of ventrals. *Boa constrictor* (Fig. 547) has more midbody dorsal scale rows, lacks a loreal pit, and attains a larger size.

REMARKS This snake is active primarily at night, especially after rain. Although once thought to be rare, judging from the large series in museum collections from the vicinities of Pisté, Yucatán, and Pueblo Nuevo X-cán, Quintana Roo, this species appears to be abundant at least locally.

REFERENCES Barrera, 1963; Boulenger, 1896; Campbell, 1976; Duellman, 1965a; Dundee et al., 1986; Lee, 1980; Martín del Campo, 1935, 1937a, 1950; McCranie and Porras, 1978; P. Müller, 1973; Schmidt and Andrews, 1936; H. M. Smith 1941a, 1944c; H. M. Smith and Taylor, 1945, 1950b; Velasco, 1895.

# Rattlesnakes

## Genus *Crotalus* Linnaeus, 1758

The genus *Crotalus* (family Viperidae) is composed of 26 species, 2 of which are extralimital to Latin America. The other 24 species all occur in Mexico, with the Mexican Plateau and its fringing mountains possessing the greatest diversity of rattlesnakes. One species, *C. durissus*, ranges south of the Isthmus of Tehuantepec through much of Central and South America, reaching northern Argentina. Members of the genus *Crotalus* exist in a myriad of habitats, ranging from the Sonoran Desert of northwestern Mexico to alpine and cloud forest habitats in central and southern Mexico. They occur from below sea level in desert basins in California to over 4,300 m in the Transverse Volcanic Cordillera of central Mexico.

Rattlesnakes vary in size from diminutive species that reach only 500–600 mm in total length (*C. intermedius*, *C. pricei*, *C. transversus*) to species that exceed 1,500 mm (*C. atrox*, *C. basiliscus*, *C. durissus*).

The presence of a rattle on the end of the tail makes rattlesnakes one of the most distinctive groups of reptiles. Rarely, the rattle may be missing as the result of an accident; in several island populations, including *C. catalinensis* on Isla de Santa Catalina and usually *C. ruber lorenzoensis* on Isla San Lorenzo del Sur, the loose rattle segments are lost.

Two genera of rattlesnakes are recognized on the basis of the presence or absence of 9 large symmetrical head plates. These head plates are present in the genus *Sistrurus*, although occasionally the parietals may be divided. In the genus *Crotalus*, however, the parietals are fragmented into many smaller scales, as is the frontal, and usually the scales in the internasal-prefrontal region.

*Crotalus basiliscus*, *C. durissus*, and *C. molossus* most frequently have a pair of large triangular internasals and a pair of large quadrangular prefrontals in contact medially that cover the top of the snout. *Crotalus pusillus* and an occasional specimen of *C. pricei* or *C. triseriatus* also have 4 large scales in the internasal-prefrontal region. In other species of rattlesnakes the internasal-prefrontal region is covered with smaller scales; some of the species that have the most finely divided snout scales are *C. exsul* with 17–40, *C. mitchellii* with 13–51, and *C. willardi* with 20–40. The number of intersupraoculars may be relatively small, ranging from usually about 2 in *C. scutulatus* and some of the smaller montane species to usually 6 or more in *C. exsul*, *C. ruber*, and *C. willardi*.

The rostral is usually wider than high in many of the desert species inhabiting northwestern Mexico or Baja California (*C. cerastes*, *C. enyo*, *C. mitchellii*, *C. tigris*) and in many of the montane species (*C. intermedius*, *C. lannomi*, *C. lepidus*, *C. pricei*, *C. pusillus*, *C. transversus*, and usually *C. triseriatus*). In other species it may be conspicuously higher than wide. The first supralabial is most often in broad contact with the prenasal; however, a forward extension of prefoveals may partially or completely preclude prenasal-supralabial contact in *C. basiliscus*, *C. exsul*, *C. mitchellii*, *C. molossus*, and *C. viridis*. The number of loreals varies from 1 to 9, with 1 or 2 most frequently present. The loreal(s) and outer edge of the posterior canthal (often deflected downward) separate the postnasal from the upper preocular in most individuals of most species; a notable exception is *C. atrox*. Usually in *C. intermedius*, *C. pricei*, *C. pusillus*, *C. transversus*, *C. triseriatus*, and often *C. lepidus*, the anterior subocular touches the supralabial series; in other species one or more interoculabials intervene to separate these scales. For specific characteristics of cephalic scalation, refer to Table 32.

The genus *Crotalus* is characterized by members that possess, collectively, 8–20 supralabials, 8–21 infralabials (the first pair of which is usually transversely divided in *C. ruber* and in *C. durissus* from the Yucatán Peninsula), 19–33 midbody dorsal scale rows, 132–206 ventrals, and 14–45 subcaudals that are mostly undivided. In general, larger species possess more numerous scales.

The ground color of rattlesnakes often matches their environment and is usually some hue of brown, gray, green, red, pink, or yellow. Most species have a dark pattern consisting of subelliptical, rhombic, or diamond-shaped middorsal blotches and 1–3 series of smaller lateral blotches. In a few species the dorsal markings are relatively short and wide, and they often merge with a lateral series of blotches to form crossbands (*C. tigris*, *C. transversus*, and some populations of *C. lepidus*). In two species there is a tendency for paravertebral blotches rather than a single middorsal series: in *C. polystictus* the paravertebral blotches are large and oval or subelliptical in shape; in *C. pricei* these blotches are small, usually irregular in outline, and about as wide as long. Some individuals of certain species may become essentially patternless as adults (*C. basiliscus*, *C. intermedius gloydi*) or have a pattern of pale flecks on a darker background (*C. basiliscus*, *C. durissus*, *C. molossus*).

The everted hemipenes are 8–12 subcaudals long in most species of *Crotalus*, although they are often a little shorter than this in some specimens of the smaller species, e.g., *C. cerastes*, *C. lepidus*, *C. pricei*, *C. pusillus*, and *C. willardi*. The organ is divided deeply; the sulcus spermaticus bifurcates at the level of subcaudal 1 or 2, with a branch extending to the apex of each lobe. The lobes are generally subcylindrical but may be slightly to greatly tapered (*C. atrox*, *C. basiliscus*, *C. durissus*), somewhat bulbous distally (*C. basiliscus*, *C. triseriatus*), somewhat constricted distally (some *C. molossus*), or greatly compressed mediolaterally (*C. stejnegeri*). The lobes may be straight and thick, straight and slender, or diverge from one another to varying degrees; in some specimens the lobes of everted hemipenes have a strongly lyriform shape. The crotch tends to be V shaped or U shaped; it is especially broad in *C. scutulatus* and *C. viridis*.

The number of large basal spines on each lobe (exclusive of smaller spinules) is highly variable: there are more than 100 in *C. polystictus* and *C. stejnegeri*; between 25 and 50 in *C. basiliscus*, *C. cerastes*, *C. molossus*, *C. pricei*, *C. scutulatus*, *C. viridis*, *C. willardi*, and *C. atrox* (sometimes more than 50 in the latter); 15–25 in *C. intermedius*, *C. pusillus*, and *C. triseriatus* (southern populations); and 7–15 in *C. lepidus* and *C. triseriatus* (northern populations). The distribution of basal spines tends to be mostly on the shoulders of the organ, but they may barely extend distally on the proximal third or less of the lobes in many species; in *C. cerastes*, *C. polystictus*, and *C. stejnegeri* basal spines extend distally for more than one-third the length of the lobe. Mesial spines may be absent or present. If present, they may be restricted to the asulcomedial surface (*C. scutulatus* and some *C. molossus*), they may be large and well developed (*C. basiliscus*, *C. cerastes*, *C. durissus*, *C. intermedius*, *C. pricei*, *C. willardi*), or they may be represented by numerous small spines (*C. polystictus*, *C. stejnegeri*). In *C. lepidus* and *C. triseriatus* mesial spines are absent, but calyces tend to become spinulate in this region. Mesial spines are usually absent in *C. atrox*, *C. pusillus*, and *C. viridis*.

The distal portion of the lobes is covered by papillate calyces. These calyces often extend further in the region flanking the sulcus than elsewhere. In species lacking mesial spines, calyces often extend to the crotch. In *C. stejnegeri* the proximal calyces are weakly papillate and distally the calyces are reduced to low smooth ridges. A few species, including *C. polystictus*, are remarkable in having especially large calyces with low ridges on the distal asulcate portion of the lobes and a soft papilla on the apex of each lobe.

In most *Crotalus* there is a rather sharp boundary between basal spines and calyces; however, in *C. polystictus* and *C. stejnegeri* the spines tend to grade into calyces.

### *Crotalus atrox* Baird and Girard

(Figs. 317, 318, 444, 445; Map 92)

LOCAL NAMES Víbora de cascabel, víbora serrana.

ENGLISH NAME Western diamondback rattlesnake.

DISTRIBUTION United States and Mexico. In the United States the range of this species extends from western Arkansas westward through Oklahoma exclusive of the northeastern and north-central part of the state and the high plains of the panhandle, through Texas exclusive of the northern panhandle and eastern part of the state, and into southern and central New Mexico and Arizona, the extreme southern tip of Nevada, and southeastern California. In Mexico it occurs westward through most of Nuevo León, Coahuila, and Chihuahua, through much of Sonora to extreme northeastern Baja California del Norte, thence southward to northern Sinaloa and much of the northern plateau region, the Sierra Madre Oriental (exclusive of the higher elevations), and the northern coastal plain of the Gulf of Mexico; its range includes northeastern Durango and Zacatecas, most of San Luis Potosí, and northern Veracruz, Hidalgo, and Querétaro.

The presence of this species as far south as the Río Tulancingo (Metztitlán) Valley in east-central Hidalgo has been documented recently (UTA R-12566) 7.1 km south of Venados. However, of even greater biogeographic interest is the existence of several populations of *C. atrox* isolated far to the south of Hidalgo. Representatives from one such population in the mountains to the northwest of Tehuantepec, Oaxaca, have been collected on at least a dozen separate occasions by four different collectors; consequently, there appears to be little doubt that a relictual population of this species was present in the Tehuantepec region as recently as the 1940s, but to our knowledge no specimens have been collected since then. Evidence of another isolated population is provided by a single specimen (KU 24129) collected near the Río Blanco, 20 km west-northwest of Piedras Negras in central Veracruz. *Crotalus atrox* is also found on the following islands in the Gulf of California: San Pedro Mártir, Santa Cruz, Santa María, Tiburón, and Turner (Map 92). In the United States, this species has been reported from extreme southeastern Kansas and southeastern and southwestern Missouri, but its presence in these areas is doubtful. The vertical distribution of this species is from near sea level (actually below sea level in the Salton Basin of California) to about 2,440 m at Alvarez, San Luis Potosí, Mexico; however, over most of its range *C. atrox* does not ascend above the 1,500-m contour.

HABITAT This snake may be found in terrain ranging from flat coastal plains to steep rocky hillsides and canyons and in a variety of vegetation types including mesquite-grassland, desert, and pine-oak forests; along the southern part of its range it occurs in tropical deciduous forest and thorn forest. It is most abundant in lowland regions that are xeric or seasonally dry.

DESCRIPTION This is one of the largest rattlesnakes, exceeded in size only by *C. adamanteus* (eastern diamondback rattlesnake) of the southeastern United States. Specimens of *C. atrox* over 1,200 mm long are relatively common, however, snakes exceeding 1,500 mm are infrequently encountered, and those over 1,800

**Table 32**
Variation of selected cephalic scale characteristics in members of the genus *Crotalus*

| *Species* | *Rostral* | *Internasals* | *Prefrontals* | *Intersupra-oculars* | *Prenasal-supralabial contact* | *Loreals (per side)* | *Postnasal–upper preocular contact* | *Supralabials* | *Scales in internasal-prefrontal region* |
|---|---|---|---|---|---|---|---|---|---|
| *C. atrox* | Higher than wide | 2, small | Absent | 3–7, usually 4–5 | Usually | Usually 1 | Usually | 12–18, usually 15–16 | 11–32 |
| *C. basilicus* | Higher than wide | 2, large | Present | 2–3, usually 2 | Variable | 1–5, usually 2 | Rarely | 13–18, usually 15 | Usually 4–6, rarely up to 9 |
| *C. catalinensis* | Higher than wide | 2, kidney-shaped | Absent | 4–5 | Yes | Usually 1 | No | 13–16, usually 14–15 | More than 8 |
| *C. cerastes* | Wider than high | 2, moderate in size | Absent | 4–6 | Yes | Usually 1 | No | 10–15, usually 12–13 | 12–34 |
| *C. durissus* | Usually slightly higher than wide | 2, large | Present | 2–5, usually 2 | Usually | 1–8, usually 2–3 | Rarely | 11–18, usually 13–16 | Usually 4–6, up to 10 |
| *C. enyo* | Usually wider than high | 2, small to moderate in size | Absent | 2–6, usually 4–5 | Usually | 1–5, usually 2–3 | Rarely | 12–15, usually 13–14 | 13–25 |
| *C. exsul* | Usually higher than wide | 2, small | Absent | 6–9, usually 7–8 | Infrequently | Usually 2 | No | 14–19, usually 16–17 | 17–40 |
| *C. intermedius* | Wider than high | 2, large | Usually absent | 2–4 | Yes | Usually 1 | No | 8–11, usually 9 | 4–8 |
| *C. lannomi* | Wider than high | 2, moderately sized | Absent | 2 | Yes | 3 | No | 14–15 | 7 |
| *C. lepidus* | Usually wider than high | 2, large | Absent | 1–4, usually 2 | Yes | 1–2, usually 1 | No | 10–15, usually 12–13 | 5–15 |
| *C. mitchellii* | Usually wider than high | 2–4, usually 2, small | Absent | 1–8 | Variable | 0–5, usually 2 | No | 12–19, usually 15–17 | 13–51 |
| *C. molossus* | Usually slightly higher than wide | 2, large | Usually present | 2–5, usually 2–3 | Rarely | 1–9, usually 2–4 | Rarely | 13–20, usually 16–18 | 4–18, usually 6 or fewer |
| *C. polystictus* | Higher than wide | 2–4, variable in size | Absent | 2–5, usually 3 | Yes | Usually 2 | No | 12–15, usually 13–14 | 6–8 |
| *C. pricei* | Usually wider than high | 2, large | Usually absent | 2–3 | Yes | Usually 1 | No | 8–10, usually 9 | 4–11 |
| *C. pusillus* | Wider than high | 2, large | Present | 1–4, usually 3 | Yes | Usually 1 | No | 11–13, usually 12 | 4 |
| *C. ruber* | Variable | 2, small | Absent | 4–10, usually 6 or more | Usually | 1 or 2 | Rarely | 12–19, usually 15–17 | — |
| *C. scutulatus* | Usually higher than wide | 2, small | Absent | Usually 2 | Yes | Usually 1 | Infrequently | 12–18, usually 13–15 | 6–21 |

| | | | | | | | | | |
|---|---|---|---|---|---|---|---|---|---|
| *C. stejnegeri* | About as high as wide | 2, large | Absent | 5–8 | Yes | 2–5 | No | 14–16 | 10–21 |
| *C. tigris* | Wider than high | 2, small | Absent | 3–8 | Usually | 1–2, usually 1 | Rarely | 11–16, usually 12–14 | 11–37 |
| *C. tortugensis* | Usually higher than wide | 2, small | Absent | 4–5, usually 4 | Yes | Usually 1 | Rarely | 14–18, usually 15–16 | 8+ |
| *C. transversus* | Wider than high | 2, large | Absent | 2–3 | Yes | 1 | No | 8–10, usually 9 | 5–6 |
| *C. triseriatus* | Variable | 2, large | Absent | 2–5, usually 3 | Yes | 1 | No | 9–15, usually 12–13 | 4–12 |
| *C. viridis* | Usually higher than wide | 1–8, usually 4, small to moderately sized | Absent | 1–10, usually 4–6 | Variable | 1–3, usually 1 | Rarely | 10–18, usually 14–15 | 7–45, usually 15–30 |
| *C. willardi* | Higher than wide | 2, small | Absent | 6–9 | Yes | 1–2, usually 2 | No | 12–17, usually 13–15 | 20–40 |

*Note.* For additional information refer to individual species accounts. Rarely = less than 5% of specimens; infrequently = more than 5%, less than 25%; usually = more than 75%.

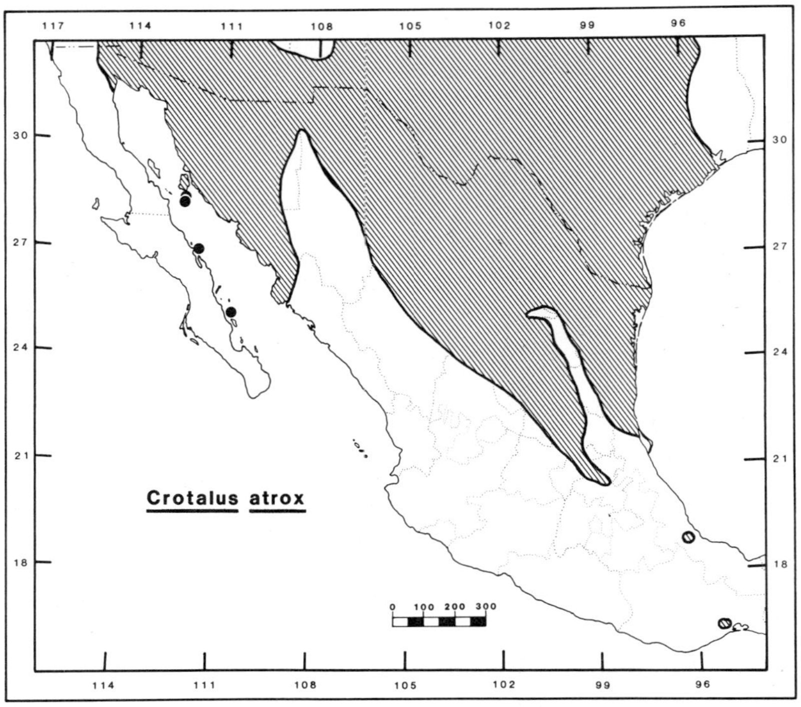


**Map 92.** Distribution of *Crotalus atrox* in Mexico and the adjacent United States. This species occurs on several islands in the Gulf of California, including (from north to south) Tiburón, Turner, San Pedro Mártir, Santa María, and Santa Cruz. See text for discussion of the status of two isolated populations in southern Mexico.

mm are very rare. The maximum reported length thought to be reliable for this species is 2,130 mm.

The ground color most often is gray-brown with an overall dusty-looking appearance, but it may be pinkish brown, brick red, yellowish, or chalky white. The ground color usually is marked by numerous dark brown or black punctations. The 24–45 dorsal body blotches are dark gray-brown to brown. The first body blotch may be in the form of a pair of short paravertebral stripes that extend posteriorly from the back of the head and coalesce with each other at their posterior ends. Several of the anteriormost blotches may be somewhat rectangular in outline, but become roughly hexagonal on the anterior third of the body and posteriorly take on a nearly diamond shape. These dorsal blotches are bordered most often with dark brown to black, which is edged partially with white, at least on the anterior two-thirds of the body; dorsal blotches tend to be separated middorsally by white or pale gray. Several series of small-to-large dark blotches may be present on the sides; these often are indistinct. A broad smoky gray to dark gray-brown postocular stripe extends diagonally from the lower edge of the eye across the side of the head; it is usually bordered below (anteriorly) by a white stripe extending from the upper preocular downward to those supralabials lying directly below or just behind the eye; in some snakes it then runs posteriorly along the upper lip margin. The upper (posterior) white border extends from the upper postocular downward across the temporals to the penultimate or antepenultimate supralabial, where it may merge with the white running along the supralabials, if white is present. The top of the head may be marked irregularly with dark pigment; sometimes a pale transverse line is present across each supraocular.

The tail has 2–8 (usually 4–6) black "rings." (These are more properly termed bands because they are incomplete ventrally). These rings occasionally may be incomplete dorsally or be staggered so they do not merge across the midline, but form vertical bars on each side of the tail. The black rings are usually as wide or a little wider than the ash-white or pale gray interspaces dividing them. The interspaces are decidedly paler than the ground color on the posterior part of the body. The proximal rattle segment is black, at least dorsally.

The mental and anterior infralabials may have a fine dusting of gray pigment, but the gular region and belly are mostly pale (whitish, yellowish, or pinkish) with dark pigment restricted to fine stippling or mottling that is on the lateral portions of the ventrals, often on their anterior edge. Anteriorly, the ventrals are most frequently bright white but become progressively more off-white posteriorly. The pale color of the ventrals extends dorsally to partially cover or to narrowly outline the first 2–3 dorsal scale rows. Except for where the black tail marking encroaches ventrally, the subcaudals are pale with a light dusting of gray.

Many snakes from southwestern New Mexico, southeastern Arizona, northeastern Sonora, and northern Chihuahua have a decidedly reddish to pinkish gray to buckskin ground color. The dorsal blotches are only a little darker than the ground color and often lack the distinctive dark borders; white edging, if present at all, is most prominent at middorsum between the blotches. The dark postocular stripe is ill-defined and often does not have white borders. Snakes from the lava flows in central New Mexico tend to be melanistic.

The rostral is higher than wide. There are 2 internasals in contact with the rostral, 11–32 scales in the internasal-prefrontal region, and 3–7 (usually 4 or 5) intersupraoculars. The prenasal and first supralabial usually make contact with each other, although they may be partially separated by the anteriormost prefoveals. The posterior canthal is large and laterally is strongly deflected downward at almost a 90° angle to partially intervene between the upper preocular and postnasal, which usually are in contact with each other. Most frequently, a single triangular loreal is present on each side; it is situated below the preocular-postnasal suture and partially intervenes between these scales. One or 2 interoculabials separate the anterior subocular from the supralabials. There are 12–18 (usually 15 or 16) supralabials, 14–20 (usually 16 or 17) infralabials (first pair infrequently transversely divided), 23–29 (mode 25) midbody dorsal scale rows, 168–196 ventrals, and 16–32 subcaudals.

SIMILAR SPECIES The wide-ranging *C. atrox* is sympatric in portions of its range with many other species of rattlesnakes. In *C. scutulatus* the pale and black tail rings stand in strong contrast to one another, but the black rings are narrow relative to the pale rings; 2 (sometimes 3) intersupraoculars usually are present; a crescent-shaped scale borders the posterior-inward side of each supraocular; and a white stripe extends from the posterior edge of the eye across the temporal region to a point above the rictus. The range of *C. ruber* is contiguous with that of *C. atrox* at the eastern base of the San Jacinto Mountains, California, but no region of sympatry has been revealed; in this species the ground color is reddish brown to pink; 29 midbody dorsal scale rows usually are present; and the first pair of infralabials is usually transversely divided. *Crotalus mitchellii* can be distinguished by several features: the ground color is usually distinctly speckled with black; the dark tail rings are obscure or, if sharply defined, the black rings are not as broad as the pale ones; the prenasals are separated from the rostral by a series of small scales; and the supraoculars are pitted, have deep furrows, or have irregular outer edges.

In *C. viridis* more than 2 internasals usually are in contact with the rostral, the color of the pale tail rings is the same as the ground color on the posterior of the body, and the pale line extending from the posterior edge of the eye passes above the rictus. *Crotalus molossus* has a tail that is uniformly dark, or at least the tail rings are indistinctly indicated and the internasal-prefrontal region usually has 4–6 scales. In *C. basiliscus* 27 midbody dorsal scale rows are usually present, the internasal-prefrontal region has 4–6 scales, and the tail is mostly dark with tail rings obscure or absent. The dorsal pattern of *C. tigris* consists of crossbands, the head is proportionally small and the rattles large, and the pale and dark tail rings are not in strong contrast with one another; In *C. durissus* the midbody blotches are usually diamond shaped (rather than hexagonal); the internasal-prefrontal area usually has 4–6 scales; the tail lacks rings and is usually uniformly gray; and a distinctive pair of paravertebral nape stripes extends posteriorly from the parietal region.

REMARKS *Crotalus atrox* will often gather in dens during the colder months, when they become relatively inactive. Dens harboring large numbers of snakes appear to be most prevalent in the northern part of the range and in rocky regions. Snakes occurring in flat areas devoid of rocky outcroppings tend to utilize mammal burrows to escape direct exposure to the extreme temperatures of winter.

This species' activity patterns appear to be more affected by temperature than light. For example, during the early spring this snake may be found crawling by day or at dusk, and only rarely is it found after dark when temperatures are cool. Conversely, during the hot summer months its activity seems largely confined to the hours of darkness.

*Crotalus atrox* possesses several attributes that make it one of the most medically important North American snakes: it has a large geographic range, a penchant for quickly defending itself, and a large size coupled with a relatively potent venom. It is responsible for more human deaths within its range than any other snake. Symptoms usually include an intense, fiery pain at the site of envenomation that eventually radiates in all directions, swelling and edema, discoloration of the tissues, an increase or decrease in pulse rate, changes in blood pressure, and nausea and vomiting.

REFERENCES Amaral, 1927g; Armstrong and Murphy, 1979; Axtell, 1956, 1959; Baird and Girard, 1853; Baker and Webb, 1967; Bogert and Oliver, 1945; A. E. Brown, 1901, 1903a; B. C. Brown, 1950; Burger and Hensley, 1949; Chrapliwy and Fugler, 1955; Cliff, 1954; Conant, 1975; Cope, 1860c, 1886, 1887; Coues, 1875; Cowles, 1941; Crimmins, 1927; Cuesta Terron, 1920, 1921a, 1921b, 1931; Curran, 1935; Dixon et al., 1962, 1972; Dugès, 1869, 1896; Dunkle and Smith, 1937; Fugler and Webb, 1956; Garman, 1884a; Gates, 1957; Gehlbach, 1956; Gloyd, 1937, 1940; Groombridge, 1986; Haller, 1971; Hallowell, 1852; Hardy and McDiarmid, 1969; Hartweg and Oliver, 1940; Hulse, 1973; Humphrey, 1936; Jacob et al., 1987; Jameson and Flury, 1949; Kennicott, 1861; Klauber, 1927, 1930a, 1931a, 1936b, 1952, 1971, 1972; Klemmer, 1963; Landreth, 1976; Lewis, 1950, 1951; Lindsay, 1962, 1966; Liner, 1964; Linsdale, 1932; Little and Keller, 1937; Lowe, 1964; Lowe et al., 1986; Martin, 1958; Martín del Campo, 1935, 1937a, 1937b, 1950, 1953; McCoy, 1984; Milstead et al., 1950; Minton, 1959; Minton and Weinstein, 1986; Mocquard, 1908–1909; Mosauer, 1932b, 1933; R. W. Murphy, 1983a, 1983b; Murphy and Ottley, 1984; Neill, 1958; Nelson, 1922; Ortenburger and Ortenburger, 1927; Pianka and Smith, 1959; Pope, 1944–1945; Raun and Gehlbach, 1972; Reynolds, 1982; Ruthven, 1907; Savage, 1960; Schmidt, 1922; Schmidt and Owens, 1944; Schmidt and Smith, 1944; Shannon and Smith, 1950; H. M. Smith, 1939, 1943; H. M. Smith and Taylor, 1945; H. M. Smith et al., 1963; P. W. Smith and Darling, 1952; P. W. Smith and Hensley, 1958; Soulé and Sloan, 1966; Stebbins, 1985; Stejneger, 1895, 1902; Stejneger and Barbour, 1943; Strecker, 1909; Strecker and Johnson, 1935; Tanner, 1985; E. H. Taylor, 1938a, 1938b, 1949, 1952; Tennant, 1984; Van Denburgh, 1895a, 1922b, 1924; Velasco-Torres, 1970; Williams et al., 1961; Woodbury and Woodbury, 1944; Woodin, 1953; Wright and Wright, 1957; Zweifel and Norris, 1955.

### *Crotalus basiliscus* (Cope)

(Figs. 319–323; Map 93)

LOCAL NAMES Saye (Cora Indians in Nayarit), teuhtlacozauhqui (Náhuatl), víbora de cascabel.

ENGLISH NAME Mexican west-coast rattlesnake.

DISTRIBUTION Mexico. The range of this species extends from the Río del Fuerte drainage in extreme

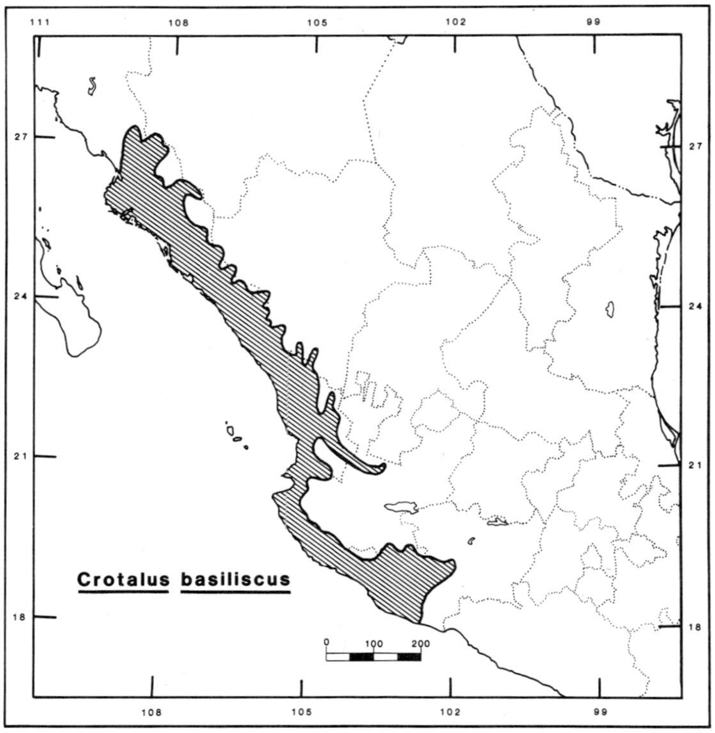


**Map 93.** Distribution of *Crotalus basiliscus* in western Mexico. The range of this species appears to be largely complementary with that of *C. molossus* (see Map 100).

southern Sonora, southward along the coastal plain, foothills, and valleys of Sinaloa, Nayarit, Jalisco, Colima, and northwestern Michoacán, including the middle Río Tepalcatepec Valley (Map 93). In the northern part of its range this species appears to occur mostly below 600 m (see Remarks for *Crotalus molossus*). In the south it ranges from near sea level well up into the Sierra de Coalcomán, Michoacán: UCM 51313 was collected at 2,225 m near Dos Aguas and UTA R-6120 was found at about 2,400 m on Cerro Barolosa.

HABITAT This species inhabits thorn forest, tropical deciduous forest, and the ecotonal belt between tropical deciduous forest and pine-oak forest; in the Sierra de Coalcomán it ranges well up into the pine-oak forest, almost to fir forest.

DESCRIPTION This is one of the largest rattlesnakes; specimens exceeding 1,500 mm are not rare, and the maximum size reported is a little over 2,000 mm. Large specimens have a prominent spinal ridge on the anterior part of the body shaped by high neural spines, but this ridge is not as well developed as in *C. durissus*.

The ground color of adults is olive-green, olive-gray, brownish green, or yellowish brown; usually the larger snakes have a more conspicuous greenish cast. Dark punctuations are absent from the ground color. Juveniles are reddish brown. The pattern is reminiscent of that of some populations of *C. molossus* in that most individual dorsals tend to be unicolored without elements of pattern cutting across them; the major exception is the pale borders of the dorsal blotches, which may consist of scales that are pale only distally. The dorsal pattern consists of 26–41 diamond-shaped blotches; these usually are enclosed laterally by a pale border and do not coalesce with the lateral series of blotches. The pale border of the dorsal blotches usually involves diagonal series of scales that are pale at least distally. In juveniles and young adults the dorsal blotches are usually reddish brown with paler centers. With age these blotches fade out somewhat; in very large or very old specimens they may become indistinguishable from the overall ground color, and the entire dorsum appears unicolored except perhaps for a few pale and/or dark scales. In juveniles pale-bordered, reddish brown ventrolateral blotches offset the lateral points of the dorsal blotches. Another series of small lateral blotches may alternate between the primary lateral series and the dorsal series; these usually consist of a small group of reddish brown scales. In many adults, except for a few dark scales, most traces of the lateral marking may vanish.

The top of the head is pale; an indistinct dark pattern is present in young snakes, but this usually disappears in adults except for a few dark scales. A dark postocular stripe about 3 scales wide extends from behind and below the eye to a point directly above the rictus, where it is 1 scale wide. The pale borders of the dark postocular stripe are usually not sharply defined, are irregular, and are often discontinuous. Like other body markings, the postocular stripe becomes obscure with age. The tail is gray with a series of 5–12 darker rings. Anteriorly, the venter is whitish, yellowish, or cream colored with a faint suffusion of gray; the belly becomes darker posteriorly, with gray mottling or blotches often in evidence.

The rostral is higher than wide. The internasal-prefrontal region usually does not have more than 4–6 scales, including 2 large triangular internasals in contact with the rostral, 2 large quadrangular prefrontals (anterior canthals) in contact with each other medially, and 2 small posterior canthals, each one lying behind the upper loreal (s) and interposed between the prefrontal and supraocular. Very rarely scales in the internasal-prefrontal region are fragmented irregularly, producing up to about 9 scales on the snout. Two or 3 (usually 2) intersupraoculars are present and the scales in the parietal and occipital regions are small and keeled. The first supralabial may be in broad contact with the prenasal or may be partially or completely separated by the forward extension of prefoveals. Two loreals (an upper and a lower) are usually present which separate the postnasal from the upper preocular. The number of loreals per side may be as low as 1 or as high as 5; occasionally, when only a lower loreal is present, the upper preocular touches the postnasal. One or more small scales (post upper loreals) often intervene posteriorly to the upper loreal to partially or completely separate the prefrontal from the upper preocular. One to 3 (usually 2) interoculabials separate the anterior subocular from the supralabials. The first pair of infralabials is not divided transversely. There are 13–18 (usually 15) supralabials, 13–19 (usually 16) infralabials, 24–29 (usually 27) midbody dorsal scale rows, 178–206 ventrals, and 18–36 subcaudals.

SIMILAR SPECIES *Crotalus atrox* is sympatric with *C. basiliscus* in southern Sonora and northern Sinaloa, but the former may be distinguished by a gray-brown ground color heavily punctated with dark brown or black; a pale stripe extending from the upper postocular downward to the lip margin 2–3 supralabials in front of the rictus; a tail with sharply contrasting, alternating black and ash-white rings; more than 9 scales in the internasal-prefrontal region, including anterior canthals that are not in contact with each other; and a large posterior canthal on each side that extends over the canthus rostralis to take the place of an upper loreal. *Crotalus durissus* is sympatric with *C. basiliscus* in Michoacán but may be distinguished by a ground color that usually does not have a greenish or reddish cast, a sharply defined pair of narrow paravertebral stripes, dorsal blotches with distinct dark borders, a tail with little or no trace of darker crossbands in adults, and usually 29 or more midbody dorsal scale rows.

A more perplexing problem of identification involves *C. basiliscus* and *C. molossus*. Anyone seeing a large *C. basiliscus* from the coastal lowlands of Sinaloa and an adult *C. molossus* from one of the many rocky canyons of central Durango would have little trouble distinguishing these species from one another. However, the situation is not nearly so clear-cut because these species appear to hydridize freely wherever they come into contact. A rather broad elevational belt where these species hybridize occurs in eastern Sinaloa and northeastern Nayarit; in most areas this hybrid zone corresponds roughly to an elevation between 600 and 1,500 m, but in southern Sonora these species apparently hybridize at even lower elevations. Attempting to define sharply the distributional boundaries between these species hardly seems a worthwhile (or possible) endeavor and range maps should be considered nothing more than approximations based on what we consider the more salient diagnostic features for each. Certain characteristics serve to distinguish *C. molossus* from *C. basiliscus*: it is smaller (*C. molossus* rarely exceeds 1,200 mm); its dorsal blotches are distinctly darker and have contrasting pale interiors; the pale margins of dorsal blotches are usually made up of scales that are uniformly pale; the dorsal blotches often coalesce with lateral blotches to form crossbands on the body; the top of the head is dark at least anterior to the supraoculars; and the tail usually is uniformly dark in adults without evidence of darker crossbands.

REMARKS This species is most active during the rainy summer months and most snakes have been found crossing roads at night. However, we have encountered a few basking during the early morning.

It is possible that an old report of rattlesnakes from Isla María Magdalena of the Islas Marías is referable to this species, although no specimen has been collected yet. This species commonly has been confused in the literature with *C. molossus* and vice versa. An old record for this species from Chapala, Jalisco, is almost certainly referrable to *C. molossus*. Previously, the large rattlesnakes inhabiting the highlands of central Oaxaca have been considered to be members of a rather distantly isolated population of *C. basiliscus*. This population apparently is more closely related to populations of *C. molossus* on the southern portion of the Mexican Plateau. For a discussion of the distribution and affinities of these snakes see Remarks for *C. molossus*.

The everted hemipenes of *C. basiliscus* are 12–14 subcaudals long and somewhat lyriform in shape. Each lobe tapers slightly toward the distal end and the tip of each lobe is slightly bulbous. The proximal third of each lobe possesses 30–40 enlarged spines inclusive of the large mesial spines, which are always present. The hemipenes of *C. basiliscus* and the southern populations of *C. molossus* are quite similar in morphology. The major differences between these two species are the length of the organ (usually 8–10 subcaudals in *C. molossus*) and the greater development of the basal and mesial spines in *C. basiliscus*.

REFERENCES Armstrong and Murphy, 1979; Bogert and Oliver, 1945; Brattstrom, 1964; Casas-Andreu, 1981; Cope, 1864, 1885b, 1887, 1895, 1896, 1900; Cuesta Terron, 1921b; Davis and Dixon, 1957; Dixon et al., 1962; Duellman, 1954, 1958, 1961, 1965b; Dugès, 1876–1877, 1888, 1896; Ferrari-Perez, 1886; Fouquette and Rossman, 1963; Fugler and Dixon, 1961; Gloyd, 1936a, 1940, 1948; Groombridge, 1986; Günther, 1885–1902; Hardy and McDiarmid, 1969; Herrera, 1890, 1891, 1899, 1904; Hoge and Romano, 1971a; Klauber, 1936b, 1952, 1971, 1972; Malkin, 1958; Martín del Campo, 1935, 1937a, 1950; McCranie, 1981; Mocquard, 1899; Ocaranza, 1930; Oliver, 1937; Peters, 1954, 1960b; Pope, 1944–1945; Schmidt and Shannon, 1947; H. M. Smith, 1943, 1970; H. M. Smith and Lynch, 1967; H. M. Smith and Taylor, 1945; H. M. Smith and Van Gelder, 1955; Spieth, 1950; Stejneger, 1899; E. H. Taylor, 1938b; Van Denburgh and Slevin, 1914; Webb, 1984; Zweifel, 1959b, 1960.

### *Crotalus catalinensis* Cliff

(Figs. 324, 325; Map 98)

LOCAL NAME Víbora de cascabel.

ENGLISH NAME Santa Catalina Island rattleless rattlesnake.

DISTRIBUTION Mexico. This species is endemic to Isla de Santa Catalina off the east coast of Baja California del Sur in the Gulf of California (see Map 98).

HABITAT Desert; the terrain of this island is rocky and sparsely covered with brush and cacti.

DESCRIPTION This is a relatively slender, stunted species; the largest measured specimen is a female 731 mm in total length.

The ground color is tan to pale gray-brown with few dark punctations. There are 34–40 medium-brown dorsal body blotches; these possess a dark brown to black border about 1 scale wide, with a cream-colored edging also about 1 scale in width. Middorsally 1 or 2 pale scales separate adjacent blotches. On the posterior portion of the body both the pale and dark margins of blotches become indistinct. Anteriorly the dorsal blotches are longitudinally elongated and may be somewhat quadrangular; at midbody they become roughly hexagonal or diamond shaped. The dorsum of the head is pale gray-brown punctated or irregularly marked with dark brown. The supraoculars have a relatively broad transverse pale streak through their centers. The pale stripes bordering the dark postocular stripe are broad but not sharply defined; the lower (anterior) pale stripe extends from the upper preocular to the supralabials under the eye, the upper (posterior) from the upper postocular to near the rictus. Of the three series of dark lateral blotches, the series with the largest blotches is below the lateral extensions of the dorsal blotches; the two smaller series are situated along an imaginary vertical line about half-way between successive lateral blotches, one series above and one below the large series. The dorsum of the tail has 5 or 6 black rings that encroach on the lateral portions of the subcaudals; the black rings are 4–5 scales wide dorsomedially, but reduced laterally. The ash-gray pale interspaces are a little narrower than the black rings along the dorsal midline and strongly contrast with the ground color on the posterior portion of the body. The proximal rattle segment is brown to black.

A pair of oddly shaped internasals is in contact with the rostral; these internasals are roughly kidney shaped and about three times longer than wide. The small anterior canthals touch each other medially, are longer than wide, and partially border the concavity of the kidney-shaped internasals. There are more than 8 scales in the internasal-prefrontal region and 4 or 5 intersupraoculars. On each side the prenasal is in broad contact with the first supralabial. The posterior canthals are large relative to the anterior canthals and the lateral portion of each scale extends ventrally over the canthus rostralis; together with the single vertically elongated loreal (in the position of a lower loreal), the lateral portion of the posterior canthal precludes the postnasal from contacting the upper preocular. A single interoculabial separates the anterior subocular from the supralabials. The first pair of infralabials is not transversely divided and there are no interchinshields or submental. There are 13–16 (usually 14 or 15) supralabials, 13–17 (usually 14 or 15) infralabials, 25 midbody dorsal scale rows, 177–189 ventrals, and 18–28 subcaudals. One of the most distinctive features of this rattlesnake is the absence of any rattles other than the proximal segment. The lobes and grooves of the proximal segment are so poorly developed in this species that a rattle segment is lost every time the snake sheds its skin—in other rattlesnakes a new segment is added.

SIMILAR SPECIES *Crotalus catalinensis* is the only rattlesnake inhabiting the Isla de Santa Catalina in the Gulf of California (not to be confused with the Island of Santa Catalina off the California coast of the United States, which is inhabited by *C. viridis*). *Crotalus catalinensis* is readily distinguished from most other populations of rattlesnakes (other than juveniles) in that individuals tend to have no rattles other than the proximal segment. In *C. ruber* the first pair of infralabials are usually divided transversely and it is a larger species; mainland specimens commonly exceed 1 m in length and usually possess at least 27 midbody dorsal scale rows. In *C. scutulatus* the black tail rings are conspicuously narrower than the pale interspaces, only 2 intersupraoculars are usually present, an enlarged crescent-shaped scale often borders the posteromedial side of each supraocular, and the upper (posterior) pale stripe bordering the dark postocular stripe extends posteriorly *above* the rictus.

REMARKS The phylogenetic relationships of *C. catalinensis* have been proposed to be with either *C. ruber* or *C. scutulatus*; the preponderance of data, morphological, biogeographic, and biochemical, suggests that *C. ruber* is its closest relative.

*Crotalus catalinensis* is reported to be quite agile and sometimes climbs in vegetation to a height of 1 m or more.

REFERENCES Armstrong and Murphy, 1979; Cliff, 1954; Hoge and Romano, 1971a; Klauber, 1963, 1971, 1972; Lindsay, 1962, 1964; R. W. Murphy, 1983a, 1983b; R. W. Murphy and Crabtree, 1985; R. W. Murphy and Ottley, 1984; Orr, 1965, 1976; Radcliffe and Maslin, 1975; Shaw, 1964a; H. M. Smith and Taylor, 1966; Soulé and Sloan, 1966.

## *Crotalus cerastes* Hallowell

(Figs. 326, 327; Map 98)

LOCAL NAMES Víbora cornuda, víbora de cascabel.

ENGLISH NAME Sidewinder.

DISTRIBUTION The United States and Mexico. In the United States this species occurs in extreme southwestern Utah, southern Nevada, southeastern California, and western and south-central Arizona; in Mexico it is found in northwestern Sonora to about the Llanos de San Juan Bautista, which lie to the southwest of Hermosillo, and in eastern Baja California del Norte to the Llano de San Pedro; it also occurs on Isla Tiburón (see Map 98). This species occurs from below sea level in desert basins to nearly 1,830 m, but usually is found below 1,200 m.

HABITAT This species inhabits desert; it is often encountered in regions of fine wind-blown sand. However, it is not restricted to this type of habitat and may be encountered in a variety of situations, including hard rocky terrain, although specimens are found most frequently in low-lying flats in the vicinity of sand hummocks or sandy washes. This species appears to be most abundant where there is little vegetation.

DESCRIPTION Most adults are 500–800 mm in total length; the largest specimen measures 824 mm. Unlike most other rattlesnakes, in *C. cerastes* it is the females that attain the greatest lengths. A spinal ridge is evident and the dorsals are strongly keeled and tuberculate, the vertebral row being the most accentuated.

The ground color is cream, buff, tan, yellowish brown, pink, or ash-gray. The 28–47 dorsal blotches on the body are subrhombic or subelliptical, usually broader than long, and grayish, pale brown, yellowish brown, or occasionally brilliant orange. These blotches have indefinitely and irregularly outlined borders; the middorsal interspace between them is often paler than the overall ground color and may be yellow or orangish in hue. Three series of lateral spots, often indistinct, lie opposite and alternate to the dorsal blotches. A pale crossbar extends transversely across the supraocular to its distal tip. A few small, irregular dark spots may be present in the parietal region, followed posteriorly by a pair of broad short occipital blotches. The first 1 or 2 dorsal blotches may be divided into small paravertebral blotches. The dark brown postocular stripe extends from behind the eye to just above the rictus. A small dark spot is often present on the supralabials below the eye. The infralabials may have a fine dusting of brown pigment, but other than this the infracephalic scales and anterior ventrals are immaculate. The belly is mostly whitish or yellowish; however, some dark markings are present on the ventrals, especially laterally. Of the 2–7 dark tail rings, the distal 2 or 3 are black or very dark brown. Specimens from Mexico tend to have a black proximal rattle segment, although in those from the southern part of the range, the proximal rattle segment may be only partly, rather than entirely, black.

The rostral is wider than high. There are 2 internasals in contact with the rostral, 12–34 scales in the internasal-prefrontal region, and 4–6 intersupraoculars. The supraoculars form a hornlike process that is greatly upturned and obtusely pointed at the tip. The prenasal and lacunals are in broad contact with the supralabials, the nasals are usually conjoined above the nostril, a single large loreal broadly separates the upper preocular from the postnasal, and 2 interoculabials usually are found between the anterior subocular and supralabials. There are 10–15 (usually 12 or 13) supralabials, 10–17 infralabials (mode 13), 19–25 midbody dorsal scale rows (snakes from Baja California and the panhandle of extreme northwestern Sonora usually have 23; those from farther east in Sonora usually have 21), 132–154 ventrals, and 14–26 subcaudals.

SIMILAR SPECIES The unique supraoculars of *C. cerastes*, distinctly raised into hornlike projections, should immediately serve to distinguish this species from any of its congeners. The supraoculars may be raised moderately (but do not form projections) in *C. enyo*, which apparently is sympatric with *C. cerastes* only in southeastern Baja California del Norte. Furthermore, *C. enyo* has clearly defined, black-edged dorsal blotches, knobby scales in the prefrontal-frontal region, usually 3 or more loreals, and usually 25 or more midbody dorsal scale rows.

REMARKS Two poorly differentiated subspecies of *C. cerastes* occur in Mexico; one subspecies is extralimital. *Crotalus c. laterorepens* (Fig. 327) occurs in Baja California and the panhandle of extreme northwestern Sonora; *C. c. cercobombus* (Fig. 326) occurs in the remainder of the species' range to the east in Sonora.

This species is mostly nocturnal but may be active diurnally during the early spring and late fall. It often utilizes rodent burrows or makes its own depression in sand to escape the heat of the day, or it may be encountered resting in the shade at the bases of bushes, especially where wind-blown sand has accumulated.

This snake employs a rather remarkable mode of locomotion known as sidewinding, whence it derives its common name. The biomechanics of sidewinding are extremely complex, but the snake moves essentially in an undulating S-shaped curve by repeatedly throwing a loop of its body in front of its head.

REFERENCES Amaral, 1927g; Armstrong and Murphy, 1979; Baird, 1859; Bogert and Oliver, 1945; Boundy and Balgooyen, 1988; Brattstrom, 1952; T. W. Brown, 1970; Bullock and Cowles, 1952; Burger and Hensley, 1949; Camp, 1916; Cope, 1860c, 1900; Coues, 1875; Cowles, 1941, 1945, 1953; Cowles and Bogert, 1936; Croulet, 1963; Cuesta Terron, 1931; Curran, 1935; Dice, 1939; Ditmars, 1907, 1910, 1930, 1936, 1937; Funk, 1965; Garman, 1884a; Gates, 1957; Gloyd, 1937, 1940; Hallowell, 1854a; Hoge, 1966; Hoge and Romano, 1971a; C. F. Kauffeld, 1943; Klauber, 1927, 1931a, 1936b, 1944, 1952, 1971, 1972; Langebartel and Smith, 1954; Linsdale, 1932, 1940; Lowe, 1964; Lowe and Norris, 1954; Lowe et al., 1986; Lowell, 1957; Malkin, 1962; Martín del Campo, 1935, 1937a, 1938b, 1950; Meek, 1906; Miller and Stebbins, 1964; Minton and Minton, 1980; Moore, 1976, 1978; Mosauer, 1932a, 1933; R. W. Murphy, 1983a, 1983b; R. W. Murphy and Ottley, 1984; Murray, 1955; Norris, 1967; Norris and Lowe, 1964; Savage, 1960; Savage and Cliff, 1953; Schmidt, 1922; H. M. Smith and Taylor, 1945, 1966; P. W. Smith and Hensley, 1958; Soulé and Sloan, 1966; Stebbins, 1985; Stejneger, 1893, 1895; Van Denburgh and Slevin, 1921a; Welsh and Bury, 1984; Wright and Wright, 1957.

### *Crotalus durissus* Linnaeus

(Figs. 328–346, 446, 447; Maps 94–96)

LOCAL NAMES Cascabel, cascabela, víbora de cascabel. Argentina: campanilla; cascabela; mbói-chiné, mbói-chiní (Guaraní tribal names); víbora de cascabel; viborón. Aruba: cascabel, colebra. Belize: rattlesnake.

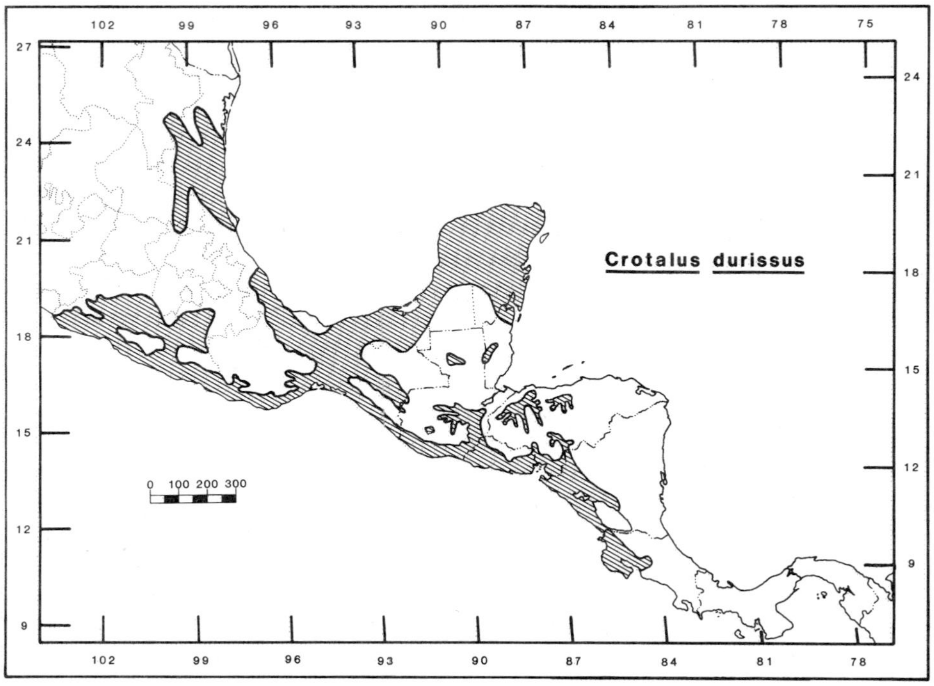


**Map 94.** Distribution of *Crotalus durissus* in Mexico and Central America. The species is apparently absent from most of Isthmian Central America, but has an extensive distribution in South America (see Maps 95 and 96).

Bolivia: cascabel chonono. Brazil: boiçininga (Amazonas), boiçinunga, boiçuninga, boiçununga, boiquira (south and southeast), cascavel, cascavel de cuatro ventas (northeast), cobra de guizo (Rio Grande do Sul), maracá, maraca-bóia (Amazonas and Central). Colombia: cascabel. Costa Rica: cascabela. Mexico: cascabel tropical, víbora real (Chiapas); shunu (Zapotec name in Isthmus of Tehuantepec region); tecuhtlacozauqui, tepocolcóatl, teuhtlacozauhqui, tlilcóatl (Náhuatl); tzab-can (Mayan name in Yucatán Peninsula). Paraguay: mboi chi-ni, víbora cascabel. Peru: cascabel, serpiente de cascabel. Uruguay: cascabel, víbora de cascabel. Venezuela: cascabel; cascabel común; cascabel de monagas, cascabel de uracoa, cascabel enana, cascabel monaguesa (names used in Monagas and Anzoátegui for *C. d. vegrandis*); cazadora; crótalo; culebra; ma-ára (tribal name in Zulia).

ENGLISH NAME Neotropical rattlesnake.

DISTRIBUTION This species is the most widely distributed rattlesnake, ranging discontinuously from Mexico to Argentina. In Mexico and Central America *C. durissus* occurs from southwestern Michoacán southward

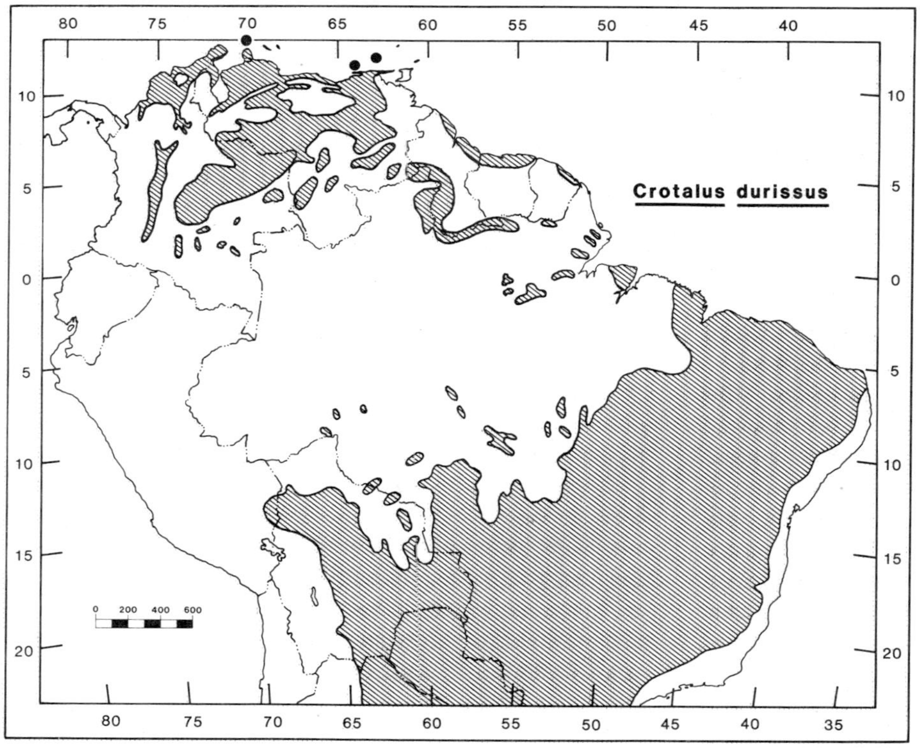


**Map 95.** Distribution of *Crotalus durissus* in northern South America. Dots represent island records for (from east to west) Aruba, Isla de Margarita, and Islas los Testigos. Small isolated areas on the mainland contain suitable habitat, but specimens have not been recorded from all of these.

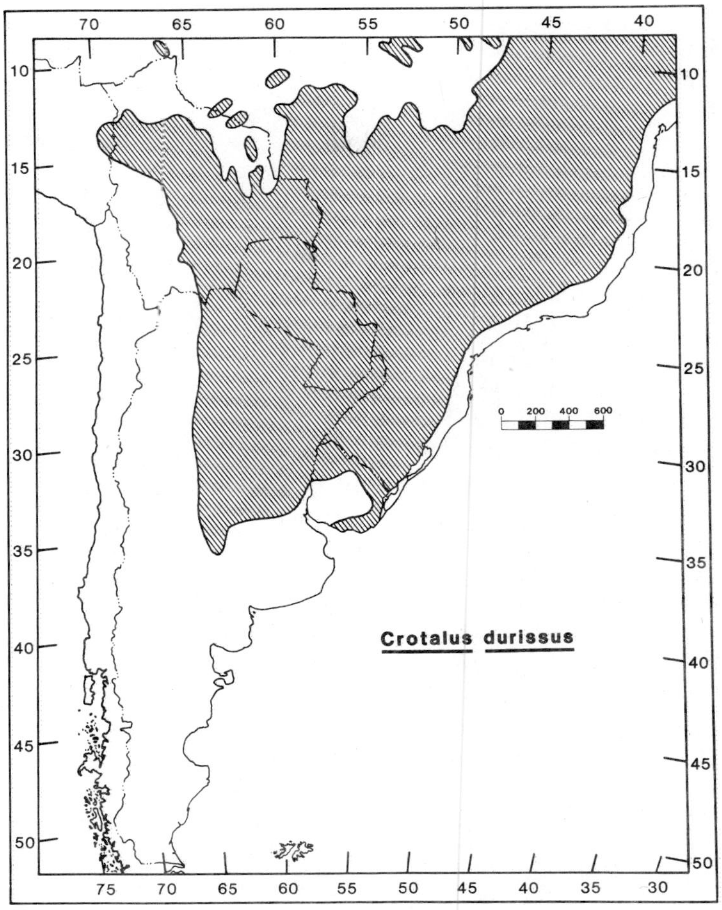


**Map 96.** Distribution of *Crotalus durissus* in southern South America. Some of the isolated areas represent suitable habitat from which specimens have not yet been recorded.

along the Pacific coastal plain and foothills through Mexico, Belize, Guatemala, El Salvador, Honduras, and Nicaragua, to the extreme western portion of the Meseta Central, province of San José, in west-central Costa Rica. There is an isolated population in northeastern Mexico from central Nuevo León through southern Tamaulipas, northern Veracruz, eastern San Luis Potosí, and northern Querétaro. In the southern Gulf of Mexico lowlands this species ranges from central Veracruz southward in Mexico (crossing the Isthmus of Tehuantepec to the Pacific) through the Yucatán Peninsula, thence eastward along the Atlantic drainage of parts of northern and eastern Guatemala, Belize, and northwestern Honduras. This species has not been recorded from Panama, although it has been alleged to exist in the dry tablelands of Veraguas and Chiriquí (Map 94).

In South America, *C. durissus* occurs in all mainland countries except Ecuador (see Remarks) and Chile; it is found also in the Antilles on Morro de la Iguana and Tamarindo (Islas Los Testigos), and on Isla Margarita (Los Frailes). Another population exists on Aruba. It has been reported once, probably in error, from the island of Curaçao, but no additional specimens have been forthcoming from this locality. In Colombia *C. durissus* ranges through the Caribbean lowlands from the Departamento de Córdoba northeastward through the Departamento de la Guajira. In the Río Magdalena Valley this species ranges at least as far south as Garzón, Departamento de Huila. East of the Andes *C. durissus* is found throughout the llanos, primarily north of the Río Guayabero/Guaviare, although we are aware of specimens from the Comisaría del Guaviare and suitable habitat exists in Guainía as well. In Venezuela *C. durissus* is distributed throughout the northern half of the country, with isolated populations in the savannas of southern Anzoátegui and Monagas and in the Guiana highlands of extreme southeastern Bolívar. Additional populations of *C. durissus* probably exist wherever suitable habitat occurs in southern Venezuela.

In the Guianas, *C. durissus* is found along the coastal lowlands from central Guyana to eastern French Guiana, where it is said to be common in the savannas of the Kourou region. Isolated populations exist in west-central and southwest Guyana and southern Suriname. A population of *C. durissus* in the territory of Amapá, Brazil, may be contiguous with the coastal Guianan population. *Crotalus durissus* exists throughout Brazil with the exceptions of Acre, Espírito Santo, and Rio de Janeiro, where it has not been recorded. In the northern half of the country *C. durissus* exists in isolated populations in Amazonas, Roraima, Pará, Amapá, and on the Ilha de Marajó. In Roraima and northern Pará populations are associated with the Guiana Massif and occur at the borders of Venezuela, Guyana, and Suriname, respectively. *Crotalus durissus* is distributed more-or-less continuously from Ceará and Rio Grande do Norte south to Rio Grande do Sul and west into Piauí and Goiás with extensions into Mato Grosso and Rondônia. This species is absent in the Atlantic coastal mountains of Brazil.

*Crotalus durissus* is absent over most of Uruguay,

being found only in the extreme north and northwest (Tacuarembó, Artigas, and Maldonado), and continuing inland into Argentina, where it occurs as far south as Mendoza, San Luis, and possibly northwestern La Pampa. The range includes all of northern Argentina exclusive of the Andean highlands, and virtually all of Paraguay (records are lacking in extreme northeast Paraguay in the Pantanal). In Bolivia *C. durissus* is restricted to the eastern lowlands (actually central Bolivia, east of the Andes), and the range continues northward into the upper Río Beni–Río Madre de Dios drainage, including a small portion of adjacent Puno, Peru. See Remarks and Maps 95 and 96 for further information on geographic races and their distribution.

This species is usually found at elevations below 700 m, but in Middle America populations occurring between, 1,500 and 2,200 m are known from Mexico in the Gómez Farías region of Tamaulipas, the Sierra de Coalcomán in Michoacán, near Comitán in Chiapas, and on the steep slopes bordering the northern side of Lago de Atitlán in Guatemala. In Costa Rica it occurs to nearly 1,000 m on the Meseta Central.

There is a record from 2,040 m in the Sierra Nevada de Santa Marta, Colombia, and *C. durissus* reputedly occurs in the semi-arid highlands of Boyacá at similar elevations. In Venezuela and the Guianas this species is recorded reliably to nearly 2,500 m (Pico Naiguatá, Venezuela), and it has been reported as high as 2,800 m. In the Sandia region of southern Peru, *C. durissus* has been found at 2,300 m.

HABITAT This species is usually found in semi-arid regions, including dry to very dry tropical forest and thorn woodland, but also in relatively dry open areas within mesic forests. Other habitats occupied in various parts of the range include tropical deciduous forest; pine-oak forest; arid tropical scrub; grass (*Trachipogon*), pine, or palm savannas (including those bordered by rainforest); and, rarely, natural breaks in cloud forest. *Crotalus durissus* is encountered infrequently in dense forest, and it is largely absent from rainforest, as reflected by its distribution.

DESCRIPTION *Crotalus durissus* is a stout terrestrial rattlesnake commonly reaching about 1,000 mm in length. Large males in some populations may attain lengths of 1,400–1,600 mm, and the maximum is at least 1,800 mm. Specimens approaching this size have been recorded from Middle America, northern South America, and (questionably) Uruguay. Some South American populations apparently are dwarfed, including those in the savannas of northeastern Venezuela, the highlands of southeastern Venezuela, the savannas of southwestern Guyana, and the Island of Aruba, where the largest specimens do not exceed 1 m in total length.

This species possesses a conspicuous spinal ridge, especially in large adults; it is most evident on the anterior part of the body, because of the height of the neural spines. Specimens from northeastern Mexico show less development of this feature. In adults, the dorsals covering the spinal ridge are notable for their prominent high tubercular keels; the degree of rugosity found in *C. durissus* is unrivaled by any other species of rattlesnake.

The ground color may be gray-brown, brown, reddish brown, yellowish gray, pale blue-gray, greenish gray, yellowish olive, straw-yellow, orangish, or nearly black. There are no dark punctations in the ground color. As a broad generality (with many exceptions), the ground color of snakes from densely forested regions—such as the Pacific lowlands of Guatemala or parts of northern South America—tends to be considerably darker than in snakes from more arid regions—such as the Río de las Balsas or Río Motagua valleys in Mexico and Guatemala, respectively. The pattern often consists of scales that are nearly all unicolored, at least on the anterior part of the body; however, the scales constituting the pale borders around the dorsal blotches may occasionally be pale distally and have dark bases. Snakes from northeastern Venezuela have a gray, tan, or reddish brown ground color with large white flecks that may outline a pattern typical of *C. durissus*, described below, or these flecks may be profuse enough to obliterate the pattern.

There are 18–35 rhombic or diamond-shaped dorsal body blotches; the population in northeastern Mexico has the highest average number (about 30) with a range of 27–35. The dorsal blotches may be too vaguely defined in adults from Aruba to allow an accurate assessment of the number. Middorsally the blotches are separated by 1 or 2 pale scales. The body blotches, at least anteriorly, are reddish brown, dark brown, or black; the interiors of these blotches are paler, usually tan to pale gray-brown, except in some southern South American snakes. Posteriorly the dorsal blotches tend to become shorter, wider, and more obscure, often coalescing with the lateral body blotches. The lateral blotches are below the lateral points of the dorsal series and usually comprise groups of 3–7 dark scales bordered by pale scales. This primary series of lateral blotches frequently engages scale rows 2–5, but in some populations, including those in northeastern Mexico and northern South America, this series may be situated somewhat more ventrally and may reach the lateral edges of the ventrals. Another secondary series of lateral blotches alternates between the primary lateral series; this series is usually paler than the primary series and involves the outer edges of the ventrals. The secondary series of blotches is often indistinct and may be absent in snakes from northeastern and southwestern Mexico.

The head pattern is fairly intricate in most populations and usually consists of a transverse dark bar across the anterior portions of the supraoculars, the posterior part of the prefrontals, and the anterior intersupraoculars (sometimes interrupted medially); a dark streak extending posteriorly from the loreal pit to the upper part of supralabials 6–9; a dark postocular stripe extending from behind the eye to the rictus or angle of the jaw; often a pair of upper temporal stripes extending diagonally from the posterior portion of the supraocular to above the angle of the jaw; and a pair of parietal stripes extending from the posterior portion of the supraocular (where they usually merge with the upper temporal stripe) to the back of the head, where they become narrower and continue onto the body as paravertebral stripes. Some or all of these head markings are pale bordered, but the extent and intensity of these markings varies considerably.

The paravertebral stripes are usually 1–4 times longer than the head, but may be shorter than this in some specimens from east central Brazil and parts of Venezuela. Throughout most of the range of *C. durissus*, each paravertebral stripe is usually 2–3 dorsal scales wide, but it is mostly 1 scale wide in snakes from southwestern Mexico and 4 scales wide in southeast Venezuelan specimens. Paravertebral stripes tend to be short and ill-defined in snakes from northeastern Mexico, or they are separated from each other by an irregular pale midvertebral stripe that varies in width from one to several scales along its length. Each supraocular is marked by a prominent pale transverse crossbar (sometimes connected across the frontal region) or subcircular spot (reported to be triangular in snakes from southwestern Guyana). The tail of adults may be uniformly gray, gray-brown, blackish, or like that of juveniles, in which 4–11 darker crossbands may be vaguely evident. The proximal rattle segment is dark gray, but tan in young snakes.

The ventral side of the head tends to be uniformly white or yellowish, although some populations bear a few punctations on the mental and anterior infralabials. The belly is usually whitish, yellowish, or buff, and varies from nearly immaculate (the usual condition) to white with pale gray blotches becoming darker posteriorly, or encroached upon by the lateral series of dark blotches, or stippled and suffused laterally with yellow, orange, or gray.

Most frequently the internasal-prefrontal region comprises 4–6 scales, including 2 large triangular internasals in contact with the rostral, followed by 2 large quadrangular prefrontals (anterior canthals) in contact with each other along the midline, and sometimes a pair of small posterior canthals. The posterior canthals, if present, are located directly behind the upper loreal and are sometimes considered post upper loreals. Snakes from Pacific Mexico, north of the isthmus, are characterized by a tendency for a relatively greater subdivision of scales in the internasal-prefrontal region; the range for these snakes is 4–10, with the prefrontals being the scales most frequently fragmented into smaller canthals and intercanthals. It is possible to encounter specimens from anywhere within the range that may have irregularly divided plates on the head; one snake from South America had 11 small scales in the internasal-prefrontal area. Anteriorly there are 2–5 (usually 2, except in Colombia and southwestern Mexico, where the mode is 3) intersupraoculars. The parietal and occipital regions usually are covered with small keeled scales; however, large, flat, somewhat irregular vestigial parietals are sometimes present in snakes from northeastern Mexico.

The first supralabial usually is in broad contact with the prenasal; however, in snakes from southwestern Mexico it is not rare (about one specimen in five) for the first supralabial to be separated from the prenasal by a row of foveals. In many Mexican populations, a single small prefoveal (postrostral) is often isolated between the rostral, prenasal, and first supralabial. The number of prefoveals varies from 3 to 11, with 6–8 most often present in all populations—except that in northeastern Mexico, whose members usually have 3 or 4. Most frequently the pre- and sublacunal are separated from the supralabials by the interposition of a row of foveals, but in about half of the snakes we have examined from southwestern Mexico and the Yucatán Peninsula the lacunals make contact with the supralabials. The lateral portions of the prefrontals (anterior canthals) are usually not deflected downward over the canthus rostralis. There are 1–6 loreals (usually 2 or 3, except in snakes from southwestern Mexico, which normally have 4 or 5 and a range of 3–8) per side; there is usually only 1 lower loreal and 1 or more upper loreals that preclude postnasal–upper preocular contact. When there is more than a single upper loreal, the extra scales are located posterior to the upper loreal (post upper loreals) and are between the prefrontal and upper preoculars, usually preventing their contact. One or 2 (usually 1) interoculabials separate the anterior suboculars from the supralabials. The first pair of infralabials are most frequently divided in specimens from the Yucatán Peninsula; commonly divided in snakes from southwestern Mexico; and divided in about one-half of South American snakes. Infracephalic scales such as submentals and interchinshields are rarely present in this species.

There are 2–5 intersupraoculars; 11–18 (usually 13–16) supralabials; 12–20 (usually 14–17) infralabials; 25–33 midbody dorsal scale rows (usually 25 in northeastern Mexico, 27 in most of South America, and 29 elsewhere in the range; there is a questionable report of 23 midbody dorsals); 155–195 ventrals (the population in northeastern Mexico has a high average number, snakes from South America have a low average number; there is an unverified record of 199 ventrals, however, from South America); and 18–34 subcaudals, 0–10 (usually 1 or 2) of which are divided.

SIMILAR SPECIES Throughout most of its vast range *C. durissus* is the only species of rattlesnake; thus confusing it with any other is out of the question. Only in Mexico north of the Isthmus of Tehuantepec does its range overlap or approach that of other species of rattlesnakes. In regions of sympatry, *C. durissus* may be distinguished from all other rattlesnakes by its conspicuous dark paravertebral stripes.

*Crotalus atrox* and *C. scutulatus* have tails with strikingly contrasting black (dark brown) and ash-white rings, a dark postocular stripe that is distinctly bordered by narrow pale stripes on either side, and usually at least 8 scales in the internasal-prefrontal area.

*Crotalus basiliscus* usually has a ground color with a greenish cast (reddish in juveniles), dorsal blotches that do not have dark borders sharply contrasting with their centers, a gray tail that has darker crossbands plainly evident, and usually 27 midbody dorsal scale rows (usually 29 in *C. durissus* from southwestern Mexico, the zone of sympatry).

Certain *C. molossus* specimens closely resemble

members of the C. *durissus* population of northeastern Mexico, the only region where these two species come into contact. Indeed, specimens from northeastern Querétaro (TCWC collection) appear to have traits of both C. *durissus* and C. *molossus* and provide strong evidence of hybridization between the two species. The following traits characterize C. *molossus* and may help distinguish it from sympatric C. *durissus*: (1) paired parietal or occipital stripes may sometimes be present, but these are even more obscure and ill-defined than in individuals of C. *durissus* occurring in northeastern Mexico, and they continue only for a short distance onto the neck; (2) the dorsal blotches tend to be coalesced more often with the primary lateral series, forming dorsal crossbands; and (3) the dorsum of the head is usually quite dark and without any intricate markings such as a dark prefrontal crossbar or pale supraocular spots or bars.

REMARKS This is the most widely distributed rattlesnake and, not surprisingly, it exhibits a considerable amount of geographic variation. We recognize 14 subspecies. One subspecific name, C. *d. neoleonensis*, is a nomen nudum. *Crotalus pifanorum*, described from Guárico, Venezuela, cannot be distinguished at present and is tentatively considered to be either a junior synonym of C. *d. cumanensis* or an intergrade.

*Crotalus d. unicolor* and C. *d. vegrandis* have often been accorded full specific status. Because both of these subspecies appear to be comparatively recently derived from an ancestor shared with northern South American populations of C. *durissus*, but not with populations in Central America and Mexico, recognizing them as full species makes C. *durissus* a likely paraphyletic species, an untenable situation to us. It seems a reasonable assumption that C. *durissus* evolved in North America and subsequently dispersed into Central and South America. It further seems reasonable to assume that this dispersal did not occur prior to the formation of the lower Central American land bridge, generally thought to have been established during the Pliocene, some 3–6 million years ago.

By the time C. *durissus* entered South America it is probable—given the distances and dispersal time involved, and a changing environment—that populations at either extreme of the range were already considerably differentiated from one another. Subsequent to the South American invasion, rattlesnakes colonized Aruba Island, probably by successfully traversing the narrow marine barrier between Aruba and the Paraguaná Peninsula. Alternatively, a land bridge may have existed between the island and mainland.

Another population became isolated geographically in the Sabanas de Maturín, Venezuela, probably at a time when changing climate greatly altered the distribution of rattlesnakes in South America. Today, other isolated rattlesnake populations exist in open dry habitats, such as savannas, all across South America—evidence of their once greater distribution. Because the great forests of South America did not exist until the late Pliocene-Pleistocene, it is possible that C. *durissus* was present in the region prior to this time and that the vicariance of C. *durissus* resulted from the emerging forests. Whether the events that isolated C. *d. unicolor* or C. *d. vegrandis* occurred before or after the vicariance event that separated South American populations from those to the north in Central America and Mexico remains to be ascertained.

The various subspecies of C. *durissus* and their geographic distributions follow: *Crotalus d. totonacus* (Fig. 341) occurs in northeastern Mexico in southern Tamaulipas, southeastern San Luis Potosí, and northern Veracruz. *Crotalus d. culminatus* (Fig. 332) inhabits southwestern Mexico from southern Michoacán to about the Isthmus of Tehuantepec. *Crotalus d. tzabcan* (Fig. 343) occurs in Mexico in the Yucatán Peninsula south to northern Belize and northern Guatemala. *Crotalus d. durissus* (Figs. 328, 329, 446, 447) ranges from Mexico to Costa Rica; it occurs on the Atlantic versant from about central Veracruz, Mexico, to western Honduras, including many interior valleys (Río Grijalva, Río Negro, Río Motagua, Río Ulúa-Chamelecón, Río Aguán), and on the Pacific from about the Isthmus of Tehuantepec to south-central Costa Rica. *Crotalus d. cumanensis* (Figs. 333, 334) occurs in Colombia and Venezuela, and is distributed along the Caribbean coastal plain from the Departamento de Córdoba, Colombia, eastward to extreme eastern Venezuela and perhaps western Guyana. In inter-Andean Colombia, this subspecies occurs south to near the headwaters of the Río Magdalena. East and south of the Andes, this subspecies is found throughout the llanos of both countries. There may be an isolated population on the high plains of Boyacá, Colombia. The populations from eastern Colombia appear to be distinguishable from those along the Caribbean Coast of Colombia. This race also occurs on the Islas Los Testigos (on Morro de la Iguana and Tamarindo) and on the Islas Los Frailes (Isla de Margarita).

*Crotalus d. unicolor* (Figs. 344, 345) inhabits the island of Aruba off the coast of Venezuela. *Crotalus d. vegrandis* (Fig. 346) is restricted to Venezuela, in southern Anzoátegui and southern Monagas (the Maturín Savanna). *Crotalus d. ruruima* (Fig. 337) occurs in Venezuela and Brazil and is known from the slopes of Mt. Roraima and Mt. Cariman-Perú, state of Bolívar, Venezuela; a single specimen has been recorded from the territory of Roraima, Brazil. This race probably occurs in adjacent Guyana as well. *Crotalus d. dryinas* (Figs. 335, 336) inhabits the northern coastal portions of Guyana, Suriname, and French Guiana, and the interior of the territory of Amapá, Brazil. The affinities of the Brazilian and French Guianan population are uncertain and it is placed tentatively with C. *d. dryinas*. *Crotalus d. trigonicus* (Fig. 342) is known with certainty only from the Rupununi Savannas in southwestern Guyana, and probably from the adjacent territory of Roraima, Brazil. There is a single puzzling report of this subspecies in the Savannas of Tiriós, Amapá, Brazil. The validity of C. *d. trigonicus* has recently been called into question

*Crotalus d. marajoensis* occurs in Pará, Brazil, and is restricted to the savannas of the Ilha de Marajó. *Crotalus d. cascavella* (Fig. 330), from Brazil, is found in the dry

Caatinga region from southern Maranhão, Piauí, Ceará, Rio Grande do Norte, south through Paraíba, Pernambuco, Alagoas, Sergipe, Bahia, and northeastern Minas Gerais. *Crotalus d. collilineatus* (Fig. 331) occurs in the central and northeastern region of Brazil, including parts of Rondônia, Mato Grosso, Goiás, southwestern Bahia, western Minas Gerais, São Paulo (where it intergrades with *C. d. terrificus*), and probably extends southward into western Paraná. There is an unsubstantiated report of this subspecies in Bolivia. *Crotalus d. terrificus* (Figs. 339, 340) ranges from the Cordillera de Carabaya in the Puno-Madre de Dios region of Peru, southward across central Bolivia, through most of Paraguay, northern Uruguay, northern Argentina, and southeastern Brazil from Rio Grande do Sul and Mato Grosso do Sul north to Minas Gerais.

For the most part, the various subspecies of *C. durissus* have been distinguished on the basis of pattern, size, color, and, to a lesser extent, squamation. The closest relatives of *C. durissus* appear to be *C. molossus* and *C. basiliscus*.

The status of isolated Brazilian populations in the Campos de Humaitá (Amazonas) and the Serra do Cachimbo and Santarém (Pará) is uncertain. *Crotalus durissus* is rumored to exist in the Departamento de Huánuco, Perú, but we are unaware of specimens from this region. Additionally, local informants maintain that rattlesnakes occur in southwest Ecuador and adjacent Peru, where suitable habitat exists. Again, there are no specimens on record, but we are aware of a pre-Columbian ceramic from western Ecuador with a graphic depiction of a rattlesnake.

As alluded to previously, an interesting aspect of the distribution of *C. durissus* is its apparent absence from Panama, although it occurs on both sides of this country in Costa Rica and Colombia. Several reports allege that it occurs in the dry tablelands of the province of Chiriquí and Veraguas. Inasmuch as this region contains what appears to be suitable habitat for *C. durissus*, it would not be astonishing if this species was eventually discovered in Panama.

The defensive coil in *C. durissus* is spectacular, with the head and anterior third of the body lifted high off the ground, the neck bent like a shepherd's crook, and the snake facing its antagonist. This species is an important cause of snakebite mortality throughout most of its range. Reports of human envenomation by *C. durissus* can be divided into two distinct clinical pictures represented by *C. d. durissus* in southern Mexico and Central America and *C. d. terrificus* in South America.

In 21 cases of *C. d. durissus* envenomation, 10 victims developed swelling of the entire extremity, 3 had hypofibrinogenuria, and 3 had local necrosis. All had a satisfactory recovery and there was no case of neurotoxicity or renal failure. This clinical picture was similar to mild to moderate envenomation by *Bothrops* and *Crotalus* species of North America. The concept that *C. d. durissus* envenomation was similar to that by *C. d. terrificus* in producing neuromuscular paralysis apparently originated with March's (1928b) case report of neck muscle "paralysis" following *C. d. durissus* envenomation; however, no similar cases have been reported since, and other reports substantiate that envenomation by individuals of the Middle America populations of *C. durissus* does not produce this effect.

A detailed description of clinical venom effects by *C. d. terrificus* in Brazil emphasized the findings of progressive neuromuscular paralysis, and hemolysis of red cells with resultant renal failure. A mortality incidence of 72% without treatment was reduced to 12% with treatment. In the most recent large series reported (1966–1973), fatality was further reduced to 6%. In addition to respiratory paralysis and renal failure, recent investigators have reported hypotension (shock), afibrinogenemia, and myonecrosis and myoglobinuria with acute renal failure. Uniformly, reports indicate a lack of swelling or other significant local effects of the venom. There is no documented report that envenomation by any other species of pitviper produces clinically significant paralysis, although the venoms of several *Crotalus* species contain "neurotoxins."

REFERENCES Abuys, 1987c; Abalos, 1961, 1977; Abalos and Bucher, 1970; Abalos and Mischis, 1975; Abalos and Pirosky, 1963; Abalos et al., 1964; Achával, 1976; Achával et al., 1976, 1978; Acosta-Solís, 1944; Alemán G., 1953; Allen and Neill, 1957; Alvarez del Toro, 1983; Amaral, 1925b, 1926d, 1928, 1929d, 1930b, 1931a, 1931b, 1931c, 1934a, 1938, 1944d, 1948b, 1974, 1978; Andrews, 1937; Angel, 1983; Armstrong and Murphy, 1979; Ayerbe, 1979; Ayerbe et al., 1977, 1979; Azevedo-Marques et al., 1985; Barrera, 1963; Barrio, 1961a; W. Beebe, 1946; Bellairs, 1969; Bertoni, 1914, 1939; Bolaños, 1971, 1982, 1983, 1984; Bolaños et al., 1981; Boulenger, 1896; Brongersma, 1940, 1967; J. H. Brown, 1973; Canese, 1966; Cardoso and Brando, 1982; Carrillo de Espinoza, 1970, 1983; Chippaux, 1987; H. C. Clark, 1925, 1942; Cochrane and Jones, 1981; Cope, 1860a, 1860c, 1861, 1876a, 1887; Cordeiro and Hoge, 1974; Cunha and Nascimento, 1982a; Curran, 1935; Daniel, 1949; Da Silva et al., 1979; Davis and Dixon, 1959; Davis and Smith, 1953; Devincenzi, 1925; Ditmars, 1905, 1928b, 1930; Dixon, 1979; Dixon et al., 1972; Duellman, 1961, 1965a, 1965b; Dugand, 1975; Dugès, 1896; Duke, 1967; Dundee et al., 1986; Dunn, 1944a, 1951; Dunn and Emlen, 1932; Eichelbaum, 1927; Elton, 1948; Fernández Barrán and Freiberg, 1951; Ferrari-Perez, 1886; Flores Villela et al., 1987; Fonseca, 1949; Freiberg, 1968, 1984; Fugler, 1960; Gadow, 1905, 1908; Gaige, 1936; Gallardo, 1977, 1979; Gann and Gann, 1939; García-López and Sandner-Montilla, 1962; Garman, 1884a; Gasc and Rodrigues, 1980; Gatti, 1955; George, 1930a, 1930b; Gliesch, 1925; Gloyd, 1936c, 1940; Gloyd and Kauffeld, 1940; Gray, 1829; Grocott and Sadler, 1958; Groombridge, 1986; Grzimek, 1975; Günther, 1861; Gutiérrez et al., 1979; Hagmann, 1909; Harris and Simmons, 1972a, 1972b, 1978a, 1978b; Hartweg and Oliver, 1940; Henderson and Hoevers, 1975; Hoevers, 1967; Hoge, 1953a, 1953b, 1966, 1967, 1979; Hoge and Lancini, 1962; Hoge and Romano, 1973; Hoge and Romano-Hoge, 1981a, 1981b; Hoge, Romano, and Cordeiro, 1977; Hoge et al., 1975, 1981; Hoogmoed, 1979, 1983; Hoogmoed and Gruber, 1983; Hummelinck, 1940; Ihering, 1911; Jan, 1859b; Jan and Sordelli, 1870–1881; Jansen et al., 1982; C. F. Kauffeld and Gloyd, 1939; I. Kauffeld, 1940; Kempff-Mercado, 1975; Klappenbach and Orejas-Miranda, 1969; Klauber, 1936b, 1941, 1952, 1971, 1972; Klemmer, 1963; Koslowsky, 1898; Lacerda, 1884; Lancini, 1962c, 1967, 1970, 1979; Lancini V., 1983; Laurent and Teran, 1981; Laurenti, 1768; Lee, 1980; Lema, 1971b, 1983; Lema and Fabián-Beurmann, 1977; Lema et al., 1980; Lyman, 1949; Machado, 1945b; Maclean et al., 1977; Magalhães, 1925; March, 1928b; Marcuzzi, 1950; Martin, 1955a, 1958; Martín del Campo, 1935, 1937a, 1950, 1984; McCranie, 1984, 1986; Medem, 1969; Meek, 1910; Meneses, 1974a, 1974b; Mertens, 1952b; Meyer, 1969; Migone, 1929; Milá de la Roca, 1932; Minton and de Cervantes, 1977; Minton et al., 1968; Moonen, 1982; Moonen et al., 1978; L. Müller, 1927; P. Müller, 1968, 1969a, 1969b, 1971, 1973; J.

B. Murphy et al., 1979; Neill, 1960, 1962, 1965; Neill and Allen, 1959a, 1959b, 1960; Nicéforo-María, 1929b, 1930b, 1933, 1942; Orcés, 1942, 1943, 1948; Parker, 1935; Pérez-Higadera [*sic*] et al., 1987; Pérez-Higareda, 1978; Pérez-Santos, 1986a, 1986b; Pérez-Santos and Moreno, 1986; Peters and Orejas-Miranda, 1970; Picado T., 1931; Powell and Parmerlee, 1980; Quelch, 1898; Ramírez-Bautista et al., 1981; Renjifo, 1979; Rivero-Blanco and Dixon, 1979; Rodas, 1938; Rohl, 1949; Rooij, 1922; Rosado-López and Laviada-Arrigunada, 1977; Rosenfeld, 1971; Roze, 1952, 1964, 1966a, 1970a; Rubio, 1972; Ruthven, 1922, 1923; Sage and Capredoni, 1971; Sandner-Montilla, 1975, 1980, 1985a; Savage, 1980; Schmidt and Andrews, 1936; Schmidt and Walker, 1943a; Schouten, 1931, 1937; Scott, 1969, 1983b; Scott and Lovett, 1975; Shreve, 1947a; H. M. Smith, 1938; H. M. Smith and Taylor, 1945, 1966; Stuart, 1935, 1948, 1950, 1954a, 1963, 1966; Sumichrast, 1873, 1880, 1881–1882, 1882; Tada and Villa, 1975; Talbot, n.d.; E. H. Taylor, 1950, 1951, 1954; R. T. Taylor et al., 1974; Tinoco, 1978; Trejos, 1937; Troschel, 1855; Vanzolini, 1947, 1948; Vanzolini et al., 1980; Vaz-Ferreira and Sierra de Soriano, 1960; Velasco, 1895; Vellard, 1941, 1943, 1946; Vetencourt Finol., 1960; Villa, 1962, 1984; Wagler, 1824; Wagner, 1985; Wettstein, 1934; Wilson, 1983; Wilson and Meyer, 1985; Wilson et al., 1979; Woodbury and Woodbury, 1944.

## *Crotalus enyo* (Cope)

(Figs. 347–349; Map 97)

LOCAL NAME Víbora de cascabel.

ENGLISH NAME Baja California rattlesnake.

DISTRIBUTION Mexico. This species occupies the Peninsula of Baja California in the north from about Río San Telmo, Baja California del Norte, on the Pacific Coast, and the mainland opposite Isla Angel de la Guarda on the Gulf of California, southward to Cabo San Lucas. It is found on a number of islands including (from north to south) San Marcos, Carmen, San José, San Francisco, Partida del Sur, Espíritu Santo, and Cerralvo in the Gulf of California, and Santa Margarita in the Pacific Ocean (Map 97).

HABITAT This species usually frequents desert but also occurs in chaparral (coastal sage) in the northwestern part of its range and extends into tropical deciduous forest and pine-oak forest (Sierra San Lázaro) in the cape region. This snake is often found in rocky areas with a vegetation consisting of cacti and arid thornscrub.

DESCRIPTION This rattlesnake is not known to exceed 1 m in total length; the record size is 898 mm. The eyes and rattle are proportionally large and the head is remarkably small and narrow.

The ground color is tan, pale to dark brown, gray-brown, or silvery gray, and may become paler posteriorly. Snakes in the northern part of the range tend to be darker than those in the south. The ground color is punctated with gray. The 28–42 clearly defined dorsal body blotches are reddish to yellowish brown, black edged, and subrectangular anteriorly but change to hexagons by midbody. The primary lateral blotches are dark, often black, and frequently coalesce with dorsal blotches, especially on the posterior half of the body, forming crossbands. These lateral blotches often engage the lateral portions of the ventrals. A small, somewhat indistinct series of lateral blotches that alternates with the primary series is sometimes present; these also involve the lateral portions of the ventrals, but do not extend up on the sides as high as the primary series.

A distinct pale bar extends across the supraoculars, curving forward medially. Usually a pair of small dark spots are present in the anterior parietal area. A pair of longitudinally elongated outer parietal blotches extend from behind the supraoculars to the posterior parietal region; these are followed by a pair of nape stripes that extend onto the neck and may or may not engage the first dorsal blotch. Often the posterior part of the parietal blotches merges with the anterior portion of the respective nape stripes, forming a pair of large irregular stripes that extend from the supraocular well onto the body. The postocular stripe extends posteriorly behind the eye to the angle of the jaw, passing above the rictus.

Often the labials, especially the infralabials, are suffused with gray. The infralabials and gulars may also be spotted with one spot below the pit and another situated 3 or 4 scales anterior to the rictus. The belly is cream colored or buff and heavily mottled or dotted with gray or brown. The tail lacks strongly contrasting pale and dark rings, but possesses 4–8 brownish rings on a ground color heavily suffused with gray. The proximal rattle segment is usually black.

The rostral is usually wider than high. Two internasals are in contact with the rostral; 13–25 scales cover the internasal-prefrontal area, and 2–6 (usually 4 or 5) intersupraoculars are present. The scales in the prefrontal-frontal area tend to be rough and knobby. Laterally the supraoculars are slanted upward and supraocular sutures are absent. The rostral is in contact with the prenasal and the prenasal is usually in contact with the first supralabial, but such contact may be prevented by anterior prefoveals in an occasional specimen. The lacunals may be in broad contact with the supralabials or they may be wholly or partially separated by 1–3 subfoveals. The upper preocular usually is not in contact with the postnasal, such contact prevented by the presence of 1–5 loreals (usually 2 or 3—a lower, an upper, and a post upper). The lower loreal, if present, is always larger than the upper. The 1 or 2 (usually 1) interoculabials intervene between the anterior subocular and supralabials. The first pair of infralabials are not transversely divided and there are no interchinshields or submental. There are 12–15 (usually 13 or 14) supralabials, 11–16 (usually 13 or 14) infralabials, 23–27 (usually 25) midbody dorsal scale rows, 157–181 ventrals (specimens from Isla Cerralvo have a higher average number than individuals from the mainland), and 18–31 subcaudals (Cerralvo individuals have a higher average number).

SIMILAR SPECIES Three species of rattlesnakes are sympatric with *C. enyo*. *Crotalus ruber* has contrasting black and ash-white bands on the tail, a top of the head with little or no pattern, usually 27 or more midbody dorsal scale rows, and 181 or more ventrals. In *C. viridis* more than 2 internasals are in contact with the rostral,

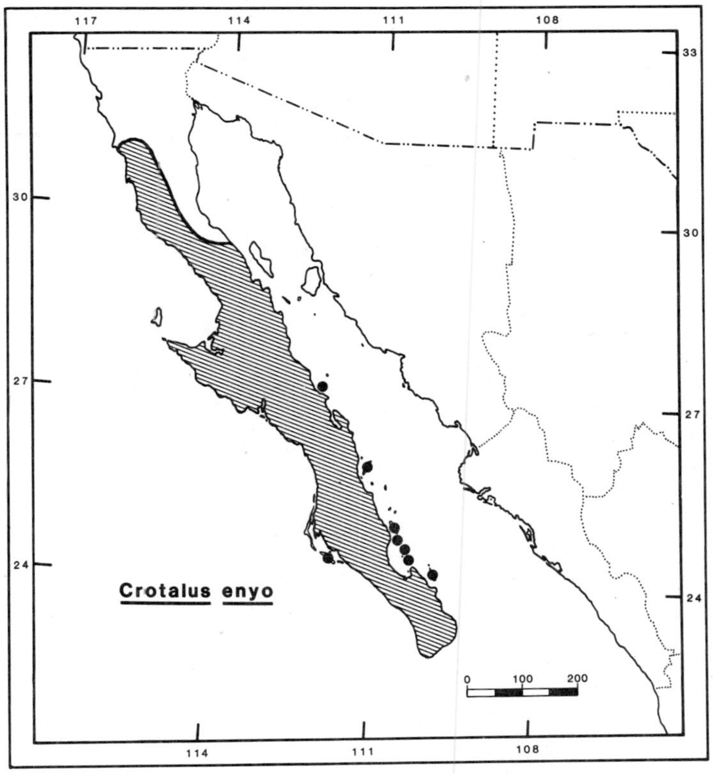


**Map 97.** Distribution of *Crotalus enyo* in the Baja California Peninsula. This species inhabits a number of islands in the Gulf of California, including (from north to south) San Marcos, Carmen, San José, San Francisco, Partida del Sur, Espíritu Santo, and Cerralvo; it also inhabits Isla Santa Margarita off the west coast.

and there are dark brown to blackish dorsal blotches with boldly contrasting pale margins. *Crotalus mitchellii* has strongly contrasting black and ash-white bands on the tail, prenasals that are usually separated from the rostral by a series of small scales, and upper preoculars that are often divided vertically and/or horizontally.

REMARKS Three subspecies are recognized: *C. e. enyo* (Fig. 347), from about El Rosario southward through the Peninsula of Baja California, including several offshore islands (see Distribution); *C. e. cerralvensis* (Fig. 348), endemic to Isla Cerralvo; and *C. e. furvus* (Fig. 349), from Río San Telmo to about El Rosario.

REFERENCES Amaral, 1929c; Armstrong and Murphy, 1979; Banks, 1962; Belding, 1887; Bostic, 1971; Cliff, 1954; Cope, 1861, 1887, 1896; Cuesta Terron, 1920, 1921a, 1931; Ditmars, 1930; Etheridge, 1961; Gloyd, 1940; Hoge and Romano, 1971a; Hoge and Romano-Hoge, 1981a; Klauber, 1931b, 1936b, 1952, 1971, 1972; Leviton and Banta, 1964; Lindsay, 1962, 1964; Linsdale, 1932; Lowe and Norris, 1954; Martín del Campo, 1935, 1937a, 1950; R. W. Murphy, 1983a, 1983b; R. W. Murphy and Ottley, 1984; Murray, 1955; Nelson, 1922; Savage, 1960; Schmidt, 1922; H. M. Smith and Taylor, 1945, 1966; Soulé and Sloan, 1966; Stejneger and Barbour, 1943; Van Denburgh, 1895a, 1922b; Van Denburgh and Slevin, 1921a; Wright and Wright, 1957; Yarrow, 1875.

## *Crotalus exsul* Garman

(Figs. 350, 351; Map 98)

LOCAL NAME Víbora de cascabel.

ENGLISH NAME Cedros Island diamond rattlesnake.

DISTRIBUTION This species is endemic to Isla de Cedros (sometimes called Cerros) off the Pacific Coast of Baja California del Norte, Mexico (Map 98).

HABITAT This species occurs mainly in rocky terrain covered with desert vegetation. This island may be enshrouded in fog for weeks at a time.

DESCRIPTION As is typical of many island species, *C. exsul* appears to be somewhat stunted in comparison with closely related mainland forms. Large adult males are usually no more than 900 mm in total length; the largest measured specimen was 940 mm.

The ground color is pale reddish gray to pinkish. The 30–37 dorsal blotches are usually reddish brown and often ill-defined in large adults; they are subcircular or roughly hexagonal on the anterior one-half to two-thirds of the body and may become transversely elongated, forming crossbands on the posterior part of the body. Color and pattern are subject to a considerable amount of ontogenetic change. In young snakes the dorsal blotches are outlined with dark brown, but in adults the blotches are usually nearly uniformly pigmented and become somewhat paler. Dorsal blotches usually have inconspicuous pale edging. In adults this is restricted to a narrow margin along the posterior border of the blotches on the anterior part of the body; it may be particularly evident at midbody. Irregular dark markings are usually present on the dorsum of the head in juveniles; adults exhibit little or no dark marking and the top of the head is more-or-less uniformly colored. The supraoculars possess a pale transverse bar in young snakes, but this disappears in adults. A dark postocular stripe is evident in young snakes and the pale lines bordering this stripe are similar in their placement to those of *C. ruber*, but tend not to be as bright; in many adults the postocular stripe becomes faded and all but a slight trace of the anterior pale border disappears. Lateral blotches are dark in juveniles, but become obscure

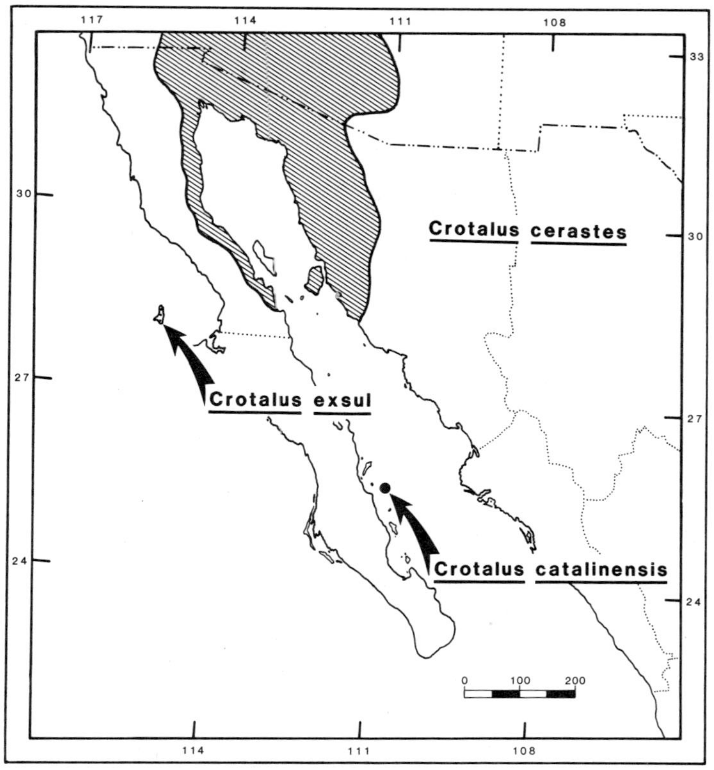


**Map 98.** Distribution of *Crotalus catalinensis* (*dot*), *C. cerastes* (*diagonal lines*), and *C. exsul* (*stipples*) in northwestern Mexico and the adjacent United States. *Crotalus exsul* is restricted to Isla de Cedros off the Pacific Coast; *C. catalinensis* is found only on Isla Santa Catalina in the Gulf of California.

in adults. The tail is marked with strongly contrasting ash-gray to whitish and black rings; the 3–5 black rings are as wide as or a little wider than the pale rings separating them and often are broken laterally. The proximal rattle segment is black.

The rostral is usually higher than wide. There are 2 internasals in contact with the rostral, 17–40 scales in the internasal-prefrontal region, and 6–9 (usually 7 or 8) intersupraoculars. The prenasal and first supralabial usually do not touch each other, their contact prevented by prefoveals that extend forward to the rostral. Usually 2 loreals per side separate the postnasal from the upper preocular. The 1 or 2 interoculabials separate the anterior subocular from the supralabials. A pair of interchinshields is usually present. There are 14–19 (usually 16 or 17) supralabials, 15–19 (usually 16 or 17) infralabials (the first pair is almost invariably transversely divided), 27–30 (mode 27) midbody dorsal scale rows, 188–201 ventrals, and 17–26 subcaudals.

SIMILAR SPECIES *Crotalus exsul* is the only rattlesnake known from Isla Cedros. *Crotalus ruber* of the mainland differs from *C. exsul* in having the prenasals usually in contact with the first pair of supralabials, tail rings that are complete or broken at midline (but usually not laterally), an adult total length that commonly exceeds 1,000 mm, and an absence of interchinshields.

REMARKS This population appears to be poorly differentiated from and may be conspecific with *C. ruber*, in which case the name *C. exsul* would have priority.

REFERENCES Garman, 1884a; Gloyd, 1940; Grinnell and Camp, 1917; Klauber, 1930a, 1936b, 1971, 1972; Martín del Campo, 1935, 1937a, 1950; Murray, 1955; Nelson, 1922; Osorio Tafall, 1948; Savage, 1967; Schmidt, 1922; Slevin, 1926; Smith and Taylor, 1945; Stejneger and Barbour, 1943; Van Denburgh, 1895a, 1905, 1922b; Van Denburgh and Slevin, 1914, 1921a; Wright and Wright, 1957.

## *Crotalus intermedius* Troschel

(Figs. 352–355, 452, 453; Map 105)

LOCAL NAMES Colcóatl, víbora de cascabel, víbora sorda (highlands of central Oaxaca, this name may also refer to other species of snakes), viborilla.

ENGLISH NAME Mexican small-headed rattlesnake.

DISTRIBUTION Several disjunct populations occur in highland regions of Mexico. In east-central Mexico this species is known from southeastern Hidalgo, northeastern and central Puebla, southwestern Tlaxcala, and west-central Veracruz; in Oaxaca it is known from the Sierra Juárez, Cerro San Felipe and its associated ridges, Sierra de Cuatro Venados, Sierra Madre del Sur, and Sierra de Miahuatlán. It is recorded in Guerrero from several localities west of Chilpancingo including the vicinity of Omilteme, San Vicente, and Filo de Caballo (see Map 105). Its vertical distribution is from about 2,000 to over 3,000 m.

HABITAT Most of this species' range is covered by seasonally dry pine-oak forest; however, we have seen this snake in cloud forest near Omilteme, Guerrero, and in desert near Cacaloapan, Puebla, and Pachuca, Hidalgo.

DESCRIPTION Large adult males of this relatively small rattlesnake are generally between 500 and 600 mm in total length; females are somewhat smaller.

The dorsal ground color is gray, pale blue-gray, or brownish gray with 38–61 medium brown, reddish brown, or dark gray body blotches. These blotches are distinctly edged with black and are 3–7 (usually about 5) scales wide and 1½–3 (usually about 2) scales long. A dark crossbar extends across the top of the head between the anterior portions of the supraoculars. (This crossbar is sometimes not particularly evident in Oaxacan specimens). A pair of conspicuous nape blotches are sometimes fused anteriorly. A broad dark brown postocular stripe extends from the lower posterior margin of the eye to the angle of the jaw. The pattern may be virtually absent in large old individuals from Oaxaca. Below this stripe the posterior supralabials tend to be mostly creamy white; anteriorly black pigment broadly encroaches along the vertical supralabial sutures and margins of the lip. The infralabials and mental are mostly dark, but often have pale central spots. The bellies of snakes from the highlands of Guerrero are strongly stippled with gray or black, sometimes so heavily as to appear uniformly dark. Specimens from central Oaxaca may also have mostly dark ventrals, but more frequently the ventrals are pale with only a moderate amount of gray stippling. The subcaudals are colored similarly to the ventrals, but distally a few may be pale.

The rostral is wider than high. Four large flat scales—a pair of large internasals and a pair of prefrontals—may cover the anterior portion of the snout, but the prefrontals are most often fragmented into a pair of canthals and smaller intercanthals. The range of scales in the internasal-prefrontal area is 4–8, and there are 2–4 intersupraoculars. The prenasal is in contact with the first supralabial and extends over the top of the postnasal. A single loreal is usually present on each side, which precludes postnasal–upper preocular contact. Directly below the loreal a single prefoveal is usually present. (This is sometimes considered a lower loreal). The supralabials and suboculars make contact with one another below the eye. There are 8–11 (mode 9) supralabials, 8–11 (mode 9) infralabials, 21 midbody dorsal scale rows, 151–185 ventrals, 18–29 subcaudals (0–11 may be divided), and 8–10 rattle-fringe scales.

SIMILAR SPECIES Only two other species of small montane rattlesnake may occur within parts of the range of *C. intermedius*. *Crotalus triseriatus* has at least 1 lower loreal intervening between the upper loreal and supralabials, and usually at least 23 dorsal scale rows anteriorly and at midbody. The top of the head of *Sistrurus ravus* is covered with large flat plates, including a pair of internasals, a pair of prefrontals, a single frontal, and usually a pair of parietals; *S. ravus* usually possesses fewer ventrals (136–152 vs. 151–185) and body blotches (22–44 vs. 38–61) than *C. intermedius*.

REMARKS The oft-cited record of *C. intermedius* from Cerro Tancítaro in Michoacán is based on a single specimen (FMNH 39115); a reexamination of this specimen reveals that it is probably either conspecific with or closely related to *C. transversus* rather than *C. intermedius*.

Three subspecies of *C. intermedius* are recognized. In *C. i. intermedius* (Figs. 352, 353), from east-central Mexico, the postnasal is in contact with both the first and second supralabial, although contact with the second may be narrow. In *C. i. gloydi* (Figs. 354, 452, 453), from the highlands of Oaxaca, the second supralabial usually fails to touch the postnasal. *Crotalus i. omiltemanus* (Fig. 355), from the highlands of Guerrero, may be distinguished from the other subspecies by having a higher number of ventrals—164 or more in males and 170 or more in females.

These snakes are infrequently encountered during the dry season. They are diurnal and on sunny days during the wet season (June to November) they may be seen basking or crawling near rocky outcroppings.

REFERENCES Amaral, 1927f; Armstrong and Murphy, 1979; Campbell, 1982a; Campbell and Armstrong, 1979; Cope, 1887; Cuesta Terron, 1921b; Davis and Dixon, 1957, 1959; Duellman, 1961, 1965b; Fischer, 1882; Gloyd, 1940; Günther, 1885–1902; Klauber, 1952, 1971, 1972; Lynch and Smith, 1965, 1966; Martín del Campo, 1950; Muñoz Alonso, 1988; Ocaranza, 1930; Pianka and Smith, 1959; Sánchez-Herrera and López-Ortega, 1987; Schmidt and Shannon, 1947; Smith, 1946a, 1970; Smith and Taylor, 1945, 1966; E. H. Taylor, 1941; Troschel, 1866.

## *Crotalus lannomi* Tanner

(Fig. 356; Map 103)

LOCAL NAME Víbora de cascabel.

ENGLISH NAME Autlán rattlesnake.

DISTRIBUTION This species is known from a single specimen collected "1.8 miles [2.9 km] west of the pass, Puerto los Mazos, or 22 miles [35.2 km] west by road from Rio Tuxcacuesco, a branch of the Rio Armería on Mexican Highway No. 80, Jalisco, Mexico" (see Map 103). This locality lies at about 1,400 m on the ridge connecting two peaks, Cerro del Varón and Cerro del Muñeco. The region is sometimes considered the southwesternmost portion of the Mexican Plateau, but it is effectively isolated from the highlands to the east by the deep entrenchment of the Río Armería and its tributaries.

HABITAT This species occupies a transitional zone between tropical deciduous forest and pine-oak forest; the area is characterized by an abundant understory of grasses and small bamboos. Many rock outcroppings dot the landscape.

DESCRIPTION The single known specimen of *C. lannomi* is 638 mm in total length. The slender 69 mm tail comprises 10.8% of the total. The rattle is relatively small, the dorsoventral width of the proximal rattle being 2.6 mm.

In preservative the ground color is gray with 31 dark chocolate brown blotches that are 9–12 scales wide and 3–5 scales long. The middorsal blotches are usually separated narrowly from one another by 1–1½ scales; a few coalesce with each other. The pattern becomes obscure on the posterior third of the body and the dorsum of the tail is nearly uniformly gray. The dorsal blotches are edged with darker brown or black. Of the two series of dark brown lateral spots, one alternates with the larger median row. The lower lateral row of blotches sometimes extends to the lateral margins of the ventrals. The belly has two highly irregular series of spots near the lateral margin of the ventrals. Spotting on the posterior ventrals is faint and the subcaudals are uniformly colored.

The rostral is wider than high; there are 7 scales in the internasal-prefrontal region. The prenasal is in contact with the first supralabial, and 3 loreals per side preclude postnasal–upper preocular contact. There are 14–15 supralabials, 15–17 infralabials, 27 midbody dorsal scale rows, 176 ventrals, 37 subcaudals, and 8 rattle-fringe scales.

SIMILAR SPECIES *Crotalus lannomi* differs from *C. stejnegeri* in having a rostral that is wider than high, fewer prefoveals (4 vs. 7), fewer intersupraoculars (2 vs. 5–8), and fewer middorsal body blotches (31 vs. 35–43). *Crotalus lannomi* differs from *C. triseriatus* and *C. pusillus* in having more numerous midbody dorsal scale rows (27 vs. 21–25), ventrals (176 vs. 162 or fewer), subcaudals (37 vs. 34 or fewer), and infralabials (15–17 vs. 9–14). It further differs from *C. pusillus* in having more supralabials (14 or 15 vs. 11–13) and fewer body blotches (31 vs. 33–50). *Crotalus lannomi* is most easily distinguished from *C. basiliscus* and *C. durissus* by its high number of subcaudals (37 vs. 36 or fewer).

REMARKS It has been suggested that *C. lannomi* is most closely related to *C. stejnegeri*; however, *C. lannomi* is a much stouter snake with a proportionately stouter head.

Despite intensive collecting near the type locality of *C. lannomi*, the only rattlesnakes that we have encountered there have been *C. triseriatus* and *C. basiliscus*.

REFERENCES Collins, 1982; Klauber, 1972; Tanner, 1966, 1986.

### *Crotalus lepidus* (Kennicott)

(Figs. 357–370, 454, 455; Map 106)

LOCAL NAMES Víbora, víbora de cascabel, víbora verde de cascabel.

ENGLISH NAME Rock rattlesnake.

DISTRIBUTION This species occurs from southeastern Arizona, southern New Mexico, and southwestern Texas through most of the Sierra Madre Occidental and northern portion of the Mexican Plateau (Mesa del Norte), and the northern portion of the Sierra Madre Oriental. Its range in Mexico includes northeastern Sonora, Chihuahua, Durango, east-central and southeastern Sinaloa, Zacatecas, probably eastern Nayarit, northern Jalisco, Aguascalientes, western San Luis Potosí, western Nuevo Léon, Coahuila, and southwestern Tamaulipas (see Map 106). Its vertical distribution is from about 300 to 3,000 m.

HABITAT This snake is found in a variety of habitats, including pine-oak forests, mesquite-grassland, and desert (only Chihuahuan, not Sonoran); in eastern Sinaloa it occurs in areas transitional between pine-oak and tropical deciduous forest.

DESCRIPTION Large adult males are 600–700 mm in total length, and females are smaller; the largest specimens may exceed 800 mm.

This rattlesnake is one of the most variable in color and pattern; a striking amount of interpopulational, ontogenetic, and sexual variation occurs. Snakes from the western portion of the Mexican Plateau, much of the Sierra Madre Occidental, Arizona, southwestern New Mexico, and extreme west Texas possess a pattern of 13–21 dark brown to black crossbands that are widely and more-or-less regularly spaced. These crossbands are much wider middorsally than laterally and in northern snakes may extend down the sides to the ventrals; in the south (Durango, Zacatecas, Jalisco) the crossbands (or blotches) may extend only to the sixth or seventh scale row. The borders of the bands have an irregular outline and are distinctly edged with white. The interspaces between crossbands contain little to moderate amounts of mottling. The postocular stripe is usually vague or absent, but occasionally may be fairly well defined, especially in snakes from the southern portion of the range. The paired nape blotches are usually merged across the midline and the top of the head is without much black pigment. Of the 1–6 tail rings, the posterior ones often become vague and hard to count. These snakes are usually strongly sexually dimorphic: the ground color of males has a greenish cast (greenish gray, bluish green, greenish tan), whereas that of females is grayish (pale gray, bluish gray, pinkish gray). The distal portion of the tail, particularly in males, is often reddish or orangish, as is the proximal rattle segment. The amount of mottling on the belly is subject to considerable variation.

Specimens from near the Sinaloa-Durango border possess a series of 23–38 small middorsal spots, often longer than wide; these may be edged irregularly in white, at least on the anterior part of the body, and do not form crossbands except sometimes on the tail. The ground color is brownish gray or dark gray with irregular mottling of dark brown on the sides and dorsum between the primary series of spots. The tail frequently has a reddish gray cast. The postocular stripe is well defined and sometimes white edged above. The venter is heavily pigmented. The top of the head is devoid of any conspicuous dark mottling and the paired nape blotches are small and do not merge with each other. The proximal rattle segment is reddish brown or gray.

Snakes from southwestern Texas (exclusive of the El Paso area) and the eastern portion of the Mexican Plateau have 13–24 dark crossbands and a highly variable ground color that may be gray, greenish gray, reddish brown, pale brown, or pinkish. Anteriorly the crossbands are often only slightly darker than the ground color, but they become more distinct posteriorly. The interspaces between the crossbands usually contain a considerable amount of gray mottling or spotting, which sometimes forms from 1 to 3 series of irregular lateral blotches or accessory (secondary) crossbands between the primary ones. The nape blotches are most frequently paired and not in contact with each other anywhere along their length. The distal portion of the tail is pinkish, reddish, or yellowish, and the proximal rattle is orangish or buff. The distinctness and amount of ventral mottling are highly variable.

Specimens from the Sierra Madre Oriental have 24–34 dark brown body blotches that often have relatively smooth edges. These blotches are usually edged with white, sometimes broadly (1 scale wide). The ground color is pale to dark gray, often with a distinctly orangish cast. Laterally there is considerable mottling. The postocular stripe is well defined and pale bordered above and below. Paired nape blotches usually do not merge with each other at any point, and the top of the head is darkly pigmented, often with a pair of wing-shaped blotches in the parietal–upper temporal region. The proximal rattle segment is dark gray.

The rostral is usually wider than high. The number of scales in the internasal-prefrontal region varies from 5 to 15, including a large pair of internasals that are in contact medially, a single canthal on each side, and a variable number of intercanthals. There are 1–4 (usually 2) intersupraoculars, 1 or 2 (usually 1) loreal(s), and 2–5 prefoveals. The prenasal is in contact with the first supralabial; the postnasal and upper preocular are not in contact. The nasals are usually conjoined above the nostril. One of the most distinctive features of this species is an upper preocular that is vertically divided; the anterior portion is situated higher on the head than the portion adjacent to the eye and is curved over the canthus rostralis in front of the supraocular. The population inhabiting the Sierra Madre Oriental is unique in that most specimens do not have divided upper preoculars. Whether or not the anterior subocular makes contact with the supralabials is highly variable; in general, snakes from the eastern portion of the Mexican Plateau and the Sierra Madre Oriental have a complete row of interoculabials separating these scales and snakes from the western portion of the plateau and the Sierra Madre Occidental have the anterior subocular and supralabials in contact. There are 10–15 (usually 12 or 13) supralabials, 9–13 (usually 11 or 12) infralabials, 21–25 (usually 23) midbody dorsal scale rows, 149–172 ventrals, and 16–33 subcaudals. Snakes from west of the range have 10–13 (usually 12) rattle-fringe scales; those snakes from the Sinaloa-Durango border and the northern portion of the Sierra Madre Oriental have 8–12 (usually 10) and a proportionately smaller rattle.

SIMILAR SPECIES *Crotalus lepidus* may be sympatric within parts of its range, or geographically at least closely approach four other species of small montane rattlesnakes. *Crotalus pricei* usually has a pattern of 39–64 pairs of paravertebral blotches on a gray ground color, an upper preocular that is not vertically divided, and usually fewer midbody dorsal scale rows, supralabials, and infralabials than *C. lepidus*. *Crotalus stejnegeri* possesses a distinctive head pattern, the first pair of infralabials are distinctively shaped, the ventrals and subcaudals are more numerous, and the tail is exceptionally slender with a tiny rattle. *Crotalus triseriatus* occurs to the southeast of *C. lepidus* and the two species do not appear to be sympatric anywhere within their ranges. In the regions where these two species most closely approach each other *C. triseriatus* differs from *C. lepidus* in possessing 24 or more middorsal body blotches, dorsal body blotches that are longer middorsally than the adjacent interspaces, and an upper preocular that is not divided vertically. *Crotalus willardi* has 6–9 intersupraoculars, usually 25 or 27 midbody dorsal scale rows, an undivided upper preocular, 20 or more scales in the internasal-prefrontal region, and usually a distinctive pattern of white facial stripes.

REMARKS This species mostly inhabits mountains and rugged broken terrain in the vicinity of rocky outcroppings and slides. Within forests it appears to prefer open or relatively barren areas subject to intense sunlight.

Four subspecies are currently recognized: *Crotalus l. lepidus* (Fig. 357) ranges from southeastern New Mexico and southwestern Texas (exclusive of the El Paso area) across much of the eastern portion of the Mexican Plateau to San Luis Potosí. *Crotalus l. klauberi* (Figs. 358–363, 454, 455) occurs from southeastern Arizona, southwestern New Mexico, and extreme southwestern Texas southward across much of the western portion of the Mexican Plateau to northern Jalisco. *Crotalus l. maculosus* (Figs. 364–366) is found in the western drainages of the Sierra Madre Occidental in Durango and Sinaloa. *Crotalus l. morulus* (Figs. 367–370) occupies the Sierra Madre Oriental in southwestern Tamaulipas, central Nuevo León, and southeastern Coahuila. *Crotalus l. castaneus* appears to be a junior synonym of *C. l. lepidus*.

REFERENCES Amaral, 1927g; Anderson and Lidicker, 1963; Armstrong and Murphy, 1979; Axtell, 1959; Baker et al., 1967; Bogert and Degenhardt, 1961; Bogert and Oliver, 1945; Boulenger, 1896; A. E. Brown, 1903a; B. C. Brown, 1950; Campbell et al., 1989; Cope, 1900; Crimmins, 1927; Cuesta Terron, 1921b, 1931; Dixon, 1956; Drake, 1958; Dunkle and Smith, 1937; Garman, 1884a, 1887a; Gehlbach, 1972; Gloyd, 1936b, 1937, 1940; Gloyd and Smith, 1942; Groombridge, 1986; Günther, 1895–1902; Hardy and McDiarmid, 1969; Jacob and Altenbach, 1977; Juliá-Zertuche and Treviño, 1978; Kauffeld, 1943; Kennicott, 1861; Klauber, 1936b, 1940b, 1940c, 1952, 1971, 1972; Liner and Olson, 1973; Lowe, 1964; Lowe et al., 1986; Martin, 1955a, 1955b, 1958; Martín del Campo, 1935, 1937a, 1950, 1953: McCoy, 1984; Mellink et al., 1987; Milstead, 1960b; Milstead et al., 1950; Minton, 1959; Mocquard, 1899, 1908–1909; Reynolds, 1982; Schmidt and Owens, 1944; Schmidt and Smith, 1944; H. M. Smith, 1943, 1944a, 1946a; H. M. Smith and Buechner, 1947; H. M. Smith and Taylor, 1945, 1966; Stejneger, 1895, 1902; Stejneger and Barbour, 1943; Strecker, 1909; Tanner, 1985; Tanner et al., 1972; E. H. Taylor, 1949, 1952; Van Denburgh, 1924; Van Devender and Lowe, 1977; Webb, 1984; Wilson and McCranie, 1979; Woodin, 1953; Wright and Wright, 1957; Zweifel, 1954.

## *Crotalus mitchellii* (Cope)

(Figs. 371–379; Map 99)

LOCAL NAMES Víbora blanca, víbora de cascabel.

ENGLISH NAME Speckled rattlesnake.

DISTRIBUTION In the United States this species ranges from east-central California, southwestern Nevada, and extreme southwestern Utah, southward through most of southern California and western Arizona. In Mexico it occurs in the northern (Pinacate) portion of the panhandle in northwestern Sonora and throughout the Peninsula of Baja California, exclusive of the desert region east of the Sierra de Juárez in Baja California del Norte and most of the Vizcaíno Desert. It occurs on numerous islands in the Gulf of California, including, from north to south, El Muerto, Angel de la Guarda, Smith, Piojo, Salsipuedes, Carmen, Monserrate, San José, Espíritu Santo, Partida del Sur, and Cerralvo. In the Pacific it occurs on Isla de Santa Margarita (Map 99). The vertical distribution is from near sea level to about 2,440 m.

HABITAT This species is mostly found in desert, but also in chaparral in northwestern Baja California del Norte, in tropical deciduous forest in the cape region, and in pine-oak forest in the Sierra de Juárez, Sierra San Pedro Mártir, and Sierra de San Lázaro. It is most frequently found in rugged rocky terrain, but may sometimes also occur in brushy lowland flats or arenicolous washes devoid of rocks.

DESCRIPTION Individuals of this species generally do not exceed 1 m in total length; large adult males are between 900 and 1,000 mm. The population on Isla Angel de la Guarda is longer, with a maximum recorded length of 1,367 mm, and the population on Isla El Muerto is dwarfed, with a maximum known length of 637 mm.

The ground color of snakes in the southern half of the Peninsula of Baja California is pale gray, tan, or yellowish gray, and the dorsal body blotches are dark gray or brown. Snakes from the northern half of the peninsula are extremely variable, with a cream, tan, buff, yellowish, pink, salmon, orange, gray, or pale brown ground color and reddish, orangish, gray, brown, or black blotches. An individual's ground color frequently matches the particular environment (soil, rocks) in which it lives. The number of dorsal blotches ranges from 23 to 46 (the population on Isla Angel de La Guarda has a higher average number than that on the mainland). Dorsal blotches may be hexagonal or diamond shaped on the anterior part of the body, but posteriorly they coalesce with the lateral series of blotches to form crossbands. The dorsum of this species is punctated liberally with dark pigment, especially within the blotches. The scales composing the row that bounds the anterior edge of a dorsal blotch are often dark brown or black tipped distally. Head markings are usually present but often ill-defined. Sometimes there are elongated paired occipital blotches and upper temporal streaks; a postocular stripe, if present, extends from the posterior edge of the eye to above the rictus. The infracephalic scales, especially the mental and anterior infralabials, are dusted or spotted with black pigment. The belly is pink, pinkish cinnamon, reddish, or orangish and heavily mottled with dark brown. The subcaudals are also heavily mottled. The 3–9 dark tail bands are widely separated, are wider and darker dorsally, and become darker (usually black) distally. The proximal segment of the rattle is black.

The rostral is usually wider than high and contacts 2 (rarely 4) small internasals. The 13–51 scales in the internasal-prefrontal region tend to be somewhat knobby, whereas those located more posteriorly on the head are flat and keeled. There are 1–8 intersupraoculars and the supraoculars may have short irregular sutures along their outer edges. The rostral is usually separated from the prenasals by the interposition of one to a series of smaller scales. The front edges of the prenasals are often chipped and sutured. The prenasal may or may not be in contact with the first supralabial (such contact is usually precluded by the forward extension of prefoveals in snakes in the south; in the north, the prenasal often contacts the first supralabial), and the lacunals may or may not be in contact with the supralabials. The number of loreals is highly variable (0–5), but most frequently there are 2; these preclude upper preocular–postnasal contact. The upper preocular is often divided vertically and/or horizontally. Two interoculabials usually separate the anterior subocular and supralabial series. Usually no interchinshields or submentals are present, and the first pair of infralabials are not transversely divided.

There are 12–19 supralabials (usually 15–17, except in snakes from Angel de la Guarda, which average about 14), 13–19 infralabials (usually 15–17), 21–27 midbody dorsal scale rows (usually 25 on the mainland, 23 on Isla El Muerto, and 27 on Angel de la Guarda), 156–190 ventrals (snakes from the southern portion of the Peninsula of Baja California average a low number, and snakes from Isla Angel de la Guarda have a high average), and 16–28 subcaudals.

SIMILAR SPECIES Specimens of *Crotalus mitchellii* from Mexico usually possess two unique characteristics, either one of which should serve to identify this snake: a rostral that is separated from the prenasal by one to a series of intervening scales; and a preocular that is divided, often irregularly, vertically and/or horizontally.

Other rattlesnakes may be confused with *C. mitchellii*. *Crotalus atrox*, sympatric in Mexico only in extreme northwestern Sonora, has strongly contrasting black and ash-white rings on the tail, a pale stripe that usually extends from the upper postocular downward to the penultimate or antepenultimate supralabial, and a belly that is mostly pale without extensive or heavy dark mottling. *Crotalus cerastes*, sympatric in northwestern Sonora and the Gulf of California side of Baja California del Norte, has supraoculars dramatically elevated into hornlike processes, nasals usually conjoined above the

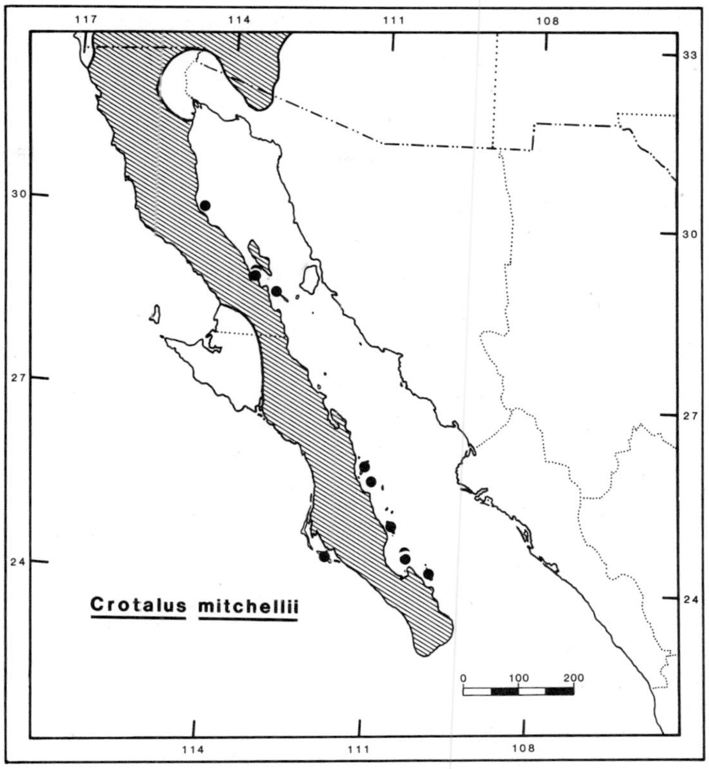


**Map 99.** Distribution of *Crotalus mitchellii* in the Baja California Peninsula and adjacent Mexico and United States. This species inhabits a number of islands in the Gulf of California, including (from north to south) El Muerto, Ángel de la Guarda, Smith, Piojo, Salsipuedes, Carmen, Monserrate, San José, Espíritu Santo, Partida del Sur, and Cerralvo. This species also inhabits Isla Santa Margarita off the west coast.

nostril, usually 21–23 midbody dorsal scale rows, and 154 or fewer ventrals. *Crotalus enyo*, broadly sympatric over much of the Peninsula of Baja California, has dorsal body blotches clearly defined with black edging, a distinct pale bar on the supraocular that curves forward medially, and a pair of distinct nape stripes that often engage the first dorsal blotch. *Crotalus ruber*, sympatric throughout most of Baja California, has a broad dark postocular stripe that is bordered by narrower pale stripes, dorsal blotches with pale borders, and a first pair of infralabials that is transversely divided. *Crotalus scutulatus*, sympatric only in northwestern Sonora, has strongly contrasting dark and pale tail rings, a broad dark postorbital stripe that is bordered by distinct narrow pale stripes, a nearly immaculate belly with only a little pigment encroaching on the lateral portions of the ventrals, usually no more than 2 intersupraoculars, and 6–21 scales in the internasal-prefrontal region. *Crotalus tigris*, which is probably not sympatric anywhere in Mexico except possibly in the panhandle of northwestern Sonora, has a proportionally much smaller head than *C. mitchellii*, a pattern of crossbands that extends from the anterior part of the body to the tail, and 23 or fewer midbody dorsal scale rows. *Crotalus viridis*, sympatric along the Pacific drainage of Baja California del Norte, has a pale brownish gray ground color, diamond-shaped blotches that are edged in black and bordered by a single row of pale scales, and 3 or more internasals.

REMARKS Five subspecies are recognized; one of these is extralimital. *Crotalus m. mitchellii* (Figs. 371–373) and *C. m. pyrrhus* (Figs. 377–379) occur in the southern and northern halves of the Peninsula of Baja California, respectively; *Crotalus m. angelensis* (Figs. 374, 375) and *C. m. muertensis* (Fig. 376) occur on the Isla Angel de la Guarda and Isla El Muerto, respectively, in the Gulf of California.

This species is mostly nocturnal during midsummer, but may be diurnal in early spring and late fall. It has a reputation for being nervous and quick to bite.

Symptoms of a bite reportedly include sharp pain at the site of envenomation—which becomes intense by 1 hour after envenomation—discoloration, and bleb formation.

REFERENCES Amaral, 1927e, 1927g, 1929a; Armstrong and Murphy, 1979; Banks, 1962; Belding, 1887; Bogert and Oliver, 1945; Bostic, 1971; Bullock and Cowles, 1952; Camp, 1916; Cliff, 1954; Cope, 1861, 1887, 1896, 1900; Coues, 1875; Cowles, 1941; Cuesta Terron, 1931; Ditmars, 1930; Etheridge, 1961; Gates, 1957; Gloyd, 1940; Grinnell and Camp, 1917; Groombridge, 1986; Hartnett, 1931; Hoge and Romano, 1971a; Klauber, 1927, 1930b, 1931a, 1931b, 1936a, 1936b, 1949b, 1952, 1963, 1971, 1972; Leviton and Banta, 1964; Lindsay, 1962, 1964, 1966; Linsdale, 1932, 1940; Lowe, 1964; Lowe et al., 1986; Martín del Campo, 1937a, 1950; McCrystal and McCoid, 1986; Meek, 1906; Miller and Stebbins, 1964; Moore, 1976, 1978; R. C. Murphy, 1917; R. W. Murphy, 1983a, 1983b; R. W. Murphy and Ottley, 1984; Murray, 1955; Neill, 1958; Norris, 1967; Orr, 1965; Pope, 1944–1945; Savage, 1960; Schmidt, 1922; Seib, 1978; H. M. Smith, 1944c; H. M. Smith and Taylor, 1945, 1966; P. W. Smith and Hensley, 1958; Soulé and Sloan, 1966; Stebbins, 1985; Stejneger, 1893, 1895; Stejneger and Barbour, 1943; Streets, 1877; Van Denburgh, 1894, 1895a, 1897, 1905, 1922b; Van Denburgh and Slevin, 1914, 1921a; Welsh and Bury, 1984; Werner, 1922; Wright and Wright, 1957; Yarrow, 1875.

### *Crotalus molossus* Baird and Girard

(Figs. 380–391; Map 100)

LOCAL NAMES Palanca, palancacóatl (southern Puebla); tecutlacotzauhqui, tepecolcóatl, teuhtlacot-

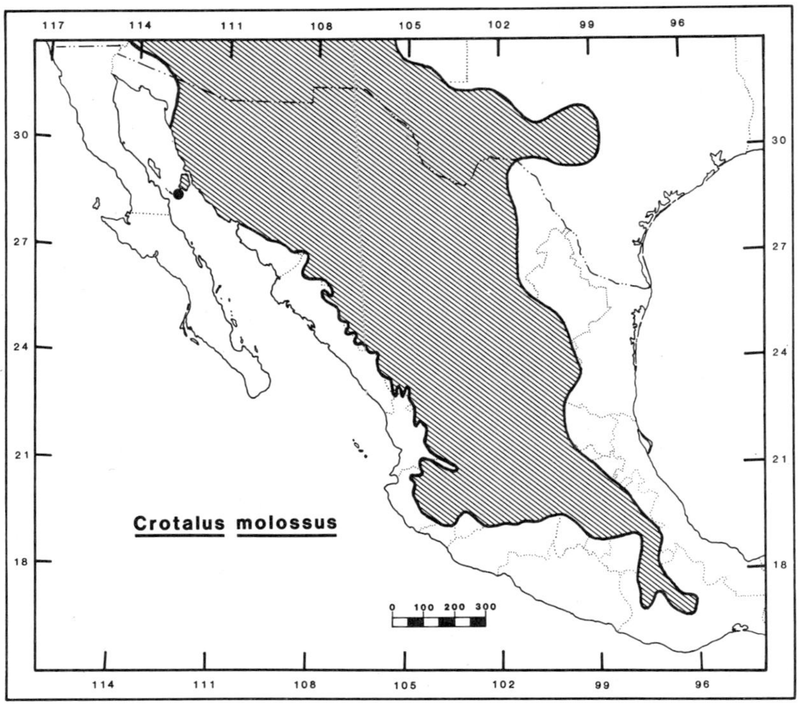


**Map 100.** Distribution of *Crotalus molossus* in Mexico and the adjacent United States. This species also inhabits Isla Tiburón and Isla de San Esteban in the Gulf of California. This species has a range that is largely complementary with that of *C. basiliscus* (Map 93).

zauhqui, teuhtlacozauhqui, tleua (Náhuatl derivatives—Valley of Mexico, Guanajuato, Jalisco); víbora, víbora de cascabel; víbora de cascabel de cola negra.

ENGLISH NAME Black-tailed rattlesnake.

DISTRIBUTION United States and Mexico. In the United States this species ranges from western and northern Arizona southward and eastward through southern Arizona, central and southern New Mexico, and west Texas, to the Edwards Plateau of central Texas; and in Mexico, from Sonora eastward through most of Chihuahua and Coahuila, southward to the southern part of the Mexican Plateau and Mesa del Sur in central Oaxaca. This snake inhabits Isla Tiburón and Isla de San Esteban in the Gulf of California (Map 100). Its vertical distribution is from near sea level to about 2,930 m.

HABITAT Pine-oak forest, boreal forest, mesquite-grassland, upland Sonoran desert, chaparral, tropical deciduous forest, and probably thorn forest.

DESCRIPTION Large specimens of this medium-sized rattlesnake usually do not greatly exceed 1 m in total length; the largest specimen known measured 1,257 mm. Populations on islands in the Gulf of California do not reach 1 m.

There is considerable north-south and east-west clinal variation for a number of characteristics in this wide-ranging species. Discordant variation in other characteristics, much individual variation within most populations, and a rather striking ontogenetic variation for tail color and pattern confuse the situation. For the purpose of describing the variation of some traits, it is convenient to broadly bisect the range of this snake into the "north" and "south" using about 25°N latitude as the dividing line.

Snakes in the north are usually paler than those to the south and have a greenish gray, steel gray, grayish olive, olive-green, yellow-green, sulphur yellow, orange-yellow, rust-colored, or cream ground color. The 20–41 rhombic dorsal blotches are chestnut brown to black; on the anterior one-half to two-thirds of the body the interiors of these blotches tend to contain several pale scales to each side of the midline. The dorsal blotches may be separated from one another by a group of scales on the midline that are considerably paler than the ground color. The first dorsal blotch often extends anteriorly as a pair of paravertebral stripes. On the anterior part of the body the blotches are rhombic to diamond shaped; more posteriorly, the dorsal blotches become progressively wider transversely and often coalesce with lateral blotches to form vertical bars that extend downward to the ventrals. The pale margins of the dorsal blotches open laterally to border each side of these vertical bars. The top of the head from the rostral to about the supraoculars is often black; the back of the head is paler (about the same as the general ground color of the body) and may have irregularly placed dark scales. The tail is dark brown to black; the dark pigment does not extend forward onto the posterior part of the body and terminates rather abruptly at about the level of the anus. The belly is whitish, yellowish, or pale gray with a subtle infusion or indistinct mottling of gray. Members of the population inhabiting Isla San Esteban tend to resemble snakes from the northern mainland of Mexico but have a high number of dorsal blotches (39–43) and indistinct dark tail rings that remain evident in adults.

The general ground color of southern *C. molossus* may be brownish olive, yellowish olive, or brownish gray. Posteriorly the ground color becomes more darkly suffused with brownish black to black pigment, which extends onto the tail; in most snakes the pattern on the posterior one-third to one-half of the body is completely obscured by the dark pigmentation. Some snakes are essentially totally black and all elements of the dorsal pattern are obscured except for the pale borders of the blotches. Twenty-four to 34 dark brown or black rhomboidal or diamond-shaped blotches are bordered by yellow or yellowish gray scales and the pale borders of adjacent blotches are usually in contact at middorsum. A few pale scales may be grouped within each blotch; pale scales are distributed primarily to either side of the midline, but sometimes come together across the dorsum. Usually fewer dorsal blotches coalesce with lateral blotches than in northern snakes; however, this is not an infrequent occurrence, especially on the posterior part of the body.

In southern snakes the top of the head, including the parietal-occipital area, is often dark with a few pale longitudinal streaks or groups of scales; alternatively, the head is brown or gray with darker markings that include upper temporal and parietal stripes. Usually a dark postocular stripe is clearly evident. It extends from beneath and behind the eye, where it is about 3–4 scales wide, to a point above the rictus, where it narrows to a single scale. The lower margin of this stripe extends along the scale row above the supralabials. The dark postocular stripe is bordered by pale lines. The lower (anterior) pale line curves from the upper preocular downward under the eye to a point on the lip margin 3–5 supralabials anterior to the rictus, and thence continues to the ultimate supralabial. The upper (posterior) pale line extends diagonally from about the upper posterior corner of the eye to just behind, or just above, the rictus. The belly is cream colored to pale yellow with a moderate amount of mottling or suffusion of dark pigment laterally; the ventrals become darker on the posterior part of the body.

The ground color in *C. molossus* includes no dark punctations, and it is not unusual for the dark dorsal body blotches to coalesce on the anterior part of the body. One peculiarity of pattern in this species is the marked tendency for each dorsal to be more-or-less unicolored; the elements of pattern do not cut across individual scales as is typical in most other rattlesnakes. Melanistic specimens are known from regions of dark volcanic rock in New Mexico and the southwestern portions of the Mexican Plateau. In juveniles 4–9 dark crossbands are evident on the tail. Throughout most of the range, the tail is uniformly dark in adults; occasionally individual specimens have dark gray tails with indistinct black rings. However, most members of southern populations in Puebla and Oaxaca retain the tail rings as adults, although they may become somewhat obscure.

The rostral is usually slightly higher than wide. Most frequently 6 scales in the internasal-prefrontal area include 2 large triangular internasals in contact with the rostral, followed by 2 large quadrangular prefrontals (anterior canthals) in contact with each other along the midline, and a pair of small posterior canthals that lie posterolaterally to the prefrontals and partially intervene between this scale and the supraoculars. Sometimes the posterior canthals are absent, leaving only 4 large scales on the dorsum of the snout. Some snakes in the northern part of the range exhibit a good deal of scale fragmentation in the internasal-prefrontal region, making the total range of variation 4–18. Anteriorly there are 2–5 intersupraoculars, with a tendency for 2 in the south and 3 in the north. Snakes from the south also tend to have larger scales in the parietal region, with a large elongated scale often present behind the posteromedial edge of the supraocular. The number and extent of the prefoveals is highly variable: snakes in the north average about 10, those in the south only 6 or 7. The first supralabial may be in broad contact with the prenasal or it may be partially separated from it by the anteriormost prefoveals, but prenasal–first supralabial contact usually is precluded completely by the forward extension of prefoveals that reach the rostral. In those instances when the prenasal and first supralabial do make contact, they frequently isolate an anterior prefoveal from the other prefoveals. (This isolated foveal has sometimes been called a postrostral).

The lateral portions of the prefrontals (anterior canthals) are usually not deflected downward over the canthus rostralis. However, contact between the postnasal and the upper preocular is almost always prevented by the presence of 1–9 loreals (usually 2–4). Snakes from throughout the range usually have an upper and a lower loreal per side, and northern snakes tend to have a greater number of loreals than snakes from the south. One to 3 (usually 2) interoculabials separate the anterior suboculars from the supralabials. Very rarely the interchinshields or the first pair of infralabials are divided transversely. There are 13–20 supralabials (usually 17 or 18 in the north, 16 or 17 in the south), 14–21 infralabials (usually 17 or 18 in the north, 16 or 17 in the south), 23–31 midbody dorsal scale rows (usually 27 in the north, 25 in the south), 166–199 ventrals (average number higher in the north), and 16–30 subcaudals, 0–19 (usually 1–3) of which are divided. The average number of subcaudals in males is lower in the central part of the range than at the northern or southern extremes.

SIMILAR SPECIES This species usually may be distinguished from other rattlesnakes in regions of sympatry by a combination of characteristics: (1) a dark tail with dark tail rings obfuscated or only vaguely indicated in adults, (2) usually no more than 6 scales in the internasal-prefrontal area, (3) the interior of the dark dorsal blotches with pale scales, often to each side of the midline, (4) dorsal scales that tend to be more-or-less unicolored, with the pattern not cutting across individual scales, and (5) parietal stripes, if present, that are obscure and irregular in outline.

REMARKS Most recent investigators have recognized three subspecies of *C. molossus*: *C. m. molossus* (Figs. 380–384) from the southwestern United States, much of northern Mexico, and Isla Tiburón; *C. m. nigrescens* (Figs. 386–389) from the southern portion of the

Mexican Plateau; and *C. m. estebanensis* (Fig. 385) from Isla de San Esteban in the Gulf of California. Additionally, we herein recognize a new combination, *C. molossus oaxacus* (Figs. 390, 391), for the population of large rattlesnakes inhabiting central Oaxaca and Puebla. Heretofore, this population has been thought to have its affinites with *C. basiliscus*, primarily on the basis of plesiomorphic color and pattern. In a number of characteristics, however—including a relatively low number of ventrals, a higher average number of labials, a lower average number of body blotches, and hemipenial morphology—these snakes more closely resemble *C. molossus*. The banded tail pattern characteristic of juvenile *C. molossus* is retained in many adult Oaxacan specimens; however, the tails of some snakes become uniformly dark, as is typical of snakes to the north.

*C. molossus* exhibits obvious clinal differences in hemipenial morphology. In snakes from northern Mexico and the United States, the lobes are straight, thick, and stubby. More than 50 relatively small spines are present on the basal part of the organ below each lobe, and these spines do not or only barely extend onto the lobes. The lobes are covered by papillate calyces that extend on the medial surfaces of the lobes down to the crotch; there are no mesial spines.

In snakes from the southern portion of the Mexican Plateau, north of the Transverse Volcanic Cordillera, the spines on the shoulders and proximal part of the lobes are slightly larger than those found in snakes to the north; also, spines are fewer, between 25 and 50. The distal portion of the lobes is covered by papillate calyces, but these do not extend to the crotch. Occasionally, there are a few soft spinules in the mesial area, but no large spines.

In snakes from Puebla and Oaxaca the lobes are relatively slender and often take on a lyriform shape when in the everted position. The basal spines are much larger than those in snakes from the north. There are 25–40 spines on the shoulders and up to the proximal third of each lobe. In most snakes, large mesial spines encroach on the asulcomedial surface of each lobe; however, in some snakes the spines terminate on the asulcate side of the organ.

In the foothills along the northwestern coast of Mexico, *C. molossus* apparently hybridizes freely with *C. basiliscus*. Most specimens from above about 1,500 m in eastern Sinaloa and western Durango clearly appear to be *C. molossus*; snakes from below 600 m are allocatable to *C. basiliscus*. However, many specimens from moderate elevations (600–1,500 m) possess traits of both species.

This species may be nocturnal during hot weather or in relatively xeric highland habitats such as southern Puebla, but it is frequently encountered by day, especially in the early morning or late afternoon. It is generally considered to be mild mannered, although a few that we have found active during the early morning have been quick to rattle and to raise their heads high off the ground into a striking position. We have encountered this species in trees up to heights of several meters.

REFERENCES Allen, 1933; Amaral, 1927g, 1929d; Anderson and Lidicker, 1963; Armstrong and Murphy, 1979; Axtell, 1959; Baird, 1859; Baird and Girard, 1853; Bogert and Oliver, 1945; A. E. Brown, 1901, 1903a; B. C. Brown, 1950; B. C. Brown and Mittleman, 1947; Bucherl and Buckley, 1971; Burchfield et al., 1982; Chrapliwy and Fugler, 1955; Cliff, 1954; Conant, 1975; Cope, 1860c, 1900; Coues, 1875; Crimmins, 1927; Cuesta Terron, 1931; Curran, 1935; Ditmars, 1930, 1936, 1937; Dixon et al., 1962, 1972; Drake, 1958; Duellman, 1961, 1965b; Dugès, 1869, 1876–1877; Dunkle and Smith, 1937; Engelhardt, 1932; Ferrari-Perez, 1886; Fouquette and Rossman, 1963; Fugler and Webb, 1956; Garman, 1884a, 1887a; Gates, 1957; Gehlbach, 1956, 1965, 1972; Gehlbach and Collette, 1957; Gloyd, 1936a, 1937, 1940, 1948; Gloyd and Smith, 1942; Grant and Smith, 1959; Greene, 1972; Hardy and McDiarmid, 1969; Hoge and Romano, 1971a; Hulse, 1973; Jameson and Flury, 1949; Kauffeld, 1943; Klauber, 1936b, 1938, 1940b, 1949b, 1952, 1971, 1972; Lewis, 1950; Lindsay, 1966; Liner, 1964; Little and Keller, 1937; Lowe, 1964; Lowe and Norris, 1954, 1955; Lowe et al., 1986; Martin, 1958; Martín del Campo, 1935, 1937a, 1938b, 1942, 1950, 1953, 1955; McCoy, 1984; Mellink et al., 1987; Milstead, 1960b; Milstead et al., 1950; Minton, 1959; Minton and Cervantes, 1977; Mosauer, 1932b; R. W. Murphy, 1983b; R. W. Murphy and Ottley, 1984; Ortenburger and Ortenburger, 1927; Pope, 1944–1945; Pough, 1966; Price, 1980; Reynolds, 1982; Schmidt, 1922; Schmidt and Owens, 1944; Schmidt and Smith, 1944; H. M. Smith, 1943, 1944a, 1970; H. M. Smith and Buechner, 1947; H. M. Smith and Taylor, 1945, 1966; Soulé and Sloan, 1966; Spengler et al., 1982; Stebbins, 1985; Stejneger, 1895, 1902; Stejneger and Barbour, 1943; Tanner, 1985; E. H. Taylor, 1938a, 1949; E. H. Taylor and Knobloch, 1940; Tennant, 1984; Townsend, 1916; Van Denburgh, 1924; T. R. Van Devender and Lowe, 1977; Webb, 1984; Webb and Baker, 1962; Wilson and McCranie, 1979; Woodin, 1953; Wright and Wright, 1957; Yarrow, 1875, 1883.

## *Crotalus polystictus* (Cope)

(Figs. 392, 393; Map 107)

LOCAL NAMES Chiauhcóatl, chiáuitl, tlehua (Náhuatl); hocico de puerco; tziripa (Tarascan); víbora de cascabel.

ENGLISH NAME Mexican lance-headed rattlesnake.

DISTRIBUTION This rattlesnake occupies the southern portion of the Mexican Plateau from west-central Veracruz westward across central Puebla, México, the Distrito Federal, northern Michoacán, southwestern Querétaro, southern Guanajuato, central and eastern Jalisco, and southern Zacatecas (see Map 107). The species has not been documented by specimens from several intervening or adjacent states, but probably occurs or occurred until recently in Colima, Tlaxcala, and Aguascalientes; literature reports exist for these states and Hidalgo. Most of the range of this species lies within the Mesa Central, but in the northwest it occurs in the eastern outlying ranges of the southern portion of the Sierra Madre Occidental, and possibly may occur as far north as southern Durango. Its vertical distribution is from about 1,450 to 2,600 m.

HABITAT This snake inhabits the broad valleys, high gently rolling plains, and grassy meadows of the highlands of the Mexican Plateau. It occurs in mesquite-grassland, pine-oak forests, and openings in forests consisting mostly of pine, often in rocky outcroppings or old lava flows.

DESCRIPTION This medium-sized rattlesnake usually attains an adult length of 700–800 mm, although exceptional specimens may approach 1 m in total length. The head of this species is particularly slender, its width being less than 60% of its length, whereas most other rattlesnakes have head widths that are 70–80% of the head length.

The ground color is buff, tan, pale brown, or pale gray to almost white, often becoming pale golden or reddish brown middorsally. The dark brown pattern is distinctive and unique among rattlesnakes. A series of 30–47 horizontally elongated, subelliptical or oval body blotches are present; anteriorly, these tend to be arranged in paravertebral pairs, but posteriorly blotches usually become more circular and may or may not merge across the midline to form individual middorsal blotches. The paravertebral blotches as well as other blotches are black edged. In addition to the paravertebral blotches, there are 2 series of large lateral blotches and a series of small ventrolateral blotches. The blotches of the uppermost lateral series are usually horizontally elongated anteriorly but become subcircular by midbody; the lower lateral series comprises subcircular or vertically elongated blotches. The blotches of the ventrolateral series tend to be roundish. The tail has 4–7 crossbands; the proximal bands are separated by the ground color of the body, and distal bands are separated by pale gray.

Markings on the side of the head include a large spot below the pit that extends to the infralabials, a large spot extending from the lower margin of the eye to almost the margin of the upper lip, and a broad postocular stripe that extends from near the posterior edge of the eye to, or over, the rictus. The top of the head is marked with a pair of prefrontal spots, often somewhat triangular; a pair of smaller parietal spots; and a pair of broad upper temporal streaks that extend anteriorly to the supraoculars, and posteriorly usually to a level above the third or fourth to the last supralabial. The upper temporal streaks sometimes may extend posteriorly to a level past the rictus. The color separating the prefrontal spots and upper temporal streaks is pale, forming a prominent transverse bar across the center of each supraocular. A large spot is present on the side of the head posterior to the rictus; either the postocular or upper temporal stripe may merge with this spot in some specimens.

There are 2–4 small dark spots and irregular dark brown stippling along the infralabials. On the anterior fifth of the belly the ventrals are mostly white or yellow; but posteriorly they become heavily stippled or mottled with dark brown pigment, which is frequently concentrated medially along the anterior margin of each ventral. The subcaudals are yellowish with dark stippling and have irregular large dark spots that fall mostly at levels between the dark crossbands on the dorsum of the tail. The upper third of the iris is yellow or tan, the lower two-thirds is darkly speckled with black. The proximal rattle segment is dark brown to black. The tongue is black.

The rostral is higher than wide. A pair of large internasals may meet each other at the midline or, more frequently, a small medial scale or a pair of small medial internasals separating a pair of large crescent-shaped internasals that lie over the nasals. A single canthal is located on each side; canthals are often separated from one another by 2 elongated intercanthals. The internasal-prefrontal area is thus typically covered by 2–4 internasals, 2 canthals, and 2 intercanthals for a total of 6–8 scales. There almost always are 3 intersupraoculars between the anterior edges of the supraoculars; the range is 2–5. The most lateral internasal is in contact with the upper loreal; the upper preocular is not vertically divided; usually 2 subequal loreals on each side do not reach the supralabials but do intervene to preclude postnasal–upper preocular contact. Usually the anterior subocular is in contact with supralabials 4 and 5. The prenasal is in contact with the first supralabial. There are 1–3 prefoveals, 12–15 (usually 13 or 14) supralabials, 11–16 (mode 14) infralabials, 25–28 (usually 27) midbody dorsal scale rows, 161–187 ventrals, 17–29 subcaudals, and usually 10 rattle-fringe scales, the posterior tips of which may be serrated.

REMARKS We have found this species active by day and at night. It appears to be especially common in rocky regions or areas with numerous gopher burrows, in which it may take refuge.

REFERENCES Armstrong and Murphy, 1979; Beebe, 1905; Boulenger, 1896; Campbell, 1979b; Cope, 1860a, 1865, 1875, 1879, 1884, 1885a, 1887; Cuesta Terron, 1921b, 1931; Duellman, 1961, 1965b; Dugès, 1869, 1876–77, 1888, 1889, 1890, 1896; Gloyd, 1940; Günther, 1885–1905; Groombridge, 1986; Herrera, 1890, 1891; Klauber, 1936b, 1938, 1940a, 1952, 1971, 1972; León, 1889; Martín del Campo, 1935, 1937a, 1940a, 1950, 1984; McCranie, 1976; Mocquard, 1908–1909; H. M. Smith, 1943, 1970; H. M. Smith and Necker, 1944; H. M. Smith and Smith, 1969; H. M. Smith and Taylor, 1945; Troschel, 1866; Velasco, 1890a, 1890b; Wilson and McCranie, 1979.

### *Crotalus pricei* Van Denburgh

(Figs. 394–399; Map 105)

LOCAL NAME Víbora de cascabel.

ENGLISH NAME Twin-spotted rattlesnake.

DISTRIBUTION In the western portion of its range this species occurs from the mountainous regions of southeastern Arizona southward through the Sierra Madre Occidental in Mexico, including northeastern Sonora and western Chihuahua and Durango. In the east, this species is known from the Sierra Madre Oriental of southeastern Coahuila, southern Nuevo León, and southwestern Tamaulipas (see Map 105). It has been suggested that *C. pricei* may occur in eastern Sinaloa and northern Nayarit, but no specimens have yet been collected in these areas. A record for Aguascalientes has recently been verified (see Remarks and Fig. 399). The vertical distribution is from 1,900 to over 3,000 m.

HABITAT Pine-oak and boreal forests.

DESCRIPTION This is a small rattlesnake that generally reaches an adult length of no more than 500–600 mm; the largest specimen known is 660 mm.

The ground color is gray, bluish gray, brownish gray, or medium to reddish brown, generally with a fine brown speckling. The middorsal blotches tend to be divided medially, forming a pattern of 39–64 pairs of small dark brown or gray paravertebral blotches. The dorsal blotches of specimens from the Sierra Madre Oriental and, less frequently, those in snakes from the Sierra Madre Occidental, may be undivided medially. Dorsal blotches are often bordered with dark brown or black which is edged with white. There are 5–10 indistinct crossbands on the tail and the basal segment of the rattle is orange to reddish orange. Laterally the three alternating series of dark spots tend to become obscure in adults. Some specimens lack the contrasting borders of the dorsal spots and, more rarely, in others the blotches are absent altogether. A dark postocular stripe extends from the lower posterior edge of the eye to the angle of the jaw. The labials are white, cream, or pinkish and heavily stippled with gray or black, especially anteriorly. The throat is usually pale also, but the ventrals become increasingly more suffused with black and posteriorly may be almost entirely black.

The rostral is usually wider than high. There are 2 large internasals. A single canthal (rarely 2) is usually present on each side, and there are 4–11 scales in the internasal-prefrontal area. From 2 to 3 scales separate the supraoculars. The prenasal curves over the top of the postnasal, and the first supralabial is in broad contact with both the prenasal and postnasal. One or 2 (usually 1) loreals are present on each side; the postnasal and upper preocular fail to make contact. The upper preocular is not divided vertically and the anterior subocular touches several supralabials (usually the third and fourth) under the eye. There are 8–10 (usually 9) supralabials, 8–11 (usually 10) infralabials, 19–23 (usually 21) midbody dorsal scale rows, 137–171 ventrals, and 18–33 subcaudals.

SIMILAR SPECIES Several other species of small montane rattlesnakes may occur sympatrically with or geographically close to *C. pricei*. *Crotalus willardi* may be distinguished from *C. pricei* by its sharp canthus rostralis and more numerous midbody dorsal scale rows (25–29), supralabials (12–17), and infralabials (12–16). Many populations of *C. willardi* possess distinctive pale facial stripes that further serve to distinguish this species from *C. pricei*. *Crotalus lepidus* usually has a pattern of widely spaced crossbands or large middorsal blotches; specimens from along the Sinaloa-Durango border may have small dorsal spots, but these are not arranged in paravertebral pairs. Unlike *C. pricei*, *C. lepidus* has an upper preocular that is usually vertically divided (in the region of sympatry) and usually has more midbody dorsal scale rows, supralabials, and infralabials (see Table 32). There are 13–38 primary body blotches in *C. lepidus* and 39–64 (usually arranged in pairs) in *C. pricei*. *Crotalus triseriatus* is not known to be sympatric with *C. pricei* but their ranges are almost parapatric in the vicinity of the Nayarit-Durango border. *Crotalus triseriatus* possesses unpaired dorsal blotches and usually more midbody dorsal scale rows than *C. pricei*.

REMARKS A specimen (UMMZ 110878) from west of Rincón de Ramos in the Sierra Fría, Aguascalientes, was hypothesized to be representative of an isolated population of *C. pricei* or to be a novel taxon. Recently collected material (see Fig. 399) has validated the former notion.

Two subspecies of *C. pricei* are recognized: *C. p. pricei* (Figs. 394–397) of the Sierra Madre Occidental and *C. p. miquihuanus* (Fig. 398) of the Sierra Madre Oriental. The characteristics purported to distinguish *C. p. miquihuanus* from *C. p. pricei* are a brown rather than gray ground color, middorsal blotches less frequently divided medially, less subdivision of the head plates, and fewer ventrals. The last characteristic is perhaps the most reliable for purposes of identification; there are 137–143 ventrals in *C. p. miquihuanus*, and 149–171 in *C. p. pricei*.

REFERENCES Amaral, 1927f, 1927g; Armstrong and Murphy, 1979; Axtell and Sabath, 1963; Bogert and Oliver, 1945; Chrapliwy and Fugler, 1955; Drake, 1958; Dunn, 1936; Gloyd, 1937, 1940; Kauffeld, 1943; Klauber, 1952, 1971, 1972; Leviton, 1953; Lowe, 1964; Lowe et al., 1986; Martín del Campo, 1937a, 1953; McCranie, 1980; H. M. Smith, 1939, 1944a, 1946a; H. M. Smith and Taylor, 1945, 1966; Stebbins, 1985; Stejneger, 1902; Stejneger and Barbour, 1943; Tanner, 1985; E. H. Taylor and Knobloch, 1940; Van Denburgh, 1895b, 1924; Van Devender and Lowe, 1977; Webb, 1984; Webb and Baker, 1962; Wilson and McCranie, 1979; Woodin, 1953; Wright and Wright, 1957.

### *Crotalus pusillus* Klauber

(Figs. 400, 401; Map 108)

LOCAL NAME Víbora de cascabel.

ENGLISH NAME Tancitaran dusky rattlesnake.

DISTRIBUTION Mexico. This species occurs in the highlands of the Sierra de Coalcomán in southwestern Michoacán and the western portion of the Transverse Volcanic Cordillera from the Nevado de Colima (and probably the Volcán de Colima) in south-central Jalisco across the Sierra de los Tarascos to near Carápan in Michoacán (see Map 108). A major hiatus in the distribution of this species occurs where the Sierra de Coalcomán is separated from the highlands of the Mexican Plateau by the headwaters of the Río Tepalcatepec and the Río Ahuijullo Depression. The vertical distribution is from 1,525 to 2,380 m.

HABITAT Pine-oak forest, usually in areas of volcanic rock or extensive limestone outcroppings.

DESCRIPTION Large adult males may exceed 500 mm in total length; females are smaller. The largest specimen known (FMNH 37048) is 682 mm in overall length.

The ground color is gray-brown or, rarely, fawn. A reddish brown cast may intervene between the 33–50 dark brown middorsal body blotches. Dorsal blotches are sometimes bordered with black and narrowly and irregularly edged with white. A dark brown postocular stripe extends from the lower posterior edge of the eye to the angle of the jaw. The postocular stripe is distinctly pale bordered above and below; the supralabials below this stripe usually are mostly pale with fine brown peppering, and anteriorly the supralabials become heavily stippled with dark pigment. A distinctive primary series of dark brown lateral blotches is present; each of these lateral blotches lies opposite a dorsal blotch, from which it is separated by a pale interspace. Two other series of lateral blotches may be present, both lying on a vertical line running between the dorsal blotches, one series above and the other series below the level of the primary series of lateral blotches; however, these two accessory series of lateral blotches tend to be indistinct or absent in many specimens. A dark brown subocular spot usually borders the lip margin and a pair of nape blotches precedes the middorsal series of blotches. Head markings are often present, including a pair of occipital spots, an upper temporal streak on either side, and an ill-defined bar across the top of the snout in front of the eyes. The infralabials are mostly pale, with fine brown peppering and clumps of pigment forming spots that often lie along the interinfralabial sutures. The gular region and anterior ventrals are finely speckled with brown pigment that becomes progressively heavier and darker posteriorly, so that the subcaudals become dark gray to black. The iris is golden to copper colored above and dark brown below; the proximal rattle segment is dark gray to black.

The rostral is wider than high. The anterior portion of the snout is covered by 4 scales: 2 internasals and 2 prefrontals (canthals). The prefrontals most often are bordered posteriorly by 3 intersupraoculars, but sometimes by 1, 2, or 4. The anterior subocular is in contact with the supralabials, usually 4 and 5; the single loreal does not touch the supralabials; there are 1–5 prefoveals; and the prenasal is not in contact with the loreal. There are 11–13 (usually 12) supralabials, 10–13 (usually 11) infralabials, 23–25 (usually 23) midbody dorsal scale rows, 150–162 ventrals, 25–33 subcaudals, and usually 8 rattle-fringe scales.

SIMILAR SPECIES *Crotalus pusillus* bears a striking resemblance to *C. triseriatus*, and these species are sympatric in a portion of their ranges. The most salient characteristic that distinguishes these two species is the presence of 2 more-or-less symmetrical prefrontals in *C. pusillus*, whereas in *C. triseriatus* there are 3 or more irregular scales immediately posterior to the internasals.

REMARKS We have seen this snake abroad only by day; nighttime temperatures within its range are cool and apparently restrict its activity.

The only small montane rattlesnake other than *C. triseriatus* that is sympatric with *C. pusillus* is a population of uncertain status on Cerro Tancítaro (see Remarks for *C. transversus*).

REFERENCES Armstrong and Murphy, 1979; Campbell, 1979b; Capocaccia, 1961; Duellman, 1961, 1965b; Klauber, 1952, 1971, 1972; Schmidt and Shannon, 1947; H. M. Smith and Taylor, 1966; Wilson and McCranie, 1979.

## *Crotalus ruber* Cope

(Figs. 402–406; Map 101)

LOCAL NAME Víbora de cascabel.

ENGLISH NAME Red diamond rattlesnake.

DISTRIBUTION This species occupies extreme southwestern California from near Pioneertown and Morongo Valley of San Bernardino County and southeastern Los Angeles County southward through the Peninsula of Baja California, Mexico, exclusive of the desert east of the Sierra de Juárez in northeastern Baja California del Norte, to the Cabo San Lucas. It occurs on either side of the peninsular mountain ranges and on a number of islands in the Gulf of California, including, from north to south, Angel de la Guarda, Pond, San Lorenzo del Sur, San Marcos, Danzante, Monserrate, and San José. In the Pacific Ocean, *C. ruber* occurs on Isla de Santa Margarita (Map 101). Its vertical distribution is from near sea level to about 1,500 m, but it is usually encountered below 1,200 m.

HABITAT This species inhabits desert, chaparral, pine-oak woodland, and tropical deciduous forest. It is most frequently found in rocky areas or heavy brush.

DESCRIPTION *Crotalus ruber* is a moderately large rattlesnake; mainland specimens commonly exceed 1 m in total length, and large males may reach 1,400 mm. However, snakes over 1,500 mm are quite rare, and the largest specimen reported measured 1,620 mm. Apparently some island populations are stunted and do not reach 1 m in length; the largest island specimen known, from Isla San Lorenzo Sur, is only 872 mm in total length.

The ground color of specimens from the northern part of the range is pale reddish brown, pale pinkish gray, pale brick-red, or tan. The 29–42 rhombic or diamond-shaped dorsal blotches are usually dark reddish brown and uniformly pigmented without pale centers. On the anterior one-half to two-thirds of the body the dorsal blotches are distinctly separated from one another middorsally by white or buff; this pale edging becomes very narrow or incomplete along the lateral margins of the dorsal blotches. The top of the head has little or no pattern and is usually nearly unicolored. A dark brown or reddish brown postocular stripe extends diagonally from the lower edge of the eye to over the posterior part of the mouth; it is bordered anteriorly by a broad stripe,

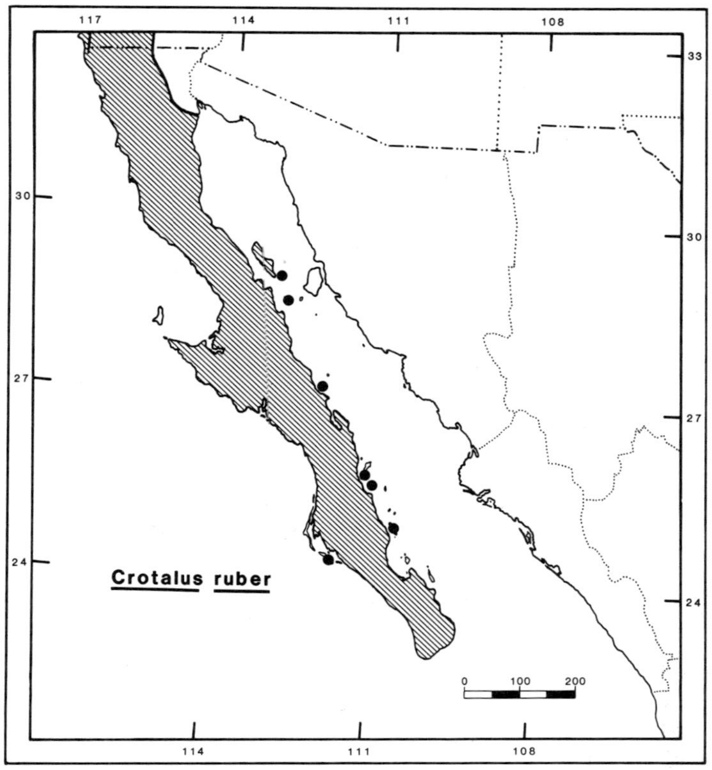


**Map 101.** Distribution of *Crotalus ruber* in the Baja California Peninsula and the adjacent United States. The islands in the Gulf of California inhabited by this species are (from north to south) Ángel de la Guarda, Pond, San Lorenzo del Sur, San Marcos, Danzante, Monserrate, and San José; it also occurs on Isla Santa Margarita off the Pacific Coast.

about 2 scales wide, that extends from the upper preocular to the supralabials lying below the eye and thence usually along the margin of the lip to the rictus. The upper (posterior) pale line bordering the dark postocular stripe is often incomplete, indistinct, or absent; when present, it extends diagonally across the temporal region to make contact with one of the last 3 supralabials. The lateral blotches tend to be obscure, consisting of 1–4 dark reddish brown scales.

Snakes from the southern half of the Peninsula of Baja California (from about Loreto to the cape) tend to have an olive-brown, yellowish brown, or straw-colored ground color. There are 20–39 brown dorsal blotches with dark brown to almost black borders and distinctly paler centers. The yellowish white to buff edging around the dorsal blotches is more prominent than in snakes from the north and tends to completely surround each blotch. The borders of the dorsal blotches are somewhat irregular compared with those from northern snakes. The top of the head possesses conspicuous dark spots. The dark postocular stripe is bordered by a preocular (anterior or lower) pale stripe 2–3 or more scales wide and a postocular (posterior or upper) pale stripe that is usually well defined. The 2–3 series of lateral blotches are relatively distinct and usually consist of groups of 2–4 dark brown scales.

In *C. ruber* the tail is pale gray with 2–7 black rings that are 2–3 scales in width laterally and conspicuously wider dorsally than the pale interspaces dividing them; the black tail rings are broken infrequently laterally. The belly is immaculate and many scales in dorsal scale rows 1–3 are whitish or narrowly edged with white. The subcaudals are black where encroached upon by the black tail rings, otherwise they are pale with a heavy suffusion of black peppering. Juveniles have a gray ground color.

The shape of the rostral is highly variable; snakes in the southern portion of the Peninsula of Baja California usually have a rostral that is higher than wide, whereas that of more northerly snakes is often wider than high. Two internasals contact the rostral, with more than 8 scales in the internasal-prefrontal regions, and 4–10 (usually 6 or more) intersupraoculars. The prenasal usually touches the first supralabial. The posterior canthal is large and angles over the canthus rostralis to intervene partially between the upper preocular and postnasal and to occupy the space of an upper loreal. There may be 1 or 2 loreals; snakes from the southern half of the Peninsula of Baja California typically have 2, those from farther north most frequently have 1. The presence of the loreal(s) and/or intervening portion of the canthal almost always precludes contact between the upper preocular and postnasal. One to 3 interoculabials separate the anterior subocular from the supralabials. A pair of interchinshields is usually absent. There are 12–19 (mode 16) supralabials, 13–21 (usually 17 or 18) infralabials (first pair usually divided transversely), 25–33 midbody dorsal scale rows (mode 29 in northern snakes, 27 in southern snakes, 25 in snakes from Isla San Lorenzo Sur), 179–206 ventrals, 15–29 subcaudals, and usually 12–13 rattle-fringe scales.

SIMILAR SPECIES Four other rattlesnakes are sympatric with *C. ruber*. In *C. viridis* usually more than 2 internasals contact the rostral, the black tail rings are conspicuously narrower than the pale interspaces dividing them, and the pale interspaces on the tail are of the same color as the ground color on the posterior part of the body. In *C. mitchellii* the ground color is distinctly speckled with black, the dark tail rings are obscure or, if sharply defined, are not as broad as the pale ones, the prenasals are separated from the rostral by a series of small scales, and the supraoculars are pitted, deeply furrowed, or have irregular outer edges. In *C. enyo* the supraoculars are inclined considerably upward toward the lateral side of the head, the tail lacks strongly contrasting pale and dark rings, and the scales in the frontal region are knobby. *Crotalus atrox* appears to be parapatric with *C. ruber* in southern California and northeastern Baja California del Norte, but the ground color is usually pale gray-brown, the first pair of infralabials usually is not transversely divided, and the postnasal and upper preocular touch each other.

REMARKS Three subspecies are recognized: *C. r. ruber* (Figs. 402, 403) in southern California and the northern part of the Peninsula of Baja California; *C. r. lucasensis* (Fig. 404) in the southern portion of the Peninsula; and *C. r. lorenzoensis* (Figs. 405, 406) on the Isla San Lorenzo Sur. The populations occurring on Isla Monserrate and Isla Angel de la Guarda were recognized as endemic subspecies by Harris and Simmons (1978b). However, the justification for doing so was so feeble that their recommendations have not been taken seriously by subsequent investigators.

Despite an apparently close relationship to the irascible *C. atrox*, *C. ruber* has a reputation as being among the most placid rattlesnakes; and often one must prod a specimen in order to elicit a rattle.

The rattle matrix is somewhat shrunken in the population from Isla San Lorenzo del Sur; therefore, the string of rattles is often missing in individual snakes.

This species has been observed to be active at relatively cool temperatures (18°C). Not surprisingly, *C. ruber* tends to be more nocturnal in the desert foothills, where its thermal maximum may be quickly exceeded by day, than along the Pacific Coast of southern California and Baja California, where temperatures tend to be considerably milder.

REFERENCES Amaral, 1927g, 1929b; Armstrong and Murphy, 1979; Beddard, 1907; Bostic, 1971; Brown, 1901; Bullock and Cowles, 1952; Clarke, 1961; Cliff, 1954; Cope, 1861; Cuesta Terron, 1931; Gloyd, 1940; Goodrich et al., 1978; Harris and Simmons, 1978b; Hoard, 1939; Klauber, 1927, 1930a, 1930b, 1931a, 1936b, 1949a, 1971, 1972; Leviton and Banta, 1964; Lindsay, 1962, 1964, 1966; Linsdale, 1932; Lowe and Norris, 1954; Martín del Campo, 1935, 1937a, 1950; Meek, 1906; Mosauer, 1936; R. W. Murphy, 1983a, 1983b; Murphy and Ottley, 1984; Murray, 1955; Neill, 1958; Nelson, 1922; Orr, 1961; Pope, 1944–1945; Radcliff and Maslin, 1975; Savage, 1960; Schmidt, 1922; H. M. Smith, 1944c; H. M. Smith and Holland, 1971; H. M. Smith and Taylor, 1945, 1966; Soulé and Sloan, 1966; Stebbins, 1985; Stejneger, 1895; Stejneger and Barbour, 1943; Tevis, 1943, 1944; Van Denburgh, 1896, 1920, 1922b; Van Denburgh and Slevin, 1921a; Welsh and Bury, 1984; Wright and Wright, 1957.

### *Crotalus scutulatus* (Kennicott)

(Figs. 407–409, 448, 449; Map 102)

LOCAL NAMES Chiauhcóatl (Náhuatl), víbora de cascabel, víbora.

ENGLISH NAME Mojave rattlesnake (see Remarks).

DISTRIBUTION United States and Mexico. In the United States this species occurs from the western edge of the Mojave Desert in southern California and southern Nevada through western and southern Arizona and the extreme southwestern tip of New Mexico to the Chihuahuan Desert of Trans-Pecos Texas; in Mexico, from northern Sonora eastward through Chihuahua and Coahuila to western Nuevo León, southward through most of Durango and Zacatecas, southern Nuevo León, southwestern Tamaulipas, western San Luis Potosí, northern and eastern Jalisco, most of Aguascalientes, northern Guanajuato, central Querétaro, southern Hidalgo, possibly northeastern México, much of Tlaxcala, northern Puebla, and southwestern Veracruz (Map 102). Its vertical distribution is from about sea level to over 2,500 m; in the southern part of its range it is restricted to elevations above 1,800 m.

HABITAT This species frequents desert, mesquite-grassland, and, in the southern portion of its range, pine-oak forest. Throughout its range in Mexico, this snake occurs mostly in relatively flat terrain such as the bottoms of broad open valleys or high plains. In the extreme south this species is often found in rocky habitats such as old lava flows; in the north it may be found in a variety of situations.

DESCRIPTION Large specimens of this medium-sized rattlesnake usually do not greatly exceed 1 meter in length; the largest specimen measured 1,231 mm.

This species exhibits a fair amount of north-south clinal variation over its extensive range, and it is convenient to refer to southern versus northern snakes. In our discussion, this division corresponds roughly to the ranges of the two subspecies (see Remarks). However, some features such as color and pattern are highly discordant.

In northern snakes the ground color is greenish gray, olive-green, greenish brown, greenish yellow, brownish, or yellowish. The 27–44 dark dorsal blotches are yellowish olive to dark brown, hexagonal to diamond shaped, and bordered by a single pale row of scales that may be incomplete. A pair of dark occipital blotches is usually present; anteriorly the dorsum of the head is nearly uniformly colored, except for the posterior edges of the supraoculars, which may be dark. The lower (anterior) pale stripe bordering the dark postorbital stripe extends from the upper preocular downward to the lip margin *behind* the posterior edge of the eye, thence along the supralabials to the rictus. The upper (posterior) pale stripe extends diagonally from the upper postocular across a point immediately *above* the ultimate supralabials. The pale tail rings are ash-gray and stand in sharp contrast to the ground color on the posterior part of the body. Two to 8 dark tail rings proximally may be about the same color as or a little darker than the dorsal blotches, but distally they become considerably darker and may be almost black. In this species the dark tail rings are narrower than the pale interspaces, especially in northern populations. The dorsal portion of the proximal rattle segment is black.

In southern snakes the ground color is pale olive-gray to straw colored. Thirty to 35 brownish olive to black subrhombic dorsal blotches appear on the body; no con-

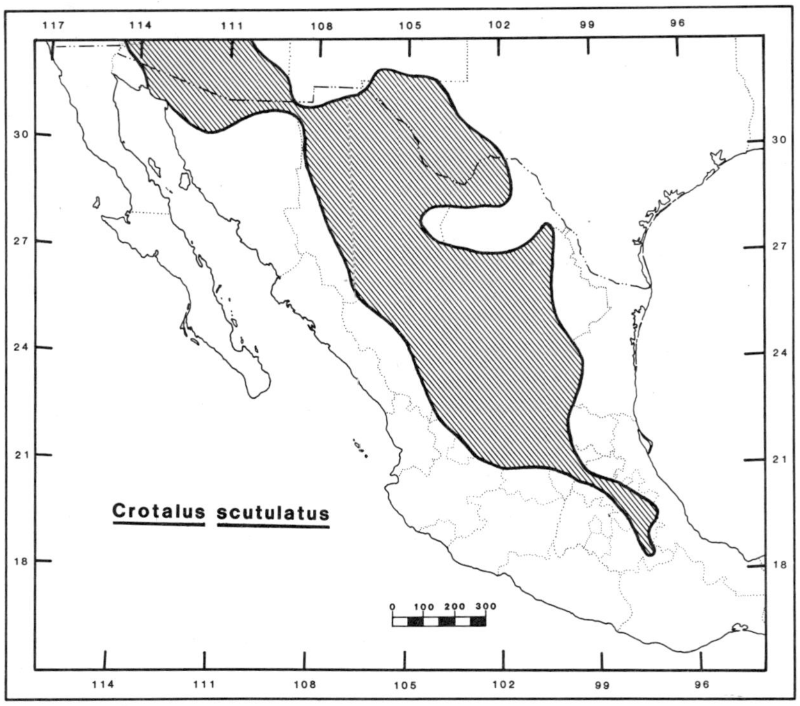


**Map 102.** Distribution of *Crotalus scutulatus* in Mexico and the adjacent United States.

trasting narrow pale border is evident around the margins of the dorsal blotches. The dorsum of the head may be pale and colored similarly to the ground color of the body, irregularly marked with dark pigment, or almost uniformly black. The dark postocular stripe, if present, is very much reduced, extending only 2–4 scales from the lower edge of the eye and not reaching the margin of the lip; it may be black or indistinct. Other than dark postocular and temporal stripes that may or may not be present, the side of the head is pale and the pale stripes bordering the dark postorbital stripe are broad with irregular margins (Fig. 448). The top of the head may have a pair of occipital blotches, or these may be obscured by heavy pigmentation. The 4–6 dark tail rings distally do not become darker than the dorsal markings. The pale interspaces separating the dark tail rings are about the same color as that on the posterior part of the body. The dorsal portion of the proximal rattle segment is only slightly darkened with brown pigment.

The belly of *C. scutulatus* is a whitish or yellowish hue and nearly immaculate except for a little dark pigment encroaching on the lateral portions of the ventrals in some snakes. The subcaudals are pale with dark gray or black flecking.

The rostral is usually higher than wide. Two internasals contact the rostral. There are 6–21 scales in the internasal-prefrontal region; snakes from the south have 9 or fewer, whereas populations in the north are highly variable but tend to have higher average numbers than those to the south. The number of intersupraoculars is rarely more than 2. The prenasal is in broad contact with the first supralabials. Frequently, a large crescent-shaped scale borders the posteromedial edge of each supraocular; this scale is divided in some specimens. The posterior canthals are large and their lateral portions extend ventrally over the canthus rostralis to take the place of an upper loreal and to intervene between the upper preocular and postnasal. A posterior canthal along with the single loreal on each side (in the position of a lower loreal) serve to preclude contact between the postnasal and upper preocular. Usually 1 interoculabial separates the anterior subocular from the supralabials. There are 12–18 supralabials (usually 13–14 in the south, 15 in the north), 12–18 infralabials (usually 14 in the south, 15 or 16 in the north), 21–29 (mode 25) midbody dorsal scale rows, 165–192 ventrals (the average number for both males and females is lower in the southern part of the range), and 15–29 subcaudals.

SIMILAR SPECIES *Crotalus scutulatus* has an extensive distribution and may be confused with many other species of rattlesnakes. In *C. atrox* the upper (posterior) pale line that borders the dark postocular stripe is narrow (less than 1 scale wide) and extends to just in front of the rictus; in the regions of sympatry, the dark tail rings are relatively wider, usually 3 or more scales wide as opposed to 2 or less; the scales on top of the head are more numerous (usually 4 or more intersupraoculars); and the upper preocular usually contacts the postnasal. In *C. viridis* (possibly sympatric with *C. scutulatus* in west Texas in the United States, and northern Coahuila and Chihuahua in Mexico), the pale interspaces separating dark tail rings are about the same color as the ground color on the posterior part of the body, and there are more than 2 internasals. In *C. molossus* 4 (rarely 6) scales in the internasal-prefrontal region include a large pair of prefrontals in contact with each other medially. In *C. mitchellii* the prenasal is separated from the rostral by a series of small scales, the ground color is heavily punctated with black, and the supraoculars are pitted, have deep furrows, or possess irregular outer edges. In *C. tigris* the dorsal pattern consists of crossbands, and the head is proportionately small and the rattles large.

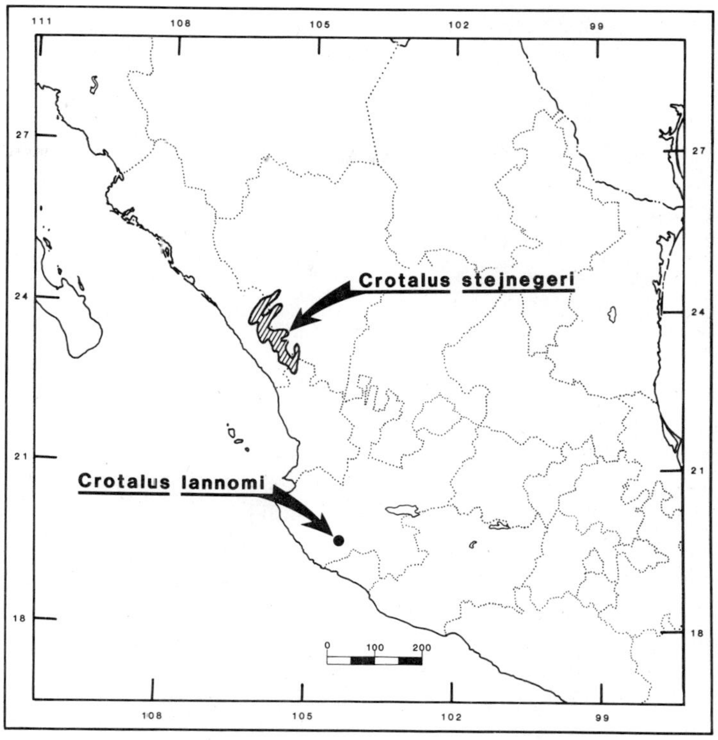


Map 103. Distributions of *Crotalus lannomi* (*dot*) and *C. stejnegeri* (*diagonal lines*) in western Mexico. *Crotalus lannomi* is still known only from the type locality.

REMARKS The common name in English for this species has been widely employed and is well known. Nevertheless, we somewhat reluctantly use the name Mojave rattlesnake because, proportionately, very little of this snake's range lies within the Mojave Desert; its distribution is actually more extensive in the Chihuahuan Desert. Some people argue that the common name for this species should be spelled "Mohave," a notion with which we disagree.

Two subspecies are recognized: *C. s. scutulatus* (Figs. 407, 408, 448, 449) in the northern part of the range from California eastward to west Texas and south to Querétaro, and *C. s. salvini* (Fig. 409) from Hidalgo through Tlaxcala and Puebla to southwestern Veracruz.

At lower elevations this snake is mostly nocturnal during the hotter months of the year. However, at high elevations and during the cooler months it is frequently found active during the daylight hours.

This snake has a highly potent venom. Symptoms of snakebite from this species are reported to include double vision and difficulty in speaking and in swallowing water.

REFERENCES Armstrong and Murphy, 1979; Banta, 1962; Bogert and Oliver, 1945; Boulenger, 1896; Brattstrom, 1964; Bravo, 1927; A. E. Brown, 1903b; B. C. Brown, 1950; Burger and Hensley, 1949; Campbell, 1979a; Cope, 1886, 1900; Coues, 1875; Croulet, 1963; Cuesta Terron, 1921b; Ditmars, 1930, 1937; Dixon et al., 1962, 1972; Dugès, 1896; Dunkel and Smith, 1937; Gadow, 1905; Garman, 1884a; Gates, 1957; Gehlbach, 1956; Gloyd, 1937, 1940; Groombridge, 1986; Günther, 1885–1902; Hahn and May, 1972; Hensley, 1950; Hoge and Romano, 1971a; Jacob et al., 1987; Jameson and Flury, 1949; Kauffeld, 1943; Kennicott, 1861; Klauber, 1930b, 1936b, 1952, 1971, 1972; Liner, 1964; Liner et al., 1976; Linsdale, 1940; Lowe, 1964; Lowe et al., 1986; Martín del Campo, 1937a, 1950; McCoy, 1984; Mellink et al., 1987; Miller and Stebbins, 1964; Minton, 1959; Mocquard, 1908–1909; Ocaranza, 1930; Pope, 1944–1945; Price, 1982; Raun and Gehlbach, 1972; Reese, 1971; Reynolds, 1982; Sánchez-Herrera and López-Ortega, 1987; H. M. Smith, 1943, 1970; H. M. Smith and Buechner, 1947; H. M. Smith and Mittleman, 1943; H. M. Smith and Taylor, 1945; P. W. Smith and Darling, 1952; P. W. Smith and Hensley, 1958; Stebbins, 1985; Stejneger and Barbour, 1943; Tanner, 1985; E. H. Taylor, 1949; T. R. Van Devender and Lowe, 1977; Webb, 1984; Woodin, 1953; Wright and Wright, 1957.

## *Crotalus stejnegeri* Dunn

(Fig. 410; Map 103)

LOCAL NAME Víbora de cascabel.

ENGLISH NAME Long-tailed rattlesnake.

DISTRIBUTION This snake is found in the rugged canyons and foothills of the western portion of the Sierra Madre Occidental in western Durango and southeastern Sinaloa, Mexico (see Map 103). It has been collected within a few kilometers of the Nayarit border and almost certainly occurs in the northern part of this state. The vertical distribution of *C. stejnegeri* is from about 500 to 1,200 m.

HABITAT This species frequents tropical deciduous and pine-oak forests; most of the specimens with which we are familiar have come from the ecotone between these two forest types.

DESCRIPTION This is a relatively small rattlesnake, usually not exceeding much over 600 mm in total length; the largest specimen known is 724 mm. The tail is slender and proportionately long, in adults comprising 11.0–14.8% of the total in males and 9.8–12.5% in females. The rattle is tiny.

The ground color is pale gray-brown or pale buckskin, becoming somewhat darker (usually dark gray) on the posterior part of the body and the tail. The conspicuous dark brown markings on top of the head often include a pair of spots in the prefrontal region, a dark bar between the supraoculars, a pair of small parietal spots bordered by a pair of elongated crescent-shaped blotches, a pair of stripes in the upper temporal region, and a pair of nape stripes that may continue unbroken onto the body. A dark brown postocular stripe extends from the lower posterior border of the eye to the rictus. The nape blotches are followed by 32–43 medium brown, black-edged middorsal body blotches. Three series of lateral body blotches alternate: the larger median series is sometimes bordered by large orange flecks and is offset from the middorsal blotches, sometimes coalescing with these on the posterior of the body; both a small upper series on scale rows 6–8 and a small lower series on scale rows 1–3 are located on a vertical line about halfway between middorsal blotches. The tail has 8–15 crossbands that become indistinct distally. The infralabials and gular region are white, almost immaculate; the belly is white with irregular roundish gray-to-brown blotches toward the lateral edges of the ventrals and faint brown speckling that becomes heavier posteriorly; and the subcaudals are pale gray. The proximal segment of the rattle is dark gray to black. The iris is yellow with fine black peppering, and the tongue is black with white tips.

The rostral is usually about as high as wide; there are 2 large, triangular internasals, and 10–21 scales occupy the internasal-prefrontal region. Five to 8 intersupraoculars, 2–5 loreals, and 1 or 2 canthals are evident on each side between the internasal and supraocular. Two interoculabials separate the suboculars from the supralabials, except for the anterior subocular, which is generally separated by only 1 scale. The prenasal is in broad contact with the first supralabial, and the postnasal is precluded from contact with the upper preocular by the intervening loreals. The first pair of infralabials are enlarged, extend backward, and are broadly in contact with each other behind the mental; they often partially or completely separate the second pair of infralabials from the chinshields. The posterior ends of the first pair of infralabials are blunt and do not intervene between the chinshields. There are 14–16 supralabials, 14–18 infralabials, 23–29 (mode 27) midbody dorsal scale rows, 171–178 ventrals, 36–48 subcaudals (0–7 divided distally), and 7–10 rattle-fringe scales.

SIMILAR SPECIES It would take a vivid imagination to mistake this species for any other. Of the other small montane rattlesnakes inhabiting the Sierra Madre Occidental, we are aware of only one, *C. lepidus*, that is sympatric with this species; *C. pricei* and *C. willardi* occur at higher elevations in this mountain system. The distinctive head pattern, shape of the first pair of infralabials, high number of ventrals and subcaudals, and slender tail with diminutive rattle serve to distinguish *C. stejnegeri* from these species. A large rattlesnake, tentatively considered to be a hybrid between *C. basiliscus* and *C. molossus* (see Remarks for *C. basiliscus*), has been collected on the same slopes as *C. stejnegeri*. It may be distinguished from *C. stejnegeri* by its pale-bordered middorsal diamonds, a pair of large prefrontals, fewer than 5 intersupraoculars, thick tail with fewer subcaudals, and relatively large size. The rattlesnake that perhaps most closely resembles *C. stejnegeri* is *C. lannomi*, known only from one locality in Jalisco. It differs from *C. stejnegeri* in having a rostral that is wider than high, fewer prefoveals (4 vs. 7), and only 2 intersupraoculars.

REMARKS This rare rattlesnake is known from only about a dozen specimens. This species has been found crawling after dark, but also basks during the early morning.

REFERENCES Armstrong and Murphy, 1979; Boulenger, 1896; Cochran, 1961; Collins, 1982; Dunn, 1919; Gloyd, 1940; Groombridge, 1986; Hardy and McDiarmid, 1969; Klauber, 1936b, 1940c, 1952, 1972; Martín del Campo, 1935, 1937a, 1950; McDiarmid et al., 1976; H. M. Smith, 1943; H. M. Smith and Taylor, 1945, 1950b; Tanner, 1966; Webb, 1984.

### *Crotalus tigris* Kennicott

(Figs. 411, 412; Map 104)

LOCAL NAME Víbora de cascabel.

ENGLISH NAME Tiger rattlesnake.

DISTRIBUTION This species ranges from south-central Arizona in the United States southward through most of Sonora, Mexico, exclusive of the panhandle in the northwest and the high mountains in the eastern portion of the state. It also occurs on Isla Tiburón in the Gulf of California (Map 104). Its vertical distribution is from near sea level to about 1,465 m.

HABITAT This species inhabits Sonoran desert and mesquite-grassland, barely entering tropical deciduous forest in southern Sonora. It is found almost exclusively in rugged, rocky country.

DESCRIPTION This species reaches less than 1 m in total length; the largest measured specimen is 885 mm. The rattles are relatively large and the head is small.

The ground color may be gray, lavender, blue-gray, pink, or buff, and usually turns to pink, pale orange, or cream on the sides. The dorsal pattern consists of 35–52 crossbands that are dark gray or brown in color and that consist largely of heavy punctations. These crossbands have vague borders, are wider middorsally than laterally, and are wider at the middorsum than the interspaces; crossbands become more clearly defined and darker on the posterior part of the body. Both the ground color and the crossbands are heavily punctated with dark pigment; the ground color tends to be paler posteriorly and thus the dark crossbands stand in greater contrast there. A series of small lateral blotches alternates between the crossbands and is located on the first 2–3

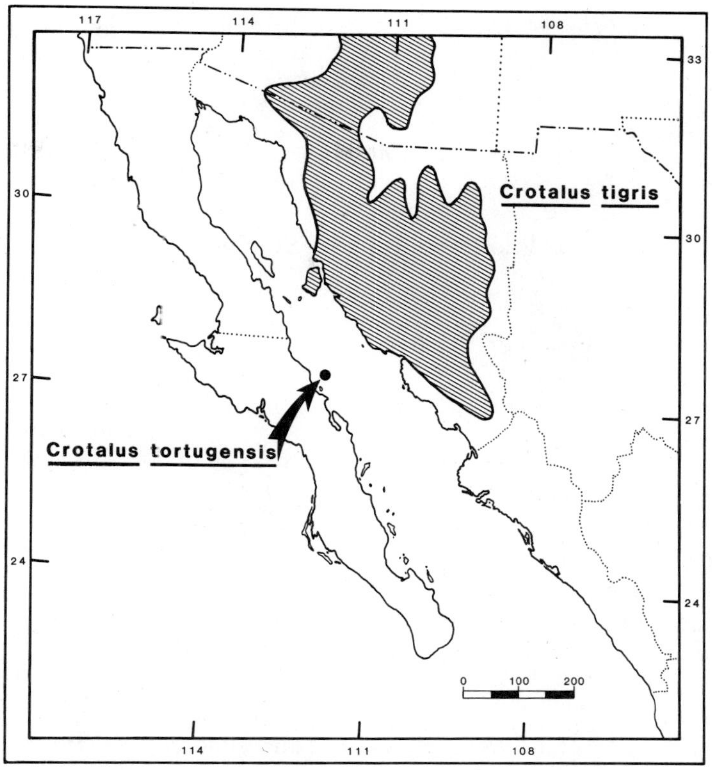


**Map 104.** Distributions of *Crotalus tigris* (*diagonal lines*) and *C. tortugensis* (*dot*) in northwestern Mexico and the adjacent United States. *Crotalus tigris* occurs on Isla Tiburón as well as the mainland; *C. tortugensis* is restricted to Isla de Tortuga in the Gulf of California.

scale rows; lateral blotches are more distinct posteriorly. Head markings are vague and irregular, but the back of the head has a few dark markings that may be arranged as paired occipital blotches and upper temporal streaks. Pale transverse bars are sometimes present on the supraoculars; these bars tend to curve forward medially. An ill-defined dark postocular stripe extends from the posterior edge of the eye to above the rictus; it is rarely bordered along its upper margin by a narrow pale stripe. The tail has 4–10 dark brown, indistinct, speckled crossbands. The caudal crossbands are wider than the adjacent interspaces along the middorsum. The infracephalic scales are mostly pale except for heavy punctations on the mental and infralabials. The belly is straw colored, yellow, or pink and moderately to heavily mottled or flecked with gray or brown pigment. The proximal rattle segment is tan or brown.

The rostral is wider than high, and 2 internasals are in contact with the rostral. There are 11–37 scales in the internasal-prefrontal area and 3–8 intersupraoculars. The prenasals are in broad contact with the rostral and usually the first supralabial. There is usually only a single loreal per side, less frequently 2. The contact of the posterior canthal with a loreal usually prevents the upper preocular from touching the postnasal. Most frequently there is one interoculabial, but in some specimens the anterior subocular is in contact with the supralabial series. There are 11–16 (usually 12–14) supralabials, 11–16 (usually 13–15) infralabials, 20–27 (usually 23) midbody dorsal scale rows, 156–177 ventrals, and 16–27 subcaudals.

SIMILAR SPECIES *Crotalus tigris* may be distinguished from other species of rattlesnakes by the presence of crossbands on the anterior part of the body. Four other species of rattlesnakes occur within the range of *C. tigris*. *Crotalus atrox* has conspicuously contrasting pale and dark tail rings, a pale postocular stripe extending from the upper postocular to a point in front of the rictus, and usually 25 or more midbody dorsal scale rows. *Crotalus cerastes* has supraoculars that form hornlike projections and 154 or fewer ventrals. *Crotalus mitchellii*, sympatric in one limited area in Arizona, has scales separating the rostral from the prenasals and usually 25 or more midbody dorsal scale rows. Though believed to be closely related to *C. tigris*, *C. mitchellii* has a proportionately much larger head. In *C. molossus* the ground color and blotches are not punctated with dark pigment, the tail of adults is nearly uniformly dark, usually 2 large prefrontals are in contact with each other medially, and 25 or more midbody dorsal scale rows are present. *Crotalus scutulatus* has conspicuously contrasting pale and dark tail rings, a broad dark postocular stripe that is bordered above and below by narrow pale stripes, usually 2 intersupraoculars, and usually 25 or more midbody dorsal scale rows.

REMARKS This species may be active any time of the day, but like all rattlesnakes, it will avoid prolonged exposure to direct sunlight during the hotter period of the day. It tends to be especially active after summer rains.

REFERENCES Allen, 1933; Amaral, 1927g, 1929a, 1929b; Armstrong and Murphy, 1979; Baird, 1859; Bogert and Oliver, 1945; Boulenger, 1896; Brattstrom, 1964; Brown, 1901; Camp, 1916; Cope, 1860c; Coues, 1875; Cuesta Terron, 1921b; Davis and Dixon, 1957; Ditmars, 1930; Dixon et al., 1962; Garman, 1884a; Gehlbach, 1956; Gloyd, 1937, 1940; Grinnell and Camp, 1917; Hoge and Romano, 1971a; Humphrey, 1936; Kauffeld, 1943; Klauber, 1927, 1930b, 1931b, 1936a, 1938, 1952, 1971, 1972; Lowe, 1964; Lowe et al., 1986; Martín del Campo, 1935, 1937a, 1950; Meek, 1906; R. W. Murphy, 1983a, 1983b; Murphy and Ottley, 1984; Ortenburger and Ortenburger, 1927; Pope, 1944–1945; Smith and Chrapliwy, 1958; Smith and Taylor, 1945; Stebbins, 1985; Stejneger, 1893, 1895; Stejneger and Barbour, 1943; E. H. Taylor, 1938a; Troschel, 1860; Werner, 1922; Wright and Wright, 1957; Zweifel and Norris, 1955.

## *Crotalus tortugensis* Van Denburgh and Slevin

(Figs. 413, 414; Map 104)

LOCAL NAME Víbora de cascabel.

ENGLISH NAME Tortuga Island diamond rattlesnake.

DISTRIBUTION This species is endemic to Isla Tortuga off the east coast of Baja California del Sur in the Gulf of California, Mexico (see Map 104).

HABITAT Desert; rocky, barren terrain covered with sparse brush and cacti.

DESCRIPTION This snake is smaller than its close relative, *C. atrox*. Large male *C. tortugensis* may slightly exceed 1 m in total length; the largest known specimen measured 1,058 mm. The head length is proportionately smaller relative to body length in *C. tortugensis* than in *C. atrox*; this trait is often considered an indicator of dwarfing.

The ground color is gray to gray-brown, sometimes with a slight purplish or pinkish cast. The 32–41 dark brown to purplish brown dorsal blotches are diamond shaped or hexagonal, punctated with black spots, and bordered with irregular black mottling; they tend to have pale interiors on either side of the midline and become relatively pale and ill-defined on the posterior part of the body. On the anterior two-thirds to three-fourths of the body, the dorsal blotches are edged along their middorsal portions with white or buff; this pale edging is usually absent, or at most extremely narrow, on the lateral margins of the dorsal blotches. The dorsum of the head usually has irregular black mottling or speckling. Each supraocular is marked with a transverse pale line. The dark postocular stripe is bordered by a lower (anterior) pale stripe that extends from the upper preocular to the lip margin below the eye and an upper (posterior) pale stripe that extends from the upper postocular to the lip margin near the rictus; overall, these pale lateral head markings are not particularly well defined. The tail has strongly contrasting ash-white and black rings; the 3–7 black tail rings are as wide as or wider than the pale rings. The proximal rattle segment is black.

The rostral is usually higher than wide. There are 2 internasals in contact with the rostral, more than 8 scales in the internasal-prefrontal region, and 4–5 (usually 4) intersupraoculars. The prenasal is invariably in contact with the first supralabial. The posterior canthal is large and its lateral portion extends ventrally over the canthus rostralis to partially intervene between the upper preocular and postnasal. A single loreal, the lower, is usually present on each side of the head; it is situated below the canthal, with which it usually makes contact, and thus usually separates the postnasal from the upper preocular. Two or 3 interoculabials separate the anterior subocular from the supralabials. There are 14–18 (usually 15 or 16) supralabials, 14–19 (usually 16 or 17) infralabials (the first pair of which is not transversely divided), 25–27 (usually 27) midbody dorsal scale rows, 180–190 ventrals, and 16–25 subcaudals.

SIMILAR SPECIES *Crotalus tortugensis* is the only species of rattlesnake on Isla Tortuga. *Crotalus atrox* occurs on the Mexican mainland to the northeast of Isla Tortuga and also on at least five islands in the Gulf of California. However, in *C. tortugensis* the dorsal blotches are marked differently than in *C. atrox*: the margins are much darker than the inner portions lying to both sides of the midline, which may be about the same color as the ground color. In *C. atrox* the upper preocular usually touches the postnasal; if not, contact is prevented by the presence of an upper loreal. *Crotalus ruber* occurs on the adjacent Peninsula of Baja California; it may be distinguished from *C. tortugensis* by having the first pair of infralabials transversely divided and a reddish, reddish brown, or pink ground color.

REMARKS This species is reported to be quick to rattle vigorously, but is not as irritable as its close relative, *C. atrox*. *Crotalus tortugensis* and *C. atrox* are not well differentiated from each other, and future studies may reveal that they are conspecific; one recent publication treated them as such, but provided no new information on their relationships.

REFERENCES Amaral, 1929b; Armstrong and Murphy, 1979; Cliff, 1954; Cuesta Terron, 1931; Ditmars, 1930; Gloyd, 1940; Klauber, 1930a, 1936b, 1938, 1971, 1972; Lindsay, 1962; Martín del Campo, 1935, 1937a, 1950; R. W. Murphy, 1983b; Murphy and Ottley, 1984; Schmidt, 1922; H. M. Smith and Taylor, 1945; Soulé and Sloan, 1966; Stejneger and Barbour, 1943; Van Denburgh, 1922b; Van Denburgh and Slevin, 1921b; Wright and Wright, 1957.

## *Crotalus transversus* Taylor

(Fig. 415; Map 105)

LOCAL NAME Víbora de cascabel.

ENGLISH NAME Cross-banded mountain rattlesnake.

DISTRIBUTION This rattlesnake is known only from a small portion of the Sierra Ajusco south of México City. Specimens have been taken from the hillsides surrounding the Lagunas de Zempoala in extreme northwestern Morelos, but the species probably also occurs in the states of México and the Distrito Federal (Map 105). It is known from elevations of about 2,900 m and above.

HABITAT Temperate boreal forest characterized by open areas of pine and bunch grass (*zacatón*).

DESCRIPTION This is a small species of rattlesnake; the longest specimen known, a female, is only 465 mm in total length.

Map 105. Distributions of *Crotalus intermedius* (*diagonal lines and square*), *C. pricei* (*stipples and triangle*), and *C. transversus* (*diamond*). *Crotalus pricei* occurs well north of the Cordillera Volcánica in Mexico (the triangle represents records from the Sierra Fría, Aguascalientes). *Crotalus intermedius* occurs as a number of disjunct highland populations in southern and eastern Mexico (*square* represents a single record for 3 km west-northwest of Tlaxcala, Tlaxcala). *Crotalus transversus* is known only from the Sierra Ajusco, south of Mexico City. The circle represents a single record for a specimen from Cerro Tancítaro that may be referable to *C. transversus*.

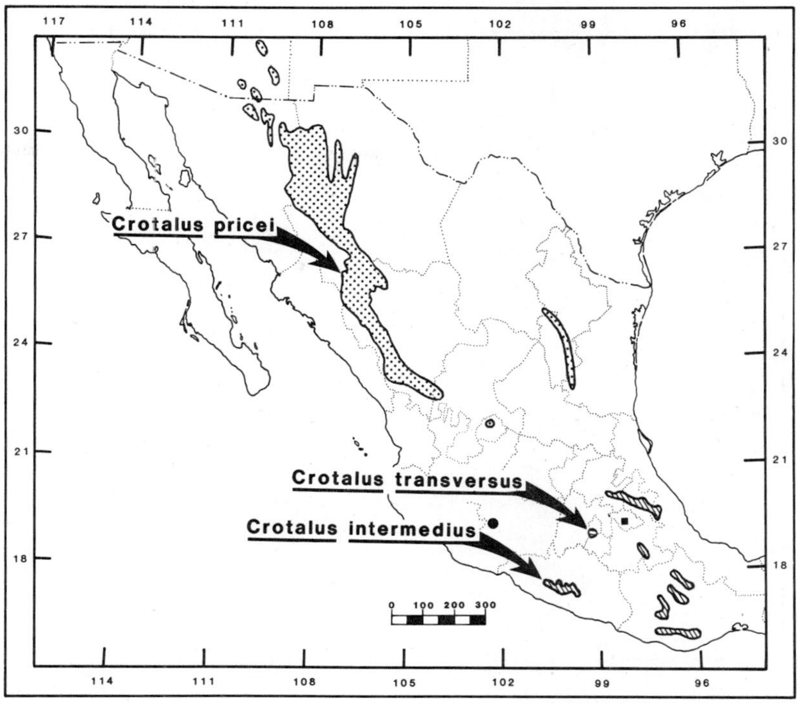


There are two different color morphs, one with an orangish ground color, the other with gray. A pair of dark nape blotches is present and a dark postocular stripe extends from the lower posterior edge of the eye past the rictus to the angle of the jaw. The supralabials tend to be pale, but have varying amounts of dark mottling, especially anteriorly and along the margin of the lip. There are 37–43 narrow dark brown to black crossbands on the body and 5–9 on the tail. The mental is dark and the infralabials are heavily mottled. The belly may be pale with scattered dark mottling or be so heavily mottled as to be almost uniformly black. The color of the basal segment of the rattle is similar to the ground color.

The rostral is wider than high. There are 2 large internasals, a single canthal on each side, 5–6 scales in the internasal-prefrontal area, 2–3 intersupraoculars, and a single loreal on each side that usually fails to make contact with the second supralabials owing to the presence of a single large prefoveal. The prenasal is in broad contact with the first supralabial; the postnasal is precluded from contact with the upper preocular by the intervening loreal. Subfoveals and postfoveals are absent. The upper preocular is not vertically divided and the lower preocular may or may not extend forward to make contact with the posterior margin of the loreal. Supralabials 3–5 usually touch the suboculars. There are 8–10 (usually 9) supralabials, 8 or 9 (usually 9) infralabials, 21 midbody dorsal scale rows, 141–152 ventrals (exclusive of preventrals), 19–27 subcaudals (the distal 3–9 are divided), and 8 rattle-fringe scales.

SIMILAR SPECIES The only rattlesnake sympatric with *C. transversus* is *C. triseriatus*. These species differ from each other most conspicuously on the basis of dorsal pattern: in *C. transversus* there are 37–43 narrow crossbands, whereas in *C. triseriatus* there are 30–57 dark middorsal blotches. *Crotalus triseriatus* differs further from *C. transversus* in possessing 2 or more prefoveals; in having the posterior edge of the loreal pointed and projecting between the anterior portions of the upper and lower preoculars; and in usually having 3 suboculars—the anteriormost in contact with 2 supralabials (usually the third and fourth), but the posterior 2 separated from the supralabials by a single row of interoculabials. *Crotalus triseriatus* usually has 23 or more midbody dorsal scale rows (vs. 21) and more numerous supralabials (9–15 vs. 8–10) and infralabials (10–14 vs. 8–9) than *C. transversus*. *Sistrurus ravus* has been taken within a few kilometers of *C. transversus* but is easily distinguished by its large symmetrical head plates, distinctive pattern, and usually more numerous labials (10–13 supralabials and 9–13 infralabials).

REMARKS This rattlesnake is known from fewer than 20 specimens. We have found it active only by day.

The status of a population of rattlesnakes from Cerro Tancítaro, Michoacán, represented by a single known specimen (FMNH 39115), is uncertain, but this population appears to be closely related to, if not actually conspecific with, *C. transversus*.

REFERENCES Armstrong and Murphy, 1979; Campbell, 1982a, 1988; Davis and Smith, 1953; Duellman, 1961, 1965b; Klauber, 1952, 1972; Martín del Campo, 1940b; H. M. Smith, 1946a; H. M. Smith and Taylor, 1945; E. H. Taylor, 1944.

## *Crotalus triseriatus* (Wagler)

(Figs. 416–427; Map 106)

LOCAL NAMES Chiauhcóatl chiáuitl, colcóatl (Náhuatl); hocico de puerco; viborita de cascabel.

ENGLISH NAME Mexican dusky rattlesnake.

DISTRIBUTION This species occurs in the highlands of the Transverse Volcanic Cordillera of Mexico from

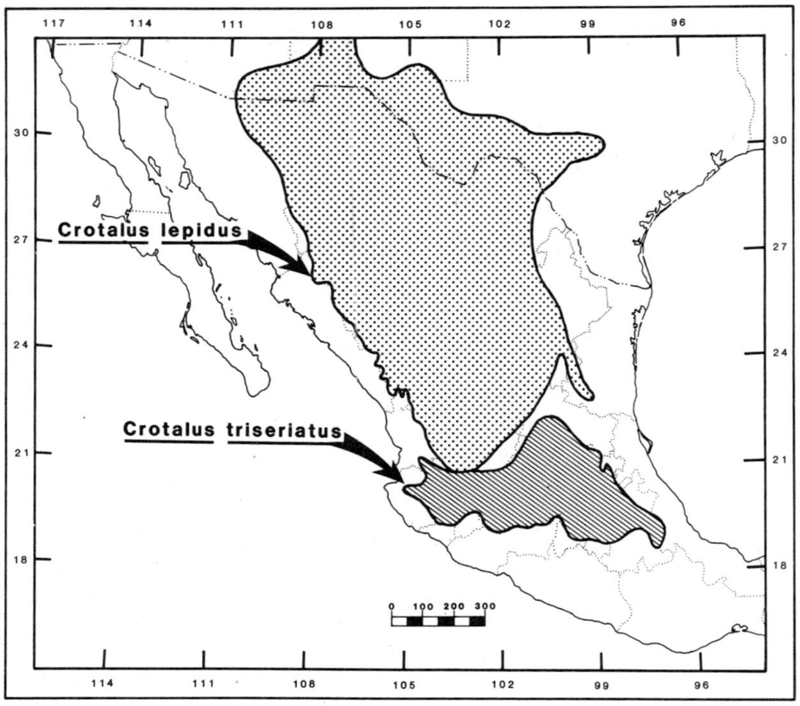


**Map 106.** Distributions of *Crotalus lepidus* (*stipples*) and *C. triseriatus* (*diagonal lines*) in Mexico and the adjacent United States.

west-central Veracruz westward to central Jalisco; in the east extending as far north on the Mesa Central as southern San Luis Potosí and in the west to the Sierra de Nayarit in Nayarit (Map 106). Its vertical distribution ranges from about 1,500 to over 4,300 m, making it the highest ranging New World snake.

HABITAT Pine-oak forest, boreal forest, and mesquite-grassland.

DESCRIPTION Large adult males commonly exceed 600 mm in total length, and females are somewhat smaller. The largest specimen reported was 683 mm in total length.

Specimens from the Transverse Volcanic Cordillera have a medium to gray-brown ground color. The ground color is darkest laterally and palest between the 30–57 dark brown middorsal blotches. The dorsal blotches are no more than 5 scales wide and frequently only 3; they may be roundish or subelliptical in shape; and most often there is an irregular pale outer edge. The postocular stripe and paired nape blotches are dark brown. Three series of small dark lateral blotches, often roundish in shape, may be reduced or indistinct. The venter usually has a pinkish cast, becoming more intense posteriorly, with varying amounts of brown-to-black mottling that tends to be concentrated toward the lateral margins of the ventrals.

In the northeastern part of its range this snake exhibits a great amount of intra- and interpopulational variation; furthermore, many populations are sexually dimorphic with regard to ground color, which may be gray to gray-green, yellowish green, or pale to reddish brown. Adult males frequently have a greenish or yellowish cast, whereas females are brownish or grayish. A dark pair of nape blotches is followed by 24–43 middorsal blotches. The dorsal blotches tend to be larger than in specimens from the Transverse Volcanic Cordillera, usually being 5–7 scales wide, and frequently are roughly quadrangular. Usually only a single series of lateral blotches is apparent. A well-defined postocular stripe may or may not be present. The venter is yellowish or pinkish with dark brown or gray mottling that becomes more intense posteriorly.

Specimens from the northwestern part of the range have a pale grayish brown, reddish brown, yellowish brown, or yellowish green ground color with 32–48 dark body blotches that are usually 5–7 dorsals wide. In pale grayish brown specimens the dorsal blotches are bordered by black with white edging, the most conspicuous of the three series of lateral blotches are often separated from the dorsal blotches by irregular pale markings, ventrolaterally the dorsals are often suffused with pink, and the venter is mostly dark. In reddish brown and yellowish green snakes, which are usually males, the dorsal blotches are not bordered by black or white edging, 1–3 series of lateral blotches are evident, and the venter is immaculate or very lightly mottled. A distinct dark postocular stripe and pair of nape blotches are present, but the latter may be indistinct in some large males.

The color of the iris in *C. triseriatus* is variable, but the upper third is much paler than below. The proximal rattle segment is reddish, gray, or dark brown.

The rostral is usually wider than high, but may sometimes be about as high or higher than wide. The anterior subocular is usually in contact with supralabials 4 and 5, but it may touch only one of these scales, touch supralabials 5 and 6, or be separated by a single interoculabial. The upper preocular may or may not be vertically divided. There are 2 large internasals, in contact; a single canthal on each side; 2 intercanthals; a total of 4–12 scales in the internasal-prefrontal area; 2–5 (usually 3) intersupraoculars; a single loreal on each side that is separated from the supralabials by foveals and that separates the upper preocular from the postnasal; 2–7 (usually 3 or 4) prefoveals; 9–15 (usually 12 or 13) supralabials; 9–14 (usually 11 or 12) infralabials; 21–26 (usually 23) midbody dorsal scale rows; 136–161 ventrals; 17–34 subcaudals; and 8–10 rattle-fringe scales.

SIMILAR SPECIES The Mexican Plateau contains a great number of rattlesnake species, some of which may be mistaken for *C. triseriatus*. *Crotalus intermedius* and *C. transversus* have 21 midbody dorsal scale rows (vs. usually 23 or more), usually 9 supralabials and infralabials (vs. 11 or 12), and 0–1 prefoveals (vs. usually 2–7); *C. polystictus* has at least 25 midbody dorsal scale rows, 162–187 ventrals (vs. 136–161), and a dorsal pattern consisting of oval paravertebral blotches; *C. pusillus* possesses 4 scales in the internasal-prefrontal area (vs. a minimum of 6); and *Sistrus ravus* has large symmetrical head plates, usually 9.

REMARKS We tentatively recognize three subspecies: *C. t. triseriatus* (Figs. 416, 417, 456, 457), with a disjunct distribution in the highlands of the Transverse Volcanic Cordillera from west-central Veracruz to the Volcán and El Nevado de Colima in southwestern Jalisco; *C. t. aquilus* (Figs. 422–427) in the eastern portion of the Mesa Central and parts of the Sierra Madre Oriental in Hidalgo and San Luis Potosí; and *C. t. armstrongi* (Figs. 418–421) in the western part of the Mesa Central and probably the southernmost extension of the Sierra Madre Occidental in Nayarit.

*Crotalus t. triseriatus* and *C. t. armstrongi* usually have more numerous (usually more than 38) and smaller dorsal blotches, a smaller rattle, and proportionately longer tail than *C. t. aquilus*. Both *C. t. triseriatus* and *C. t. armstrongi* invariably have a well-defined postocular stripe, most frequently possess 8 rattle-fringe scales, and only rarely have the upper preocular vertically divided; *C. t. aquilus* may or may not have a well-defined postocular stripe, usually possesses 10 rattle-fringe scales, and has the upper preocular vertically divided with some frequency. *Crotalus t. armstrongi* and most populations of *C. t. aquilus* are sexually dimorphic for color, but this trend is absent in *C. t. triseriatus*. *Crotalus t. armstrongi* may be further distinguished from *C. t. triseriatus* on the basis of its ground color and less numerous subcaudals in males (24–26 vs. 26–34).

A number of characteristics suggest that *C. t. aquilus* may be more closely related to *C. lepidus* than it is to *C. t. triseriatus* or *C. t. armstrongi*, making *C. triseriatus*, as presently recognized, paraphyletic. These characteristics include the condition of the upper preocular (often vertically divided), shape of the nasal (prenasal curves under postnasal), tendency toward sexual dimorphism in ground color (males greenish or yellowish), osteology (distance between outer edges of frontals comparatively narrow, squamosal more elongated with less prominent posterior processes, foramen in maxillary cavity relatively small), eye size (relatively small), rattle size (relatively large), and hemipenial spines (relatively shorter and stouter). We suspect that a thorough investigation of the relationships of these rattlesnakes would reveal that *C. t. aquilus* should be given a subspecific status with *C. lepidus* or be considered a full species.

Two other subspecies have been described: *C. t. anahuacus* and *C. t. quadrangularis* appear to be junior synonyms of *C. t. triseriatus* and *C. t. aquilus*, respectively.

As a general rule, these snakes occur in rocky areas and are active only by day, although those from elevations below 2,500 m occasionally have been found crawling at night.

Envenomation by this species is reported to cause intense pain, faintness, cold perspiration, and swelling.

REFERENCES Amaral, 1927f; Armstrong and Murphy, 1979; Boulenger, 1896; Campbell, 1979b; Campbell and Armstrong, 1979; Cope, 1864, 1879, 1885a, 1885b, 1887; Cuesta Terron, 1921b, 1930a; Davis and Smith, 1953; Dixon et al., 1972; Duellman, 1958, 1961, 1965b; Dugès, 1876–1877, 1896; Dunn, 1936; Ferrari-Perez, 1886; Gadow, 1905, 1910; Garman, 1884a; Gloyd, 1940; Greene, 1972; Groombridge, 1986; Günther, 1885–1902; Harris and Simmons, 1978b; Klauber, 1936b; 1940a, 1940b, 1940c, 1952, 1971, 1972; Leviton, 1953; Martín del Campo, 1935, 1937a, 1938b, 1940a, 1940b, 1950, 1955, 1984; Mertens, 1930; Minton and Cervantes, 1977; Mocquard, 1899, 1908–1909; Schmidt and Shannon, 1947; H. M. Smith, 1946a, 1970; H. M. Smith and Laufe, 1945; H. M. Smith and Taylor, 1945, 1966; Sumichrast, 1882; Swan, 1952; E. H. Taylor, 1941, 1949, 1953b; Werner, 1922; Wilson and McCranie, 1979.

## ***Crotalus viridis* (Rafinesque)**

(Figs. 428–430, 450, 451; Map 107)

LOCAL NAME Víbora de cascabel.

ENGLISH NAME Western rattlesnake.

DISTRIBUTION Only a small portion of this snake's range is in Mexico: northern Chihuahua, northwestern Coahuila, western Baja California del Norte, extreme northern Baja California del Sur, and Isla Coronado del Sur off the northwest coast of Baja California del Norte (Map 107). Extralimitally, this species occurs over much of the western half of the United States and ranges as far north as southwestern Canada. Its vertical distribution in Mexico is from about sea level to over 2,500 m.

HABITAT In Mexico this species inhabits mesquite-grassland, desert, (even the dunes near Samalayuca, Chihuahua), and chaparral; it enters pine-oak forest near the Continental Divide along the northern Sonoran-Chihuahuan border and the mountain ranges of northern Baja California.

DESCRIPTION Snakes from the mainland commonly exceed 1 m in total length; the largest known specimen measured 1,620 mm. Large adults from Isla Coronado del Sur are usually 600–700 mm in overall length.

In general, most populations of *C. viridis* exhibit a considerable amount of ontogenetic variation—relatively distinct patterns evident in juveniles become progressively obscured with age.

Snakes from Chihuahua to Coahuila in north-central Mexico have 33–57 brown dorsal blotches that are nar-

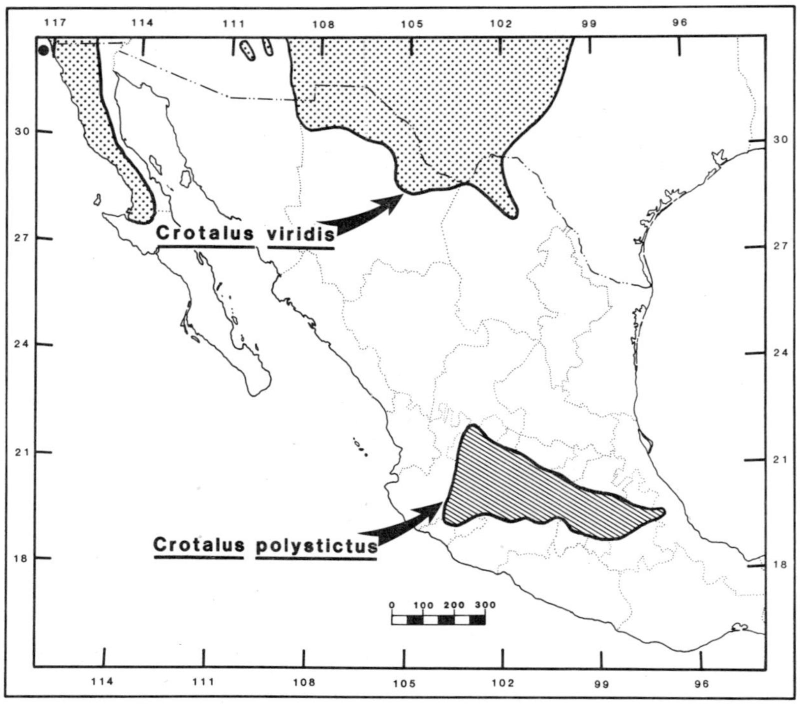


**Map 107.** Distributions of *Crotalus polystictus* (*diagonal lines*) and *C. viridis* (*stipples*) in Mexico and the adjacent United States.

rowly edged (less than 1 scale) with white on a greenish gray, greenish brown, pale brown, or straw-yellow ground color. The dorsal blotches are often indented along their anterior and/or posterior margins; however, these indentations are absent in some specimens and the blotches may appear nearly hexagonal or rectangular. Two to three series of lateral blotches are not particularly well-defined in young snakes and usually become virtually absent in large adults. A broad postocular stripe curves downward from the eye to the angle of the jaw and is bordered by two pale diagonal stripes: one passing in front of the eye from the upper preocular or posterior canthal downward to the lip margin at a point below the posterior edge of the eye, and thence along the supralabials to the rictus; the other extending from the upper postocular to a point above the angle of the jaw. Narrow transverse white stripes are present in the prefrontal and the supraocular-frontal regions; these two bars are often connected by a medial white stripe. Pale dorsal head markings are usually absent in large adults. Of the 4–10 dark tail bands, the ultimate one is usually darker than, but no longer than, the others. The proximal rattle segment is black. The venter possesses little or no dark mottling.

In juvenile to medium-sized individuals from the Baja California mainland the ground color is pale brownish gray. Twenty-seven to 43 dark brown, often diamond-shaped blotches are edged in black and bordered by a single row of pale scales. These dorsal blotches are separated from one another middorsally by 1 or 2 pale scales. Of the two series of dark brown lateral blotches, the upper is the largest. The top of the head is brown. A pale prefrontal bar connects the pale lower (anterior) borders of the dark brown to black postocular stripes on either side of the head; then a pale bar extends across the supraoculars and frontal region, followed posteriorly by a dark brown bar and a pale upper temporal streak that forms the upper (posterior) border of the postocular stripe and extends to above the angle of the jaw. The pale head markings that are so obvious in young snakes disappear in adults and the top of the head becomes uniformly dark brown or black; the body of large snakes may be blackish or very dark with an indistinct body pattern. There are 2–8 dark tail rings. The end of the tail has a long yellow or orange ring that gradually turns to gray or black as the snake matures and is one and one-half to over two times as long as the preceding black ring. The basal rattle segment is yellow or orange in juveniles and subadults, becoming black in older snakes. The venter has a moderate to heavy amount of dark mottling.

Snakes from Isla Coronado del Sur closely resemble those from the adjacent mainland; the range of dorsal blotches is 27–37.

The rostral is usually higher than wide. One of the most distinctive features of *C. viridis* is that it often possesses 3 or more internasals (range 1–8; over 90% of Mexican specimens have 3 or more, with the mode being 4). There are usually 2 canthals on each side, but sometimes 3 or, rarely, 4. The number of scales on the snout in front of a line between the anterior edges of the supraoculars is extremely variable, ranging from 7–45, but most specimens have between 15 and 30. The number of intersupraoculars is likewise variable, with a range of 1–9 (most frequently 4, 5, or 6). Usually there is a single loreal per side, but sometimes there are 2 or, very rarely, 3. The prenasal may or may not contact the first supralabial. There are 10–18 (usually 14 or 15) supralabials, 11–20 (usually 15 or 16) infralabials, 23–29 midbody dorsal scale rows (usually 25 in western Mexico and on islands, 27 in north-central Mexico), 162–196 ventrals, 15–31 subcaudals, and usually 12 rattle-fringe scales.

SIMILAR SPECIES A number of species of rattlesnakes having large dorsal blotches and reaching a mod-

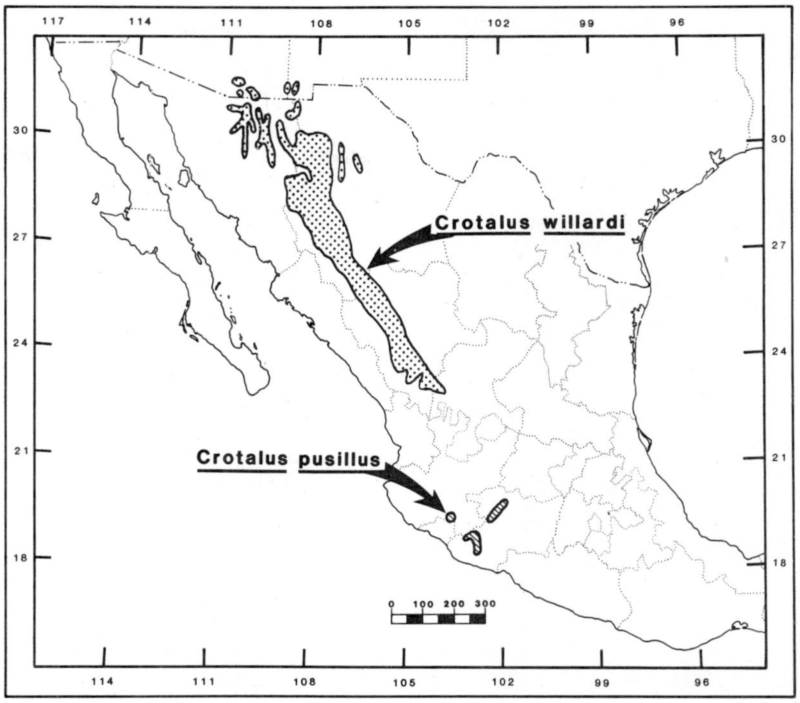


**Map 108.** Distributions of *Crotalus pusillus* (*diagonal lines*) and *C. willardi* (*stipples*) in Mexico and the adjacent United States.

erate to large length are sympatric with *C. viridis* in parts of its range; all of these normally have only 2 internasals in contact with the rostral. *Crotalus atrox* has a tail with strongly contrasting rings of white and black and the pale posterior border of the postocular stripe extends to the rictus (not to above the angle of the jaw). *Crotalus scutulatus* also possesses a tail with strongly contrasting rings of white and black and often has a crescent-shaped scale bordering the posterior-inward side of each supraocular. *Crotalus ruber* possesses a reddish ground color and the first pair of infralabials are transversely divided. *Crotalus enyo* is beetle browed with supraoculars inclined upward toward the lateral side of the head, the tail lacks strongly contrasting pale and dark rings, and the scales in the prefrontal-frontal region are knobby. *Crotalus molossus* has a uniformly dark tail with no bands or rings evident and 4–6 large flat scales in the internasal-prefrontal area. *Crotalus mitchellii* has prenasals that are not in contact with the rostral owing to the intervention of a series of small scales, and the pattern in this species is often banded rather than blotched. *Crotalus tigris* has a pattern of 35 or more crossbands on the body and members of the genus *Sistrurus* have 9 large symmetrical plates on top of the head.

REMARKS Three subspecies of *C. viridis* occur in Mexico; *C. v. viridis* (Figs. 428, 450, 451) in north-central Mexico, *C. v. helleri* (Fig. 430) along the Pacific Coast and in the mountains of about the northern half of the Peninsula of Baja California, and *C. v. caliginis* (Fig. 429) on Isla Coronado del Sur.

At high elevations this species is reported to be mainly diurnal, but throughout much of its range it is most commonly active after dark.

REFERENCES Amaral, 1929c; Armstrong and Murphy, 1979; Bogert and Oliver, 1945; Bostic, 1971; Bullock and Cowles, 1952; Cope, 1860c; Coues, 1875; Crimmins, 1927; Cuesta Terron, 1931; Curran, 1935; Garman, 1884a; Gehlbach, 1956; Girard, 1858; Gloyd, 1940; Groombridge, 1986; Hallowell, 1852; Jameson and Flury, 1949; Jones, 1981; Kauffeld, 1964; Klauber, 1927, 1930b, 1931a, 1936b, 1940c, 1949b, 1952, 1963, 1971, 1972; Klemmer, 1963; Linsdale, 1932, 1940; Lowe et al., 1986; Martín del Campo, 1935, 1937a, 1950; Meek, 1906; Minton, 1959; Mosauer, 1936; R. W. Murphy, 1983a; Murray, 1955; Ottley and Hunt, 1981; Savage, 1960, 1967; Schmidt and Owens, 1944; H. M. Smith and Brodie, 1982; H. M. Smith and Buechner, 1947; H. M. Smith and Taylor, 1945, 1966; H. M. Smith et al., 1971; Stebbins, 1985; Stejneger, 1893; Stejneger and Barbour, 1943; Tanner, 1985; Van Denburgh, 1896, 1905, 1924; Van Denburgh, and Slevin, 1914; Wright and Wright, 1957; Yarrow, 1875.

### *Crotalus willardi* Meek

(Figs. 431–436, 458, 459; Map 108)

LOCAL NAME Víbora de cascabel.

ENGLISH NAME Ridge-nosed rattlesnake.

DISTRIBUTION Mexico and the United States. Most of the range of this species lies within the highlands of the Sierra Madre Occidental and associated ranges of northwestern Mexico. It occurs in north-central and northeastern Sonora, western Chihuahua, and the Sierra del Nido complex to the east of the main mountain system. In the south, it occurs from the vicinity of Coyotes, Durango, eastward to the Cerro Candelaria in southwestern Zacatecas; its distribution is probably fragmented by the Río Mezquital Depression. In the United States, it is known only from a few ranges in southwestern New Mexico and southeastern Arizona (Map 108). The vertical distribution of this species ranges from about 1,600 to 2,750 m.

HABITAT These snakes frequent pine-oak woodland, oak scrub, and open grassy meadows within pine-oak forests; they are more abundant in humid canyon bottoms and less exposed, more mesic slopes.

DESCRIPTION Large adult males of this species may exceed 550 mm, and females are usually somewhat smaller. The largest measured specimen is 670 mm in total length (Fig. 436).

The ground color is reddish brown, rust-colored, yellowish brown, gray-brown, or gray. The 18–45 dorsal blotches are deep chestnut or chocolate brown, usually edged on their anterior and posterior margins with dark brown and/or black pigment; they are more-or-less subquadrate in shape and tend to merge with the ground color laterally. The interspaces between the middorsal blotches are paler than the lateral ground color and may form distinctive cream-colored, buff, or pale brown crossbands. There may be three series of dark brown lateral spots, however, these are frequently irregular or vague, and may be absent altogether in some specimens. The top of the head is usually marked with a few irregular dark brown or black spots, flecks, or stipples. A postocular stripe extends from the lower posterior edge of the eye to the angle of the jaw; this stripe may be ill-defined in snakes from northwestern Chihuahua and southwestern New Mexico. The proximal portion of the tail possesses 1–3 blotches or bands, whereas the distal portion is striped or unicolored with gray or brown. The anterior ventrals usually have a yellowish, cream-colored, or pinkish cast and are finely peppered with dark pigment; posteriorly the pigment often, but not invariably, tends to be distributed in clumps and is concentrated toward the lateral margins of the ventrals. The belly becomes progressively darker posteriorly. The subcaudals are pinkish, reddish, or orangish with irregular black markings. The iris is yellowish brown or bronze with heavy black peppering. The basal rattle segment is deep reddish brown, orange, gray-brown, or gray. The tongue is black with gray tips.

One of the most distinctive features of *C. willardi* is its facial pattern of pale (usually bright white) stripes; however, there is a considerable amount of variation among the various populations. In snakes from the Sierra del Nido and the states of Durango and Zacatecas, the upper stripe extends posteriorly from the prenasal across the postnasal, lower loreal (or lower portion, if only 1 loreal), lower preocular, suboculars, usually several interoculabials, and the posterior 7–8 supralabials to the rictus. The lower stripe usually begins on about infralabial 2 or 3 and extends posteriorly along the lip margin 4–7 infralabials before angling ventromedially and continuing along the gulars that are contiguous with the posterior infralabials; then it turns dorsally and merges with the upper pale stripe at the rictus. The lower stripe may also merge at several points along its length with more medially situated pale markings or stripes on the gular region. Even though the lower stripe does not extend to the anterior tip of the lower jaw, a pale streak along the lip margin of the upper jaw may involve the first 3–5 pairs of supralabials; thus a continuous pale stripe is evident along the anterior portions of the mouth when the jaws are closed. A vertical stripe is usually present on the rostral and mental; that on the mental widens as it extends posteriorly across the medial portions of the first pair of infralabials and chinshields and ultimately merges with the pale coloration of the posterior gulars and anterior ventrals.

In some specimens from northern Sonora and adjacent Arizona, there is no pale stripe along the anterior lip margin of the lower jaw. Rather, a pale stripe angles immediately inward toward the ventral midline at about the level of infralabial 8, extends along the gulars parallel to the lip, and then turns dorsally to merge with the upper stripe at the rictus.

This unique pattern of pale facial stripes is less distinct in most snakes from northeastern Sonora and western Chihuahua; in these the upper pale facial stripe does not extend anteriorly past the level of the eye. Snakes from southwestern New Mexico and the Sierra de San Luis on the Chihuahuan-Sonoran border have no distinct pattern of facial stripes, but the posterior supralabials are generally pale with some dark peppering. The postocular stripe in these snakes is poorly defined.

The rostral is higher than wide. The pair of internasals and 2/2 canthals are relatively large compared with most other scales on the crown. The canthus rostralis and tip of the snout are distinctly raised by the flared-up internasals, anterior canthals, and sometimes posterior canthals. Other than the internasals and canthals, the scales covering the top of the snout are small; there are 20–40 between the rostral and front edges of the supraoculars. There are 6–9 intersupraoculars. The prenasal is in contact with the first supralabials, and the upper preocular is not vertically divided and is not in contact with the postnasal. Most frequently there are 2 loreals on each side, the upper usually smaller than the lower; however, it is not unusual, particularly in snakes from the south, to find a single vertically elongated scale in the loreal region. The interoculabial series is most frequently reduced to a single scale between the anterior subocular and supralabials, or rarely 2. There are 12–17 (mode 14) supralabials, 12–17 (mode 14) infralabials, 25–29 midbody dorsal scale rows (usually 27, except in snakes from the northern part of the range, where 25 is more common), 146–163 ventrals, 21–36 subcaudals, and 8–10 rattle-fringe scales, which are usually sharply pointed.

SIMILAR SPECIES No other species of rattlesnake possesses the distinctive pattern of white facial stripes and the characteristic sharply raised canthus rostralis found in most populations of *C. willardi*. *Crotalus lepidus* may be further distinguished from *C. willardi* by having 1–4 intersupraoculars, usually 23 midbody dorsal scale rows, an upper preocular that is divided vertically, a single loreal, and usually fewer than 10 scales on top of the snout between the rostral and anterior edge of the supraoculars. *Crotalus pricei* usually has a gray ground color with a series of 39–64 pairs of small dark brown paravertebral blotches, a single canthal, a single loreal, no more than about 6 or 7 scales on top of the snout between the rostral and anterior edge of the supraoculars, 2 or 3 intersupraoculars, usually 21 midbody dorsal scale rows, and the anterior subocular in contact with several supralabials. *Crotalus cerastes* occurs in xeric habitats to the northwest and west of *C.*

*willardi* and is morphologically quite distinctive. *Crotalus cerastes* usually possesses 23 or fewer midbody dorsal scale rows, the supraocular is strongly shaped into a soft hornlike process, and the outline of the scales along the upper lip margin is distinctly scalloped; furthermore, male and female *C. cerastes* have fewer subcaudals than their respective sexes in *C. willardi*.

REMARKS This species is mainly diurnal and, in our experience, tends to have a mild temperament.

Five subspecies of *C. willardi* have been described. *Crotalus w. willardi* (Fig. 431) occurs in the Huachuca, Patagonia, and Santa Rita Mountains of southeastern Arizona, south into the Sierra de los Ajos, Sierra de Cananea, and Sierra Azul of northern Sonora, Mexico. *Crotalus w. amabilis* (Fig. 432) is known only from several canyons (arroyos) in the Sierra del Nido of north-central Chihuahua. *Crotalus w. meridionalis* (Figs. 433–434) occurs in southern Durango and northwestern Zacatecas, and probably occurs northward in the Sierra Madre Occidental into northwestern Durango. *Crotalus w. obscurus* (Figs. 435, 458, 459) inhabits the Animas and Peloncillo Mountains, New Mexico, and the Sierra de San Luis in extreme northeastern Sonora and northwestern Chihuahua. *Crotalus w. silus* (Fig. 436) occurs in the mountains of northeastern Sonora and western Chihuahua, including the Sierra del Tigre, Sierra de Oposura, Sierra Aconchi, and Sierra Purica, as well as to the south in the Sierra Madre Occidental.

REFERENCES Anderson, 1962; Armstrong and Murphy, 1979; Bogert and Degenhardt, 1961; Bogert and Oliver, 1945; Campbell et al., 1989; Gloyd, 1940; Harris, 1974; Harris and Simmons, 1976; Hartman, 1911; Kauffeld, 1943; Klauber, 1936b, 1949c, 1952, 1971, 1972; Leopold, 1967; Lowe, 1964; Lowe et al., 1986; Manion, 1968; Martín del Campo, 1935, 1937a; McCranie and Wilson, 1978; Meek, 1906; Rado and Rowlands, 1981; H. M. Smith and Taylor, 1945, 1966; Stejneger and Barbour, 1943; Swarth, 1921; Tanner, 1985; E. H. Taylor and Knobloch, 1940; T. R. Van Devender and Lowe, 1977; Webb, 1984; Wilson and McCranie, 1979; Woodin, 1953; Wright and Wright, 1957.

# Massasauga and Mexican Pygmy Rattlesnake

## Genus *Sistrurus* Garman, 1883

The genus *Sistrurus* (family Viperidae) includes three North American species of rattlesnake; only two of these occur within the limits of this work. The Mexican pygmy rattlesnake, *S. ravus*, is restricted to the highlands of central and southern Mexico; and the massasauga, *S. catenatus*, is largely extralimital but a few relictual populations occur in north-central and northeastern Mexico. *Sistrurus catenatus* in Mexico is confined to dry habitats, although it is usually found in the vicinity of water; *S. ravus* occurs in a great variety of conditions ranging from desert to cloud forest, generally at elevations above 1,500 m.

The following discussion of variation refers only to *S. ravus* and *S. catenatus*. The rostral is low and has a pointed apex in *S. ravus*, whereas in *S. catenatus* the rostral is higher and is rounded above. The canthus rostralis is sharp in *S. catenatus*; in *S. ravus* it is rounded. There are usually 9 large symmetrical head plates, but in some specimens of *S. ravus* the parietals may be divided transversely. There are 9–13 (usually 11 or 12) supralabials and infralabials, 21–25 (usually 21 or 23) midbody dorsal scale rows, 136–152 ventrals, and 19–36 subcaudals, most or all of which are undivided. The middorsals are keeled, and the anal plate is undivided. The middorsal body blotches are usually as long as or longer than wide in *S. ravus*, whereas they are wider than long in *S. catenatus*. Descriptions of color and pattern for members of this genus follow in the species accounts.

The hemipenes of *S. catenatus* and *S. ravus* differ from each other in a number of aspects. In *S. catenatus* the organ extends 5–8 subcaudals (up to 10 in large males) and is divided with a bifurcated sulcus spermaticus that extends to the apex of each lobe. The base of the organ and proximal portions of the lobes are covered with a total of 60–70 medium to large spines; these gradually diminish in size distally and grade into spinulate calyces which cover the distal two-thirds of each lobe. The size of the spinules on the calyces also diminishes toward the apices. Each lobe is subcylindrical throughout most of its length, but becomes bulbous near its terminus. The apex of each lobe bears a large soft papilla. In *S. ravus* the hemipenes extend 5–8 subcaudals and are divided with a bifurcated sulcus spermaticus extending to the apex of each subcylindrical lobe. Six to 8 large spines, interspersed with smaller ones, occur below each lobe. The crotch is wide and at its level there is an abrupt transition from basal spines to spinulate flounces that encircle the lobes. Distally there is a gradual transition from flounces to spinulate calyces. With respect to the number of basal spines, wide crotch, and abrupt transition from spines to the ornamentation of the lobes, *S. ravus* more closely resembles some members of the genus *Crotalus* than it does the other species of *Sistrurus*.

Despite their small size, rattlesnakes of the genus *Sistrurus* appear capable at times of producing moderate to severe envenomation and all victims of their bites should be treated accordingly.

### ***Sistrurus catenatus*** **(Rafinesque)**

(Figs. 437, 438; Map 109)

LOCAL NAME Víbora de cascabel.

ENGLISH NAME Massasauga.

DISTRIBUTION Most of the distribution of this snake is extralimital to Latin America; in the United States it occurs from southeastern Arizona, southern New Mexico, and most of Texas northeastward to central New York and southern Ontario, Canada. In Mexico this species is known from the Cuatro Ciénegas Basin, Coahuila, and from the vicinity of Aramberri, Nuevo León. It probably occurs in northern Tamaulipas, northern Chihuahua, and possibly in northeastern Sonora (Map 109). An unconfirmed report exists for Durango (see Remarks). In the southwestern United States this snake ranges from near sea level to over 1,500 m.

HABITAT The habitat for this species in the southwestern United States has been described as desert-grassland. The region about the Cuatro Ciénegas Basin where this snake has been collected is vegetated with various combinations of creosote bush, chenopods, low mesquite, desert willow, salt grass (*Distichlis*), and numerous cacti. The vegetation near Aramberri is mostly xerophytic, however, the Río Blanco and several other tributaries of the Río Soto la Marina cut through the countryside and possess luxuriant riparian vegetations. Northern Tamaulipas is covered by mesquite-grassland.

DESCRIPTION This is a relatively small rattlesnake that generally attains an adult size of a little over 500 mm, but it infrequently may approach twice this length.

The dorsal ground color is pale brown. The top of the head is generally marked with a pair of spots on the supraoculars and frontal, a single median brown spot on the parietals, and pair of nape blotches that form a

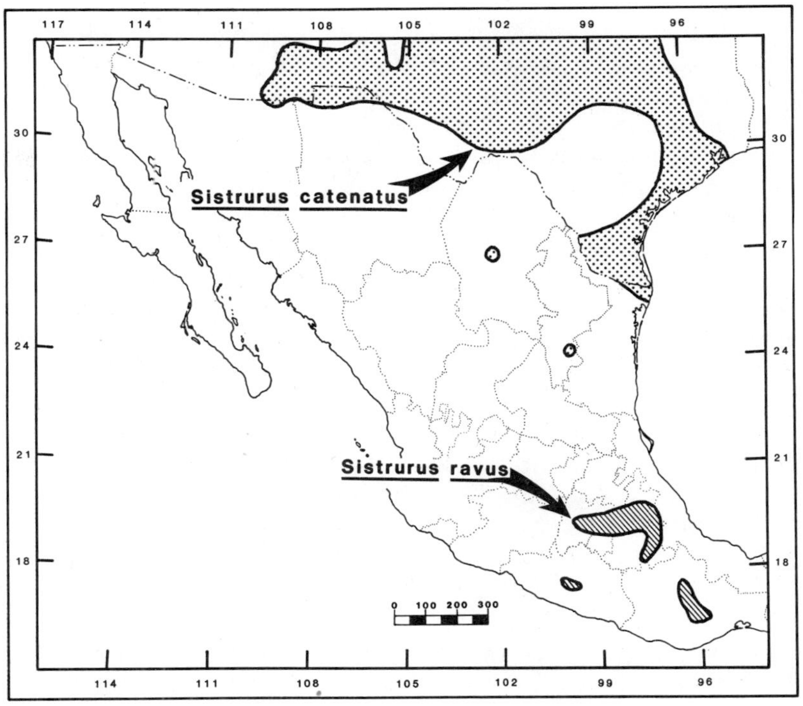


**Map 109.** Distributions of *Sistrurus catenatus* and *S. ravus* in Mexico and the adjacent United States. Several isolated populations of *S. catenatus* occur in northern Mexico in the vicinity of Cuatro Ciénegas, Coahuila, and near Aramberri, Nuevo León. This species is extinct over much of the western portion of its former range.

somewhat lyriform figure. A white line extends diagonally from the postnasal to the rictus; above this is a broad dark brown stripe. The 27–42 medium to dark brown middorsal blotches on the body are cordiform, subcircular, subovate, or subelliptical. Each blotch is bordered with blackish brown and edged narrowly with brownish white. The middorsal blotches are offset laterally by three series of alternating dark spots: an upper, median, and lower series. The lower series is usually ill-defined or absent posteriorly. The labials are stippled or mottled with brown or gray, and the mental and chinshields are white to pale brown and sometimes immaculate. The ventrals are white or cream and lightly mottled laterally with gray or brown; the ventrals in some specimens may approach a nearly immaculate condition. Juvenile snakes are paler than adults and their pattern is more distinct; their tail tips are pale yellowish white.

There are 9 large symmetrical head plates, 10–13 (usually 11 or 12) supralabials, 10–13 (usually 12) infralabials, 22–25 (usually 23) midbody dorsal scale rows, 137–153 ventrals, and 24–36 subcaudals (0–7 of the distal subcaudals may be divided).

SIMILAR SPECIES *Sistrurus catenatus* may be distinguished from all other species of rattlesnakes with which it is sympatric in Mexico by its 9 large symmetrically arranged head plates and paired elongated nape blotches (Figs. 437, 438). Additionally, several large species of rattlesnakes, including *Crotalus atrox*, *C. molossus*, *C. viridis*, and *C. scutulatus*, have more ventrals (more than 163) and usually more midbody dorsal scale rows (more than 24), supralabials (more than 13), and infralabials (more than 13) than *S. catenatus*. *Crotalus lepidus* has a dorsal pattern of 13–24 widely spaced dark crossbands. *Heterodon nasicus* (Fig. 556), a species not dangerous to man, bears a strong superficial resemblance to *S. catenatus*.

REMARKS It has been suggested that populations of *S. catenatus* in Mexico are relicts that have become isolated from those to the north since the advent of drying conditions that followed Pleistocene pluvial periods. All Mexican specimens with precise locality data have come from near permanent streams or marshes. A report of this species from an unspecified locality in Durango may represent yet another isolated population or it may be based on a misidentification.

Three subspecies of *S. catenatus* are recognized; only one of these, *S. c. edwardsi*, is known to occur in Mexico, although specimens from the Cuatro Ciénegas region are intermediate between *S. c. edwardsi* and *S. c. tergeminus* in some characteristics.

Bites may be extremely painful and may be accompanied by swelling, faintness, nausea, and a cold sweat. Hemolysin and a strong neurotoxic factor are present in this venom.


REFERENCES Amaral, 1927g; Baird, 1859; Baird and Girard, 1853; Bogert and Oliver, 1945; Brown, 1950; Buckley and Porges, 1956; Cockerell, 1896; Cope, 1860a; Coues, 1875; Crimmins, 1927; Cuesta Terron, 1921b, 1930a; Gloyd, 1940, 1955; Jan and Sordelli, 1870–1881; Klauber, 1936b, 1971, 1972; Knopf and Tinkle, 1961; Lowe, 1964; Lowe et al., 1986; Martín del Campo, 1935, 1937a, 1950; McCoy, 1984; McCoy and Minckley, 1969; McCranie, 1988; Milstead, 1960a; Minckley and Rinne, 1972; Minton, 1983; Ochoterena, 1934; H. M. Smith and Taylor, 1945, 1966; Stebbins, 1985; Stejneger, 1895, 1902, 1940; Van Denburgh, 1924; Werler, 1967; Woodin, 1953; Wright and Wright, 1957; Yarrow, 1875.


### ***Sistrurus ravus* (Cope)**

(Figs. 439–443; Map 109)

LOCAL NAMES Cascabel enana, Colcóatl, víbora de cascabel, viborita de cascabel.

ENGLISH NAME Mexican pygmy rattlesnake.

DISTRIBUTION Temperate montane regions of moderate to high elevations across the Mexican Plateau from the Volcán de Toluca (Zinantecatl) in the state of Mexico to the highlands of west-central Veracruz, southward through the Sierra de Acatepec in Puebla and extreme northern Oaxaca; the Mesa del Sur in Oaxaca including the Sierra Juárez, the mountains that extend northward from Cerro San Felipe, and the Sierra Mixe; and the Sierra Madre del Sur in Guerrero (see Map 109). The vertical distribution is from about 1,490 to slightly above 3,000 m.

HABITAT This species inhabits pine-oak forest, cloud forest, boreal forest, high and tropical scrub forest, and upper tropical deciduous forest—zones of considerable ecological diversity. It is most frequently encountered in open areas such as meadows or regions covered by low vegetation. It appears to be most abundant in relatively flat areas such as plateaus, floodplains, or alluvial fans or basins. Nevertheless, we have taken this widely ranging species from steep slopes within virgin cloud forest.

DESCRIPTION This is a moderately stout rattlesnake; adults generally reach lengths of 400–650 mm, and occasionally approach 700 mm.

The anterior portion of the top of the head is patternless; posteriorly a broad pair of nape blotches is generally evident. A postocular stripe is generally absent or only faintly indicated. The labials are yellow or peach colored and may or may not be stippled. The ground color is extremely variable, even within populations; it may be pale grayish brown, dark brown, bluish gray, or pale rust. The 22–44 reddish brown or dark brown body blotches frequently are paler in their centers. Except for rust-colored specimens from Guerrero, dorsal blotches tend to have narrow dark margins. The ground color between dorsal blotches is paler than that on the sides of the body. There are 2–8 dark tail bands. There tends to be a moderate to great amount of stippling or mottling on the ventrals and proximal subcaudals. However, some specimens from widely scattered localities tend to have almost immaculate bellies except for the darkened lateral portions of the ventrals. Large specimens tend to be darker than juveniles and melanistic specimens are known from high elevations along the transverse Volcanic Cordillera. The iris ranges from gray to copper colored.

The top of the head usually is covered by 9 symmetrically arranged head plates (Fig. 439); however, the parietals frequently are divided transversely in the Guerrero population. There are 9–13 supralabials (usually 11 or 12), 9–13 infralabials (generally 11 or 12), 21–25 middorsal scale rows (generally 23 in Oaxacan and Guerreran snakes, 21 in more northerly populations), 136–152 ventrals, and 19–30 subcaudals.

SIMILAR SPECIES This species may be distinguished from all other Mexican rattlesnakes, except for *S. catenatus*, by the presence of 9 (or 11 if parietals are divided) large head plates. *Sistrurus catenatus* is known only from two small areas well to the north of where *S. ravus* occurs (Map 109) and may be distinguished from this species by distinct markings on top of the head over and in front of the eyes, a well-defined postocular stripe, cordiform dorsal blotches (Figs. 437, 438), an upper preocular that is in contact with the postnasal, and a sharper canthus. *Crotalus pusillus*, which occurs to the west of the range of *S. ravus*, possesses relatively large anterior dorsal head scales, but the parietal region is covered by small scales, there are 150 or more ventrals, and the postocular stripe is well defined.

REMARKS Three subspecies are recognized: *S. r. ravus* (Figs. 439, 440) of the Altiplanicie Meridional, *S. r. brunneus* (Fig. 441) from the Oaxacan highlands, and *S. r. exiguus* (Figs. 442, 443) from the Sierra Madre del Sur in Guerrero.

We consider the subspecies *S. r. lutescens* to be a synonym of *S. r. ravus*, for reasons provided by Campbell and Armstrong (1979). An additional subspecies, *S. r. sinaloensis*, has been proposed, but the description is woefully incomplete and the locality data are likely suspect.

REFERENCES Campbell and Armstrong, 1979; Cope, 1865, 1875, 1885b, 1887; Davis and Smith, 1953; Dugès, 1876–1877; Gloyd, 1940; Günther, 1895–1902; Harris and Simmons, 1978b; Juliá-Zertuche, 1983; Klauber, 1952, 1972; Martín del Campo, 1935, 1937a, 1942, 1950, 1955; McCranie, 1988; Muñoz Alonso, 1988; H. M. Smith, 1970; H. M. Smith and Taylor, 1945; Sumichrast, 1882.

# Mimics of Venomous Snakes

The problem of correctly identifying dangerously venomous snakes is compounded because many harmless or mildly venomous species closely resemble dangerous species in coloration, pattern, and behavior. Additionally, in Latin America there are a number of poorly known rear-fanged species, and although no Neotropical rear-fanged snake has been clearly implicated in the fatal envenomation of a human, individual reactions to their bites vary greatly. Several species are known to produce symptoms analogous to local envenomation by a pitviper, and these effects are sometimes severe (Fig. 546; Neill, 1954; Seib, 1980; Silva and Buononato, 1984). Occasionally such symptoms may arise as the result of an allergic reaction or a secondary bacterial infection rather than snake venom; in such cases the offending snake need not be a rear-fanged species (Ellis and Smith, 1965).

It is not appropriate to describe herein all Latin American taxa that fall under the categories above, but we feel that an explanation of the problems along with a discussion of selected species may allay some of the confusion that usually accompanies encounters with snakes in the field. For convenience we have divided potentially confusing species into two groups: those species resembling *Micrurus* or *Micruroides* in pattern or behavior are herein called false coral snakes, and those species resembling pitvipers are referred to as false pitvipers. The latter group comprises snakes that resemble terrestrial pitvipers and those that resemble the green arboreal forms (Schulte, 1988). Our assemblages are arbitrary and intended to anticipate human error in identification rather than to elucidate mimetic complexes. Nonetheless, mimicry is central to the problem of similar species and accordingly we include a brief history and discussion of the concept.

## MIMICRY AND FALSE CORAL SNAKES

The term "mimicry" is derived from the Greek word *mimos*, meaning imitator. In modern usage, it refers to the close resemblance of one organism to another or to some object in its environment. The notion was formalized by Bates (1861), who was unable to distinguish between some pierid and heliconiid butterflies and sought to explain why the former failed to resemble their close relatives. His concept, which has come to be called Batesian mimicry, involves a "model," which is a noxious species, and a "mimic," which lacks noxious qualities. Five prerequisites for a case of Batesian mimicry were developed by Wallace (1867). These have varying degrees of applicability to modern theory.

1. Range overlap (now known as sympatry): model and mimic must occupy the same territory; this may include the same foraging range of a relevant predator (Hecht and Marien, 1956).
2. A difference between the mimic and its relatives.
3. Restriction of mimetic features to external characteristics.
4. Fewer mimics than models.
5. Mimics less able to defend themselves than the models.

The sharing of a common phenotype by two or more noxious species is considered to represent a second type of mimicry (Müller, 1878). In this situation, the cost and benefits are shared by more than one species, with the predator "learning only one lesson" and requiring less time to do so. This concept is referred to as Mullerian mimicry.

Many examples of these and other kinds of mimicry have been described for a multitude of plants and arthropods but few vertebrates. Common elements shared by all types of mimicry include a signal sender (the model and mimic), a signal receiver (usually a predator, sometimes the prey), and some degree of pattern generalization on the part of the receiver. Many problems are inherent in the mimicry concept, including defining limits, degree of overlap, inherent assumptions, oversimplification, and dogma.

Shortcomings in the theory of mimicry are not due to a lack of interest in the subject. Indeed, in the first century after Bates defined the concept no fewer than 1,500 papers were published on mimicry (Wickler, 1968). Our perception of mimicry is part of the foundation of modern evolutionary thought, and a consideration of the coral snake problem touches upon all of the controversies with which the mimicry theory has been beset.

Two mimetic complexes of snakes have traditionally been studied: a group of procryptically colored African vipers and their presumed mimics (Gans, 1961), and the brilliantly ringed coral snakes and similarly colored harmless varieties in southern North America and the Neotropics (Greene and McDiarmid, 1981). True coral snakes (*Micrurus* and *Micruroides*) carry potent venom and are usually ringed in various sequences of brigh colors: bicolor, tricolor, and tricolor-triad. False coral snakes fall into two groups: harmless varieties, and mildly venomous species (several genera; rear-fanged). While colored similarly to true coral snakes, false coral snakes (with notable exceptions such as *Pliocercus*) rarely possess the same tricolor combination and, with few exceptions, do not exhibit the triad pattern.

Nonetheless, the degree of superficial similarity between false and true coral snakes is at times astonishing. Their resemblance was noted before Bates had formalized his mimicry theory (Cope, 1860), and shortly thereafter the relationship was considered to be mimetic (Wallace, 1867). During the early twentieth century, Wallace's conjecture was both contested and supported. Gadow (1911), who disagreed with Wallace, made the important observation that coral snake patterns might be protective in that they disrupt body outline and deflect light. Sternfeld (1913), a Wallace supporter, noted the size similarity between true and false coral snakes.

Observations, theories, and dissenting views accrued during the ensuing years, with much controversy over whether mimicry occurred in coral snakes, what kind (or kinds) might be involved (Darlington, 1938; Dunn, 1954), and whether coral snake patterns might serve other (procryptic, disruptive) purposes (Brattstrom, 1955; Cott, 1940; Dunn, 1954; Thayer, 1918). The idea that coral snake colors and patterns might have an aposematic function was introduced by Dunn (1954) and challenged by Brattstrom (1955), who made a good case for the disruptive and/or illusory effect of bands or rings. He attributed observable similarities among species to convergent evolution.

The increasing diversity of opinion regarding mimicry led to a broad-based synthesis (Hecht and Marien, 1956) in which color pattern was viewed as the product of several selective forces working for or against one another in the determination of gene frequencies. This departure from the "single selective force" approach led the authors to the conclusion that the primary function of coral snake patterns was aposematic. It was suggested that a Mullerian mimetic complex, with some Batesian overlap, accounted for the relationship between coral snake models and mimics. The possibility that sympatry might be with a common predator, rather than between model and mimic, was introduced.

Data indicating the presence of a much higher number of mimics than models in Brazil led Mertens (1956, 1957) to postulate the rear-fanged forms to be the models, with both *Micrurus* and nonvenomous varieties constituting the mimics. Mertens mentioned, but did not discuss, possible instinctive avoidance of coral snakes by some predators. Wickler (1968) supported Mertens' theory, modified it slightly, and coined the term Mertensian mimicry. He visualized rear-fanged species as models, nonvenomous varieties as Batesian mimics, and *Micrurus* as Mullerian mimics. Wickler also discounted the possibility of innate pattern recognition.

Brower (1958, 1960), working with butterflies and starlings, showed that no strategy is absolute. Green, a nonwarning color, was used to mark distasteful mealworms, and experience with this proved inhibitory when the starlings were subsequently confronted with similarly colored but palatable butterflies. Thus, support was added to the notion that mimics might numerically exceed models. Gans (1961), while working with African egg-eating snakes (*Dasypeltis*), suggested that selection upon predator behavior, rather than a learning process, might be the basis for avoidance of certain prey items.

Mullerian mimicry was commonly envisaged as having arisen via convergence of color pattern between two previously developed models. Huheey (1961) argued for the possibility of a Batesian mimetic origin for Mullerian mimics. Reasoning that selection would operate against any restriction in the number of mimics by the number of models, and that the cost at the outset would be great for the evolution of noxious qualities, he felt that a Batesian mimic could evolve such qualities while being "protected" by the model. Emsley (1966) cautioned against interpreting mainland South American species of *Erythrolamprus* as Batesian or Mullerian mimics; he suggested that the phenomenon might be highly localized and thus necessitate a "sliding scale" type of analysis. Tobago lacks *Micrurus* but hosts a race of *Erythrolamprus aesculapii* that lacks rings, a condition in marked contrast to the ringed mainland forms. Emsley provisionally considered this ringless pattern to have a procryptic function.

The determination of mimetic complexes in coral snakes is further complicated because bright colors on these snakes may not be strictly aposematic (Gehlbach, 1970, 1972). Coral snakes may escape predators via behavior designed to startle and/or confuse; such defense is known as "self-mimicry" (Gehlbach, 1972) and consists of raising and curling the tail and moving it in tandem with the head, thereby creating the appearance of two snakes. Other possible defense mechanisms utilized by coral snakes include erratic behavior, death feigning, extrusion of the hemipenes, and cloacal popping (Allen, 1940; Azevedo, 1960; Gehlbach, 1970). The evolution of such behavior as well as of bright colors is considered by some to have occurred independently of mimicry. The aposematic value of color pattern in snakes thought to be nocturnal and secretive has been called into question (Schmidt and Inger, 1957).

The problem of sympatry between model and mimic was referred to by Echternacht (1973) with regard to a polymorphic false coral of the genus *Sonora*, and he raised the possibility of Pleistocene sympatry between ancestors of presently allopatric species. Echternacht viewed *Sonora michoacanensis* as an imperfect Batesian mimic of *Micrurus*, intermediate between a bicolored ancestor and an eventual tricolored mimic.

Greene and Pyburn (1973) commented on several aspects of the mimicry controversy and offered alternative suggestions to support the hypothesis that coral snake coloration has an aposematic function. They supported a cryptic role for coral snake coloration but felt that coral snakes would bite defensively with probable serious results. Mertensian mimicry was regarded by them as doubtful because of the unsubstantiated defensive capabilities that it assumes for mildly venomous forms. They proposed further consideration of the idea that selection on predators of coral snakes is for innate avoidance behavior.

S. M. Smith (1975, 1977), in an important series of experiments, demonstrated an innate response of birds to the coral snake color pattern (see also Caldwell and Rubinoff, 1983). She further showed that stimulus generalization accompanied this innate response, a fact that might allow more alternatives in the evolution of Batesian and Mullerian mimics. Concurrently, a hypothesis based on the notion that selective pressures leading to aposematism and mimicry among secretive snakes would not occur was brought forth by Grobman (1978). He proposed that, in the absence of such pressures, a wide array of bright color patterns arose among various species, some bearing a close resemblance to one another. In areas where these species are sympatric (e.g., *Cemophora*, *Lampropeltis*, and *Micrurus*), they could be said to be "pseudomimics."

Greene and McDiarmid (1981) analyzed pertinent experimental evidence and added compelling field observations detailing the concordant variation of color pattern involving several venomous and nonvenomous species. They made a strong case for the existence of a mimetic relationship between some species of coral snakes and false coral snakes by providing evidence of diurnal activity in *Micrurus*, coupled with the innate avoidance by potential predators demonstrated previously (Gehlbach, 1972; S. M. Smith, 1975, 1977). Their observations of pattern variation in the colubrid genera *Atractus*, *Erythrolamprus*, *Lampropeltis*, and *Pliocercus*, when viewed in relation to sympatric *Micrurus* or *Micruroides*, strongly imply a Batesian or perhaps Mullerian mimetic relationship. Furthermore, their evidence was not supportive of Mertensian mimicry or of pseudomimicry.

Our field observations corroborate those of Greene and McDiarmid (1981). We attribute difficulty in encountering *Micrurus* to habitat preferences; they are not necessarily as uncommon as Gadow believed. The ringed pattern, aside from its aposematic functions, appears to us to serve a procryptic function by disrupting body outline and deflecting light in an illusory fashion. We have collected large specimens of *M. spixii* exposed in sunlit leaf litter and found them to be very difficult to perceive; when viewed in motion, their patterns sometimes seem to make them "disappear."

Many species of *Micrurus* are forest dwellers; they can carry out diurnal activity while remaining "semiconcealed" in leaf litter. This, coupled with the fact that many coral snakes with bicolored or nonringed body patterns defensively display brightly colored head and tail rings, leads us to doubt the notion that coral snake color patterns play a passive role in defense (Grobman, 1978).

It has been our experience that even diminutive specimens of *Micrurus* can and will bite defensively; one of us, while in the field, sustained a double bite from an *M. filiformis* less than 200 mm in total length. We are aware of a chicken (*Gallus gallus*) that died after ingesting a *M. mipartitus* specimen that bit it internally (Santiago Ayerbe, personal communication). Reflexive biting action could conceivably enable a tiny *Micrurus* to deliver a lethal bite to the tender mouth parts of a large predator. Although there are exceptions, such as *Pliocercus* (Seib, 1980) and *Hydrodynastes* (personal observation), evidence suggests that mildly venomous false coral snakes normally do not inflict serious bites. Many species of false coral snakes, in fact, are reluctant to bite at all. Data are lacking on the perception of color at night, both by animals with chromatic and those with achromatic vision. Red pigment in a species of fish was described as murky gray by moonlit night (Taylor and Taylor, 1981), resembling the creature's surroundings.

It seems clear that potential predators, for whatever reason, may be discouraged by the bright color patterns displayed by *Micrurus* and *Micruroides*, and that other broadly sympatric venomous and harmless snake species derive benefit by being colored similarly. The concordant variation seen in widely ranging species of *Erythrolamprus* and *Pliocercus* is remarkable. *Erythrolamprus aesculapii* may be similar in appearance to *Micrurus hemprichii* in eastern Colombia (Figs. 471 and 59, respectively), while resembling *M. lemniscatus* in Suriname (Figs. 473 and 68, respectively) or *M. spixii* in southern Peru (Figs. 472 and 99, respectively). *Pliocercus euryzonus* (Fig. 517) and *P. elapoides* (Figs. 510–516) are unsurpassed in the degree to which they can resemble *Micrurus*. We have observed concordant altitudinal variation within a small area between *M. hippocrepis* (Figs. 60, 61) and sympatric *P. elapoides* (Figs. 514, 515). Resemblance to coral snakes may be related to ontogeny: in some species of *Lampropeltis triangulum* only the juveniles resemble *Micrurus*, while in others (such as some *Oxyrhopus*) the reverse is true. Individuals of many populations of *O. petola* are bicolored black and white at birth but accrue red pigment with age, beginning posteriorly and proceding anteriorly.

The efficacy of the coral snakes' behavioral repertoire when confronted by a potential predator is little-documented owing to the difficulty of making such observations in nature (Pough, 1964; N. G. Smith, 1969). We had the good fortune to see a *Micrurus filiformis* attacked by a South American trumpeter (*Psophia crepitans*). Trumpeters are highly efficient predators that routinely consume small vertebrates, but in this instance the adult bird was successfully held at bay by a snake less than 250 mm in total length. The behavior consisted of the usual sequence of dorsoventral flattening of the head and body, self-mimicry, and erratic behavior.

A similar defense strategy is used by a number of false coral snakes. While such tactics may serve collectively as a teaching mechanism, it seems to us that empathic learning (or the "predator learning experience" suggested by Brattstrom, 1955) is likely to account for a smaller reduction in predation than selection for innate avoidance on the part of the predator. While it seems clear that some sort of mimicry occurs among the coral snakes, it remains difficult to assign a specific complex anywhere, and a multitude of questions remain unanswered. Ironically, the problem was most clearly per-

**Table 33**
Distributions of false coral snakes by genus in Mexico and Central America

| | *Mexico* | *Belize* | *Guatemala* | *Honduras* | *El Salvador* | *Nicaragua* | *Costa Rica* | *Panama* |
|---|---|---|---|---|---|---|---|---|
| *Atractus* | | | | | | | | X |
| *Chilomeniscus* | X | | | | | | | |
| *Chionactis* | X | | | | | | | |
| *Clelia* | X | X | X | X | X | X | X | X |
| *Dipsas* | | | | | | X | X | X |
| *Elaphe* | X | X | X | X | X | X | | |
| *Erythrolamprus* | | | | X | X | X | X | X |
| *Geophis* | X | X | X | X | X | X | X | |
| *Gyalopion* | X | | | | | | | |
| *Lampropeltis* | X | X | X | X | X | X | X | X |
| *Liophis* | | | | | | | X | X |
| *Ninia* | X | X | X | X | X | X | X | X |
| *Oxyrhopus* | X | X | X | X | X | X | X | X |
| *Phyllorhynchus* | X | | | | | | | |
| *Pliocercus* | X | X | X | X | X | X | X | X |
| *Pseudoboa* | | | | | | | | X |
| *Rhinobothryum* | | | ? | X | | X | X | X |
| *Scaphiodontophis* | X | X | X | X | X | X | X | X |
| *Scolecophis* | | | X | X | X | X | X | |
| *Sibon* | X | X | X | X | X | X | X | X |
| *Sonora* | X | | | | | | | |
| *Stenorrhina* | X | X | X | X | X | X | X | X |
| *Sympholis* | X | | | | | | | |
| *Tantilla* | | | | | | | X | X |
| *Tripanurgos* | | | | | | | X | X |

ceived by its discoverer: "The process by which a mimetic analogy is brought about in nature is a problem which involves that of the origin of all species and all adaptations" (Bates, 1861).

Regardless of any natural benefits such pattern mimicry might bestow, there is no question that humans are deceived by brightly colored snakes, including those that are red dorsally. The key at the end of this section is intended to facilitate generic assignment of false coral snakes in Latin America. It encompasses the majority of relevant species, although it is by no means exhaustive. For information regarding the distribution of false coral snakes within these genera, refer to Tables 33 and 34.

## FALSE PITVIPERS

Dorsal patterns of Latin American pitvipers may be grossly stated to be less distinctive than those of coral snakes. This factor, coupled with the considerable variation in size and external morphology of the pitvipers, renders a detailed discussion of similar but harmless species impractical. Moreover, to the majority of persons unfamiliar with snakes, practically all species tend to look alike. Although harmless or mildly venomous species of snakes tend to be encountered more frequently than dangerous varieties, some are capable of envenomating humans and require some degree of consideration.

Snakes in the following genera have been known to produce bites that may involve local pain, swelling, and discoloration: *Conophis* (Fig. 549), *Heterodon* (Fig. 556), *Leptodeira* (Figs. 557–559), *Leptophis* (Figs. 540, 541), *Oxybelis* (Fig. 543), *Philodryas* (Figs. 544–546), *Tachymenis*, and *Trimorphodon* (Fig. 562). It should be noted that symptoms can vary from nonexistent to pronounced according to the degree (primary or secondary) of envenomation. Boid snakes of the genera *Boa* (Fig. 547), *Corallus* (Figs. 538, 550, 551), *Epicrates* (Fig. 555), and *Eunectes* are capable of producing painful bites owing to their long teeth, some of which may be of fanglike proportions.

Many tropical snakes are green dorsally, among them species of the genera *Chironius* (Figs. 535–537), *Corallus* (Fig. 538), *Drymobius* (Fig. 539), *Leptophis* (Figs. 540, 541), *Liophis* (Fig. 542), *Oxybelis* (Fig. 543), and *Philodryas* (Figs. 544, 545). Careful perusal of their external morphology should distinguish them from dangerously venomous species.

Among those snakes resembling terrestrial pitvipers, the *Boa constrictor* (Fig. 547) is frequently encountered by humans. This species has a wide distribution, occurs in a variety of habitats, and often is found near areas of human activity. Owing to its large head and coloration, it is often thought to be venomous, but this species may be distinguished from pitvipers in that it lacks the loreal pit. Boids of the genera *Corallus* (Figs. 550, 551) and *Epicrates* (Fig. 555) possess labial pits, but there are several present on each side of the head and none are found in the loreal region.

Many snakes species, some of which bear only a superficial resemblance to pitvipers, may cause concern because of their vigorous defensive behavior (*Chironius*, Fig. 548; *Xenodon*, Figs. 563–567; *Waglerophis*, Fig. 568; and others). Snakes of the genera *Lystrophis* (Fig. 560), *Pseudotomodon*, *Tomodon*, *Waglerophis* (Fig. 568), and *Xenodon* (Figs. 563–567) show a high degree of similarity to various species of pitvipers throughout their range, as do some members of the genus *Dipsas* (Figs. 553, 554). Numerous genera (including *Cryophis*, Fig. 552, and *Thamnodynastes*, Fig. 561) contain species that simply have a venomous appearance owing to dorsal patterns, prominent eyes with elliptical pupils, or large heads. Many harmless and venomous snake species vibrate the tail or hiss to produce a sound simi-

**Table 34**
Distributions of false coral snakes by genus in South America

| | *Colombia* | *Venezuela* | *Trinidad* | *Guyana* | *Suriname* | *French Guiana* | *Brazil* | *Ecuador* | *Peru* | *Bolivia* | *Paraguay* | *Uruguay* | *Argentina* |
|---|---|---|---|---|---|---|---|---|---|---|---|---|---|
| *Anilius* | X | X | | X | X | X | X | X | X | X | | | |
| *Apostolepis* | | | | X | | | X | | X | X | X | | X |
| *Atractus* | X | X | | X | X | X | X | X | X | X | | | |
| *Clelia* | X | X | X | X | X | X | X | X | X | X | X | X | X |
| *Dipsas* | X | X | | X | X | X | X | X | X | X | | | |
| *Drepanoides* | X | | | | | | X | X | X | X | | | |
| *Elapomorphus* | | | | | | | X | | | | X | X | X |
| *Erythrolamprus* | X | X | X | X | X | X | X | X | X | X | X | | X |
| *Helicops* | X | X | X | X | X | X | X | X | X | X | X | X | X |
| *Hydrodynastes* | X | X | | X | X | X | X | X | | | | | |
| *Hydrops* | X | X | X | X | X | X | X | X | X | X | | | |
| *Lampropeltis* | X | X | | | | | | X | | | | | |
| *Liophis* | X | X | X | X | X | X | X | X | X | X | X | X | X |
| *Lystrophis* | | | | | | | X | | | X | X | X | X |
| *Oxyrhopus* | X | X | X | X | X | X | X | X | X | X | X | X | X |
| *Phimophis* | X | X | | X | X | X | | | | | | | |
| *Pliocercus* | X | | | | | | X | X | | | | | |
| *Pseudoboa* | X | X | X | X | X | X | X | X | X | X | X | | X |
| *Rhinobothryum* | X | X | | X | X | X | X | X | X | X | X | | |
| *Scaphiodontophis* | X | | | | | | | | | | | | |
| *Simophis* | | | | | | | X | | | | X | | |
| *Stenorrhina* | X | X | | | | | | X | | | | | |
| *Tantilla* | X | | | | | | | | | | | | |
| *Tripanurgos* | X | X | X | X | X | X | X | X | X | X | X | | |

lar to that made by a rattlesnake (Kardong, 1980). In every case, caution and clear judgment will help to minimize the confusion that so frequently accompanies encounters with snakes.

*Literature Cited*


Allen, C. E. 1940. Behavior of *Micrurus frontalis frontalis*. Copeia 1940:51–52.

Azevedo, A. C. P. 1960. Notes on coral snakes (I–II). (Serpentes, Elapidae). I. About the eggs of coral snakes. II. A new observation of the behavior of *Micrurus frontalis multicinctus* and its relationship with folklore. Iheringia, Zool. 14:1–13.

Bates, H. W. 1861. Contribution to an insect fauna of the Amazonas Valley. Lepidoptera: Heliconidae. Trans. Linn. Soc. London 23:495–566.

Boos, H. 1975. Report on the effect of the venom of the colubrid snake the "Ratonel" *Pseudoboa neuwiedii*. J. Trinidad Tobago Field Nat. Club: 28–30.

Brattstrom, B. H. 1955. The coral snake "mimic" problem and protective coloration. Evolution 9:217–219.

Brower, J. V. Z. 1958. Experimental studies of mimicry in some North American butterflies I. Evolution 12:32–47.

Brower, J. V. Z. 1960. Experimental studies in mimicry IV. The reactions of starlings to different proportions of models and mimics. Am. Nat. 94:271–281.

Caldwell, G. S., and R. W. Rubinoff. 1983. Avoidance of venomous sea snakes by naive herons and egrets. Auk 100:195–198.

Cope, E. D. 1860. Catalogue of the colubrid snakes in the museum of the Academy of Natural Sciences in Philadelphia. Proc. Acad. Nat. Sci. Philadelphia 12:241–266.

Cott, H. B. 1940. Adaptive coloration in animals. London, Methuen. 508 pp.

Darlington, P. J. 1938. Experiments on mimicry in Cuba, with suggestions for future study. Trans. Roy. Entomol. Soc. London 87:681–695.

Dunn, E. R. 1954. The coral snake "mimic" problem in Panama. Evolution 8:97–102.

Echternacht, A. C. 1973. The color pattern of *Sonora michoacanensis* (Dugès) (Serpentes: Colubridae) and its bearing on the origin of the species. Breviora 410:1–18.

Ellis, E. F., and R. T. Smith. 1965. Systemic anaphylaxis after rattlesnake bite. J. Am. Med. Assoc. 193:401–402.

Emsley, M. G. 1966. The mimetic significance of *Erythrolamprus aesculapii ocellatus* Peters, from Tobago. Evolution 20:663–664.

Gadow, H. 1911. Isotely and coral snakes. Zool. Jahrb., Abt. Syst. 31:1–27.

Gans, C. 1961. Mimicry in procryptically colored snakes of the genus *Dasypeltis*. Evolution 15:72–91.

Gelbach, F. R. 1970. Death-feigning and erratic behavior in Leptotyphlopid, Colubrid, and Elapid snakes. Herpetologica 26:24–34.

Gelbach, F. R. 1972. Coral snake mimicry reconsidered: The strategy of self-mimicry. Forma et Functio 5:311–320.

Greene, H. W. 1969. Unusual pattern and coloration in snakes of the genus *Pliocercus* from Veracruz. J. Herpetol. 3:27–31.

Greene, H. W., and R. W. McDiarmid. 1981. Coral snake mimicry: Does it occur? Science, Washington, D.C. 213:1207–1212.

Greene, H. W., and W. F. Pyburn. 1973. Comments on aposematism and mimicry among coral snakes. Biologist 55:144–148.

Grobman, A. B. 1978. An alternative solution to the coral snake mimic problem (Reptilia, Serpentes, Elapidae). J. Herpetol. 12:1–11.

Hecht, M. K., and D. Marien. 1956. The coral snake mimic problem: a reinterpretation. J. Morphol. 98:325–365.

Huheey, J. E. 1961. Studies in warning coloration and mimicry. III. Evolution of Mullerian mimicry. Evolution 15:567–568.

Kardong, K. V. 1980. Gopher snakes and rattlesnakes: Presumptive Batesian mimicry. Northwest Science 54:1–4.

Mertens, R. 1956. Das Problem der Mimikry bei Korallenschlangen. Zool. Jahrb., Abt. Syst. 84:541–576.

Mertens, R. 1957. Gibt es Mimikry bei Korallenschlangen? Nat. Volk 87:56–66.

Müller, F. 1878. Katalog der im Museum und Universitätskabinet zu Basel aufgestellen Amphibien und Reptilien nebst Anmerkungen. Verh. Naturforsch. Ges. Basel 6:557–709.

Neill. W. T. 1954. Evidence of venom in snakes of the genera *Alsophis* and *Rhadinaea*. Copeia 1954:59–60.

Pough, F. H., Jr. 1964. A coral snake "mimic" eaten by a bird. Copeia 1964:223.

Roosevelt, T. 1921. Through the Brazilian wilderness. 5th ed. New York, Scribner's. 410 pp.

Schmidt, K. P., and R. F. Inger. 1957. Living reptiles of the world. Garden City, Hanover House.

Schulte, R. 1988. Observaciones sobre la boa verde, *Corallus caninus*, en el Departamento San Martín-Perú. Bol. Lima 55:21–26.

Sieb, R. L. 1980. Human envenomation from the bite of an aglyphous false coral snake, *Pliocercus elapoides* (Serpentes: Colubridae). Toxicon 18:399–401.

Silva, M. V. da, and M. A. Buononato. 1984 [dated 1983/84]. Relato clínico de envenenamento humano por *Philodryas olfersi*. Mem. Inst. Butantan 47/48:121–126.

Smith, N.G. 1969. Avian predation of coral snakes. Copeia 1969: 402–404.

Smith, S. M. 1975. Innate recognition of coral snake pattern by a possible avian predator. Science, Washington, D.C. 187:759–760.

Smith, S. M. 1977. Coral snake pattern recognition and stimulus generalization by naive great kiskadees (Aves: Tyrannidae). Nature 265:535–536.

Sternfeld, R. 1913. Die erschienungen der Mimikry bei den Schlangen. Schr. Ges. Naturforsch. Freunde Berlin 1913:98–117.

Taylor, R., and V. Taylor, 1981. Paradise beneath the sea. Nat. Geogr. Mag. 159:654.

Thayer, G. H. 1918. Concealing coloration in the animal kingdom. 2d ed. New York, Macmillan. 260 pp.

Wallace, A. R. 1867. Mimicry and other protective resemblances among animals. Westminster Rev. (July): 45–129.

Wickler, W. 1968. Mimicry in plants and animals. New York, McGraw-Hill. 255 pp.


## Key to Latin American False Coral Snakes[1] by Genus

1. Body pattern not ringed or banded ........ 2
   Body pattern ringed, banded, or appearing so ........ 16
2. Anal plate divided ........ 3
   Anal plate single ........ 8
3. Midbody dorsal scale rows 26 or more ........ *Elaphe* (Fig. 469)
   Midbody dorsal scale rows fewer than 26 ........ 4

1. The term "false coral snakes" as used here applies to those species that are brightly colored with rings, bands, or large amounts of red pigment in their patterns. Snakes that are solid red or nearly so have been included, as they are routinely mistaken for venomous coral snakes.

4. Midbody dorsal scale rows 17; anterior nasal fused with internasal................ .......................................................................*Stenorrhina* (Fig. 532)
Midbody dorsal scale rows fewer than 17; nasal not fused with internasal.....5
5. Loreal usually present....................................................*Sonora* (Fig. 531)
Loreal usually absent ..............................................................................6
6. Dorsum, excluding head and tail, primarily black .........venomous coral snake
Dorsum variable but not black ...............................................................7
7. Internasals distinct from prefrontals.......................*Elapomorphus* (Fig. 470)
Internasals fused with prefrontals...............................*Apostolepis* (Fig. 461)
8. Midbody dorsal scale rows fewer than 17 ................................*Drepanoides*
Midbody dorsal scale rows 17 or more ....................................................9
9. Midbody dorsal scale rows 17...............................................................12
Midbody dorsal scale rows 19 or more ..................................................10
10. Dorsals mostly smooth.........................................................................11
Dorsals keeled..............................................................*Ninia* (Fig. 501)
11. Rostral sharply pointed and upturned .......................................*Phimophis*
Rostral normal.................................................*Oxyrhopus* (Figs. 502–508)
12. Subcaudals single..................................................*Pseudoboa* (Fig. 518)
Subcaudals divided...............................................................................13
13. Dorsals smooth.....................................................................................14
Dorsals keeled..............................................................*Ninia* (Fig. 501)
14. Rostral modified and upturned...................................*Gyalopion* (Fig. 486)
Rostral normal.......................................................................................15
15. More than 200 ventrals.......................................................*Clelia* (Fig. 466)
Fewer than 200 ventrals................................................*Atractus* (Fig. 462)
16. Anal plate single...................................................................................17
Anal plate divided ................................................................................34
17. Midbody dorsal scale rows 17 or more ..................................................18
Midbody dorsal scale rows 17 or fewer..................................................24
18. Subcaudals all or mostly single.......................*Rhinocheilus* (Figs. 520–521)
Subcaudals all or mostly divided..........................................................19
19. Nasals and prefrontals fused ...............................................................20
Nasals and prefrontals distinct.............................................................21
20. Ventrals only slightly larger than dorsals; eye beneath pentagonal scale.......... ..........................................................................*Anilius* (Fig. 460)
Ventrals much larger than dorsals; eye not beneath pentagonal scale............. ....................................................................................*Sympholis*
21. Vertebral row of dorsals enlarged; head flattened and broad......................... ...................................................................*Tripanurgos* (Fig. 534)
Vertebral row of dorsals not enlarged; head not as above..........................22
22. Rostral enlarged into a wedge-shaped protuberance separating nasals and part of prefrontals; pupil elliptical ............................*Phyllorhynchus* (Fig. 509)
Rostral normal; pupil round or elliptical.................................................23
23. Supralabials 4 and 5 forming lower border of eye; pupil vertical................... ..........................................................*Oxyrhopus* (Figs. 502–508)
Supralabials 3 and 4 forming lower border of eye; pupil round..................... ........................................................*Lampropeltis* (Figs. 489–498)
24. Dorsals all or mostly keeled.................................................................33
Dorsals all or mostly smooth.................................................................25
25. Loreal absent........................................................................................26
Loreal present ......................................................................................27
26. Rostral modified and upturned...................................*Gyalopion* (Fig. 486)
Rostral normal.........................................................venomous coral snake
27. Vertebral scale row distinctly enlarged; mental groove absent ...................... ....................................................................*Dipsas* (Figs. 467, 468)
Vertebral scale row normal; mental groove present..................................28
28. Anterior temporal absent .......................................*Geophis* (Figs. 483–485)
Anterior temporal present ....................................................................29

29. Supralabial below anterior temporal considerably larger than adjacent supralabials ............ *Sibon*[2] (Figs. 527–529)
Supralabials nearly equal in size ............ 30

30. Eye completely separated from supralabials ............ *Hydrodynastes* (Fig. 487)
Eye in contact with one or more supralabials ............ 31

31. Dorsal scale rows 17; found north of Panama ............ *Geophis* (Figs. 483–485)
Dorsal scale rows 15–17; found from Panama southward ............ 32

32. One preocular; apical pits present; pupil elliptical ............ *Oxryhopus* (Figs. 502–508)
No preoculars; apical pits absent; pupil round ............ *Atractus* (Fig. 462)

33. Midbody dorsal scale rows 19 ............ *Ninia* (Fig. 501)
Midbody dorsal scale rows 17 or fewer ............ *Sibon*[2] (Figs. 527–529)

34. Some or all dorsals keeled ............ 35
Dorsals smooth ............ 37

35. Single internasal ............ *Helicops*
Two internasals ............ 36

36. Midbody dorsal scale rows 26 or more; pattern consists of dorsal blotches or bands ............ *Elaphe* (Fig. 469)
Midbody dorsal scale rows fewer than 26; pattern consists of rings ............ *Rhinobothryum* (Fig. 519)

37. Dorsal scale rows 15, unreduced ............ 38
Dorsal scale rows not as above ............ 40

38. Snout sharply pointed, with a projecting horizontal cutting ridge ............ *Chionactis* (Figs. 464, 465)
Snout normal ............ 39

39. Loreal usually present ............ *Sonora* (Fig. 531)
Loreal absent ............ *Tantilla* (Fig. 533)

40. Rostral modified, sometimes upturned ............ 41
Rostral normal, not upturned ............ 43

41. Dorsal scale rows 13, unreduced ............ *Chilomeniscus* (Fig. 463)
Dorsal scales rows 15–21, reduced posteriorly ............ 42

42. Snout distinctly upturned; midbody dorsal scale rows 19–21 ............ *Lystrophis* (Fig. 500)
Snout protuberant, but not upturned; midbody dorsal scale rows 15–17 ............ *Simophis* (Fig. 530)

43. Dorsal scale rows 17–19, unreduced ............ 49
Dorsal scale rows 17, reduced; or fewer rows, with or without reduction ............ 44

44. Third and fourth supralabials in contact with eye ............ 45
Only fourth supralabial in contact with eye ............ 48

45. Vertebral region with an orange caste; remainder of pattern consisting of black and white rings ............ *Scolecophis* (Fig. 526)
Vertebral region not distinct from rest of dorsum; pattern tricolored or bicolored ............ 46

46. Loreal absent ............ venomous coral snake
Loreal present ............ 47

47. Dorsal scale rows 17 or fewer, unreduced; apical pits absent; pattern usually of distinct rings ............ *Erythrolamprus* (Figs. 471–482)
Dorsal scale rows 17 or more, reduced; apical pits usually present; pattern often indistinct ............ *Liophis*[3] (Fig. 499)

48. Subcaudals 40 or fewer ............ venomous coral snake
Subcaudals more than 40 ............ *Hydrops* (Fig. 488)

49. Dorsal *rings* extending across venter ............ *Pliocercus* (Figs. 510–517)
Dorsal *bands* not extending across venter ... *Scaphiodontophis* (Figs. 522–525)

2. As used here, the genus *Sibon* includes those species that were formerly included in the genus *Tropidodipsas*.

3. As used here, the genus *Liophis* includes those species that were formerly assigned to *Dromicus*, *Leimadophis*, and *Lygophis*.

# Glossary

Some of the scientific and medical terms used in this book, particularly those in the keys and species descriptions, are defined in the following glossary. We have made no effort to provide a comprehensive listing of herpetological/biological terms; instead, we have defined those terms that we think readers will need to understand in order to use the keys. These definitions are often somewhat restricted and apply only to our usage of the terms within this book.

**Acuminate** Pointed.

**Afibrinogenemia** An absence of plasma fibrinogen. This abnormality of the blood-clotting mechanism may result in prolonged bleeding. Venom from a snakebite can break down fibrinogen, sometimes inducing afibrinogenemia.

**Allopatric** Living apart; two species whose ranges do not overlap at any point are said to be allopatric.

**Anal** The ventrally located plate immediately preceding the anus. In snakes it is larger than other scales of the ventral series and may be single or divided by a diagonal suture. This scale should not be included in the ventral series. The body of a snake is measured from the rostral to the posterior edge of the anal plate.

**Angle of the jaw** The angle formed by the articulation of the quadrate bone of the skull and the compound bone of the lower jaw.

**Annulus** See **Ring.**

**Arenicolous** Inhabiting sandy areas.

**Arid tropical scrub** See **Tropical arid forest.**

**Asulcate** The side of a hemipenis opposite to the side bearing the sulcus spermaticus.

**Band** An element of skin pattern that is darker or paler than the ground color and that runs perpendicularly across the vertebral line; it may or may not extend onto the ventrals but does not completely encircle the body (see **Ring**). Synonymous with crossband.

**Bifid** Divided into two lobes or branches.

**Bifurcate** To branch or divide into two parts.

**Bleb** A small blister containing serum or blood.

**Blotch** A discrete area that differs from the ground color, either darker or paler, is generally as long or longer than wide, and is not transversely widened to form a band or ring. Many snakes have a primary series of blotches along the dorsum and one to several smaller series of blotches laterally. Counts of body blotches in pitvipers do not include paired nape blotches (if present) nor those on the tail.

**Boreal forest** A type of vegetation occurring only on the tops of a few high peaks in central and northern Mexico. Some of the dominant trees of this forest are firs (*Abies* and *Pseudotsuga*), pines (*Pinus*), junipers (*Juniperus*), and alders (*Alnus*). Various coarse bunch grasses (*Agrostis, Festuca, Muhlenbergia*) often form a dense understory.

**Bradycardia** An abnormally slow heart rate.

**Bulla** (plural, bullae) A large (usually greater than 2 cm in diameter) blister, typically containing serum or blood. See also **Bleb.**

**Button** The first and smallest permanent rattle segment acquired by a young rattlesnake. As a rattlesnake matures, the button usually breaks off. At birth rattlesnakes possess a "prebutton," which is lost at the time of the first shedding, exposing the button.

**Calyces** The small pockets surrounded by ridges on the distal portion of the hemipenes of many snakes.

**Calyculate** Having small superficial pockets or sunken interspaces between the retiform ridges, as found on the apices of the hemipenial lobes of many snakes.

**Canthal** The scale or scales situated along the upper surface of the canthus rostralis. These scales lie behind the level of the prenasal and postnasal suture and in front of the supraocular. If these scales are large and in contact along the midline, they are more properly called prefrontals.

**Canthus rostralis** The area between the supraocular and the rostral where the dorsum of the snout turns downward on the side. It is delimited as a sharp ridge in many vipers, but is rounded in most rattlesnakes and in coral snakes.

**Capitate** Pertaining to a snake hemipenis whose apical region is clearly separated from the basal part of the organ by a groove.

**Ceja de la montaña** Spanish for "brow of the mountain." A vegetation type that covers the upper parts (1,000–3,350 m) of the eastern slopes of the Andes in Peru and Bolivia. It occurs in areas of great rainfall and is composed of cloud forest vegetation.

**Chaparral** A vegetation type restricted in Latin America to the western coast of the Peninsula of Baja California. The dominant shrubs in this dry habitat are chamise (*Adenostoma*), manzanita (*Arctostaphylos*), sage (*Artemisia*), coyote bush (*Baccharis*), wild lilac (*Ceanothus*), and scrub oaks (*Quercus*).

**Chinshield** A large, elongated scale lying directly behind the first pair of infralabials along either side of the midline on the ventral surface of the head. Chinshields are always arranged in pairs, with a single pair most frequently present in snakes.

**Cline** A geographic character gradient. A character that continuously varies geographically is said to be clinal.

**Cloud forest** A montane forest type characterized by cool temperatures, frequent fogs and high humidity, and lush, dense vegetation that includes numerous hardwood tree species. Cloud forest usually occurs above 1,000 m on the windward escarpments of tropical mountains. The lower belt of cloud forest is sometimes referred to as subtropical wet forest and the higher belt as lower montane wet forest or montane rainforest. The biological diversity of cloud forests is greater than that of any other habitat, with the possible exception of the great lowland rainforests.

**Coagulopathy** A disorder of the blood-clotting mechanism.

**Colubrid** A snake of the family Colubridae. Most members of this family are considered harmless, although many species have enlarged teeth on the rear of the maxilla (opisthoglyphic dentition) and a few species are known to produce a venom dangerous to humans.

**Congener** Of the same genus.

**Crotch** The V- or U-shaped area where the two lobes bifurcate from one another on the hemipenes of some snakes.

**Crown** The anterior part of the top of the head, usually corresponding to the anterior portion of the frontal area forward to the tip of the snout.

**Deciduous forest** See **Tropical deciduous forest.**

**Dentary** One of the major bones of the lower jaw in reptiles. In snakes and lizards this bone bears the teeth of the lower jaw.

**Discordant** Dissimilar with respect to one or more characters.

**Distal** Pertaining to the part of a structure, such as the tail or hemipenis, that is farther removed from the center of the body than some other part of that structure.

**Dorsal scale row number** The number of longitudinal scale rows encircling the body of a snake at a certain point, exclusive of the ventrals. Often counts are made at three points along a snake's body: a head's length behind the head, at midbody, and a head's length in front of the anus. A dorsal scale formula of 23–21–19 reflect's these three counts. If only one figure is given, it is the midbody count. The dorsal scale rows are most easily counted in oblique or diagonal series, starting with a paraventral.

**Dorsum** The upper surface of an animal or part thereof; for example, the dorsum of a snake head extends from the internasals through the parietal regions.

**Dysarthria** A difficulty in articulating words, usually caused by a disturbance of the motor neurons.

**Dysphagia** A difficulty in swallowing.

**Ecchymosis** The escape of blood from ruptured blood vessels into the tissues, resulting in severe purple or black coloration of the skin.

**Elapid** A snake of the family Elapidae. In the New World, this family includes the coral snakes (*Micruroides, Micrurus*) and the pelagic sea snake (*Pelamis platurus*). All members of this family are proteroglyphous, and all New World species should be considered dangerous. Some authorities have placed the sea snakes in a separate family, the Hydrophiidae.

**Emarginate** Pertaining to a margin that is notched or scalloped in outline.

**Erythemia** A greater than normal number of erythrocytes in the blood.

**Evergreen forest** See **Tropical evergreen forest.**

**Fang** Any hollow or grooved tooth borne on the maxillary bone of the upper jaw in snakes that is longer than other teeth and serves in the conduction of venom.

**Fibrinogenolytic** Able to destroy fibrinogen, usually by means of an enzyme.

**Foramen** Any small opening or perforation, such as that found in a bone.

**Foveal** Any of the small scales surrounding the loreal pit of viperid snakes that have no other regular designations. These scales usually lie exterior to the lacunals, above the supralabials, below the loreal, and anterior to the level of the eye. More specifically, the prefoveals usually lie within the area bordered by the nasals, loreal, prelacunal, and supralabials, and may extend forward between the nasals and supralabials to make contact with the rostral. The subfoveals lie below the pit between the lacunals and supralabials; and the postfoveals lie along the lower posterior border of the pit, between the sublacunal and supralabials, but in front of the interoculabials.

**Frontal** The scale or scales lying on top of the head between the supraoculars; or pertaining to this region. In many snakes—including coral snakes, *Agkistrodon,* and *Sistrurus*—there is a single large, flat, symmetrical scale in this region; however, in most pitvipers a number of irregularly disposed scales, keeled or not, occupy this space (see **Intersupraoculars**).

**Gallery forest** A forest growing along a watercourse in a region otherwise mostly devoid of trees.

**Grasslands** See **Savanna.**

**Ground color** The basic color between the various elements of pattern; the background color. The ground color is referred to in those snakes with spots, blotches, or bands; in ringed snakes, such as some coral snakes, no ground color is identifiable.

**Gular** Pertaining to the throat region or ventral surface of the neck; or a scale in this region not having other designations.

**Head cap** In coral snakes, the black pigment that extends posteriorly from the top of the snout often to cover most or all of the parietal scales.

**Hematemesis** The vomiting of blood.

**Hematuria** The presence of blood in the urine.

**Hemipenis** One of the copulatory organs in snakes or lizards. There are two of these structures; when inverted, they lie ventrolaterally in the base of the tail. Hemipenes (plural) tend to be ornate with spines and calyces, thereby providing useful taxonomic characteristics.

**Hypofibrinogenemia** A deficiency of plasma fibrinogen.

**Hypofibrinogenuria** A deficiency of fibrinogen in the urine.

**Hypotension** Low blood pressure.

**Hypovolemia** The decrease in volume of circulating blood.

**Imbricate** Overlapping, as the shingles of a roof. Used in reference to the scales in reptiles that have their posterior margins overlapping adjacent scales.

**Infracephalic** Pertaining to the venter of the head.

**Infralabials** The series of scales along the lip of the lower jaw exclusive of the anterior median mental. The notation 9/9 indicates 9 infralabials each on the right and left sides, respectively.

**Intercanthals** The scales on top of the snout between the canthals.

**Interchinshields** The scales lying between the paired elongated chinshields. These scales are present in a few species of rattlesnakes.

**Intergrade** The offspring of individuals of two different subspecies or populations of the same species. Many of the characteristics that distinguish the parental populations are often intermediate in intergrades.

**Internasals** The scales or plates in snakes and lizards that run across the top of the front of the snout between the prenasals and make contact with the prenasals and/or the rostral. Most frequently there are two internasals in snakes.

**Interoculabials** The scales between, but not including, the suboculars and supralabials. The fewest of these usually occur below the anteriormost subocular. In some species the interoculabial series is incomplete or absent, with the suboculars and supralabials in contact or the supralabials reaching the eye.

**Intersupraoculars** The scales lying on top of the head between the supraoculars. The scales in this area often are disposed in an irregular fashion. The number of intersupraoculars lying between the supraoculars is generally taken as the lowest number of contiguous scales. If only one large scale is present, it is called the frontal.

**Jacobson's organ** A sensory structure located in the roof of the mouth of some reptiles such as snakes and lizards. Sensory particles are picked up from the surrounding environment by the tongue, which is then protruded into the blind sac that is the Jacobson's organ.

**Juxtaposed** Disposed in a side-by-side fashion.

**Keeled** Pertaining to scales that possess a median ridge. The ridge may or may not extend to the tip of the scale.

**Labial** See **Infralabial** and **Supralabial.**

**Lacunal** Any one of the scales that form the inner border of the loreal pit in crotaline snakes. These scales are usually large and curve outward to form part of the outer border of the pit as well. Small scales lying near but entirely outside of the pit and having no other designation (e.g., supralabials, loreals, preoculars) are called foveals. The external aperture of the pit is generally triangular, with one apex pointing posteriorly toward the eye. In front the pit is bounded by the prelacunal, below by the sublacunal, and above by the supralacunal.

**Lacunolabial** The single large scale that is formed in some crotaline snakes from the fusion of the prelacunal and the second (or, rarely, the third) supralabial. It is often said of snakes having this condition that "the second labial enters the pit."

**Lateral** Pertaining to a position away from the midline of the body.

**Lepidosis** The arrangement and pattern of the scales (synonym, scutellation).

**Llanos** Extensive grassy plains, usually with few trees except along watercourses. This habitat is widespread in eastern Colombia and Venezuela.

**Loreal** The scales lying on the side of the head between the postnasal and preoculars. There is much variation in the location and number of these scales: in most coral snakes loreals are absent, most crotalines have at least 1 per side, and many have 2 or more. In some snakes, the postnasal and upper preocular may make contact with each other, displacing the loreal(s) to above or below the point of contact.

**Loreal pit** A deep depression on the side of the head of crotaline snakes, thus the name pitviper. The pit is located behind the nostril and in front of the eye, but most of it lies below a line drawn from the nostril to the center of the eye. The loreal pit is the external opening of an extremely sensitive infrared-detecting organ.

**Lorilabials** In lizards, one or more scales arranged in a longitudinal row between the supralabials and loreals.

**Matrix** The fleshy tip of the tail in rattlesnakes upon which each successive rattle is formed. In a few populations, the matrix is shriveled or withered, precluding development of a string of rattles.

**Medial** Pertaining to a position toward the midline of the body.

**Melanic** See **Melanistic.**

**Melanistic** Characterized by the development of black or nearly black skin. This condition occurs either as a characteristic of a species or as an individual variation. As used in this text, melanistic refers to a condition affecting overall pattern, whereas melanic or melanized refers to an element of a pattern, such as a melanic ring.

**Melena** A black, tarry stool caused by upper gastrointestinal bleeding.

**Mental** The median triangular scale at the anterior edge of the lower jaw in snakes and lizards. This scale is bordered on both sides by the first infralabials.

**Meristic** Divided into discrete entities; features that are countable (such as scales) are said to be meristic.

**Mesial spines** Those spines located just above the crotch of the hemipenis of certain snakes.

**Mesquite-grassland** A seasonally dry vegetation type occurring on the high tableland of Mexico at elevations of 1,500–2,100 m. This habitat is also found on the Gulf Coast of northeastern Mexico and along the foothills of eastern and southern Sonora. Characteristic plants include grasses (*Andropogon, Bouteloua, Spartina*), mesquite (*Prosopis*), legumes (*Acacia, Mimosa*), cacti (*Opuntia*), and agaves.

**Monovalent** Pertaining to an antivenom effective against the venom of only one species.

**Montane** Of, or relating to, mountains.

**Montane dry forest** A type of vegetation usually found between elevations of 600 and 1,500 m and characterized by thorny shrubs and low deciduous trees, agaves and cacti, and many kinds of grasses. Many of the rainshadow valleys of Middle America contain this type of forest. Portions of montane dry forest are sometimes referred to as subtropical dry forest or lower montane dry forest.

**Montane moist forest** A type of forest found mostly at elevations above 1,000 m. This forest experiences a well-defined dry season and receives an amount of rainfall intermediate between that received by montane dry and montane wet forests. In Mexico and northern Central America, **lower montane moist forest** lies just below montane moist forest and is generally equivalent to **pine-oak forest.**

**Montane wet forest** A type of very humid forest usually found at elevations well above 1,500 m and corresponding to the upper portion of the cloud forest; the lower portion of cloud forest is often referred to as **subtropical** or **lower montane wet forest**. See also **Cloud forest.**

**Myoglobinuria** The presence of myoglobin in the urine.

**Myonecrosis** The death of muscle tissue.

**Naked** In reference to snake hemipenes, devoid of ornamentation such as spines on the basal area and proximal portion of the lobes.

**Nape** The dorsal part of the neck. In snakes, nape generally refers to the part of the neck just behind the head and may be used as an adjective (e.g., nape blotch).

**Nasals** See **Postnasal** and **Prenasal.**

**Necrosis** The death of tissue.

**Norther** A cold front from the midlatitude frontal storms of the westerly wind belt. Mexico, Central America, and even northern South America are subject to these cold fronts from October to May.

**Nuchal** Pertaining to the region immediately behind the head.

**Ocellus** (plural, ocelli) An element of pattern that resembles an eye.

**Oculoplegia** Paralysis of the eyes.

**Oropel** The local name in parts of Nicaragua, Costa Rica, and Panama for the yellow color phase of *Bothriechis schlegelii.*

**Osteoderm** A small dermal bone that is located under an epidermal scale of *Heloderma*. Osteoderms are found in many lizards and crocodilians.

**Palpebral ptosis** The drooping of the upper eyelid, often caused by paralysis of the oculomotor nerve.

**Papillate** Bearing small nipplelike projections; sometimes used in reference to the micro-ornamentation of hemipenes.

**Páramo** Isolated cold, humid meadows occurring above the treeline (2,600 to 3,800 m) in the northern Andes and Mérida Andes (in Colombia, Ecuador, Peru, and Venezuela). This vegetation type is characterized by grasses (*Calamagrostis, Festuca*), *Baccharis, Diplostephium*, and, perhaps the most distinctive páramo plant genus, *Espeletia*.

**Paraphyletic group** A group comprising a common ancestor and some, but not all, of its descendants.

**Paraventrals** The scales composing the longitudinal series that are situated on either side of the ventrals. The paraventrals are usually slightly larger than the scales more dorsally located. In snakes with most of the dorsals keeled, the paraventrals are usually smooth or weakly keeled. Paraventral also refers to the area on either side of the ventrals.

**Paravertebral** Lying to either side of the vertebral line; often used in reference to the rows of dorsals lying to either side of the vertebral row.

**Parietal eye** A sensory structure that opens by means of the parietal foramen, a hole in the top of the skull. This opening lies along the middorsal line in the parietal or frontoparietal region. The parietal eye is thought to detect temperature, and in some species of lizards, it is capable of light reception.

**Parietals** Typically, a pair of large scales on the back of the dorsum of a snake's head. In most vipers, the parietals are fragmented into many small scales. The parietal region is located on top of the head posterior to the frontal region and the supraoculars.

**Pine-oak forest** A widespread forest occurring mostly at elevations above 1,000 m in the seasonally dry highlands of Mexico and northern Central America. This vegetation type comprises many communities, including oak scrub, pine forest, pine-oak woodland, and piñon-juniper woodland, among others. See also **Montane moist forest.**

**Plates** Large, usually flat, scales; typically used in reference to the enlarged scales on top of a snake's head or on its belly.

**Polyvalent** Pertaining to an antivenom effective against the venoms of multiple species.

**Postnasal** The scale bordering the posterior margin of the nostril. It may be conjoined above and/or below with the prenasal.

**Postocular** The scale or scales bordering the posterior periphery of the eye.

**Prefoveal** See **Foveal.**

**Prefrontals** The scales on top of the snout behind the internasals and in front of the frontal(s). The scales in this region may be paired and meet at the midline or may be fragmented into numerous smaller scales, including the canthals and intercanthals.

**Prehensile** Adapted for seizing by wrapping around; the arboreal pitvipers have a prehensile tail.

**Premontane** Pertaining to the lower piedmont region or foothills of a mountain or mountain range; used to describe several types of forest that occur in these areas.

**Prenasal** The scale bordering the anterior margin of the nostril. It may be conjoined above and/or below with the postnasal.

**Preocular** The scale or scales bordering the anterior periphery of the eye.

**Preventrals** The scales lying anteriorly in the ventral series, wider than long, but not in contact on both sides with the paraventral row of dorsals.

**Proteroglyph** A snake with fangs attached to a relatively akinetic maxillary bone that is located in the front of the mouth. At rest, the fangs are not folded against the roof of the mouth. See also **Solenoglyph.**

**Proximal** Pertaining to the part of a structure, such as the tail or hemipenis, that is closer to the center of the body than some other part of that structure.

**Puna** An essentially treeless, windswept vegetation type occurring at elevations of about 3,400 to 4,400 m and even higher on the dry tableland region of the high Andes (from southern Ecuador to northern Argentina). The dominant plants are bunch grasses (*Festuca, Poa, Stipa*), low shrubs (*Adesmia, Parastephia*), and sometimes small, scattered trees (*Polylepis*). In some areas along the eastern side of the Altiplano, the puna is more humid, and bromeliads (*Puya, Tillandsia*) may be abundant.

**Rainforest** A humid, tropical, relatively aseasonal vegetation type characterized by gigantic trees, lianas, palms, and epiphytes. Rainforest occurs throughout much of the Middle American Caribbean lowlands from Veracruz, Mexico, to Panama; it is also found locally on the Pacific coast in Guatemala, Costa Rica, and Panama. In South America, rainforest occurs along the Pacific lowlands from Colombia through Ecuador to extreme northern Peru, in the lower Río Orinoco Basin and Trinidad, throughout most of the Amazon Basin, and along an Atlantic corridor in Brazil from the state of Rio Grande do Norte to Santa Catarina.

**Rainshadow** Used in reference to the dry conditions found on the leeward side of some mountain ranges. Where rainshadow effects exist, the warm, moisture-laden air coming off a large body of water (e.g., an ocean) rises as it is swept up the windward slopes of mountains. As it rises, the air cools, condensing the water vapor, and most of the moisture is lost on the windward side of the mountain range, often creating luxuriant cloud forest vegetation. By the time the air reaches the leeward side of the mountain, it is relatively dry and promotes xeric or rainshadow vegetation.

**Rattle** The sound-producing appendage on the tail of rattlesnakes.

**Rattle matrix** The fleshy tip of the tail of rattlesnakes upon which each new rattle is formed.

**Rictus** The point, somewhat anterior to the angle of the jaw, where the lips of the upper and lower jaws come together.

**Ring** An element of pattern consisting of a solid color that completely encircles the body of a snake. Rings have been described as broad, wide, narrow, or long; because of their orientation around the long axis of the body, we prefer the last-named term. Counts of black body rings in coral snakes include the nape ring. (Synonymous with annulus, annuli.)

**Rostral** The median scale covering the anterior tip of the snout in snakes and lizards. This scale is usually bordered by the first supralabials, the prenasals, and the internasals.

**Rugose** Rough, wrinkled. The dorsal aspect of some pitvipers is rugose owing to the presence of heavy keels and high neural spines.

**Saddle** A dorsal blotch that extends down the sides but is longer along the midline than it is laterally.

**Savanna** A large grassy plain often containing scattered groves of trees, palms, or palmettos. Savannas may occur on flat coastal plains or in interior drainages. They are sometimes the result of clearing by humans, but many savannas are thought to be relatively old and to be caused by edaphic conditions.

**Scutellation** See **Lepidosis.**

**Shoulders** The proximal outer basal margins of a divided hemipenis, such as that found in pitvipers.

**Solenoglyph** A snake with fangs attached to a relatively kinetic maxillary bone that is located in the front of the mouth. At rest, the fangs are folded against the roof of the mouth. See also **Proteroglyph.**

**Subcaudals** The scales lying on the ventral side of the tail in snakes, extending from immediately behind the anal plate to (but not including) the tail spine. In some snakes these scales are entire (undivided), whereas in other species they are paired (divided).

**Subocular** A scale bordering the lower periphery of the eye, but not the margin of the upper lip (in which case it would be considered a supralabial). Many species of pitvipers have several suboculars, but some snakes possess a single elongated scale.

**Subtropical dry forest** See **Montane dry forest.**

**Subtropical moist forest** See **Montane moist forest.**

**Subtropical wet forest** See **Montane wet forest.**

**Sulcate** Pertaining to the side of the hemipenis bearing the sulcus spermaticus.

**Sulcus spermaticus** A well-defined longitudinal groove on the outer surface of the everted hemipenis that serves to transport spermatozoa. In species with divided hemipenes, this groove is also divided, with a branch extending to the apex of each hemipenial lobe.

**Superciliary** Any one of a small series of scales lying above the eye and along the outer edge of the supraocular. In *Bothriechis schlegelii*, some of these scales are raised into spinelike projections.

**Supra-anal keels** Well-developed keels on the scales covering the lateral portion of the body above the anus. These keels occur in certain species of coral snakes and typically only in males; however, in some species large females also develop keels in this region. Sometimes called supra-anal tubercles.

**Supracephalic** On top of the head, such as scales.

**Supralabials** The series of scales along the lip of the upper jaw, exclusive of the anterior median rostral. The notation $^9/_9$ indicates 9 supralabials each on the right and left sides, respectively.

**Supraocular** In snakes, usually a large plate that lies on top of the head over either eye. In some species (e.g., *Porthidium nummifer, P. picadoi*) this scale may be either fragmented into many small scales or reduced to a small elongated scale. In other species (e.g., *Ophryacus undulatus, P. melanurum*), the supraocular is divided into many small scales, one or several of which may form a spine or hornlike process above the eye.

**Sympatric** Coexistent; two species living in the same general region are said to be sympatric.

**Tachycardia** A rapid heart rate.

**Tail length** In snakes, the distance from the posterior edge of the anal plate to the tip of the tail.

**Tail spine** The terminal scale on the tip of the tail in snakes. In most species, it is elongated and spinelike, but in some (e.g., *Bothriechis*), it is short and blunt; it is of course absent in rattlesnakes, where it is replaced by a rattle. The tail spine varies in size and shape among individuals of a species, and it usually becomes longer and more pointed with age.

**Temporal** The scale or scales lying behind the postoculars, above the supralabials, and below the parietals. The temporals are often arranged in two vertical rows, the anterior and posterior temporals, named according to their location. The notation 1 + 2 indicates a snake has 1 anterior and 2 posterior temporals on each side of the head.

**Tepui** Any one of a series of tabletop mountains of the Guiana Shield. These mountains are erosional remnants of the Cretaceous and Tertiary uplifts.

**Thorn forest** A relatively short scrubby forest occurring along portions of the western coast of Mexico, at the northern end of the Yucatán Peninsula, in a few interior valleys in Central America, and in the Caribbean coastal plain of northern South America. Leguminous trees (*Acacia, Caesalpinia, Cassia, Mimosa*) are characteristic.

**Thrombin** A proteolytic enzyme that facilitates the clotting of blood by promoting the conversion of fibrinogen to fibrin.

**Thrombocytopenia** A persistent decrease in the number of blood platelets, usually associated with hemorrhagic conditions.

**Total length** (TL) The distance from the front face of the rostral to the tip of the tail; in other words, the combined head-body length and tail length.

**Transversely divided** Used in reference to a scale that is partitioned across its long axis into two smaller scales. Examples are the upper preocular in most *Crotalus lepidus* and the first infralabial in *C. ruber* and some populations of *C. durissus*.

**Triad** A grouping of three similar items. This term is frequently applied to the groups of black rings found in the pattern of some coral snakes and their mimics in which sequences of *black*-yellow-*black*-yellow-*black* rings are separated from one another by red rings.

**Tropical arid forest** A type of xeric vegetation, sometimes called arid tropical scrub in Mexico, that is characteristic of the lower elevations (100–600 m) of the driest rainshadow valleys in Mexico and northern Central America. This forest experiences an extended, harsh dry season and usually receives less than 1,000 mm of precipatation each year. The vegetation is sparse and comprises various grasses, cacti, and thorny leguminous shrubs.

**Tropical deciduous forest** A vegetation type occurring at low elevations in the semi-arid tropics which is characterized by species of trees (belonging to the genera *Bursera, Ipomoea, Lysiloma, Tabebuia*) that lose their leaves during the dry season. This type of forest is widespread, occurring principally along the western coast of Mexico and parts of Central America and at scattered locales in South America.

**Tropical evergreen forest** A vegetation type occurring at low elevations in the semihumid tropics which is characterized by species of trees (belonging to the *Bursera, Cedrela, Ceiba*) that are not deciduous. This type of forest is not as wet, dense, or tall as rainforest, and it usually experiences at least a short but well-defined dry season.

**Tropical moist forest** See **Rainforest.**

**Type locality** The geographic locality at which a holotype (a specimen designated by an author as type in the original description), lectotype (a specimen chosen as type if the author failed to designate type in the original description), or neotype (a specimen chosen as type to replace a type that has been lost or destroyed) was collected.

**Venter** The undersurface of an animal.

**Ventral** In snakes, one of the large, transversely elongated plates covering the belly from the neck to the anal plate. When the ventral series are counted, the first ventral is the anteriormost scale bordered on either side by the continuous, longitudinal row of dorsals that is adjacent to the ventrals more posteriorly (paraventrals); the anal plate is not counted in the ventral series.

**Viperid** A snake of the family Viperidae. In the New World, this family includes the cantil and copperhead (*Agkistrodon*), palm-pitvipers (*Bothriechis*), forest-pitvipers (*Bothriopsis*), lanceheads (*Bothrops*), bushmaster (*Lachesis*), Mexican horned pitviper (*Ophryacus*), hognosed and montane pitvipers (*Porthidium*), and rattlesnakes (*Crotalus* and *Sistrurus*). Members of this family are solenoglyphous, and all should be considered potentially dangerous.

**Xanthic** Possessing yellow pigment or tending toward a yellow color.

# References

Authors' surnames are cited as they appear on the original publication; variant spellings have not been standardized here or in the lists of reference citations following the species accounts. Consequently, the same author may be cited more than one way (e.g., Lancini, 1967; Lancini V., 1983). Works that were published later than the date printed on the publication are listed here with the actual date of publication first, followed by the purported date of publication in square brackets (see, e.g., Abalos and Baez, 1963).


Abalos, J. W. 1961. Distribución y densidad de las serpientes venenosas de Santiago del Estero. Acta Krausi Cuad. Inst. Nac. Microbiol. Buenos Aires 3:69–70.

Abalos, J. W. 1977. ¿Qué sabe usted de víboras? Buenos Aires, Edit. Losada. 175 pp.

Abalos, J. W., and E. C. Baez. 1963 [dated 1961]. Variaciones del diseño en "*Bothrops neuwiedii meridionalis*" de Santiago del Estero. Acta Zool. Lilloana 19:479–486.

Abalos, J. W., E. C. Baez, and R. Nader. 1964. Serpientes de Santiago del Estero. Acta Zool. Lilloana 20:211–283.

Abalos, J. W., and E. Bucher. 1970. Zoo-epidemiología del ofidismo en Santiago del Estero. Bol. Acad. Nac. Cienc. (Córdoba) 47:259–272.

Abalos, J. W., and C. C. Mischis. 1975. Elenco sistemático de los ofidios Argentinos. Bol. Acad. Nac. Cienc. (Córdoba) 51:55–76.

Abalos, J. W., and R. Nader. 1962. La coral *Micrurus lemniscatus frontalis* de Santiago del Estero. An. Inst. Nac. Microbiol. (Buenos Aires) 1:83–94.

Abalos, J. W., and I. Pirosky. 1963. Venomous Argentine serpents ophidism and snake antivenin. Pp. 363–371 in H. L. Keegan and W. V. MacFarlane, eds. Venomous and poisonous animals and noxious plants of the Pacific region. Oxford, Pergamon Press.

Abuys, A. 1982. Enige korrekties en aanvullende gegevens t.a.v. het boekje "Surinaamse slangen in kleur" van Joep Moonen e. a., 1979. Litt. Serp. 2:34–42.

Abuys, A. 1987a. A new coral snake (genus *Micrurus*) from Surinam [*sic*]. Litt. Serp. 7:215–220.

Abuys, A. 1987b. The snakes of Surinam [*sic*], part XVIII: family Elapidae, subfamily Micrurinae. Litt. Serp. 7:221–242.

Abuys, A. 1987c. The snakes of Surinam [*sic*], part XIX: family Viperidae, subfamily Crotalinae (genus *Crotalus*). Litt. Serp. 7:282–296.

Achával, F. 1976. Reptiles. Pp. 26–29 in A. Langguth, ed. Lista de las especies de vertebrados del Uruguay (Reptiles). Mus. Nac. Hist. Nat. Montevideo.

Achával, F. 1979 [dated 1977]. Lista comentada de los reptiles que habitan en la zona de influencia de la represa de Salto Grande. Sem. Medio Ambiente y Represas (Montevideo) 1:173–181.

Achával, F., A. Melgarejo, and M. Meneghel. 1976. Víboras venenosas del Uruguay. Inst. Inves. Cienc. Biol. Montevideo. Pp. 1–6.

Achával, F., A. R. Melgarejo, and M. Meneghel. 1978. Ofidios del area de influencia de Salto Grande (Aspectos biológicos y referencias sobre ofidismo). V Reunión sobre Aspectos de Desarrollo Ambiental. 31 pp.

Acosta-Solís, M. 1944. Nuevas contribuciones al conocimiento de la provincia de Esmeraldas. Quito, Editorial Ecuador. 606 pp.

Ahl, E. 1927. Zwei neue Korallenottern der Gattung *Elaps*. Zool. Anz. 70:251–252.

Albritton, D. C., H. M. Parrish, and E. R. Allen. 1970. Venenation by the Mexican beaded lizard (*Heloderma horridum*): Report of a case. S. Dakota J. Med. 23:9–11.

Alemán G., C. 1953. Contribución al estudio de los reptiles y batracios de la Sierra de Perijá. Mem. Soc. Cienc. Nat. La Salle (Caracas) 13:205–225.

Allen, C. E. 1940. Behavior of *Micrurus frontalis frontalis*. Copeia 1940:51–52.

Allen, E. R. 1949. Observations on the feeding habits of the juvenile cantil. Copeia 1949:225–226.

Allen, E. R., and W. T. Neill. 1957. Some interesting rattlesnakes from southern British Guiana. Herpetologica 13:67–74.

Allen, M. J. 1933. Report on a collection of amphibians and reptiles from Sonora, Mexico, with a description of a new lizard. Occas. Pap. Mus. Zool. Univ. Michigan no. 259:1–15.

Altini, G. 1942. I rettili dei Laghi Chapala, Patzcuaro e Peten raccolti nel 1932 dal Prof. Allesandro Ghigi e dal Prof. Alula Taibel. Atti Soc. Ital. Sci. Nat. Mus. Civ. Stor. Nat. Milano 81:153–195.

Alvarez del Toro, M. 1972. Los Reptiles de Chiapas. 2d ed. Chiapas, Mexico, Tuxtla Gutiérrez. 178 pp.

Alvarez del Toro, M. 1983 [dated 1982]. Los reptiles de Chiapas. 3d ed. Tuxtla Gutiérrez, Chiapas, Mexico, Publicación del Instituto de Historia Natural. 248 pp.

Alvarez del Toro, M., and H. M. Smith. 1956. Notulae herpetologicae Chiapasiae I. Herpetologica 12:3–17.

Amaral, A. do. 1921a. Contribuição para o conhecimento dos ofídios do Brasil—A. Parte 1. Anex. Mem. Inst. Butantan 1:1–38.

Amaral, A. do. 1921b. Contribuição para o conhecimento dos ofídios do Brasil—A. Parte II. Biologia da nova espécie, *Lachesis insularis*. Anex. Mem. Inst. Butantan 1:39–44.

Amaral, A. do. 1922 [dated 1921]. Contribution towards the knowledge of snakes in Brazil—A. Part I. Four new species of Brazilian snakes. Anex. Mem. Inst. Butantan. 1:49–81.

Amaral, A. do. 1923. New genera and species of snakes. Proc. New England Zool. Club 8:85–105.

Amaral, A. do. 1925a. A general consideration of snake poisoning and observations on Neotropical pit-vipers. Contr. Harvard Inst. Trop. Biol. Med. 2:1–64.

Amaral, A. do. 1925b. South American snakes in the collection of the United States National Museum. Proc. U.S. Natl. Mus. 67:1–30.

Amaral, A. do. 1925c. On the oviparity of *Lachesis muta* Daudin, 1803. Copeia 1925:93–94.

Amaral, A. do. 1926a. Novos gêneros e espécies de ophídios brasileiros. Arch. Mus. Nac. Rio de Janeiro 26:97–121.

Amaral, A. do. 1926b. Ophidia from South America in the Carnegie Museum: A critique of Dr. L. E. Griffin's "Catalog of the Ophidia from South America at present (June, 1916) contained in the Carnegie Museum." Ann. Carnegie Mus. 16:319–323.

Amaral, A. do. 1926c. Studies of Neotropical ophidia. II. On *Micrurus mipartitus* and allied forms. Proc. New England Zool. Club. 9:61–66.

Amaral, A. do. 1926d. Nomes vulgares de ophídios do Brasil. Bol. Mus. Nac., Rio de Janeiro 2:19–29.

Amaral, A. do. 1926e. Notas de ophiologia. 1.ª nota de ophiologia. Sobre a invalidez de um genero e algumas espécies de ophídios sul-Americanos. Rev. Mus. Paulista, São Paulo, 14:17–33.

Amaral, A. do. 1927a. Studies of Neotropical ophidia. IV. A new form of Crotalidae from Bolivia. Bull. Antivenin Inst. Am. 1:5–6.

Amaral, A. do. 1927b. Studies of Neotropical ophidia. V. Notes on *Bothrops lansbergii* and *B. brachystoma*. Bull. Antivenin Inst. Am. 1:22.

Amaral, A. do. 1927c. The snake-bite problem in the United States and in Central America. Bull. Antivenin Inst. Am. 1:31–35.

Amaral, A. do. 1927d. Studies of Neotropical ophidia VII. An interesting collection of snakes from west Colombia. Bull. Antivenin Inst. Am. 1:44–47.

Amaral, A. do. 1927e. Studies on Nearctic ophidia. I. *Crotalus godmani* Schmidt 1922, a synonym of *C. mitchelli* Cope 1961. Bull. Antivenin Inst. Am. 1:47–48.

Amaral, A. do. 1927f. Studies of Nearctic ophidia II. *Crotalus pricei* Van Denburgh 1896, a synonym of *C. triseriatus* (Wagler, 1830). Bull. Antivenin Inst. Am. 1:48–54.

Amaral, A. do. 1927g. Notes on Nearctic poisonous snakes and treatment of their bites. Bull. Antivenin Inst. Am. 1:61–76.

Amaral, A. do. 1928. Studies of Neotropical ophidia XI. Snakes from the Santa Marta region, Colombia. Bull. Antivenin Inst. Am. 2:7–8.

Amaral, A. do. 1929a. Studies on Nearctic ophidia. III. Notes on *Crotalus tigris* Kennicott, 1859. Bull. Antivenin Inst. Am. 2:82–85.

Amaral, A. do. 1929b. Studies of Nearctic ophidia. IV. On *Crotalus tortugensis* Vandenburgh and Slevin 1921, *Crotalus atrox elegans* Schmidt 1922, and *Crotalus atrox lucasensis* (Vandenburgh 1920). Bull. Antivenin Inst. Am. 2:85–86.

Amaral, A. do. 1929c. Studies of Nearctic ophidia. V. On *Crotalus confluentus* Say, 1823, and its allied forms. Bull. Antivenin Inst. Am. 2:86–97.

Amaral, A. do. 1929d. Studies of Nearctic ophidia. VI. Phylogeny of the rattlesnakes. Bull. Antivenin Inst. Am. 3:6–8.

Amaral, A. do. 1929e. Studies of Neotropical ophidia. XII. On the *Bothrops lansbergi* group. Bull. Antivenin Inst. Am. 3:19–27.

Amaral, A. do. 1930a [dated 1929]. Estudos sôbre ophidios neotrópicos XVII. Valor sistemático de varias formas de ophídios neotrópicos. Mem. Inst. Butantan 4:3–68.

Amaral, A. do. 1930b [dated 1929]. Contribuição ao conhecimento dos ophídios do Brasil. IV. Lista remissiva dos ophídios do Brasil. Mem. Inst. Butantan 4:71–125.

Amaral, A. do. 1930c [dated 1929]. Estudos sôbre ophídios neotrópicos. XVIII-Lista remissiva dos ophídios da região neotrópica. Mem. Inst. Butantan 4:129–271.

Amaral, A. do. 1930d. Studies of Neotropical ophidia. XXV. A new race of *Bothrops neuwiedii*. Bull. Antivenin Inst. Am. 4:65–67.

Amaral, A. do. 1931a. Studies of Neotropical ophidia. XXIII. Additional notes on Colombian snakes. Bull. Antivenin Inst. Am. 4:85–89.

Amaral, A. do. 1931b. Studies of Neotropical ophidia. XXVI. Ophidia of Colombia. Bull. Antivenin Inst. Am. 4:89–94.

Amaral, A. do. 1931c [dated 1930]. Animaes venenosos do Brasil. Instituto Butantan. São Paulo, Typografia Levi. 65 pp.

Amaral, A. do. 1932. Estudos sôbre ophídios neotrópicos XXIX. Novas notas sôbre especies da Colombia. Mem. Inst. Butantan, 7:103–123.

Amaral, A. do. 1933 [dated 1932]. Contribuição ao conhecimento dos ophídios do Brasil. 5. Uma nova raça de *Bothrops neuwiedii*. Mem. Inst. Butantan 7:97–98.

Amaral, A. do. 1934a [dated 1933/34]. Notas sôbre chromatismo de ophídios III. Um caso de xanthismo e um novo de albinismo observados no Brasil. Mem. Inst. Butantan 8:151–153.

Amaral, A. do. 1934b [dated 1933/34]. Estudos sôbre ophídios neotrópicos. 31. Sôbre a espécie *Bothrops alternata* D. & B., 1854 (Crotalidae). Variações. Redescripção. Mem. Inst. Butantan 8:161–182.

Amaral, A. do. 1935. Estudios sôbre ophídios Neotrópicos. XXXIII. Novas especies de ophídios da Colombia. Mem. Inst. Butantan 9:219–223.

Amaral, A. do. 1937a. New species of ophidians from Colombia. Comptes Rendus. XII Congr. Inst. Zool. (Lisbonne 1935) 3:1762–67.

Amaral, A. do. 1937b. Remarks on the ophiological fauna of Colombia. Comptes Rendus. XII Congr. Int. Zool. (Lisbonne 1935) 3:1768–1776.

Amaral, A. do. 1938 [dated 1937]. Contribuição ao conhecimento dos ofídios do Brasil. 11. Synopse das crotalideas do Brasil. Mem. Inst. Butantan 11:217–229.

Amaral, A. do. 1944a. Notas sôbre a ofiología neotrópica e brasílica. II. Sobre *Bothrops lansbergii lansbergii* (Schlegel 1841); *Trimeresurus dunni* Hartweg and Oliver 1938; *T. lansbergii annectens* Schmidt 1936. Pap. Avulsos Dep. Zool., São Paulo 5:7–12.

Amaral, A. do. 1944b. Notas sôbre a ofiología neotrópica e brasílica. IV. Da invalidez da espécie *Bothrops pessoai* A. Prado 1939. Pap. Avulsos Dep. Zool., São Paulo 5:19–28.

Amaral, A. do. 1944c. Notas sôbre a ofiología neotrópica e brasílica. XI. Subespécies de *Micrurus lemniscatus* (L.) e suas afinidades com *M. frontalis* (Dm. e. Bibr.). Pap. Avulsos Dep. Zool., São Paulo 5:83–94.

Amaral, A. do. 1944d. Notas sôbre a ofiología neotrópica e brasílica. V. Sôbre a invalidez específica de *Crotalus unicolor*. Pap. Avulsos. Dep. Zool., São Paulo 5:29–40.

Amaral, A. do. 1948a. Ofídios de Mato Grosso (Contribuição II para o conhecimento dos ofídios do Brasil). Com. Linh. Telegr. Estrat. Mato Grosso Amazonas. Publicação n. 84; Anexos n. 5: Hist. Nat. Zool. 43 pp.

Amaral, A. do. 1948b. Ofídios do Pará. Bol. Mus. Paraense E. Goeldi 10:149–159.

Amaral, A. do. 1955a [dated 1954]. Contribuição ao conhecimento dos ofídios Neotrópicos. 35. A propósito da revalidação de *Coluber lanceolatus* Lacepéde, 1789. Mem. Inst. Butantan 26:207–214.

Amaral, A. do. 1955b [dated 1954]. Contribuição ao conhecimento dos ofídios do Brasil 15. Situação taxonómica de algumas formas de *Crotalidae, Lachesinae*, recentemente descritas. Mem. Inst. Butantan 26:215–220.

Amaral, A. do. 1955c [dated 1954]. Contribuição ao conhecimento dos ofídios neotrópicos. 36. Redescrição da espécie *Bothrops hyoprora* Amaral, 1935. Mem. Inst. Butantan 26:221–225.

Amaral, A. do. 1974 [dated 1973]. Ofionimia ameríndia na ofiología Brasiliense. Mem. Inst. Butantan 37:1–15.

Amaral, A. do. 1978. Serpentes do Brasil: Iconografía colorida. 2d ed. Ed. da Univ. de São Paulo. 246 pp.

Ambrose, M. S. 1956. Snakebite in Central America. Pp. 323–329 in E. E. Buckley and N. Porges, eds. Venoms. Washington, D.C., American Association for the Advancement of Science.

Anderson, J. D. 1962. A new subspecies of the ridged-nosed rattlesnake, *Crotalus willardi*, from Chihuahua, Mexico. Copeia 1962:160–163.

Anderson, J. D., and W. Z. Lidicker, Jr. 1963. A contribution to our knowledge of the herpetofauna of the Mexican state of Aguascalientes. Herpetologica 19:40–51.

Andersson, L. G. 1899. Catalogue of Linnean type-specimens of snakes in the Royal Museum in Stockholm. Bih. K. Svenska Vetensk. Akad. Handl. 24:1–35.

Andrews, E. W. 1937. Notes on snakes from the Yucatán Peninsula. Field Mus. Nat. Hist. Publ., Zool. Ser. 20:355–359.

Andrle, R. F. 1964. A biogeographical investigation of the Sierra de Tuxtla in Veracruz, Mexico. Ph.D. Diss., Louisiana State University. 236 pp. Ann Arbor, Mich., University Microfilms. Diss. Abstr. 64–13, 244.

Angel M., R. 1983. Serpientes de Colombia. Guia práctica para su clasificación y tratamiento del envenenamiento causado por sus mordeduras. Rev. Fac. Nac. Agron. (Medellín) 36:1–171.

Anonymous. 1870. [*Heloderma horridum* from Guaymas.] Proc. California Acad. Sci. 4:55.

Antonio, F. B. 1980. Mating behavior and reproduction of the eyelash viper (*Bothrops schlegeli*) in captivity. Herpetologica 36:231–233.

Appun, K. F. 1961. En los trópicos. Caracas, Imprenta Universitaria, Univ. Central de Venezuela. 519 pp.

Armstrong, B. L., and J. B. Murphy. 1979. The natural history of Mexican rattlesnakes. Univ. Kansas Mus. Nat. Hist. Spec. Publ. 5:1–88.

Arrington, O. N. 1930. Notes on the two poisonous lizards with special reference to *Heloderma suspectum*. Bull. Antivenin Inst. Am. 4:29–35.

Atkinson, D. A. 1907. Notes on a collection of batrachians and reptiles from Central America. Ohio Nat. 7:151–157.

Axtell, R. W. 1956. [Size maxima in the western diamond-backed rattlesnake.] Texas J. Sci. 8:frontis.

Axtell, R. W. 1959. Amphibians and reptiles of the Black Gap Wildlife Management Area, Brewster County, Texas. Southwest Nat. 4:88–109.

Axtell, R. W., and M. D. Sabath. 1963. *Crotalus pricei miquihuanus* from the Sierra Madre of Coahuila, Mexico. Copeia 1964:161–164.

Axtell, R. W., and O. Wasserman. 1953. Interesting herpetological records from southern Texas and northern Mexico. Herpetologica 9:1–6.

Ayerbe, S. 1979. Pautas para el manejo de las mordeduras de serpiente. Cuad. Med. Popayán (Colombia) 4:46–55.

Ayerbe, S., L. M. Otero, D. Galvez, and A. Paredes. 1977. Estudio retrospectivo sobre ofidiotoxicosis en el Departmento del Cauca. 1a Parte. Cuad. Med. Popayán (Colombia) 2:1–7.

Ayerbe, S., A. Paredes, and D. A. Gálvez. 1979. Estudio retrospectivo sobre ofidiotoxicosis en el Departamento del Cauca. 2a Parte. Aspectos clinicos, epidemiológicos y complicaciones. Cuad. Med. Popayán (Colombia) 4:28–45.

Azevedo, A. C. P. 1960. Notes on coral snakes (I–II). (Serpentes, Elapidae). I. About the eggs of coral snakes. II. A new observation of the behavior of *Micrurus frontalis multicinctus* and its relationship with folklore. Iheringia, Zool. 14:1–13.

Azevedo, A. C. P. 1962a. Anomalias observadas em serpentes do gênero *Micrurus* Wagler, 1824 (Serpentes, Elapidae). Iheringia, Zool. 26:1–6.

Azevedo, A. C. P. 1962b. Sôbre uma população de *Micrurus frontalis frontalis* (D. & B., 1854) de Lagoa Santa, Minas Gerais, Brasil. (Serpentes, Elapidae). Iheringia, Zool. 27:1–3.

Azevedo A. C. P. 1964. Variações cromáticas em *Micrurus corallinus* (Wied, 1820). Serpentes: Elapidae. Iheringia, Ser. Zool. 34:1–15.

Azevedo-Marques, M. M., P. Cupo, T. M. Coimbra, S. E. Hering, M. A. Rossi, and C. J. Laure. 1985. Myonecrosis, myoglobinuria and acute renal failure induced by South American rattlesnake (*Crotalus durissus terrificus*) envenomation in Brazil. Toxicon 23:621–636.

Baird, S. F. 1859. Reptiles of the boundary, with notes by the naturalists on the survey. United States and Mexican Boundary Survey under the order of Lieut. Col. W. H. Emory 3:1–35.

Baird, S. F. 1875. Affinities of *Heloderma horridum*. Annual Rec. 1874:308.

Baird, S. F., and C. Girard. 1853. Catalogue of North American reptiles in the Museum of the Smithsonian Institution. Part I: Serpents. Washington, D.C., GPO. 172 pp.

Baker, R. H., and R. G. Webb. 1967 [dated 1966]. Notas acerca de los anfibios, reptiles, y mamíferos de la Pesca, Tamaulipas. Rev. Soc. Mex. Hist. Nat. 27:179–190.

Baker, R. H., R. G. Webb, and P. Dalby. 1967. Notes on reptiles and mammals from southern Zacatecas. Am. Midl. Nat. 77:223–226.

Baker, R. H., R. G. Webb, and E. Stern. 1971. Amphibians, reptiles, and mammals from north-central Chiapas. An. Inst. Biol. Univ. Nac. Auton. Mex. Ser. Zool. 42:77–86.

Bancroft, E. 1769. An essay on the natural history of Guiana. London, T. Becket and P. A. DeHondt. 402 pp.

Banks, R. C. 1962. A history of explorations for vertebrates on Cerralvo Island, Baja California. Proc. California Acad. Sci. Ser. 4, 30:117–125.

Banta, B. H. 1962. The amphibians and reptiles from the state of Aguascalientes, Mexico, in the collections of the California Academy of Sciences. Wasmann J. Biol. 20:99–105.

Barbour, T. 1905. The vertebrata of Gorgona Island, Colombia. V. Reptilia and Amphibia. Bull. Mus. Comp. Zool. 46:98–102.

Barbour, T. 1906. Vertebrata from the savanna of Panama IV. Reptilia and Amphibia. Bull. Mus. Comp. Zool. 46:224–229.

Barbour, T. 1913. Reptiles collected by the Yale Peruvian expedition of 1912. Proc. Acad. Nat. Sci. Philadelphia 65:505–507.

Barbour, T. 1914. A contribution to the zoogeography of the West Indies, with special reference to amphibians and reptiles. Mem. Mus. Comp. Zool. 64:209–347.

Barbour, T. 1916. Amphibians and reptiles from Tobago. Proc. Biol. Soc. Washington 29:221–224.

Barbour, T. 1923. Notes on reptiles and amphibians from Panama. Occas. Pap. Mus. Zool. Univ. Michigan 129:1–16.

Barbour, T. 1928. Reptiles from the Bay Islands. Proc. New England Zool. Club. 10:55–61.

Barbour, T. 1930. The bushmaster in the Canal Zone. Bull Antivenin Inst. Am. 4:11.

Barbour, T., and A. do Amaral. 1924. Notes on some Central American snakes. Occas. Pap. Boston Soc. Nat. Hist. 5:129–132.

Barbour, T., and A. do Amaral. 1928. A new elapid from western Panama. Bull. Antivenin Inst. Am. 1:100.

Barbour, T., and W. S. Brooks. 1923. The Sapo Mountains and the Sambú Valley. A biological reconnaissance in southeastern Panama. Geogr. Rev. 13:211–222.

Barbour, T., and A. Loveridge. 1929a. On *Bothrops atrox* (Linné). Bull. Antivenin Inst. Am. 2:108.

Barbour, T., and A. Loveridge. 1929b. On some Honduranian and Guatemalan snakes with the description of a new arboreal pit viper of the genus *Bothrops*. Bull. Antivenin Inst. Am. 3:1–3.

Barbour, T., and A. Loveridge. 1929c. Reptiles and amphibians. Vertebrates from the Corn Islands. Bull. Mus. Comp. Zool. 69:138–146.

Barbour, T., and G. K. Noble. 1920. Amphibians and reptiles from southern Peru collected by the Peruvian expedition of 1914–1915 under the auspices of Yale University and the National Geographic Society. Proc. U.S. Natl. Mus. 58:609–620.

Barrera, A. 1963 [dated 1962]. La península de Yucatán como provincia biótica. Rev. Soc. Mex. Hist. Nat. 23:71–105.

Barrio, A. 1961a [dated 1960]. Consideraciones en torno a *Crotalus terrificus crotaminicus* Moura Goncalves. Physis (Buenos Aires) 22:141–147.

Barrio, A. 1961b [dated 1960]. Distribución del género *Bothrops* Wagler (Ophidia, Crotalidae) en la provincia de Buenos Aires. Physis (Buenos Aires) 22:211–215.

Barrio, A., and M. E. Miranda. 1967a [dated 1966]. Estudio comparativo morfológico e inmunológico entre diferentes entidades del género *Micrurus* Wagler (Ophidia, Elapidae) de la Argentina. Mem. Inst. Butantan 33:869–880.

Barrio, A., and M. E. Miranda. 1967b [dated 1966]. Las diferentes poblaciones de *Bothrops alternata* Duméril y Bibron (Ophidia, Crotalidae) de la Argentina, consideradas desde el punto de vista morfológico y antigénico. Mem. Inst. Butantan 33:887–892.

Bates, L. B. 1928. Snakes and snake-bite accidents of the Panama Canal Zone. Bull. Antivenin Inst. Am. 2:31–33.

Beddard, F. E. 1907. Contributions to the knowledge of the systematic arrangement and anatomy of certain genera and species of Squamata. Proc. Zool. Soc. London 1907:36–68.

Beebe, C. W. 1905. Two bird-lovers in Mexico. Boston, Houghton-Mifflin. 407 pp.

Beebe, W. 1946. Field notes on the snakes of Kartabo, British Guiana and Caripito, Venezuela. Zoologica, New York 31: 11–52.

Beebe, W. 1947. Snake skins and color. Copeia 1947:205–206.

Belding, L. 1887. Reptiles of the cape region of lower California. W. Am. Sc. 3:97–99.

Bellairs, A. 1969. The life of reptiles. 2 vols. London, Weidenfeld and Nicolson.

Berthold, A. A. 1846. Ueber verschiedene neue oder seltene Reptilien aus New Granada und Crustacien aus China. Abh. Ges. Wiss. Göttingen 3:3–32.

Bertoni, A. W. 1914. Fauna Paraguayana. Catálogos sistemáticos de los vertebrados del Paraguay. Peces, batracios, reptiles, aves y mamíferos conocidos hasta 1913. Pp. 1–83 in M. S. Bertoni, ed. Descripción física y económica del Paraguay. Vol. 59. Asunción, Gob. Paraguay.

Bertoni, A. de W. 1939. Catálogos sistemáticos de los vertebrados del Paraguay. Rev. Soc. Cient. Paraguay 4:47–49.

Biasi, P. de, H. E. Belluomini, and W. Fernandes. 1977a [dated 1976/77]. Quantidades de veneno obtidas na extração de serpentes *Bothrops pradoi* (Hoge 1948). (Serpentes, Viperidae, Crotalinae). Mem. Inst. Butantan 40/41:155–166.

Biasi, P. de, S. Hyakutake, H. E. Belluomini, and C. A. Santa Rosa. 1977b [dated 1976/77]. Contribuição ao estudo epidemiológico das Leptospiroses em serpentes do Brazil: 1—Levantamento sorológico em *Bothrops pradoi* Hoge 1948 (Viperidae: Crotalinae). Mem. Inst. Butantan 40/41:173–180.

Blanchard, R. 1889. Remarques critiques sur les serpents du genre *Thanatophis* Posada-Arango. Bull. Soc. Zool. France 14:346–349.

Blaney, R. M., and P. K. Blaney. 1978. Notes on three species of *Micrurus* (Serpentes: Elapidae) from Mexico. Herpetol. Rev. 9:92.

Blaney, R. M., and P. K. Blaney. 1979. Variation in the coral snake, *Micrurus diastema*, in Quintana Roo, Mexico. Herpetologica 35:276–278.

Bocourt, M. F. 1868. Descriptions de quelques crotaliens nouveaux appartenant au genre *Bothrops*, recueillis dans le Guatémala. Ann. Sci. Nat. Paris, Ser. 5, 10:201–202.

Bocourt, M. F. 1875. Observations sur les moeurs de l'*Heloderma horridum* Wiegmann par M. F. Sumichrast. C. R. Hebd. Séances Acad. Sci., Paris 80:676–679.

Bocourt, M. F. 1876. Note sur quelques reptiles de l'isthme de Tehuantepec (Mexique) donnés par M. Sumichrast au muséum. J. Zool., Paris 5:386–411.

Bocourt, M. F. 1878. Etudes sur les reptiles. Mission scientifique au Mexique et dans l'Amérique Centrale-Recherches Zooloques. Paris, Imprimerie Impériale. Livr. 5:281–360.

Bogert, C. M. 1956. The world's only venomous lizard. Anim. Kingdom 59:105–109.

Bogert, C. M. 1959. The Gila monster. Audubon Mag. 61:160–163.

Bogert, C. M. 1968. A new arboreal pit viper of the genus *Bothrops* from the Isthmus of Tehuantepec, Mexico. Am. Mus. Novit. no. 2341:1–14.

Bogert, C. M., and W. G. Degenhardt. 1961. An addition to the fauna of the United States, the Chihuahua ridge-nosed rattlesnake in New Mexico. Am. Mus. Novit. no. 2064:1–15.

Bogert, C. M., and R. Martín del Campo. 1956. The Gila monster and its allies. The relationships, habits, and behavior of the lizards of the family Helodermatidae. Bull. Am. Mus. Nat. Hist. 109:1–238.

Bogert, C. M., and J. A. Oliver. 1945. A preliminary analysis of the herpetofauna of Sonora. Bull. Am. Mus. Nat. Hist. 83: 297–426.

Bolaños, R. 1971. Nuevos recursos contra el ofidismo en Centroamérica, 2d ed. Costa Rica, Ministerio de Salubridad Pública. 29 pp.

Bolaños, R. 1972. Toxicity of Costa Rican snake venoms for the white mouse. Am. J. Trop. Med. Hyg. 21:260–263.

Bolaños, R. 1982. Las serpientes venenosas de Centro América y el problema del ofidismo. Primera Parte. Aspectos zoológicos, epidemiológicos y biomédicos. Rev. Costarric. Cienc. Med. 3:165–184.

Bolaños, R. 1983 [dated 1982]. Serpientes venenosas de Centro America: distribución, características y patrones cariológicos. Mem. Inst. Butantan 46:275–291.

Bolaños R. 1984. Serpientes, venenos y ofidismo en Centroamérica. San José, Costa Rica, Editorial Universidad de Costa Rica. 136 pp.

Bolaños, R., A. Flores, R. T. Taylor, and L. Cerdas. 1974. Color patterns and venom characteristics in *Pelamis platurus*. Copeia 1974:909–912.

Bolaños, R., O. Marin, E. Mora Medina, and E. A. Alfaro. 1981. El accidente ofidico por cascabela (*Crotalus durissus durissus*) en Costa Rica. Acta Med. Costarric. 24:211–214.

Bolaños, R., and J. R. Montero. 1970. *Agkistrodon bilineatus* Günther from Costa Rica. Rev. Biol. Tropical 16:277–279.

Bolaños, R., G. Muñoz, and L. Cerdas. 1978. Toxicidad, neutralización e inmunoelectroforesis de los venenos de *Lachesis muta* de Costa Rica y Colombia. Toxicon 16:295–300.

Bolaños, R., O. Rojas, and C. E. Ulloa Flores. 1982. Aspectos biomédicos de cuatro casos de mordedura de serpiente por *Lachesis muta* (Ophidia: Viperidae) en Costa Rica. Rev. Biol. Tropical 30:53–58.

Boos, H. 1975. Check list of Trinidad snakes. J. Trinidad and Tobago Field Nat. Club 1975:22–28.

Boos, H. 1984a [dated 1983/84]. A consideration of the terrestrial reptile fauna on some offshore islands north west of Trinidad. Living World Journal. J. Trinidad and Tobago Field Nat. Club 1983/84:19–26.

Boos, H. 1984b. The status and distribution of important reptiles and amphibians in Trinidad and Tobago. New York, FAO United Nations. 19 pp.

Boos, H., and V. Quesnel. 1968. Reptiles of Trinidad and Tobago. Publ. Branch, Minis. Educ. Cult. Trinidad and Tobago. 39 pp.

Booth, E. S. 1959. Amphibians and reptiles collected in Mexico and Central America from 1952 to 1958. Walla Walla Coll. Publ., Dep. Biol. Sci. no. 24:1–9.

Bostic, D. L. 1971. Herpetofauna of the Pacific coast of north central Baja California, Mexico, with a description of a new subspecies of *Phyllodactylus xanti*. Trans. San Diego Soc. Nat. Hist. 16:237–263.

Boulenger, G. A. 1885. Catalogue of lizards in the British Museum (Natural History). 2d ed. 2 vols. London, Taylor and Francis.

Boulenger, G. A. 1891. The anatomy of *Heloderma*. Nature 44:444.

Boulenger, G. A. 1896. Catalogue of the snakes in the British Museum (Natural History). Vol. 3. London, Taylor and Francis. 727 pp.

Boulenger, G. A. 1898a. A list of the reptiles and batrachians collected by the late Prof. L. Balzan in Bolivia. Ann. Mus. Civ. Stor. Nat. Genova no. 2 19:128–133.

Boulenger, G. A. 1898b. An account of the reptiles and batrachians collected by Mr. W. F. H. Rosenberg in western Ecuador. Proc. Zool. Soc. London 1898:107–126.

Boulenger, G. A. 1902a. Descriptions of new batrachians and reptiles from north-western Ecuador. Ann. Mag. Nat. Hist. Ser. 7, 9:51–57.

Boulenger, G. A. 1902b. Descriptions of new batrachians and reptiles from the Andes of Peru and Bolivia. Ann. Mag. Nat. Hist. Ser. 7, 10:394–402.

Boulenger, G. A. 1903. Descriptions of new snakes in the collection of the British Museum. Ann. Mag. Nat. Hist. Ser. 7, 12:350–354.

Boulenger, G. A. 1905. Descriptions of new snakes in the collection of the British Museum. Ann. Mag. Nat. Hist. Ser. 7, 15:453–456.

Boulenger, G. A. 1907. Description of a new pit-viper from Brazil. Ann. Mag. Nat. Hist. Ser. 7, 20:338.

Boulenger, G. A. 1912. Descriptions of new reptiles from the Andes of South America preserved in the British Museum. Ann. Mag. Nat. Hist. Ser. 8, 10:420–424.

Boulenger, G. A. 1913. On a collection of batrachians and reptiles made by Dr. H. G. F. Spurrell, F.Z.S. in the Chocó, Colombia. Proc. Zool. Soc. London 1913:1019–1038.

Boulenger, G. A. 1914. On a second collection of batrachians and reptiles made by Dr. H. G. F. Spurrell, F.Z.S. in the Chocó, Colombia. Proc. Zool. Soc. London 1914:813–817.

Boulenger, G. A. 1920. Descriptions of four new snakes in the collection of the British Museum. Ann. Mag. Nat. Hist. Ser. 9, 6:108–111.

Boundy, J., and T. G. Balgooyen. 1988. Record lengths for some amphibians and reptiles from the western United States. Herpetol. Rev. 19:26–27.

Brattstrom, B. H. 1952. Diurnal activities of a nocturnal animal. Herpetologica 8:61–63.

Brattstrom, B. H. 1964. Evolution of the pit vipers. Trans. San Diego Soc. Nat. Hist. 13:185–267.

Brattstrom, B. H., and T. R. Howell. 1954. Notes on some collections of reptiles and amphibians from Nicaragua. Herpetologica 10:114–123.

Bravo, H. 1927. Flagelados encontrados en batracios y reptiles del Valle de México. Mem. Rev. Soc. Cient. Antonio Alzate 48:385–390.

Brazil, V. 1914. La défense contre l'ophidisme. Traduction française par le Professeur J. Maibon. Saint-Paul (S. Paulo), Pocai-Weiss & C. 319 pp.

Breder, C. M., Jr. 1946. Amphibians and reptiles of the Rio Chucunaque drainage, Darien, Panama, with notes on their life histories and habits. Bull. Am. Mus. Nat. Hist. 86:377–453.

Brongersma, L. D. 1940. Snakes from the Leeward Group, Venezuela and eastern Colombia. Pp. 116–137 in P. W. Hummelinck, ed. Studies on the fauna of Curaçao, Aruba, Bonaire, and the Venezuelan islands. Vol. 2. Utrecht, N. V. Drukkerij P. Den Boer.

Brongersma, L. D. 1966. Note on *Leptomicrurus collaris* (Schlegel) (Reptilia, Serpentes). Zool. Meded., Leiden 41:243–254.

Brongersma, L. D. 1967 [dated 1966]. Poisonous snakes of Surinam. Mem. Inst. Butantan 33:73–79.

Brown, A. E. 1893. Notes on some snakes from Tropical America lately living in the collection of the zoological society of Philadelphia. Proc. Acad. Nat. Sci. Philadelphia 45:429–435.

Brown, A. E. 1901. A review of the genera and species of American snakes, north of Mexico. Proc. Acad. Nat. Sci. Philadelphia 53:10–110.

Brown, A. E. 1903a. Texas reptiles and their faunal relations. Proc. Acad. Nat. Sci. Philadelphia 55:543–558.

Brown, A. E. 1903b. Note on *Crotalus scutulatus* Kenn. Proc. Acad. Nat. Sci. Philadelphia 55:625.

Brown, B. C. 1950. An annotated check list of the reptiles and amphibians of Texas. Waco, Baylor University. 257 pp.

Brown, B. C., and L. M. Brown. 1967. Notable records of Tamaulipan snakes. Texas J. Sci. 19:323–326.

Brown, B. C., and M. B. Mittleman. 1947. A range extension for *Crotalus m. molossus* Baird and Girard in Texas. Herpetologica 4:23–24.

Brown, B. C., and H. M. Smith. 1942. A new subspecies of Mexican coral snake. Proc. Biol. Soc. Washington 55:63–66.

Brown, J. H. 1973. Toxicology and pharmacology of venoms from poisonous snakes. Springfield, Ill., Charles C. Thomas. 184 pp.

Brown, T. W. 1970. Autecology of the sidewinder (*Crotalus cerastes*) at Kelso Dunes, Mojave Desert, California. Diss. Abstr. B31:6336–6337.

Bucherl, W., and E. E. Buckley, eds. 1971. Venomous animals and their venoms. Vol. 2: Venomous vertebrates. N.Y., Academic Press. 687 pp.

Buckley, E., and N. Porges, eds. 1956. Venoms. Papers presented at the first international conference on venoms, December 27–30, 1954, at the annual meeting of the American Association for the Advancement of Science, Berkeley, California. Publ. no. 44. Am. Assoc. Adv. Sci. Abstr. Pap. Nat. Meet. 467 pp.

Bullock, T. H., and R. B. Cowles. 1952. Physiology of an infrared receptor: The facial pit of pit vipers. Science, Washington, D.C. 115:541–543.

Burchfield, P. M., T. F. Beimler, and C. D. Hairston. 1982. A range extension for *Crotalus molossus nigrescens* in Tamaulipas, Mexico. Herpetol. Rev. 13:131–132.

Burger, W. L. 1950. A preliminary study of the subspecies of the jumping viper *Bothrops nummifer*. Bull. Chicago Acad. Sci. 9:59–67.

Burger, W. L. 1955. A new subspecies of the coral snake *Micrurus lemniscatus*, from Venezuela, British Guiana, and Trinidad; and a key for the identification of associated species of coral snakes. Bol. Mus. Cienc. Nat. (Caracas). 1:35–51.

Burger, W. L. 1971. Genera of pitvipers (Serpentes: Crotalidae). Ph.D. diss. University of Kansas. Ann Arbor, Mich., University Microfilms. 186 pp. Diss. Abstr. Int. B32:6119.

Burger, W. L., and M. M. Hensley. 1949. Notes on a collection of reptiles and amphibians from northwestern Sonora. Chicago Acad. Nat. Hist. Misc. Chicago no. 35:1–6.

Burger, W. L., and W. B. Robertson. 1951. A new subspecies of the Mexican moccasin, *Agkistrodon bilineatus*. Univ. Kansas Sci. Bull. 24:213–218.

Burger, W. L., and P. W. Smith. 1950. The coloration of the tail tip of young fer-de-lances: Sexual dimorphism rather than adaptive coloration. Science, Washington, D.C. 112:431–433.

Burt, C. E., and G. S. Myers. 1942. Neotropical lizards in the collection of the Natural History Museum of Stanford University. Stanford Univ. Publ. Biol. Sci. 8:273–324.

Caballero y Caballero, E. 1954. Estudios helmintológicos de la región oncocercosa de México y de la República de Guatemala. Nemátoda. 8a Parte. An. Inst. Biol. Univ. Mex. 25:259–274.

Camarillo Rangel, J. L., R. Aguilar Cortés, and A. González Ruíz. 1985. Distributional records of amphibians and reptiles from the state of Mexico. Herpetol. Rev. 16:85.

Cameron, H. A. 1898. *Heloderma horridum (suspectum)*. J. Homeop. 1:295–306.

Camp, C. L. 1916. Notes on the local distribution and habits of the amphibians and reptiles of southeastern California in the vicinity of the Turtle Mountains. Univ. California Publs. Zool. 12:503–544.

Camp, C. L. 1923. Classification of the lizards. Bull. Am. Mus. Nat. Hist. 48:289–481.

Campbell, J. A. 1973. Life history: *Bothrops bilineatus*. HISS News—J. 1:191.

Campbell, J. A. 1976. A new terrestrial pit viper of the genus *Bothrops* (Reptilia, Serpentes, Crotalidae) from western Mexico. J. Herpetol. 10:151–160.

Campbell, J. A. 1977. The distribution, variation, and natural history of the Middle American highland pitvipers, *Bothrops barbouri* and *Bothrops godmani*. M.A. Thesis, Univ. of Texas at Arlington. 152 pp.

Campbell, J. A. 1979a. *Crotalus scutulatus* (Viperidae) in Jalisco, Mexico. Southwest Nat. 24:693–694.

Campbell, J. A. 1979b. A new rattlesnake (Reptilia, Serpentes, Viperidae) from Jalisco, Mexico. Trans. Kansas Acad. Sci 81:365–369.

Campbell, J. A. 1982a. A confusing specimen of rattlesnake from Cerro Tancítaro, Michoacán, Mexico. Southwest Nat. 27:353.

Campbell, J. A. 1982b. The biogeography of the cloud forest herpetofauna of Middle America, with special reference to the Sierra de las Minas of Guatemala. Ph.D. diss. University of Kansas. Ann Arbor, Michigan, University Microfilms. 322 pp. Diss. Abstr. Int. B Sci. Eng. 44:1025.

Campbell, J. A. 1985. A new species of highland pitviper of the genus *Bothrops* from southern Mexico. J. Herpetol. 19:48–54.

Campbell, J. A. 1988. *Crotalus transversus*. Cat. Am. Amph. Rept. 450.1–450.3.

Campbell, J. A. 1989. The distribution, variation, and natural history of *Porthidium barbouri*. Acta Zool. Mex. Nueva Ser. 26:1–32.

Campbell, J. A., and B. L. Armstrong. 1979. Geographic variation in the Mexican Pygmy Rattlesnake, *Sistrurus ravus*, with the description of a new subspecies. Herpetologica 35:304–317.

Campbell, J. A., E. D. Brodie, Jr., D. G. Barker, and A. H. Price. 1989. An apparent natural hybrid rattlesnake and *Crotalus willardi* (Viperidae: Crotalinae) from the Peloncillo Mountains of New Mexico. Herpetologica 45:In press.

Campbell, J. A., and J. P. Vannini. 1988. A new subspecies of beaded lizard, *Heloderma horridum* (Sauria: Helodermatidae), from the Motagua Valley of Guatemala. J. Herpetol. 22:457–468.

Canese, A. 1966. Animales venenosos del Paraguay. Rev. Paraguay. Microbiol. 1:56–72.

Capocaccia, L. 1961. Catalogo dei tipi de rettili del Museo Civico di Storia Naturale di Genova. Ann. Mus. Civ. Stor. Nat. Genova 72:86–111.

Cardoso, J. L., and R. B. Brando. 1982. Acidentes por animais peçonhentos clinica e tratamento. São Paulo, Livraria e Editória Santos.

Carrillo de Espinoza, N. 1970. Contribución al conocimiento de los reptiles del Perú (Squamata, Crocodylia, Testudinata: Reptilia). Publ. Mus. Hist. Nat. 'Javier Prado' Ser. A Zool. no. 22. Pp. 1–64.

Carrillo de Espinoza, N. 1977. Arañas y serpientes muy venenosas en el Departamento de Lima. Publ. Mus. Hist. Nat. 'Javier Prado' Ser. de Divul. no. 8. Pp. 1–8.

Carrillo de Espinoza, N. 1983. Contribución al conocimiento de las serpientes venenosas del Peru de las familias Viperidae, Elapidae e Hydrophiidae (Ophidia: Reptilia). Publ. Mus. Hist. Nat. 'Javier Prado' Ser. A Zool. no. 30. Pp. 1–55.

Casas-Andreu, G. 1981. Lista preliminar de los anfibios y reptiles de la costa de Jalisco. Inst. Biol. Univ. Nat. Auton. Mexico. 5 pp. Mimeo.

Casas-Andreu, G., and W. López-Forment C. 1978. Notas sobre *Micrurus browni taylori* Schmidt and Smith, en Guerrero, México. An. Inst. Biol. Univ. Nat. Auton. Mexico 49:291–294.

Castro, F., G. Kattan K., and C. Murcia D. 1982. Serpientes corales verdaderas y falsas del Valle del Cauca. COAGRO 4:15–21.

Cei, J. M. 1975. *Liolaemus melanops* Burmeister and the subspecific status of the *Liolaemus fitzingeri* group (Sauria-Iguanidae). J. Herpetol. 9:217–222.

Cei, J. M. 1979. The Patagonian Herpetofauna. Pp. 309–339 in W. E. Duellman, ed. The South American Herpetofauna: Its origin, evolution, and dispersal. Mus. Nat. Hist. Univ. Kansas, Monogr. no. 7.

Cei, J. M. 1987 [dated 1986]. Reptiles del centro, centro-oeste y sur de la Argentina. Herpetofauna de las zonas áridas y semiáridas. Mus. Reg. Sci. Nat. Boll. Monogr. no. 4. 527 pp.

Cendrero, L., F. de Buen, M. A. Freiberg, C. C. Olrog, and J. Yepes. 1972. Zoología Hispanoamericana. Vertebrados. Mexico, Edit. Porrúa. 1160 pp.

Chippaux, J-P. 1987 [dated 1986]. Les serpents de la Guyane française. Coll. Faune Tropicale no. 27. Paris, Editions de l'Orstom. 165 pp.

Chrapliwy, P. S., and C. M. Fugler. 1955. Amphibians and reptiles collected in Mexico in the summer of 1953. Herpetologica 11:121–128.

Clark, H. C. 1925. Snakes of the Ulua River Valley. Annual Report United Fruit Company Medical Department no. 14. Pp. 286–297.

Clark, H. C. 1942. Venomous snakes. Some Central American records: incidence of snake-bite accidents. Am. J. Trop. Med. 22:37–49.

Clark, H. C. 1951. Annual report of the Gorgas Memorial Laboratory, 1951. Washington, D.C., U.S. GPO. 36 pp.

Clark, P. J., and R. F. Inger. 1942. Scale reduction studies in certain non-Colubrid snakes. Copeia 1942:230–232.

Clarke, G. K. 1961. Report on a bite by a red diamond rattlesnake, *Crotalus ruber ruber*. Copeia 1961:418–422.

Cliff, F. S. 1954. Snakes of the islands in the Gulf of California, Mexico. Trans. San Diego Soc. Nat. Hist. 12:67–98.

Cochran, D. M. 1943. Poisonous reptiles of the world: A wartime handbook. Smithson. Inst. War Background Stud. no. 10. Pp. 1–37.

Cochran, D. M. 1946. Notes on the herpetology of the Pearl Islands, Panama. Smithson. Misc. Collect. 106:1–8.

Cochran, D. M. 1961. Type specimens of reptiles and amphibians in the United States National Museum. Bull. U.S. Natl. Mus. no. 220. Pp. 1–291.

Cochrane, T. T., and P. G. Jones. 1981. Savannas, forests and wet season potential evapotranspiration in tropical South America. Trop. Agric. Trinidad 58:185–190.

Cockerell, T. D. A. 1896. Reptiles and batrachians of Mesilla Valley, N. Mex. Am. Nat. 30:325–327.

Cogger, H. G. 1983. Reptiles and Amphibians of Australia, 3d ed. Sanibel, FL, Ralph Curtis Books. 660 pp.

Cohen, P., and E. B. Seligmann, Jr. 1967 [dated 1966]. Immunological studies of coral snake venom. Mem. Inst. Butantan 33:339–347.

Collins, J. T. 1982. *Crotalus stejnegeri*. Cat. Am. Amph. Rept. Pp. 303.1–303.2.

Conant, R. 1975. A field guide to reptiles and amphibians of eastern and central North America. 2d ed. Boston, Houghton-Mifflin. 429 pp.

Conant, R. 1982. The origin of the name "cantil" for *Agkistrodon bilineatus*. Herpetol. Rev. 13:118.

Conant, R. 1984. A new subspecies of the pit viper *Agkistrodon bilineatus* (Reptilia: Viperidae) from Central America. Proc. Biol. Soc. Washington 97:135–141.

Cooper, J. E. 1972. Review of Studies on the cavernicole fauna of Mexico, by J. R. Reddell and R. W. Mitchell, eds. Herpetol. Rev. 4:75.

Cope, E. D. 1860a. An enumeration of the genera and species of rattlesnakes, with synonymy and references. Smithson. Contrib. Knowl. 12:119–126.

Cope, E. D. 1860b. Supplement to "A catalogue of the venomous serpents in the museum of the Academy of Natural Sciences of Philadelphia, with notes on the families, genera, and species." Proc. Acad. Nat. Sci. Philadelphia 1860:72–74.

Cope, E. D. 1860c [dated 1859]. Catalogue of the venomous serpents in the museum of the Academy of Natural Sciences of Philadelphia, with notes on the families, genera, and species. Proc. Acad. Nat. Sci. Philadelphia 1859:332–347.

Cope, E. D. 1861. Contributions to the ophiology of lower California, Mexico, and Central America. Proc. Acad. Nat. Sci. Philadelphia 13:292–306.

Cope, E. D. 1862. Catalogues of the reptiles obtained during the explorations of the Paraná, Paraguay, Vermejo and Uraguay [*sic*] rivers by Capt. Thos. J. Page, U.S.N., and those procured by Lieut. N. Michler, U.S. Top. Eng., commander of the expedition conducting the survey of the Atrato river. Proc. Acad. Nat. Sci. Philadelphia 1862:346–359.

Cope, E. D. 1864. Contributions to the herpetology of tropical America. Proc. Acad. Nat. Sci. Philadelphia 16:166–181.

Cope, E. D. 1865. Third contribution to the herpetology of tropical America. Proc. Acad. Nat. Sci. Philadelphia 17:185–189.

Cope, D. E. 1868. An examination of the reptilia and batrachia obtained by the Orton expedition to Equador [*sic*] and the upper Amazon, with notes on other species. Proc. Acad. Nat. Sci. Philadelphia 1868:96–119.

Cope, E. D. 1869. Remarks on *Heloderma suspectum*. Proc. Acad. Nat. Sci. Philadelphia 21:5.

Cope, E. D. 1870 [dated 1869]. Seventh contribution to the herpetology of tropical America. Proc. Am. Philos. Soc. 11:147–169.

Cope, E. D. 1871. Ninth contribution to the herpetology of tropical America. Proc. Acad. Nat. Sci. Philadelphia 23:200–224.

Cope, E. D. 1874. Description of some species of reptiles obtained by Dr. John F. Bransford, assistant surgeon, United States Navy, while attached to the Nicaraguan surveying expedition in 1873. Proc. Acad. Nat. Sci. Philadelphia 26:64–72.

Cope, E. D. 1875. Check-list of North American batrachia and reptilia with a systematic list of the higher groups, and an essay on geographical distribution based on specimens contained in the U. S. National Museum. Washington, D.C., U.S. GPO. 1–104.

Cope, E. D. 1876a [dated 1875]. On the Batrachia and Reptilia of Costa Rica. J. Acad. Nat. Sci. Philadelphia Ser. 2, 8:93–154.

Cope, E. D. 1876b. Report on the reptiles brought by Professor James Orton from the middle and upper Amazon, and western Peru. J. Acad. Nat. Sci. Philadelphia Ser. 2, 8:159–188.

Cope, E. D. 1877. Synopsis of the cold-blooded vertebrata procured by Prof. James Orton during his exploration of Peru in 1876–77. Proc. Am. Philos. Soc. 17:33–49.

Cope, E. D. 1879. Eleventh contribution to the herpetology of tropical America. Proc. Am. Philos. Soc. 18:261–277.

Cope, E. D. 1884. [Review of] Garman's North American reptiles and batrachians. Am. Nat. 18:513–515.

Cope, E. D. 1885a [dated 1884]. Twelfth contribution to the herpetology of tropical America. Proc. Am. Philos. Soc. 22:167–194.

Cope, E. D. 1885b. A contribution to the herpetology of Mexico. Proc. Am. Philos. Soc. 22:379–404.

Cope, E. D. 1886 [dated 1885]. Thirteenth contribution to the herpetology of tropical America. Proc. Am. Philos. Soc. 23:271–287.

Cope, E. D. 1887. Catalogue of batrachians and reptiles of Central America and Mexico. Bull. U.S. Natl. Mus. 32:1–98.

Cope, E. D. 1892. A critical review of the characters and variations of the snakes of North America. Proc. U.S. Natl. Mus. 14:589–694.

Cope, E. D. 1895 [dated 1894]. The classification of the Ophidia. Trans. Am. Philos. Soc. 18:186–219.

Cope, E. D. 1896. The geographical distribution of Batrachia and Reptilia in North America. Am. Nat. 30:886–902, 1003–1026.

Cope, E. D. 1900. The crocodilians, lizards, and snakes of North America. Rep. U.S. Natl. Mus. 1898:153–1270.

Cordeiro, C. L., and A. R. Hoge. 1974 [dated 1973]. Contribuição ao conhecimento das serpentes do estado de Pernambuco. Mem. Inst. Butantan 37:261–290.

Coues, E. 1875. Synopsis of the reptiles and batrachians of Arizona; with critical and field notes, and on extensive synonymy. Rep. Geog. Geol. Explor. Surv. West 100th Merid. by Geo. M. Wheeler 5:585–633.

Cowles, R. B. 1941. Observations on the winter activities of desert reptiles. Ecology 22:125–140.

Cowles, R. B. 1945. Some of the activities of the sidewinder. Copeia 1945:220–222.

Cowles, R. B. 1953. The sidewinder: Master of desert travel. Pacif. Discovery 6:12–15.

Cowles, R. B., and C. M. Bogert. 1936. The herpetology of the Boulder Dam region (Nevada, Arizona, Utah). Herpetologica 1:33–42.

Crimmins, M. L. 1927. Notes on the Texas rattlesnakes. Bull. Antivenin Inst. Am. 1:23–24.

Cross, J. K., and M. S. Rand. 1979. Climbing activity in wild-ranging Gila monsters, *Heloderma suspectum* (Helodermatidae). Southwest Nat. 24:703–705.

Croulet, C. 1963. A taste of the tropics. Bull. Philadelphia Herpetol. Soc. 11:1–5.

Cruz, G. A., L. D. Wilson, and J. Espinosa. 1979. Two additions to the reptile fauna of Honduras, *Eumeces managuae* Dunn and *Agkistrodon bilineatus* (Gunther) [*sic*], with comments on *Pelamis platurus* (Linnaeus). Herpetol. Rev. 10:26–27.

Cuesta Terron, C. 1920 [dated 1919]. Datos para una monografía sobre la fauna erpetológica de la península de la Baja California. Bol. Dir. Estud. Biol. Mex. 2:398–402.

Cuesta Terron, C. 1921a. Datos para una monografía de la fauna erpetológica de la península de la Baja California. Mem. Rev. Soc. Cient. Antonio Alzate 39:161–171.

Cuesta Terron, C. 1921b. Los crotalianos mexicanos. Mem. Rev. Soc. Cient. Antonio Alzate 39:173–194.

Cuesta Terron, C. 1930a. Los crotalianos mexicanos: su clasificación, ecología y distribución geográfica. An. Inst. Biol. Univ. Auton. Mexico 1:187–199.

Cuesta Terron, C. 1930b. Los reptiles ponzoñosos mexicanos. 1. El escorpión (*Heloderma horridum* Wiegmann). Folletos Divulg. Cient. Inst. Biol., Mexico no. 2. Pp. 1–11.

Cuesta Terron, C. 1931. Los crotalianos mexicanos. An. Inst. Biol. Univ. Mex. 2:47–72.

Cuesta Terron, C. 1932. Los coralillos mexicanos. An. Inst. Biol. Univ. Mex. 3:5–14.

Cunha, O. R. da. 1967. Ofídios da Amazônia. 1-A ocorrência de *Bothrops bilineatus bilineatus* (Wied) nas matas dos arredores de Belém, Pará (Ophidia, Crotalidae). Bol. Mus. Para. Emilio Goeldi (n.s.) Zool. no. 66. Pp. 1–12.

Cunha, O. R. da, and F. P. Nascimento. 1972. Ofídios da Amazônia. 3. Sôbre a ocorrência de *Bothrops lichenosus* Roze, 1958 no Brasil (Ophidia, Crotalidae). Rev. Bras. Biol. 32:27–32.

Cunha, O. R. da, and F. P. Nascimento. 1973. Ofídios da Amazônia. 4. As cobras corais (Gênero *Micrurus*) da região leste do Pará. (Ophidia, Elapidae). -Nota preliminar. Mus. Emilio Goeldi Publ. Avulsas no. 20:273–286.

Cunha, O. R. da, and F. P. Nascimento. 1975a. Ofídios da Amazônia. 5. *Bothrops lichenosus* Roze, 1958, sinonimo de *Bothrops castelnaudi* Duméril, Bibron e Duméril, 1854, com nova descrição e comentários. Bol. Mus. Para. Emilio Goeldi (n.s.) Zool. no. 80. Pp. 1–15.

Cunha, O. R. da, and F. P. Nascimento. 1975b. Ofídos da Amazônia. VII. -As serpentes peçonhentas do gênero *Bothrops* (Jararacas) e *Lachesis* (Surucucu) da região leste do Pará. (Ophidia, Viperidae). Bol. Mus. Para. Emilio Goeldi (n.s.) Zool. no. Pp. 1–42.

Cunha, O. R. da, and F. P. Nascimento. 1978. Ofídios da Amazônia. X. As cobras da região leste do Pará, Belém. Mus. Para. Emilio Goeldi Publ. Avulsas no. 31. 218 pp.

Cunha, O. R. da, and F. P. Nascimento. 1982a. Ofídios da Amazônia, XIV.-As especies de *Micrurus, Bothrops, Lachesis* e *Crotalus* do sul do Pará e oeste do Maranhão, incluindo áreas de cerrado deste estado. (Ophidia: Elapidae e Viperidae). Bol. Mus. Para. Emilio Goeldi (n.s.) Zool. no. 112. Pp. 1–58.

Cunha, O. R. da, and F. P. do Nascimento. 1982b. Ofídios da Amazônia XVII. Revalidação de *Micrurus ornatissimus* (Jan. 1858) diferenciada de *M. langsdorffi* (Wagler 1824) e distribuição geográfica das duas espécies (Ophidia: Elapidae). Bol. Mus. Para. Emilio Goeldi (n.s.) Zool. no. 116. Pp. 1–17.

Cunha, O. R. da, F. P. do Nascimiento, and T. C. S. Avila-Pires. 1985. Contribuições do Museu Paraense Emílio Goeldi ao Projeto Carajás. Os répteis da área de Carajás, Pará, Brasil (Testudines e Squamata). Mus. Emilio Goeldi Publ. Avulsas no. 40. Pp. 9–87.

Curran, C. H. 1935. Rattlesnakes. Nat. Hist., New York 36:331–340.

Curran, C. H., and C. Kauffeld. 1937. Snakes and their ways. N.Y., Harper and Bros. 285 pp.

D'Alessandro, A. 1972. Tratamiento de las mordeduras de víboras. Acta Med. Valle 3:74–76.

Daniel, Hno. 1949. Las serpientes en Colombia. Rev. Fac. Nac. Agron. Medellín 9:301–333.

Daniel, Hno. 1959. La Colgadora y sus actividades. Progreso, Medellín no. 27, 38–42.

Da Silva, O. A., M. López, and P. Godoy. 1979. Intensive care unit treatment of acute renal failure following snake bite. Am. J. Trop. Med. Hyg. 28:401–407.

Daudin, F. M. 1803. Histoire naturelle générale et particulière des reptiles. Vol. 8. Paris, F. Dufort. 439 pp.

Davis, W. B., and J. R. Dixon. 1957. Notes on Mexican snakes (Ophidia). Southwest Nat. 2:19–27.

Davis, W. B., and J. R. Dixon. 1959. Snakes of the Chilpancingo region, Mexico. Proc. Biol. Soc. Washington 72:79–92.

Davis, W. B., and J. R. Dixon. 1961. Reptiles (exclusive of snakes) from the Chilpancingo region, Mexico. Proc. Biol. Soc. Washington 74:37–56.

Davis, W. B., and H. M. Smith. 1953. Snakes of the Mexican state of Morelos. Herpetologica 8:133–143.

Despax, R. 1911. Reptiles et batraciens de l'Equateur recueillis par M. le Dr. Rivet. Pp. 17–44, in Ministère de l'Instruction Publique. Mission du Service Geógraphique de l'Armée pour la mesure d'un Arc de Méridien Equatorial en Amérique du Sud (1899–1906). Vol. 9. Paris, Gauthier-Villars.

Devincenzi, G. J. 1925. Fauna erpetológica del Uruguay. An. Mus. Nac. Hist. Nat. Montev. Ser. 2, 2:1–65.

Díaz-Gómez, O. 1971. Accidentes por animales ponzoñsos. Trib. Med. (Bogotá) 1971:6–12.

Dice, L. R. 1939. The Sonoran biotic province. Ecology 20:118–129.

Ditmars, R. L. 1905. A new species of rattlesnake. Ninth Ann. Rep., New York Zool. Soc. 1904:197–200.

Ditmars, R. L. 1907. The reptile book: A comprehensive popularized work on the structure and habits of the turtles, tortoises, crocodilians, lizards and snakes which inhabit the United States and northern Mexico. N.Y., Doubleday Page. 472 pp.

Ditmars, R. L. 1910. Reptiles of the world: Tortoises and turtles, crocodilians, lizards and snakes of the eastern and western hemispheres. N.Y., Sturgis and Walton Co. 373 pp.

Ditmars, R. L. 1928a. The lizards. Bull. New York Zool. Soc. 33:79–132.

Ditmars, R. L. 1928b. A reptile reconnaissance in Honduras. Bull. Antivenin Inst. Am. 2:25–29.

Ditmars, R. L. 1930. The poisonous serpents of the New World. Bull. New York Zool. Soc. 33:79–132.

Ditmars, R. L. 1936. The reptiles of North America. A review of the crocodilians, lizards, snakes, turtles and tortoises inhabiting the United States and northern Mexico. N.Y., Doubleday Doran. 476 pp.

Ditmars, R. L. 1937. Snakes of the World. 5th ed. N.Y., Macmillan. 207 pp.

Dixon, J. R. 1956. The mottled rock rattlesnake *Crotalus lepidus lepidus*, in Edwards County, Texas. Copeia 1956:126–127.

Dixon, J. R. 1979. Origin and distribution of reptiles in lowland tropical rainforests of South America. Pp. 217–240 in W. E. Duellman, ed. The South American herpetofauna: Its origin, evolution, and dispersal. Monogr. Mus. Nat. Hist. Univ. Kansas No. 7.

Dixon, J. R., C. A. Ketchersid, and C. S. Lieb. 1972. The herpetofauna of Querétaro, Mexico with remarks on taxonomic problems. Southwest Nat. 16:225–237.

Dixon, J. R., and P. A. Medica. 1965. Noteworthy records of reptiles from New Mexico. Herpetologica 21:72–75.

Dixon, J. R., M. Sabbath, and R. Worthington. 1962. Comments on snakes from central and western Mexico. Herpetologica 18:91–100.

Dixon, J. R., and P. Soini. 1986. The reptiles of the upper Amazon basin, Iquitos region, Peru. 2d ed. Milwaukee Publ. Mus. 154 pp.

Dixon, J. R., and R. G. Webb. 1965. *Micrurus laticollaris* Peters, from Jalisco, Mexico. Southwest Nat. 10:77.

Doello-Jurado, M. 1916. Cual es la serpiente mencionada por Darwin con el nombre de "Trigonocephalus crepitans?" Physis 2:287–290.

Donoso-Barros, R. 1966. Reptiles de Chile. Santiago, Ediciones de la Univ. de Chile. 458 pp.

Dowling, H. G. 1965. The puzzle of the *Bothrops*; or, a tangle of serpents. Anim. Kingdom 68:18–21.

Drake, J. J. 1958. The brush mouse *Peromyscus boylii* in southern Durango. Publ. Mus. Michigan State Univ. Biol. Ser. 1. Pp. 99–132.

Duellman, W. E. 1954. The amphibians and reptiles of Jorullo Volcano, Michoacán, México. Occas. Pap. Mus. Zool. Univ. Michigan no. 560. Pp. 1–24.

Duellman, W. E. 1957. Notes on snakes from the Mexican state of Sinaloa. Herpetologica 13:237–40.

Duellman, W. E. 1958. A preliminary analysis of the herpetofauna of Colima, Mexico. Occas. Pap. Mus. Zool. Univ. Michigan no. 589. Pp. 1–22.

Duellman, W. E. 1961. The amphibians and reptiles of Michoacán, Mexico. Univ. Kansas Publ. Mus. Nat. Hist. 15:1–148.

Duellman, W. E. 1963. Amphibians and reptiles of the rainforests of southern El Petén, Guatemala. Univ. Kansas. Publ. Mus. Nat. Hist. 15:205–249.

Duellman, W. E. 1965a. Amphibians and reptiles from the Yucatan Peninsula, México. Univ. Kansas Publ. Mus. Nat. Hist. 15:577–614.

Duellman, W. E. 1965b. A biogeographic account of the herpetofauna of Michoacán, Mexico. Univ. Kansas Publ. Mus. Nat. Hist. 15:627–709.

Duellman, W. E. 1978. The biology of an equatorial herpetofauna in Amazonian Ecuador. Misc. Publ. Mus. Nat. Hist. Univ. Kansas no. 65. Pp. 1–352.

Duellman, W. E. 1979. The herpetofauna of the Andes: Patterns of distribution, origin, differentiation, and present communities. Pp. 371–459 in W. E. Duellman, ed. The South American herpetofauna: Its origin, evolution, and dispersal. Monogr. Mus. Nat. Hist. Univ. Kansas no. 7.

Dugand, A. 1975. Serpentifauna de la llanura costera del Caribe. Caldasia 11:61–82.

Dugès, A. A. D. 1869. Catálogo de animales vertebrados observados en la república Mexicana. Naturaleza 1:137–145, erratas p. 414.

Dugès, A. A. D. 1876–77. Apuntes para la monografía de los crótalos de México. Naturaleza, Mexico 4:1–29.

Dugès, A. A. D. 1878. Programa de un curso de zoología. Guanajuato, Justo Palencia. 256 pp.

Dugès, A. A. D. 1885. Nota sobre las coralillas (*Elaps* Schneider). Naturaleza, Mexico 7:200–203.

Dugès, A. A. D. 1888. Erpetología del Valle De México. Naturaleza, Mexico, Ser. 2, 1:97–146.

Dugès, A. A. D. 1889. Un punto curioso de geografía zoológica. Naturaleza, Mexico, Ser. 2, 1:209–211.

Dugès, A. A. D. 1890. Fauna del estado de Guanajuato. Pp. 287–295 in A. L. Velasco, ed. Geografía y estadística del estado de Guanajuato. Vol. 5 of Geografía y estadística de la República Mexicana. México, D.F., Secr. Fomento.

Dugès, A. A. D. 1891. *Elaps diastema* var. *Michoacanensis* A. Dug. Naturaleza, Mexico, Ser. 2, 1:487.

Dugès, A. A. D. 1894. Lista de algunas reptiles y batracios de Tabasco y Chiapas. Naturaleza, Mexico, Ser. 2, 2:375–377.

Dugès, A. A. D. 1896. Reptiles y batracios de los E.U. Mexicanos. Naturaleza, Mexico, Ser. 2, 2:479–485.

Dugès, A. A. D. 1897. Sur l'*Heloderma horridum* Wiegm. Acta. Soc. Scient. Chili 7:113–117.

Dugès, A. A. D. 1899a. Venin de l'*Heloderma horridum* (Wiegm.). Cinquantenaire de la Société de Biologie. Vol. Jubilaire. Paris, Masson. 740 pp.

Dugès, A. A. D. 1899b. Contribución al estudio del escorpión, *Heloderma horridum*. Anu. Acad. Méx. Cienc. Exact. Fís. Nat. 5:85–91.

Dugès, A. A. D. 1901. Contribución al estudio del escorpión. Anu. Acad. Méx. Cienc. Exact. Fís. Nat. 5:85–91.

Duke, J. A. 1967. Herpetological Dietary. Bioenvironmental and radiological-safety feasibility studies, Atlantic-Pacific interoceanic canal. Columbus, Ohio, Battelle Mem. Inst. Pp. 1–35.

Duméril, A. M. C., G. Bibron, and A. Duméril. 1854. Erpétologie générale ou histoire naturelle complète des reptiles. Pp. 781–1536. Vol. 7. Paris, Librairie Encyclopédique de Roret.

Dundee, H. A., D. A. White, and V. Rico-Gray. 1986. Observations on the distribution and biology of some Yucatan Peninsula amphibians and reptiles. Bull. Maryland Herpetol. Soc. 22:37–50.

Dunkle, D. H., and H. M. Smith. 1937. Notes on some Mexican ophidians. Occas. Pap. Mus. Zool. Univ. Michigan no. 363. Pp. 1–15.

Dunn, E. R. 1919. Two new crotaline snakes from western Mexico. Proc. Biol. Soc. Washington 32:213–216.

Dunn, E. R. 1923. Some snakes from northwestern Peru. Proc. Biol. Soc. Washington 36:185–188.

Dunn, E. R. 1928. Notes on *Bothrops lansbergi* and *Bothrops ophryomegas*. Bull. Antivenin Ins. Am. 2:29–30.

Dunn, E. R. 1933. Amphibians and reptiles from El Valle de Anton, Panama. Occas. Pap. Boston Soc. Nat. Hist. 8:65–79.

Dunn, E. R. 1936. The amphibians and reptiles of the Mexican expedition of 1934. Proc. Acad. Nat. Sci. Philadelphia 88:471–477.

Dunn, E. R. 1937. Notes on some Colombian reptiles. Proc. Biol. Soc. Washington 50:11–14.

Dunn, E. R. 1939. A new pit viper from Costa Rica. Proc. Biol. Soc. Washington 52:165–166.

Dunn, E. R. 1940a. New and noteworthy herpetological material from Panama. Proc. Acad. Nat. Sci. Philadelphia 92:105–123.

Dunn, E. R. 1940b. Some aspects of herpetology in lower Central America. Trans. New York Acad. Sci. Ser. 2, 2:156–158.

Dunn, E. R. 1942. New or noteworthy snakes from Panama. Not. Nat., Philadelphia 108:1–8.

Dunn, E. R. 1944a. Los generos de anfibios y reptiles de Colombia, III. Tercera parte: Reptiles, Orden de las Serpientes. Caldasia 3:155–224.

Dunn, E. R. 1944b. Herpetology of the Bogotá area. Rev. Acad. Colomb. Cienc. Exactas Fís. Nat. 6:68–81.

Dunn, E. R. 1946. A small herpetological collection from eastern Peru. Proc. Biol. Soc. Washington 59:17–20.

Dunn, E. R. 1947. Snakes of the Lerida Farm (Chiriqui Volcano, western Panamá). Copeia 1947:153–157.

Dunn, E. R. 1949. Relative abundance of some Panamanian snakes. Ecology 30:39–57.

Dunn, E. R. 1951. Venomous reptiles of the tropics. Pp. 741–754 in G. C. Shattuck, ed. Diseases of the tropics. N.Y., Appleton-Century-Crofts. 803 pp.

Dunn, E. R., and J. R. Bailey, 1939. Snakes from the uplands of the Canal Zone and of Darien. Bull. Mus. Comp. Zool. 86:1–22.

Dunn, E. R., and J. T. Emlen, Jr. 1932. Reptiles and amphibians from Honduras. Proc. Acad. Nat. Sci. Philadelphia 84:21–32.

Dunn, E. R., and L. C. Stuart. 1951. Comments on some recent restrictions of type localities of certain South and Central American amphibians and reptiles. Copeia 1951:55–61.

Dunson, W. A., ed. 1975. The biology of sea snakes. Baltimore, Md., University Park Press. 530 pp.

Echternacht, A. A. 1973. The color pattern of *Sonora michoacanensis* (Dugès) (Serpentes, Colubridae) and its bearing on the origin of the species. Breviora 410:1–18.

Eichelbaum, H. R. 1927. Cases of snake-bite treated in Almirante Hospital, Panama, the years 1922–26, inclusive. Bull. Antivenin Inst. Am. 1:35–36.

Elton, N. W. 1948. The venomous snakes of Panama. Safety Zone, Panama C. July 1948, 1–7.

Emsley, M. 1977. Snakes, and Trinidad and Tobago. Bull. Maryland Herpetol. Soc. 13:201–304.

Englehardt, G. P. 1932. Notes on poisonous snakes in Texas. Copeia 1932:37–38.

Ernst, C. H. 1965. Fang length comparisons of American *Agkistrodon*. Trans. Kentucky Acad. Sci. 26:12–18.

Etheridge, R. 1961. Additions to the herpetological fauna of Isla Cerralvo in the Gulf of California, Mexico. Herpetologica 17:57–60.

Evans, H. E. 1947. Notes on Panamanian reptiles and amphibians. Copeia 1947:166–170.

Fernández Barrán, E., and M. A. Freiberg. 1951. Nombres vulgares de reptiles y batracios de la Argentina. Physis 20:303–319.

Ferrari-Perez, F. 1886. Catalogue of animals collected by the geographical and exploring commission of the Republic of Mexico. Part III: Reptiles and Amphibians. Pp. 182–199. Proc. U.S. Natl. Mus. 9:125–199.

Fischer, J. G. 1880. Neue Amphibien und Reptilien. Arch. Naturgesch. 46:215–227.

Fischer, J. G. 1882. Herpetologische Bemerkungen vorzugsweise uber Stücke der Sammlung des Naturhistorischen Museums in Bremen. Abh. Naturwiss. Ver. Bremen 7:225–238.

Fitch, H. S. 1960. Autecology of the copperhead. Univ. Kansas Publ. Mus. Nat. Hist. 13:85–288.

Flores Villela, O., G. Pérez-Higadera [*sic*], R. C. Vogt, and M. Palma Muñoz. 1987. Claves para los géneros y las especies de anfibios y reptiles de la región de los Tuxtlas. Mexico, D.F., Univ. Nac. Auton. Mexico. 27 pp.

Flury, A. G. 1949. Range extensions for two west Texas snakes. Copeia 1949:293.

Fonseca, F. da. 1949. Animais peçonhentos. Inst. Butantan, São Paulo. 376 pp.

Fountain, P. 1902. The great mountains and forests of South America. London, Longmans, Green, and Co. 306 pp.

Fouquette, M. J., Jr., and D. A. Rossman. 1963. Noteworthy records of Mexican amphibians and reptiles in the Florida State Museum and the Texas Natural History collection. Herpetologica 19:185–201.

Fraser, D. F. 1964. *Micrurus limbatus,* a new coral snake from Veracruz, Mexico. Copeia 1964:570–573.

Fraser, D. F. 1973. Variation in the coral snake, *Micrurus diastema.* Copeia 1973:1–17.

Freiberg, M. A. 1968. Ofidios ponzoñosos de la Argentina. Cienc. Invest. (Buenos Aires) 24:338–353.

Freiberg, M. A. 1982. Snakes of South America. Neptune, N.J., T.F.H. Publications. 189 pp.

Freiberg, M. A. 1984. El mundo de los ofidios. Buenos Aires, Ed. Albatross. 152 pp.

Frost, D., and S. Aird. 1978. Geographic distribution: *Micrurus laticollaris.* Herpetol. Rev. 9:62.

Fugler, C. M. 1960. New herpetological records for British Honduras. Texas J. Sci. 12:8–13.

Fugler, C. M., and J. R. Dixon. 1961. Notes on the herpetofauna of the El Dorado area of Sinaloa, Mexico. Publ. Mus. Michigan State Biol. Ser. 2:1–21.

Fugler, C. M., and A. B. Walls. 1978. Snakes of the Upano Valley of Amazonian Ecuador. J. Tennessee Acad. Sci. 53:81–87.

Fugler, C. M., and R. G. Webb. 1956. Distributional notes on some reptiles and amphibians from southern and central Coahuila. Herpetologica 12:167–171.

Fukada, H. 1964. A small collection of snakes of the Kyoto University expedition to the upper Amazon. Bull. Kyoto Gakugei Univ. Ser. B. Math. Nat. Sci. no. 23 Pp. 19–26.

Funk, R. S. 1965. Food of *Crotalus cerastes laterorepens* in Yuma County, Arizona. Herpetologica 21:15–17.

Funk, R. S. 1966. Notes about *Heloderma suspectum* along the western extremity of its range. Herpetologica 22:254–258.

Gadow, H. 1905. The distribution of Mexican amphibians and reptiles. Proc. Zool. Soc. London 1905:191–244.

Gadow, H. 1908. Through southern Mexico. London, Witherly and Co. 527 pp.

Gadow, H. 1910. The effect of altitude upon the distribution of Mexican amphibians and reptiles. Zool. Jahrb., Abt. Syst. 29:689–714.

Gaige, H. T. 1936. Some reptiles and amphibians from Yucatan and Campeche, Mexico. Publ. Carnegie Inst. no. 457. Pp. 289–304.

Gaige, H. T., N. Hartweg, and L. C. Stuart. 1937. Notes on a collection of amphibians and reptiles from eastern Nicaragua. Occas. Pap. Mus. Zool. Univ. Michigan no. 357. Pp. 1–8.

Gallardo, J. M. 1977. Reptiles de los alrededores de Buenos Aires. Editorial Universitaria de Buenos Aires. 213 pp.

Gallardo, J. M. 1979. Composición, distribución y origen de la herpetofauna Chaqueña. Pp. 299–307 in W. E. Duellman, ed. The South American Herpetofauna: Its origin, evolution, and dispersal. Monogr. Mus. Nat. Hist. Univ. Kansas no. 7.

Gann, T., and M. Gann. 1939. Archeological investigations in the Corozal District of British Honduras. Smithson. Inst. Bull. Bureau Am. Ethnol. 123:1–66.

García, E. 1896. Los ofidios venenosos del Cauca. Métodos empíricos y racionales empleados contra los accidentes producidos por la mordedura de esos reptiles. Cali, Colombia, Librería Colombiana. 102 pp.

García-López, R., and F. Sandner-Montilla. 1962. Estudio bioquímico y electroforético de las ponzoñas de las principales serpientes de la fam. crotalidae venezolanas y su actividad biologica en el hombre. Mem. Soc. Cienc. Nat. La Salle 22:5–33.

Garman, S. 1877 [dated 1876]. Reptiles and batrachians collected by Allen Lesley, Esq., on the Isthmus of Panama. Proc. Boston Soc. Nat. Hist. 18:402–413.

Garman, S. 1881. New and little-known reptiles and fishes in the museum collections. Bull. Mus Comp. Zool. 8:85–93.

Garman, S. 1884a [dated 1883]. The reptiles and batrachians of North America. Mem. Mus. Comp. Zool. 8:1–185.

Garman, S. 1884b. The North American reptiles and batrachians. A list of the species occurring north of the Isthmus of Tehuantepec, with references. Bull. Essex Inst. 16:1–46.

Garman, S. 1887a. Reptiles and batrachians from Texas and Mexico. Bull. Essex Inst. 19:119–138.

Garman, S. 1887b. On West Indian reptiles in the Museum of Comparative Zoology, at Cambridge, Mass. Proc. Am. Philos. Soc. 24:278–286.

Garman, S. 1891 [dated 1890]. On the "Gila monster" (*Heloderma suspectum*). Bull. Essex Inst. 22:60–69.

Garman, S. 1892a. The reptiles of the Galapagos islands from the collections of Dr. Geo. Baur. Bull. Essex Inst. 24:73–87.

Garman, S. 1892b. On reptiles collected by Dr. Geo. Baur near Guayaquil, Ecuador. Bull. Essex Inst. 24:88–95.

Garman, S. 1908. The reptiles of Easter Island. Bull. Mus. Comp. Zool. 52:1–13.

Gasc, J.-P., and M. T. Rodrigues. 1980. Liste préliminaire des serpents de la Guyane française. Bull. Mus. Natl. Hist. Nat., Paris, Ser. 4, 2:559–598.

Gates, G. O. 1956a. A record length for the Arizona coral snake. Herpetologica 12:155.

Gates, G. O. 1956b. Mating habits of the Gila monster. Herpetologica 12:184.

Gates, G. O. 1957. A study of the herpetofauna in the vicinity of Wickenburg, Maricopa County, Arizona. Trans. Kansas Acad. Sci. 60:403–418.

Gatti, C. 1955. Las culebras venenosas del Paraguay. Rev. Med. Paraguay 1:81–100.

Gehlbach, F. R. 1956. Annotated records of southwestern amphibians and reptiles. Trans. Kansas Acad. Sci. 59:364–372.

Gehlbach, F. R. 1965. Herpetology of the Zuni Mountains region, northwestern New Mexico. Proc. U.S. Natl. Mus. 116:243–332.

Gehlbach, F. R. 1972. Coral snake mimicry reconsidered: The strategy of self-mimicry. Forma et Functio 5:311–320.

Gehlbach, F. R., and B. B. Collette. 1957. A contribution to the herpetofauna of the highlands of Oaxaca and Puebla, Mexico. Herpetologica 13:227–231.

George, I. D. 1930a. Notes on the extraction of venom at the serpentarium of the Antivenin Institute at Tela, Honduras. Bull. Antivenin Inst. Am. 4:57–59.

George, I. D. 1930b. Short report of work on the snake farm at Lancetilla, Tela, Honduras. Rep. United Fruit Company Medical Department, Boston, Mass. 18:326–332.

Girard, C. F. 1858. Herpetology. United States Exploring Expedition during the years 1838, 1839, 1840, 1841, 1842, under the command of Charles Wilkes, U.S.N. 20:1–496, atlas of 32 plates. Reprint 1858. Philadelphia, J. B. Lippincott and Co.

Gliesch, R. 1925. As cobras do Estado do Rio Grande do Sul. Almanak Agric. Brasil. 1925:97–118.

Gliesch, R. 1931. A Urutu (*Lachesis-Bothrops-alternata* D. e B). Egatea—Revista da escola de engenharia de Pôrto Alegre 16:96–102.

Gloyd, H. K. 1936a. A Mexican subspecies of *Crotalus molossus* Baird and Girard. Occas. Pap. Mus. Zool. Univ. Michigan no. 325. Pp. 1–5.

Gloyd, H. K. 1936b. The subspecies of *Crotalus lepidus.* Occas. Pap. Mus. Zool. Univ. Michigan no. 337. Pp. 1–5.

Gloyd, H. K. 1936c. The status of *Crotalus unicolor* Van Lidth de Jeude and *Crotalus pulvis* Ditmars. Herpetologica 1:65–68.

Gloyd, H. K. 1937. A herpetological consideration of faunal areas in southern Arizona. Bull. Chicago Acad. Sci 5:79–136.

Gloyd, H. K. 1938. A case of poisoning from the bite of a black coral snake. Herpetologica 1:121–124.

Gloyd, H. K. 1940. The rattlesnakes, genera *Sistrurus* and *Crotalus.* A study in zoogeography and evolution. Spec. Publ. Chicago Acad. Sci. no. 4. Pp. 1–270.

Gloyd, H. K. 1948. Description of a neglected subspecies of rattlesnake from Mexico. Nat. Hist. Misc., Chicago no. 17. Pp. 1–4.

Gloyd, H. K. 1955. A review of the massasaugas, *Sistrurus catenatus,* of the southwestern United States. Bull. Chicago Acad. Sci. 10:83–98.

Gloyd, H. K. 1956. Distribution of the Mexican moccasin: A correction. Copeia 1956:259.

Gloyd, H. K. 1972. A subspecies of *Agkistrodon bilineatus* (Serpentes: Crotalidae) on the Yucatan Peninsula, México. Proc. Biol. Soc. Washington 84:327–334.

Gloyd, H. K., and R. Conant. 1943. A synopsis of the American forms of *Agkistrodon* (copperheads and moccasins). Bull. Chicago Acad. Sci. 7:147–170.

Gloyd, H. K., and C. F. Kauffeld. 1940. A new rattlesnake from Mexico. Bull. Chicago Acad. Sci. 6:11–14.

Gloyd, H. K., and H. M. Smith. 1942. Amphibians and reptiles from the Carmen Mountains, Coahuila. Bull. Chicago Acad. Sci. 6:231–235.

Golay, P. 1985. Checklist and keys to the terrestrial proteroglyphs of the World. Geneva, Switzerland, Gilbert Rey. 90 pp.

Goldman, I. 1979. The Cubeo. 2d ed. Chicago, Univ. of Illinois Press. 315 pp.

Gomes, J. F. 1913. Uma nova cobra venenosa do Brasil. Ann. Paulistas Med. Cir. (São Paulo) 1:65–67.

Gomes, J. F. 1918a. Contribuição para o conhecimento dos ophídios do Brasil. II. Ophídios do Museu Rocha (Ceará). Rev. Mus. Paulista, São Paulo. 10:503–527.

Gomes, J. F. 1918b. Contribuição para o conhecimento dos ophídios do Brasil. III (1).1.—Ophídios do Museu Paraense. Mem. Inst. Butantan 1:57–77.

Goodrich, R. L., R. W. Murphy, J. Nyhan, and M. J. Wong. 1978. Geographic distribution: *Crotalus ruber lucasensis*. Herpetol. Rev. 9:108.

Gosner, K. L. 1987. Observations on Lesser Antillean pit vipers. J. Herpetol. 21:78–80.

Grant, C., and H. M. Smith. 1959. Herptiles from San Luis Potosi. Herpetologica 15:54–56.

Gray, J. E. 1829. Synopsis generum reptilium et amphibiorum. Isis von Oken 22:187–206.

Gray, J. E. 1842. Synopsis of the species of rattle-snakes, or family of Crotalidae. Zool. Misc. Parts 2/3:47–51.

Gray, J. E. 1845. Catalogue of the specimens of lizards in the collection of the British Museum. London, Taylor and Francis. 289 pp.

Greene, H. W. 1972. Mexican reptiles in the Senckenberg Museum. Pittsburg, Penn., Carnegie Mus. 15 pp.

Greene, H. W. 1973. Defensive tail display by snakes and amphisbaenians. J. Herpetol. 7:143–161.

Greene, H. W. 1986. Natural history and evolutionary biology. Pp. 99–108 in M. E. Feder, and G. V. Lauder, eds. Predator-prey relationships: Perspectives and approaches from the study of lower vertebrates. Chicago, Univ. Chicago Press.

Greene, H. W., and J. A. Campbell. 1972. Notes on the use of caudal lures by arboreal green pit vipers. Herpetologica 28:32–34.

Greene, H. W., and R. W. McDiarmid. 1981. Coral snake mimicry: Does it occur? Science, Washington, D.C. 213:1207–1212.

Greene, H. W., and W. F. Pyburn. 1973. Comments on aposematism and mimicry among coral snakes. Biologist 55: 144–148.

Greene, H. W., and M. A. Santana. 1983. Field studies of hunting behavior by bushmasters. Am. Zool. 23:897.

Greene, H. W., and R. L. Seib. 1983. *Micrurus nigrocinctus* (corál, coral snake, coralillo). Pp. 406–408 in D. H. Janzen, ed. Costa Rican Natural History. Chicago, Univ. of Chicago Press.

Griffin, L. E. 1916. A catalog of the ophidia from South America at present (June 1916) contained in the Carnegie Museum with descriptions of some new species. Mem. Carnegie Mus. 7:163–228.

Grinnell, J., and C. L. Camp. 1917. A distributional list of the amphibians and reptiles of California. Univ. California Publ. Zool. 17:127–208.

Grocott, R. G., and G. G. Sadler. 1958. The poisonous snakes of Panama. Mt. Hope, Canal Zone, Panama Canal Printing Plant. 38 pp.

Groombridge, B. 1986. Comments on the *M. pterygoideus glandulae* of crotaline snakes (Reptilia: Viperidae). Herpetologica 42:449–457.

Grzimek, B., ed. 1975. Grzimek's animal life encyclopedia. Vol. 6: Reptiles. N.Y., Van Nostrand Reinhold. 589 pp.

Gumilla, S. J. 1741. El Orinoco ilustrado, historia natural, civil, y geográfica de este gran Río y de sus caudalosas vertientes. Vols. 1–2. Madrid, Manuel Fernández. 580 pp.

Günther, A. C. L. G. 1859. On the genus *Elaps* of Wagler. Proc. Zool. Soc. London 1859:79–89.

Günther, A. C. L. G. 1861. Account of the reptiles sent by Dr. Wucherer from Bahia. Proc. Zool. Soc. London 1861:12–18.

Günther, A. C. L. G. 1863. Third account of the snakes in the collection of the British Museum. Ann. Mag. Nat. Hist. Ser. 3, 12:348–365.

Günther, A. C. L. G. 1868. Sixth account of new species of snakes in the collection of the British Museum. Ann. Mag. Nat. Hist. Ser. 4, 1:413–429.

Günther, A. C. L. G. 1895–1902. Biologia Centrali-Americana. Reptilia and Batrachia. London, Porter. 326 pp.

Gütiérrez, J. M., and R. Bolaños. 1979. Cariotipos de los principales serpientes coral (Elapidae: *Micrurus*) de Costa Rica. Rev. Biol. Tropical 27:57–73.

Gutiérrez, J. M., and R. Bolaños. 1980. Karyotype of the yellow-bellied sea snake, *Pelamis platurus*. J. Herpetol. 14:161–165.

Gutiérrez, J. M., and R. Bolaños. 1981. Polimorfismo cromosómico intraespecífico en la serpiente de coral *Micrurus nigrocinctus* (Ophidia: Elapidae). Rev. Biol. Tropical 29: 115–122.

Gutiérrez, J. M., F. Chaves, and R. Bolaños. 1980. Estudio comparativo de venenos de ejemplares recién nacidos y adultos de *Bothrops asper*. Rev. Biol. Tropical 28:311–351.

Gutiérrez, J. M., A. Solórzano, L. Cerdas, and J. P. Vannini. 1988. Karyotypes of five species of coral snakes (*Micrurus*). J. Herpetol. 22:109–112.

Gutiérrez, J. M., R. T. Taylor, and R. Bolaños. 1979. Cariotipos de diez especies costarricenses de la familia Viperidae. Rev. Biol. Tropical 27:309–319.

Hadley, W. F., and C. Gans. 1972. Convergent ontogenetic change of color pattern in *Elaphe climacophora* (Colubridae: Reptilia). J. Herpetol. 6:75–78.

Hagmann, G. 1909. Die Reptilien der Insel Mexiana, Amazonestrom. Zool. Jahrb., Abt. Syst. 28:473–504.

Hahn, D. E. 1971. Noteworthy herpetological records from Honduras. Herpetol. Rev. 3:111–112.

Hahn, D. E., and C. J. May. 1972. Noteworthy Arizona herpetofaunal records. Herpetol. Rev. 4:91–92.

Hall, E. R., and W. W. Dalquest. 1963. The mammals of Veracruz. Univ. Kansas Publ. Mus. Nat. Hist. 14:165–362.

Haller, R. 1971. The diamondback rattlesnakes. Herpetology 5:1–34.

Hallowell, E. 1845. Description of reptiles from South America, supposed to be new. Proc. Acad. Nat. Sci. Philadelphia 2:241–247.

Hallowell, E. 1852. Descriptions of new species of reptiles inhabiting North America. Proc. Acad. Nat. Sci. Philadelphia 6:177–182.

Hallowell, E. 1854a. Descriptions of new reptiles from California. Proc. Acad. Nat. Sci. Philadelphia 7:91–97.

Hallowell, E. 1854b. Remarks on the geographical distribution of reptiles, with descriptions of several species supposed to be new, and corrections of former papers. Proc. Acad. Nat. Sci. Philadelphia 7:98–105.

Hallowell, E. 1861. Report upon the reptilia of the north Pacific exploring expedition, under command of Capt. John Rogers, U.S.N. Proc. Acad. Nat. Sci. Philadelphia 12:480–510.

Halstead, B. W., ed. 1970. Poisonous and venomous marine animals of the world. Vol. 3. Washington, D.C., G.P.O. 1006 pp.

Hardy, L. M., and R. W. McDiarmid. 1969. The amphibians and reptiles of Sinaloa, Mexico. Univ. Kansas Publ. Mus. Nat. Hist. 18:39–252.

Harris, H. S., Jr. 1974. The New Mexican ridge-nosed rattlesnake. Natl. Parks Conserv. Mag. 48:22–24.

Harris, H. S., Jr., and R. S. Simmons. 1972a. A checklist of the rattlesnakes (*Crotalus durissus* group) of South America. Bull. Maryland Herpetol. Soc. 8:27–32.

Harris, H. S., Jr., and R. S. Simmons. 1972b. Keys to the Neotropical species and subspecies of the *Crotalus durissus* group. Bull. Maryland Herpetol. Soc. 8:33–40.

Harris, H. S., Jr., and R. S. Simmons. 1976. The paleogeography and evolution of *Crotalus willardi*, with a formal description of a new subspecies from New Mexico, United States. Bull. Maryland Herpetol. Soc. 12:1–22.

Harris, H. S., Jr., and R. S. Simmons. 1978a [dated 1976/77]. A new subspecies of *Crotalus durissus* (Serpentes: Crotalidae) from the Rupununi Savanna of southwestern Guyana. Mem. Inst. Butantan 40/41:305–311.

Harris, H. S., Jr., and R. S. Simmons. 1978b. A preliminary account of the rattlesnakes with the descriptions of four new subspecies. Bull. Maryland Herpetol. Soc. 14:105–211.

Hartman, F. A. 1911. Description of a little-known rattlesnake, *Crotalus willardi*, from Arizona. Proc. U.S. Natl. Mus. 39:569–570.

Hartnett, W. G. 1931. Poisonous snake bite: Etiology and treatment with case report. Ohio State Med. J. 27:636–639.

Hartweg, N., and J. A. Oliver. 1938. A contribution to the herpetology of the Isthmus of Tehuantepec. III. Three new snakes from the Pacific slope. Occas. Pap. Mus. Zool. Michigan no. 390. Pp. 1–9.

Hartweg, N., and J. A. Oliver. 1940. A contribution to the herpetology of the Isthmus of Tehuantepec. IV. Misc. Pub. Mus. Zool. Univ. Michigan no. 47. Pp. 1–31.

Hatt, R. T. 1930. Collectors' days and nights in Yucatán. Nat. Hist., New York 30:617–626.

Heatwole, H. 1987. Sea snakes. Kensington, New South Wales Univ. Press. 85 pp.

Hecht, M. K., C. Kropach, and B. M. Hecht. 1974. Distribution of the yellow-bellied sea snake, *Pelamis platurus*, and its significance in relation to the fossil record. Herpetologica 30:387–396.

Henderson, R. W. 1978. Notes on *Agkistrodon bilineatus* (Reptilia, Serpentes, Viperidae) in Belize. J. Herpetol. 12:412–413.

Henderson, R. W., and L. G. Hoevers. 1975. A checklist and key to the amphibians and reptiles of Belize, Central America. Milwaukee Public Mus. Contrib. Biol. Geol. 5:1–63.

Henderson, R. W., M. N. Nickerson, and S. Ketcham. 1976. Short term movements of the snakes *Chironius carinatus, Helicops angulatus*, and *Bothrops atrox* in Amazonian Peru. Herpetologica 32:304–310.

Hensley, M. M. 1949. Mammal diet of *Heloderma*. Herpetologica 5:152.

Hensley, M. M. 1950. Results of a herpetological reconnaissance in extreme southwestern Arizona and adjacent Sonora, with a description of a new subspecies of the Sonoran whipsnake, *Masticophis bilineatus*. Trans. Kansas Acad. Sci. 53:270–288.

Hensley, M. M., and P. W. Smith. 1962. Noteworthy herpetological records from the Mexican states of Hidalgo and Tabasco. Herpetologica 18:70–71.

Herrera, A. L. 1890. Notas acerca de los vertebrados del Valle de México. Naturaleza, Mexico, Ser. 2, 1:299–342.

Herrera, A. L. 1891. El clima del Valle de México y la biología de los vertebrados. Part 1. Naturaleza, Mexico, Ser. 2, 2:38–86.

Herrera, A. L. 1899. Sinonimia vulgar y científica de los principales vertebrados mexicanos. Mexico, Secr. Fomento. 31 pp.

Herrera, A. L. 1904. Catálogo de la colección de reptiles y batracios del Museo Nacional. 2d ed. Mexico, D.F., Museo Nacional. 65 pp.

Heyer, W. R. 1967. A herpetofaunal study of an ecological transect through the Cordillera de Tilaran, Costa Rica. Copeia 1967:259–271.

Hidalgo, H. 1980. Occurrence of *Pelamis platurus* (Linnaeus) in El Salvador. Herpetol. Rev. 11:117.

Higgins, S. B. 1870. Culebras i reptiles venenosos. Bogotá, Imprenta de Gaitán. 167 pp.

Hirth, H. F. 1964. Observations of the fer-de-lance, *Bothrops atrox*, in coastal Costa Rica. Copeia 1964:453–454.

Hoard, R. S. 1939. New Lower California reptile records. J. Ent. Zool. 31:4–5.

Hoevers, L. 1967. Herpetological collections from the Atkinson-Maduni-Laluni area, east Demerara, Guyana. TIMEHRI 43:34–50.

Hoevers, L. G., and R. W. Henderson. 1974. Additions to the herpetofauna of Belize (British Honduras). Milwaukee Public Mus. Contrib. Biol. Geol. 2:1–6.

Hoffstetter, R. 1962. Revue des récentes acquisitions concernant l'histoire et la systématique des squamates. Colloq. Int. Cent. Nat. Rech. Sci. no. 104. Pp. 243–279.

Hoge, A. R. 1948a [dated 1947]. Notas erpetológicas. 3. Uma nova espécie de *Trimeresurus*. Mem. Inst. Butantan 20:193–202.

Hoge, A. R. 1948b. Notas erpetológicas 7. Sôbre a ocorrência de *Trimeresurus hyoprora* (Amaral) no Brasil. Bol. Mus. Para. Emilio Goeldi 10:325–329.

Hoge, A. R. 1950. Notas erpetológicas. 7. Fauna erpetológica da Ilha da Queimada Grande. Mem. Inst. Butantan 22:151–172.

Hoge, A. R. 1953a [dated 1952]. Notas erpetológicas. 1. Contribuição ao conhecimento dos ofídios do Brasil central. Mem. Inst. Butantan 24:179–214.

Hoge, A. R. 1953b [dated 1952]. Notas erpetológicas. 2a. Contribuição ao conhecimento dos ofídios do Brasil central. Mem. Inst. Butantan 24:215–223.

Hoge, A. R. 1953c [dated 1952]. Snakes from the Uaupés Region. Mem. Inst. Butantan 24:225–230.

Hoge, A. R. 1953d [dated 1952]. Notas erpetológicas. Revalidação de *Bothrops lanceolata* (Lacépede). Mem. Inst. Butantan 24:231–236.

Hoge, A. R. 1953e [dated 1952]. Notas erpetológicas. Anomalia na lepidose e pigmentação das escamas dorsais em *B. jararaca* e *B. alternata*. Mem. Inst. Butantan 24:237–240.

Hoge, A. R. 1954 [dated 1953]. A new *Bothrops* from Brazil—*Bothrops brazili*, sp. nov. Mem. Inst. Butantan 25:15–21.

Hoge, A. R. 1956 [dated 1955]. Uma nova espécie de *Micrurus* (Serpentes—Elapidae) do Brasil. Mem. Inst. Butantan 27: 67–72.

Hoge, A. R. 1958. Três notas sôbre serpentes brasileiras. I. Sôbre à posição genérica de *Coluber bicinctus* Hermann, 1804 e *Xenodon gigas* Duméril, 1853 (Colubridae). II. Sôbre a posição sistemática de *Enicognathus joberti* Sauvage, 1884 (Colubridae). III. Dimorfismo sexual em *Micrurus s. surinamensis* (Cuvier, 1817) (Elapidae). Pap. Avulsos Zool., São Paulo 13:221–224.

Hoge, A. R. 1959 [dated 1957/58]. Note sur la position systematique de *Trigonocephalus (Bothrops) pubescens* Cope 1869. Mem. Inst. Butantan 28:83–84.

Hoge, A. R. 1964 [dated 1960/62]. Serpentes da Fundação "Surinaam Museum." Mem. Inst. Butantan 30:51–64.

Hoge, A. R. 1966 [dated 1965]. Preliminary account on Neotropical Crotalinae (Serpentes, Viperidae). Mem. Inst. Butantan 32:109–184.

Hoge, A. R. 1967. Serpentes do Território Federal do Amapá. Atas Simp. Biota Amaz. 5:217–223.

Hoge, A. R. 1979. Distribuição e dispersão de *Crotalus durissus*. An. Acad. Brasil. Cienc. 51:570–571.

Hoge, A. R., and H. E. Belluomini. 1959 [dated 1957/58]. Uma nova espécie de *Bothrops* do Brasil (Serpentes). Mem. Inst. Butantan 28:195–206.

Hoge, A. R., and H. E. Belluomini. 1964 [dated 1960/62]. Notas sôbre *Bothrops fonsecai* Hoge e Belluomini, *Bothrops alternatus* Duméril, Bibron et Duméril e *Bothrops cotiara* Gomes. Mem. Inst. Butantan 30:97–102.

Hoge, A. R., H. E. Belluomini, and W. Fernandes. 1977 [dated 1976/77]. Variação do número de placas ventrais de *Bothrops jararaca* em função dos climas. (Viperidae, Crotalinae). Mem. Inst. Butantan 40/41:11–17.

Hoge, A. R., H. Belluomini, G. Schreiber, and A. M. Penha. 1960 [dated 1959]. Sexual abnormalities in *Bothrops insularis* (Amaral) 1921. Mem. Inst. Butantan 29:17–88.

Hoge, A. R., C. L. Cordeiro, and S. A. R. W. D. L. Romano. 1976. A new species of *Micrurus* from Brazil (Serpentes Elapidae). Soc. Bras. Prog. Cienc. 28:417–418.

Hoge, A. R., C. L. Cordeiro, and S. A. R. W. D. L. Romano. 1977 [dated 1976/77]. Redescription of *Micrurus donosoi* Hoge, Cordeiro et Romano (Serpentes: Elapinae). Mem. Inst. Butantan 40/41:71–73.

Hoge, A. R., and A. R. Lancini. 1960 [dated 1959]. Nota sôbre *Micrurus surinamensis nattereri* Schmidt e *Micrurus pyrrhocryptus* Cope. Mem. Inst. Butantan 29:9–13.

Hoge, A. R., and A. R. Lancini. 1962. Sinopsis de las serpientes venenosas de Venezuela. Publ. Ocas. Mus. Cienc. Nat. Caracas Zool. 1:1–24.

Hoge, A. R., and S. A. R. W. D. L. Romano. 1966 [dated 1965]. *Leptomicrurus* in Brasil (Serpentes-Elapidae). Mem. Inst. Butantan 32:1–8.

Hoge, A. R., and S. A. R. W. D. L. Romano. 1969. Espécies registradas para o Brasil (Serpentes). Cienc. Cult., Suppl. 21:454.

Hoge, A. R., and S. A. R. W. D. L. Romano. 1971a. Neotropical pit vipers, sea snakes, and coral snakes. Pp. 211–293 in W. Bucherl and E. Buckley, eds. Venomous animals and their venoms. Vol. 2: Venomous vertebrates. N.Y., Academic Press.

Hoge, A. R., and S. A. R. W. D. L. Romano. 1971b. *Micrurus hemprichii hemprichii* recorded for Brazil. Mem. Inst. Butantan 35:107–109.

Hoge, A. R., and S. A. R. W. D. L. Romano. 1973 [dated 1972]. Sinopse das serpentes peçonhentas do Brasil. Serpentes, Elapidae e Viperidae. Mem. Inst. Butantan 36:109–207.

Hoge, A. R., and S. A. R. W. D. L. Romano-Hoge. 1981a [dated 1978/79]. Poisonous snakes of the world. Part 1: Check list of the pit vipers, Viperoidea, Viperidae, Crotalinae. Mem. Inst. Butantan 42/43:179–309.

Hoge, A. R., and S. A. R. W. D. L. Romano-Hoge. 1981b [dated 1978/79]. Sinopse das serpentes peçonhentas do Brasil. Mem. Inst. Butantan 42/43:373–496.

Hoge, A. R., S. A. R. W. D. L. Romano, and C. L. Cordeiro. 1977 [dated 1976/77]. Contribuição ao conhecimento das serpentes do Maranhão, Brasil [Serpentes: Boidae, Colubridae e Viperidae]. Mem. Inst. Butantan 40/41:37–52.

Hoge, A. R., S. A. R. W. D. L. Romano, P. A. Federsoni-Junior, and C. L. S. Cordeiro. 1975 [dated 1974]. Nota prévia. Lista das espécies de serpentes coletadas na região da usina hidroelétrica de Ilha Solteira-Brasil. Mem. Inst. Butantan 38:167–178.

Hoge, A. R., C. R. Russo, M. C. Santos, and M. F. D. Furtado. 1981 [dated 1978/79]. Snakes collected by "Projeto Rondon XXII" to Piauí, Brazil. Mem. Inst. Butantan 42/43:87–94.

Hoge, A. R., N. P. Santos, C. Heitor, L. A. Lopes, and I. M. de Souza. 1973 [dated 1972]. Serpentes coletadas pelo projeto Rondon VII em Iauareté, Brasil. Mem. Inst. Butantan 36:221–232.

Holdridge, L. R. 1964. Life zone ecology. Tropical Science Center. San José, Costa Rica, 124 pp.

Hoogmoed, M. S. 1979. The Herpetofauna of the Guianan Region. Pp. 241–279 in W. E. Duellman, ed. The South American Herpetofauna: Its origin, evolution, and dispersal. Monogr. Mus. Nat. Hist. Univ. Kansas, no. 7.

Hoogmoed, M. S. 1983 [dated 1982]. Snakes of the Guianan region. Mem. Inst. Butantan 46:219–254.

Hoogmoed, M. S., and U. Gruber. 1983. Spix and Wagler type specimens of reptiles and amphibians in the Natural History Musea in Munich (Germany) and Leiden (The Netherlands). Spixiana, Suppl. 9:319–415.

Hulse, A. C. 1973. Herpetofauna of the Fort Apache Indian reservation, east central Arizona. J. Herpetol. 7:275–282.

Hummelinck, P. W. 1940. A survey of the mammals, lizards and mollusks. Pp. 1–129 in P. W. Hummelinck, ed. Studies on the fauna of Curaçao, Aruba, Bonaire and the Venezuelan islands. Utrecht, N.V. Drukkerij P. Den Boer nos. 1–3.

Humphrey, R. R. 1936. Notes on altitudinal distribution of rattlesnakes. Ecology 17:328–329.

Ihering, R. von. 1911 [dated 1910]. As cobras do Brazil. Primeira parte. Rev. Mus. Paulista, São Paulo 8:273–379.

Jacob, J. S., and J. S. Altenbach. 1977. Sexual color dimorphism in *Crotalus lepidus klauberi* Gloyd (Reptilia, Serpentes, Viperidae), J. Herpetol. 11:81–84.

Jacob, J. S., S. R. Williams, and R. P. Reynolds. 1987. Reproductive activity of male *Crotalus atrox* and *C. scutulatus* (Reptilia: Viperidae) in northeastern Chihuahua, Mexico. Southwest Nat. 32:273–276.

Jameson, D. L., and A. G. Flury. 1949. The reptiles and amphibians of the Sierra Vieja range of southwestern Texas. Texas J. Sci. 1:54–77.

Jan, G. 1858. Plan d'une iconographie descriptive des ophidiens et description sommaire de nouvelles espèces de serpents. Rev. Mag. Zool., Paris 2:438–449, 514–527.

Jan, G. 1859a. Plan d'une iconographie descriptive des ophidiens et description sommaire de nouvelles espèces de serpents. Rev. Mag. Zool., Paris 10:122–130, 148–157.

Jan, G. 1859b. Spix' Serpentes brasilienses beurtheilt nach Autopsie der original Exemplare und auf die Nomenclatur von Dumeril und Bibron zurückgeführt. Arch. Naturg esch. 25:272–275.

Jan, G. 1863. Elenco sistematico degli ofidi descritti e disegnati per l'iconografia generale. Milan, A. Lombardi. 143 pp.

Jan, G., and F. Sordelli. 1870–1881. Iconographie générale des ophidiens. Vol. 3, Livraisons 35–50, Milan, chez les auteurs.

Jansen, E., I. Kristensen, J. Maduro, V. Rooze, and R. Stanley, eds. 1982. Discover Aruba's wildlife. STINAPA 26:1–61.

Jiménez-Porras, J. M. 1964. Intraspecific variations in composition of venom of the jumping viper, *Bothrops nummifera*. Toxicon 2:187–195.

Jiménez-Porras, J. M. 1967. Differentiation between *Bothrops nummifer* and *Bothrops picadoi* by means of the biochemical properties of their venoms. Pp. 307–321 in Animal Toxins. Oxford, Pergamon Press.

Johnson, J. D. 1974 [dated 1973]. New records of reptiles and amphibians from Chiapas, Mexico. Trans. Kansas Acad. Sci. 76:223–224.

Johnson, J. D., and J. R. Dixon. 1984. Taxonomic status of the Venezuelan macagua, *Bothrops colombiensis*. J. Herpetol. 18:329–332.

Johnson, M. L. 1952. Herpetological notes from north-eastern Brazil. Copeia 1952:283–284.

Jones, L. L. C. 1981. Geographic distribution: *Crotalus viridis helleri*. Herpetol. Rev. 12:65.

Juliá-Zertuche, J. 1983 [dated 1982]. Una nueva subespecie de víbora de cascabel pigmea de la Sierra de Sinaloa. Resumenes del Sexto Congreso Nacional de Zoología, Mazatlán, Sinaloa, México: no pagination (1 page).

Juliá-Zertuche, J., and C. H. Treviño. 1978. Una nueva subespecie de *Crotalus lepidus* encontrada en Nuevo León. Resumenes del Segundo Congreso Nacional de Zoología, Monterrey, Nuevo León, México: 60.

Juliá-Zertuche, J., and M. Varela-J. 1978. Una *Bothrops* de México, nueva para la ciéncia. Mem. Primer Congreso Nacional Zool., Escuela Nac. Agric. (Univ. Auton. Chapingo) 1977: 209–210.

Kaiser, E., and H. Michl. 1971. Chemistry, biochemistry, pharmacology and toxicology of *Bothrops* and *Lachesis*. Pp. 307–318 in W. Bucherl and E. Buckley, eds. Venomous animals and their venoms, Vol. 2: Venomous Vertebrates. N.Y., Academic Press.

Kauffeld, C. F. 1943. Field notes on some Arizona reptiles and amphibians. Am. Midl. Nat. 29:342–359.

Kauffeld, C. F. 1964. Coronado Island rattlesnake. Animaland 17:2–4.

Kauffeld, C. F., and H. K. Gloyd. 1939. Notes on the Aruba rattlesnake, *Crotalus unicolor*. Herpetologica 1:156–160.

Kauffeld, I. 1940. A glimpse into Mexico. News Bull. Staten Island Zool. Soc. 7:3–4.

Kaup, J. J. 1865. Einige Nachtrage zur Gattung *Heloderma horridum* Wiegm. Arch. Naturgesch. 31:33–40.

Kempff-Mercado, N. 1975. Ofidios de Bolivia. La Paz, Acad. Nac. Cienc. Bolivia. 46 pp.

Kennicott, R. 1860. Descriptions of new species of North American serpents in the museum of the Smithsonian Institution, Washington. Proc. Acad. Nat. Sci. Philadelphia 12:328–338.

Kennicott, R. 1861. On three new forms of rattlesnakes. Proc. Acad. Nat. Sci. Philadelphia 13:204–208.

Klappenbach, M. A., and B. Orejas-Miranda. 1969. Anfibios y Reptiles. Nuestra Tierra, Montevideo no. 11. 68 pp.

Klauber, L. M. 1927. Some observations on the rattlesnakes of the extreme southwest. Bull. Antivenin Inst. Am. 1:7–21.

Klauber, L. M. 1930a. Differential characteristics of the southwestern rattlesnakes allied to *Crotalus atrox*. Bull. Zool. Soc. San Diego no. 6. Pp. 1–72.

Klauber, L. M. 1930b. New and renamed subspecies of *Crotalus confluentus*. Say, with remarks on related species. Trans. San Diego Soc. Nat. Hist. 6:95–144.

Klauber, L. M. 1931a. A statistical survey of the snakes of the southern border of California. Bull. Zool. Soc. San Diego no. 8. Pp. 1–93.

Klauber, L. M. 1931b. *Crotalus tigris* and *Crotalus enyo*, two little known rattlesnakes of the southwest. Trans. San Diego Soc. Nat. Hist. 6:353–370.

Klauber, L. M. 1936a. *Crotalus mitchelli*, the speckled rattlesnake. Trans. San Diego Soc. Nat. Hist. 8:149–184.

Klauber, L. M. 1936b. Key to the rattlesnakes with summary of characteristics. Trans. San Diego Soc. Nat. Hist. 8:185–276.

Klauber, L. M. 1938. A statistical study of the rattlesnakes. V. Head dimensions. Occas. Pap. San Diego Soc. Nat. Hist. 4:1–53.

Klauber, L. M. 1940a. Notes from a herpetological diary, II. Copeia 1940:15–18.

Klauber, L. M. 1940b. [Review of] The rattlesnakes, genera *Sistrurus* and *Crotalus*: A study in zoogeography and evolution. Copeia 1940:206–207.

Klauber, L. M. 1940c. A statistical study of the rattlesnakes. VII. The rattle. Occas. Pap. San Diego Soc. Nat. Hist. no. 6. Pp. 1–62.

Klauber, L. M. 1941. A new species of rattlesnake from Venezuela. Trans. San Diego Soc. Nat. Hist. 9:333–336.

Klauber, L. M. 1944. The sidewinder, *Crotalus cerastes*, with a description of a new subspecies. Trans. San Diego Soc. Nat. Hist. 10:91–126.

Klauber, L. M. 1949a. The relationship of *Crotalus ruber* and *Crotalus lucasensis*. Trans. San Diego Soc. Nat. Hist. 11:57–60.

Klauber, L. M. 1949b. Some new and revived subspecies of rattlesnakes. Trans. San Diego Soc. Nat. Hist. 11:61–116.

Klauber, L. M. 1949c. The subspecies of the ridge-nosed rattlesnake, *Crotalus willardi*. Trans. San Diego Soc. Nat. Hist. 11:121–140.

Klauber, L. M. 1952. Taxonomic studies of the rattlesnakes of mainland Mexico. Bull. Zool. Soc. San Diego no. 26. Pp. 1–143.

Klauber, L. M. 1963. A new insular subspecies of the speckled rattlesnake. Trans. San Diego Soc. Nat. Hist. 13:73–80.

Klauber, L. M. 1971. Classification, distribution, and biology of the venomous snakes of northern Mexico, the United States, and Canada: *Crotalus* and *Sistrurus*. Pp. 115–156 in W. Bucherl and E. Buckley, eds. Venomous animals and their venoms. Vol. 2: Venomous vertebrates. N.Y., Academic Press.

Klauber, L. M. 1972. Rattlesnakes: Their habits, life histories and influence on mankind. 2d ed. 2 vols. Berkeley and Los Angeles, Univ. California Press. 1533 pp.

Klawe, W. L. 1964. Food of the black and yellow sea snake, *Pelamis platurus* from Ecuadorian coastal waters. Copeia 1964:712–713.

Klemmer, K. 1963. Liste der rezenten Giftschlangen: Elapidae, Hydropheidae, Viperidae und Crotalidae. Pp. 255–264 in Die Giftschlangen der Erde. Marburg, N. G. Elwert Universitäts-und Verlags-Buchhandlung.

Knopf, G. N., and D. W. Tinkle. 1961. The distribution and habits of *Sistrurus catenatus* in northwest Texas. Herpetologica 17:126–131.

Koslowsky, J. 1895. Batracios y reptiles de Rioja y Catamarca (Republica Argentina) recogidos durante los meses de Febrero a Mayo de 1895 (expedición del director del museo). Rev. Mus. La Plata 6:357–370.

Koslowsky, J. 1898. Ofidios de Mato-Grosso (Brasil). Rev. Mus. La Plata 8:3–32.

Koster, W. J. 1951. The distribution of the Gila monster in New Mexico. Herpetologica 7:97–101.

Krochmal, L., and P. C. Anderson. 1976. Copperhead bites: Update on therapy. Missouri Med. 73:169–172, 178.

Kropach, C. 1971a. Sea snake (*Pelamis platurus*) aggregations on slicks in Panama. Herpetologica 27:131–135.

Kropach, C. 1971b. Another color variety of the sea snake *Pelamis platurus* from Panama Bay. Herpetologica 27:326–327.

Kropach, C. 1972. *Pelamis platurus* as a potential colonizer of the Caribbean Sea. Bull. Biol. Soc. Washington 2:267–269.

Kropach, C. 1975. The yellow bellied sea snake, *Pelamis*, in the eastern Pacific. Pp. 185–213 in W. A. Dunson, ed. The biology of sea-snakes. Baltimore, Md. Univ. Park Press.

Lacerda, J. B. 1884. Leçons sur le venin des serpents du Brésil et sur la méthode de traitement des morsures venimeuses par le permanganate de potasse. Rio de Janeiro, Lombaerts & C. 194 pp.

Lalung, H. de. 1934. Le serpent de la Martinique, sa légende, ses moeurs, ses ennemis: Comment les caraibes et les nègres soignaient ses piqûres. Paris, Laboratories Corbiere. 77 pp.

Lancini, A. R. 1962a. Una nueva especie de serpiente coral (Serpentes: Elapidae) del Peru. Publ. Ocas. Mus. Cienc. Nat. Caracas Zool. no. 2. 3 pp.

Lancini, A. R. 1962b. Un cambio de nombre para una serpiente coral (Elapidae: *Micrurus*) del Peru. Publ. Ocas. Mus. Cienc. Nat. Caracas Zool. no. 3. 1 p.

Lancini, A. R. 1962c. Contribución al conocimiento de los ofidios del cordon litoral. Los ofidios de Curupao, Estado Miranda (Venezuela). Acta Biol. Venezuelica 3:161–172.

Lancini, A. R. 1962d. Notas taxonomicas sobre una pequeña colección de serpientes del Río Palmar, Estado Zulia (Venezuela). Acta Biol. Venezuelica 3:195–200.

Lancini, A. R. 1967 [dated 1966]. *Crotalus vegrandis* Klauber. Redescripción y distribución. Mem. Inst. Butantan 33:725–734.

Lancini, A. R. 1970. Los ofidios. Oficina central de información (Venezuela). 21 pp.

Lancini, A. R. 1978. Un nuevo record de serpiente "Mapanare" para Venezuela. Natura, Caracas 65:16–17.

Lancini, A. R. 1979. Serpientes de Venezuela. Caracas, Edit. Ernesto Armitano. 262 pp.

Lancini V., A. R. 1983 [dated 1982]. Serpientes de Venezuela: Distribución geográfica y altitudinal de generos de serpientes en Venezuela. Mem. Inst. Butantan 46:95–103.

Landreth, H. F. 1976. Orientation and behavior of the rattlesnake, *Crotalus atrox*. Copeia 1976:26–31.

Landy, M. J., D. A. Langebartel, E. O. Moll, and H. M. Smith. 1966. A collection of snakes from Volcán Tacaná, Chiapas, Mexico. J. Ohio Herpetol. Soc. 5:93–101.

Langebartel, D. A., and H. M. Smith. 1954. Summary of the Norris collection of reptiles and amphibians from Sonora, Mexico. Herpetologica 10:125–136.

Laurent, R. F., and E. M. Teran. 1981. Lista de anfibios y reptiles de la Provincia de Tucumán. Fund. Miguel Lillo, Misc. 71:1–15.

Laurenti, J. N. 1768. Specimen medicum exhibens Synopsin Reptilium emendatum cum experimentis circa venena et antidota reptilium austriacorum. Vienna, Joan. Thom. Trattnern. 214 pp.

Lazell, J. D., Jr. 1964. The lesser Antillean representatives of *Bothrops* and *Constrictor*. Bull. Mus. Comp. Zool. 132:245–273.

Lee, J. C. 1980. An ecogeographic analysis of the herpetofauna of the Yucatan Peninsula. Misc. Publ. Mus. Nat. Hist. Univ. Kansas no. 67. Pp. 1–75.

Leloup, P. 1975. Observations sur la reproduction de *Bothrops moojeni* Hoge en captivite. Acta. Zool. Pathol. Antverp. no. 62. Pp. 173–201.

Lema, T. 1960a. Sôbre a espécie *Bothrops cotiara* (Gomes 1913) e sua ocorrência no estado do Rio Grande do Sul (Serpentes: Crotalidae). Iheringia, Zool. 13:6–10.

Lema, T. 1960b. Notas sôbre os répteis do estado do Rio Grande do Sul, Brasil. Notas V–VIII. Iheringia, Zool. 13:1–36.

Lema, T. 1962. Sôbre a espécie *Bothrops itapetiningae* (Boulenger, 1907) e sua ocorrência no Estado do Rio Grande do Sul, Brasil (Serpentes, Crotalidae). Iheringia, Zool. 21:1–12.

Lema, T. 1971a. Análise geográfica dos répteis do Río Grande do Sul. Arq. Mus. Nac., Rio de Janeiro 54:61–62.

Lema, T. 1971b. Serpentes peçonhentas do Rio Grande do Sul. Iheringia, Divulg. 1:25–32.

Lema, T. 1972. Sôbre *Micrurus putumayensis* Lancini, 1962 e sua ocorrência no Brasil—(Serpentes, Elapidae). Iheringia, Zool. 41:35–58.

Lema, T. 1983 [dated 1982]. Fauna de serpentes da província pampeana e inter-relações com as províncias limitrofes. Mem. Inst. Butantan 46:173–182.

Lema, T., and A. C. P. Azevedo. 1969. Ocorrência de *Micrurus decoratus* (Jan) no Rio Grande do Sul, Brasil, (Serpentes, Elapidae). Iheringia, Zool. 37:113–117.

Lema, T., and M. E. Fabián-Beurmann. 1977. Levantamento preliminar dos répteis da região da fronteira Brasil-Uruguai. Iheringia, Zool. 50:61–92.

Lema, T., M. E. Fabián-Beurmann, M. Leitão de Araujo, M. L. M. Alves, and M. I. Vieira. 1980. Lista de répteis encontrados na região da Grande Pôrto Alegre, Estado do Río Grande do Sul, Brasil. Iheringia, Zool. 55:27–36.

Lema, T., and M. Leitão de Araujo. 1980. Sôbre *Bothrops jararacussu* Lacerda, 1884 do extremo sul do Brasil e sua ocorrência no Estado do Rio Grande do Sul (Ophidia, Viperidae). Iheringia, Zool. 56:63–70.

León, N. 1889. Nombres de animales en Tarasco y Castellano, con su correspondiente clasificación científica. An. Mus. Michoacana 2:186–192.

Leopold, A. S. 1967. Grizzlies of the Sierra del Nido. Pacific Disc. 20:30–32.

Lescure, J., and J. P. Gasc. 1986. Partage de l'espace forestier par les amphibiens et les reptiles en Amazonie du nord-ouest. Caldasia 15:707–723.

Leviton, A. E. 1953. Catalogue of the amphibian and reptile types in the Natural History Museum of Stanford University. Herpetologica 8:121–132.

Leviton, A. E., and B. H. Banta. 1964. Midwinter reconnaissance of the herpetofauna of the cape region of Baja California, Mexico. Proc. California Acad. Sci. Ser. 4, 30:127–156.

Lewis, T. H. 1950. The herpetofauna of the Tularosa Basin and Organ Mountains of New Mexico with some ecological features of the Chihuahuan desert. Herpetologica 6:1–10.

Lewis, T. H. 1951. Dark coloration in the reptiles of the malpais of the Mexican border. Copeia 1951:311–312.

Leybold, F. 1873. Escursion a las pampas argentinas. Hojas de mi diario. Santiago, Imprenta Nacional. 107 pp.

Lindsay, G. E. 1962. The Belvedere expedition to the Gulf of California. Trans. San Diego Soc. Nat. Hist. 13:1–44.

Lindsay, G. E. 1964. Sea of Cortez expedition of the California Academy of Sciences. Proc. California Acad. Sci. Ser. 4, 30:211–242.

Lindsay, G. E. 1966. The Gulf Islands expedition of 1966. Proc. California Acad. Sci. Ser. 4, 30:309–355.

Liner, E. A. 1964. Notes on four small herpetological collections from Mexico. I. Introduction, turtles and snakes. Southwest Nat. 8:221–227.

Liner, E. A., and A. H. Chaney, 1974. Life history: *Micrurus fulvius tenere*. HISS News J. 1:186.

Liner, E. A., R. M. Johnson, and A. H. Chaney. 1976. Geographic distribution: *Crotalus scutulatus scutulatus*. Herpetol. Rev. 7:177.

Liner, E. A., and R. E. Olson. 1973. Adults of the lizard *Sceloporus torquatus binocularis* Dunn. Herpetologica 29:53–55.

Linnaeus, C. 1758. Systema naturae. 10th ed. Stockholm, Laurentii Salvii. Reprint 1956, Great Britain, Unwin Brothers Limited.

Linsdale, J. M. 1932. Amphibians and reptiles from lower California. Univ. California Publ. Zool. 38:345–386.

Linsdale, J. M. 1940. Amphibians and reptiles in Nevada. Proc. Am. Acad. Arts Sci. 73:197–257.

Little, E. L., and J. G. Keller. 1937. Amphibians and reptiles of the Jornada Experimental Range, New Mexico. Copeia 1937: 216–222.

Loeb, L., C. L. Alsberg, E. Cooke, E. P. Corson-White, M. S. Fleisher, H. Fox, T. S. Githens, S. Leopold, M. K. Meyers, M. E. Rehfuss, D. Rivas, and L. Tuttle. 1913. The venom of *Heloderma*. Publ. Carnegie Inst. Washington no. 177. Pp. 1–244.

Long, E. G. 1974. The serpent's tale. Reptiles and amphibians of St. Lucia. IOUANALOA Ser. 2. St. Lucia, Univ. West Indies Extramural Dept. 46 pp.

Lönnberg, E. 1902. On a collection of snakes from north-western Argentine and Bolivia, containing new species. Ann. Mag. Nat. Hist. 10:457–462.

Loveridge, A. 1928a. Note on *Agkistrodon bilineatus* Günther. Bull. Antivenin Inst. Am. 2:52.

Loveridge, A. 1928b. On *Bothrops lansbergii* (Schlegel). Bull. Antivenin Inst. Am. 2:64–65.

Lowe, C. H., Jr. 1948. Effects of venom of *Micruroides* upon *Xantusia vigilis*. Herpetologica 4:136.

Lowe, C. H., Jr. 1955. The eastern limit of the Sonoran Desert in the United States with additions to the known herpetofauna of New Mexico. Ecology 36:343–345.

Lowe, C. H., Jr. 1964. The vertebrates of Arizona. Tucson, Univ. Arizona Press. 259 pp.

Lowe, C. H., Jr., and K. S. Norris. 1954. Analysis of the herpetofauna of Baja California, Mexico. Trans. San Diego Soc. Nat. Hist. 12:47–64.

Lowe, C. H., Jr., and K. S. Norris. 1955. Analysis of the herpetofauna of Baja California, Mexico. III. New and revived reptilian subspecies of Isla de San Estéban, Gulf of California, Sonora, Mexico, with notes on other satellite islands of Isla Tiburón. Herpetologica 11:89–96.

Lowe, C. H., Jr., C. R. Schwalbe, and T. B. Johnson. 1986. The venomous reptiles of Arizona. Phoenix, Ariz., Arizona Game and Fish Dept. 115 pp.

Lowell, J. A. 1957. A bite by a sidewinder rattlesnake. Herpetologica 13:135–136.

Luján Medina, F. 1973. Nota sobre *Bothrops pictus* Tschudi. Rebiol. 2:191–201.

Lutz, A., and O. de Mello. 1922. *Elaps ezequieli* e *Rhinostoma bimaculatum*, cobras novas do estado de Minas Geraes. Mem. Inst. Oswaldo Cruz, Rio de Janeiro 15:235–239.

Lutz, A., and O. Mello. 1923. Duas novas espécies de colubrideos brasileiros. Folia Med. (Rio de Janeiro) 4:2–3.

Lyman, V. A. 1949. Incidence of rattlesnakes in Panama. Herpetologica 5:44.

Lynch, J. D., and H. M. Smith. 1965. New or unusual amphibians and reptiles from Oaxaca, Mexico. Herpetologica 21: 168–177.

Lynch, J. D., and H. M. Smith. 1966. New or unusual amphibians and reptiles from Oaxaca, Mexico. II. Trans. Kansas Acad. Sci. 69:58–75.

MacDougall, T. 1971. The Chima wilderness. Explor. J. 49:86–103.

Machado, O. 1945a. Estudo comparativo das Elapideas do Brasil. Bol. Inst. Vital Brasil 5:37–46.

Machado, O. 1945b. Estudo comparativo das Crotalideas do Brasil. Bol. Inst. Vital Brazil 5:47–66.

Machado, O. 1945c. Variacões do desenho da *Bothrops jararaca*. Bol. Inst. Vital Brazil 5:75–76.

Maclean, W. P. 1968. A case of intersexuality in *Bothrops moojeni* Hoge. Copeia 1:170.

Maclean, W. P., R. Kellner, and H. Dennis. 1977. Island lists of West Indian amphibians and reptiles. Smithson. Herpetol. Inform. Serv. 40:1–47.

Macphail, N. P. 1929. A case report. Bull. Antivenin Inst. Am. 2:81–82.

Magalhães, O. 1925. Contribuição para o estudo dos ophidios brasileiros (1). Mem. Inst. Oswaldo Cruz, Rio de Janeiro 18:151–155.

Malkin, B. 1956. Seri ethnozoology: A preliminary report. Davidson J. Anth. 2:73–83.

Malkin, B. 1958. Cora ethnozoology, herpetological knowledge; A bio-ecological and cross cultural approach. Anthropol. Q. 31:73–90.

Malkin, B. 1962. Seri ethnology. Occas. Pap. Idaho State College Mus. no. 7. Pp. 1–59.

Manion, S. 1968. *Crotalus willardi*—The Arizona ridge-nosed rattlesnake. Herpetology 2:27–30.

Mao, S-H., and B-Y. Chen. 1980. Sea snakes of Taiwan. NSC Spec. Pub. no. 4. Taipei, Taiwan, Nat. Sci. Council. 64 pp.

March, D. D. H. 1928a. Field notes on Barba Amarilla (*Bothrops atrox*). Bull. Antivenin Inst. Am. 1:92–97.

March, D. D. H. 1928b. Field notes on the Neotropical rattlesnake (*Crotalus terrificus*). Bull. Antivenin Inst. Am. 2:55–61.

March, D. D. H. 1929a. Notes on *Bothrops nummifera*, mano de piedra or timbo. Bull. Antivenin Inst. Am. 3:27–29.

March, D. D. H. 1929b. Notes on *Bothrops nigroviridis*. Bull. Antivenin Inst. Am. 3:58.

Marcuzzi, G. 1950. Ofidios existentes en las colecciones de los museos de Caracas (Venezuela). Noved. Cient. Contrib. Ocas. Mus. Hist. Nat. La Salle Caracas Ser. Zool. no. 3. Pp. 1–20.

Marinkelle, C. J. 1966. Accidents by venomous animals in Colombia. Industrial. Med. Surg. 1966:988–992.

Martin, P. S. 1955a. Zonal distribution of vertebrates in a Mexican cloud forest. Am. Nat. 89:347–361.

Martin, P. S. 1955b. Herpetological records from the Gómez Farías region of southwestern Tamaulipas, Mexico. Copeia 1955:173–180.

Martin, P. S. 1958. A biogeography of reptiles and amphibians in the Gómez Farías region, Tamaulipas, Mexico. Misc. Publ. Mus. Zool. Univ. Michigan 101:1–102.

Martín del Campo, R. 1935. Nota acerca de la distribución geográfica de los reptiles ponzoñosos en México. An. Inst. Biol. Univ. Mexico 6:291–300.

Martín del Campo, R. 1937a. Reptiles ponzoñosos de México. Las víboras de Cascabel. Folletos Divulg. Cient. Inst. Biol., Mexico 27:1–18.

Martín del Campo. R. 1937b. Contribución al conocimiento de los batracios y reptiles del Valle del Mezquital, Hgo. An. Inst. Biol. Univ. Mexico 7:489–512.

Martín del Campo, R. 1938a. Tres *Bothrops* de Chiapas, dos de ellas nuevas para la fauna de México. An. Inst. Biol. Univ. Mexico 9:227–229.

Martín del Campo, R. 1938b. Ensayo de interpretación del libro undécimo de la Historia de Sahagún. An. Inst. Biol. Univ. Mexico 9:379–391.

Martín del Campo, R. 1940a. Los vertebrados de Pátzcuaro. An. Inst. Biol. Univ. Mexico 11:481–492.

Martín del Campo, R. 1940b. Nota acerca de algunos vertebrados de las lagunas de Cempoala y sus alrededores. An. Inst. Biol. Univ. Mexico 11:741–743.

Martín del Campo, R. 1942 [dated 1941]. Nota sobre el segundo hallazgo de *Sistrurus ravus* en el Distrito Federal. An. Inst. Biol. Univ. Mexico 12:762.

Martín del Campo, R. 1950. Serpientes ponzoñosas de México. Rev. Mex. Cienc. Med. Biol. 8:103–115.

Martín del Campo, R. 1953. Contribución al conocimiento de la herpetología de Nuevo León. Universidad, Monterrey 11:115–152.

Martín del Campo, R. 1955. Productos biológicas del Valle de México. Rev. Mex. Estud. Antrop. 14:53–77.

Martín del Campo, R. 1979. Un manuscrito inédito de Alfredo Dugès. An. Inst. Biol. Univ. Nat. Auton. Mexico 50:665–672.

Martín del Campo, R. 1984 [dated 1983]. Herpetología Mexicana antigua. II. Nomenclatura y taxonomicá de las serpientes. An. Inst. Biol. Univ. Nat. Auton. Mexico 54, Ser. Zool. no. 1. Pp. 177–198.

Martínez, V. and R. Bolaños. 1982. The bushmaster, *Lachesis muta muta* (Linnaeus) [Ophidia: Viperidae] in Panamá. Rev. Biol. Tropical 30:100–101.

McCoy, C. J. 1971 [dated 1970]. The snake fauna of Middlesex, British Honduras. J. Herpetol. 4:135–140.

McCoy, C. J. 1984. Ecological and zoogeographic relationships of amphibians and reptiles of the Cuatro Cienegas Basin. J. Arizona-Nevada Acad. Sci. 19:49–59.

McCoy, C. J., Jr., and W. L. Minckley. 1969. *Sistrurus catenatus* (Reptilia: Crotalidae) from the Cuatro Ciénegas Basin, Coahuila, México. Herpetologica 25:152–153.

McCoy, C. J. Jr., and N. D. Richmond. 1966. Herpetological type-specimens in Carnegie Museum. Ann. Carnegie Mus. 38:233–264.

McCranie, J. R. 1976. *Crotalus polystictus*. Cat. Am. Amph. Rept. Pp. 180.1–180.2.

McCranie, J. R. 1980. *Crotalus pricei*. Cat. Am. Amph. Rept. Pp. 266.1–266.2.

McCranie, J. R. 1981. *Crotalus basiliscus*. Cat. Am. Amph. Rept. Pp. 283.1–283.2.

McCranie, J. R. 1984. *Crotalus vegrandis*. Cat. Am. Amph. Rept. Pp. 350.1–350.2.

McCranie, J. R. 1986. *Crotalus unicolor*. Cat. Am. Amph. Rept. Pp. 389.1–389.2.

McCranie, J. R. 1988. Description of the hemipenis of *Sistrurus ravus* (Serpentes: Viperidae). Herpetologica 44:123–126.

McCranie, J. R., and L. Porras. 1978. Geographic distribution: *Bothrops yucatanicus*. Herpetol. Rev. 9:108.

McCranie, J. R., and L. D. Wilson. 1978. A second Mexican specimen of *Crotalus willardi obscurus* from the Sierra San Luis, Chihuahua, with comments on other members of the herpetofauna. Herpetol. Rev. 9:108–109.

McCrystal, H. K., and M. J. McCoid. 1986. *Crotalus mitchellii*. Cat Am. Amph. Rept. Pp. 388.1–388.4.

McDiarmid, R. W. 1963. A collection of reptiles and amphibians from the highland faunal assemblage of western Mexico. Contrib. Sci. Nat. Hist. Mus. Los Angeles Co. no. 68. Pp. 1–15.

McDiarmid, R. W., J. F. Copp, and D. E. Breedlove. 1976. Notes on the herpetofauna of western México: New records from Sinaloa and the Tres Marías Islands. Contrib. Sci. Nat. Hist. Mus. Los Angeles Co. no. 275. Pp. 1–17.

McDiarmid, R. W., and M. F. Foster. 1987. Additions to the reptile fauna of Paraguay, with notes on a small herpetological collection from Amambay. Stud. Neotrop. Fauna Environ. 22:1–9.

Mebs, D. 1968. Some studies on the biochemistry of the venom gland of *Heloderma horridum*. Toxicon 5:225–226.

Medem, F. 1965. Bibliografía comentada de reptiles colombianos. Rev. Acad. Colomb. Cienc. Exactas Fís. Nat. 12:299–346.

Medem, F. 1969 [dated 1968]. El desarrollo de la herpetología en Colombia. Rev. Acad. Colomb. Cienc. Exactas Fís Nat. 13:149–199.

Medem, F. 1979. Los anfibios y reptiles de las Islas Gorgona y Gorgonilla. Pp. 189–218 in H. Prahl, F. Guhl, and M. Grogl, eds. Gorgona. Bogotá, Univ. de Los Andes. 179 pp.

Meek, S. E. 1906 [dated 1905]. An annotated list of a collection of reptiles from southern California and northern Lower California. Field Mus. Nat. Hist. Publ., Zool. Ser. 7:1–19.

Meek, S. E. 1910. Notes on batrachians and reptiles from the islands north of Venezuela. Field Mus. Nat. Hist. Publ., Zool. Ser. 7:415–418.

Meise, W. 1938. Eine neue Korallenschlange aus dem Amazonasgebeit. Zool. Anz. 123:20–22.

Melgarejo, A. R. 1977. Observaciones sobre nacimiento en el laboratorio de *Bothrops neuwiedi pubescens* (Cope, 1870) (Ophidia, Crotalinae). Rev. Biol. Uruguay 5:35–41.

Melgarejo, A. R., M. D. Meneghel, and F. Achával. 1980. Sobre un ejemplar de *Bothrops alternatus* (Serpentes: Viperidae) con aberraciones cromáticas y morfológicas; estudio revisivo de la especie para Uruguay. Abstract. Pp. 142–143 in 8th Cong. Latinoamer. Zool., Mérida.

Mellink, E., J. R. Aguírre-Rivera, and E. García-Moya. 1987. Ethnozoology of the San Luis Potosi-Zacatecas Plateau, Mexico. Cont. Pap. 2d Symp. Res. Chihuahuan Desert Reg. no. 6. Pp. 1–16.

Meneses, O. 1974a. Ofidios y ofidismo en el Peru. I. Las serpientes venenosas del Perú. Rev. Inst. Zoonos. Invest. Pecuar. 2:69–77.

Meneses, O. 1974b. Ofidios y ofidismo en el Peru. II. Aspectos ecologicos de la fauna ofidica ponzoñosa. Rev. Inst. Zoonos. Invest. Pecuar. 2:79–84.

Merrem, B. 1820. Versuch eines Systems der Amphibien. Marburg, Johann Christian Krieger. 191 pp.

Mertens, R. 1929. Herpetologische Mitteilungen: XXIII–XXV. Zool. Anz. 86:57–68.

Mertens, R. 1930. Bemerkungen über die von Herrn Dr. K. Lafrentz in Mexico gesammelten Amphibien und Reptilien. Abh. Ber. Mus. Nat. Heimatkd. Magdeburg 6:153–161.

Mertens, R. 1941. Eine neue Korallennatter aus Mexico. Senckenb. Biol. 23:216–217.

Mertens, R. 1942. Amphibien und Reptilien I. Ausbeute der Hamburger Sudperu-Expedition. Pp. 277–287 in E. Titschack, ed. Beitrage zur Fauna Perus vol. 2. Hamburg.

Mertens, R. 1952a. Neues über die Reptilienfauna von El Salvador. Zool. Anz. 148:87–94.

Mertens, R. 1952b. Die Amphibien und Reptilien von El Salvador auf Grund der Reisen von R. Mertens und A. Zilch. Abh. Senckenb. Naturforsch. Ges. 487:1–83.

Mertens, R. 1956. Das Problem der Mimikry bei Korallenschlangen. Zool. Jahrb., Abt. Syst. 84:541–576.

Mertens, R. 1957. Gibt es eine Mimikry bei Korallenschlangen? Nat. Volk 87:56–66.

Mertens, R. 1963. Liste der rezenten Amphibien und Reptilien. Helodermatidae, Varanidae, Lanthanotidae. Das Tierreich (Berlin) 79:1–26.

Mertens, R. 1966. Ueber die Inselotter, *Bothrops insularis*. Salamandra 2:72–74.

Meyer, J. R. 1969. A biogeographic study of the amphibians and reptiles of Honduras. Ph.D. diss., Univ. of S. California. 589 pp. Ann Arbor, Mich., Univ. Microfilms. Diss. Abstr. B Sci. Eng. 70:5222.

Meyer, J. R., and L. D. Wilson. 1971. Taxonomic studies and notes on some Honduran amphibians and reptiles. Bull. S. California Acad. Sci. 70:106–114.

Migone, L. E. 1929. Apuntes de climatología y nosografía médica del Paraguay. Rev. Soc. Cient. Parag. 2:203–222.

Milá de la Roca, F. 1932. Introducción al estudio de los ofidios de Venezuela. Bol. Soc. Venezolana Cienc. Nat. 1:381–392.

Milá de la Roca, F. 1935. Notas sobre ofidios venenosos Venezolanos. Descripción provisional de la "Tigra Mariposa." Caracas Med. 2:319–333.

Miller, A. H., and R. C. Stebbins. 1964. The lives of desert animals in Joshua Tree National Monument. Berkeley, Univ. California Press. 452 pp.

Milstead, W. W. 1960a. Relict species of the Chihuahuan Desert. Southwest Nat. 5:75–88.

Milstead, W. W. 1960b. Supplementary notes on the herpetofauna of the Stockton Plateau. Texas J. Sci. 12:228–231.

Milstead, W. W., J. S. Mecham, and H. McClintock. 1950. The amphibians and reptiles of the Stockton Plateau in northern Terrell County, Texas. Texas J. Sci. 2:543–562.

Minckley, C. O., and W. E. Rinne. 1972. Another massasauga from Mexico. Texas J. Sci. 23:432–433.

Minton, S. A., Jr. 1959 [dated 1958]. Observations of amphibians and reptiles of the Big Bend region of Texas. Southwest Nat. 3:28–54.

Minton, S. A. 1983. *Sisturus catenatus*. Cat. Am. Amph. Rept.: 332.1–332.2.

Minton, S. A., and B. M. de Cervantes. 1977. Observations on the snakes of Querétaro, México. Bull. Chicago Herpetol. Soc. 12:69–74.

Minton, S. A., H. G. Dowling, and F. E. Russell. 1968. Poisonous snakes of the world. A manual for use by the U.S. amphibious forces. Washington, D.C. U.S. GPO. 212 pp.

Minton, S. A., and M. R. Minton. 1980. Venomous reptiles. Rev. Ed. N.Y., Charles Scribner's Sons. 308 pp.

Minton, S. A., and S. A. Weinstein. 1986. Geographic and ontogenetic variation in venom of the western diamondback rattlesnake (*Crotalus atrox*). Toxicon 24:71–80.

Minton de Cervantes, B. and S. A. Minton. 1975. Geographic distribution: *Micrurus fulvius microgalbineus*. Herpetol. Rev. 6:116.

Miranda, M. E., G. A. Couturier, and J. D. Williams. 1983. Guía de los ofidios bonaerenses, 2d ed. Asoc. Coop. Jard. Zool. de La Plata (Buenos Aires). 72 pp.

Miranda Ribeiro, A. 1915. *Lachesis lutzi*, uma variedade de *L. pictus* Tschudi. Arch. Mus. Nac. Rio de Janeiro 17:3–4.

Mittleman, M. B., and H. M. Smith. 1949. Remarks on the Mexican subspecies of the coral snake *Micrurus nigrocinctus*. Trans. Kansas Acad. Sci. 52:86–88.

Miyata, K. 1982. A check list of the amphibians and reptiles of Ecuador with a bibliography of Ecuadorian herpetology. Smithson. Herpetol. Inform. Serv. 54:1–70.

Mocquard, M. F. 1899. Reptiles et batraciens recueillis au Mexique par M. León Diguet en 1896 et 1897. Bull. Soc. Philomath. Paris Ser. 9, 4:154–169.

Mocquard, M. F. 1908–1909. Etudes sur les reptiles. Mission scientifique au Mexique et dans l'Amérique Centrale . . . Recherches zoologiques. Part 3. Paris, Imprimerie Impériale. [Livraison 16, 1908, pp. 861–932, plates 69–74; Livraison 17, 1909, pp. 933–1012, plates 75–77].

Mole, R. R. 1914. Trinidad Snakes. Proc. Agric. Soc. Trinidad Tobago 14:363–369.

Mole, R. R. 1924. The Trinidad Snakes. Proc. Zool. Soc. London: 235–278.

Moonen, J. 1982. De Boomowroekoekoe *Bothrops castelnaudi* Dumeril, Bibron & Dumeril 1854, een weinig bekende gifslang uit zuidelijk Suriname. Paramaribo Zoo Med. no. 1. 4 pp.

Moonen, J., W. Eriks, and K. van deursen. 1978. Surinaamse Slangeninkleur. Paramaribo, C. Kersten & Co. 119 pp.

Moore, R. G. 1976. Seasonal and daily activity patterns and thermoregulation in the southwestern speckled rattlesnake (*Crotalus mitchelli pyrrhus*) and the Colorado desert sidewinder (*Crotalus cerastes lateroreprens*). Diss. Abstr. B37: 1099–1100.

Moore, R. G. 1978. Seasonal and daily activity patterns and thermoregulation in the southwestern speckled rattlesnake (*Crotalus mitchelli pyrrhus*) and the Colorado desert sidewinder (*Crotalus cerastes laterorepens*). Copeia 1978:439–442.

Moreno, A. 1873. El tepotzo. Nota sobre este reptil. Naturaleza, Mexico 2:336–338.

Mosauer, W. 1932a. Adaptive convergence in the sand reptiles of the Sahara and of California: A study in structure and behavior. Copeia 1932:72–78.

Mosauer, W. 1932b. The amphibians and reptiles of the Guadalupe Mountains of New Mexico and Texas. Occas. Pap. Mus. Zool. Univ. Michigan no. 246. Pp. 1–18.

Mosauer, W. 1933. Locomotion and diurnal range of *Sonora occipitalis, Crotalus cerastes*, and *Crotalus atrox* as seen from their tracks. Copeia 1933:14–16.

Mosauer, W. 1936. The reptilian fauna of sand dune areas of the Vizcaino Desert and of northwestern Lower California. Occas. Pap. Mus. Zool. Univ. Michigan no. 329. Pp. 1–22.

Müller, F. 1878. Mitteilungen aus der herpetologischen Sammlung des Basler Museums. Verh. Naturforsch. Ges. Basel 6:389–427.

Müller, F. 1882. Zweiter Nachtrag zum Katalog der herpetologischen Sammlung des Basler Museums. Verh. Naturforsch. Ges. Basel 7:166–174.

Müller, F. 1885. Vierter Nachtrag zum Katalog der herpetologischen Sammlung des Basler Museums. Verh. Naturforsch. Ges. Basel 7:668–717.

Müller, L. 1923. Ueber neue oder seltene mittel-und südamerikanische Amphibien und Reptilien. Mitt. Zool. Mus. Berlin 11:77–93.

Müller, L. 1926. Neue Reptilien und Batrachier der zoologischen Sammlung der Bayerischen Staates. Zool. Anz. 65: 193–200.

Müller, L. 1927. Amphibien und Reptilien der Ausbeute Prof. Breslau's in Brasilien 1913–14. Abh. Senckenb. Naturforsch. Ges. 40:259–304.

Müller, P. 1968. Die Herpetofauna der Insel von São Sebastião (Brasilien). Saarbrucken, Saarbrucher Zeitung Verl. und Druckerei GmbH. 68 pp.

Müller, P. 1969a. Vertebratenfaunen Brasilianischer Inseln als Indikatoren für glaziale und postglaziale Vegetationsfluktuationen. Zool. Anz. Suppl. 33:97–107.

Müller, P. 1969b. Herpetologische Beobachtungen auf der Insel Marajo. DATZ 22:117–121.

Müller, P. 1971. Herpetologische Reiseeindrucke aus Brasilien. Salamandra 7:9–30.

Müller, P. 1973. The dispersal centres of terrestrial vertebrates in the neotropical realm. The Hague, Dr. W. Junk. 244 pp.

Muñoz Alonso, L. A. 1988. Estudio herpetofaunistico del Parque Ecológico Estatal de Omiltemi, Mpio. de Chilpancingo, Guerrero. Thesis. Univ. Nac. Aut. Mexico. Ciudad Universitaria, D.F. 111 pp.

Murphy, J. B., L. A. Mitchell, and J. A. Campbell. 1979. Miscellaneous notes on the reproductive biology of reptiles. III. The Uracoan rattlesnake, *Crotalus vegrandis* Klauber (Serpentes, Viperidae). J. Herpetol. 13:373–374.

Murphy, R. C. 1917. Natural history observations from the Mexican portion of the Colorado desert, with a note on the Lower California pronghorn and a list of birds. Proc. Linn. Soc. New York nos. 28/29. Pp. 43–101.

Murphy, R. W. 1983a. Paleobiogeography and genetic differentiation of the Baja California herpetofauna. Occ. Pap. California Acad. Sci. no. 137. Pp. 1–48.

Murphy, R. W. 1983b. The reptiles: Origin and evolution. Pp. 130–158 and appendices 6.1 and 6.2 in T. J. Case, and M. L. Cody, eds. Island biogeography in the Sea of Cortez. Berkeley, Univ. of California Press.

Murphy, R. W., and B. Crabtree. 1985. Genetic relationships of the Santa Catalina Island rattleless Rattlesnake, *Crotalus catalinensis* (Serpentes: Viperidae). Acta Zool. Mex. Nueva Ser. no. 9. Pp. 1–16.

Murphy, R. W., and J. R. Ottley. 1984. Distribution of amphibians and reptiles on islands in the Gulf of California. Ann. Carnegie Mus. 53:207–230.

Murray, K. F. 1955. Herpetological collections from Baja California. Herpetologica 11:33–48.

Myers, C. W. 1969. The ecological geography of cloud forest in Panama. Am. Mus. Novit., no. 2396. Pp. 1–52.

Myers, C. W. 1972. The status of herpetology in Panamá. Bull. Biol. Soc. Washington 2:199–209.

Myers, C. W., and A. S. Rand. 1969. Checklist of amphibians and reptiles of Barro Colorado Island, Panama, with comments on faunal change and sampling. Smithson. Contrib. Zool., no. 19. Pp. 1–11.

Myers, G. S. 1945. Nocturnal observations on sea-snakes in Bahia Honda, Panama. Herpetologica 3:22–23.

Nahas, L., A. S. Kamiguti, and M. A. R. Barros. 1979. Thrombin-like and factor X-activator components of *Bothrops* snake venoms. Thrombos. Haemostasis. (Stuttg.) 41:314–328.

Nascimento, F. P., T. C. S. Avila-Pires, and O. R. Rodrigues da Cunha. 1987. Os répteis da área de Carajás, Pará, Brasil (Squamata). II. Bol. Mus. Para. Emilio Goeldi Ser. Zool. 3:33–65.

Neill, W. T. 1957. The vipers of Queimada Grande. Nature Mag. 1957:188–191.

Neill, W. T. 1958. The occurrence of amphibians and reptiles in saltwater areas, and a bibliography. Bull. Mar. Sci. Gulf Caribb. 8:1–97.

Neill, W. T. 1960. Nature and man in British Honduras. Maryland Natur. 30:2–14.

Neill, W. T. 1962. The reproductive cycle of snakes in a tropical region, British Honduras. Q. J. Florida Acad. Sci. 25:234–253.

Neill, W. T. 1963. Polychromatism in snakes. Q. J. Florida Acad. Sci. 26:194–216.

Neill, W. T. 1965. New and noteworthy amphibians and reptiles from British Honduras. Bull. Florida St. Mus., Biol. Sci. 9:77–130.

Neill, W. T. 1966. Notes on *Bothrops hyoprora* (Serpentes, Crotalidae). Herpetologica 22:235–239.

Neill, W. T., and R. Allen. 1959a. Studies on the amphibians and reptiles of British Honduras. Publ. Research Div., Ross Allen's Reptile Inst. 2:1–76.

Neill, W. T., and R. Allen. 1959b. Additions to the British Honduras herpetofaunal list. Herpetologica 15:235–240.

Neill, W. T., and E. R. Allen. 1960. Noteworthy snakes from British Honduras. Herpetologica 16:145–162.

Neill, W. T., and E. R. Allen. 1962. Reptiles of the Cambridge Expedition to British Honduras, 1959–1960. Herpetologica 18:79–91.

Nelson, E. W. 1922. Lower California and its natural resources. Mem. Natl. Acad. Sci. Washington 16:1–194.

Nemuras, K. 1967. Notes on the herpetology of Panama. Part 4. Bull. Maryland Herpetol. Soc. 3:63–71.

Nicéforo-María, Hno. 1929a. Rabo de Chucha del Chocó. Rev. Soc. Colomb. Cienc. Nat. 4:185–188.

Nicéforo-María, Hno. 1929b. Observaciones acerca de algunos nombres científicos que emplea el Dr. Evaristo García en su obra titulada "Los Ofidios venenosos del Cauca." Rev. Soc. Colomb. Cienc. Nat. 18:189–191.

Nicéforo-María, Hno. 1930a. La colgadora o víbora: *Bothrops schlegelii*. Bol. Inst. La Salle (Bogotá) 17:129–132.

Nicéforo-María, Hno. 1930b. Los reptiles de Villavicencio en el Museo de La Salle. Rev. Soc. Colomb. Cienc. Nat. 19:40–54.

Nicéforo-María, Hno. 1930c. Los reptiles y batracios de Honda (Tolima) en el Museo de La Salle. Rev. Soc. Colomb. Cienc. Nat. 19:96–104.

Nicéforo-María, Hno. 1933. Las serpientes de Villavicencio. Pp. 199–237 in Libro Conmemorativo del Segundo Centenario de don José Celestino Bruno Mutis y Bosio, 1732–1932. Bogotá, Imprenta Nacional.

Nicéforo-María, Hno. 1938. Las serpientes colombianas de hocico proboscidiforme, grupo *Bothrops lansbergii-nasuta-hyoprora*. Rev. Acad. Colomb. Cienc. Exactas Fis. Nat. 2: 417–421.

Nicéforo-María, Hno. 1939. Contribución al estudio de la ofiología Colombiana. Rev. Acad. Colomb. Cienc. Exactas Fis. Nat. 3:91–94.

Nicéforo-María, Hno. 1942. Los ofidios de Colombia. Rev. Acad. Colomb. Cienc. Exactas Fis. Nat. 5:84–101.

Nicéforo-María, Hno. 1964. Herpetologia. Bol. Inst. La Salle (Bogotá) 204:129–135.

Nicéforo-María, Hno. 1975. Contribución al estudio de las serpientes de Colombia II. Bol. Inst. La Salle (Bogotá) no. 215. Pp. 1–4.

Nickerson, M. A., and C. E. Mays. 1970. A preliminary herpetofaunal analysis of the Graham (Pinaleno) mountain region, Graham Co., Arizona with ecological comments. Trans. Kansas Acad. Sci. 72:492–505.

Nickerson, M. A., R. A. Sajdak, R. W. Henderson, and S. Ketcham. 1978. Notes on the movements of some Neotropical snakes (Reptilia, Serpentes). J. Herpetol. 12:419–422.

Noguchi, H. 1909. Snake venoms. An investigation of venomous snakes with special reference to the phenomena of their venoms. Washington, D.C., Carnegie Inst. 315 pp.

Norris, K. S. 1967. Color adaptations in desert reptiles and its thermal relationships. Pp. 162–229 in W. W. Milstead, ed. Lizard ecology: A symposium. Columbia, Univ. Missouri Press. 300 pp.

Norris, K. S., and C. H. Lowe. 1964. An analysis of background color matching in amphibians and reptiles. Ecology 45:565–580.

Nutter, R. B. 1927. Report of snake-bite cases. Bull. Antivenin Inst. Am. 1:38–39.

Ocaranza, F. 1930. Sistemática de los animales ponzoñosos de la América Latina y acción biológica de sus venenos. Medicina 10:357–374.

Ochoterena, I. 1934. Distribución geográfica de los animales de México. Reseñ. Cient. Soc. Esp. Hist. Nat. 6:23–41.

Odermatt, C. 1940. Beitrage zur Kenntniss des Gebisses von *Heloderma*. Vjschr. Naturf. Ges. Zurich 85:98–141.

Oliver, J. A. 1937. Notes on a collection of amphibians and reptiles from the state of Colima, Mexico. Occas. Pap. Mus. Zool. Univ. Michigan no. 360. Pp. 1–30.

Orcés, G. 1942. Los ofidios venenosos del Ecuador. Flora (Quito), 2:147–155.

Orcés, G. 1943. Los ofidios venenosos del Ecuador. Flora (Quito), 3:165–170.

Orcés, G. 1948. Notas sobre los ofidios venenosos del Ecuador. Rev. Filos. Letr., Quito, 3:231–250.

Orr, R. T. 1961. Vertebrate biology. Philadelphia, W. B. Saunders Co. 400 pp.

Orr, R. T. 1965. An expedition to the sea of Cortez. Animals 6:86–91.

Orr, R. T. 1976. Vertebrate biology. 4th ed. Philadelphia, W. B. Saunders Co. 472 pp.

Ortenburger, A. I., and R. D. Ortenburger. 1927 [dated 1926]. Field observations on some amphibians and reptiles of Pima County, Arizona. Proc. Oklahoma Acad. Sci. 6:101–121.

Orton, J. 1876. The Andes and the Amazon; or, across the continent of South America. 3d ed. N.Y., Harper and Brothers. 645 pp.

Osorio Tafall, B. F. 1948. La Isla de Cedros, Baja California. Ensayo monográfico. Bol. Soc. Mex. Geogr. Estad. 66:318–402.

Ottley, J. R. 1981a. Geographic distribution: *Heloderma horridum exasperatum*. Herpetol. Rev. 12:64.

Ottley, J. R. 1981b. Geographic distribution: *Heloderma suspectum suspectum*. Herpetol. Rev. 12:65.

Ottley, J. R., and L. E. Hunt. 1981. Geographic distribution: *Crotalus viridis helleri*. Herpetol. Rev. 12:65.

Parker, H. W. 1926. The reptiles and batrachians of Gorgona Island, Colombia. Ann. Mag. Nat. Hist. Ser. (9) 17:549–554.

Parker, H. W. 1930. Two new reptiles from southern Ecuador. Ann. Mag. Nat. Hist. Ser. (10) 5:568–571.

Parker, H. W. 1932. Some new or rare reptiles and amphibians from southern Ecuador. Ann. Mag. Nat. Hist. Ser. (10) 9:21–26.

Parker, H. W. 1934. Reptiles and amphibians from southern Ecuador. Ann. Mag. Nat. Hist. Ser. (10) 14:264–273.

Parker, H. W. 1935. The frogs, lizards, and snakes of British Guiana. Proc. Zool. Soc. London 1935:505–530.

Parker, H. W. 1938. The vertical distribution of some reptiles and amphibians in southern Ecuador. Ann. Mag. Nat. Hist. Ser. (11) 2:438–450.

Parrish, H. M., and C. A. Carr. 1967. Bites by copperheads (*Ancistrodon contortrix*) in the United States. J. Am. Med. Assoc. 201:927–932.

Patzelt, E. 1979. Fauna del Ecuador. 2d ed. Quito, Edit. Las Casas. 198 pp. (unnumbered).

Pawley, R. 1969. Observations on a prolonged food refusal period of an adult fer-de-lance. Int. Zoo Yearb. 9:58–59.

Pefaur, J. E., J. Davila, E. Lopez, and A. Nuñez. 1978. Distribución y clasificación de los reptiles del Departamento de Arequipa. Bull. Inst. Fr.—El And. 7:129–139.

Peracca, M. G. 1897. Viaggio del Dott. Alfredo Borelli nel Chaco Boliviano e nella Repubblica Argentina. Rettili ed anfibi. Bol. Mus. Zool. Anat. Comp. Univ. Torino vol. 12. 19 pp.

Peracca, M. G. 1910. Descrizione di alcune nuove specie di ofidii del Museo Zoologico della R. Universitá di Napoli. Ann. Mus. Zool. Univ. Napoli n.s. 3:1–3.

Pérez-Higadera [*sic*], G., R. C. Vogt, and O. A. Flores Villela. 1987. Lista anotada de los anfibios y reptiles de la región de los Tuxtlas, Veracruz. Univ. Nac. Auton. Mexico. 23 pp.

Pérez-Higareda, G. 1978. Reptiles and amphibians from the Estación de Biología Tropical "Los Tuxtlas" (U.N.A.M.), Veracruz, Mexico. Bull. Maryland Herpetol. Soc. 14:67–74.

Pérez-Higareda, G. 1980. Additions to and notes on the known snake fauna of the Estación de Biología Tropical "Los Tuxtlas," Veracruz, México. Bull. Maryland Herpetol. Soc. 16: 23–26.

Pérez-Higareda, G., H. M. Smith, and J. Juliá-Zertuche. 1985. A new jumping viper, *Porthidium olmec*, from southern Veracruz, México (Serpentes: Viperidae). Bull. Maryland Herpetol. Soc. 21:97–106.

Pérez-Santos, C. 1986a. Las serpientes del Atlántico. Madrid, Mus. Nac. Cien. Nat. 83 pp.

Pérez-Santos, C. 1986b. Las serpientes del Tolima. Madrid, T. Torreblanca. 96 pp.

Pérez-Santos, C. and A. G. Moreno. 1986. Distribución altitudinal de las serpientes en Colombia. Rev. Españ. Herpetol. 1:11–27.

Pesce, H., and H. Lumbreras. 1965. Ofidismo de Lima por *Bothrops pictus*. An. Fac. Med., Lima 39:1153–1188.

Peters, J. A. 1953. Snakes and lizards from Quintana Roo, Mexico. Lloydia 16:227–232.

Peters, J. A. 1954. The amphibians and reptiles of the coast and coastal sierra of Michoacán, Mexico. Occas. Pap. Mus. Zool. Univ. Michigan no. 554. Pp. 1–37.

Peters, J. A. 1955. Herpetological type localities in Ecuador. Rev. Ecuat. Entomol. Parasitol. 2:335–352.

Peters, J. A. 1960a. The snakes of Ecuador. A check list and key. Bull. Mus. Comp. Zool. 122:491–541.

Peters, J. A. 1960b. Notes on the faunistics of southwestern and coastal Michoacan, with lists of reptilia and amphibia collected in 1950 and 1951. Pp. 319–334 in P. D. Brand, ed. Coalcoman and Motines del Oro, and ex-distrito of Michoacán Mexico. Austin, Texas, Institute for Latin American Studies, Univ. Texas.

Peters, J. A. 1968. A replacement name for *Bothrops lansbergii venezuelensis* Roze. 1959 (Viperidae, Serpentes). Proc. Biol. Soc. Washington 81:319–322.

Peters, J. A., and B. Orejas-Miranda. 1970. Catalogue of the Neotropical Squamata: Part I. Snakes. Bull. U.S. Natl. Mus. 297:1–347.

Peters, W. C. H. 1861. Über eine Sammlung von Schlangen aus Huanusco in Mexico welche das Königl. zoologische Museum kurzlich von Dr. Hille erworden hat. Monatsber. Preuss. Akad. Wiss. Berlin 1861:460–462.

Peters, W. C. H. 1863 [dated 1862]. Ueber die craniologischen Verschiedenheiten der Grubenottern (Trigonocephali) und ueber eine neue Art der Gattung *Bothriechis*. Monatsber. Preuss. Akad. Wiss. Berlin 1862:670–674.

Peters, W. C. H. 1869. Eine Mittheilung über Mexicanische Amphibien, welche Hr. Berkenbusch in Puebla auf Veranlassung des Hrn. Legationsraths von Schlozer dem zoologischen Museum zugesandt hat. Monatsber. Preuss. Akad. Wiss. Berlin. 1869:874–881.

Peters, W. C. H. 1871. Ueber eine von hrn. Dr. Robert Abendroth in dem Hochlande von Peru gemachte Sammlung von Amphibien, welche derselbe dem Königl. zoologischen Museum geschenkt hat. Monatsber. Preuss. Akad. Wiss. Berlin 1871:397–404.

Peterson, H. W., and H. M. Smith. 1974. Observations on sea snakes in the vicinity of Acapulco, Guerrero, Mexico. Bull. Chicago Herpetol. Soc. 8:29.

Pettigrew, L. C., and J. P. Glass. 1985. Neurologic complications of a coral snake bite. Neurology 35:589–592.

Pianka, E. R., and H. M. Smith. 1959. Distributional records for certain Mexican and Guatemalan reptiles. Herpetologica 15:119–120.

Picado T., C. 1930. Venom of Costa Rican arboreal vipers. Bull. Antivenin Inst. Am. 4:1–3.

Picado T., C. 1931. Serpientes venenosas de Costa Rica. San José, Costa Rica, Secretaría de Salubridad y Protección Social. 219 pp.

Picado T., C. 1936 [dated 1933/34]. Serpentes venenosas occorrêntes em Costa Rica. Mem. Inst. Butantan 8:389–397.

Pickwell, G. V., R. L. Bezy, and J. E. Fitch. 1983. Northern occurrences of the sea snake, *Pelamis platurus*, in the eastern Pacific, with a record of predation on the species. California Fish Game 69:172–177.

Pickwell, G. V., and W. A. Culotta. 1980. *Pelamis, P. platurus*. Cat. Am. Amph. Rept.:255.1–255.4.

Pifano C., F., and M. Romer. 1949a. Ofidios ponzoñosos de Venezuela. 1.-Nueva comprobación en Venezuela del *Bothrops medusa* (Sternfeld, 1920) Amaral, 1929 y redescripción de la especie. Arch. Venez. Patol. Trop. Parasitol. Med. 1:277–300.

Pifano C., F., and M. Romer. 1949b. Ofidios ponzoñosos de Venezuela. II. Sobre las serpientes ponzoñosas venezolanas del grupo *Bothrops lansbergii*. Arch. Venez. Patol. Trop. Parasitol. Med. 1:301–326.

Pifano C., F., Romer, M., and F. Sandner-Montilla. 1950. Serpientes ponzoñosas de Venezuela III-*Bothrops schlegelii* (Berthold, 1846) Jan., 1875: Su existencia en Venezuela. Arch. Venez. Patol. Trop. Parasitol. Med. 2:261–264.

Pope, C. H. 1944–45. The poisonous snakes of the New World. Bull. New York Zool. Soc. 47(1944): 83–90, 111–120, 143–152; idem, 48(1945): 17–23, 44–47.

Porras, L., J. R. McCranie, and L. D. Wilson. 1981. The systematics and distribution of the Hognose Viper *Bothrops nasuta* Bocourt (Serpentes: Viperidae). Tulane Stud. Zool. 22:85–107.

Posada-Arango, A. 1889a. Apuntamientos para la ofiología colombiana. An. Acad. Med. Medellín 2:45–49.

Posada-Arango, A. 1889b. Note sur quelques solénoglyphes de Colombie. Bull. Soc. Zool. France 14:343–345.

Pough, H. 1966. Ecological relationships of rattlesnakes in southeastern Arizona with notes on other species. Copeia 1966:676–683.

Powell, R. and J. Parmerlee. 1980. Geographic distribution: *Crotalus durissus*. Herpetol. Rev. 11:116.

Prado, A. 1939 [dated 1938/39]. Notas ofiológicas. I. Sôbre as serpentes do grupo *Bothrops lansbergii*, com a descrição de uma nova espécie. Mem. Inst. Butantan 12:1–4.

Prado, A. 1945. Serpentes do Brasil. São Paulo, Edit. Sítios e Fazendas, Biblioteca Agro-Pecuária. 134 pp.

Prado, A., and A. R. Hoge. 1948 [dated 1947]. Notas ofiológicas. 21. Observações sôbre serpentes do Perú. Mem. Inst. Butantan 20:283–296.

Pregill, G. K., J. A. Gauthier, and H. W. Greene. 1986. The evolution of helodermatid squamates, with the description of a new taxon and an overview of Varanoidea. Trans. San Diego Soc. Nat. Hist. 21:167–202.

Price, A. H. 1980. *Crotalus molossus*. Cat. Am. Amph. Rept.: Pp. 242.1–242.2.

Price, A. H. 1982. *Crotalus scutulatus*. Cat. Am. Amph. Rept.: Pp. 291.1–291.2.

Procter, J. B. 1918. On the variation of the pit viper, *Lachesis atrox*. Proc. Zool. Soc. London 1918:163–182.

Quelch, J. J. 1898. The poisonous snakes of British Guiana. Timehri 2:26–36.

Quintini N., J. 1927. Contribución a la geografía médica del ferrocarril de Santa Bárbara al vigía en los Estados Zulia y Mérida. Chap.: Los animales ponzoñosos. Mem. V. Congr. Venez. Medic. (Caracas) 1:305–311.

Quintini N., J. 1936. Contribución al estudio del género *Bothrops* en el Estado Trujillo. Sobre un ejemplar del grupo *B. lansbergii*. Caracas Medico 3:493–498.

Radcliffe, W. C., and T. P. Maslin. 1975. A new subspecies of the Red Rattlesnake, *Crotalus ruber*, from San Lorenzo Sur Island, Baja California Norte, Mexico. Copeia 1975:490–493.

Rado, T. A., and P. G. Rowlands. 1981. A range extension and low elevational record for the Arizona ridge-nosed rattlesnake (*Crotalus w. willardi*). Herpetol. Rev. 12:15.

Ramírez-Bautista, A., G. Pérez-Higareda, and G. Casas-Andreu. 1981. Lista preliminar de los anfibios y reptiles de la region de Los Tuxtlas, Veracruz. Instituto de Biología, Univ. Nat. Auton. Mexico. 6 pp.

Raun, G. G., and F. R. Gehlbach. 1972. Amphibians and reptiles in Texas. Bull. Dallas Mus. Nat. Hist. 2:1–61.

Ravenau de Lussan. 1690. Journal du voyage fait a la mer de sud, avec les filibustiers de l'Amerique en 1684. & années suivantes. Paris. 272 pp.

Reddell, J. R., and R. W. Mitchell, eds. 1971. Studies on the cavernicole fauna of Mexico. Bull. Assoc. Mexican Cave Stud. 4:1–239.

Reese, R. W. 1971. Notes on a small herpetological collection from northeastern Mexico. J. Herpetol. 5:67–69.

Reichel-Dolmatoff, G. 1968. Desana. Bogotá, Colombia, Univ. Los Andes. 270 pp.

Rendahl, H. 1937. Einige reptilien aus Ecuador und Bolivia. Ark. Zool. 29A:1–19.

Rendahl, H., and G. Vestergren. 1940. Notes on Colombian snakes. Ark. Zool. 33A:1–16.

Rendahl, H., and G. Vestergren. 1941. On a small collection of snakes from Ecuador. Ark. Zool. 33A:1–16.

Renjifo, J. M. 1979. Systematics and distribution of crotalid snakes in Colombia. M.S. thesis, Univ. of Kansas, Lawrence. 64 pp.

Reyes, D. S. 1889. El lagarto de costra. Naturaleza, Mexico, Ser. 2, 1:277–278.

Reynolds, R. P. 1982. Seasonal incidence of snakes in northeastern Chihuahua, Mexico. Southwest Nat. 27:161–166.

Reynolds, R. P., and G. V. Pickwell, 1984. Records of the yellow-bellied sea snake, *Pelamis platurus*, from the Galápagos Islands. Copeia 1984:786–789.

Rivero-Blanco, C., and J. R. Dixon. 1979. Origin and distribution of the herpetofauna of the dry lowland regions of northern South America. Pp. 281–298 in W. E. Duellman, ed. The South American Herpetofauna: Its origin, evolution, and dispersal. Monogr. Mus. Nat. Hist. Univ. Kansas no. 7.

Rodas J., T. 1938. Contribución al estudio de las serpientes venenosas de Guatemala. Guatemala City, Tipografía Nacional. 152 pp.

Roge [*sic*], A. R., and S. A. R. W. D. L. Romano. 1977 [dated 1976/77]. *Lachesis muta rhombeata* [Serpentes: Viperidae: Crotalinae]. Mem. Inst. Butantan 40/41:53–54.

Rohl, E. 1949. Fauna descriptiva de Venezuela (vertebrados). 2d ed. Caracas, Tipografía Americana.

Rokosky, E. J. 1941. Notes on new-born jumping vipers, *Bothrops nummifera*. Copeia 1941:267.

Rokosky, E. J. 1942. Notes on *Trimeresurus nigroviridis marchi*. Copeia 1943:260.

Romano, S. A. R. W. D. L. 1972 [dated 1971]. Notes on *Leptomicrurus* Schmidt (Serpentes Elapidae). Mem. Inst. Butantan 35:111–115.

Romer, A. S. 1956. Osteology of the reptiles. Chicago, Univ. Chicago Press. 772 pp.

Rooij, N. de. 1922. Reptiles and amphibians of Curacao. Bijdr. Dierkd. 1922:249–253.

Rosado-López, L., and F. A. Laviada-Arrigunada. 1977. Accidente ofídico. Communicación de 38 casos. Prensa Med. Mex. 42:409–412.

Rosenfeld, G. 1971. Symptomatology, pathology, and treatment of snake bite in South America. Pp. 345–384 in W. Bucherl and E. E. Buckley, eds. Venomous animals and their venoms, Vol. 2. N.Y., Academic Press.

Roux-Esteve, R. 1983 [dated 1982]. Les spécimens-types du genre *Micrurus* (Elapidae) conservés au Muséum National D'Histoire Naturelle de Paris. Mem. Inst. Butantan 46:79–94.

Roze, J. A. 1952. Colección de reptiles del Profesor Scorza, de Venezuela. Acta Biol. Venezuelica 1:93–114.

Roze, J. A. 1954. Nota preliminar sobre los ofidios de la expedición Franco-Venezolana al alto Orinoco. Arch. Venez. Patol. Trop. Parasitol. Med. 2:227–234.

Roze, J. A. 1955. Revision de las corales (Serpentes: Elapidae) de Venezuela. Acta Biol. Venezuelica 1:453–500.

Roze, J. A. 1957 [dated 1955]. Ofidios coleccionados por la expedición Franco-Venezolana al Alto Orinoco, 1951 a 1952. Bol. Mus. Cienc. Nat. Caracas 1:179–195.

Roze, J. A. 1958a. On Hallowell's type specimens of reptiles from Venezuela in the collection of the Academy of Natural Science of Philadelphia. Not. Nat., Philadelphia no. 309. Pp. 1–4.

Roze, J. A. 1958b. Resultados zoológicos de la expedición de la Universidad Central de Venezuela a la región del Auyantepui en la Guayana Venezolana, Abril 1956. 5. Los reptiles del Auyantepui, Venezuela, basándose en las colecciones de las expediciones de Phelps-Tate, del American Museum of Natural History, 1937–1938, y de la Universidad Central de Venezuela, 1956. Acta Biol. Venezuelica 2:243–270.

Roze, J. A. 1958c. Los reptiles del Chimantá Tepui (Estado Bolívar, Venezuela) colectados por la expedición botánica del Chicago Natural History Museum. Acta Biol. Venezuelica 2:299–314.

Roze, J. A. 1959. Taxonomic notes on a collection of Venezuelan reptiles in the American Museum of Natural History. Am. Mus. Novit. 1934:1–14.

Roze, J. A. 1964. La herpetología de la Isla de Margarita, Venezuela. Mem. Soc. Cienc. Nat. La Salle 24:209–241.

Roze, J. A. 1966a. La taxonomía y zoogeografía de los ofídios en Venezuela. Univ. Central Venezuela, Caracas, Edit. Biblioteca 28. 362 pp.

Roze, J. A. 1966b. On the synonymy and type specimens of the coral snakes *Micrurus corallinus* and *M. ibiboboca* (Marcgravii). Copeia 1966:369–371.

Roze, J. A. 1967. A checklist of the New World venomous coral snakes (Elapidae), with descriptions of new forms. Am. Mus. Novit. no. 2287. Pp. 1–60.

Roze, J. A. 1970a. Ciencia y fantasía sobre las serpientes de Venezuela. Caracas, Edit. Fondo de Cultura Científica. 162 pp.

Roze, J. A. 1970b. *Micrurus*. Pp. 196–220 in J. A. Peters and B. Orejas-Miranda, eds. Catalogue of Neotropical Squamata. Part 1: Snakes. Bull. U.S. Natl. Mus. no. 297.

Roze, J. A. 1974. *Micruroides, M. euryxanthus*. Cat. Am. Amph. Rept. Pp. 163.1–163.4.

Roze, J. A. 1983 [dated 1982]. New World Coral Snakes (Elapidae): A taxonomic and biological summary. Mem. Inst. Butantan 46:305–338.

Roze, J. A. 1987. Summary of coral snakes (Elapidae) from Cerro de la Neblina, Venezuela, with description of a new subspecies. Rev. Fr. Aquariol. Herpetol. 14:109–112.

Roze, J. A., and A. Bernal-Carlo. In press. Las serpientes corales venenosas del genero *Leptomicrurus* (serpentes, elapidae) de Suramerica con descripción de una nueva subespecie. Boll. Mus. Sci. Torino. 5.

Roze, J. A., and G. M. Tilger. 1983. *Micrurus fulvius*. Cat. Am. Amph. Rept. Pp. 316.1–316.4.

Roze, J. A., and C. P. Trebbau M. 1958. Un nuevo género de corales venenosas (*Leptomicrurus*) para Venezuela. Acta Cient. Venez. 9:128–130.

Rubio, M. V. 1972. In search of the rare cascabel. Bull. New York Herpetol. Soc. 8:6–15.

Rüppell, E. 1845. Verzeichniss der in dem Museum der Senckenbergischen Gesselshaft aufgestellten Sammlung. Amphibien. Mus. Senckenb. 3:293–316.

Russell, F. E. 1967. Bites by the Sonoran coral snake, *Micruroides euryxanthus*. Toxicon 5:39–42.

Russell, F. E., and C. M. Bogert. 1981. Gila monster: Its biology, venom and bite—a review. Toxicon 19:341–359.

Ruthven, A. G. 1907. A collection of reptiles and amphibians from southern New Mexico and Arizona. Bull. Am. Mus. Nat. Hist. 23:483–603.

Ruthven, A. G. 1912. The amphibians and reptiles collected by the University of Michigan-Walker Expedition in Southern Vera Cruz, Mexico. Zool. Jahrb., Abt. Syst. 32:295–332.

Ruthven, A. G. 1922. The amphibians and reptiles of the Sierra Nevada de Santa Marta, Colombia. Misc. Publ. Mus. Zool. Univ. Michigan 8:1–69.

Ruthven, A. G. 1923. The reptiles of the Dutch Leeward Islands. Occas. Pap. Mus. Zool. Univ. Michigan no. 143. Pp. 1–10.

Saavedra R., D., A. Restrepo M., and N. Caro M. 1975. Ofidiotoxicosis botrópica en Colombia. Parte 1: Aspectos clinicos y hematologicos. Antioquia Med. 25:13–26.

Sage, R. D., and E. E. Capredoni. 1971. La distribución de la cascabel (*Crotalus durissus terrificus* (Laurentius) en Argentina y su significado zoogeográfico (Reptilia, Serpentes). Neotropica 17:133–136.

Salvin, O. 1860. On the reptiles of Guatemala. Proc. Zool. Soc. London 1860:451–461.

Sanborn, S. S., and R. B. Loomis. 1976. Keys to the amphibians and reptiles of Baja California, Mexico, including the adjacent islands. Long Beach, California State University. 26 pp.

Sánchez-Herrera, O., and G. López-Ortega. 1987. Noteworthy records of amphibians and reptiles from Tlaxcala, Mexico. Herpetol. Rev. 18:41.

Sandner-Montilla, F. 1952. Serpientes *Bothrops* de Venezuela. Monogr. Cient. Inst. Terap. Exper. Lab. "Veros," Bogotá no. 9. 4 pp.

Sandner-Montilla, F. 1961. Ofidios ponzoñosos de Venezuela *Bothrops venezuelae* Sp. nov. Noved. Cient. Mus. Hist. Nat. La Salle Caracas Ser. Zool., no. 30. Pp. 1–36.

Sandner-Montilla, F. 1966. El caso de anomalía en *Bothrops venezuelae*. Inst. Invest. Ofidiologia Venez. (Caracas) no. 1. 17 pp.

Sandner-Montilla, F. 1975. Manual de las serpientes ponzoñosas de Venezuela. Caracas, Talleres Tipo. Miguel Angel García y hijo. 112 pp.

Sandner-Montilla, F. 1976. Una nueva especie del género *Bothrops* (Serpientes: Crotalidae, Lachesinae) de la Gran Sabana, Edo. Bolívar, Venezuela. Mem. Cien. Ofidiologia 1:1–4.

Sandner-Montilla, F. 1978. *Bothrops castelnaudi* Duméril, Bribron [*sic*] et Duméril, 1854. Su existencia en Venezuela y el paso a sinonimía de *Bothrops lichenosus* Roze, 1958. Mem. Cien. Ofidiologia 2:1–8.

Sandner-Montilla, F. 1979a. La necesaria revalidación de *Bothrops lanceolatus* (Lacepede, 1789) y el paso a sinonimía de *B. colombiensis* (Hallowell 1845). Mem. Cien. Ofidiologia no. 3. Pp. 1–7.

Sandner-Montilla, F. 1979b. Una nueva especie del género *Bothrops* (Serpentes, Crotalidae, Bothropinae) de la region de Guanare, Estado Portuguesa, Venezuela. Mem. Cien. Ofidiologia no. 4. Pp. 1–19.

Sandner-Montilla, F. 1980. Una nueva especie del género *Crotalus* (Serpentes, Crotalidae, Crotalinae) del sur del estado Guárico, Venezuela. Mem. Cient. Ofidiología no. 5. Pp. 1–12.

Sandner-Montilla, F. 1981. Una nueva subespecie de *Bothrops lanceolatus* (Lacépede, 1789) Fam. Crotalidae. Mem. Cien. Ofidiologia. no. 6. Pp. 1–15.

Sandner-Montilla, F. 1983 [dated 1982]. Serpientes Crotalinae de Venezuela. Mem. Inst. Butantan 46:193–194.

Sandner-Montilla, F. 1985a. Edición dedicada al más insigne herpetólogo de todos los tiempos: el profesor doctor Afranio do Amaral. Mem. Cien. Ofidiologia 7:1–77.

Sandner-Montilla, F. 1985b. La creación de la familia Micruridae Fam. Nov. para las corales de America de la superfamilia Elapoidea y la proposición para la creación de la familia Oxyuranidae de la misma superfamilia, para proteroglifas australianas. Mem. Cient. Ofidiología no. 8. Pp. 1–22.

Sandner-Montilla, F., and M. Romer. 1961. Ofidios ponzoñosos de Venezuela, *Bothrops pifanoi* Sp. nov. Noved. Cient. Mus. Hist. La Salle Caracas Ser. Zool. no. 29. Pp. 1–15.

Santiago, Q. S. 1979. Diagnostic and therapeutic measure for copperhead snake bite. West Virginia Med. 75:62–64.

Santos, E. 1981. Anfíbios e répteis do Brasil (vida e costumbres). 3d ed. Belo Horizonte, Edit. Itatiaia. 263 pp.

Savage, J. M. 1960. Evolution of a peninsular herpetofauna. Syst. Zool. 9:184–211.

Savage, J. M. 1967. Evolution of the insular herpetofaunas. Proc. Symposium Biol. California Isl., Santa Barbara Botanic Garden:219–227.

Savage, J. M. 1980. A handlist with preliminary keys to the herpetofauna of Costa Rica. Allan Hancock Foundation, Univ. S. California. 111 pp.

Savage, J. M., and F. S. Cliff. 1953. A new subspecies of sidewinder, *Crotalus cerastes* from Arizona. Nat. Hist. Misc., Chicago no. 119:1–7.

Savage, J. M., and J. L. Vial. 1974. The venomous coral snakes (genus *Micrurus*) of Costa Rica. Rev. Biol. Tropical 21:295–349.

Sazima, I. 1987. Biologia comportamental da jararaca. An. Acad. Brasil. Cienc. 59:134–135.

Schätti, B. 1986 [dated 1985]. Catalogue des types et des exemplaires figures du Musee d'Histoire Naturelle de Neuchatel. II. Ophidiens. Biblio. Mus. Ville de Neuchatel 1985: 98–108.

Schmidt, K. P. 1922. The amphibians and reptiles of Lower California and the neighboring islands. Bull. Am. Mus. Nat. Hist. 46:607–707.

Schmidt, K. P. 1928a. Notes on American coral snakes. Bull. Antivenin Inst. Am. 2:63–64.

Schmidt, K. P. 1928b. Reptiles collected in Salvador for the California Institute of Technology. Field Mus. Nat. Hist. Publ., Zool. Ser. 12:193–201.

Schmidt, K. P. 1932. A new subspecies of coral snake from Guatemala. Proc. California Acad. Sci. Ser. (4) 20:265–267.

Schmidt, K. P. 1933a. Preliminary account of the coral snakes of Central America and Mexico. Field Mus. Nat. Hist. Publ., Zool. Ser. 20:29–40.

Schmidt, K. P. 1933b. Amphibians and reptiles collected by the Smithsonian biological survey of the Panama Canal Zone. Smithson. Misc. Collect. 89:1–20.

Schmidt, K. P. 1936a. A preliminary account of coral snakes of South America. Field. Mus. Nat. Hist. Publ., Zool. Ser. 20: 189–203.

Schmidt, K. P. 1936b. Notes on Central American and Mexican coral snakes. Field Mus. Nat. Hist. Publ., Zool. Ser. 20:205–216.

Schmidt, K. P. 1937. The history of *Elaps collaris* Schlegel, 1837–1937. Field Mus. Nat. Hist. Publ., Zool. Ser. 20:361–364.

Schmidt, K. P. 1939. A new coral snake from British Guiana. Field Mus. Nat. Hist. Publ., Zool. Ser. 24:45–47.

Schmidt, K. P. 1941. The amphibians and reptiles of British Honduras. Field Mus. Nat. Hist. Publ., Zool. Ser. 22:475–510.

Schmidt, K. P. 1952. The Surinam coral snake *Micrurus surinamensis*. Fieldiana: Zool. 34:25–34.

Schmidt, K. P. 1953a. Hemprich's coral snake, *Micrurus hemprichi*. Fieldiana: Zool. 34:165–170.

Schmidt, K. P. 1953b. The Amazonian coral snake, *Micrurus spixi*. Fieldiana: Zool. 34:171–180.

Schmidt, K. P. 1954. The annellated coral snake, *Micrurus annellatus* Peters. Fieldiana: Zool. 34:319–325.

Schmidt, K. P. 1955. Coral snakes of the genus *Micrurus* in Colombia. Fieldiana: Zool. 34:337–359.

Schmidt, K. P. 1957a. The venomous coral snakes of Trinidad. Fieldiana: Zool. 39:55–63.

Schmidt, K. P. 1957b. Anent the "dangerous" Bushmaster. Copeia 1957:233.

Schmidt, K. P. 1958. Some rare or little-known Mexican coral snakes. Fieldiana: Zool. 39:201–212.

Schmidt, K. P., and E. W. Andrews. 1936. Notes on snakes from Yucatan. Field Mus. Nat. Hist. Publ., Zool. Ser. 20:167–187.

Schmidt, K. P., and R. F. Inger. 1951. Amphibians and reptiles of the Hopkins-Branner expedition to Brazil. Fieldiana: Zool. 31:439–465.

Schmidt, K. P., and D. W. Owens. 1944. Amphibians and reptiles of northern Coahuila, México. Field Mus. Nat. Hist. Publ., Zool. Ser. 29:97–115.

Schmidt, K. P., and F. J. W. Schmidt. 1925. New coral snakes from Peru. Report on results of the Captain Marshall Field expeditions. Field Mus. Nat. Hist. Publ., Zool. Ser. 12:129–134.

Schmidt, K. P., and F. A. Shannon. 1947. Notes on the amphibians and reptiles of Michoacan, Mexico. Fieldiana: Zool. 31:63–85.

Schmidt, K. P., and H. M. Smith. 1943. Notes on coral snakes from Mexico. Field Museum Nat. Hist. Publ., Zool. Ser. 29:25–31.

Schmidt, K. P., and T. F. Smith. 1944. Amphibians and reptiles of the Big Bend region of Texas. Field Mus. Nat. Hist. Publ., Zool. Ser. 29:75–96.

Schmidt, K. P., and W. F. Walker. 1943a. Peruvian snakes from the University of Arequipa. Field Mus. Nat. Hist. Publ., Zool. Ser. 24:279–296.

Schmidt, K. P., and W. F. Walker. 1943b. Snakes of the Peruvian coastal region. Field Mus. Nat. Hist. Publ., Zool. Ser. 24:297–324.

Schouten, G. B. 1931. Contribuciones al conocimiento de la fauna herpetológica del Paraguay y de los paises limítrofes. Rev. Soc. Cient. Parag. 3:5–32.

Schouten, G. B. 1937. Fauna herpetológica del Paraguay. Novena Reunión Soc. Argent. Patol. Reg. 2:1218–1232.

Schreiber, G., A. R. Hoge, H. E. Belluomini, and A. M. Penha. 1958. Further researches on intersexuality in a highly isolated population of snakes. Proc. 10th Int. Congr. Genet. (Montreal 1958) 2:254–255.

Schulte, R. 1988. Observaciones sobre la boa verde, *Corallus caninus*, en el Departamento San Martín-Perú. Bol. Lima 55:21–26.

Schwartz, A., and R. W. Henderson. 1985. A guide to the identification of the amphibians and reptiles of the West Indies exclusive of Hispaniola. Milwaukee, Wis., Milwaukee Public Museum. 165 pp.

Schwartz, A., and R. Thomas. 1975. A check-list of West Indian amphibians and reptiles. Carnegie Mus. Nat. Hist. Spec. Publ. 1:1–216.

Scott, N. J. 1969. A zoogeographic analysis of the snakes of Costa Rica. Ph.D. Diss. Univ. S. California, 390 pp. Ann Arbor, Mich., University Microfilms. Diss. Abstr. B Sci. Eng. 69:17, 891.

Scott, N. J. 1983a. *Bothrops asper* (Terciopelo, fer-de-lance). Pp. 383–384 in D. H. Janzen, ed. Costa Rican natural history. Chicago, Univ. Chicago Press.

Scott, N. J. 1983b. *Crotalus durissus* (Cascabel, tropical rattlesnake). Pp. 393–394 in D. H. Janzen, ed. Costa Rican natural history. Chicago, Univ. Chicago Press.

Scott, N. J., and J. W. Lovett. 1975. A collection of reptiles and amphibians from the Chaco of Paraguay. Univ. Connecticut Occas. Pap., Biol. Sci. 2:257–266.

Seib, R. L. 1978. Geographic distribution: *Crotalus mitchelli pyrrhus*. Herpetol. Rev. 9:22.

Seifert, R. P. 1983. *Bothrops schlegelii* (Oropel [Gold Morph], Bocaracá, eyelash viper, palm viper). Pp. 384–385 in D. H. Janzen, ed. Costa Rican natural history, Chicago, Univ. Chicago Press.

Seifert, W. 1972. Habitat, variations, and intergradation of the Trans Pecos copperhead *Agkistrodon contortrix pictigaster* in Texas. Dallas Mus. Nat. Hist. Bull. 2:1–10.

Sexton, O. J. 1958 [dated 1956/57]. The distribution of *Bothrops atrox* in relation to food supply. Bol. Mus. Cienc. Nat. (Caracas) no. 2/3:47–54.

Sexton, O. J. and H. Heatwole. 1965. Life history notes on some Panamanian snakes. Caribb. J. Sci. 5:39–43.

Shannon, F. A. 1951. Notes on a herpetological collection from Oaxaca and other localities in Mexico. Proc. U.S. Natl. Mus. 101:465–484.

Shannon, F. A. 1953. Case reports of two Gila monster bites. Herpetologica 9:125–127.

Shannon, F. A., and H. M. Smith. 1950 [dated 1949]. Herpetological results of the University of Illinois Field Expedition, Spring 1949. I. Introduction, Testudines, Serpentes. Trans. Kansas Acad. Sci. 52:499–514.

Shaw, C. E. 1964a. A snake easily ruffled but unrattled. Zoonooz, San Diego. 37:1–7.

Shaw, C. E. 1964b. Beaded lizards-dreaded but seldom deadly. Zoonooz, San Diego. 37:10–15.

Shaw, C. E. 1971. The coral snakes, genera *Micrurus* and *Micruroides*, of the United States and northern Mexico. Pp. 156–172 in W. Bucherl and E. E. Buckley, eds. Venomous animals and their venoms. Vol. 2: Venomous vertebrates. N.Y., Academic Press.

Shreve, B. 1934. Notes on Ecuadorian snakes. Occas. Pap. Boston Soc. Nat. Hist. 8:125–132.

Shreve, B. 1938. A new *Agkistrodon* from Mexico. Copeia 1938:9.

Shreve, B. 1947a. On Venezuelan reptiles and amphibians collected by Dr. H. G. Kugler. Bull. Mus. Comp. Zool. 99:519–537.

Shreve, B. 1947b. On Colombian reptiles and amphibians collected by Dr. R. E. Schultes. Caldasia 4:311–316.

Shreve, B. 1953. Notes on the races of *Micrurus frontalis* (Duméril, Duméril and Bibron). Breviora 16:1–6.

Shuntov, V. P. 1963. Sea-snakes. Priroda (Mosc.) 3:103–104.

Shuntov, V. P. 1971. Sea snakes of the north Australian shelf. Ekologiya 1971:65–72. (Consultants Bureau English Translation, 1972).

Silva Haad, J. 1982a [dated 1980/81]. Accidentes humanos por los serpientes de los géneros *Bothrops* y *Lachesis*. Mem. Inst. Butantan 44/45:403–423.

Silva Haad, J. 1982b. Las serpientes del género *Bothrops* en la Amazonia Colombiana. Amazonia 1982:45–50.

Silva Haad, J., and R. A. Rodríguez R. 1985. Las serpientes *Micrurus* de la Amazonia Colombiana. Amazonia 1985:26–28.

Slevin, J. R. 1926. Expedition to the Revillagigedo Islands, Mexico in 1925, III. Notes on a collection of reptiles and amphibians from Tres Marias and Revillagigedo Islands, and west coast of Mexico, with description of a new species of *Tantilla*. Proc. California Acad. Sci. Ser. 4, 15:195–207.

Slevin, J. R. 1939. Notes on a collection of reptiles and amphibians from Guatemala. 1. Snakes. Proc. California Acad. Sci. Ser. 4, 23:393–414.

Smith, H. M. 1935. Miscellaneous notes on Mexican lizards. Univ. Kansas Sci. Bull. 22:119–155.

Smith, H. M. 1938. Notes on reptiles and amphibians from Yucatan and Campeche, Mexico. Occas. Pap. Mus. Zool. Univ. Michigan no. 388. Pp. 1–22.

Smith, H. M. 1939. An annotated list of the Mexican amphibians and reptiles in the Carnegie Museum. Ann. Carnegie Mus. 27:311–320.

Smith, H. M. 1940. Descriptions of new lizards and snakes from Mexico and Guatemala. Proc. Biol. Soc. Washington 53:55–64.

Smith, H. M. 1941a. Notes on Mexican snakes of the genus *Trimeresurus*. Zoologica, New York 26:61–64.

Smith, H. M. 1941b. On the Mexican snakes of the genus *Pliocercus*. Proc. Biol. Soc. Washington 54:119–124.

Smith, H. M. 1942. Additional notes on Mexican snakes of the genus *Pliocercus*. Proc. Biol. Soc. Washington 55:159–164.

Smith, H. M. 1943. Summary of the collections of snakes and crocodilians made in Mexico under the Walter Rathbone Traveling Scholarship. Proc. U.S. Natl. Mus. 93:393–504.

Smith, H. M. 1944a. Snakes of the Hoogstraal expeditions to northern Mexico. Field Mus. Nat. Hist. Publ., Zool. Ser. 29:135–152.

Smith, H. M. 1944b. Notes on a small collection of reptiles and amphibians from Tabasco, Mexico. J. Washington Acad. Sci. 34:154–156.

Smith, H. M. 1944c. Additions to the list of Mexican amphibians and reptiles in the Carnegie Museum. Ann. Carnegie Mus. 30:89–92.

Smith, H. M. 1946a. Preliminary notes and speculations on the *Triseriatus* group of rattlesnakes in Mexico. Univ. Kansas Sci. Bull. 31:75–101.

Smith, H. M. 1946b. Handbook of lizards: Lizards of the United States and of Canada. Ithaca, N.Y., Comstock Publishing Co. 557 pp.

Smith, H. M. 1947a [dated 1946]. Notas sobre una colección de reptiles y anfibios de Chiapas, Mex. Rev. Soc. Mex. Hist. Nat. 7:63–74.

Smith, H. M. 1947b. Notes on Mexican amphibians and reptiles. J. Washington Acad. Sci. 37:408–412.

Smith, H. M. 1958. Handlist of the snakes of Panama. Herpetologica 14:222–224.

Smith, H. M. 1960a [dated 1959]. New and noteworthy reptiles from Oaxaca, Mexico. Trans. Kansas Acad. Sci. 62:265–271.

Smith, H. M. 1960b. Herpetozoa from Tabasco. Herpetologica 16:222–223.

Smith, H. M. 1970 [dated 1969]. The first herpetology of Mexico. Herpetology 3:1–16.

Smith, H. M., and E. D. Brodie, Jr. 1982. A guide to field identification. Reptiles of North America. N.Y., Golden Press. 240 pp.

Smith, H. M., and H. K. Buechner. 1947. The influence of the Balcones Escarpment on the distribution of amphibians and reptiles in Texas. Bull. Chicago Acad. Sci. 8:1–16.

Smith, H. M., and P. S. Chrapliwy. 1958. New and noteworthy Mexican herptiles from the Lidicker collection. Herpetologica 13:267–271.

Smith, H. M., and C. Grant. 1958. Noteworthy herptiles from Jalisco, Mexico. Herpetologica 14:18–23.

Smith, H. M., and R. L. Holland. 1971. Noteworthy snakes and lizards from Baja California. J. Herpetol. 5:56–59.

Smith, H. M., R. L. Holland, and R. L. Brown. 1971. The prairie rattlesnake in Baja California del Sur. J. Herpetol. 5:200.

Smith, H. M., and M. J. Landy. 1965. New and unusual snakes of the genus *Pliocercus* from Oaxaca, Mexico. Chicago Acad. Sci. Nat. Hist. Misc. no. 183. Pp. 1–4.

Smith, H. M., and D. A. Langebartel. 1949. Notes on a collection of reptiles and amphibians from the Isthmus of Tehuantepec, Oaxaca. J. Washington Acad. Sci. 39:409–416.

Smith, H. M., and L. E. Laufe. 1945. Mexican amphibians and reptiles in the Texas Cooperative Wildlife Collections. Trans. Kansas Acad. Sci. 48:325–354.

Smith, H. M., and J. D. Lynch. 1967. A new cryptic lizard (Iguanidae: *Sceloporus*) with comments on other reptiles from Oaxaca, Mexico. Herpetologica 23:18–29.

Smith, H. M., and M. B. Mittleman. 1943. Notes of the Mansfield Museum's Mexican reptiles collected by Wilkinson. Trans. Kansas Acad. Sci. 46:342–349.

Smith, H. M., and E. O. Moll. 1969. A taxonomic rearrangement of the pit vipers of the *Bothrops nigroviridis* complex of southern Mexico. J. Herpetol. 3:151–155.

Smith, H. M., and W. L. Necker. 1944 [dated 1943]. Alfredo Dugès' types of Mexican reptiles and amphibians. An. Esc. Nac. Cienc. Biol. Mex. 3:179–233.

Smith, H. M., and R. B. Smith. 1969. Early foundations of Mexican herpetology: An annotated and indexed bibliography of the herpetological publications of Alfredo Dugès, 1826–1910. Urbana, Univ. Illinois Press. 87 pp.

Smith, H. M., and E. H. Taylor. 1945. An annotated checklist and key to the snakes of Mexico. Bull. U.S. Natl. Mus. no. 187. Pp. 1–239.

Smith, H. M., and E. H. Taylor. 1950a. An annotated checklist and key to the reptiles of Mexico exclusive of the snakes. Bull. U.S. Natl. Mus. no. 199:1–253.

Smith, H. M., and E. H. Taylor. 1950b. Type localities of Mexican reptiles and amphibians. Univ. Kansas Sci. Bull. 33: 313–380.

Smith, H. M., and E. H. Taylor. 1966. Herpetology of Mexico. Annotated checklists and keys to the amphibians and reptiles. A reprint of Bulletins 187, 194, and 199 of the U.S. National Museum with a list of subsequent taxonomic innovations. Ashton, Md., Eric Lundberg. 239, 118, and 253 pp.

Smith, H. M., and R. Van Gelder. 1955. New and noteworthy amphibians and reptiles from Sinaloa and Puebla, Mexico. Herpetologica 11:145–149.

Smith, H. M., K. L. Williams, and E. O. Moll. 1963. Herpetological explorations on the Río Conchos, Chihuahua, Mexico. Herpetologica 19:205–215.

Smith, M. 1926. Monograph of the sea-snakes (Hydrophiidae). London, Trustees of the British Museum. 130 pp.

Smith, P. W., and D. M. Darling. 1952. Results of a herpetological collection from eastern central Mexico. Herpetologica 8:81–86.

Smith, P. W., and M. M. Hensley. 1958. Notes on a small collection of amphibians and reptiles from the vicinity of Pinacate lava cap in northwestern Sonora, Mexico. Trans. Kansas Acad. Sci. 61:64–76.

Soini, P. 1973. Notes on an upper Amazonian coral snake, *Micrurus putumayensis* Lancini. J. Herpetol. 7:306–307.

Soini, P. 1974a. Polychromatism in a population of *Micrurus langsdorffi*. J. Herpetol. 8:267–269.

Soini, P. 1974b. Ofidios venenosos del nor-oriente Peruano. Copy of unpublished manuscript. Univ. of Texas at Arlington Collection of Vertebrates, Arlington, Texas. 93 pp.

Solórzano, A., and L. Cerdas. 1984. Confirmación de la presencia de *Micrurus clarki* Schmidt (Elapidae) en Costa Rica. Rev. Biol. Tropical 32:317–318.

Solórzano, A., and L. Cerdas. 1986. A new subspecies of the bushmaster, *Lachesis muta*, from southeastern Costa Rica. J. Herpetol. 20:463–466.

Soulé, M., and A. J. Sloan. 1966. Biogeography and distribution of the reptiles and amphibians on islands in the Gulf of California, Mexico. Trans. San Diego Soc. Nat. Hist. 14:137–156.

Spengler, J. C., H. M. Smith, D. Chiszar, and G. Casas-Andreu. 1982. Geographic distribution: *Crotalus basiliscus oaxacus*. Herpetol. Rev. 13:25.

Spieth, H. T. 1950. The David Rockefeller Mexican Expedition of the American Museum of Natural History. Introductory Account. Am. Mus. Novit. no. 1454. Pp. 1–67.

Stadelman, R. 1940. Maize cultivation in northwestern Guatemala. Contrib. Am. Anthrop. and Hist., Carnegie Inst. Washington no. 4, 33:82–264.

Stebbins, R. C. 1985. A field guide to western reptiles and amphibians. Boston, Houghton Mifflin Co. 336 pp.

Steindachner, F. 1870. Herpetologische notizen (II). II. Über einige neue oder seltene Reptilien des Wiener Museums. Sitzungsber. Akad. Wiss. Wein, Math. Naturwiss. Kl. 61:11–25.

Stejneger, L. H. 1893. Annotated list of the reptiles and batrachians collected by the Death Valley expedition in 1891, with descriptions of new species. N. Am. Fauna 7:159–228.

Stejneger, L. H. 1895. The poisonous snakes of North America. Ann. Rep. U.S. Natl. Mus. 1893:337–487.

Stejneger, L. H. 1899. Reptiles of the Tres Marías and Isabel islands. N. Am. Fauna 14:63–71.

Stejneger, L. H. 1902. The reptiles of the Huachuca Mountains, Arizona. Proc. U.S. Natl. Mus. 25:149–158.

Stejneger, L. H. 1940. "Sonora" as the locality of the Graham-Clark reptile collections of 1851. Copeia 1940:204–205.

Stejneger, L. H., and T. Barbour. 1943. A check list of North American amphibians and reptiles. Bull. Mus. Comp. Zool. 93:260 pp.

Sternfeld, R. 1920. Eine neue Schlange der Gattung *Lachesis* aus Südamerika. Senckenb. Biol. 2:179–181.

Stevan, L. J., and E. B. Seligmann, Jr. 1970. Agar-gel and acrylamide-disc electrophoresis of coral snake venom. Toxicon 8:11–14.

Storer, T. I. 1931. *Heloderma* poisoning in man. Bull. Antivenin Inst. Am. 5:12–15.

Strecker, J. K., Jr. 1909. Reptiles and amphibians collected in Brewster County, Texas. Baylor Univ. Bull. 12:1–20.

Strecker, J. K., Jr. 1928. The copperhead west of the Pecos River. Contrib. Baylor Univ. Mus. 15:9.

Strecker, J. K., and J. E. Johnson, Jr. 1935. Notes on the herpetology of Wilson County, Texas. Baylor Univ. Bull. 38:17–23.

Streets, T. H. 1877. Contributions to the natural history of the Hawaiian and Fanning Islands and Lower California. Bull. U.S. Natl. Mus. no. 7. Pp. 1–172.

Stuart, L. C. 1934. A contribution to a knowledge of the herpetological fauna of El Petén, Guatemala. Occas. Pap. Mus. Zool. Univ. Michigan no. 292. Pp. 1–18.

Stuart, L. C. 1935. A contribution to a knowledge of the herpetology of a portion of the savanna region of central Petén, Guatemala. Misc. Publ. Mus. Zool. Univ. Michigan no. 29. Pp. 1–56.

Stuart, L. C. 1937. Some further notes on the amphibians and reptiles of the Petén forest of northern Guatemala. Copeia 1937:67–70.

Stuart, L. C. 1943. Comments on the herpetofauna of the Sierra de los Cuchumatanes of Guatemala. Occas. Pap. Mus. Zool. Univ. Michigan no. 471. Pp. 1–28.

Stuart, L. C. 1948. The amphibians and reptiles of Alta Verapaz, Guatemala. Misc. Publ. Mus. Zool. Univ. Michigan no. 69. Pp. 1–109.

Stuart, L. C. 1950. A geographic study of the herpetofauna of Alta Verapaz, Guatemala. Contrib. Lab. Vertebr. Biol. Univ. Michigan no. 45. Pp. 1–77.

Stuart, L. C. 1951. The herpetofauna of the Guatemalan Plateau, with special reference to its distribution on the southwestern highlands. Contrib. Lab. Vertebr. Biol. Univ. Michigan no. 49. Pp. 1–71.

Stuart, L. C. 1954a. A description of a subhumid corridor across northern Central America, with comments on its herpetofaunal indicators. Contrib. Lab. Vertebr. Biol. Univ. Michigan no. 65. Pp. 1–26.

Stuart, L. C. 1954b. Herpetofauna of the southeastern highlands of Guatemala. Contrib. Lab. Vertebr. Biol. Univ. Michigan no. 68. Pp. 1–65.

Stuart, L. C. 1958. A study of the herpetofauna of the Uaxactun-Tikal area of northern El Petén, Guatemala. Contrib. Lab. Vertebr. Biol. Univ. Michigan no. 75. Pp. 1–30.

Stuart, L. C. 1963. A checklist of the herpetofauna of Guatemala. Misc. Publ. Mus. Zool. Univ. Michigan no. 122. Pp. 1–150.

Stuart, L. C. 1964. Fauna of Middle America. Pp. 316–362 in R. Wauchope and R. C. West, eds. Handbook of Middle American Indians. Vol. 1, Austin, Univ. Texas Press.

Stuart, L. C. 1966. The environment of the Central American cold-blooded vertebrate fauna. Copeia 1966:684–699.

Sumichrast, F. 1864a. Notes on the habits of some Mexican reptiles. Ann. Mag. Nat. Hist. Ser. 3, 13:497–507.

Sumichrast, F. 1864b. Notes sur les moeurs de quelques reptiles du Mexique. Arch. Sci. Phys. Nat. 19:45–61.

Sumichrast, F. 1870. Notas sobre las costumbres de algunos reptiles de México. Familia de los varanideos. Naturaleza, Mexico 1:221–223.

Sumichrast, F. 1873. Coup d'oeil sur la distribution géographique des reptiles au Mexique. Arch. Sci. Phys. Nat. 46:233–250.

Sumichrast, F. 1875. Observations sur les moeurs de l'*Heloderma horridum*. C. R. Hebd. Séances Acad. Sci., Paris 80:676–679.

Sumichrast, F. 1880. Contribution à l'histoire naturelle du Mexique. I. Notes sur une collection de reptiles et de batraciens de la partie occidentale de l'Isthme de Tehuantepec. Bull. Soc. Zool. France 5:162–190.

Sumichrast, F. 1881–1882. Contribución a la historia natural de México. I. Notas acerca de una colección de reptiles y batracios de la parte occidental del Istmo de Tehuantepec. Naturaleza, Mexico 5:268–293. (1881: 268–270; 1882: 271–293.)

Sumichrast, F. 1882. Enumeración de las especies de reptiles observados en la parte meridional de la República Mexicana. Naturaleza, Mexico 6:31–45.

Swan, L. W. 1952. Some environmental conditions influencing life at high altitudes. Ecology 33:109–111.

Swanson, P. L. 1945. Herpetological notes from Panama. Copeia 1945:210–216.

Swaroop, S., and B. Grab. 1954. Snakebite mortality in the world. Bull. World Health Org. 10:35–76.

Swarth, H. S. 1921. The type locality of *Crotalus willardi* Meek. Copeia 1921:83.

Tada, I. di, and J. Villa. 1975. The serpentarium at Córdoba, Argentina. Herpetol. Rev. 6:76–77.

Talbot, J. J. n.d. Una nueva lista sistematica de reptiles del Paraguay. Informes Cient. 2:88–90.

Tanner, W. W. 1957. Notes on a collection of amphibians and reptiles from Southern Mexico, with a description of a new *Hyla*. Great Basin Nat. 17:52–56.

Tanner, W. W. 1966. A new rattlesnake from western Mexico. Herpetologica 22:298–302.

Tanner, W. W. 1985. Snakes of western Chihuahua. Great Basin Nat. 45:615–676.

Tanner, W. W. 1986. *Crotalus lannomi*. Cat. Am. Amph. Rept. Pp. 384.1.

Tanner, W. W., J. R. Dixon, and H. S. Harris, Jr. 1972. A new subspecies of *Crotalus lepidus* from western Mexico. Great Basin Nat. 32:16–24.

Taylor, E. H. 1938a [dated 1936]. Notes on the herpetological fauna of the Mexican state of Sonora. Univ. Kansas Sci. Bull. 24:475–503.

Taylor, E. H. 1938b [dated 1936]. Notes on the herpetological fauna of the Mexican state of Sinaloa. Univ. Kansas Sci. Bull. 24:505–537.

Taylor, E. H. 1940 [dated 1939]. Some Mexican serpents. Univ. Kansas Sci. Bull. 26:445–487.

Taylor, E. H. 1941. Herpetological miscellany. No. II. Univ. Kansas Sci. Bull. 27:105–139.

Taylor, E. H. 1943. "Island" faunas of the Mexican Plateau. Proc. 8th Am. Scientific Congress 3:503–504.

Taylor, E. H. 1944. Two new species of crotalid snakes from Mexico. Univ. Kansas Sci. Bull. 30:47–56.

Taylor, E. H. 1949. A preliminary account of the herpetology of the state of San Luis Potosí, Mexico. Univ. Kansas Sci. Bull. 33:169–215.

Taylor, E. H. 1950. Second contribution to the herpetology of San Luis Potosí. Univ. Kansas Sci. Bull. 33:441–457.

Taylor, E. H. 1951. A brief review of the snakes of Costa Rica. Univ. Kansas Sci. Bull. 34:1–188.

Taylor, E. H. 1952. Third contribution to the herpetology of the Mexican state of San Luis Potosí. Univ. Kansas Sci. Bull. 34:793–815.

Taylor, E. H. 1953a. Early records of the seasnake, *Pelamis platurus* in Latin America. Copeia 1953:124.

Taylor, E. H. 1953b. Fourth contribution to the herpetology of San Luis Potosí. Univ. Kansas Sci. Bull. 35:1587–1614.

Taylor, E. H. 1954. Further studies on the serpents of Costa Rica. Univ. Kansas Sci. Bull. 36:673–801.

Taylor, E. H., and I. W. Knobloch. 1940. Report on a herpetological collection from the Sierra Madre Mountains of Chihuahua. Proc. Biol. Soc. Washington 53:125–130.

Taylor, R. T., A. Flores, G. Flores, and R. Bolaños. 1974. Geographical distribution of Viperidae, Elapidae and Hydrophidae in Costa Rica. Rev. Biol. Tropical 21:383–397.

Tennant, A. 1984. The Snakes of Texas. Austin, Texas, Texas Monthly Press. 561 pp.

Test, F. H., O. J. Sexton, and H. Heatwole. 1966. Reptiles of Rancho Grande and vicinity, Estado Aragua, Venezuela. Misc. Publ. Mus. Zool. Univ. Michigan no. 128. Pp. 1–63.

Tevis, L. 1943. Field notes on a red rattlesnake in Lower California. Copeia 1943:241–245.

Tevis, L. 1944. Herpetological notes from Lower California. Copeia 1944:6–18.

Thompson, J. C. 1913. The correct status of *Elaps collaris*. Notes Leyden Mus. 35:171–175.

Tiedemann, F., and M. Haupl. 1980. Typenkatalog der herpetologischen Sammlung. Teil II: Reptilia. Kat. Wiss. Samml. Naturlist. Mus. Wien. 4(Vertebrata 2):1–80.

Timmerman, W. W., and M. P. Hayes. 1981. The reptiles and amphibians of Monteverde: An annotated check list to the herpetofauna of Monteverde, Costa Rica. Monteverde, Pensión Quetzal in cooperation with the Tropical Science Center, San José. 32 pp.

Tinkham, E. R. 1971a. The biology of the Gila monster. Pp. 387–413 in W. Bucherl and E. E. Buckley, eds. Venomous animals and their venoms. Vol. 2: Venomous vertebrates. N.Y., Academic Press.

Tinkham, E. R. 1971b. The venom of the Gila monster. Pp. 415–422 in W. Bucherl and E. E. Buckley, eds. Venomous animals and their venoms. Vol. 2:Venomous vertebrates. N.Y., Academic Press.

Tinoco, R. A. 1978. Las serpientes de Colombia, ciencia, mitos y leyendas. Barranquilla, Edic. Ed. Mejoras. 105 pp.

Touzet, J. M. 1983. Los ofidios de la region lojana segun las relaciones de 1808. Cultura 5:481–488.

Townsend, C. H. T. 1916. Voyage of the 'Albatross' to the Gulf of California in 1911. Bull. Am. Mus. Nat. Hist. 35:399–476.

Trejos, J. F. 1937. Geografía de Costa Rica, física, política y económica. San José, Imprenta Universal. 346 pp.

Troschel, F. H. 1853. Ueber *Heloderma horridum* Wiegm. Arch. Naturgesch. 19:294–315.

Troschel, F. H. 1855. Bericht über die Leistungen in der Herpetologie während des Jahres 1854. Arch. Naturgesch. 21:411–425.

Troschel, F. H. 1860. Bericht über die Leistungen in der Herpetologie während des Jahres 1859. Arch. Naturgesch. 26: 265–278.

Troschel, F. H. 1866. Bericht über die Leistungen in der Herpetologie während des Jahres 1865. Arch. Naturgesch. 32: 180–192.

Trutnau, L. 1970. Die Skorpion-Krustenechse *Heloderma horridum* (Wiegmann). Aquar. Terr. Z. 17:228–231.

Tschudi, J. J. Von. 1845. Reptilium conspectum quae in Republica Peruana reperiuntur et pleraque observata vel collecta sunt in itinere a Dr. J. J. de Tschudi. Arch. Naturgesch. 11:150–170.

Tu, A. T. 1976. Investigation of the sea snake, *Pelamis platurus* (Reptilia, Serpentes, Hydrophiidae), on the Pacific coast of Costa Rica, Central America. J. Herpetol. 10:13–18.

Tyler, R. E. 1849. Notes on the serpents of St. Lucia. Proc. Zool. Soc. London 1849:100–104.

Underwood, G. 1962. Reptiles of the eastern Caribbean. Dept. Extra-mural Stud., Univ. West Indies, Port-of-Spain, Caribb. Affairs n.s. 1:1–192.

Uzzell, T. M., Jr., and P. Starrett. 1958. Snakes from El Salvador. Copeia 1958:339–342.

Van Bourgondien, T. M., and R. C. Bothner. 1969. A comparative study of the arterial systems of some New World Crotalinae (Reptilia: Ophidia). Am. Midl. Nat. 81:107–147.

Van Denburgh, J. 1894. Notes on *Crotalus mitchelli* and "*Crotalus pyrrhus*." Proc. California Acad. Sci. Ser. 2, 4:450–455.

Van Denburgh, J. 1895a. A review of the herpetology of Lower California. Part I: Reptiles. Proc. California Acad. Sci. Ser. 2, 5:77–163.

Van Denburgh, J. 1895b. Description of a new rattlesnake (*Crotalus pricei*) from Arizona. Proc. California Acad. Sci. Ser. 2, 5:856–857.

Van Denburgh, J. 1896. Additional notes on the herpetology of Lower California. Proc. California Acad. Sci. Ser. 2, 5:1004–1008.

Van Denburgh, J. 1897. The reptiles of the Pacific coast and Great Basin: An account of the species known to inhabit California,

and Oregon, Washington, Idaho and Nevada. Occas. Pap. California Acad. Sci. 5:1–236.
Van Denburgh, J. 1905. The reptiles and amphibians of the islands of the Pacific Coast of North America from the Farallons to Cape San Lucas and the Revilla Gigedos. Proc. California Acad. Sci. Ser. 3, 4:1–40.
Van Denburgh, J. 1920. Description of a new species of rattlesnake (*Crotalus lucasensis*) from Lower California. Proc. California Acad. Sci. Ser. 4, 10:29–30.
Van Denburgh, J. 1922a. The reptiles of western North America. Part I. Lizards. Occas. Pap. California Acad. Sci. 10:1–611.
Van Denburgh, J. 1922b. The reptiles of western North America. Part II. Snakes and turtles. Occas. Pap. California Acad. Sci. 10:617–1028.
Van Denburgh, J. 1924. Notes on the herpetology of New Mexico, with a list of species known from that state. Proc. California Acad. Sci. Ser. 4, 8:189–230.
Van Denburgh, J., and J. R. Slevin. 1914. Reptiles and amphibians of the islands of the west coast of North America. Proc. California Acad. Sci. Ser. 4, 4:129–152.
Van Denburgh, J., and J. R. Slevin. 1921a. A list of amphibians and reptiles of the peninsula of Lower California, with notes on the species in the collection of the Academy. Proc. California Acad. Sci. Ser. 4, 11:49–72.
Van Denburgh, J., and J. R. Slevin. 1921b. Preliminary diagnoses of more new species of reptiles from islands in the Gulf of California, Mexico. Proc. California Acad. Sci. Ser. 4, 11:395–398.
Van Devender, R. W. 1980. Preliminary checklist of the herpetofauna of Monteverde, Puntarenas Province, Costa Rica and vicinity. Brenesia 17:319–326.
Van Devender, T. R., and C. H. Lowe, Jr. 1977. Amphibians and reptiles of Yepómera, Chihuahua, Mexico. J. Herpetol. 11: 41–50.
Vanzolini, P. E. 1946. Regressão do peso sôbre o comprimento em *Bothrops jararaca* e sua variação sexual e estacional. Pap. Avulsos Zool., São Paulo 7:271–292.
Vanzolini, P. E. 1947. Notas sôbre um deródimo de *Crotalus durissus terrificus* (Laur.). Pap. Avulsos Zool., São Paulo 8:273–283.
Vanzolini, P. E. 1948. Notas sôbre os ofídios e lagartos da Cachoeira de Emas, no município de Pirassununga, estado de São Paulo. Rev. Brasil Biol. 8:377–400.
Vanzolini, P. E. 1953. On the type locality of some Brazilian reptiles and amphibians collected by H. H. Smith and described by E. D. Cope. Copeia 1953:124–125.
Vanzolini, P. E. 1985. *Micrurus averyi* Schmidt, 1939, in central Amazonia (Serpentes, Elapidae). Pap. Avulsos Zool., São Paulo 36:77–85.
Vanzolini, P. E., and J. H. Ferreira Brandão. 1946 [dated 1944/45]. Notas sôbre algumas diferencas sexuais na folidose de *Bothrops alternata* D. & B., 1854, e sua variação geográfica. Mem. Inst. Butantan 18:251–258.
Vanzolini, P. E., A. M. M. Ramos-Costa, and L. J. Vitt. 1980. Repteis das Caatingas. Acad. Bras. Cienc. Rio de Janeiro. 161 pp.
Vaz-Ferreira, R., and B. Sierra de Soriano. 1960. Notas sobre reptiles del Uruguay. Rev. Fac. Human. Cienc. (Montevideo) 18:1–55.
Velasco, A. L. 1890a. Geografía y estadística del estado de Guanajuato. Fauna pp. 53–55, 287–295 in vol. 5 of Geografía y estadística de la República Mexicana. Mexico, D.F., Secr. Fomento. 300 pp.
Velasco, A. L. 1890b. Geografía y estadística del estado de Morelos. Reptiles and amphibians, p. 52 in vol. 7 of Geografía y estadística de la República Mexicana. Mexico, D.F., Secr. Fomento. 140 pp.
Velasco, A. L. 1895. Geografía y estadística del estado de Campeche. Reptiles and amphibians, pp. 37–39 in vol. 16 of Geografía y estadística de la República Mexicana. Mexico, D.F., Secr. Fomento. 140 pp.
Velasco-Torres, J. J. 1970. Contribución al conocimiento de la herpetología del norte de Nuevo León, México. Diss., Univ. Nuevo León. Monterrey, Nuevo León. 69 pp.
Vellard, J. 1941. Serpents venimeux du Venezuela. Ann. Sci. Nat., Paris 3:193–225.
Vellard, J. 1943. Diferenciación biológica de la Cascabel Sudamericana. Acta. Zool. Lilloana 1:55–88.
Vellard, J. 1946. Morfología del hemipenis y evolución de los ofídios. Acta. Zool. Lilloana 3:263–288.
Vellard, J. 1948. El veneno de *Lachesis muta* (L.). Publ. Mus. Hist. Nat. 'Javier Prado' Ser. A. Zool. no. 1. Pp. 1–51.
Verteuil, L. A. A. de. 1884. Trinidad: Its geography, natural resources, administration, present condition, and prospects. 2d ed. London, Cassell and Co. 484 pp.
Vetencourt Finol., H. 1960 [dated 1959/60]. Ofidios venenosos de Venezuela. Rev. Med. Vet. Parasitol. (Maracay) 18:161–192.
Vial, J. L., and J. M. Jimenez-Porras. 1967. The ecogeography of the bushmaster, *Lachesis muta*, in Central America. Am. Midl. Nat. 78:182–187.
Villa, J. 1962. Las serpientes venenosas de Nicaragua. Managua, Editorial Novedades. 93 pp.
Villa, J. 1971. Notes on some Nicaraguan reptiles. J. Herpetol. 5:45–48.
Villa, J. 1972a. Un coral (*Micrurus*) blanco y negro de Costa Rica. Brenesia 1:10–13.
Villa, J. 1972b. Snakes of the Corn Islands, Caribbean Nicaragua. Brenesia 1:14–18.
Villa, J. 1984. The venomous snakes of Nicaragua: A synopsis. Milwaukee Public Mus. Contrib. Biol. Geol. 59:1–41.
Vital Brazil, O. 1980. Venenos ofídicos neurotóxicos. Rev. Assoc. Med. Bras. 26:212–218.
Vitt, L. J., and A. C. Hulse. 1973. Observations of feeding habits and tail display of the Sonoran coral snake, *Micruroides euryxanthus*. Herpetologica 29:302–304.
Voris, H. K. 1983. *Pelamis platurus* (Culebra del Mar, Pelagic sea Snake). Pp. 411–412 in D. H. Janzen, ed. Costa Rican Natural History, Chicago, Univ. of Chicago Press.
Wagler, J. 1824. Serpentum Brasiliensium species novae. . . . In J. de Spix. Animalia nova sive species novae. Monaco, Typis Franc. Seraph. Hübschmanni. 75 pp.
Wagner, V. 1985. Crotoxin: A review of the physiological effects of South American rattlesnake venom. J. NOAH 11:9–28.
Walters, V. 1953. Notes on reptiles and amphibians from El Volcán de Chiriqui, Panama. Copeia 1953:125–127.
Webb, R. G. 1966. The lizard *Sceloporus bulleri* in western Mexico. Yearb. Am. Philos. Soc. 1965:356–357.
Webb, R. G. 1984. Herpetogeography in the Mazatlán-Durango Region of the Sierra Madre Occidental, Mexico. Pp. 217–241 in R. A. Seigel et al., eds. Vertebrate ecology and systematics. Univ. Kansas Mus. Nat. Hist. no. 10.
Webb, R. G., and R. H. Baker. 1962. Terrestrial vertebrates of the Pueblo Nuevo area of southwestern Durango, Mexico. Am. Midl. Nat. 68:325–333.
Webb, R. G., and C. M. Fugler. 1957. Selected comments on amphibians and reptiles from the Mexican state of Puebla. Herpetologica 13:33–36.
Wehekind, L. 1960. Trinidad snakes. Occas. Pap. R. Victoria Inst. Mus. (Trinidad) no. 1. Pp. 1–8.
Welch, K. R. G. 1980. On a collection of reptiles from Trinidad. S. W. Herpetol. Soc. Bull. (San Diego)3:1–6.
Welsh, H. H., and R. B. Bury. 1984. Additions to the herpetofauna of the south Colorado Desert, Baja California, with comments on the relationships of *Lichanura trivirgata*. Herpetol. Rev. 15:53–56.
Werler, J. E. 1967. Poisonous snakes of Texas and first aid treatment of their bites. Texas Parks and Wildlife Dept. Bull. no. 31. Pp. 1–62.
Werler, J. E., and H. M. Smith. 1952. Notes on a collection of reptiles and amphibians from Mexico, 1951–1952. Texas J. Sci. 4:551–573.
Werman, S. D. 1984a. *Bothrops schlegelii* (Eyelash viper). Coloration. Herpetol. Rev. 15:17–18.
Werman, S. D. 1984b. Taxonomic comments on the Costa Rican pit viper, *Bothrops picadoi* (Dunn). J. Herpetol. 18:207–210.
Werman, S. D. 1984c. The taxonomic status of *Bothrops supraciliaris* Taylor. J. Herpetol. 18:484–486.
Werner, F. 1896. Beitrage zur Kenntniss der Reptilien und

Batrachier von Centralamerika und Chile, sowie einiger seltener Schlangenarten. Verh. Zool. Bot. Ges. Wien. 46:344–365.

Werner, F. 1897. Über einige neue oder seltene Reptilien und Frösche der zoologischen Sammlung des Staates in Munchen. Sitzungsber. Bayer Akad. Wiss., Munich 27:203–220.

Werner, F. 1900. Ueber Reptilien und Batrachier aus Columbien und Trinidad. II. Verh. Zod. Bot. Ges. Wien 50:262–272.

Werner, F. 1901a. Ueber Reptilien und Batrachier aus Ecuador und Neu-Guinea. Verh. Zool. Bot. Ges. Wien 51:593–614.

Werner, F. 1901b. Reptilien und Batrachier aus Peru und Bolivier. Abh. Ber. K. Zool. Anthro. Ethno. Mus. Dresden 9:1–14.

Werner, F. 1903. Neue Reptilien und Batrachier aus dem naturhistorischen Museum in Brüssel. Zool. Anz. 26:246–253.

Werner, F. 1922. Synopsis der Schlangen-Familien der Amblycephalidae und Viperidae nebst uebersicht über die kleineren Familien und die Colubriden der Acrochordineugruppe. Auf Grund des Boulenger'schen Schlangenkatologs (1893–1896). Arch. Naturgesch. 88:185–244.

Werner, F. 1927. Neue oder wenig bekannte Schlangen aus dem Wiener naturhistorischen Staatsmuseum (III. Teil). Sitzungsber. Akad. Wiss. Wien, Math. Naturwiss. Kl. (Abt. 1) 135:243–257.

Wettstein, O. 1934. Ergebnisse der Österreichischen biologischen Costa Rica-Expedition 1930. Die Amphibien und Reptilien. Sitzungsber. Akad. Wiss. Wien, Math. Naturwiss. Kl. 143:1–39.

Wied-Neuwied, M. 1820. Ueber die Cobra Coral oder Cobra Coraes der Brasilianer. Nova Acta Acad. Caesar. Leop. Carol., Halle 10:105–110.

Wiegmann, A. F. A. 1834. Herpetologica Mexicana seu descriptio amphibiorum Novae Hispaniae. Pars prima. Saurorum species. Berlin, Luderitz. 54 pp.

Williams, K. L., P. S. Chrapliwy, and H. M. Smith. 1961. Snakes from northern Mexico. Nat.Hist.Misc.,Chicago no. 177. Pp. 1–8.

Wilson, L. D. 1983. Update on the list of amphibians and reptiles known from Honduras. Herpetol. Rev. 14:125–126.

Wilson, L. D., and D. E. Hahn. 1973. The herpetofauna of the Islas de la Bahia, Honduras. Bull. Florida State Mus., Biol. Sci. 17:93–150.

Wilson, L. D., and J. R. McCranie. 1979. Notes on the herpetofauna of two mountain ranges in Mexico (Sierra Fría, Aguascalientes, and Sierra Morones, Zacatecas). J. Herpetol. 13:271–278.

Wilson, L. D., and J. R. McCranie. 1984. *Bothrops nasuta*. Cat. Am. Amph. Rept. Pp. 349.1–349.2.

Wilson, L. D., J. R. McCranie, and L. Porras. 1978. Two snakes, *Leptophis modestus* and *Pelamis platurus*, new to the herpetofauna of Honduras. Herpetol. Rev. 9:63–64.

Wilson, L. D., J. R. McCranie, and L. Porras. 1979. New departmental records for reptiles and amphibians from Honduras. Herpetol. Rev. 10:25.

Wilson, L. D., and J. R. Meyer. 1972. The coral snake *Micrurus nigrocinctus* in Honduras. Bull. S. California Acad. Sci. 71:139–145.

Wilson, L. D., and J. R. Meyer. 1985. The Snakes of Honduras. 2d ed. Milwaukee, Wis., Milwaukee Pub. Mus. 150 pp.

Woodbury, A. M. 1931. A descriptive catalogue of the reptiles of Utah. Bull. Univ. Utah, Biol. Ser. 21:1–129.

Woodbury, A. M., and D. M. Woodbury. 1944. Notes on Mexican snakes from Oaxaca. J. Washington Acad. Sci. 34:360–373.

Woodin, W. H. 1953. Notes on some reptiles from the Huachuca area of southeastern Arizona. Bull. Chicago Acad. Sci. 9:285–296.

Wright, A. H., and A. A. Wright. 1957. Handbook of snakes of the United States and Canada, vol. 2. Ithaca, N.Y., Comstock Publishing. Pp. 565–1105.

Yarrow, H. C. 1875. Report upon the collections of batrachians and reptiles made in portions of Nevada, Utah, California, Colorado, New Mexico, and Arizona, during the years 1871, 1872, 1873 and 1874. Rep. Geog. Geol. Expl. Surv. W. 100th Merid. Geo. M. Wheeler 5:509–584.

Yarrow, H. C. 1883 [dated 1982]. Check list of North American Reptilia and Batrachia, with catalogue of specimens in the United States Museum. Bull. U.S. Natl. Mus. 24:1–249.

Zweifel, R. G. 1954. Notes on the distribution of some reptiles in western Mexico. Herpetologica 10:145–149.

Zweifel, R. G. 1959a. The provenance of reptiles and amphibians collected in Mexico by J. J. Major. Am. Mus. Novit. 1949:1–9.

Zweifel, R. G. 1959b. Additions to the herpetofauna of Nayarit, Mexico. Am. Mus. Novit. 1953. Pp. 1–13.

Zweifel, R. G. 1960. Results of the Puritan-American Museum of Natural History expedition to western Mexico. 9. Herpetology of the Tres Marias Islands. Bull. Am. Mus. Nat. Hist. 119:77–128.

Zweifel, R. G., and K. S. Norris. 1955. Contributions to the herpetology of Sonora, Mexico: Descriptions of new subspecies of snakes (*Micruroides euryxanthus* and *Lampropeltis getulus*) and miscellaneous collecting notes. Am. Midl. Nat. 54:230–249.

# Index

This index contains the scientific, local, and English names of reptiles discussed in this book. Page numbers in boldface type indicate the location of the principal description.